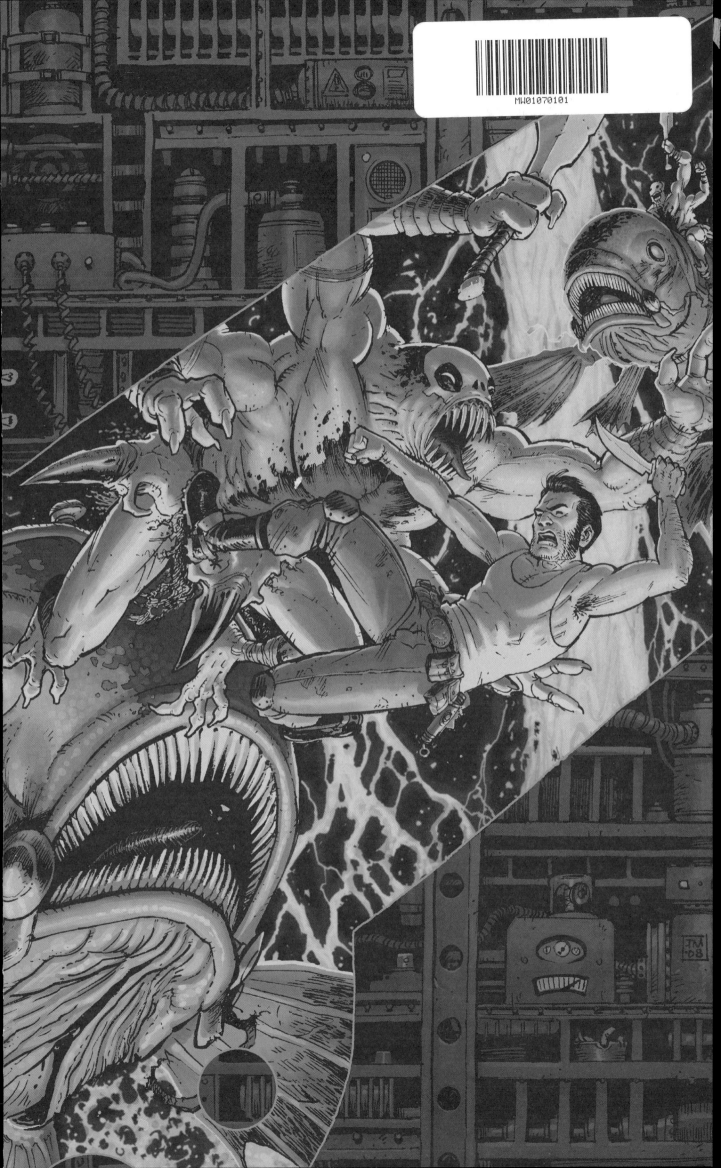

FEAR AGENT™

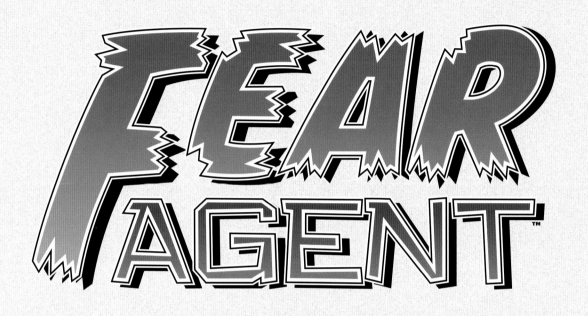

SENSES-SHATTERING!

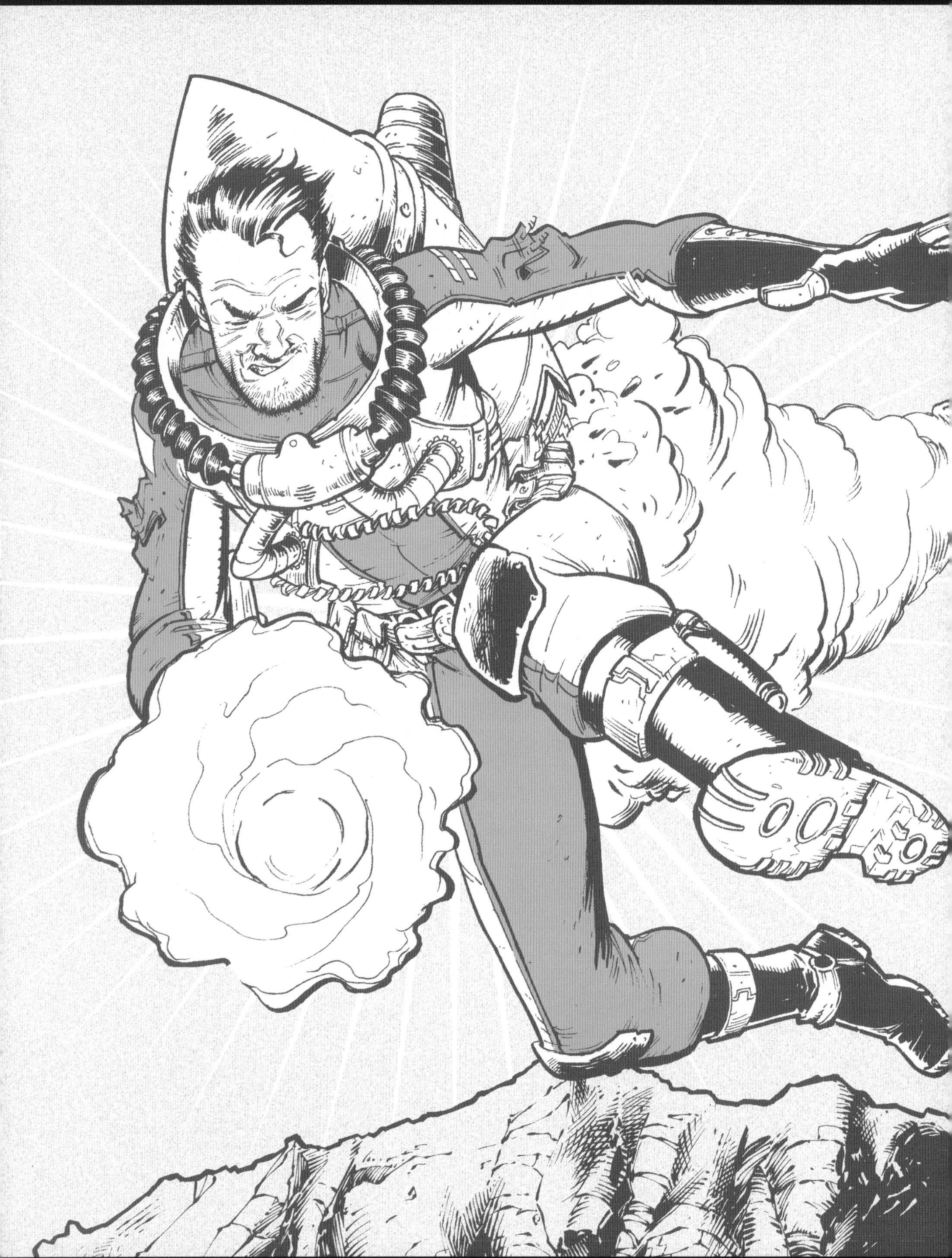

Space thrills and chills

FEAR AGENT™

Volume Two

HATCHET JOB
I AGAINST I
OUT OF STEP

DARK HORSE BOOKS

Publisher ⁄⁄ Mike Richardson

Designers ⁄⁄ M. Joshua Elliott & Tina Alessi

Series Editor ⁄⁄ Dave Land

Assistant Series Editors ⁄⁄ Katie Moody & Patrick Thorpe

Assistant Collection Editor ⁄⁄ Everett Patterson

Collection Editor ⁄⁄ Patrick Thorpe

SPECIAL THANKS TO Mike Hawthorne, John Lucas, Dave Land, and Scott Allie

Dark Horse Books
A division of Dark Horse Comics, Inc.
10956 SE Main Street
Milwaukie, OR 97222

DarkHorse.com

To find a comics shop in your area call the Comic Shop
Locator Service toll-free at (888) 266-4226

First edition: March 2014
ISBN 978-1-61655-103-2

1 3 5 7 9 10 8 6 4 2
Printed in China

FEAR AGENT LIBRARY EDITION VOLUME 2

This book collects issues #17 through #32 of the comic-book series *Fear Agent*, published by Dark Horse Comics.

MIKE RICHARDSON President and Publisher • NEIL HANKERSON Executive Vice President • Tom Weddle Chief Financial Officer • RANDY STRADLEY Vice President of Publishing • MICHAEL MARTENS Vice President of Book Trade Sales • ANITA NELSON Vice President of Business Affairs • SCOTT ALLIE Editor in Chief • MATT PARKINSON Vice President of Marketing • DAVID SCROGGY Vice President of Product Development • DALE LaFOUNTAIN Vice President of Information Technology • DARLENE VOGEL Senior Director of Print, Design, and Production • KEN LIZZI General Counsel • DAVEY ESTRADA Editorial Director • CHRIS WARNER Senior Books Editor • DIANA SCHUTZ Executive Editor • CARY GRAZZINI Director of Print and Development • LIA RIBACCHI Art Director • CARA NIECE Director of Scheduling • TIM WIESCH Director of International Licensing • MARK BERNARDI Director of Digital Publishing

☆ ☆ ☆ CONTENTS ☆ ☆ ☆

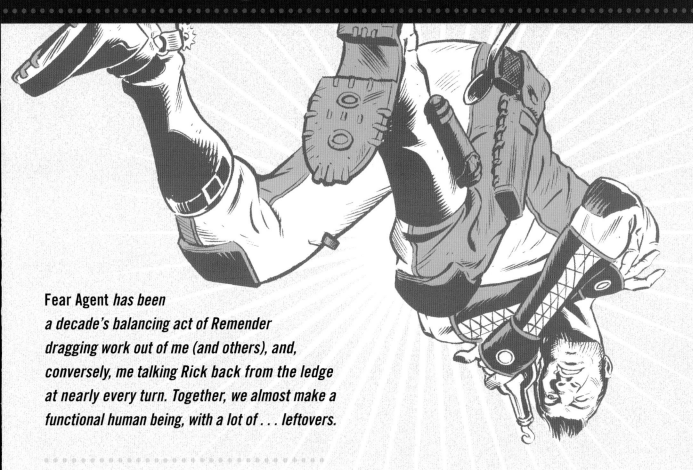

Fear Agent has been a decade's balancing act of Remender dragging work out of me (and others), and, conversely, me talking Rick back from the ledge at nearly every turn. Together, we almost make a functional human being, with a lot of . . . leftovers.

Setting the Stage

Last round, your friend and mine Rick Remender gave us his perspective on the birth of our be-stubbled spaceman love child. Rick is a brilliant writer and one of the most wildly creative folks I know. That's what attracted me to his work, and ultimately we fed off each other's energy, which made *Fear Agent* one of the most special projects either of us would ever put our names on. We were on the same page creatively, which made the work a joy and easy to become invested in.

In the year 2000, I was in college in Kentucky and toiling away on my first-ever comic, with a child-hood friend. Growing up on a farm, I'd been in-grained with a strong DIY mindset, and as I got older and more culturally aware, I saw how this translated to the world of music and art, and found that most of my favorite things were made by folks who went against the will of the mainstream powers that be and created from their inscrutable personal need to create what they wanted to see, rather than accepting the preapproved dreck that had been laid before them. I'd always been a fan of the perverse humor of underground comics and had a strong disdain for the establishment, so when I saw that there was this guy who was putting together a beautifully drawn series of some of the most irreverent filth ever printed and, because of one of his parodies, was getting the hammer dropped on him by a certain mermaid coffee shop turned urban virus, of course, I had to find out how to get in on the action. I concocted a couple of weird shorts which were added to the publication, and thus, Kieron Dwyer and, by extension, his kewpie-haired Salacious Crumb, Rick Remender, became some of my first industry friends.

The Kentucky crew prepared to take our first-ever book to our first-ever San Diego Comic-Con, and literally not knowing *anyone* else, we requested to be placed near Rick and Kieron. Little did we green-horns know that we'd be relegated to the ass end of the convention, on the other side of the pornography section, where presumably we were expected to die. Rather, we commiserated with our new (and only) friends, and Rick taught me that cartoonists sometimes drink to alleviate anger and pain.

Rick and I went our separate ways but stayed in touch to commiserate over the years, as the cartoonist's life delivered its gut-churning and devastating blows to each of us. We grew up in different scenes, but we were both very by-your-own-bootstraps kinda guys and had more in common than we ever could have known. We'd each found ourselves on the shit end of the stick more than a few times, and because of that, I think we found relief and comfort in trusting each other. The primordial soup of our love was rich and ready. All it needed was a spark to bring it to life.

A New Gang of Idiots

I had been doing covers for various projects and had just finished one that involved a bubble-helmeted guy fighting a big, tentacled space monster, with an old sci-fi-style rocket crashed in the background on a bleak lunar landscape. Rick reached out to me one day to tell me how much he enjoyed it, and we started talking at length about the joys of old EC comics. I literally learned to read from *Mad* magazines that my uncle had left around the house when I was a kid, and as I got older, found myself digging through the back-issue bins to find more Jack Davis, John Severin, and Will Elder. I had amassed a nice little trove of reprints, mostly from EC's *Tales from the Crypt*, *Two-Fisted Tales*, *Frontline Combat*, and *Shock SuspenStories* books. Rick was more in tune with the sci-fi stuff that Wally Wood and Al Williamson had done for *Weird Science* and *Weird Fantasy*, and urged me to dig them up. Next thing I knew, we were two full-blown EC junkies, cooking up our way to embrace that pioneering aesthetic and create a wild science fantasy that filled that hole in the modern publishing landscape as we saw it. Within a couple of feverishly giddy phone calls, *Fear Agent* was pretty much developed, stem to stern.

We proceeded to pour ourselves into it, and little did we realize how much. We were stepping into an unfilled niche, and this brand of sci-fi had more or less proven itself to be commercially nonviable. As we were nearing the point of diving in, I was offered a good paying job on another book, which I had to take. We hunted for a collaborator, and after a few candidates washed out, we found Jerome Opeña, whose work absolutely blew me away. He stepped in and made *Fear Agent* something truly special. I tried to juggle both my new jobs and excelled at neither. We were faced with hardships from without and within, but Rick, much like the bull-headed hero we created, would not give up so easily. He reached out to a lot of friends, who helped us along in ways large and small. Despite some truly harrowing passes, we managed to get Heath's story out and on the stands. Our friendships were tested and battle hardened, and our love manifested itself into the tale of this booze-soaked old space soldier. Our hopes and fears played out in his pages. Our frailties and bravado, rejection and isolation, our victories turned to ash, our oppressors and friends in the shadows—all took flight as often thinly veiled metaphors, if hidden at all. Despite every repeated sign from the universe that this book was not meant to exist, we managed, somehow, to get his story told the way we'd always wanted.

And so, here you have it—a five-hundred-and-some-page tome, serving as pretty damn strong evidence that there is indeed, as the saying goes, some kind of Providence that protects idiots, drunkards, and children.

Thanks for coming along for the ride.

—Tony Moore

FOREWORD

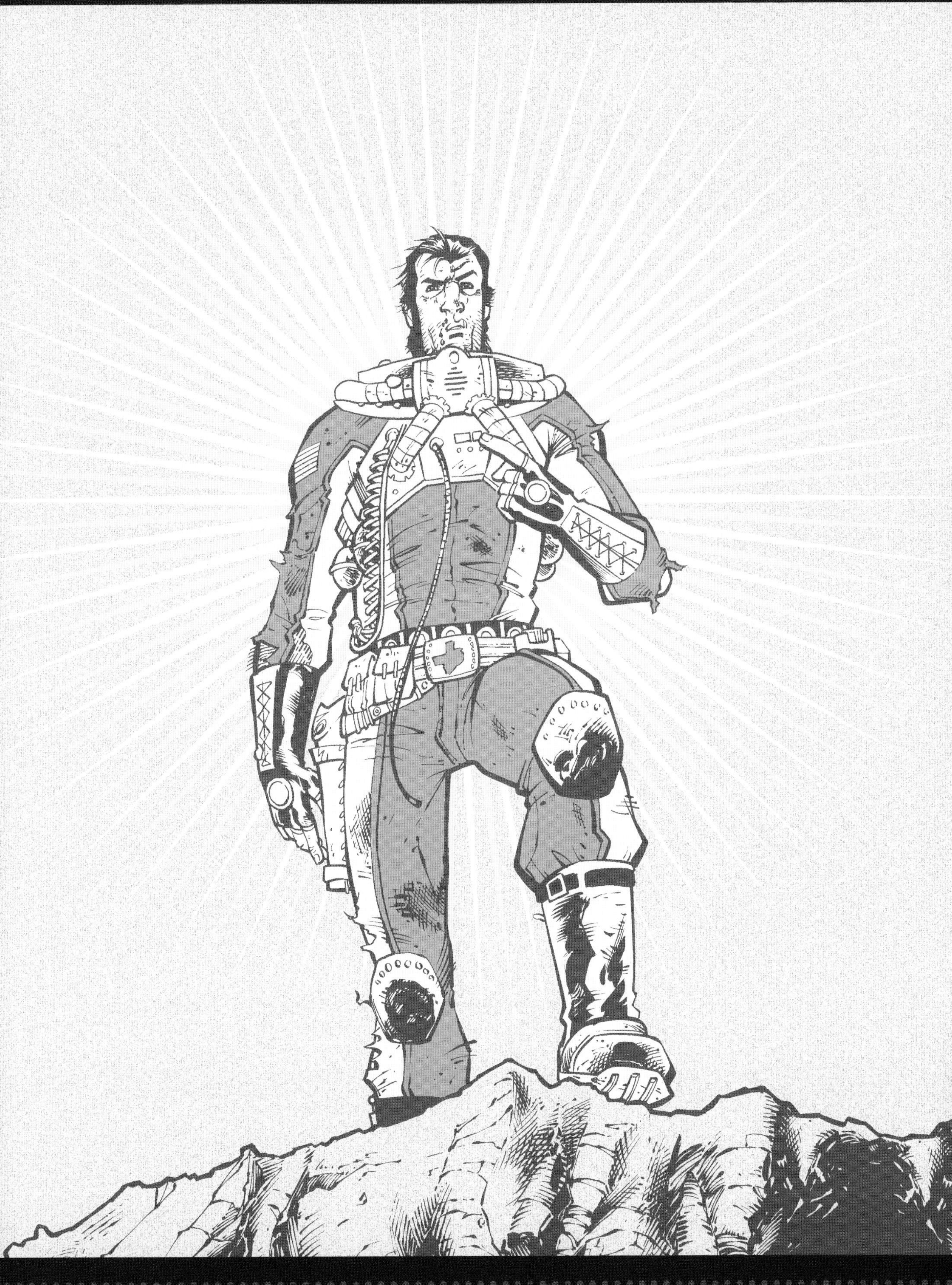

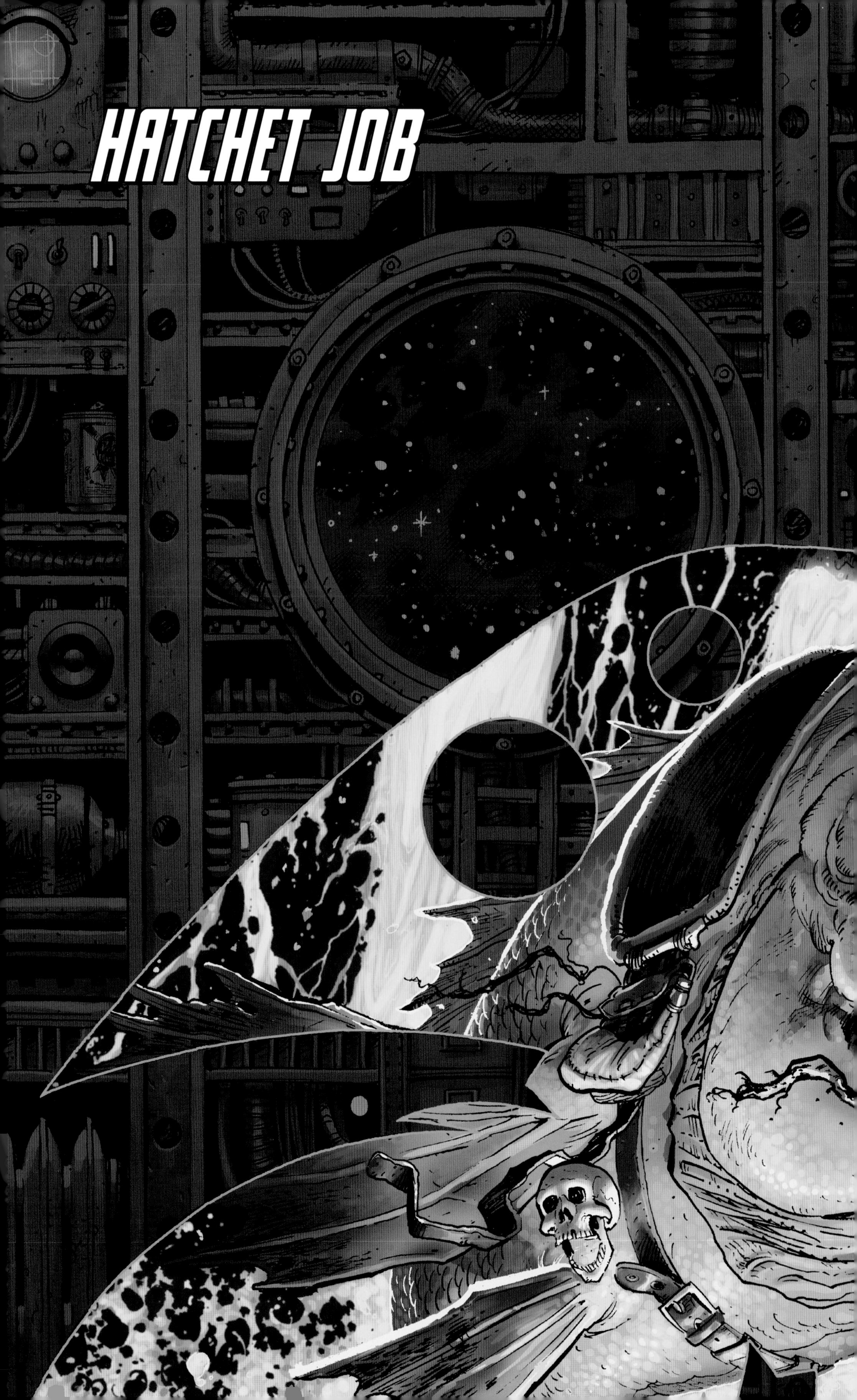
HATCHET JOB

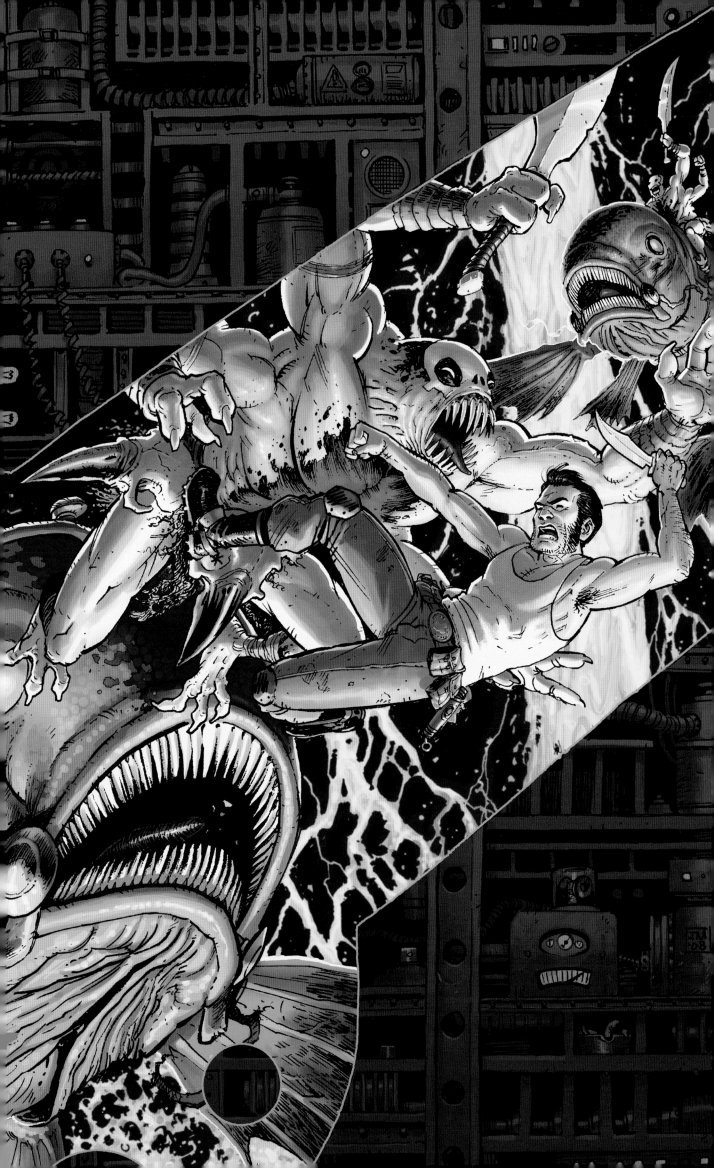

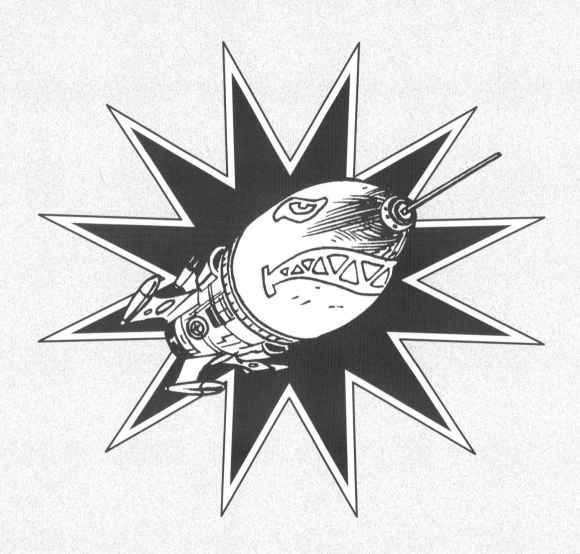

CHAPTER 1

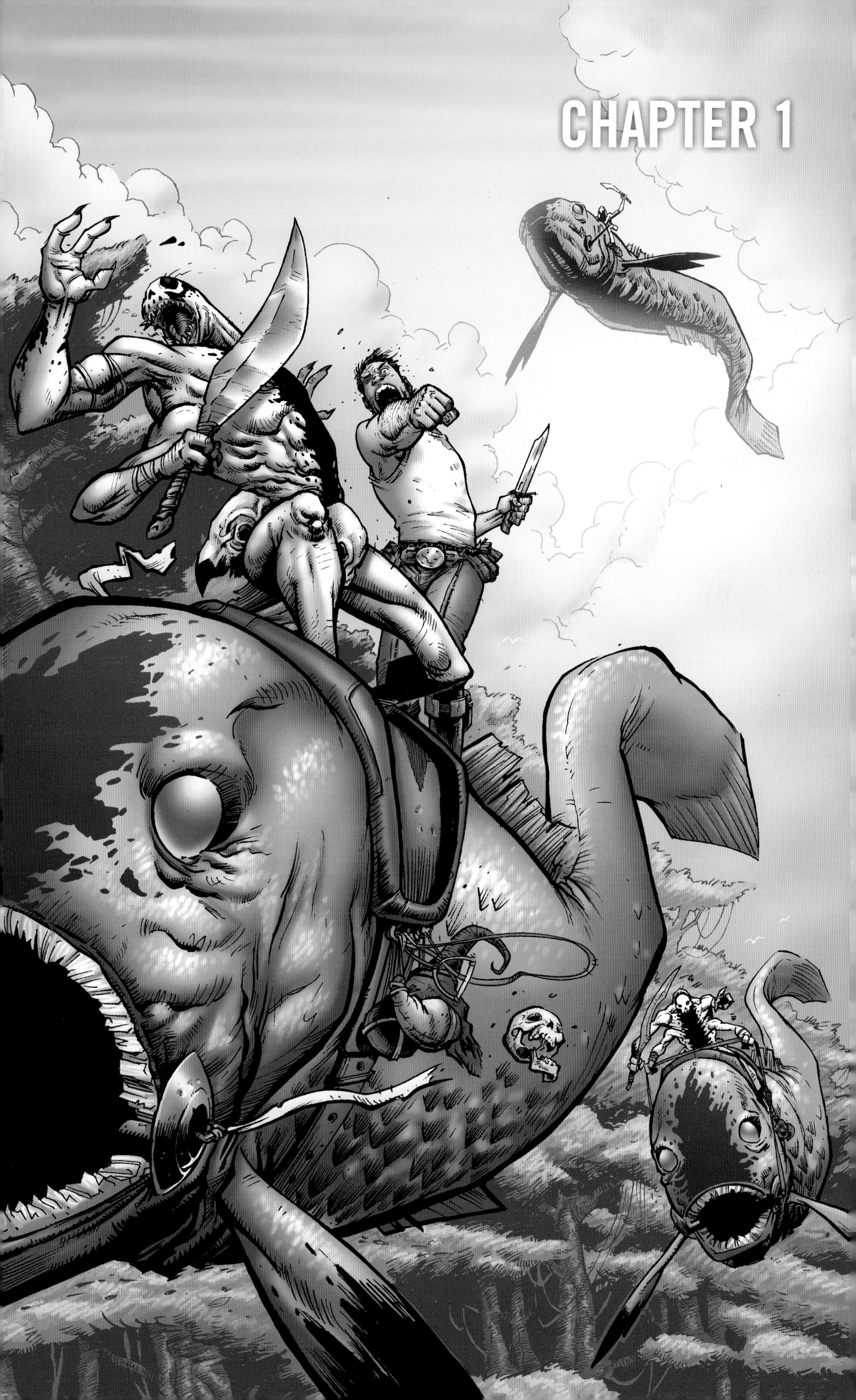

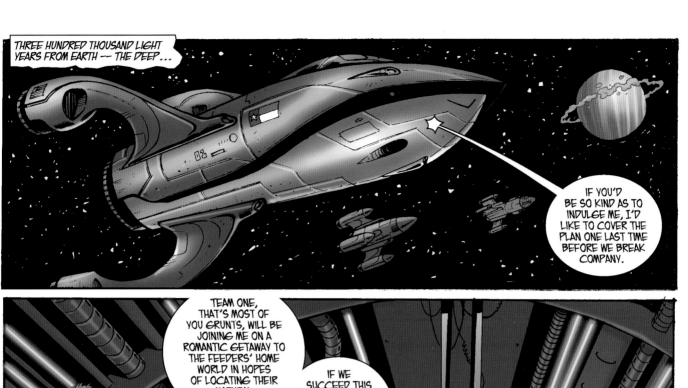

THREE HUNDRED THOUSAND LIGHT YEARS FROM EARTH -- THE DEEP...

IF YOU'D BE SO KIND AS TO INDULGE ME, I'D LIKE TO COVER THE PLAN ONE LAST TIME BEFORE WE BREAK COMPANY.

TEAM ONE, THAT'S MOST OF YOU GRUNTS, WILL BE JOINING ME ON A ROMANTIC GETAWAY TO THE FEEDERS' HOME WORLD IN HOPES OF LOCATING THEIR NATURAL PREDATOR.

IF WE SUCCEED THIS MAY WELL PROVE TO BE THE KEY TO RECLAIMING EARTH FROM THE FEEDERS.

OBVIOUSLY, GIVEN THE HIGH PROBABILITY OF FAILURE, IT'D BE RECKLESS TO THROW ALL HUMANITY'S EGGS IN THIS ONE BASKET.

HIGH PROBABILITY OF FAILURE... WAY TO MOTIVATE THE TROOPS, GENERAL MACARTHUR.

CHARLOTTE WILL HEAD A SECOND MISSION, IN THE HUNT FOR INHABITABLE PLANETS TO RELOCATE WHAT REMAINS OF OUR SPECIES.

COMMUNICATIONS WILL BE DEAD AT THESE DISTANCES, SO REMEMBER--WE RENDEZVOUS BACK HERE IN TWO MONTHS.

DUE TO HER TRAVELS AND KNOWLEDGE OF THESE AREAS, MARA HAS REQUESTED TO SERVE AS CHIEF NAVIGATION OFFICER FOR TEAM TWO.

WHAT?

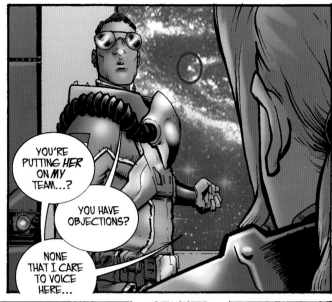

YOU'RE PUTTING *HER* ON *MY* TEAM...?

YOU HAVE OBJECTIONS?

NONE THAT I CARE TO VOICE HERE...

YOU STILL COMIN' WITH US, HUSTON?

I RECKON SO.

GUESS THAT LEAVES ME AS THE ONLY GAL YOU'LL NEED TA KEEP CONTENTED.

THEN SISTER, I HOPE YOU CAN OBTAIN CONTENTMENT FROM A HALF-SAIL WHISKY DICK.

AH, *COME ON!* I'M SITTIN' RIGHT HERE.

HAH!

OKAY, SAY YOUR GOODBYES, PEOPLE.

WE SPLIT COMPANIES AT FOURTEEN HUNDRED HOURS.

HEATH, YOU STILL UP FOR A FOOD RUN ONCE WE SPLIT?

NOT MUCH CHOICE IN THE MATTER--ANNIE'S THE ONLY SHIP BUILT FOR A FAST LAND.

PERFECT, SO YOU DON'T MIND IF I TAG ALONG?

GIVE US SOME TIME TO GET TO KNOW EACH OTHER.

YEAH, *GREAT*... WE'LL PAINT EACH OTHER'S NAILS AN' TALK ABOUT BOYS...

IF YOU'LL EXCUSE ME NOW...

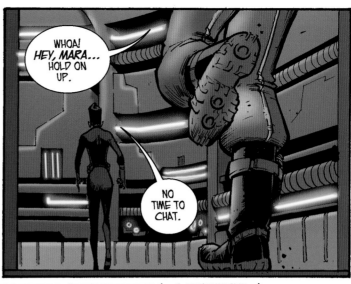

WHOA! *HEY, MARA*... HOLD ON UP.

NO TIME TO CHAT.

DAMMIT, MARA-- ENOUGH COLD SHOULDER.

LISTEN-- WHERE I'M GOING... WELL, IT'S JUST ABOUT THE WORST PLACE IN THE UNIVERSE.

I CAN'T HANDLE IT WITH THIS DRAMA RENTIN' SPACE IN MY HEAD.

BABY, CHAR'S IN MY PAST...

ONLY BECAUSE *SHE* MOVED ON.

AND IF WE SURVIVE THIS IDIOCY, I PLAN ON DOING THE SAME... HOPEFULLY WITH YOU BY MY SIDE.

WHADDAYA SAY? PLANT ONE ON ME FER GOOD LUCK?

HEATH, I...

I...I'M SORRY.

I'VE HAD ENOUGH OF YOUR LUCK FOR ONE LIFETIME.

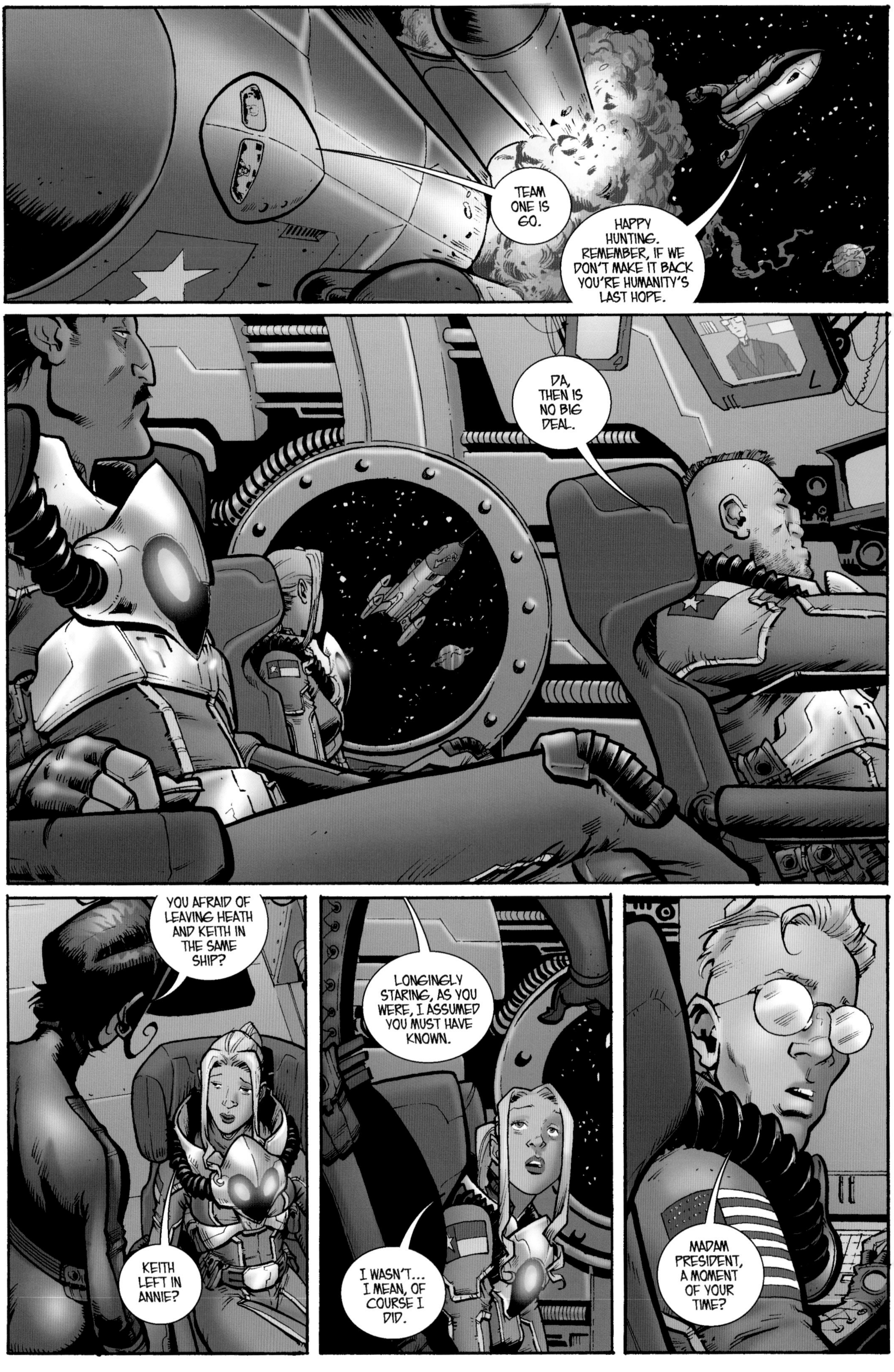
TEAM ONE IS GO.
HAPPY HUNTING. REMEMBER, IF WE DON'T MAKE IT BACK YOU'RE HUMANITY'S LAST HOPE.
DA, THEN IS NO BIG DEAL.
YOU AFRAID OF LEAVING HEATH AND KEITH IN THE SAME SHIP?
KEITH LEFT IN ANNIE?
LONGINGLY STARING, AS YOU WERE, I ASSUMED YOU MUST HAVE KNOWN.
I WASN'T... I MEAN, OF COURSE I DID.
MADAM PRESIDENT, A MOMENT OF YOUR TIME?

WE'VE GOT A FEW OPTIONS NEARBY. OLIVER AND HIS PEOPLE WERE HEADED HERE TO FLIN.
ACCORDIN' TA HEATHROW, AIN'T NOT BUT FLY-PEOPLE AND GIANT SPIDERS THERE.
THIS GREENISH PLANET HERE ISN'T LISTED ON THE UNITED SYSTEMS LOGS, SO IT'S NOT A MEMBER AND COULD BE UNINHABITED.
WHOA--! SCOTT, PULL IN ON IT.
IS THAT...? WELL I'LL BE A MONKEY'S UNCLE, IT SURE IS.
WHAT YOU'RE LOOKING AT IS A WORLD KNOWN AS THE BOG.
THE BOG...?
THAT PLACE IS PACKED TO THE GILLS WITH VICIOUS, AMPHIBIAN CREATURES, BAD JUJU.
OVER HERE, NEAVSIVIA... THIS IS THE ONE WE WANT.
WELL, WE'LL HAVE TA START SOMEWHERE.
ANDI, SET A COURSE TO NEAVSIVIA.
IMMEDIATELY, MADAM PRESIDENT.
SNIFF-SNIFF...

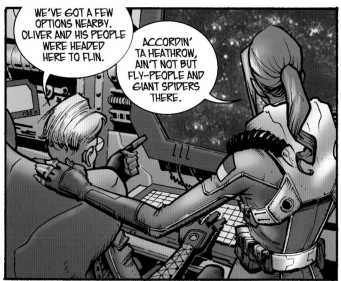

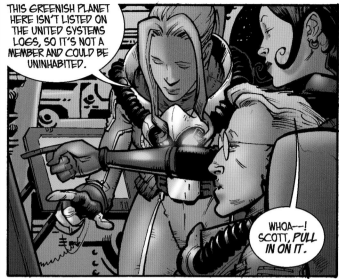

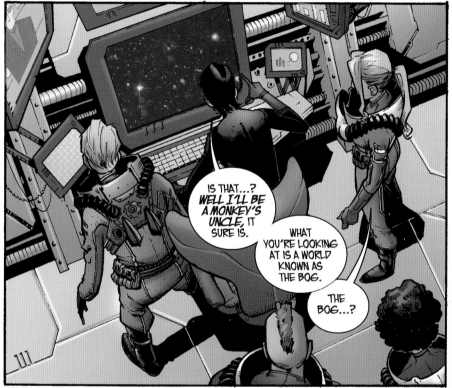

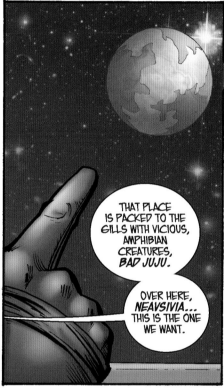

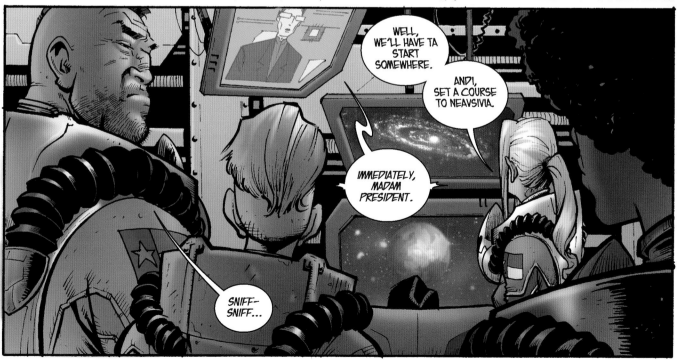

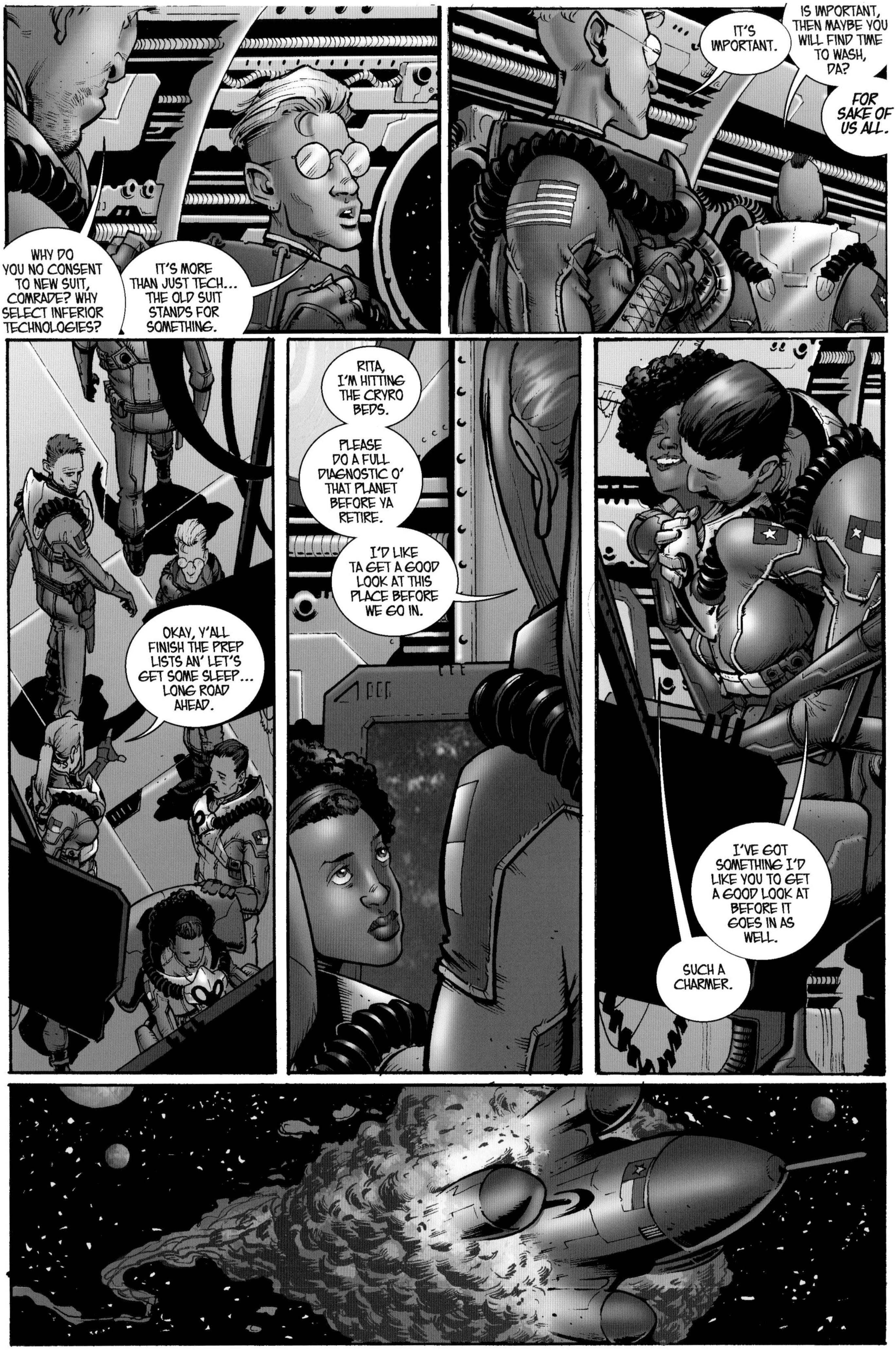
WHY DO YOU NO CONSENT TO NEW SUIT, COMRADE? WHY SELECT INFERIOR TECHNOLOGIES?
IT'S MORE THAN JUST TECH... THE OLD SUIT STANDS FOR SOMETHING.
IT'S IMPORTANT.
IS IMPORTANT, THEN MAYBE YOU WILL FIND TIME TO WASH, DA?
FOR SAKE OF US ALL.
OKAY, Y'ALL FINISH THE PREP LISTS AN' LET'S GET SOME SLEEP... LONG ROAD AHEAD.
RITA, I'M HITTING THE CRYRO BEDS.
PLEASE DO A FULL DIAGNOSTIC O' THAT PLANET BEFORE YA RETIRE.
I'D LIKE TA GET A GOOD LOOK AT THIS PLACE BEFORE WE GO IN.
I'VE GOT SOMETHING I'D LIKE YOU TO GET A GOOD LOOK AT BEFORE IT GOES IN AS WELL.
SUCH A CHARMER.

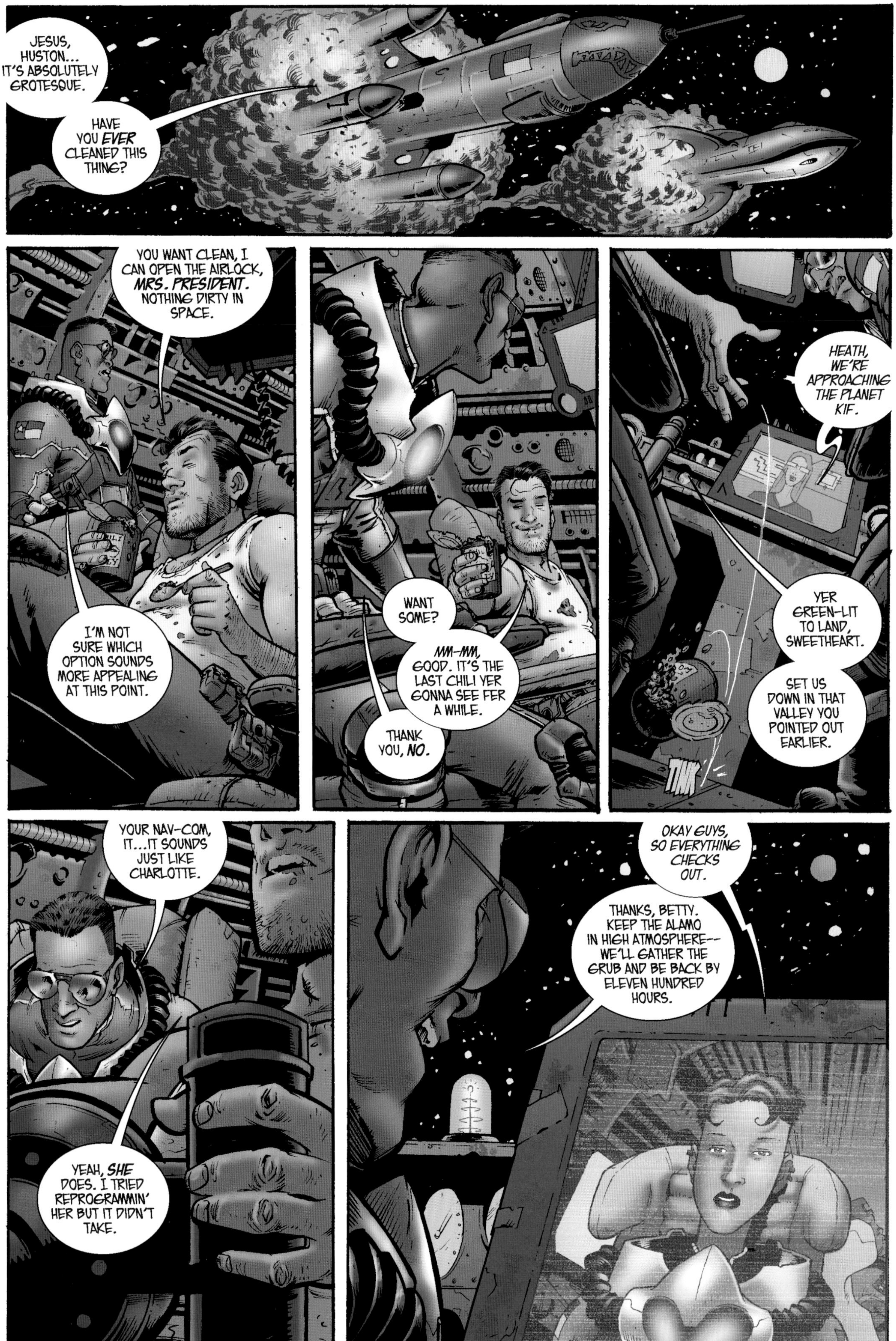
JESUS, HUSTON... IT'S ABSOLUTELY GROTESQUE.
HAVE YOU EVER CLEANED THIS THING?
YOU WANT CLEAN, I CAN OPEN THE AIRLOCK, MRS. PRESIDENT. NOTHING DIRTY IN SPACE.
I'M NOT SURE WHICH OPTION SOUNDS MORE APPEALING AT THIS POINT.
WANT SOME?
MM-MM, GOOD. IT'S THE LAST CHILI YER GONNA SEE FER A WHILE.
THANK YOU, NO.
HEATH, WE'RE APPROACHING THE PLANET KIF.
YER GREEN-LIT TO LAND, SWEETHEART.
SET US DOWN IN THAT VALLEY YOU POINTED OUT EARLIER.
TINK
YOUR NAV-COM, IT...IT SOUNDS JUST LIKE CHARLOTTE.
YEAH, SHE DOES. I TRIED REPROGRAMMIN' HER BUT IT DIDN'T TAKE.
OKAY GUYS, SO EVERYTHING CHECKS OUT.
THANKS, BETTY. KEEP THE ALAMO IN HIGH ATMOSPHERE-- WE'LL GATHER THE GRUB AND BE BACK BY ELEVEN HUNDRED HOURS.

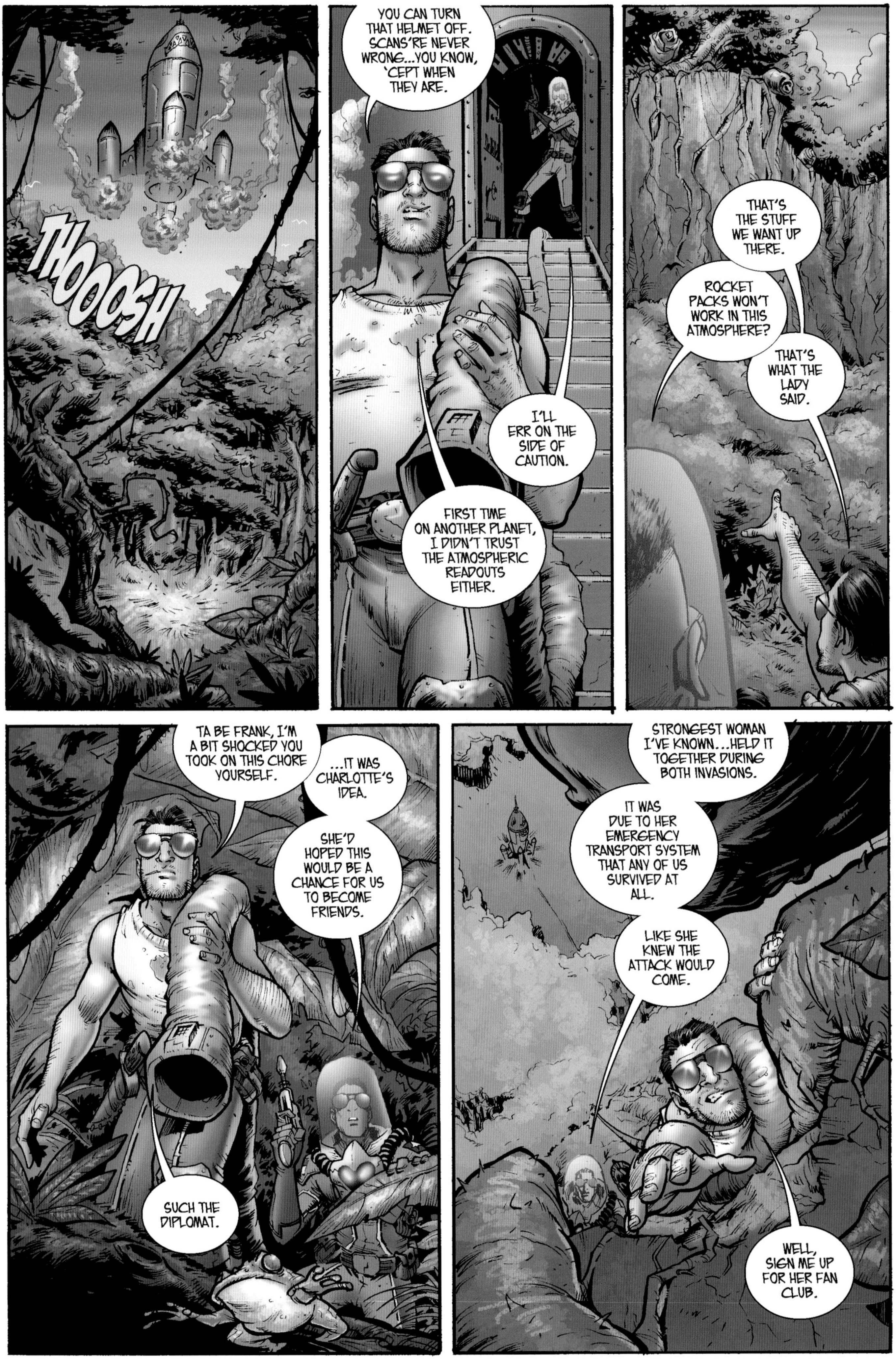
THOOOSH
YOU CAN TURN THAT HELMET OFF. SCANS'RE NEVER WRONG...YOU KNOW, 'CEPT WHEN THEY ARE.
I'LL ERR ON THE SIDE OF CAUTION.
FIRST TIME ON ANOTHER PLANET, I DIDN'T TRUST THE ATMOSPHERIC READOUTS EITHER.
THAT'S THE STUFF WE WANT UP THERE.
ROCKET PACKS WON'T WORK IN THIS ATMOSPHERE?
THAT'S WHAT THE LADY SAID.
TA BE FRANK, I'M A BIT SHOCKED YOU TOOK ON THIS CHORE YOURSELF.
...IT WAS CHARLOTTE'S IDEA.
SHE'D HOPED THIS WOULD BE A CHANCE FOR US TO BECOME FRIENDS.
SUCH THE DIPLOMAT.
STRONGEST WOMAN I'VE KNOWN...HELD IT TOGETHER DURING BOTH INVASIONS.
IT WAS DUE TO HER EMERGENCY TRANSPORT SYSTEM THAT ANY OF US SURVIVED AT ALL.
LIKE SHE KNEW THE ATTACK WOULD COME.
WELL, SIGN ME UP FOR HER FAN CLUB.

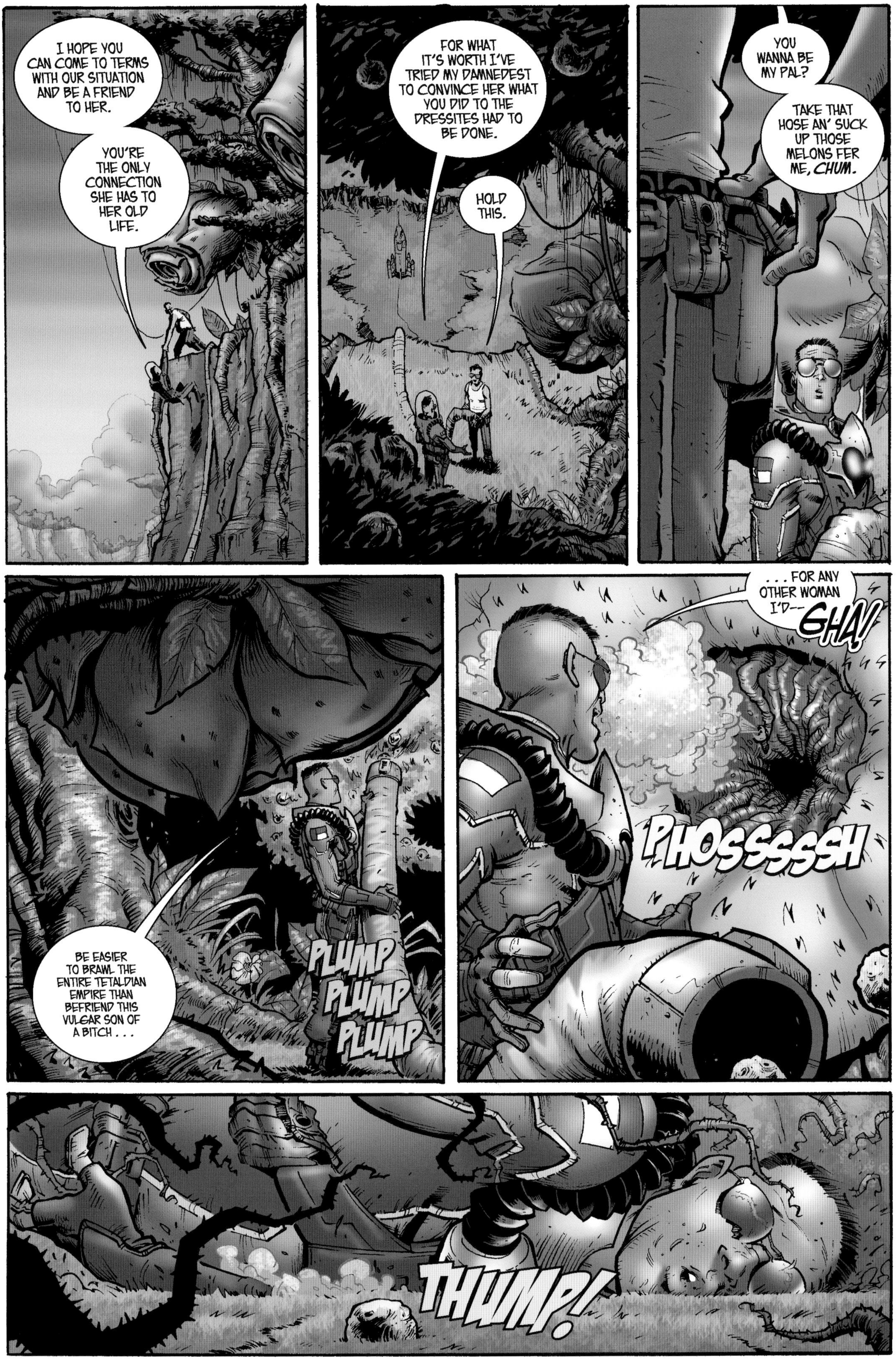
I HOPE YOU CAN COME TO TERMS WITH OUR SITUATION AND BE A FRIEND TO HER.
YOU'RE THE ONLY CONNECTION SHE HAS TO HER OLD LIFE.
FOR WHAT IT'S WORTH I'VE TRIED MY DAMNEDEST TO CONVINCE HER WHAT YOU DID TO THE DRESSITES HAD TO BE DONE.
HOLD THIS.
YOU WANNA BE MY PAL?
TAKE THAT HOSE AN' SUCK UP THOSE MELONS FER ME, CHUM.
BE EASIER TO BRAWL THE ENTIRE TETALDIAN EMPIRE THAN BEFRIEND THIS VULGAR SON OF A BITCH . . .
PLUMP
PLUMP
PLUMP
. . . FOR ANY OTHER WOMAN I'D--GHA!
PHOSSSSSH
THUMP!

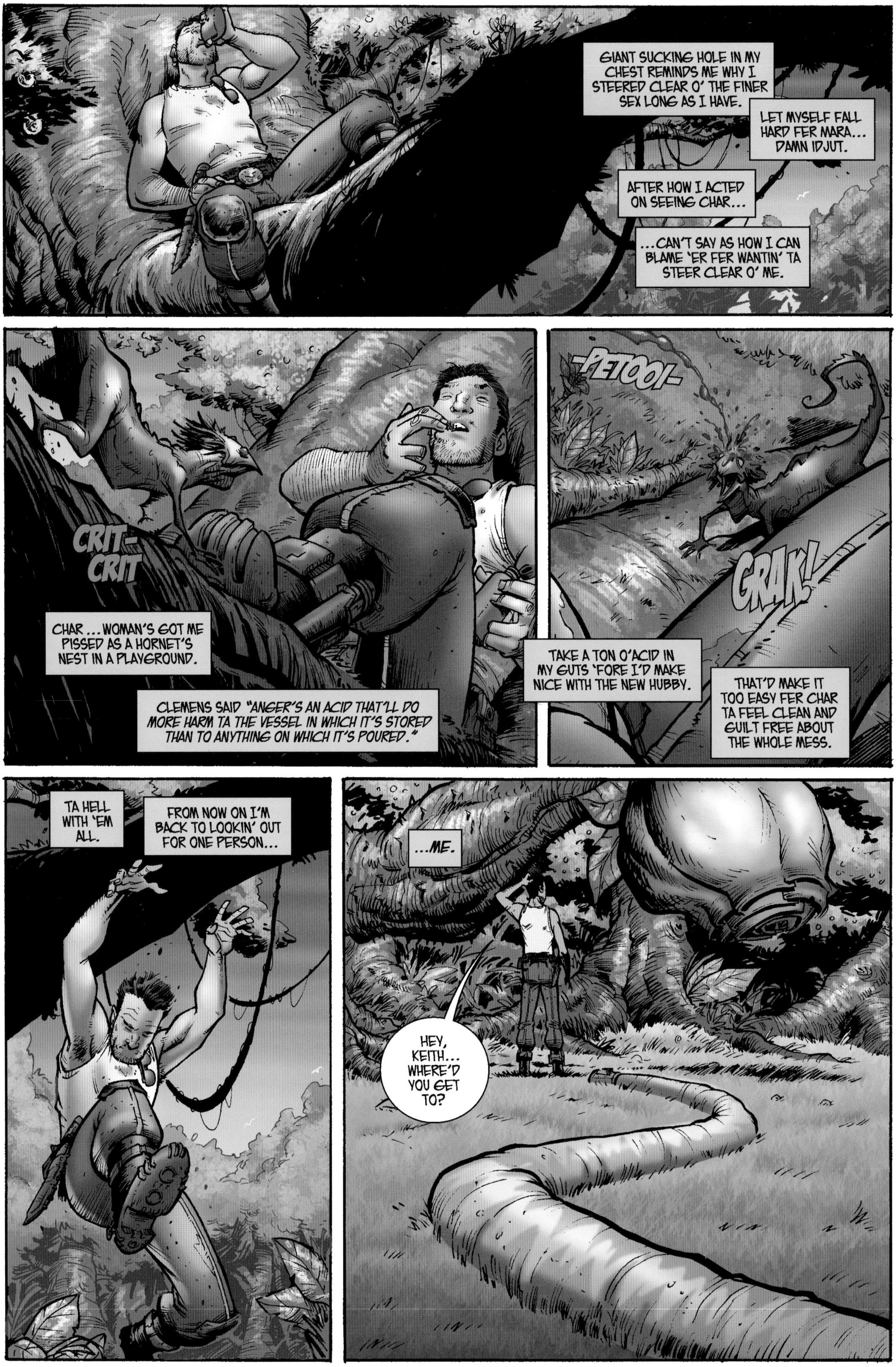
GIANT SUCKING HOLE IN MY CHEST REMINDS ME WHY I STEERED CLEAR O' THE FINER SEX LONG AS I HAVE.
LET MYSELF FALL HARD FER MARA... DAMN IDJUT.
AFTER HOW I ACTED ON SEEING CHAR...
...CAN'T SAY AS HOW I CAN BLAME 'ER FER WANTIN' TA STEER CLEAR O' ME.
CRIT-CRIT
CHAR... WOMAN'S GOT ME PISSED AS A HORNET'S NEST IN A PLAYGROUND.
CLEMENS SAID "ANGER'S AN ACID THAT'LL DO MORE HARM TA THE VESSEL IN WHICH IT'S STORED THAN TO ANYTHING ON WHICH IT'S POURED."
-PETOOI-
GRAK!
TAKE A TON O'ACID IN MY GUTS 'FORE I'D MAKE NICE WITH THE NEW HUBBY.
THAT'D MAKE IT TOO EASY FER CHAR TA FEEL CLEAN AND GUILT FREE ABOUT THE WHOLE MESS.
TA HELL WITH 'EM ALL.
FROM NOW ON I'M BACK TO LOOKIN' OUT FOR ONE PERSON...
...ME.
HEY, KEITH... WHERE'D YOU GET TO?

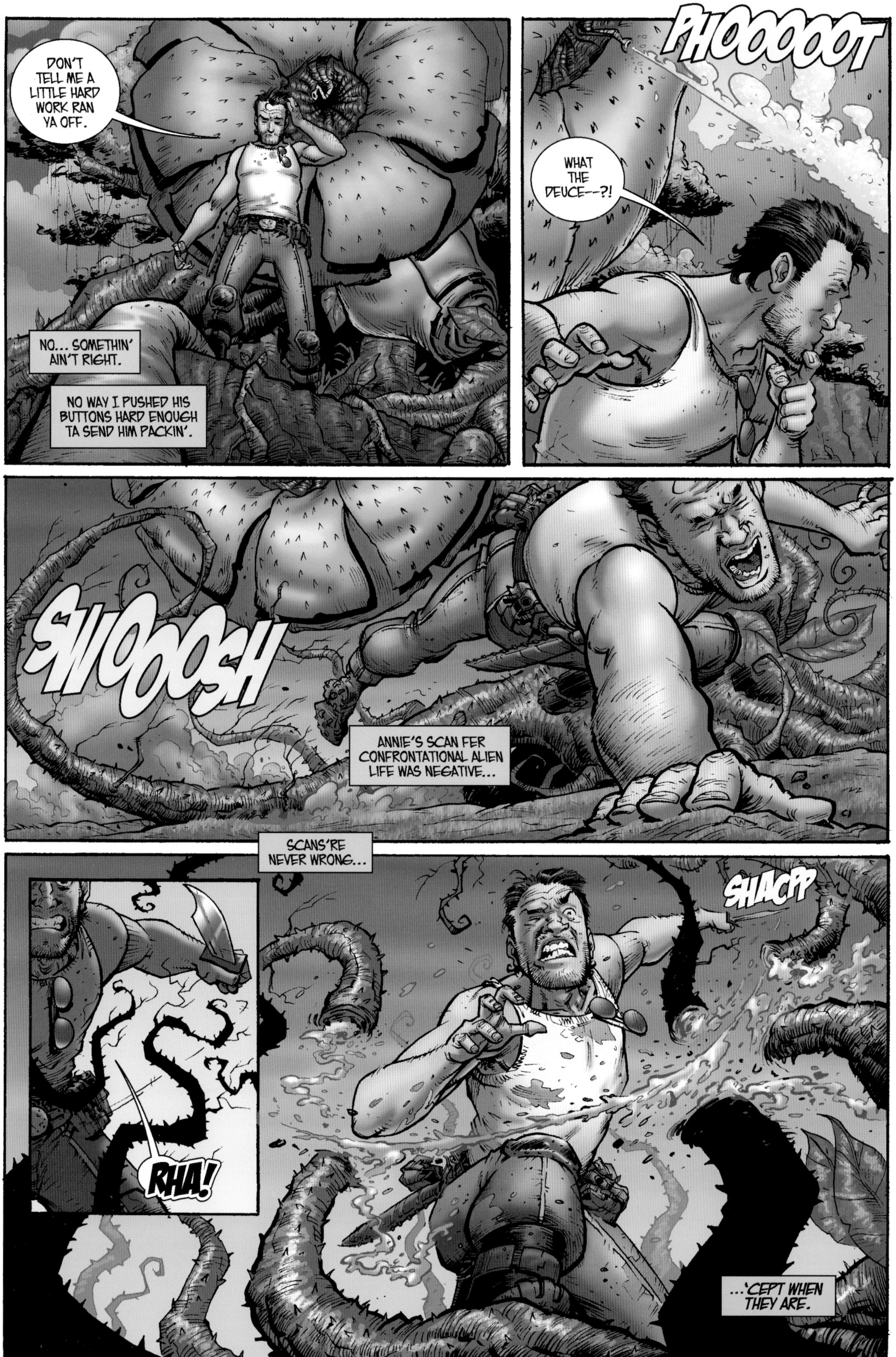
DON'T TELL ME A LITTLE HARD WORK RAN YA OFF.
NO... SOMETHIN' AIN'T RIGHT.
NO WAY I PUSHED HIS BUTTONS HARD ENOUGH TA SEND HIM PACKIN'.
PHOOOOOT
WHAT THE DEUCE--?!
SWOOOSH
ANNIE'S SCAN FER CONFRONTATIONAL ALIEN LIFE WAS NEGATIVE...
SCANS'RE NEVER WRONG...
RHA!
SHACPP
...'CEPT WHEN THEY ARE.

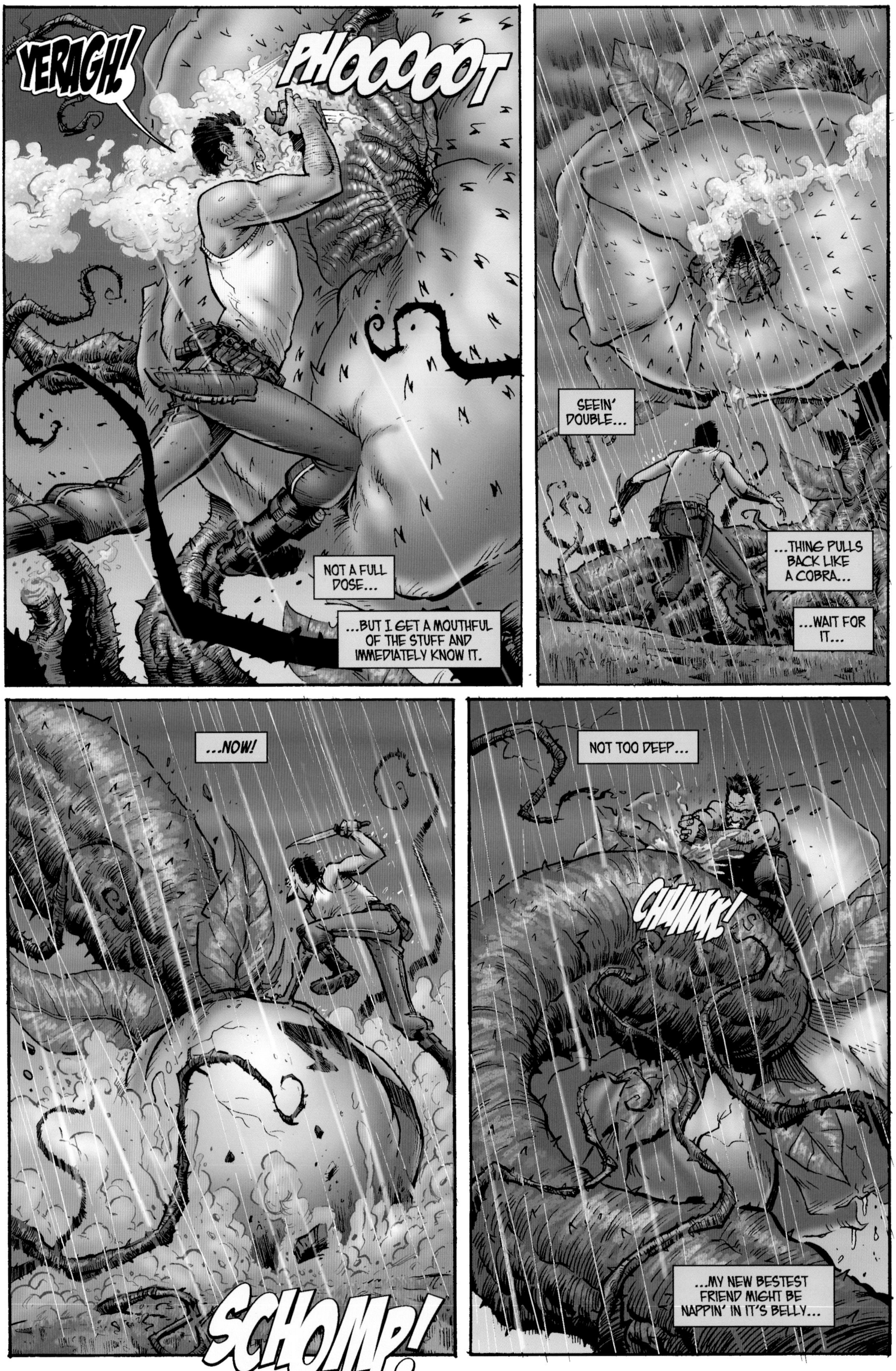
YERAGH!
PHOOOOOT
NOT A FULL DOSE...
...BUT I GET A MOUTHFUL OF THE STUFF AND IMMEDIATELY KNOW IT.
SEEIN' DOUBLE...
...THING PULLS BACK LIKE A COBRA...
...WAIT FOR IT...
...NOW!
SCHOMP!
NOT TOO DEEP...
CHUNKK!
...MY NEW BESTEST FRIEND MIGHT BE NAPPIN' IN IT'S BELLY...

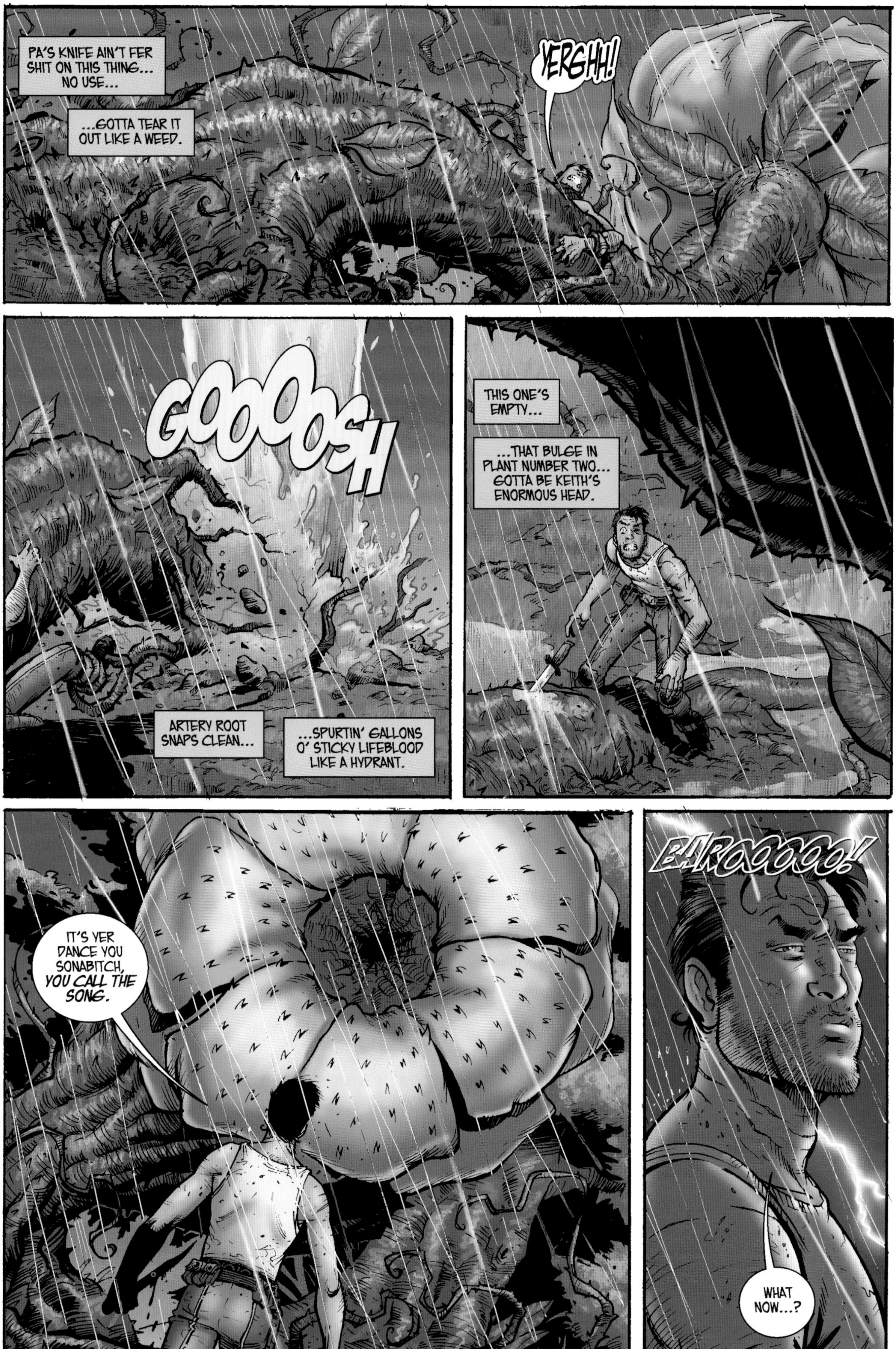
PA'S KNIFE AIN'T FER SHIT ON THIS THING... NO USE...
...GOTTA TEAR IT OUT LIKE A WEED.
YERGHH!
GOOOOSH
ARTERY ROOT SNAPS CLEAN...
...SPURTIN' GALLONS O' STICKY LIFEBLOOD LIKE A HYDRANT.
THIS ONE'S EMPTY...
...THAT BULGE IN PLANT NUMBER TWO... GOTTA BE KEITH'S ENORMOUS HEAD.
IT'S YER DANCE YOU SONABITCH, YOU CALL THE SONG.
BAROOOOOO!
WHAT NOW...?

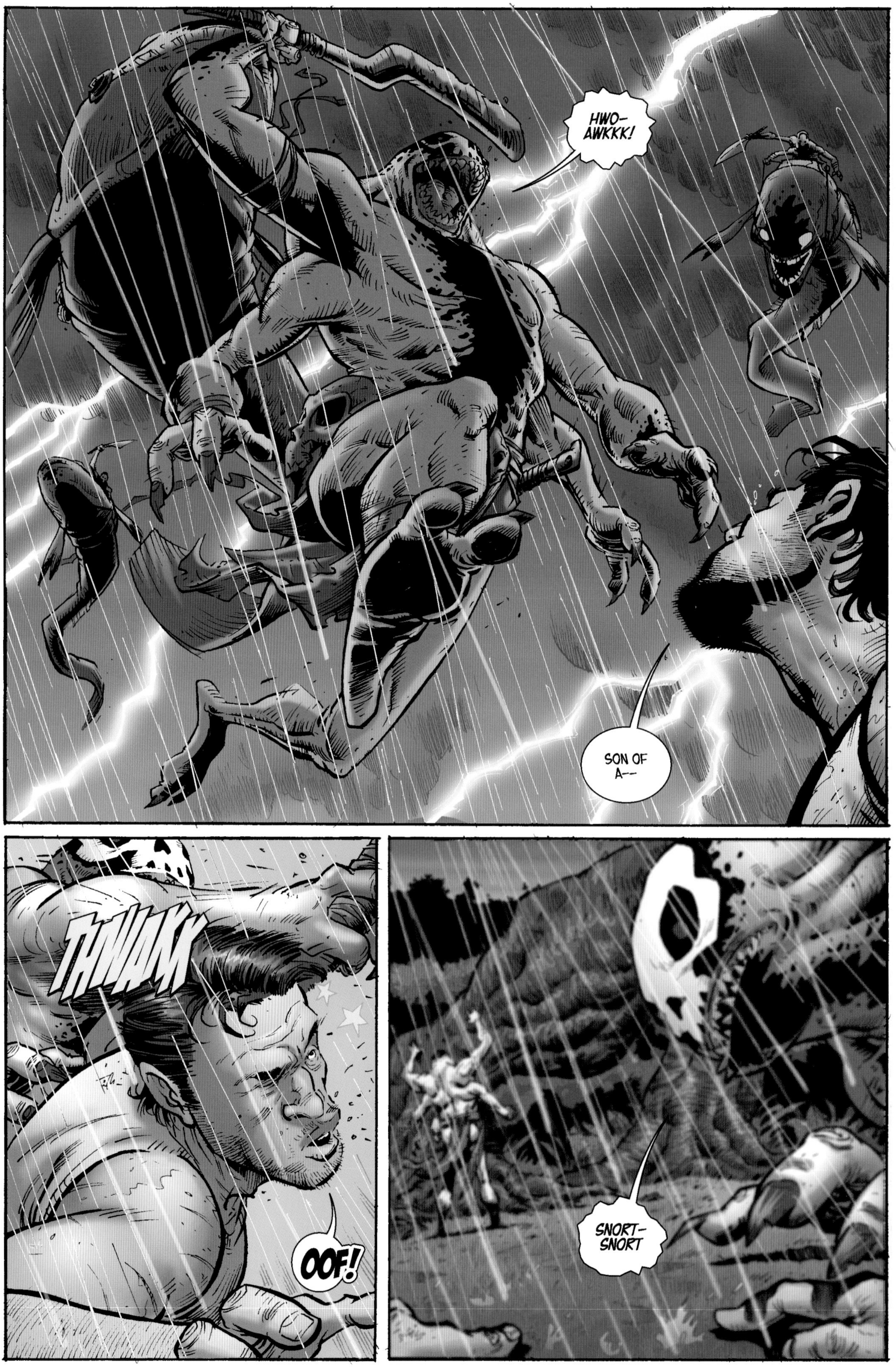
HWO-
AWKKK!
SON OF
A--
THWAKK
OOF!
SNORT-
SNORT

LATER...

GHA--!

FLOATIN' A MILE ABOVE GROUND WITH A BROKEN JAW...

FILE UNDER "BAD WAYS TO WAKE UP."

THINK UP THREE DIFFERENT WAYS TO ESCAPE WHEN I SEE KEITH.

HE'S A RIGHT TOOL, BUT I CAN'T ABANDON HIM TO THIS.

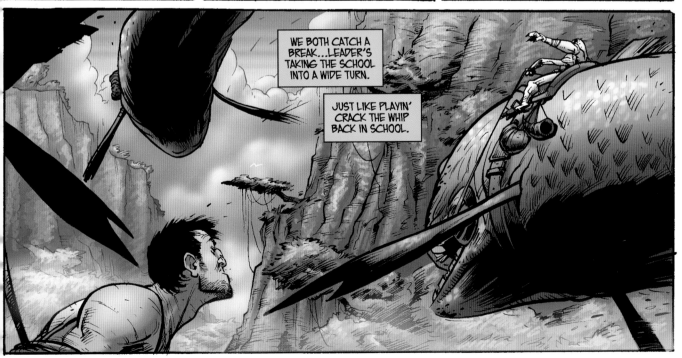

WE BOTH CATCH A BREAK...LEADER'S TAKING THE SCHOOL INTO A WIDE TURN.

JUST LIKE PLAYIN' CRACK THE WHIP BACK IN SCHOOL.

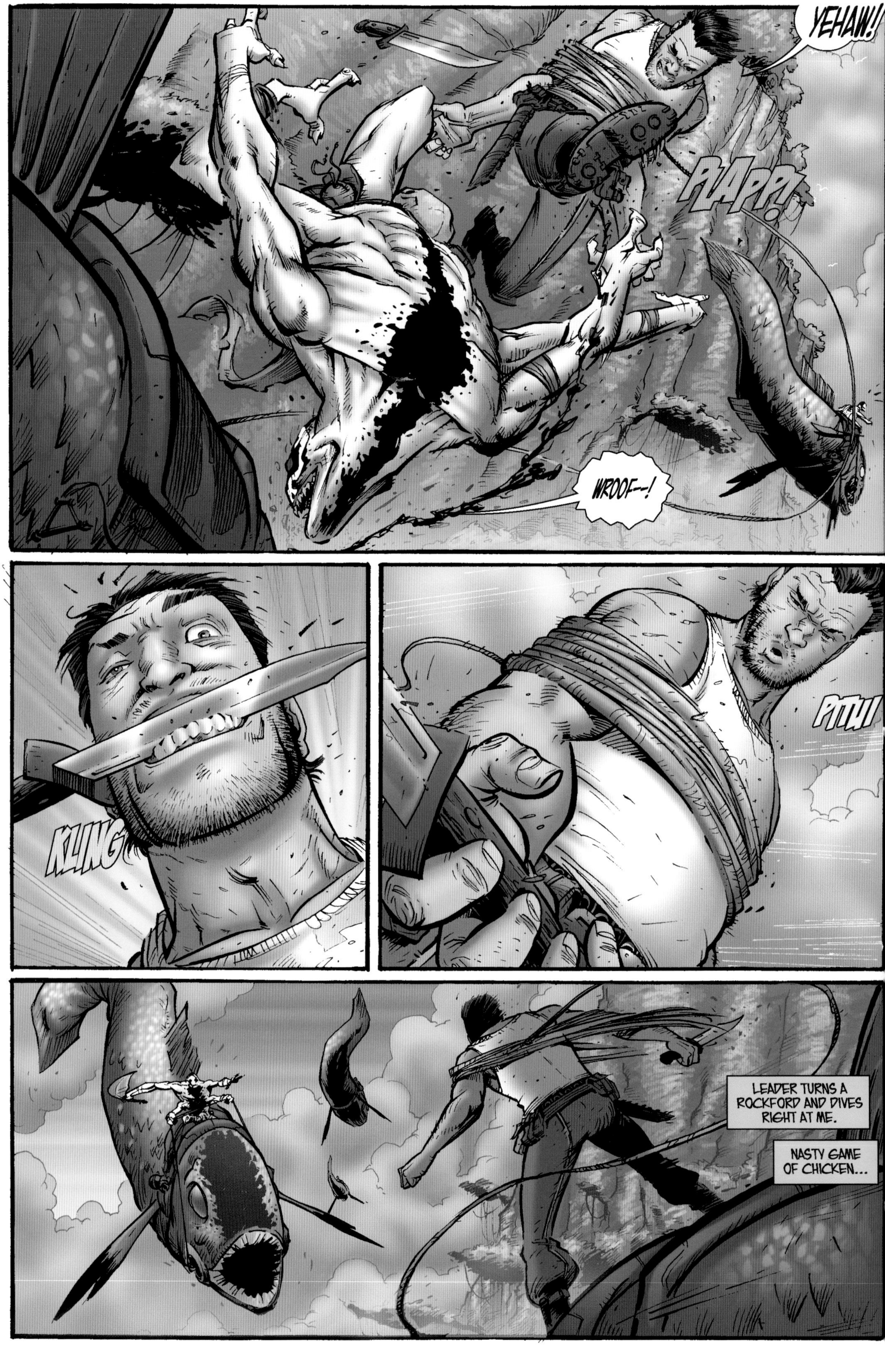
YEHAW!
PLAPP!
WROOF--!
KLING
PTUI
LEADER TURNS A ROCKFORD AND DIVES RIGHT AT ME.
NASTY GAME OF CHICKEN...

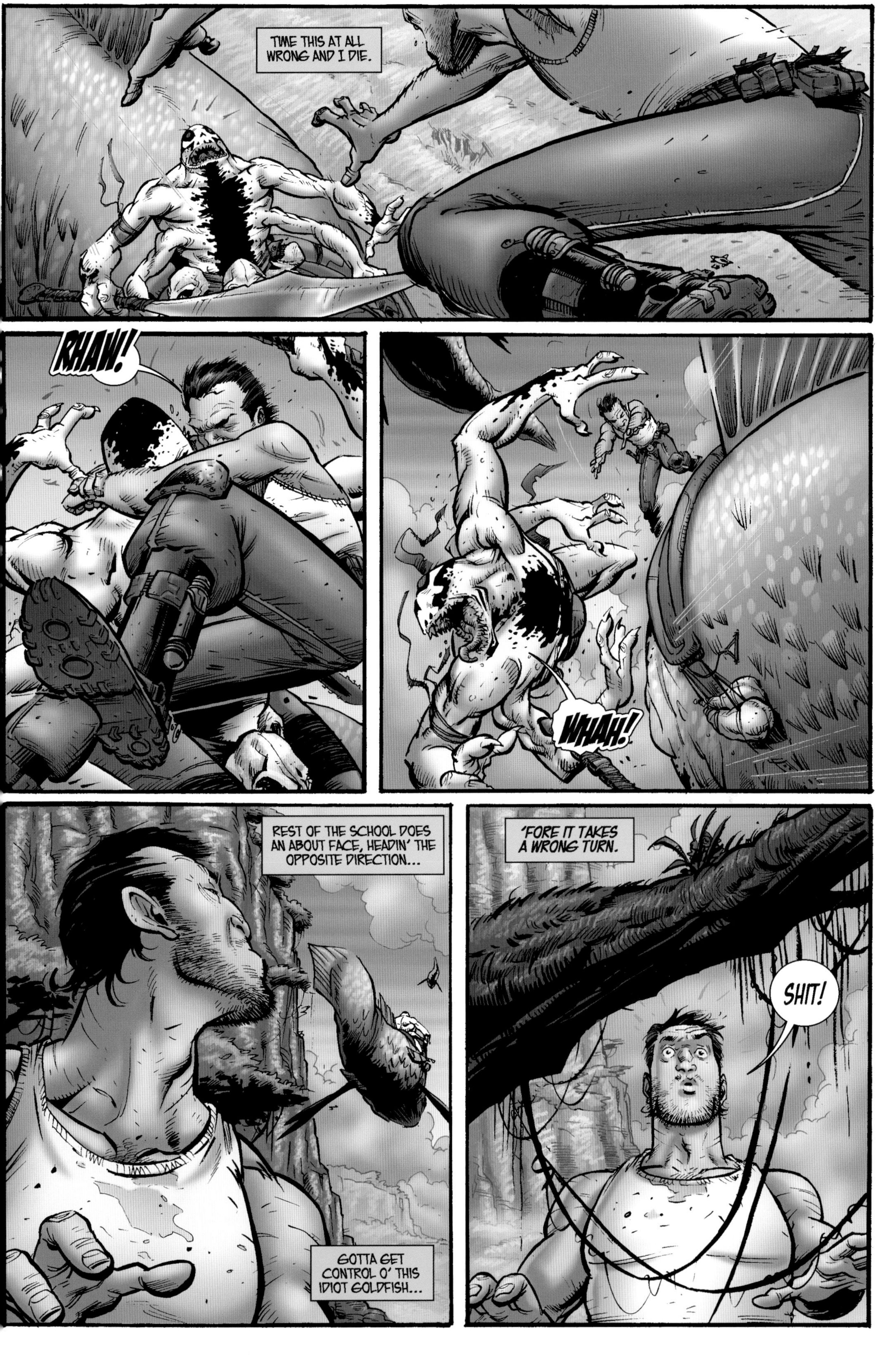

TIME THIS AT ALL WRONG AND I DIE.
RHAW!
WHAH!
REST OF THE SCHOOL DOES AN ABOUT FACE, HEADIN' THE OPPOSITE DIRECTION...
GOTTA GET CONTROL O' THIS IDIOT GOLDFISH...
'FORE IT TAKES A WRONG TURN.
SHIT!

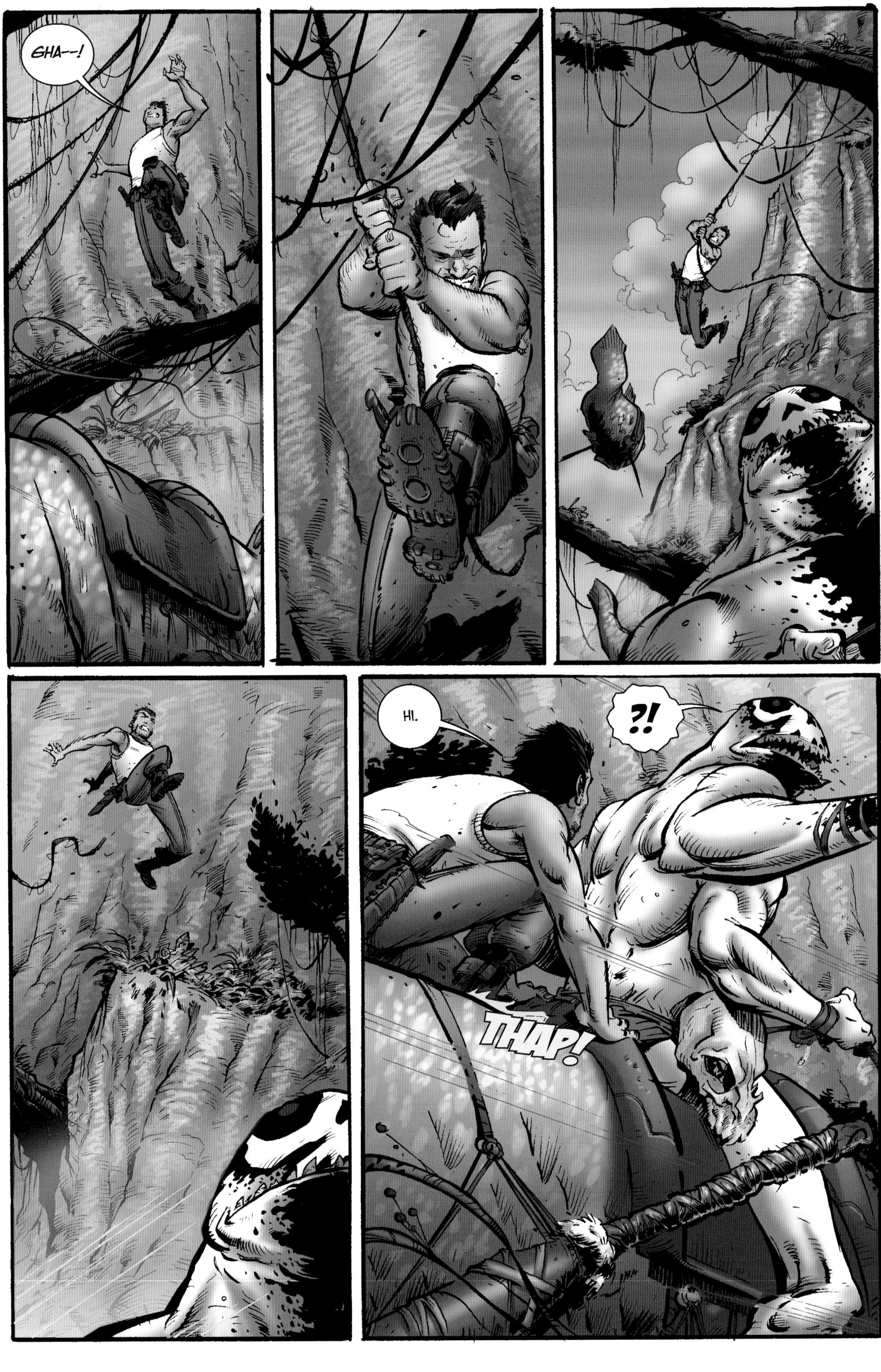
GHA--!
HI.
?!
THAP!

BASTARD AIN'T GOIN' EASY...

...TAKES US INTO A HARD DIVE.

SON-OF-A-BITCH!

STALACTITE NEARLY KNOCKS ME GALLEY WEST...

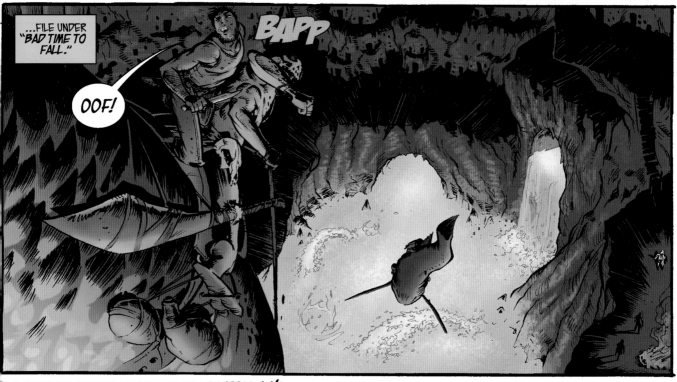

...FILE UNDER "BAD TIME TO FALL."

BAPP

OOF!

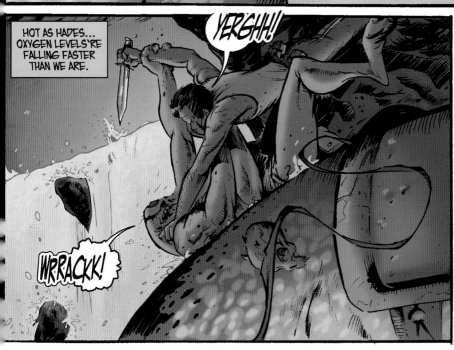

HOT AS HADES... OXYGEN LEVELS'RE FALLING FASTER THAN WE ARE.

YERGH!!

WRRACKK!

...TWO FEET CLOSER AN' BREATHIN' WON'T BE A CONCERN O' MINE...

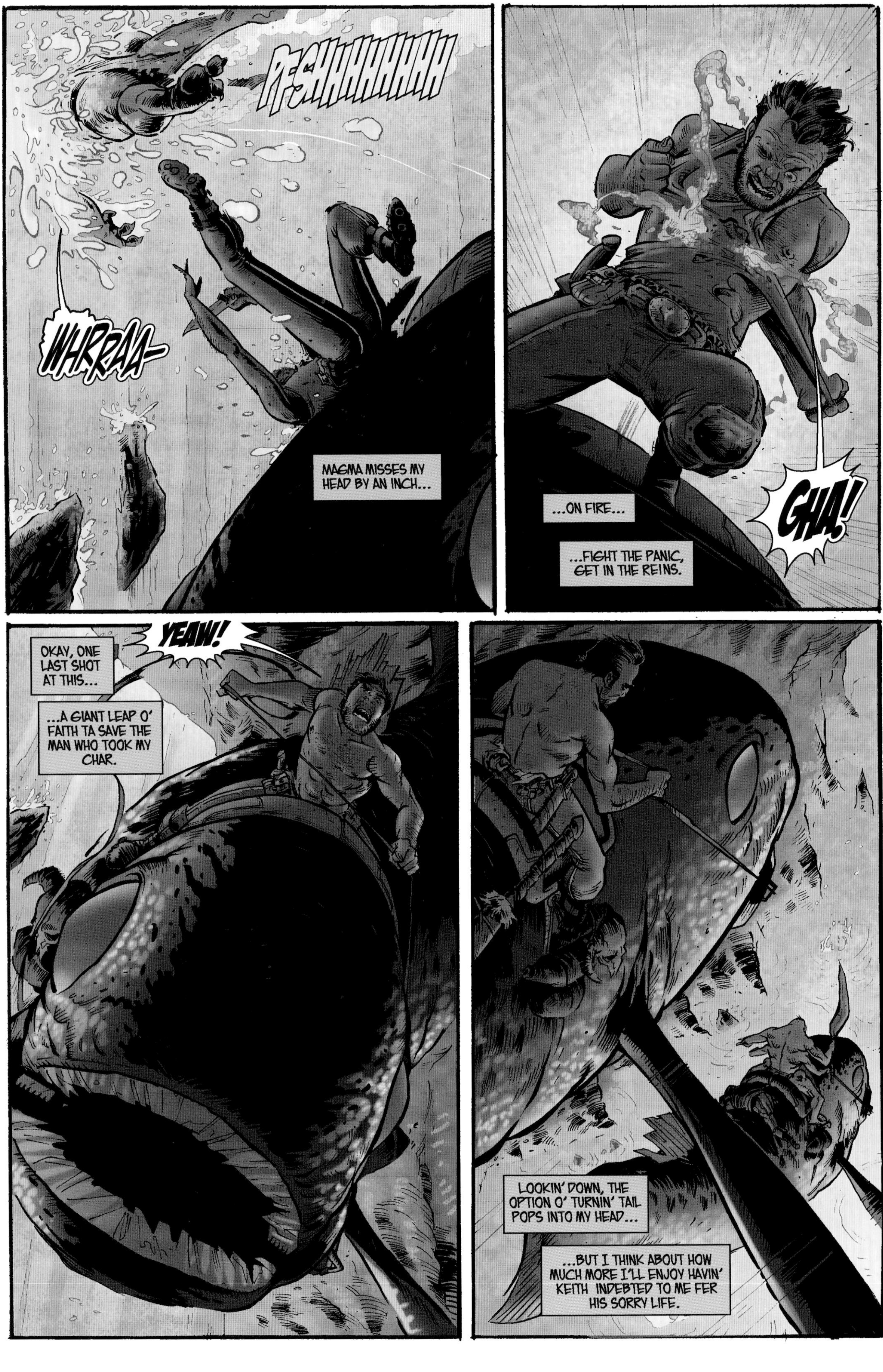
PFSHHHHHHHH
WHRRAA—
MAGMA MISSES MY HEAD BY AN INCH...
...ON FIRE...
...FIGHT THE PANIC, GET IN THE REINS.
GHA!
OKAY, ONE LAST SHOT AT THIS...
...A GIANT LEAP O' FAITH TA SAVE THE MAN WHO TOOK MY CHAR.
YEAW!
LOOKIN' DOWN, THE OPTION O' TURNIN' TAIL POPS INTO MY HEAD...
...BUT I THINK ABOUT HOW MUCH MORE I'LL ENJOY HAVIN' KEITH INDEBTED TO ME FER HIS SORRY LIFE.

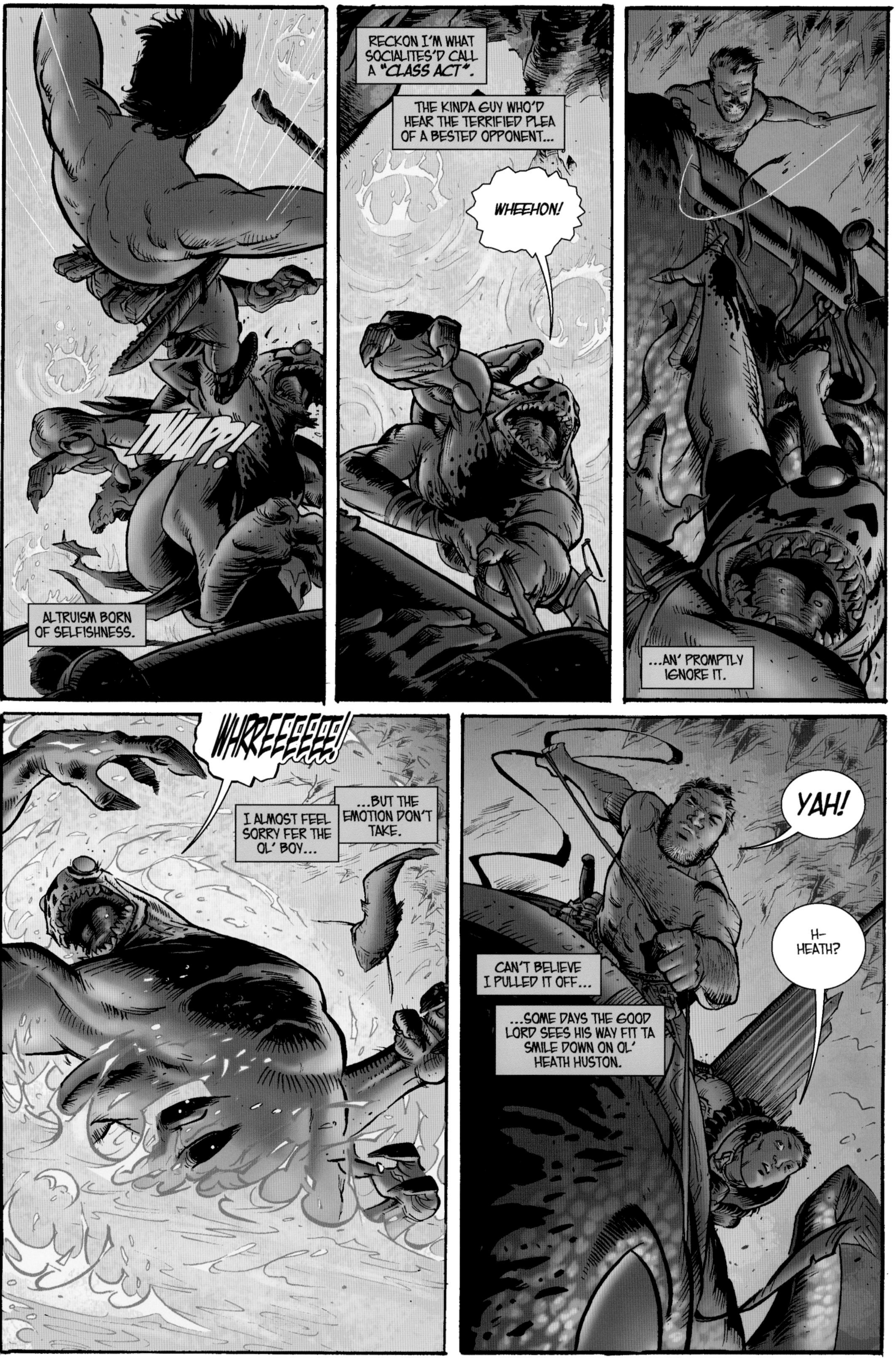
THWAPP!
ALTRUISM BORN OF SELFISHNESS.
RECKON I'M WHAT SOCIALITES'D CALL A "CLASS ACT".
THE KINDA GUY WHO'D HEAR THE TERRIFIED PLEA OF A BESTED OPPONENT...
WHEEHON!
...AN' PROMPTLY IGNORE IT.
WHRREEEEEEE!
I ALMOST FEEL SORRY FER THE OL' BOY...
...BUT THE EMOTION DON'T TAKE.
YAH!
CAN'T BELIEVE I PULLED IT OFF...
...SOME DAYS THE GOOD LORD SEES HIS WAY FIT TA SMILE DOWN ON OL' HEATH HUSTON.
H-HEATH?

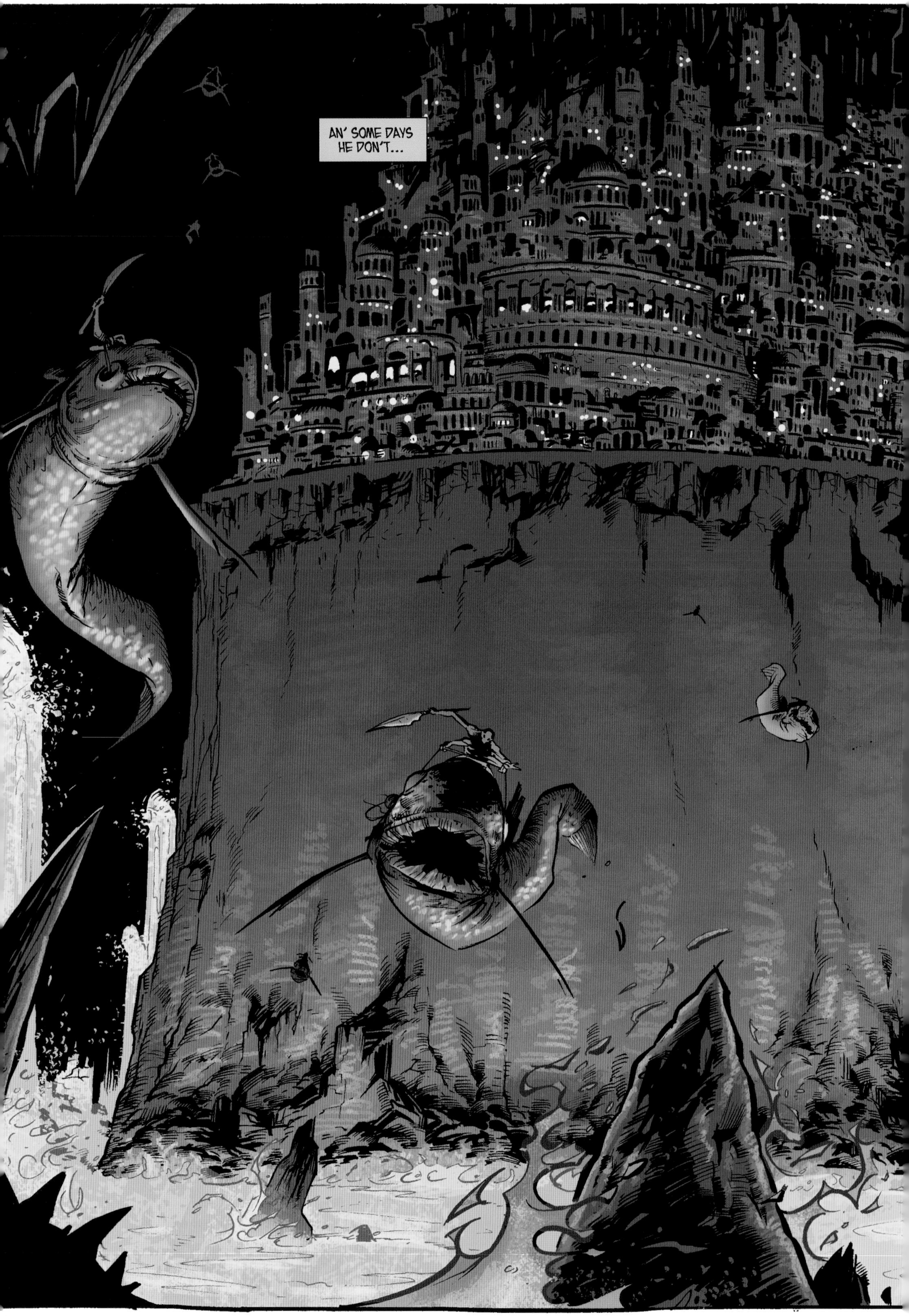
AN' SOME DAYS
HE DON'T...

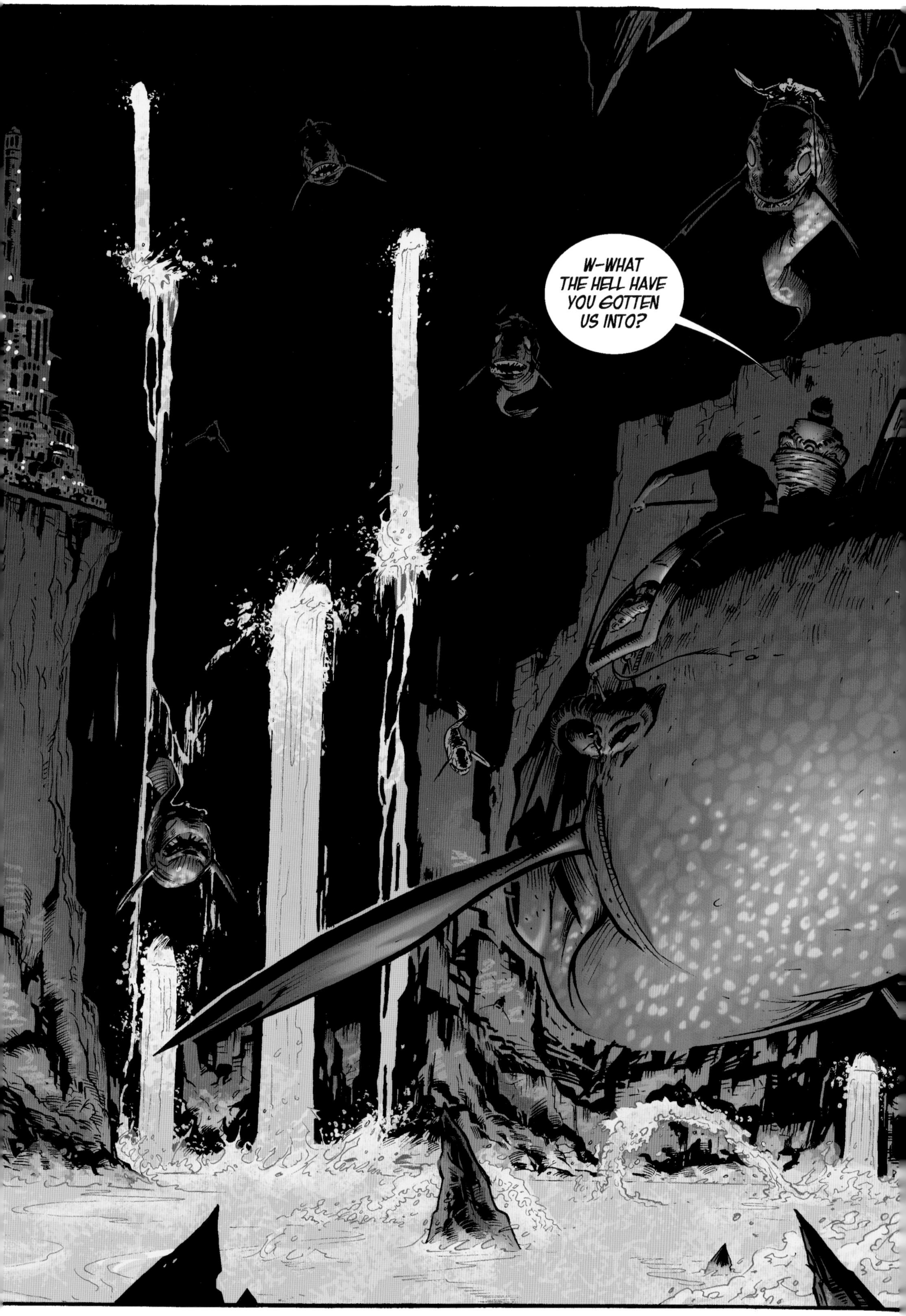
W-WHAT THE HELL HAVE YOU GOTTEN US INTO?

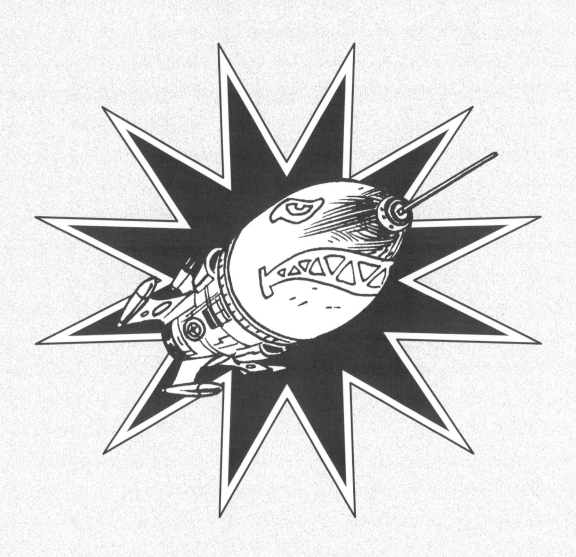

CHAPTER 2

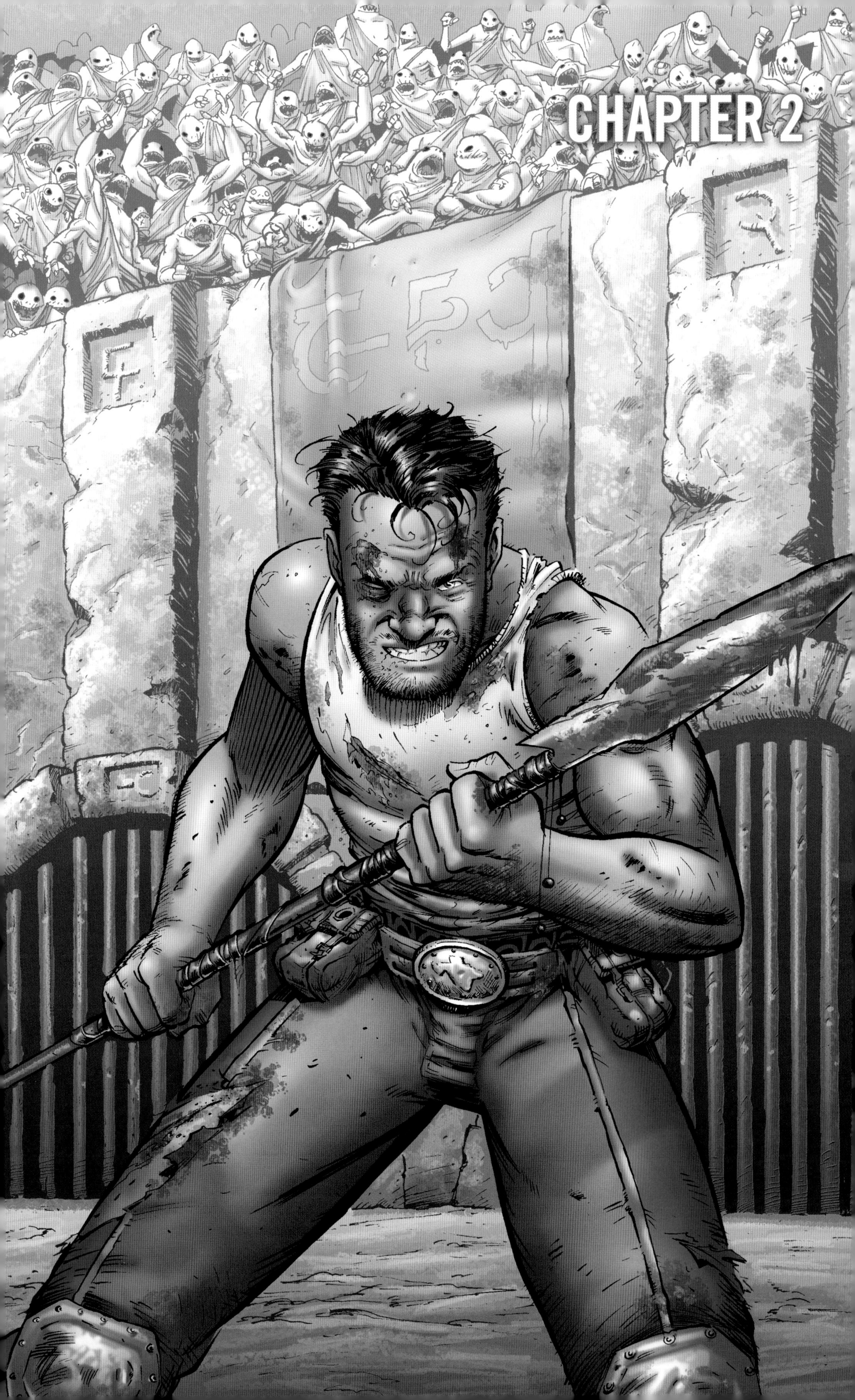

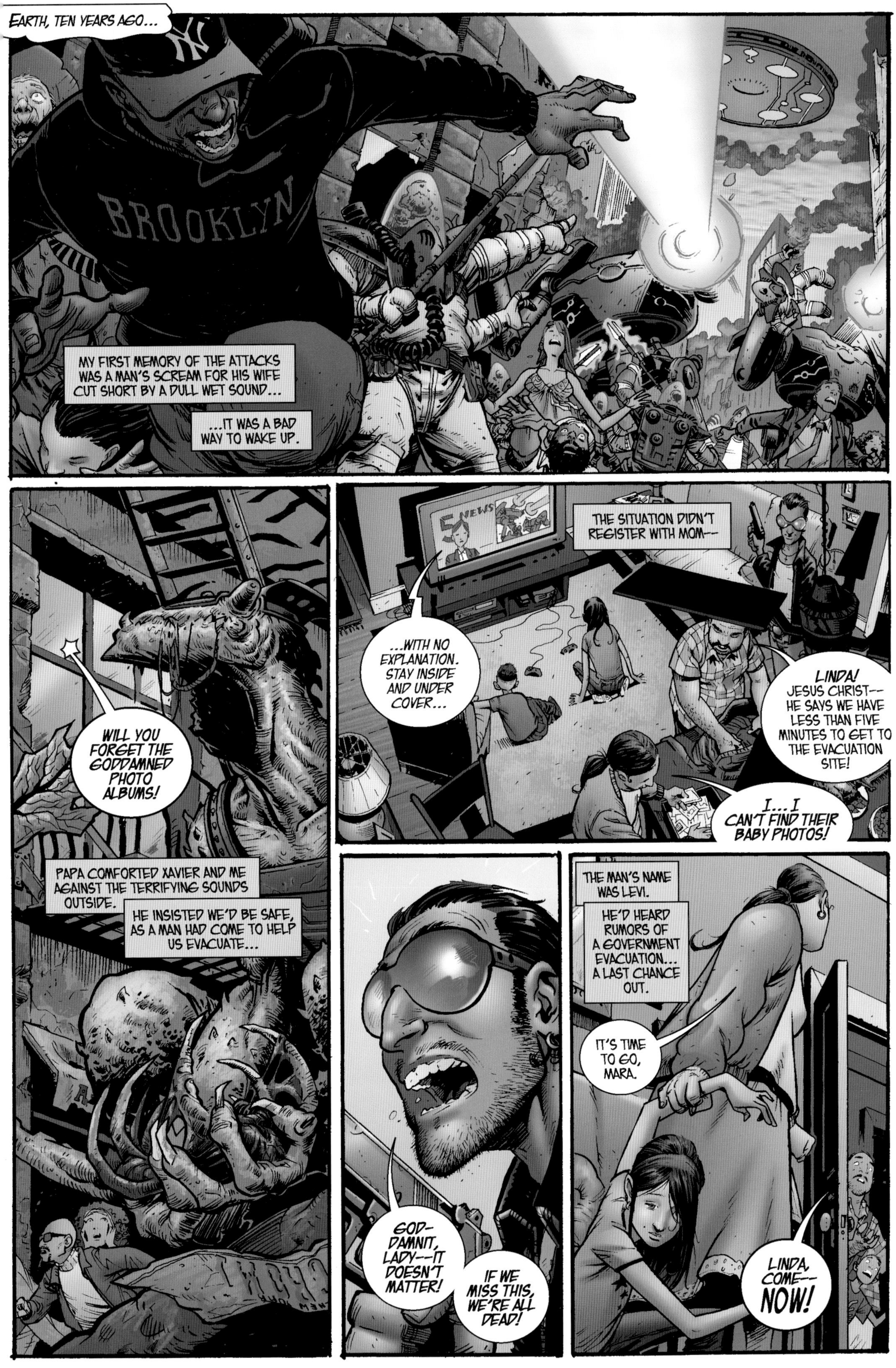
EARTH, TEN YEARS AGO...
BROOKLYN
MY FIRST MEMORY OF THE ATTACKS WAS A MAN'S SCREAM FOR HIS WIFE CUT SHORT BY A DULL WET SOUND...
...IT WAS A BAD WAY TO WAKE UP.
WILL YOU FORGET THE GODDAMNED PHOTO ALBUMS!
THE SITUATION DIDN'T REGISTER WITH MOM--
...WITH NO EXPLANATION. STAY INSIDE AND UNDER COVER...
LINDA! JESUS CHRIST-- HE SAYS WE HAVE LESS THAN FIVE MINUTES TO GET TO THE EVACUATION SITE!
I... I CAN'T FIND THEIR BABY PHOTOS!
PAPA COMFORTED XAVIER AND ME AGAINST THE TERRIFYING SOUNDS OUTSIDE.
HE INSISTED WE'D BE SAFE, AS A MAN HAD COME TO HELP US EVACUATE...
GOD-DAMNIT, LADY--IT DOESN'T MATTER!
IF WE MISS THIS, WE'RE ALL DEAD!
THE MAN'S NAME WAS LEVI.
HE'D HEARD RUMORS OF A GOVERNMENT EVACUATION... A LAST CHANCE OUT.
IT'S TIME TO GO, MARA.
LINDA, COME-- NOW!

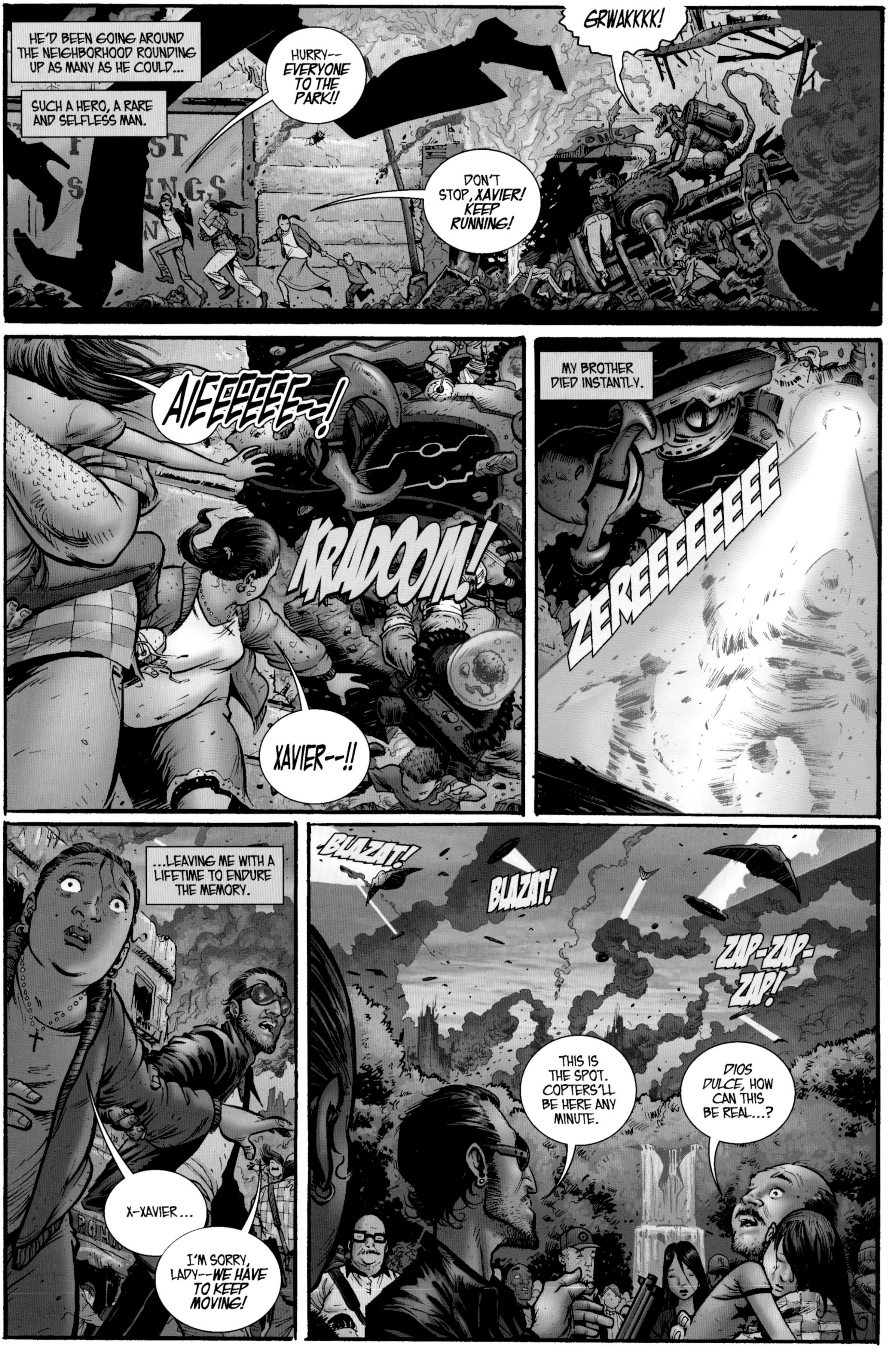

HE'D BEEN GOING AROUND THE NEIGHBORHOOD ROUNDING UP AS MANY AS HE COULD...
SUCH A HERO, A RARE AND SELFLESS MAN.
HURRY-- EVERYONE TO THE PARK!!
GRWAKKKK!
DON'T STOP, XAVIER! KEEP RUNNING!
AIEEEEEEE--!
KRADOOM!
XAVIER--!!
MY BROTHER DIED INSTANTLY.
ZEREEEEEEEEE
...LEAVING ME WITH A LIFETIME TO ENDURE THE MEMORY.
X-XAVIER...
I'M SORRY, LADY--WE HAVE TO KEEP MOVING!
BLAZAT!
BLAZAT!
ZAP-ZAP-ZAP!
THIS IS THE SPOT. COPTERS'LL BE HERE ANY MINUTE.
DIOS DULCE, HOW CAN THIS BE REAL...?

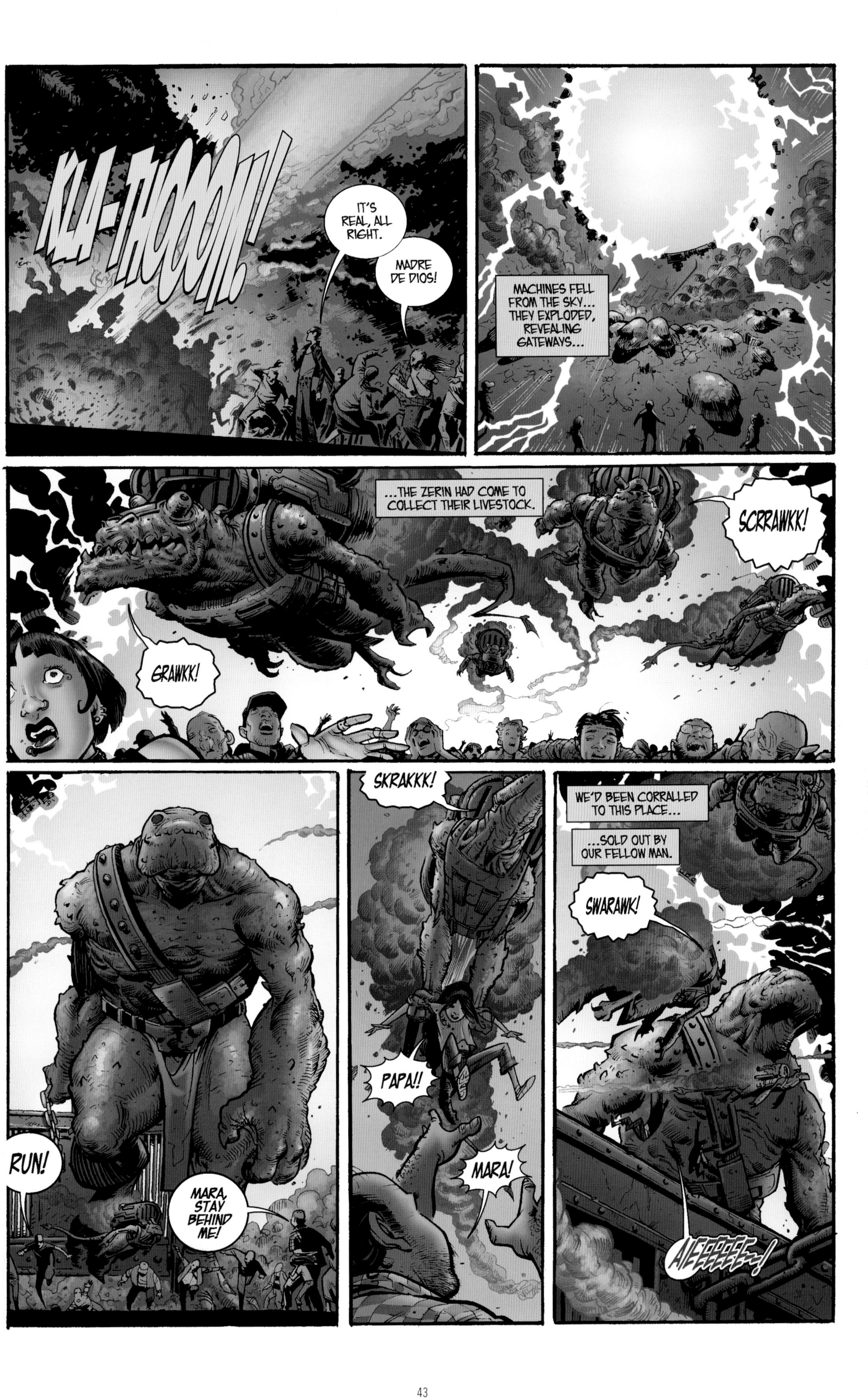
KLA-THOOOM!!
IT'S REAL, ALL RIGHT.
MADRE DE DIOS!
MACHINES FELL FROM THE SKY... THEY EXPLODED, REVEALING GATEWAYS...
...THE ZERIN HAD COME TO COLLECT THEIR LIVESTOCK.
SCRRAWKK!
GRAWKK!
RUN!
MARA, STAY BEHIND ME!
SKRAKKK!
PAPA!!
MARA!
WE'D BEEN CORRALLED TO THIS PLACE...
...SOLD OUT BY OUR FELLOW MAN.
SWARAWK!
AIEEEEEE--!

I'VE TRIED TO EXPLAIN THE INVASION AND WHAT HAPPENED TO MY FAMILY AFTERWARDS...

...BUT THE WORDS WERE VACANT. THERE IS NO LANGUAGE ADEQUATE TO REPRESENT THE DREADFULNESS OF IT.

≈SOB≈ M-MARA... PLEASE, PLEASE, GOD, NO!!

MAMA!!

YO, I'M LOOKIN' TA COLLECT SOME UNI-CREDS FROM GENERAL ROWLL...

...WHERE'S THE GUY IN CHARGE?

GRWAKK?

WHOA! L-LOOK AT THE CARD!

I'M ONE OF THE ROUNDUP GUYS, YA KNUCKLEHEAD!

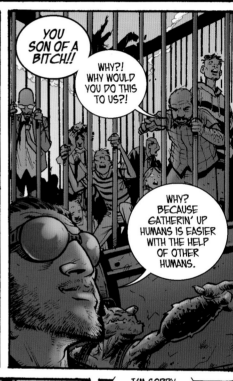

YOU SON OF A BITCH!!

WHY?! WHY WOULD YOU DO THIS TO US?!

WHY? BECAUSE GATHERIN' UP HUMANS IS EASIER WITH THE HELP OF OTHER HUMANS.

OH, YOU MEANT "WHY" AS IN "WHY WOULD I DO WORK AS CRUEL AS THIS."

HELL, I'M JUST A GALACTIC RAPSCALLION LOOKIN' TA MAKE AN EASY BUCK, FRIEND.

YOU GARBAGE! I-I'LL KILL YOU!

KILL ME? HA! YOU SHOULD THANK ME. YOU GOT IT LUCKY, BROTHER!

WHILE THE TETALDIAN EMPIRE ANNIHILATES EVERY SOUL ON YOUR PLANET, YOU'LL BE GRAZING ON ZERINIA FOR MONTHS BEFORE THEY FINALLY...

...AH, HELL, IT AIN'T IMPORTANT...

≈SOB≈

I'M SORRY FOR YOUR PLANET'S BAD LUCK, FRIEND.

BUT, YOU CAN'T BLAME A GUY FOR MAKING A QUICK BUCK OFF THE INEVITABLE.

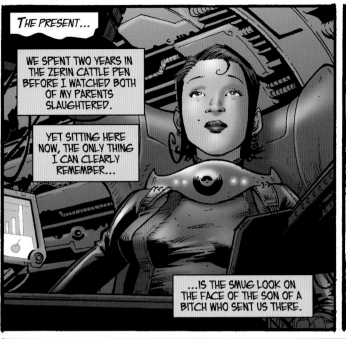

THE PRESENT...

WE SPENT TWO YEARS IN THE ZERIN CATTLE PEN BEFORE I WATCHED BOTH OF MY PARENTS SLAUGHTERED.

YET SITTING HERE NOW, THE ONLY THING I CAN CLEARLY REMEMBER...

...IS THE SMUG LOOK ON THE FACE OF THE SON OF A BITCH WHO SENT US THERE.

RED ALERT!

WIPING THAT FACE CLEAN IS THE ONLY THING I'VE HAD TO LIVE FOR SINCE THE INVASION.

THE REASON I BREATHE. A FANATICAL OBSESSION...

...THE KIND YOU'D GO TO ANY LENGTHS TO REALIZE.

IN MY, CASE "ANY LENGTHS" WAS SELLING SECRETS TO THE DRESSITES FOR THE LOCATION OF THE MAN INSIDE THAT SHIP.

A MAN NAMED LEVI DIABLO...

THE BLACK GALLEON

RED ALERT, WAR CRAFT APPROACHING. IMPLEMENTING EMERGENCY THAW OF ALL BEDS.

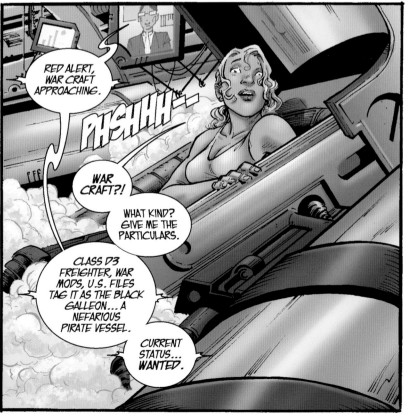

RED ALERT, WAR CRAFT APPROACHING.

PHSHHH!

WAR CRAFT?!

WHAT KIND? GIVE ME THE PARTICULARS.

CLASS D3 FREIGHTER, WAR MODS, U.S. FILES TAG IT AS THE BLACK GALLEON... A NEFARIOUS PIRATE VESSEL.

CURRENT STATUS... WANTED.

HOW IN THE HELL DID THEY GET SO CLOSE?!

WE'D JUST REACHED NEAVSIVIA WHEN THEY DID A SLINGSHOT AT US FROM THE OTHER SIDE OF THE PLANET.

THEY'VE OPENED A CHANNEL... I'M PATCHING INTO IT NOW.

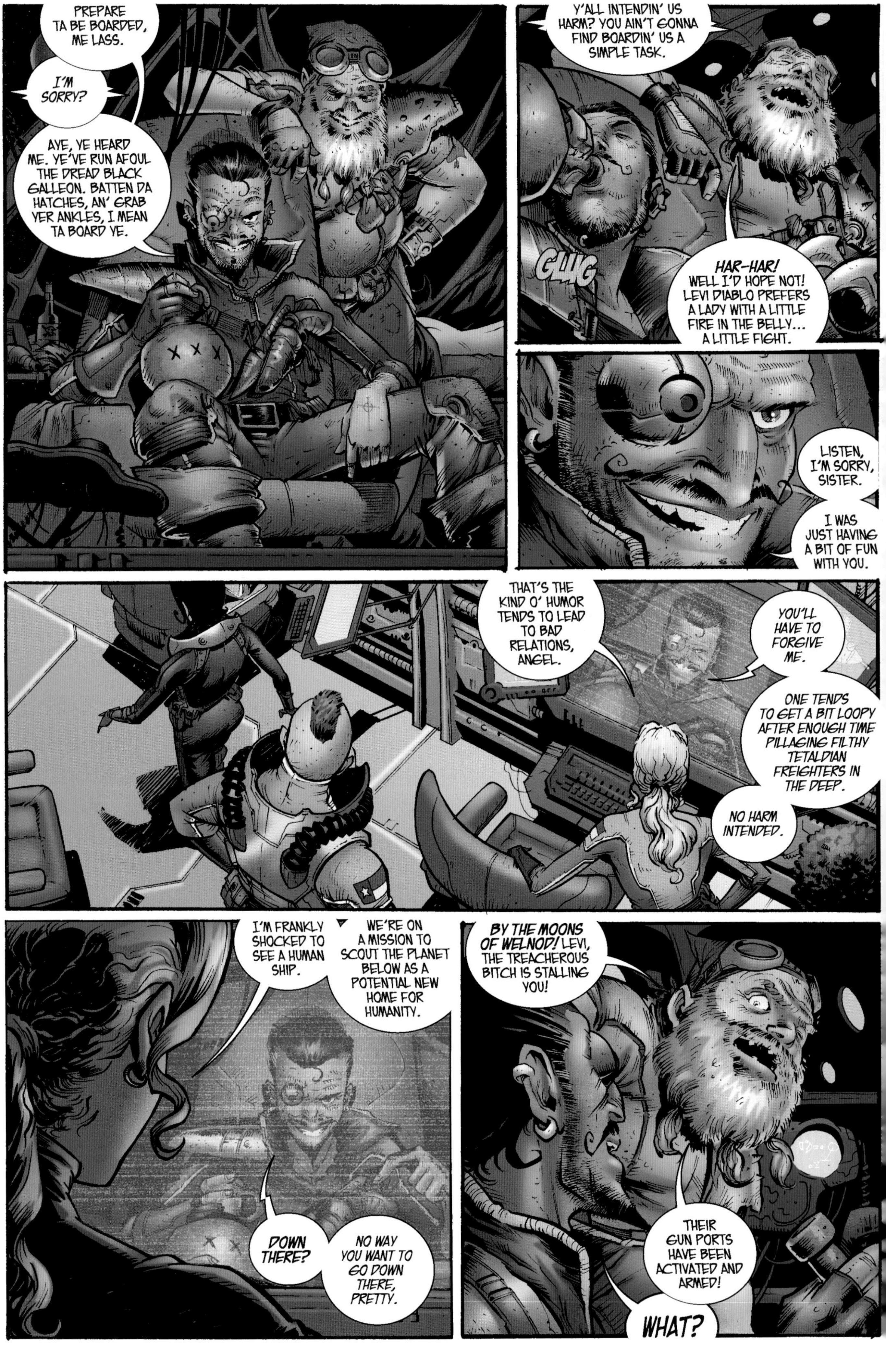
PREPARE TA BE BOARDED, ME LASS.
I'M SORRY?
AYE, YE HEARD ME. YE'VE RUN AFOUL THE DREAD BLACK GALLEON. BATTEN DA HATCHES, AN' GRAB YER ANKLES, I MEAN TA BOARD YE.
Y'ALL INTENDIN' US HARM? YOU AIN'T GONNA FIND BOARDIN' US A SIMPLE TASK.
GLUG
HAR-HAR! WELL I'D HOPE NOT! LEVI DIABLO PREFERS A LADY WITH A LITTLE FIRE IN THE BELLY... A LITTLE FIGHT.
LISTEN, I'M SORRY, SISTER.
I WAS JUST HAVING A BIT OF FUN WITH YOU.
THAT'S THE KIND O' HUMOR TENDS TO LEAD TO BAD RELATIONS, ANGEL.
YOU'LL HAVE TO FORGIVE ME.
ONE TENDS TO GET A BIT LOOPY AFTER ENOUGH TIME PILLAGING FILTHY TETALDIAN FREIGHTERS IN THE DEEP.
NO HARM INTENDED.
I'M FRANKLY SHOCKED TO SEE A HUMAN SHIP.
WE'RE ON A MISSION TO SCOUT THE PLANET BELOW AS A POTENTIAL NEW HOME FOR HUMANITY.
DOWN THERE?
NO WAY YOU WANT TO GO DOWN THERE, PRETTY.
BY THE MOONS OF WELNOD! LEVI, THE TREACHEROUS BITCH IS STALLING YOU!
THEIR GUN PORTS HAVE BEEN ACTIVATED AND ARMED!
WHAT?

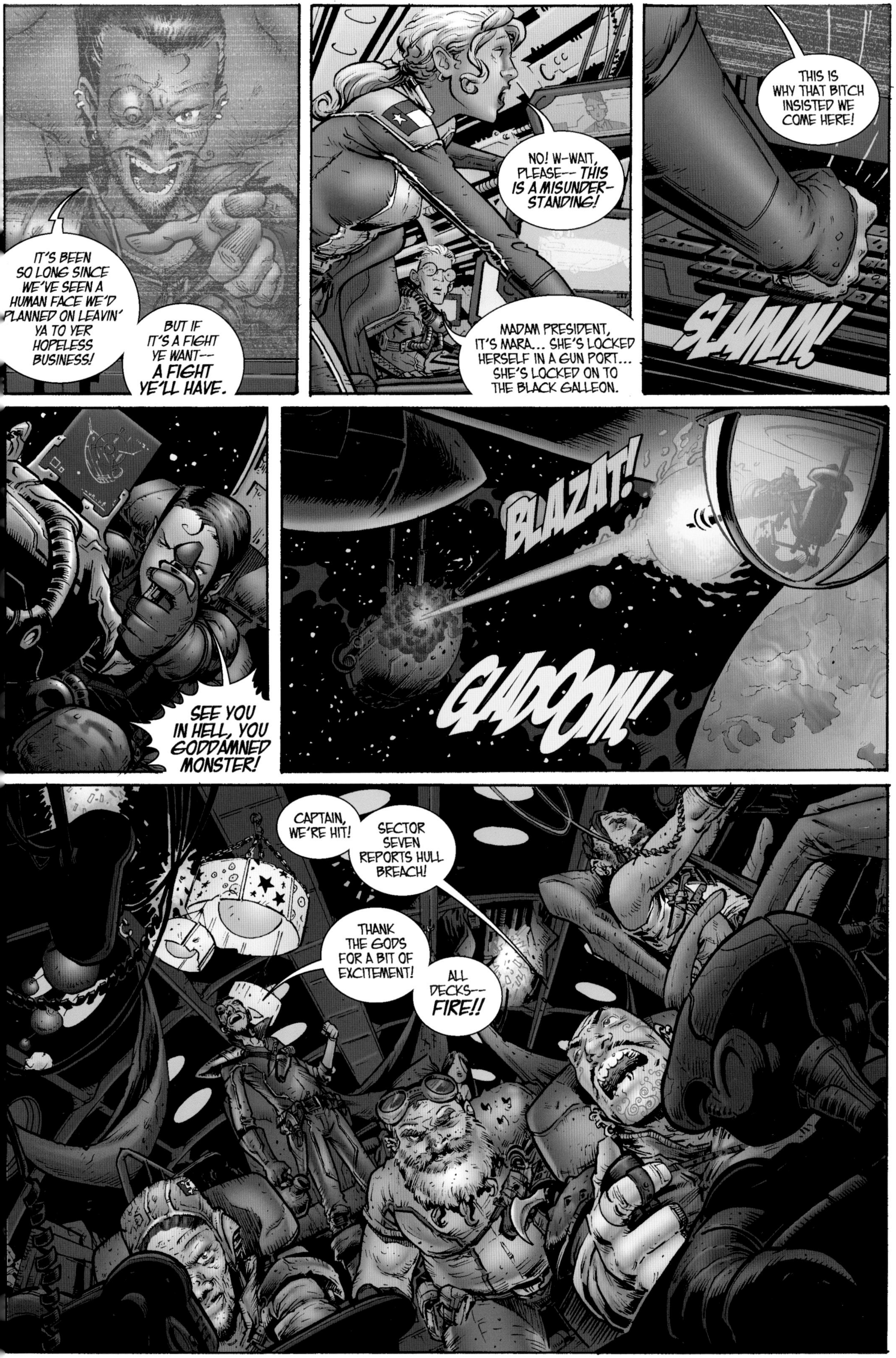
IT'S BEEN SO LONG SINCE WE'VE SEEN A HUMAN FACE WE'D PLANNED ON LEAVIN' YA TO YER HOPELESS BUSINESS!
BUT IF IT'S A FIGHT YE WANT-- A FIGHT YE'LL HAVE.
NO! W-WAIT, PLEASE-- THIS IS A MISUNDER-STANDING!
MADAM PRESIDENT, IT'S MARA... SHE'S LOCKED HERSELF IN A GUN PORT... SHE'S LOCKED ON TO THE BLACK GALLEON.
THIS IS WHY THAT BITCH INSISTED WE COME HERE!
SLAMM!
SEE YOU IN HELL, YOU GODDAMNED MONSTER!
BLAZAT!
GLADOOM!
CAPTAIN, WE'RE HIT!
SECTOR SEVEN REPORTS HULL BREACH!
THANK THE GODS FOR A BIT OF EXCITEMENT!
ALL DECKS-- FIRE!!

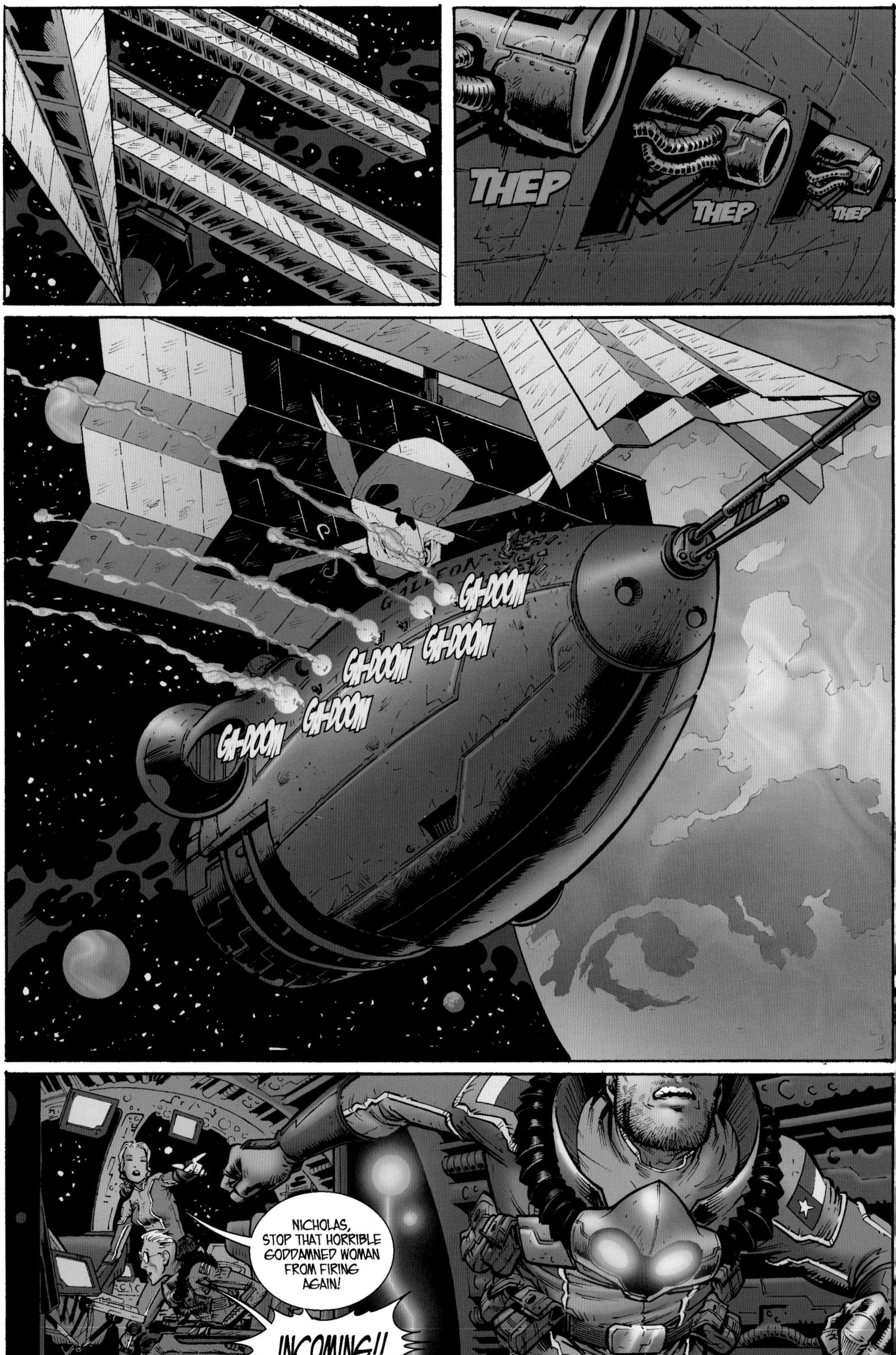
THEP
THEP
THEP
GA-DOOM
GA-DOOM
GA-DOOM
GA-DOOM
GA-DOOM
NICHOLAS, STOP THAT HORRIBLE GODDAMNED WOMAN FROM FIRING AGAIN!
INCOMING!!

THRAGGOOOM!

NICHOLAS, TIE HER DOWN! EVERYONE INTO CRASH POSITIONS!

LET ME GO!

LUCKY I NOT SNAP NECK!

ALL SYSTEMS OFFLINE!

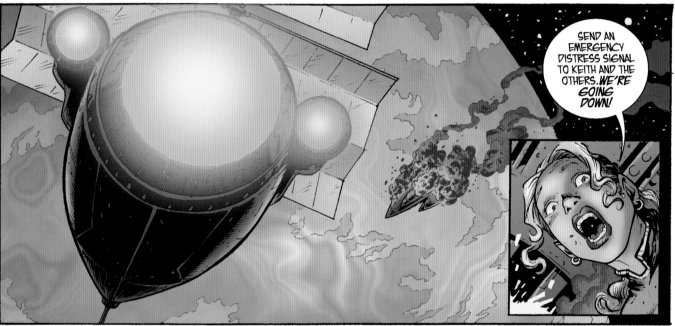

SEND AN EMERGENCY DISTRESS SIGNAL TO KEITH AND THE OTHERS. WE'RE GOING DOWN!

BHA! THE EARTHER SHIP IS GOING DOWN... NO CHALLENGE AT ALL.

TO ATTACK IN SUCH HALFHEARTED FASHION WITH AN INFERIOR SHIP...

...STRANGE BEHAVIOR FROM THOSE PURPORTING TO BE THE LAST BASTION OF HUMANITY.

I ACTED ON EMOTION--DIDN'T EVEN CONSIDER THEY'D HAVE SUCH HIGH-GRADE ARMOR.

AFTER ALL I'VE GONE THROUGH TO GET HERE, TO GET TO THIS MOMENT...

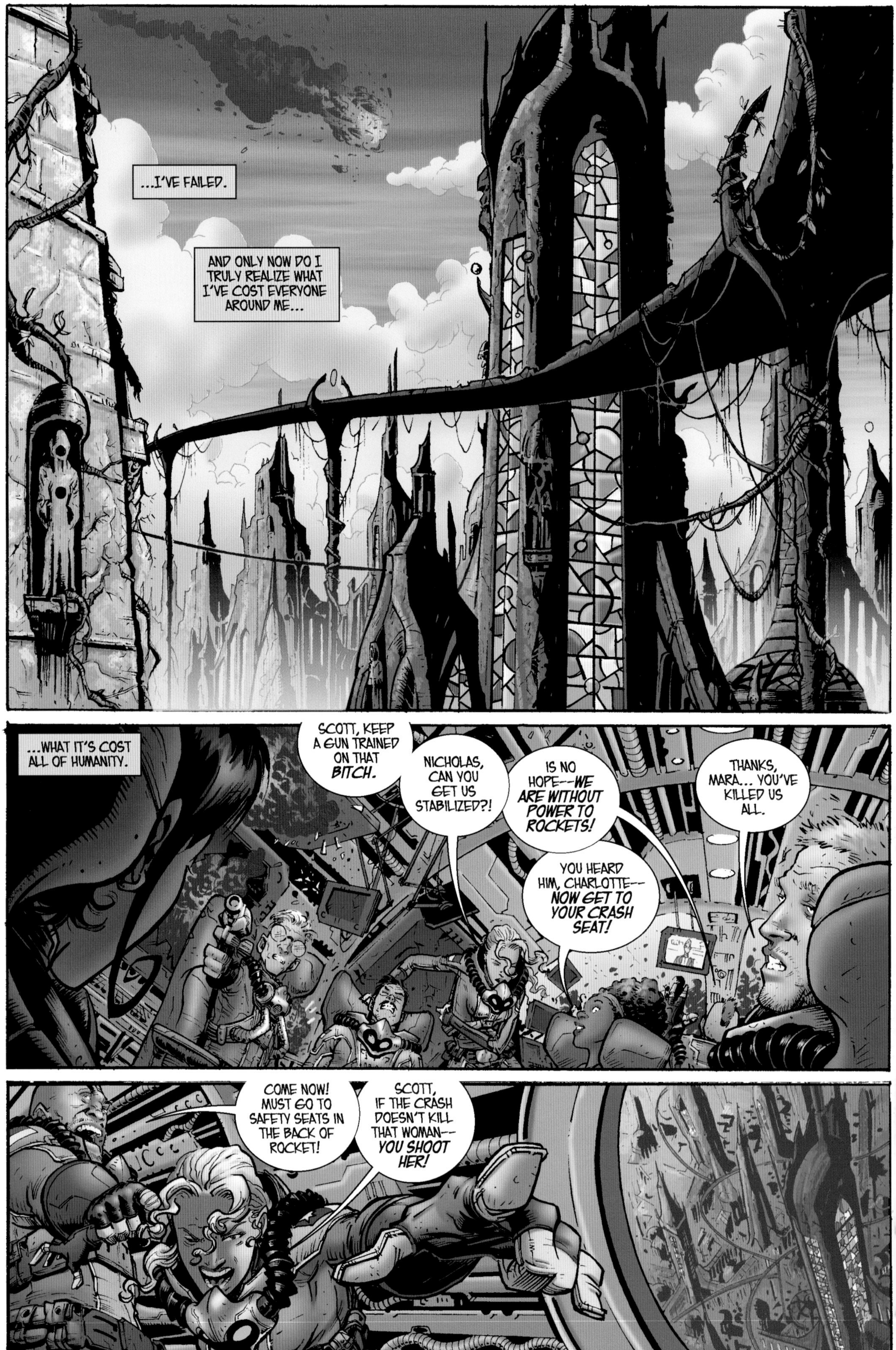

...I'VE FAILED.
AND ONLY NOW DO I TRULY REALIZE WHAT I'VE COST EVERYONE AROUND ME...
...WHAT IT'S COST ALL OF HUMANITY.
SCOTT, KEEP A GUN TRAINED ON THAT BITCH.
NICHOLAS, CAN YOU GET US STABILIZED?!
IS NO HOPE--WE ARE WITHOUT POWER TO ROCKETS!
THANKS, MARA... YOU'VE KILLED US ALL.
YOU HEARD HIM, CHARLOTTE--NOW GET TO YOUR CRASH SEAT!
COME NOW! MUST GO TO SAFETY SEATS IN THE BACK OF ROCKET!
SCOTT, IF THE CRASH DOESN'T KILL THAT WOMAN--YOU SHOOT HER!

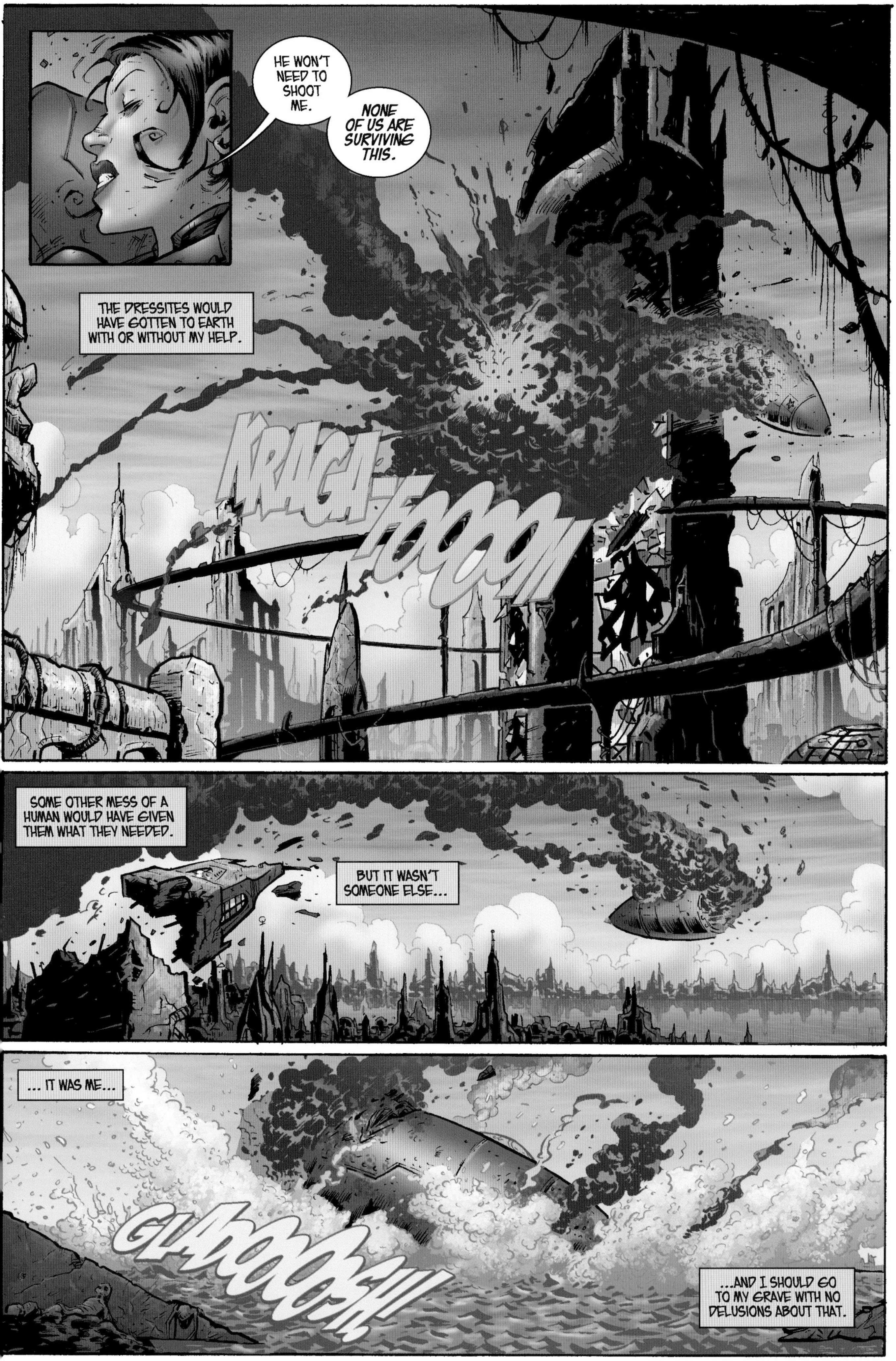
HE WON'T NEED TO SHOOT ME.
NONE OF US ARE SURVIVING THIS.
THE DRESSITES WOULD HAVE GOTTEN TO EARTH WITH OR WITHOUT MY HELP.
KRAGA-FOOOOM
SOME OTHER MESS OF A HUMAN WOULD HAVE GIVEN THEM WHAT THEY NEEDED.
BUT IT WASN'T SOMEONE ELSE...
... IT WAS ME...
GLABOOOOSH!!
...AND I SHOULD GO TO MY GRAVE WITH NO DELUSIONS ABOUT THAT.

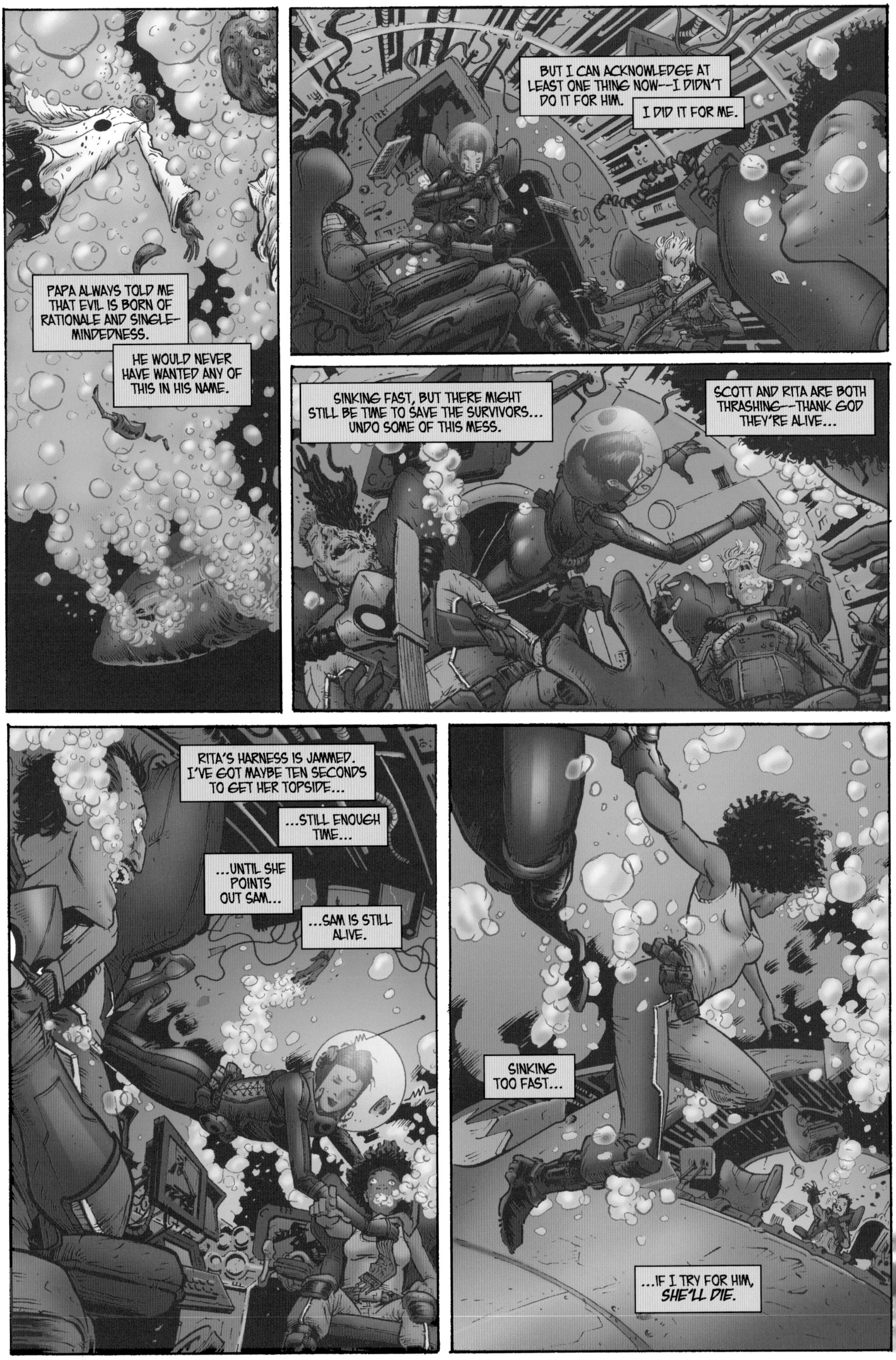

PAPA ALWAYS TOLD ME THAT EVIL IS BORN OF RATIONALE AND SINGLE-MINDEDNESS.
HE WOULD NEVER HAVE WANTED ANY OF THIS IN HIS NAME.
BUT I CAN ACKNOWLEDGE AT LEAST ONE THING NOW--I DIDN'T DO IT FOR HIM.
I DID IT FOR ME.
SINKING FAST, BUT THERE MIGHT STILL BE TIME TO SAVE THE SURVIVORS... UNDO SOME OF THIS MESS.
SCOTT AND RITA ARE BOTH THRASHING--THANK GOD THEY'RE ALIVE...
RITA'S HARNESS IS JAMMED. I'VE GOT MAYBE TEN SECONDS TO GET HER TOPSIDE...
...STILL ENOUGH TIME...
...UNTIL SHE POINTS OUT SAM...
...SAM IS STILL ALIVE.
SINKING TOO FAST...
...IF I TRY FOR HIM, *SHE'LL DIE.*

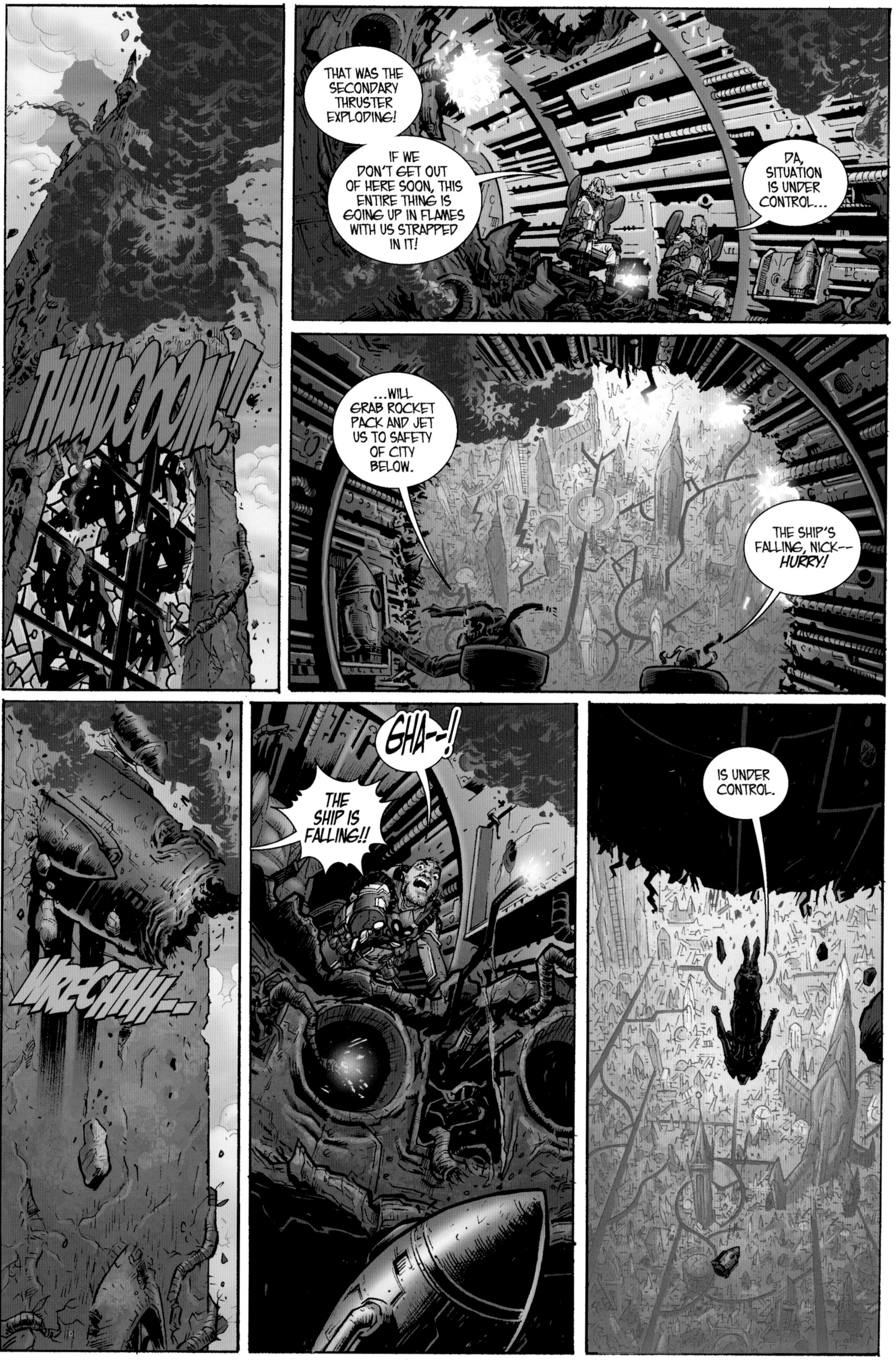
THUDOOOM..!!
THAT WAS THE SECONDARY THRUSTER EXPLODING!
IF WE DON'T GET OUT OF HERE SOON, THIS ENTIRE THING IS GOING UP IN FLAMES WITH US STRAPPED IN IT!
DA, SITUATION IS UNDER CONTROL...
...WILL GRAB ROCKET PACK AND JET US TO SAFETY OF CITY BELOW.
THE SHIP'S FALLING, NICK-- HURRY!
WRECHHH--
THE SHIP IS FALLING!!
GHA--!
IS UNDER CONTROL.

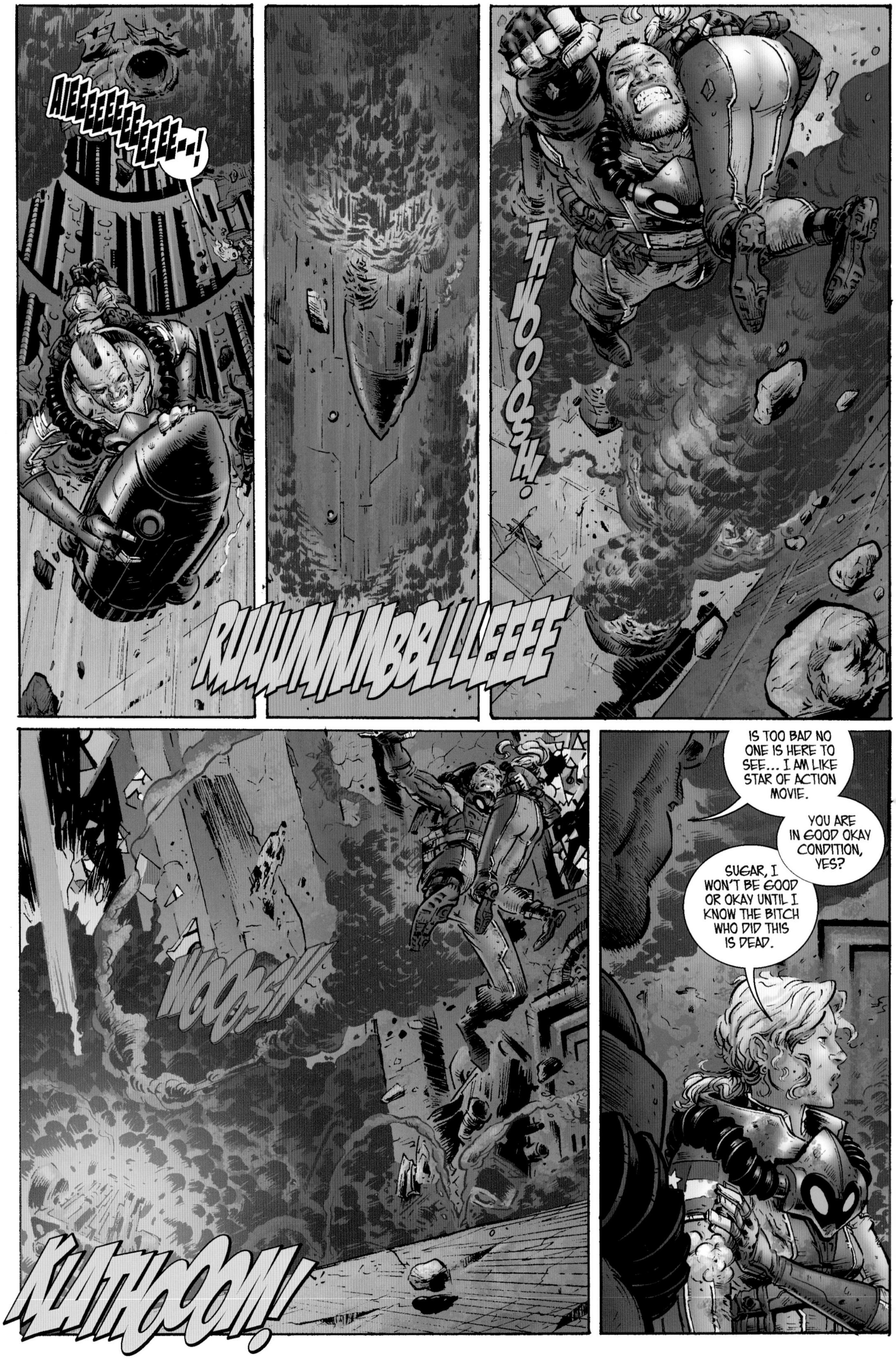
AIEEEEEEEEEEEEE--!
RUUUMMMBBLLLEEEE
THWOOOOSH!
WOOOSH
KLATHOOOM!
IS TOO BAD NO ONE IS HERE TO SEE... I AM LIKE STAR OF ACTION MOVIE.
YOU ARE IN GOOD OKAY CONDITION, YES?
SUGAR, I WON'T BE GOOD OR OKAY UNTIL I KNOW THE BITCH WHO DID THIS IS DEAD.

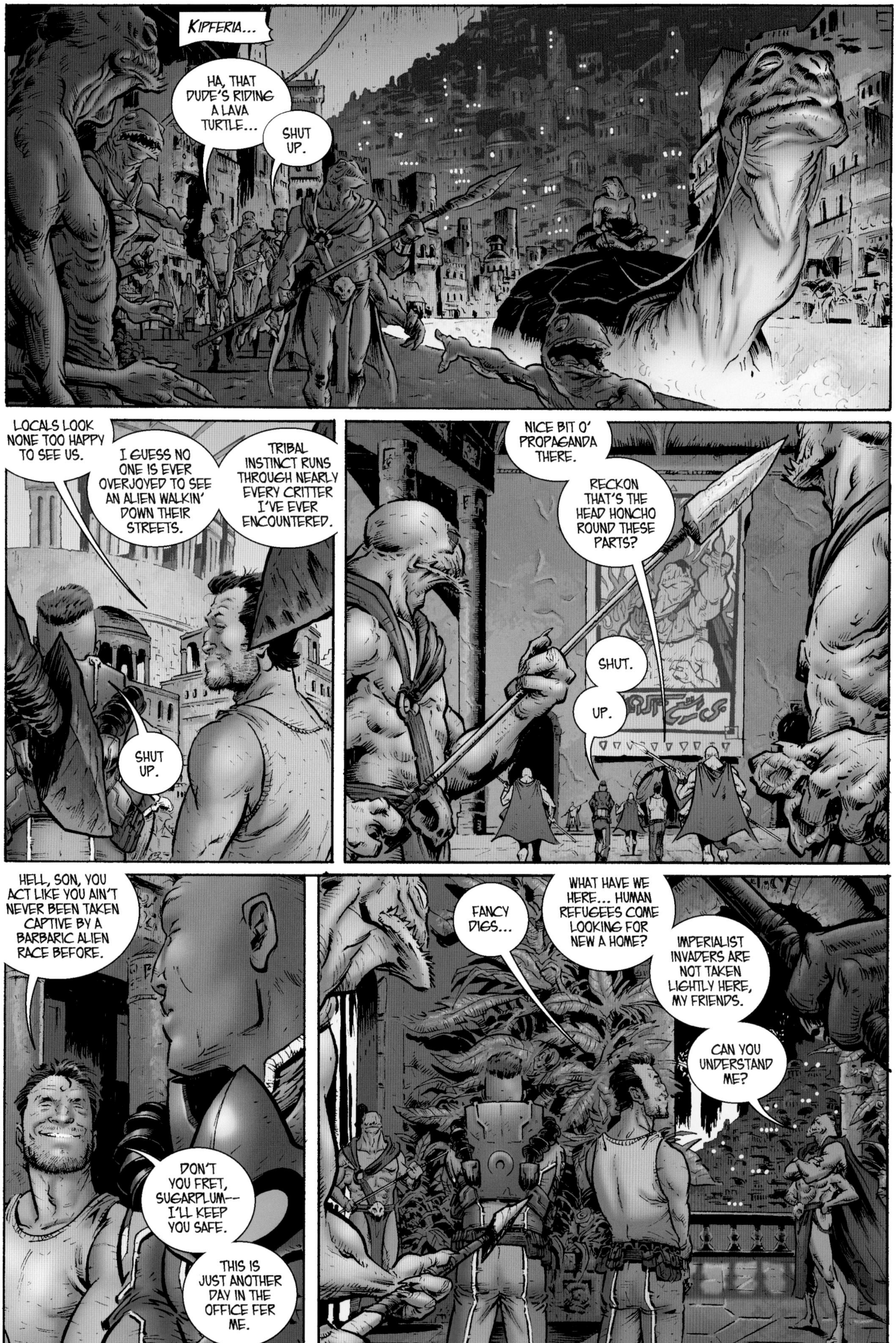

KIPFERIA...
HA, THAT DUDE'S RIDING A LAVA TURTLE...
SHUT UP.
LOCALS LOOK NONE TOO HAPPY TO SEE US.
I GUESS NO ONE IS EVER OVERJOYED TO SEE AN ALIEN WALKIN' DOWN THEIR STREETS.
TRIBAL INSTINCT RUNS THROUGH NEARLY EVERY CRITTER I'VE EVER ENCOUNTERED.
SHUT UP.
NICE BIT O' PROPAGANDA THERE.
RECKON THAT'S THE HEAD HONCHO ROUND THESE PARTS?
SHUT.
UP.
HELL, SON, YOU ACT LIKE YOU AIN'T NEVER BEEN TAKEN CAPTIVE BY A BARBARIC ALIEN RACE BEFORE.
DON'T YOU FRET, SUGARPLUM-- I'LL KEEP YOU SAFE.
THIS IS JUST ANOTHER DAY IN THE OFFICE FER ME.
FANCY DIGS...
WHAT HAVE WE HERE... HUMAN REFUGEES COME LOOKING FOR NEW A HOME?
IMPERIALIST INVADERS ARE NOT TAKEN LIGHTLY HERE, MY FRIENDS.
CAN YOU UNDERSTAND ME?

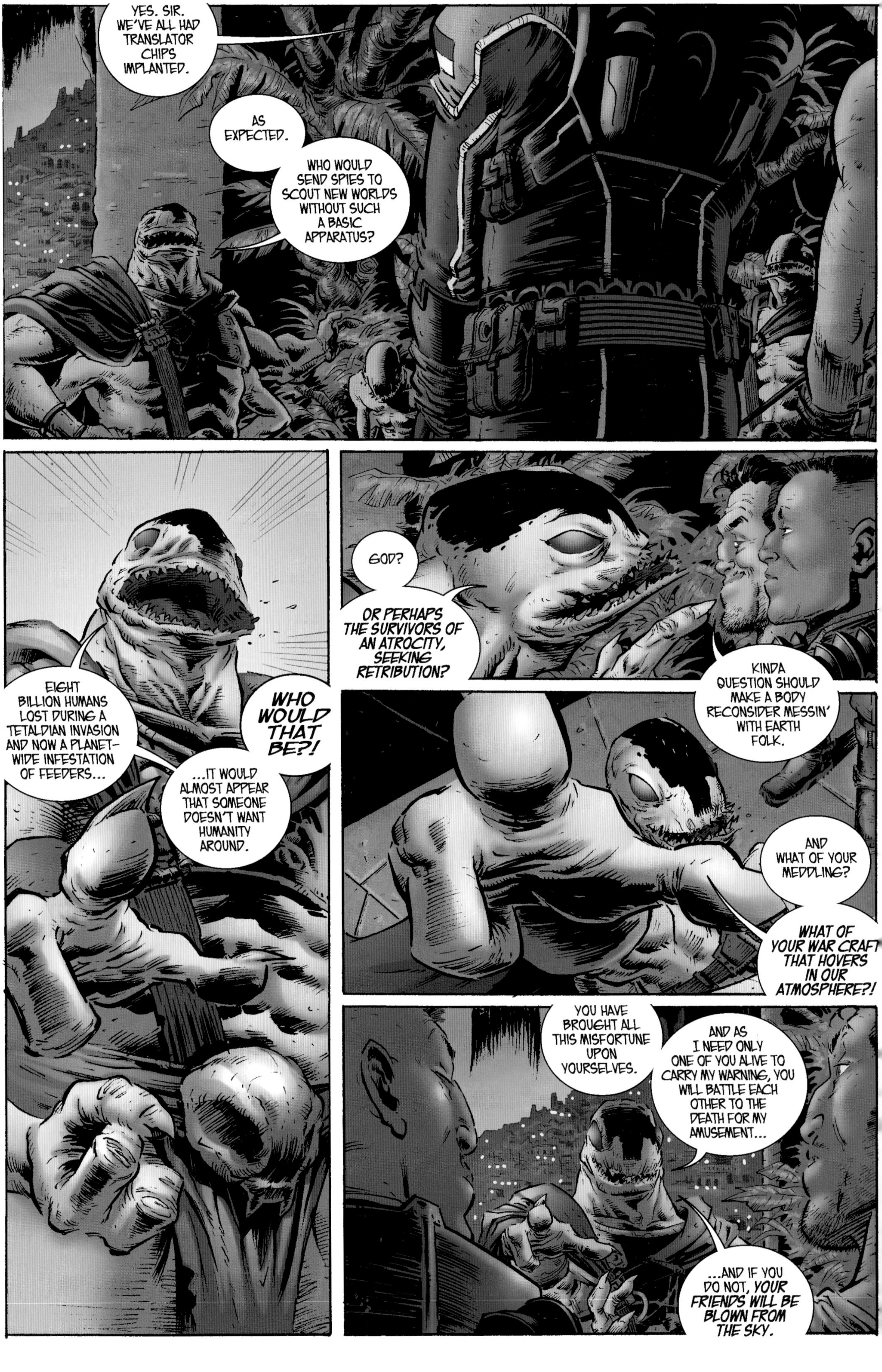
YES. SIR. WE'VE ALL HAD TRANSLATOR CHIPS IMPLANTED.
AS EXPECTED.
WHO WOULD SEND SPIES TO SCOUT NEW WORLDS WITHOUT SUCH A BASIC APPARATUS?
EIGHT BILLION HUMANS LOST DURING A TETALDIAN INVASION AND NOW A PLANET-WIDE INFESTATION OF FEEDERS...
...IT WOULD ALMOST APPEAR THAT SOMEONE DOESN'T WANT HUMANITY AROUND.
WHO WOULD THAT BE?!
GOD?
OR PERHAPS THE SURVIVORS OF AN ATROCITY, SEEKING RETRIBUTION?
KINDA QUESTION SHOULD MAKE A BODY RECONSIDER MESSIN' WITH EARTH FOLK.
AND WHAT OF YOUR MEDDLING?
WHAT OF YOUR WAR CRAFT THAT HOVERS IN OUR ATMOSPHERE?!
YOU HAVE BROUGHT ALL THIS MISFORTUNE UPON YOURSELVES.
AND AS I NEED ONLY ONE OF YOU ALIVE TO CARRY MY WARNING, YOU WILL BATTLE EACH OTHER TO THE DEATH FOR MY AMUSEMENT...
...AND IF YOU DO NOT, YOUR FRIENDS WILL BE BLOWN FROM THE SKY.

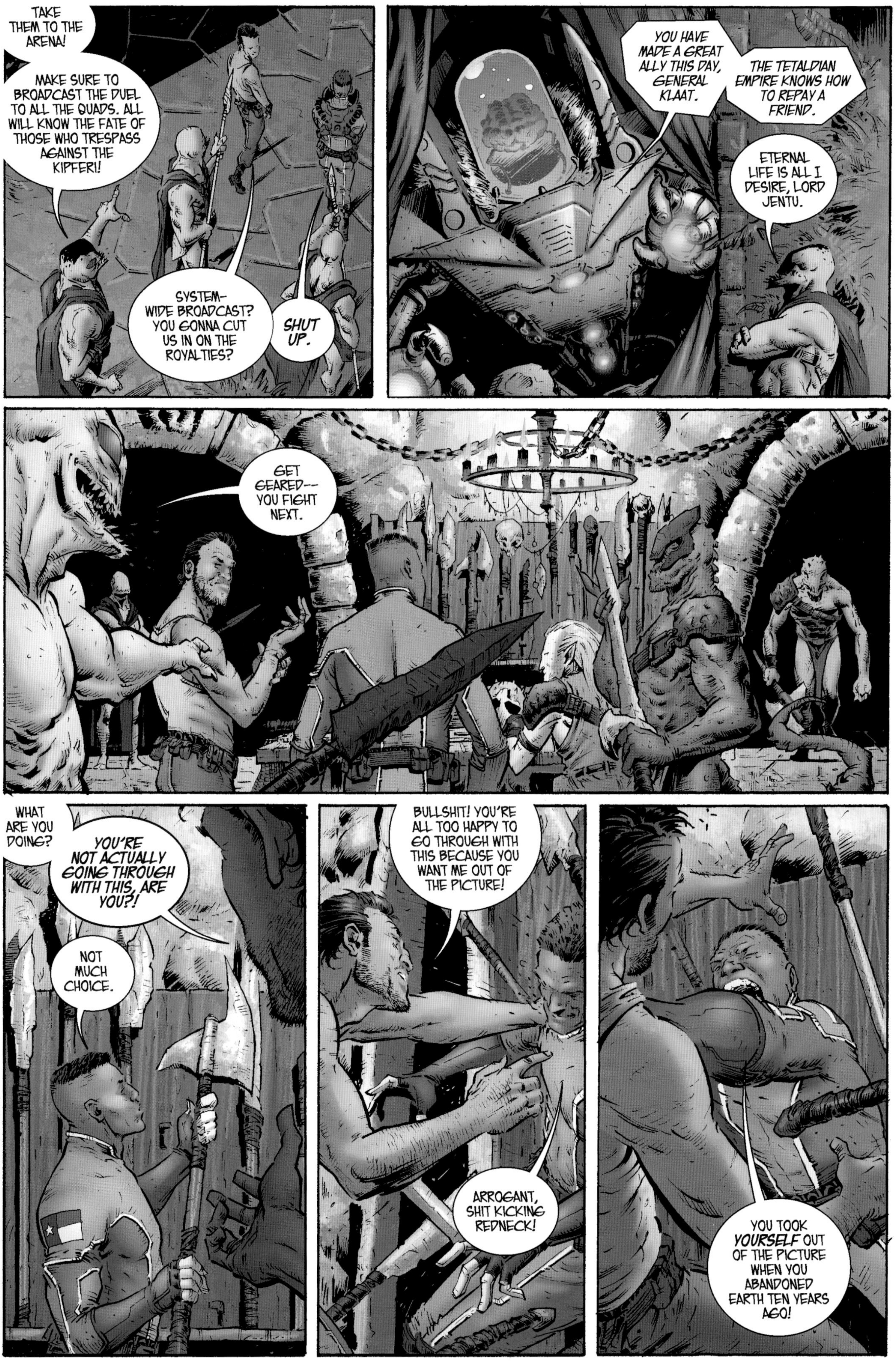
TAKE THEM TO THE ARENA!
MAKE SURE TO BROADCAST THE DUEL TO ALL THE QUADS. ALL WILL KNOW THE FATE OF THOSE WHO TRESPASS AGAINST THE KIPFERI!
SYSTEM-WIDE BROADCAST? YOU GONNA CUT US IN ON THE ROYALTIES?
SHUT UP.
YOU HAVE MADE A GREAT ALLY THIS DAY, GENERAL KLAAT.
THE TETALDIAN EMPIRE KNOWS HOW TO REPAY A FRIEND.
ETERNAL LIFE IS ALL I DESIRE, LORD JENTU.
GET GEARED--YOU FIGHT NEXT.
WHAT ARE YOU DOING?
YOU'RE NOT ACTUALLY GOING THROUGH WITH THIS, ARE YOU?!
NOT MUCH CHOICE.
BULLSHIT! YOU'RE ALL TOO HAPPY TO GO THROUGH WITH THIS BECAUSE YOU WANT ME OUT OF THE PICTURE!
ARROGANT, SHIT KICKING REDNECK!
YOU TOOK YOURSELF OUT OF THE PICTURE WHEN YOU ABANDONED EARTH TEN YEARS AGO!

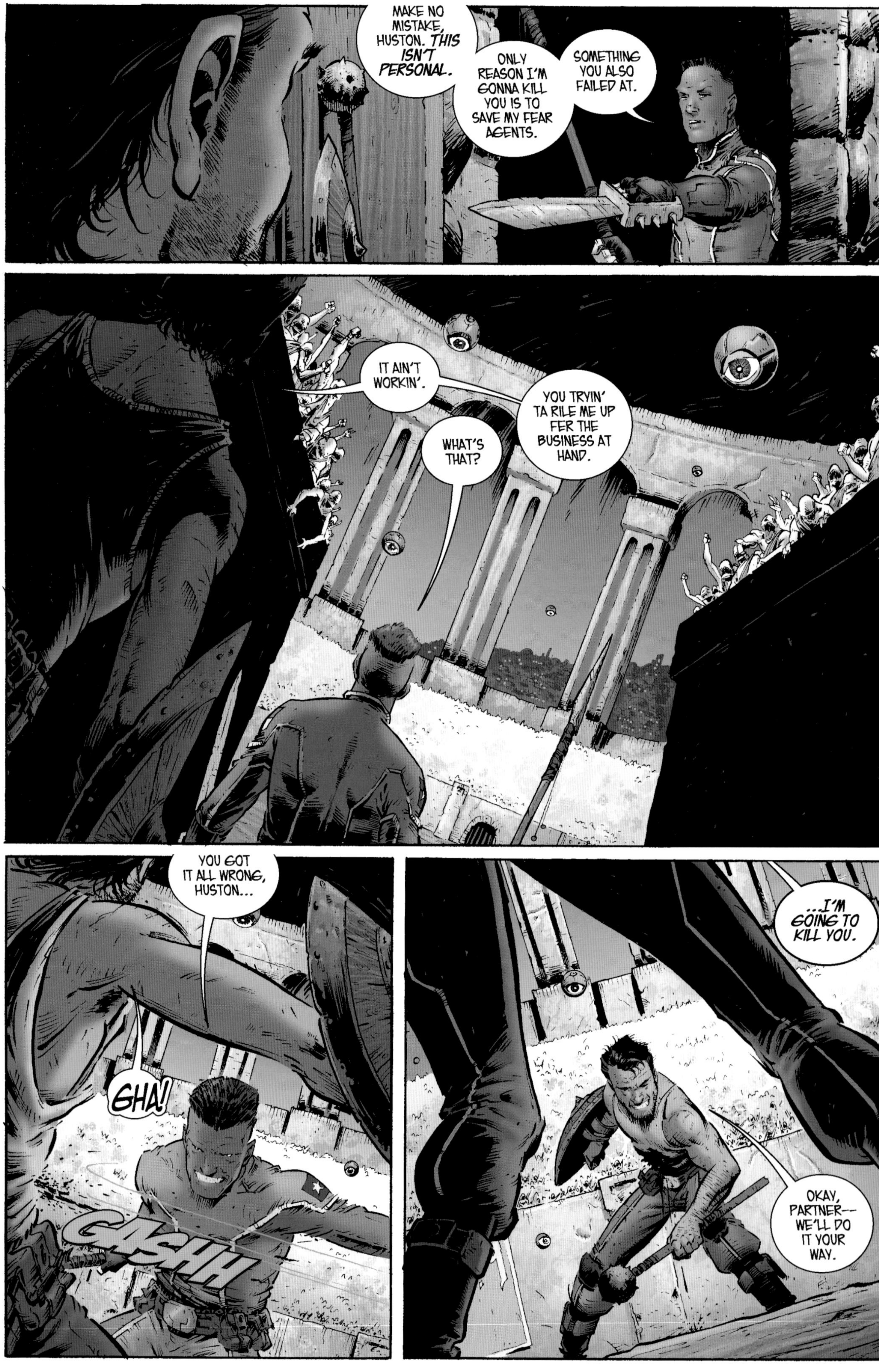
MAKE NO MISTAKE, HUSTON. THIS ISN'T PERSONAL.
ONLY REASON I'M GONNA KILL YOU IS TO SAVE MY FEAR AGENTS.
SOMETHING YOU ALSO FAILED AT.
IT AIN'T WORKIN'.
WHAT'S THAT?
YOU TRYIN' TA RILE ME UP FER THE BUSINESS AT HAND.
YOU GOT IT ALL WRONG, HUSTON...
GHA!
GASHH
...I'M GOING TO KILL YOU.
OKAY, PARTNER-- WE'LL DO IT YOUR WAY.

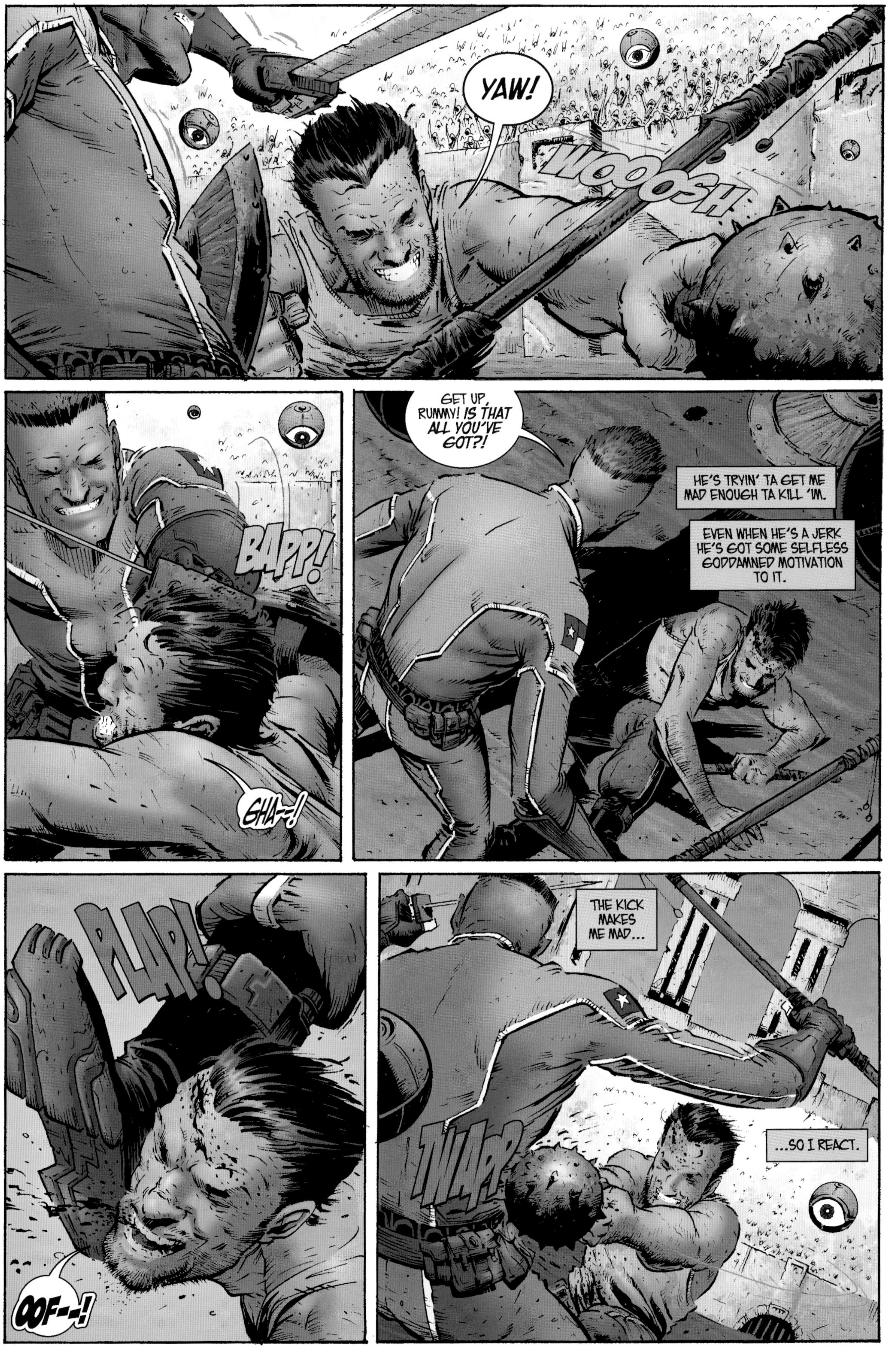
YAW!
WOOOSH
BAPP!
GHA--!
GET UP, RUMMY! IS THAT ALL YOU'VE GOT?!
HE'S TRYIN' TA GET ME MAD ENOUGH TA KILL 'IM.
EVEN WHEN HE'S A JERK HE'S GOT SOME SELFLESS GODDAMNED MOTIVATION TO IT.
PLAP!
OOF--!
THE KICK MAKES ME MAD...
TWAP!
...SO I REACT.

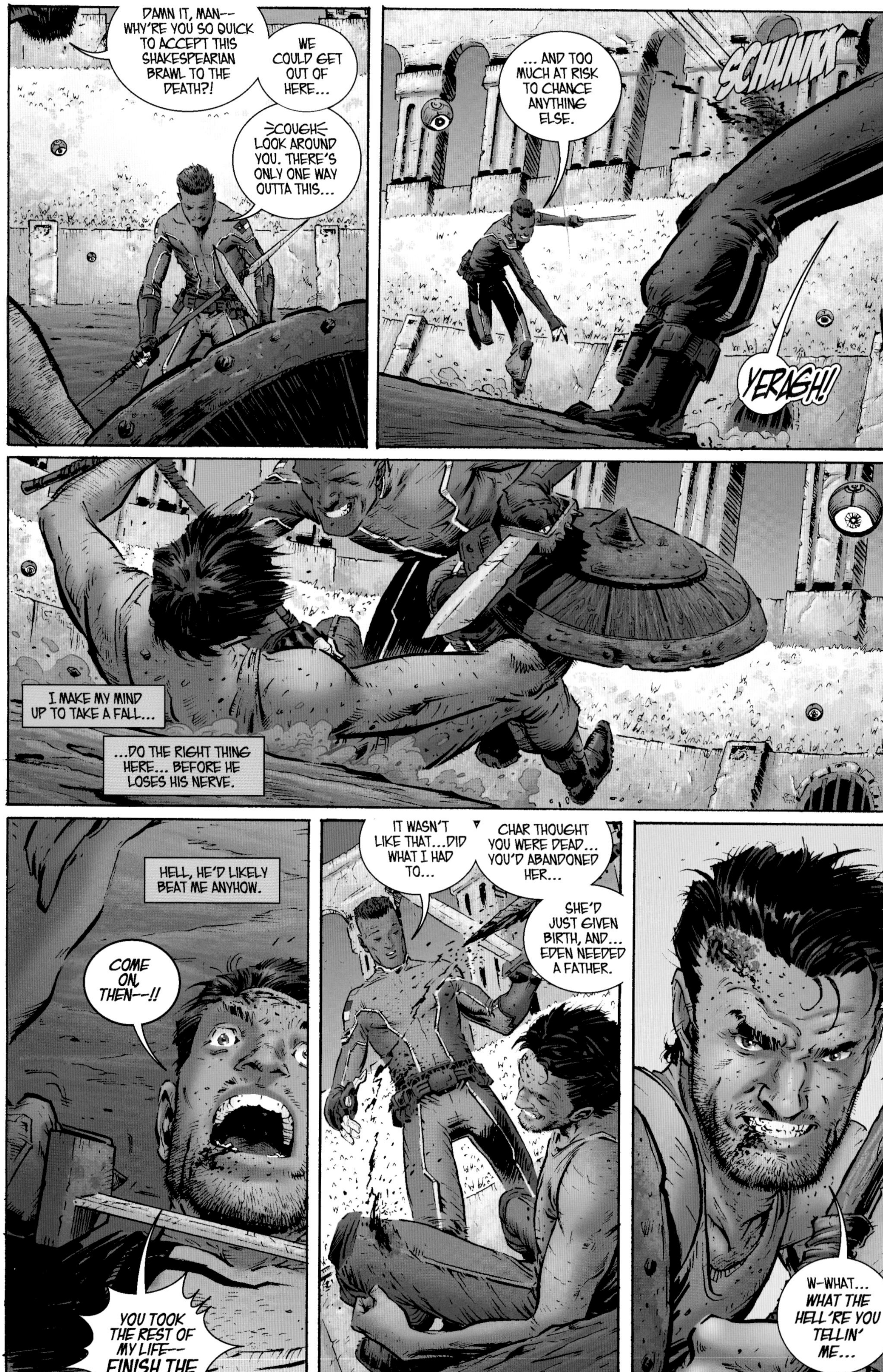
DAMN IT, MAN-- WHY'RE YOU SO QUICK TO ACCEPT THIS SHAKESPEARIAN BRAWL TO THE DEATH?!
WE COULD GET OUT OF HERE...
COUGH LOOK AROUND YOU. THERE'S ONLY ONE WAY OUTTA THIS...
... AND TOO MUCH AT RISK TO CHANCE ANYTHING ELSE.
SCHUNKK
YERAGH!
I MAKE MY MIND UP TO TAKE A FALL...
...DO THE RIGHT THING HERE... BEFORE HE LOSES HIS NERVE.
HELL, HE'D LIKELY BEAT ME ANYHOW.
COME ON, THEN--!!
YOU TOOK THE REST OF MY LIFE-- FINISH THE JOB!!
IT WASN'T LIKE THAT...DID WHAT I HAD TO...
CHAR THOUGHT YOU WERE DEAD... YOU'D ABANDONED HER...
SHE'D JUST GIVEN BIRTH, AND... EDEN NEEDED A FATHER.
W-WHAT... WHAT THE HELL'RE YOU TELLIN' ME...

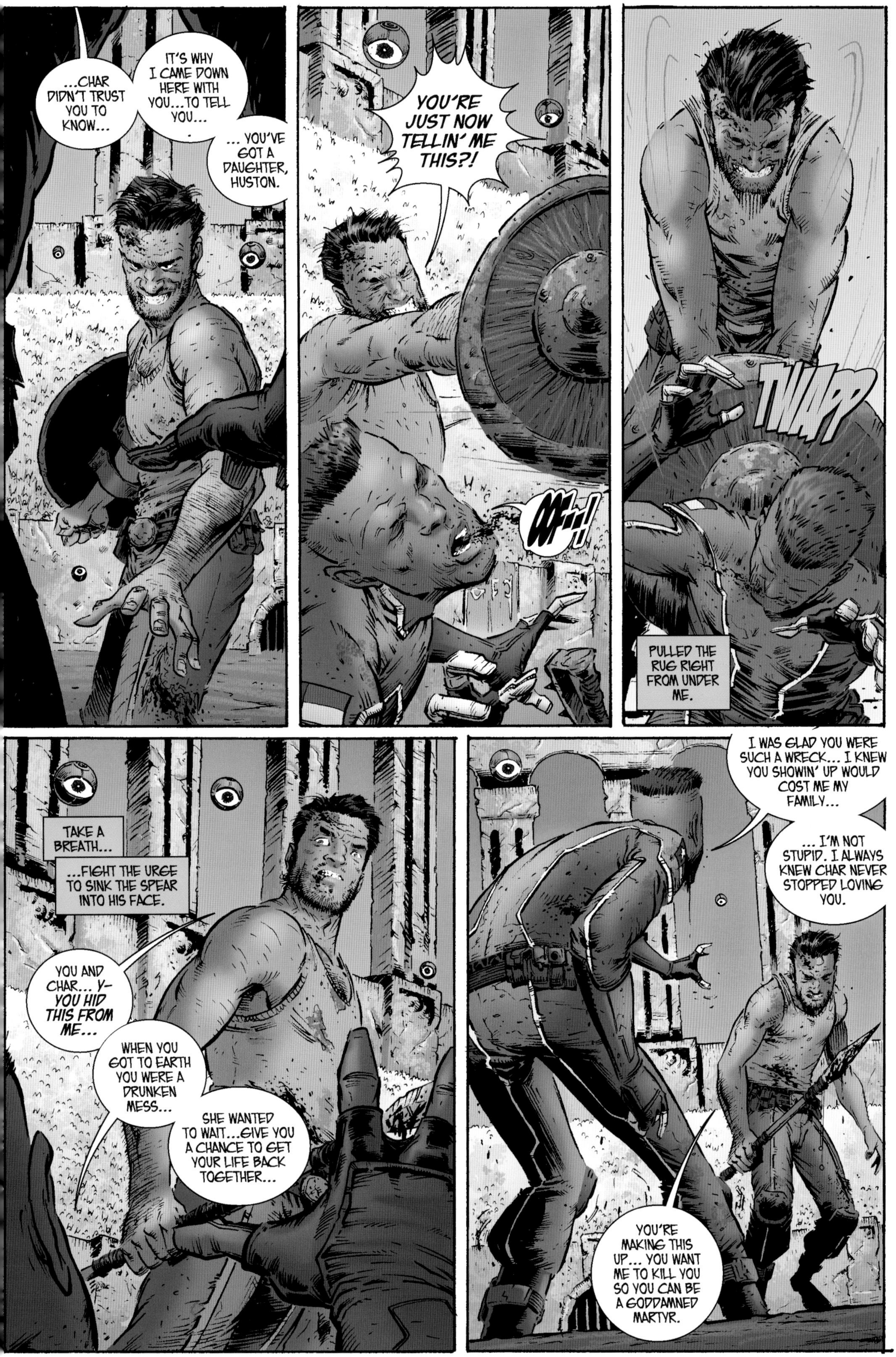
...CHAR DIDN'T TRUST YOU TO KNOW...
IT'S WHY I CAME DOWN HERE WITH YOU...TO TELL YOU...
... YOU'VE GOT A DAUGHTER, HUSTON.
YOU'RE JUST NOW TELLIN' ME THIS?!
OOF!!
TWAPP
PULLED THE RUG RIGHT FROM UNDER ME.
TAKE A BREATH...
...FIGHT THE URGE TO SINK THE SPEAR INTO HIS FACE.
YOU AND CHAR... Y-YOU HID THIS FROM ME...
WHEN YOU GOT TO EARTH YOU WERE A DRUNKEN MESS...
SHE WANTED TO WAIT...GIVE YOU A CHANCE TO GET YOUR LIFE BACK TOGETHER...
I WAS GLAD YOU WERE SUCH A WRECK... I KNEW YOU SHOWIN' UP WOULD COST ME MY FAMILY...
... I'M NOT STUPID. I ALWAYS KNEW CHAR NEVER STOPPED LOVING YOU.
YOU'RE MAKING THIS UP... YOU WANT ME TO KILL YOU SO YOU CAN BE A GODDAMNED MARTYR.

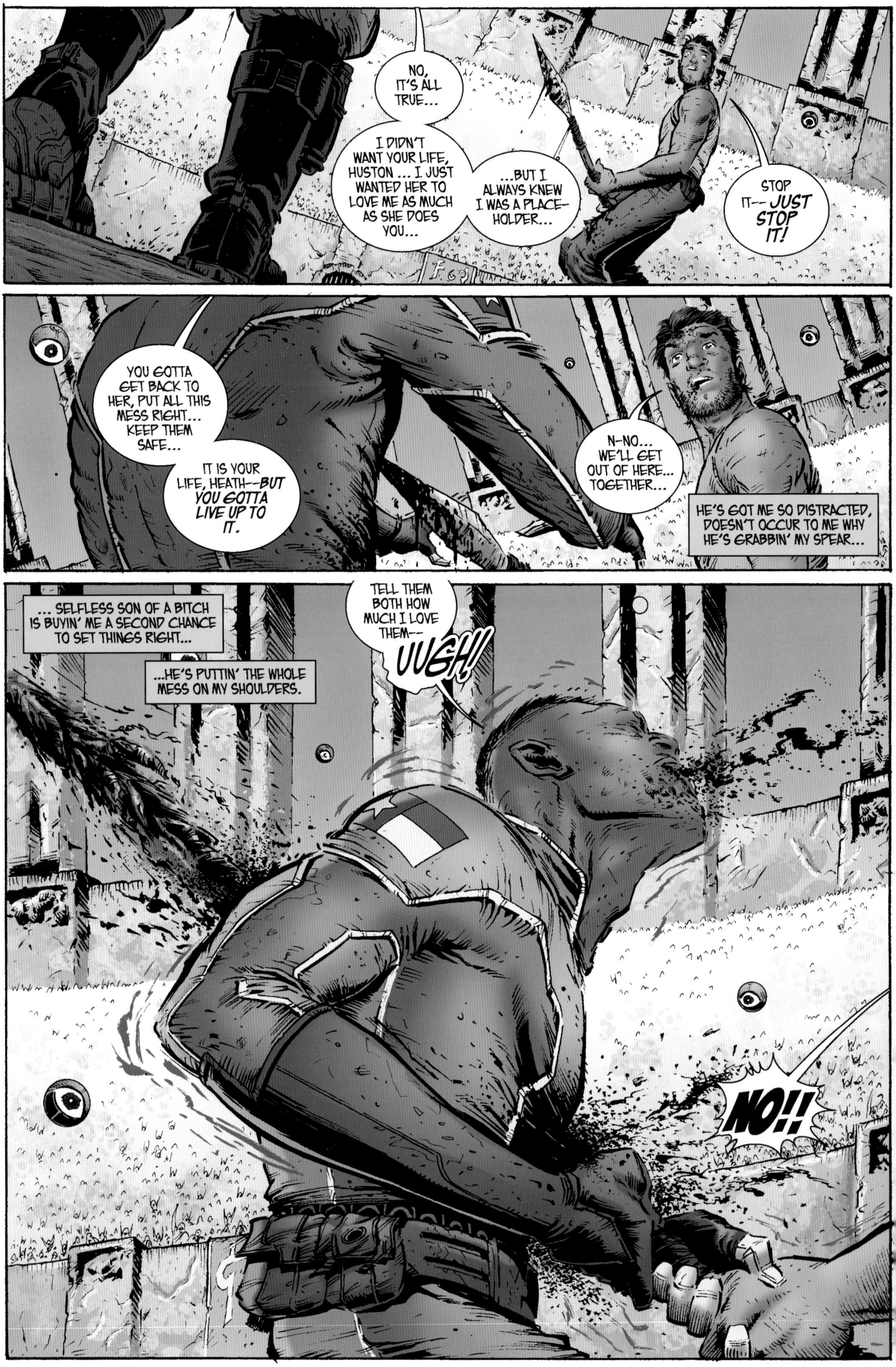
NO, IT'S ALL TRUE...
I DIDN'T WANT YOUR LIFE, HUSTON ... I JUST WANTED HER TO LOVE ME AS MUCH AS SHE DOES YOU...
...BUT I ALWAYS KNEW I WAS A PLACE-HOLDER...
STOP IT-- JUST STOP IT!
YOU GOTTA GET BACK TO HER, PUT ALL THIS MESS RIGHT... KEEP THEM SAFE...
IT IS YOUR LIFE, HEATH--BUT YOU GOTTA LIVE UP TO IT.
N-NO... WE'LL GET OUT OF HERE... TOGETHER...
HE'S GOT ME SO DISTRACTED, DOESN'T OCCUR TO ME WHY HE'S GRABBIN' MY SPEAR...
... SELFLESS SON OF A BITCH IS BUYIN' ME A SECOND CHANCE TO SET THINGS RIGHT...
...HE'S PUTTIN' THE WHOLE MESS ON MY SHOULDERS.
TELL THEM BOTH HOW MUCH I LOVE THEM--
UUGH!
NO!!

CHAPTER 3

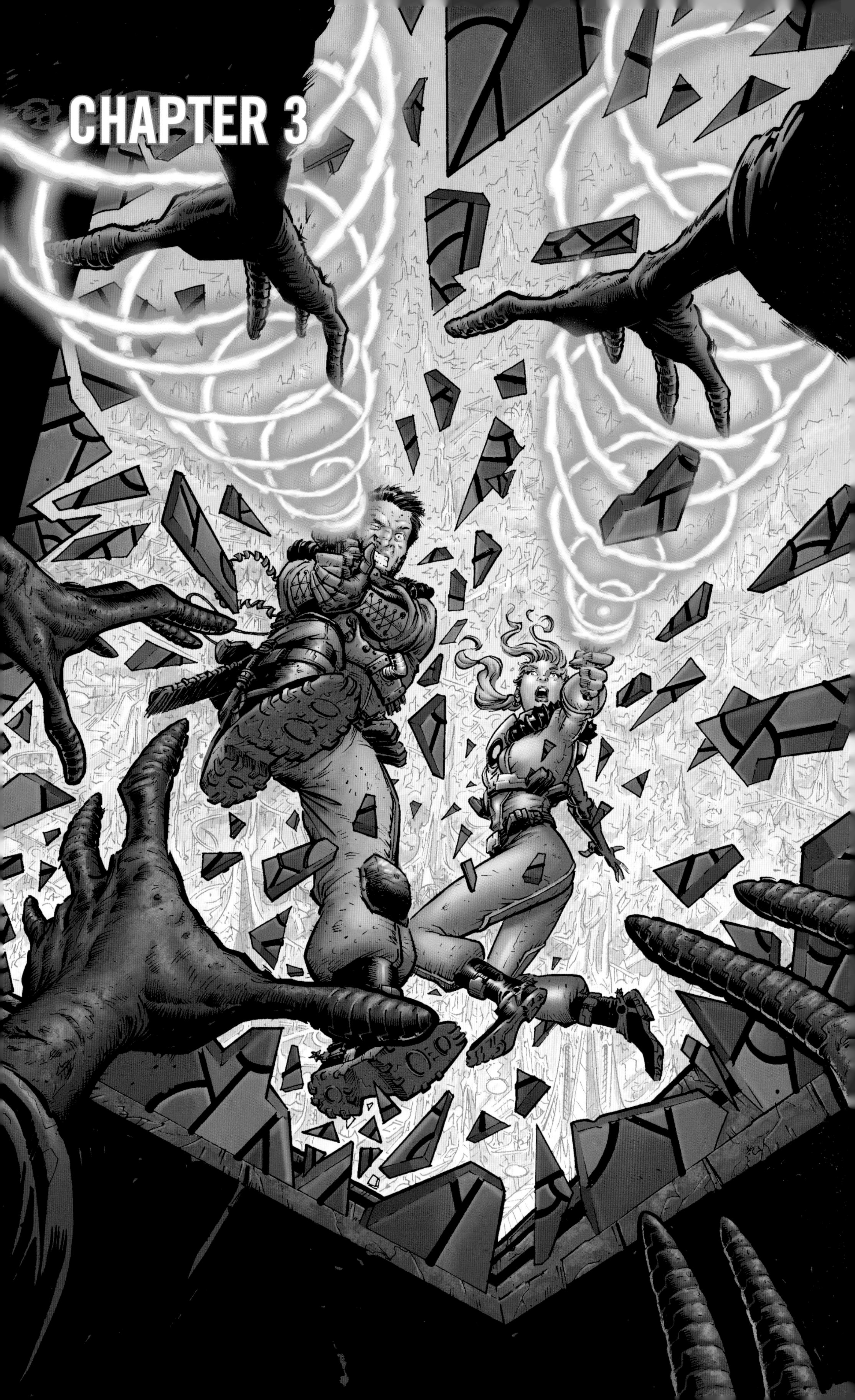

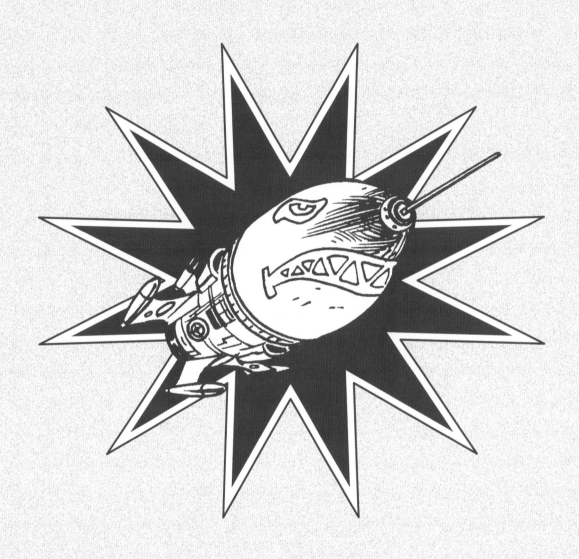

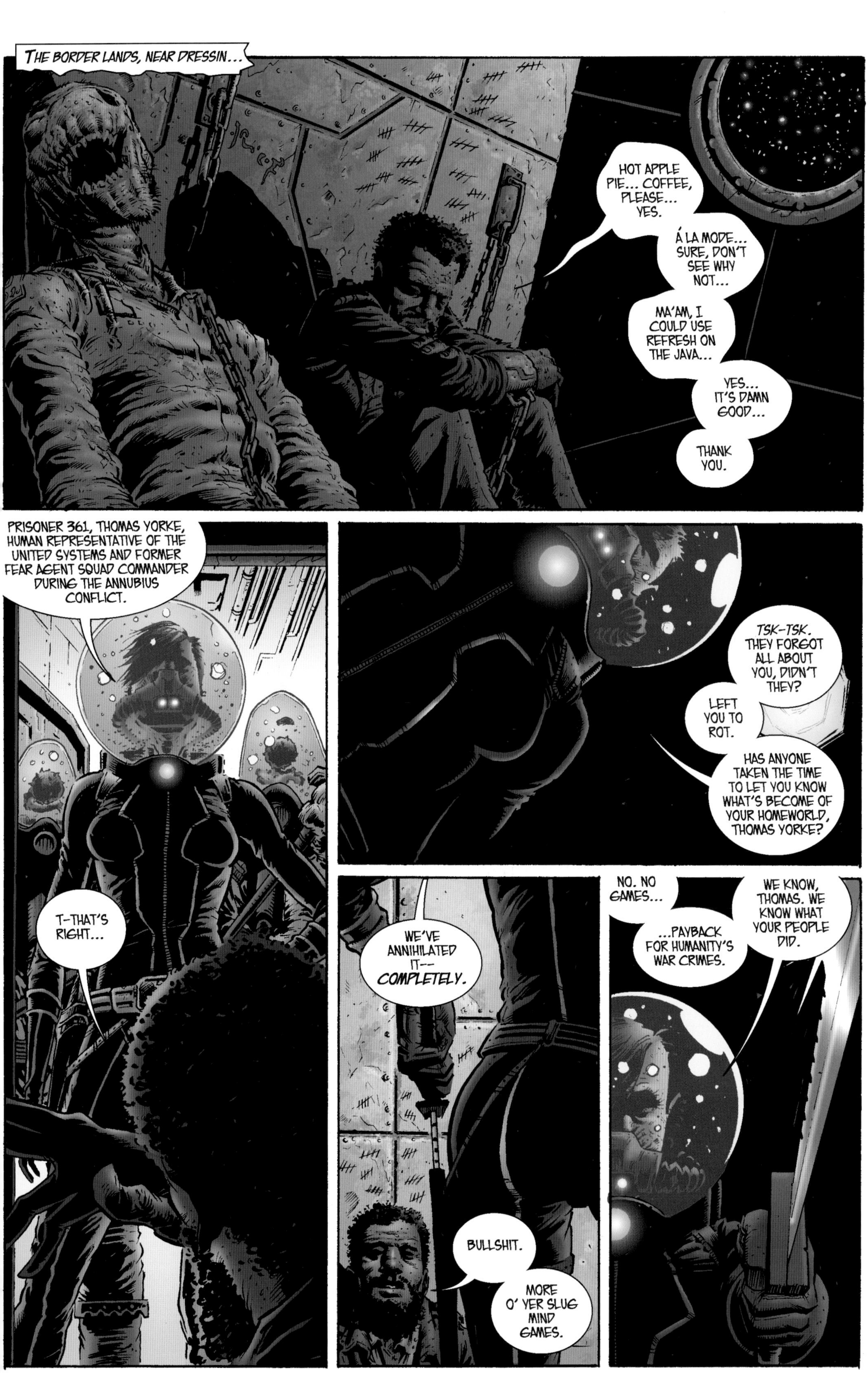
THE BORDER LANDS, NEAR DRESSIN...
HOT APPLE PIE... COFFEE, PLEASE... YES.
Á LA MODE... SURE, DON'T SEE WHY NOT...
MA'AM, I COULD USE REFRESH ON THE JAVA...
YES... IT'S DAMN GOOD...
THANK YOU.
PRISONER 361, THOMAS YORKE, HUMAN REPRESENTATIVE OF THE UNITED SYSTEMS AND FORMER FEAR AGENT SQUAD COMMANDER DURING THE ANNUBIUS CONFLICT.
T-THAT'S RIGHT...
TSK-TSK. THEY FORGOT ALL ABOUT YOU, DIDN'T THEY?
LEFT YOU TO ROT.
HAS ANYONE TAKEN THE TIME TO LET YOU KNOW WHAT'S BECOME OF YOUR HOMEWORLD, THOMAS YORKE?
WE'VE ANNIHILATED IT-- COMPLETELY.
BULLSHIT.
MORE O' YER SLUG MIND GAMES.
NO. NO GAMES...
...PAYBACK FOR HUMANITY'S WAR CRIMES.
WE KNOW, THOMAS. WE KNOW WHAT YOUR PEOPLE DID.

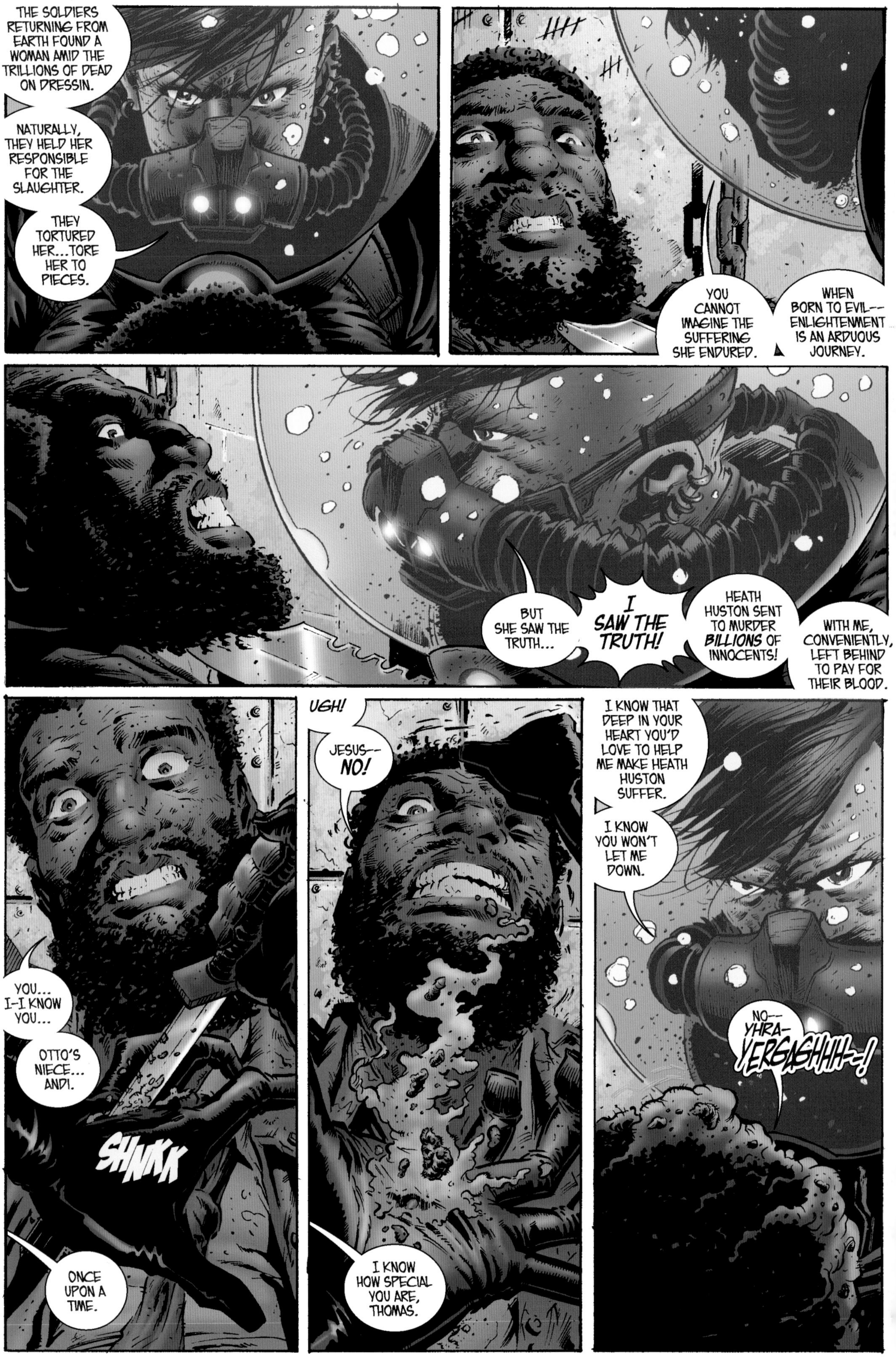
THE SOLDIERS RETURNING FROM EARTH FOUND A WOMAN AMID THE TRILLIONS OF DEAD ON DRESSIN.
NATURALLY, THEY HELD HER RESPONSIBLE FOR THE SLAUGHTER.
THEY TORTURED HER...TORE HER TO PIECES.
YOU CANNOT IMAGINE THE SUFFERING SHE ENDURED.
WHEN BORN TO EVIL-- ENLIGHTENMENT IS AN ARDUOUS JOURNEY.
BUT SHE SAW THE TRUTH...
I SAW THE TRUTH!
HEATH HUSTON SENT TO MURDER BILLIONS OF INNOCENTS!
WITH ME, CONVENIENTLY, LEFT BEHIND TO PAY FOR THEIR BLOOD.
YOU... I-I KNOW YOU...
OTTO'S NIECE... ANDI.
SHNKK
ONCE UPON A TIME.
UGH!
JESUS-- NO!
I KNOW HOW SPECIAL YOU ARE, THOMAS.
I KNOW THAT DEEP IN YOUR HEART YOU'D LOVE TO HELP ME MAKE HEATH HUSTON SUFFER.
I KNOW YOU WON'T LET ME DOWN.
NO-- YHRA- YERGASHHH--!

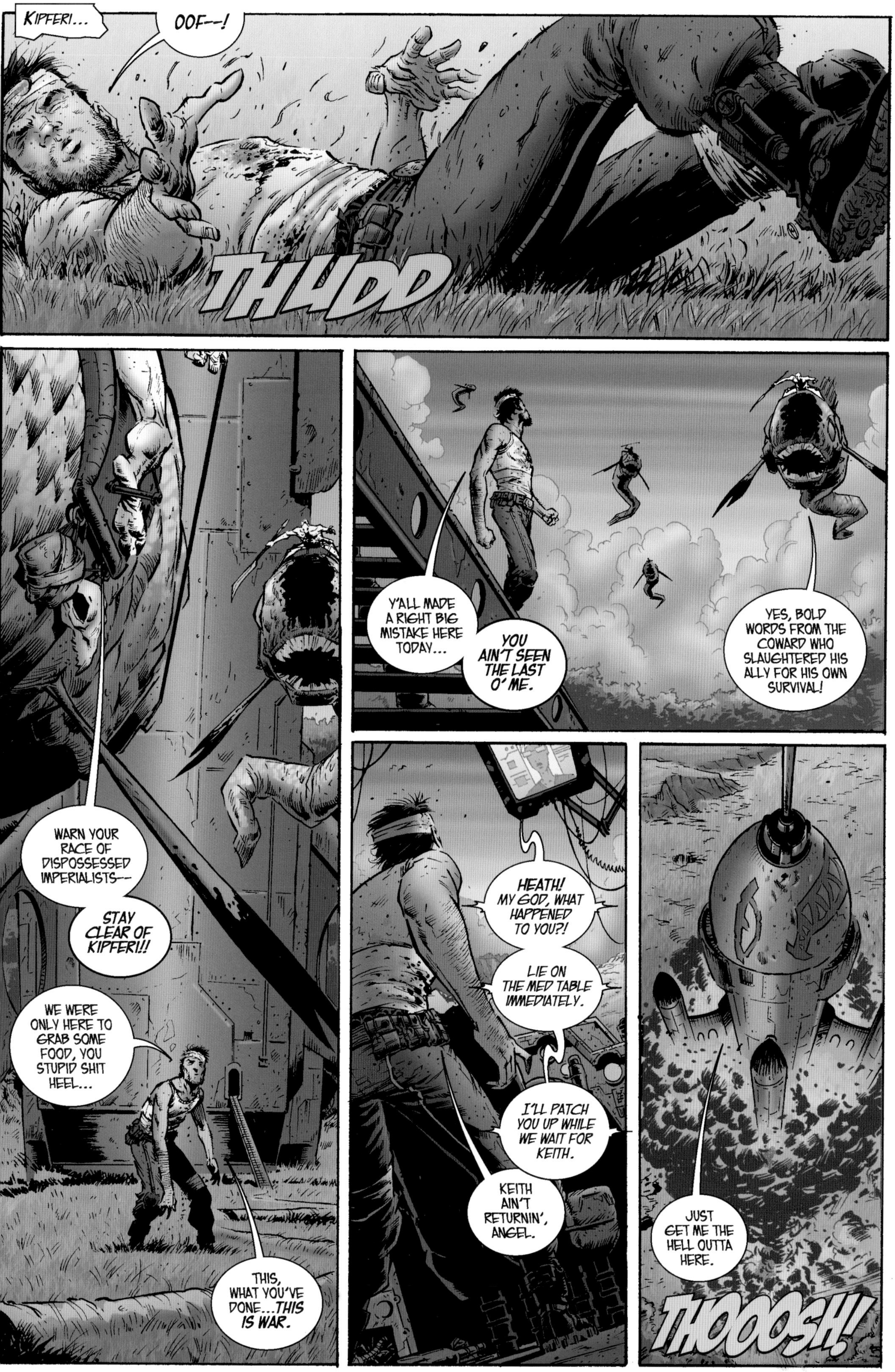

KIPFERI...
OOF--!
THUDD
Y'ALL MADE A RIGHT BIG MISTAKE HERE TODAY...
YOU AIN'T SEEN THE LAST O' ME.
YES, BOLD WORDS FROM THE COWARD WHO SLAUGHTERED HIS ALLY FOR HIS OWN SURVIVAL!
WARN YOUR RACE OF DISPOSSESSED IMPERIALISTS--
STAY CLEAR OF KIPFERI!!
WE WERE ONLY HERE TO GRAB SOME FOOD, YOU STUPID SHIT HEEL...
THIS, WHAT YOU'VE DONE...THIS IS WAR.
HEATH! MY GOD, WHAT HAPPENED TO YOU?!
LIE ON THE MED TABLE IMMEDIATELY.
I'LL PATCH YOU UP WHILE WE WAIT FOR KEITH.
KEITH AIN'T RETURNIN', ANGEL.
JUST GET ME THE HELL OUTTA HERE.
THOOOSH!

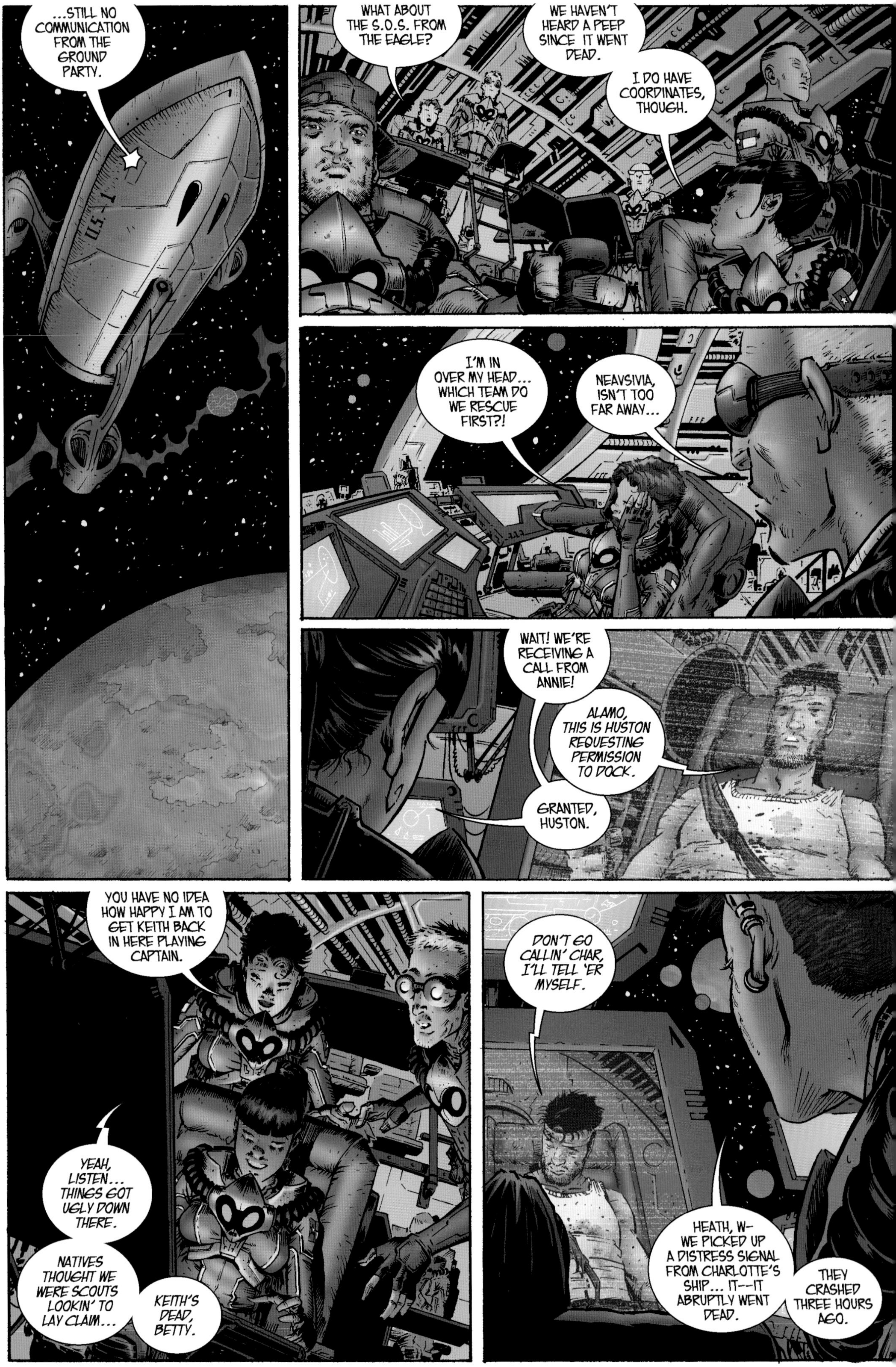
...STILL NO COMMUNICATION FROM THE GROUND PARTY.
U.S. 1
WHAT ABOUT THE S.O.S. FROM THE EAGLE?
WE HAVEN'T HEARD A PEEP SINCE IT WENT DEAD.
I DO HAVE COORDINATES, THOUGH.
I'M IN OVER MY HEAD... WHICH TEAM DO WE RESCUE FIRST?!
NEAVSIVIA, ISN'T TOO FAR AWAY...
WAIT! WE'RE RECEIVING A CALL FROM ANNIE!
ALAMO, THIS IS HUSTON REQUESTING PERMISSION TO DOCK.
GRANTED, HUSTON.
YOU HAVE NO IDEA HOW HAPPY I AM TO GET KEITH BACK IN HERE PLAYING CAPTAIN.
YEAH, LISTEN... THINGS GOT UGLY DOWN THERE.
NATIVES THOUGHT WE WERE SCOUTS LOOKIN' TO LAY CLAIM...
KEITH'S DEAD, BETTY.
DON'T GO CALLIN' CHAR, I'LL TELL 'ER MYSELF.
HEATH, W-WE PICKED UP A DISTRESS SIGNAL FROM CHARLOTTE'S SHIP... IT--IT ABRUPTLY WENT DEAD.
THEY CRASHED THREE HOURS AGO.

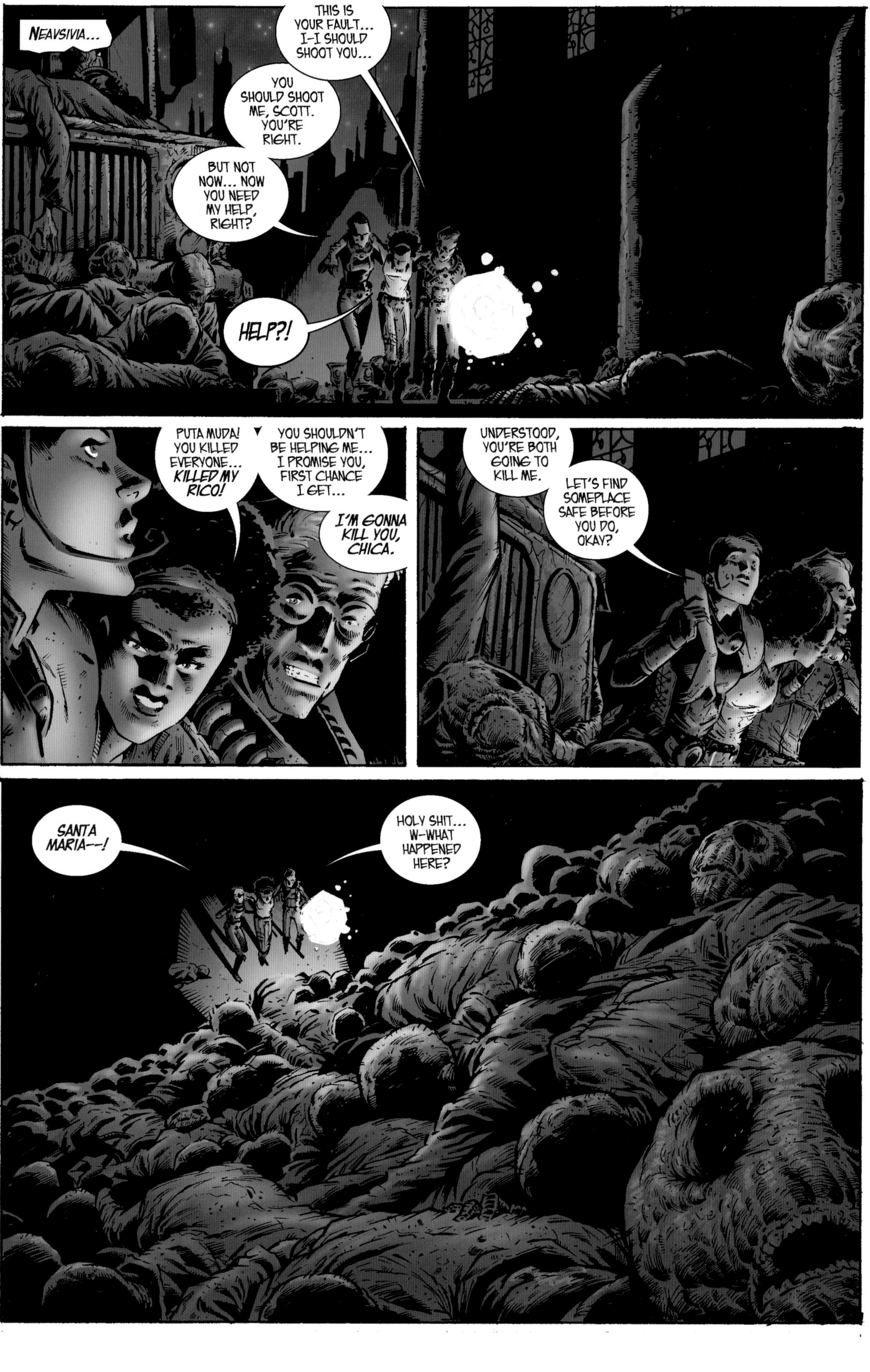
NEAVSIVIA...
THIS IS YOUR FAULT... I-I SHOULD SHOOT YOU...
YOU SHOULD SHOOT ME, SCOTT. YOU'RE RIGHT.
BUT NOT NOW... NOW YOU NEED MY HELP, RIGHT?
HELP?!
PUTA MUDA! YOU KILLED EVERYONE... KILLED MY RICO!
YOU SHOULDN'T BE HELPING ME... I PROMISE YOU, FIRST CHANCE I GET...
I'M GONNA KILL YOU, CHICA.
UNDERSTOOD, YOU'RE BOTH GOING TO KILL ME.
LET'S FIND SOMEPLACE SAFE BEFORE YOU DO, OKAY?
SANTA MARIA--!
HOLY SHIT... W-WHAT HAPPENED HERE?

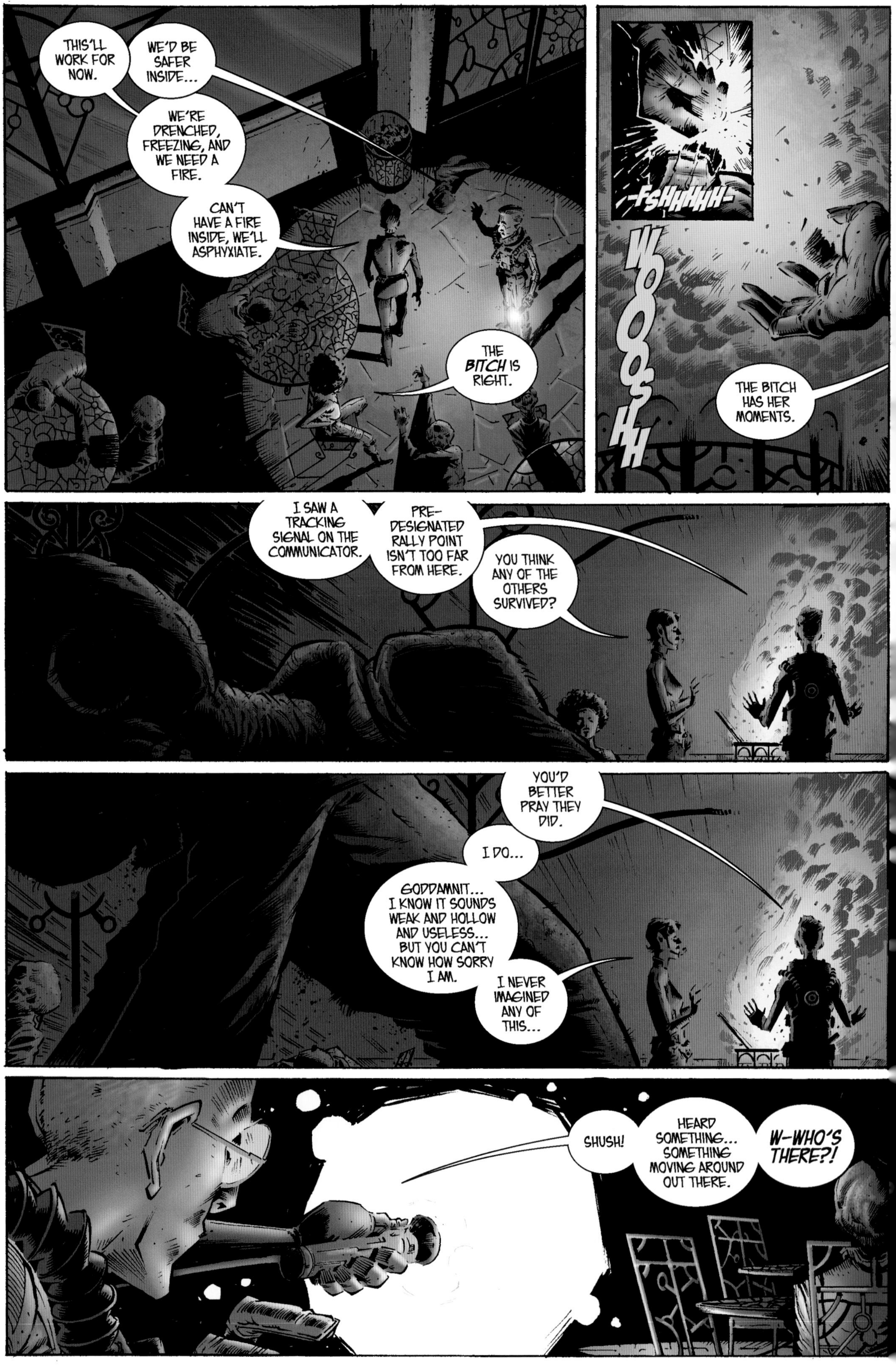
THIS'LL WORK FOR NOW.
WE'D BE SAFER INSIDE...
WE'RE DRENCHED, FREEZING, AND WE NEED A FIRE.
CAN'T HAVE A FIRE INSIDE, WE'LL ASPHYXIATE.
THE *BITCH* IS RIGHT.
-FSHHHHH-
WOOOOSHHH
THE BITCH HAS HER MOMENTS.
I SAW A TRACKING SIGNAL ON THE COMMUNICATOR.
PRE-DESIGNATED RALLY POINT ISN'T TOO FAR FROM HERE.
YOU THINK ANY OF THE OTHERS SURVIVED?
YOU'D BETTER PRAY THEY DID.
I DO...
GODDAMNIT... I KNOW IT SOUNDS WEAK AND HOLLOW AND USELESS... BUT YOU CAN'T KNOW HOW SORRY I AM.
I NEVER IMAGINED ANY OF THIS...
SHUSH!
HEARD SOMETHING... SOMETHING MOVING AROUND OUT THERE.
W-WHO'S THERE?!

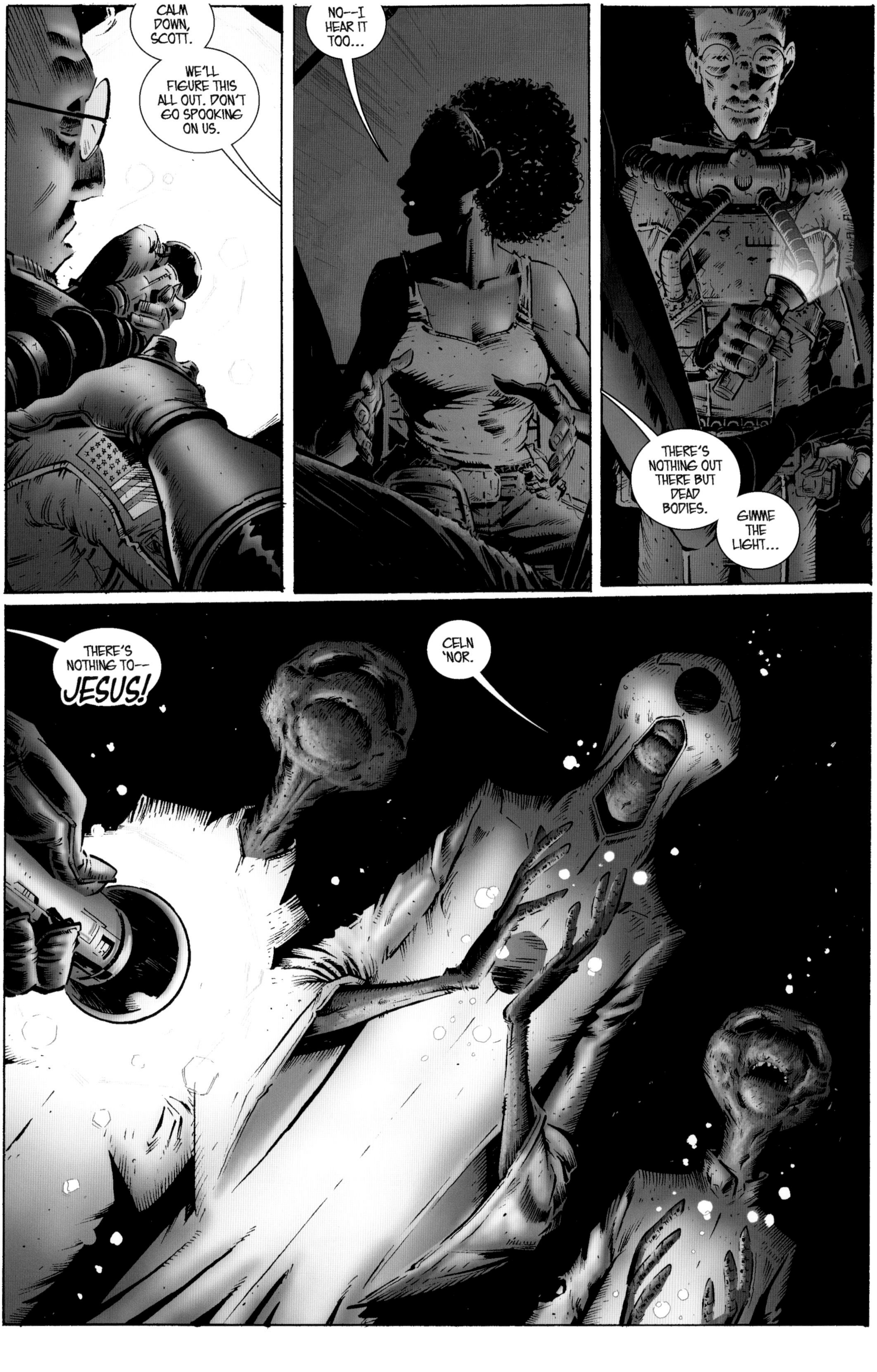
CALM DOWN, SCOTT.
WE'LL FIGURE THIS ALL OUT. DON'T GO SPOOKING ON US.
NO--I HEAR IT TOO...
THERE'S NOTHING OUT THERE BUT DEAD BODIES.
GIMME THE LIGHT...
THERE'S NOTHING TO-- JESUS!
CELN 'NOR.

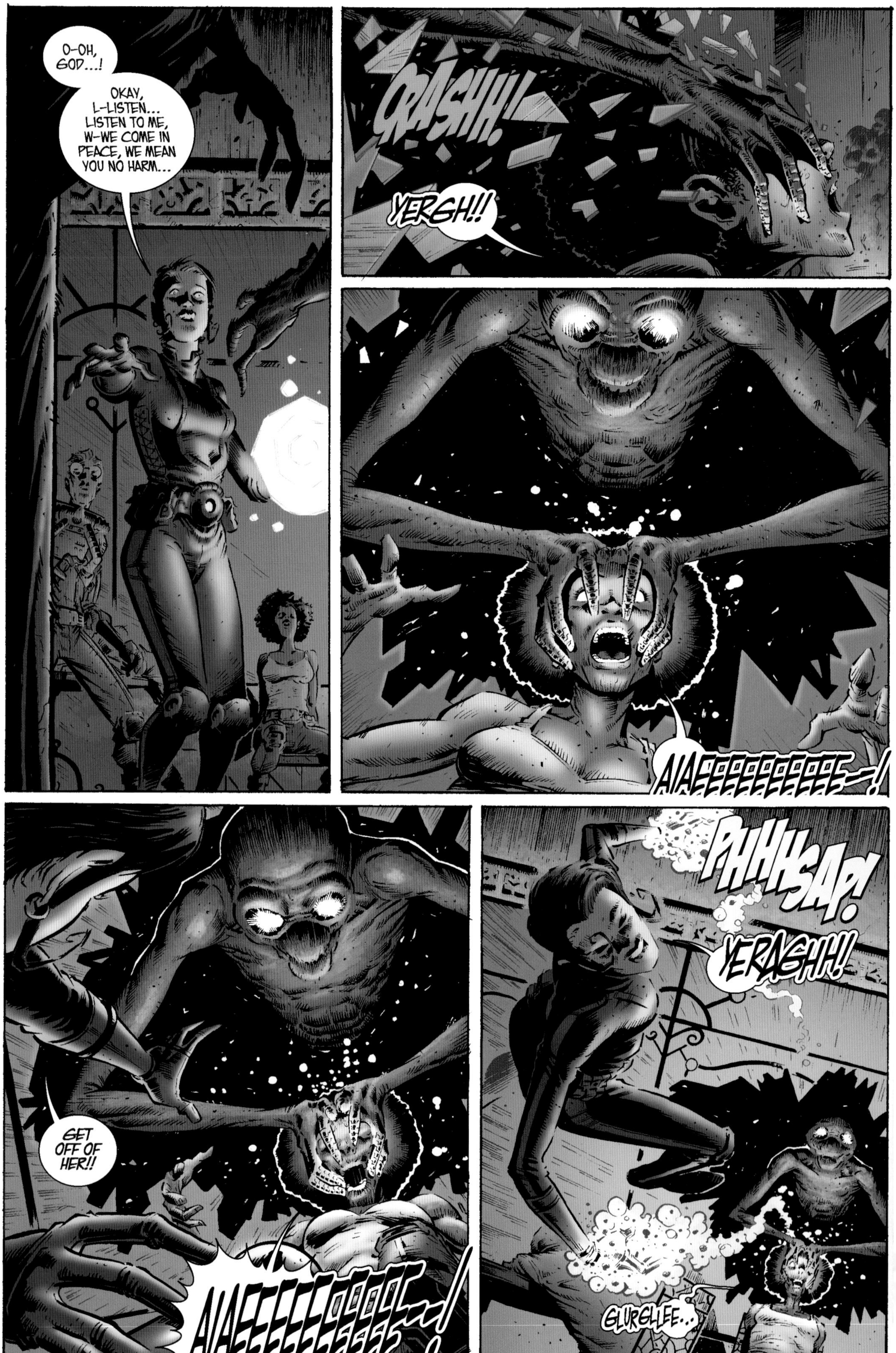
O-OH, GOD...!
OKAY, L-LISTEN... LISTEN TO ME, W-WE COME IN PEACE, WE MEAN YOU NO HARM...
CRASHH!
YERGH!!
AIAEEEEEEEEEEEE--!
GET OFF OF HER!!
AIAEEEEEEEEEEEEEEEE--!
PHHHSAP!
YERASHH!
GLURGLEE...

WHOOOSH!

GHRAH! GET AWAY FROM HER!

RUN!

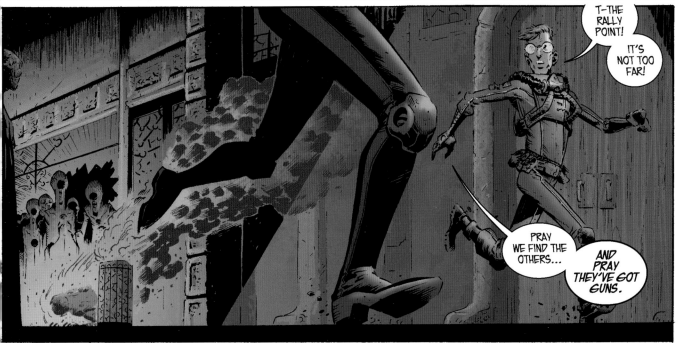

T-THE RALLY POINT!

IT'S NOT TOO FAR!

PRAY WE FIND THE OTHERS...

AND PRAY THEY'VE GOT GUNS.

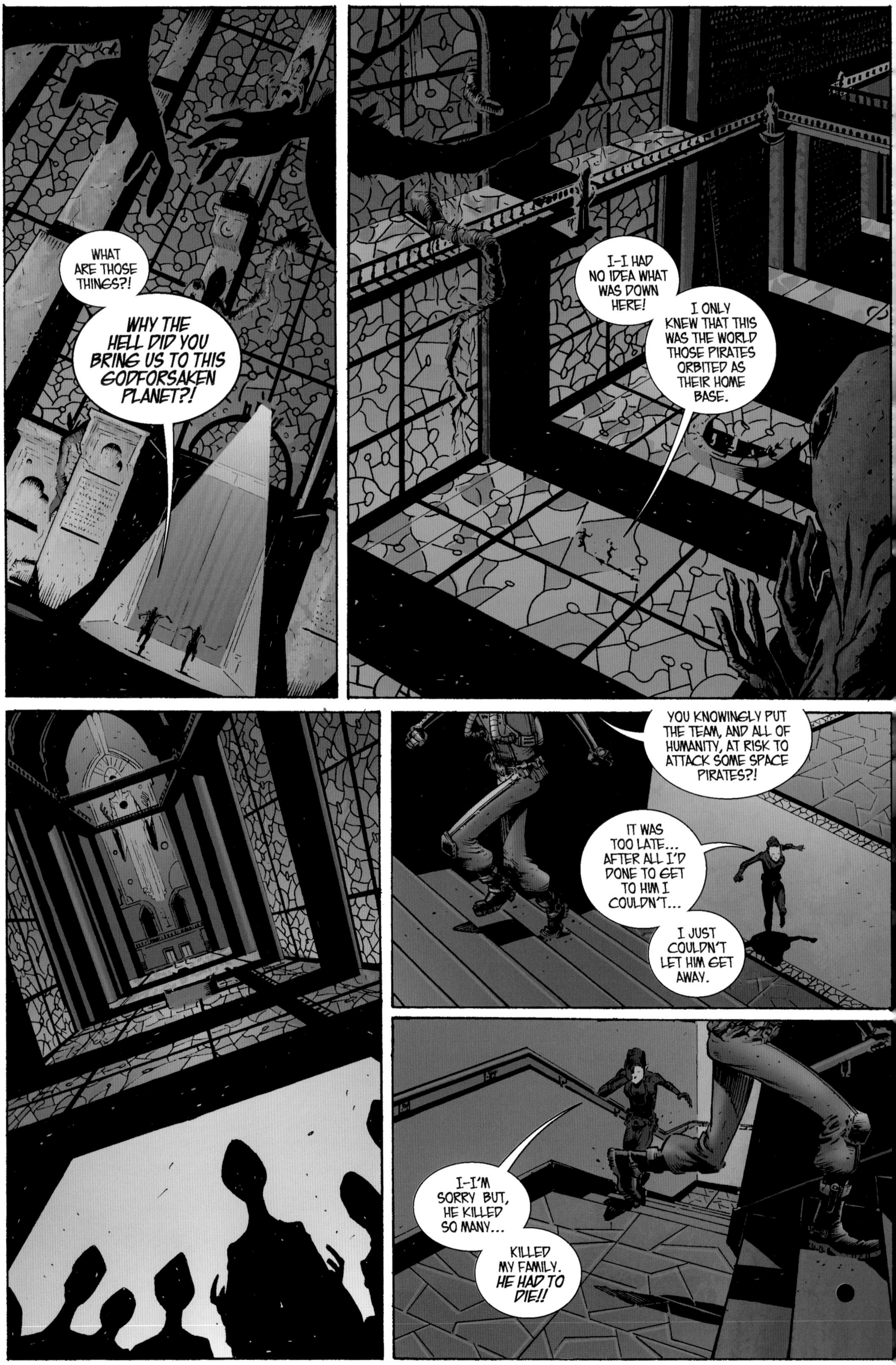
WHAT ARE THOSE THINGS?!
WHY THE HELL DID YOU BRING US TO THIS GODFORSAKEN PLANET?!
I-I HAD NO IDEA WHAT WAS DOWN HERE!
I ONLY KNEW THAT THIS WAS THE WORLD THOSE PIRATES ORBITED AS THEIR HOME BASE.
YOU KNOWINGLY PUT THE TEAM, AND ALL OF HUMANITY, AT RISK TO ATTACK SOME SPACE PIRATES?!
IT WAS TOO LATE... AFTER ALL I'D DONE TO GET TO HIM I COULDN'T...
I JUST COULDN'T LET HIM GET AWAY.
I-I'M SORRY BUT, HE KILLED SO MANY...
KILLED MY FAMILY. HE HAD TO DIE!!

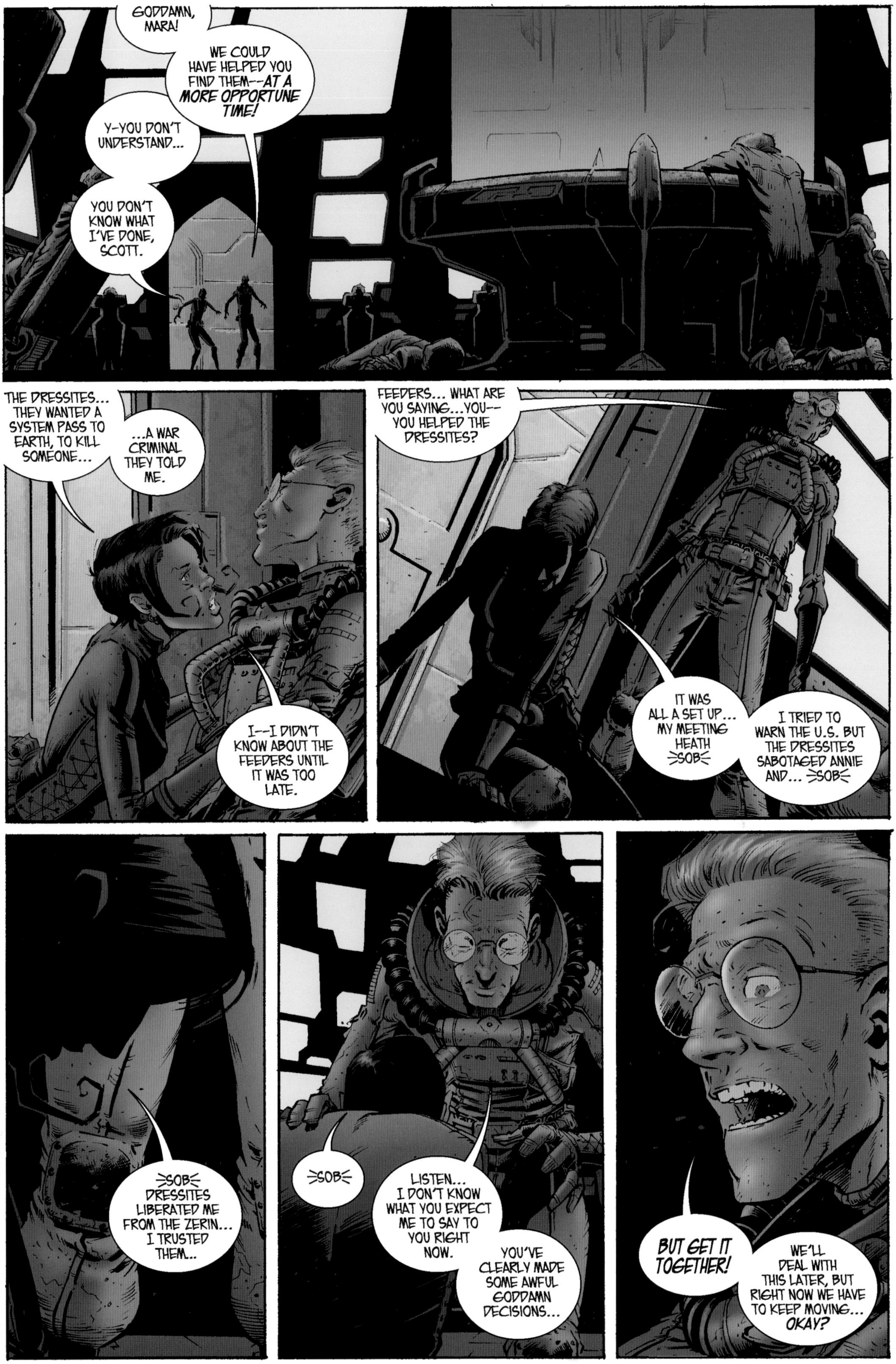

GODDAMN, MARA!
WE COULD HAVE HELPED YOU FIND THEM--AT A MORE OPPORTUNE TIME!
Y-YOU DON'T UNDERSTAND...
YOU DON'T KNOW WHAT I'VE DONE, SCOTT.
THE DRESSITES... THEY WANTED A SYSTEM PASS TO EARTH, TO KILL SOMEONE...
...A WAR CRIMINAL THEY TOLD ME.
I--I DIDN'T KNOW ABOUT THE FEEDERS UNTIL IT WAS TOO LATE.
FEEDERS... WHAT ARE YOU SAYING...YOU--YOU HELPED THE DRESSITES?
IT WAS ALL A SET UP... MY MEETING HEATH ≥SOB≤
I TRIED TO WARN THE U.S. BUT THE DRESSITES SABOTAGED ANNIE AND... ≥SOB≤
≥SOB≤ DRESSITES LIBERATED ME FROM THE ZERIN... I TRUSTED THEM...
≥SOB≤
LISTEN... I DON'T KNOW WHAT YOU EXPECT ME TO SAY TO YOU RIGHT NOW.
YOU'VE CLEARLY MADE SOME AWFUL GODDAMN DECISIONS...
BUT GET IT TOGETHER!
WE'LL DEAL WITH THIS LATER, BUT RIGHT NOW WE HAVE TO KEEP MOVING... OKAY?

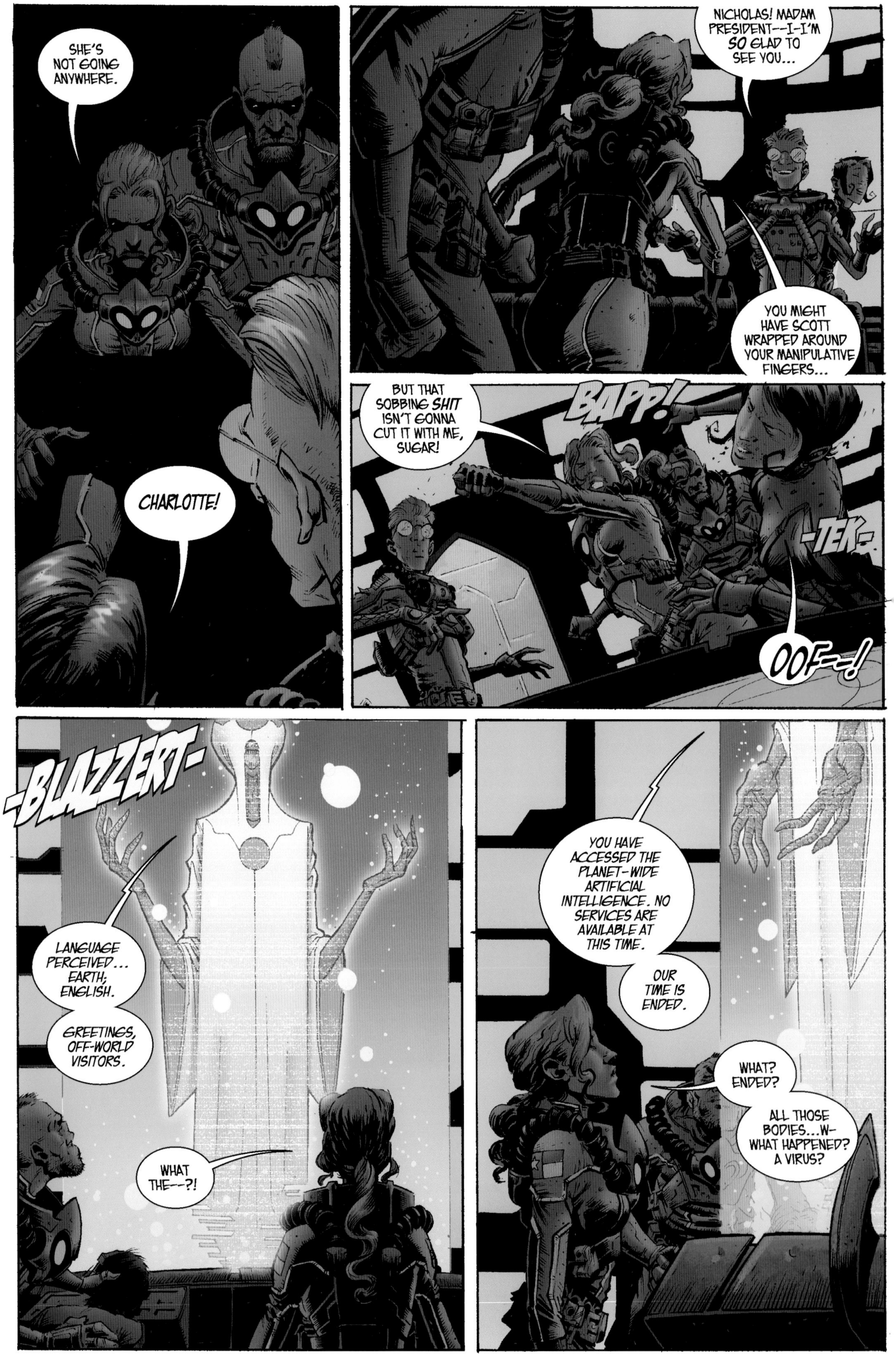
SHE'S NOT GOING ANYWHERE.
CHARLOTTE!
NICHOLAS! MADAM PRESIDENT--I-I'M SO GLAD TO SEE YOU...
YOU MIGHT HAVE SCOTT WRAPPED AROUND YOUR MANIPULATIVE FINGERS...
BUT THAT SOBBING SHIT ISN'T GONNA CUT IT WITH ME, SUGAR!
BAPP!
-TEK-
OOF--!
-BLAZZERT-
LANGUAGE PERCEIVED... EARTH; ENGLISH.
GREETINGS, OFF-WORLD VISITORS.
WHAT THE--?!
YOU HAVE ACCESSED THE PLANET-WIDE ARTIFICIAL INTELLIGENCE. NO SERVICES ARE AVAILABLE AT THIS TIME.
OUR TIME IS ENDED.
WHAT? ENDED?
ALL THOSE BODIES...W-WHAT HAPPENED? A VIRUS?

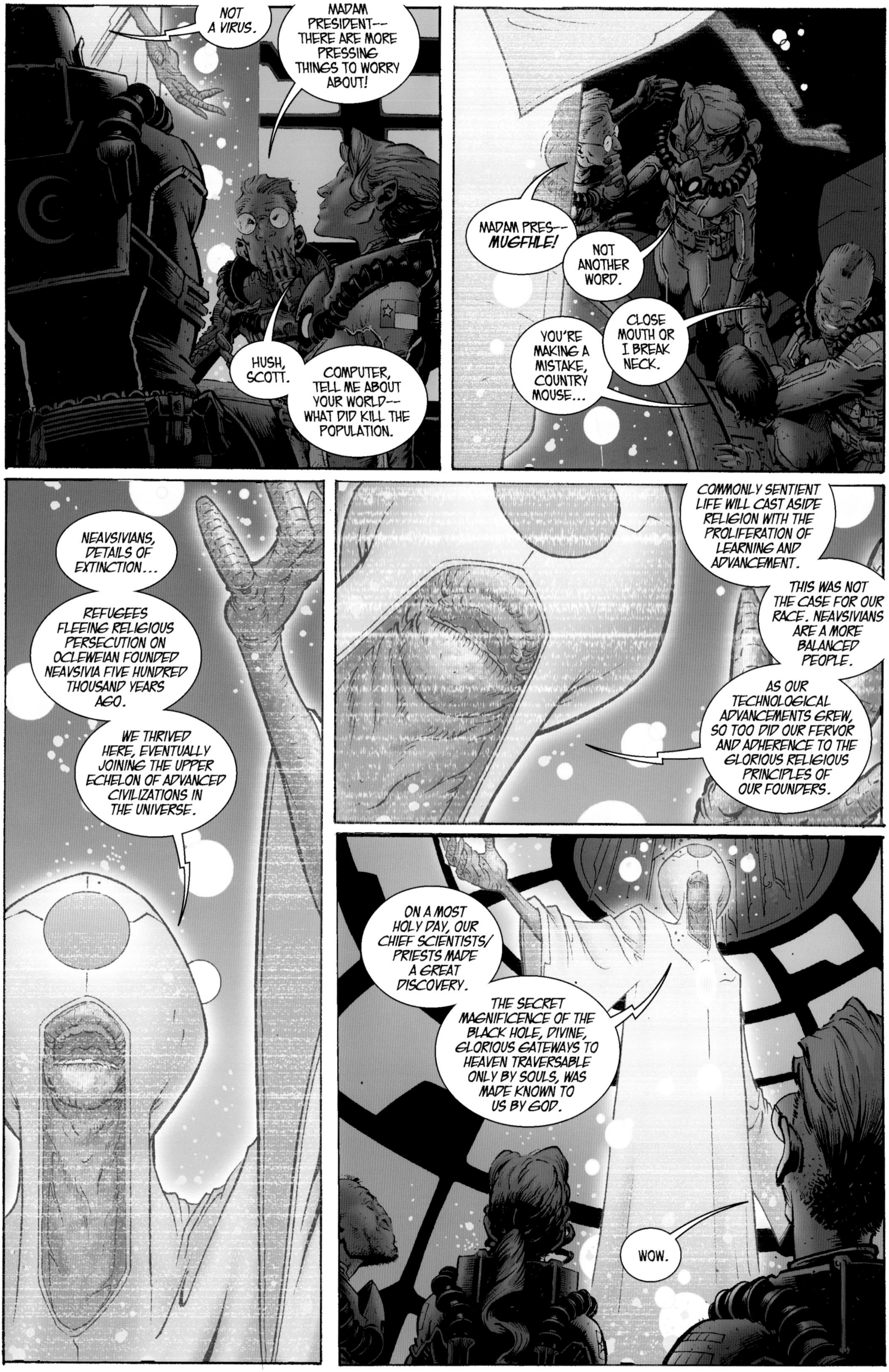
NOT A VIRUS.
MADAM PRESIDENT--- THERE ARE MORE PRESSING THINGS TO WORRY ABOUT!
HUSH, SCOTT.
COMPUTER, TELL ME ABOUT YOUR WORLD--- WHAT DID KILL THE POPULATION.
MADAM PRES--- MUGFHLE!
NOT ANOTHER WORD.
CLOSE MOUTH OR I BREAK NECK.
YOU'RE MAKING A MISTAKE, COUNTRY MOUSE...
NEAVSIVIANS, DETAILS OF EXTINCTION...
REFUGEES FLEEING RELIGIOUS PERSECUTION ON OCLEWEIAN FOUNDED NEAVSIVIA FIVE HUNDRED THOUSAND YEARS AGO.
WE THRIVED HERE, EVENTUALLY JOINING THE UPPER ECHELON OF ADVANCED CIVILIZATIONS IN THE UNIVERSE.
COMMONLY SENTIENT LIFE WILL CAST ASIDE RELIGION WITH THE PROLIFERATION OF LEARNING AND ADVANCEMENT.
THIS WAS NOT THE CASE FOR OUR RACE. NEAVSIVIANS ARE A MORE BALANCED PEOPLE.
AS OUR TECHNOLOGICAL ADVANCEMENTS GREW, SO TOO DID OUR FERVOR AND ADHERENCE TO THE GLORIOUS RELIGIOUS PRINCIPLES OF OUR FOUNDERS.
ON A MOST HOLY DAY, OUR CHIEF SCIENTISTS/ PRIESTS MADE A GREAT DISCOVERY.
THE SECRET MAGNIFICENCE OF THE BLACK HOLE, DIVINE, GLORIOUS GATEWAYS TO HEAVEN TRAVERSABLE ONLY BY SOULS, WAS MADE KNOWN TO US BY GOD.
WOW.

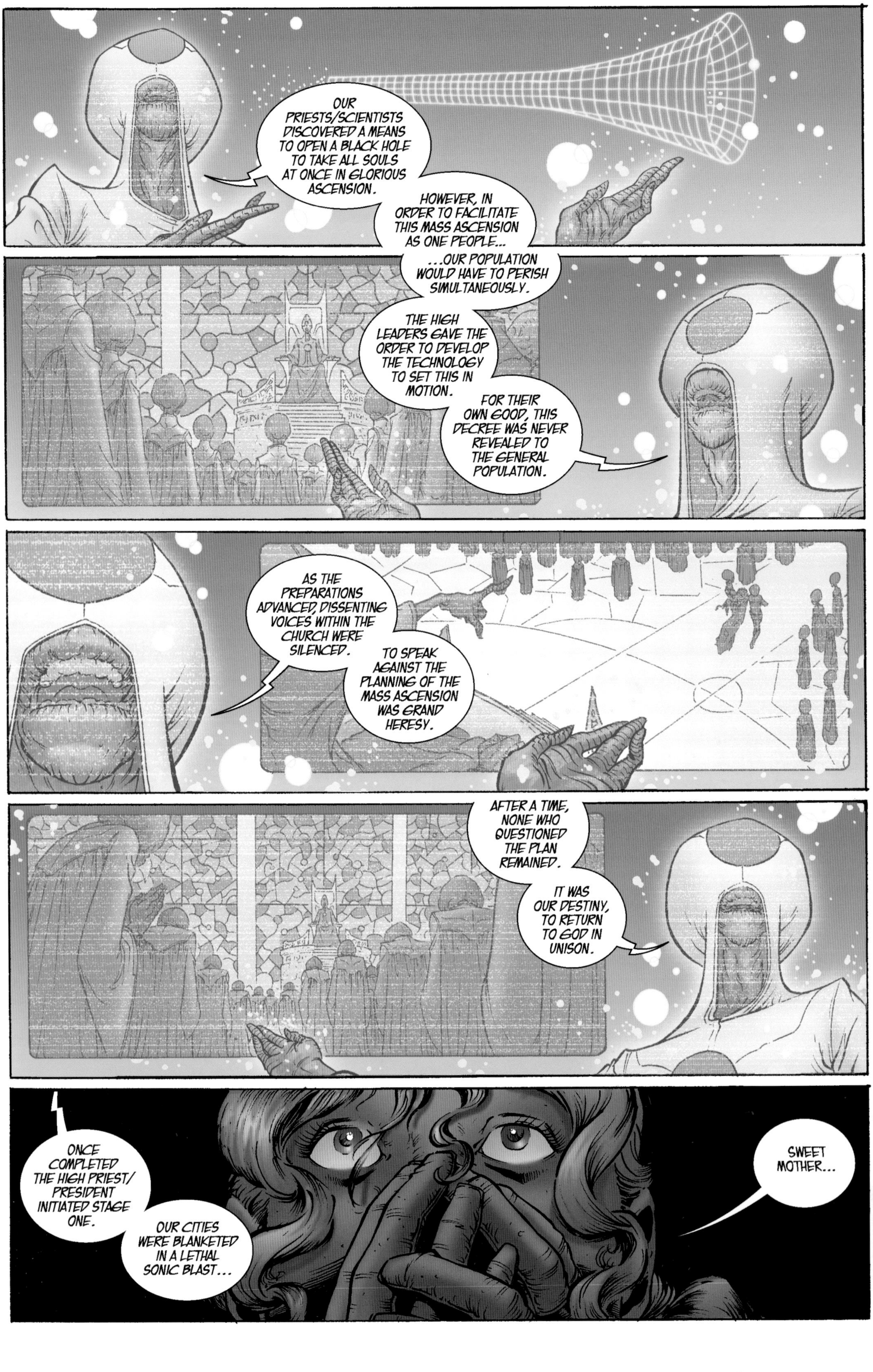

OUR PRIESTS/SCIENTISTS DISCOVERED A MEANS TO OPEN A BLACK HOLE TO TAKE ALL SOULS AT ONCE IN GLORIOUS ASCENSION.
HOWEVER, IN ORDER TO FACILITATE THIS MASS ASCENSION AS ONE PEOPLE...
...OUR POPULATION WOULD HAVE TO PERISH SIMULTANEOUSLY.
THE HIGH LEADERS GAVE THE ORDER TO DEVELOP THE TECHNOLOGY TO SET THIS IN MOTION.
FOR THEIR OWN GOOD, THIS DECREE WAS NEVER REVEALED TO THE GENERAL POPULATION.
AS THE PREPARATIONS ADVANCED, DISSENTING VOICES WITHIN THE CHURCH WERE SILENCED.
TO SPEAK AGAINST THE PLANNING OF THE MASS ASCENSION WAS GRAND HERESY.
AFTER A TIME, NONE WHO QUESTIONED THE PLAN REMAINED.
IT WAS OUR DESTINY, TO RETURN TO GOD IN UNISON.
ONCE COMPLETED THE HIGH PRIEST/ PRESIDENT INITIATED STAGE ONE.
OUR CITIES WERE BLANKETED IN A LETHAL SONIC BLAST...
SWEET MOTHER...

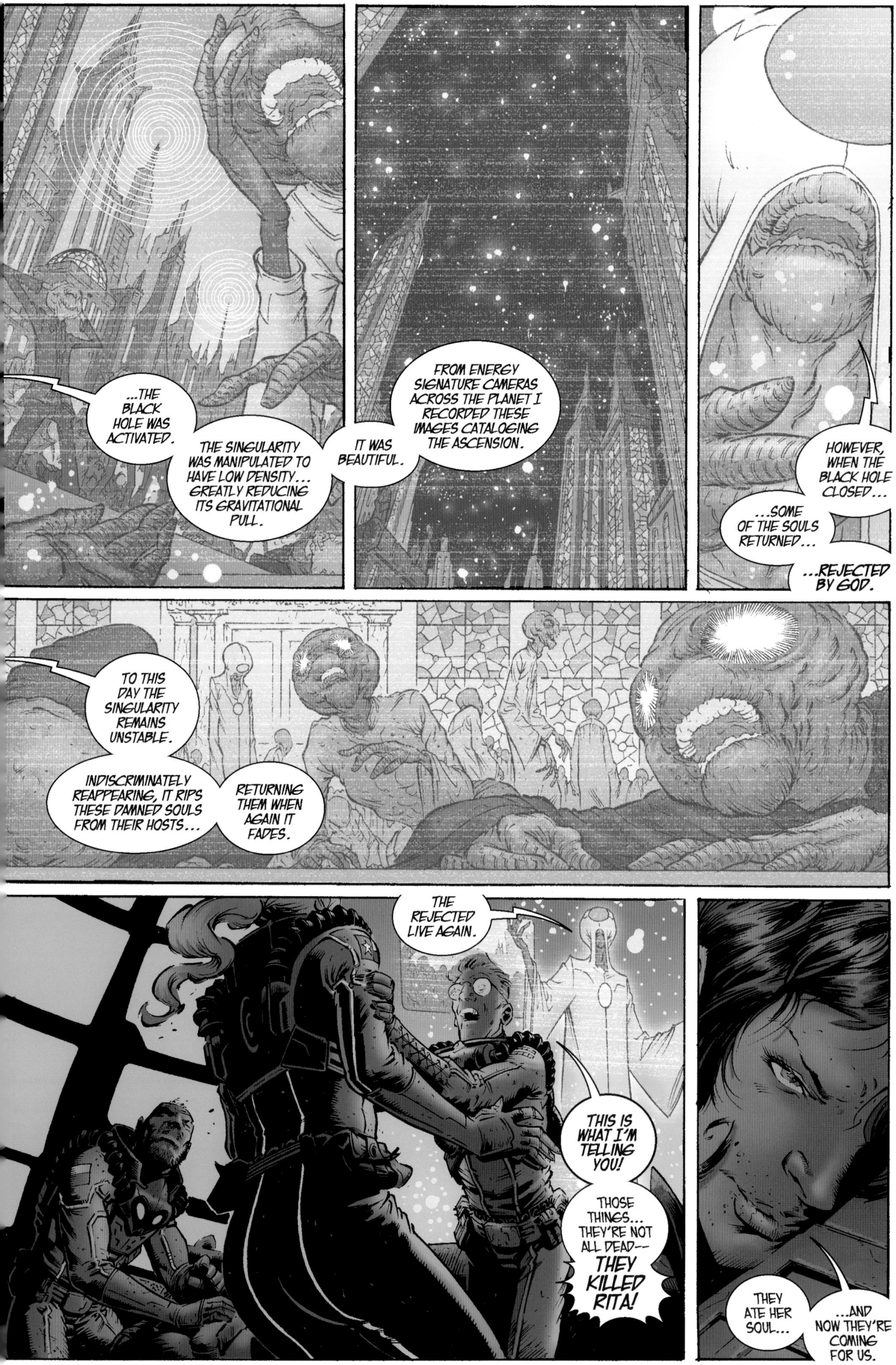
...THE BLACK HOLE WAS ACTIVATED.
THE SINGULARITY WAS MANIPULATED TO HAVE LOW DENSITY... GREATLY REDUCING ITS GRAVITATIONAL PULL.
IT WAS BEAUTIFUL.
FROM ENERGY SIGNATURE CAMERAS ACROSS THE PLANET I RECORDED THESE IMAGES CATALOGING THE ASCENSION.
HOWEVER, WHEN THE BLACK HOLE CLOSED...
...SOME OF THE SOULS RETURNED...
...REJECTED BY GOD.
TO THIS DAY THE SINGULARITY REMAINS UNSTABLE.
INDISCRIMINATELY REAPPEARING, IT RIPS THESE DAMNED SOULS FROM THEIR HOSTS...
RETURNING THEM WHEN AGAIN IT FADES.
THE REJECTED LIVE AGAIN.
THIS IS WHAT I'M TELLING YOU!
THOSE THINGS... THEY'RE NOT ALL DEAD-- THEY KILLED RITA!
THEY ATE HER SOUL...
...AND NOW THEY'RE COMING FOR US.

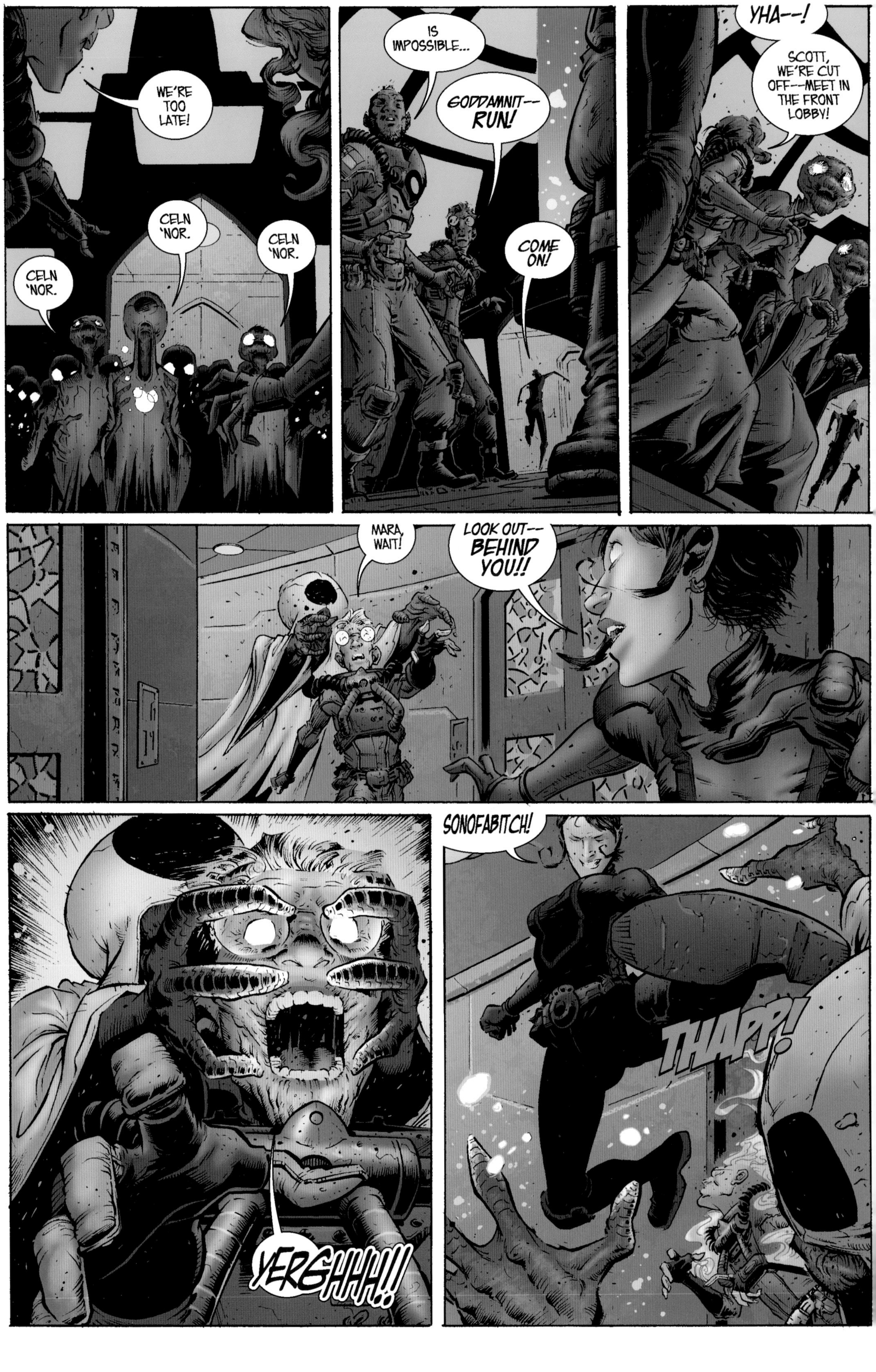

WE'RE TOO LATE!
CELN 'NOR.
CELN 'NOR.
CELN 'NOR.
IS IMPOSSIBLE...
GODDAMNIT-- RUN!
COME ON!
YHA--!
SCOTT, WE'RE CUT OFF--MEET IN THE FRONT LOBBY!
MARA, WAIT!
LOOK OUT-- BEHIND YOU!!
YERGHHH!!
SONOFABITCH!
THAPP!

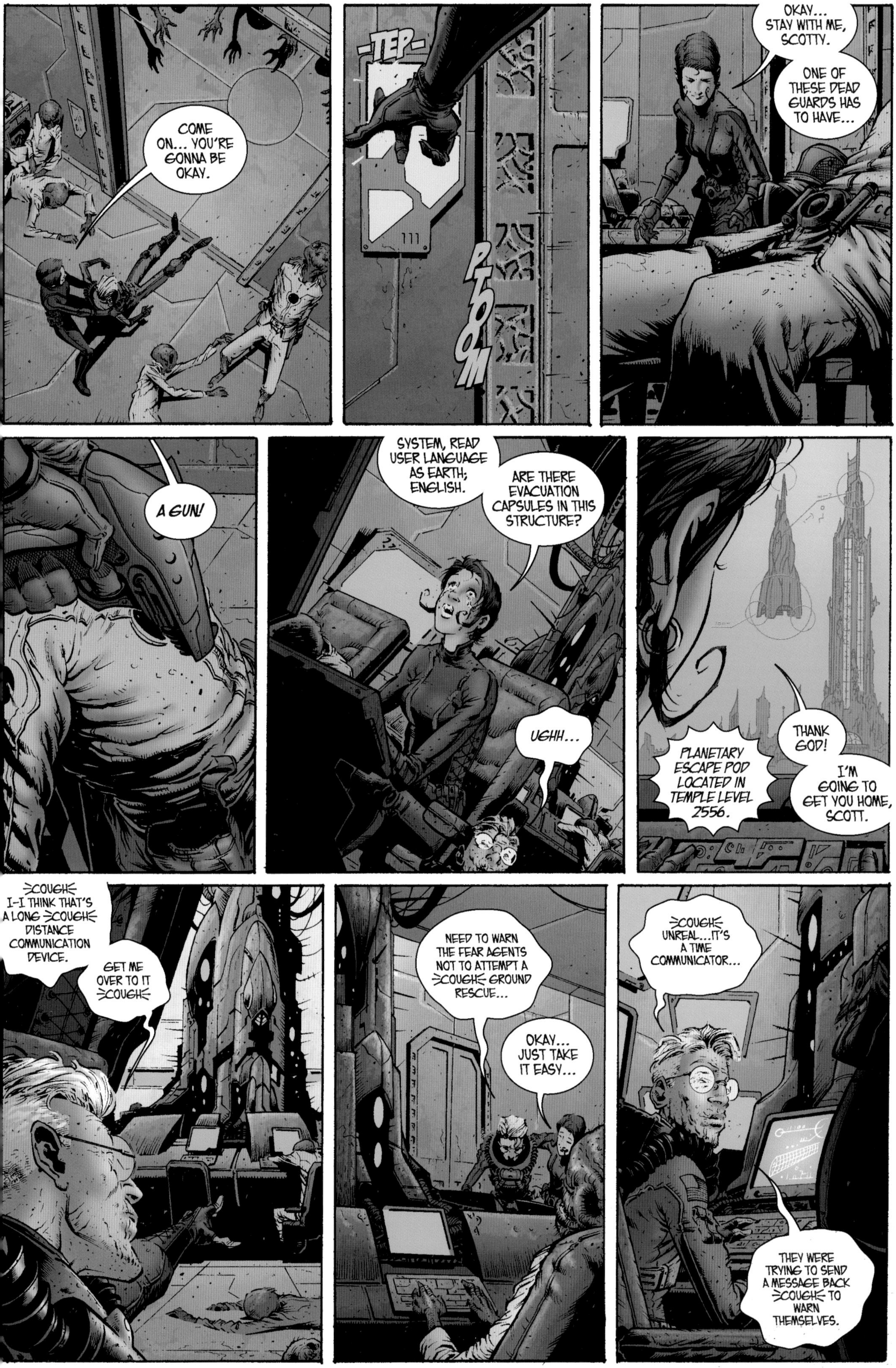
COME ON... YOU'RE GONNA BE OKAY.
-TEP-
PTOOM
OKAY... STAY WITH ME, SCOTTY.
ONE OF THESE DEAD GUARDS HAS TO HAVE...
A GUN!
SYSTEM, READ USER LANGUAGE AS EARTH; ENGLISH.
ARE THERE EVACUATION CAPSULES IN THIS STRUCTURE?
UGHH...
PLANETARY ESCAPE POD LOCATED IN TEMPLE LEVEL 2556.
THANK GOD!
I'M GOING TO GET YOU HOME, SCOTT.
COUGH I-I THINK THAT'S A LONG COUGH DISTANCE COMMUNICATION DEVICE.
GET ME OVER TO IT COUGH
NEED TO WARN THE FEAR AGENTS NOT TO ATTEMPT A COUGH GROUND RESCUE...
OKAY... JUST TAKE IT EASY...
COUGH UNREAL...IT'S A TIME COMMUNICATOR...
THEY WERE TRYING TO SEND A MESSAGE BACK COUGH TO WARN THEMSELVES.

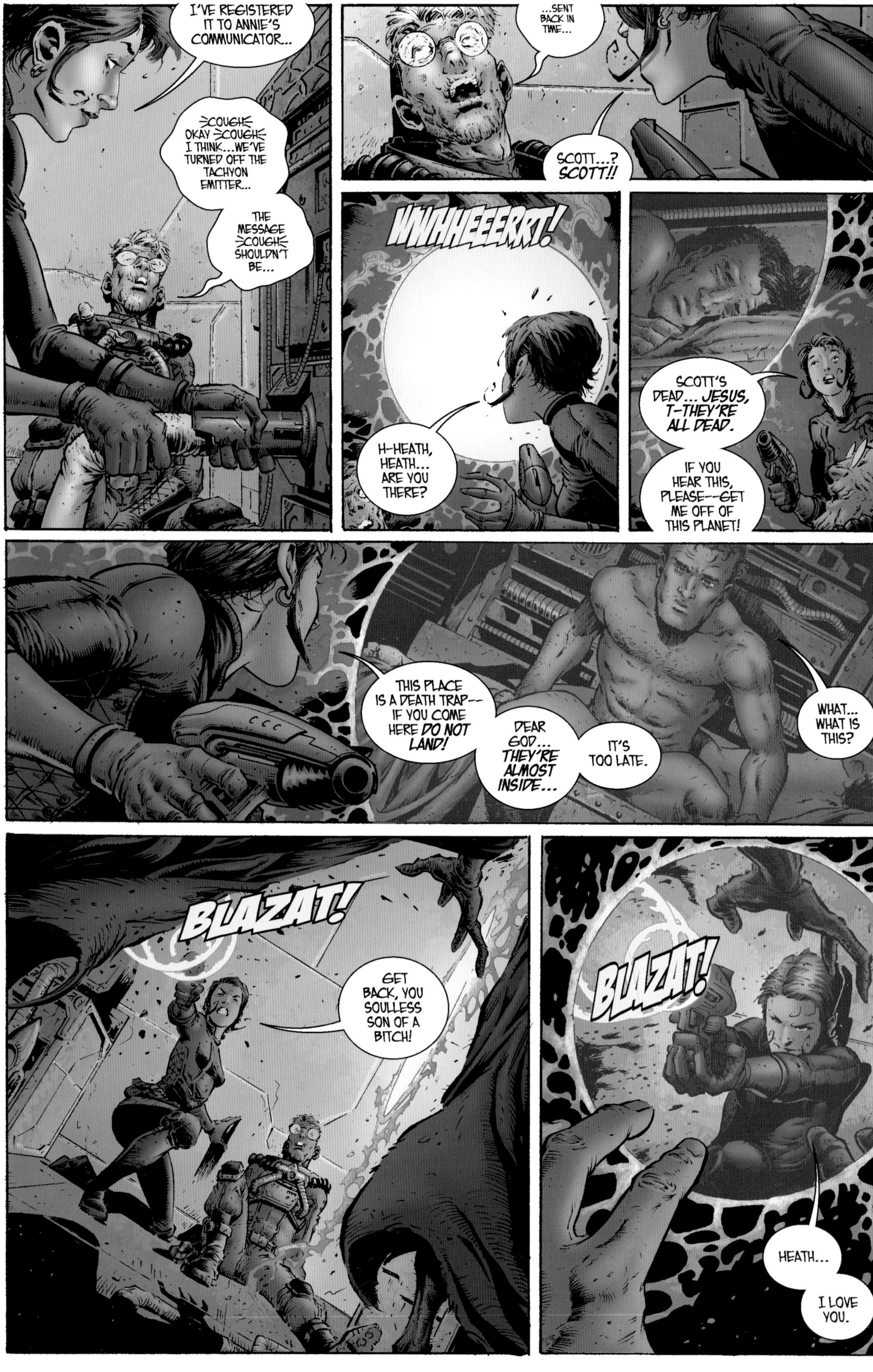

I'VE REGISTERED IT TO ANNIE'S COMMUNICATOR...
≶COUGH≶ OKAY ≶COUGH≶ I THINK...WE'VE TURNED OFF THE TACHYON EMITTER...
THE MESSAGE ≶COUGH≶ SHOULDN'T BE...
...SENT BACK IN TIME...
SCOTT...? SCOTT!!
WWHHEEERRT!
H-HEATH, HEATH... ARE YOU THERE?
SCOTT'S DEAD... JESUS, T-THEY'RE ALL DEAD.
IF YOU HEAR THIS, PLEASE--GET ME OFF OF THIS PLANET!
THIS PLACE IS A DEATH TRAP-- IF YOU COME HERE DO NOT LAND!
DEAR GOD... THEY'RE ALMOST INSIDE...
IT'S TOO LATE.
WHAT... WHAT IS THIS?
BLAZAT!
GET BACK, YOU SOULLESS SON OF A BITCH!
BLAZAT!
HEATH...
I LOVE YOU.

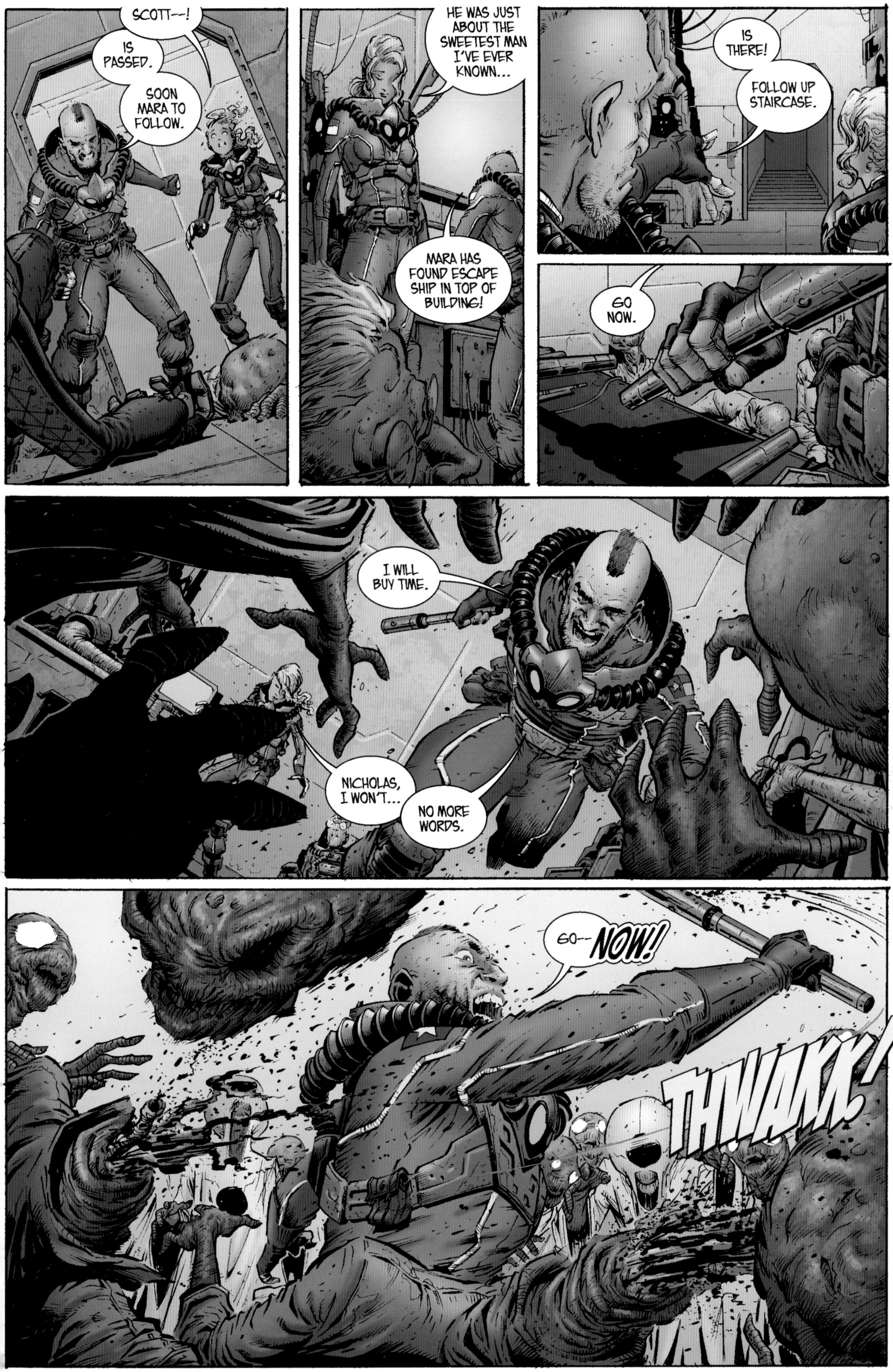
SCOTT--!
IS PASSED.
SOON MARA TO FOLLOW.
HE WAS JUST ABOUT THE SWEETEST MAN I'VE EVER KNOWN...
MARA HAS FOUND ESCAPE SHIP IN TOP OF BUILDING!
IS THERE!
FOLLOW UP STAIRCASE.
GO NOW.
I WILL BUY TIME.
NICHOLAS, I WON'T...
NO MORE WORDS.
GO--NOW!
THWAKK!

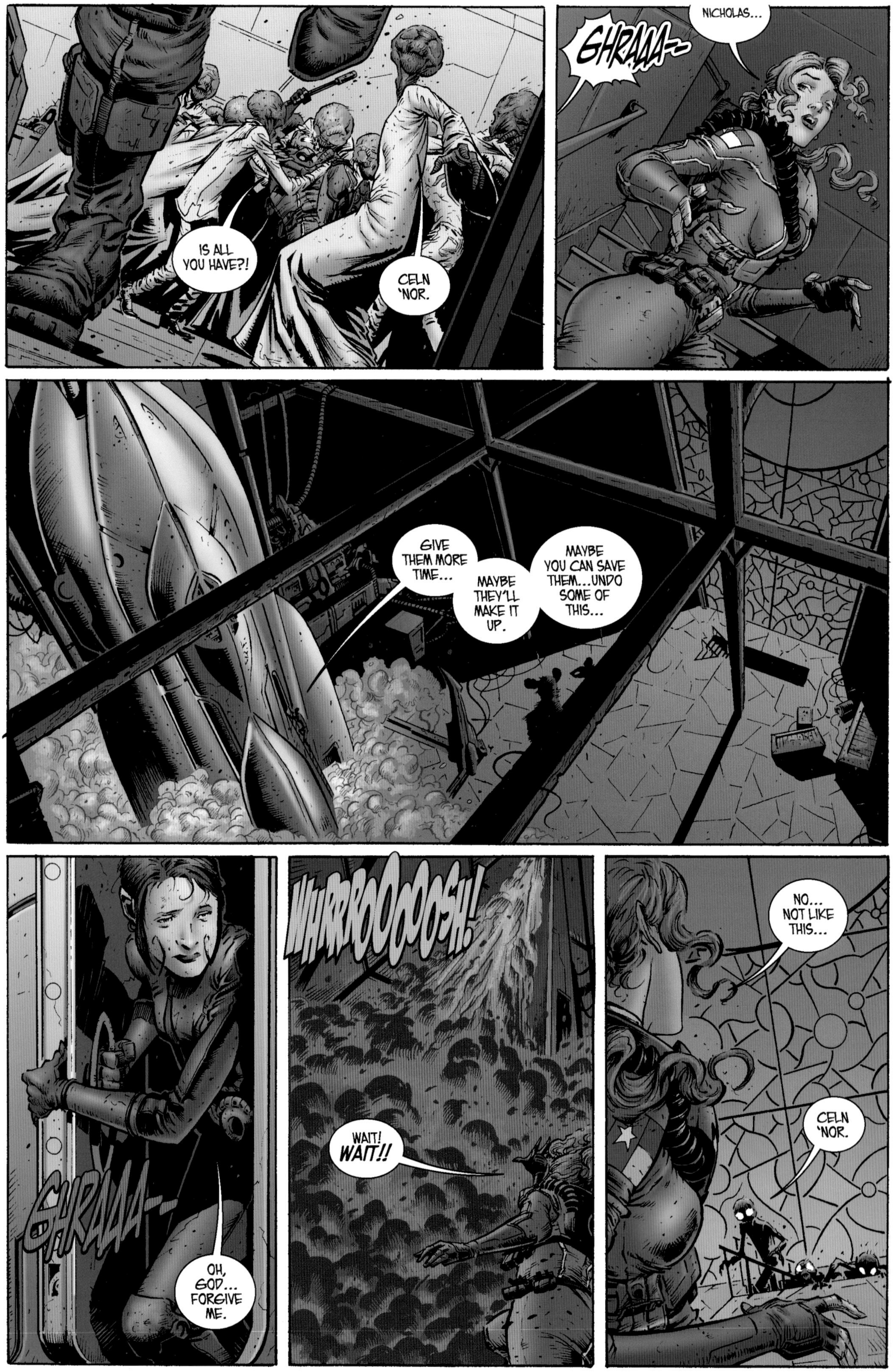
IS ALL YOU HAVE?!
CELN 'NOR.
GHRAAA--
NICHOLAS...
GIVE THEM MORE TIME...
MAYBE THEY'LL MAKE IT UP.
MAYBE YOU CAN SAVE THEM...UNDO SOME OF THIS...
GHRAAA--
OH, GOD... FORGIVE ME.
WHRRROOOOOSH!
WAIT! WAIT!!
NO... NOT LIKE THIS...
CELN 'NOR.

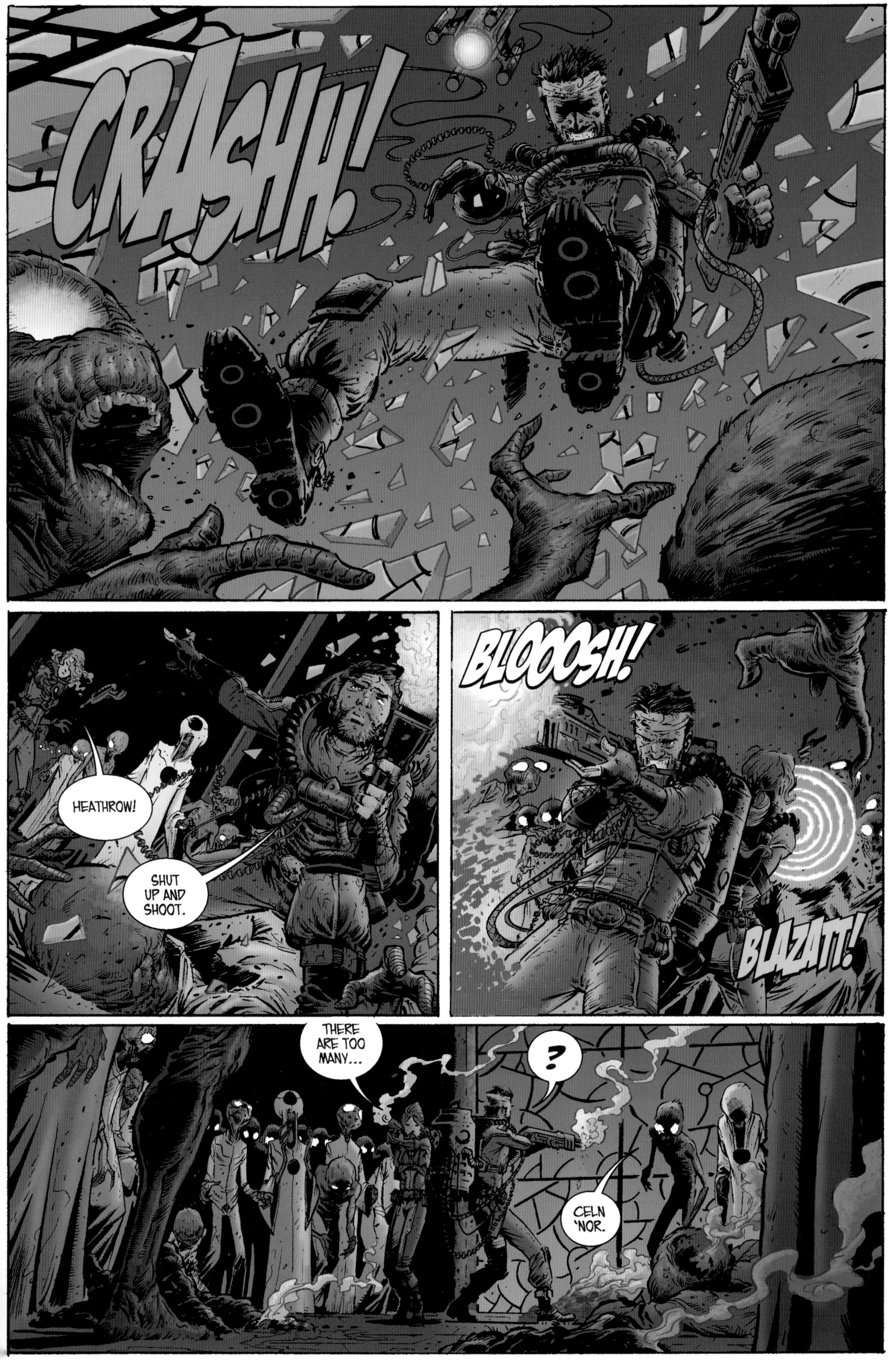
CRASHH!
HEATHROW!
SHUT UP AND SHOOT.
BLOOOSH!
BLAZATT!
THERE ARE TOO MANY...
?
CELN 'NOR.

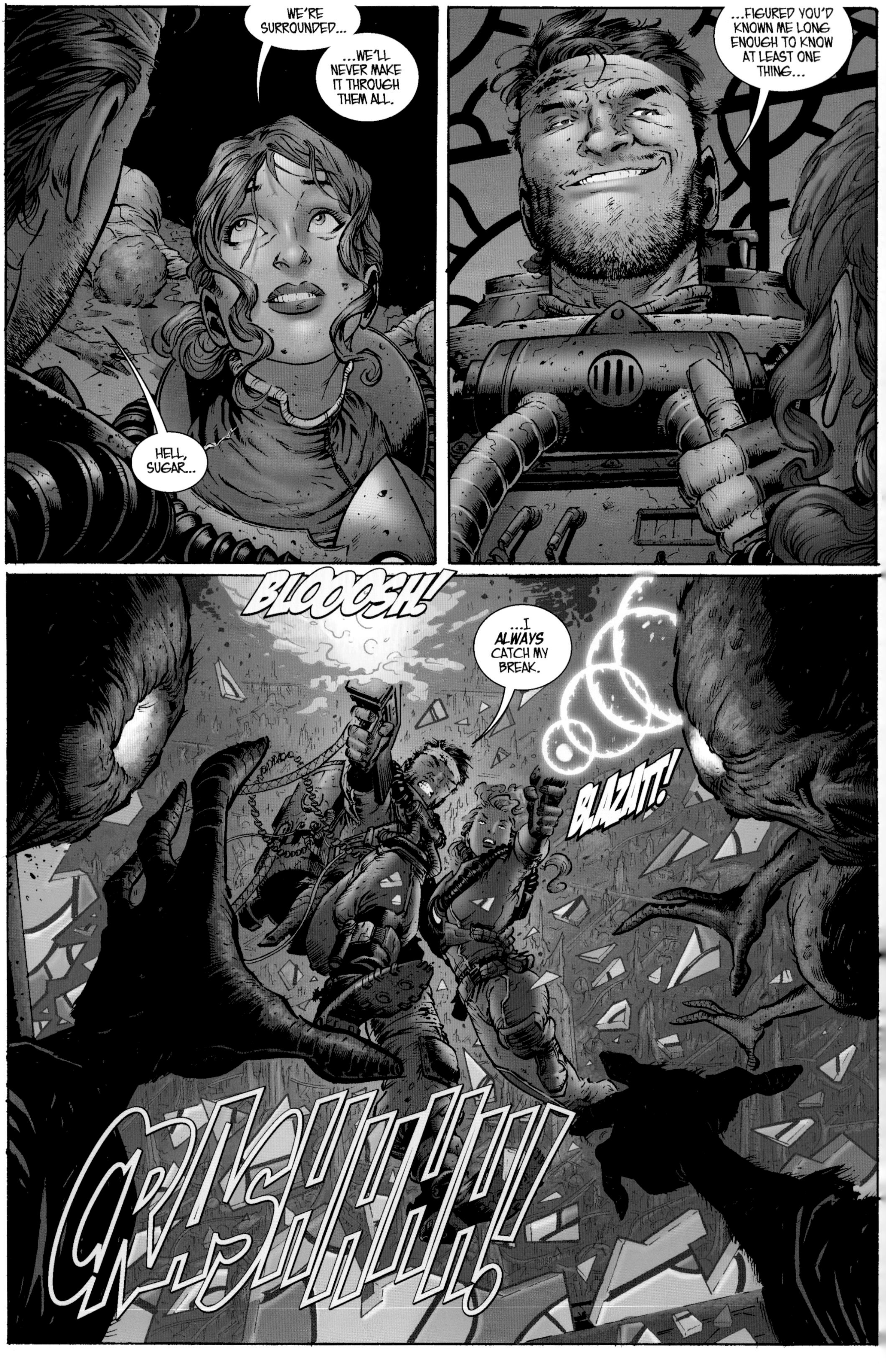
WE'RE SURROUNDED...
...WE'LL NEVER MAKE IT THROUGH THEM ALL.
HELL, SUGAR...
...FIGURED YOU'D KNOWN ME LONG ENOUGH TO KNOW AT LEAST ONE THING...
BLOOOSH!
...I ALWAYS CATCH MY BREAK.
BLAZATT!
CRSHHHH!

CHAPTER 4

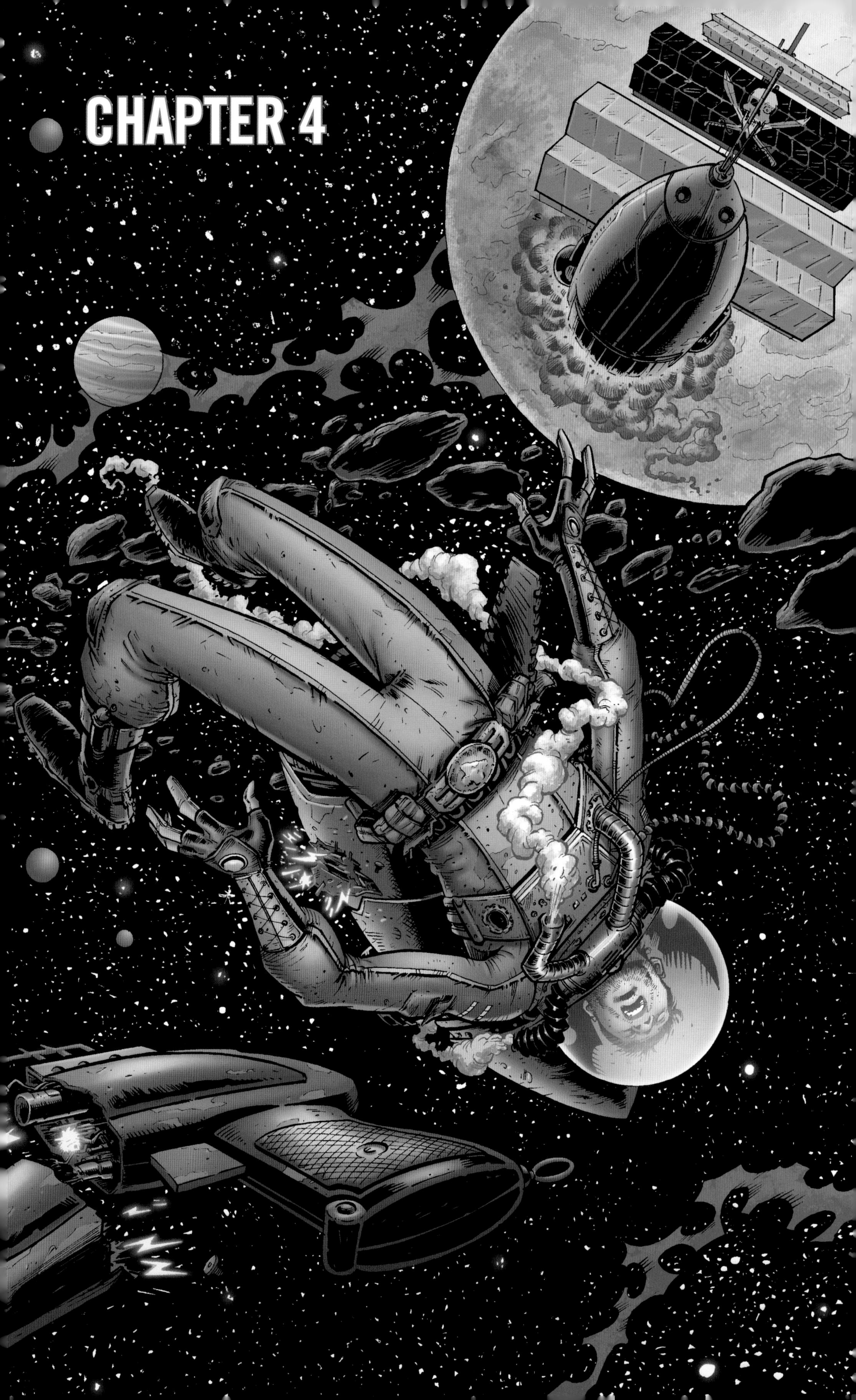

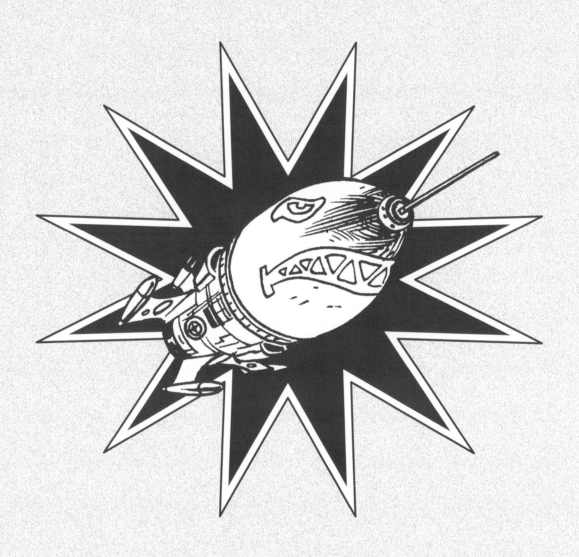

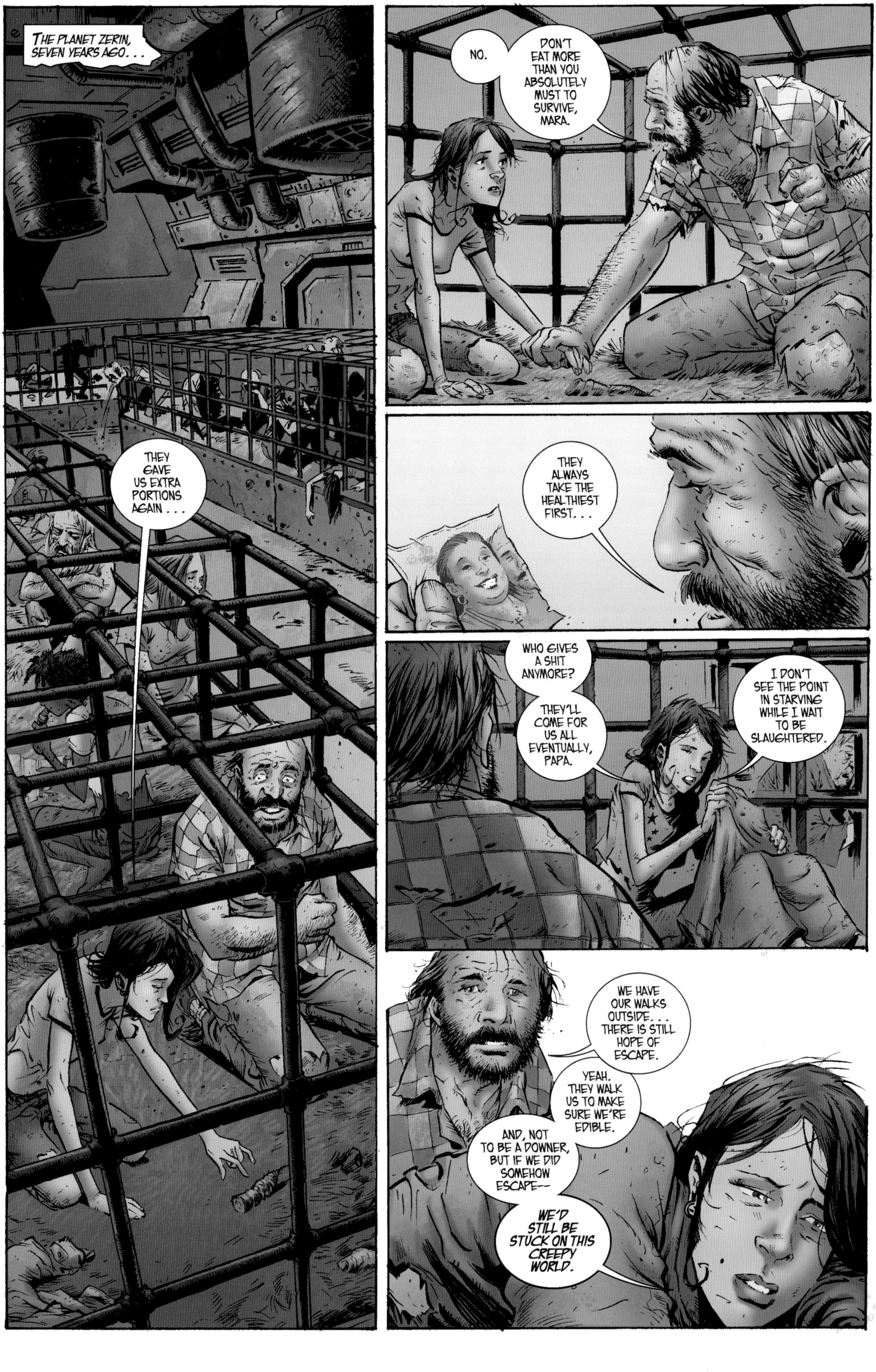
THE PLANET ZERIN, SEVEN YEARS AGO. . .
THEY GAVE US EXTRA PORTIONS AGAIN . . .
NO.
DON'T EAT MORE THAN YOU ABSOLUTELY MUST TO SURVIVE, MARA.
THEY ALWAYS TAKE THE HEALTHIEST FIRST. . .
WHO GIVES A SHIT ANYMORE?
THEY'LL COME FOR US ALL EVENTUALLY, PAPA.
I DON'T SEE THE POINT IN STARVING WHILE I WAIT TO BE SLAUGHTERED.
WE HAVE OUR WALKS OUTSIDE. . . THERE IS STILL HOPE OF ESCAPE.
YEAH. THEY WALK US TO MAKE SURE WE'RE EDIBLE.
AND, NOT TO BE A DOWNER, BUT IF WE DID SOMEHOW ESCAPE--
WE'D STILL BE STUCK ON THIS CREEPY WORLD.

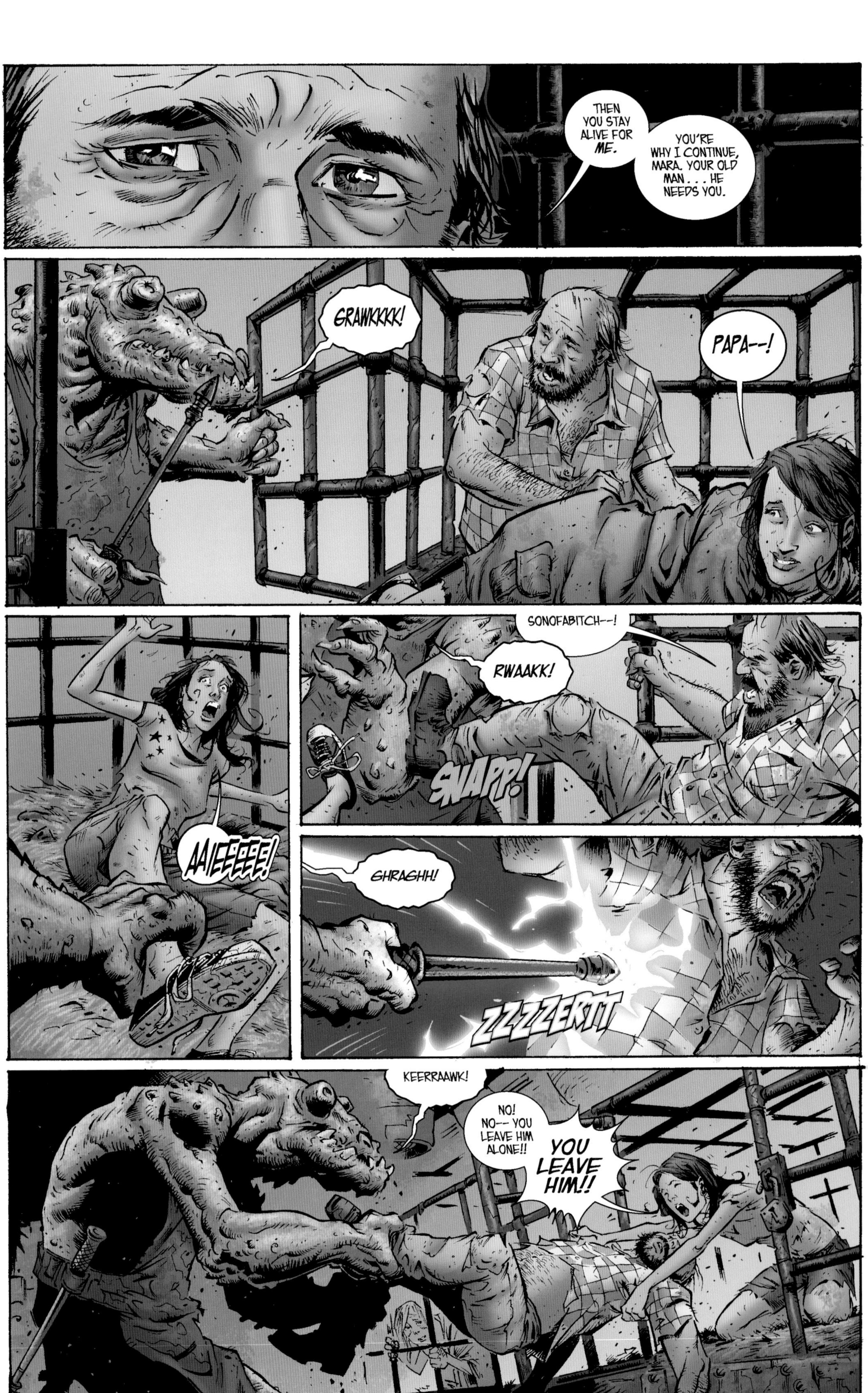
THEN YOU STAY ALIVE FOR ME.
YOU'RE WHY I CONTINUE, MARA. YOUR OLD MAN . . . HE NEEDS YOU.
GRAWKKKK!
PAPA--!
AAIEEEEEE!
SONOFABITCH--!
RWAAKK!
SNAPP!
GHRAGHH!
ZZZZERTT
KEERRAAWK!
NO! NO-- YOU LEAVE HIM ALONE!!
YOU LEAVE HIM!!

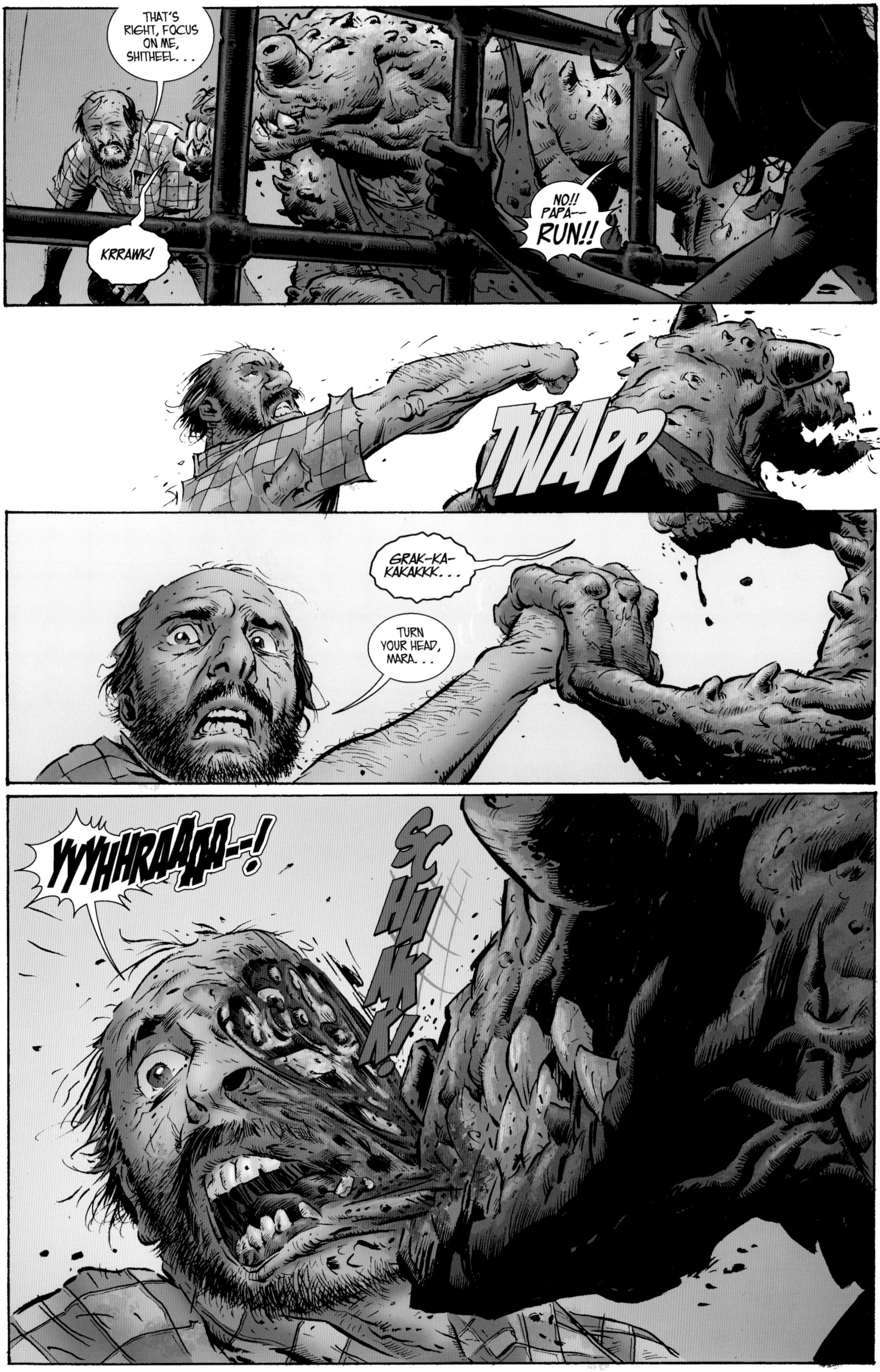

THAT'S RIGHT, FOCUS ON ME, SHITHEEL. . .
KRRAWK!
NO!! PAPA-- RUN!!
TWAPP
GRAK-KA-KAKAKKK. . .
TURN YOUR HEAD, MARA. . .
YYYHHRAAAA--!
SCHUKK!

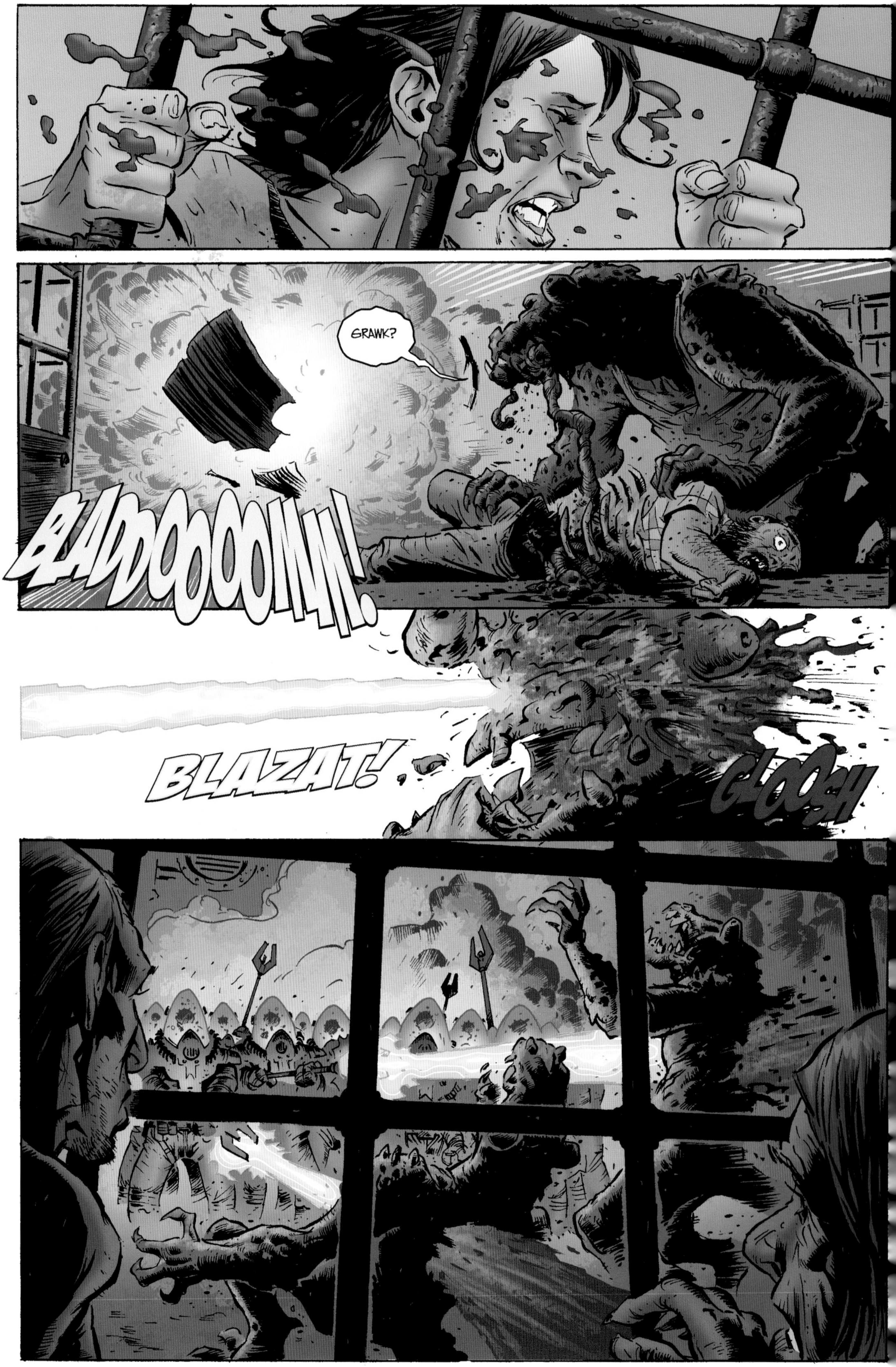
GRAWK?
BLADOOOOMM!
BLAZAT!
GLOOSH

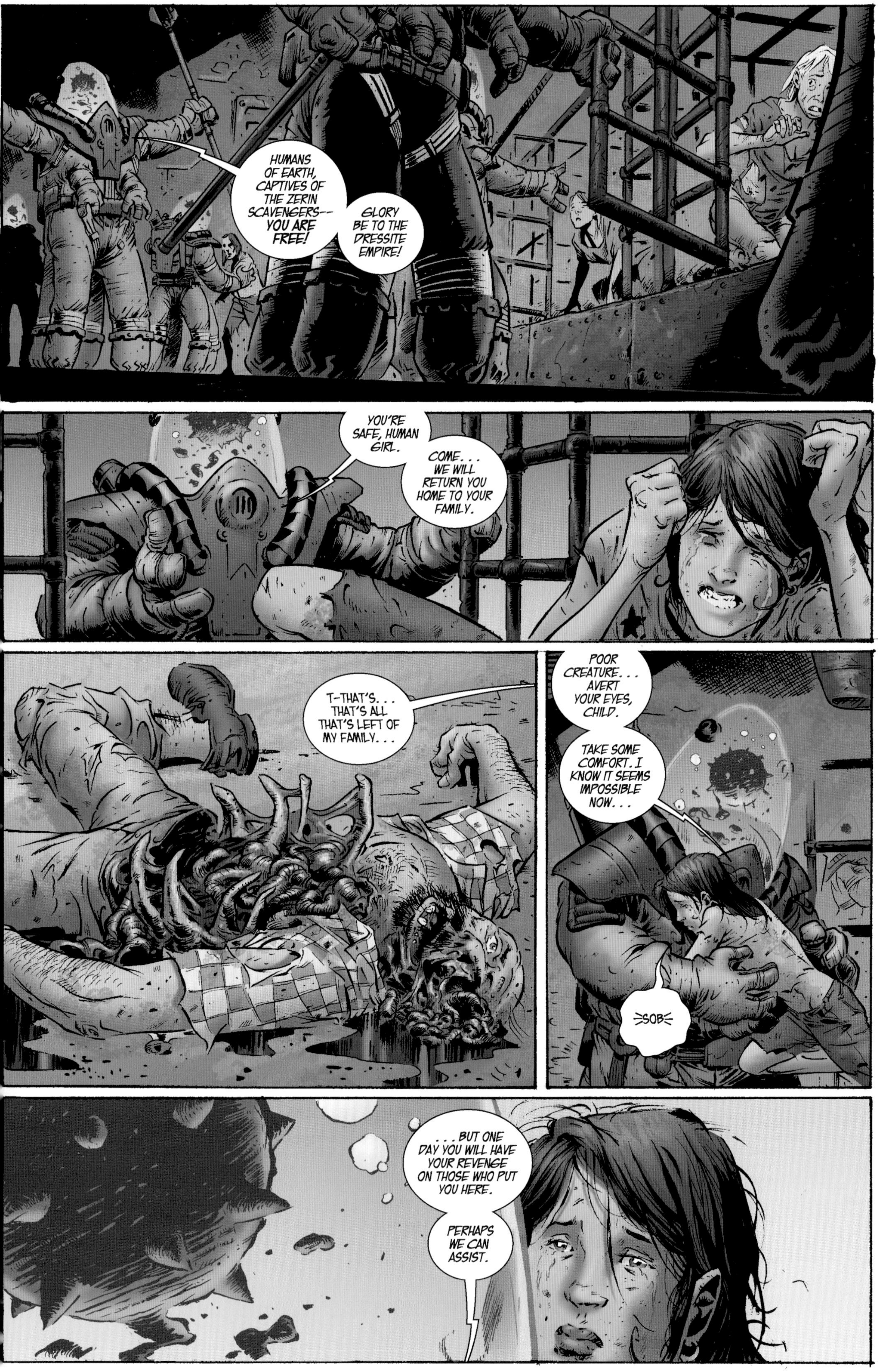
HUMANS OF EARTH, CAPTIVES OF THE ZERIN SCAVENGERS-- YOU ARE FREE!
GLORY BE TO THE DRESSITE EMPIRE!
YOU'RE SAFE, HUMAN GIRL.
COME... WE WILL RETURN YOU HOME TO YOUR FAMILY.
T-THAT'S... THAT'S ALL THAT'S LEFT OF MY FAMILY...
POOR CREATURE... AVERT YOUR EYES, CHILD.
TAKE SOME COMFORT. I KNOW IT SEEMS IMPOSSIBLE NOW...
SOB
...BUT ONE DAY YOU WILL HAVE YOUR REVENGE ON THOSE WHO PUT YOU HERE.
PERHAPS WE CAN ASSIST.

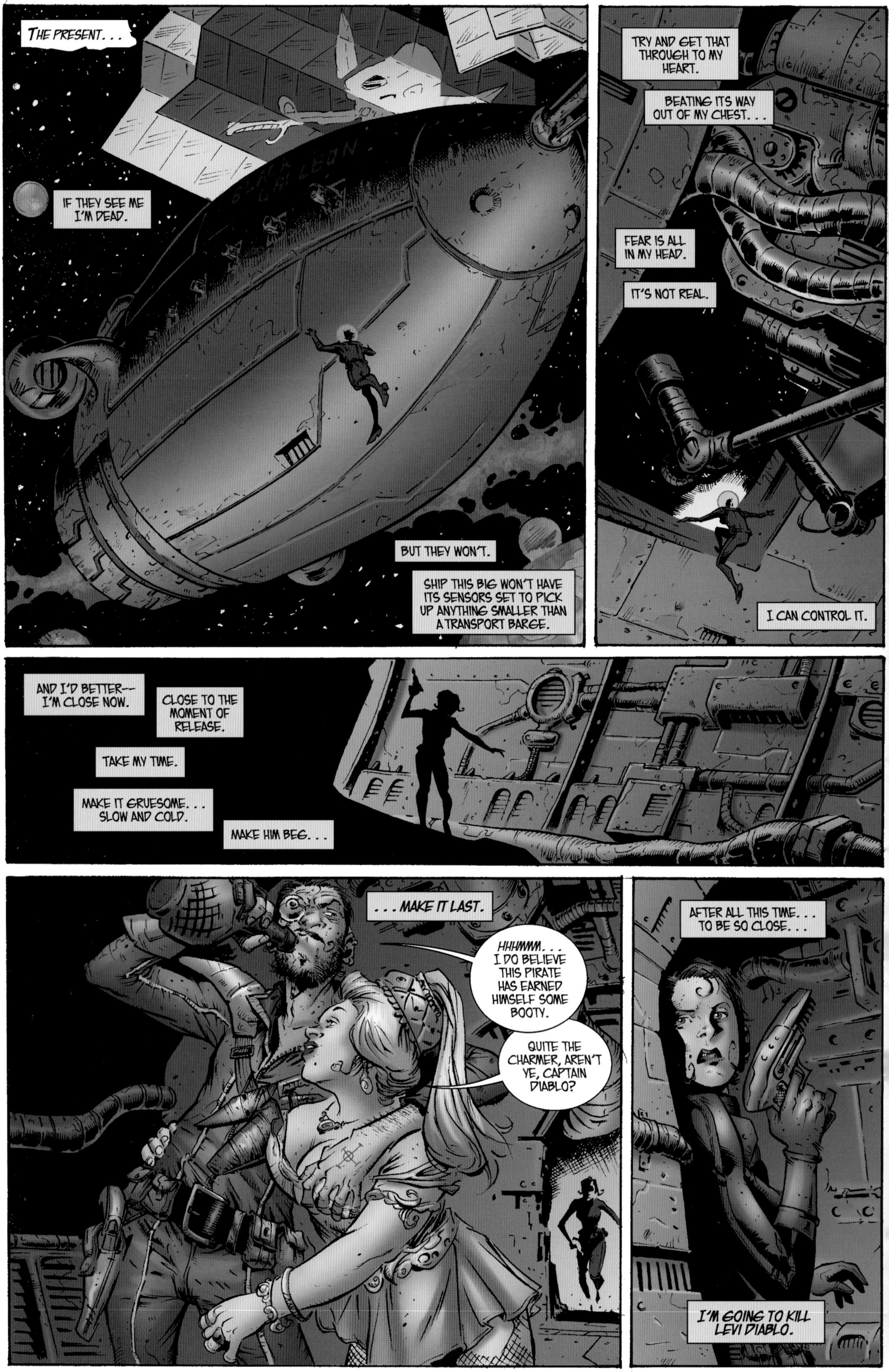
THE PRESENT...
IF THEY SEE ME I'M DEAD.
BUT THEY WON'T.
SHIP THIS BIG WON'T HAVE ITS SENSORS SET TO PICK UP ANYTHING SMALLER THAN A TRANSPORT BARGE.
TRY AND GET THAT THROUGH TO MY HEART.
BEATING ITS WAY OUT OF MY CHEST...
FEAR IS ALL IN MY HEAD.
IT'S NOT REAL.
I CAN CONTROL IT.
AND I'D BETTER-- I'M CLOSE NOW.
CLOSE TO THE MOMENT OF RELEASE.
TAKE MY TIME.
MAKE IT GRUESOME... SLOW AND COLD.
MAKE HIM BEG...
...MAKE IT LAST.
HHHMMM... I DO BELIEVE THIS PIRATE HAS EARNED HIMSELF SOME BOOTY.
QUITE THE CHARMER, AREN'T YE, CAPTAIN DIABLO?
AFTER ALL THIS TIME... TO BE SO CLOSE...
I'M GOING TO KILL LEVI DIABLO.

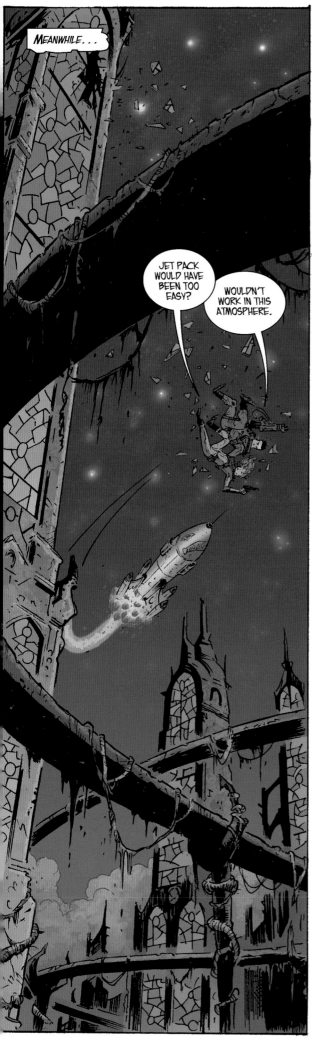

MEANWHILE...

JET PACK WOULD HAVE BEEN TOO EASY?

WOULDN'T WORK IN THIS ATMOSPHERE.

FLEPP!

HANG ON.

WHO ELSE IS DOWN HERE?

NO ONE. THEY'RE ALL DEAD...

...DEAD BECAUSE OF YOUR NEW GIRLFRIEND.

HELLO, CHARLOTTE. IT'S GOOD TO SEE YOU. WE WERE VERY CONCERNED.

ANNIE.

NO OTHER SURVIVORS.

GET US TO THE OTHER SIDE OF THE PLANET--

AVOID THAT PIRATE SHIP WE SCANNED ON THE WAY IN.

I KNOW MARA, WE'VE BEEN THROUGH SOME TERRIBLE SHIT TOGETHER...

...IT'S GOTTA BE A MISUNDER-STANDIN'.

WELL, THERE'S CLEARLY PLENTY YOU DON'T KNOW.

HOW CAN YOU BE SO BLIND?!

THAT PIRATE SHIP YOU SCANNED-- SHE AMBUSHED IT!

ATTACKED A CLASS D-3 WARSHIP AND GOT US BLOWN TO HELL!

SHE KILLED MY ENTIRE TEAM!!

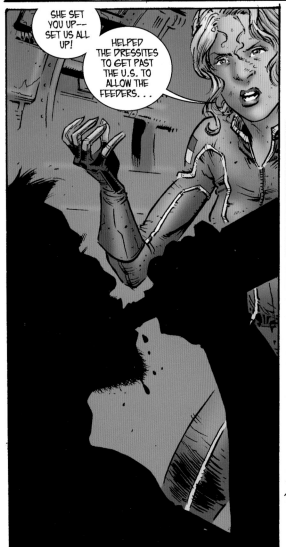

SHE SET YOU UP-- SET US ALL UP!

HELPED THE DRESSITES TO GET PAST THE U.S. TO ALLOW THE FEEDERS...

NO-- DON'T YOU DARE DRINK YOUR WAY THROUGH THIS!!

DASHH!

OKAY, OKAY...

I WANT YOU SOBER ENOUGH TO FEEL WHAT IS HAPPENING HERE.

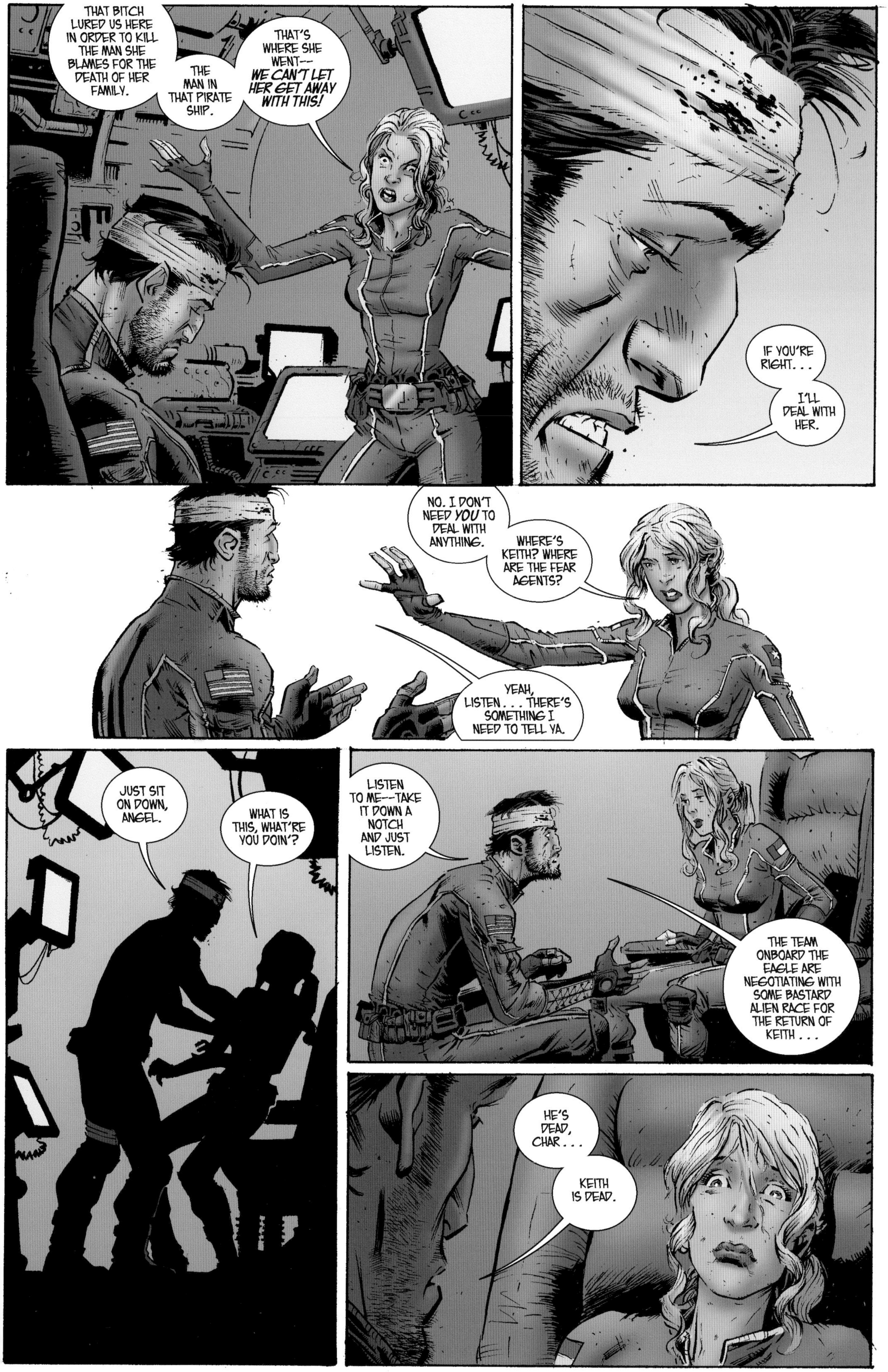
THAT BITCH LURED US HERE IN ORDER TO KILL THE MAN SHE BLAMES FOR THE DEATH OF HER FAMILY.
THE MAN IN THAT PIRATE SHIP.
THAT'S WHERE SHE WENT-- WE CAN'T LET HER GET AWAY WITH THIS!
IF YOU'RE RIGHT. . .
I'LL DEAL WITH HER.
NO. I DON'T NEED YOU TO DEAL WITH ANYTHING.
WHERE'S KEITH? WHERE ARE THE FEAR AGENTS?
YEAH, LISTEN. . . THERE'S SOMETHING I NEED TO TELL YA.
JUST SIT ON DOWN, ANGEL.
WHAT IS THIS, WHAT'RE YOU DOIN'?
LISTEN TO ME--TAKE IT DOWN A NOTCH AND JUST LISTEN.
THE TEAM ONBOARD THE EAGLE ARE NEGOTIATING WITH SOME BASTARD ALIEN RACE FOR THE RETURN OF KEITH . . .
HE'S DEAD, CHAR . . .
KEITH IS DEAD.

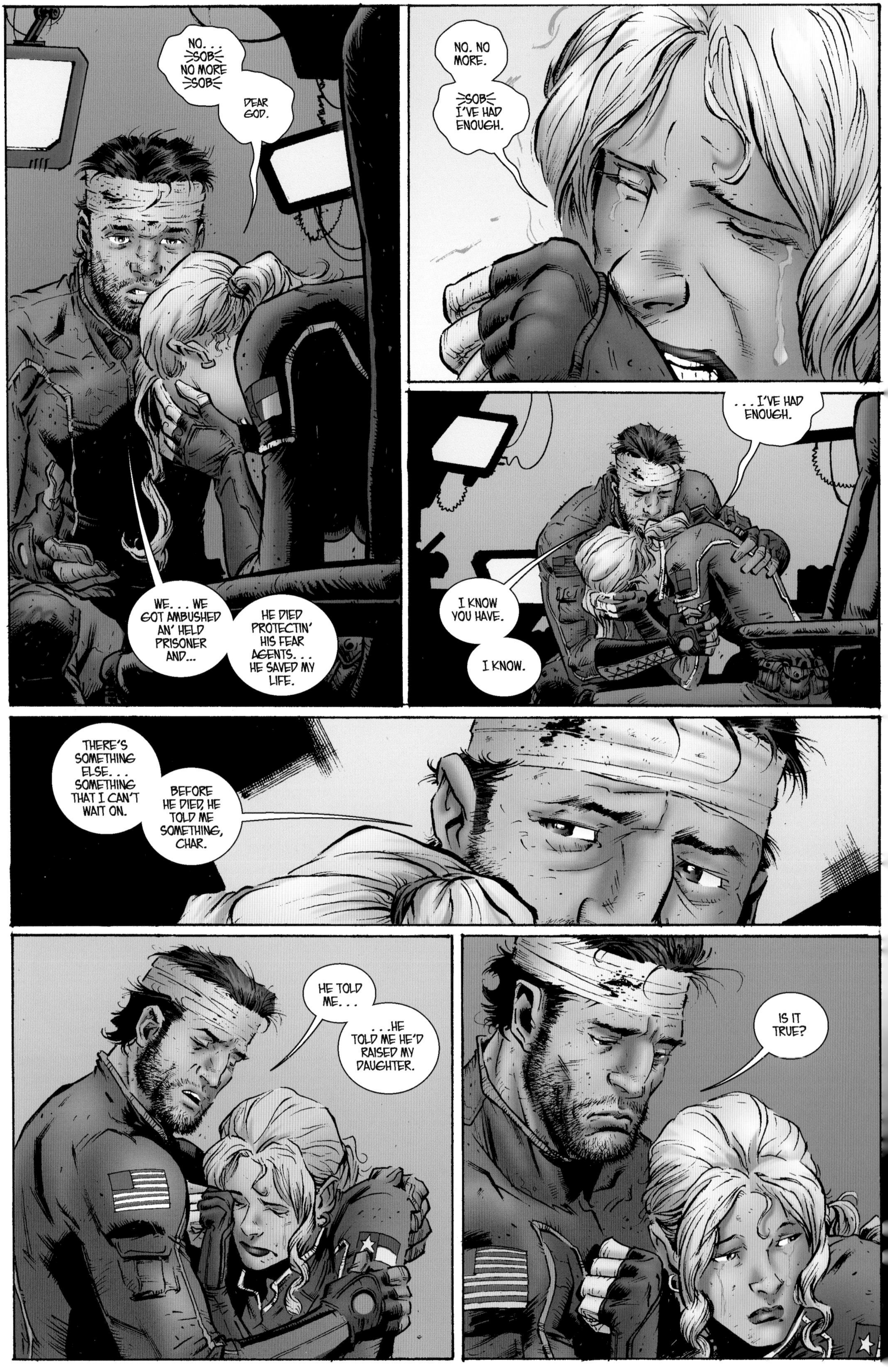
NO. . . ≶SOB≷ NO MORE ≶SOB≷
DEAR GOD.
NO. NO MORE.
≶SOB≷ I'VE HAD ENOUGH.
WE. . . WE GOT AMBUSHED AN' HELD PRISONER AND...
HE DIED PROTECTIN' HIS FEAR AGENTS. . . HE SAVED MY LIFE.
. . . I'VE HAD ENOUGH.
I KNOW YOU HAVE.
I KNOW.
THERE'S SOMETHING ELSE. . . SOMETHING THAT I CAN'T WAIT ON.
BEFORE HE DIED, HE TOLD ME SOMETHING, CHAR.
HE TOLD ME. . .
. . .HE TOLD ME HE'D RAISED MY DAUGHTER.
IS IT TRUE?

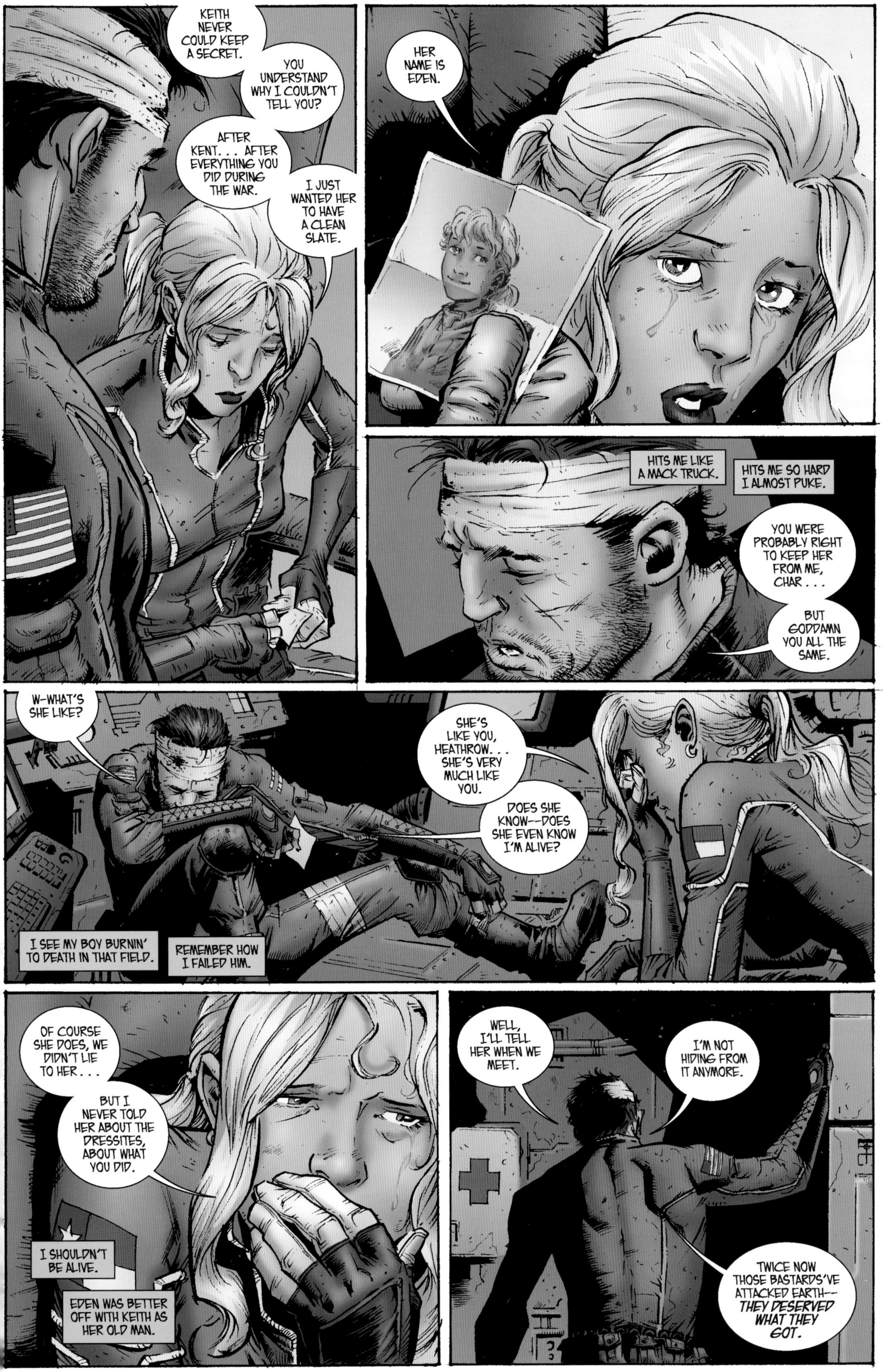

KEITH NEVER COULD KEEP A SECRET.
YOU UNDERSTAND WHY I COULDN'T TELL YOU?
AFTER KENT. . . AFTER EVERYTHING YOU DID DURING THE WAR.
I JUST WANTED HER TO HAVE A CLEAN SLATE.
HER NAME IS EDEN.
HITS ME LIKE A MACK TRUCK.
HITS ME SO HARD I ALMOST PUKE.
YOU WERE PROBABLY RIGHT TO KEEP HER FROM ME, CHAR . . .
BUT GODDAMN YOU ALL THE SAME.
W-WHAT'S SHE LIKE?
SHE'S LIKE YOU, HEATHROW. . . SHE'S VERY MUCH LIKE YOU.
DOES SHE KNOW--DOES SHE EVEN KNOW I'M ALIVE?
I SEE MY BOY BURNIN' TO DEATH IN THAT FIELD.
REMEMBER HOW I FAILED HIM.
OF COURSE SHE DOES, WE DIDN'T LIE TO HER . . .
BUT I NEVER TOLD HER ABOUT THE DRESSITES, ABOUT WHAT YOU DID.
I SHOULDN'T BE ALIVE.
EDEN WAS BETTER OFF WITH KEITH AS HER OLD MAN.
WELL, I'LL TELL HER WHEN WE MEET.
I'M NOT HIDING FROM IT ANYMORE.
TWICE NOW THOSE BASTARDS'VE ATTACKED EARTH-- *THEY DESERVED WHAT THEY GOT.*

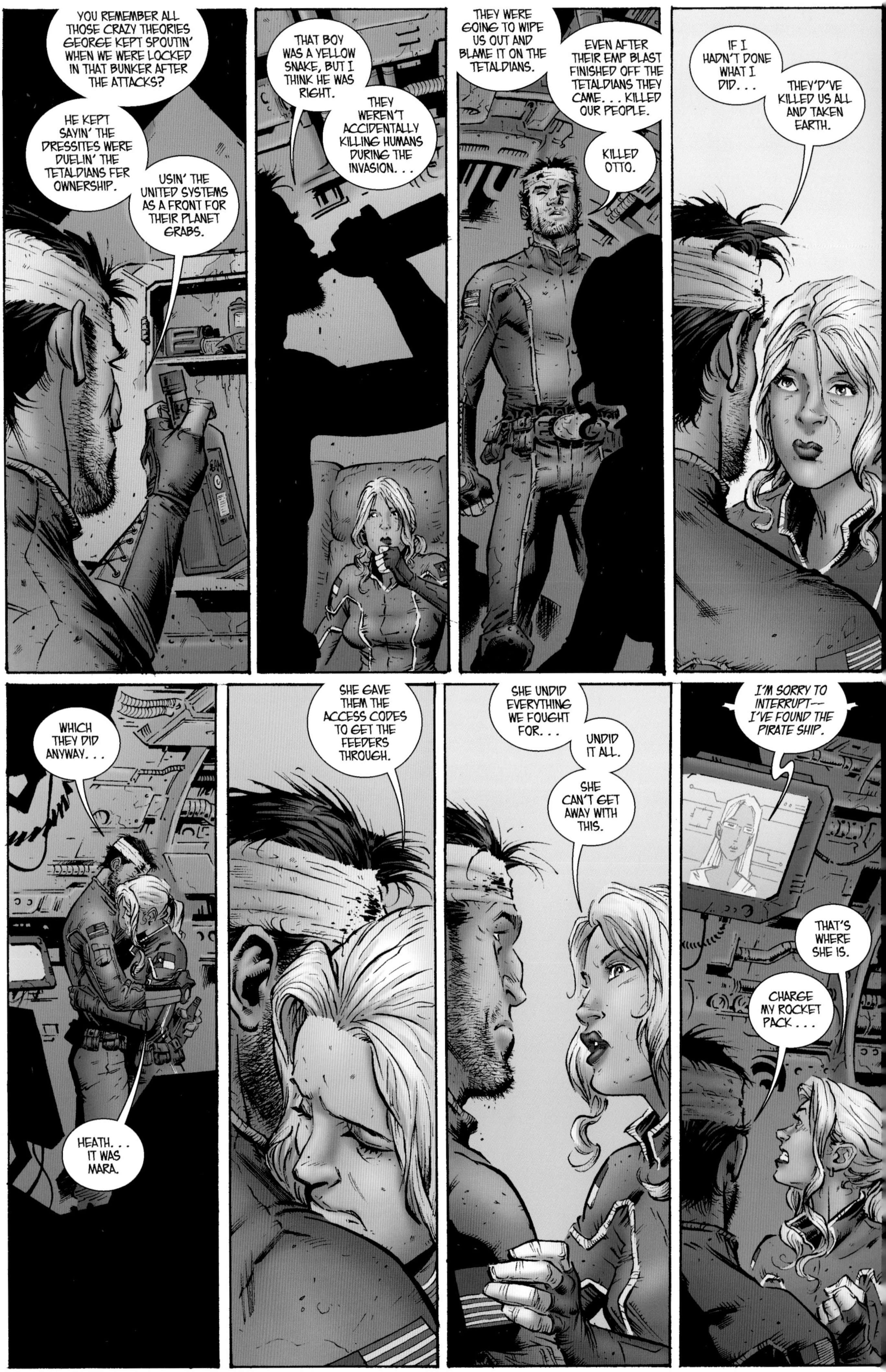
YOU REMEMBER ALL THOSE CRAZY THEORIES GEORGE KEPT SPOUTIN' WHEN WE WERE LOCKED IN THAT BUNKER AFTER THE ATTACKS?
HE KEPT SAYIN' THE DRESSITES WERE DUELIN' THE TETALDIANS FER OWNERSHIP.
USIN' THE UNITED SYSTEMS AS A FRONT FOR THEIR PLANET GRABS.
THAT BOY WAS A YELLOW SNAKE, BUT I THINK HE WAS RIGHT.
THEY WEREN'T ACCIDENTALLY KILLING HUMANS DURING THE INVASION. . .
THEY WERE GOING TO WIPE US OUT AND BLAME IT ON THE TETALDIANS.
EVEN AFTER THEIR EMP BLAST FINISHED OFF THE TETALDIANS THEY CAME. . . KILLED OUR PEOPLE.
KILLED OTTO.
IF I HADN'T DONE WHAT I DID. . .
THEY'D'VE KILLED US ALL AND TAKEN EARTH.
WHICH THEY DID ANYWAY. . .
HEATH. . . IT WAS MARA.
SHE GAVE THEM THE ACCESS CODES TO GET THE FEEDERS THROUGH.
SHE UNDID EVERYTHING WE FOUGHT FOR. . .
UNDID IT ALL.
SHE CAN'T GET AWAY WITH THIS.
I'M SORRY TO INTERRUPT-- I'VE FOUND THE PIRATE SHIP.
THAT'S WHERE SHE IS.
CHARGE MY ROCKET PACK. . .

"...I'LL DEAL WITH HER."

≥GLUG!≤

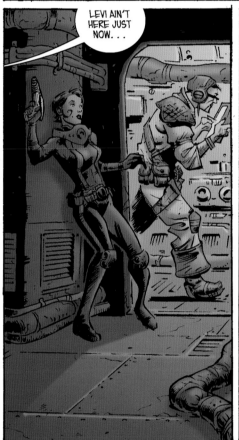

LEVI AIN'T HERE JUST NOW...

WHAT SAY YE MAKE WITH THE MESSAGE SO I KIN RETURN TA ME DEBAUCHERY.

THERE IS A MAN IN YOUR REGION WITH A SIZABLE BOUNTY ON HIS HEAD.

HIS NAME IS HEATH HUSTON, HUMAN ARCHITECT OF THE GENOCIDE ON DRESSIN.

IT IS BELIEVED HE AND HIS FEMALE ACCOMPLICE WILL SEEK YOU OUT... THE WOMAN HAS BUSINESS WITH LEVI.

IT IS A DELICATE JOB, AND AS SUCH, THE DRESSITE EMPIRE IS PREPARED TO OFFER SEVEN BILLION UNI-CREDS FOR HIS APPREHENSION-- ALIVE AND UNHARMED.

SHIP ARRIVED HERE AN HOUR AGO... WENT DOWN TO THE SURFACE OF NEAVSIVIA.

WE ASSUMED HE WAS ON A MISSION TO RESCUE THE DOLTS WE SHOT DOWN.

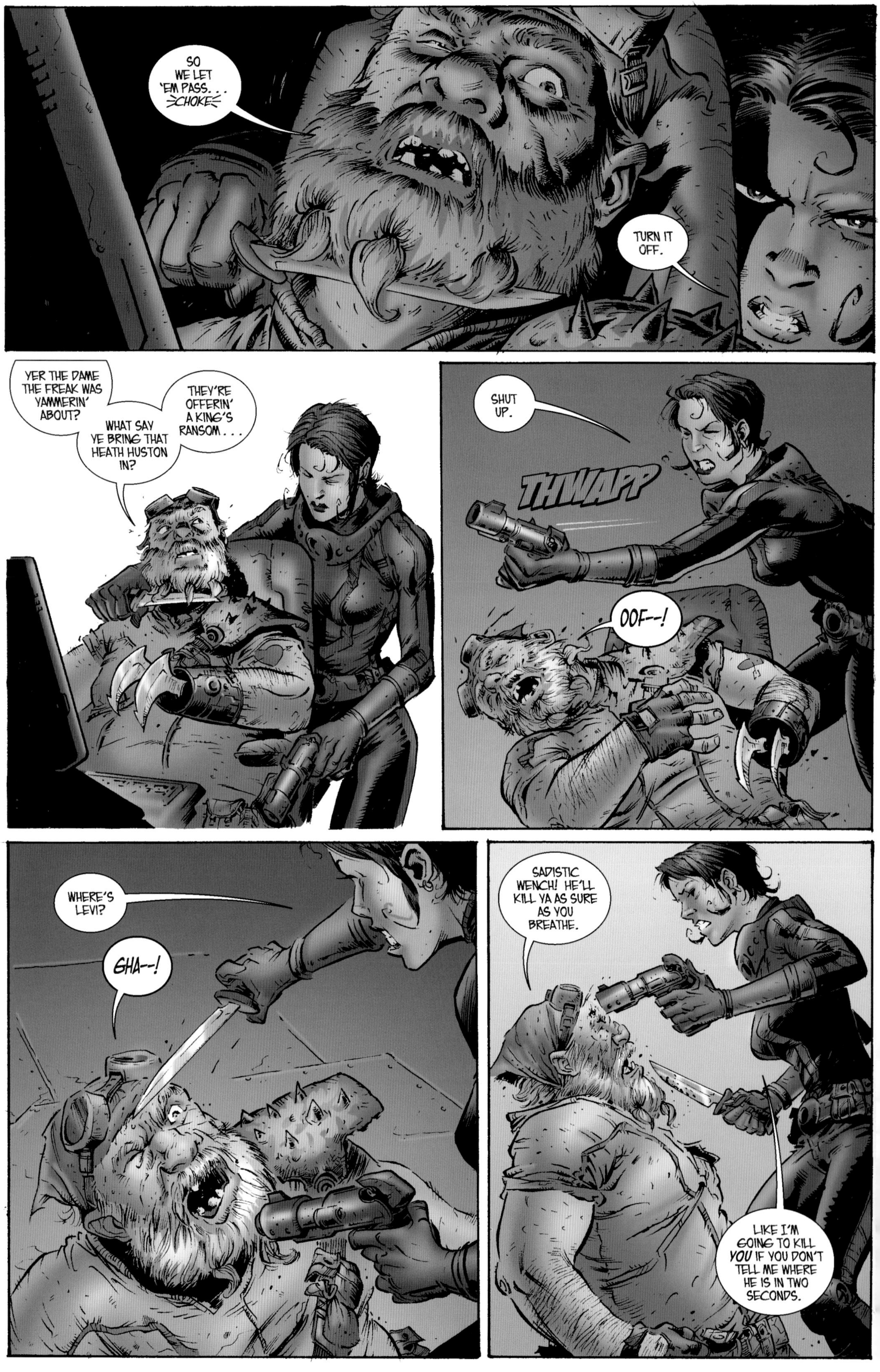
SO WE LET 'EM PASS... CHOKE
TURN IT OFF.
YER THE DAME THE FREAK WAS YAMMERIN' ABOUT?
THEY'RE OFFERIN' A KING'S RANSOM...
WHAT SAY YE BRING THAT HEATH HUSTON IN?
SHUT UP.
THWAPP
OOF--!
WHERE'S LEVI?
GHA--!
SADISTIC WENCH! HE'LL KILL YA AS SURE AS YOU BREATHE.
LIKE I'M GOING TO KILL *YOU* IF YOU DON'T TELL ME WHERE HE IS IN TWO SECONDS.

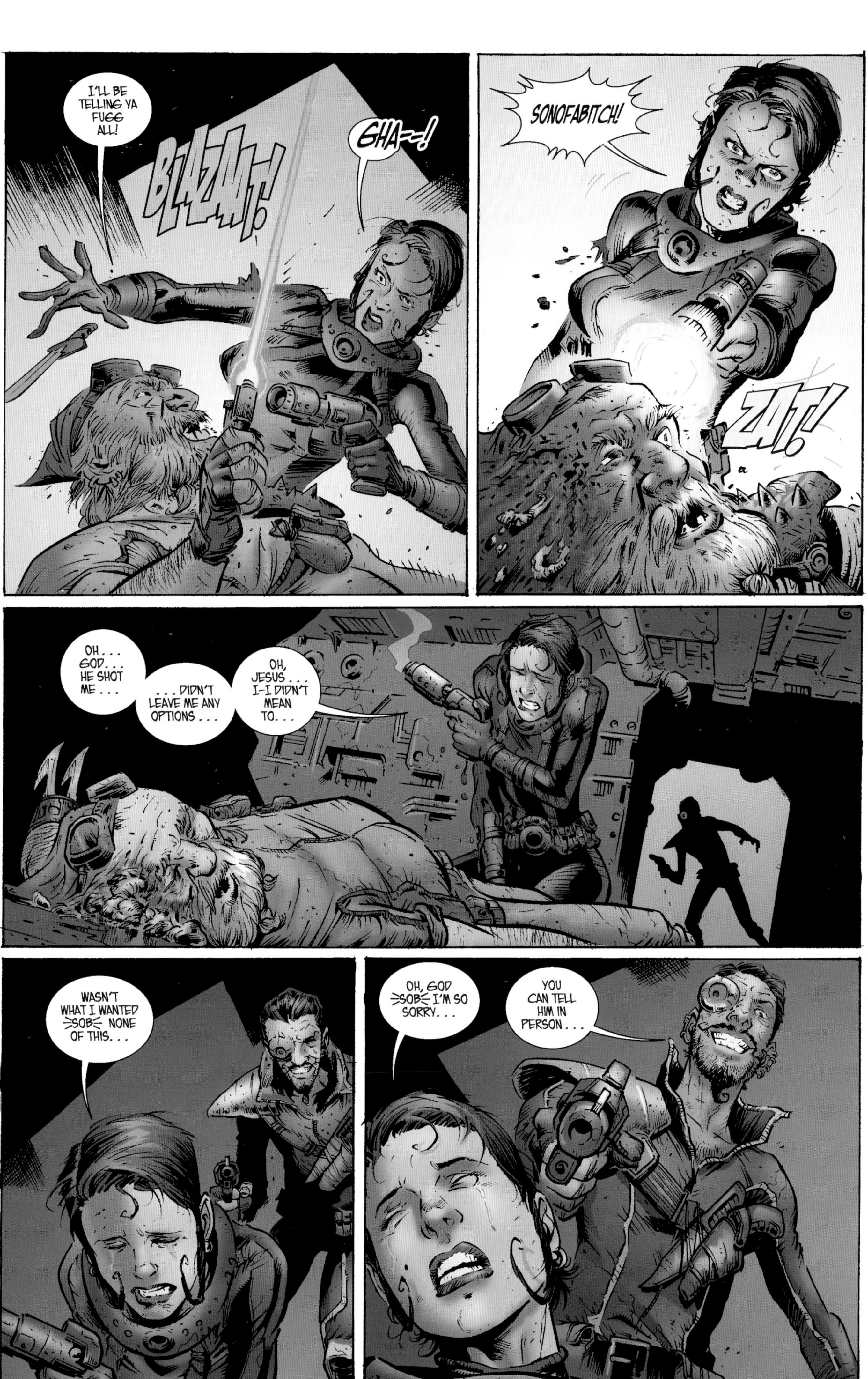
I'LL BE TELLING YA FUGG ALL!
BLAZAAT!
GHA--!
SONOFABITCH!
ZAT!
OH . . . GOD . . . HE SHOT ME . . .
. . . DIDN'T LEAVE ME ANY OPTIONS . . .
OH, JESUS . . . I-I DIDN'T MEAN TO. . .
WASN'T WHAT I WANTED ⋝SOB⋜ NONE OF THIS. . .
OH, GOD ⋝SOB⋜ I'M SO SORRY. . .
YOU CAN TELL HIM IN PERSON . . .

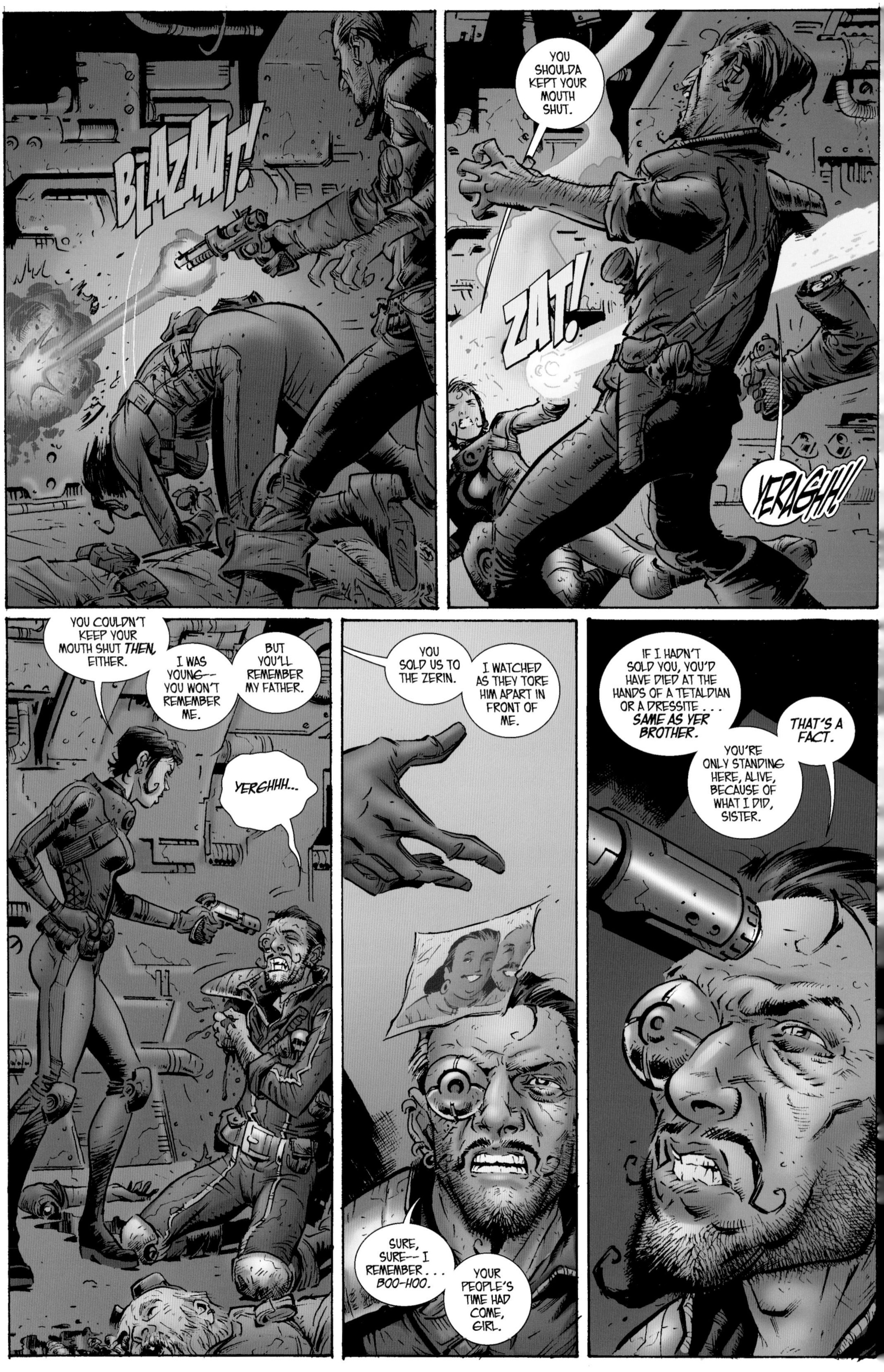
BLAZAAT!
YOU SHOULDA KEPT YOUR MOUTH SHUT.
ZAT!
YERAGHH!!
YOU COULDN'T KEEP YOUR MOUTH SHUT THEN, EITHER.
I WAS YOUNG-- YOU WON'T REMEMBER ME.
BUT YOU'LL REMEMBER MY FATHER.
YERGHHH...
YOU SOLD US TO THE ZERIN.
I WATCHED AS THEY TORE HIM APART IN FRONT OF ME.
SURE, SURE-- I REMEMBER... BOO-HOO.
YOUR PEOPLE'S TIME HAD COME, GIRL.
IF I HADN'T SOLD YOU, YOU'D HAVE DIED AT THE HANDS OF A TETALDIAN OR A DRESSITE... SAME AS YER BROTHER.
THAT'S A FACT.
YOU'RE ONLY STANDING HERE, ALIVE, BECAUSE OF WHAT I DID, SISTER.

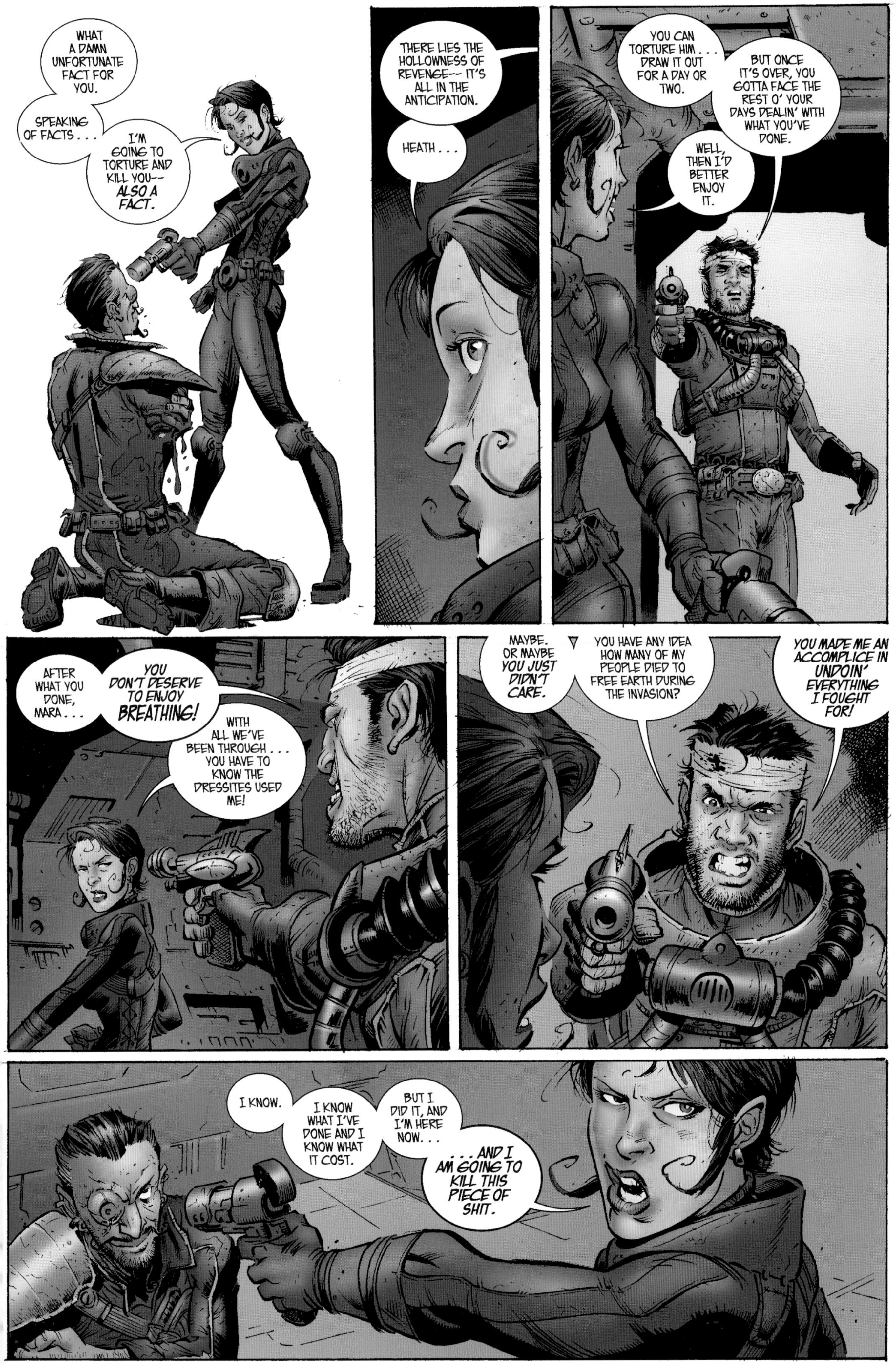
WHAT A DAMN UNFORTUNATE FACT FOR YOU.
SPEAKING OF FACTS . . .
I'M GOING TO TORTURE AND KILL YOU-- *ALSO A FACT.*
THERE LIES THE HOLLOWNESS OF REVENGE-- IT'S ALL IN THE ANTICIPATION.
HEATH . . .
YOU CAN TORTURE HIM . . . DRAW IT OUT FOR A DAY OR TWO.
BUT ONCE IT'S OVER, YOU GOTTA FACE THE REST O' YOUR DAYS DEALIN' WITH WHAT YOU'VE DONE.
WELL, THEN I'D BETTER ENJOY IT.
AFTER WHAT YOU DONE, MARA . . .
YOU DON'T DESERVE TO ENJOY **BREATHING!**
WITH ALL WE'VE BEEN THROUGH . . . YOU HAVE TO KNOW THE DRESSITES USED ME!
MAYBE. OR MAYBE *YOU JUST DIDN'T CARE.*
YOU HAVE ANY IDEA HOW MANY OF MY PEOPLE DIED TO FREE EARTH DURING THE INVASION?
YOU MADE ME AN ACCOMPLICE IN **UNDOIN'** *EVERYTHING I FOUGHT FOR!*
I KNOW.
I KNOW WHAT I'VE DONE AND I KNOW WHAT IT COST.
BUT I DID IT, AND I'M HERE NOW. . .
. . . AND I AM GOING TO KILL THIS PIECE OF SHIT.

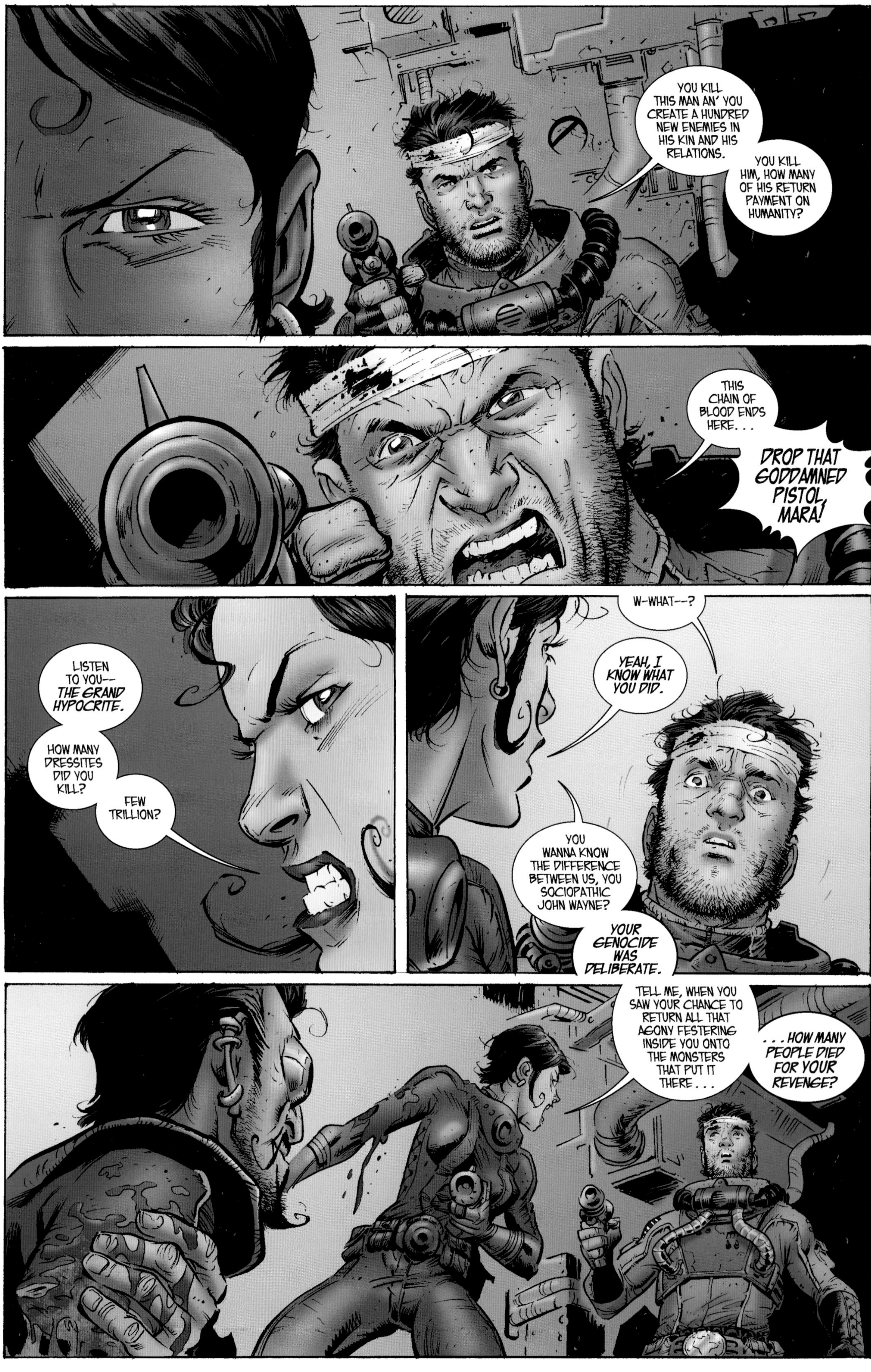
YOU KILL THIS MAN AN' YOU CREATE A HUNDRED NEW ENEMIES IN HIS KIN AND HIS RELATIONS.
YOU KILL HIM, HOW MANY OF HIS RETURN PAYMENT ON HUMANITY?
THIS CHAIN OF BLOOD ENDS HERE. . .
DROP THAT GODDAMNED PISTOL, MARA!
LISTEN TO YOU-- THE GRAND HYPOCRITE.
HOW MANY DRESSITES DID YOU KILL?
FEW TRILLION?
W-WHAT--?
YEAH, I KNOW WHAT YOU DID.
YOU WANNA KNOW THE DIFFERENCE BETWEEN US, YOU SOCIOPATHIC JOHN WAYNE?
YOUR GENOCIDE WAS DELIBERATE.
TELL ME, WHEN YOU SAW YOUR CHANCE TO RETURN ALL THAT AGONY FESTERING INSIDE YOU ONTO THE MONSTERS THAT PUT IT THERE . . .
. . . HOW MANY PEOPLE DIED FOR YOUR REVENGE?

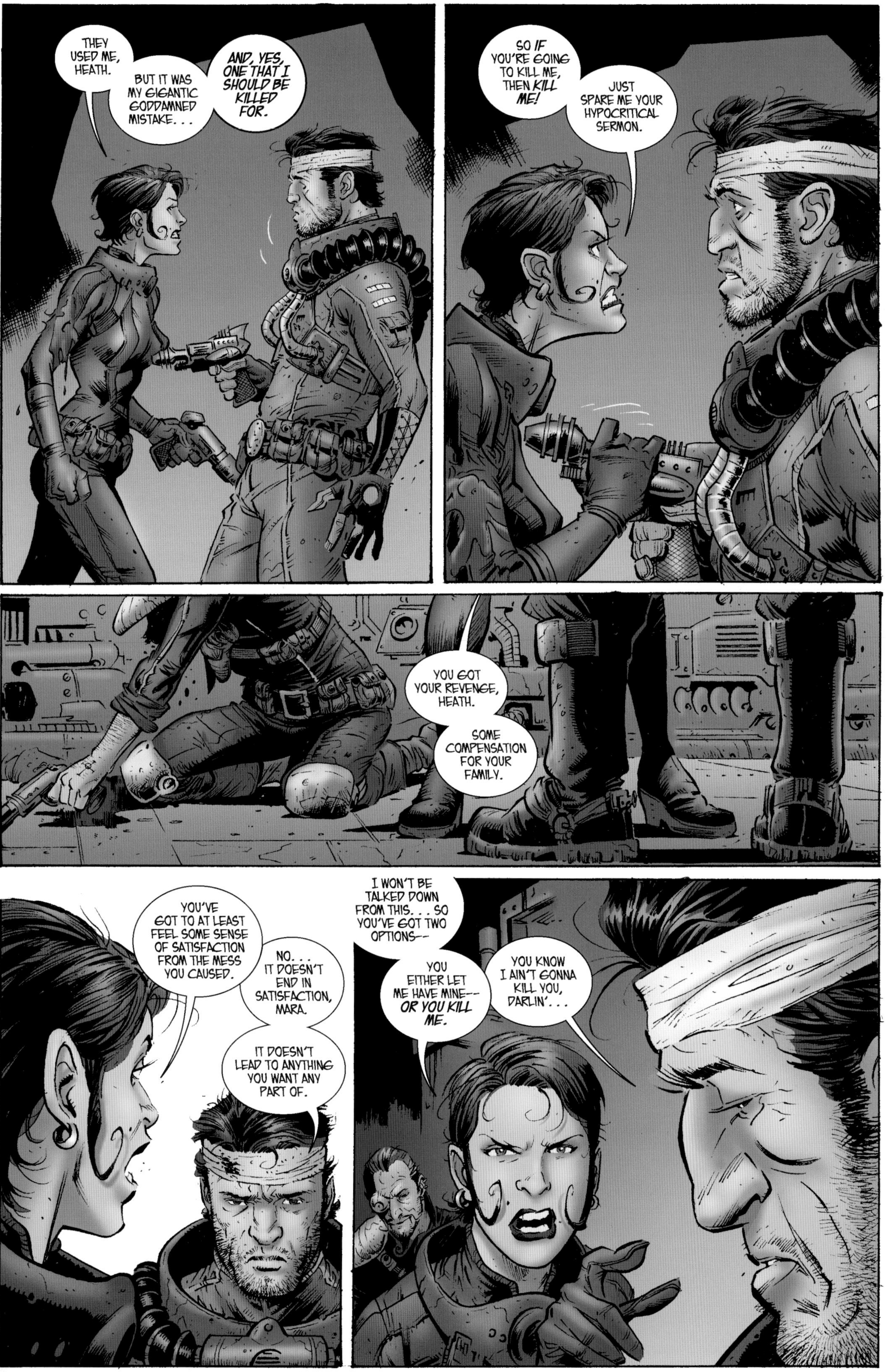
THEY USED ME, HEATH.
BUT IT WAS MY GIGANTIC GODDAMNED MISTAKE. . .
AND, YES, ONE THAT I SHOULD BE KILLED FOR.
SO IF YOU'RE GOING TO KILL ME, THEN KILL ME!
JUST SPARE ME YOUR HYPOCRITICAL SERMON.
YOU GOT YOUR REVENGE, HEATH.
SOME COMPENSATION FOR YOUR FAMILY.
YOU'VE GOT TO AT LEAST FEEL SOME SENSE OF SATISFACTION FROM THE MESS YOU CAUSED.
NO. . . IT DOESN'T END IN SATISFACTION, MARA.
IT DOESN'T LEAD TO ANYTHING YOU WANT ANY PART OF.
I WON'T BE TALKED DOWN FROM THIS. . . SO YOU'VE GOT TWO OPTIONS--
YOU EITHER LET ME HAVE MINE-- OR YOU KILL ME.
YOU KNOW I AIN'T GONNA KILL YOU, DARLIN'. . .

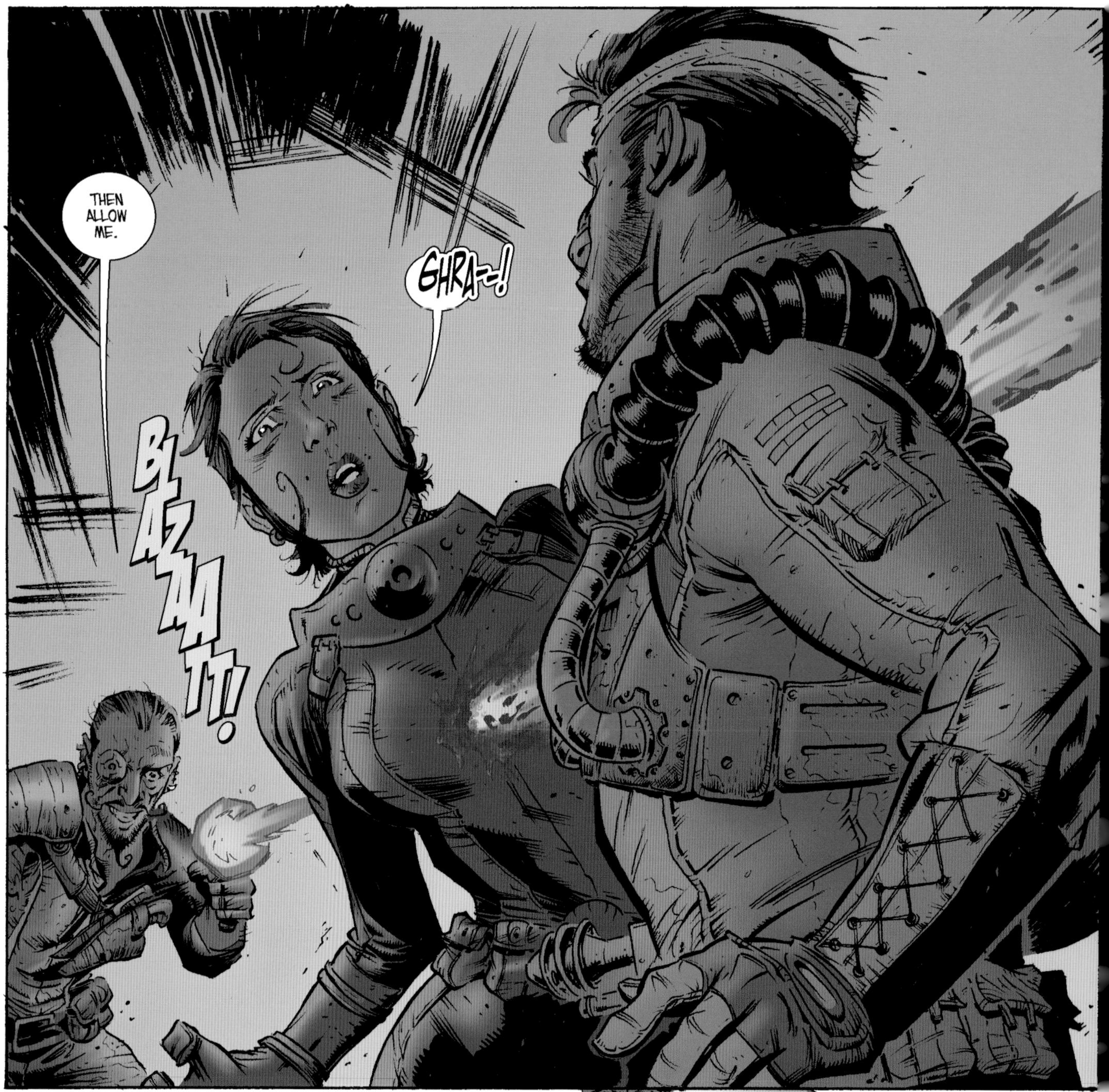
THEN ALLOW ME.
GHRA--!
BLAZAATT!

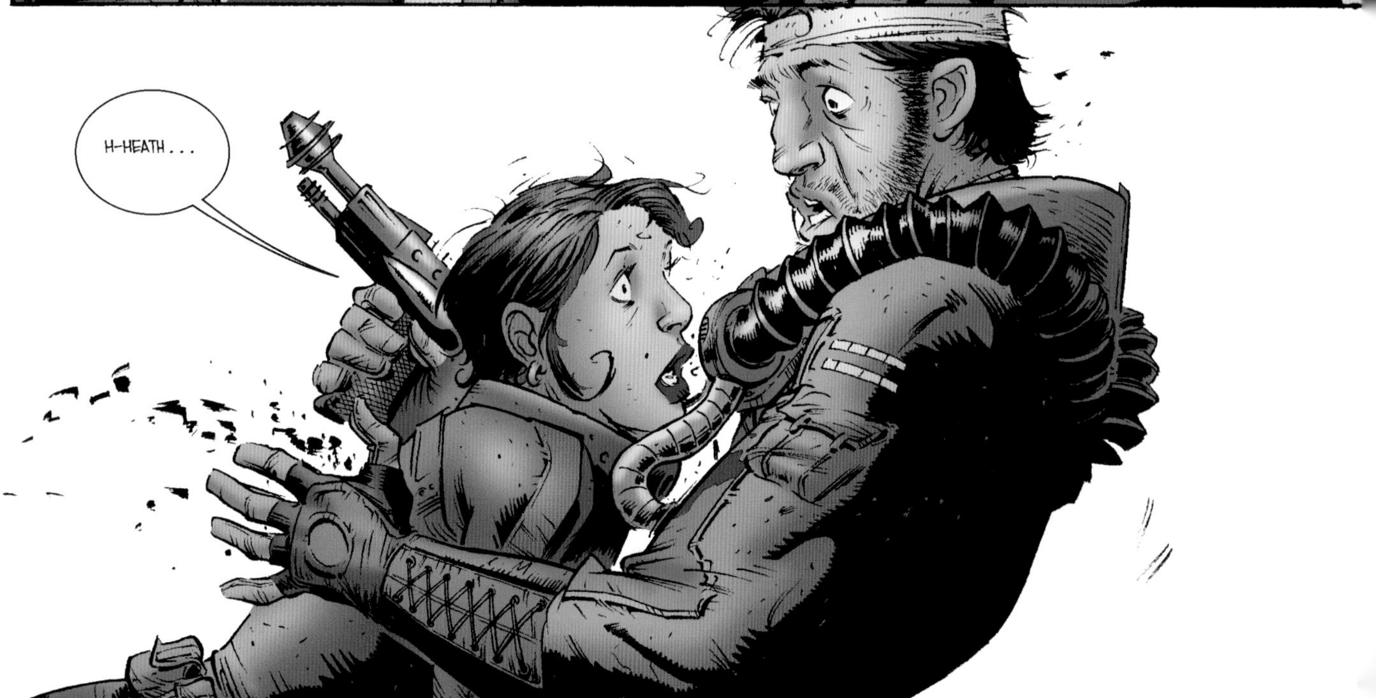
H-HEATH . . .

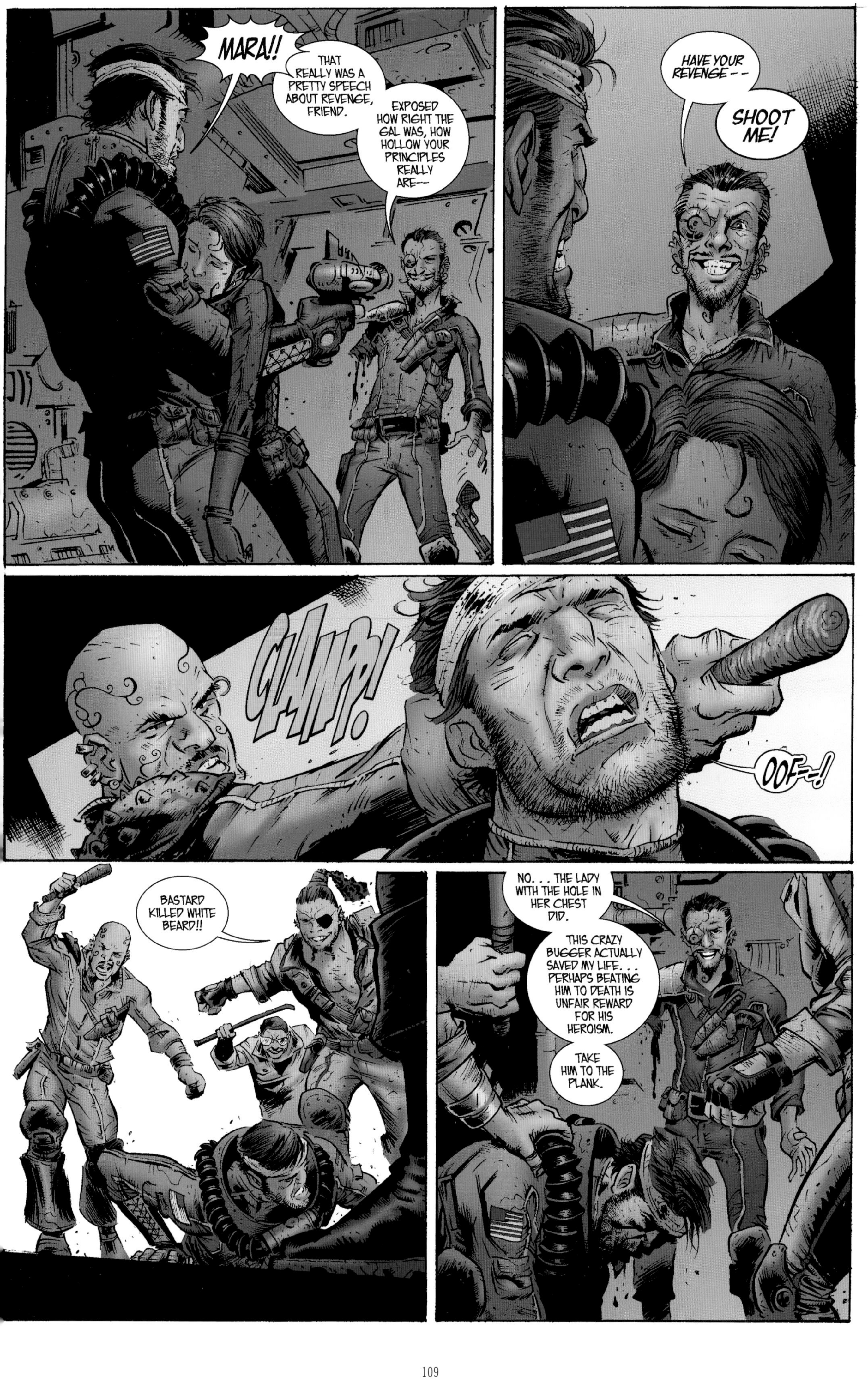
MARA!!
THAT REALLY WAS A PRETTY SPEECH ABOUT REVENGE, FRIEND.
EXPOSED HOW RIGHT THE GAL WAS, HOW HOLLOW YOUR PRINCIPLES REALLY ARE--
HAVE YOUR REVENGE --
SHOOT ME!
CLAMP!
OOF--!
BASTARD KILLED WHITE BEARD!!
NO. . . THE LADY WITH THE HOLE IN HER CHEST DID.
THIS CRAZY BUGGER ACTUALLY SAVED MY LIFE. . . PERHAPS BEATING HIM TO DEATH IS UNFAIR REWARD FOR HIS HEROISM.
TAKE HIM TO THE PLANK.

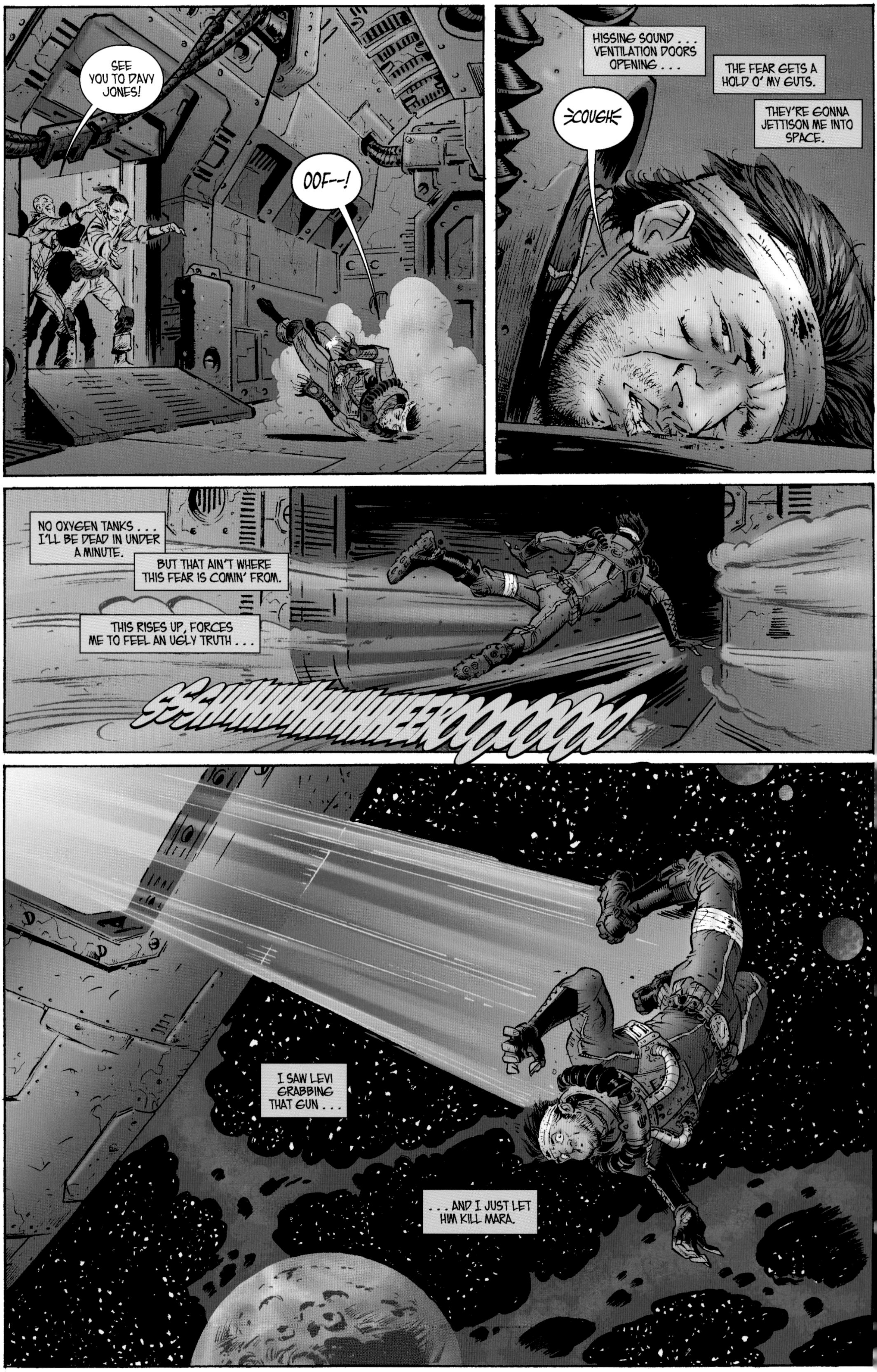

SEE YOU TO DAVY JONES!
OOF--!
HISSING SOUND . . . VENTILATION DOORS OPENING . . .
THE FEAR GETS A HOLD O' MY GUTS.
THEY'RE GONNA JETTISON ME INTO SPACE.
COUGH
NO OXYGEN TANKS . . . I'LL BE DEAD IN UNDER A MINUTE.
BUT THAT AIN'T WHERE THIS FEAR IS COMIN' FROM.
THIS RISES UP, FORCES ME TO FEEL AN UGLY TRUTH . . .
SSHHHHHHHHHHEEROOOOOOOO
I SAW LEVI GRABBING THAT GUN . . .
. . . AND I JUST LET HIM KILL MARA.

CHAPTER 5

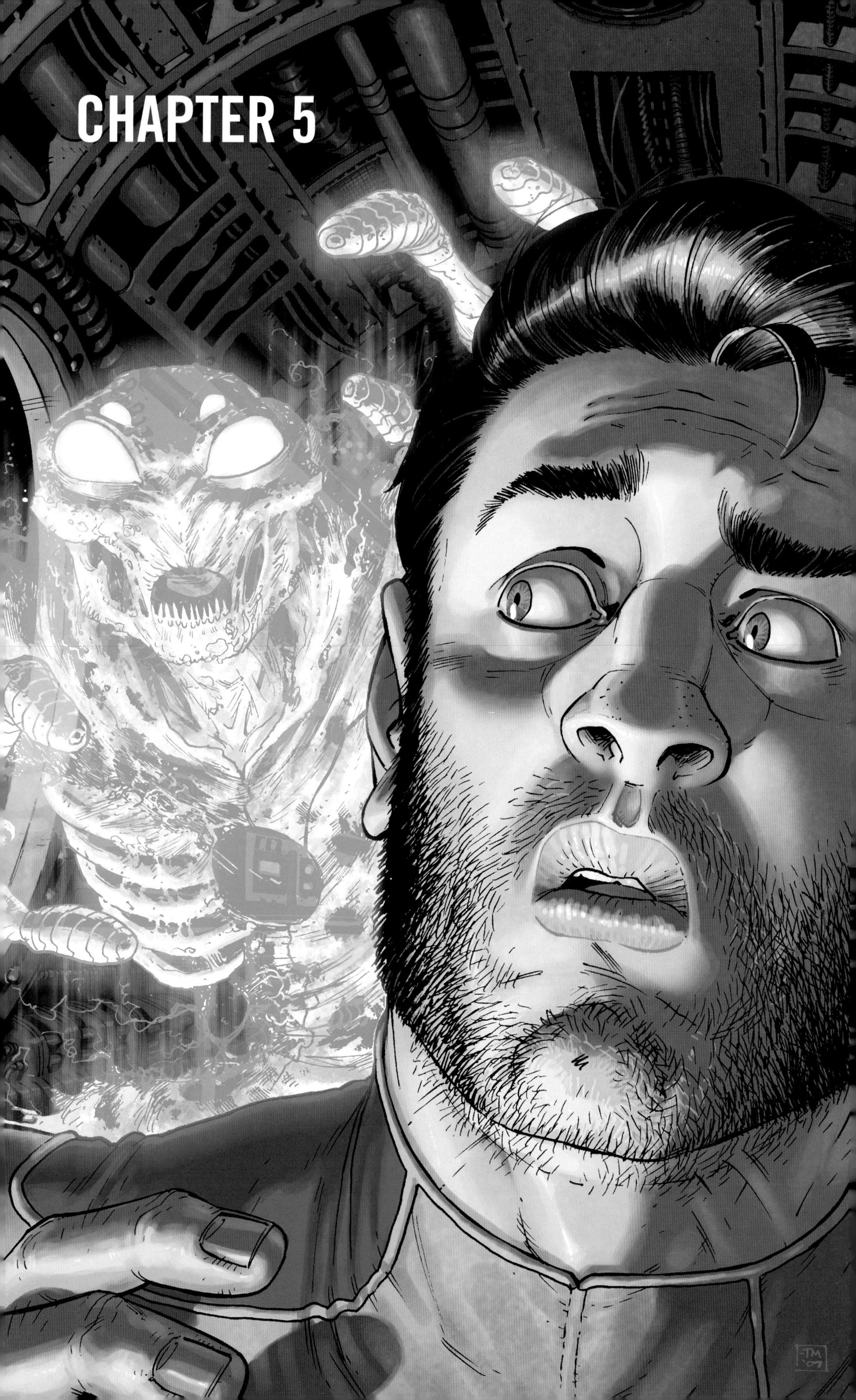

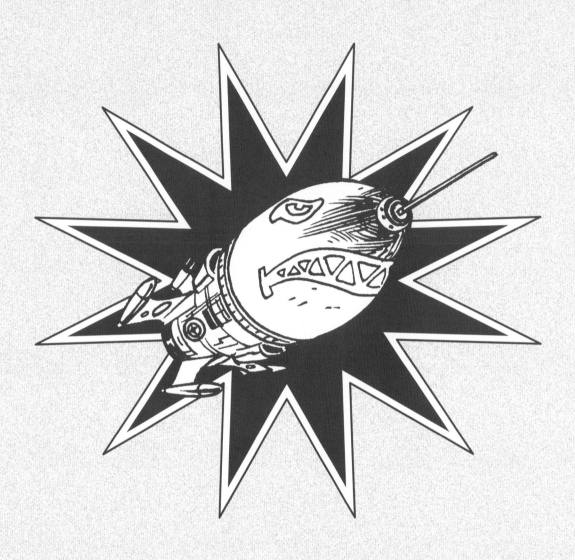

EARTH'S MOON...

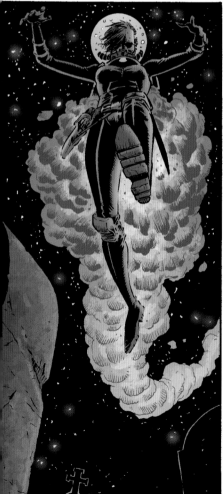

"WHEN YOU GO HOME, TELL THEM OF US AND SAY, FOR THEIR TOMORROW WE GAVE OUR TODAY"

IN MEMORY OF OTTO BIGLEY BELOVED HUSBAND, UNCLE, AND FEAT AGENT

UNCLE OTTO...

REST EASY-- HE'S GOING TO BLEED FOR WHAT HE DID TO US.

113

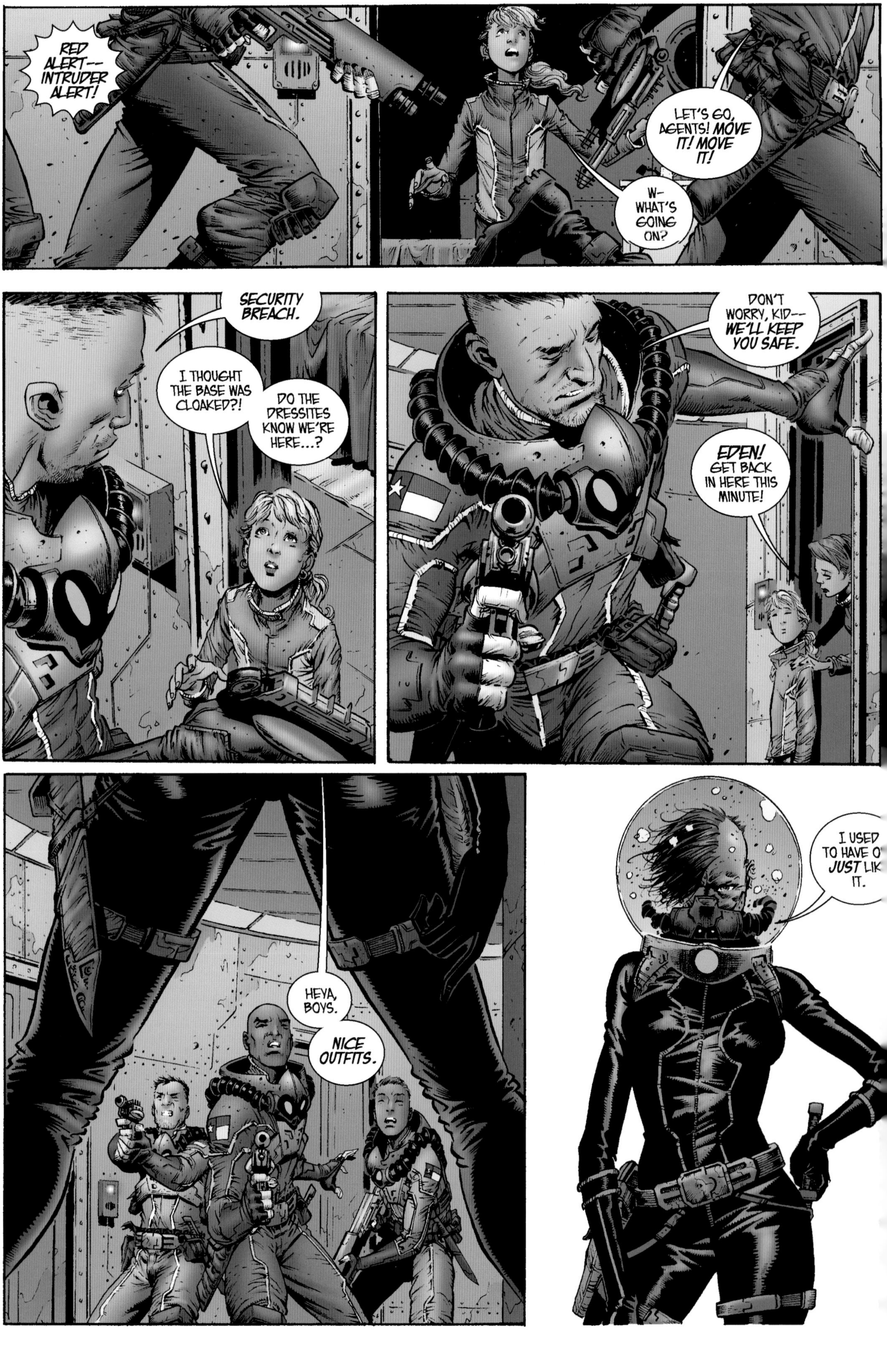
RED ALERT-- INTRUDER ALERT!
LET'S GO, AGENTS! MOVE IT! MOVE IT!
W-WHAT'S GOING ON?
SECURITY BREACH.
I THOUGHT THE BASE WAS CLOAKED?!
DO THE DRESSITES KNOW WE'RE HERE...?
DON'T WORRY, KID-- WE'LL KEEP YOU SAFE.
EDEN! GET BACK IN HERE THIS MINUTE!
HEYA, BOYS.
NICE OUTFITS.
I USED TO HAVE O JUST LIK IT.

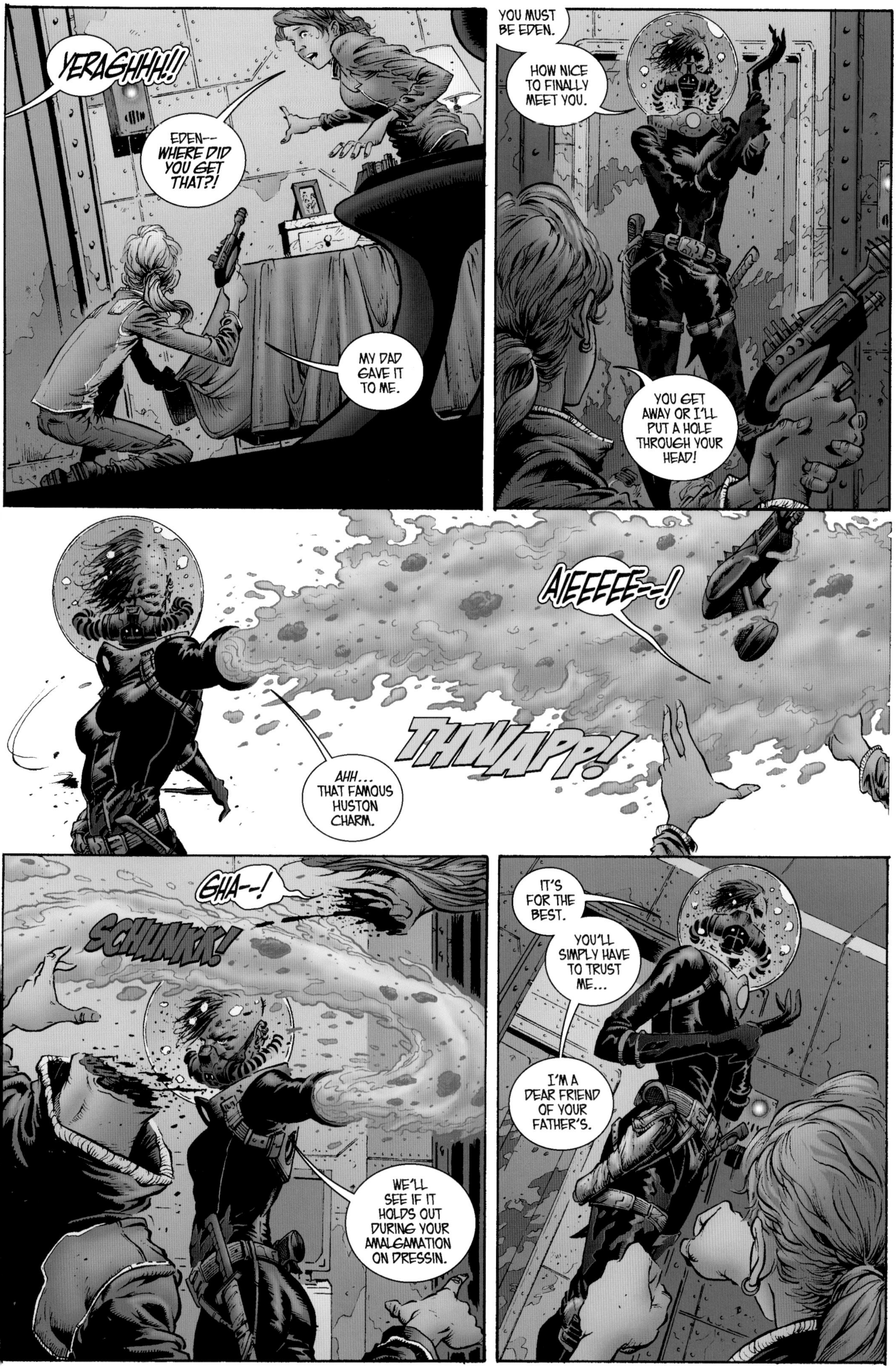
YERAGHHH!!
EDEN-- WHERE DID YOU GET THAT?!
MY DAD GAVE IT TO ME.
YOU MUST BE EDEN.
HOW NICE TO FINALLY MEET YOU.
YOU GET AWAY OR I'LL PUT A HOLE THROUGH YOUR HEAD!
AIEEEEE--!
THWAPP!
AHH... THAT FAMOUS HUSTON CHARM.
GHA--!
SCHUNKK!
WE'LL SEE IF IT HOLDS OUT DURING YOUR AMALGAMATION ON DRESSIN.
IT'S FOR THE BEST.
YOU'LL SIMPLY HAVE TO TRUST ME...
I'M A DEAR FRIEND OF YOUR FATHER'S.

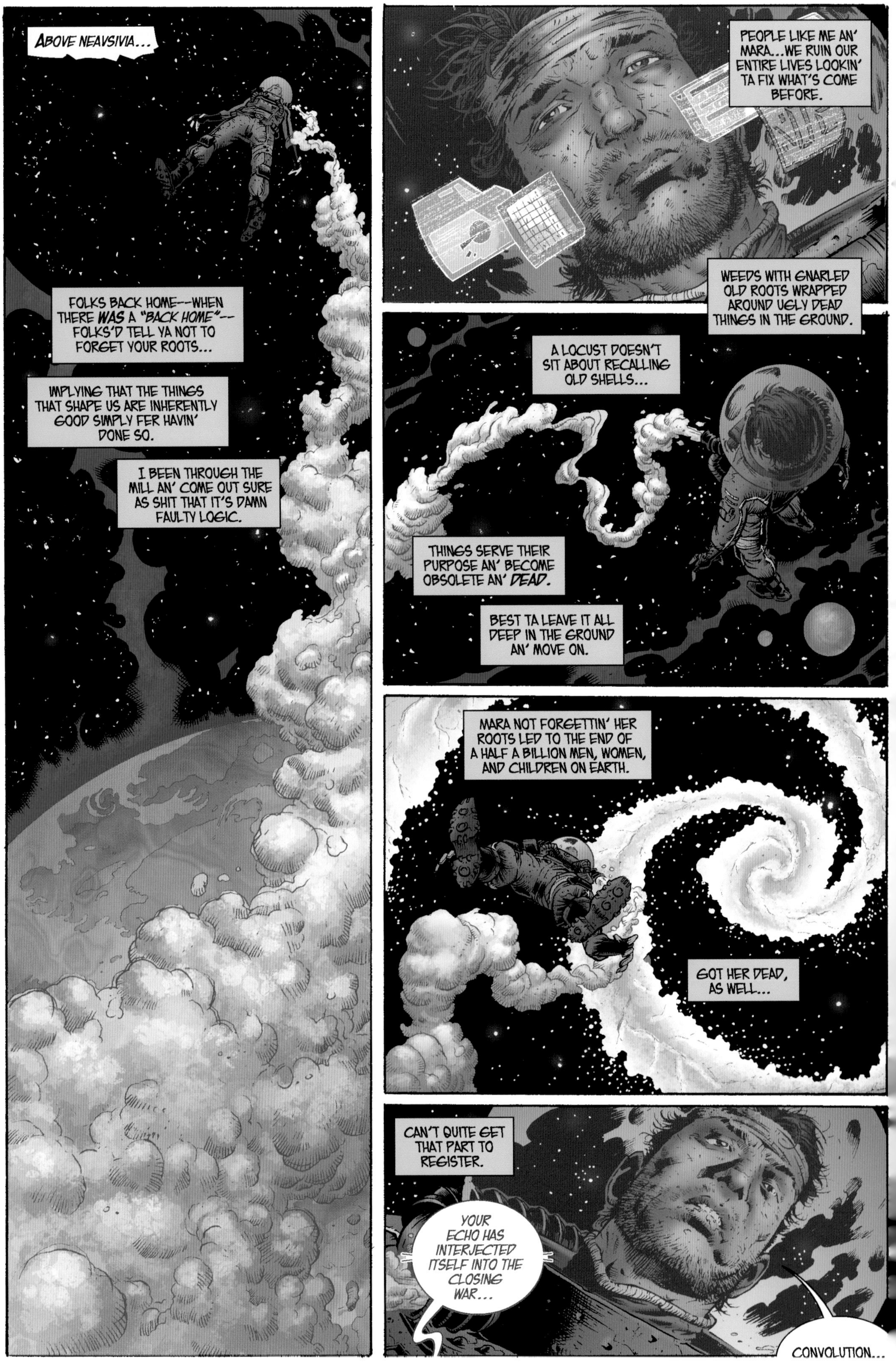
ABOVE NEAVSIVIA...
FOLKS BACK HOME--WHEN THERE WAS A "BACK HOME"--FOLKS'D TELL YA NOT TO FORGET YOUR ROOTS...
IMPLYING THAT THE THINGS THAT SHAPE US ARE INHERENTLY GOOD SIMPLY FER HAVIN' DONE SO.
I BEEN THROUGH THE MILL AN' COME OUT SURE AS SHIT THAT IT'S DAMN FAULTY LOGIC.
PEOPLE LIKE ME AN' MARA...WE RUIN OUR ENTIRE LIVES LOOKIN' TA FIX WHAT'S COME BEFORE.
WEEDS WITH GNARLED OLD ROOTS WRAPPED AROUND UGLY DEAD THINGS IN THE GROUND.
A LOCUST DOESN'T SIT ABOUT RECALLING OLD SHELLS...
THINGS SERVE THEIR PURPOSE AN' BECOME OBSOLETE AN' DEAD.
BEST TA LEAVE IT ALL DEEP IN THE GROUND AN' MOVE ON.
MARA NOT FORGETTIN' HER ROOTS LED TO THE END OF A HALF A BILLION MEN, WOMEN, AND CHILDREN ON EARTH.
GOT HER DEAD, AS WELL...
CAN'T QUITE GET THAT PART TO REGISTER.
YOUR ECHO HAS INTERJECTED ITSELF INTO THE CLOSING WAR...
CONVOLUTION...

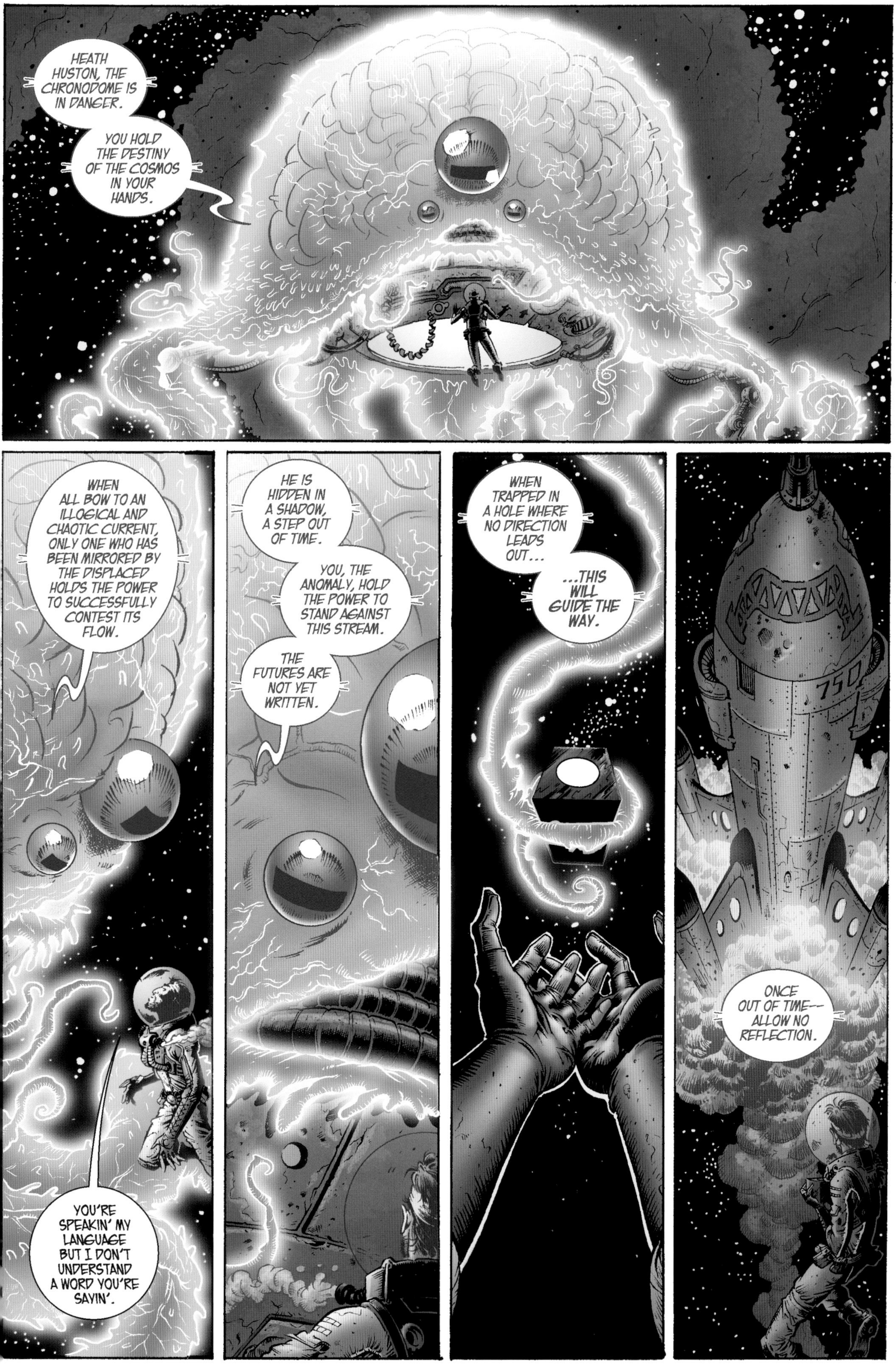
HEATH HUSTON, THE CHRONODOME IS IN DANGER.
YOU HOLD THE DESTINY OF THE COSMOS IN YOUR HANDS.
WHEN ALL BOW TO AN ILLOGICAL AND CHAOTIC CURRENT, ONLY ONE WHO HAS BEEN MIRRORED BY THE DISPLACED HOLDS THE POWER TO SUCCESSFULLY CONTEST ITS FLOW.
YOU'RE SPEAKIN' MY LANGUAGE BUT I DON'T UNDERSTAND A WORD YOU'RE SAYIN'.
HE IS HIDDEN IN A SHADOW, A STEP OUT OF TIME.
YOU, THE ANOMALY, HOLD THE POWER TO STAND AGAINST THIS STREAM.
THE FUTURES ARE NOT YET WRITTEN.
WHEN TRAPPED IN A HOLE WHERE NO DIRECTION LEADS OUT...
...THIS WILL GUIDE THE WAY.
750
ONCE OUT OF TIME-- ALLOW NO REFLECTION.

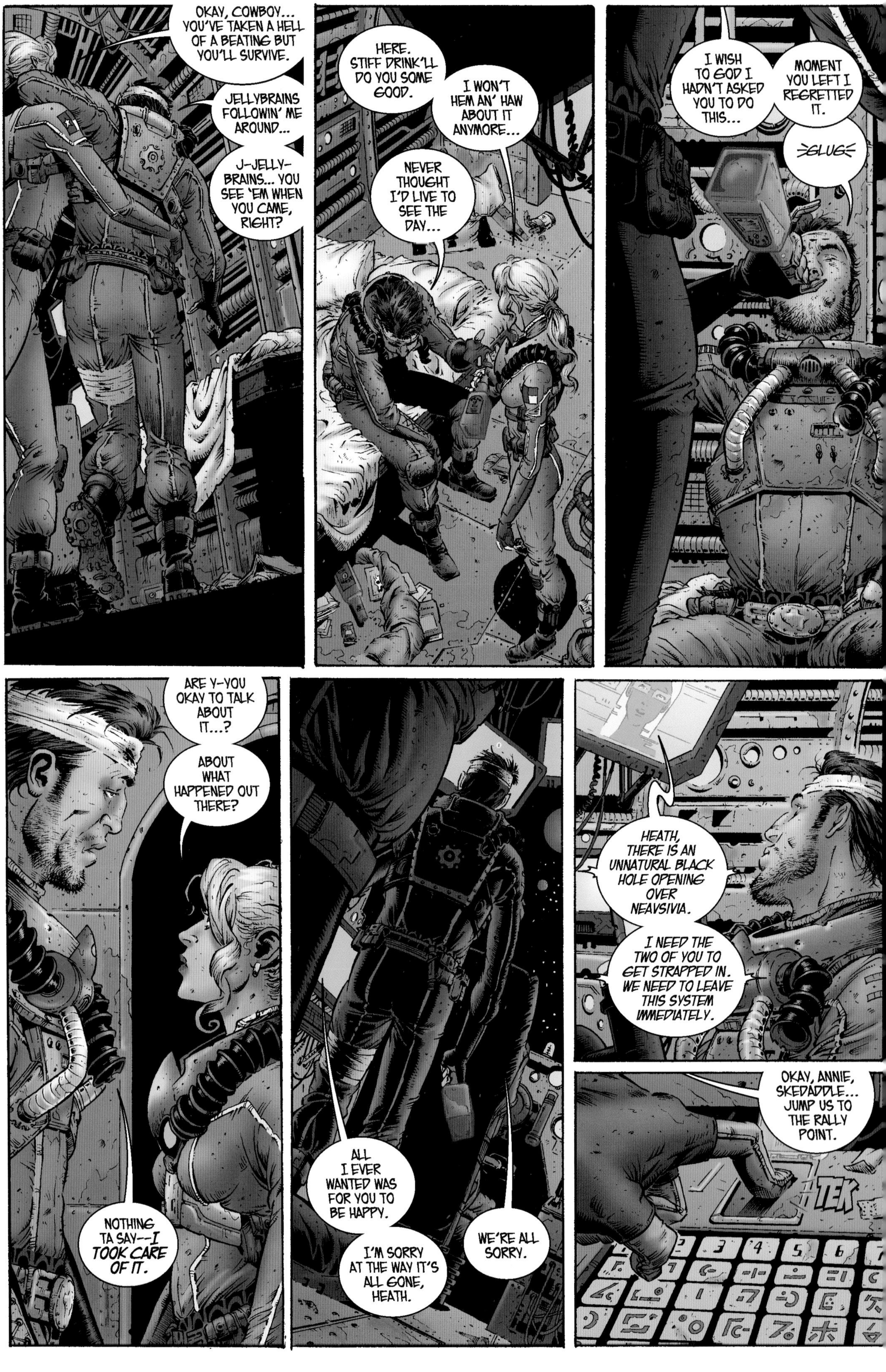
OKAY, COWBOY... YOU'VE TAKEN A HELL OF A BEATING BUT YOU'LL SURVIVE.
JELLYBRAINS FOLLOWIN' ME AROUND...
J-JELLY-BRAINS... YOU SEE 'EM WHEN YOU CAME, RIGHT?
HERE. STIFF DRINK'LL DO YOU SOME GOOD.
I WON'T HEM AN' HAW ABOUT IT ANYMORE...
NEVER THOUGHT I'D LIVE TO SEE THE DAY...
I WISH TO GOD I HADN'T ASKED YOU TO DO THIS...
MOMENT YOU LEFT I REGRETTED IT.
GLUG
ARE Y-YOU OKAY TO TALK ABOUT IT...?
ABOUT WHAT HAPPENED OUT THERE?
NOTHING TA SAY--I TOOK CARE OF IT.
ALL I EVER WANTED WAS FOR YOU TO BE HAPPY.
I'M SORRY AT THE WAY IT'S ALL GONE, HEATH.
WE'RE ALL SORRY.
HEATH, THERE IS AN UNNATURAL BLACK HOLE OPENING OVER NEAVSIVIA.
I NEED THE TWO OF YOU TO GET STRAPPED IN. WE NEED TO LEAVE THIS SYSTEM IMMEDIATELY.
OKAY, ANNIE, SKEDADDLE... JUMP US TO THE RALLY POINT.
TEK

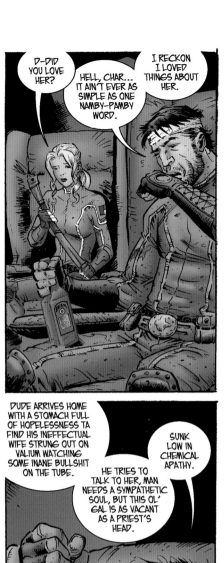

D-DID YOU LOVE HER?

HELL, CHAR... IT AIN'T EVER AS SIMPLE AS ONE NAMBY-PAMBY WORD.

I RECKON I LOVED THINGS ABOUT HER.

AFTER A FEW WEEKS HELPIN' ME DETOX SHE'D HAD ENOUGH O' MY MOPIN'.

THERE WAS A THING SHE MADE ME DO TO GET PAST THE ROTTEN TIMES WITH SOME PERSPECTIVE.

SHE'D TELL ME TA PICTURE AN AVERAGE FLABBY AMERICAN BUSINESSMAN IN HIS MID-FORTIES.

HE'S STRESSIN' THROUGH SMOGGY NEW YORK TRAFFIC ON HIS WAY HOME AFTER HIS BOSS TOLD HIM THE COMPANY IS DOWNSIZING.

DUDE ARRIVES HOME WITH A STOMACH FULL OF HOPELESSNESS TA FIND HIS INEFFECTUAL WIFE STRUNG OUT ON VALIUM WATCHING SOME INANE BULLSHIT ON THE TUBE.

HE TRIES TO TALK TO HER, MAN NEEDS A SYMPATHETIC SOUL, BUT THIS OL' GAL IS AS VACANT AS A PRIEST'S HEAD.

SUNK LOW IN CHEMICAL APATHY.

IN A RARE LUCID MOMENT HE'S SUDDENLY AWARE THAT HIS SOLE MOTIVATION IN LIFE HAS BEEN TO LIVE UP TO HIS FATHER'S INTERPRETATION OF WHAT A MAN SHOULD BE.

BUT THIS IS BETTER LEFT RUNNING IN THE BACKGROUND.

DESPERATE FOR IDENTIFICATION AND COMMISERATION THIS TIN CAN ATTEMPTS TO HAVE A HUMAN MOMENT WITH HIS SON.

THE BOY'S BEEN AN AFTERTHOUGHT FOR TOO LONG, HE WON'T EVEN OPEN HIS DOOR.

SO THE OLD MAN DRINKS DOWN A HIGHBALL, STARES AT THE HANDGUN IN HIS DRESSER FOR TWENTY MINUTES, AND FINALLY RETREATS TO THE NEUTRALITY OF HIS BED.

YEARS PASS AND HIS SON DIES OF AN OVERDOSE, HIS WIFE LEAVES HIM, HIS PARENTS AND FRIENDS BEGIN TO DIE OFF AND EVENTUALLY HE FOLLOWS SUIT.

DEAR GOD, HEATHROW. YOU FOUND COMFORT IN THIS MORBID UGLINESS?

NAH.

IT'S THE DAY AFTER THE OLD MAN'S FUNERAL THAT HELPS ME.

THE NEXT DAY WHEN THE SUN RISES AND EVERYTHING GOES ON ABOUT ITS BUSINESS AS USUAL.

SEE, EVERYTHING THAT OLD MAN DID...

EVERYTHING HE FRETTED AND BLED FOR...

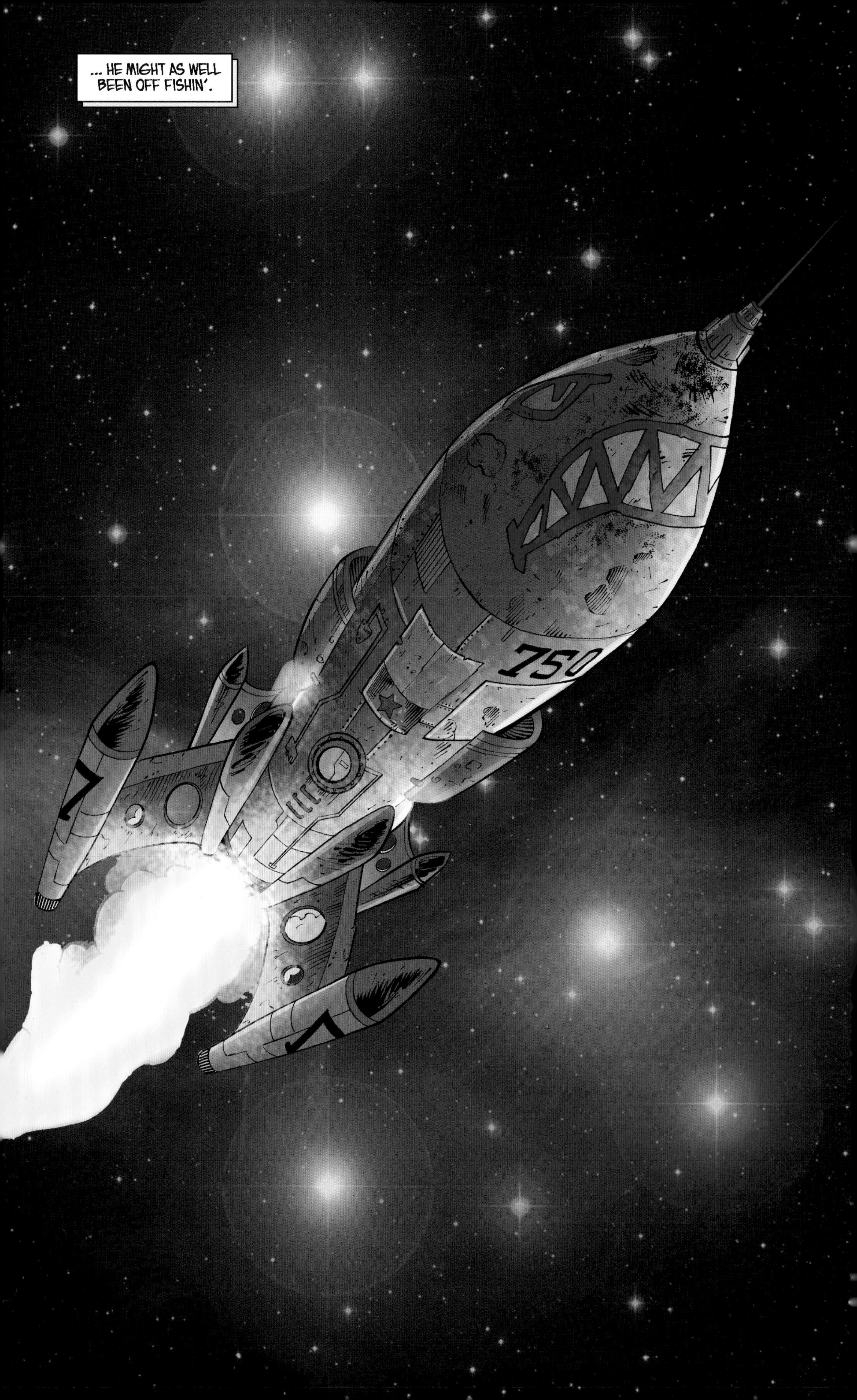
... HE MIGHT AS WELL BEEN OFF FISHIN'.
750

THE PLANET TETALDIA...

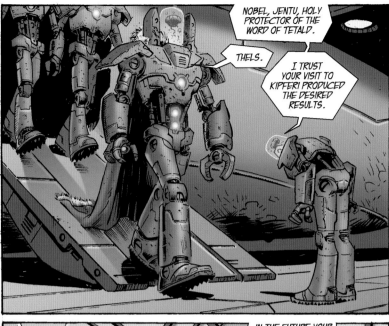

NOBEL, JENTU, HOLY PROTECTOR OF THE WORD OF TETALD.

THELS.

I TRUST YOUR VISIT TO KIPFERI PRODUCED THE DESIRED RESULTS.

IN THE FUTURE YOUR LORDSHIP NEED NOT DIRTY HIS HANDS. SUCH TASKS--

ARE TOO IMPORTANT TO TRUST TO ANYONE ELSE. IMAGINE IT... WHEN FINISHED WE'LL HAVE MAPPED OUT AN ENTIRELY NEW HISTORY FOR THE UNIVERSE.

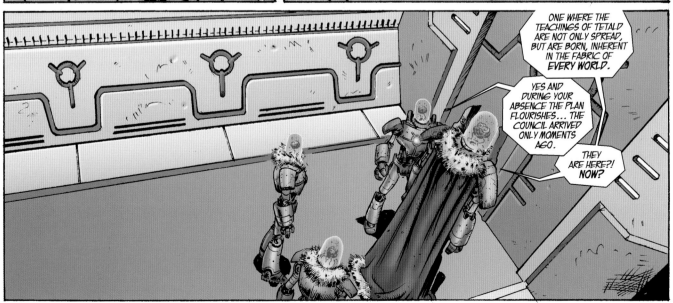

ONE WHERE THE TEACHINGS OF TETALD ARE NOT ONLY SPREAD, BUT ARE BORN, INHERENT IN THE FABRIC OF EVERY WORLD.

YES AND DURING YOUR ABSENCE THE PLAN FLOURISHES... THE COUNCIL ARRIVED ONLY MOMENTS AGO.

THEY ARE HERE?! NOW?

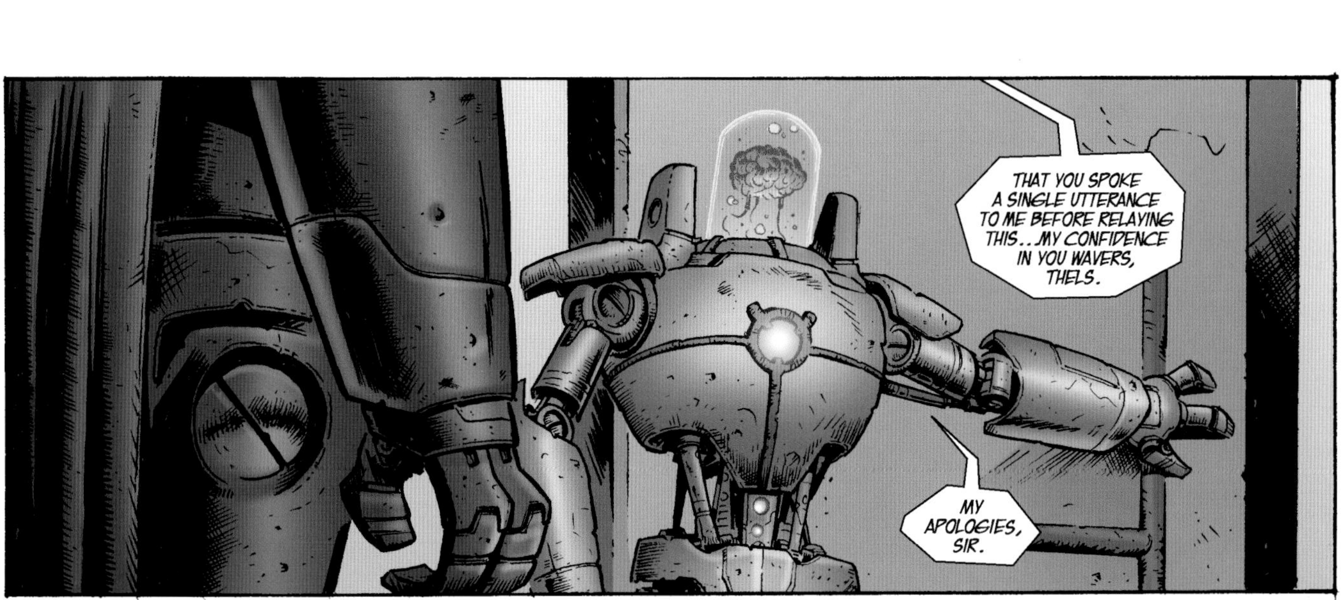
THAT YOU SPOKE A SINGLE UTTERANCE TO ME BEFORE RELAYING THIS... MY CONFIDENCE IN YOU WAVERS, THELS.
MY APOLOGIES, SIR.

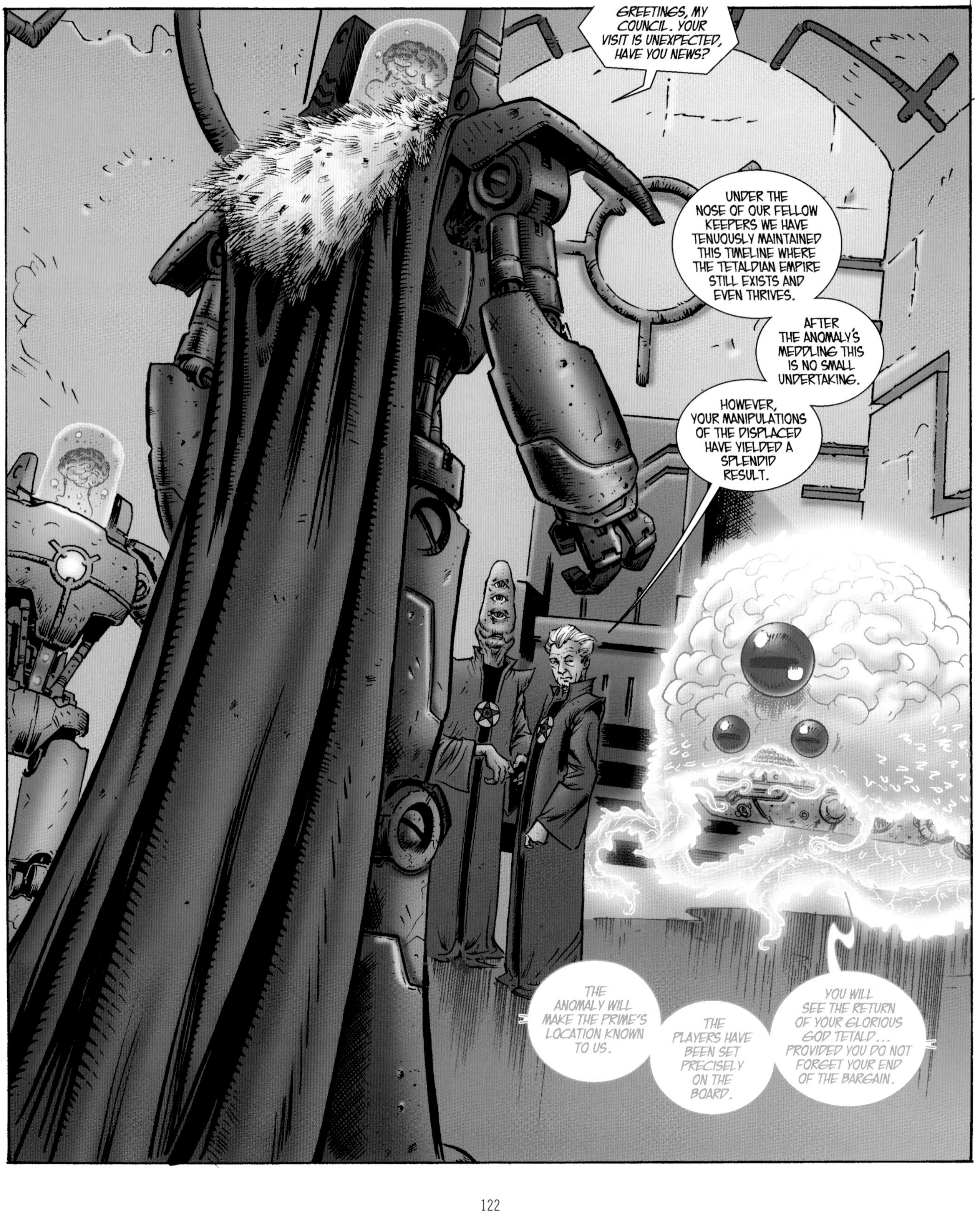
GREETINGS, MY COUNCIL. YOUR VISIT IS UNEXPECTED, HAVE YOU NEWS?
UNDER THE NOSE OF OUR FELLOW KEEPERS WE HAVE TENUOUSLY MAINTAINED THIS TIMELINE WHERE THE TETALDIAN EMPIRE STILL EXISTS AND EVEN THRIVES.
AFTER THE ANOMALY'S MEDDLING THIS IS NO SMALL UNDERTAKING.
HOWEVER, YOUR MANIPULATIONS OF THE DISPLACED HAVE YIELDED A SPLENDID RESULT.
THE ANOMALY WILL MAKE THE PRIME'S LOCATION KNOWN TO US.
THE PLAYERS HAVE BEEN SET PRECISELY ON THE BOARD.
YOU WILL SEE THE RETURN OF YOUR GLORIOUS GOD TETALD... PROVIDED YOU DO NOT FORGET YOUR END OF THE BARGAIN.

GODDAMN, IT'S GOOD TO SEE YOU...

WE LOST TOO MANY GOOD PEOPLE... MY RETURN IS NO CAUSE TO CELEBRATE.

I KNOW... I...I'M SO SORRY ABOUT KEITH.

THANK YOU, BETTY.

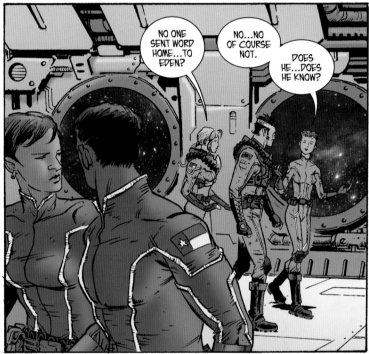

NO ONE SENT WORD HOME...TO EDEN?

NO...NO OF COURSE NOT.

DOES HE...DOES HE KNOW?

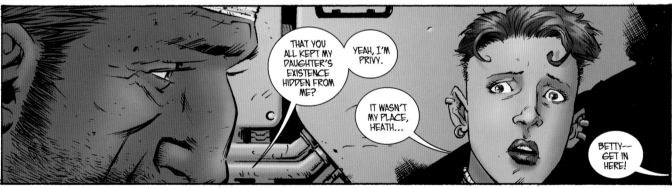

THAT YOU ALL KEPT MY DAUGHTER'S EXISTENCE HIDDEN FROM ME?

YEAH, I'M PRIVY.

IT WASN'T MY PLACE, HEATH...

BETTY-- GET IN HERE!

OKAY, WHAT'S ALL THE COMMOTION IN HERE?

JUST MORE SHITTY NEWS...

123

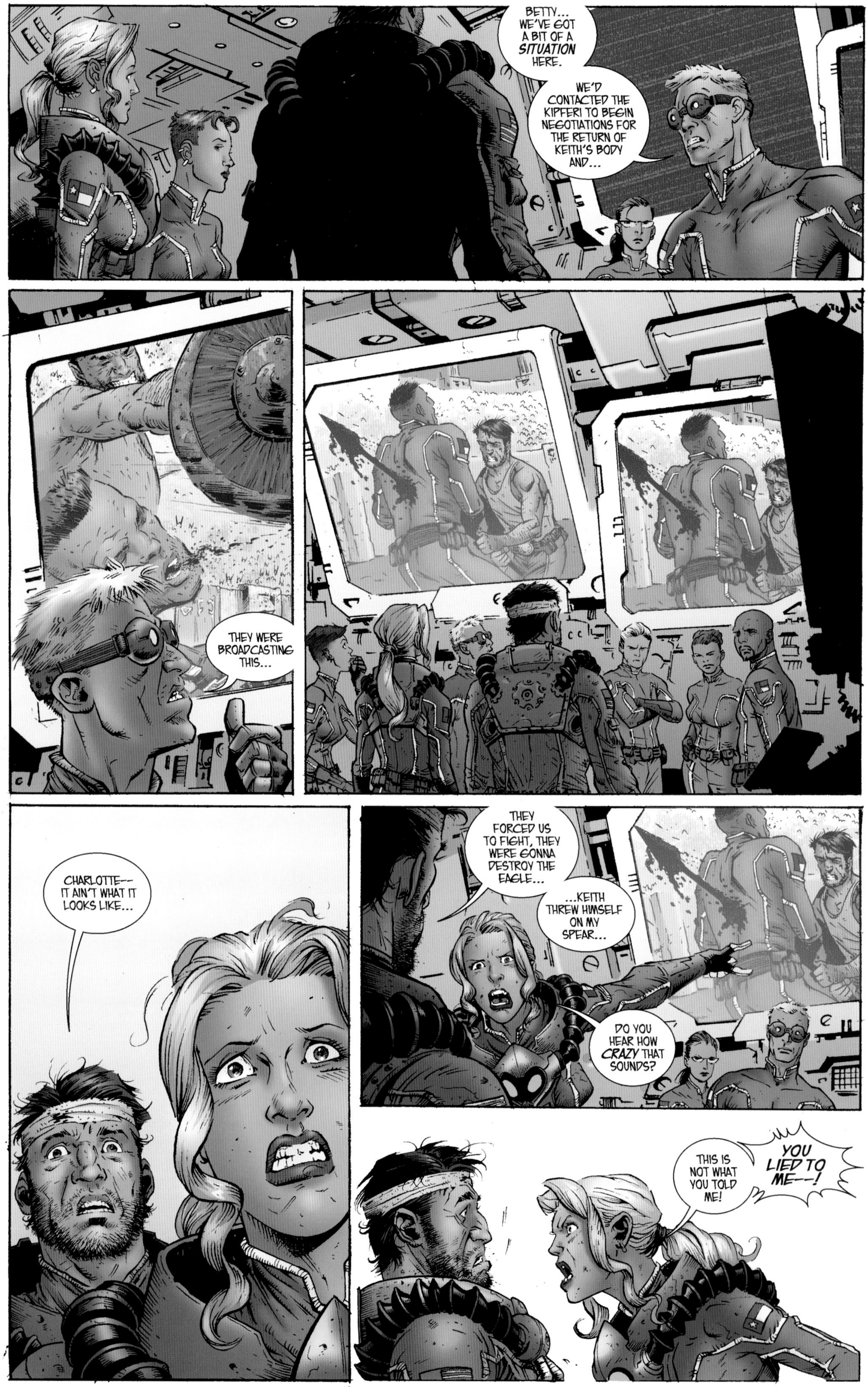
BETTY... WE'VE GOT A BIT OF A SITUATION HERE.
WE'D CONTACTED THE KIPFERI TO BEGIN NEGOTIATIONS FOR THE RETURN OF KEITH'S BODY AND...
THEY WERE BROADCASTING THIS...
CHARLOTTE-- IT AIN'T WHAT IT LOOKS LIKE...
THEY FORCED US TO FIGHT, THEY WERE GONNA DESTROY THE EAGLE...
...KEITH THREW HIMSELF ON MY SPEAR...
DO YOU HEAR HOW CRAZY THAT SOUNDS?
THIS IS NOT WHAT YOU TOLD ME!
YOU LIED TO ME--!

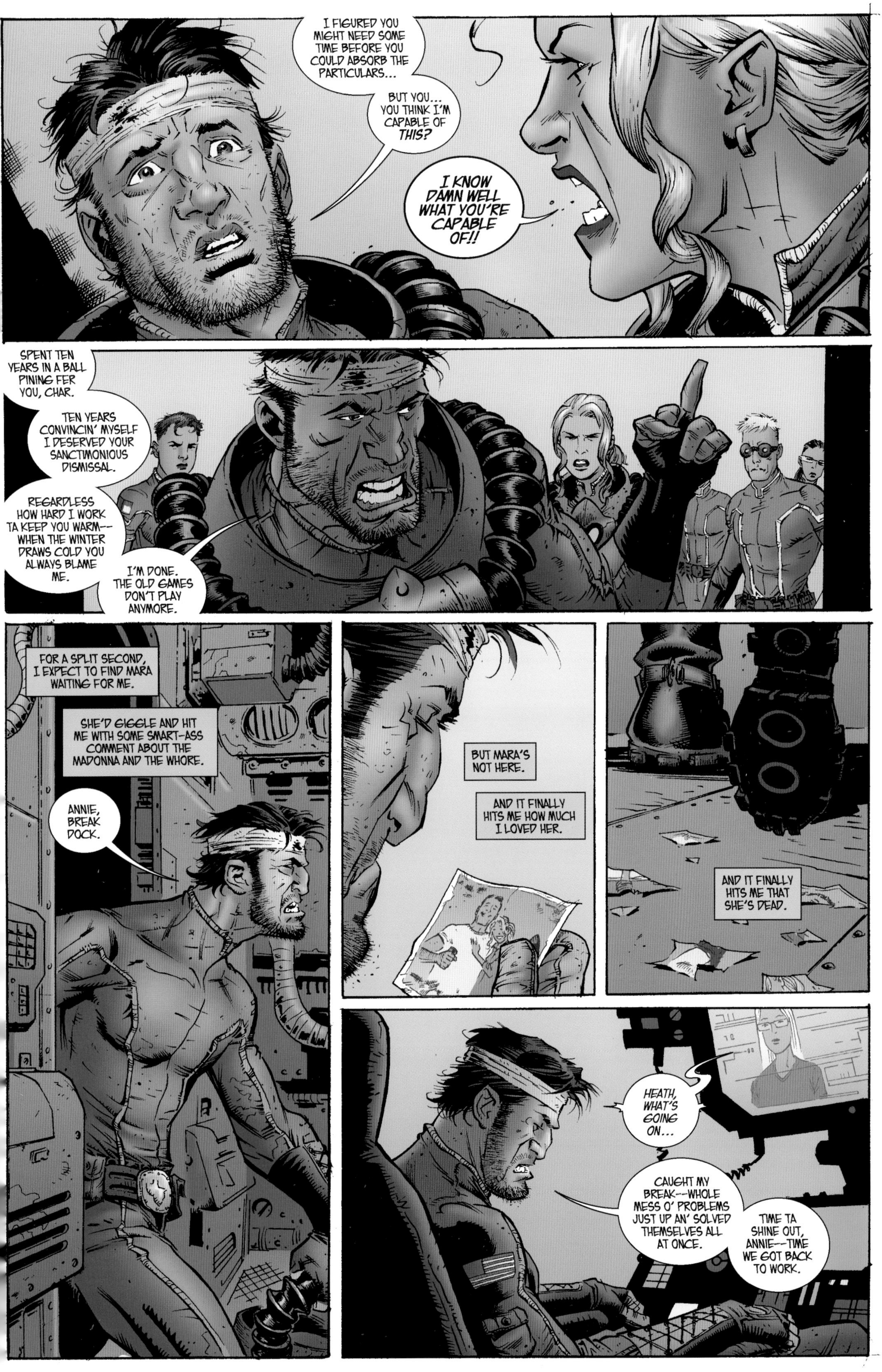
I FIGURED YOU MIGHT NEED SOME TIME BEFORE YOU COULD ABSORB THE PARTICULARS...
BUT YOU... YOU THINK I'M CAPABLE OF *THIS?*
I KNOW DAMN WELL WHAT YOU'RE CAPABLE OF!!
SPENT TEN YEARS IN A BALL PINING FER YOU, CHAR.
TEN YEARS CONVINCIN' MYSELF I DESERVED YOUR SANCTIMONIOUS DISMISSAL.
REGARDLESS HOW HARD I WORK TA KEEP YOU WARM-- WHEN THE WINTER DRAWS COLD YOU ALWAYS BLAME ME.
I'M DONE. THE OLD GAMES DON'T PLAY ANYMORE.
FOR A SPLIT SECOND, I EXPECT TO FIND MARA WAITING FOR ME.
SHE'D GIGGLE AND HIT ME WITH SOME SMART-ASS COMMENT ABOUT THE MADONNA AND THE WHORE.
ANNIE, BREAK DOCK.
BUT MARA'S NOT HERE.
AND IT FINALLY HITS ME HOW MUCH I LOVED HER.
AND IT FINALLY HITS ME THAT SHE'S DEAD.
HEATH, WHAT'S GOING ON...
CAUGHT MY BREAK--WHOLE MESS O' PROBLEMS JUST UP AN' SOLVED THEMSELVES ALL AT ONCE.
TIME TA SHINE OUT, ANNIE--TIME WE GOT BACK TO WORK.

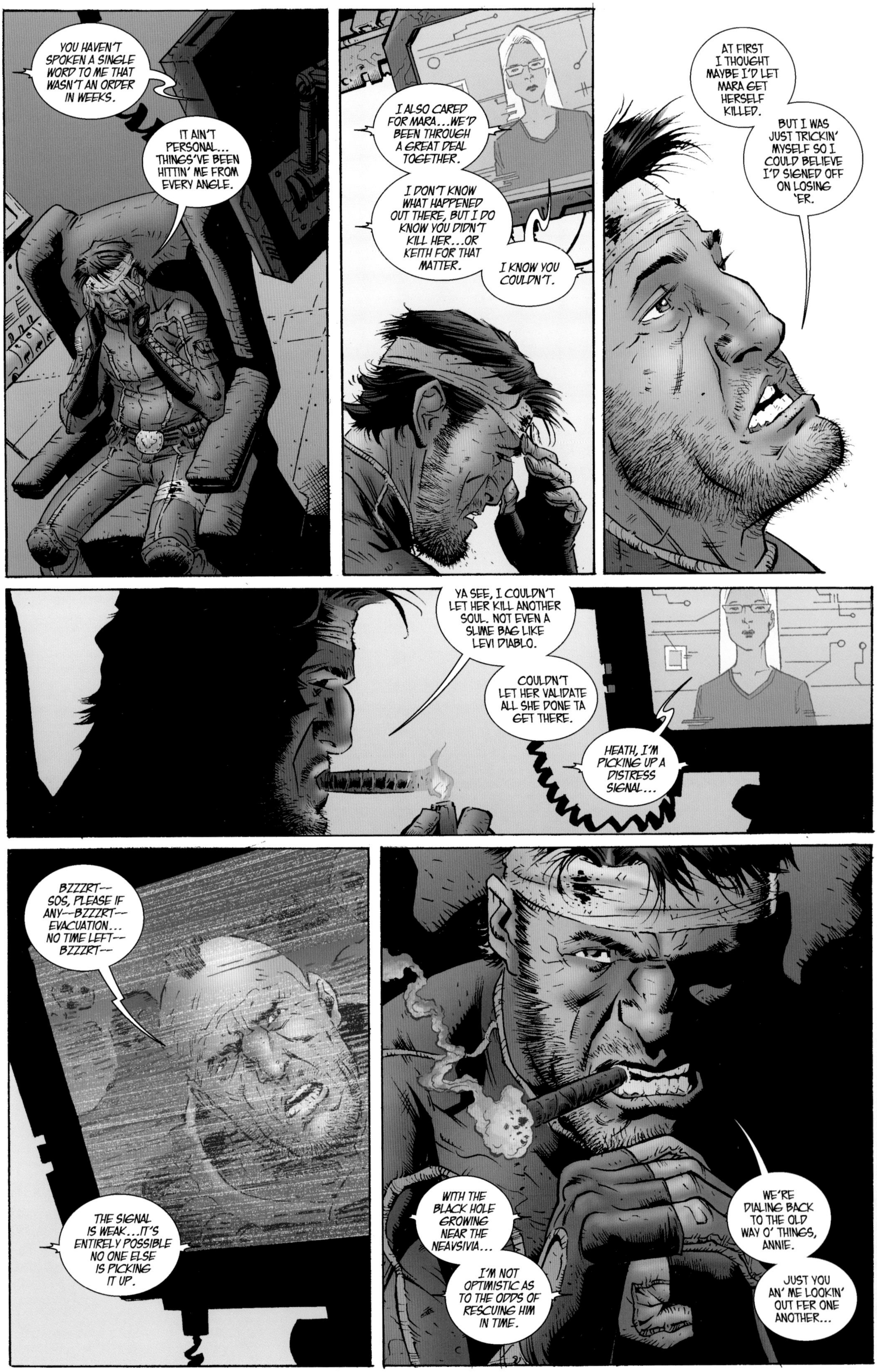
YOU HAVEN'T SPOKEN A SINGLE WORD TO ME THAT WASN'T AN ORDER IN WEEKS.
IT AIN'T PERSONAL... THINGS'VE BEEN HITTIN' ME FROM EVERY ANGLE.
I ALSO CARED FOR MARA...WE'D BEEN THROUGH A GREAT DEAL TOGETHER.
I DON'T KNOW WHAT HAPPENED OUT THERE, BUT I DO KNOW YOU DIDN'T KILL HER...OR KEITH FOR THAT MATTER.
I KNOW YOU COULDN'T.
AT FIRST I THOUGHT MAYBE I'D LET MARA GET HERSELF KILLED.
BUT I WAS JUST TRICKIN' MYSELF SO I COULD BELIEVE I'D SIGNED OFF ON LOSING 'ER.
YA SEE, I COULDN'T LET HER KILL ANOTHER SOUL. NOT EVEN A SLIME BAG LIKE LEVI DIABLO.
COULDN'T LET HER VALIDATE ALL SHE DONE TA GET THERE.
HEATH, I'M PICKING UP A DISTRESS SIGNAL...
BZZZRT-- SOS, PLEASE IF ANY--BZZZRT-- EVACUATION... NO TIME LEFT-- BZZZRT--
THE SIGNAL IS WEAK...IT'S ENTIRELY POSSIBLE NO ONE ELSE IS PICKING IT UP.
WITH THE BLACK HOLE GROWING NEAR THE NEAVSIVIA...
I'M NOT OPTIMISTIC AS TO THE ODDS OF RESCUING HIM IN TIME.
WE'RE DIALING BACK TO THE OLD WAY O' THINGS, ANNIE.
JUST YOU AN' ME LOOKIN' OUT FER ONE ANOTHER...

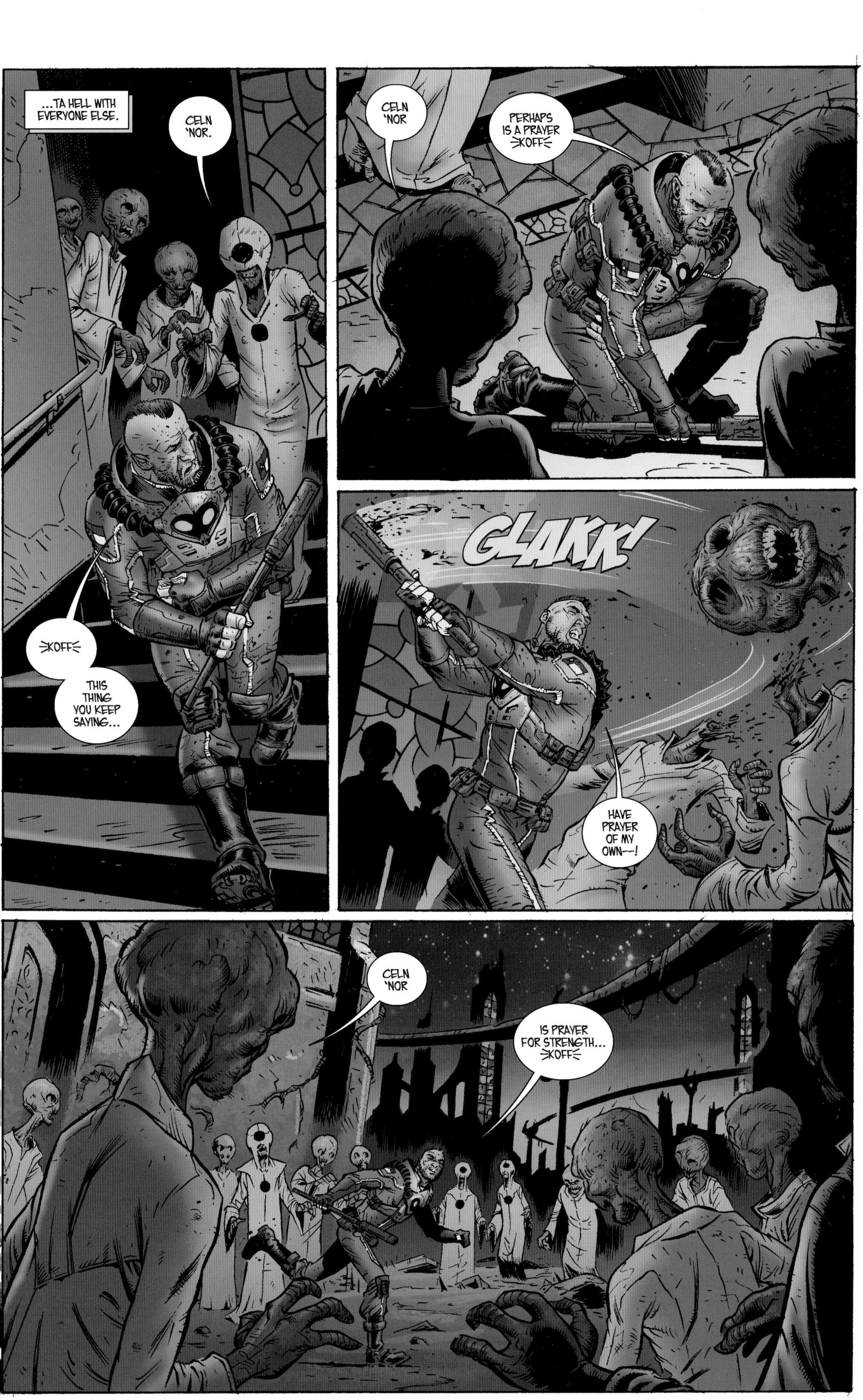
...TA HELL WITH EVERYONE ELSE.
CELN 'NOR.
⋛KOFF⋚
THIS THING YOU KEEP SAYING...
CELN 'NOR
PERHAPS IS A PRAYER ⋛KOFF⋚
GLAKK!
HAVE PRAYER OF MY OWN--!
CELN 'NOR
IS PRAYER FOR STRENGTH... ⋛KOFF⋚

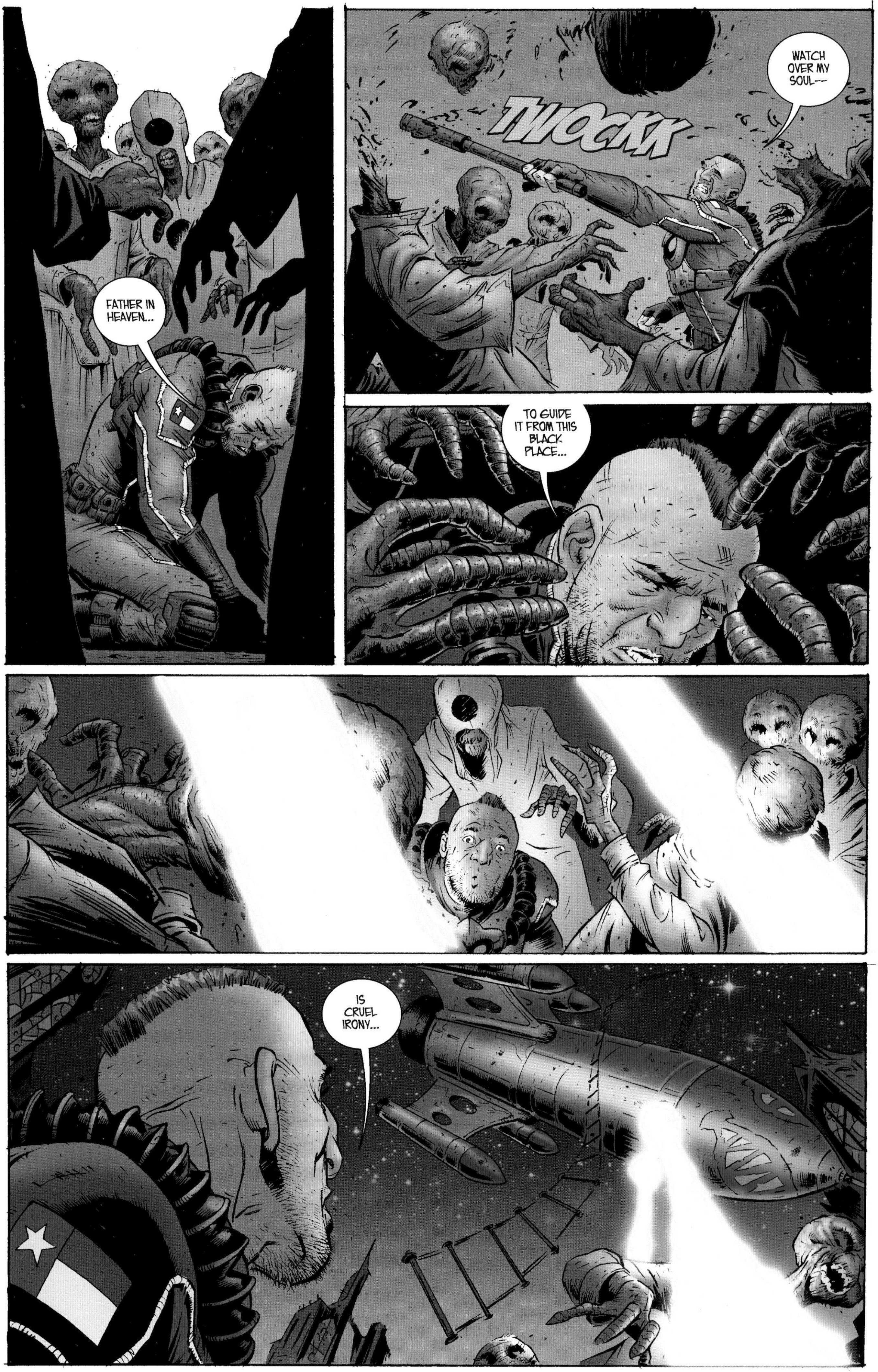
FATHER IN HEAVEN...
TWOCKK
WATCH OVER MY SOUL--
TO GUIDE IT FROM THIS BLACK PLACE...
IS CRUEL IRONY...

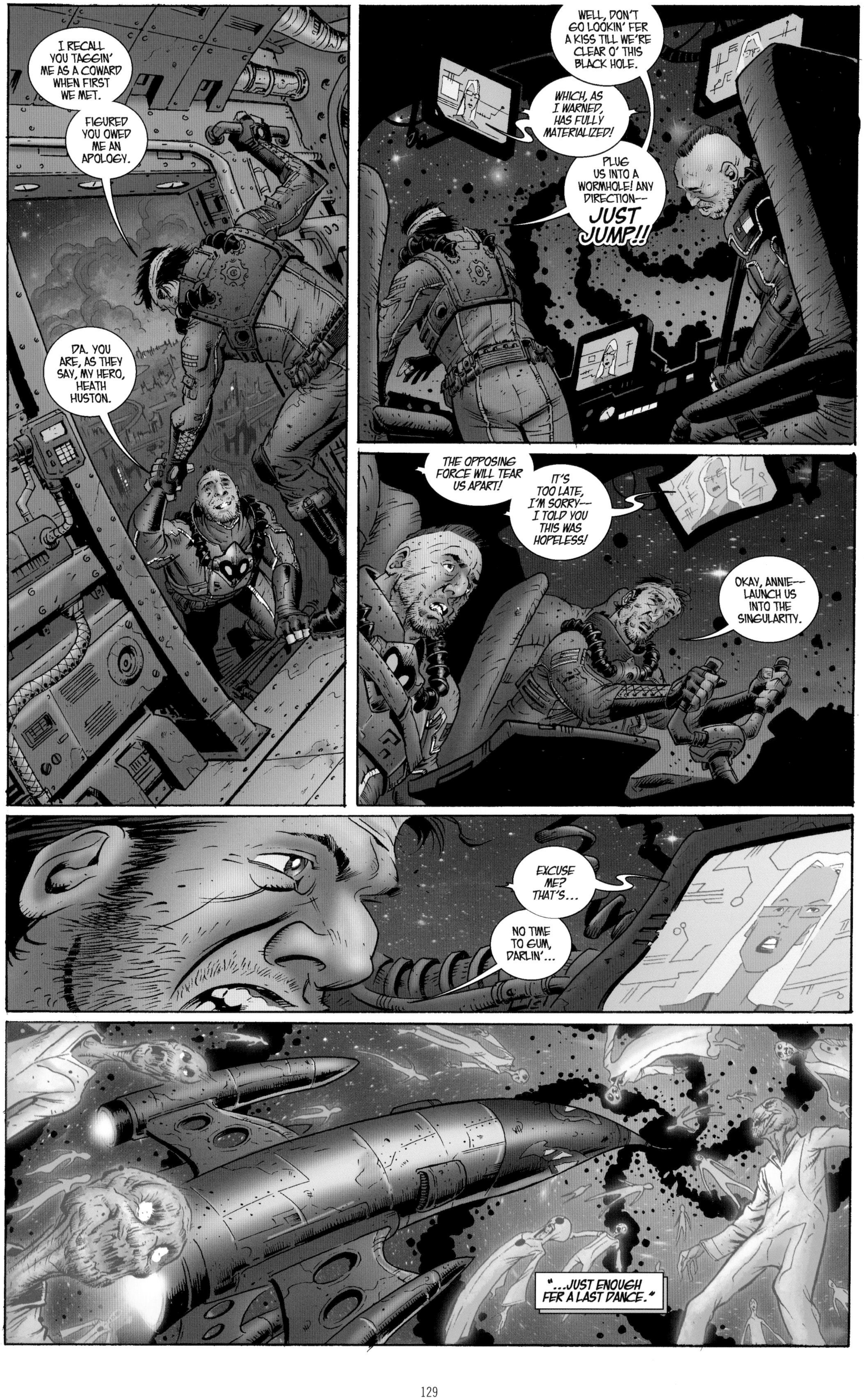
I RECALL YOU TAGGIN' ME AS A COWARD WHEN FIRST WE MET.
FIGURED YOU OWED ME AN APOLOGY.
DA. YOU ARE, AS THEY SAY, MY HERO, HEATH HUSTON.
WELL, DON'T GO LOOKIN' FER A KISS TILL WE'RE CLEAR O' THIS BLACK HOLE.
WHICH, AS I WARNED, HAS FULLY MATERIALIZED!
PLUG US INTO A WORMHOLE! ANY DIRECTION-- JUST JUMP!!
THE OPPOSING FORCE WILL TEAR US APART!
IT'S TOO LATE, I'M SORRY-- I TOLD YOU THIS WAS HOPELESS!
OKAY, ANNIE-- LAUNCH US INTO THE SINGULARITY.
EXCUSE ME? THAT'S...
NO TIME TO GUM, DARLIN'...
"...JUST ENOUGH FER A LAST DANCE."

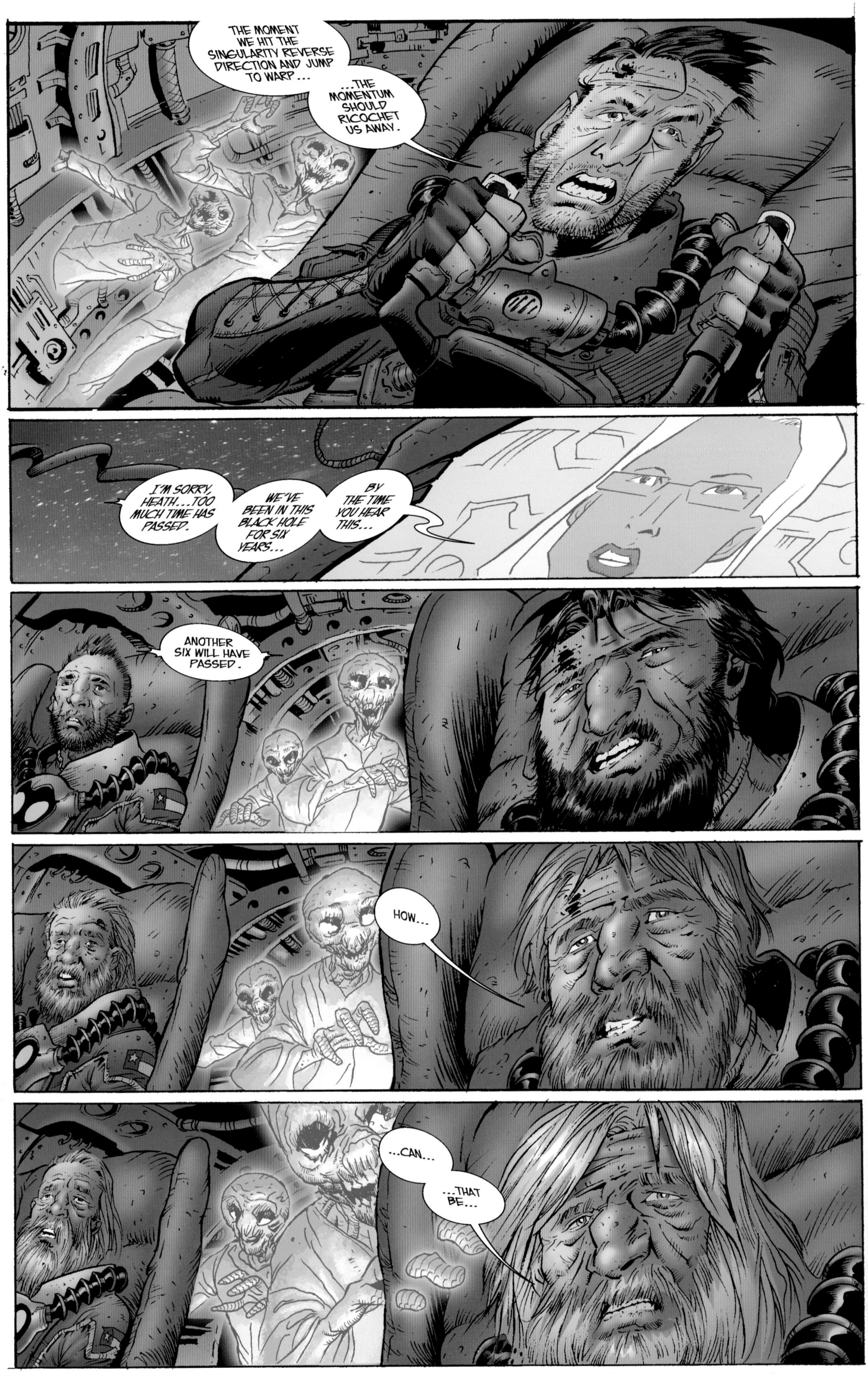
THE MOMENT WE HIT THE SINGULARITY REVERSE DIRECTION AND JUMP TO WARP...
...THE MOMENTUM SHOULD RICOCHET US AWAY.
I'M SORRY, HEATH...TOO MUCH TIME HAS PASSED.
WE'VE BEEN IN THIS BLACK HOLE FOR SIX YEARS...
BY THE TIME YOU HEAR THIS...
ANOTHER SIX WILL HAVE PASSED.
HOW...
...CAN...
...THAT BE...

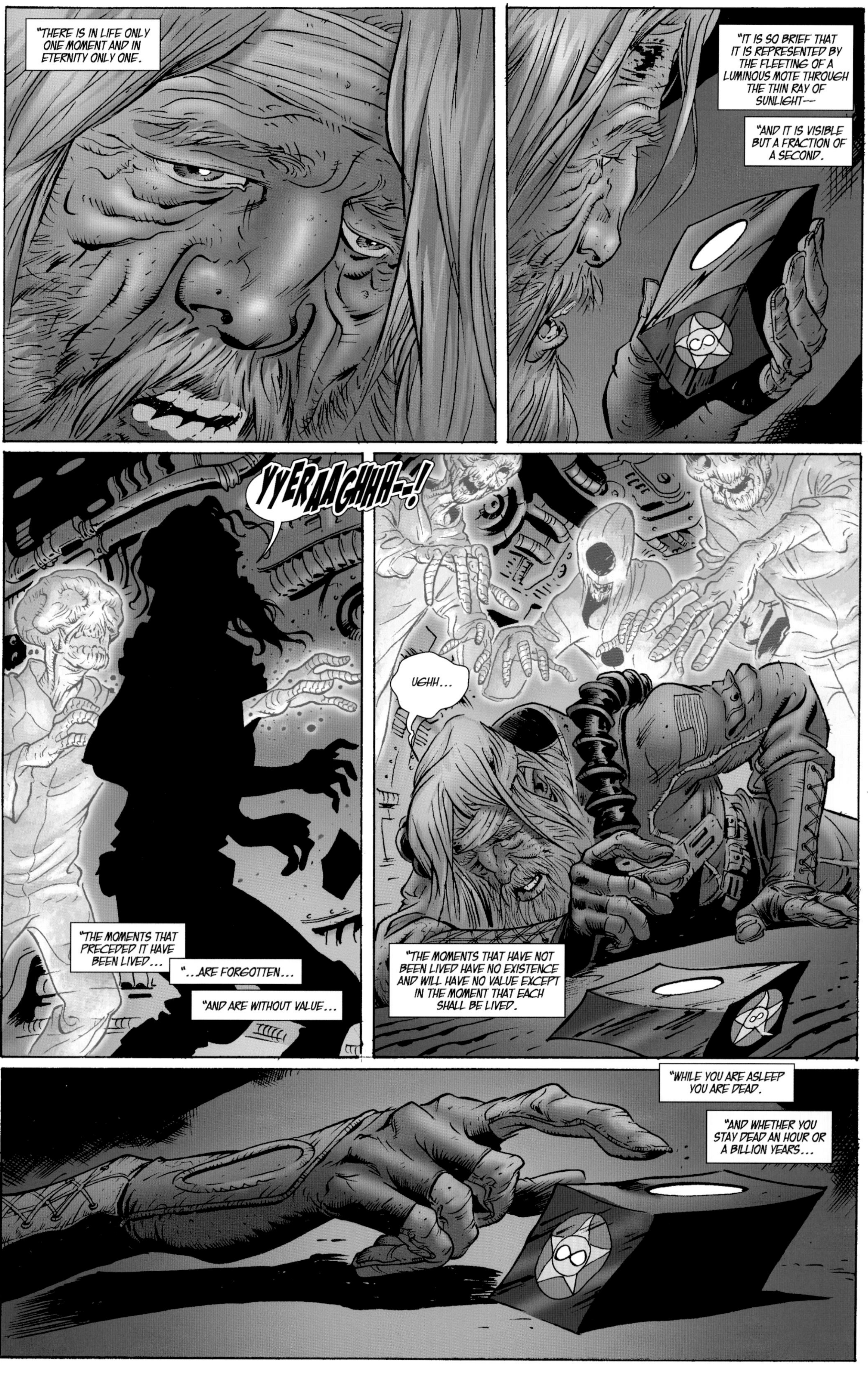
"THERE IS IN LIFE ONLY ONE MOMENT AND IN ETERNITY ONLY ONE.
"IT IS SO BRIEF THAT IT IS REPRESENTED BY THE FLEETING OF A LUMINOUS MOTE THROUGH THE THIN RAY OF SUNLIGHT--
"AND IT IS VISIBLE BUT A FRACTION OF A SECOND.
YYERAAGHHH--!
"THE MOMENTS THAT PRECEDED IT HAVE BEEN LIVED...
"...ARE FORGOTTEN...
"AND ARE WITHOUT VALUE...
UGHH...
"THE MOMENTS THAT HAVE NOT BEEN LIVED HAVE NO EXISTENCE AND WILL HAVE NO VALUE EXCEPT IN THE MOMENT THAT EACH SHALL BE LIVED.
"WHILE YOU ARE ASLEEP YOU ARE DEAD.
"AND WHETHER YOU STAY DEAD AN HOUR OR A BILLION YEARS...

"...THE TIME TO
YOU IS THE SAME."
—SAMUEL CLEMENS

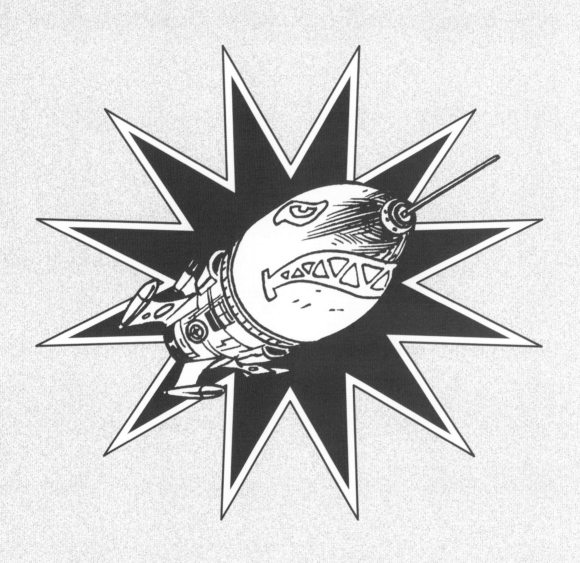

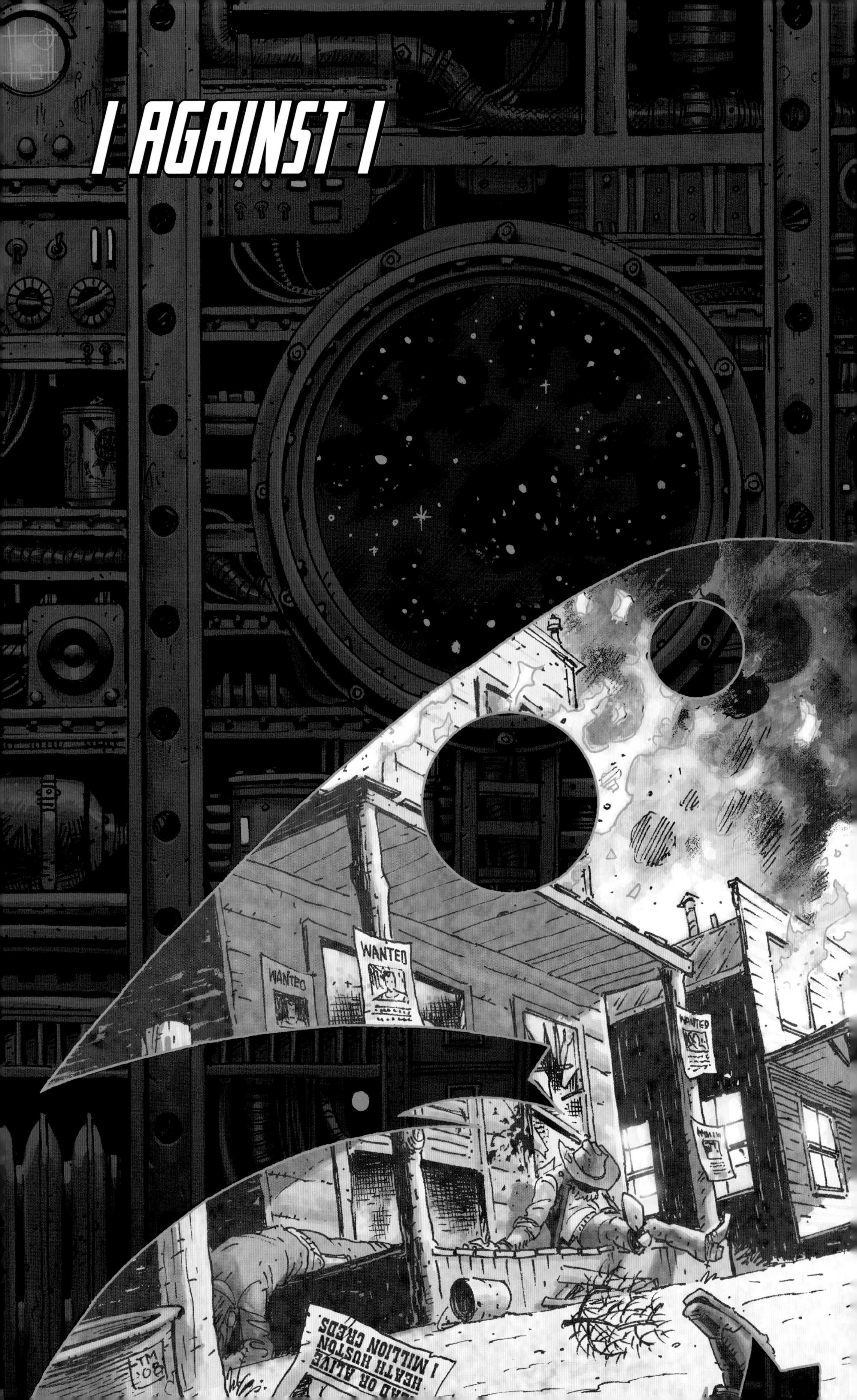
I AGAINST I
WANTED
WANTED
WANTED
HEATH HUSTON
1 MILLION CREDS
TM 08

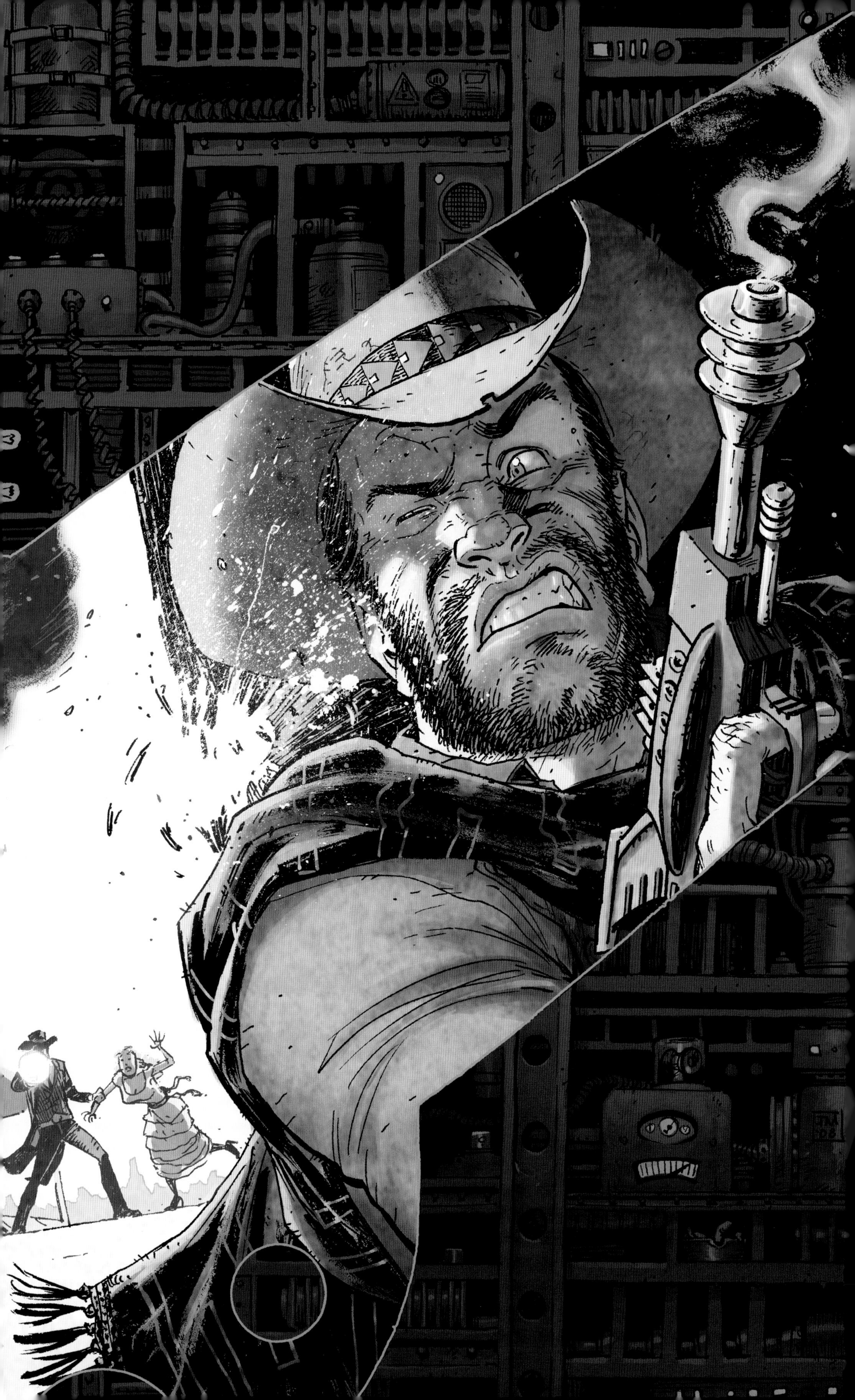

CHAPTER 1

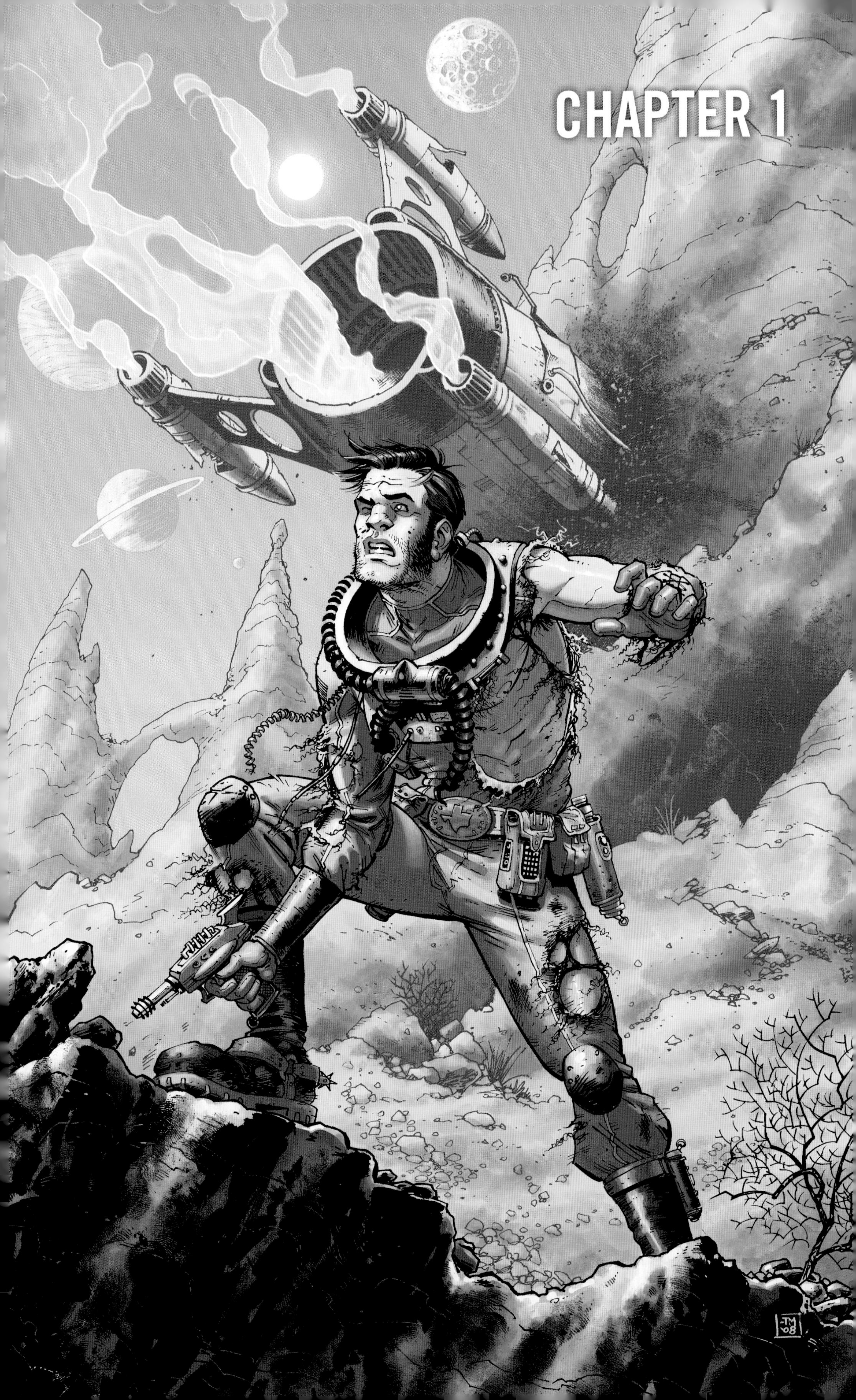

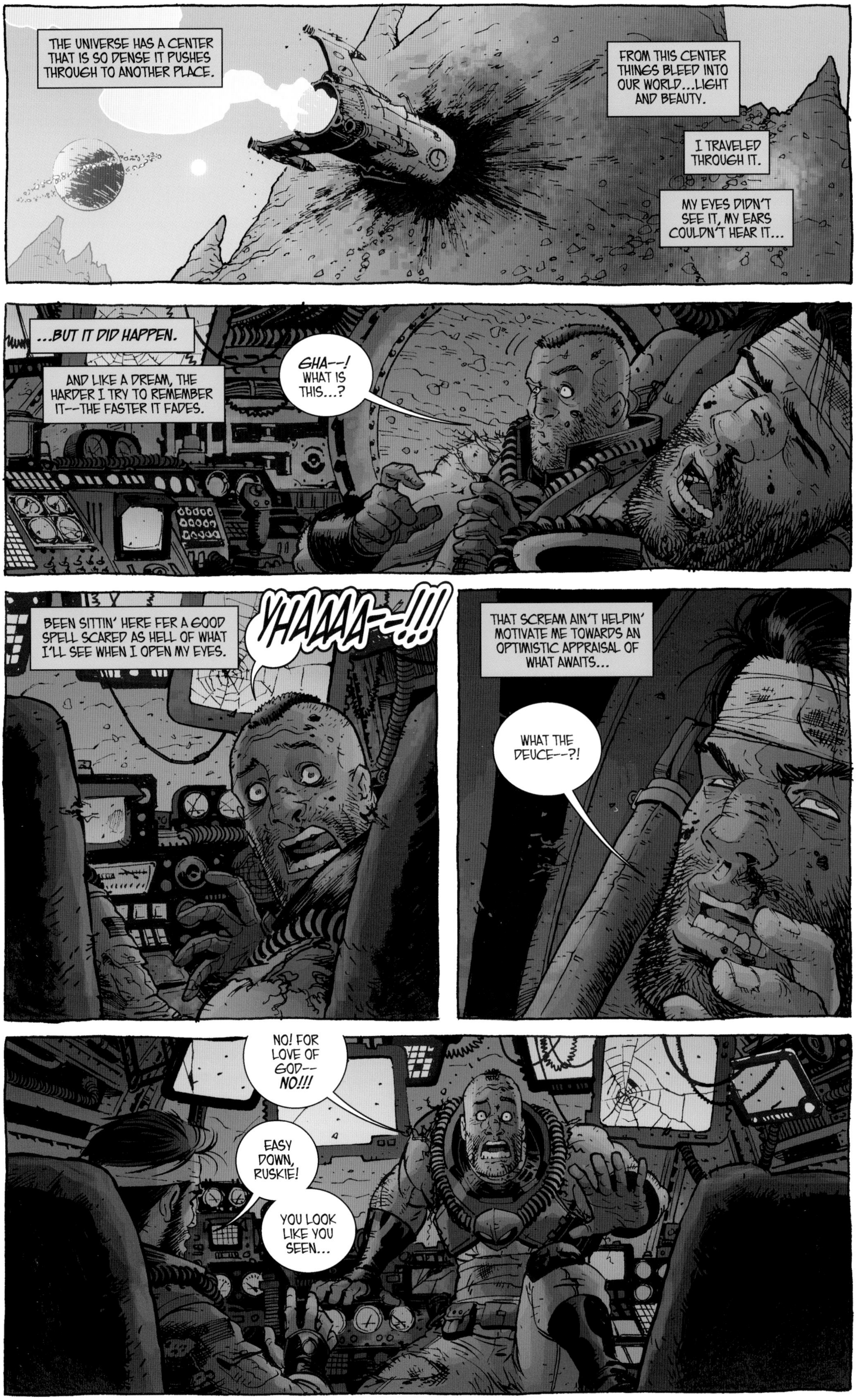
THE UNIVERSE HAS A CENTER THAT IS SO DENSE IT PUSHES THROUGH TO ANOTHER PLACE.
FROM THIS CENTER THINGS BLEED INTO OUR WORLD...LIGHT AND BEAUTY.
I TRAVELED THROUGH IT.
MY EYES DIDN'T SEE IT, MY EARS COULDN'T HEAR IT...
...BUT IT DID HAPPEN.
AND LIKE A DREAM, THE HARDER I TRY TO REMEMBER IT--THE FASTER IT FADES.
GHA--! WHAT IS THIS...?
BEEN SITTIN' HERE FER A GOOD SPELL SCARED AS HELL OF WHAT I'LL SEE WHEN I OPEN MY EYES.
YHAAAA--!!!
THAT SCREAM AIN'T HELPIN' MOTIVATE ME TOWARDS AN OPTIMISTIC APPRAISAL OF WHAT AWAITS...
WHAT THE DEUCE--?!
NO! FOR LOVE OF GOD-- NO!!!
EASY DOWN, RUSKIE!
YOU LOOK LIKE YOU SEEN...

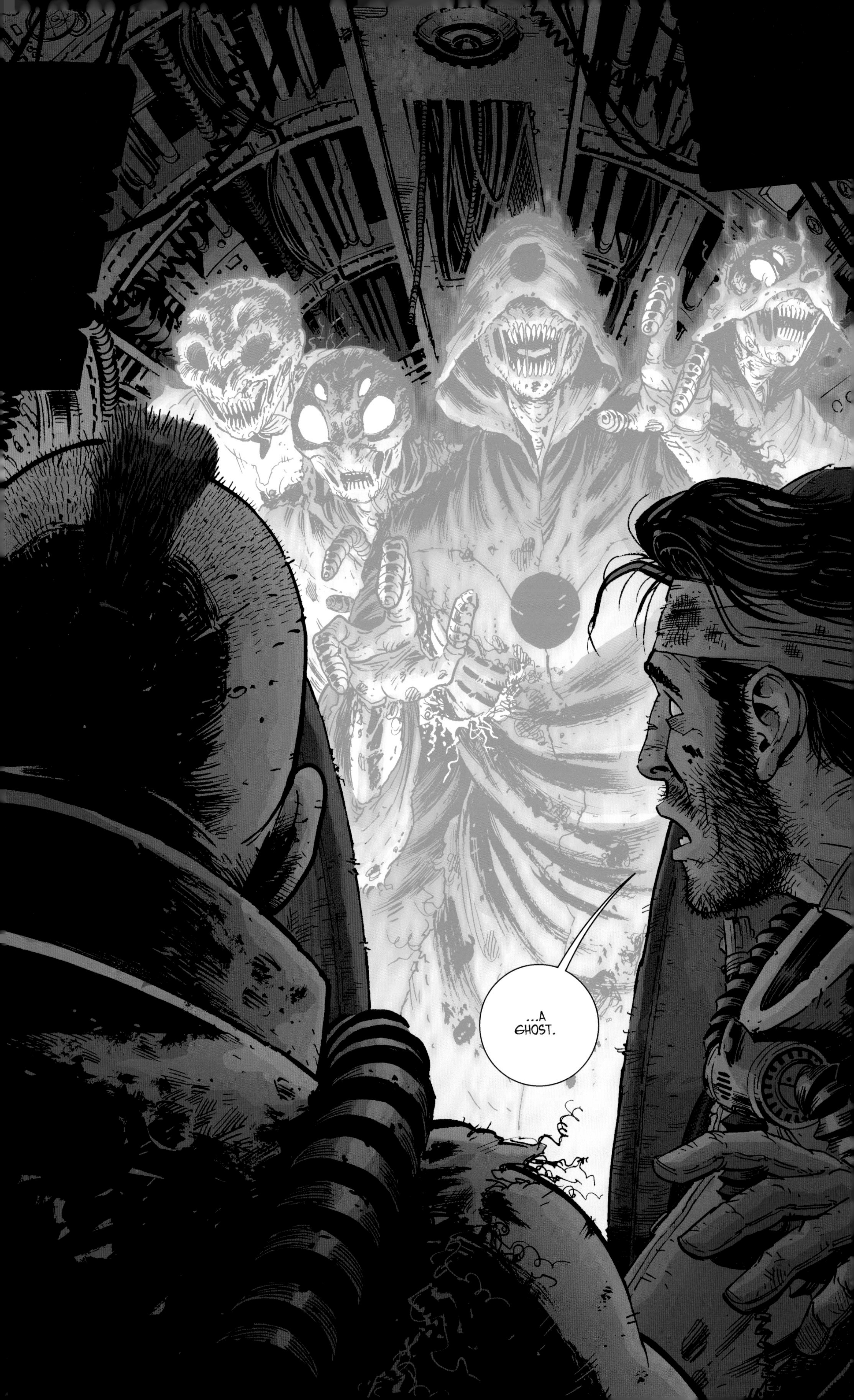
...A GHOST.

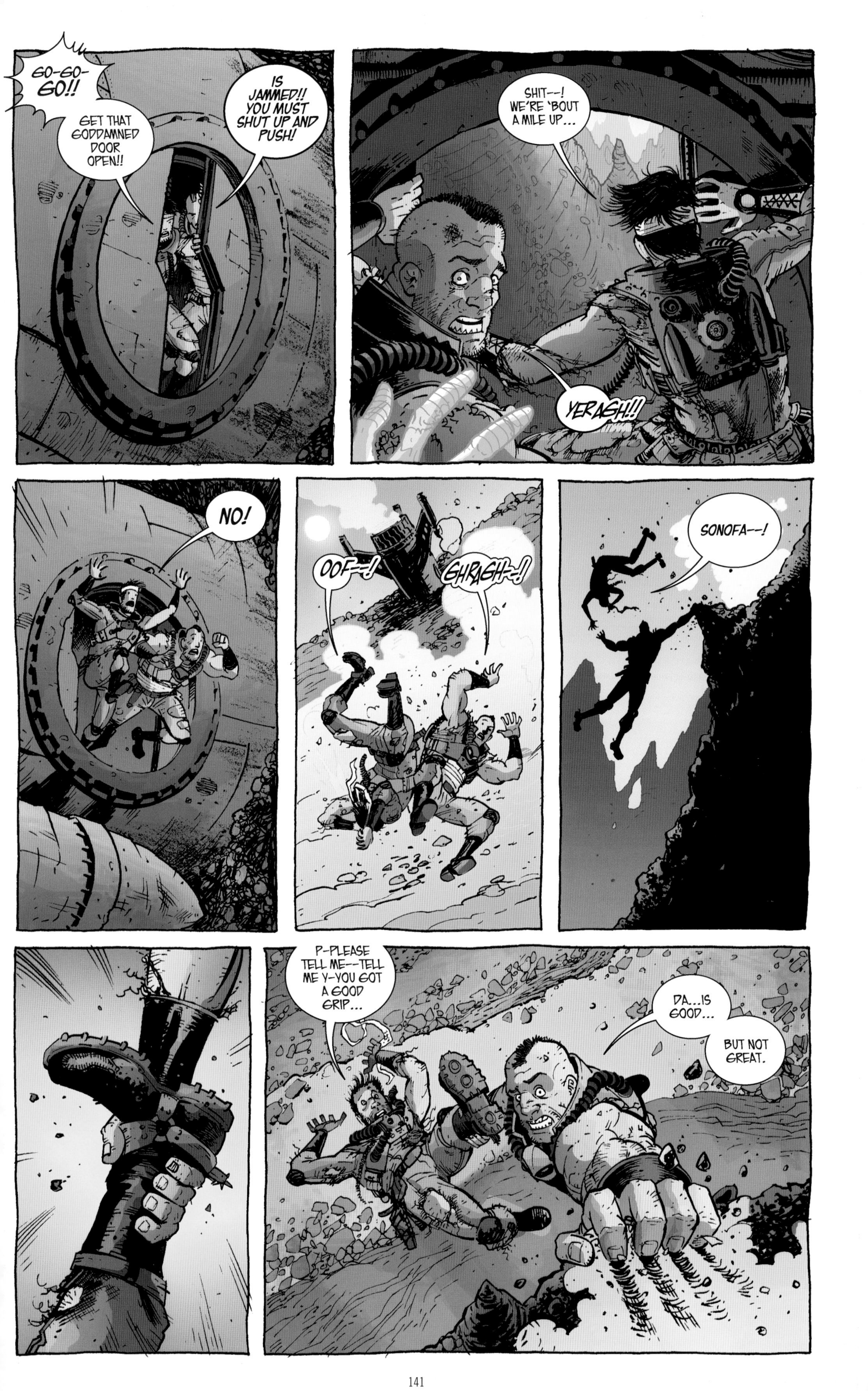
GO-GO-GO!!
GET THAT GODDAMNED DOOR OPEN!!
IS JAMMED!! YOU MUST SHUT UP AND PUSH!
SHIT--! WE'RE 'BOUT A MILE UP...
YERAGH!!
NO!
OOF--!
GHRAGH--!
SONOFA--!
P-PLEASE TELL ME--TELL ME Y-YOU GOT A GOOD GRIP...
DA...IS GOOD...
BUT NOT GREAT.

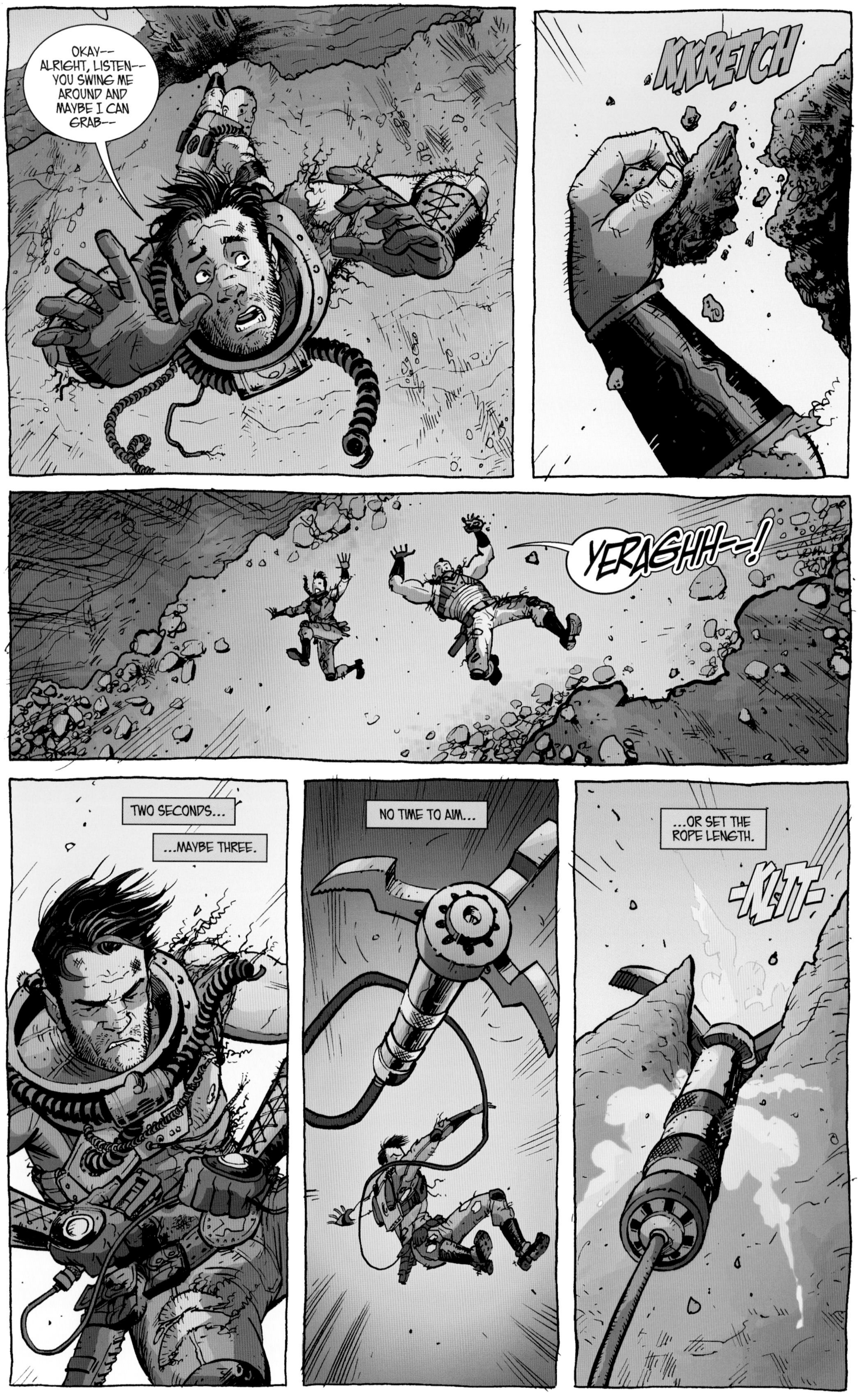
OKAY-- ALRIGHT, LISTEN-- YOU SWING ME AROUND AND MAYBE I CAN GRAB--
KKRETCH
YERAGHH--!
TWO SECONDS...
...MAYBE THREE.
NO TIME TO AIM...
...OR SET THE ROPE LENGTH.
-KLIT-

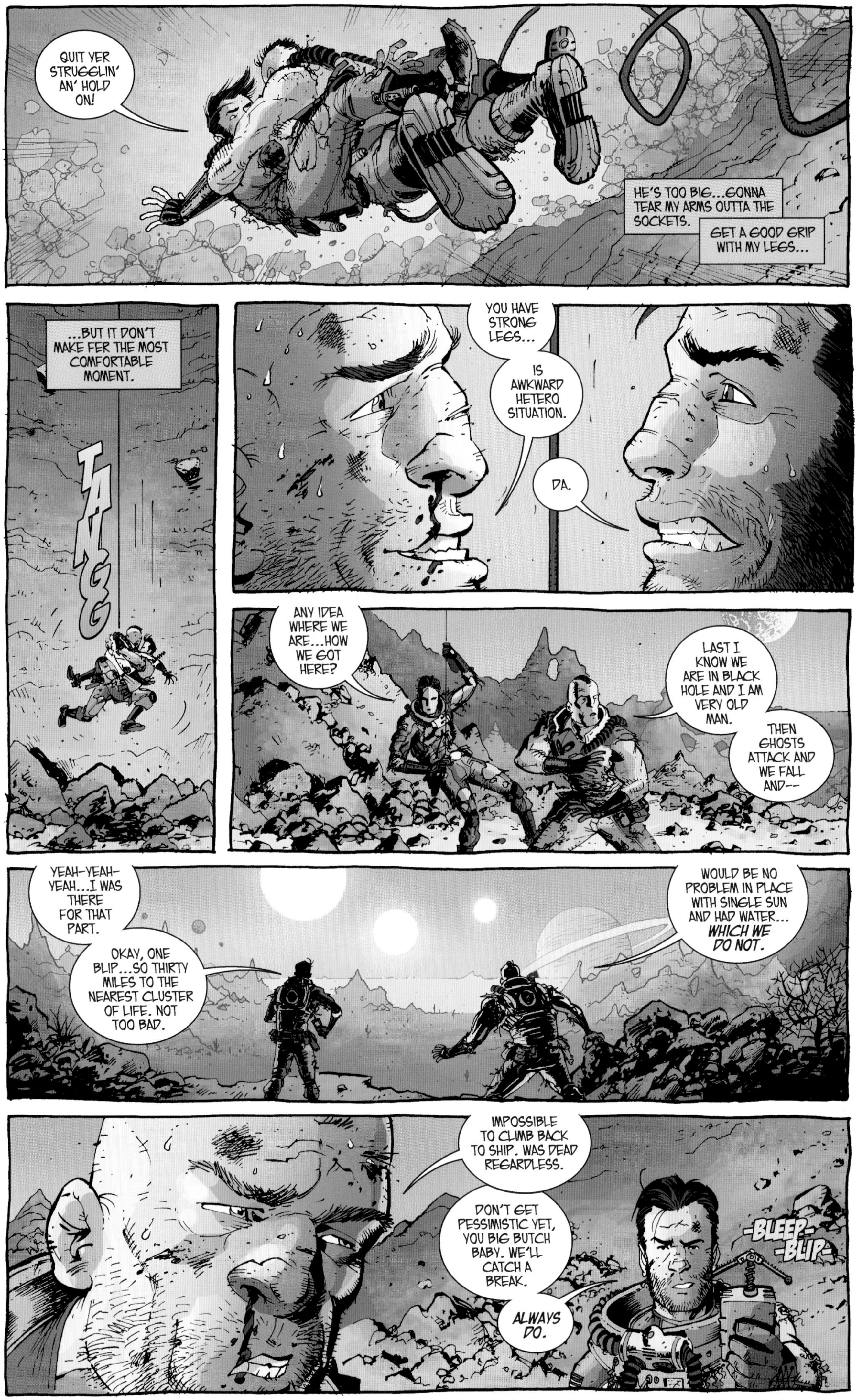
QUIT YER STRUGGLIN' AN' HOLD ON!
HE'S TOO BIG...GONNA TEAR MY ARMS OUTTA THE SOCKETS.
GET A GOOD GRIP WITH MY LEGS...
...BUT IT DON'T MAKE FER THE MOST COMFORTABLE MOMENT.
TANGG
YOU HAVE STRONG LEGS...
IS AWKWARD HETERO SITUATION.
DA.
ANY IDEA WHERE WE ARE...HOW WE GOT HERE?
LAST I KNOW WE ARE IN BLACK HOLE AND I AM VERY OLD MAN.
THEN GHOSTS ATTACK AND WE FALL AND--
YEAH-YEAH-YEAH...I WAS THERE FOR THAT PART.
OKAY, ONE BLIP...SO THIRTY MILES TO THE NEAREST CLUSTER OF LIFE. NOT TOO BAD.
WOULD BE NO PROBLEM IN PLACE WITH SINGLE SUN AND HAD WATER... *WHICH WE DO NOT.*
IMPOSSIBLE TO CLIMB BACK TO SHIP. WAS DEAD REGARDLESS.
DON'T GET PESSIMISTIC YET, YOU BIG BUTCH BABY. WE'LL CATCH A BREAK.
ALWAYS DO.
-BLEEP-
-BLIP-

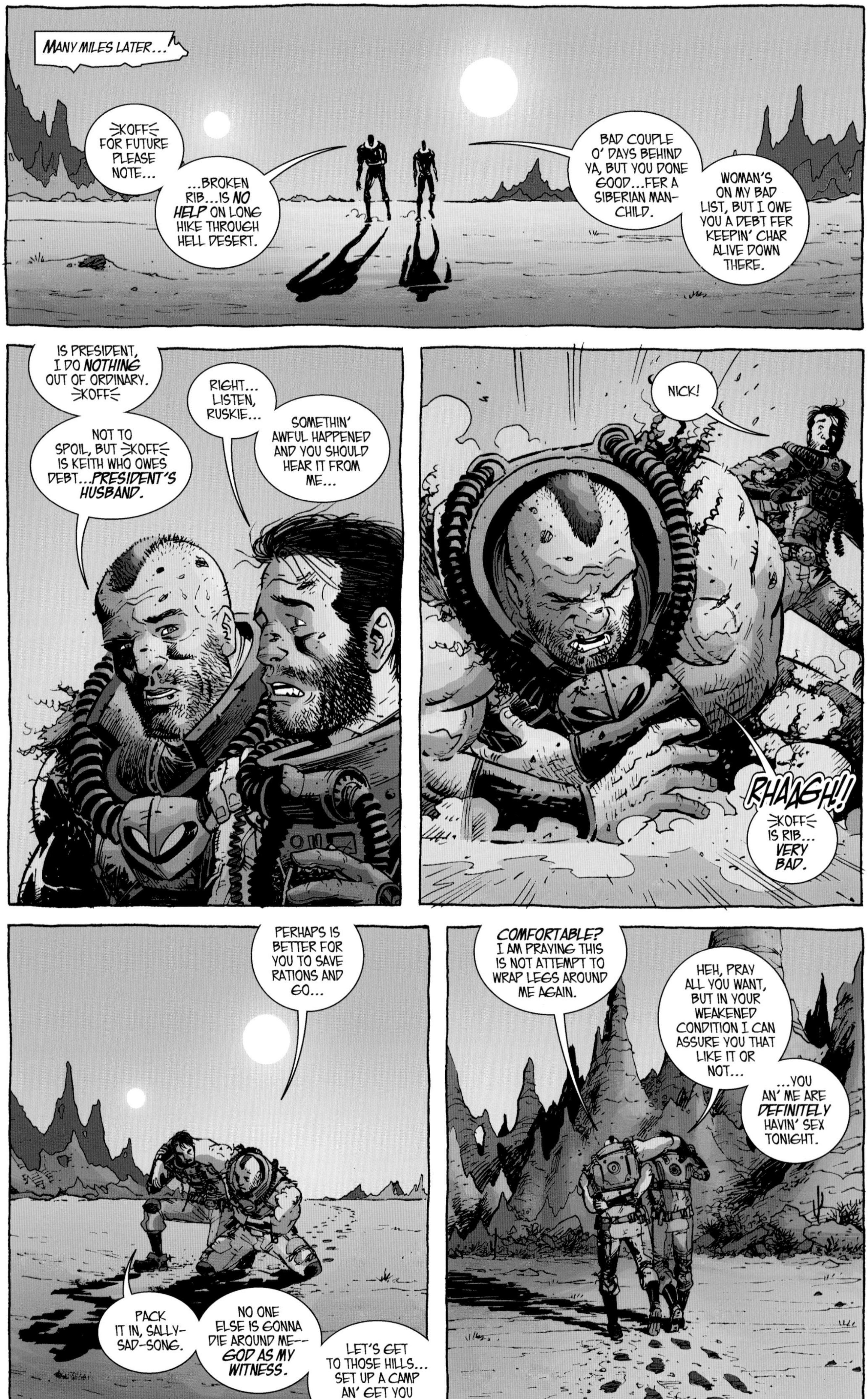
MANY MILES LATER...
⋟KOFF⋞ FOR FUTURE PLEASE NOTE...
...BROKEN RIB...IS NO HELP ON LONG HIKE THROUGH HELL DESERT.
BAD COUPLE O' DAYS BEHIND YA, BUT YOU DONE GOOD...FER A SIBERIAN MAN-CHILD.
WOMAN'S ON MY BAD LIST, BUT I OWE YOU A DEBT FER KEEPIN' CHAR ALIVE DOWN THERE.
IS PRESIDENT, I DO NOTHING OUT OF ORDINARY. ⋟KOFF⋞
NOT TO SPOIL, BUT ⋟KOFF⋞ IS KEITH WHO OWES DEBT...PRESIDENT'S HUSBAND.
RIGHT... LISTEN, RUSKIE...
SOMETHIN' AWFUL HAPPENED AND YOU SHOULD HEAR IT FROM ME...
NICK!
RHAAGH!!
⋟KOFF⋞ IS RIB... VERY BAD.
PERHAPS IS BETTER FOR YOU TO SAVE RATIONS AND GO...
PACK IT IN, SALLY-SAD-SONG.
NO ONE ELSE IS GONNA DIE AROUND ME-- GOD AS MY WITNESS.
LET'S GET TO THOSE HILLS... SET UP A CAMP AN' GET YOU COMFORTABLE.
COMFORTABLE? I AM PRAYING THIS IS NOT ATTEMPT TO WRAP LEGS AROUND ME AGAIN.
HEH, PRAY ALL YOU WANT, BUT IN YOUR WEAKENED CONDITION I CAN ASSURE YOU THAT LIKE IT OR NOT...
...YOU AN' ME ARE DEFINITELY HAVIN' SEX TONIGHT.

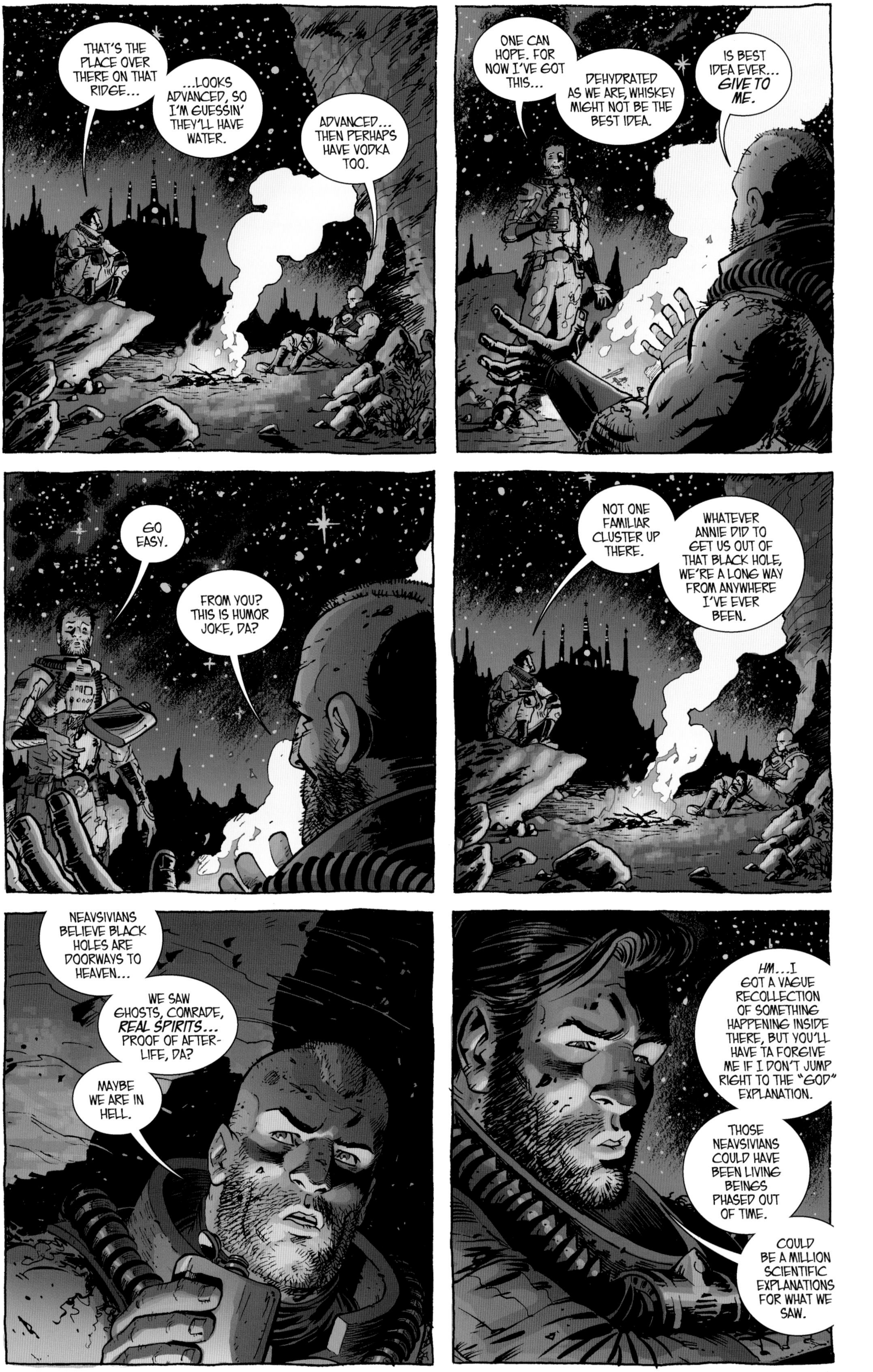
THAT'S THE PLACE OVER THERE ON THAT RIDGE...
...LOOKS ADVANCED, SO I'M GUESSIN' THEY'LL HAVE WATER.
ADVANCED... THEN PERHAPS HAVE VODKA TOO.
ONE CAN HOPE. FOR NOW I'VE GOT THIS...
DEHYDRATED AS WE ARE, WHISKEY MIGHT NOT BE THE BEST IDEA.
IS BEST IDEA EVER... *GIVE TO ME.*
GO EASY.
FROM YOU? THIS IS HUMOR JOKE, DA?
NOT ONE FAMILIAR CLUSTER UP THERE.
WHATEVER ANNIE DID TO GET US OUT OF THAT BLACK HOLE, WE'RE A LONG WAY FROM ANYWHERE I'VE EVER BEEN.
NEAVSIVIANS BELIEVE BLACK HOLES ARE DOORWAYS TO HEAVEN...
WE SAW GHOSTS, COMRADE, *REAL SPIRITS...* PROOF OF AFTER-LIFE, DA?
MAYBE WE ARE IN HELL.
HM...I GOT A VAGUE RECOLLECTION OF SOMETHING HAPPENING INSIDE THERE, BUT YOU'LL HAVE TA FORGIVE ME IF I DON'T JUMP RIGHT TO THE "GOD" EXPLANATION.
THOSE NEAVSIVIANS COULD HAVE BEEN LIVING BEINGS PHASED OUT OF TIME.
COULD BE A MILLION SCIENTIFIC EXPLANATIONS FOR WHAT WE SAW.

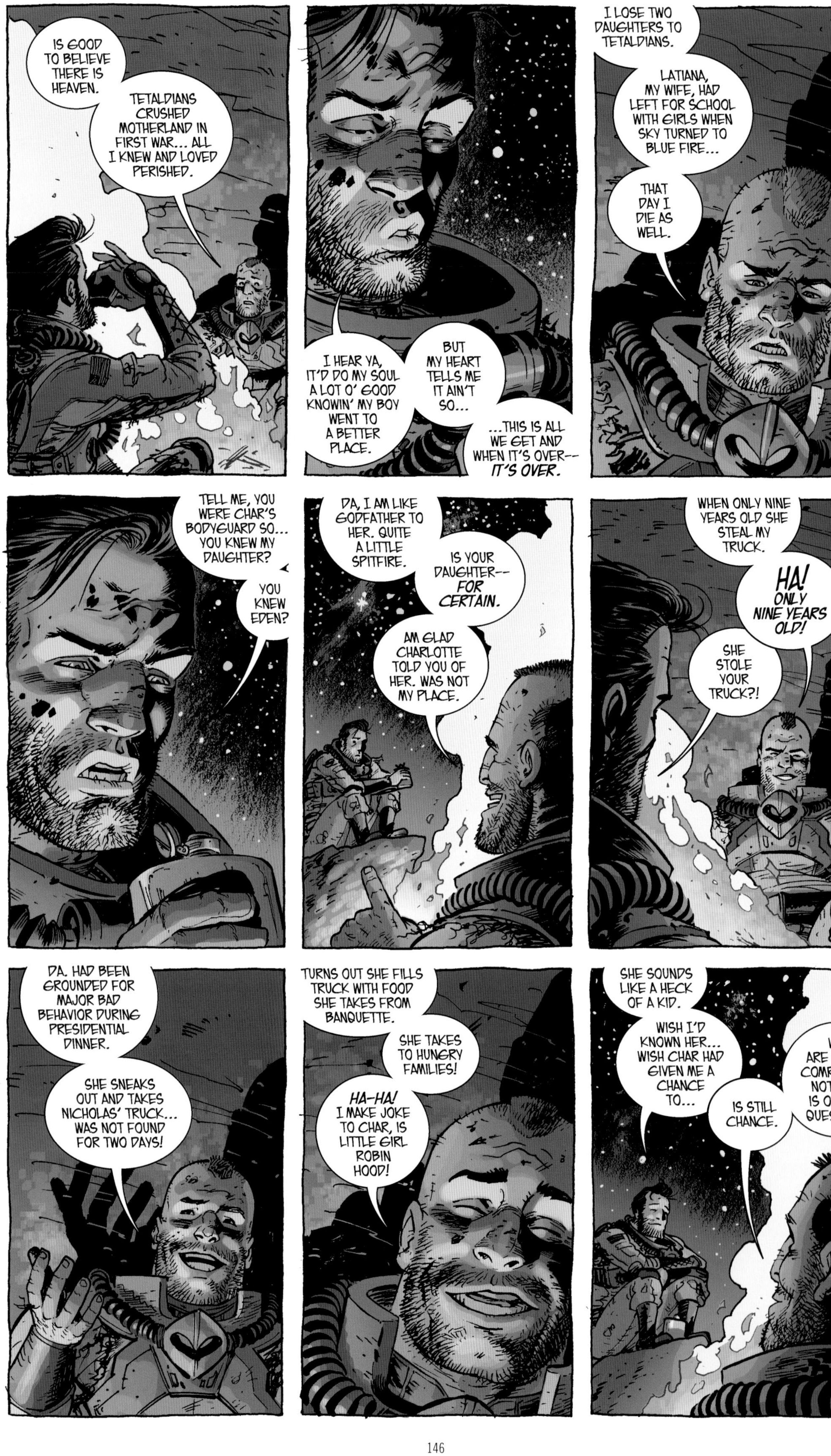
IS GOOD TO BELIEVE THERE IS HEAVEN.
TETALDIANS CRUSHED MOTHERLAND IN FIRST WAR... ALL I KNEW AND LOVED PERISHED.
I HEAR YA, IT'D DO MY SOUL A LOT O' GOOD KNOWIN' MY BOY WENT TO A BETTER PLACE.
BUT MY HEART TELLS ME IT AIN'T SO...
...THIS IS ALL WE GET AND WHEN IT'S OVER-- IT'S OVER.
I LOSE TWO DAUGHTERS TO TETALDIANS.
LATIANA, MY WIFE, HAD LEFT FOR SCHOOL WITH GIRLS WHEN SKY TURNED TO BLUE FIRE...
THAT DAY I DIE AS WELL.
TELL ME, YOU WERE CHAR'S BODYGUARD SO... YOU KNEW MY DAUGHTER?
YOU KNEW EDEN?
DA, I AM LIKE GODFATHER TO HER. QUITE A LITTLE SPITFIRE.
IS YOUR DAUGHTER-- FOR CERTAIN.
AM GLAD CHARLOTTE TOLD YOU OF HER. WAS NOT MY PLACE.
WHEN ONLY NINE YEARS OLD SHE STEAL MY TRUCK.
HA! ONLY NINE YEARS OLD!
SHE STOLE YOUR TRUCK?!
DA. HAD BEEN GROUNDED FOR MAJOR BAD BEHAVIOR DURING PRESIDENTIAL DINNER.
SHE SNEAKS OUT AND TAKES NICHOLAS' TRUCK... WAS NOT FOUND FOR TWO DAYS!
TURNS OUT SHE FILLS TRUCK WITH FOOD SHE TAKES FROM BANQUETTE.
SHE TAKES TO HUNGRY FAMILIES!
HA-HA! I MAKE JOKE TO CHAR, IS LITTLE GIRL ROBIN HOOD!
SHE SOUNDS LIKE A HECK OF A KID.
WISH I'D KNOWN HER... WISH CHAR HAD GIVEN ME A CHANCE TO...
IS STILL CHANCE.
WE ARE ALIVE, COMRADE-- NOTHING IS OUT OF QUESTION.

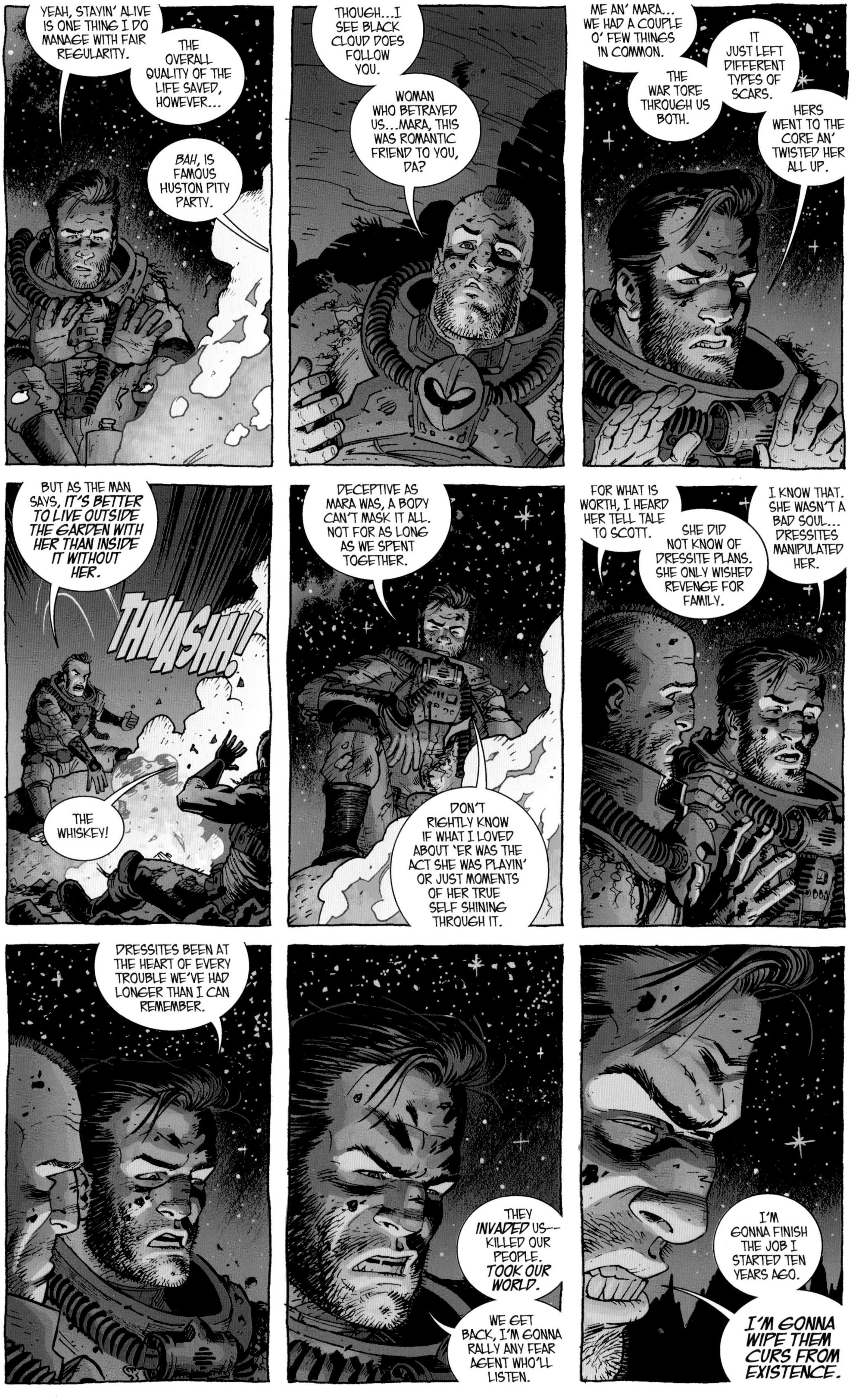
YEAH, STAYIN' ALIVE IS ONE THING I DO MANAGE WITH FAIR REGULARITY.
THE OVERALL QUALITY OF THE LIFE SAVED, HOWEVER...
BAH, IS FAMOUS HUSTON PITY PARTY.
THOUGH...I SEE BLACK CLOUD DOES FOLLOW YOU.
WOMAN WHO BETRAYED US...MARA, THIS WAS ROMANTIC FRIEND TO YOU, DA?
ME AN' MARA... WE HAD A COUPLE O' FEW THINGS IN COMMON.
THE WAR TORE THROUGH US BOTH.
IT JUST LEFT DIFFERENT TYPES OF SCARS.
HERS WENT TO THE CORE AN' TWISTED HER ALL UP.
BUT AS THE MAN SAYS, IT'S BETTER TO LIVE OUTSIDE THE GARDEN WITH HER THAN INSIDE IT WITHOUT HER.
THWASHH!
THE WHISKEY!
DECEPTIVE AS MARA WAS, A BODY CAN'T MASK IT ALL. NOT FOR AS LONG AS WE SPENT TOGETHER.
DON'T RIGHTLY KNOW IF WHAT I LOVED ABOUT 'ER WAS THE ACT SHE WAS PLAYIN' OR JUST MOMENTS OF HER TRUE SELF SHINING THROUGH IT.
FOR WHAT IS WORTH, I HEARD HER TELL TALE TO SCOTT.
SHE DID NOT KNOW OF DRESSITE PLANS. SHE ONLY WISHED REVENGE FOR FAMILY.
I KNOW THAT. SHE WASN'T A BAD SOUL... DRESSITES MANIPULATED HER.
DRESSITES BEEN AT THE HEART OF EVERY TROUBLE WE'VE HAD LONGER THAN I CAN REMEMBER.
THEY INVADED US-- KILLED OUR PEOPLE. TOOK OUR WORLD.
WE GET BACK, I'M GONNA RALLY ANY FEAR AGENT WHO'LL LISTEN.
I'M GONNA FINISH THE JOB I STARTED TEN YEARS AGO.
I'M GONNA WIPE THEM CURS FROM EXISTENCE.

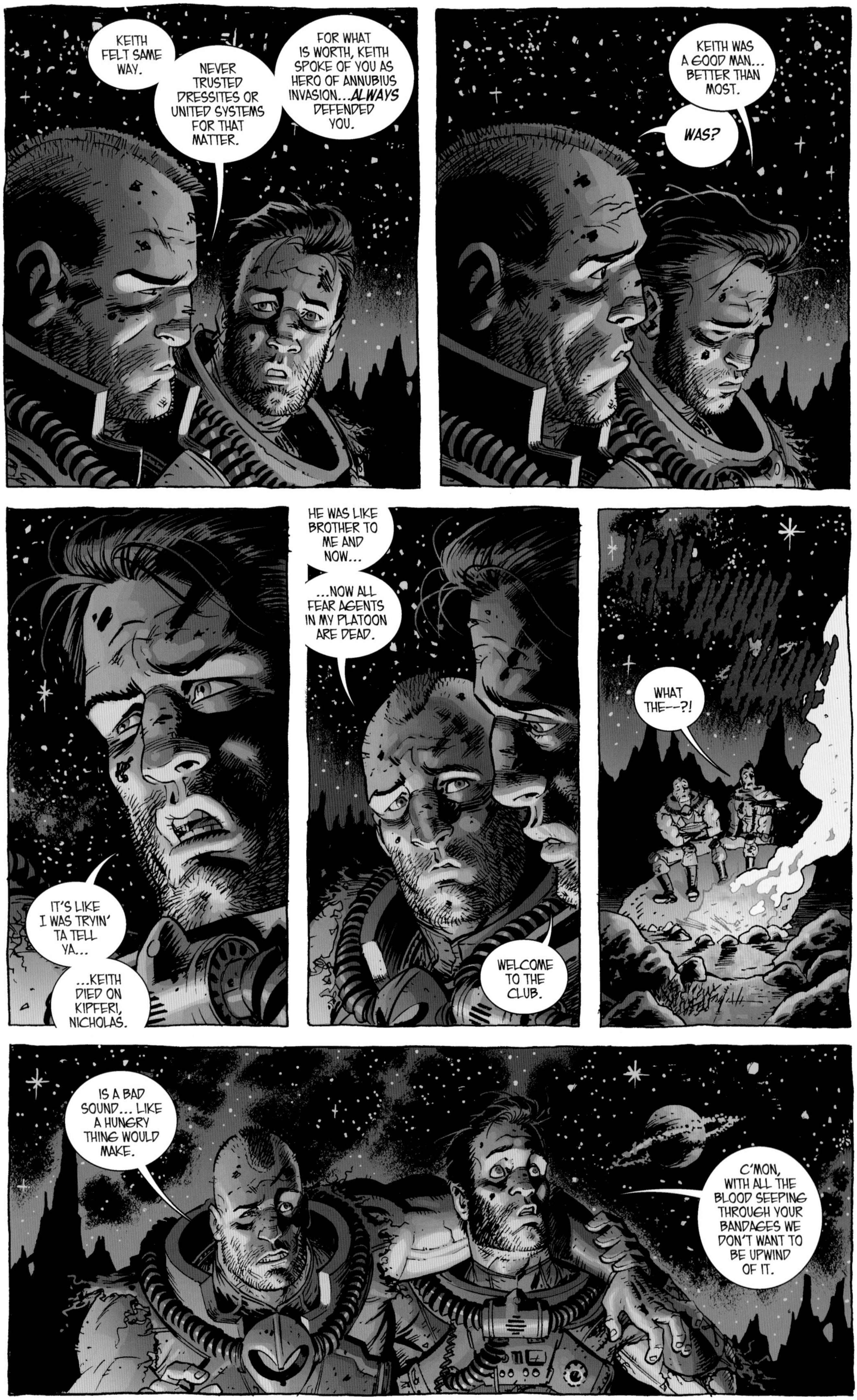

KEITH FELT SAME WAY.
NEVER TRUSTED DRESSITES OR UNITED SYSTEMS FOR THAT MATTER.
FOR WHAT IS WORTH, KEITH SPOKE OF YOU AS HERO OF ANNUBIUS INVASION...ALWAYS DEFENDED YOU.
KEITH WAS A GOOD MAN... BETTER THAN MOST.
WAS?
IT'S LIKE I WAS TRYIN' TA TELL YA...
...KEITH DIED ON KIPFERI, NICHOLAS.
HE WAS LIKE BROTHER TO ME AND NOW...
...NOW ALL FEAR AGENTS IN MY PLATOON ARE DEAD.
WELCOME TO THE CLUB.
WHAT THE--?!
IS A BAD SOUND... LIKE A HUNGRY THING WOULD MAKE.
C'MON, WITH ALL THE BLOOD SEEPING THROUGH YOUR BANDAGES WE DON'T WANT TO BE UPWIND OF IT.

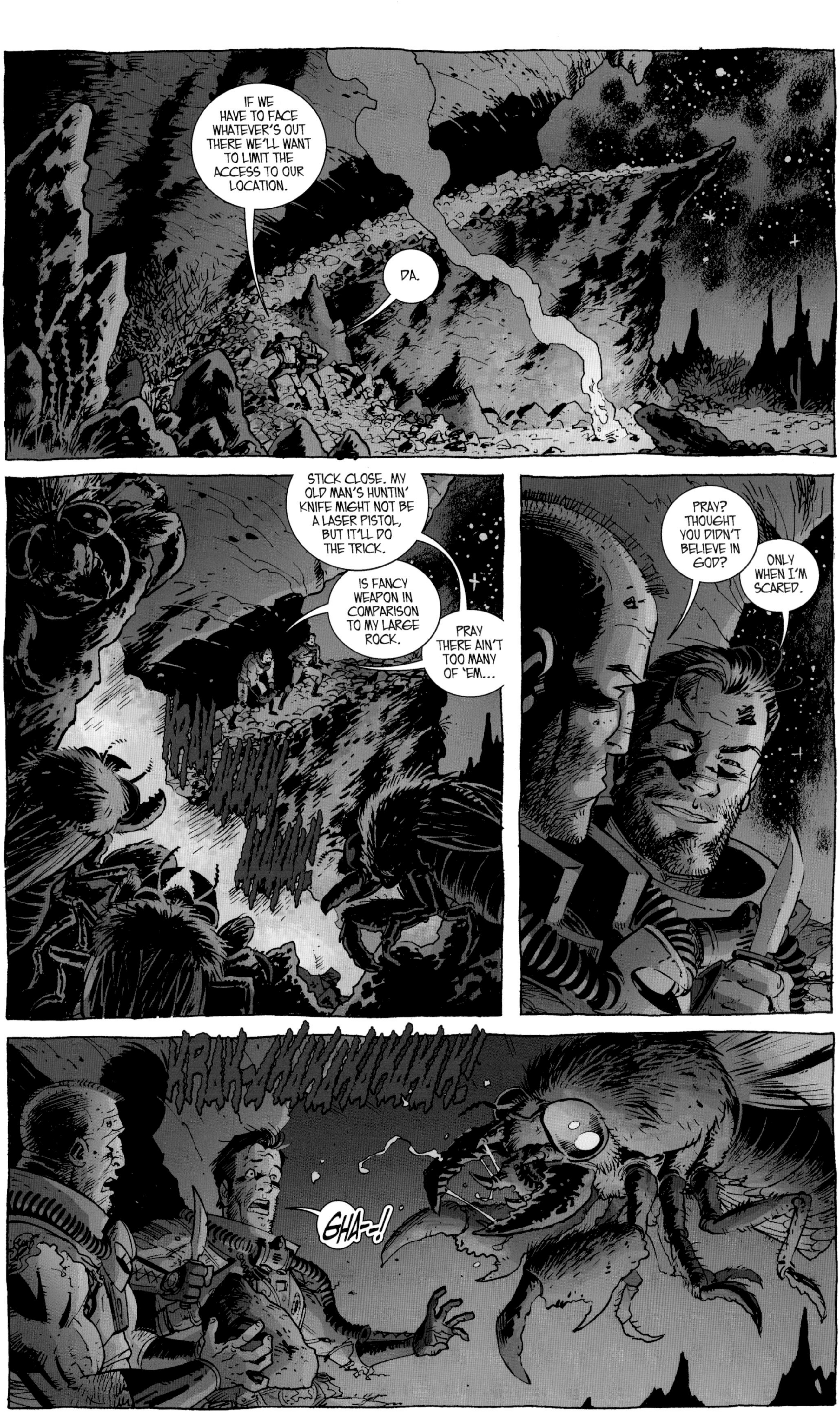

IF WE HAVE TO FACE WHATEVER'S OUT THERE WE'LL WANT TO LIMIT THE ACCESS TO OUR LOCATION.
DA.
STICK CLOSE. MY OLD MAN'S HUNTIN' KNIFE MIGHT NOT BE A LASER PISTOL, BUT IT'LL DO THE TRICK.
IS FANCY WEAPON IN COMPARISON TO MY LARGE ROCK.
PRAY THERE AIN'T TOO MANY OF 'EM...
PRAY? THOUGHT YOU DIDN'T BELIEVE IN GOD?
ONLY WHEN I'M SCARED.
GHA--!

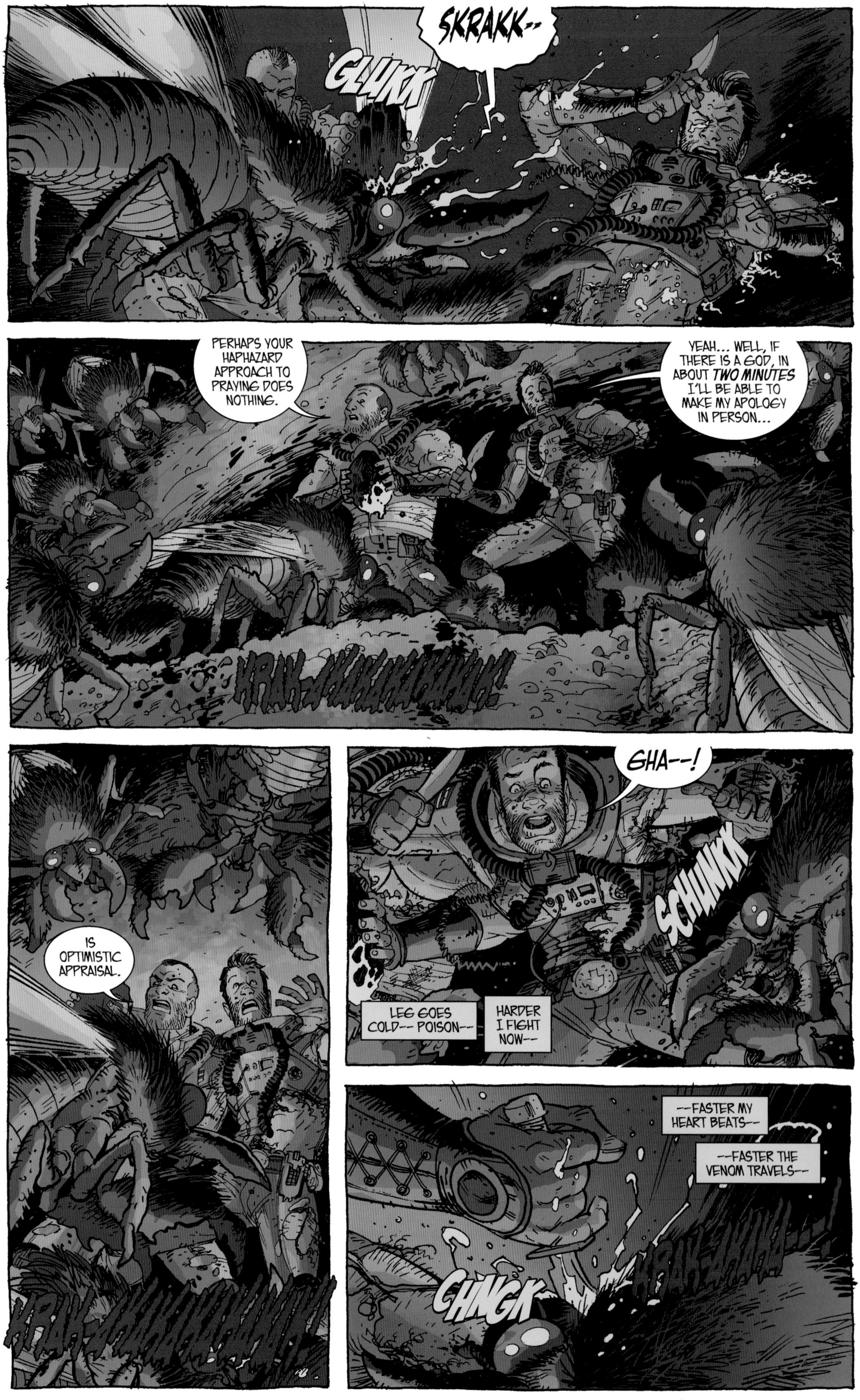
SKRAKK--
GLUKK
PERHAPS YOUR HAPHAZARD APPROACH TO PRAYING DOES NOTHING.
YEAH... WELL, IF THERE IS A GOD, IN ABOUT TWO MINUTES I'LL BE ABLE TO MAKE MY APOLOGY IN PERSON...
IS OPTIMISTIC APPRAISAL.
GHA--!
SCHUNKK
LEG GOES COLD-- POISON--
HARDER I FIGHT NOW--
--FASTER MY HEART BEATS--
--FASTER THE VENOM TRAVELS--
CHNGK

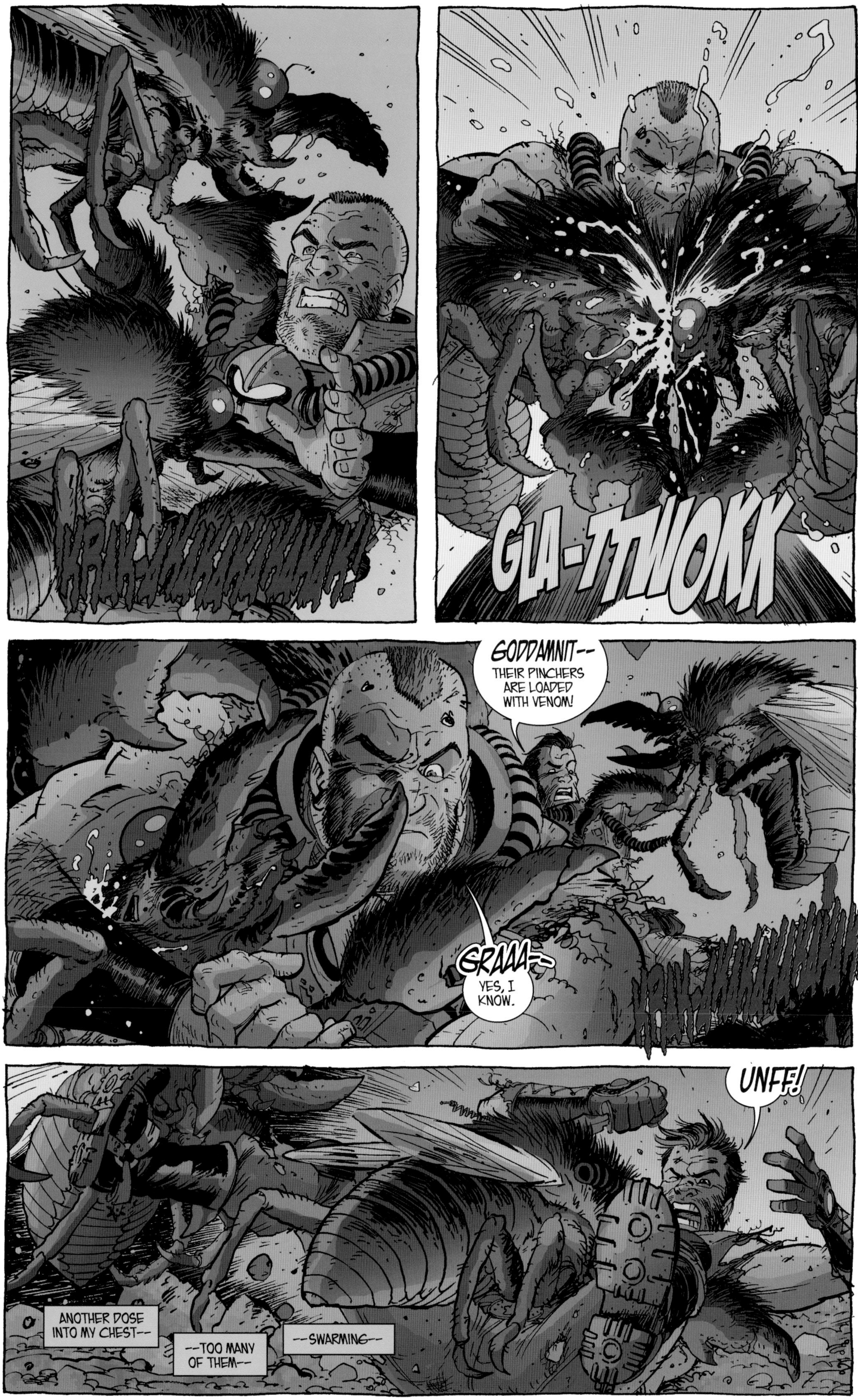
HRAH-WHAHAHAHAHAH!!
GLA-TTWOKK
GODDAMNIT-- THEIR PINCHERS ARE LOADED WITH VENOM!
GRAAA--
YES, I KNOW.
HRAH-WHAHAHAHAHAH!!
UNFF!
ANOTHER DOSE INTO MY CHEST--
--TOO MANY OF THEM--
--SWARMING--

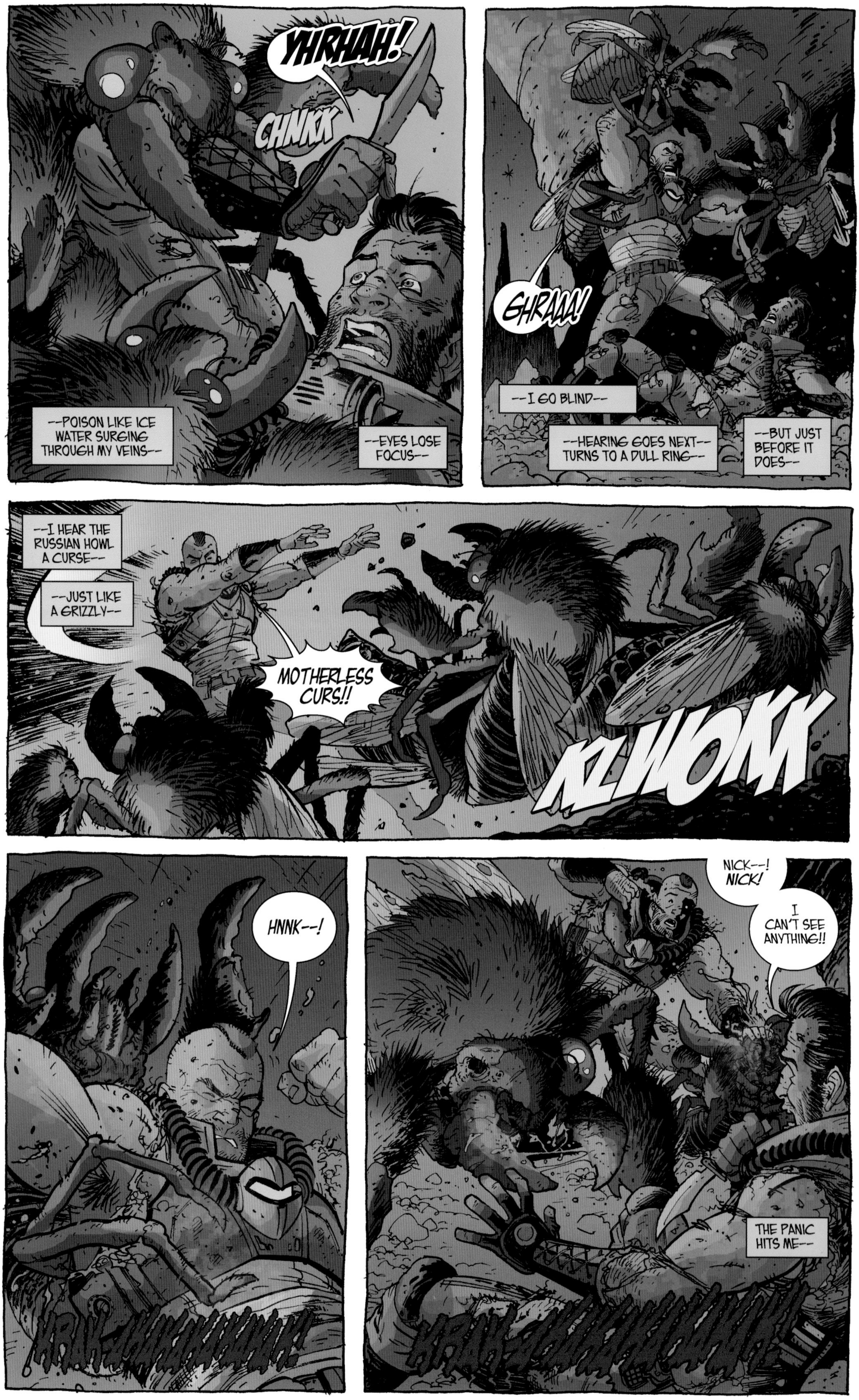
YHRHAH!
CHNKK
--POISON LIKE ICE WATER SURGING THROUGH MY VEINS--
--EYES LOSE FOCUS--
GHRAAA!
--I GO BLIND--
--HEARING GOES NEXT-- TURNS TO A DULL RING--
--BUT JUST BEFORE IT DOES--
--I HEAR THE RUSSIAN HOWL A CURSE--
--JUST LIKE A GRIZZLY--
MOTHERLESS CURS!!
KLWOKK
HNNK--!
NICK--! NICK!
I CAN'T SEE ANYTHING!!
THE PANIC HITS ME--

SOMETHING OPENS UP MY STOMACH--

SHNTT

--HOLD THE KNIFE FOR ALL I'M WORTH--

KRAKK--!

SCHUNKK

--STAB AT THE BASTARD--

GAA--!

--ANOTHER BITE-- I CATCH A FULL DOSE--

--I KNOW IT RIGHT AWAY--

SCHOPP

GRHAH!!

--BLIND--

--WAITING FOR THE FINAL STROKE--

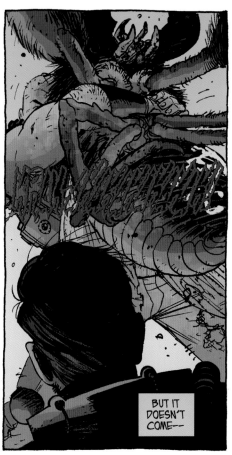

BUT IT DOESN'T COME--

RRRHHOOAAAHHH!!

--AN' BEYOND THE HUM IN MY EARS I MAKE OUT A SOUND--

CRRMBBLE....

--JUST LIKE A GRIZZLY.

SOMETHING COLD STOPS MY HEART--

--NUMBNESS GIVES WAY TO PAIN--

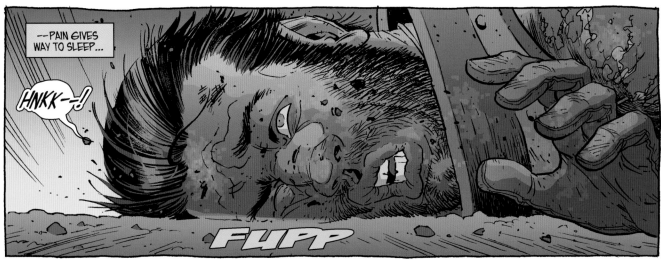

--PAIN GIVES WAY TO SLEEP...

HNKK--!

FUPP

SLEEP...

...GIVES WAY... TO...

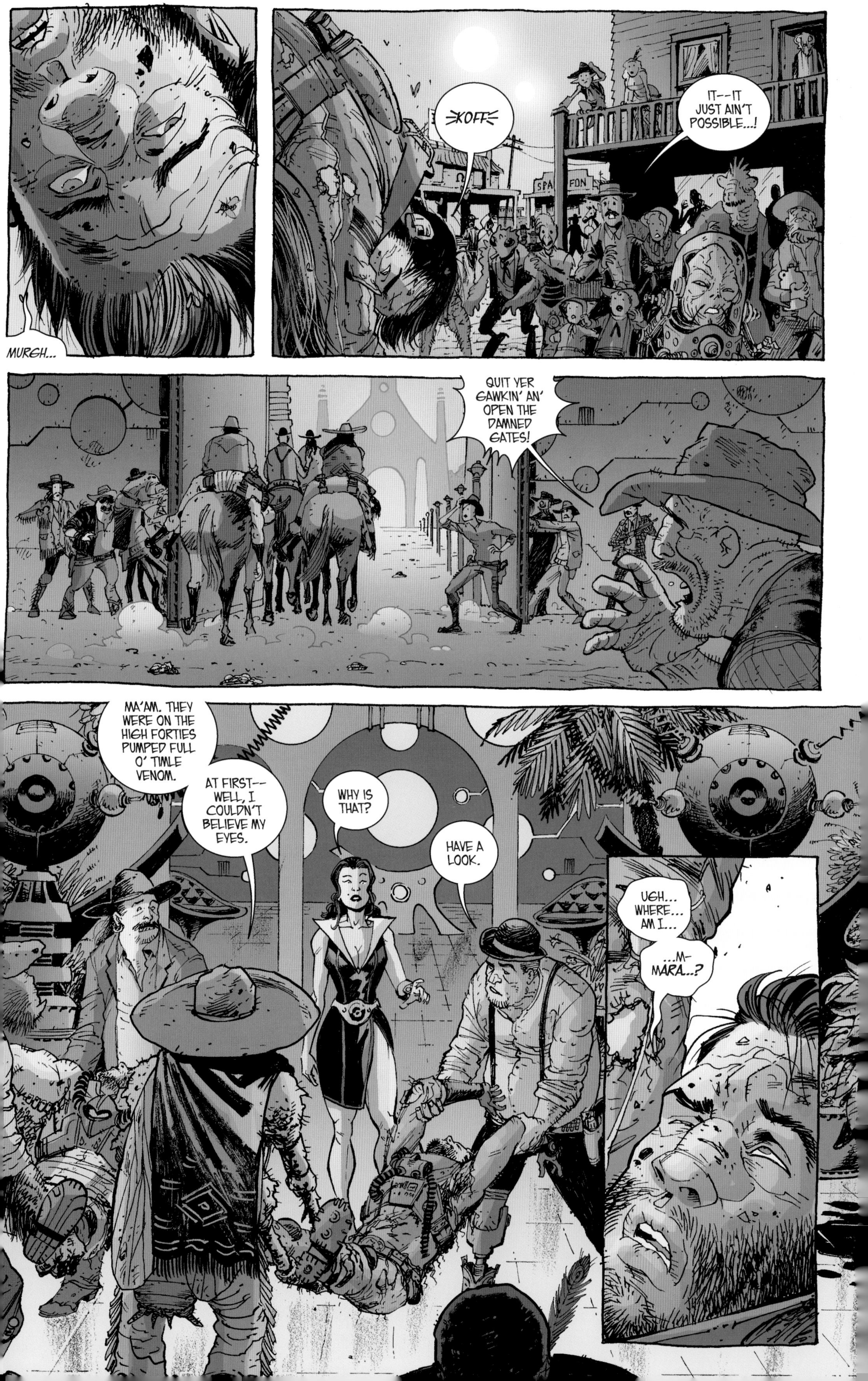
MURGH...
KOFF
IT--IT JUST AIN'T POSSIBLE...!
QUIT YER GAWKIN' AN' OPEN THE DAMNED GATES!
MA'AM. THEY WERE ON THE HIGH FORTIES PUMPED FULL O' TIMLE VENOM.
AT FIRST-- WELL, I COULDN'T BELIEVE MY EYES.
WHY IS THAT?
HAVE A LOOK.
UGH... WHERE... AM I...
...M-MARA...?

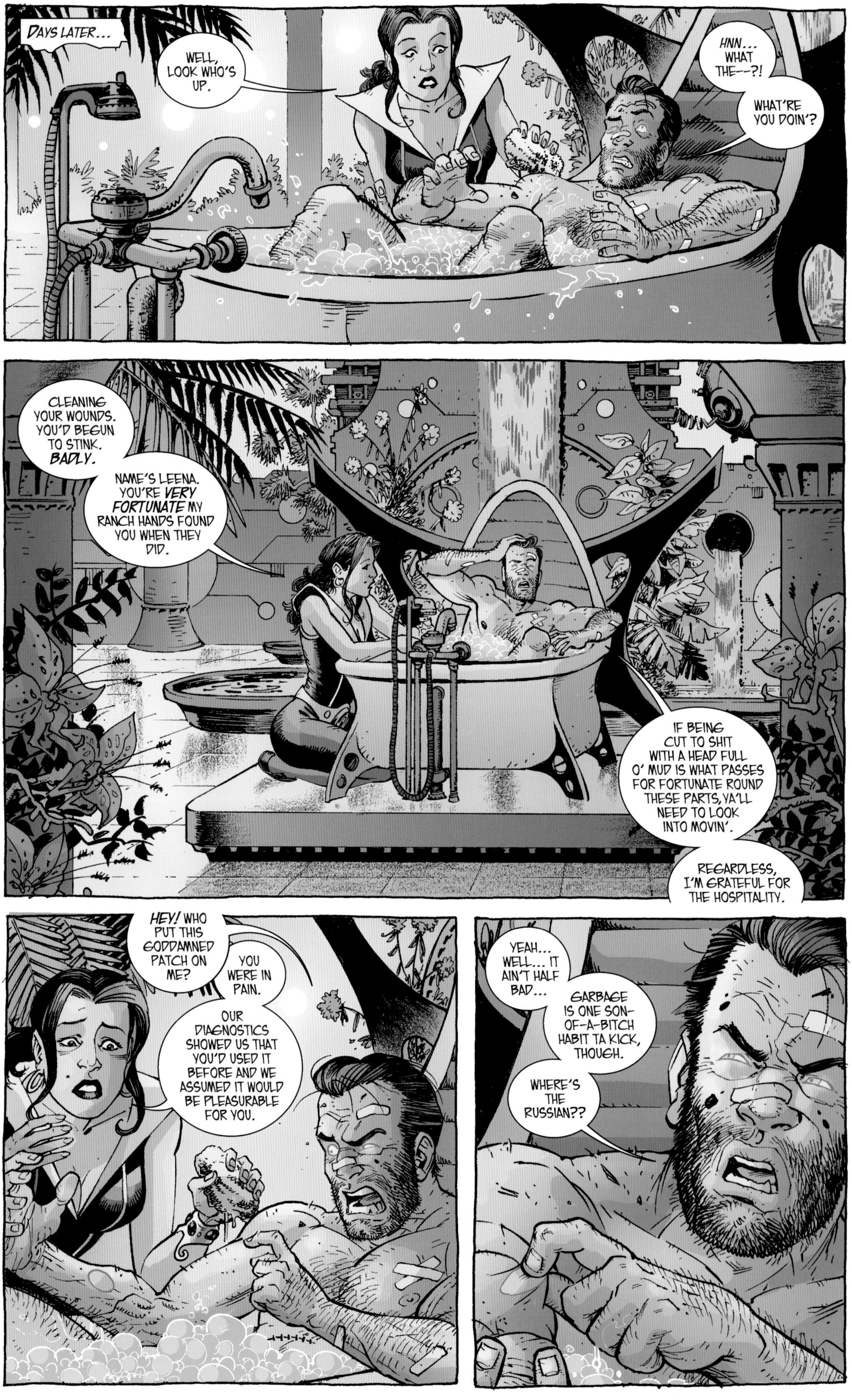
DAYS LATER...
WELL, LOOK WHO'S UP.
HNN... WHAT THE--?!
WHAT'RE YOU DOIN'?
CLEANING YOUR WOUNDS. YOU'D BEGUN TO STINK. BADLY.
NAME'S LEENA. YOU'RE VERY FORTUNATE MY RANCH HANDS FOUND YOU WHEN THEY DID.
IF BEING CUT TO SHIT WITH A HEAD FULL O' MUD IS WHAT PASSES FOR FORTUNATE ROUND THESE PARTS, YA'LL NEED TO LOOK INTO MOVIN'.
REGARDLESS, I'M GRATEFUL FOR THE HOSPITALITY.
HEY! WHO PUT THIS GODDAMNED PATCH ON ME?
YOU WERE IN PAIN.
OUR DIAGNOSTICS SHOWED US THAT YOU'D USED IT BEFORE AND WE ASSUMED IT WOULD BE PLEASURABLE FOR YOU.
YEAH... WELL... IT AIN'T HALF BAD...
GARBAGE IS ONE SON-OF-A-BITCH HABIT TA KICK, THOUGH.
WHERE'S THE RUSSIAN??

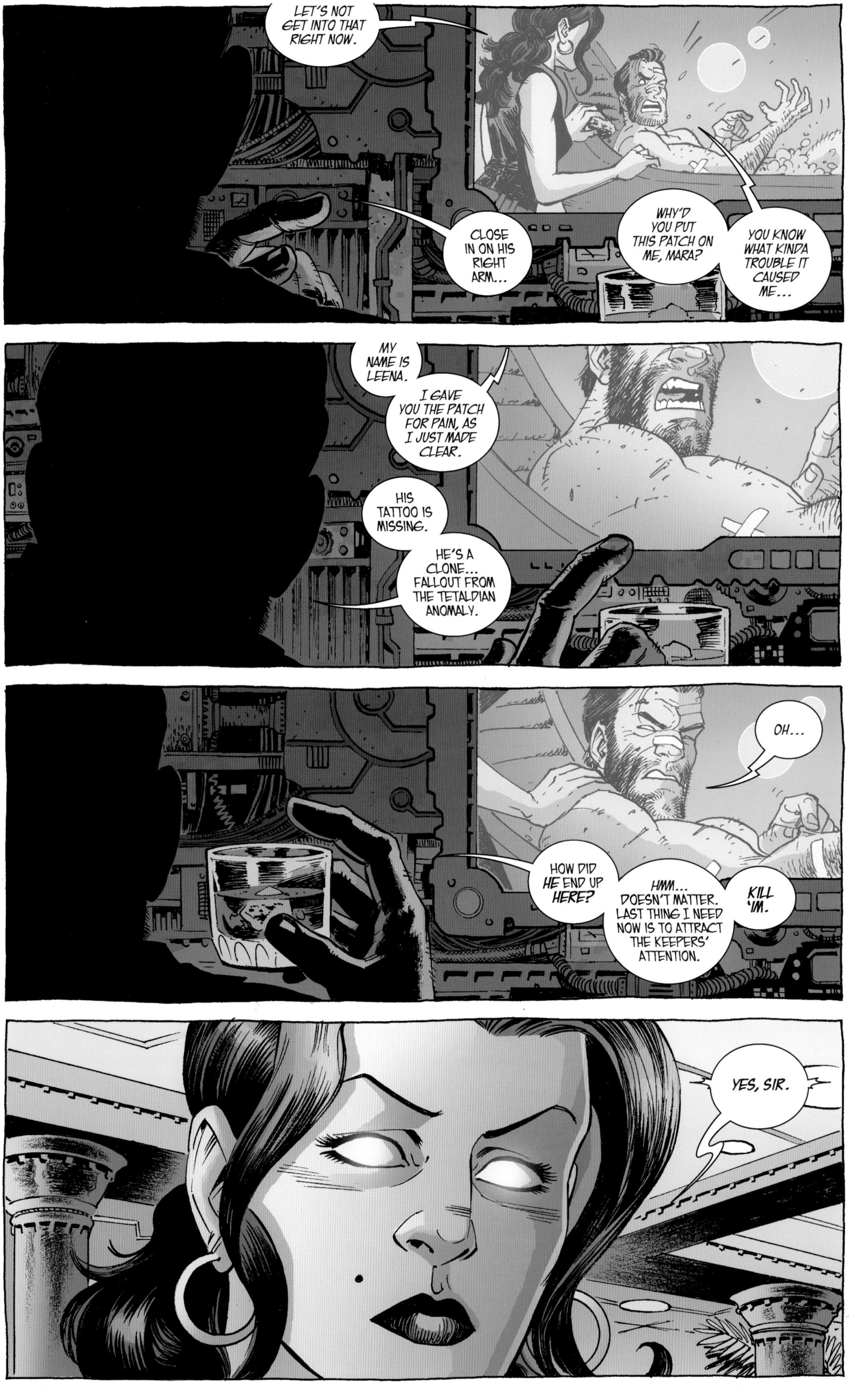
LET'S NOT GET INTO THAT RIGHT NOW.
CLOSE IN ON HIS RIGHT ARM...
WHY'D YOU PUT THIS PATCH ON ME, MARA?
YOU KNOW WHAT KINDA TROUBLE IT CAUSED ME...
MY NAME IS LEENA.
I GAVE YOU THE PATCH FOR PAIN, AS I JUST MADE CLEAR.
HIS TATTOO IS MISSING.
HE'S A CLONE... FALLOUT FROM THE TETALDIAN ANOMALY.
OH...
HOW DID HE END UP HERE?
HMM... DOESN'T MATTER. LAST THING I NEED NOW IS TO ATTRACT THE KEEPERS' ATTENTION.
KILL 'IM.
YES, SIR.

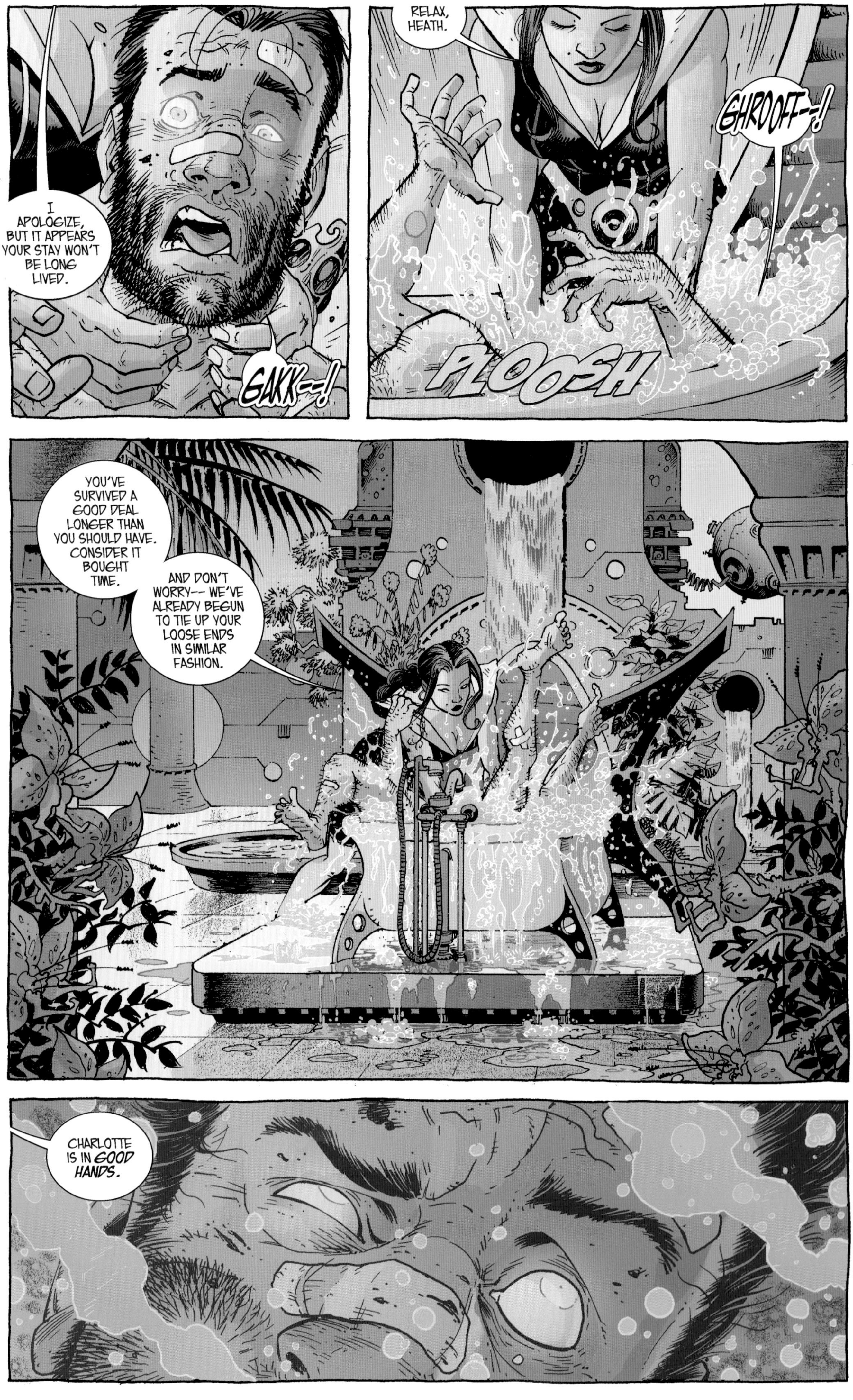
I APOLOGIZE, BUT IT APPEARS YOUR STAY WON'T BE LONG LIVED.
GAKK--!
RELAX, HEATH.
GHROOFF--!
PLOOSH
YOU'VE SURVIVED A GOOD DEAL LONGER THAN YOU SHOULD HAVE. CONSIDER IT BOUGHT TIME.
AND DON'T WORRY-- WE'VE ALREADY BEGUN TO TIE UP YOUR LOOSE ENDS IN SIMILAR FASHION.
CHARLOTTE IS IN GOOD HANDS.

CHAPTER 2

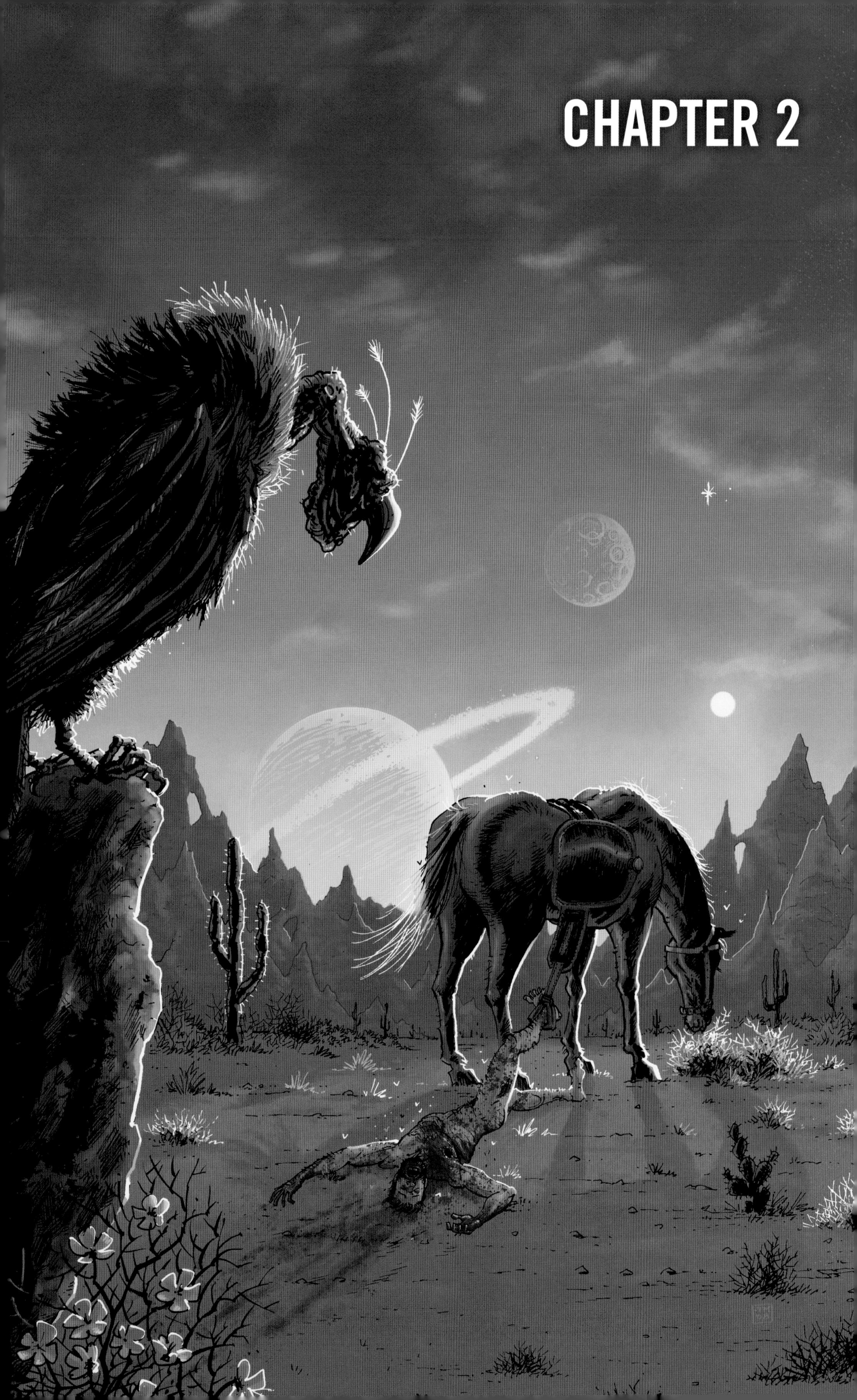

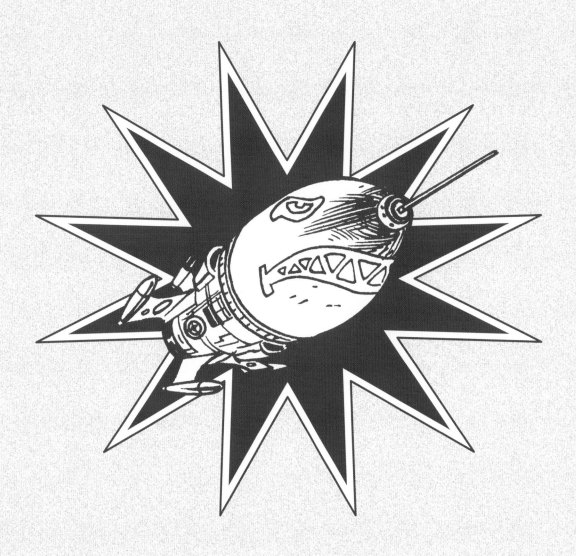

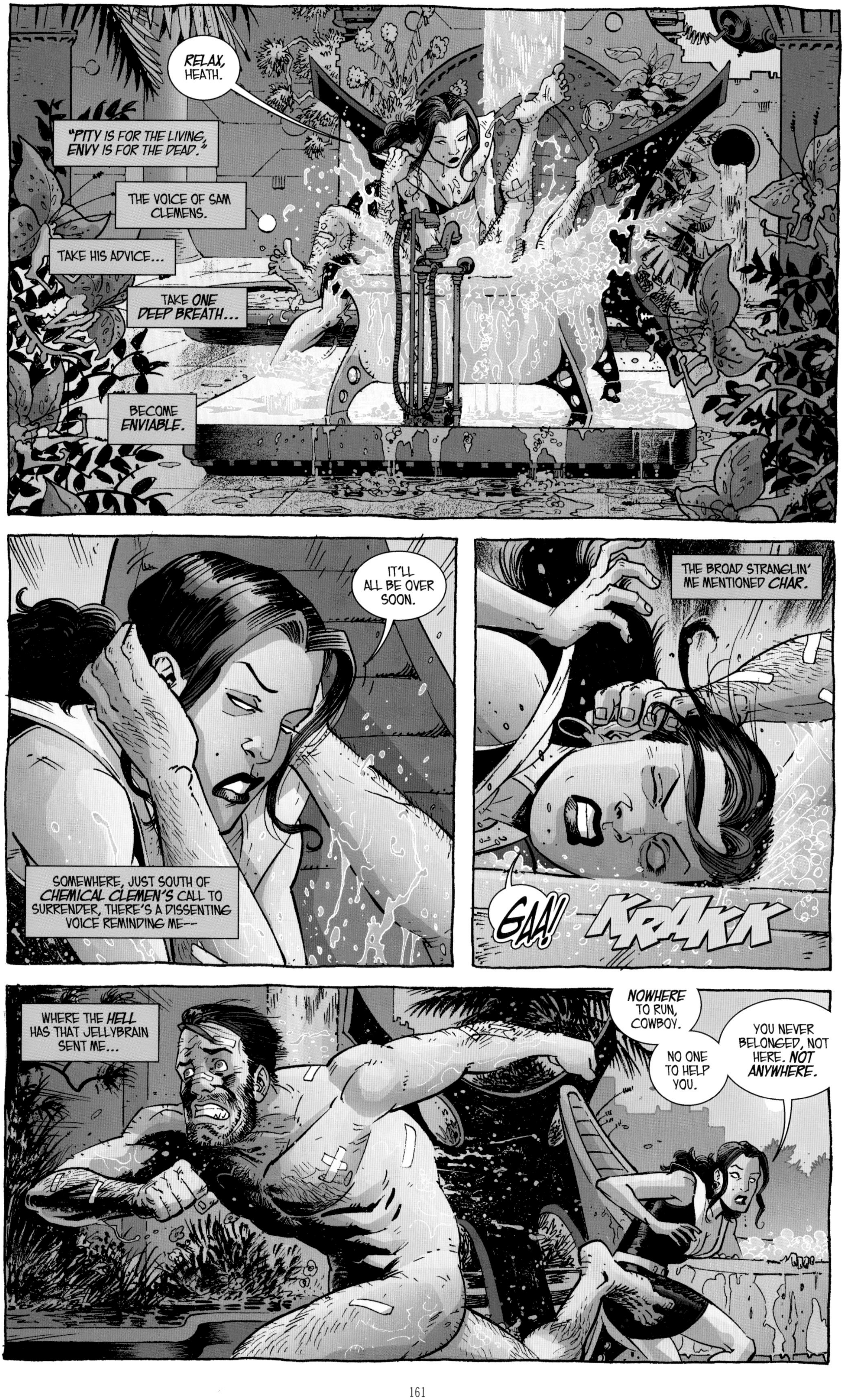
RELAX, HEATH.
"PITY IS FOR THE LIVING, ENVY IS FOR THE DEAD."
THE VOICE OF SAM CLEMENS.
TAKE HIS ADVICE...
TAKE ONE DEEP BREATH...
BECOME ENVIABLE.
IT'LL ALL BE OVER SOON.
SOMEWHERE, JUST SOUTH OF CHEMICAL CLEMEN'S CALL TO SURRENDER, THERE'S A DISSENTING VOICE REMINDING ME--
THE BROAD STRANGLIN' ME MENTIONED CHAR.
GAA!
KRAKK
WHERE THE HELL HAS THAT JELLYBRAIN SENT ME...
NOWHERE TO RUN, COWBOY.
NO ONE TO HELP YOU.
YOU NEVER BELONGED, NOT HERE. NOT ANYWHERE.

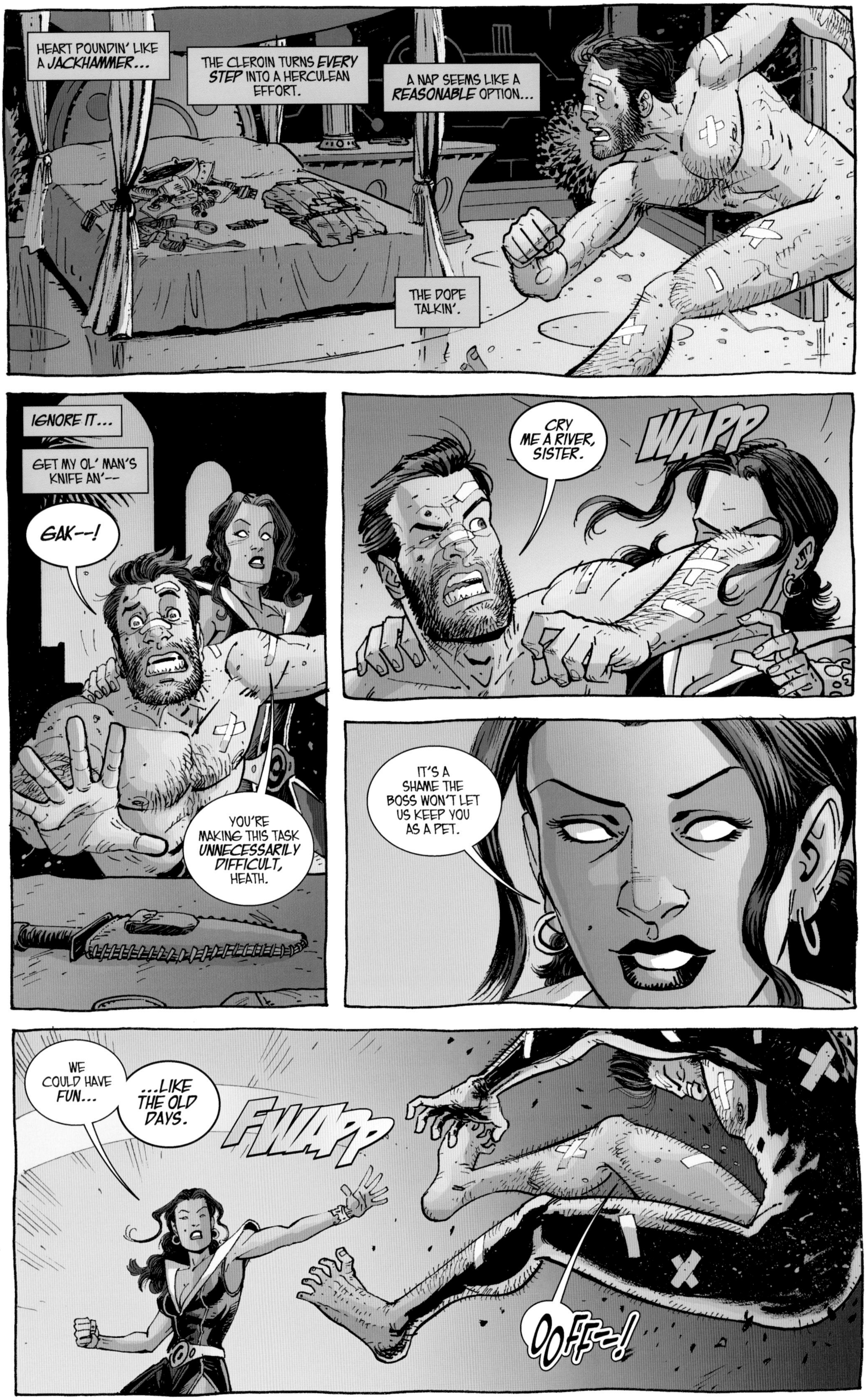
HEART POUNDIN' LIKE A JACKHAMMER...
THE CLEROIN TURNS EVERY STEP INTO A HERCULEAN EFFORT.
A NAP SEEMS LIKE A REASONABLE OPTION...
THE DOPE TALKIN'.
IGNORE IT...
GET MY OL' MAN'S KNIFE AN'--
GAK--!
YOU'RE MAKING THIS TASK UNNECESSARILY DIFFICULT, HEATH.
CRY ME A RIVER, SISTER.
WAPP
IT'S A SHAME THE BOSS WON'T LET US KEEP YOU AS A PET.
WE COULD HAVE FUN...
...LIKE THE OLD DAYS.
FWAPP
OOFF--!

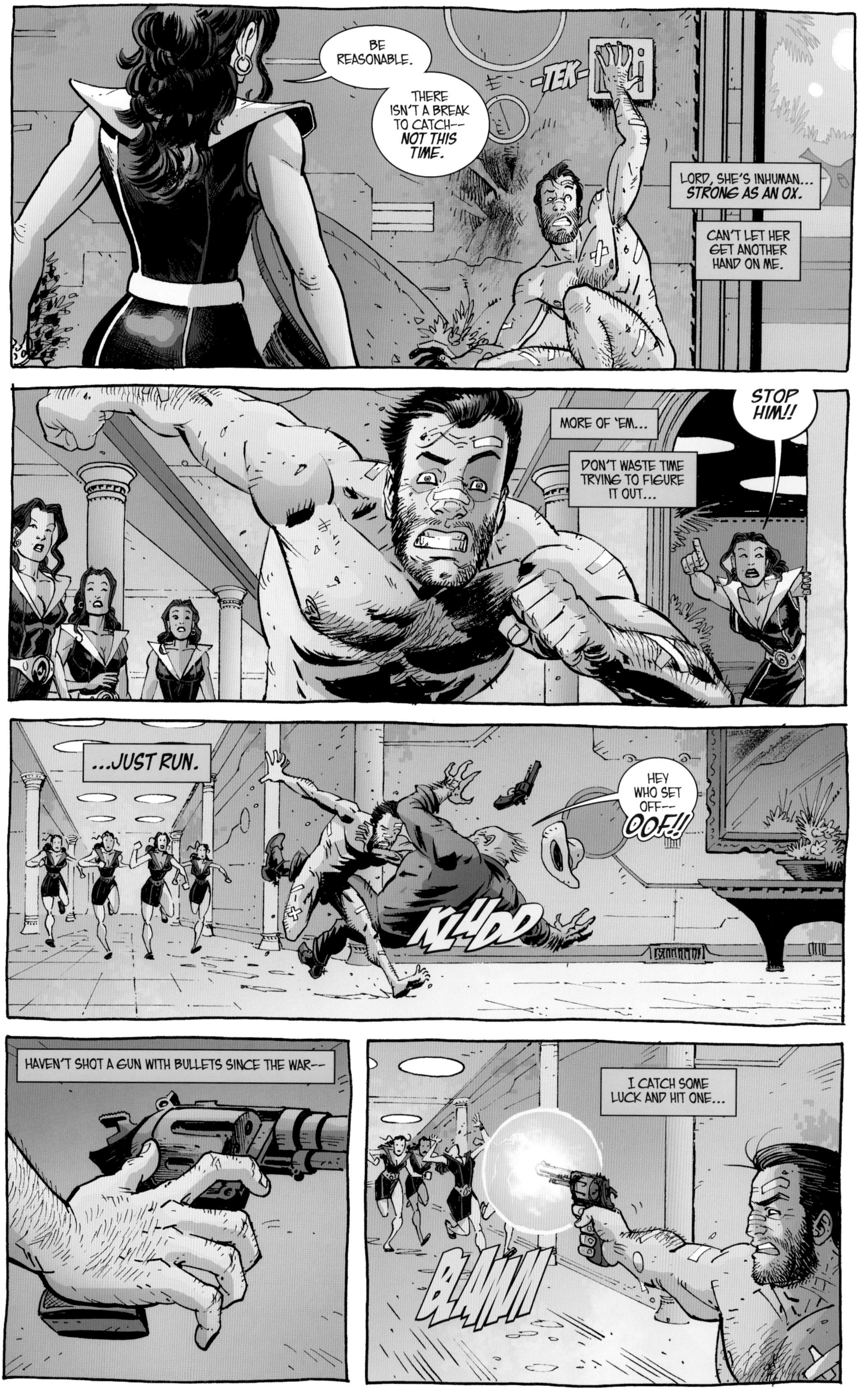
BE REASONABLE.
THERE ISN'T A BREAK TO CATCH-- NOT THIS TIME.
-TEK-
LORD, SHE'S INHUMAN... STRONG AS AN OX.
CAN'T LET HER GET ANOTHER HAND ON ME.
MORE OF 'EM...
DON'T WASTE TIME TRYING TO FIGURE IT OUT...
STOP HIM!!
...JUST RUN.
HEY WHO SET OFF-- OOF!!
KLUDD
HAVEN'T SHOT A GUN WITH BULLETS SINCE THE WAR--
I CATCH SOME LUCK AND HIT ONE...
BLAMM

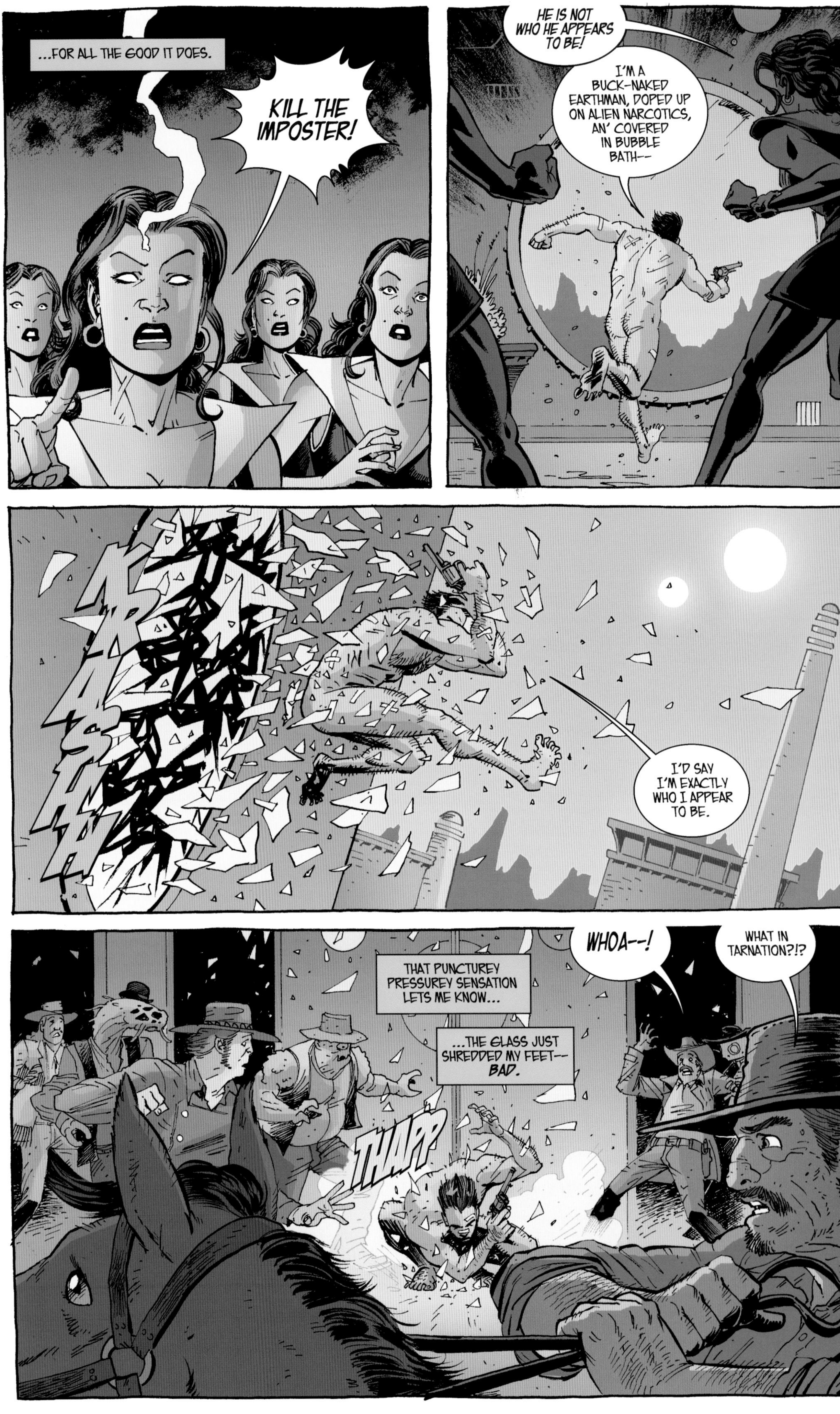
...FOR ALL THE GOOD IT DOES.
KILL THE IMPOSTER!
HE IS NOT WHO HE APPEARS TO BE!
I'M A BUCK-NAKED EARTHMAN, DOPED UP ON ALIEN NARCOTICS, AN' COVERED IN BUBBLE BATH--
I'D SAY I'M EXACTLY WHO I APPEAR TO BE.
THAT PUNCTUREY PRESSUREY SENSATION LETS ME KNOW...
...THE GLASS JUST SHREDDED MY FEET-- BAD.
THAPP
WHOA--!
WHAT IN TARNATION?!?

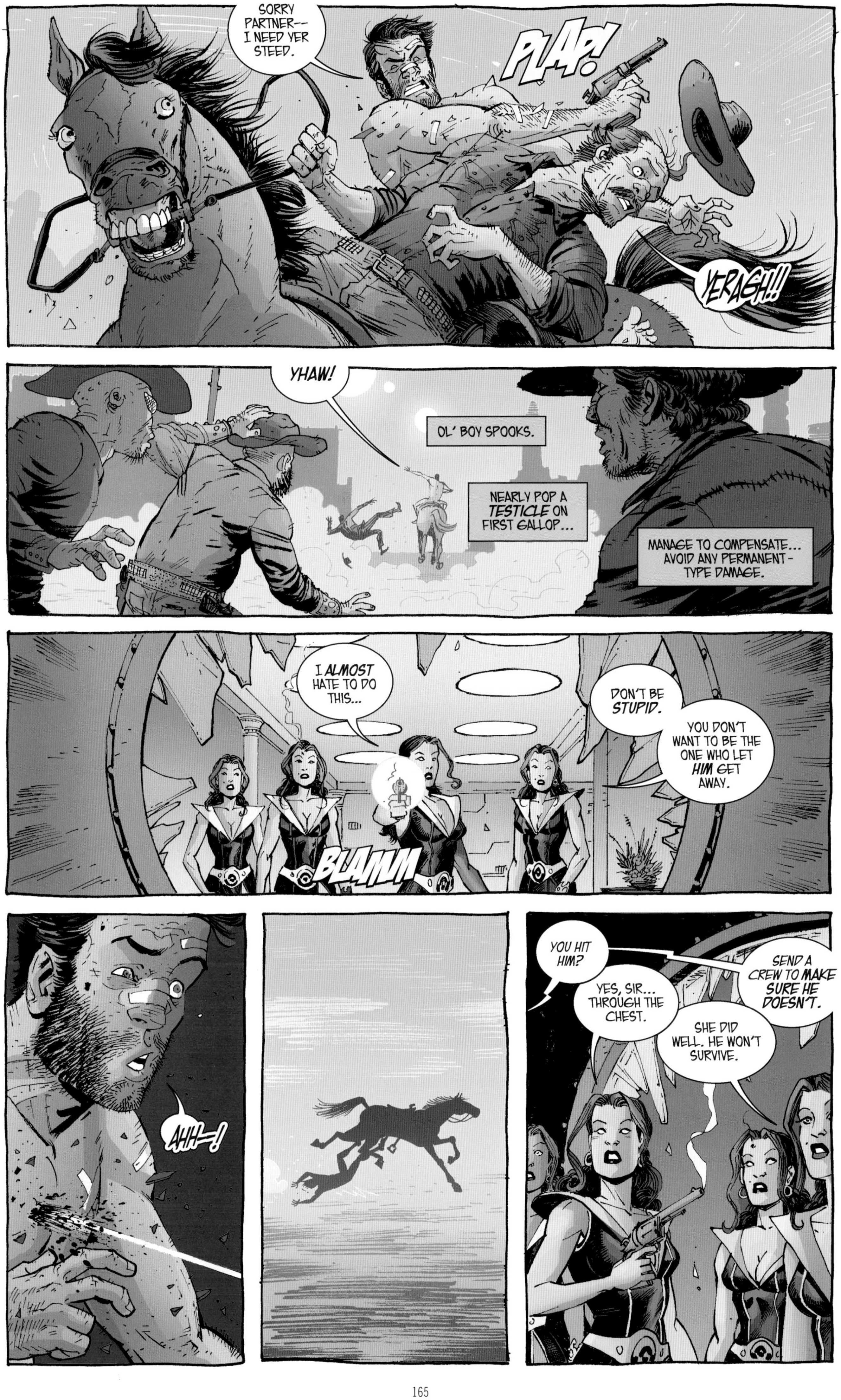
SORRY PARTNER-- I NEED YER STEED.
PLAP!
YERAGH!!
YHAW!
OL' BOY SPOOKS.
NEARLY POP A TESTICLE ON FIRST GALLOP...
MANAGE TO COMPENSATE... AVOID ANY PERMANENT-TYPE DAMAGE.
I ALMOST HATE TO DO THIS...
DON'T BE STUPID.
YOU DON'T WANT TO BE THE ONE WHO LET HIM GET AWAY.
BLAMM
AHH--!
YOU HIT HIM?
YES, SIR... THROUGH THE CHEST.
SEND A CREW TO MAKE SURE HE DOESN'T.
SHE DID WELL. HE WON'T SURVIVE.

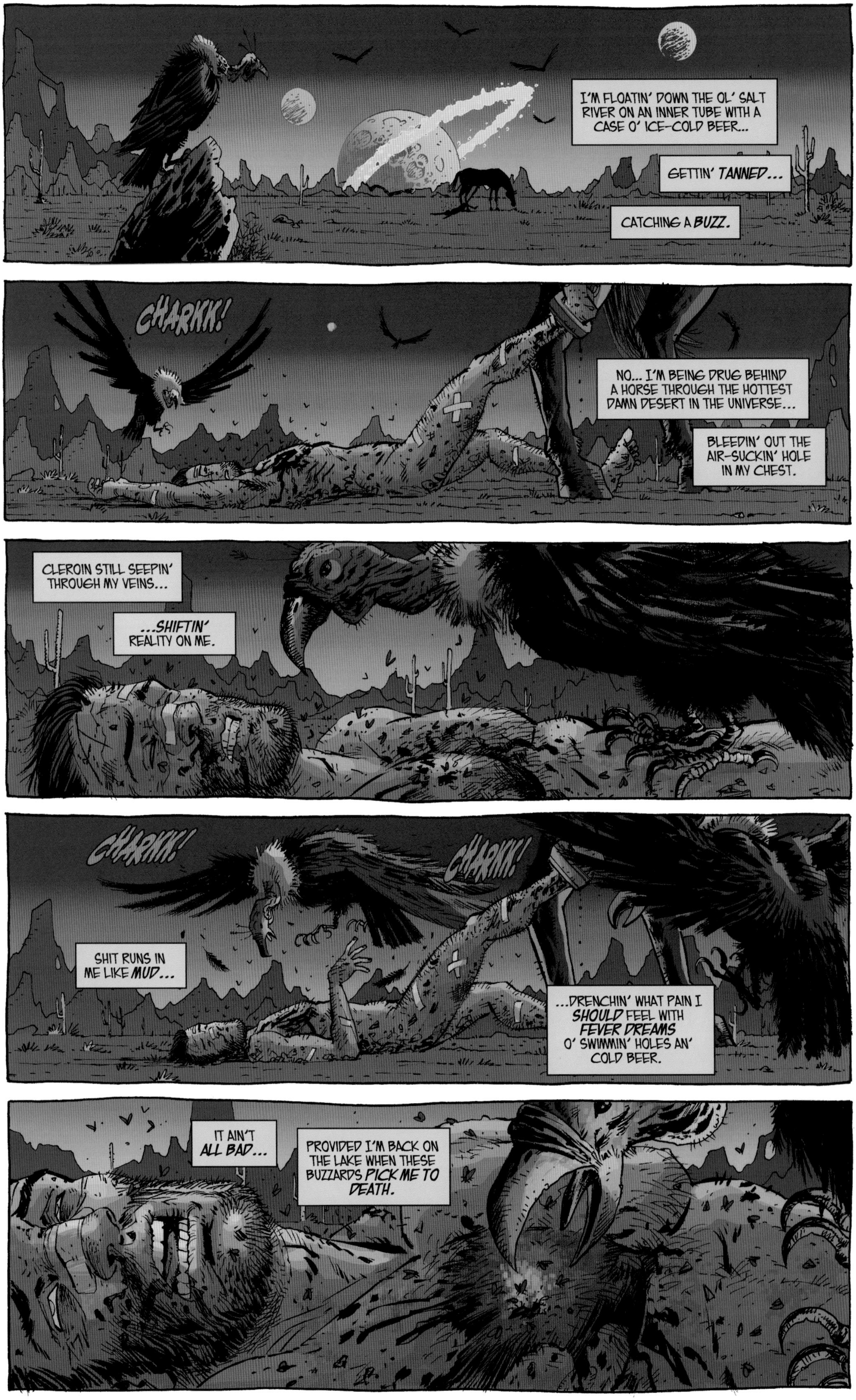
I'M FLOATIN' DOWN THE OL' SALT RIVER ON AN INNER TUBE WITH A CASE O' ICE-COLD BEER...
GETTIN' TANNED...
CATCHING A BUZZ.
CHARKK!
NO... I'M BEING DRUG BEHIND A HORSE THROUGH THE HOTTEST DAMN DESERT IN THE UNIVERSE...
BLEEDIN' OUT THE AIR-SUCKIN' HOLE IN MY CHEST.
CLEROIN STILL SEEPIN' THROUGH MY VEINS...
...SHIFTIN' REALITY ON ME.
CHARKK!
CHARKK!
SHIT RUNS IN ME LIKE MUD...
...DRENCHIN' WHAT PAIN I SHOULD FEEL WITH FEVER DREAMS O' SWIMMIN' HOLES AN' COLD BEER.
IT AIN'T ALL BAD...
PROVIDED I'M BACK ON THE LAKE WHEN THESE BUZZARDS PICK ME TO DEATH.

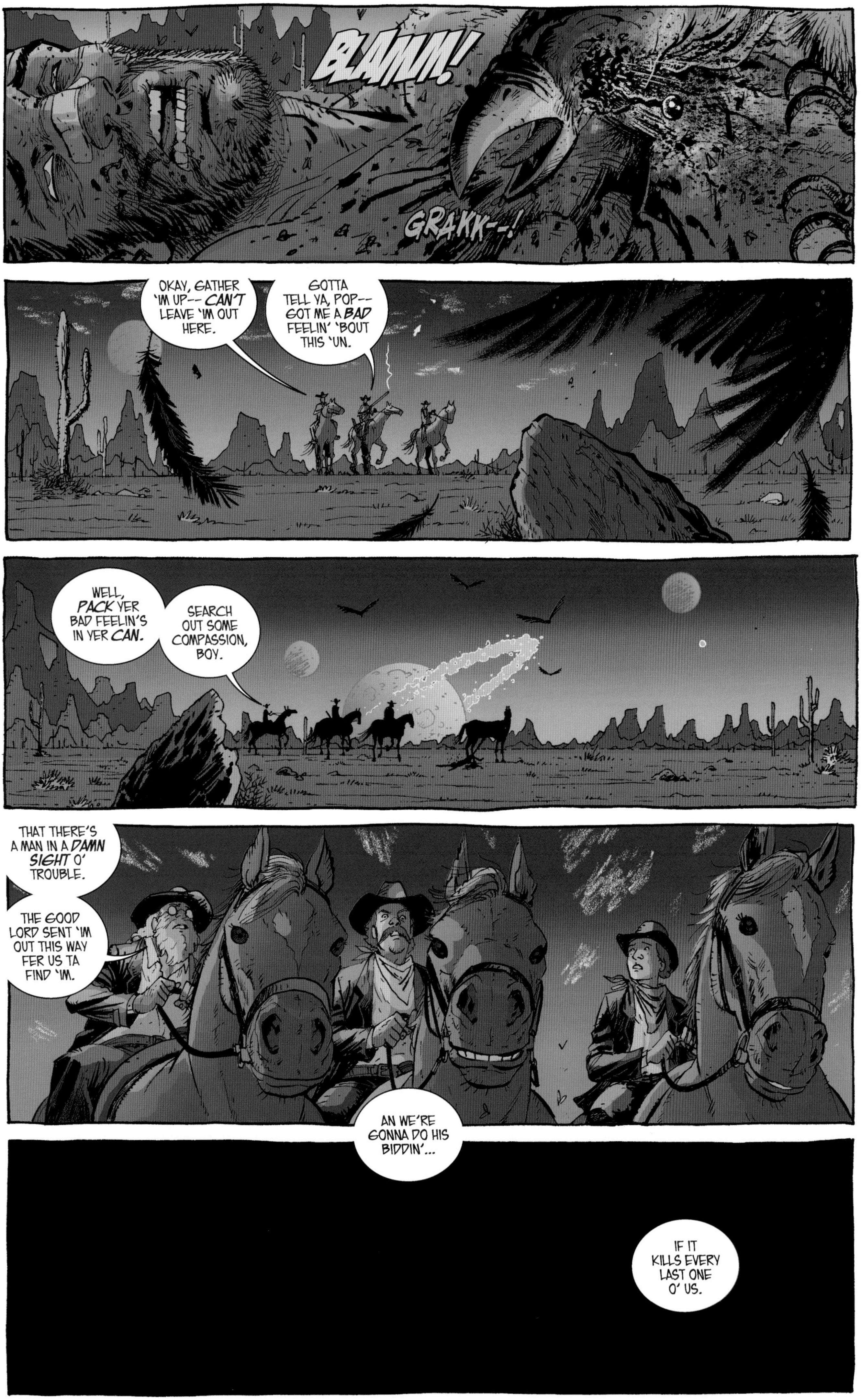
BLAMM!
GRAKK--!
OKAY, GATHER 'IM UP-- CAN'T LEAVE 'IM OUT HERE.
GOTTA TELL YA, POP-- GOT ME A BAD FEELIN' 'BOUT THIS 'UN.
WELL, PACK YER BAD FEELIN'S IN YER CAN.
SEARCH OUT SOME COMPASSION, BOY.
THAT THERE'S A MAN IN A DAMN SIGHT O' TROUBLE.
THE GOOD LORD SENT 'IM OUT THIS WAY FER US TA FIND 'IM.
AN WE'RE GONNA DO HIS BIDDIN'...
IF IT KILLS EVERY LAST ONE O' US.

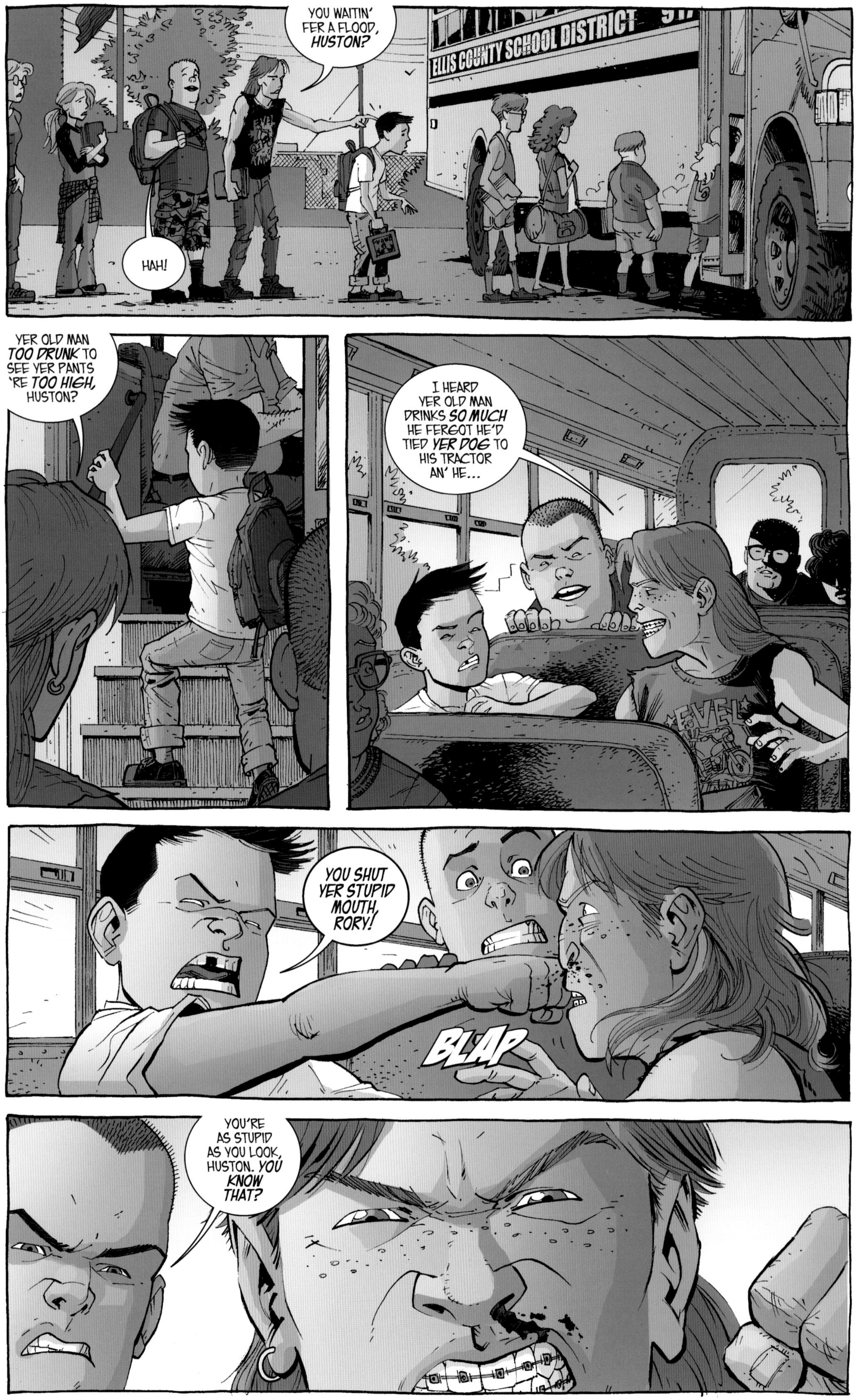
ELLIS COUNTY SCHOOL DISTRICT
YOU WAITIN' FER A FLOOD, HUSTON?
HAH!
YER OLD MAN TOO DRUNK TO SEE YER PANTS 'RE TOO HIGH, HUSTON?
I HEARD YER OLD MAN DRINKS SO MUCH HE FERGOT HE'D TIED YER DOG TO HIS TRACTOR AN' HE...
YOU SHUT YER STUPID MOUTH, RORY!
BLAP
YOU'RE AS STUPID AS YOU LOOK, HUSTON. YOU KNOW THAT?

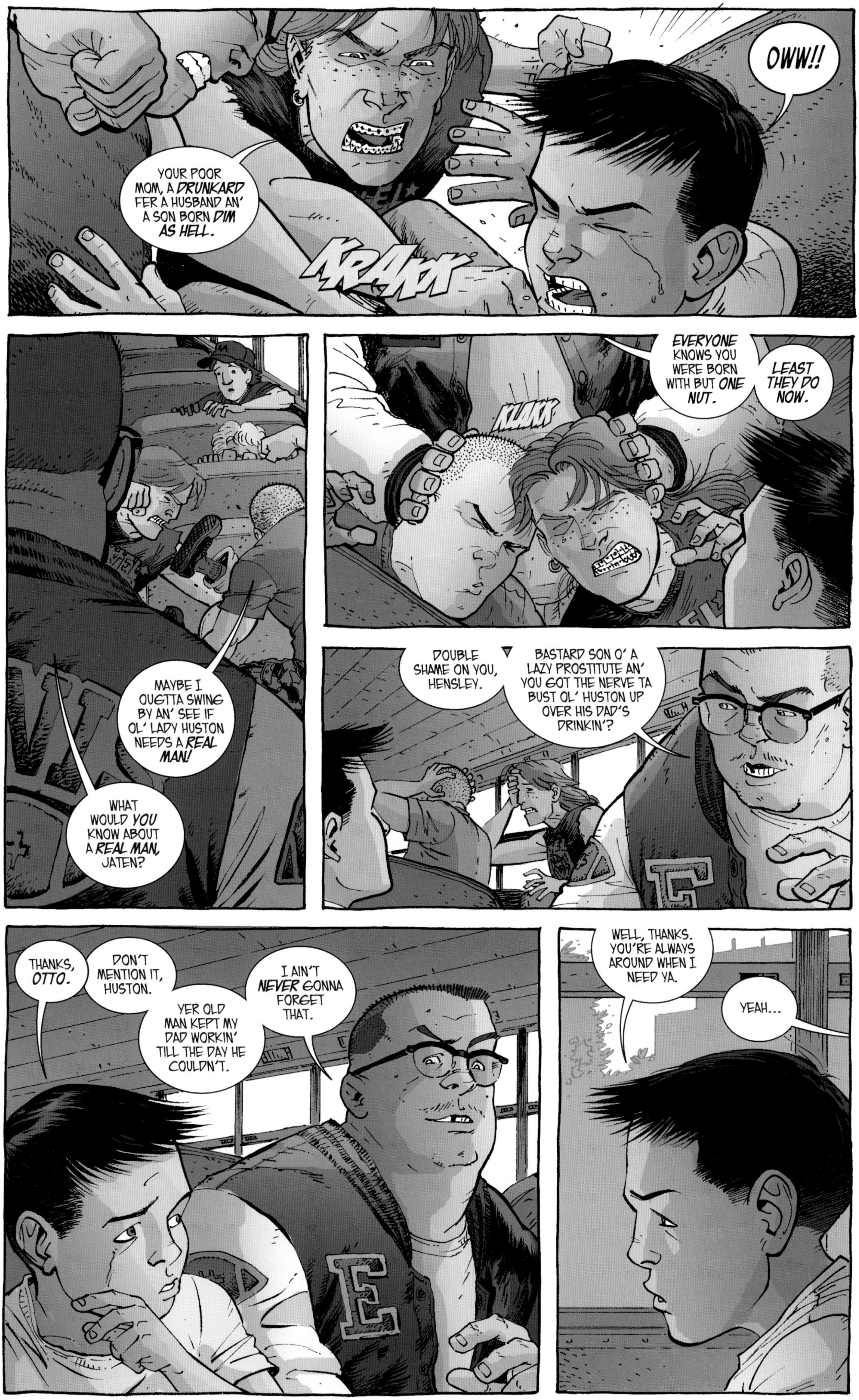
OWW!!
YOUR POOR MOM, A DRUNKARD FER A HUSBAND AN' A SON BORN DIM AS HELL.
KRAKK
EVERYONE KNOWS YOU WERE BORN WITH BUT ONE NUT.
LEAST THEY DO NOW.
KLAKK
MAYBE I OUGTTA SWING BY AN' SEE IF OL' LADY HUSTON NEEDS A REAL MAN!
WHAT WOULD YOU KNOW ABOUT A REAL MAN, JATEN?
DOUBLE SHAME ON YOU, HENSLEY.
BASTARD SON O' A LAZY PROSTITUTE AN' YOU GOT THE NERVE TA BUST OL' HUSTON UP OVER HIS DAD'S DRINKIN'?
THANKS, OTTO.
DON'T MENTION IT, HUSTON.
YER OLD MAN KEPT MY DAD WORKIN' TILL THE DAY HE COULDN'T.
I AIN'T NEVER GONNA FORGET THAT.
WELL, THANKS. YOU'RE ALWAYS AROUND WHEN I NEED YA.
YEAH...

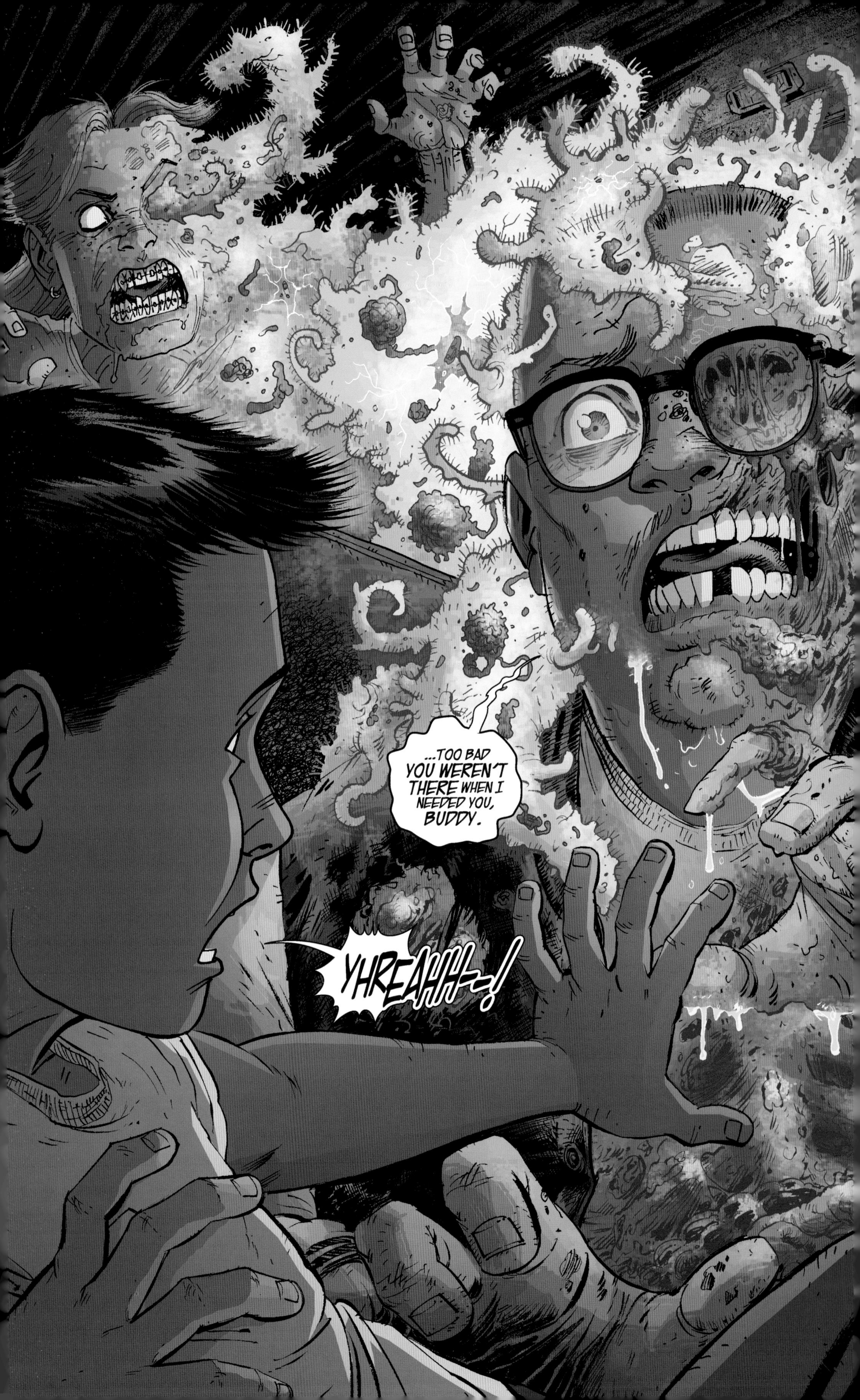
...TOO BAD YOU WEREN'T THERE WHEN I NEEDED YOU, BUDDY.
YHREAHHH--!

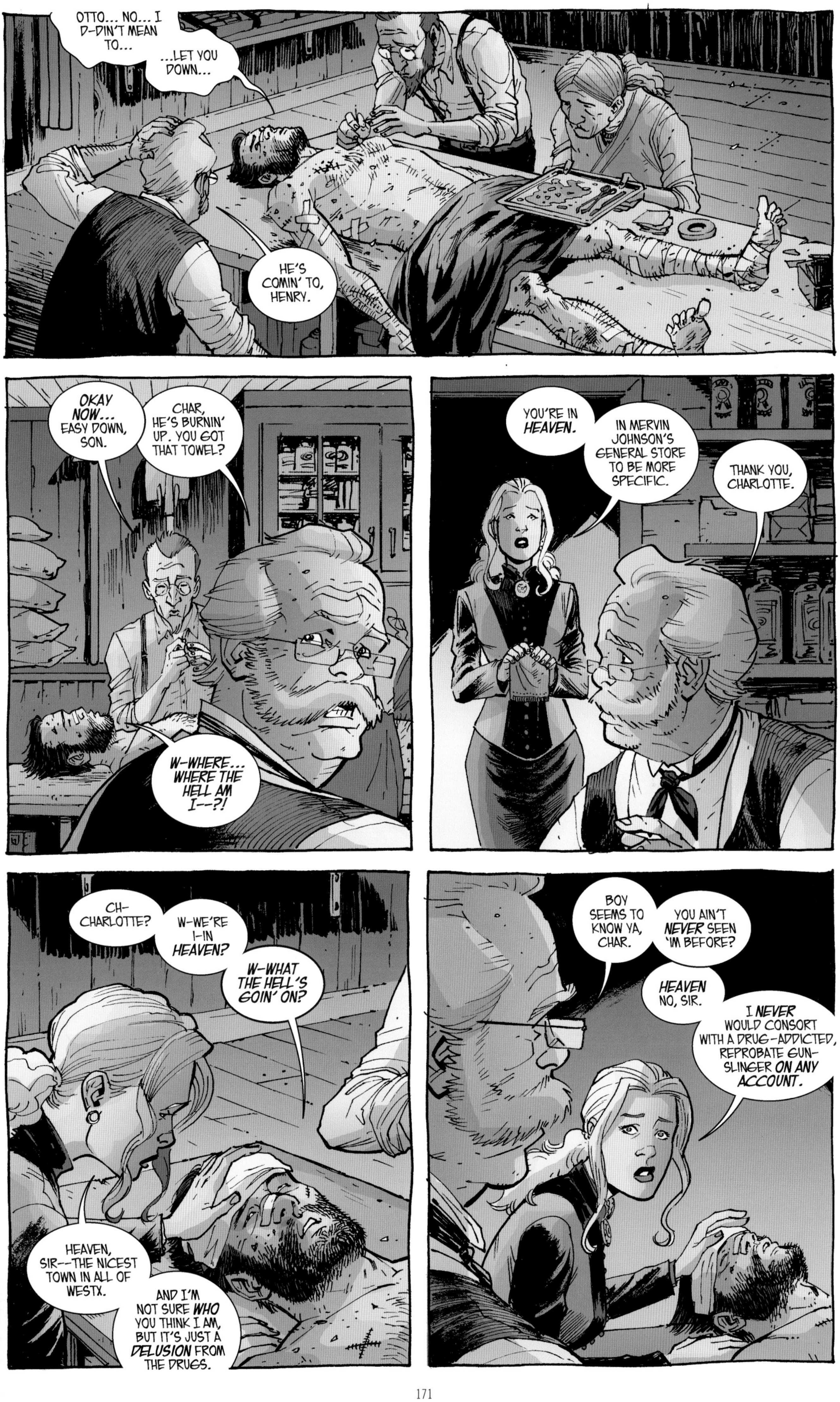
OTTO... NO... I D-DIN'T MEAN TO...
...LET YOU DOWN...
HE'S COMIN' TO, HENRY.
OKAY NOW... EASY DOWN, SON.
CHAR, HE'S BURNIN' UP. YOU GOT THAT TOWEL?
W-WHERE... WHERE THE HELL AM I--?!
YOU'RE IN HEAVEN.
IN MERVIN JOHNSON'S GENERAL STORE TO BE MORE SPECIFIC.
THANK YOU, CHARLOTTE.
CH-CHARLOTTE?
W-WE'RE I-IN HEAVEN?
W-WHAT THE HELL'S GOIN' ON?
HEAVEN, SIR--THE NICEST TOWN IN ALL OF WESTX.
AND I'M NOT SURE WHO YOU THINK I AM, BUT IT'S JUST A DELUSION FROM THE DRUGS.
BOY SEEMS TO KNOW YA, CHAR.
YOU AIN'T NEVER SEEN 'IM BEFORE?
HEAVEN NO, SIR.
I NEVER WOULD CONSORT WITH A DRUG-ADDICTED, REPROBATE GUN-SLINGER ON ANY ACCOUNT.

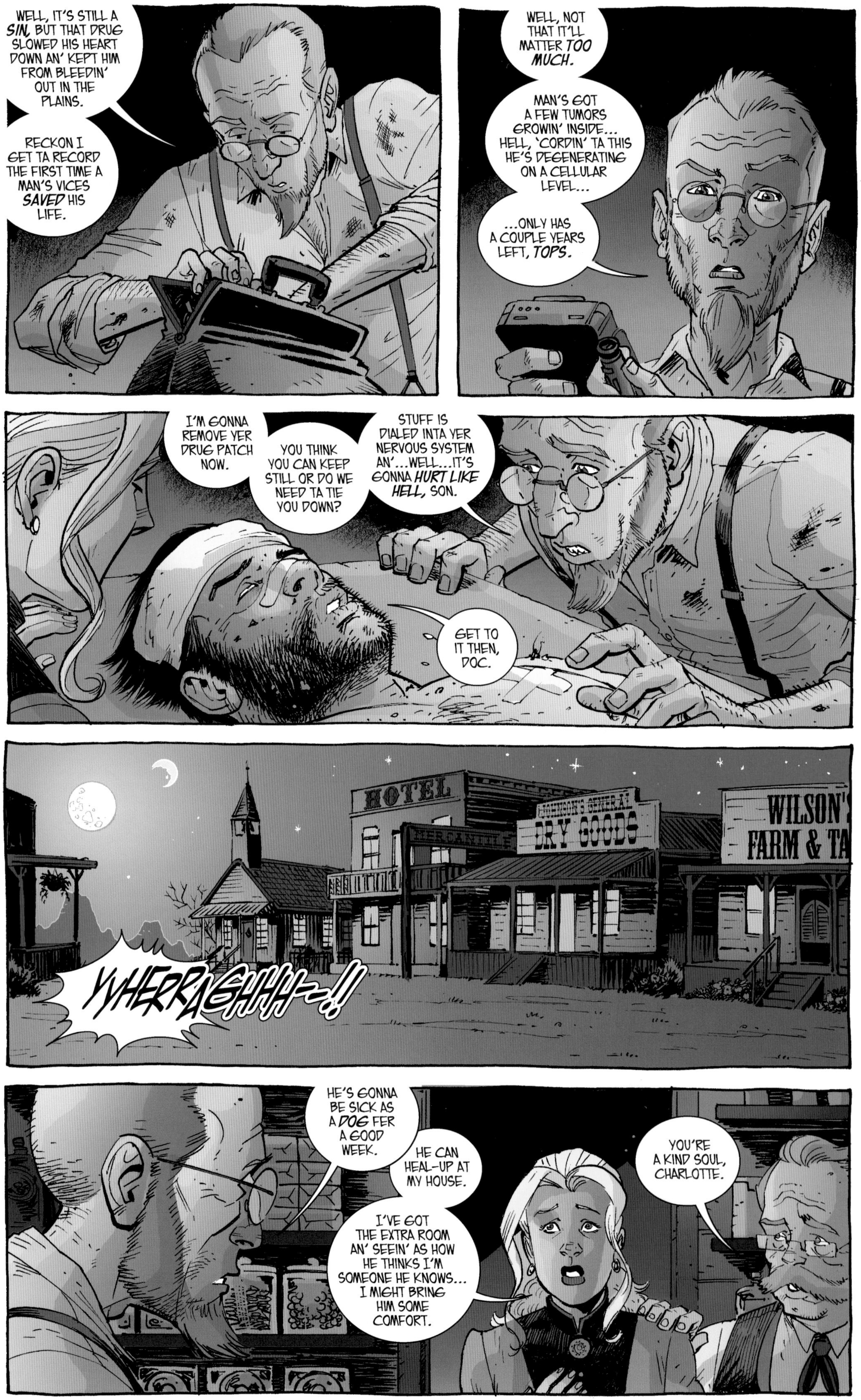

WELL, IT'S STILL A SIN, BUT THAT DRUG SLOWED HIS HEART DOWN AN' KEPT HIM FROM BLEEDIN' OUT IN THE PLAINS.
RECKON I GET TA RECORD THE FIRST TIME A MAN'S VICES SAVED HIS LIFE.
WELL, NOT THAT IT'LL MATTER TOO MUCH.
MAN'S GOT A FEW TUMORS GROWIN' INSIDE... HELL, 'CORDIN' TA THIS HE'S DEGENERATING ON A CELLULAR LEVEL...
...ONLY HAS A COUPLE YEARS LEFT, TOPS.
I'M GONNA REMOVE YER DRUG PATCH NOW.
YOU THINK YOU CAN KEEP STILL OR DO WE NEED TA TIE YOU DOWN?
STUFF IS DIALED INTA YER NERVOUS SYSTEM AN'...WELL...IT'S GONNA HURT LIKE HELL, SON.
GET TO IT THEN, DOC.
HOTEL
MERCANTILE
DRY GOODS
WILSON'S
FARM & TA
YYHERRAGHHH--!!
HE'S GONNA BE SICK AS A DOG FER A GOOD WEEK.
HE CAN HEAL-UP AT MY HOUSE.
I'VE GOT THE EXTRA ROOM AN' SEEIN' AS HOW HE THINKS I'M SOMEONE HE KNOWS... I MIGHT BRING HIM SOME COMFORT.
YOU'RE A KIND SOUL, CHARLOTTE.

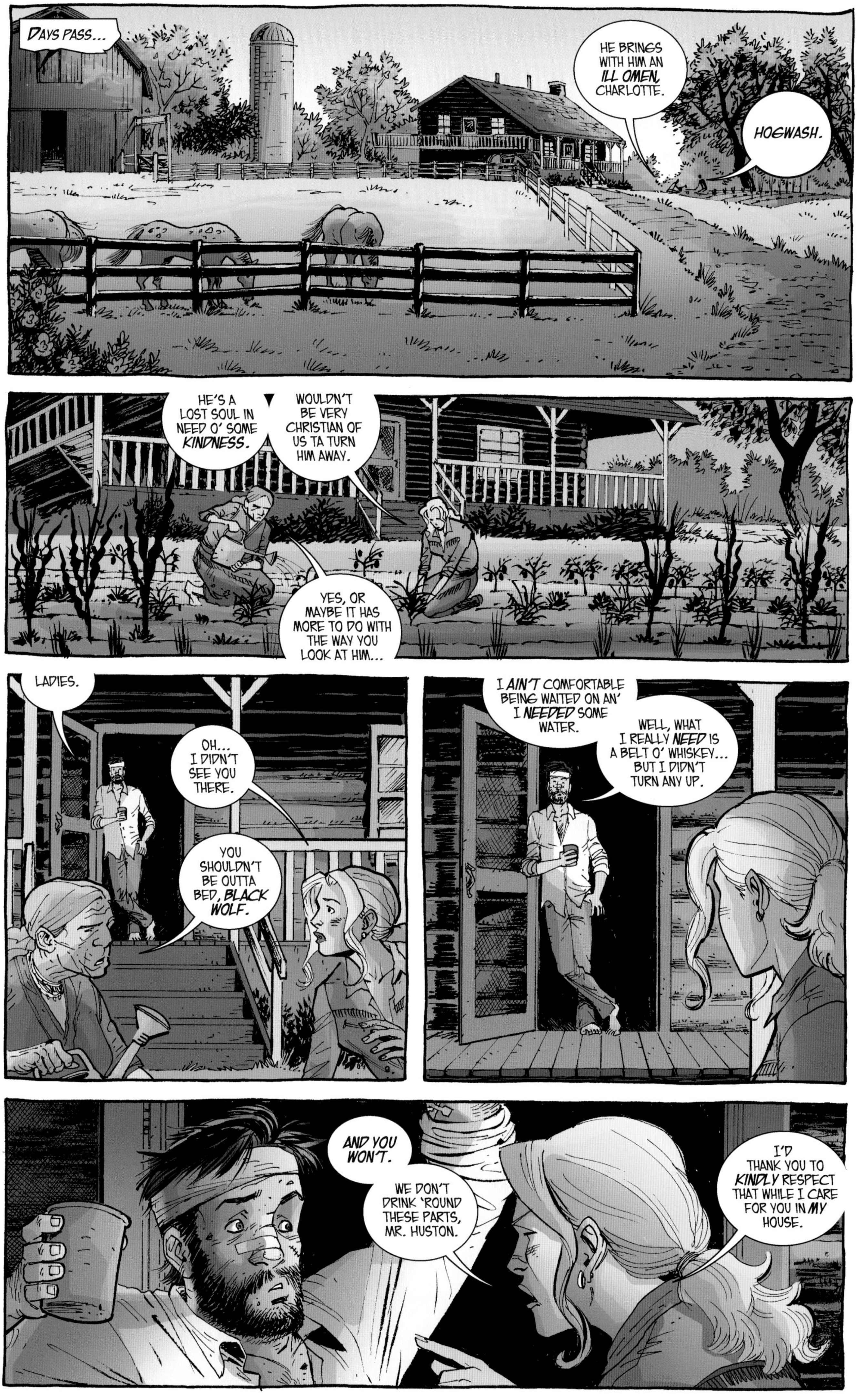
DAYS PASS...
HE BRINGS WITH HIM AN ILL OMEN, CHARLOTTE.
HOGWASH.
HE'S A LOST SOUL IN NEED O' SOME KINDNESS.
WOULDN'T BE VERY CHRISTIAN OF US TA TURN HIM AWAY.
YES, OR MAYBE IT HAS MORE TO DO WITH THE WAY YOU LOOK AT HIM...
LADIES.
OH... I DIDN'T SEE YOU THERE.
YOU SHOULDN'T BE OUTTA BED, BLACK WOLF.
I AIN'T COMFORTABLE BEING WAITED ON AN' I NEEDED SOME WATER.
WELL, WHAT I REALLY NEED IS A BELT O' WHISKEY... BUT I DIDN'T TURN ANY UP.
AND YOU WON'T.
WE DON'T DRINK 'ROUND THESE PARTS, MR. HUSTON.
I'D THANK YOU TO KINDLY RESPECT THAT WHILE I CARE FOR YOU IN MY HOUSE.

I NEED TO GO TO TOWN BEFORE IT GETS DARK. YOU NEED ANYTHING?

I AIN'T PICKY. I'D EVEN SETTLE FER SOME *GIN*.

I TAKE THAT AS A *NO*.

ALL RIGHT THEN-- IT'S JUST THE TWO OF US NOW, CHAR.

CUT THE CRAP AN' TELL ME *WHAT THE HELL IS GOIN'* ON HERE.

LIKE I TOLD YOU, YOU'VE GOT ME MIXED UP WITH SOMEONE ELSE.

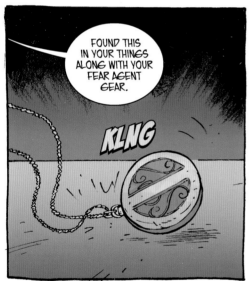

FOUND THIS IN YOUR THINGS ALONG WITH YOUR FEAR AGENT GEAR.

KLNG

YEAH, OKAY, OBVIOUSLY IT'S ME, HEATHROW.

SO YOU KNOW NOW-- *BUT THEY CAN'T.*

I DON'T KNOW EXACTLY WHAT IS GOING ON, BUT SOMETHING IN THOSE HILLS HAS THESE FOLKS *SPOOKED* AN' I DON'T WANNA BE RODE OUT ONNA RAIL.

HOW THE HELL'D YOU END UP HERE? *WHERE ARE WE?*

TWO YEARS AGO, RIGHT AFTER YOU LEFT--*AFTER OUR FIGHT--* I FOUND A SMALL BOX.

HAD A NOTE THAT SAID IT WAS FROM YOU. SAID TO PRESS THE BUTTON FOR A RECORDIN'.

SO I PRESSED IT AN' NEXT THING I KNEW I WAS HERE, IN THIS TOWN.

TWO YEARS?

AFTER I LEFT YOU I WENT BACK TO NEAVSIVIA, PICKED UP NICHOLAS...

COULDN'T O' BEEN THREE DAYS BACK...

NICHOLAS! HE'S *ALIVE?!*

YEAH, TOUGH OL' RUSKIE THAT ONE.

HE'S HERE WITH ME... LEAST HE WAS.

SORTA LOST 'IM.

SOMEONE'S PLAYIN' AT SOMETHING, HEATH.

WHATEVER IS GOIN' ON I NEED YOU TO *GET ME HOME!*

I CAN'T STAND THE THOUGHT OF EDEN ON HER OWN ALL THIS TIME...

LOOKS LIKE OUR *NEWEST* RESIDENT IS ON THE MEND.

PARDON THE INTRUSION, NAME'S *THEODORE BARNS*, LOCAL LAW 'ROUND HEAVEN.

SIXTY-FOUR GOD-FEARIN' MEN, WOMEN, AND CHILDREN PUT THEIR TRUST IN ME TO WATCH OVER 'EM.

SO WHEN A NAKED STRANGER HOPPED UP ON DRUGS SHOWS UP I RECKON I SHOULD INQUIRE 'BOUT THE PARTICULARS.

I RECKON SO, SHERIFF.

I'M HEATH, HEATH HUSTON.

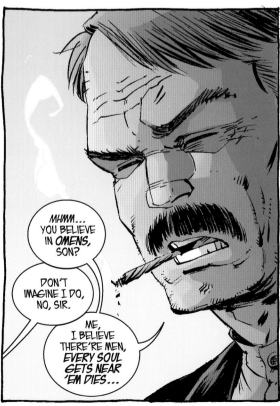

MHMM... YOU BELIEVE IN *OMENS*, SON?

DON'T IMAGINE I DO, NO, SIR.

ME, I BELIEVE THERE'RE MEN, EVERY SOUL GETS NEAR 'EM DIES...

175

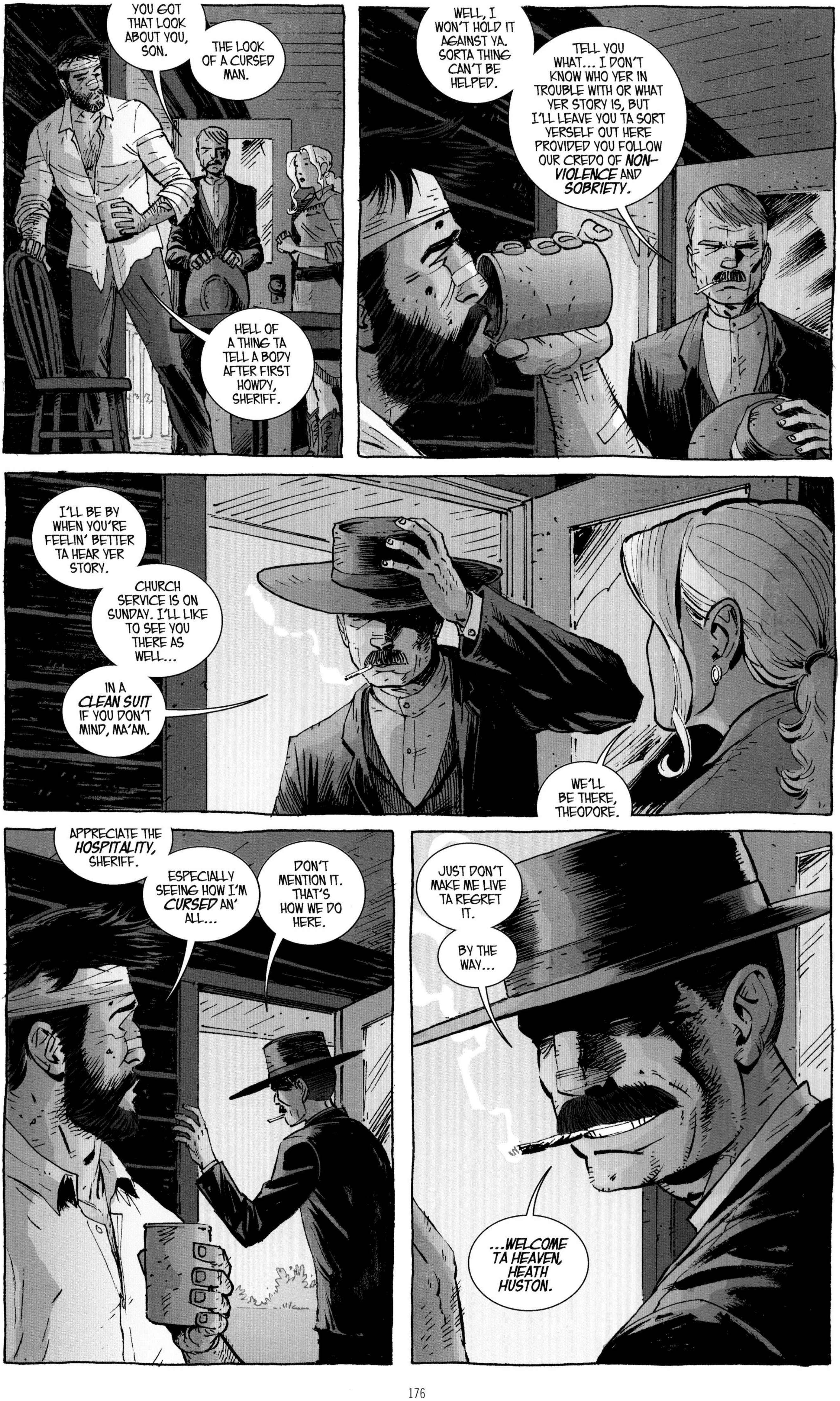
YOU GOT THAT LOOK ABOUT YOU, SON.
THE LOOK OF A CURSED MAN.
HELL OF A THING TA TELL A BODY AFTER FIRST HOWDY, SHERIFF.
WELL, I WON'T HOLD IT AGAINST YA. SORTA THING CAN'T BE HELPED.
TELL YOU WHAT... I DON'T KNOW WHO YER IN TROUBLE WITH OR WHAT YER STORY IS, BUT I'LL LEAVE YOU TA SORT YERSELF OUT HERE PROVIDED YOU FOLLOW OUR CREDO OF NON-VIOLENCE AND SOBRIETY.
I'LL BE BY WHEN YOU'RE FEELIN' BETTER TA HEAR YER STORY.
CHURCH SERVICE IS ON SUNDAY. I'LL LIKE TO SEE YOU THERE AS WELL...
IN A CLEAN SUIT IF YOU DON'T MIND, MA'AM.
WE'LL BE THERE, THEODORE.
APPRECIATE THE HOSPITALITY, SHERIFF.
ESPECIALLY SEEING HOW I'M CURSED AN' ALL...
DON'T MENTION IT. THAT'S HOW WE DO HERE.
JUST DON'T MAKE ME LIVE TA REGRET IT.
BY THE WAY...
...WELCOME TA HEAVEN, HEATH HUSTON.

CHAPTER 3

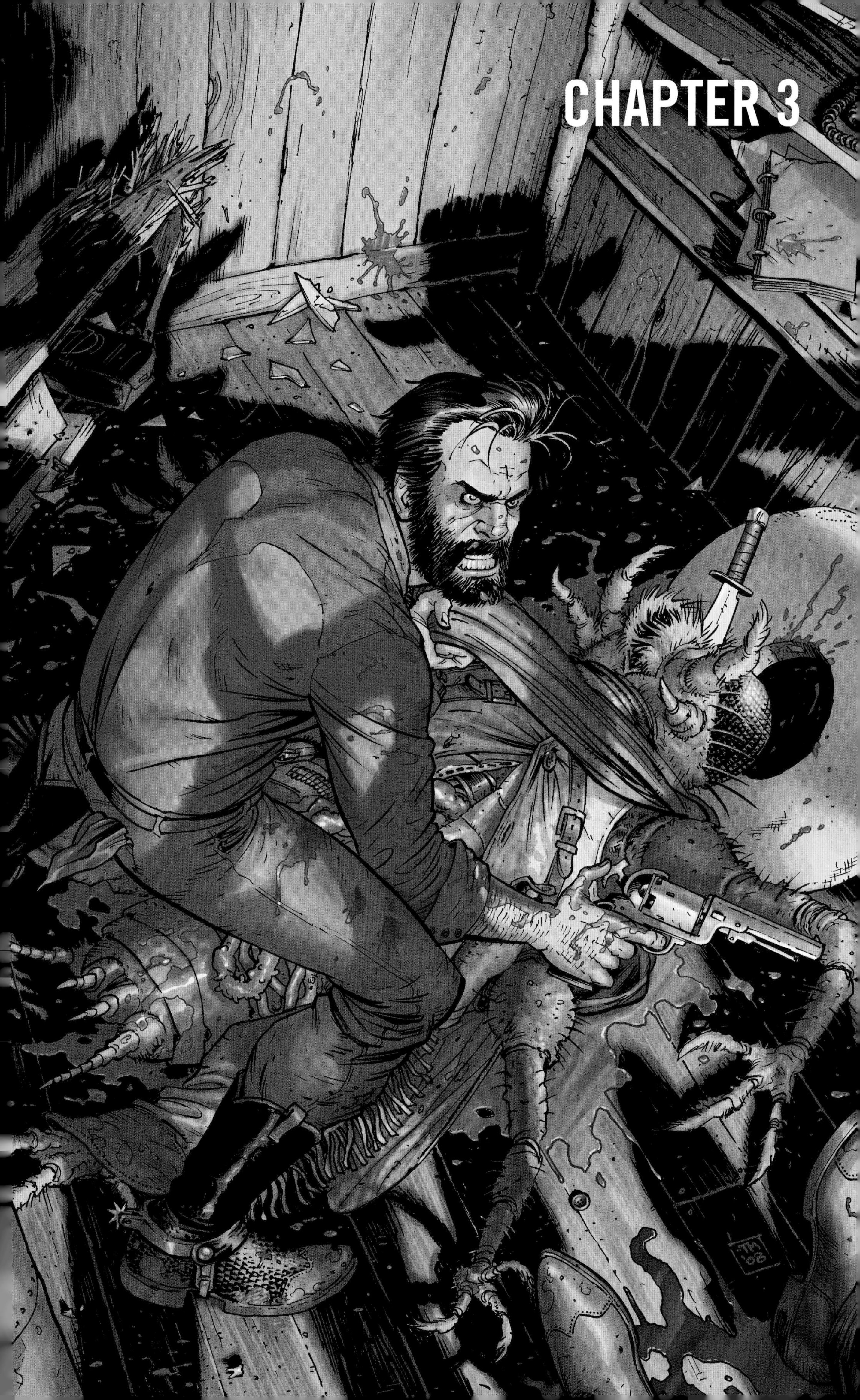

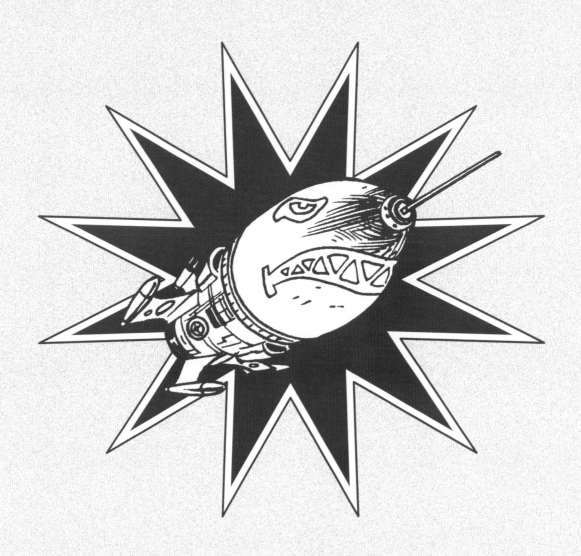

LOT O' STUPID FOLKS IN THIS WORLD, SON.

LOT O' UGLY MINDED IDIOTS MIRED IN BLOODLUST.

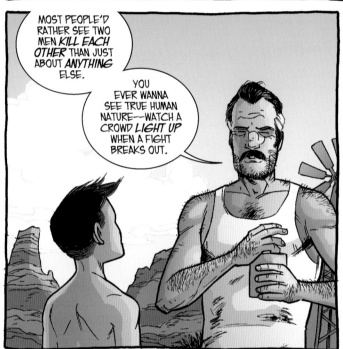

MOST PEOPLE'D RATHER SEE TWO MEN *KILL EACH OTHER* THAN JUST ABOUT *ANYTHING* ELSE.

YOU EVER WANNA SEE TRUE HUMAN NATURE--WATCH A CROWD *LIGHT UP* WHEN A FIGHT BREAKS OUT.

IF YA *NEVER* REMEMBER *ANOTHER* THING YER OLD MAN TAUGHT YA-- *REMEMBER THIS...*

PEOPLE *DON'T WANT* TO SEE OTHER PEOPLE *HAPPY.*

HELL, MOST FOLKS WON'T EVEN LET JOY INTO THEIR *OWN LIVES* MUCH LESS SOMEONE ELSE'S.

DON'T YA *EVER* COUNT ON SOMEONE PUTTIN' YOUR INTERESTS BEFORE THEIR *OWN...*

NOT EVEN YER OLD MAN.

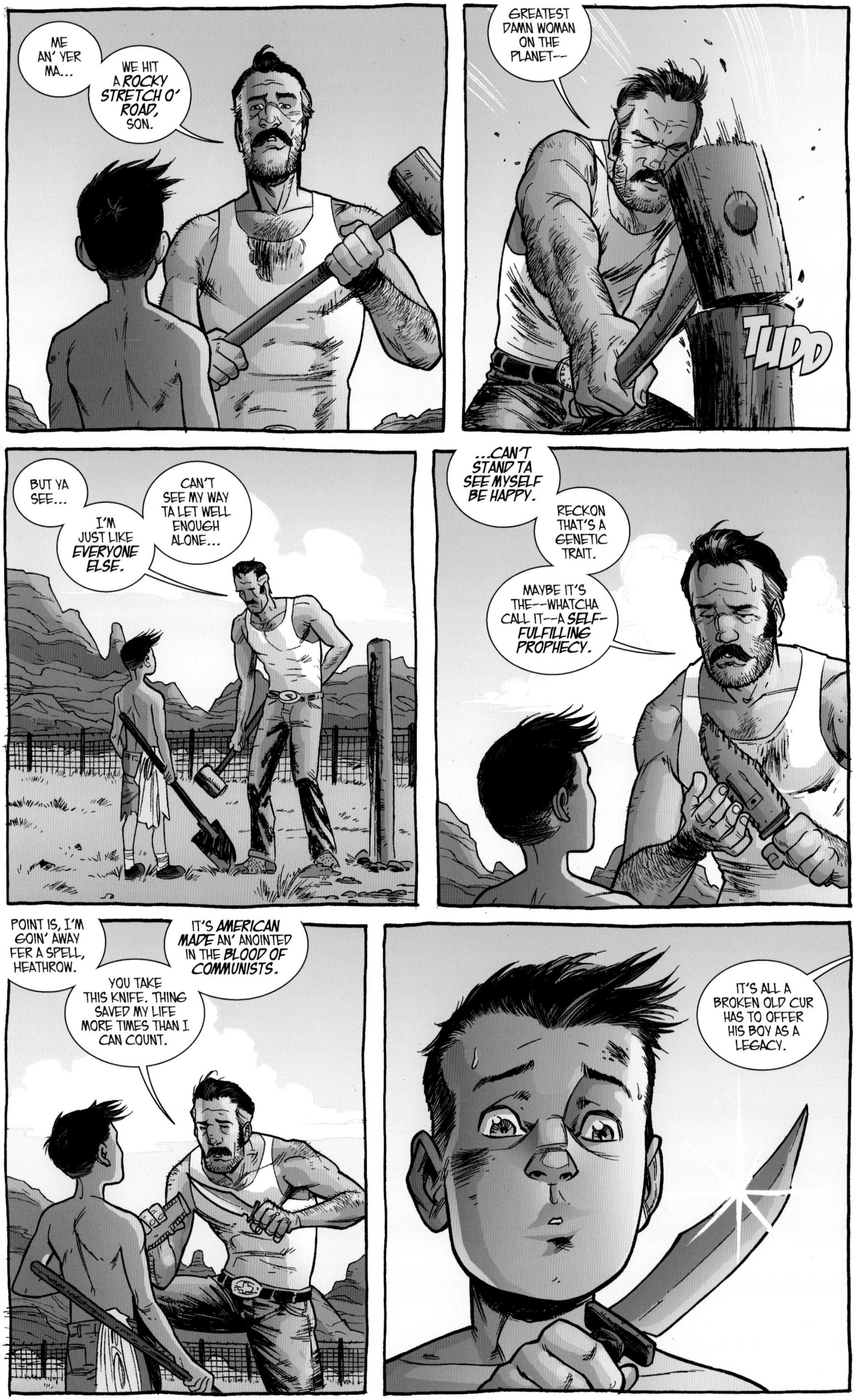
ME AN' YER MA...
WE HIT A ROCKY STRETCH O' ROAD, SON.
GREATEST DAMN WOMAN ON THE PLANET--
TUDD
BUT YA SEE...
I'M JUST LIKE EVERYONE ELSE.
CAN'T SEE MY WAY TA LET WELL ENOUGH ALONE...
...CAN'T STAND TA SEE MYSELF BE HAPPY.
RECKON THAT'S A GENETIC TRAIT.
MAYBE IT'S THE--WHATCHA CALL IT--A SELF-FULFILLING PROPHECY.
POINT IS, I'M GOIN' AWAY FER A SPELL, HEATHROW.
YOU TAKE THIS KNIFE. THING SAVED MY LIFE MORE TIMES THAN I CAN COUNT.
IT'S AMERICAN MADE AN' ANOINTED IN THE BLOOD OF COMMUNISTS.
IT'S ALL A BROKEN OLD CUR HAS TO OFFER HIS BOY AS A LEGACY.

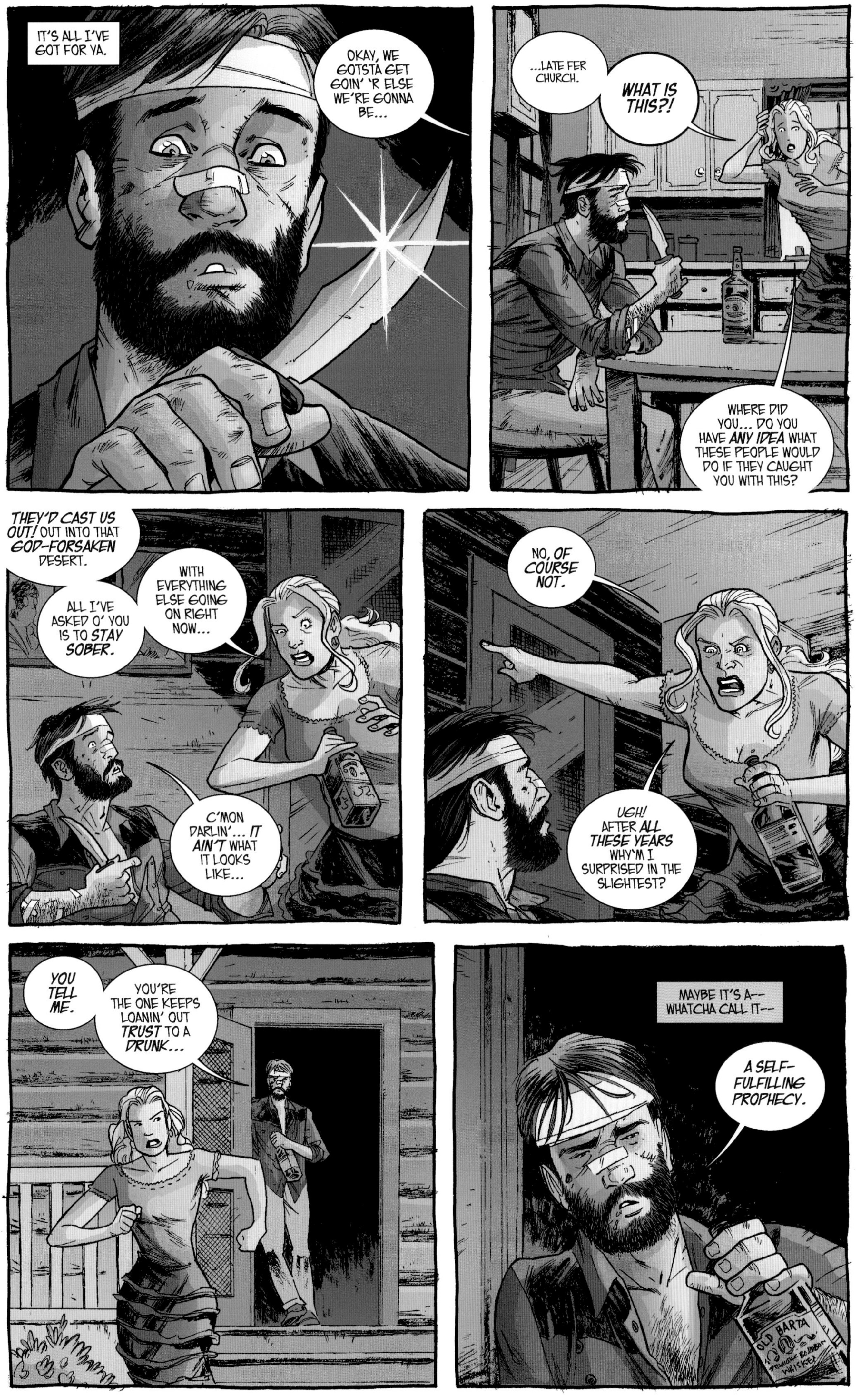
IT'S ALL I'VE GOT FOR YA.
OKAY, WE GOTSTA GET GOIN' 'R ELSE WE'RE GONNA BE...
...LATE FER CHURCH.
WHAT IS THIS?!
WHERE DID YOU... DO YOU HAVE ANY IDEA WHAT THESE PEOPLE WOULD DO IF THEY CAUGHT YOU WITH THIS?
THEY'D CAST US OUT! OUT INTO THAT GOD-FORSAKEN DESERT.
ALL I'VE ASKED O' YOU IS TO STAY SOBER.
WITH EVERYTHING ELSE GOING ON RIGHT NOW...
C'MON DARLIN'... IT AIN'T WHAT IT LOOKS LIKE...
NO, OF COURSE NOT.
UGH! AFTER ALL THESE YEARS WHY'M I SURPRISED IN THE SLIGHTEST?
YOU TELL ME.
YOU'RE THE ONE KEEPS LOANIN' OUT TRUST TO A DRUNK...
MAYBE IT'S A-- WHATCHA CALL IT--
A SELF-FULFILLING PROPHECY.
OLD BARTA

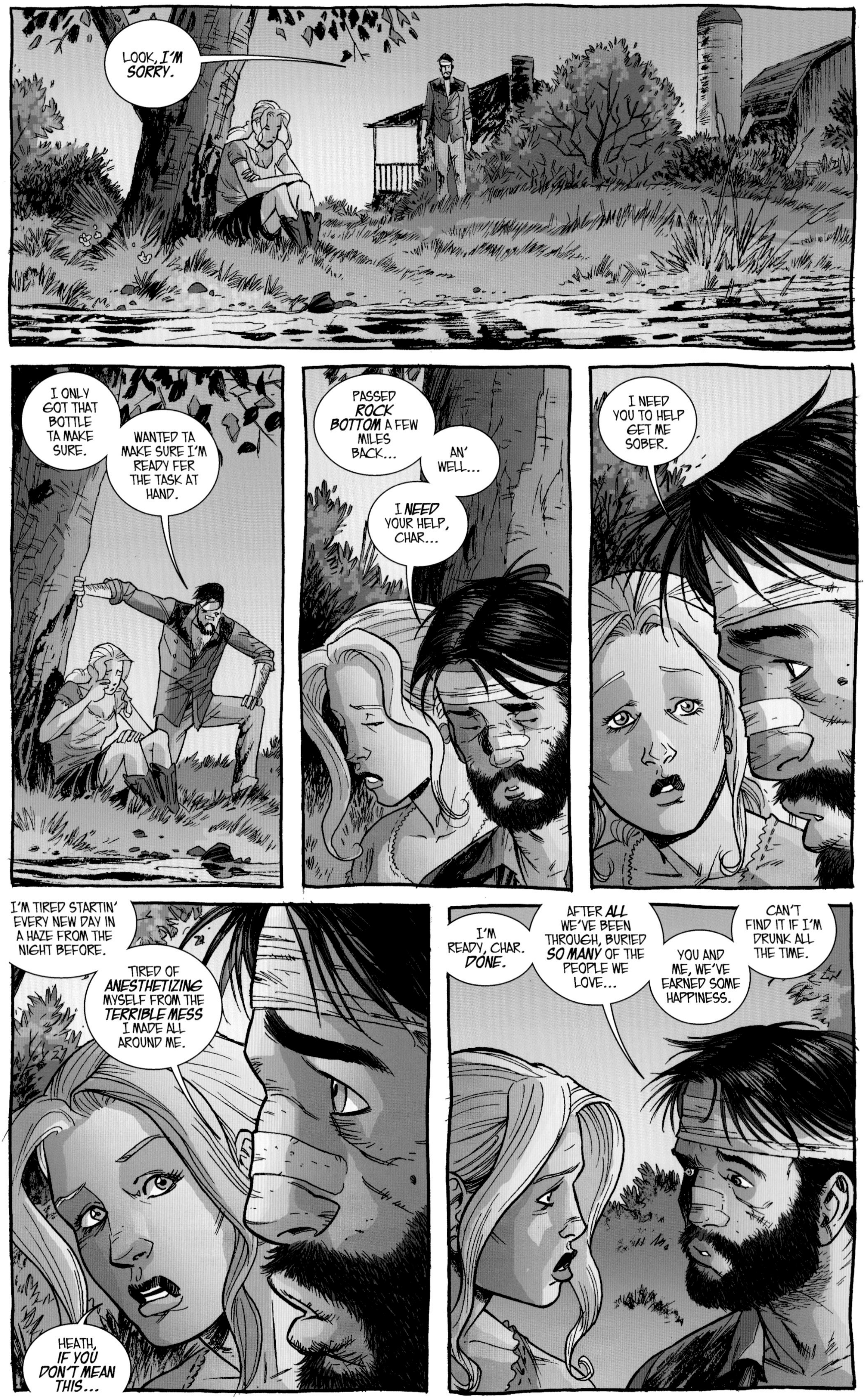
LOOK, I'M SORRY.
I ONLY GOT THAT BOTTLE TA MAKE SURE.
WANTED TA MAKE SURE I'M READY FER THE TASK AT HAND.
PASSED ROCK BOTTOM A FEW MILES BACK...
AN' WELL...
I NEED YOUR HELP, CHAR...
I NEED YOU TO HELP GET ME SOBER.
I'M TIRED STARTIN' EVERY NEW DAY IN A HAZE FROM THE NIGHT BEFORE.
TIRED OF ANESTHETIZING MYSELF FROM THE TERRIBLE MESS I MADE ALL AROUND ME.
HEATH, IF YOU DON'T MEAN THIS...
I'M READY, CHAR. DONE.
AFTER ALL WE'VE BEEN THROUGH, BURIED SO MANY OF THE PEOPLE WE LOVE...
YOU AND ME, WE'VE EARNED SOME HAPPINESS.
CAN'T FIND IT IF I'M DRUNK ALL THE TIME.

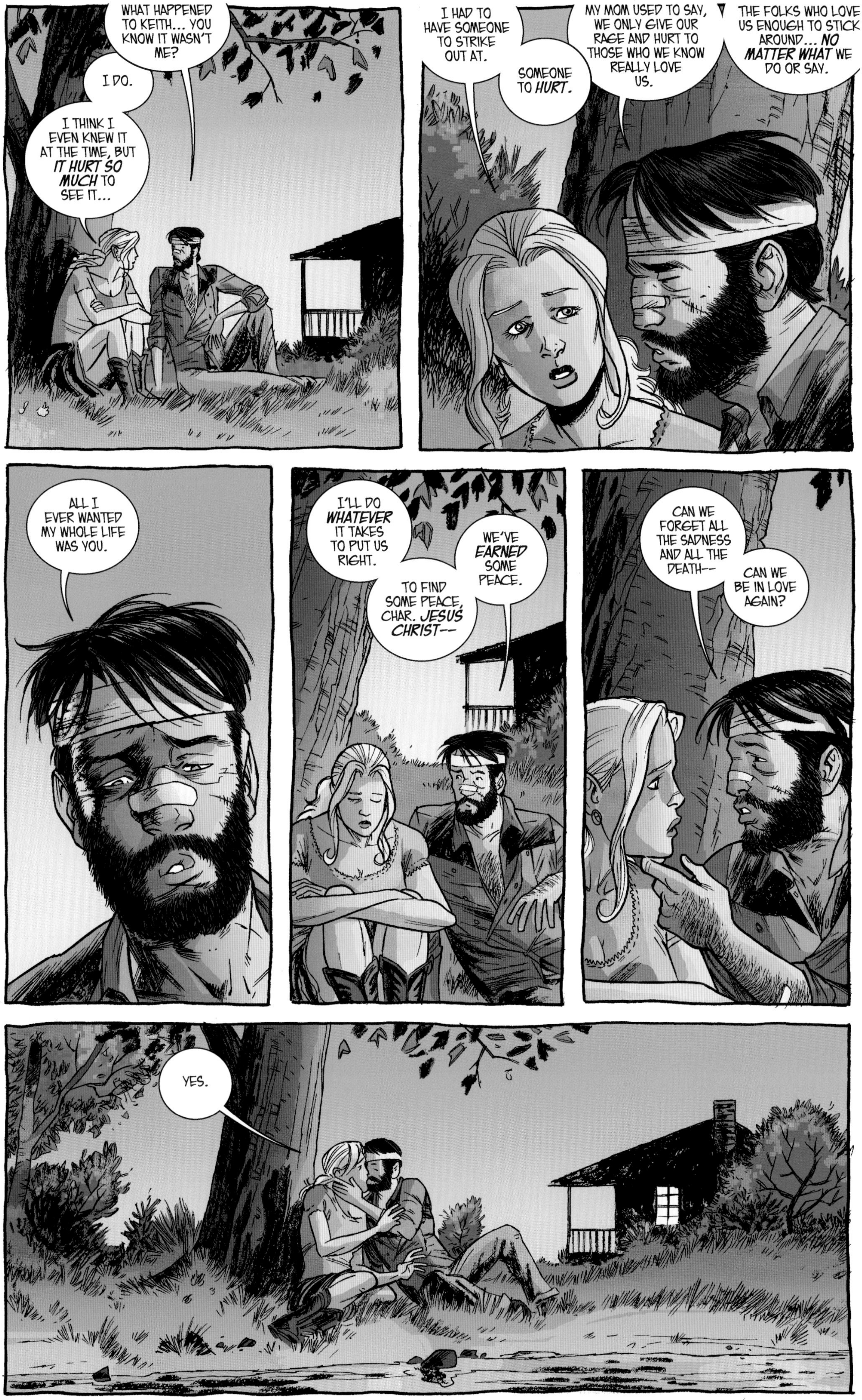
WHAT HAPPENED TO KEITH... YOU KNOW IT WASN'T ME?
I DO.
I THINK I EVEN KNEW IT AT THE TIME, BUT IT HURT SO MUCH TO SEE IT...
I HAD TO HAVE SOMEONE TO STRIKE OUT AT.
SOMEONE TO HURT.
MY MOM USED TO SAY, WE ONLY GIVE OUR RAGE AND HURT TO THOSE WHO WE KNOW REALLY LOVE US.
THE FOLKS WHO LOVE US ENOUGH TO STICK AROUND... NO MATTER WHAT WE DO OR SAY.
ALL I EVER WANTED MY WHOLE LIFE WAS YOU.
I'LL DO WHATEVER IT TAKES TO PUT US RIGHT.
TO FIND SOME PEACE, CHAR. JESUS CHRIST--
WE'VE EARNED SOME PEACE.
CAN WE FORGET ALL THE SADNESS AND ALL THE DEATH--
CAN WE BE IN LOVE AGAIN?
YES.

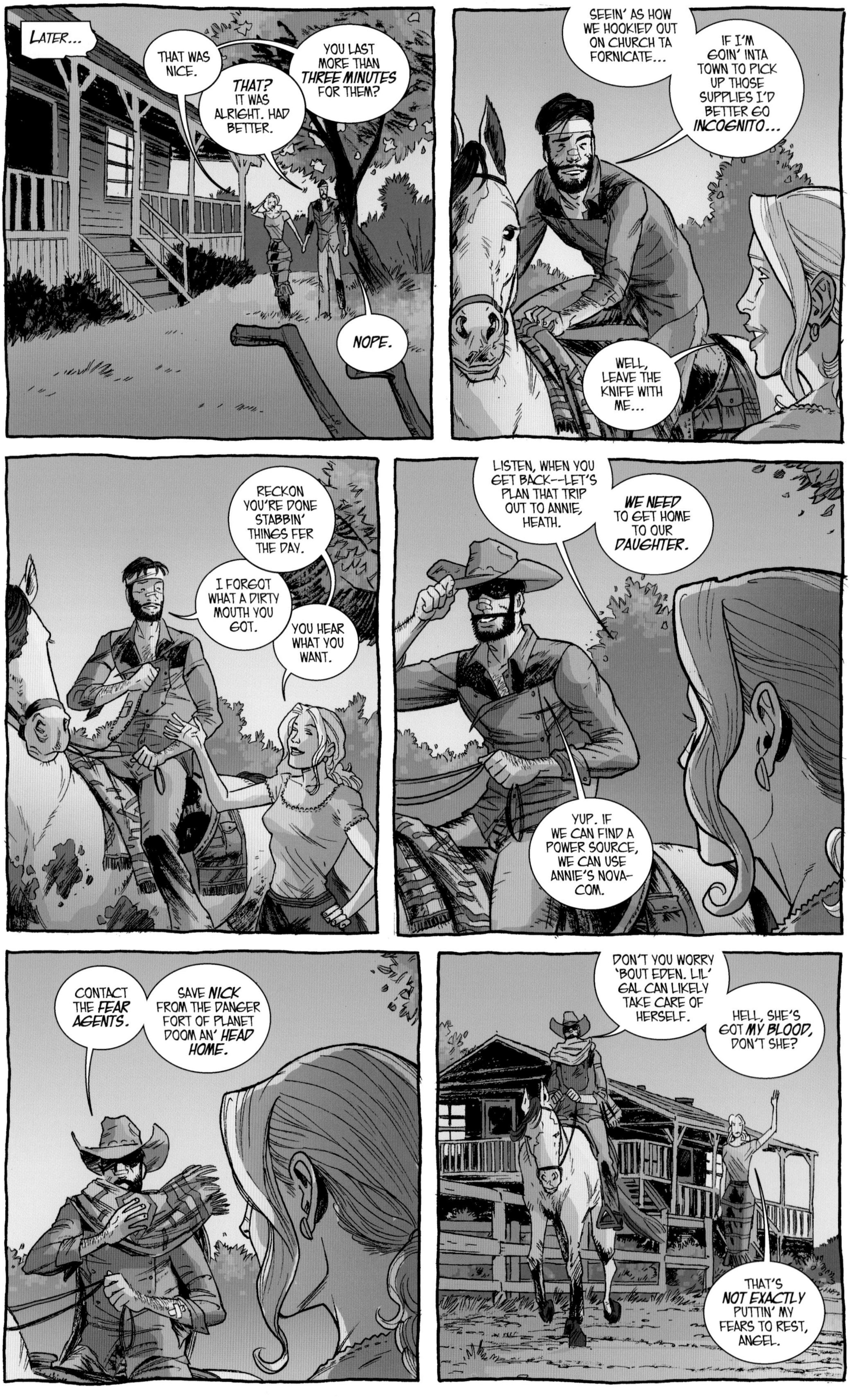
LATER...
THAT WAS NICE.
YOU LAST MORE THAN THREE MINUTES FOR THEM?
THAT? IT WAS ALRIGHT. HAD BETTER.
NOPE.
SEEIN' AS HOW WE HOOKIED OUT ON CHURCH TA FORNICATE...
IF I'M GOIN' INTA TOWN TO PICK UP THOSE SUPPLIES I'D BETTER GO INCOGNITO...
WELL, LEAVE THE KNIFE WITH ME...
RECKON YOU'RE DONE STABBIN' THINGS FER THE DAY.
I FORGOT WHAT A DIRTY MOUTH YOU GOT.
YOU HEAR WHAT YOU WANT.
LISTEN, WHEN YOU GET BACK--LET'S PLAN THAT TRIP OUT TO ANNIE, HEATH.
WE NEED TO GET HOME TO OUR DAUGHTER.
YUP. IF WE CAN FIND A POWER SOURCE, WE CAN USE ANNIE'S NOVA-COM.
CONTACT THE FEAR AGENTS.
SAVE NICK FROM THE DANGER FORT OF PLANET DOOM AN' HEAD HOME.
DON'T YOU WORRY 'BOUT EDEN. LIL' GAL CAN LIKELY TAKE CARE OF HERSELF.
HELL, SHE'S GOT MY BLOOD, DON'T SHE?
THAT'S NOT EXACTLY PUTTIN' MY FEARS TO REST, ANGEL.

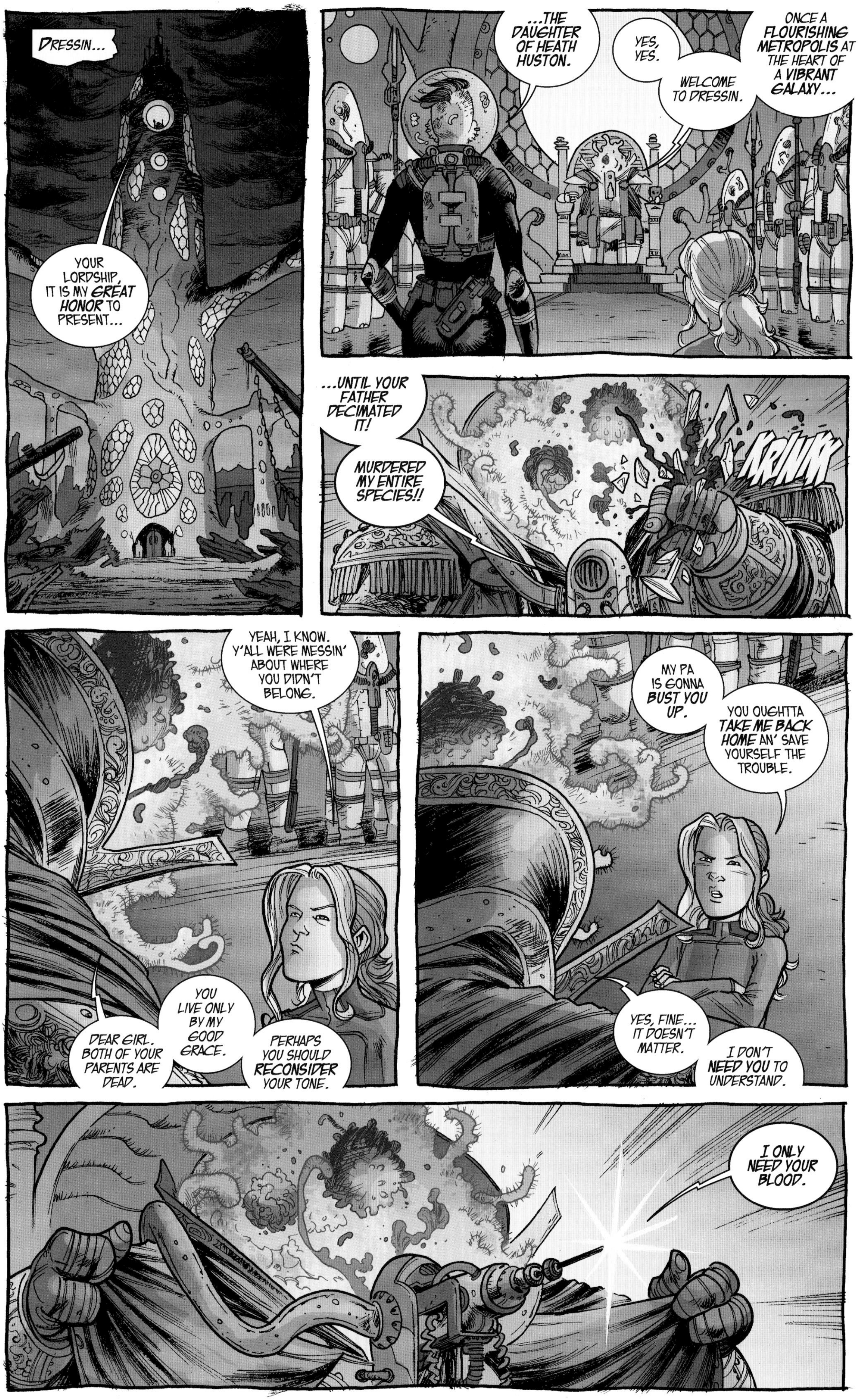
DRESSIN...
YOUR LORDSHIP, IT IS MY GREAT HONOR TO PRESENT...
...THE DAUGHTER OF HEATH HUSTON.
YES, YES.
WELCOME TO DRESSIN.
ONCE A FLOURISHING METROPOLIS AT THE HEART OF A VIBRANT GALAXY...
...UNTIL YOUR FATHER DECIMATED IT!
MURDERED MY ENTIRE SPECIES!!
KRINK
YEAH, I KNOW. Y'ALL WERE MESSIN' ABOUT WHERE YOU DIDN'T BELONG.
DEAR GIRL. BOTH OF YOUR PARENTS ARE DEAD.
YOU LIVE ONLY BY MY GOOD GRACE.
PERHAPS YOU SHOULD RECONSIDER YOUR TONE.
MY PA IS GONNA BUST YOU UP.
YOU OUGHTTA TAKE ME BACK HOME AN' SAVE YOURSELF THE TROUBLE.
YES, FINE... IT DOESN'T MATTER.
I DON'T NEED YOU TO UNDERSTAND.
I ONLY NEED YOUR BLOOD.

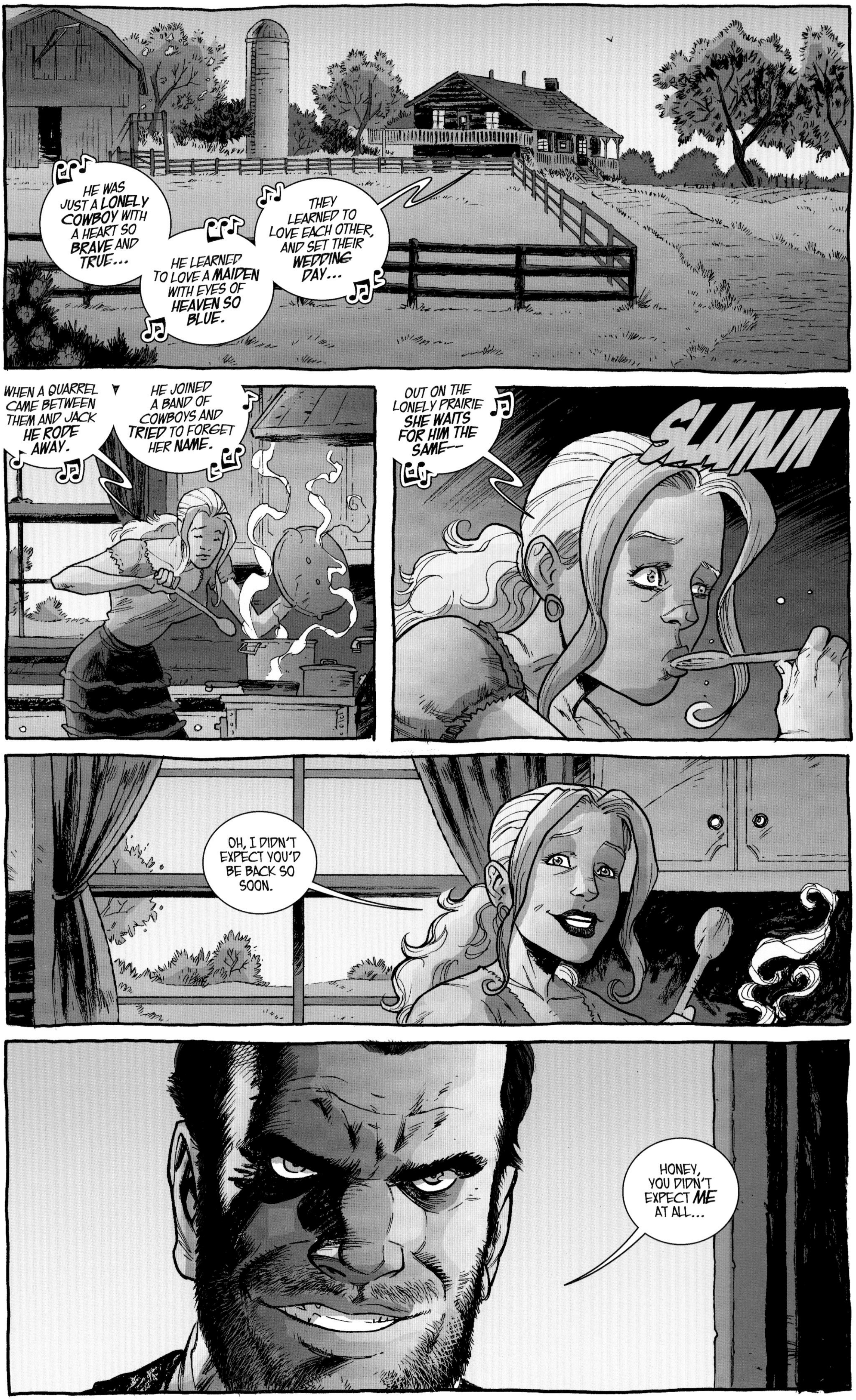
HE WAS JUST A LONELY COWBOY WITH A HEART SO BRAVE AND TRUE...
HE LEARNED TO LOVE A MAIDEN WITH EYES OF HEAVEN SO BLUE.
THEY LEARNED TO LOVE EACH OTHER, AND SET THEIR WEDDING DAY...
WHEN A QUARREL CAME BETWEEN THEM AND JACK HE RODE AWAY.
HE JOINED A BAND OF COWBOYS AND TRIED TO FORGET HER NAME.
OUT ON THE LONELY PRAIRIE SHE WAITS FOR HIM THE SAME--
SLAMM
OH, I DIDN'T EXPECT YOU'D BE BACK SO SOON.
HONEY, YOU DIDN'T EXPECT ME AT ALL...

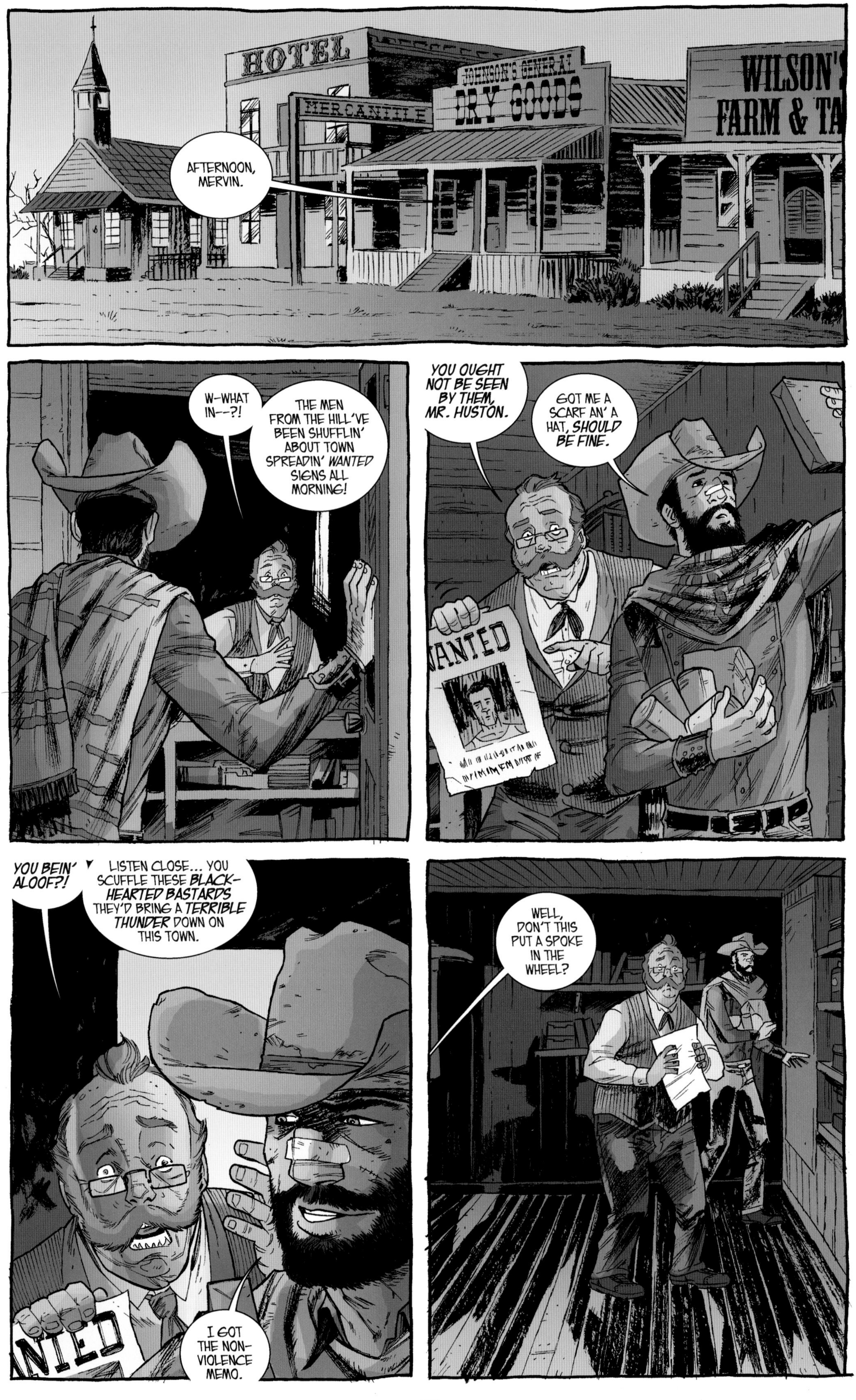
HOTEL
MERCANTILE
JOHNSON'S GENERAL
DRY GOODS
AFTERNOON, MERVIN.
W-WHAT IN--?!
THE MEN FROM THE HILL'VE BEEN SHUFFLIN' ABOUT TOWN SPREADIN' WANTED SIGNS ALL MORNING!
YOU OUGHT NOT BE SEEN BY THEM, MR. HUSTON.
GOT ME A SCARF AN' A HAT, SHOULD BE FINE.
WANTED
YOU BEIN' ALOOF?!
LISTEN CLOSE... YOU SCUFFLE THESE BLACK-HEARTED BASTARDS THEY'D BRING A TERRIBLE THUNDER DOWN ON THIS TOWN.
I GOT THE NON-VIOLENCE MEMO.
WELL, DON'T THIS PUT A SPOKE IN THE WHEEL?

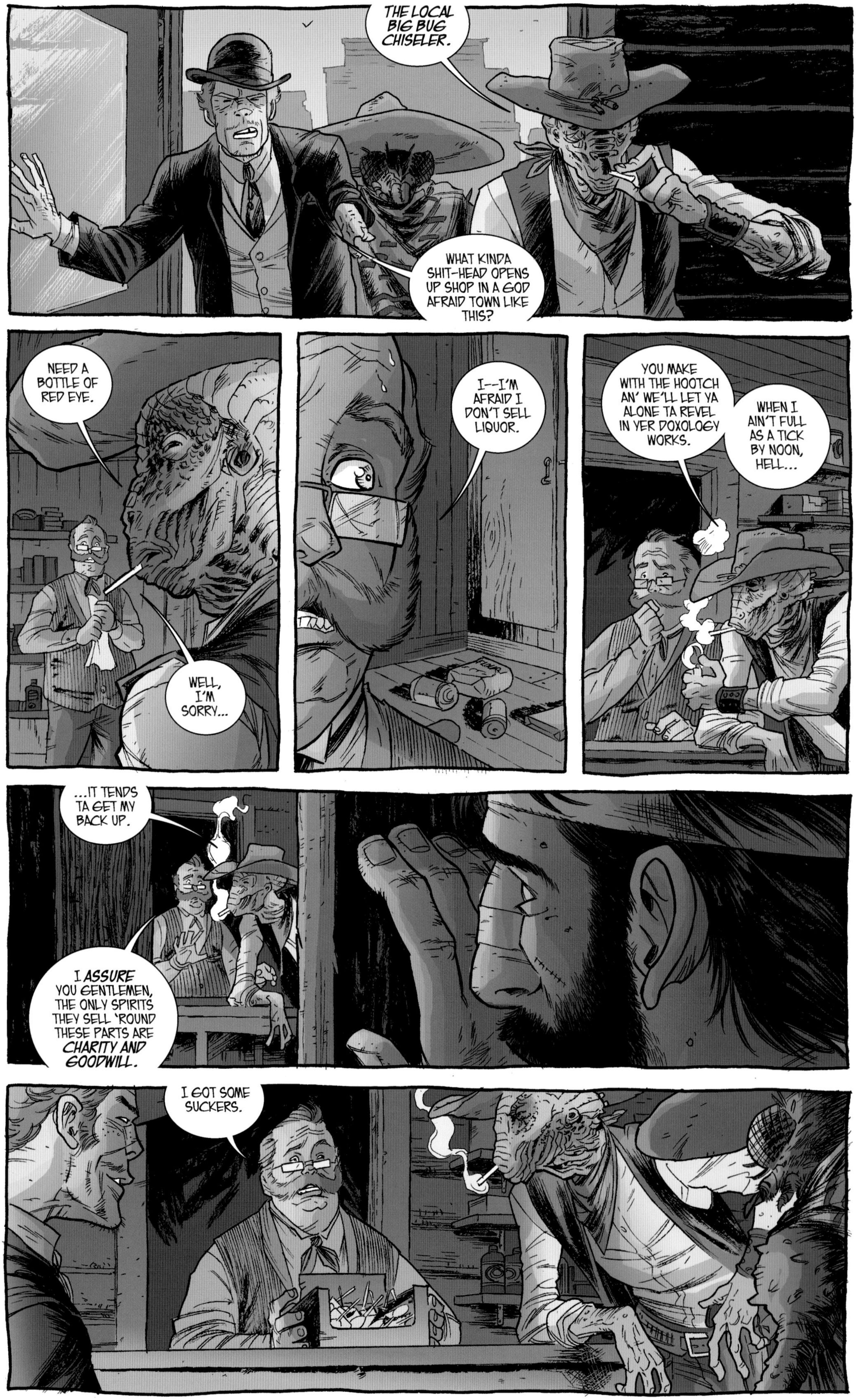
THE LOCAL BIG BUG CHISELER.
WHAT KINDA SHIT-HEAD OPENS UP SHOP IN A GOD AFRAID TOWN LIKE THIS?
NEED A BOTTLE OF RED EYE.
WELL, I'M SORRY...
I--I'M AFRAID I DON'T SELL LIQUOR.
YOU MAKE WITH THE HOOTCH AN' WE'LL LET YA ALONE TA REVEL IN YER DOXOLOGY WORKS.
WHEN I AIN'T FULL AS A TICK BY NOON, HELL...
...IT TENDS TA GET MY BACK UP.
I ASSURE YOU GENTLEMEN, THE ONLY SPIRITS THEY SELL 'ROUND THESE PARTS ARE CHARITY AND GOODWILL.
I GOT SOME SUCKERS.

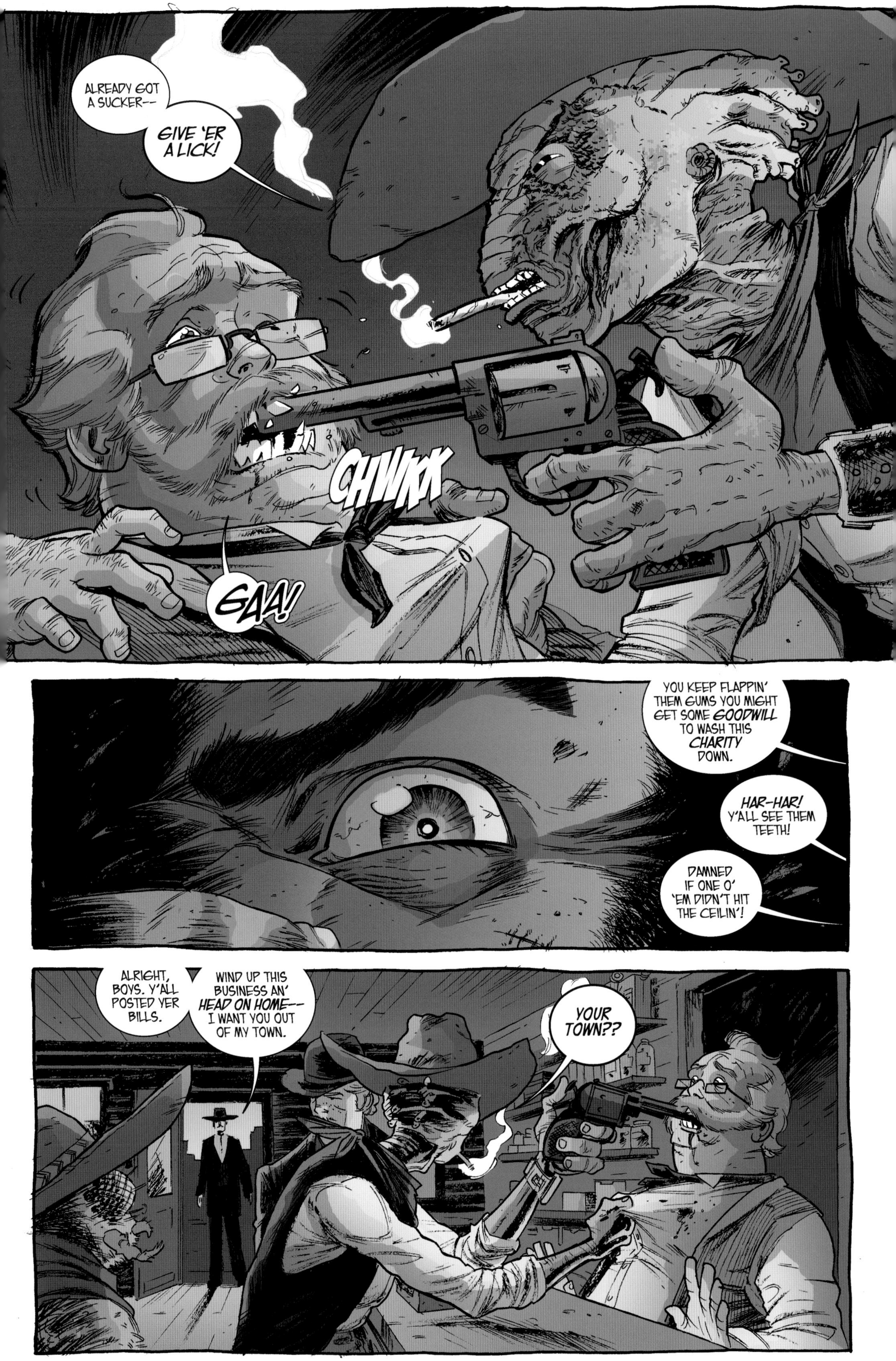
ALREADY GOT A SUCKER--
GIVE 'ER A LICK!
CHWKK
GAA!
YOU KEEP FLAPPIN' THEM GUMS YOU MIGHT GET SOME GOODWILL TO WASH THIS CHARITY DOWN.
HAR-HAR! Y'ALL SEE THEM TEETH!
DAMNED IF ONE O' 'EM DIDN'T HIT THE CEILIN'!
ALRIGHT, BOYS. Y'ALL POSTED YER BILLS.
WIND UP THIS BUSINESS AN' HEAD ON HOME-- I WANT YOU OUT OF MY TOWN.
YOUR TOWN??

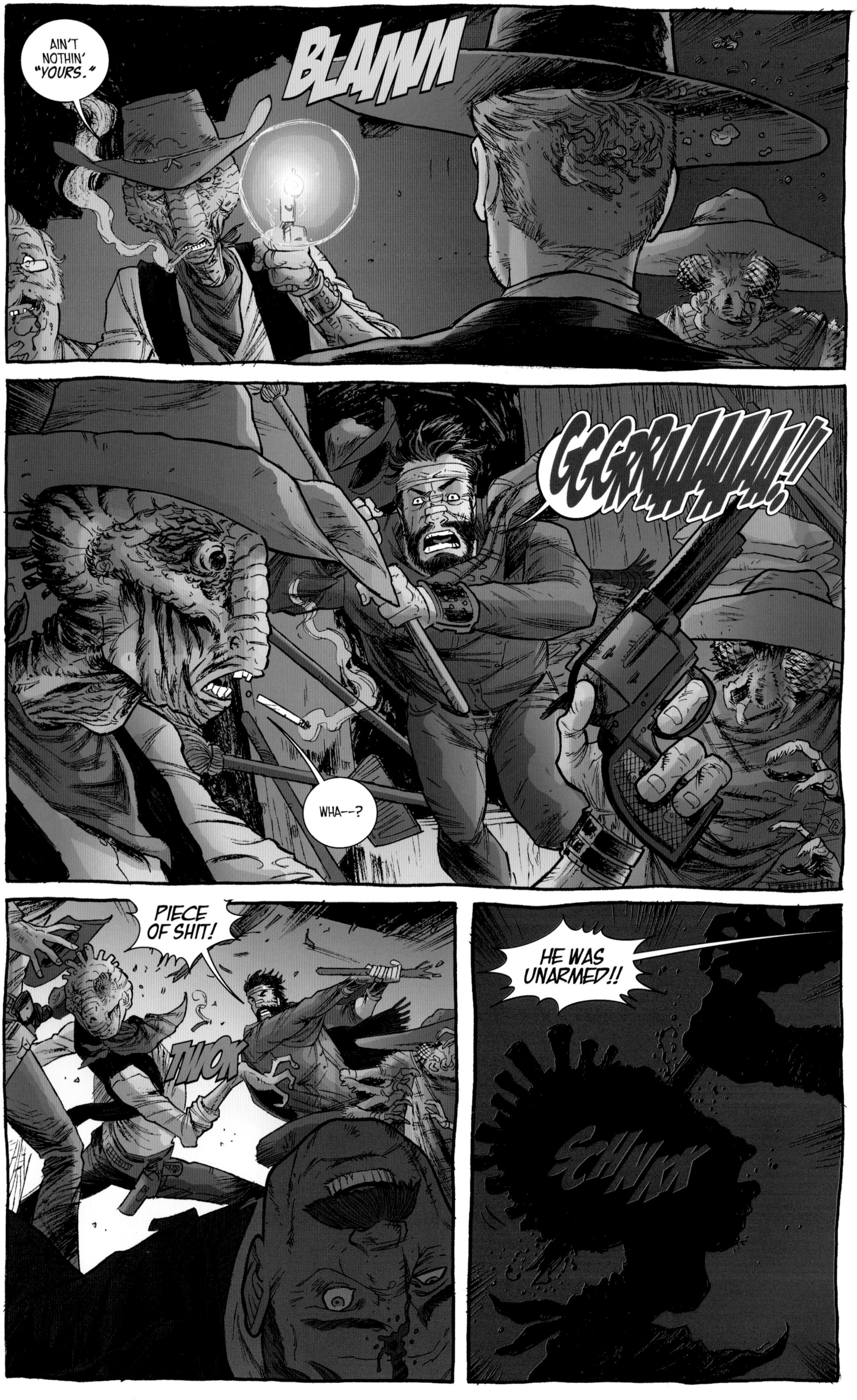
AIN'T NOTHIN' "YOURS."
BLAMM
GGGRRAAAAAAA!!
WHA--?
PIECE OF SHIT!
THOK
HE WAS UNARMED!!
SCHNKK

BLAM!

GHA!

OOF--!

KRSH!

"HE WAS UNARMED-- HE WAS UNARMED--!"

WHERE'S THAT LOUD MOUTH NOW, BOY?!

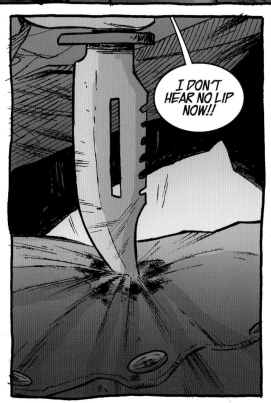

I DON'T HEAR NO LIP NOW!!

LISTEN CLOSER.

YYERAAGH!!

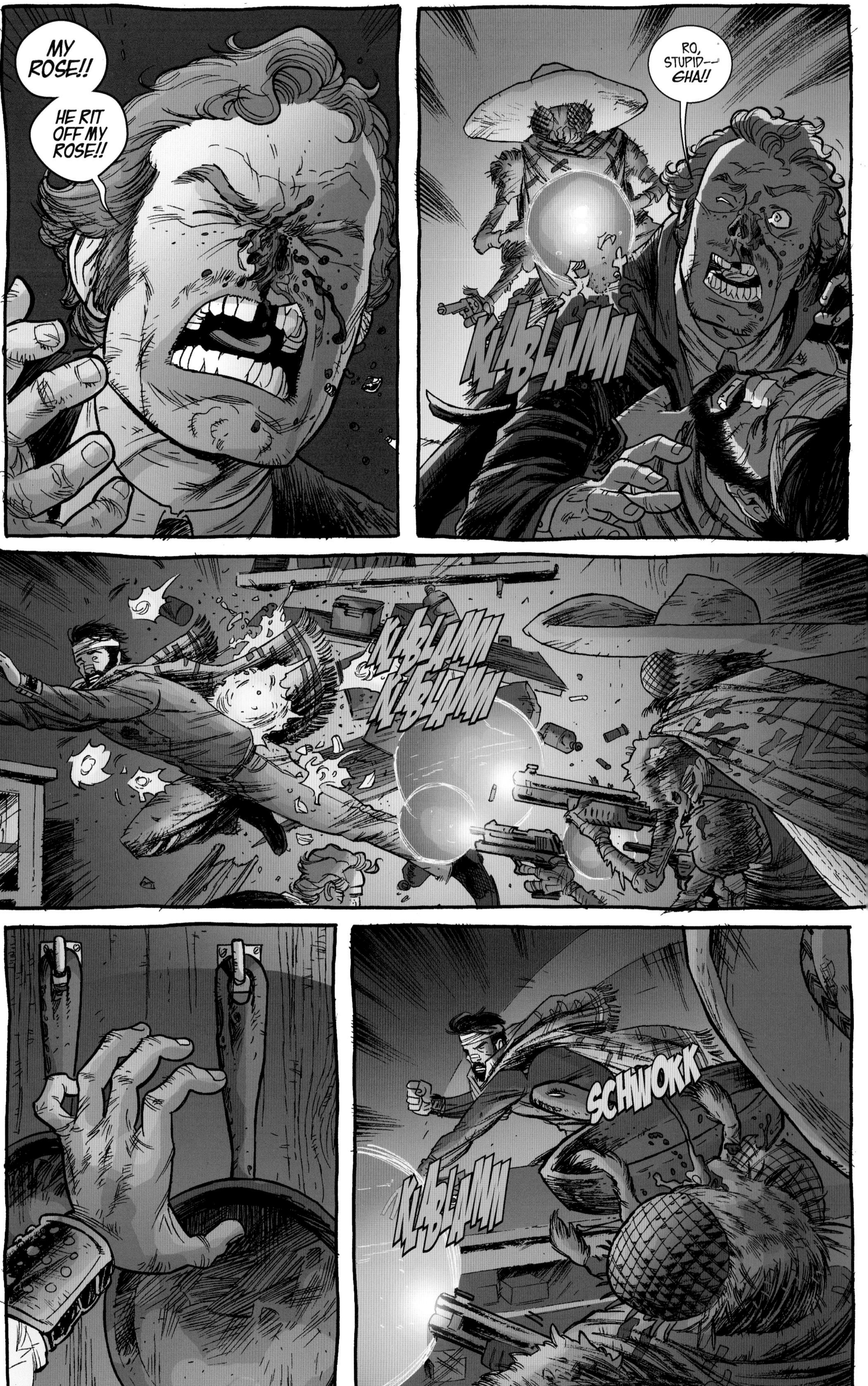
MY ROSE!!
HE RIT OFF MY ROSE!!
RO, STUPID-- GHA!!
KABLAMM
KABLAMM
KABLAMM
SCHWOKK
KABLAMM

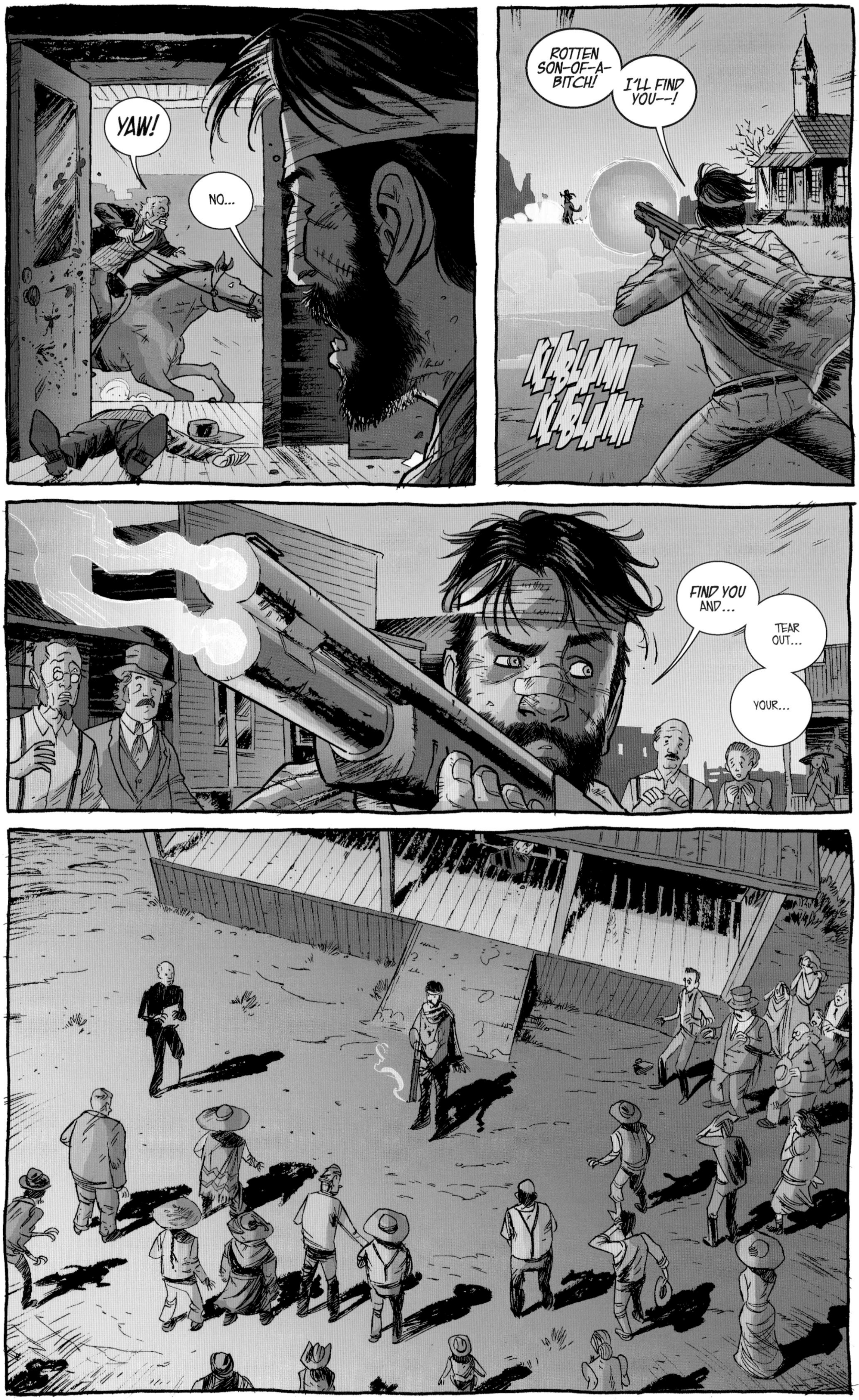
YAW!
NO...
ROTTEN SON-OF-A-BITCH!
I'LL FIND YOU--!
KABLAMM KABLAMM
FIND YOU AND...
TEAR OUT...
YOUR...

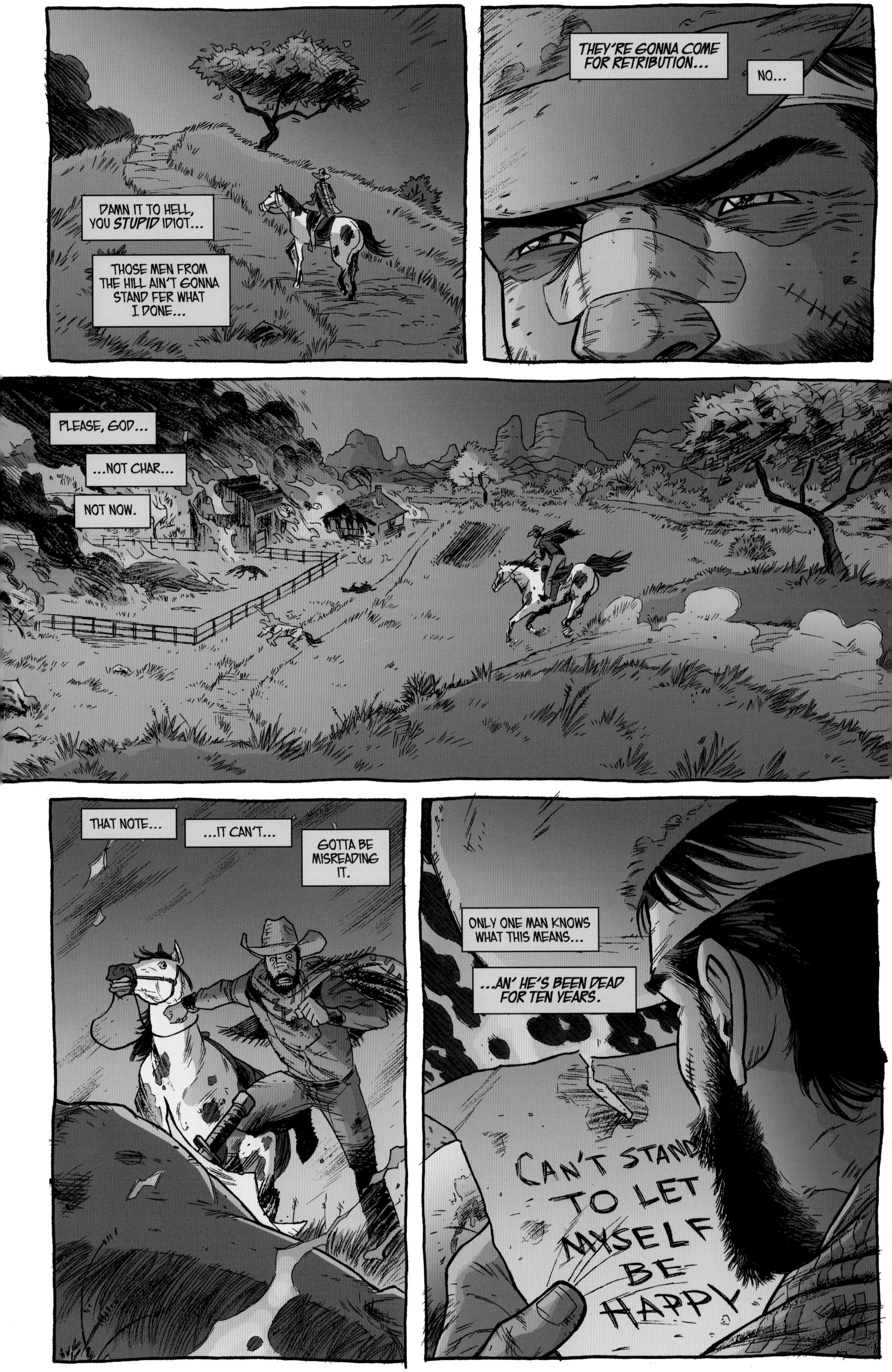
DAMN IT TO HELL, YOU STUPID IDIOT...
THOSE MEN FROM THE HILL AIN'T GONNA STAND FER WHAT I DONE...
THEY'RE GONNA COME FOR RETRIBUTION...
NO...
PLEASE, GOD...
...NOT CHAR...
NOT NOW.
THAT NOTE...
...IT CAN'T...
GOTTA BE MISREADING IT.
ONLY ONE MAN KNOWS WHAT THIS MEANS...
...AN' HE'S BEEN DEAD FOR TEN YEARS.
CAN'T STAND TO LET MYSELF BE HAPPY

CHAPTER 4

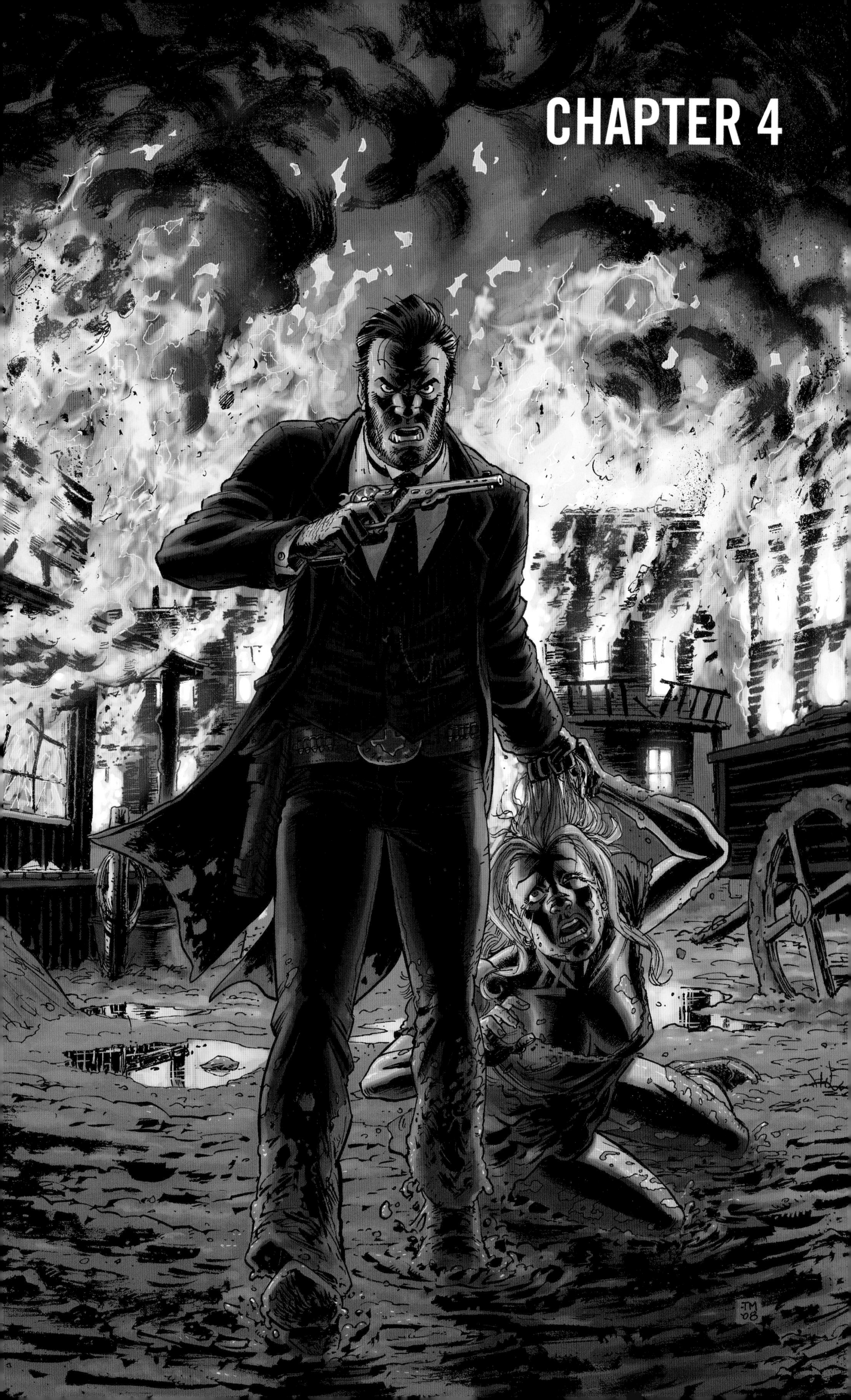

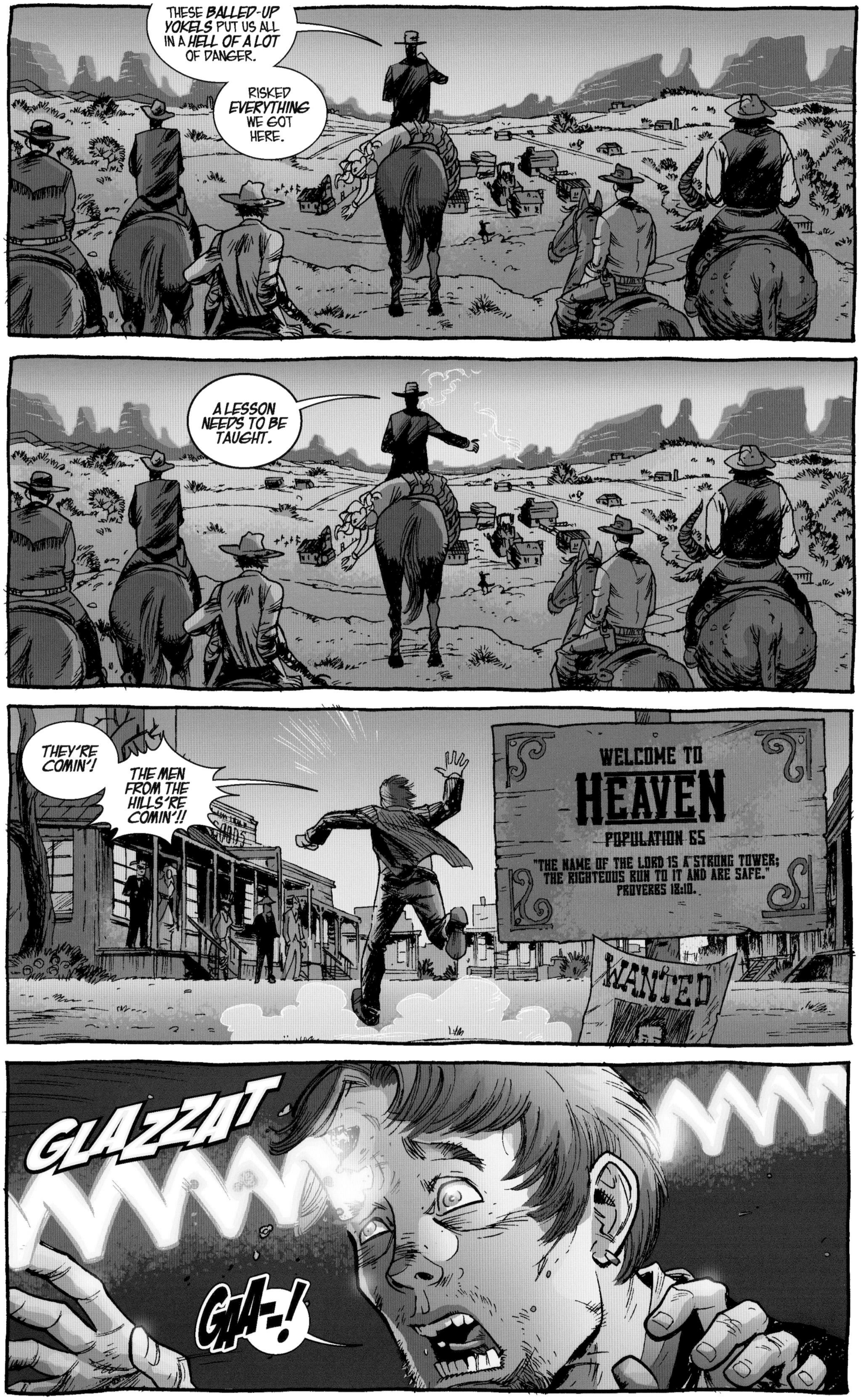

THESE BALLED-UP YOKELS PUT US ALL IN A HELL OF A LOT OF DANGER.
RISKED EVERYTHING WE GOT HERE.
A LESSON NEEDS TO BE TAUGHT.
THEY'RE COMIN'!
THE MEN FROM THE HILLS'RE COMIN'!!
WELCOME TO
HEAVEN
POPULATION 65
"THE NAME OF THE LORD IS A STRONG TOWER; THE RIGHTEOUS RUN TO IT AND ARE SAFE."
PROVERBS 18:10.
WANTED
GLAZZAT
GAA-!

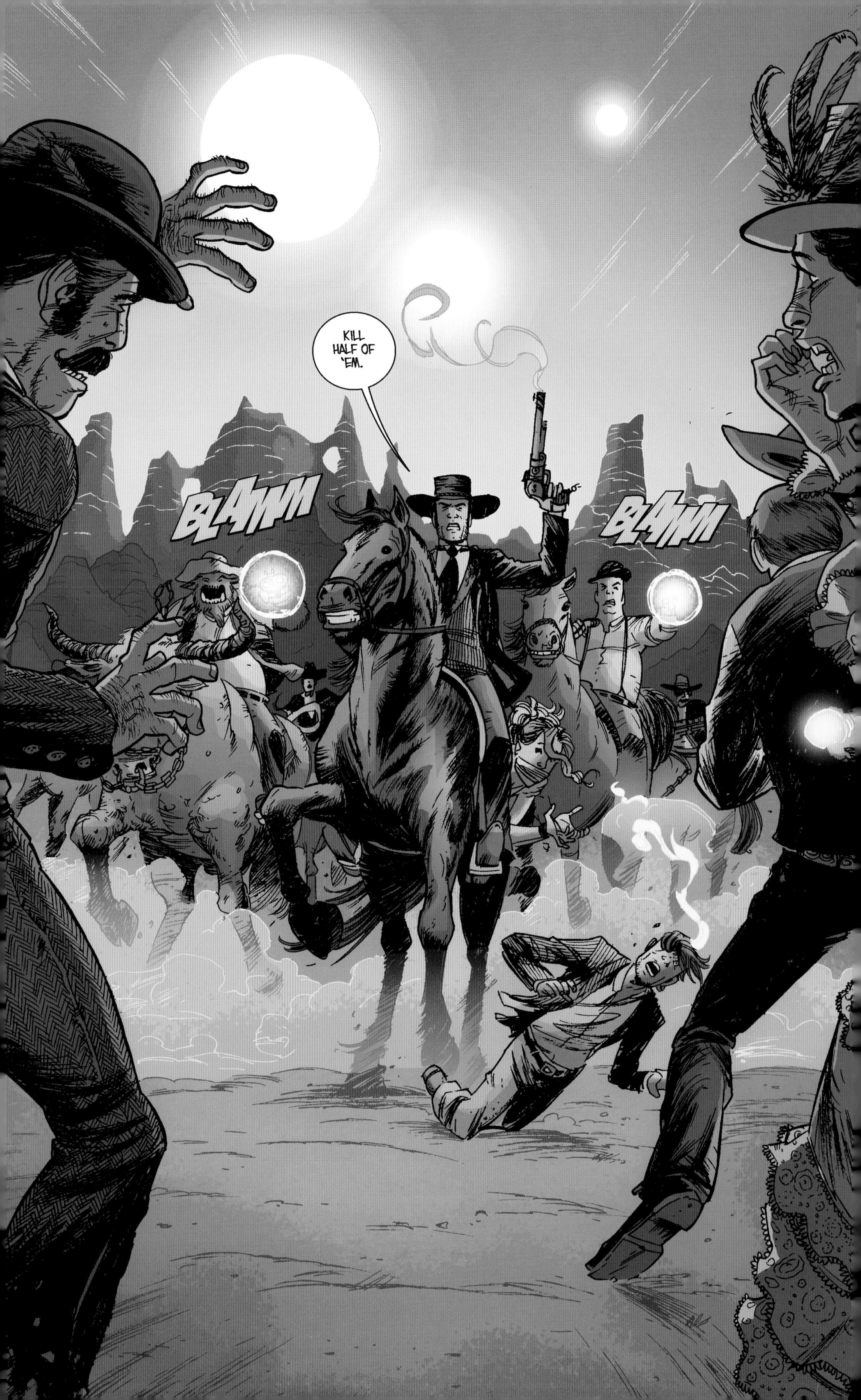
BLAMM
KILL HALF OF 'EM.
BLAMM

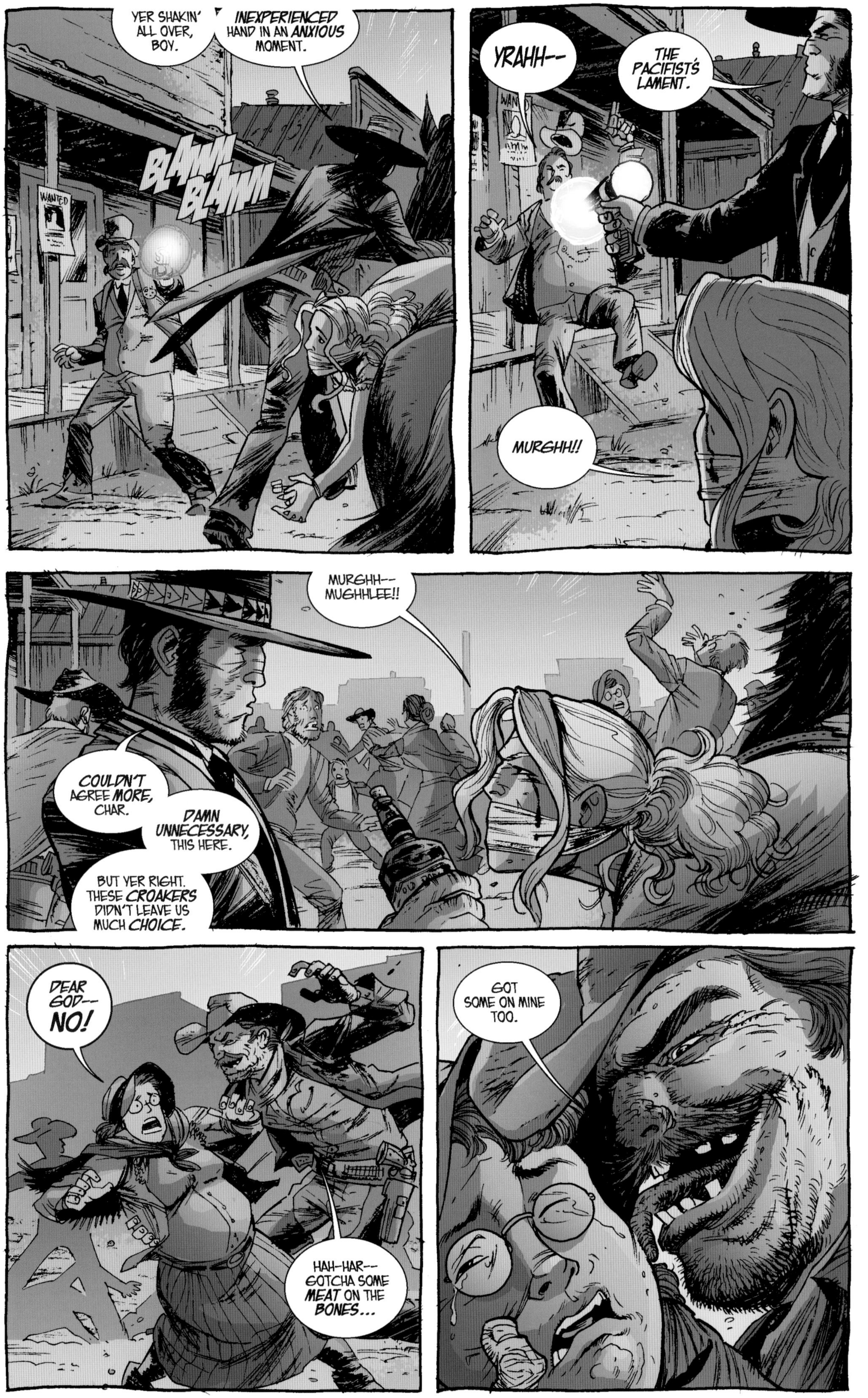
YER SHAKIN' ALL OVER, BOY.
INEXPERIENCED HAND IN AN ANXIOUS MOMENT.
BLAMM BLAMM
WANTED
YRAHH--
THE PACIFIST'S LAMENT.
MURGHH!!
MURGHH-- MUGHHLEE!!
COULDN'T AGREE MORE, CHAR.
DAMN UNNECESSARY, THIS HERE.
BUT YER RIGHT. THESE CROAKERS DIDN'T LEAVE US MUCH CHOICE.
DEAR GOD-- NO!
HAH-HAR-- GOTCHA SOME MEAT ON THE BONES...
GOT SOME ON MINE TOO.

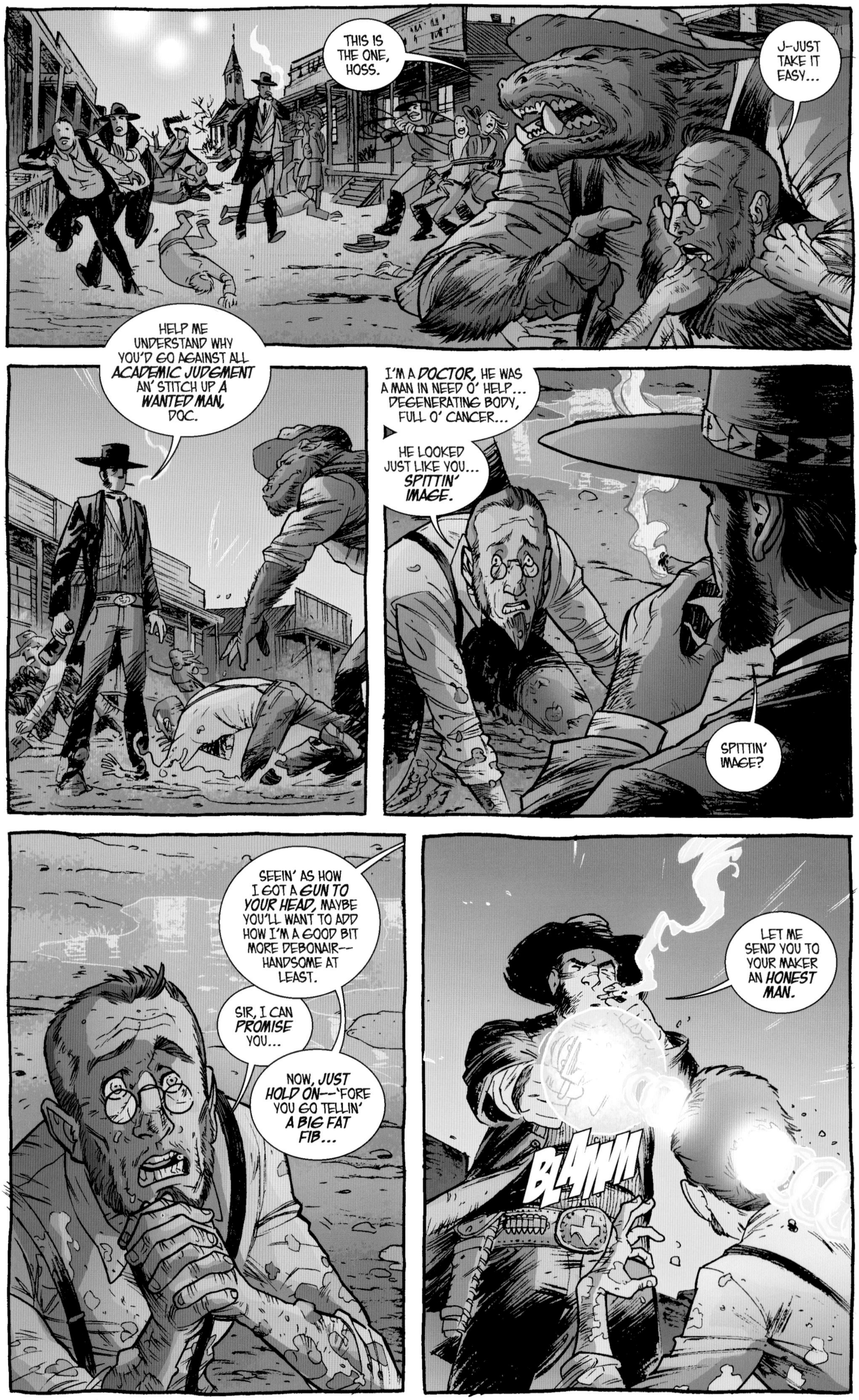
THIS IS THE ONE, HOSS.
J-JUST TAKE IT EASY...
HELP ME UNDERSTAND WHY YOU'D GO AGAINST ALL ACADEMIC JUDGMENT AN' STITCH UP A WANTED MAN, DOC.
I'M A DOCTOR, HE WAS A MAN IN NEED O' HELP... DEGENERATING BODY, FULL O' CANCER...
HE LOOKED JUST LIKE YOU... SPITTIN' IMAGE.
SPITTIN' IMAGE?
SEEIN' AS HOW I GOT A GUN TO YOUR HEAD, MAYBE YOU'LL WANT TO ADD HOW I'M A GOOD BIT MORE DEBONAIR-- HANDSOME AT LEAST.
SIR, I CAN PROMISE YOU...
NOW, JUST HOLD ON--'FORE YOU GO TELLIN' A BIG FAT FIB...
LET ME SEND YOU TO YOUR MAKER AN HONEST MAN.
BLAMM

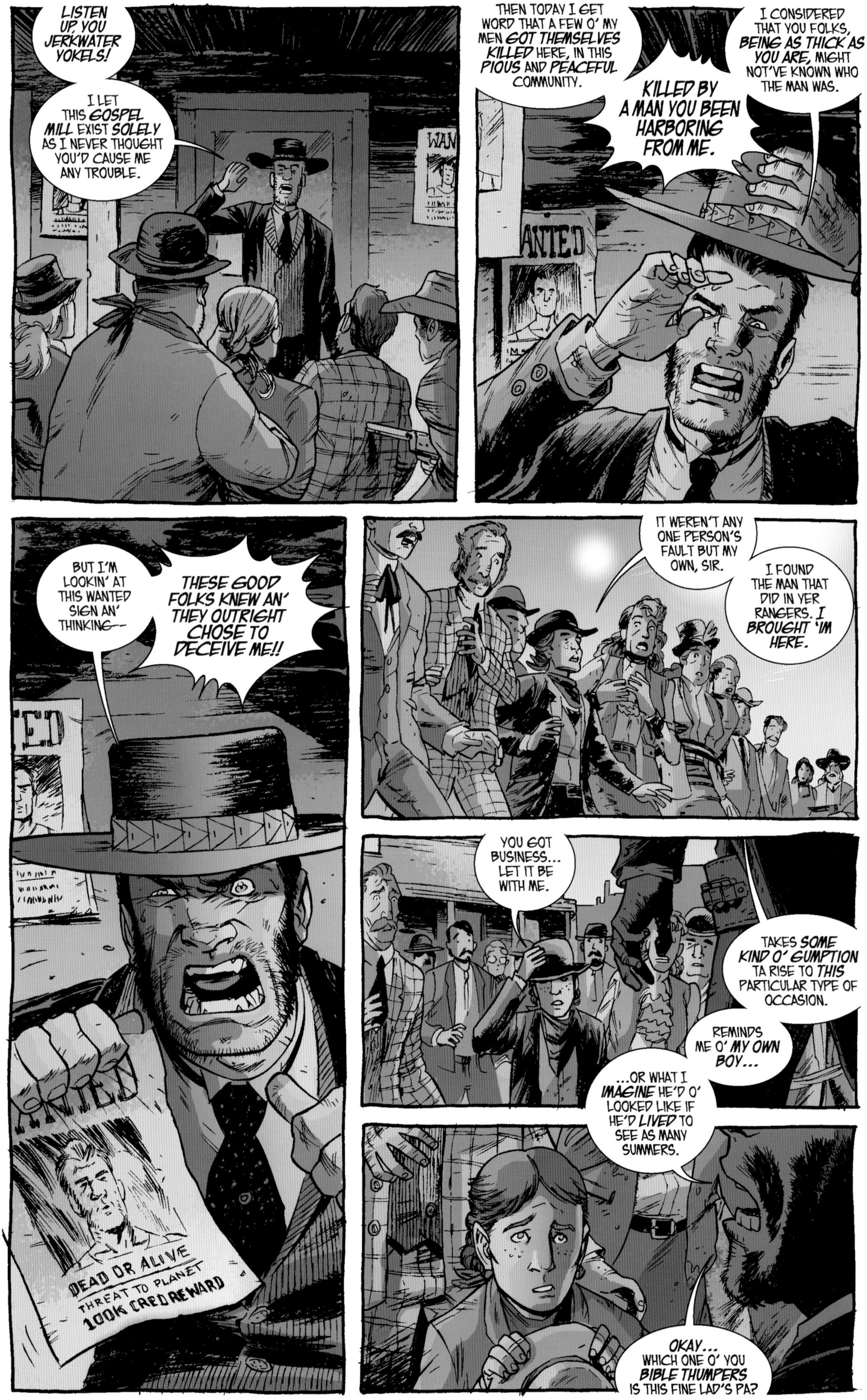

LISTEN UP YOU JERKWATER YOKELS!
I LET THIS GOSPEL MILL EXIST SOLELY AS I NEVER THOUGHT YOU'D CAUSE ME ANY TROUBLE.
THEN TODAY I GET WORD THAT A FEW O' MY MEN GOT THEMSELVES KILLED HERE, IN THIS PIOUS AND PEACEFUL COMMUNITY.
KILLED BY A MAN YOU BEEN HARBORING FROM ME.
I CONSIDERED THAT YOU FOLKS, BEING AS THICK AS YOU ARE, MIGHT NOT'VE KNOWN WHO THE MAN WAS.
WAN
ANTED
BUT I'M LOOKIN' AT THIS WANTED SIGN AN' THINKING--
THESE GOOD FOLKS KNEW AN' THEY OUTRIGHT CHOSE TO DECEIVE ME!!
DEAD OR ALIVE
THREAT TO PLANET
100K CRED REWARD
IT WEREN'T ANY ONE PERSON'S FAULT BUT MY OWN, SIR.
I FOUND THE MAN THAT DID IN YER RANGERS. I BROUGHT 'IM HERE.
YOU GOT BUSINESS... LET IT BE WITH ME.
TAKES SOME KIND O' GUMPTION TA RISE TO THIS PARTICULAR TYPE OF OCCASION.
REMINDS ME O' MY OWN BOY...
...OR WHAT I IMAGINE HE'D O' LOOKED LIKE IF HE'D LIVED TO SEE AS MANY SUMMERS.
OKAY... WHICH ONE O' YOU BIBLE THUMPERS IS THIS FINE LAD'S PA?

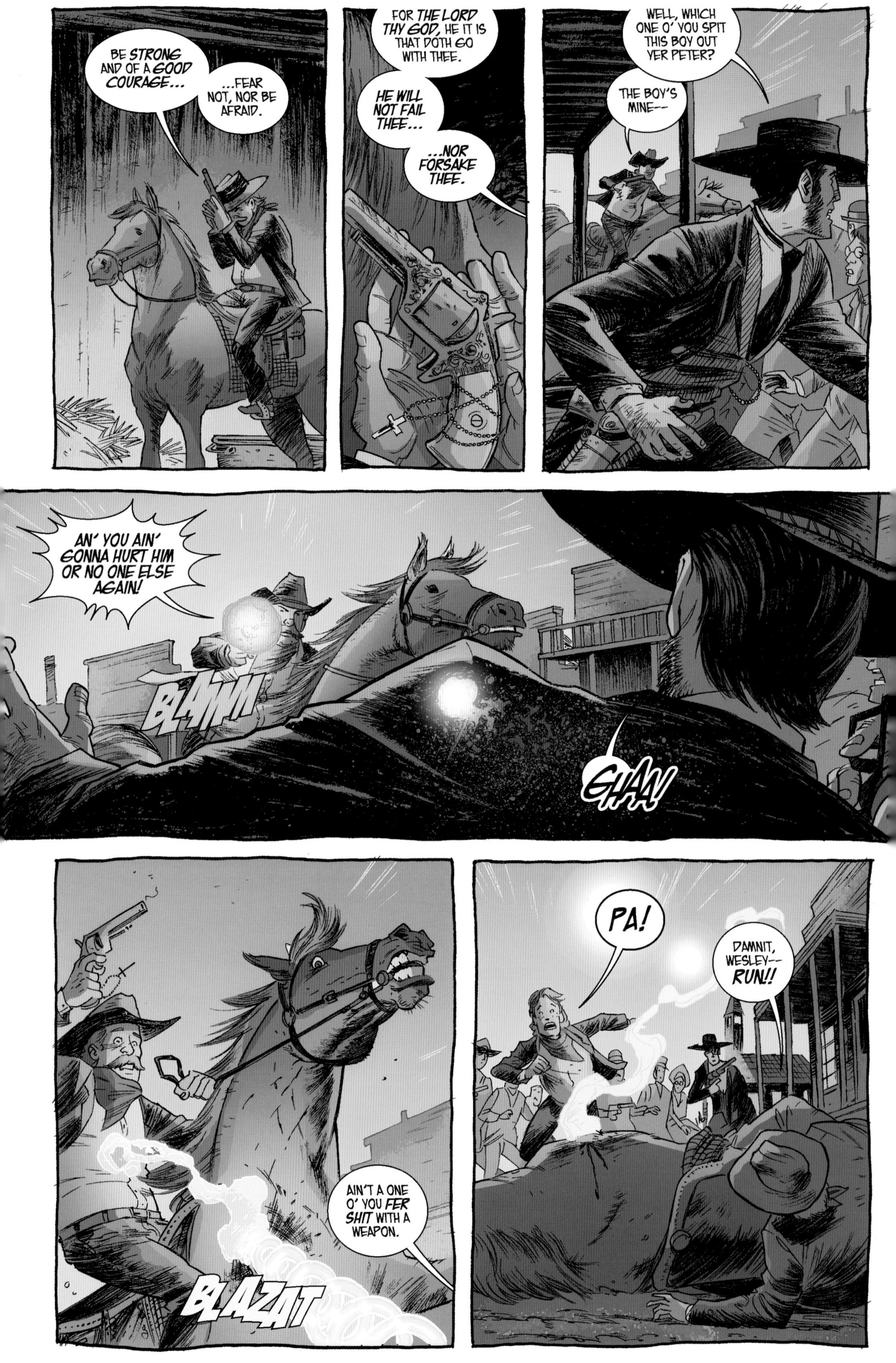
BE STRONG AND OF A GOOD COURAGE...
...FEAR NOT, NOR BE AFRAID.
FOR THE LORD THY GOD, HE IT IS THAT DOTH GO WITH THEE.
HE WILL NOT FAIL THEE...
...NOR FORSAKE THEE.
WELL, WHICH ONE O' YOU SPIT THIS BOY OUT YER PETER?
THE BOY'S MINE--
AN' YOU AIN' GONNA HURT HIM OR NO ONE ELSE AGAIN!
BLAMM
GHAA!
AIN'T A ONE O' YOU FER SHIT WITH A WEAPON.
BLAZAT
PA!
DAMNIT, WESLEY-- RUN!!

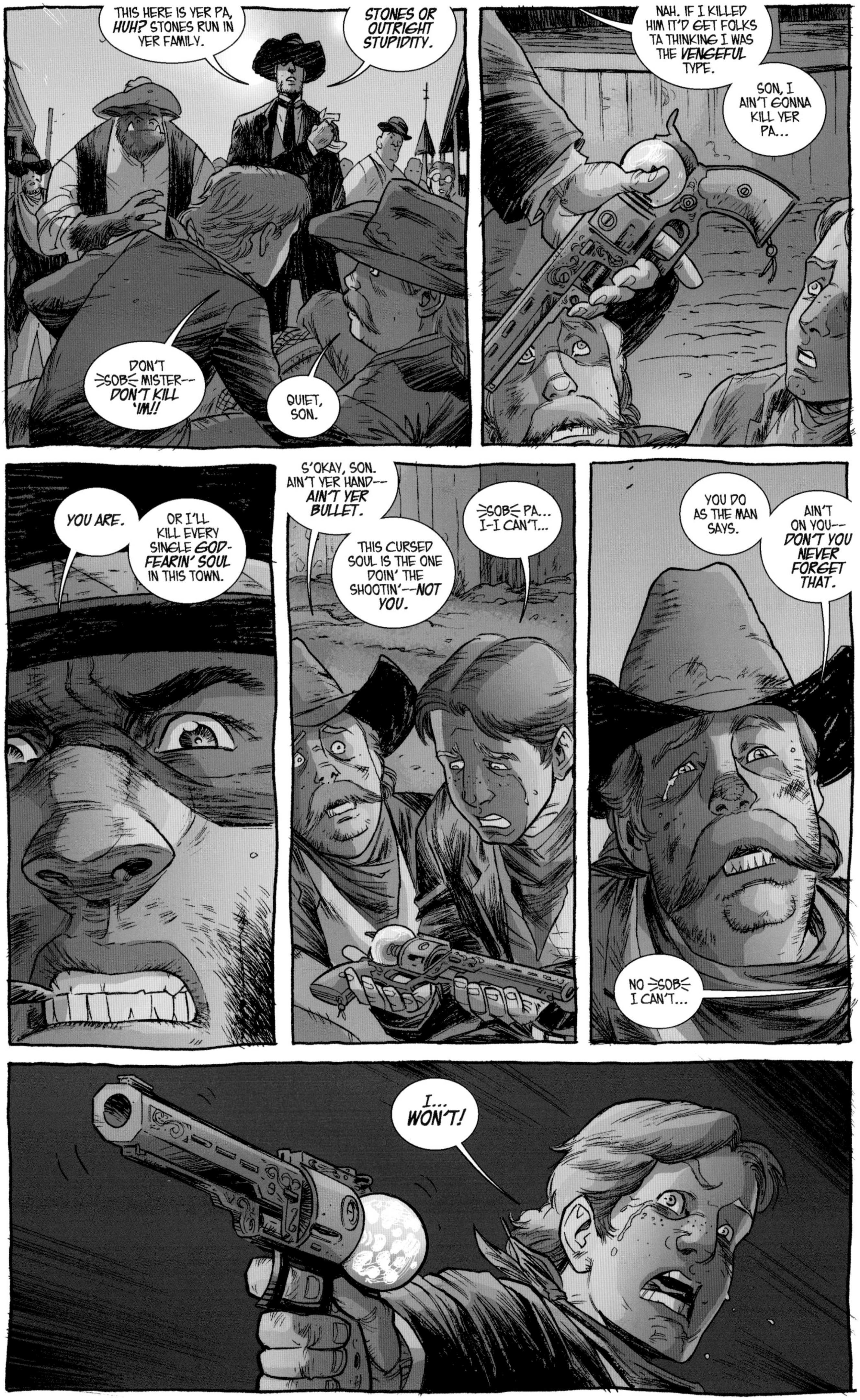
THIS HERE IS YER PA, HUH? STONES RUN IN YER FAMILY.
STONES OR OUTRIGHT STUPIDITY.
DON'T =SOB= MISTER-- DON'T KILL 'IM!!
QUIET, SON.
NAH. IF I KILLED HIM IT'D GET FOLKS TA THINKING I WAS THE VENGEFUL TYPE.
SON, I AIN'T GONNA KILL YER PA...
YOU ARE.
OR I'LL KILL EVERY SINGLE GOD-FEARIN' SOUL IN THIS TOWN.
S'OKAY, SON. AIN'T YER HAND-- AIN'T YER BULLET.
THIS CURSED SOUL IS THE ONE DOIN' THE SHOOTIN'--NOT YOU.
=SOB= PA... I-I CAN'T...
YOU DO AS THE MAN SAYS.
AIN'T ON YOU-- DON'T YOU NEVER FORGET THAT.
NO =SOB= I CAN'T...
I... WON'T!

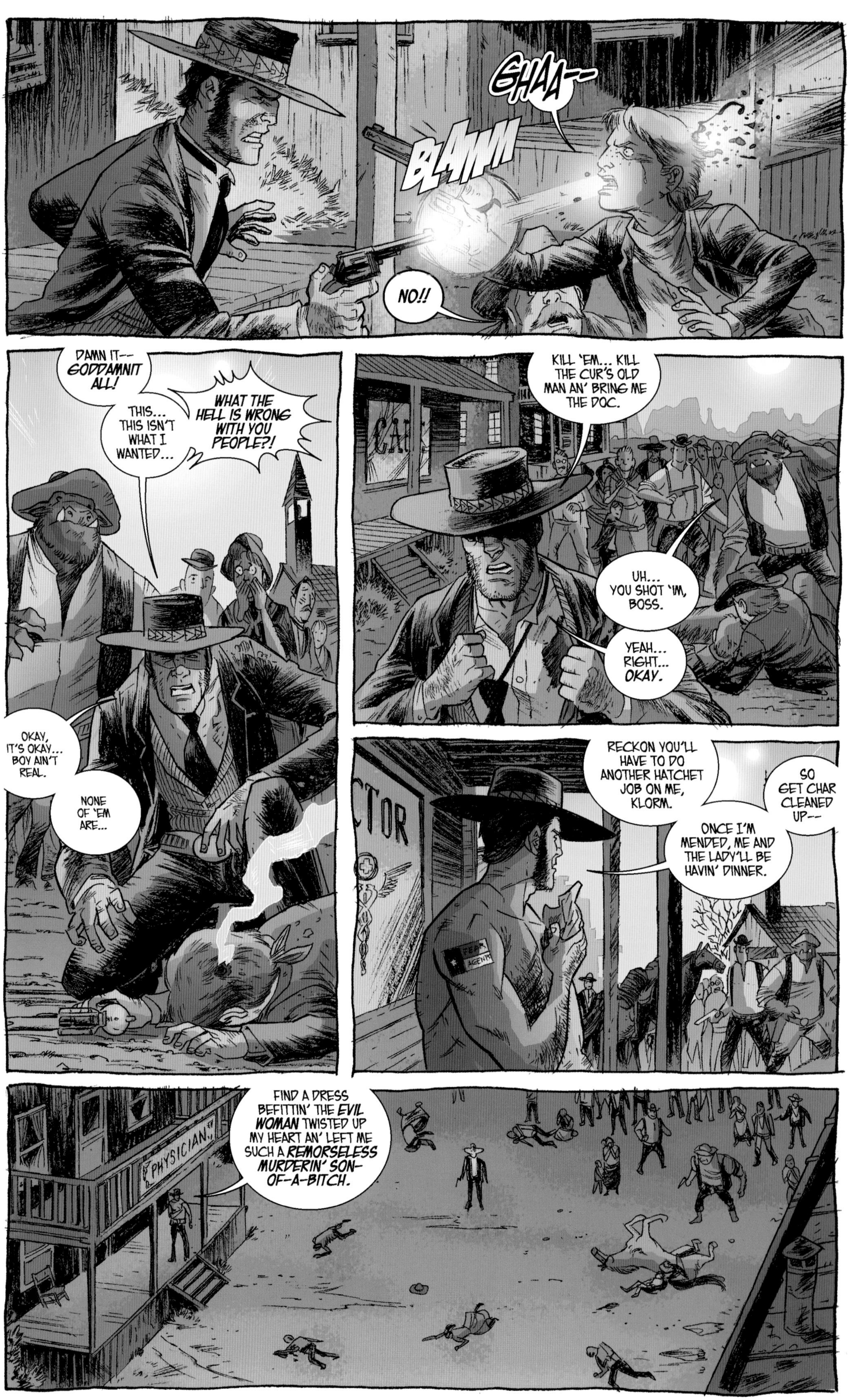
GHAA--
BLAMM
NO!!
DAMN IT-- GODDAMNIT ALL!
THIS... THIS ISN'T WHAT I WANTED...
WHAT THE HELL IS WRONG WITH YOU PEOPLE?!
OKAY, IT'S OKAY... BOY AIN'T REAL.
NONE OF 'EM ARE...
KILL 'EM... KILL THE CUR'S OLD MAN AN' BRING ME THE DOC.
UH... YOU SHOT 'IM, BOSS.
YEAH... RIGHT... OKAY.
RECKON YOU'LL HAVE TO DO ANOTHER HATCHET JOB ON ME, KLORM.
SO GET CHAR CLEANED UP--
ONCE I'M MENDED, ME AND THE LADY'LL BE HAVIN' DINNER.
FIND A DRESS BEFITTIN' THE EVIL WOMAN TWISTED UP MY HEART AN' LEFT ME SUCH A REMORSELESS MURDERIN' SON-OF-A-BITCH.
PHYSICIAN

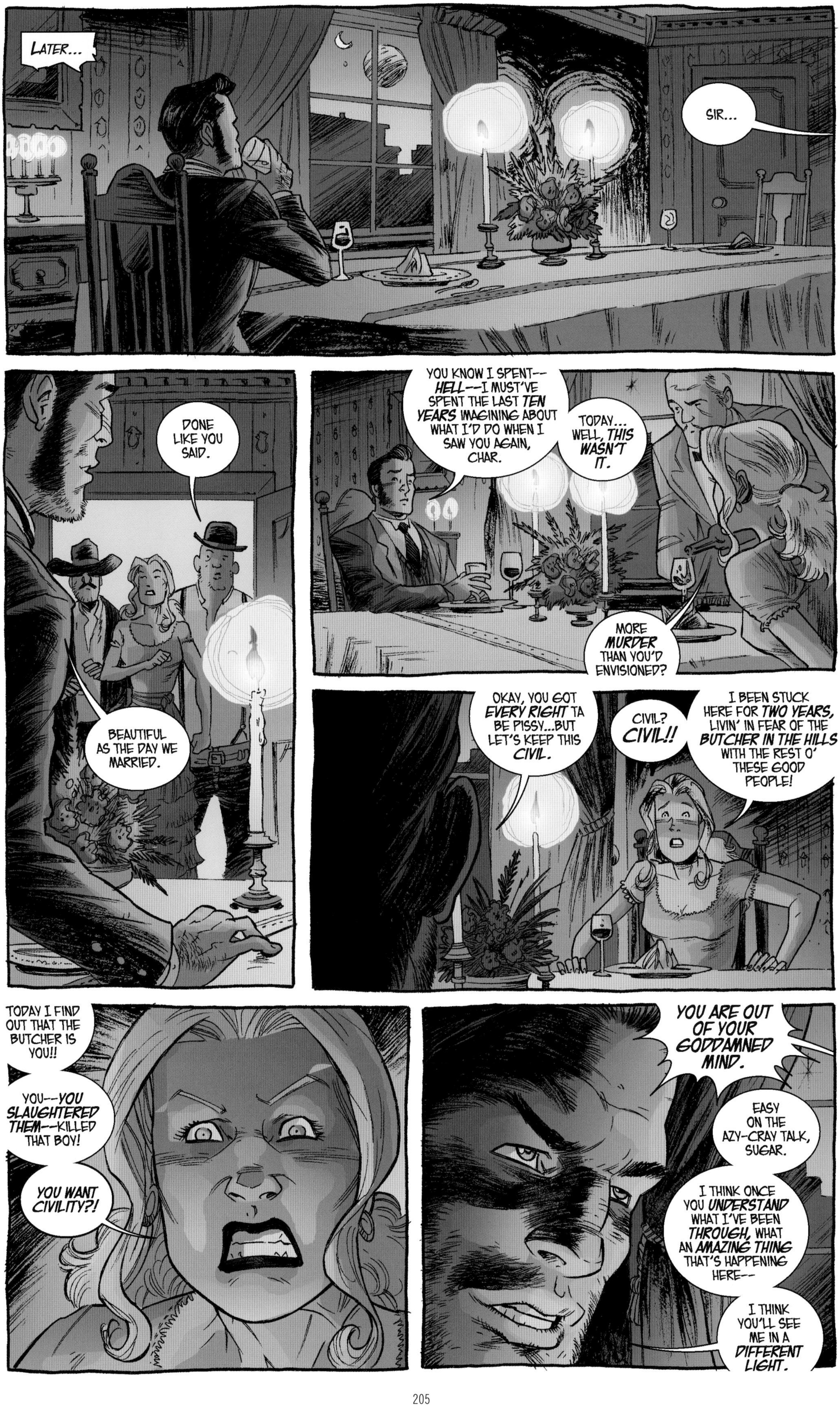
LATER...
SIR...
DONE LIKE YOU SAID.
BEAUTIFUL AS THE DAY WE MARRIED.
YOU KNOW I SPENT-- HELL--I MUST'VE SPENT THE LAST TEN YEARS IMAGINING ABOUT WHAT I'D DO WHEN I SAW YOU AGAIN, CHAR.
TODAY... WELL, THIS WASN'T IT.
MORE MURDER THAN YOU'D ENVISIONED?
OKAY, YOU GOT EVERY RIGHT TA BE PISSY...BUT LET'S KEEP THIS CIVIL.
CIVIL? CIVIL!!
I BEEN STUCK HERE FOR TWO YEARS, LIVIN' IN FEAR OF THE BUTCHER IN THE HILLS WITH THE REST O' THESE GOOD PEOPLE!
TODAY I FIND OUT THAT THE BUTCHER IS YOU!!
YOU--YOU SLAUGHTERED THEM--KILLED THAT BOY!
YOU WANT CIVILITY?!
YOU ARE OUT OF YOUR GODDAMNED MIND.
EASY ON THE AZY-CRAY TALK, SUGAR.
I THINK ONCE YOU UNDERSTAND WHAT I'VE BEEN THROUGH, WHAT AN AMAZING THING THAT'S HAPPENING HERE--
I THINK YOU'LL SEE ME IN A DIFFERENT LIGHT.

COUPLE O' FEW YEARS AFTER I LEFT EARTH, *DRESSITES* SENT ME BACK IN TIME, MAROONED ME ON THE PLANET *TETALD* AS THE *TETALDIAN* RACE WAS FORMING.

RECKON THEY FIGURED I'D PUT AN END TO THE *TETALDIANS* 'FORE THEY STARTED, SAVE *EARTH* AN' THE *ENTIRE UNIVERSE* THEIR SCOURGE.

AN' I WAS GONNA.

WENT TO THE LEADER'S PALACE-- *OL' JENTU HIMSELF*--WITH INTENT O' *KILLIN' 'IM* AND STOPPIN' THE *TIN SHIT-CAN RACE* BEFORE THEY GOT THEIR FOOTIN'.

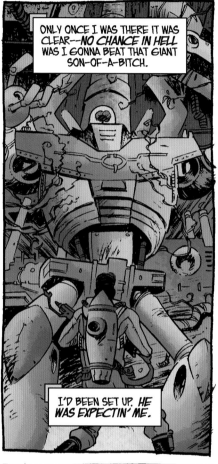

ONLY ONCE I WAS THERE IT WAS CLEAR-- *NO CHANCE IN HELL* WAS I GONNA BEAT THAT GIANT SON-OF-A-BITCH.

I'D BEEN SET UP. *HE WAS EXPECTIN' ME.*

SO INSTEAD I MADE A *DEAL.*

I'D LET 'IM IN ON WHAT THE *FUTURE HELD FER HIM* IF HIS *ROBOT RACE* PROVIDED ME A FEW THINGS--

GET ME BACK TO MY *OWN TIME* ON A WORLD *CUSTOM MADE* TO MY SPECIFICATIONS...

AND THAT HE'D BRING ME YOU.

TETALDIANS MADE ME A FEW *CYBORGS* IN THE LIKENESS OF A RECENTLY DECEASED *FRIEND* TA HELP BIDE MY TIME WHILE I *WAITED...*

NO IDEA HOW, BUT THEY CAME THROUGH.

MADE ME MY OWN PLANET USING MY MENTAL IMAGES OF PARADISE.

BEFORE I LEFT I SET A FEW EXPLOSIVE CHARGES TO SHOW THE OL' BOY MY GRATITUDE.

TOOK ANNIE A COUPLE O' FEW TIME JUMPS TO GET IT RIGHT, BUT SHE EVENTUALLY GOT US TO OUR NEW HOME HERE IN THE PRESENT...

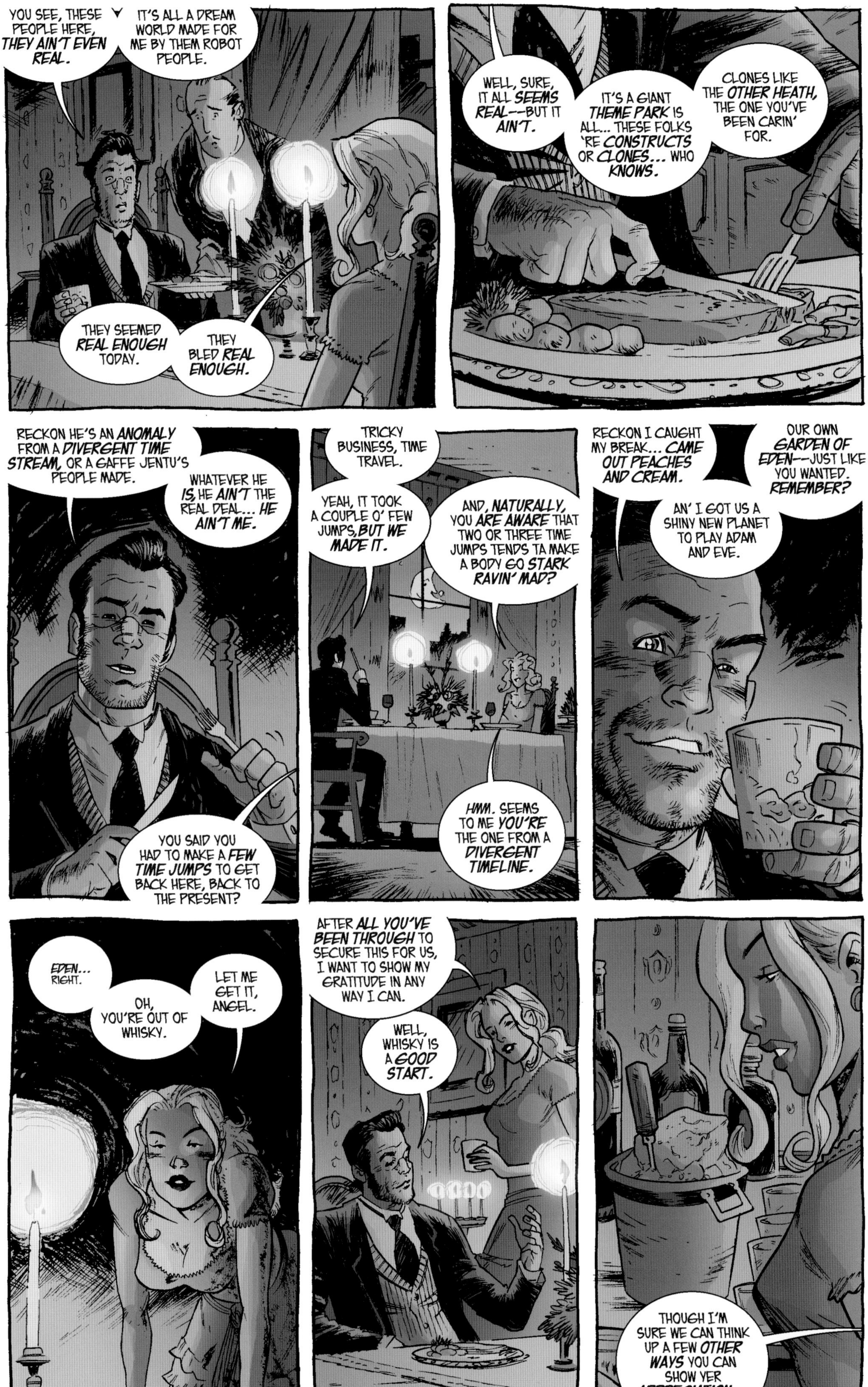

YOU SEE, THESE PEOPLE HERE, THEY AIN'T EVEN REAL.
IT'S ALL A DREAM WORLD MADE FOR ME BY THEM ROBOT PEOPLE.
THEY SEEMED REAL ENOUGH TODAY.
THEY BLED REAL ENOUGH.
WELL, SURE, IT ALL SEEMS REAL--BUT IT AIN'T.
IT'S A GIANT THEME PARK IS ALL... THESE FOLKS 'RE CONSTRUCTS OR CLONES... WHO KNOWS.
CLONES LIKE THE OTHER HEATH, THE ONE YOU'VE BEEN CARIN' FOR.
RECKON HE'S AN ANOMALY FROM A DIVERGENT TIME STREAM, OR A GAFFE JENTU'S PEOPLE MADE.
WHATEVER HE IS, HE AIN'T THE REAL DEAL... HE AIN'T ME.
YOU SAID YOU HAD TO MAKE A FEW TIME JUMPS TO GET BACK HERE, BACK TO THE PRESENT?
TRICKY BUSINESS, TIME TRAVEL.
YEAH, IT TOOK A COUPLE O' FEW JUMPS, BUT WE MADE IT.
AND, NATURALLY, YOU ARE AWARE THAT TWO OR THREE TIME JUMPS TENDS TA MAKE A BODY GO STARK RAVIN' MAD?
HMM. SEEMS TO ME YOU'RE THE ONE FROM A DIVERGENT TIMELINE.
RECKON I CAUGHT MY BREAK... CAME OUT PEACHES AND CREAM.
AN' I GOT US A SHINY NEW PLANET TO PLAY ADAM AND EVE.
OUR OWN GARDEN OF EDEN--JUST LIKE YOU WANTED. REMEMBER?
EDEN... RIGHT.
OH, YOU'RE OUT OF WHISKY.
LET ME GET IT, ANGEL.
AFTER ALL YOU'VE BEEN THROUGH TO SECURE THIS FOR US, I WANT TO SHOW MY GRATITUDE IN ANY WAY I CAN.
WELL, WHISKY IS A GOOD START.
THOUGH I'M SURE WE CAN THINK UP A FEW OTHER WAYS YOU CAN SHOW YER APPRECIATION...

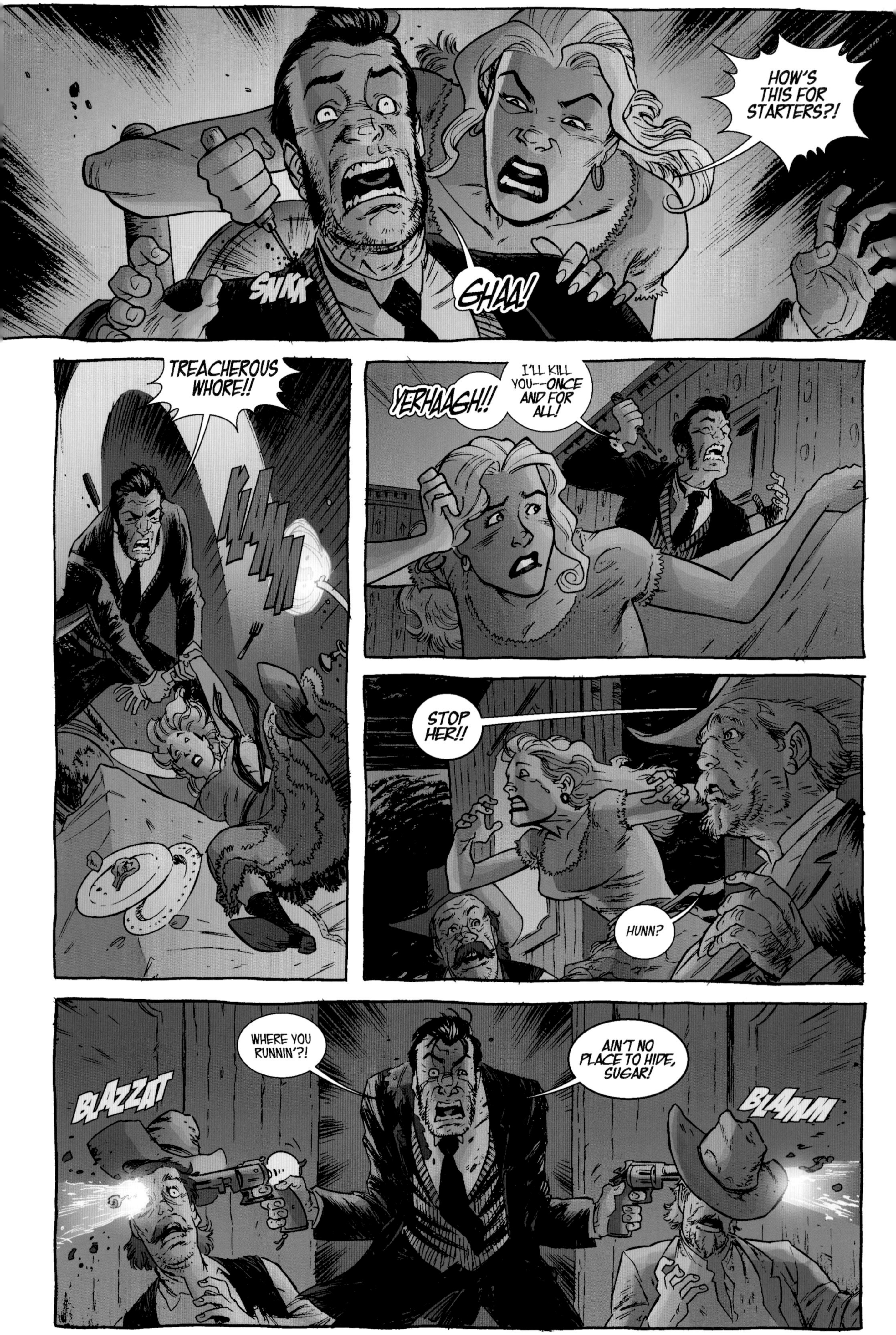
HOW'S THIS FOR STARTERS?!
SNIKK
GHAA!
TREACHEROUS WHORE!!
YERHAAGH!!
I'LL KILL YOU--ONCE AND FOR ALL!
STOP HER!!
HUNN?
WHERE YOU RUNNIN'?!
AIN'T NO PLACE TO HIDE, SUGAR!
BLAZZAT
BLAMM

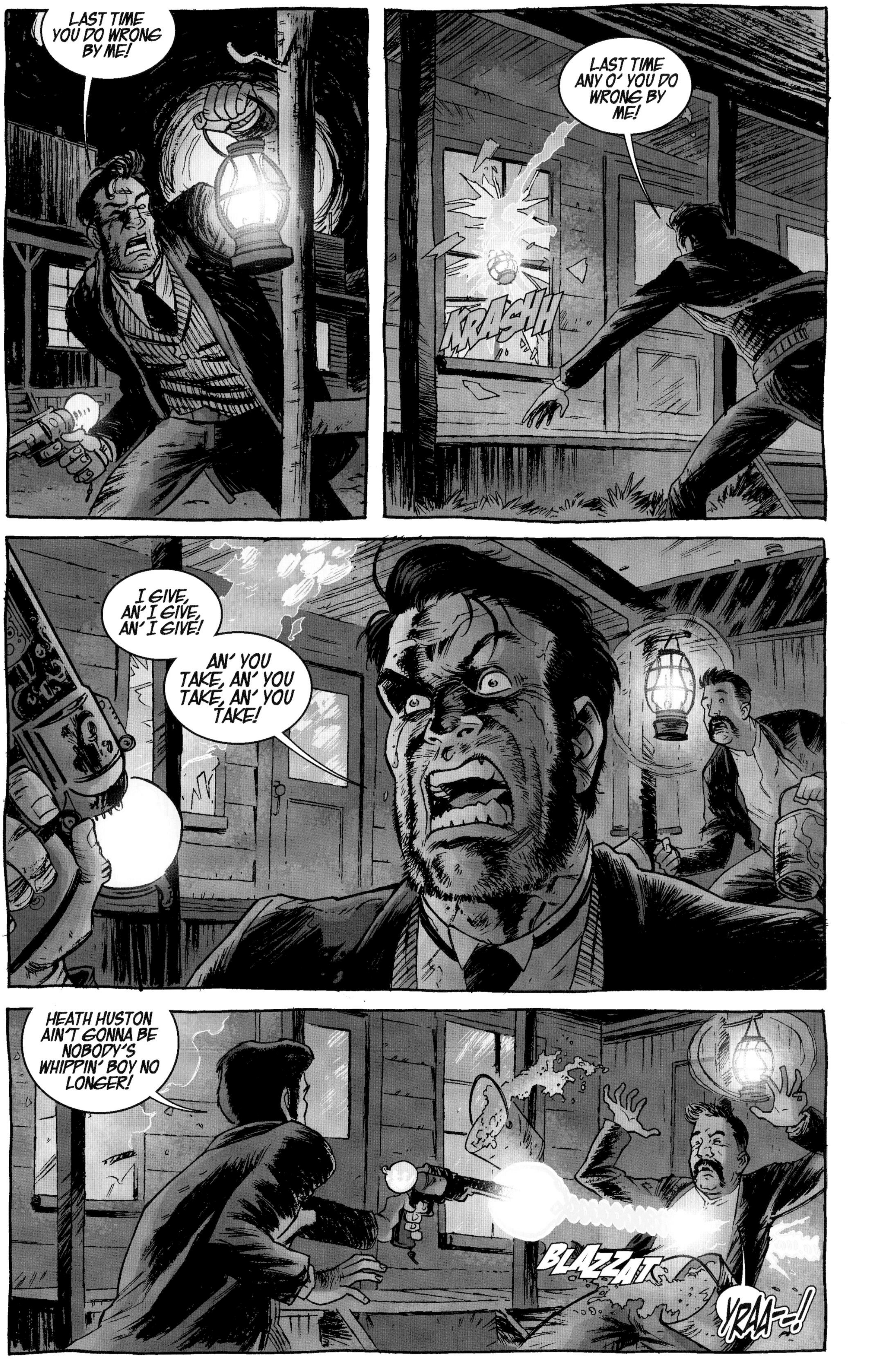
LAST TIME YOU DO WRONG BY ME!
LAST TIME ANY O' YOU DO WRONG BY ME!
KRASHH
I GIVE, AN' I GIVE, AN' I GIVE!
AN' YOU TAKE, AN' YOU TAKE, AN' YOU TAKE!
HEATH HUSTON AIN'T GONNA BE NOBODY'S WHIPPIN' BOY NO LONGER!
BLAZZAT
YRAA--!

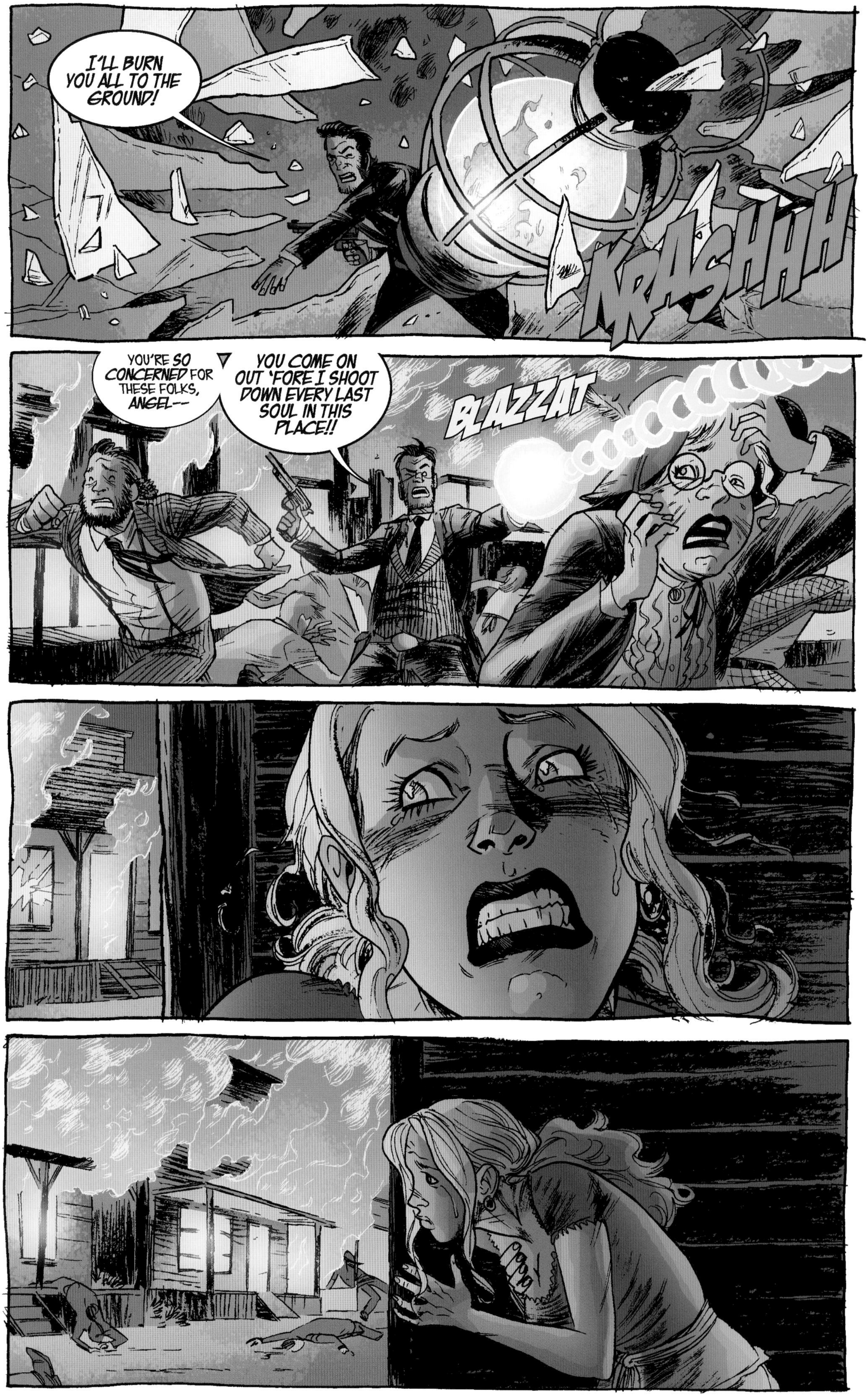
I'LL BURN YOU ALL TO THE GROUND!
KRASHHH
YOU'RE SO CONCERNED FOR THESE FOLKS, ANGEL--
YOU COME ON OUT 'FORE I SHOOT DOWN EVERY LAST SOUL IN THIS PLACE!!
BLAZZAT

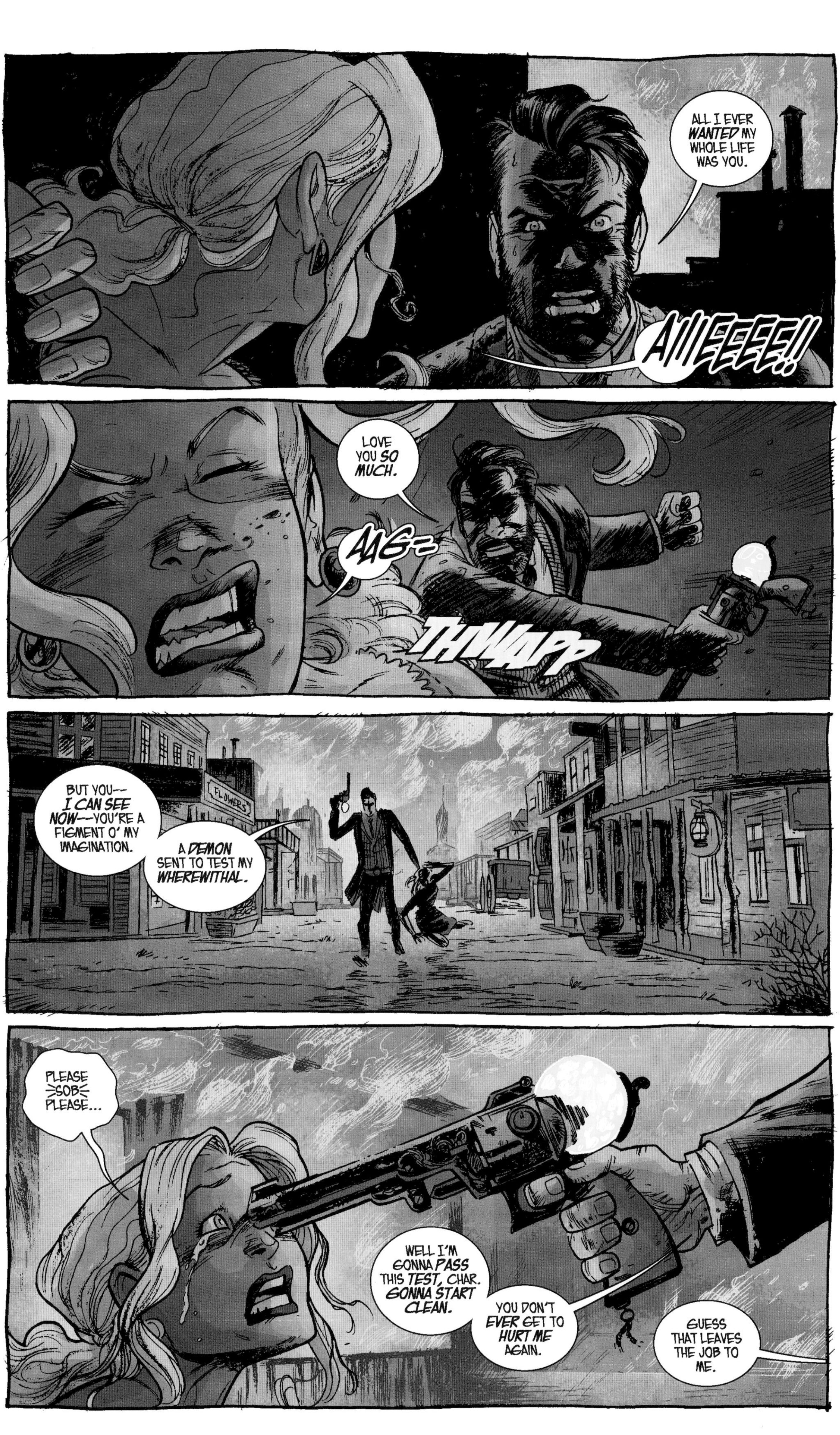
ALL I EVER WANTED MY WHOLE LIFE WAS YOU.
AIIEEEE!!
LOVE YOU SO MUCH.
AAG--
THWAPP
BUT YOU-- I CAN SEE NOW--YOU'RE A FIGMENT O' MY IMAGINATION.
A DEMON SENT TO TEST MY WHEREWITHAL.
FLOWERS
PLEASE --SOB-- PLEASE...
WELL I'M GONNA PASS THIS TEST, CHAR. GONNA START CLEAN.
YOU DON'T EVER GET TO HURT ME AGAIN.
GUESS THAT LEAVES THE JOB TO ME.

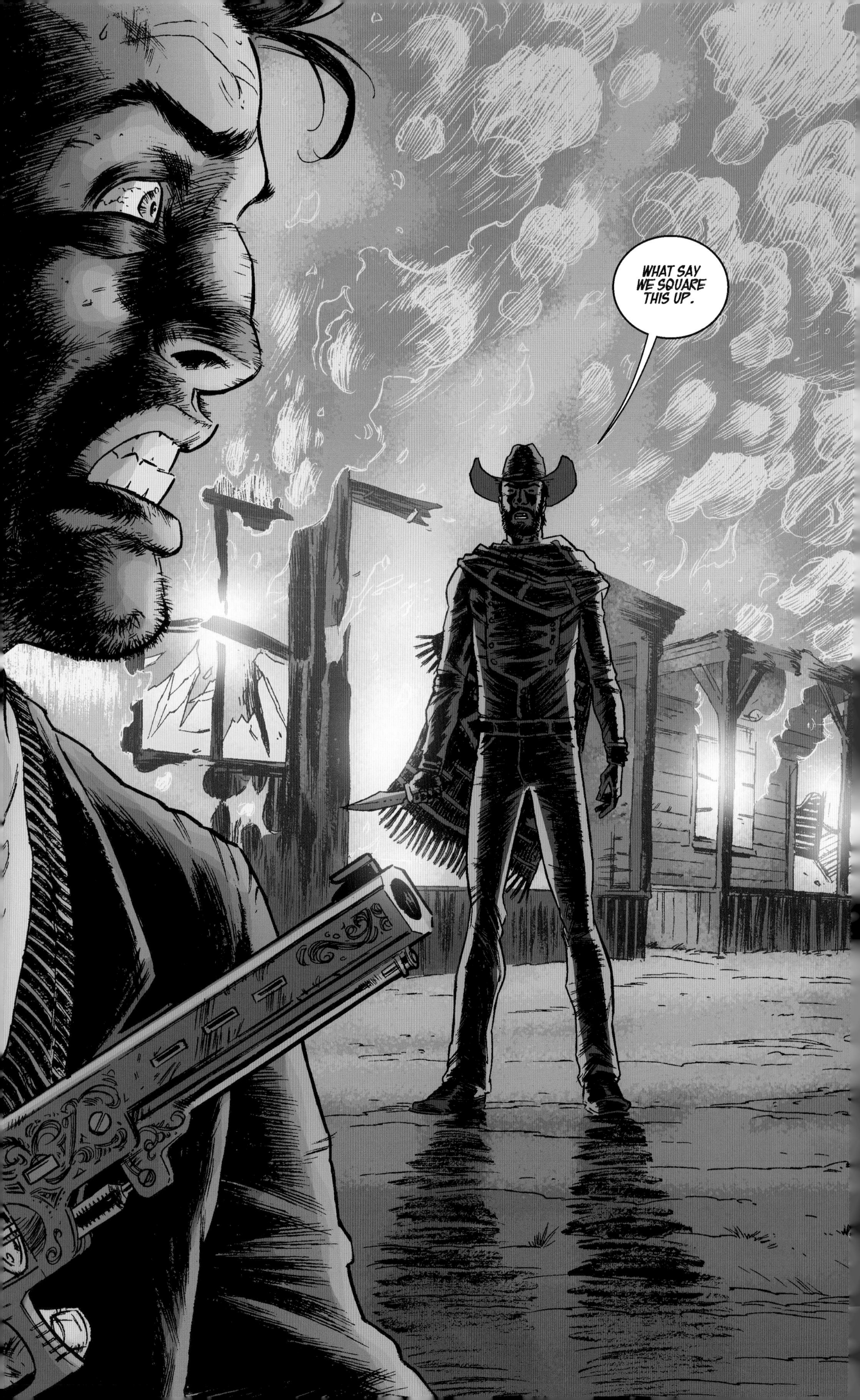
WHAT SAY WE SQUARE THIS UP.

CHAPTER 5

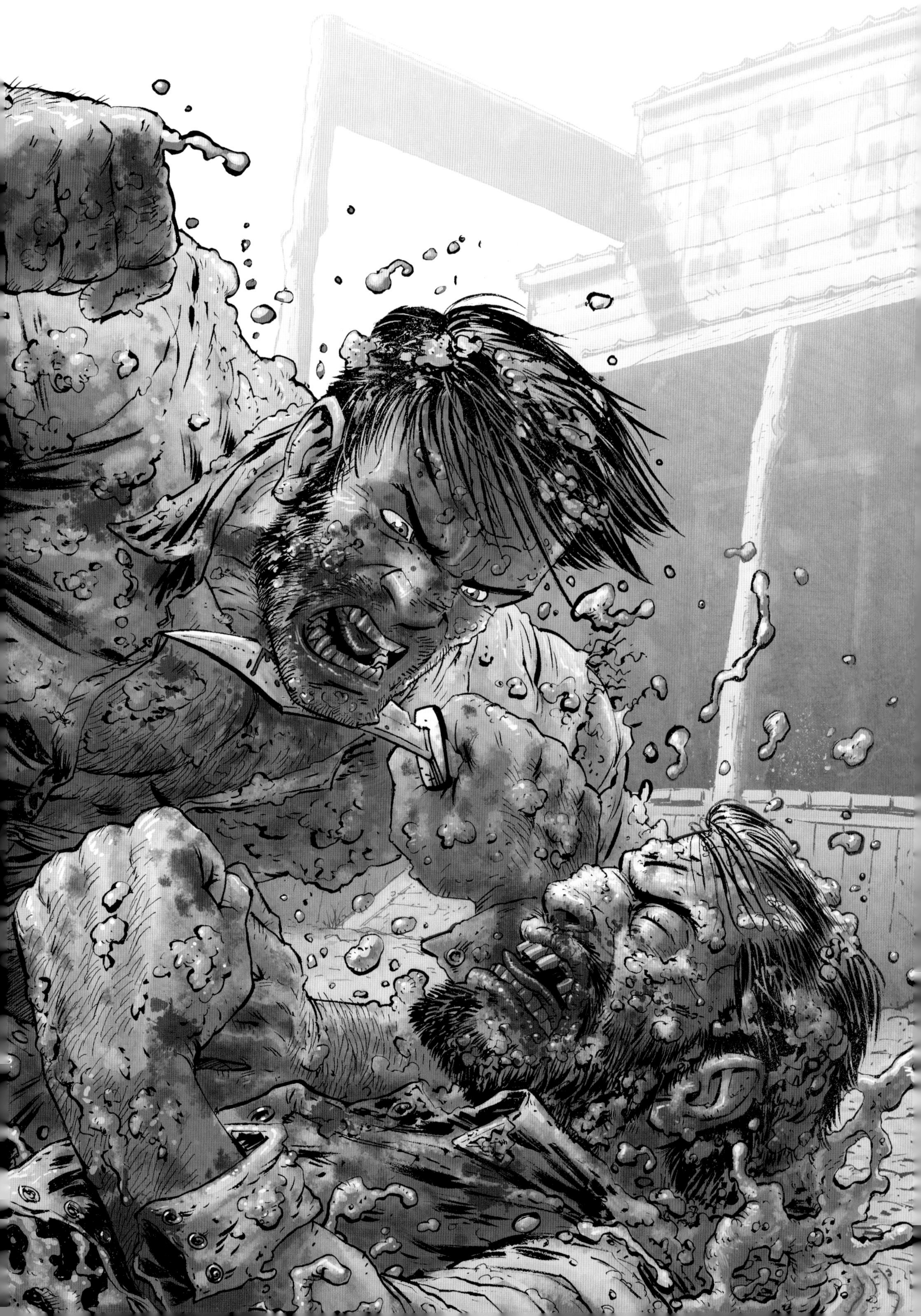

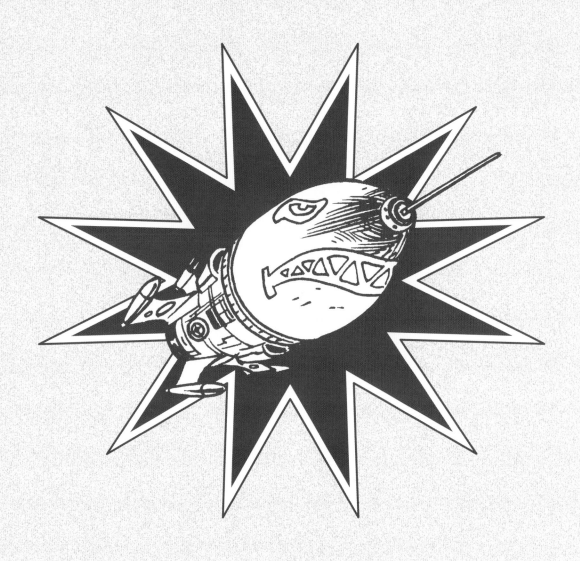

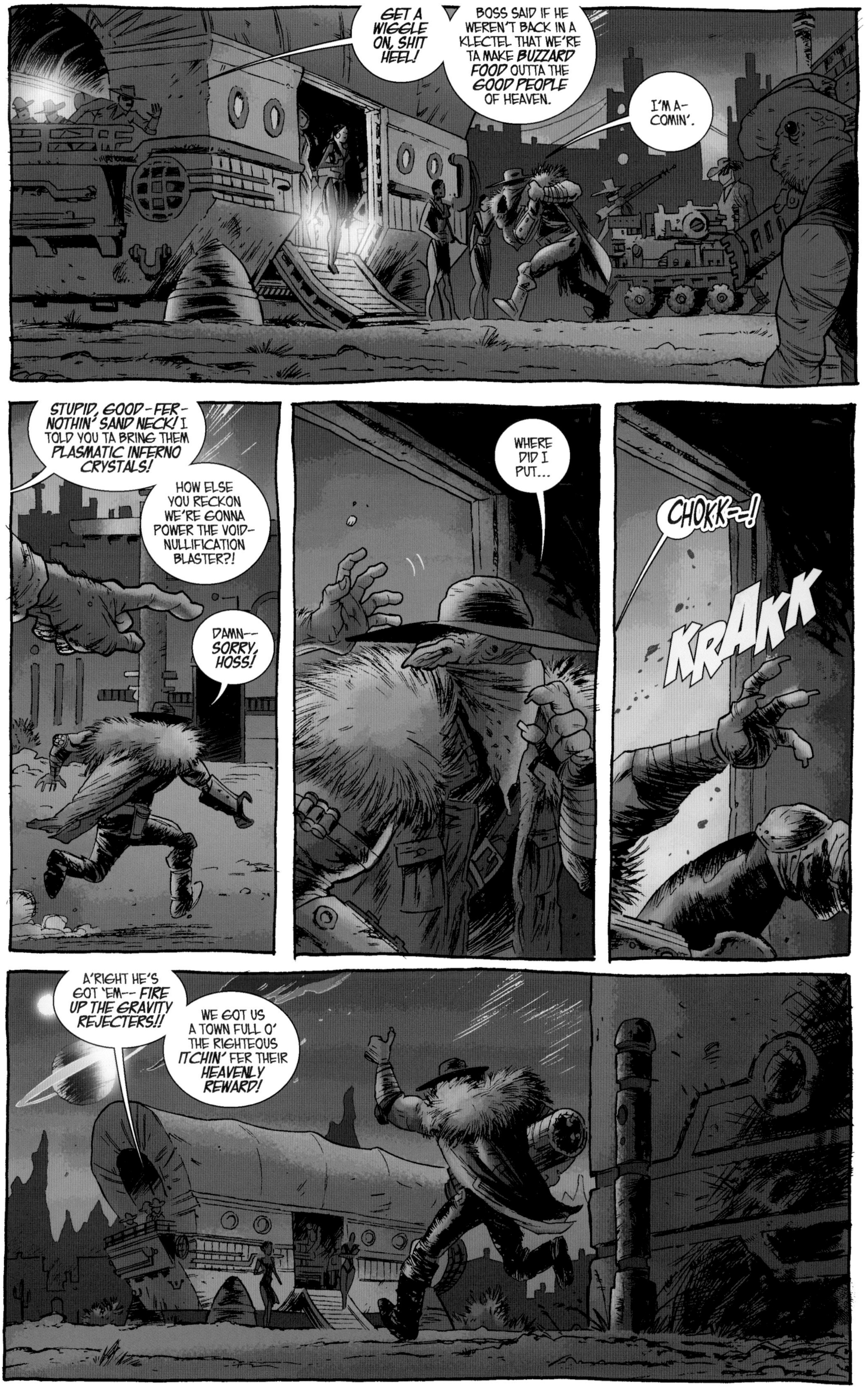
GET A WIGGLE ON, SHIT HEEL!
BOSS SAID IF HE WEREN'T BACK IN A KLECTEL THAT WE'RE TA MAKE BUZZARD FOOD OUTTA THE GOOD PEOPLE OF HEAVEN.
I'M A-COMIN'.
STUPID, GOOD-FER-NOTHIN' SAND NECK! I TOLD YOU TA BRING THEM PLASMATIC INFERNO CRYSTALS!
HOW ELSE YOU RECKON WE'RE GONNA POWER THE VOID-NULLIFICATION BLASTER?!
DAMN-- SORRY, HOSS!
WHERE DID I PUT...
CHOKK--!
KRAKK
A'RIGHT HE'S GOT 'EM-- FIRE UP THE GRAVITY REJECTERS!!
WE GOT US A TOWN FULL O' THE RIGHTEOUS ITCHIN' FER THEIR HEAVENLY REWARD!

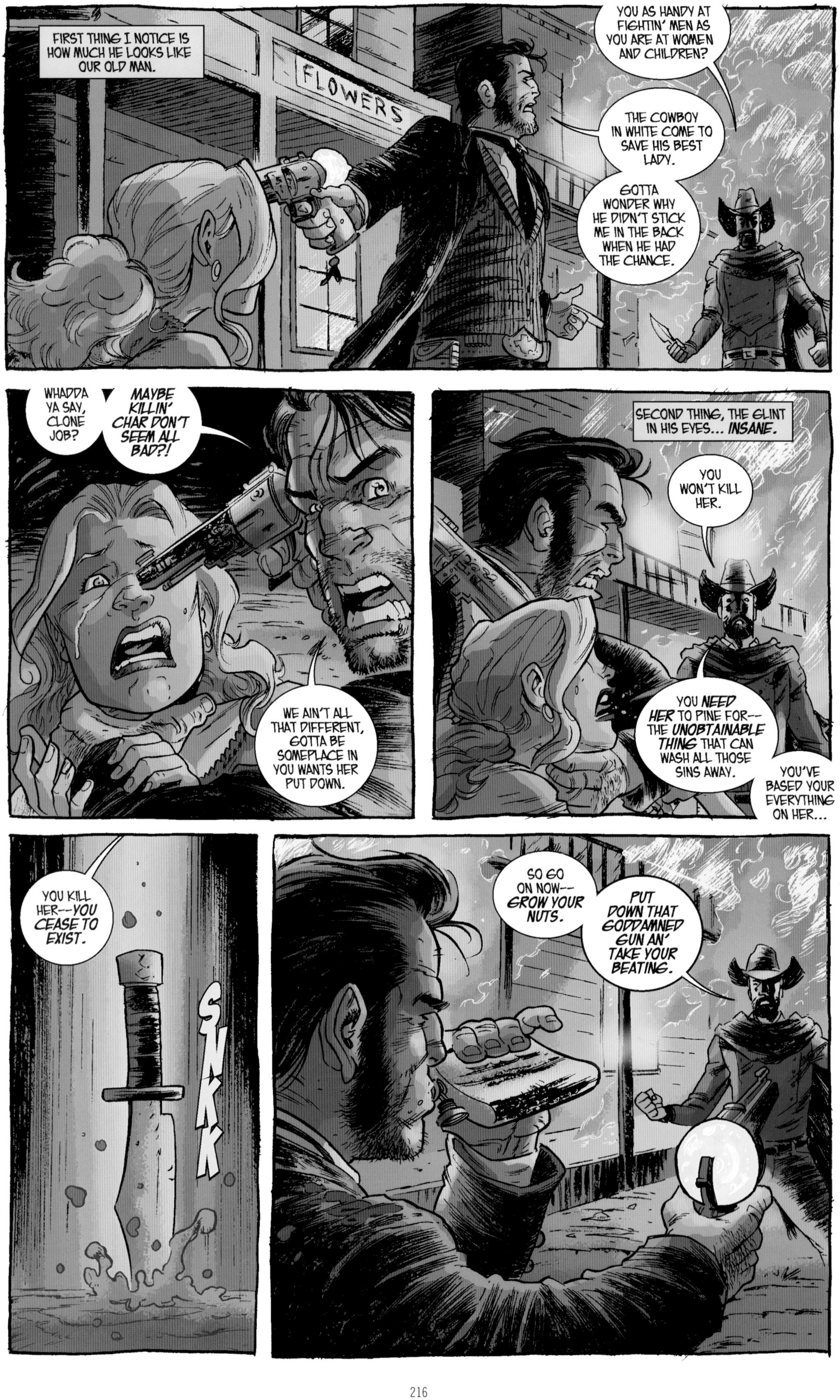
FIRST THING I NOTICE IS HOW MUCH HE LOOKS LIKE OUR OLD MAN.
FLOWERS
YOU AS HANDY AT FIGHTIN' MEN AS YOU ARE AT WOMEN AND CHILDREN?
THE COWBOY IN WHITE COME TO SAVE HIS BEST LADY.
GOTTA WONDER WHY HE DIDN'T STICK ME IN THE BACK WHEN HE HAD THE CHANCE.
WHADDA YA SAY, CLONE JOB?
MAYBE KILLIN' CHAR DON'T SEEM ALL BAD?!
WE AIN'T ALL THAT DIFFERENT, GOTTA BE SOMEPLACE IN YOU WANTS HER PUT DOWN.
SECOND THING, THE GLINT IN HIS EYES... INSANE.
YOU WON'T KILL HER.
YOU NEED HER TO PINE FOR-- THE UNOBTAINABLE THING THAT CAN WASH ALL THOSE SINS AWAY.
YOU'VE BASED YOUR EVERYTHING ON HER...
YOU KILL HER--YOU CEASE TO EXIST.
SNKK
SO GO ON NOW-- GROW YOUR NUTS.
PUT DOWN THAT GODDAMNED GUN AN' TAKE YOUR BEATING.

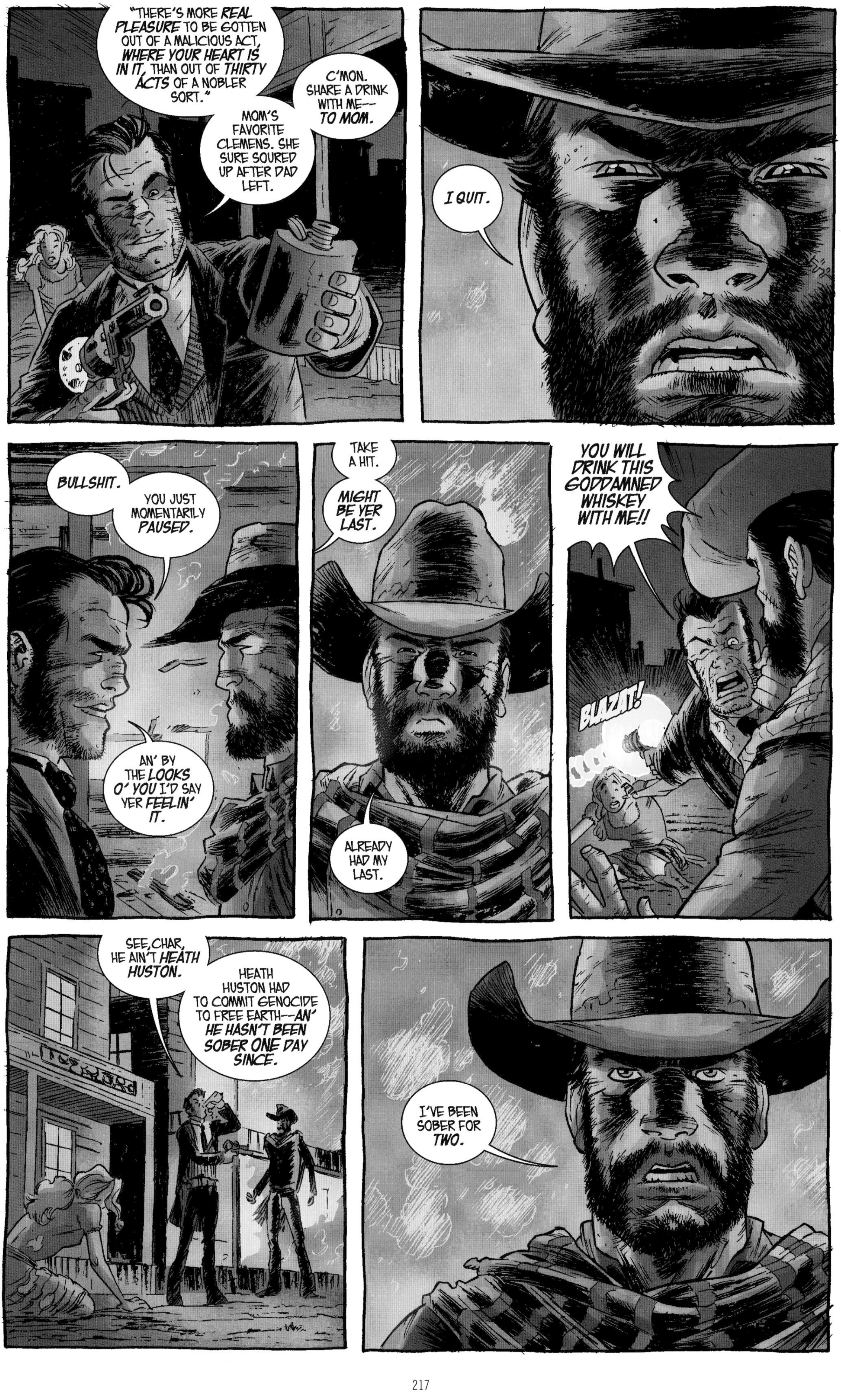
"THERE'S MORE REAL PLEASURE TO BE GOTTEN OUT OF A MALICIOUS ACT, WHERE YOUR HEART IS IN IT, THAN OUT OF THIRTY ACTS OF A NOBLER SORT."
MOM'S FAVORITE CLEMENS. SHE SURE SOURED UP AFTER DAD LEFT.
C'MON. SHARE A DRINK WITH ME-- TO MOM.
I QUIT.
BULLSHIT.
YOU JUST MOMENTARILY PAUSED.
AN' BY THE LOOKS O' YOU I'D SAY YER FEELIN' IT.
TAKE A HIT.
MIGHT BE YER LAST.
ALREADY HAD MY LAST.
YOU WILL DRINK THIS GODDAMNED WHISKEY WITH ME!!
BLAZAT!
SEE, CHAR, HE AIN'T HEATH HUSTON.
HEATH HUSTON HAD TO COMMIT GENOCIDE TO FREE EARTH--AN' HE HASN'T BEEN SOBER ONE DAY SINCE.
I'VE BEEN SOBER FOR TWO.

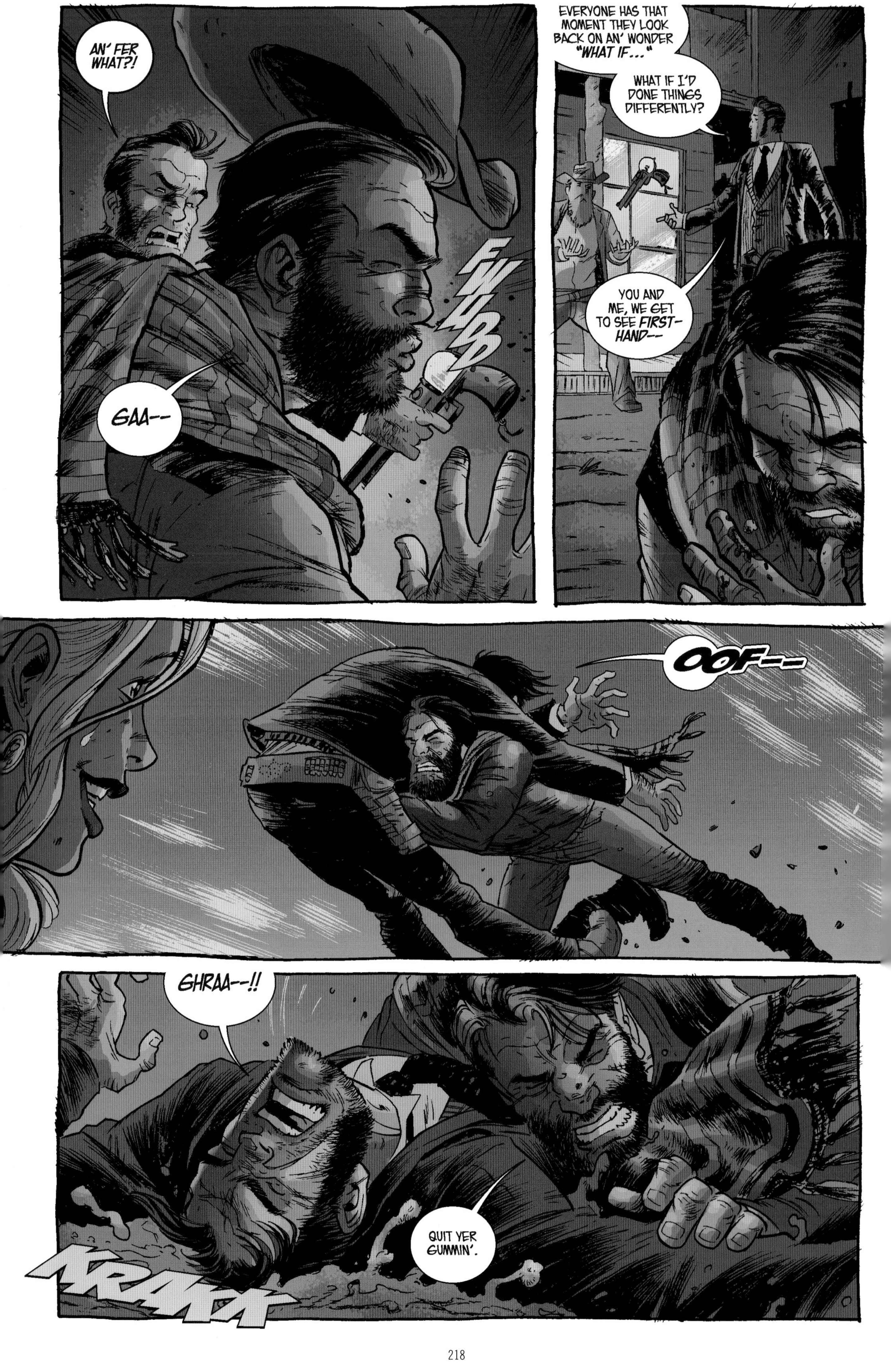
AN' FER WHAT?!
FWUD
GAA--
EVERYONE HAS THAT MOMENT THEY LOOK BACK ON AN' WONDER "WHAT IF..."
WHAT IF I'D DONE THINGS DIFFERENTLY?
YOU AND ME, WE GET TO SEE FIRST-HAND--
OOF--
GHRAA--!!
QUIT YER GUMMIN'.
KRAKA

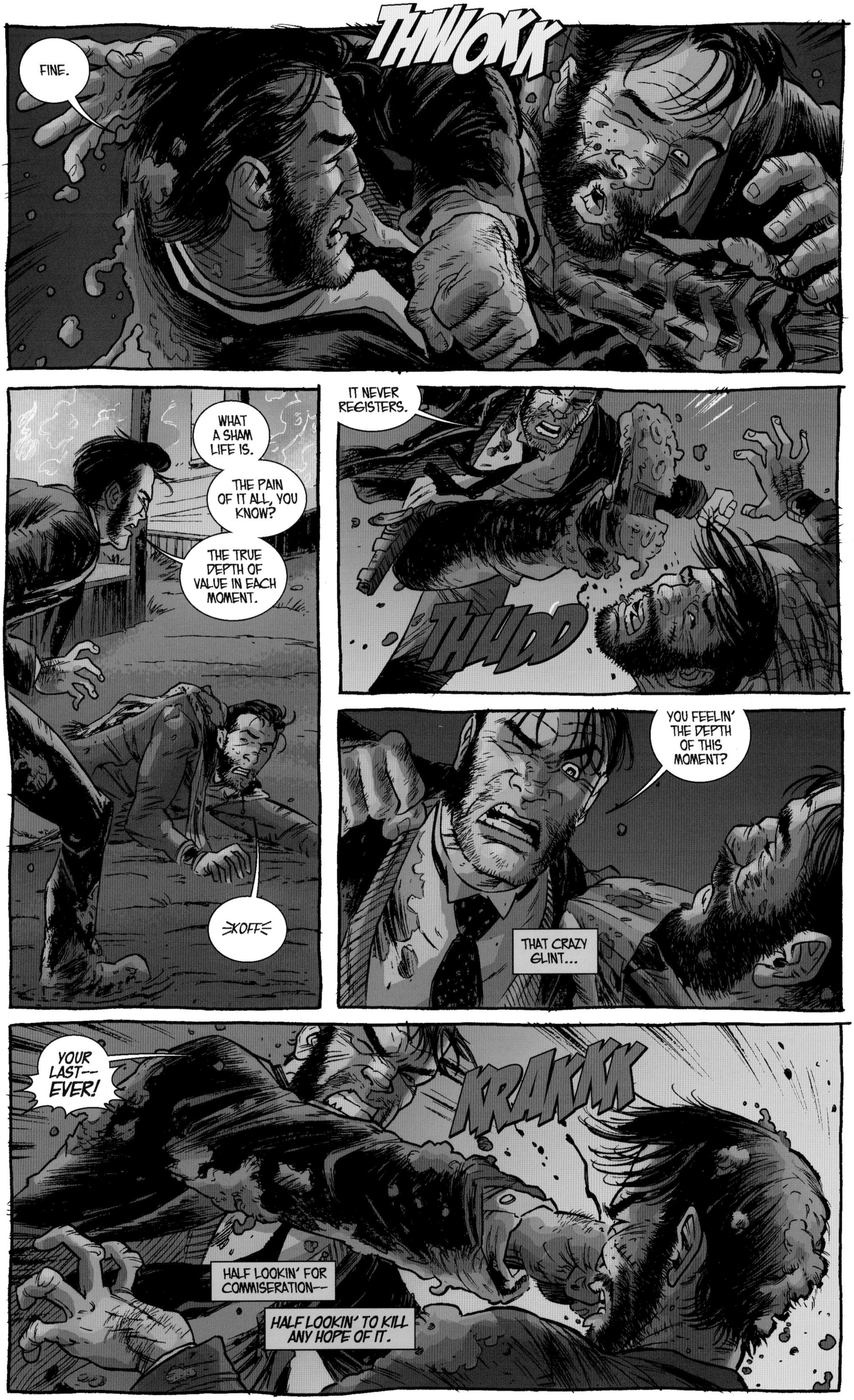
THWOKK
FINE.
WHAT A SHAM LIFE IS.
THE PAIN OF IT ALL, YOU KNOW?
THE TRUE DEPTH OF VALUE IN EACH MOMENT.
KOFF
IT NEVER REGISTERS.
THUDD
YOU FEELIN' THE DEPTH OF THIS MOMENT?
THAT CRAZY GLINT...
YOUR LAST-- EVER!
KRAKKK
HALF LOOKIN' FOR COMMISERATION--
HALF LOOKIN' TO KILL ANY HOPE OF IT.

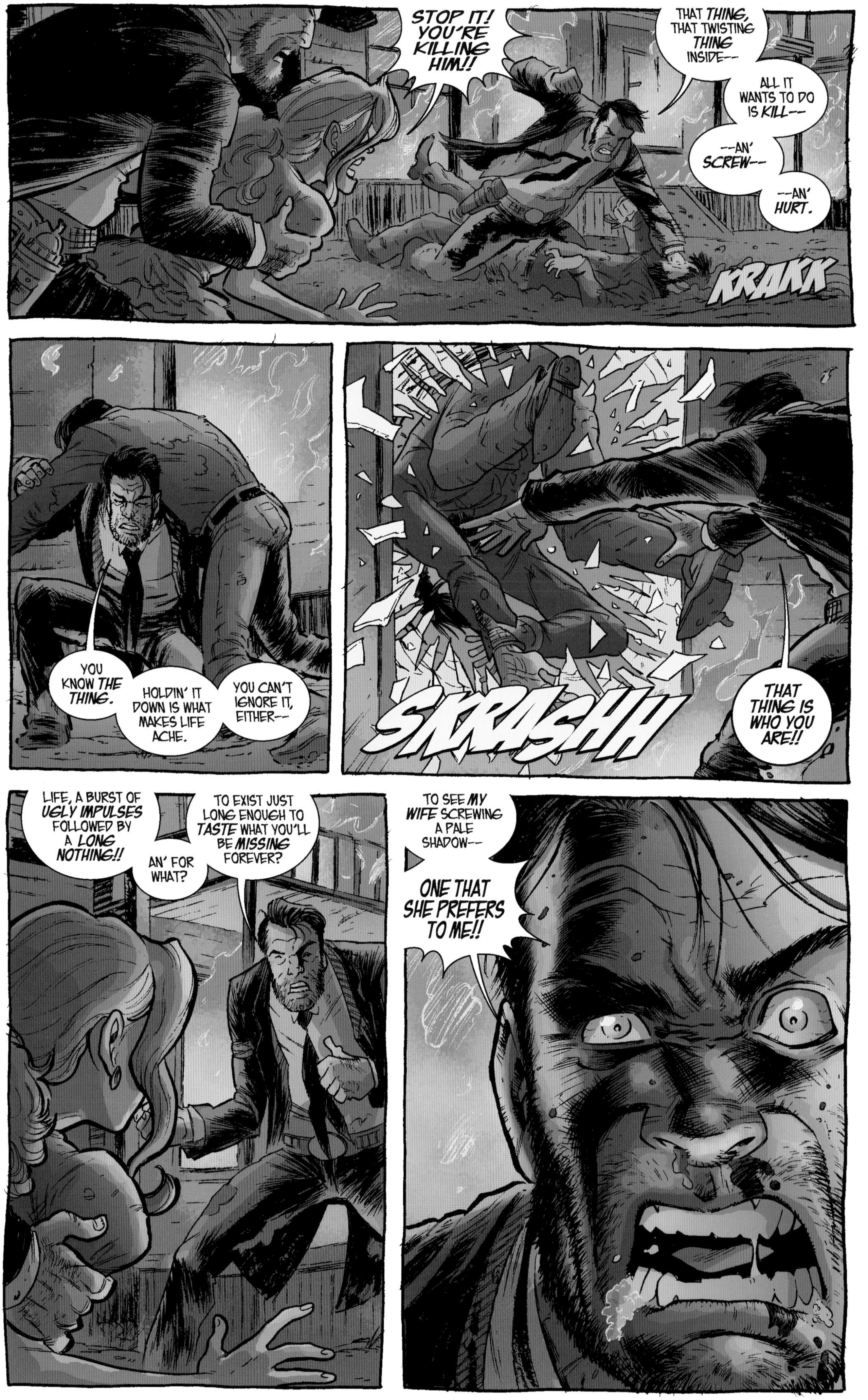
STOP IT! YOU'RE KILLING HIM!!
THAT THING, THAT TWISTING THING INSIDE--
ALL IT WANTS TO DO IS KILL--
--AN' SCREW--
--AN' HURT.
KRAKK
YOU KNOW THE THING.
HOLDIN' IT DOWN IS WHAT MAKES LIFE ACHE.
YOU CAN'T IGNORE IT, EITHER--
SKRASHH
THAT THING IS WHO YOU ARE!!
LIFE, A BURST OF UGLY IMPULSES FOLLOWED BY A LONG NOTHING!!
AN' FOR WHAT?
TO EXIST JUST LONG ENOUGH TO TASTE WHAT YOU'LL BE MISSING FOREVER?
TO SEE MY WIFE SCREWING A PALE SHADOW--
ONE THAT SHE PREFERS TO ME!!

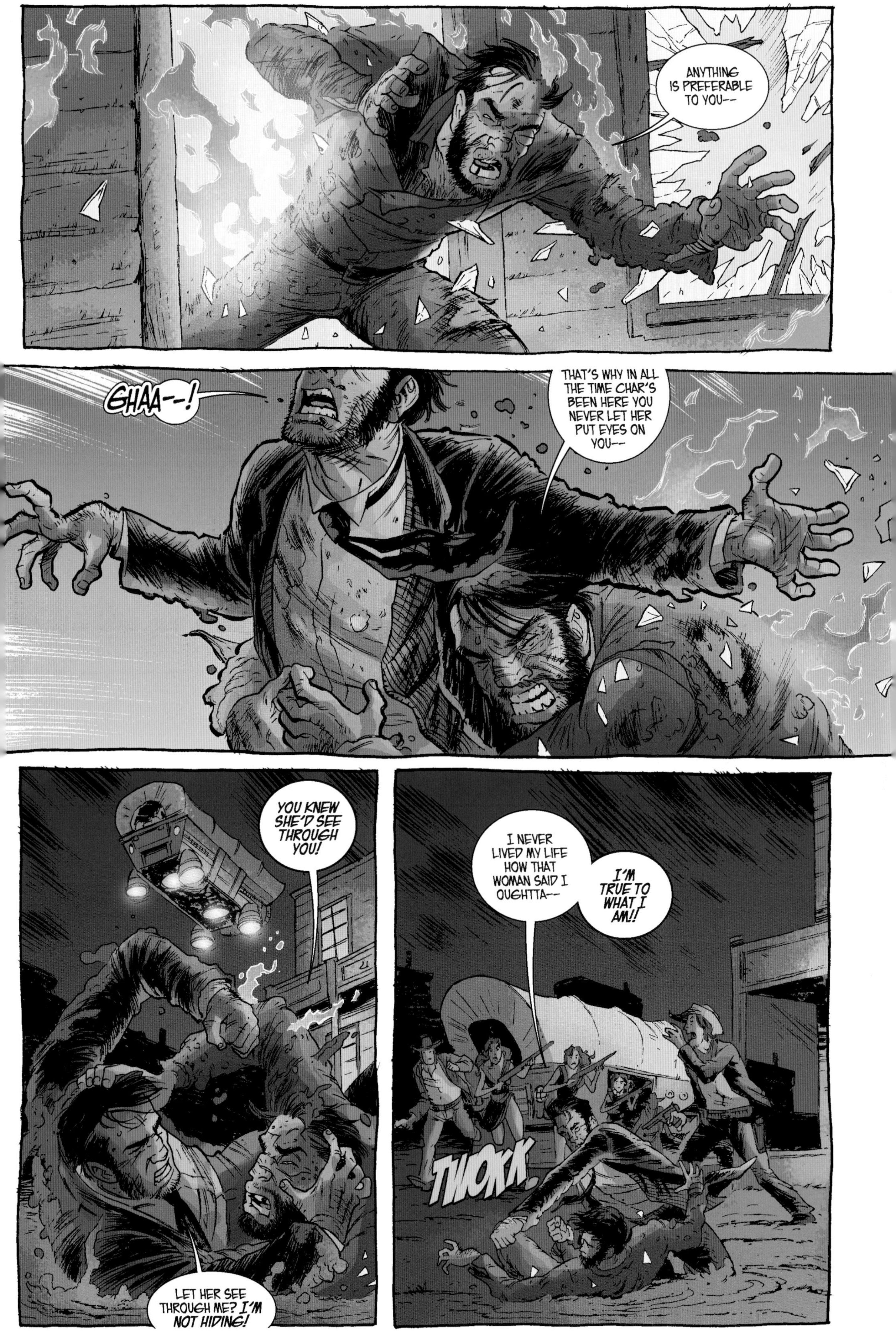
ANYTHING IS PREFERABLE TO YOU--
GHAA--!
THAT'S WHY IN ALL THE TIME CHAR'S BEEN HERE YOU NEVER LET HER PUT EYES ON YOU--
YOU KNEW SHE'D SEE THROUGH YOU!
LET HER SEE THROUGH ME? I'M NOT HIDING!
I NEVER LIVED MY LIFE HOW THAT WOMAN SAID I OUGHTTA--
I'M TRUE TO WHAT I AM!!
TWOKK

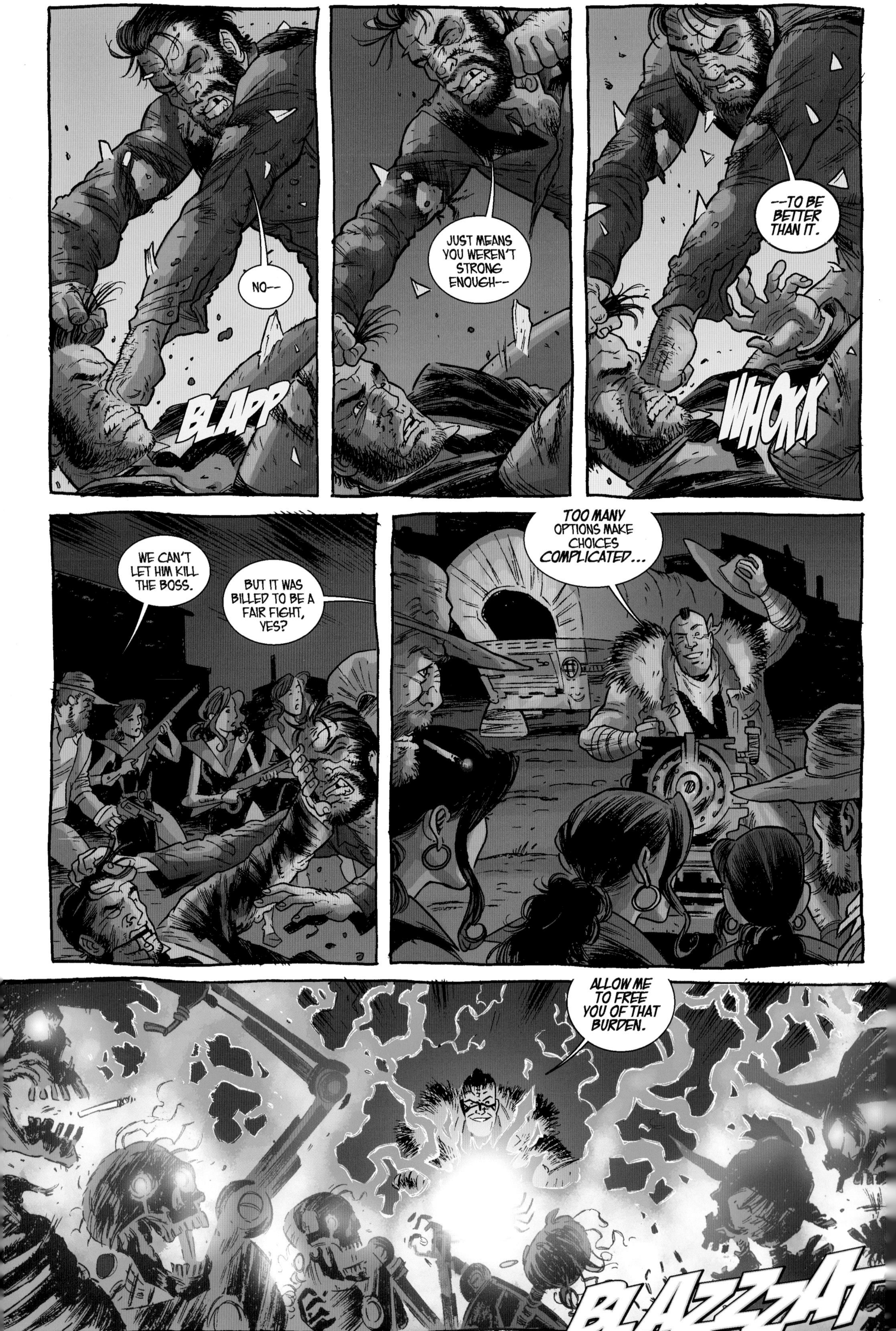
NO--
BLAPP
JUST MEANS YOU WEREN'T STRONG ENOUGH--
--TO BE BETTER THAN IT.
WHOKK
WE CAN'T LET HIM KILL THE BOSS.
BUT IT WAS BILLED TO BE A FAIR FIGHT, YES?
TOO MANY OPTIONS MAKE CHOICES COMPLICATED...
ALLOW ME TO FREE YOU OF THAT BURDEN.
BLAZZZAT

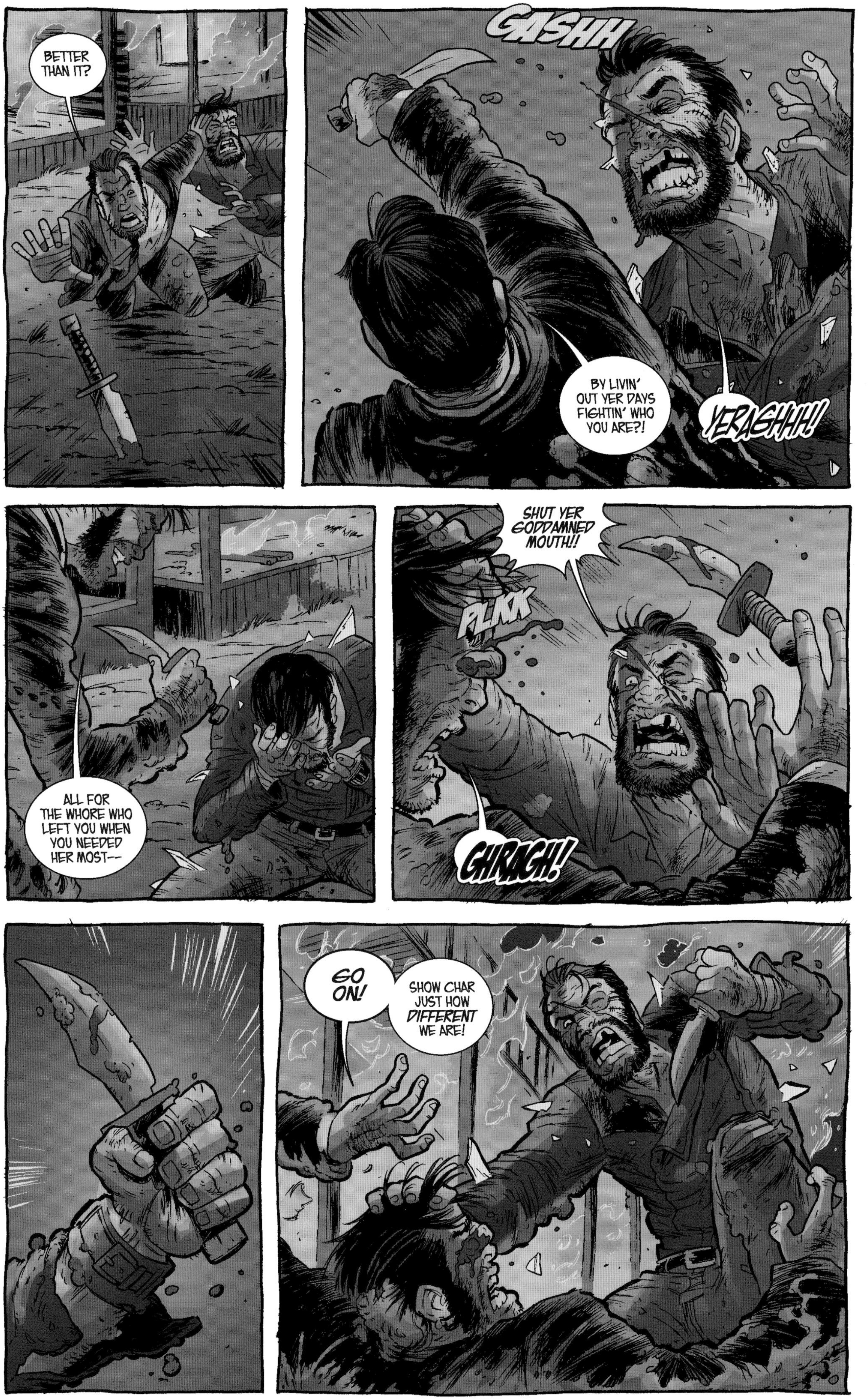
BETTER THAN IT?
GASHH
BY LIVIN' OUT YER DAYS FIGHTIN' WHO YOU ARE?!
YERASHHH!
ALL FOR THE WHORE WHO LEFT YOU WHEN YOU NEEDED HER MOST--
SHUT YER GODDAMNED MOUTH!!
PLKK
GHRAGH!
GO ON!
SHOW CHAR JUST HOW DIFFERENT WE ARE!

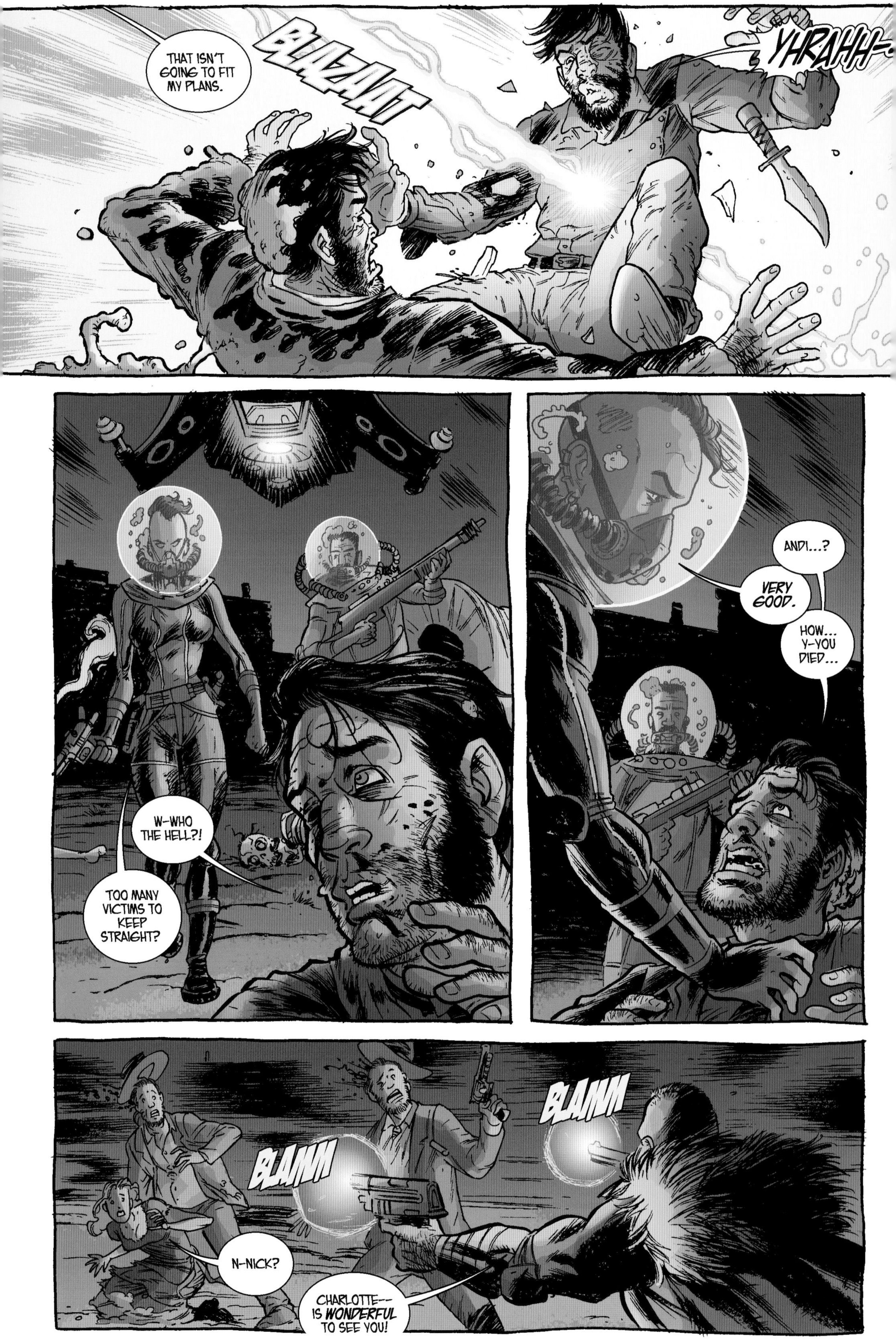
THAT ISN'T GOING TO FIT MY PLANS.
BLAZAAT
YHRAHH--
W-WHO THE HELL?!
TOO MANY VICTIMS TO KEEP STRAIGHT?
ANDI...?
VERY GOOD.
HOW... Y-YOU DIED...
BLAMM
BLAMM
N-NICK?
CHARLOTTE-- IS WONDERFUL TO SEE YOU!

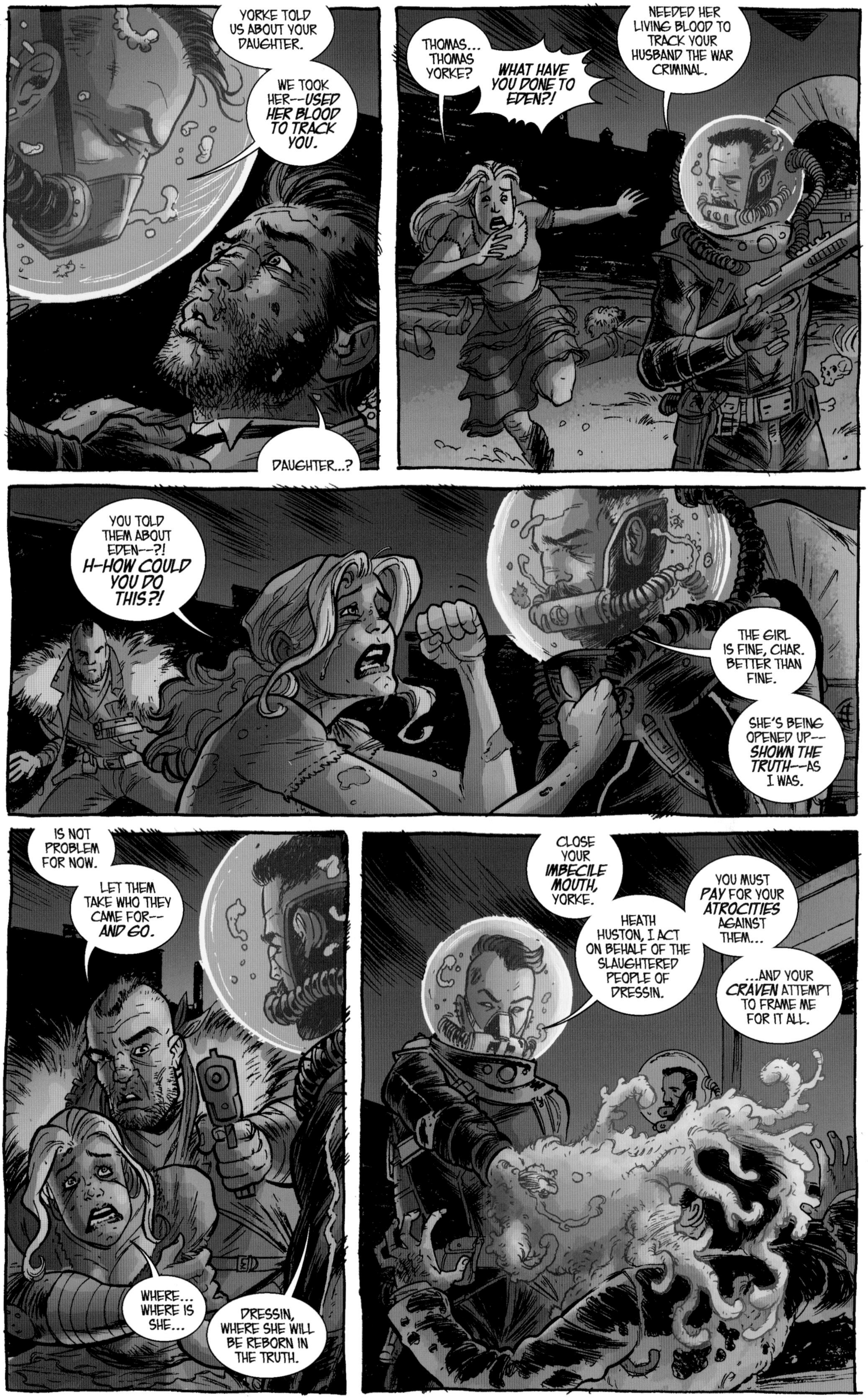
YORKE TOLD US ABOUT YOUR DAUGHTER.
WE TOOK HER--USED HER BLOOD TO TRACK YOU.
DAUGHTER...?
THOMAS... THOMAS YORKE?
WHAT HAVE YOU DONE TO EDEN?!
NEEDED HER LIVING BLOOD TO TRACK YOUR HUSBAND THE WAR CRIMINAL.
YOU TOLD THEM ABOUT EDEN--?! H-HOW COULD YOU DO THIS?!
THE GIRL IS FINE, CHAR. BETTER THAN FINE.
SHE'S BEING OPENED UP--SHOWN THE TRUTH--AS I WAS.
IS NOT PROBLEM FOR NOW.
LET THEM TAKE WHO THEY CAME FOR--AND GO.
WHERE... WHERE IS SHE...
DRESSIN, WHERE SHE WILL BE REBORN IN THE TRUTH.
CLOSE YOUR IMBECILE MOUTH, YORKE.
HEATH HUSTON, I ACT ON BEHALF OF THE SLAUGHTERED PEOPLE OF DRESSIN.
YOU MUST PAY FOR YOUR ATROCITIES AGAINST THEM...
...AND YOUR CRAVEN ATTEMPT TO FRAME ME FOR IT ALL.

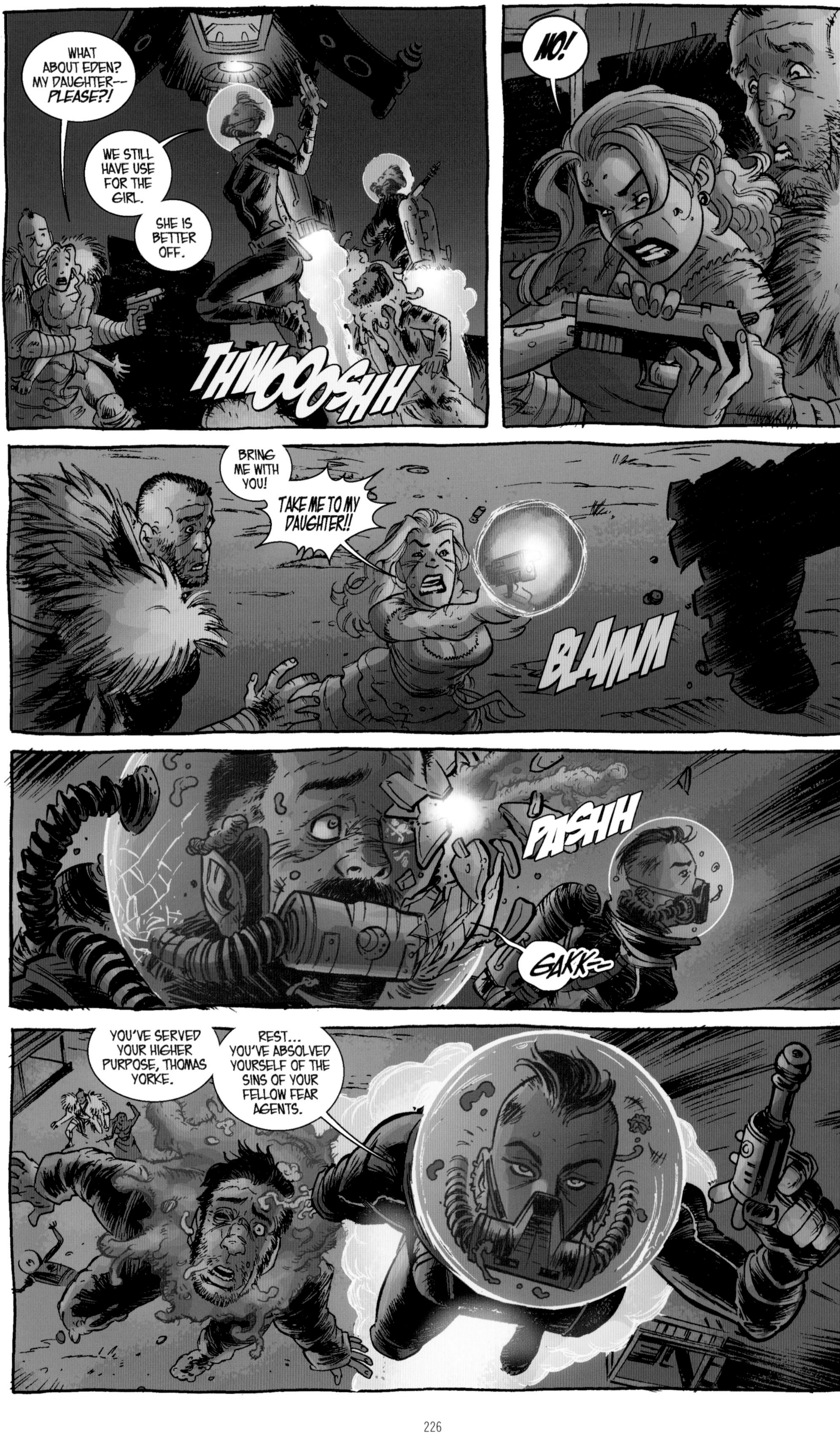
WHAT ABOUT EDEN? MY DAUGHTER-- PLEASE?!
WE STILL HAVE USE FOR THE GIRL.
SHE IS BETTER OFF.
THWOOOSHH
NO!
BRING ME WITH YOU!
TAKE ME TO MY DAUGHTER!!
BLAMM
PASHH
GAKK--
YOU'VE SERVED YOUR HIGHER PURPOSE, THOMAS YORKE.
REST... YOU'VE ABSOLVED YOURSELF OF THE SINS OF YOUR FELLOW FEAR AGENTS.

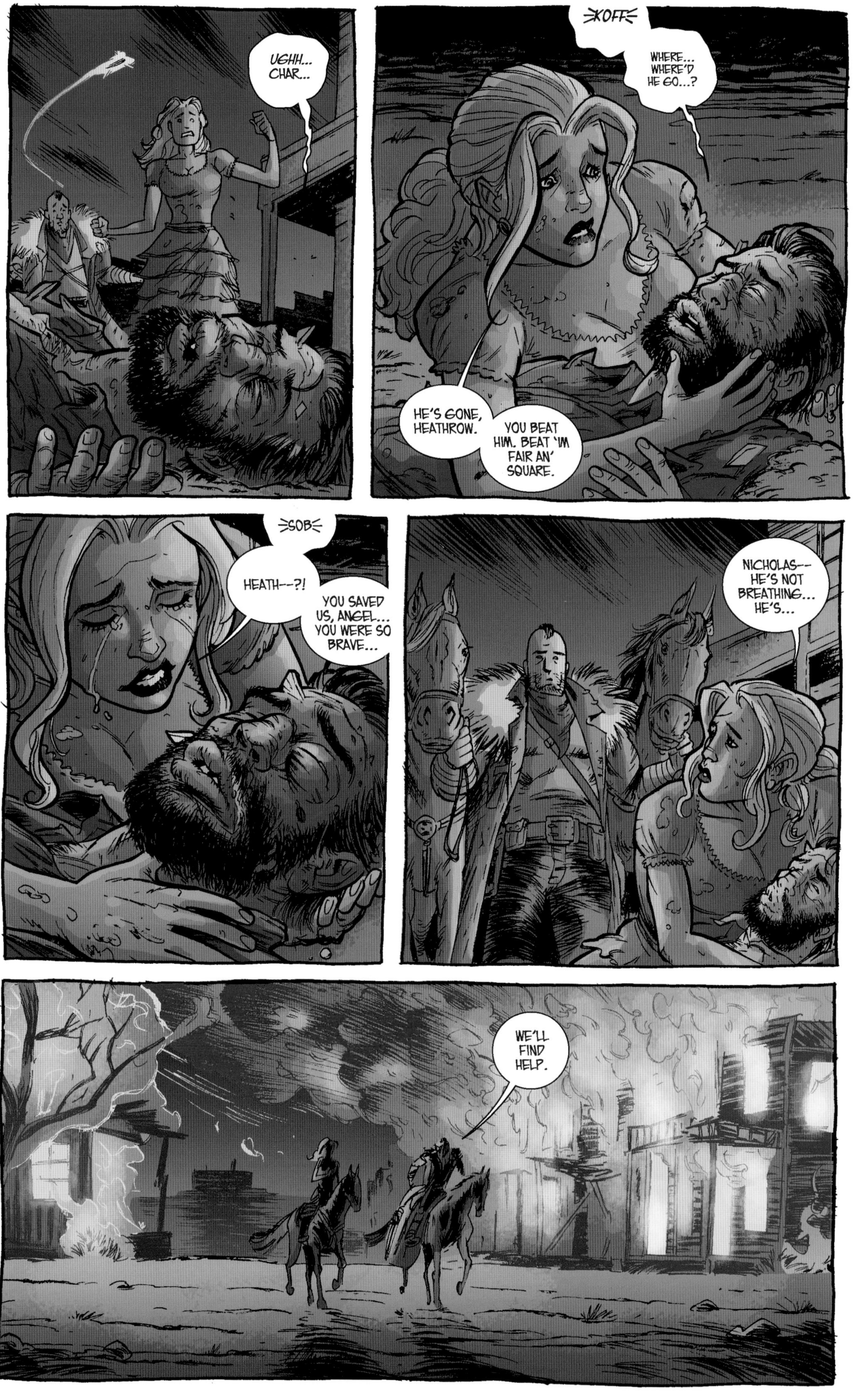
UGHH... CHAR...
KOFF
WHERE... WHERE'D HE GO...?
HE'S GONE, HEATHROW.
YOU BEAT HIM. BEAT 'IM FAIR AN' SQUARE.
SOB
HEATH--?!
YOU SAVED US, ANGEL... YOU WERE SO BRAVE...
NICHOLAS-- HE'S NOT BREATHING... HE'S...
WE'LL FIND HELP.

MONTHS PASS...

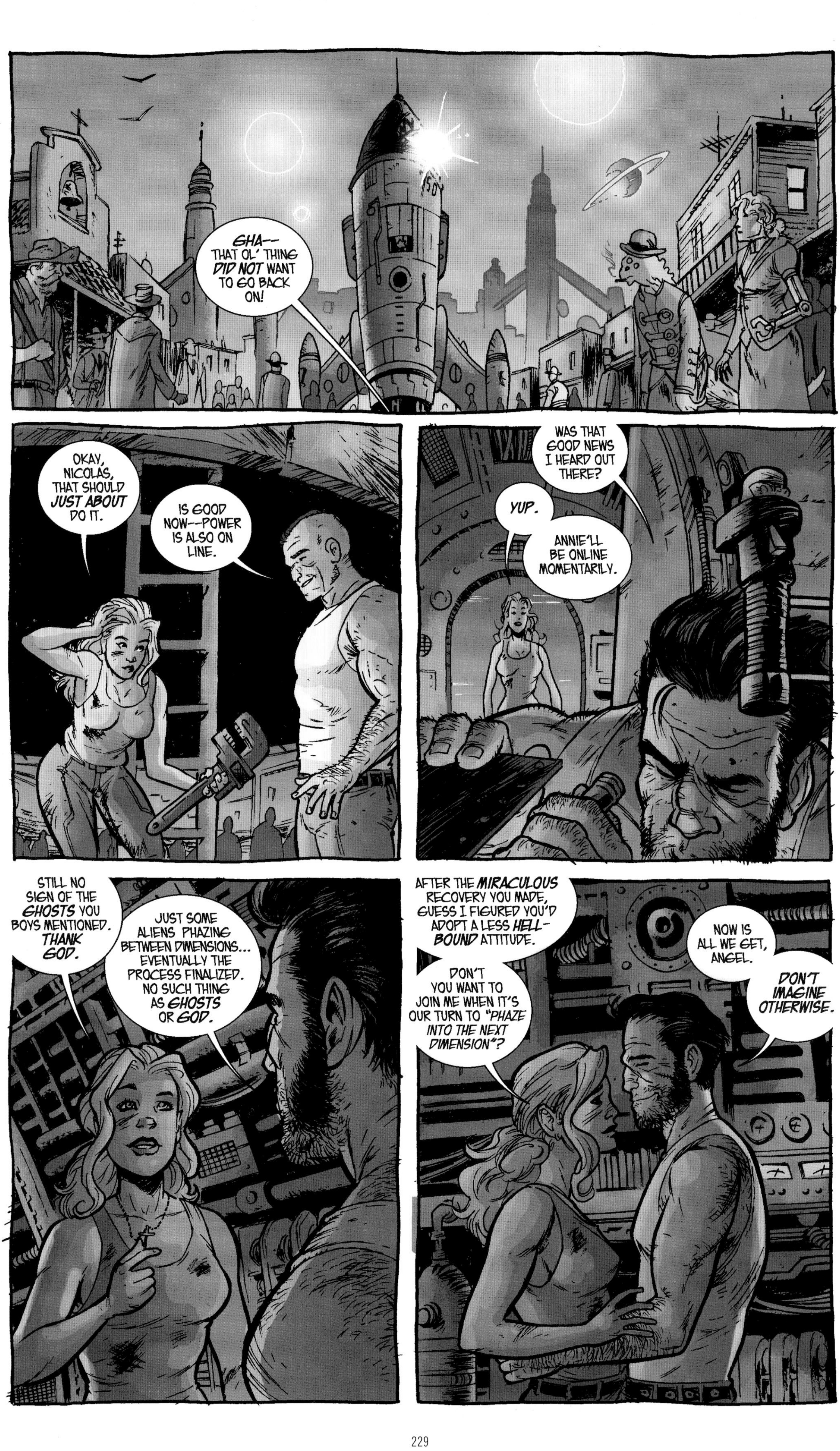
GHA--
THAT OL' THING DID NOT WANT TO GO BACK ON!
OKAY, NICOLAS, THAT SHOULD JUST ABOUT DO IT.
IS GOOD NOW--POWER IS ALSO ON LINE.
WAS THAT GOOD NEWS I HEARD OUT THERE?
YUP.
ANNIE'LL BE ONLINE MOMENTARILY.
STILL NO SIGN OF THE GHOSTS YOU BOYS MENTIONED. THANK GOD.
JUST SOME ALIENS PHAZING BETWEEN DIMENSIONS... EVENTUALLY THE PROCESS FINALIZED. NO SUCH THING AS GHOSTS OR GOD.
AFTER THE MIRACULOUS RECOVERY YOU MADE, GUESS I FIGURED YOU'D ADOPT A LESS HELL-BOUND ATTITUDE.
DON'T YOU WANT TO JOIN ME WHEN IT'S OUR TURN TO "PHAZE INTO THE NEXT DIMENSION"?
NOW IS ALL WE GET, ANGEL.
DON'T IMAGINE OTHERWISE.

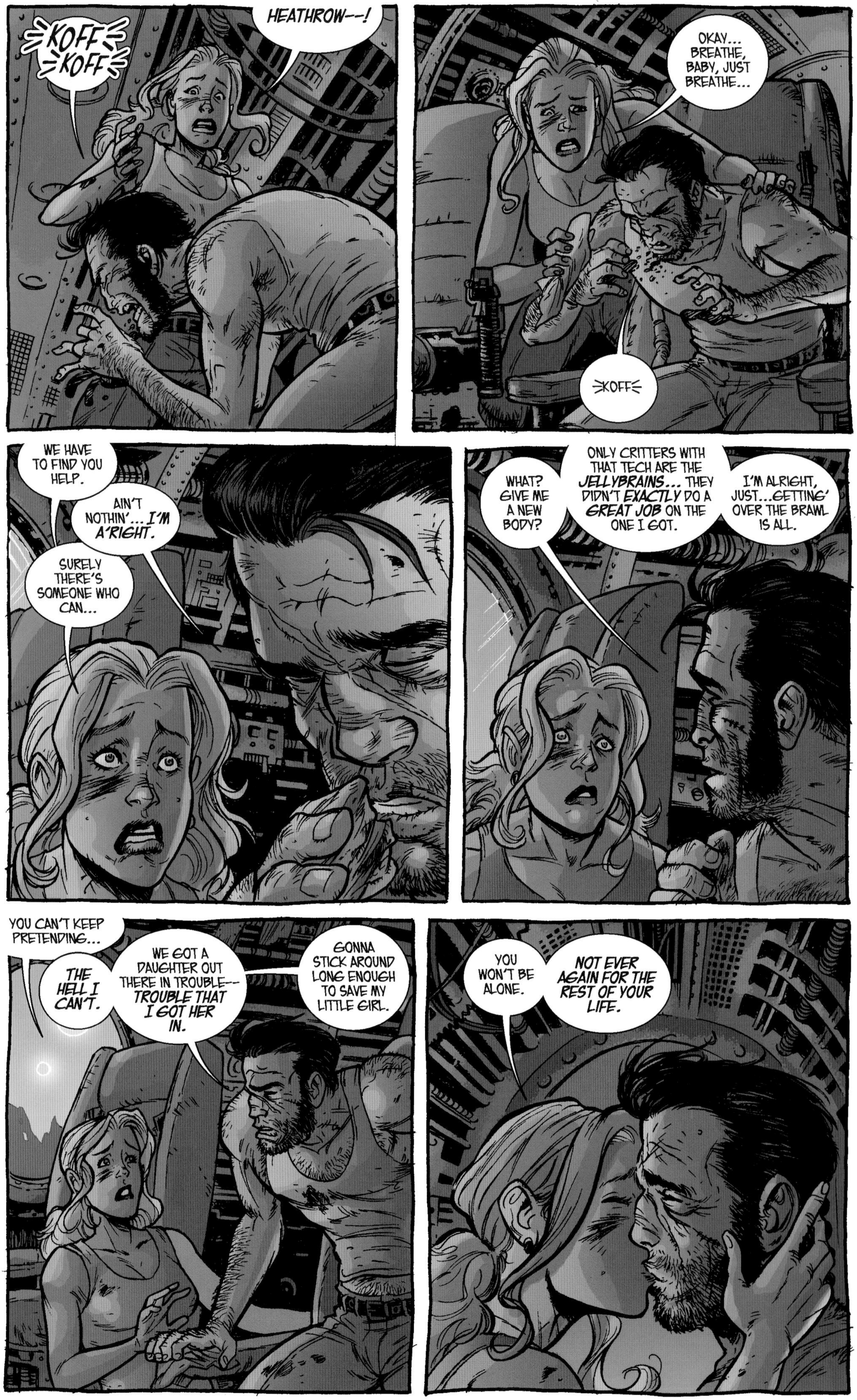
KOFF KOFF
HEATHROW--!
OKAY... BREATHE, BABY, JUST BREATHE...
KOFF
WE HAVE TO FIND YOU HELP.
AIN'T NOTHIN'... I'M A'RIGHT.
SURELY THERE'S SOMEONE WHO CAN...
WHAT? GIVE ME A NEW BODY?
ONLY CRITTERS WITH THAT TECH ARE THE JELLYBRAINS... THEY DIDN'T EXACTLY DO A GREAT JOB ON THE ONE I GOT.
I'M ALRIGHT, JUST...GETTING' OVER THE BRAWL IS ALL.
YOU CAN'T KEEP PRETENDING...
THE HELL I CAN'T.
WE GOT A DAUGHTER OUT THERE IN TROUBLE-- TROUBLE THAT I GOT HER IN.
GONNA STICK AROUND LONG ENOUGH TO SAVE MY LITTLE GIRL.
YOU WON'T BE ALONE.
NOT EVER AGAIN FOR THE REST OF YOUR LIFE.

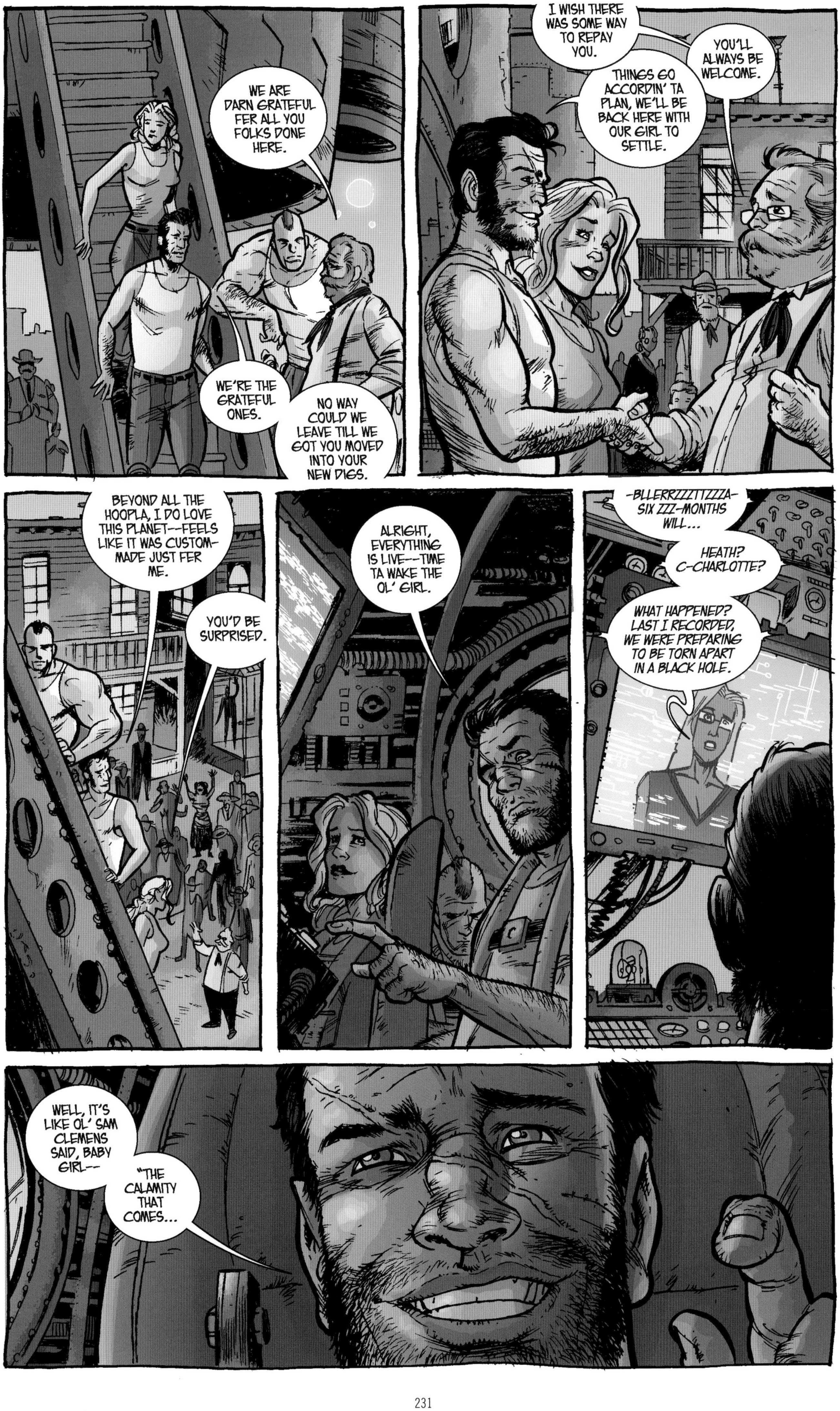
WE ARE DARN GRATEFUL FER ALL YOU FOLKS DONE HERE.
WE'RE THE GRATEFUL ONES.
NO WAY COULD WE LEAVE TILL WE GOT YOU MOVED INTO YOUR NEW DIGS.
I WISH THERE WAS SOME WAY TO REPAY YOU.
YOU'LL ALWAYS BE WELCOME.
THINGS GO ACCORDIN' TA PLAN, WE'LL BE BACK HERE WITH OUR GIRL TO SETTLE.
BEYOND ALL THE HOOPLA, I DO LOVE THIS PLANET--FEELS LIKE IT WAS CUSTOM-MADE JUST FER ME.
YOU'D BE SURPRISED.
ALRIGHT, EVERYTHING IS LIVE--TIME TA WAKE THE OL' GIRL.
-BLLERRZZZTTZZZA-SIX ZZZ-MONTHS WILL...
HEATH? C-CHARLOTTE?
WHAT HAPPENED? LAST I RECORDED, WE WERE PREPARING TO BE TORN APART IN A BLACK HOLE.
WELL, IT'S LIKE OL' SAM CLEMENS SAID, BABY GIRL--
"THE CALAMITY THAT COMES...

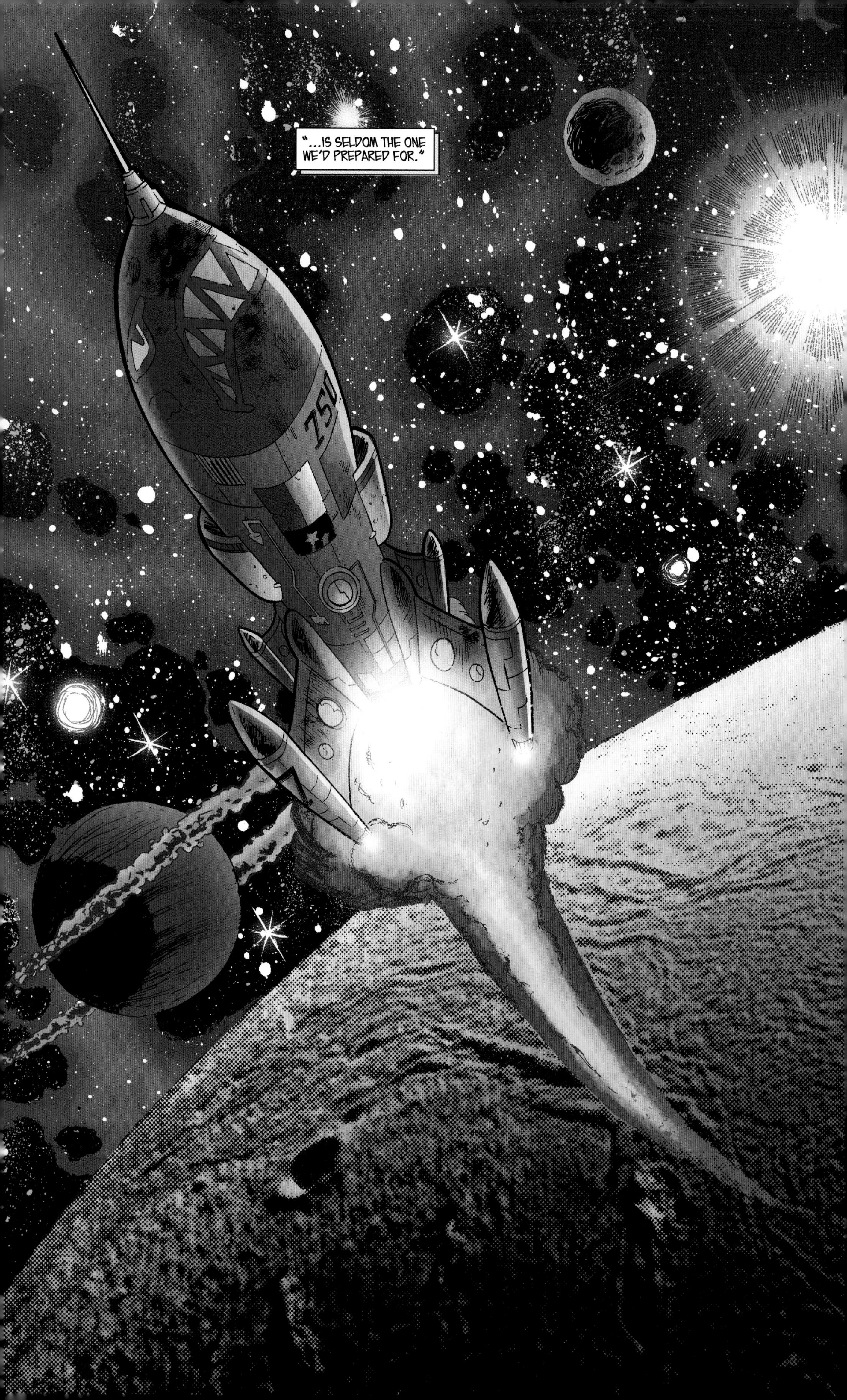
"...IS SELDOM THE ONE WE'D PREPARED FOR."
750

CHAPTER 6

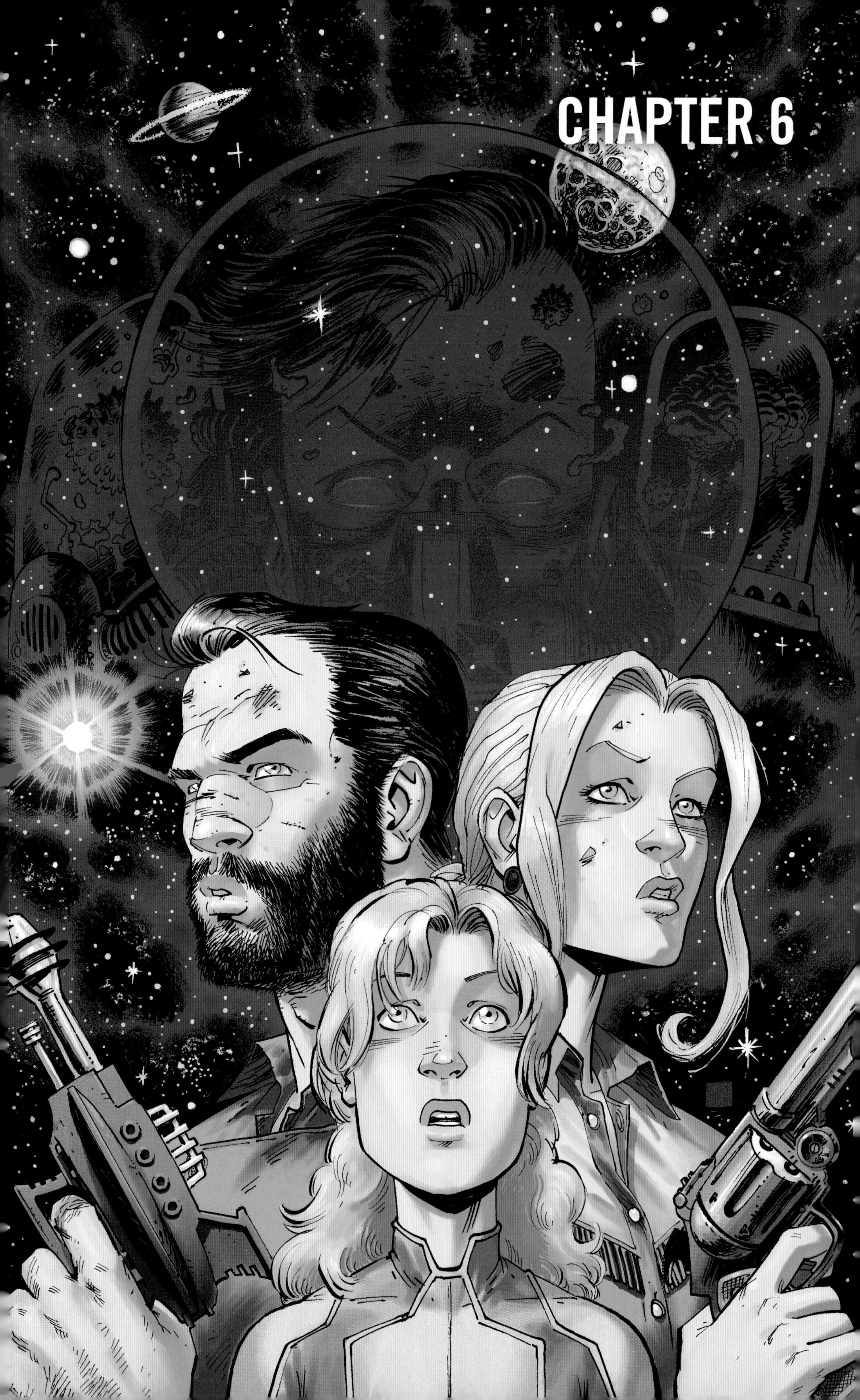

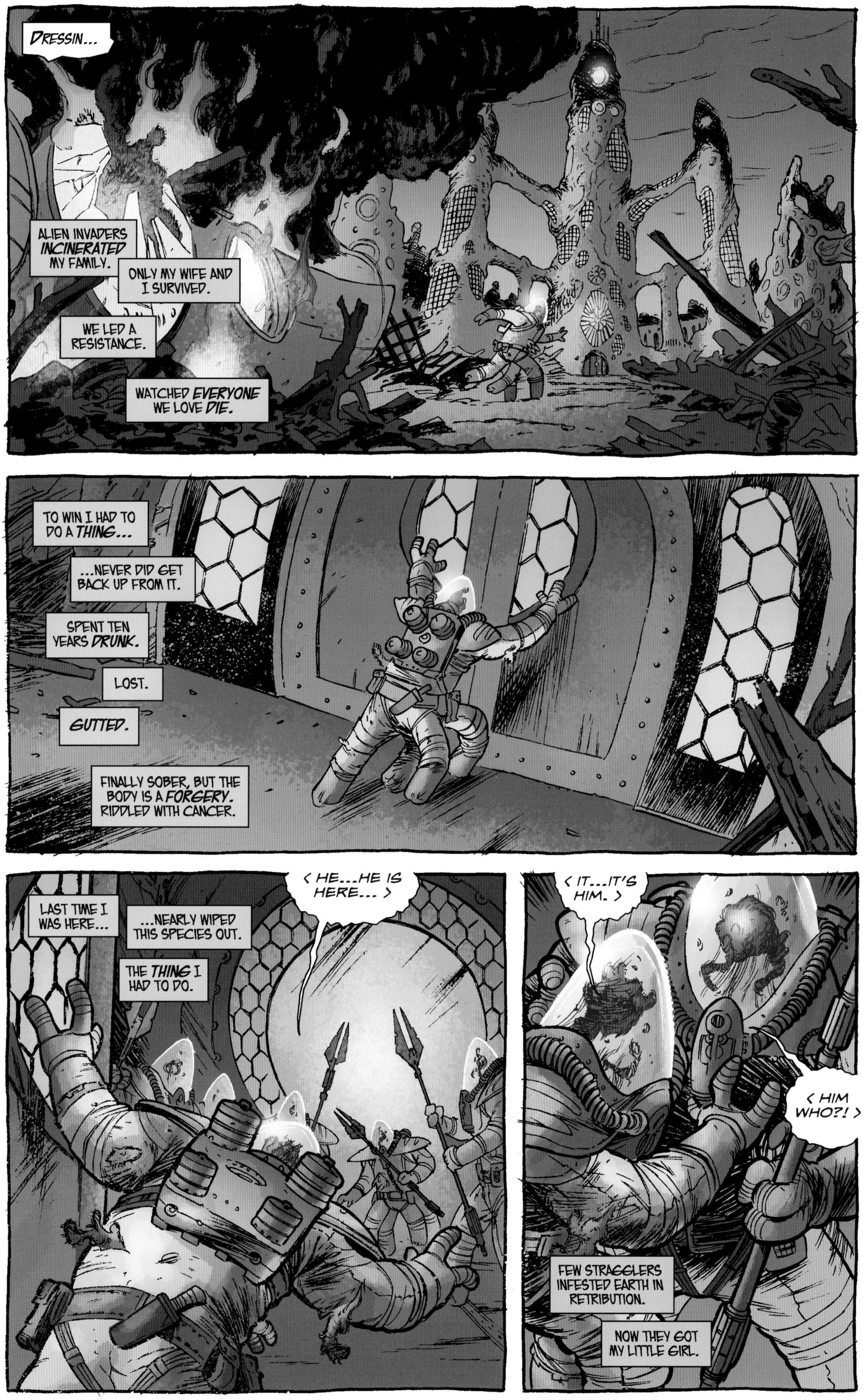
DRESSIN...
ALIEN INVADERS INCINERATED MY FAMILY.
ONLY MY WIFE AND I SURVIVED.
WE LED A RESISTANCE.
WATCHED EVERYONE WE LOVE DIE.
TO WIN I HAD TO DO A THING...
...NEVER DID GET BACK UP FROM IT.
SPENT TEN YEARS DRUNK.
LOST.
GUTTED.
FINALLY SOBER, BUT THE BODY IS A FORGERY. RIDDLED WITH CANCER.
LAST TIME I WAS HERE...
...NEARLY WIPED THIS SPECIES OUT.
THE THING I HAD TO DO.
‹ HE...HE IS HERE... ›
‹ IT...IT'S HIM. ›
‹ HIM WHO?! ›
FEW STRAGGLERS INFESTED EARTH IN RETRIBUTION.
NOW THEY GOT MY LITTLE GIRL.

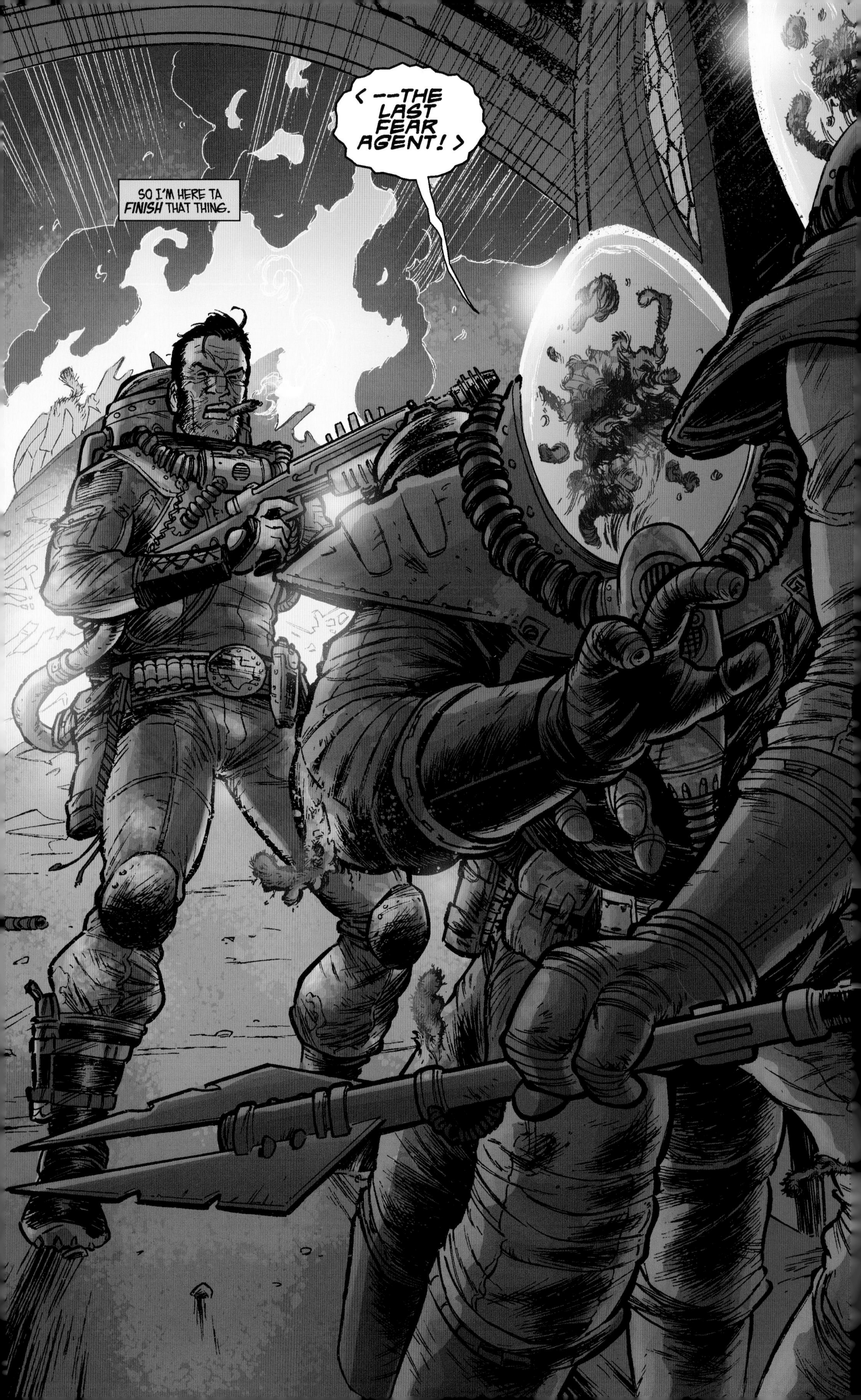
SO I'M HERE TA FINISH THAT THING.
< --THE LAST FEAR AGENT! >

THEY DIE IN FAMILIAR WAYS.
SOUNDS I'VE HEARD A MILLION TIMES BEFORE.
VARIATIONS ON A HIGH-PITCHED THEME.
TORBB!
GLAZATT
THEY DO THE SAME THINGS.
I REACT.
SECOND NATURE.
DOWN TO AN ART.
FWOOSHH
BUT THIS TIME IS DIFFERENT.
THIS IS THE LAST TIME.
THIS TIME SOMEBODY STANDS THE CLEAR WINNER.
KRAKK
GLORRBO!
GLAZZAT
AND SOMEBODY ELSE GETS ARMAGEDDON.

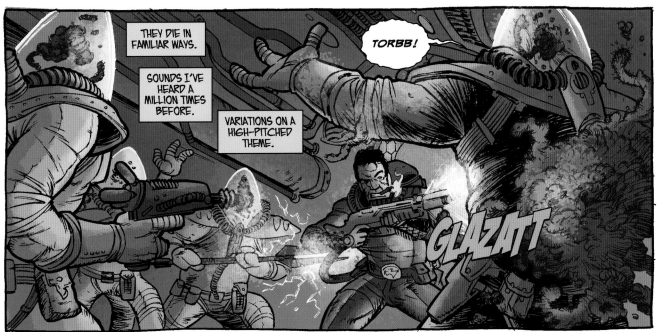

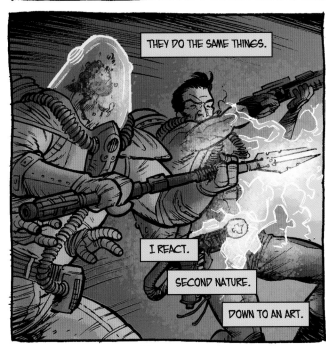

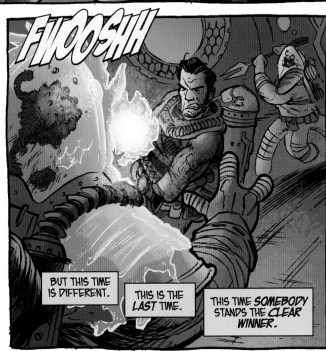

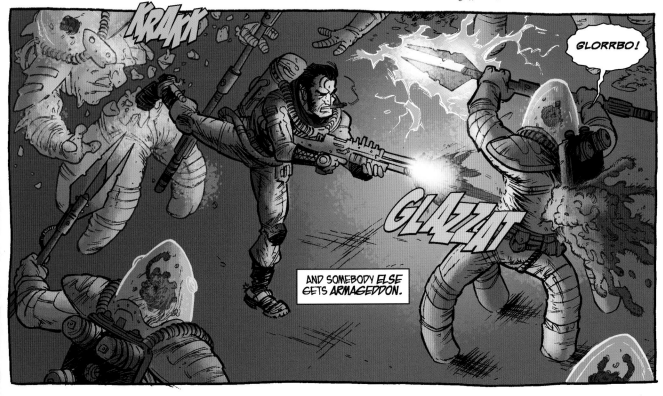

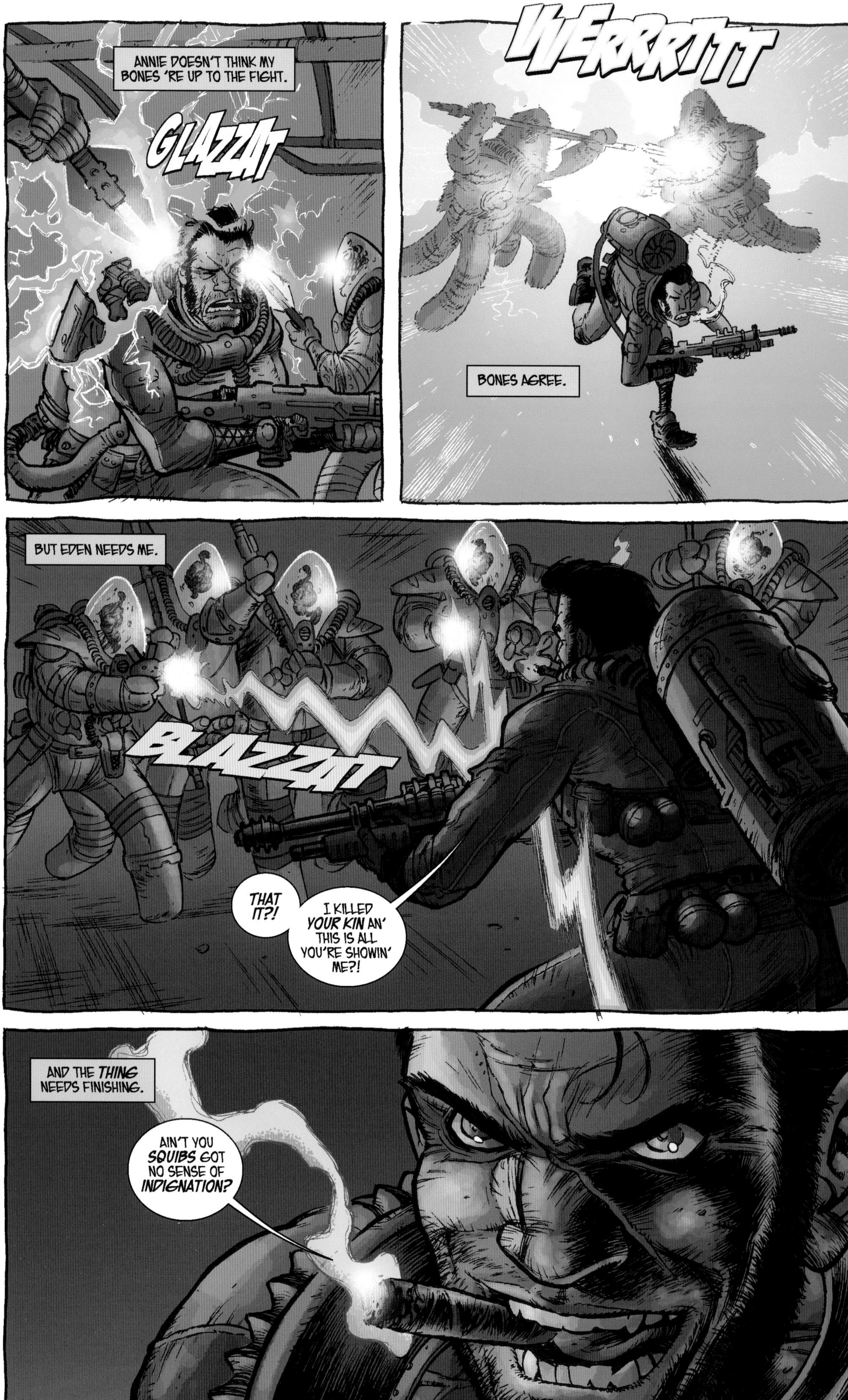
ANNIE DOESN'T THINK MY BONES 'RE UP TO THE FIGHT.
GLAZZAT
WERRRTTT
BONES AGREE.
BUT EDEN NEEDS ME.
BLAZZAT
THAT IT?!
I KILLED YOUR KIN AN' THIS IS ALL YOU'RE SHOWIN' ME?!
AND THE THING NEEDS FINISHING.
AIN'T YOU SQUIBS GOT NO SENSE OF INDIGNATION?

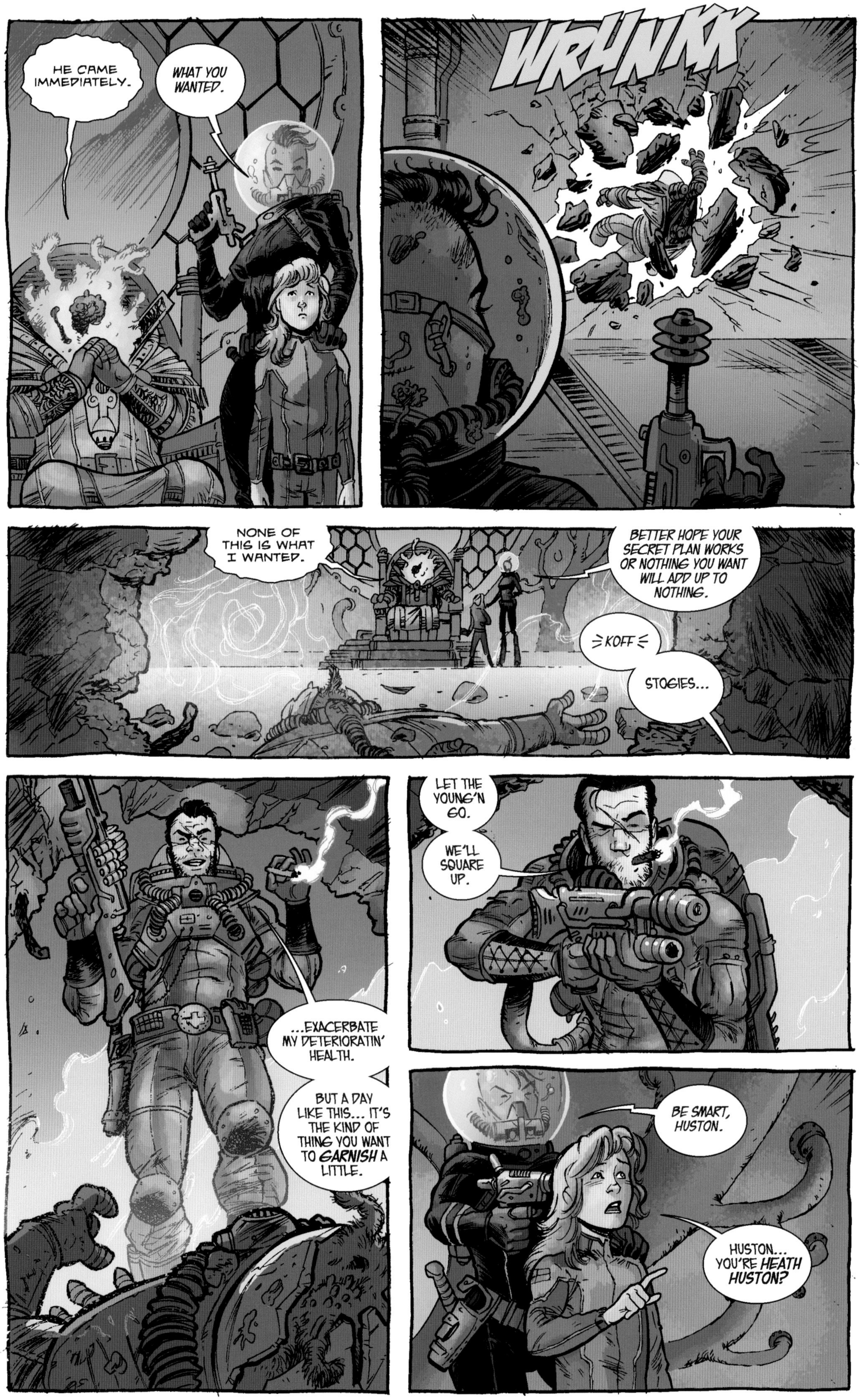
HE CAME IMMEDIATELY.
WHAT YOU WANTED.
WRUNKK
NONE OF THIS IS WHAT I WANTED.
BETTER HOPE YOUR SECRET PLAN WORKS OR NOTHING YOU WANT WILL ADD UP TO NOTHING.
KOFF
STOGIES...
...EXACERBATE MY DETERIORATIN' HEALTH.
BUT A DAY LIKE THIS... IT'S THE KIND OF THING YOU WANT TO GARNISH A LITTLE.
LET THE YOUNG'N GO.
WE'LL SQUARE UP.
BE SMART, HUSTON.
HUSTON... YOU'RE HEATH HUSTON?

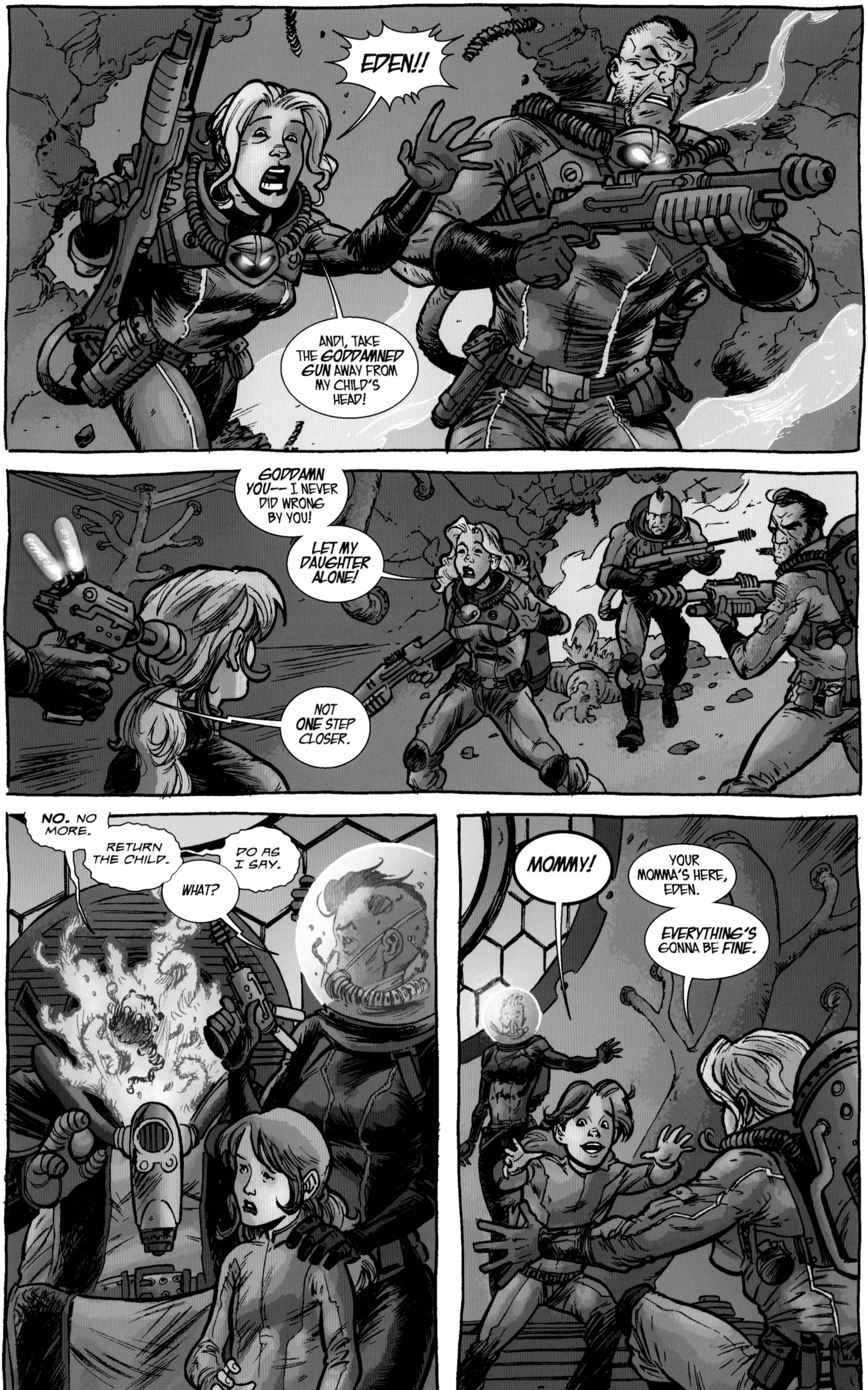
EDEN!!
ANDI, TAKE THE GODDAMNED GUN AWAY FROM MY CHILD'S HEAD!
GODDAMN YOU-- I NEVER DID WRONG BY YOU!
LET MY DAUGHTER ALONE!
NOT ONE STEP CLOSER.
NO. NO MORE.
RETURN THE CHILD.
WHAT?
DO AS I SAY.
MOMMY!
YOUR MOMMA'S HERE, EDEN.
EVERYTHING'S GONNA BE FINE.

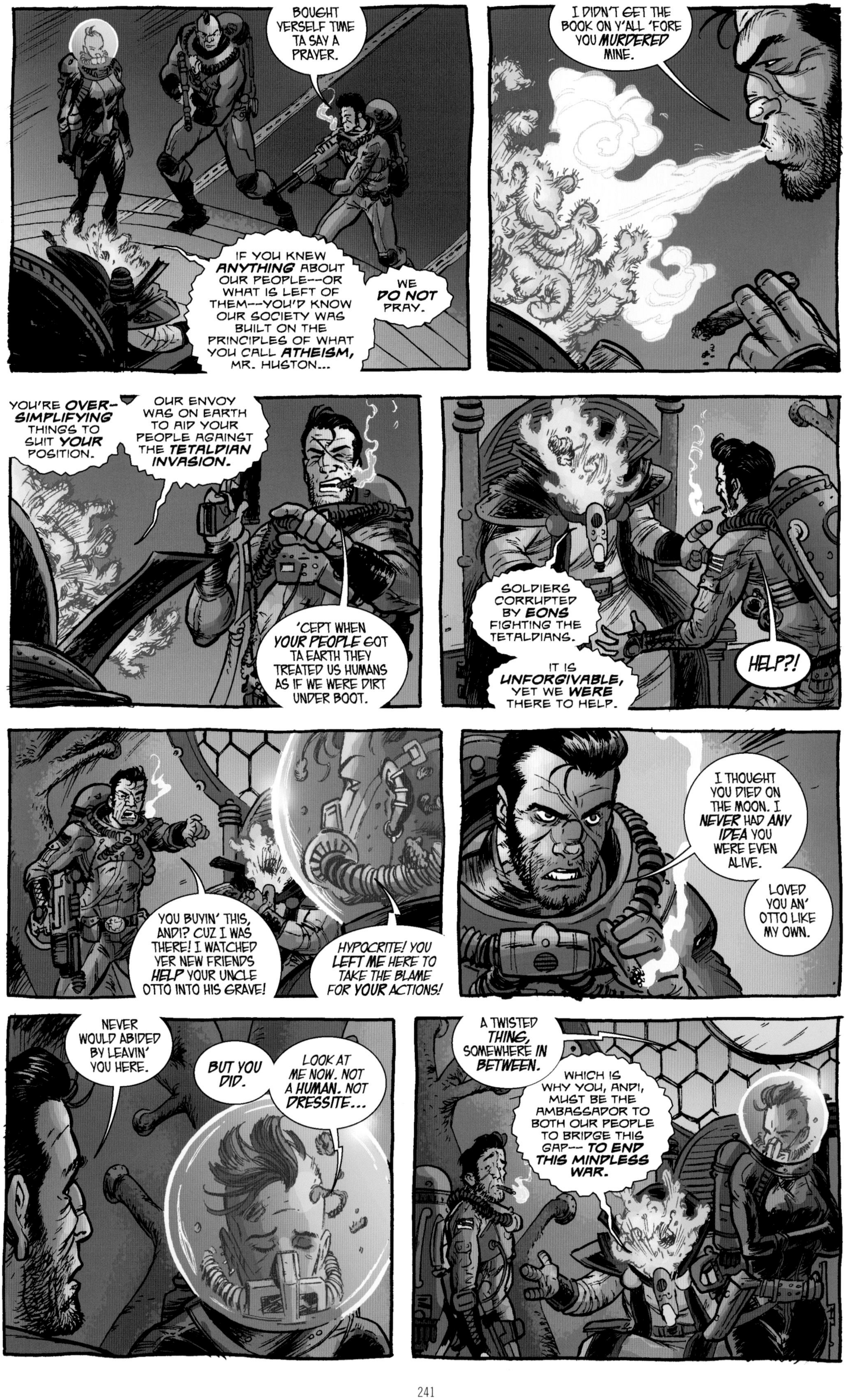
BOUGHT YERSELF TIME TA SAY A PRAYER.
IF YOU KNEW ANYTHING ABOUT OUR PEOPLE--OR WHAT IS LEFT OF THEM--YOU'D KNOW OUR SOCIETY WAS BUILT ON THE PRINCIPLES OF WHAT YOU CALL ATHEISM, MR. HUSTON...
WE DO NOT PRAY.
I DIDN'T GET THE BOOK ON Y'ALL 'FORE YOU MURDERED MINE.
YOU'RE OVER-SIMPLIFYING THINGS TO SUIT YOUR POSITION.
OUR ENVOY WAS ON EARTH TO AID YOUR PEOPLE AGAINST THE TETALDIAN INVASION.
'CEPT WHEN YOUR PEOPLE GOT TA EARTH THEY TREATED US HUMANS AS IF WE WERE DIRT UNDER BOOT.
SOLDIERS CORRUPTED BY EONS FIGHTING THE TETALDIANS.
IT IS UNFORGIVABLE, YET WE WERE THERE TO HELP.
HELP?!
YOU BUYIN' THIS, ANDI? CUZ I WAS THERE! I WATCHED YER NEW FRIENDS HELP YOUR UNCLE OTTO INTO HIS GRAVE!
HYPOCRITE! YOU LEFT ME HERE TO TAKE THE BLAME FOR YOUR ACTIONS!
I THOUGHT YOU DIED ON THE MOON. I NEVER HAD ANY IDEA YOU WERE EVEN ALIVE.
LOVED YOU AN' OTTO LIKE MY OWN.
NEVER WOULD ABIDED BY LEAVIN' YOU HERE.
BUT YOU DID.
LOOK AT ME NOW. NOT A HUMAN. NOT DRESSITE...
A TWISTED THING, SOMEWHERE IN BETWEEN.
WHICH IS WHY YOU, ANDI, MUST BE THE AMBASSADOR TO BOTH OUR PEOPLE TO BRIDGE THIS GAP-- TO END THIS MINDLESS WAR.

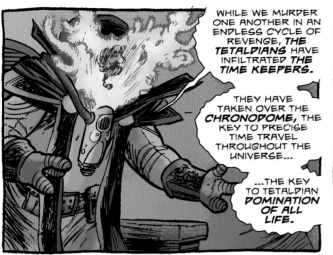

WHILE WE MURDER ONE ANOTHER IN AN ENDLESS CYCLE OF REVENGE, **THE TETALDIANS** HAVE INFILTRATED **THE TIME KEEPERS.**

THEY HAVE TAKEN OVER THE **CHRONODOME,** THE KEY TO PRECISE TIME TRAVEL THROUGHOUT THE UNIVERSE...

...THE KEY TO TETALDIAN **DOMINATION OF ALL LIFE.**

THEY **WILL** USE IT. THEY WILL SPREAD, **INFECTING** THE UNIVERSE.

THEIR GOAL **IS** WITHIN REACH.

OUR PEOPLE-- **NEARLY DECIMATED!!**

WHILE **THE TETALDIAN EMPIRE** GROWS STRONGER BY THE DAY!!

WE MUST MOVE BEYOND THIS PATH OF SELF-DESTRUCTION.

WE MUST STAND **TOGETHER** AGAINST THEM.

TOGETHER...?

I BEG YOU TO ACCEPT.

IF ONLY FOR SELF-INTEREST. IF ONLY FOR **SURVIVAL!**

ACCEPT PEACE NOW...

WE MUST UNITE.

NOW, WHEN I GOT YOU DEAD TO RIGHTS--**NOW** YOU WANT TO **PARTNER UP?**

... I WILL FREE YOUR EARTH FROM **FEEDER INFESTATION.**

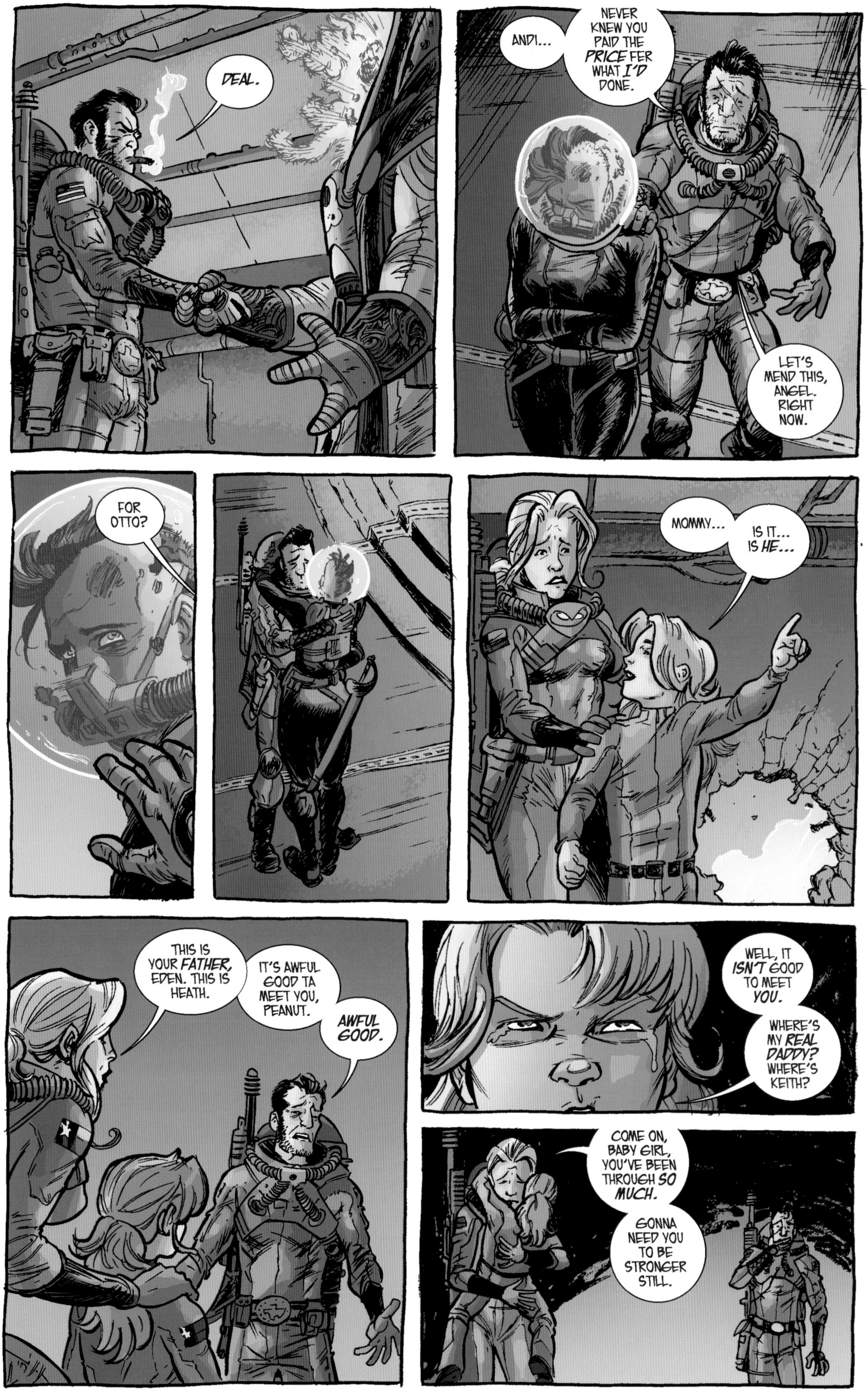
DEAL.
ANDI...
NEVER KNEW YOU PAID THE PRICE FER WHAT I'D DONE.
LET'S MEND THIS, ANGEL. RIGHT NOW.
FOR OTTO?
MOMMY...
IS IT... IS HE...
THIS IS YOUR FATHER, EDEN. THIS IS HEATH.
IT'S AWFUL GOOD TA MEET YOU, PEANUT.
AWFUL GOOD.
WELL, IT ISN'T GOOD TO MEET YOU.
WHERE'S MY REAL DADDY? WHERE'S KEITH?
COME ON, BABY GIRL, YOU'VE BEEN THROUGH SO MUCH.
GONNA NEED YOU TO BE STRONGER STILL.

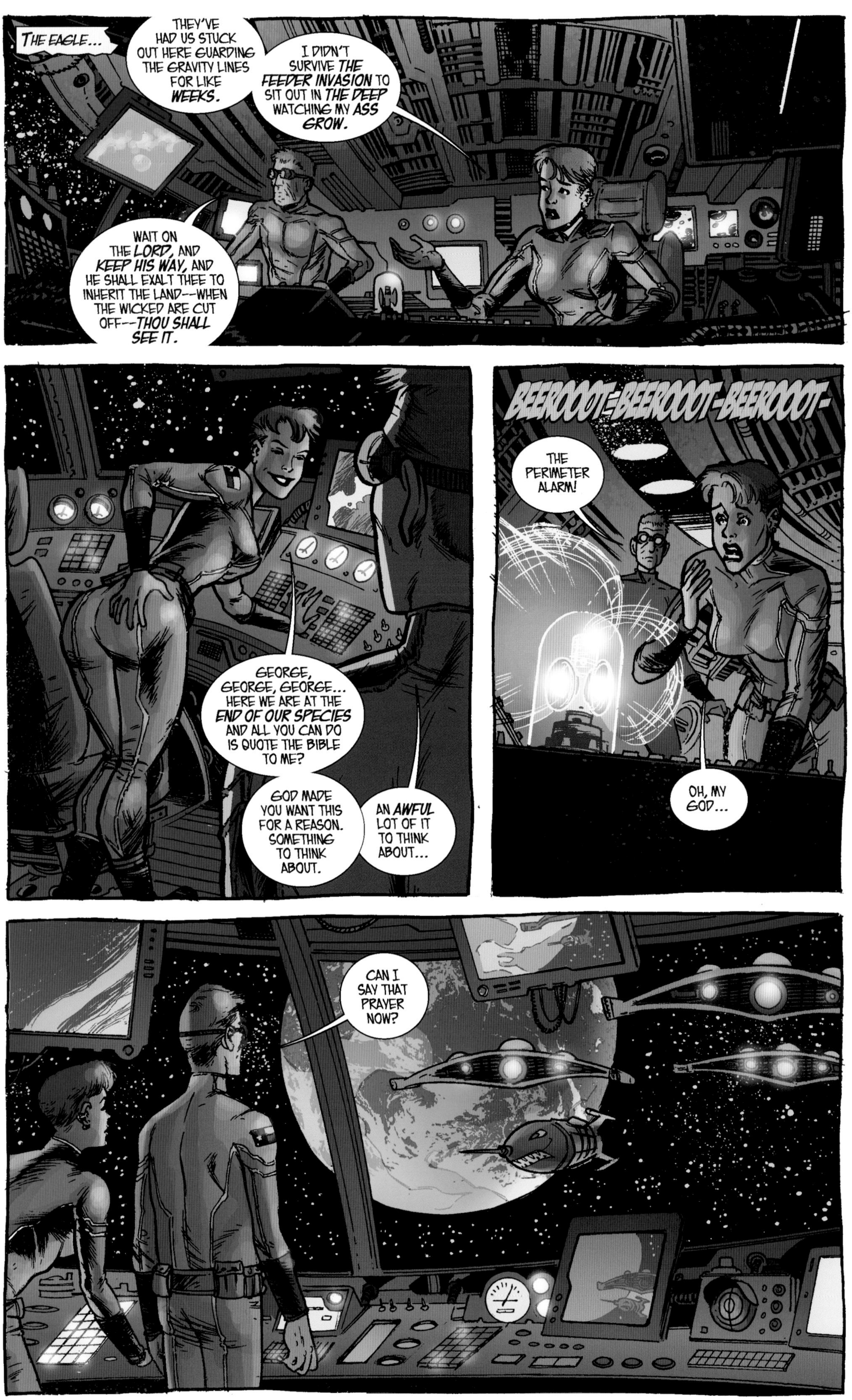
THE EAGLE...
THEY'VE HAD US STUCK OUT HERE GUARDING THE GRAVITY LINES FOR LIKE WEEKS.
I DIDN'T SURVIVE THE FEEDER INVASION TO SIT OUT IN THE DEEP WATCHING MY ASS GROW.
WAIT ON THE LORD, AND KEEP HIS WAY, AND HE SHALL EXALT THEE TO INHERIT THE LAND--WHEN THE WICKED ARE CUT OFF--THOU SHALL SEE IT.
GEORGE, GEORGE, GEORGE... HERE WE ARE AT THE END OF OUR SPECIES AND ALL YOU CAN DO IS QUOTE THE BIBLE TO ME?
GOD MADE YOU WANT THIS FOR A REASON. SOMETHING TO THINK ABOUT.
AN AWFUL LOT OF IT TO THINK ABOUT...
BEEROOOT-BEEROOOT-BEEROOOT-
THE PERIMETER ALARM!
OH, MY GOD...
CAN I SAY THAT PRAYER NOW?

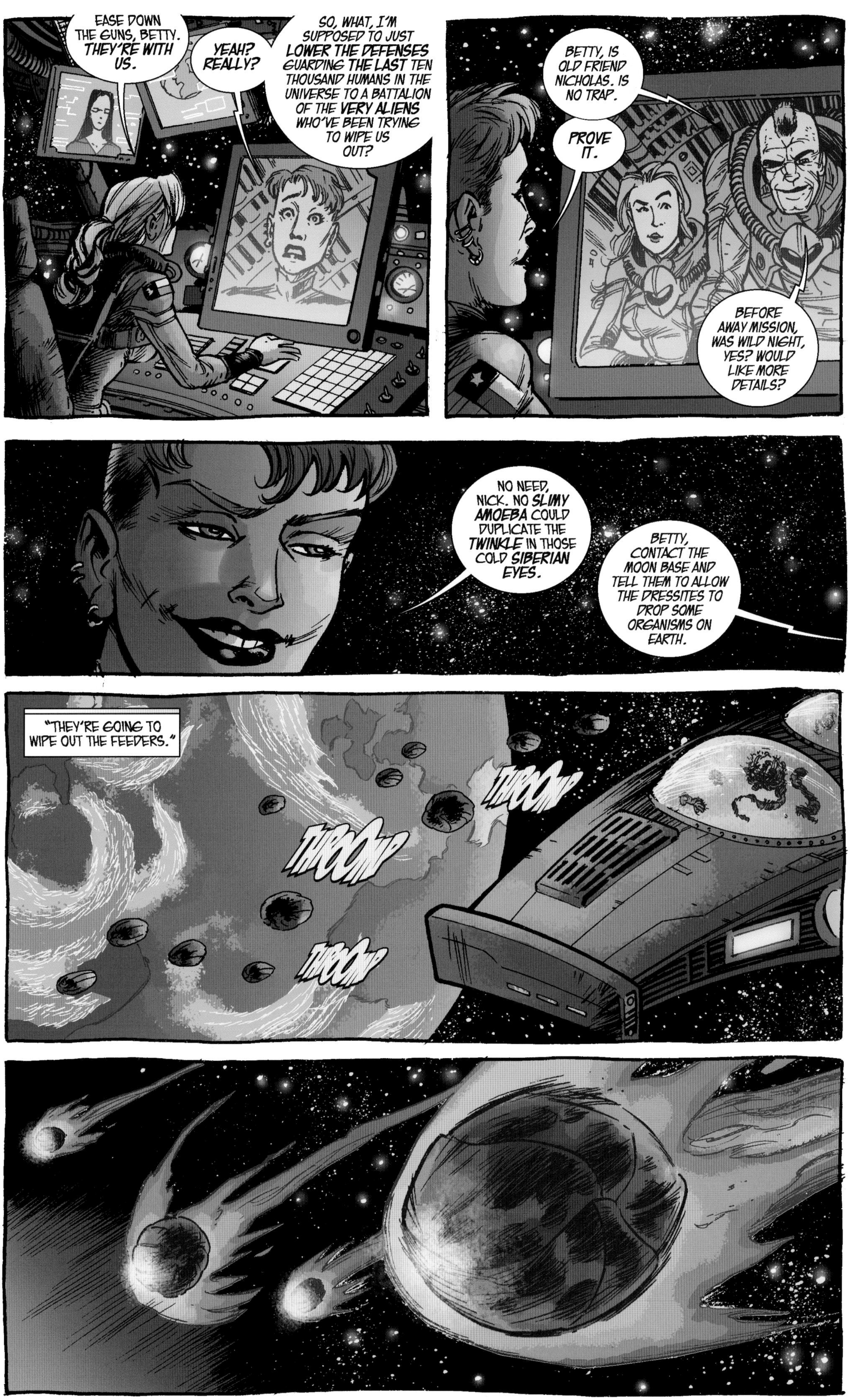
EASE DOWN THE GUNS, BETTY. THEY'RE WITH US.
YEAH? REALLY?
SO, WHAT, I'M SUPPOSED TO JUST LOWER THE DEFENSES GUARDING THE LAST TEN THOUSAND HUMANS IN THE UNIVERSE TO A BATTALION OF THE VERY ALIENS WHO'VE BEEN TRYING TO WIPE US OUT?
BETTY, IS OLD FRIEND NICHOLAS. IS NO TRAP.
PROVE IT.
BEFORE AWAY MISSION, WAS WILD NIGHT, YES? WOULD LIKE MORE DETAILS?
NO NEED, NICK. NO SLIMY AMOEBA COULD DUPLICATE THE TWINKLE IN THOSE COLD SIBERIAN EYES.
BETTY, CONTACT THE MOON BASE AND TELL THEM TO ALLOW THE DRESSITES TO DROP SOME ORGANISMS ON EARTH.
"THEY'RE GOING TO WIPE OUT THE FEEDERS."
THROOMP
THROOMP
THROOMP

THOOOM

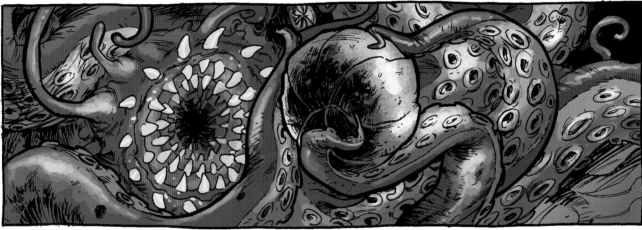

EERREKK–

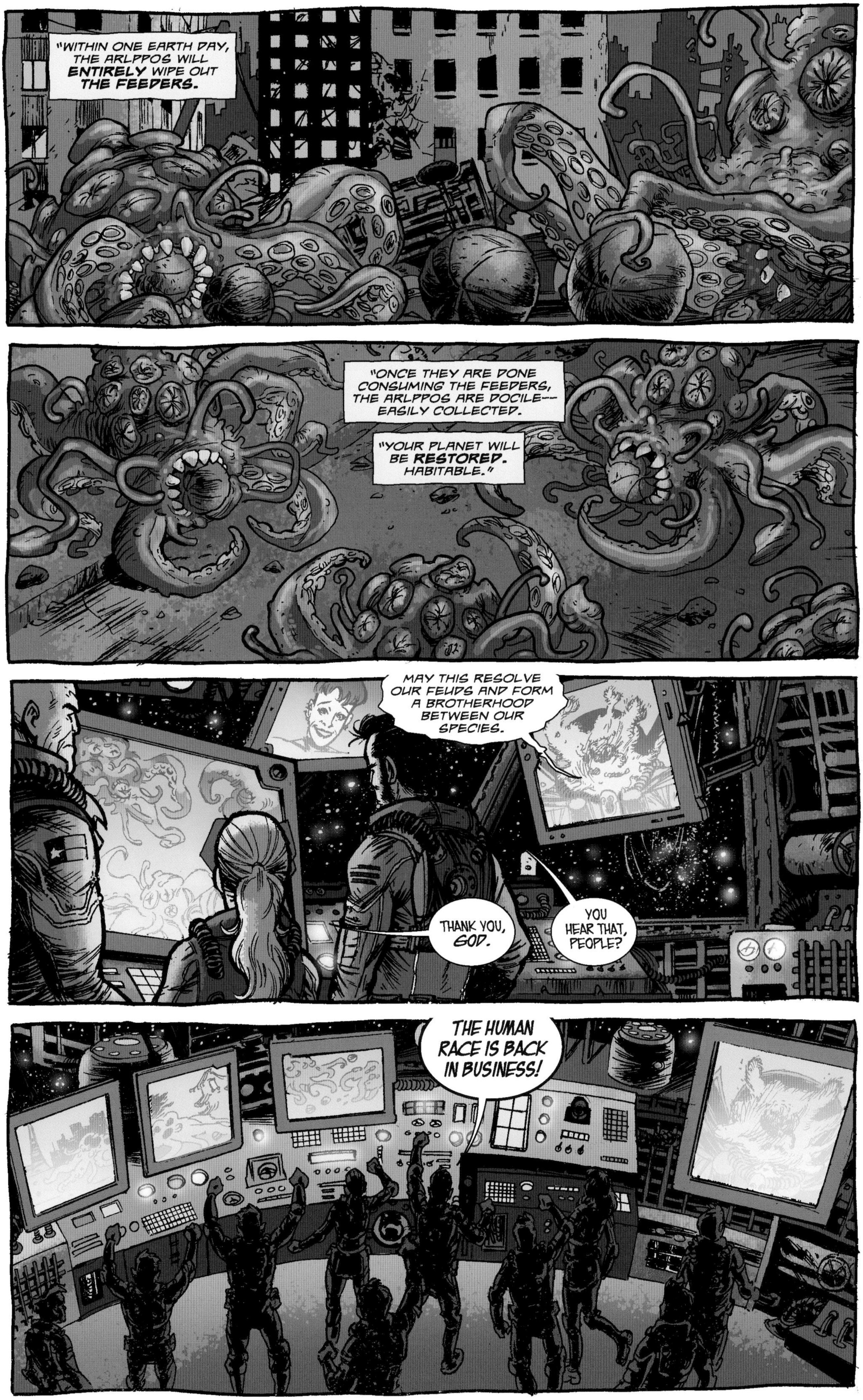
"WITHIN ONE EARTH DAY, THE ARLPPOS WILL ENTIRELY WIPE OUT THE FEEDERS.
"ONCE THEY ARE DONE CONSUMING THE FEEDERS, THE ARLPPOS ARE DOCILE-- EASILY COLLECTED.
"YOUR PLANET WILL BE RESTORED. HABITABLE."
MAY THIS RESOLVE OUR FEUDS AND FORM A BROTHERHOOD BETWEEN OUR SPECIES.
THANK YOU, GOD.
YOU HEAR THAT, PEOPLE?
THE HUMAN RACE IS BACK IN BUSINESS!

Months pass...

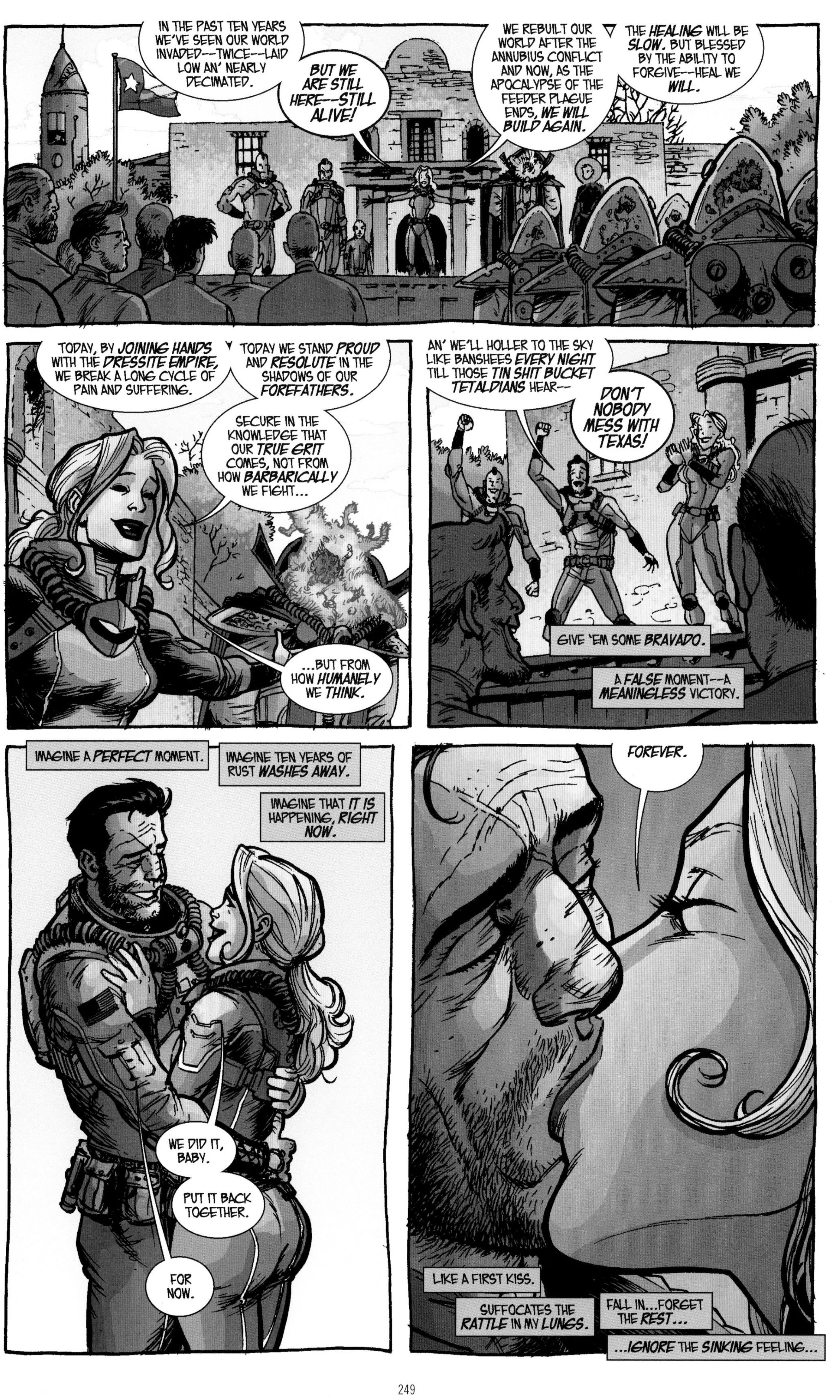
IN THE PAST TEN YEARS WE'VE SEEN OUR WORLD INVADED--TWICE--LAID LOW AN' NEARLY DECIMATED.
BUT WE ARE STILL HERE--STILL ALIVE!
WE REBUILT OUR WORLD AFTER THE ANNUBIUS CONFLICT AND NOW, AS THE APOCALYPSE OF THE FEEDER PLAGUE ENDS, WE WILL BUILD AGAIN.
THE HEALING WILL BE SLOW. BUT BLESSED BY THE ABILITY TO FORGIVE--HEAL WE WILL.
TODAY, BY JOINING HANDS WITH THE DRESSITE EMPIRE, WE BREAK A LONG CYCLE OF PAIN AND SUFFERING.
TODAY WE STAND PROUD AND RESOLUTE IN THE SHADOWS OF OUR FOREFATHERS.
SECURE IN THE KNOWLEDGE THAT OUR TRUE GRIT COMES, NOT FROM HOW BARBARICALLY WE FIGHT...
...BUT FROM HOW HUMANELY WE THINK.
AN' WE'LL HOLLER TO THE SKY LIKE BANSHEES EVERY NIGHT TILL THOSE TIN SHIT BUCKET TETALDIANS HEAR--
DON'T NOBODY MESS WITH TEXAS!
GIVE 'EM SOME BRAVADO.
A FALSE MOMENT--A MEANINGLESS VICTORY.
IMAGINE A PERFECT MOMENT.
IMAGINE TEN YEARS OF RUST WASHES AWAY.
IMAGINE THAT IT IS HAPPENING, RIGHT NOW.
WE DID IT, BABY.
PUT IT BACK TOGETHER.
FOR NOW.
FOREVER.
LIKE A FIRST KISS.
SUFFOCATES THE RATTLE IN MY LUNGS.
FALL IN...FORGET THE REST...
...IGNORE THE SINKING FEELING...

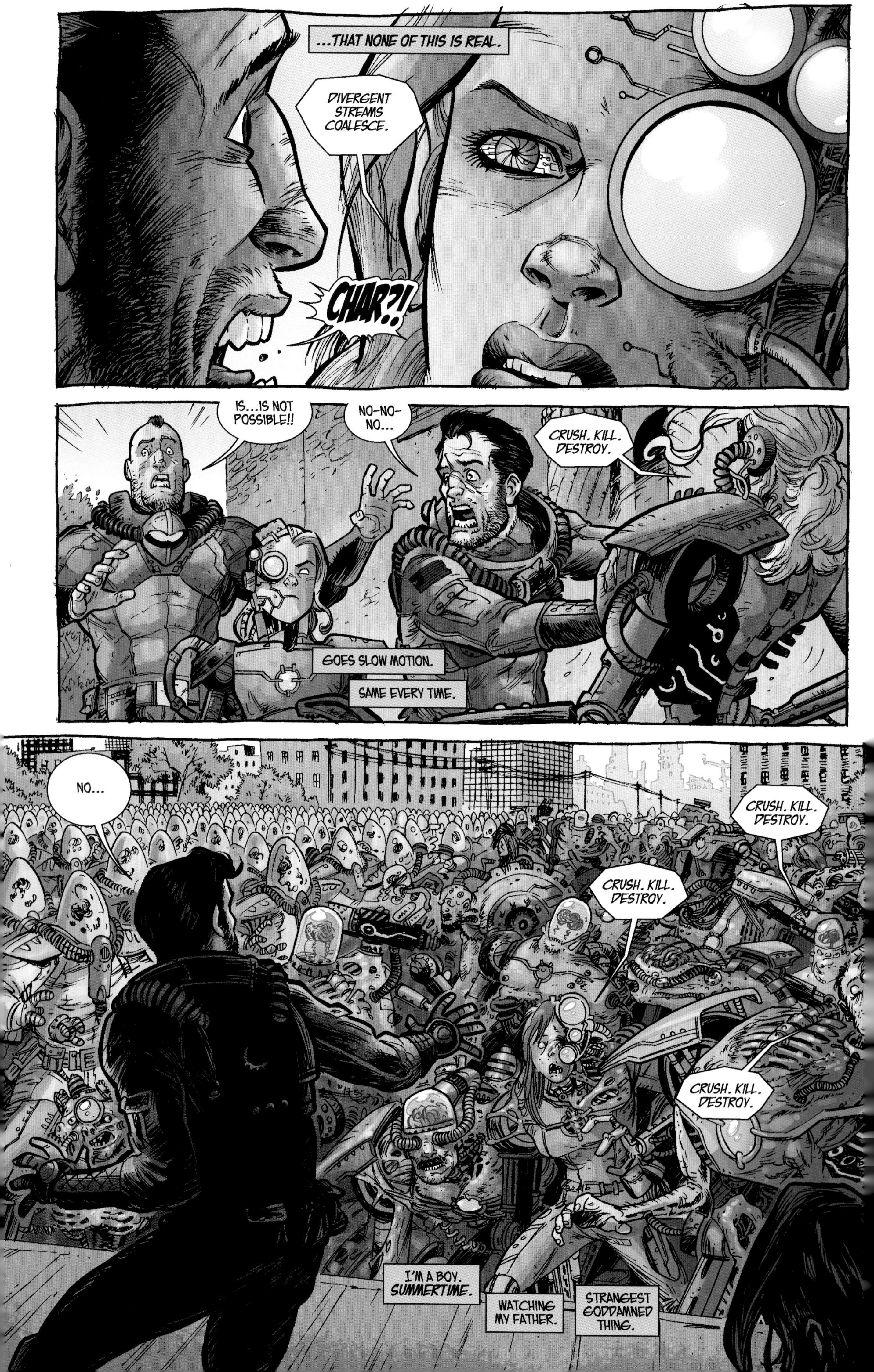
...THAT NONE OF THIS IS REAL.
DIVERGENT STREAMS COALESCE.
CHAR?!
IS...IS NOT POSSIBLE!!
NO-NO-NO...
CRUSH. KILL. DESTROY.
GOES SLOW MOTION.
SAME EVERY TIME.
NO...
CRUSH. KILL. DESTROY.
CRUSH. KILL. DESTROY.
CRUSH. KILL. DESTROY.
I'M A BOY. SUMMERTIME.
WATCHING MY FATHER.
STRANGEST GODDAMNED THING.

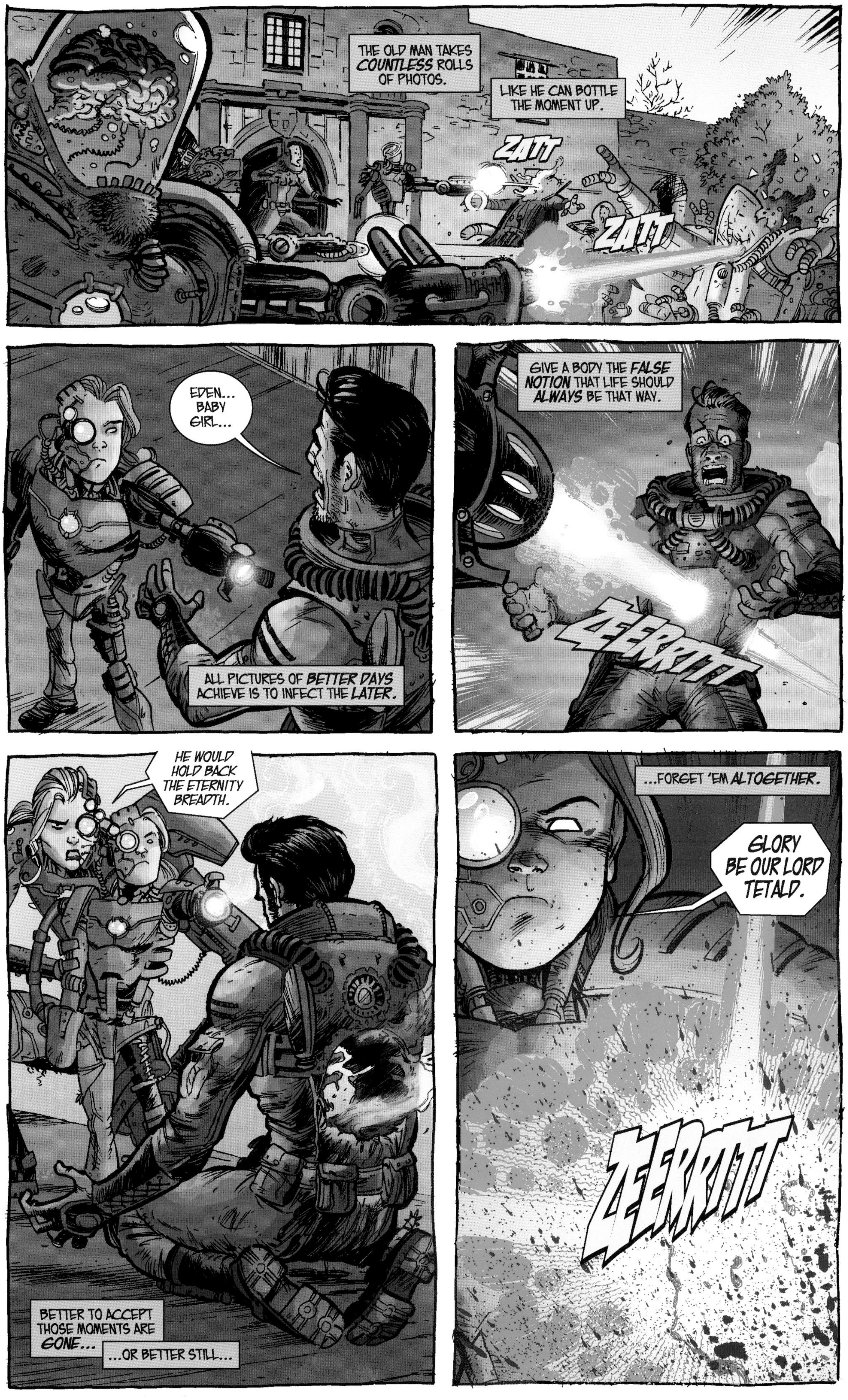
THE OLD MAN TAKES COUNTLESS ROLLS OF PHOTOS.
LIKE HE CAN BOTTLE THE MOMENT UP.
ZATT
ZATT
EDEN... BABY GIRL...
ALL PICTURES OF BETTER DAYS ACHIEVE IS TO INFECT THE LATER.
GIVE A BODY THE FALSE NOTION THAT LIFE SHOULD ALWAYS BE THAT WAY.
ZEERRTTT
HE WOULD HOLD BACK THE ETERNITY BREADTH.
BETTER TO ACCEPT THOSE MOMENTS ARE GONE...
...OR BETTER STILL...
...FORGET 'EM ALTOGETHER.
GLORY BE OUR LORD TETALD.
ZEERRTTT

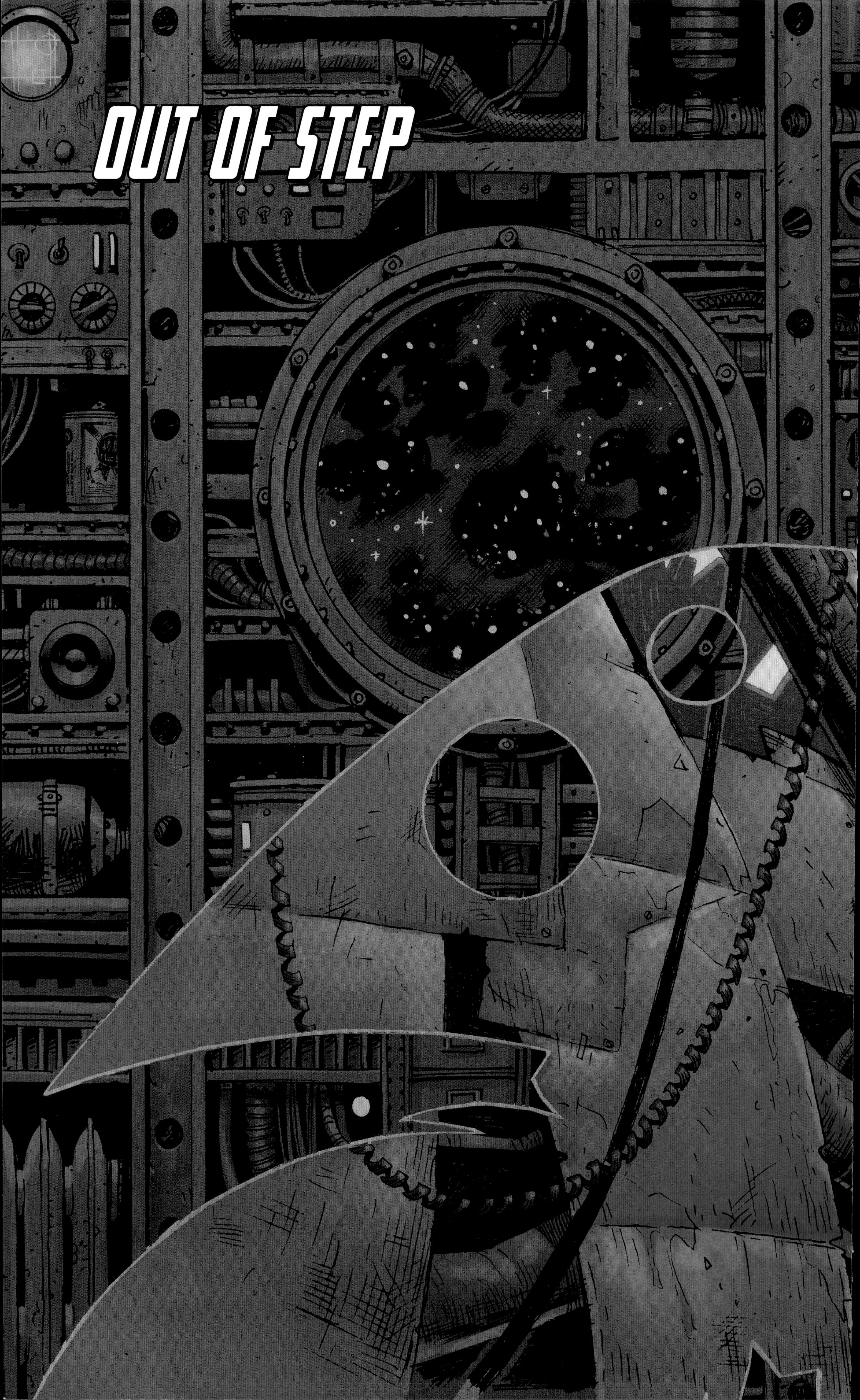
OUT OF STEP

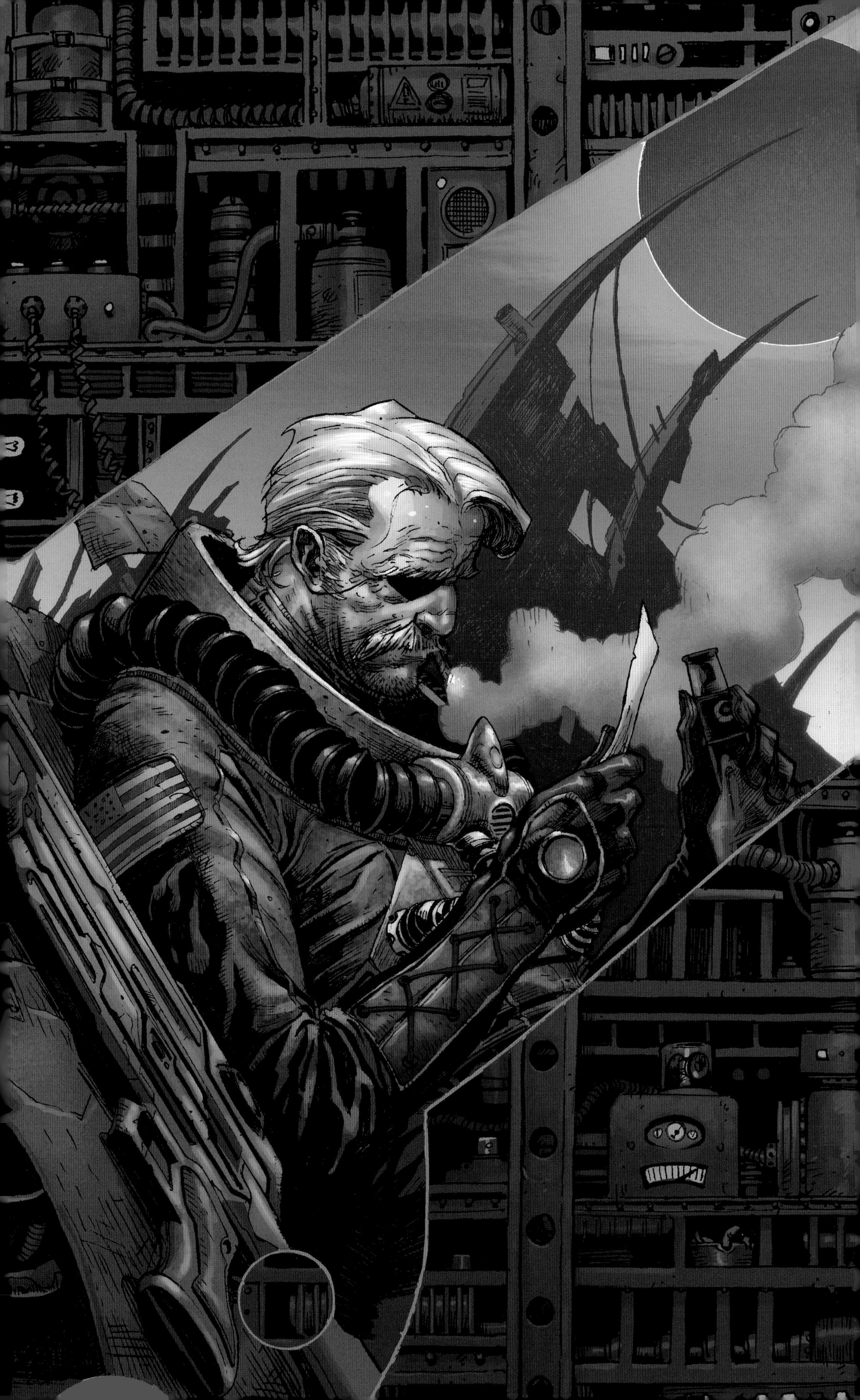

CHAPTER 1

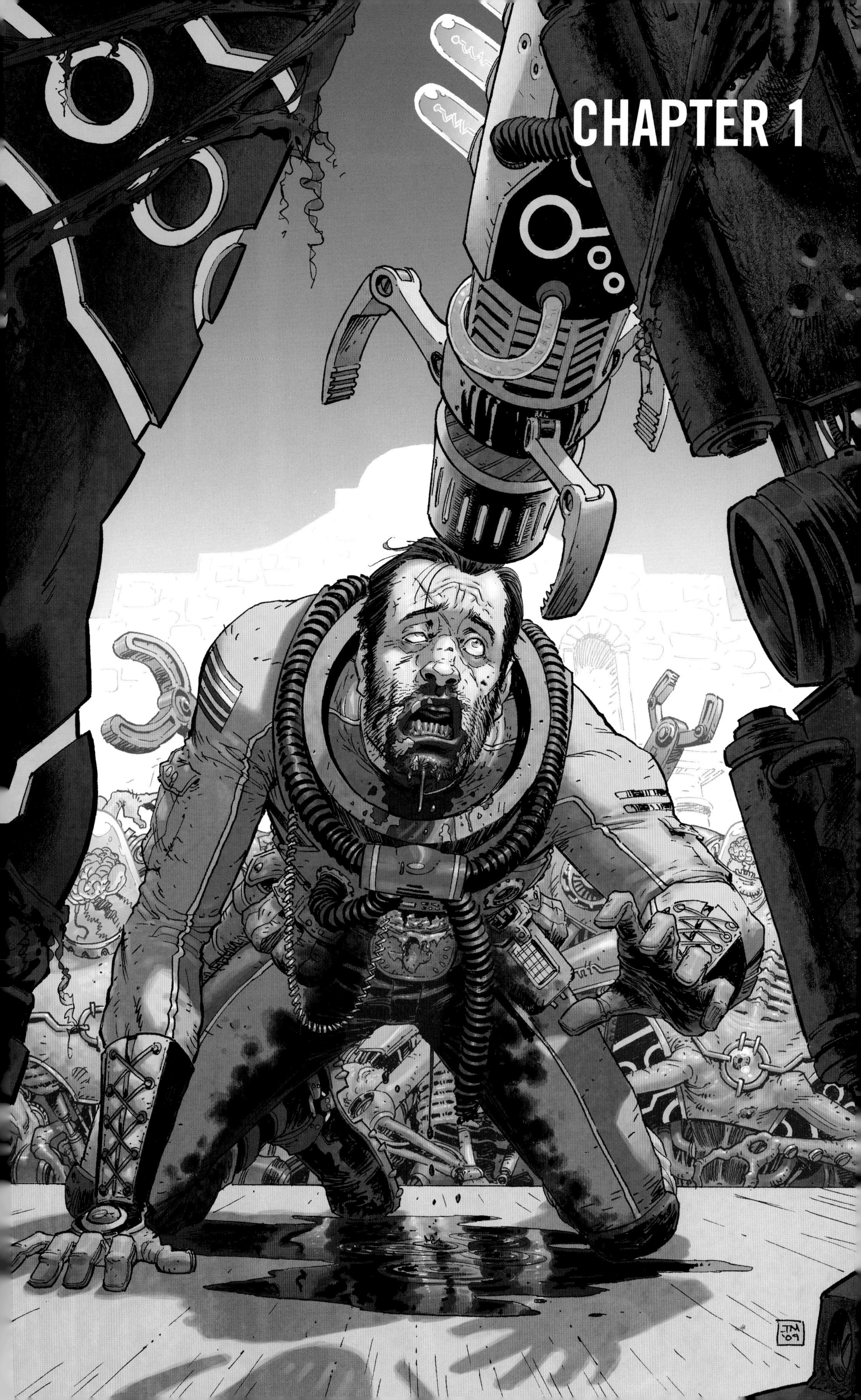

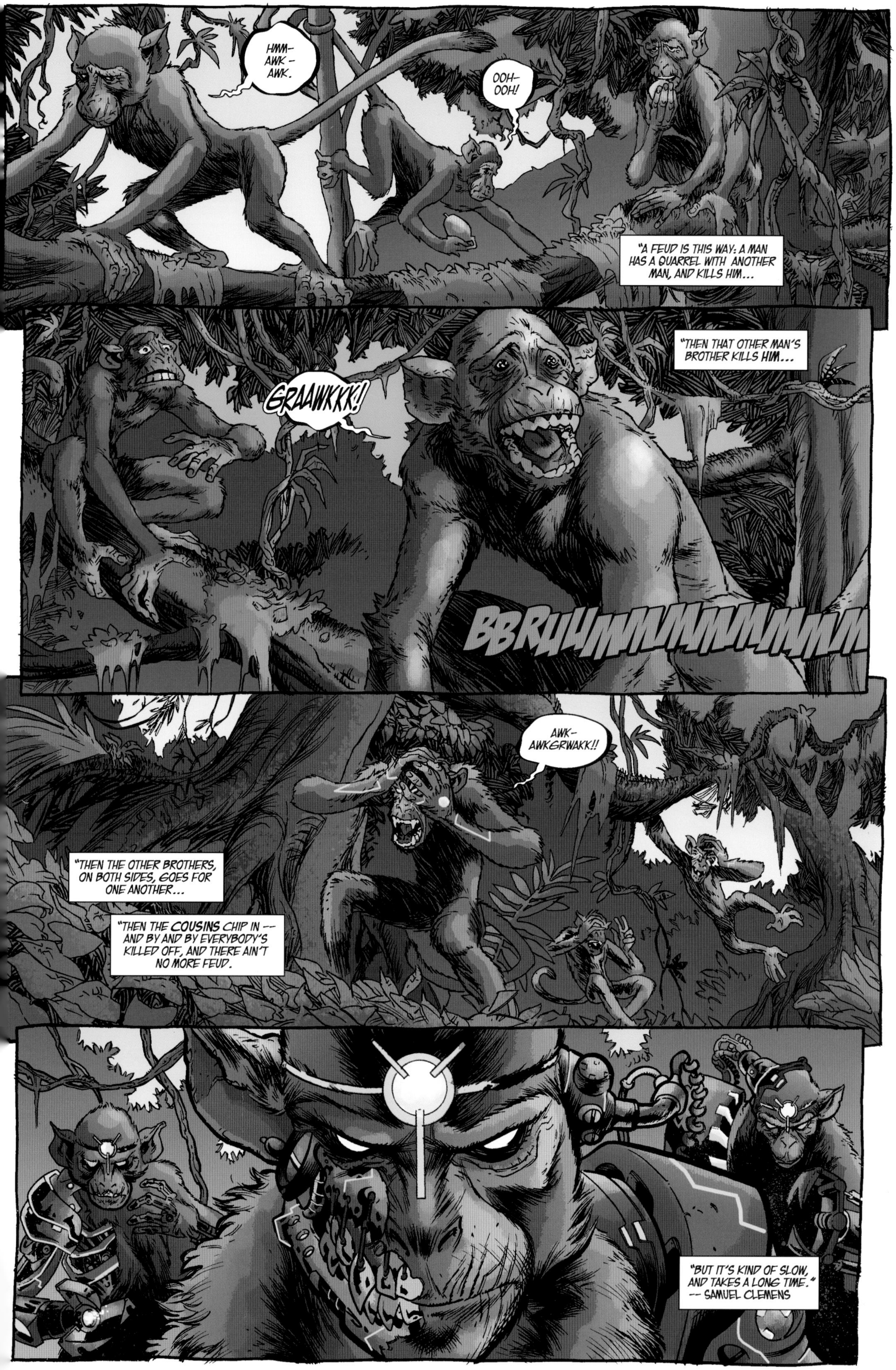
HMM-AWK-AWK.
OOH-OOH!
"A FEUD IS THIS WAY: A MAN HAS A QUARREL WITH ANOTHER MAN, AND KILLS HIM...
"THEN THAT OTHER MAN'S BROTHER KILLS HIM...
GRAAWKKK!
BBRUUMMMMMMMMMM
AWK-AWKGRWAKK!!
"THEN THE OTHER BROTHERS, ON BOTH SIDES, GOES FOR ONE ANOTHER...
"THEN THE COUSINS CHIP IN -- AND BY AND BY EVERYBODY'S KILLED OFF, AND THERE AIN'T NO MORE FEUD.
"BUT IT'S KIND OF SLOW, AND TAKES A LONG TIME."
-- SAMUEL CLEMENS

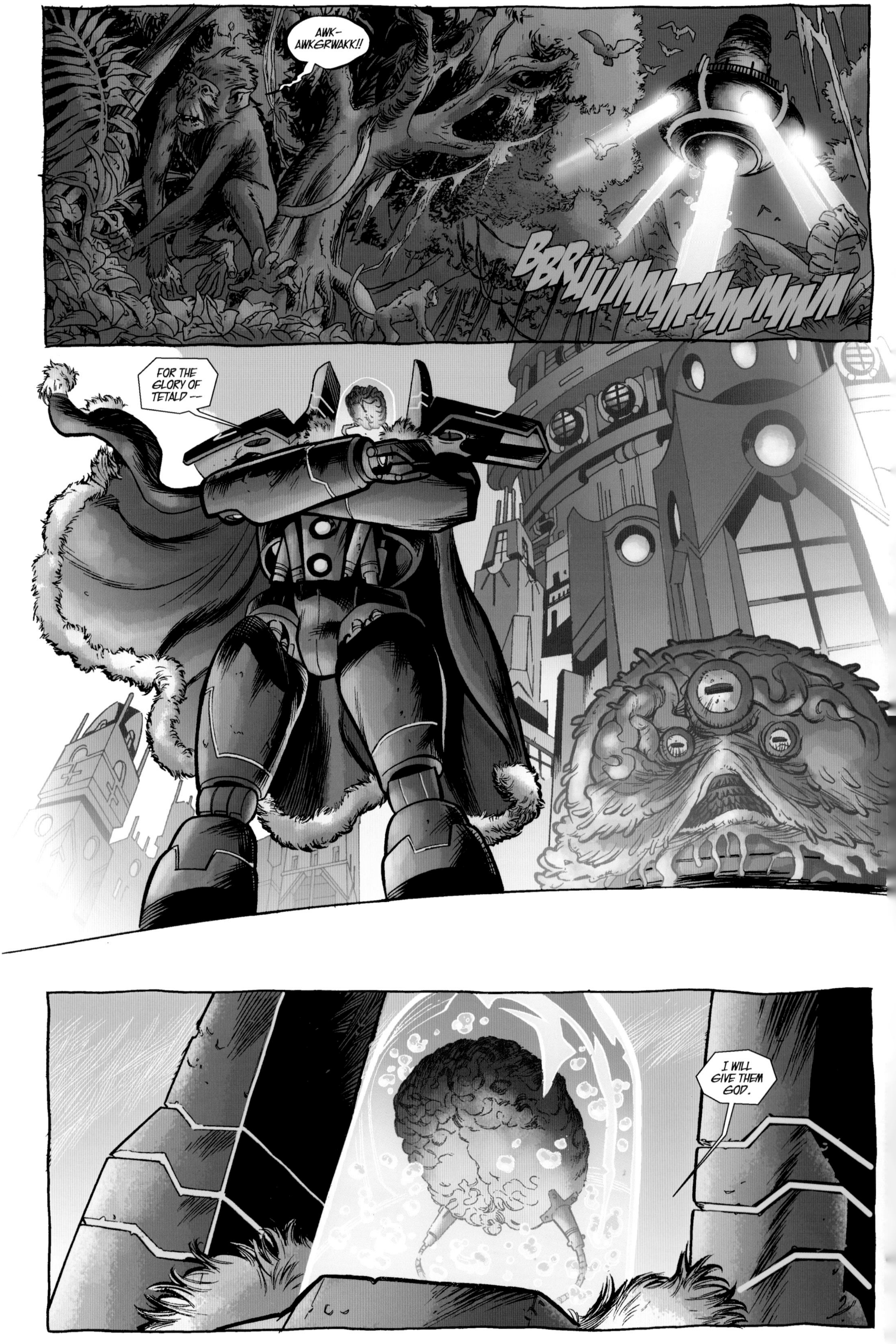
AWK-
AWKGRWAKK!!
BBRUUMMMMMMMMMM
FOR THE GLORY OF TETALD --
I WILL GIVE THEM GOD.

ONE HUNDRED AND FIFTY MILLION YEARS LATER...

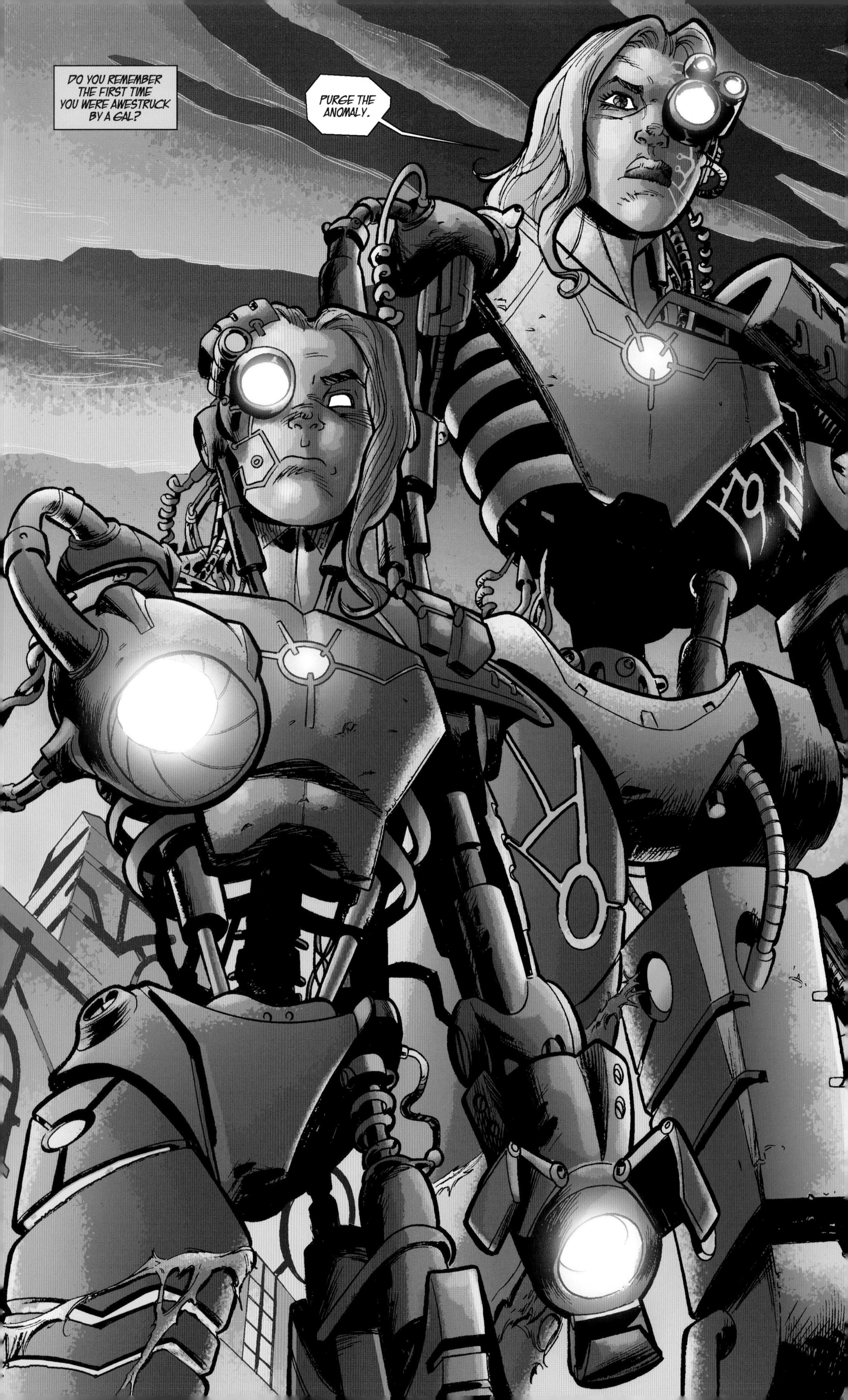
DO YOU REMEMBER THE FIRST TIME YOU WERE AWESTRUCK BY A GAL?
PURGE THE ANOMALY.

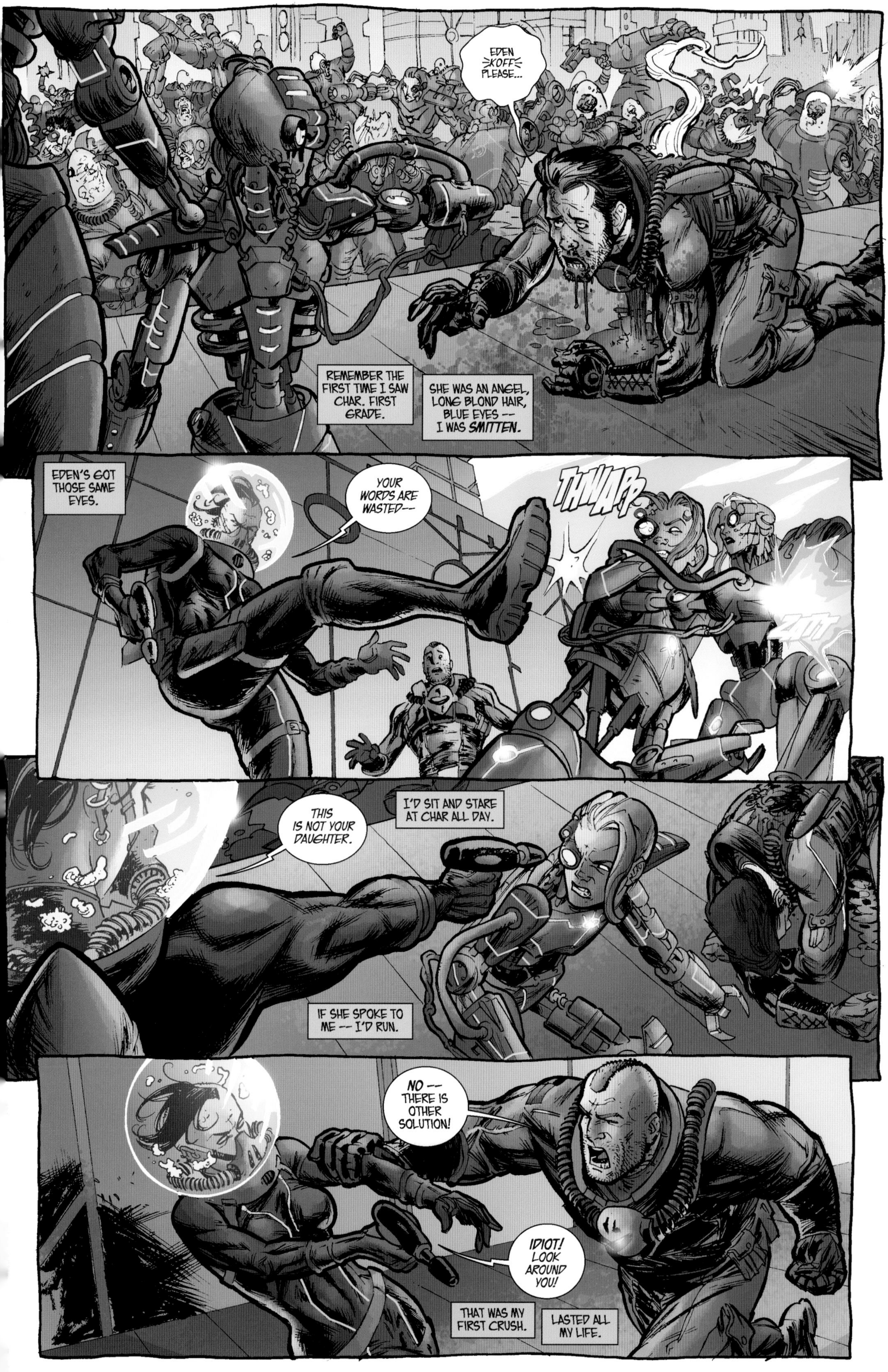
EDEN KOFF PLEASE...
REMEMBER THE FIRST TIME I SAW CHAR. FIRST GRADE.
SHE WAS AN ANGEL, LONG BLOND HAIR, BLUE EYES -- I WAS SMITTEN.
EDEN'S GOT THOSE SAME EYES.
YOUR WORDS ARE WASTED--
THWAPP
ZATT
THIS IS NOT YOUR DAUGHTER.
I'D SIT AND STARE AT CHAR ALL DAY.
IF SHE SPOKE TO ME -- I'D RUN.
NO -- THERE IS OTHER SOLUTION!
IDIOT! LOOK AROUND YOU!
THAT WAS MY FIRST CRUSH.
LASTED ALL MY LIFE.

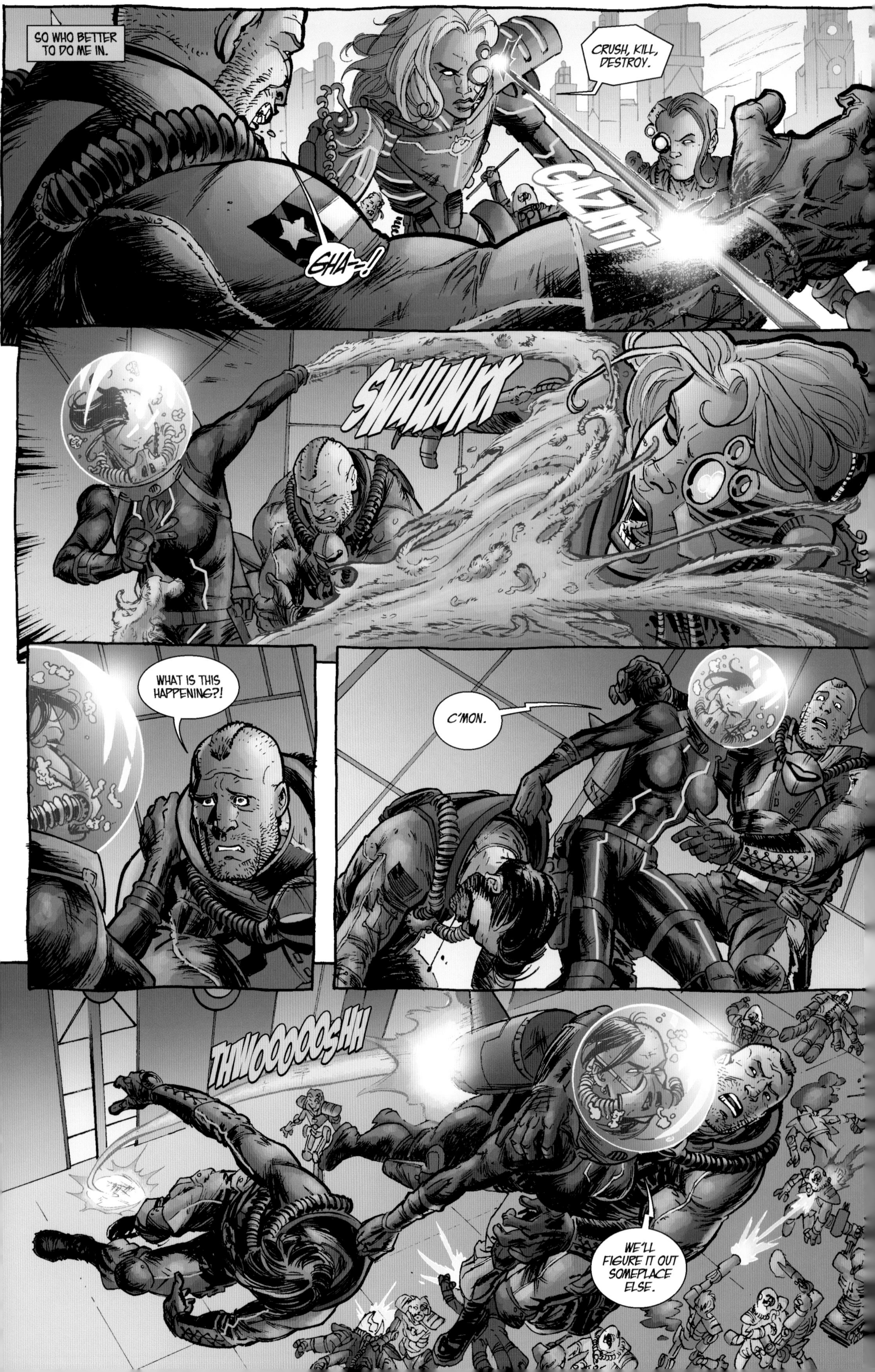
SO WHO BETTER TO DO ME IN.
CRUSH, KILL, DESTROY.
GHA--!
CAZATT
SWUNKK
WHAT IS THIS HAPPENING?!
C'MON.
THWOOOOOSHH
WE'LL FIGURE IT OUT SOMEPLACE ELSE.

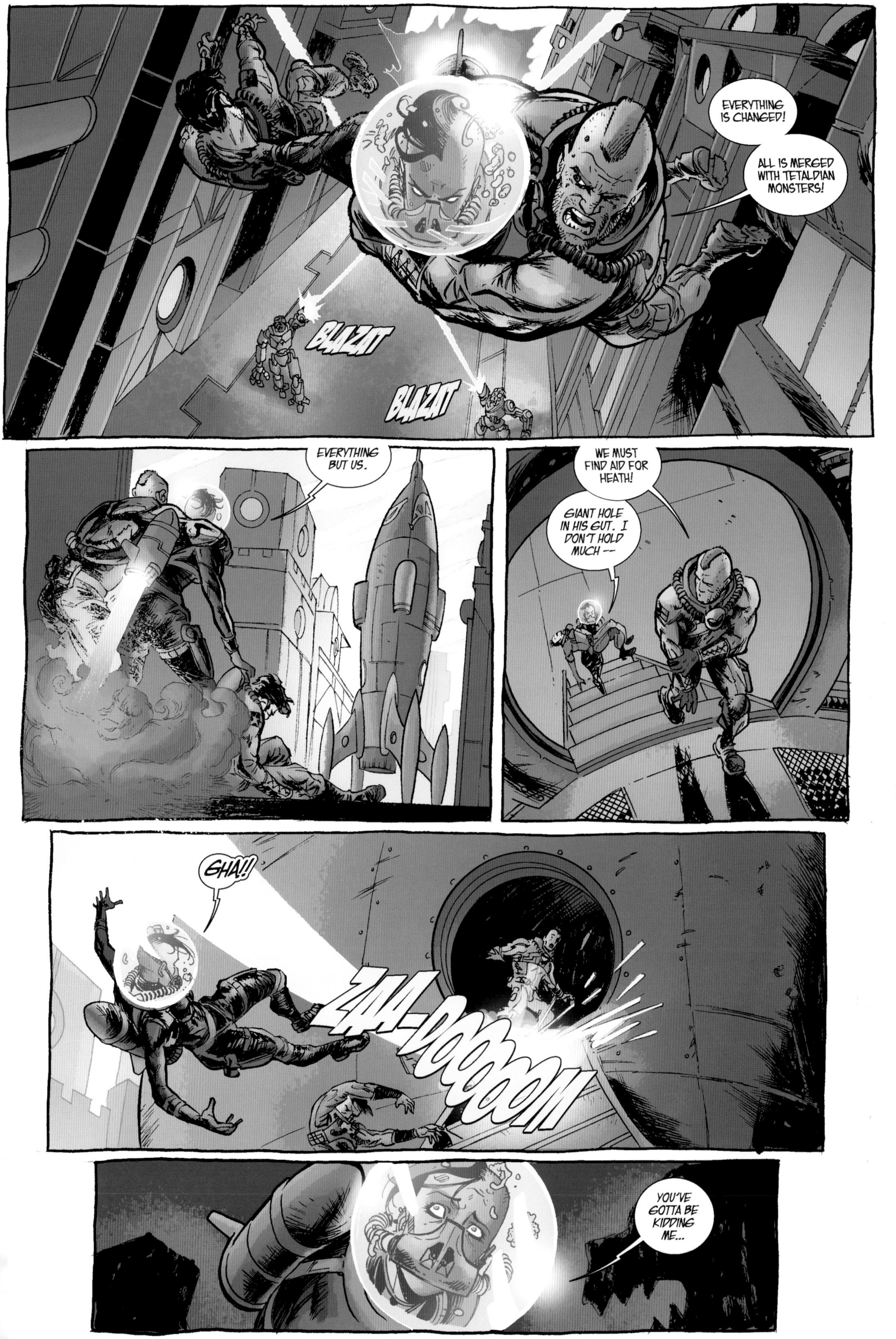
EVERYTHING IS CHANGED!
ALL IS MERGED WITH TETALDIAN MONSTERS!
BLAZAT
BLAZAT
EVERYTHING BUT US.
WE MUST FIND AID FOR HEATH!
GIANT HOLE IN HIS GUT. I DON'T HOLD MUCH --
GHA!!
ZAA-DOOOOOM
YOU'VE GOTTA BE KIDDING ME...

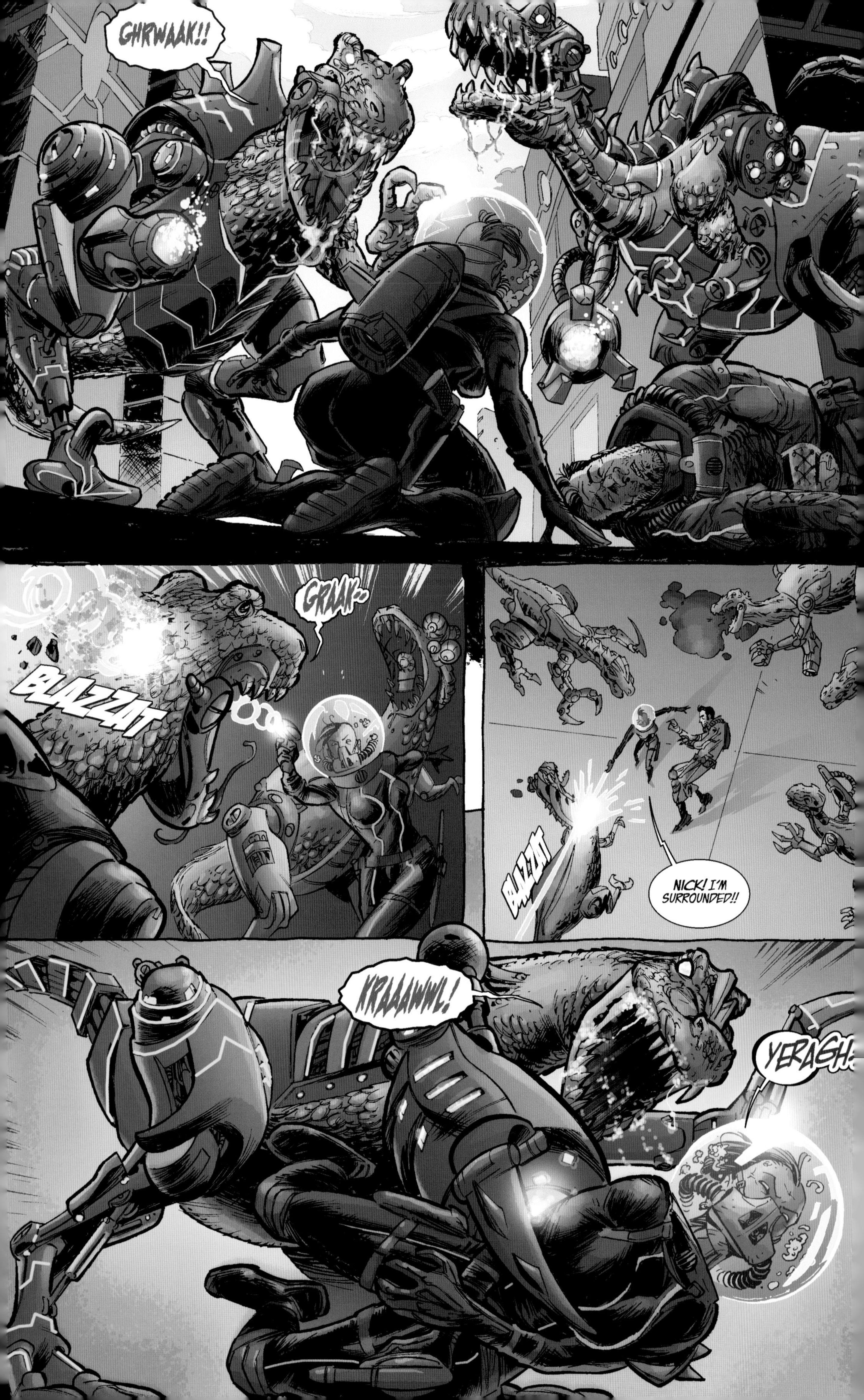
GHRWAAK!!
BLAZZAT
GRAAK
BLAZZAT
NICK! I'M SURROUNDED!!
KRAAAWWL!
YERAGH!

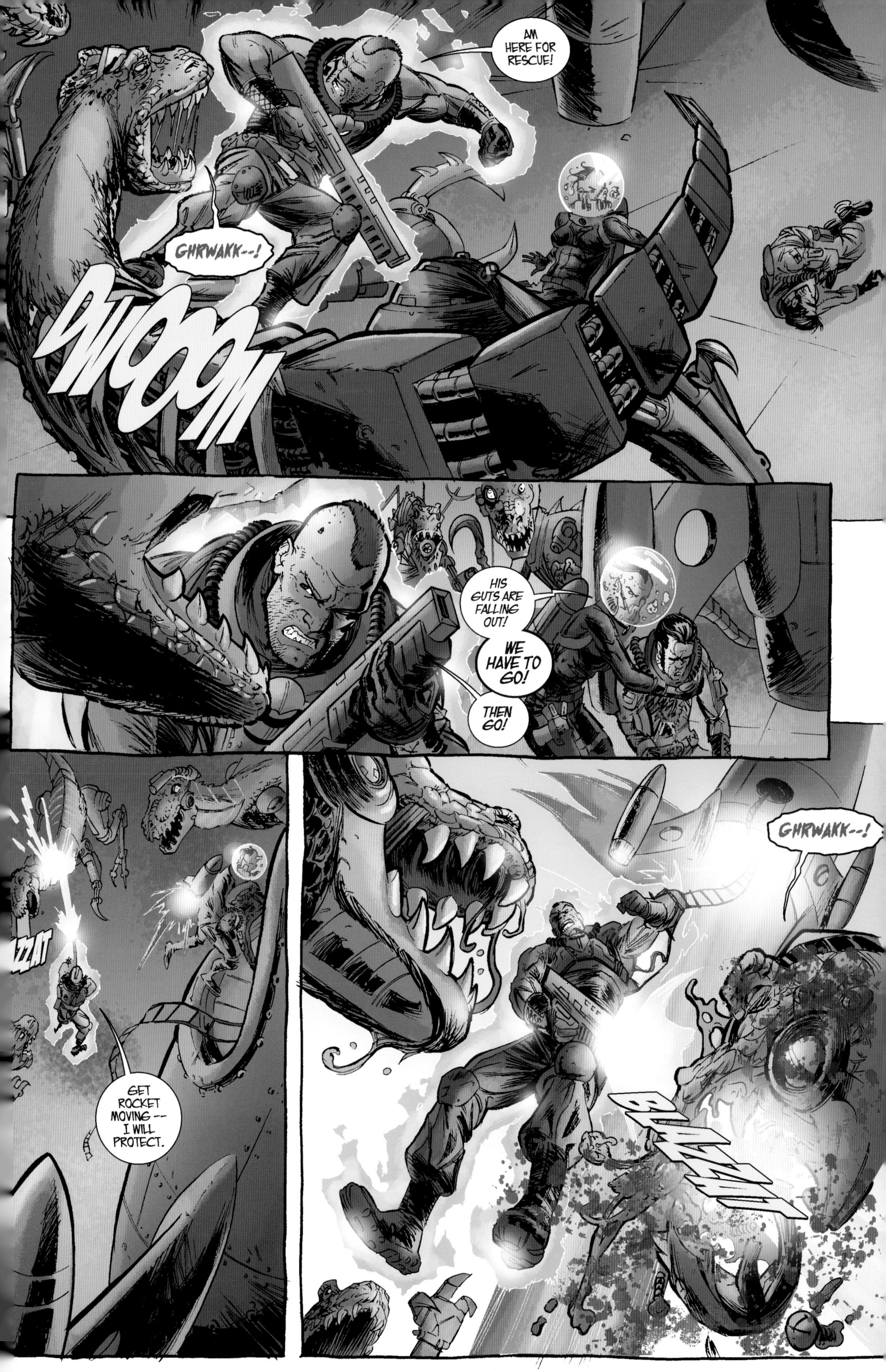
AM HERE FOR RESCUE!
GHRWAKK--!
HIS GUTS ARE FALLING OUT!
WE HAVE TO GO!
THEN GO!
GET ROCKET MOVING -- I WILL PROTECT.
GHRWAKK--!

WE ARE CLEAR.

ANNIE, DIAGNOSE FABRIC OF SPACE-TIME -- MUST KNOW WHAT HAS HAPPENED TO FIX.

WHO IS THIS PERSON? WHAT IS SHE DOING TO HEATH?!

FREEONIUM -- FILLING HIM UP WITH IT.

QUICK FREEZE, ONLY CHANCE WE HAVE OF SAVING HIS BRAIN.

THIS IS AN UNACCEPTABLE RISK!

LISTEN, SHITHEADS -- HE'S AS GOOD AS DEAD.

THIS WILL AT LEAST PRESERVE HIS BRAIN TILL WE SORT OUT WHAT TO DO.

NO. NOT UNTIL I'M SURE YOU'RE NOT PARTY TO CONSPIRACY --

LISTEN TO ME, IF YOUR FROZEN SIBERIAN BRAIN CAN GRASP THE WEIGHT OF THE SITUATION -- HEATH'S BODY IS DEAD -- HUMANITY HAS BEEN TAKEN OVER BY THE TETALDIANS.

YOU'RE OUT OF OPTIONS. I HAVE AN IDEA HOW TO SAVE HIM.

BUT YOU HAVE TO TRUST ME.

BECAUSE IF I'M IN ON THIS--

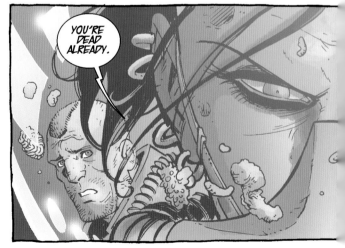

YOU'RE DEAD ALREADY.

DRESSIN...

GORTOBOR NET OL LORBO DEOLO.*

*PEACE BETWEEN OUR PEOPLE THEY SAY. TRUCE TO BE HONORED THEY DICTATE.

NO... NO, PLEASE... HURTS... HURTS...

BENORB TELBO ORNOT OTR LEBMOORE!

BUT YOU, HEATH HUSTON-- YOU ANNIHILATED MY FAMILY WHILE I FOUGHT TO PROTECT YOUR WORLD!

UGH... NO... MORE...

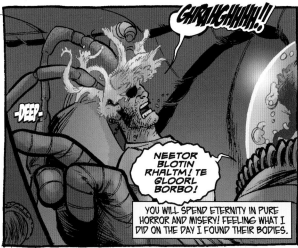

GHRAHGHHH!!

-DEEP-

NEETOR BLOTIN RHALTM! TE GLOORL BORBO!

YOU WILL SPEND ETERNITY IN PURE HORROR AND MISERY! FEELING WHAT I DID ON THE DAY I FOUND THEIR BODIES.

YERRAHGHHH!!

TEELN BOR TORO MEELO BO TORNOT.

THE ANOMALY HUSTON IS TO COME WITH US. DISCONNECT HIM-- HE IS NEEDED IMMEDIATELY.

GLORTOB! MEY HOLRO TORB!

I WAS PROMISED THIS. PROMISED BY THE HIGH LEADER HIS TORTURE WAS IN MY HANDS!

MEENO TUYO BLO MO GORB.

THERE IS A BETTER USE FOR HIM. AN ABSOLUTE PUNISHMENT.

NO MORE... NO MORE... NO MORE.

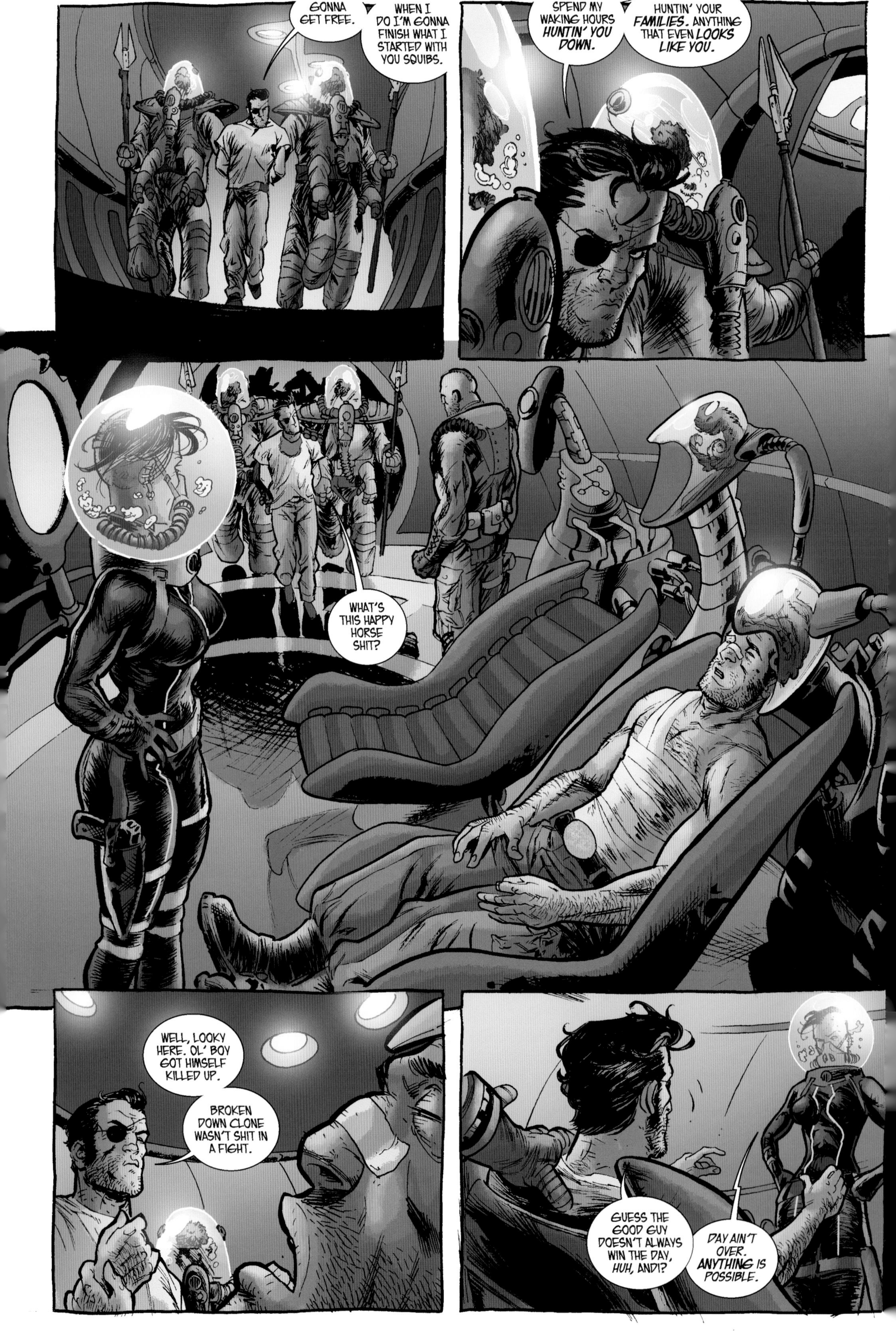
GONNA GET FREE.
WHEN I DO I'M GONNA FINISH WHAT I STARTED WITH YOU SQUIBS.
SPEND MY WAKING HOURS HUNTIN' YOU DOWN.
HUNTIN' YOUR FAMILIES. ANYTHING THAT EVEN LOOKS LIKE YOU.
WHAT'S THIS HAPPY HORSE SHIT?
WELL, LOOKY HERE. OL' BOY GOT HIMSELF KILLED UP.
BROKEN DOWN CLONE WASN'T SHIT IN A FIGHT.
GUESS THE GOOD GUY DOESN'T ALWAYS WIN THE DAY, HUH, ANDI?
DAY AIN'T OVER. ANYTHING IS POSSIBLE.

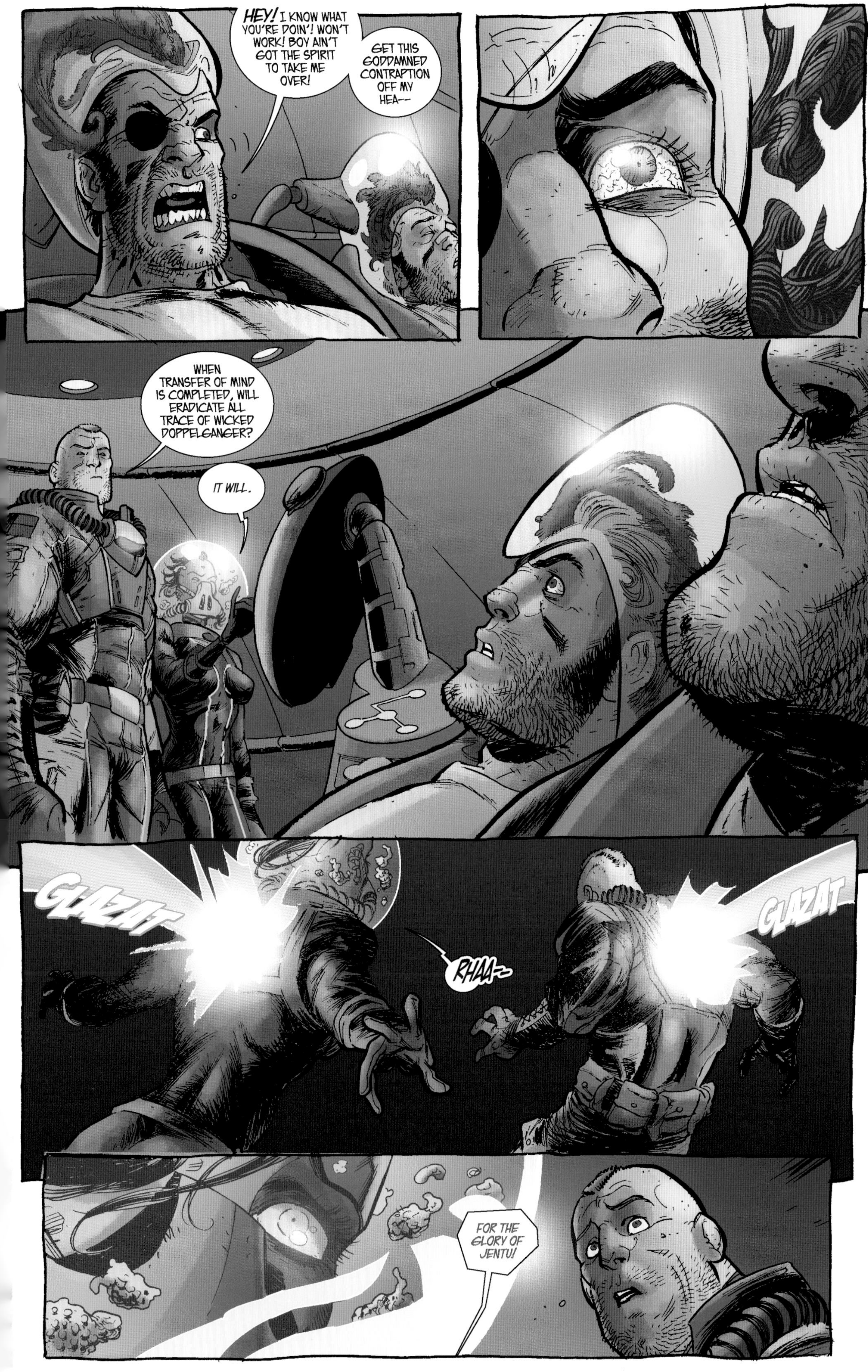
HEY! I KNOW WHAT YOU'RE DOIN'! WON'T WORK! BOY AIN'T GOT THE SPIRIT TO TAKE ME OVER!
GET THIS GODDAMNED CONTRAPTION OFF MY HEA--
WHEN TRANSFER OF MIND IS COMPLETED, WILL ERADICATE ALL TRACE OF WICKED DOPPELGANGER?
IT WILL.
GLAZAT
RHAA--
GLAZAT
FOR THE GLORY OF JENTU!

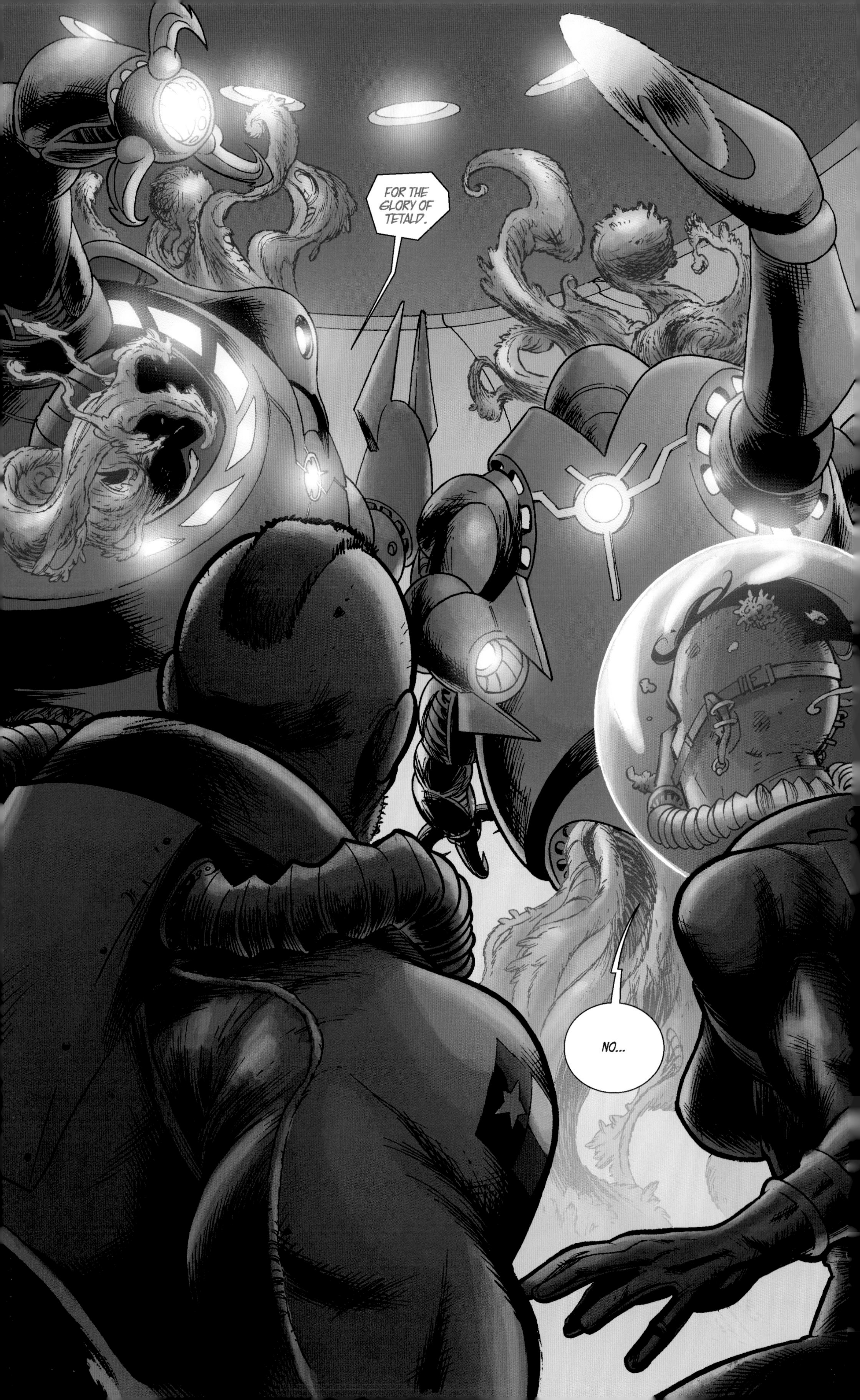
FOR THE GLORY OF TETALD.
NO...

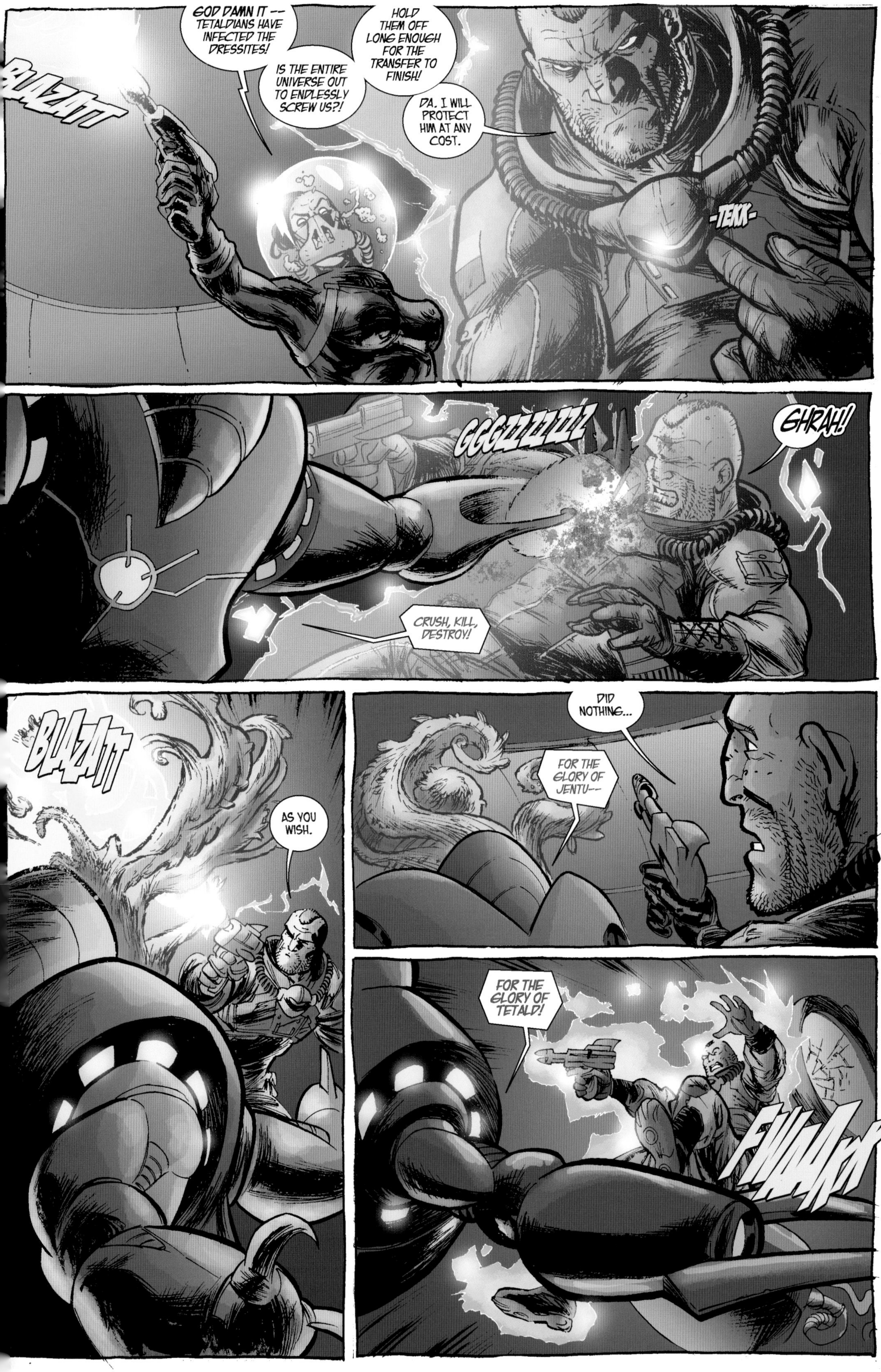
BLAZATT
GOD DAMN IT -- TETALDIANS HAVE INFECTED THE DRESSITES!
IS THE ENTIRE UNIVERSE OUT TO ENDLESSLY SCREW US?!
HOLD THEM OFF LONG ENOUGH FOR THE TRANSFER TO FINISH!
DA. I WILL PROTECT HIM AT ANY COST.
-TEKK-
GGGZZZZZZZ
GHRAH!
CRUSH, KILL, DESTROY!
BLAZATT
AS YOU WISH.
DID NOTHING...
FOR THE GLORY OF JENTU--
FOR THE GLORY OF TETALD!
FWAARK

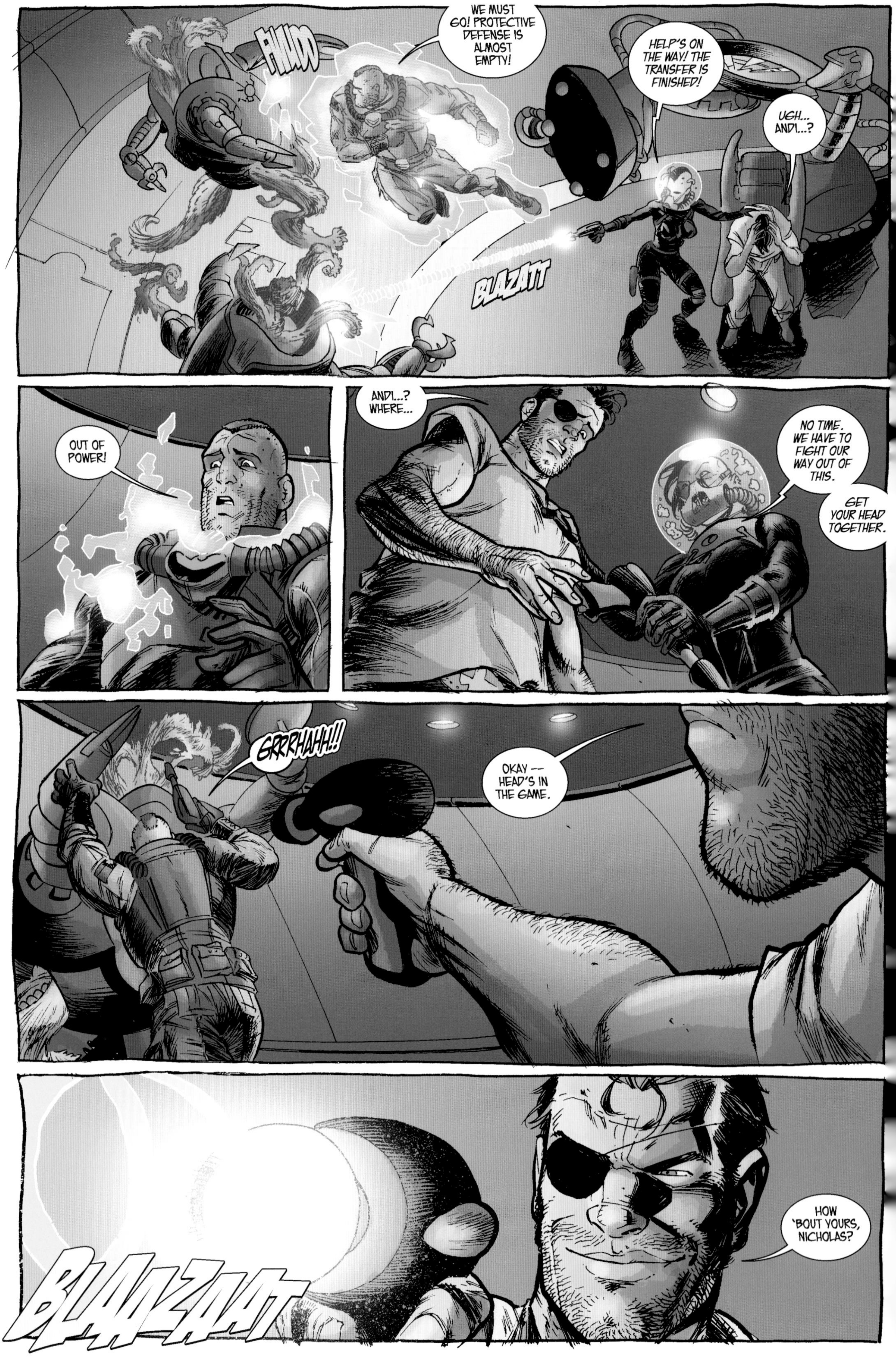
FWUDO
WE MUST GO! PROTECTIVE DEFENSE IS ALMOST EMPTY!
HELP'S ON THE WAY! THE TRANSFER IS FINISHED!
UGH... ANDI...?
BLAZATT
OUT OF POWER!
ANDI...? WHERE...
NO TIME. WE HAVE TO FIGHT OUR WAY OUT OF THIS.
GET YOUR HEAD TOGETHER.
GRRRHAHH!!
OKAY -- HEAD'S IN THE GAME.
HOW 'BOUT YOURS, NICHOLAS?
BLAAZAAT

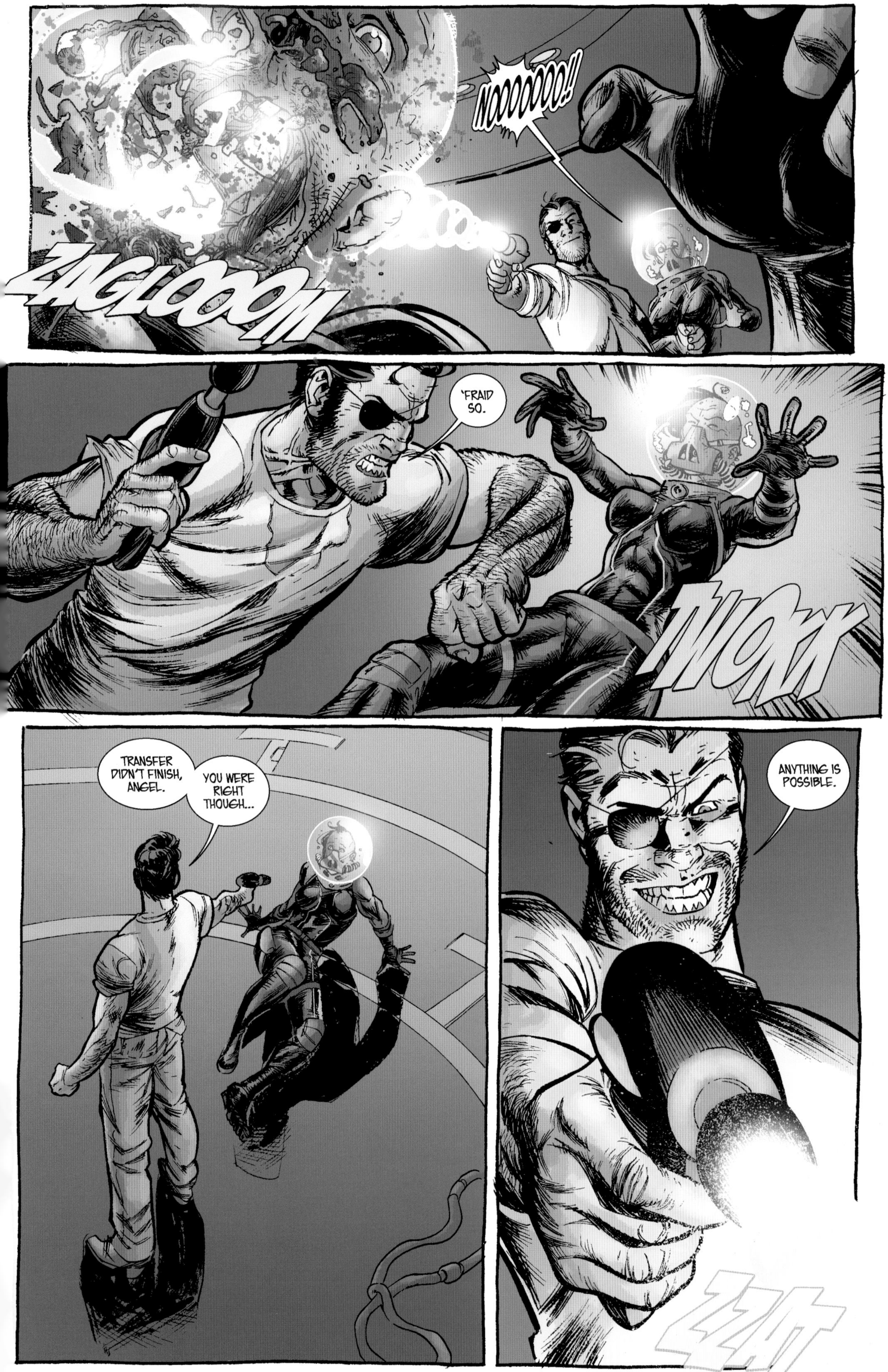
NOOOOOOO!!
ZAGLOOOM
'FRAID SO.
TWONK
TRANSFER DIDN'T FINISH, ANGEL.
YOU WERE RIGHT THOUGH...
ANYTHING IS POSSIBLE.
ZZAT

YOUR UNCLE OTTO AN' I HAD A FRIEND GROWIN' UP NAMED PETE. QUITE THE LADIES MAN, OL' PETE.

HELL, BY THIRD GRADE HE HAD A HANDFUL OF GALS WHO'D CHASE 'IM EVERY LUNCH.

CHASIN' 'IM TO SMOOCH 'IM.

AS THE KID *NOT BEING CHASED* I REMEMBER WHAT IT FELT LIKE TO WATCH.

ALL THESE CUTE GIRLS CHASE MY BUDDY WHILE I SAT SCRATCHING MY HEAD.

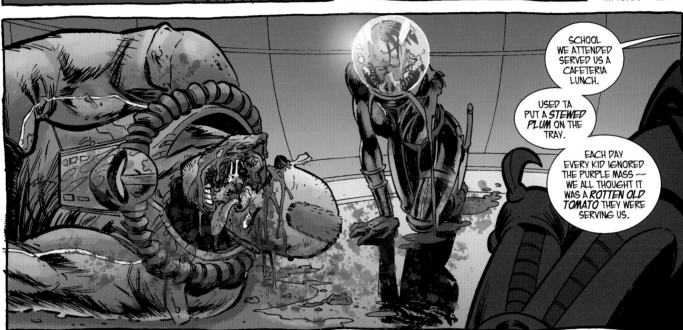

SCHOOL WE ATTENDED SERVED US A CAFETERIA LUNCH.

USED TA PUT A *STEWED PLUM* ON THE TRAY.

EACH DAY EVERY KID IGNORED THE PURPLE MASS -- WE ALL THOUGHT IT WAS A *ROTTEN OLD TOMATO* THEY WERE SERVING US.

N--NOT... NOT LIKE THIS...

PETE, HE TELLS ME IF I EAT THE FLESHY MASS OF PUTRID TORTURE HE'LL TELL ALL THEM GIRLS TO CHASE *ME* AROUND THAT DAY.

KNOW WHAT TASTES WORSE THAN THE SWEETNESS OF A *STEWED PLUM?*

WHEN YOU THINK YOU'RE EATIN' A *ROTTEN TOMATO.*

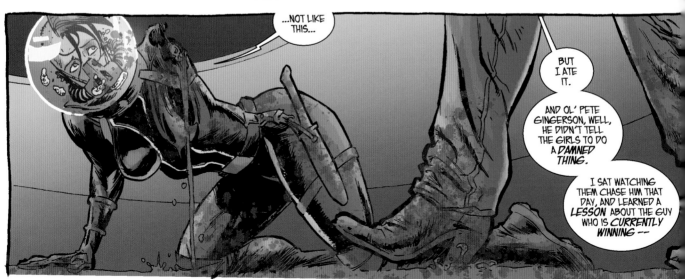

...NOT LIKE THIS...

BUT I ATE IT.

AND OL' PETE GINGERSON, WELL, HE DIDN'T TELL THE GIRLS TO DO A *DAMNED THING.*

I SAT WATCHING THEM CHASE HIM THAT DAY, AND LEARNED A *LESSON* ABOUT THE GUY WHO IS *CURRENTLY WINNING* --

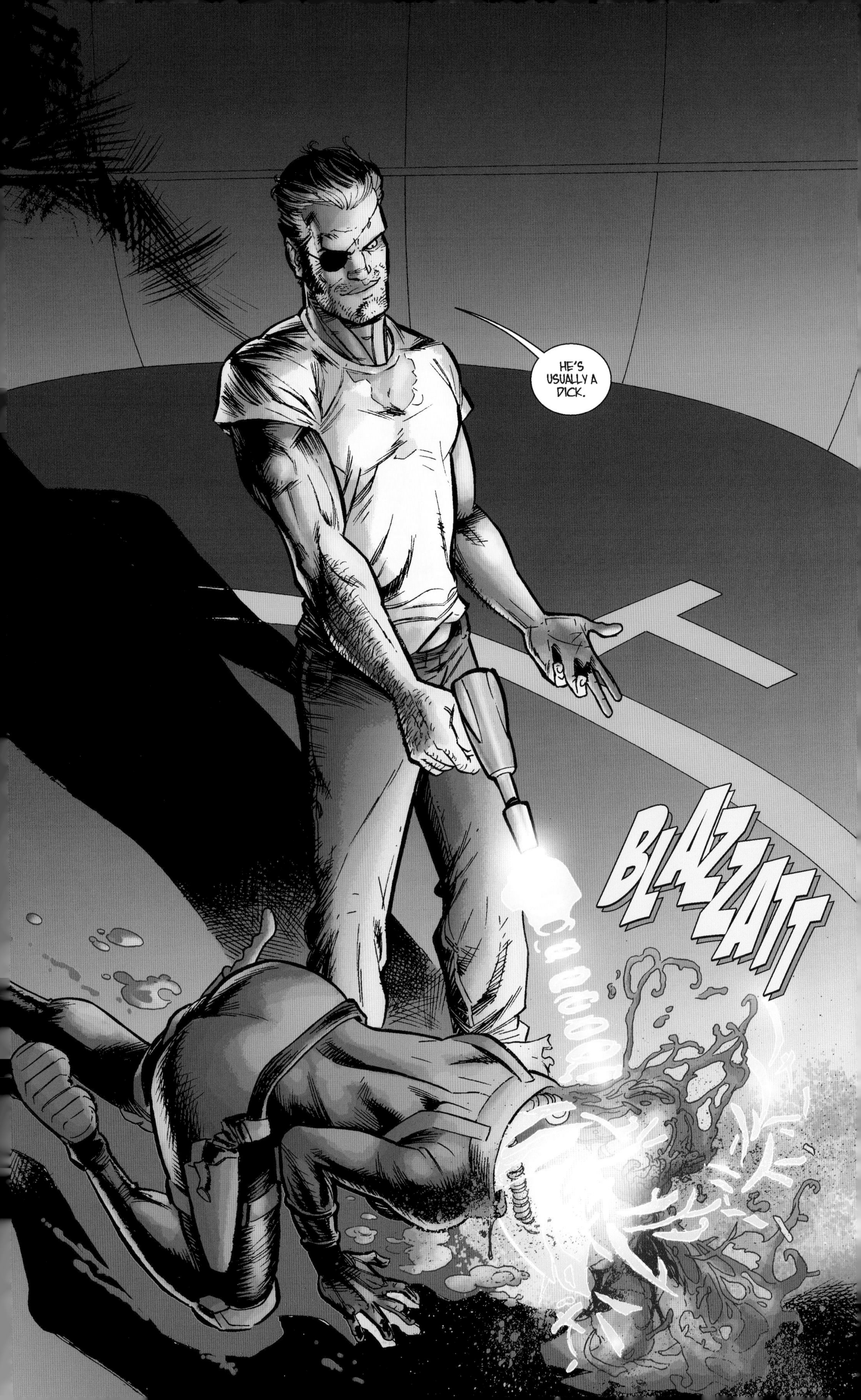
HE'S USUALLY A DICK.
BLAZZATT

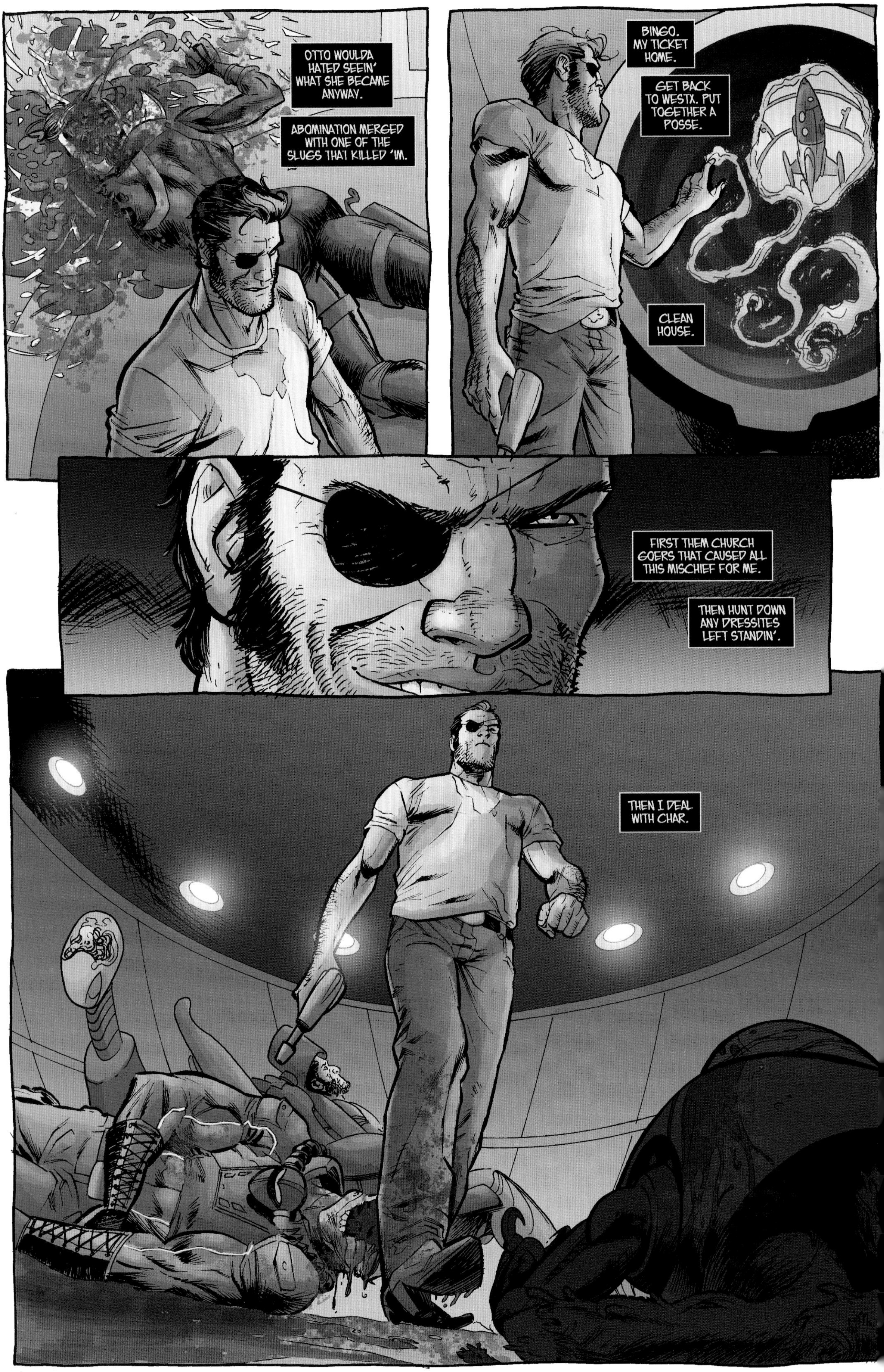
OTTO WOULDA HATED SEEIN' WHAT SHE BECAME ANYWAY.
ABOMINATION MERGED WITH ONE OF THE SLUGS THAT KILLED 'IM.
BINGO. MY TICKET HOME.
GET BACK TO WESTX. PUT TOGETHER A POSSE.
CLEAN HOUSE.
FIRST THEM CHURCH GOERS THAT CAUSED ALL THIS MISCHIEF FOR ME.
THEN HUNT DOWN ANY DRESSITES LEFT STANDIN'.
THEN I DEAL WITH CHAR.

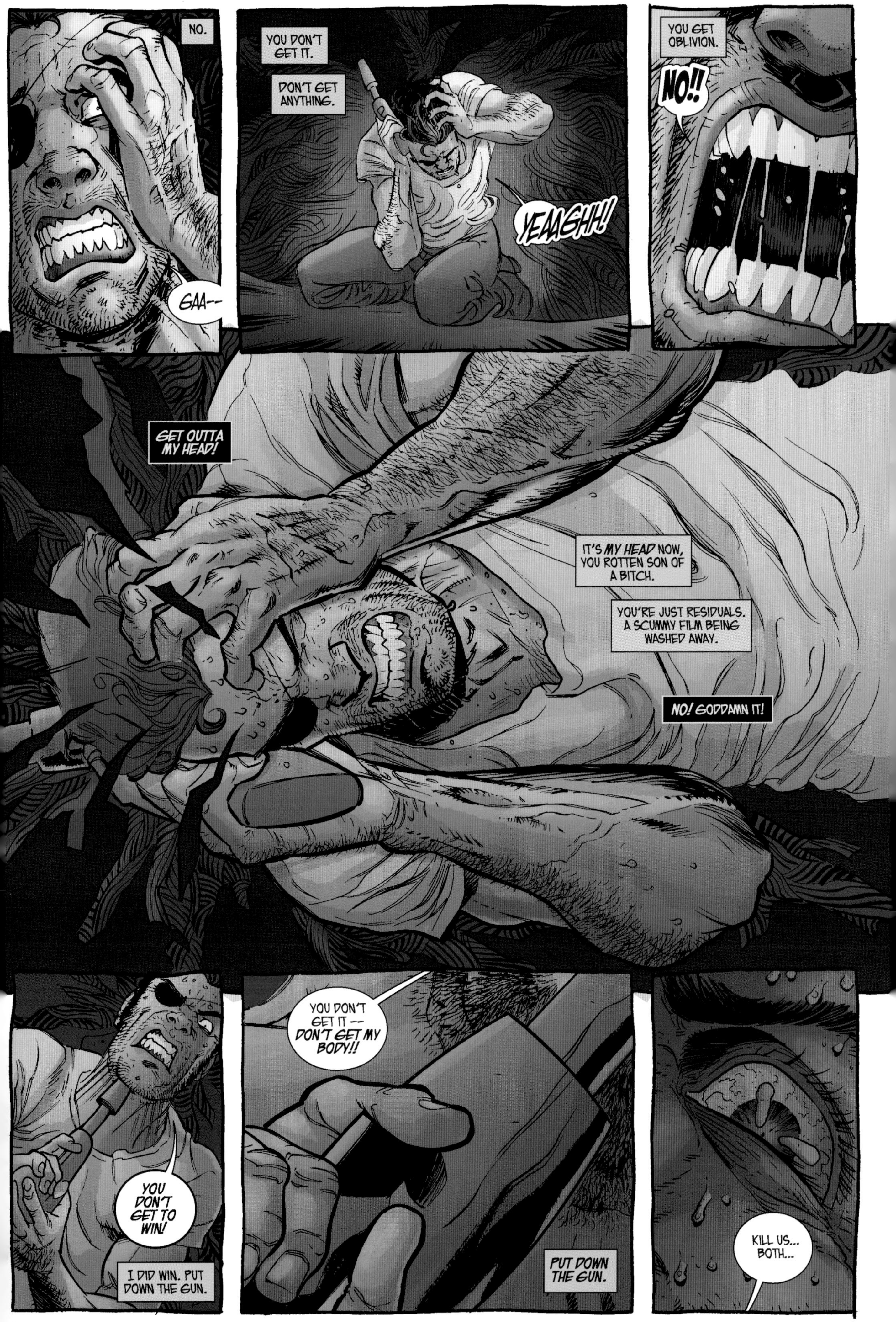
NO.
GAA--
YOU DON'T GET IT.
DON'T GET ANYTHING.
YEAAGHH!
YOU GET OBLIVION.
NO!!
GET OUTTA MY HEAD!
IT'S MY HEAD NOW, YOU ROTTEN SON OF A BITCH.
YOU'RE JUST RESIDUALS. A SCUMMY FILM BEING WASHED AWAY.
NO! GODDAMN IT!
YOU DON'T GET TO WIN!
I DID WIN. PUT DOWN THE GUN.
YOU DON'T GET IT -- DON'T GET MY BODY!!
PUT DOWN THE GUN.
KILL US... BOTH...

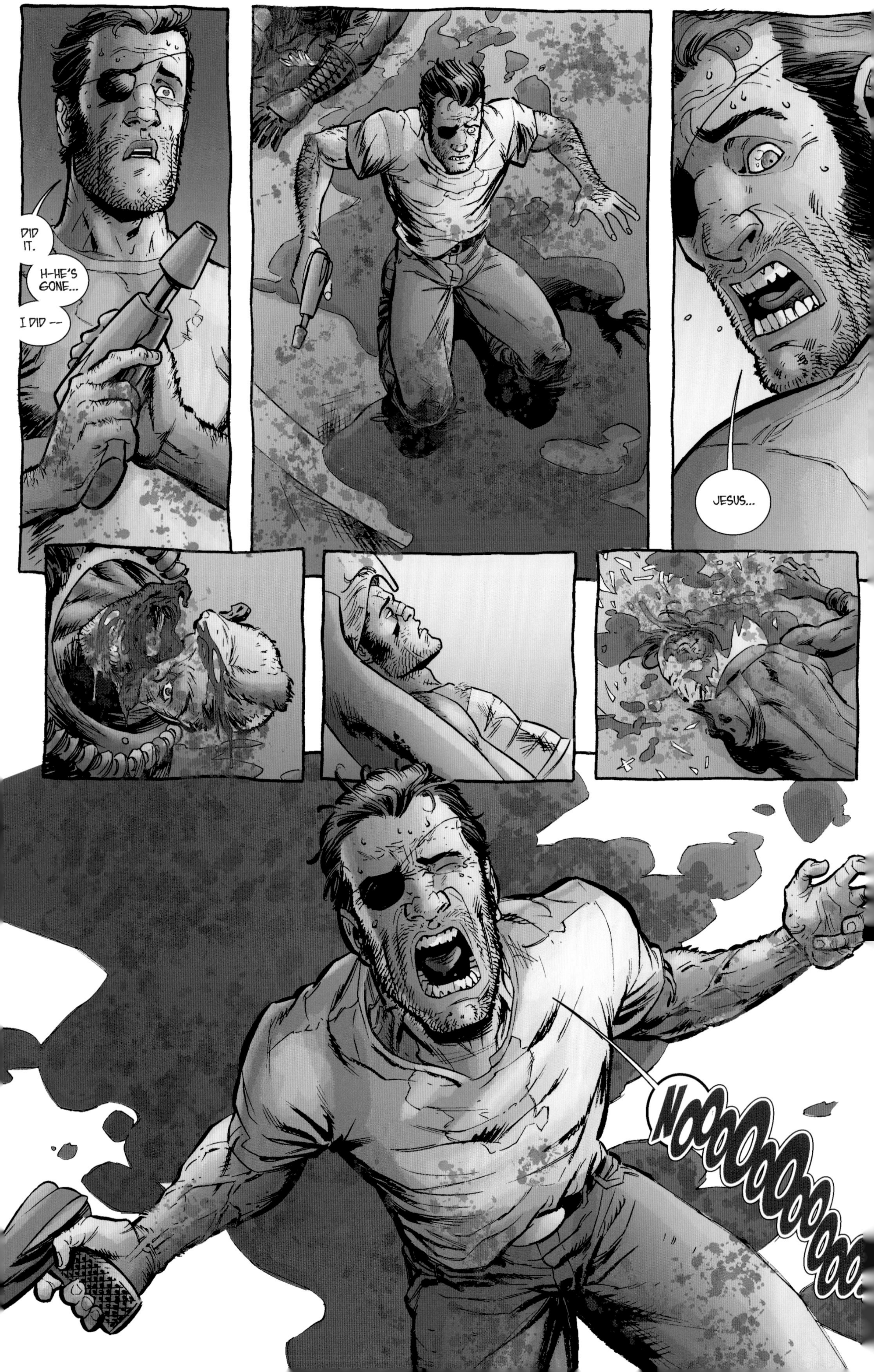

DID IT.
H-HE'S GONE...
I DID --
JESUS...
NOOOOOOOOOOO

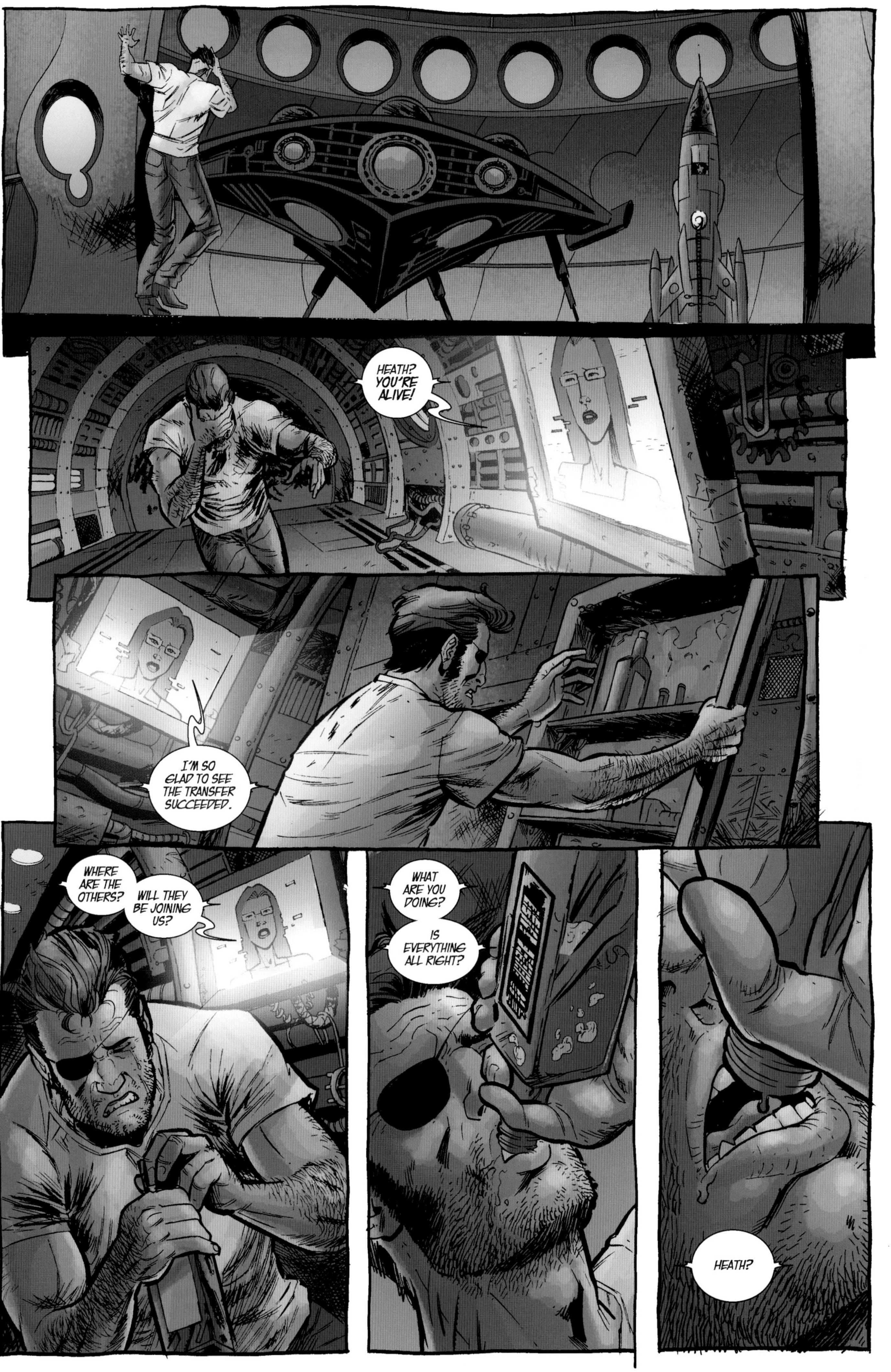
HEATH? YOU'RE ALIVE!
I'M SO GLAD TO SEE THE TRANSFER SUCCEEDED.
WHERE ARE THE OTHERS?
WILL THEY BE JOINING US?
WHAT ARE YOU DOING?
IS EVERYTHING ALL RIGHT?
HEATH?

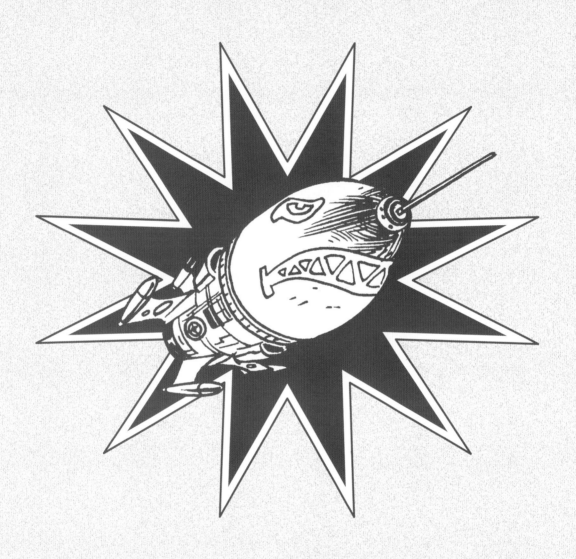

CHAPTER 2

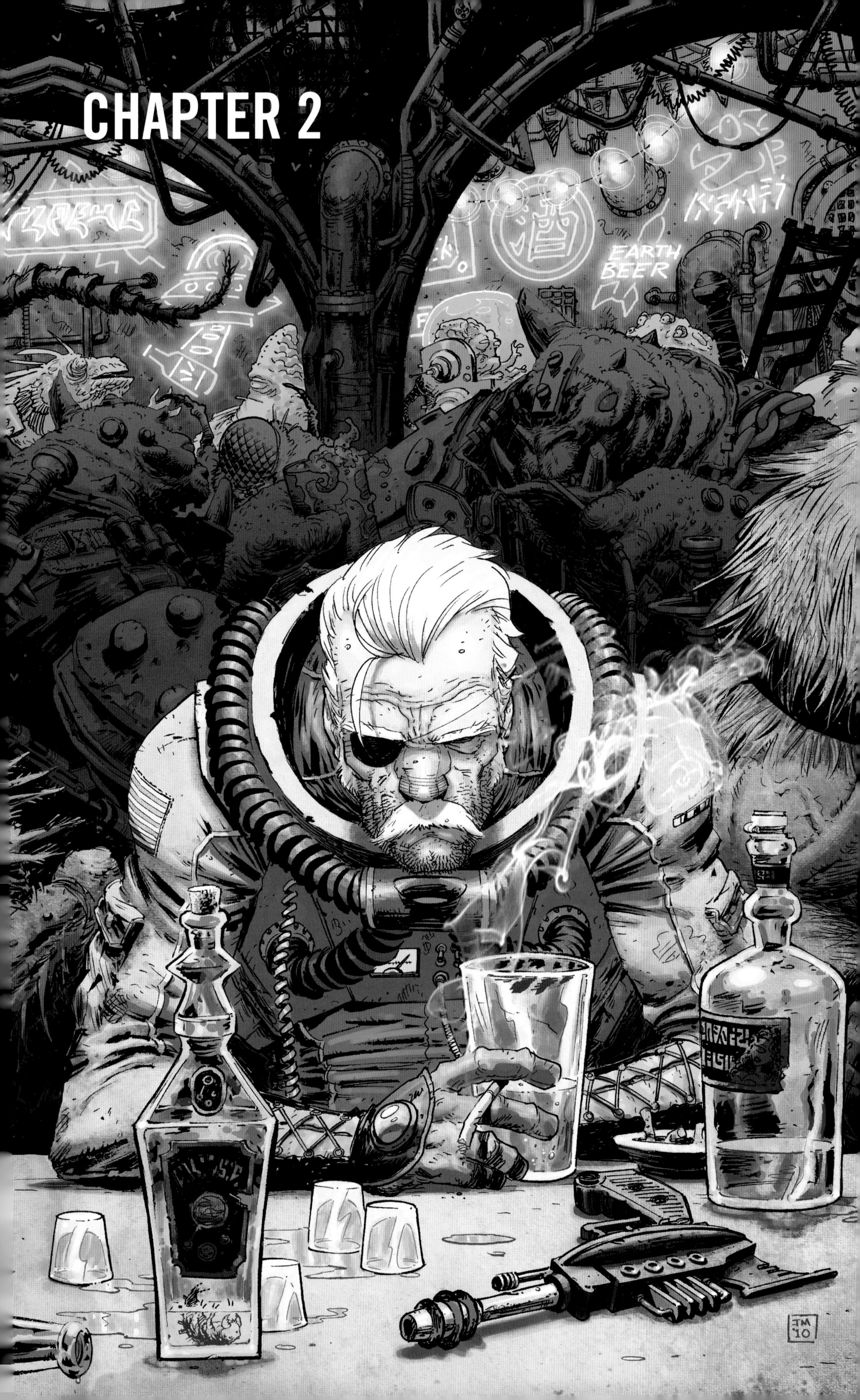
EARTH BEER

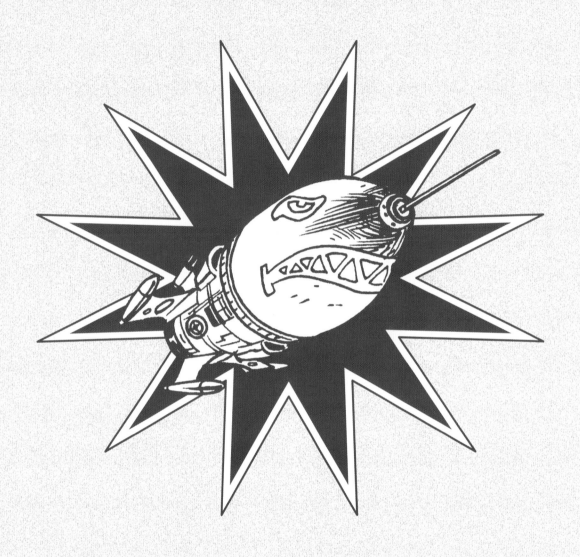

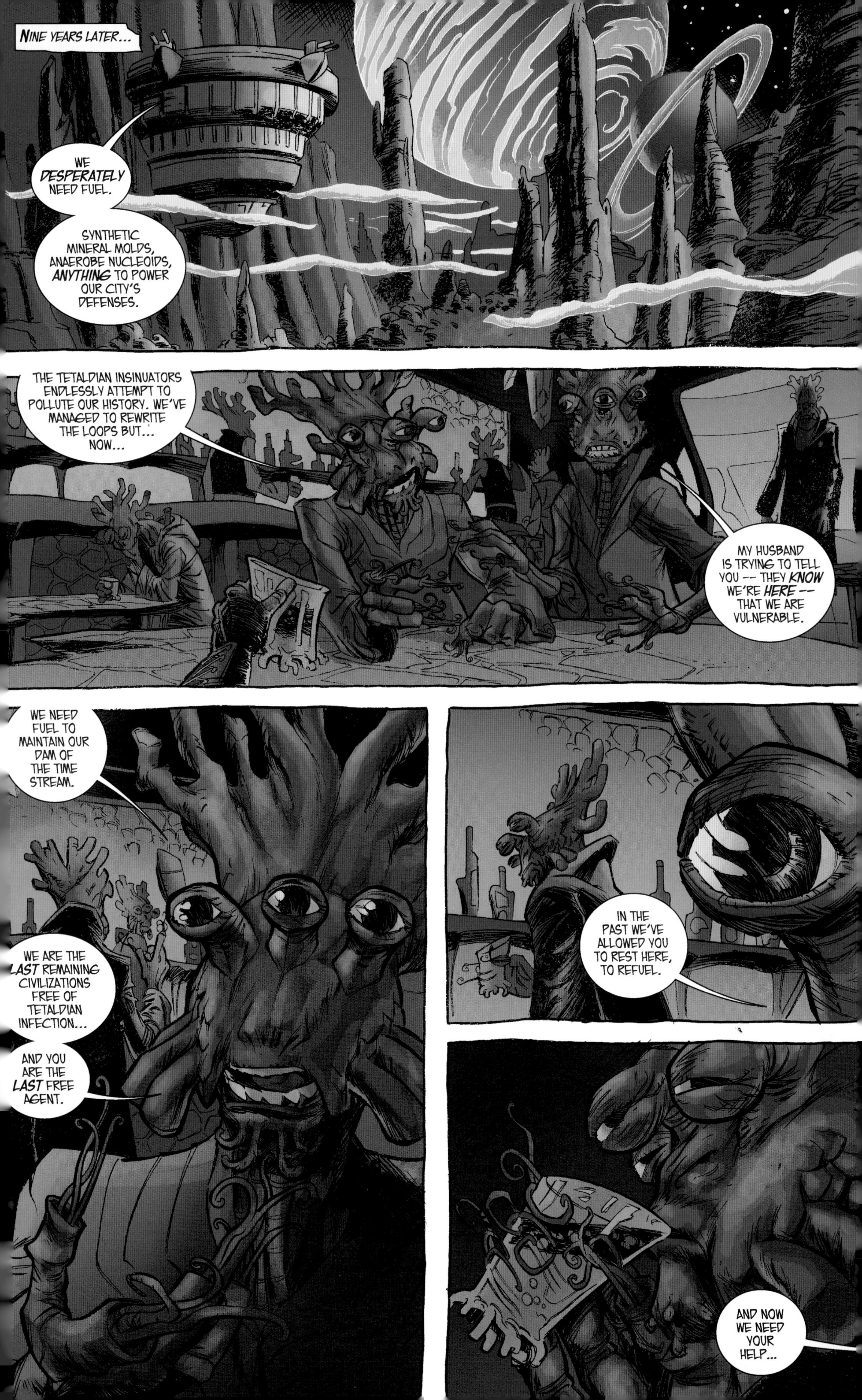
NINE YEARS LATER...
WE DESPERATELY NEED FUEL.
SYNTHETIC MINERAL MOLDS, ANAEROBE NUCLEOIDS, ANYTHING TO POWER OUR CITY'S DEFENSES.
THE TETALDIAN INSINUATORS ENDLESSLY ATTEMPT TO POLLUTE OUR HISTORY. WE'VE MANAGED TO REWRITE THE LOOPS BUT... NOW...
MY HUSBAND IS TRYING TO TELL YOU -- THEY KNOW WE'RE HERE -- THAT WE ARE VULNERABLE.
WE NEED FUEL TO MAINTAIN OUR DAM OF THE TIME STREAM.
WE ARE THE LAST REMAINING CIVILIZATIONS FREE OF TETALDIAN INFECTION...
AND YOU ARE THE LAST FREE AGENT.
IN THE PAST WE'VE ALLOWED YOU TO REST HERE, TO REFUEL.
AND NOW WE NEED YOUR HELP...

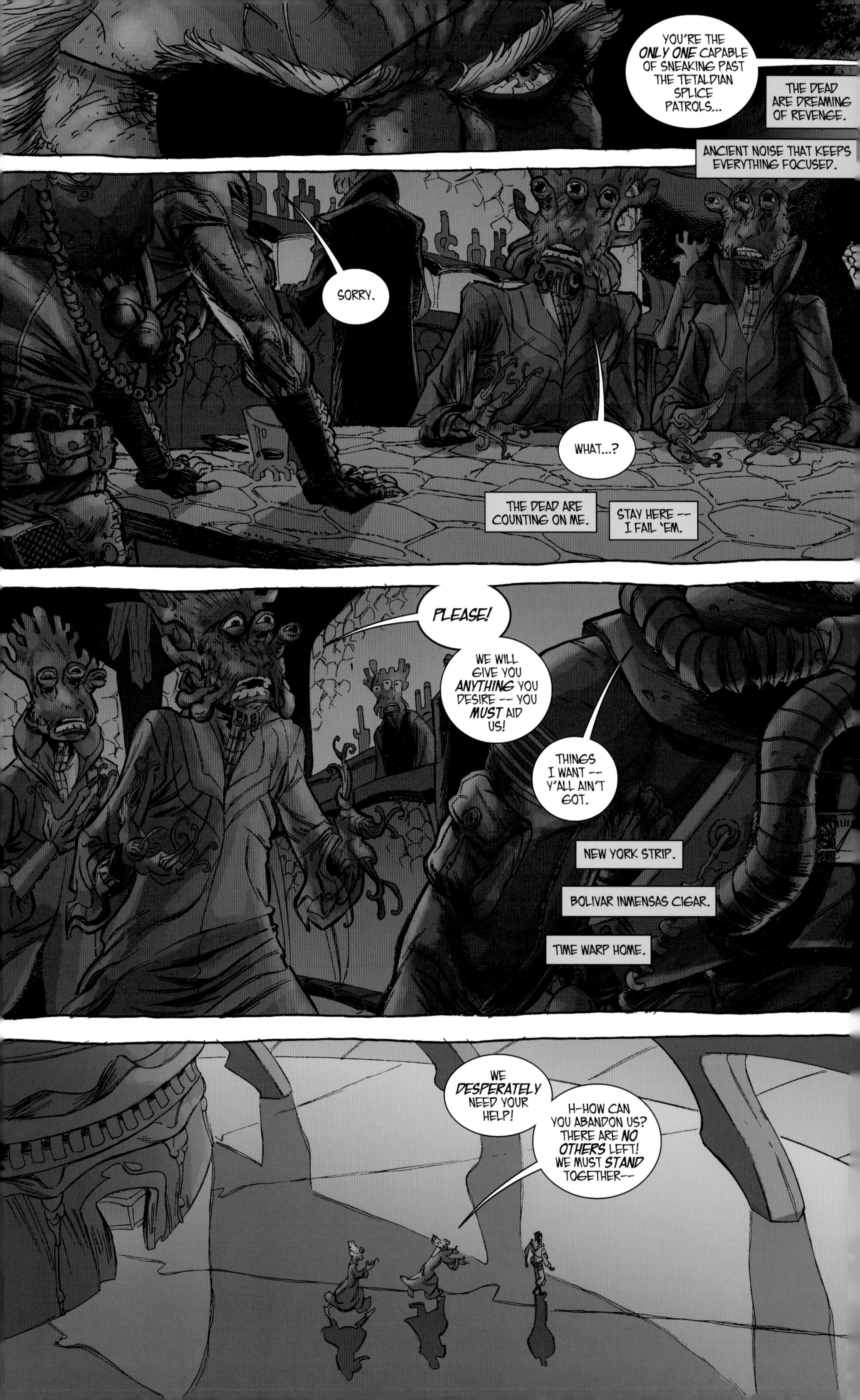
YOU'RE THE ONLY ONE CAPABLE OF SNEAKING PAST THE TETALDIAN SPLICE PATROLS...
THE DEAD ARE DREAMING OF REVENGE.
ANCIENT NOISE THAT KEEPS EVERYTHING FOCUSED.
SORRY.
WHAT...?
THE DEAD ARE COUNTING ON ME.
STAY HERE -- I FAIL 'EM.
PLEASE!
WE WILL GIVE YOU ANYTHING YOU DESIRE -- YOU MUST AID US!
THINGS I WANT -- Y'ALL AIN'T GOT.
NEW YORK STRIP.
BOLIVAR INMENSAS CIGAR.
TIME WARP HOME.
WE DESPERATELY NEED YOUR HELP!
H-HOW CAN YOU ABANDON US? THERE ARE NO OTHERS LEFT! WE MUST STAND TOGETHER--

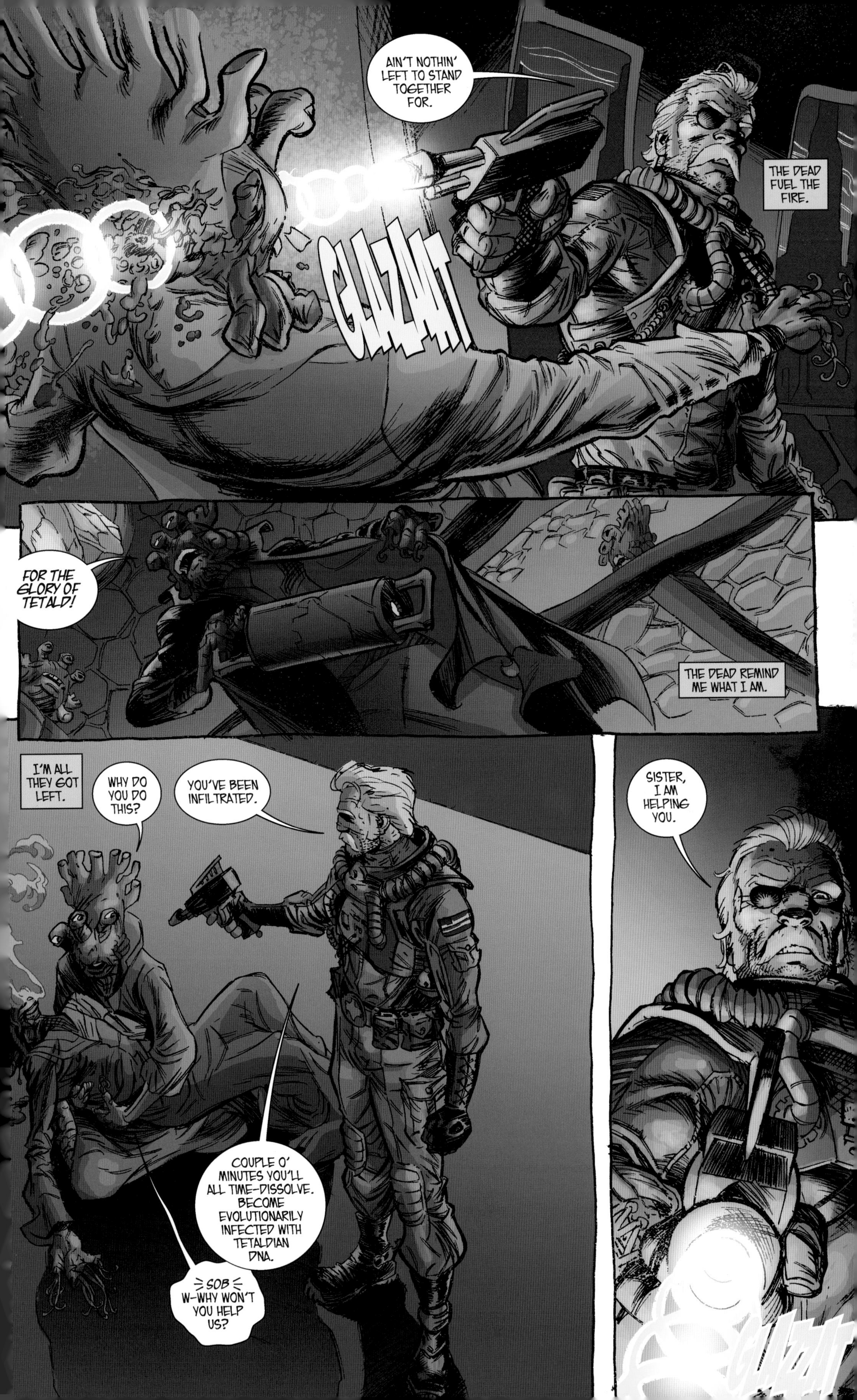
AIN'T NOTHIN' LEFT TO STAND TOGETHER FOR.
THE DEAD FUEL THE FIRE.
GLAZAT
FOR THE GLORY OF TETALD!
THE DEAD REMIND ME WHAT I AM.
I'M ALL THEY GOT LEFT.
WHY DO YOU DO THIS?
YOU'VE BEEN INFILTRATED.
COUPLE O' MINUTES YOU'LL ALL TIME-DISSOLVE. BECOME EVOLUTIONARILY INFECTED WITH TETALDIAN DNA.
SOB W-WHY WON'T YOU HELP US?
SISTER, I AM HELPING YOU.
GLAZAT

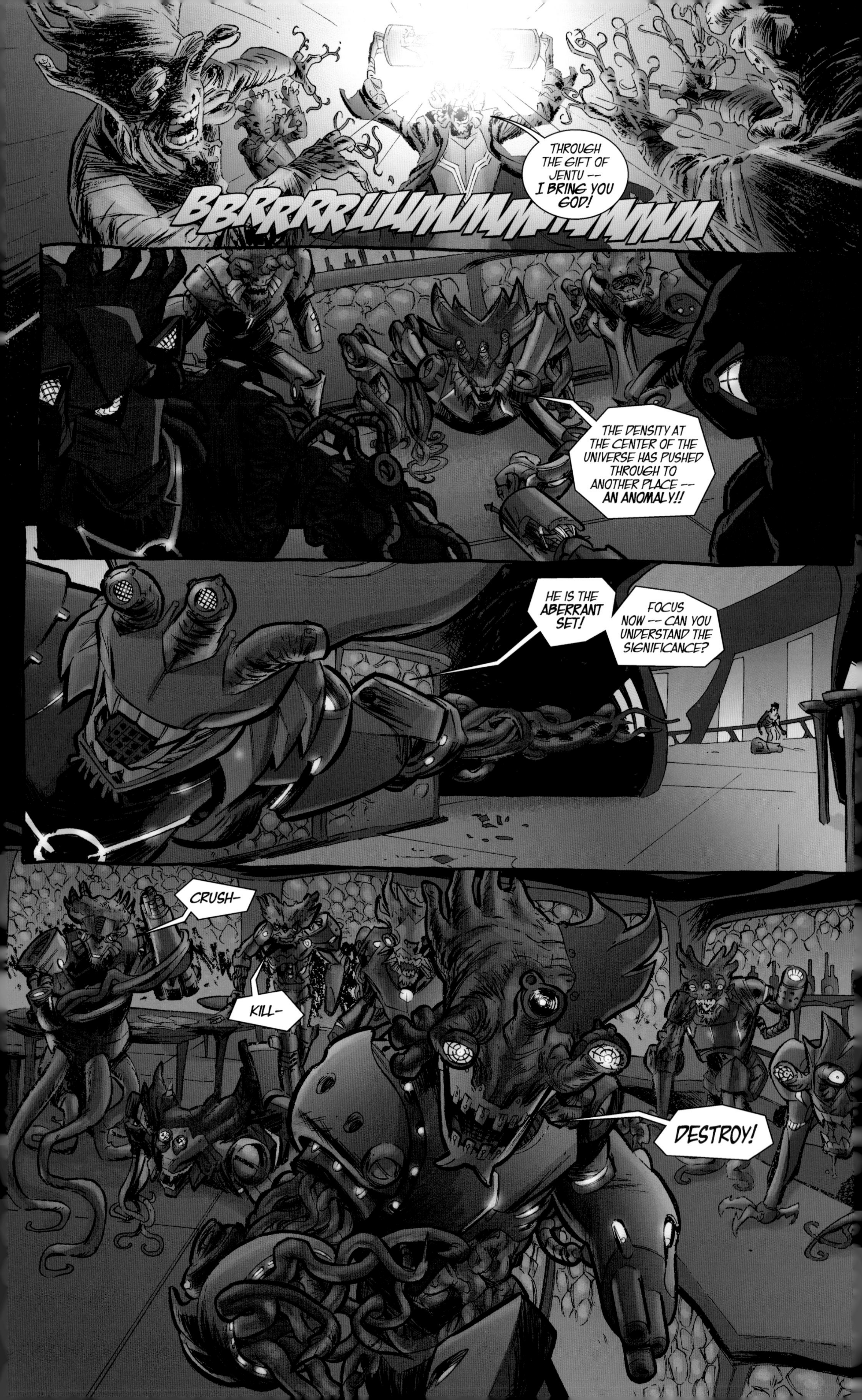
THROUGH THE GIFT OF JENTU -- I BRING YOU GOD!
BBRRRRRUUMMMMMMMM
THE DENSITY AT THE CENTER OF THE UNIVERSE HAS PUSHED THROUGH TO ANOTHER PLACE -- AN ANOMALY!!
HE IS THE ABERRANT SET!
FOCUS NOW -- CAN YOU UNDERSTAND THE SIGNIFICANCE?
CRUSH-
KILL-
DESTROY!

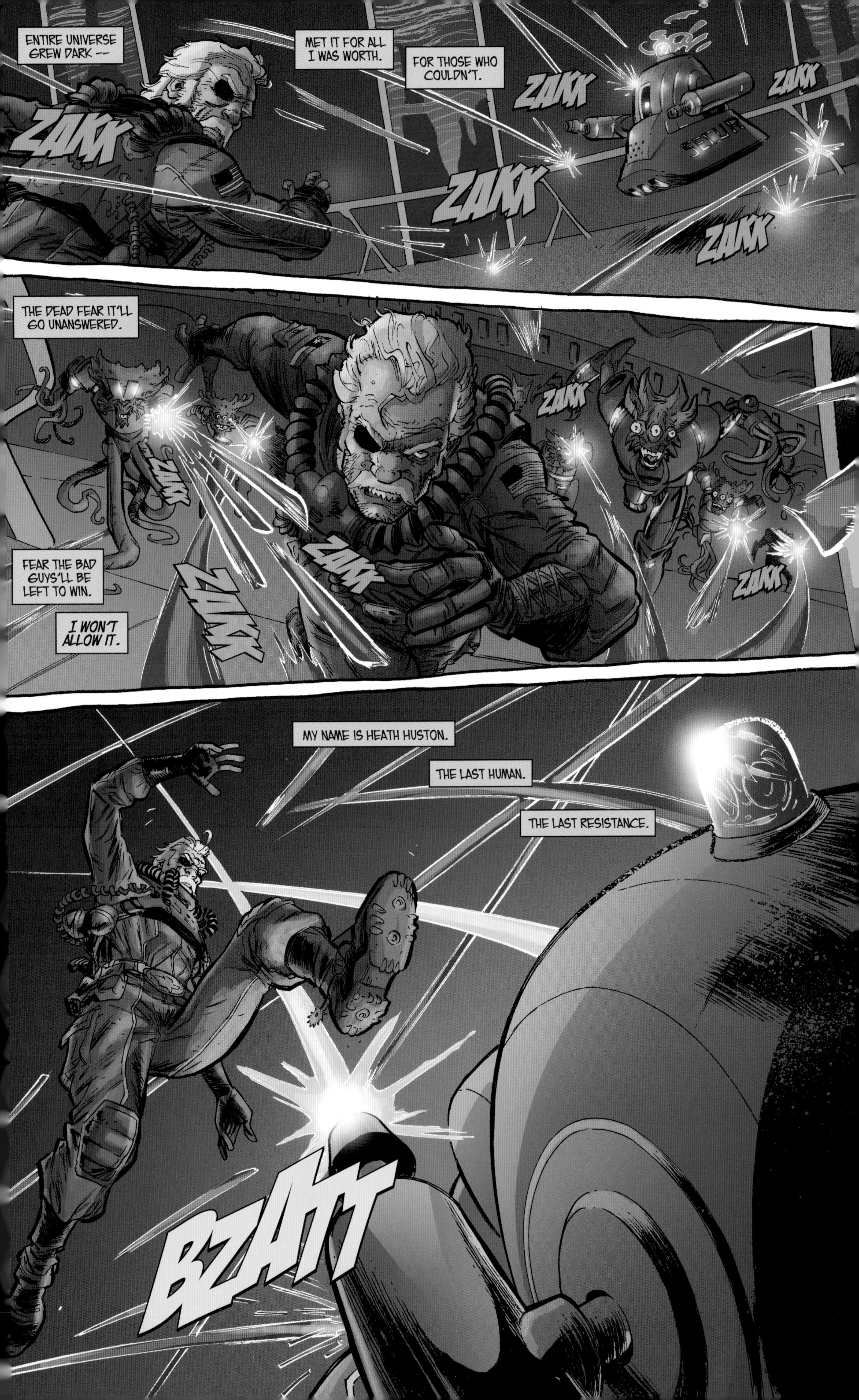
ENTIRE UNIVERSE GREW DARK --
ZAKK
MET IT FOR ALL I WAS WORTH.
FOR THOSE WHO COULDN'T.
ZAKK
ZAKK
ZAKK
ZAKK
THE DEAD FEAR IT'LL GO UNANSWERED.
ZAKK
ZAKK
ZAKK
FEAR THE BAD GUYS'LL BE LEFT TO WIN.
I WON'T ALLOW IT.
ZAKK
ZAKK
ZAKK
MY NAME IS HEATH HUSTON.
THE LAST HUMAN.
THE LAST RESISTANCE.
BZATT

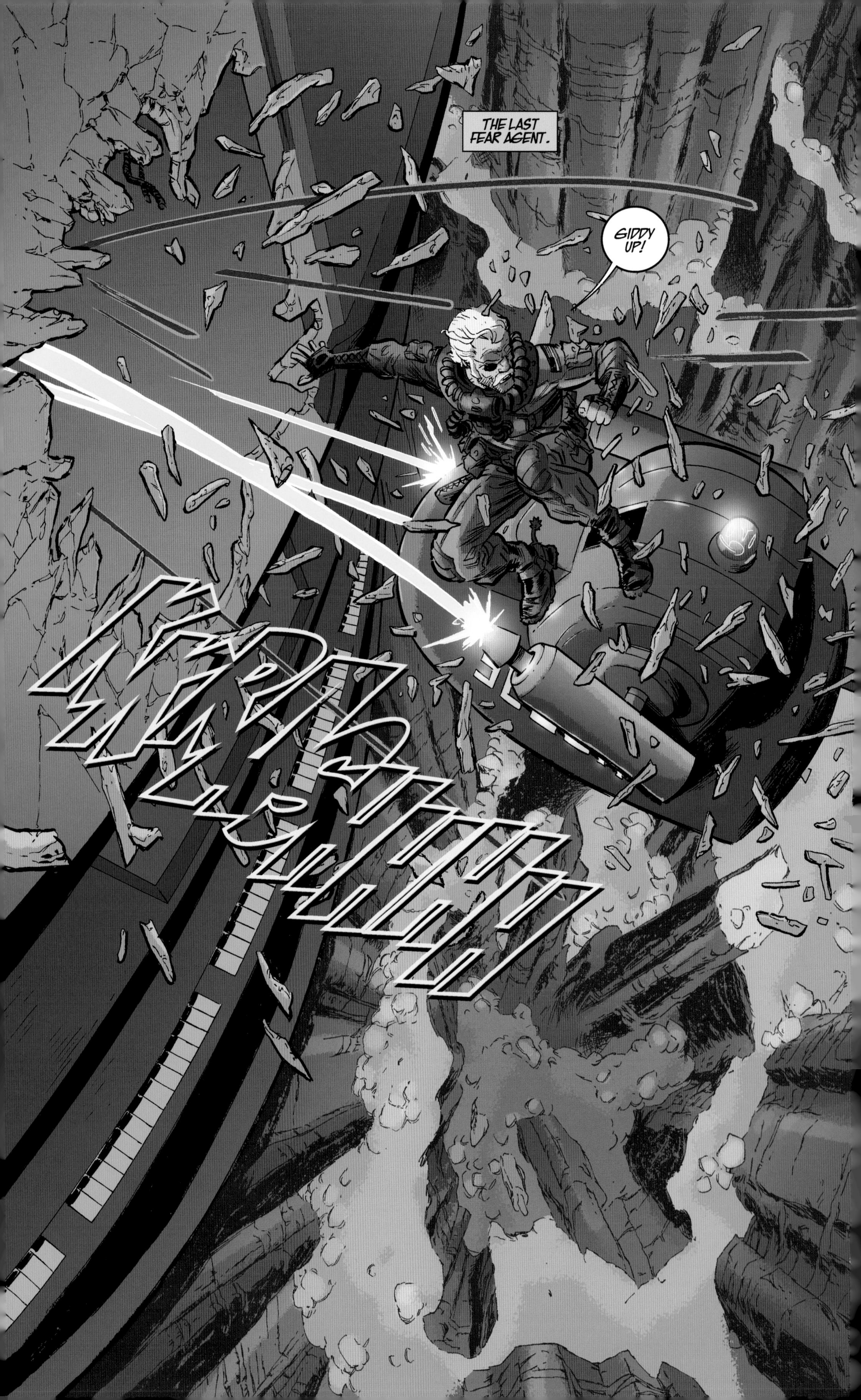
THE LAST FEAR AGENT.
GIDDY UP!

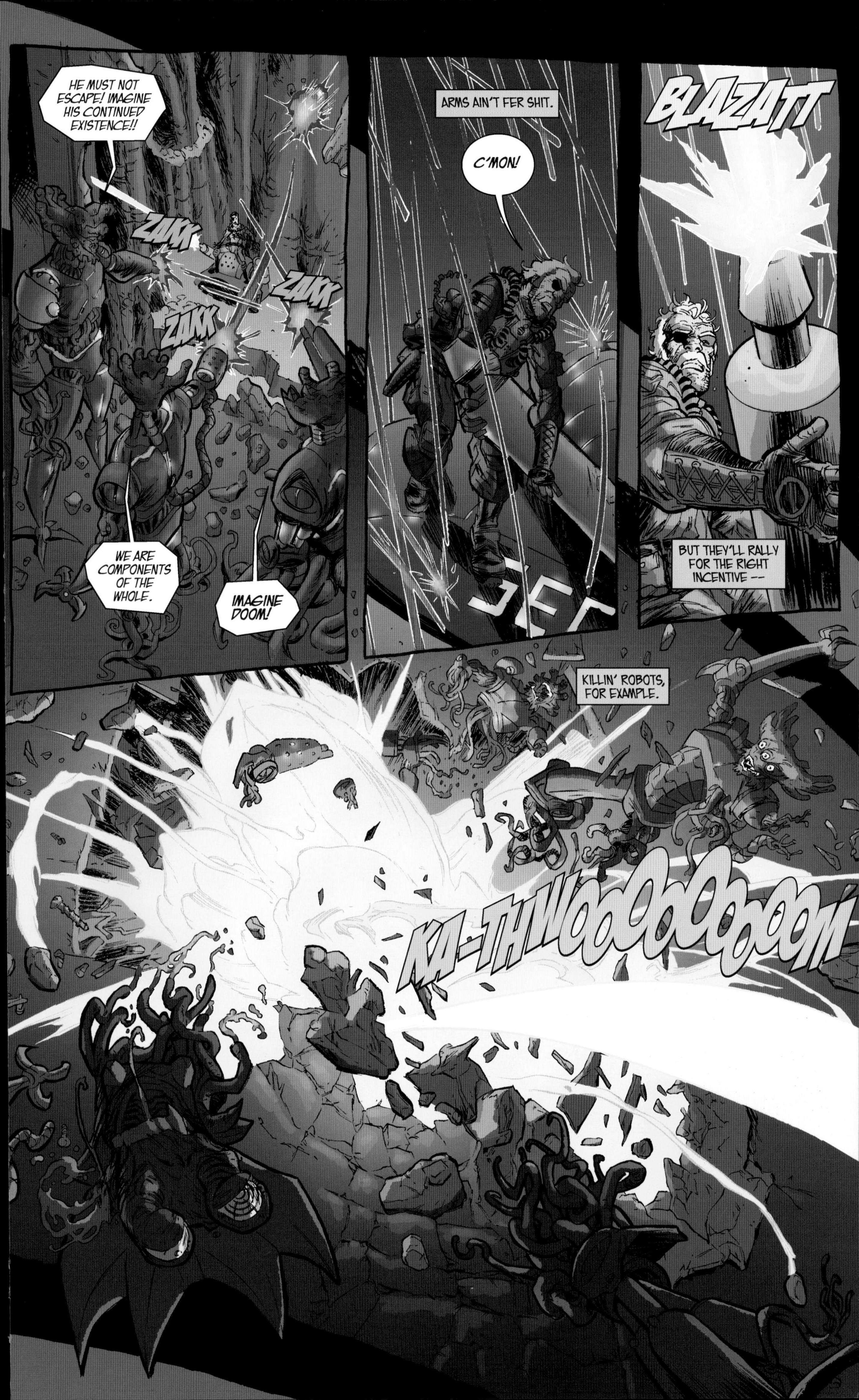

HE MUST NOT ESCAPE! IMAGINE HIS CONTINUED EXISTENCE!!
ZAKK
ZAKK
ZAKK
WE ARE COMPONENTS OF THE WHOLE.
IMAGINE DOOM!
ARMS AIN'T FER SHIT.
C'MON!
BLAZATT
BUT THEY'LL RALLY FOR THE RIGHT INCENTIVE --
KILLIN' ROBOTS, FOR EXAMPLE.
KA-THWOOOOOOOOOM

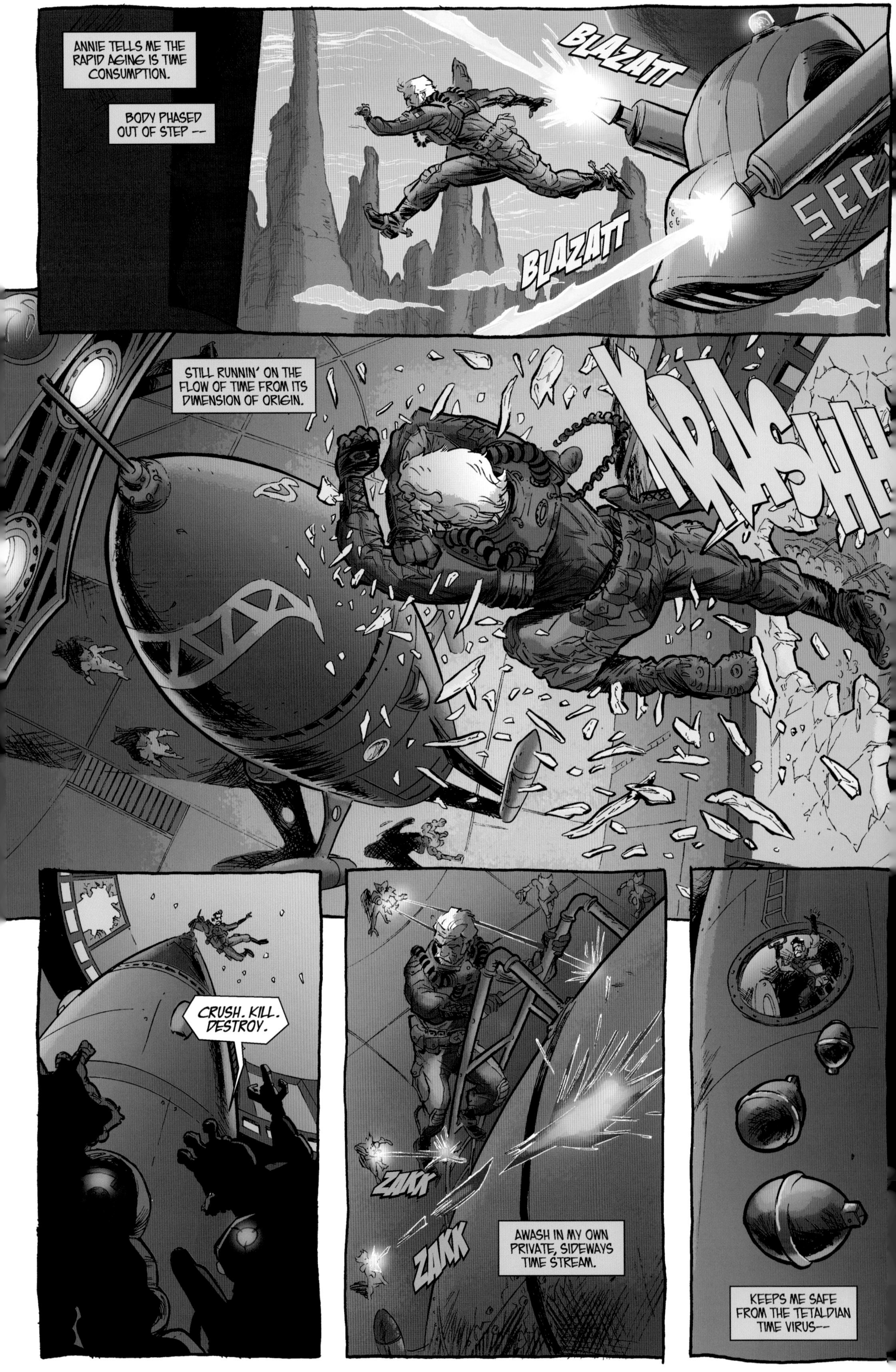

ANNIE TELLS ME THE RAPID AGING IS TIME CONSUMPTION.
BODY PHASED OUT OF STEP --
BLAZATT
BLAZATT
SEC
STILL RUNNIN' ON THE FLOW OF TIME FROM ITS DIMENSION OF ORIGIN.
KRASHH
CRUSH. KILL. DESTROY.
ZAKK
ZAKK
AWASH IN MY OWN PRIVATE, SIDEWAYS TIME STREAM.
KEEPS ME SAFE FROM THE TETALDIAN TIME VIRUS--

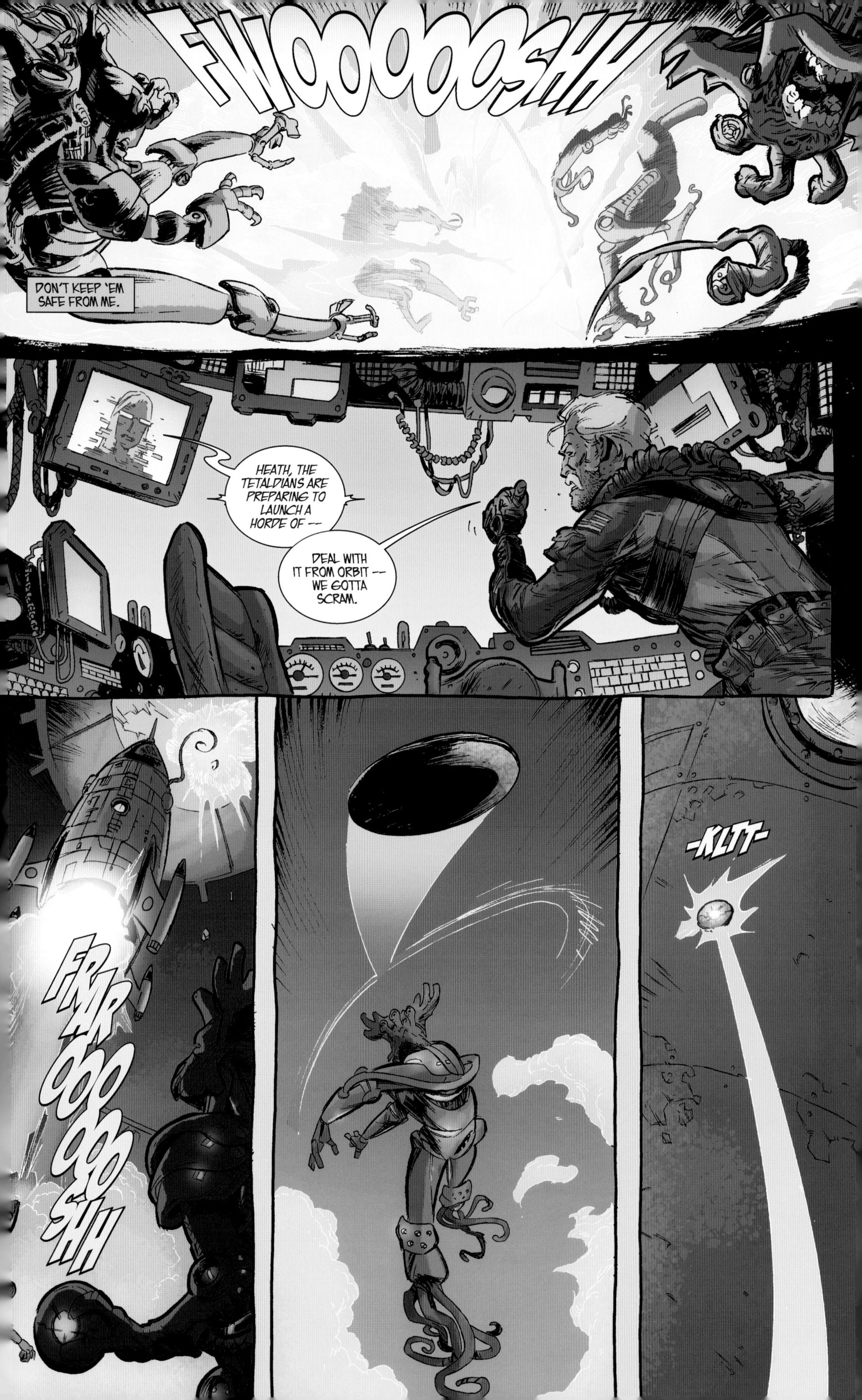
FWOOOOOSHH
DON'T KEEP 'EM SAFE FROM ME.
HEATH, THE TETALDIANS ARE PREPARING TO LAUNCH A HORDE OF --
DEAL WITH IT FROM ORBIT -- WE GOTTA SCRAM.
FRAROOOOOOSHH
-KLTT-

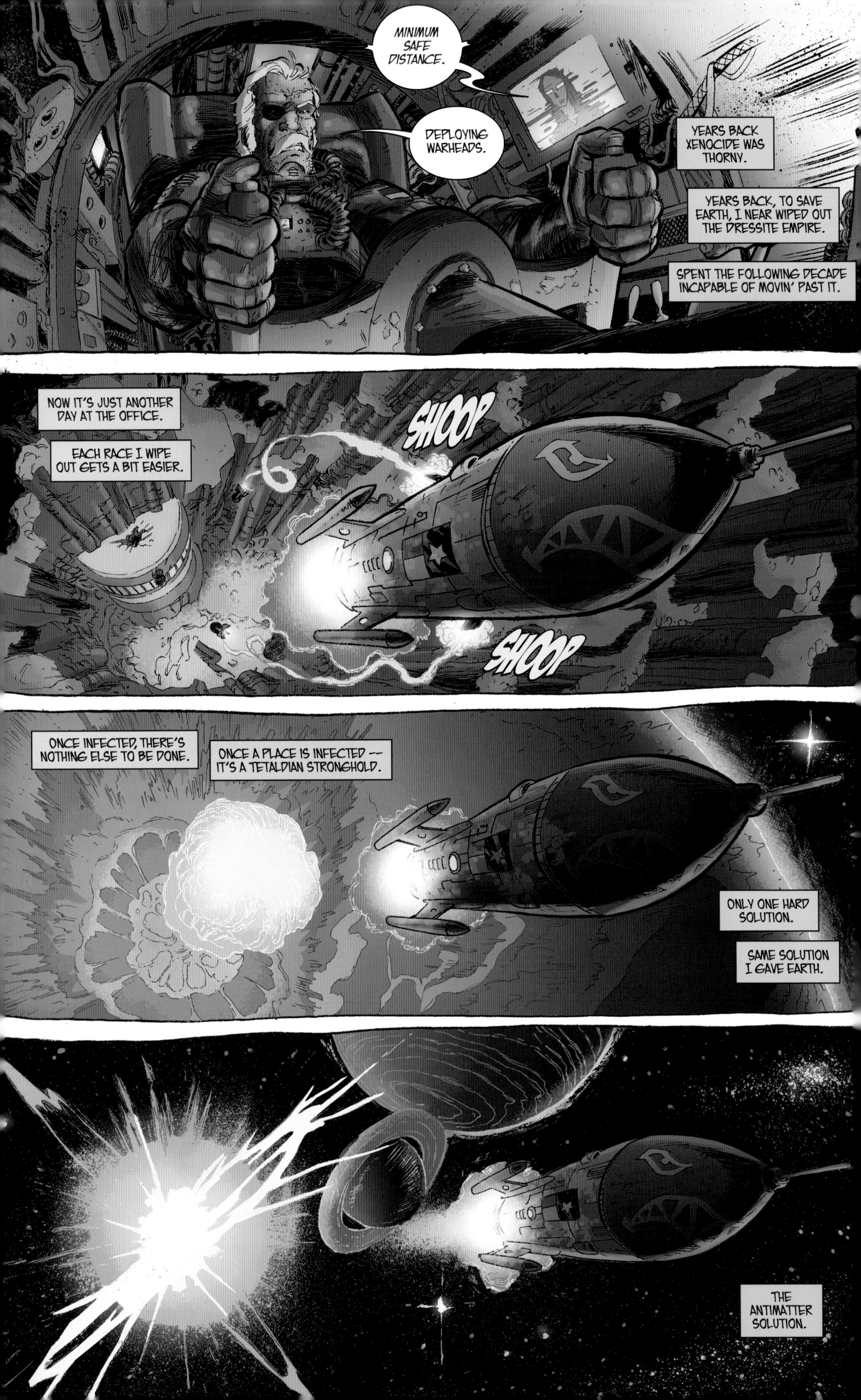
MINIMUM SAFE DISTANCE.
DEPLOYING WARHEADS.
YEARS BACK XENOCIDE WAS THORNY.
YEARS BACK, TO SAVE EARTH, I NEAR WIPED OUT THE DRESSITE EMPIRE.
SPENT THE FOLLOWING DECADE INCAPABLE OF MOVIN' PAST IT.
NOW IT'S JUST ANOTHER DAY AT THE OFFICE.
EACH RACE I WIPE OUT GETS A BIT EASIER.
SHOOP
SHOOP
ONCE INFECTED, THERE'S NOTHING ELSE TO BE DONE.
ONCE A PLACE IS INFECTED -- IT'S A TETALDIAN STRONGHOLD.
ONLY ONE HARD SOLUTION.
SAME SOLUTION I GAVE EARTH.
THE ANTIMATTER SOLUTION.

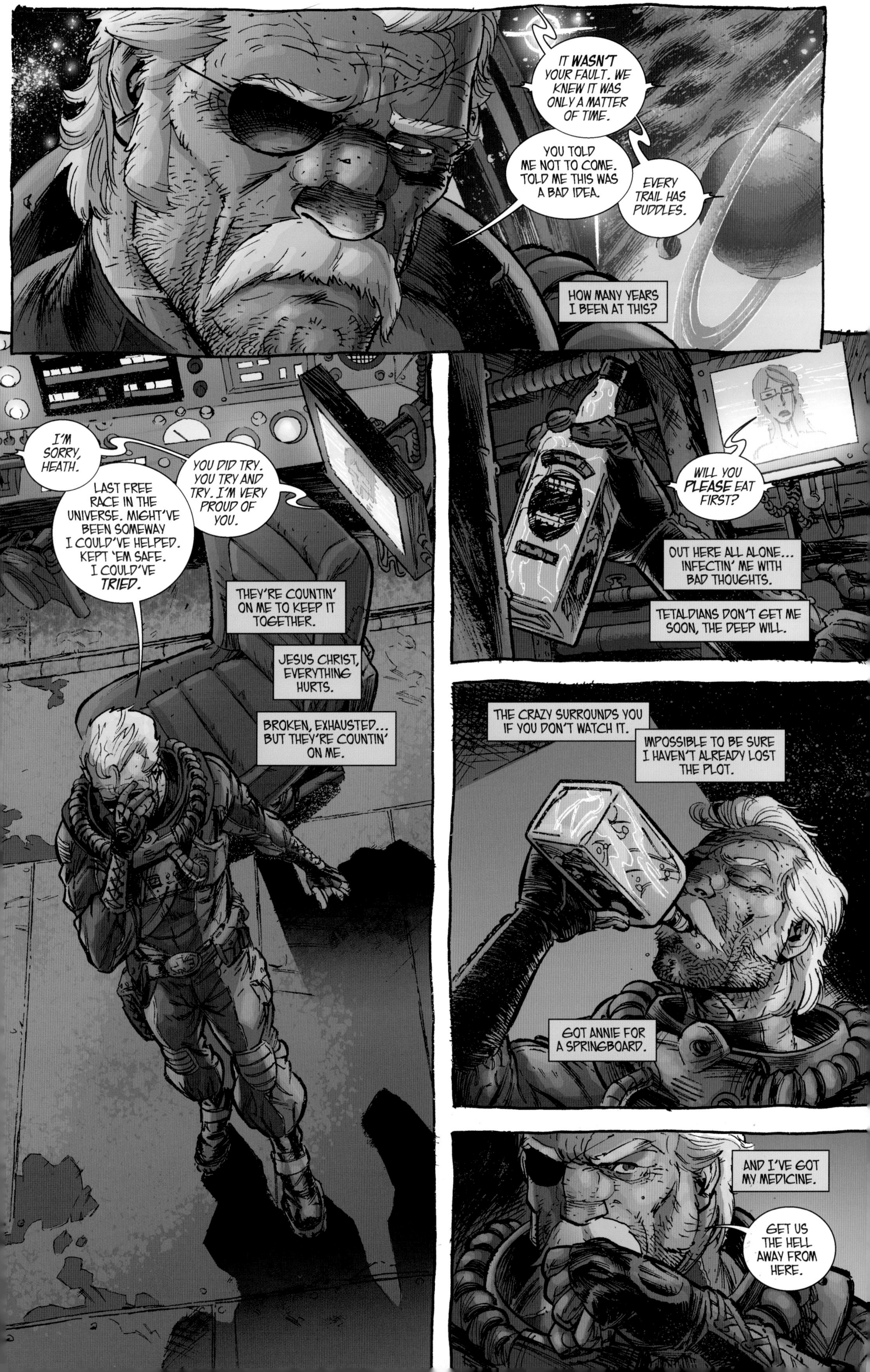
IT WASN'T YOUR FAULT. WE KNEW IT WAS ONLY A MATTER OF TIME.
YOU TOLD ME NOT TO COME. TOLD ME THIS WAS A BAD IDEA.
EVERY TRAIL HAS PUDDLES.
HOW MANY YEARS I BEEN AT THIS?
I'M SORRY, HEATH.
LAST FREE RACE IN THE UNIVERSE. MIGHT'VE BEEN SOMEWAY I COULD'VE HELPED. KEPT 'EM SAFE. I COULD'VE TRIED.
YOU DID TRY. YOU TRY AND TRY. I'M VERY PROUD OF YOU.
THEY'RE COUNTIN' ON ME TO KEEP IT TOGETHER.
JESUS CHRIST, EVERYTHING HURTS.
BROKEN, EXHAUSTED... BUT THEY'RE COUNTIN' ON ME.
WILL YOU PLEASE EAT FIRST?
OUT HERE ALL ALONE... INFECTIN' ME WITH BAD THOUGHTS.
TETALDIANS DON'T GET ME SOON, THE DEEP WILL.
THE CRAZY SURROUNDS YOU IF YOU DON'T WATCH IT.
IMPOSSIBLE TO BE SURE I HAVEN'T ALREADY LOST THE PLOT.
GOT ANNIE FOR A SPRINGBOARD.
AND I'VE GOT MY MEDICINE.
GET US THE HELL AWAY FROM HERE.

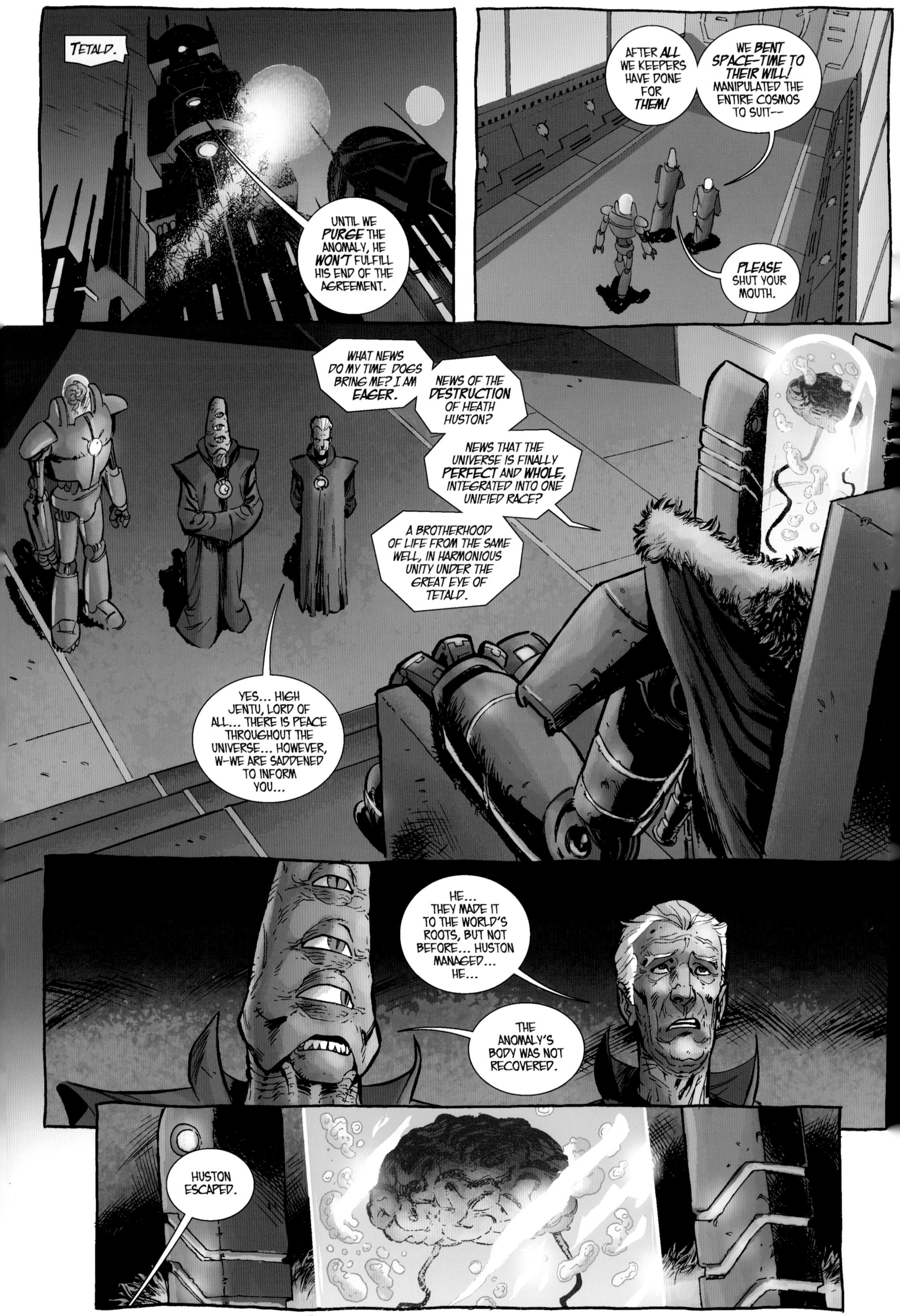
TETALD.
UNTIL WE PURGE THE ANOMALY, HE WON'T FULFILL HIS END OF THE AGREEMENT.
AFTER ALL WE KEEPERS HAVE DONE FOR THEM!
WE BENT SPACE-TIME TO THEIR WILL! MANIPULATED THE ENTIRE COSMOS TO SUIT--
PLEASE SHUT YOUR MOUTH.
WHAT NEWS DO MY TIME DOGS BRING ME? I AM EAGER.
NEWS OF THE DESTRUCTION OF HEATH HUSTON?
NEWS THAT THE UNIVERSE IS FINALLY PERFECT AND WHOLE, INTEGRATED INTO ONE UNIFIED RACE?
A BROTHERHOOD OF LIFE FROM THE SAME WELL, IN HARMONIOUS UNITY UNDER THE GREAT EYE OF TETALD.
YES... HIGH JENTU, LORD OF ALL... THERE IS PEACE THROUGHOUT THE UNIVERSE... HOWEVER, W-WE ARE SADDENED TO INFORM YOU...
HE... THEY MADE IT TO THE WORLD'S ROOTS, BUT NOT BEFORE... HUSTON MANAGED... HE...
THE ANOMALY'S BODY WAS NOT RECOVERED.
HUSTON ESCAPED.

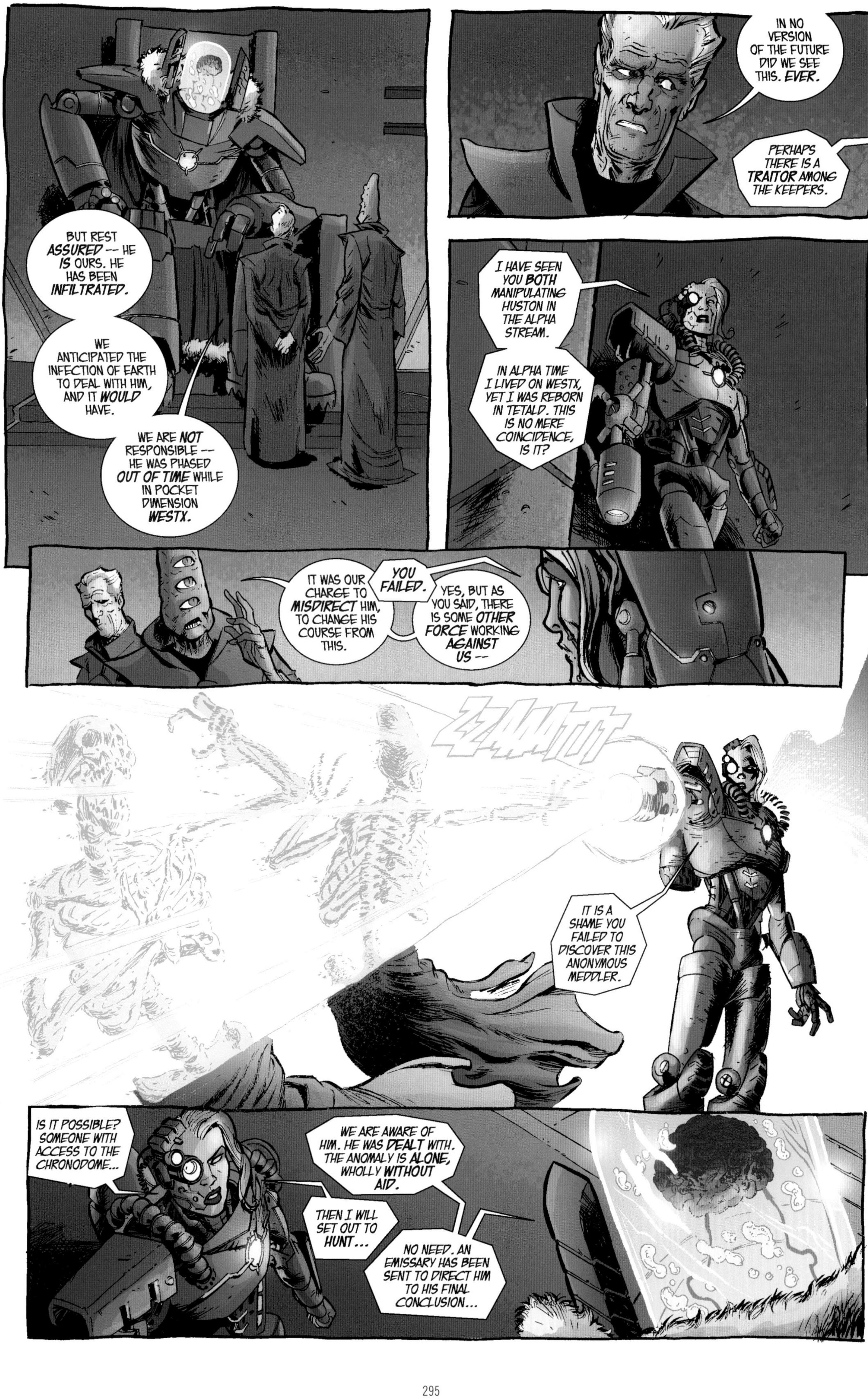
BUT REST ASSURED -- HE IS OURS. HE HAS BEEN INFILTRATED.
WE ANTICIPATED THE INFECTION OF EARTH TO DEAL WITH HIM, AND IT WOULD HAVE.
WE ARE NOT RESPONSIBLE -- HE WAS PHASED OUT OF TIME WHILE IN POCKET DIMENSION WESTX.
IN NO VERSION OF THE FUTURE DID WE SEE THIS. EVER.
PERHAPS THERE IS A TRAITOR AMONG THE KEEPERS.
I HAVE SEEN YOU BOTH MANIPULATING HUSTON IN THE ALPHA STREAM.
IN ALPHA TIME I LIVED ON WESTX, YET I WAS REBORN IN TETALD. THIS IS NO MERE COINCIDENCE, IS IT?
IT WAS OUR CHARGE TO MISDIRECT HIM, TO CHANGE HIS COURSE FROM THIS.
YOU FAILED.
YES, BUT AS YOU SAID, THERE IS SOME OTHER FORCE WORKING AGAINST US --
ZZAAAATTT
IT IS A SHAME YOU FAILED TO DISCOVER THIS ANONYMOUS MEDDLER.
IS IT POSSIBLE? SOMEONE WITH ACCESS TO THE CHRONODOME...
WE ARE AWARE OF HIM. HE WAS DEALT WITH. THE ANOMALY IS ALONE, WHOLLY WITHOUT AID.
THEN I WILL SET OUT TO HUNT...
NO NEED. AN EMISSARY HAS BEEN SENT TO DIRECT HIM TO HIS FINAL CONCLUSION...

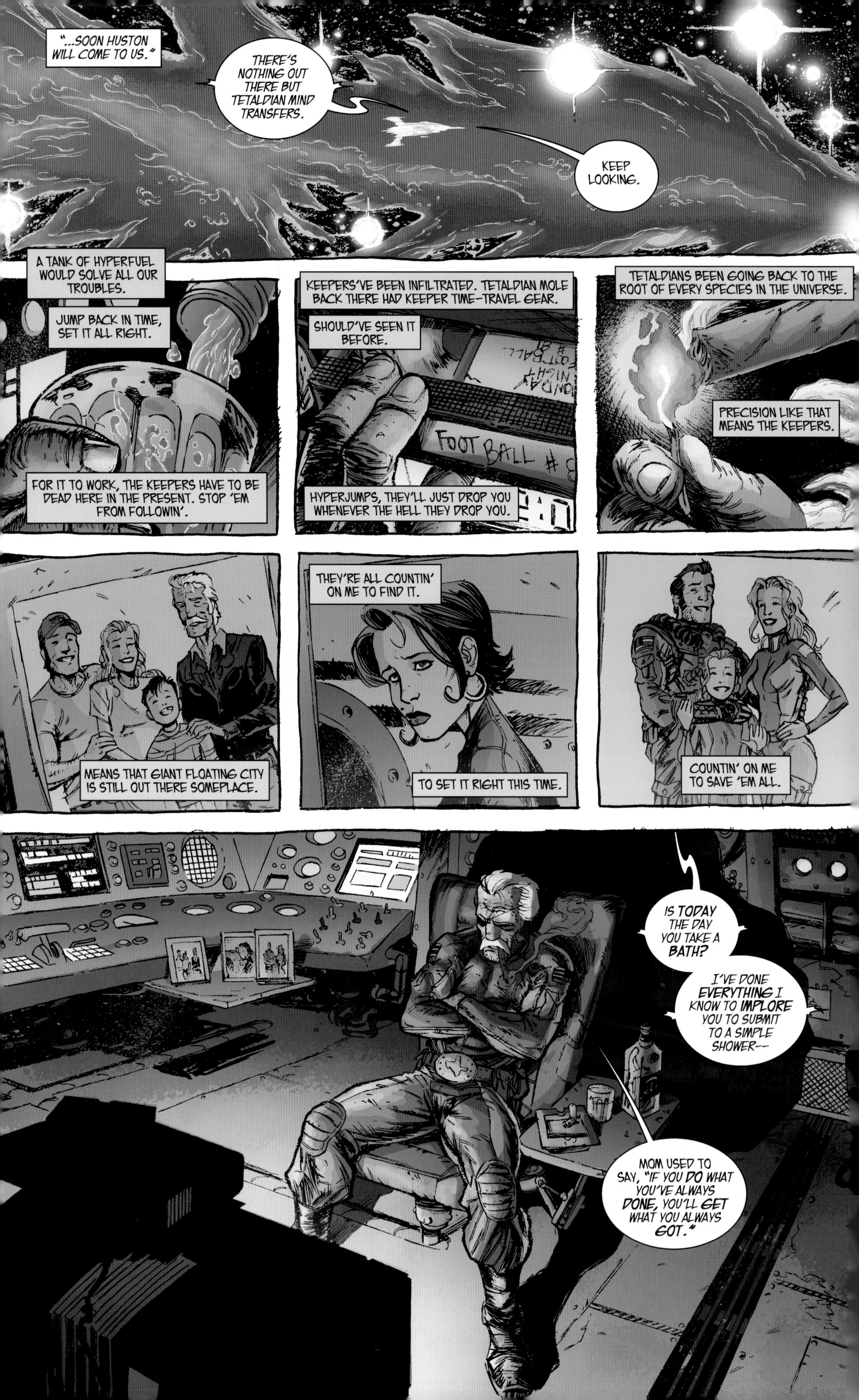
"...SOON HUSTON WILL COME TO US."
THERE'S NOTHING OUT THERE BUT TETALDIAN MIND TRANSFERS.
KEEP LOOKING.
A TANK OF HYPERFUEL WOULD SOLVE ALL OUR TROUBLES.
JUMP BACK IN TIME, SET IT ALL RIGHT.
FOR IT TO WORK, THE KEEPERS HAVE TO BE DEAD HERE IN THE PRESENT. STOP 'EM FROM FOLLOWIN'.
KEEPERS'VE BEEN INFILTRATED. TETALDIAN MOLE BACK THERE HAD KEEPER TIME-TRAVEL GEAR.
SHOULD'VE SEEN IT BEFORE.
FOOT BALL # 8
HYPERJUMPS, THEY'LL JUST DROP YOU WHENEVER THE HELL THEY DROP YOU.
TETALDIANS BEEN GOING BACK TO THE ROOT OF EVERY SPECIES IN THE UNIVERSE.
PRECISION LIKE THAT MEANS THE KEEPERS.
MEANS THAT GIANT FLOATING CITY IS STILL OUT THERE SOMEPLACE.
THEY'RE ALL COUNTIN' ON ME TO FIND IT.
TO SET IT RIGHT THIS TIME.
COUNTIN' ON ME TO SAVE 'EM ALL.
IS TODAY THE DAY YOU TAKE A BATH?
I'VE DONE EVERYTHING I KNOW TO IMPLORE YOU TO SUBMIT TO A SIMPLE SHOWER--
MOM USED TO SAY, "IF YOU DO WHAT YOU'VE ALWAYS DONE, YOU'LL GET WHAT YOU ALWAYS GOT."

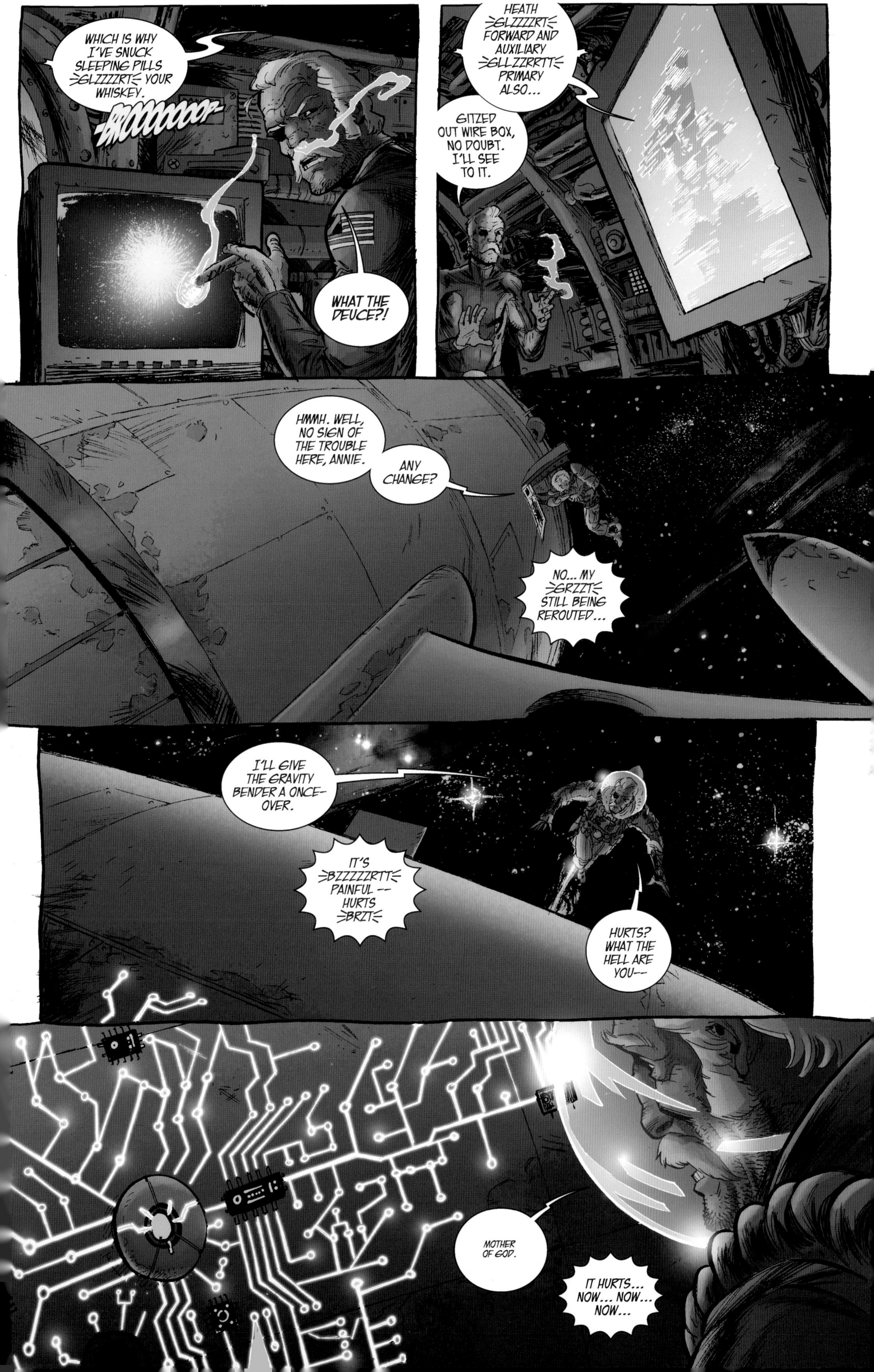
WHICH IS WHY I'VE SNUCK SLEEPING PILLS ≡GLZZZZRT≡ YOUR WHISKEY.
-BROOOOOOOP-
WHAT THE DEUCE?!
HEATH ≡GLZZZZRT≡ FORWARD AND AUXILIARY ≡GLLZZRRTT≡ PRIMARY ALSO...
GITZED OUT WIRE BOX, NO DOUBT. I'LL SEE TO IT.
HMMH. WELL, NO SIGN OF THE TROUBLE HERE, ANNIE.
ANY CHANGE?
NO... MY ≡GRZZT≡ STILL BEING REROUTED...
I'LL GIVE THE GRAVITY BENDER A ONCE-OVER.
IT'S ≡BZZZZZRTT≡ PAINFUL -- HURTS ≡BRZT≡
HURTS? WHAT THE HELL ARE YOU--
MOTHER OF GOD.
IT HURTS... NOW... NOW... NOW...

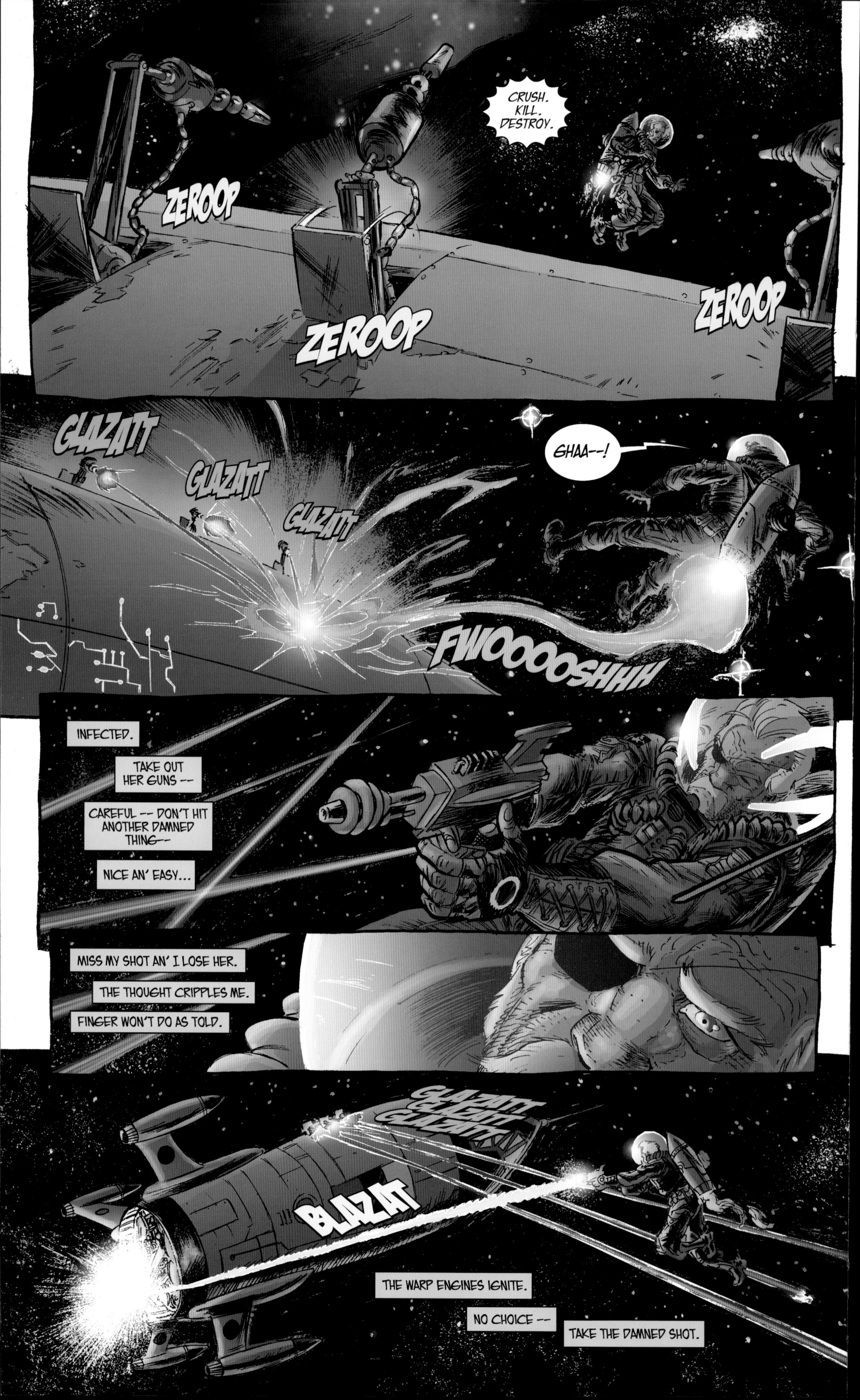
CRUSH. KILL. DESTROY.
ZEROOP
ZEROOP
ZEROOP
GLAZATT
GLAZATT
GLAZATT
GHAA--!
FWOOOOOSHHH
INFECTED.
TAKE OUT HER GUNS --
CAREFUL -- DON'T HIT ANOTHER DAMNED THING--
NICE AN' EASY...
MISS MY SHOT AN' I LOSE HER.
THE THOUGHT CRIPPLES ME.
FINGER WON'T DO AS TOLD.
GLAZATT
GLAZATT
GLAZATT
BLAZAT
THE WARP ENGINES IGNITE.
NO CHOICE --
TAKE THE DAMNED SHOT.

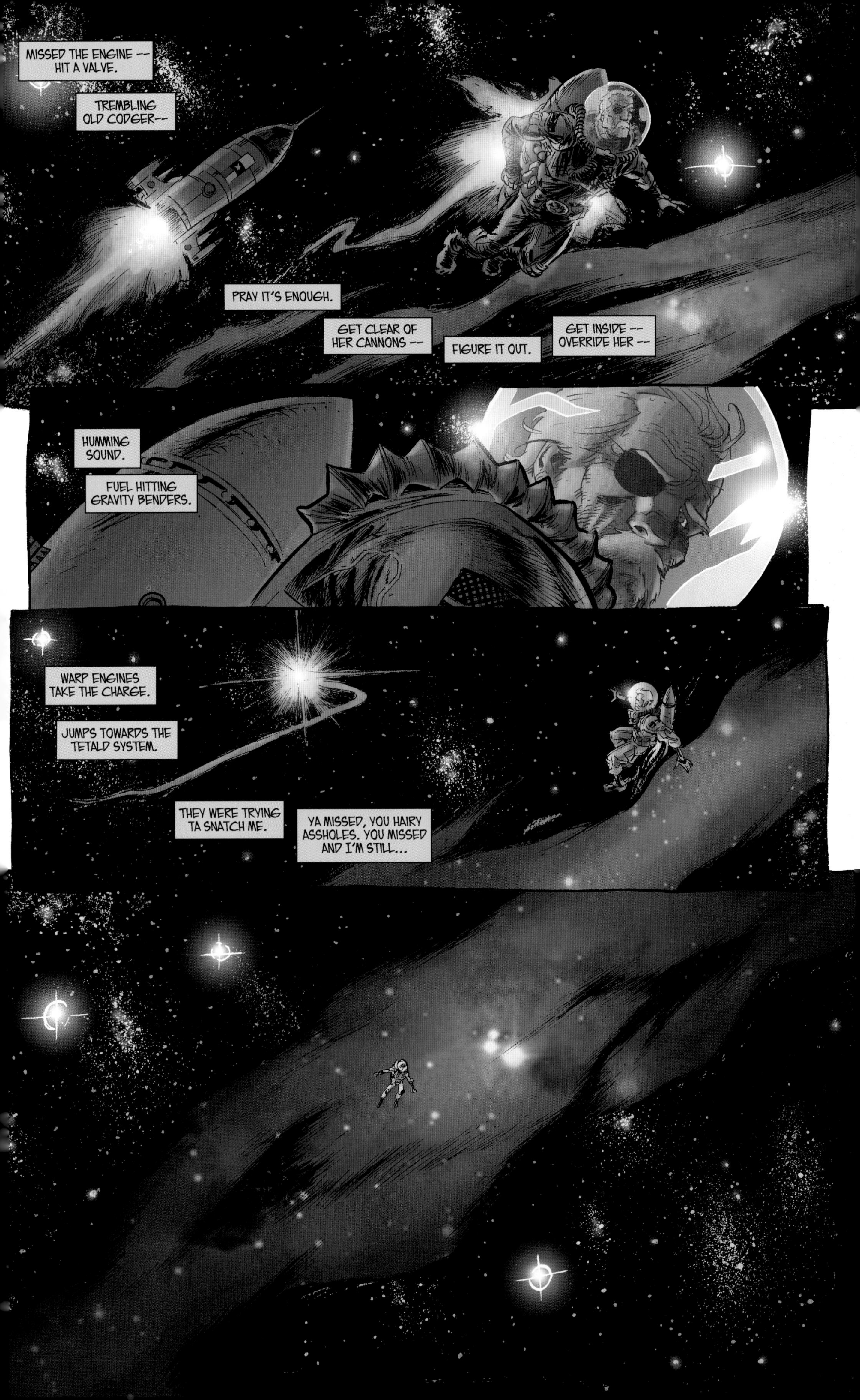
MISSED THE ENGINE -- HIT A VALVE.
TREMBLING OLD CODGER--
PRAY IT'S ENOUGH.
GET CLEAR OF HER CANNONS --
FIGURE IT OUT.
GET INSIDE -- OVERRIDE HER --
HUMMING SOUND.
FUEL HITTING GRAVITY BENDERS.
WARP ENGINES TAKE THE CHARGE.
JUMPS TOWARDS THE TETALD SYSTEM.
THEY WERE TRYING TA SNATCH ME.
YA MISSED, YOU HAIRY ASSHOLES. YOU MISSED AND I'M STILL...

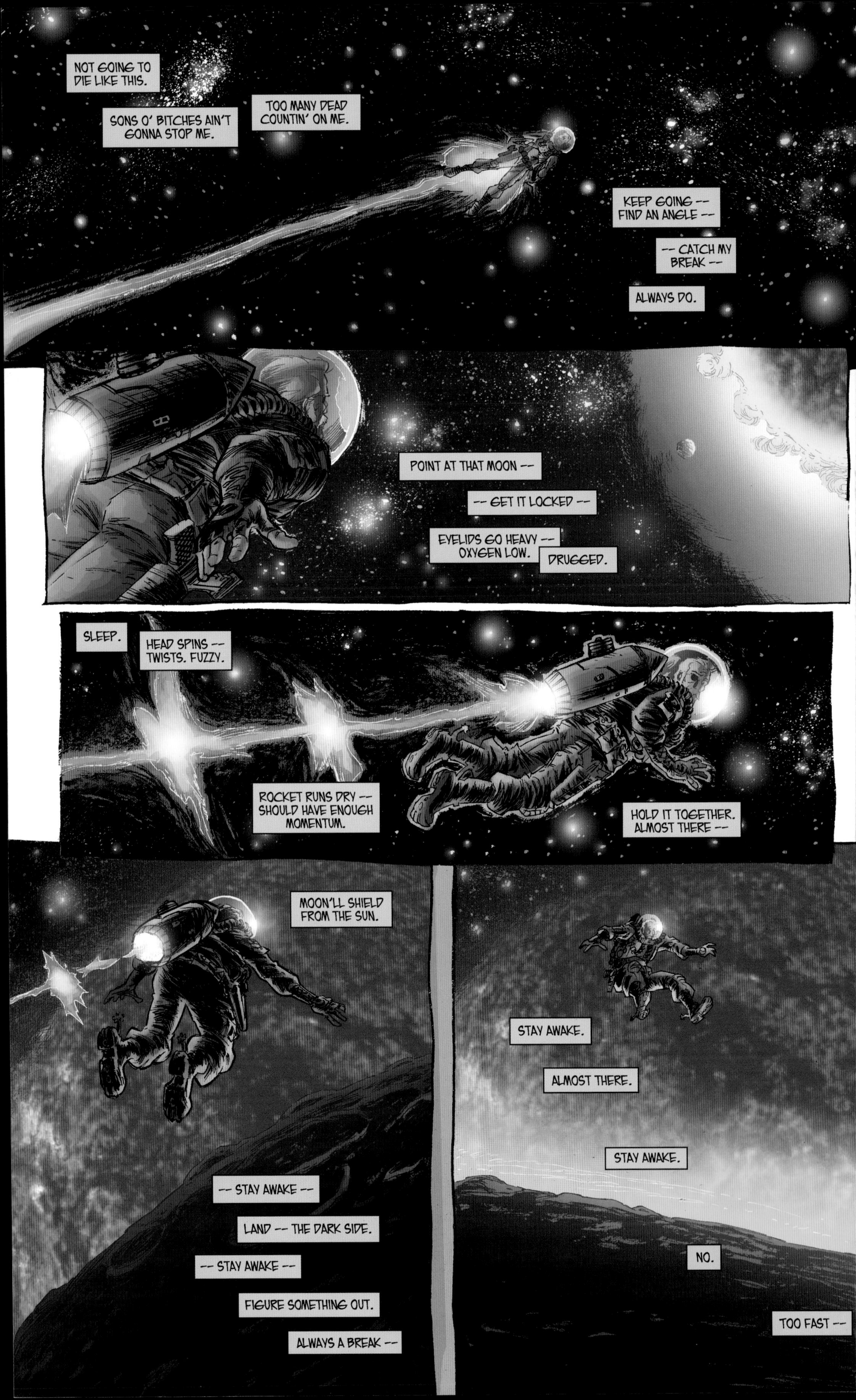
NOT GOING TO DIE LIKE THIS.
SONS O' BITCHES AIN'T GONNA STOP ME.
TOO MANY DEAD COUNTIN' ON ME.
KEEP GOING -- FIND AN ANGLE --
-- CATCH MY BREAK --
ALWAYS DO.
POINT AT THAT MOON --
-- GET IT LOCKED --
EYELIDS GO HEAVY -- OXYGEN LOW.
DRUGGED.
SLEEP.
HEAD SPINS -- TWISTS. FUZZY.
ROCKET RUNS DRY -- SHOULD HAVE ENOUGH MOMENTUM.
HOLD IT TOGETHER. ALMOST THERE --
MOON'LL SHIELD FROM THE SUN.
-- STAY AWAKE --
LAND -- THE DARK SIDE.
-- STAY AWAKE --
FIGURE SOMETHING OUT.
ALWAYS A BREAK --
STAY AWAKE.
ALMOST THERE.
STAY AWAKE.
NO.
TOO FAST --

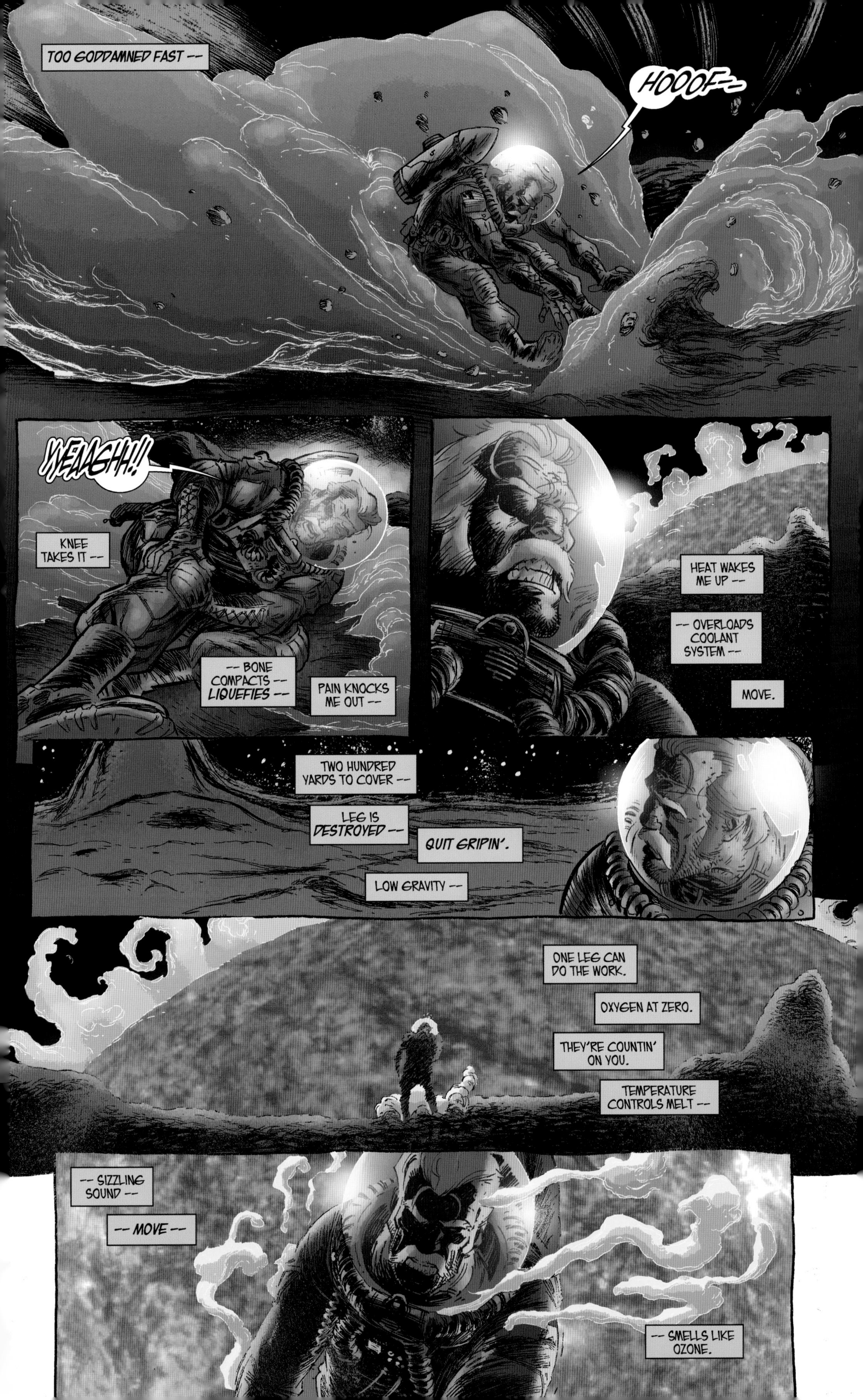

TOO GODDAMNED FAST --
HOOOF--
YYEAAGHH!!
KNEE TAKES IT --
-- BONE COMPACTS -- LIQUEFIES --
PAIN KNOCKS ME OUT --
HEAT WAKES ME UP --
-- OVERLOADS COOLANT SYSTEM --
MOVE.
TWO HUNDRED YARDS TO COVER --
LEG IS DESTROYED --
QUIT GRIPIN'.
LOW GRAVITY --
ONE LEG CAN DO THE WORK.
OXYGEN AT ZERO.
THEY'RE COUNTIN' ON YOU.
TEMPERATURE CONTROLS MELT --
-- SIZZLING SOUND --
-- MOVE --
-- SMELLS LIKE OZONE.

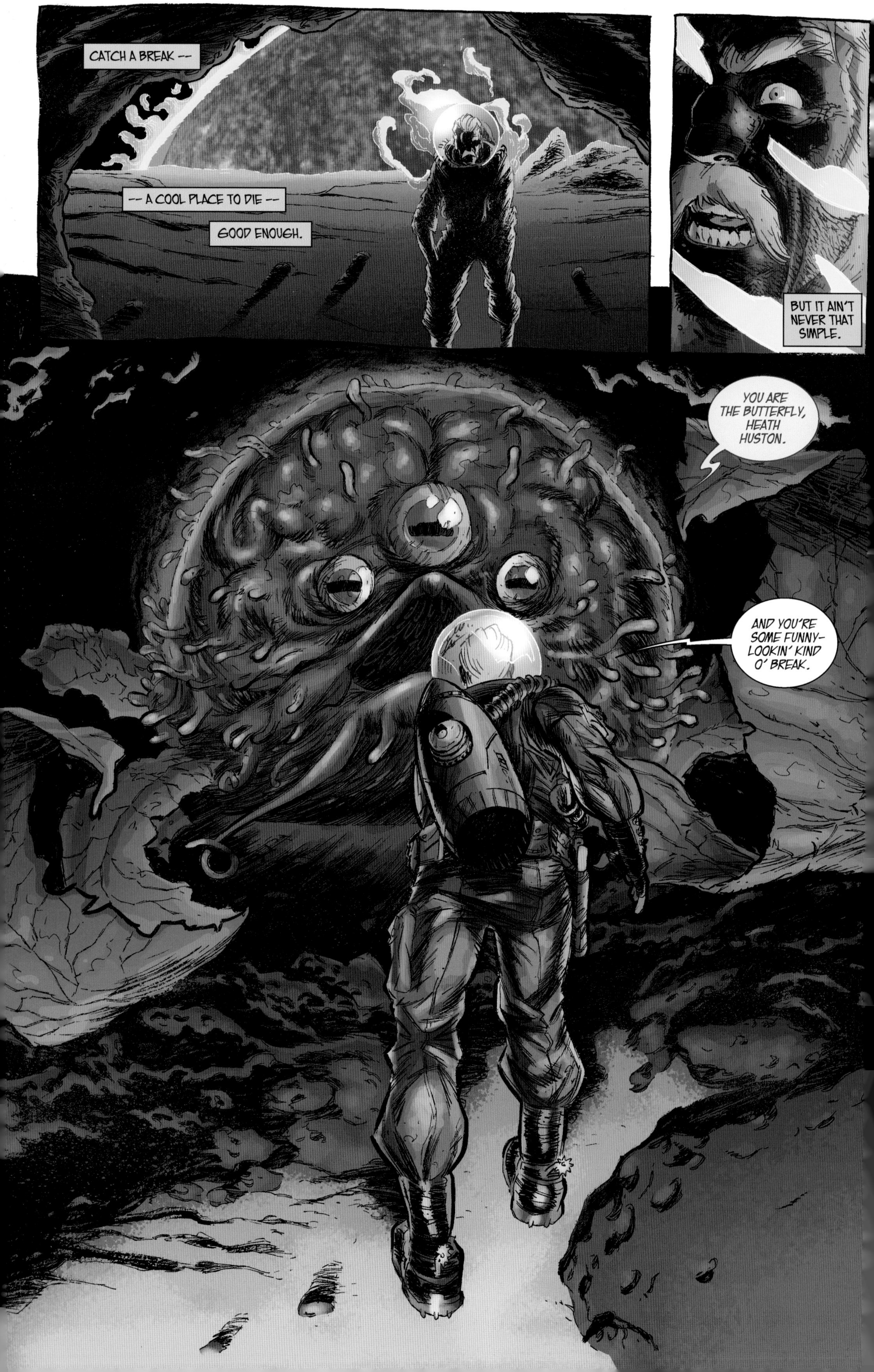
CATCH A BREAK --
-- A COOL PLACE TO DIE --
GOOD ENOUGH.
BUT IT AIN'T NEVER THAT SIMPLE.
YOU ARE THE BUTTERFLY, HEATH HUSTON.
AND YOU'RE SOME FUNNY-LOOKIN' KIND O' BREAK.

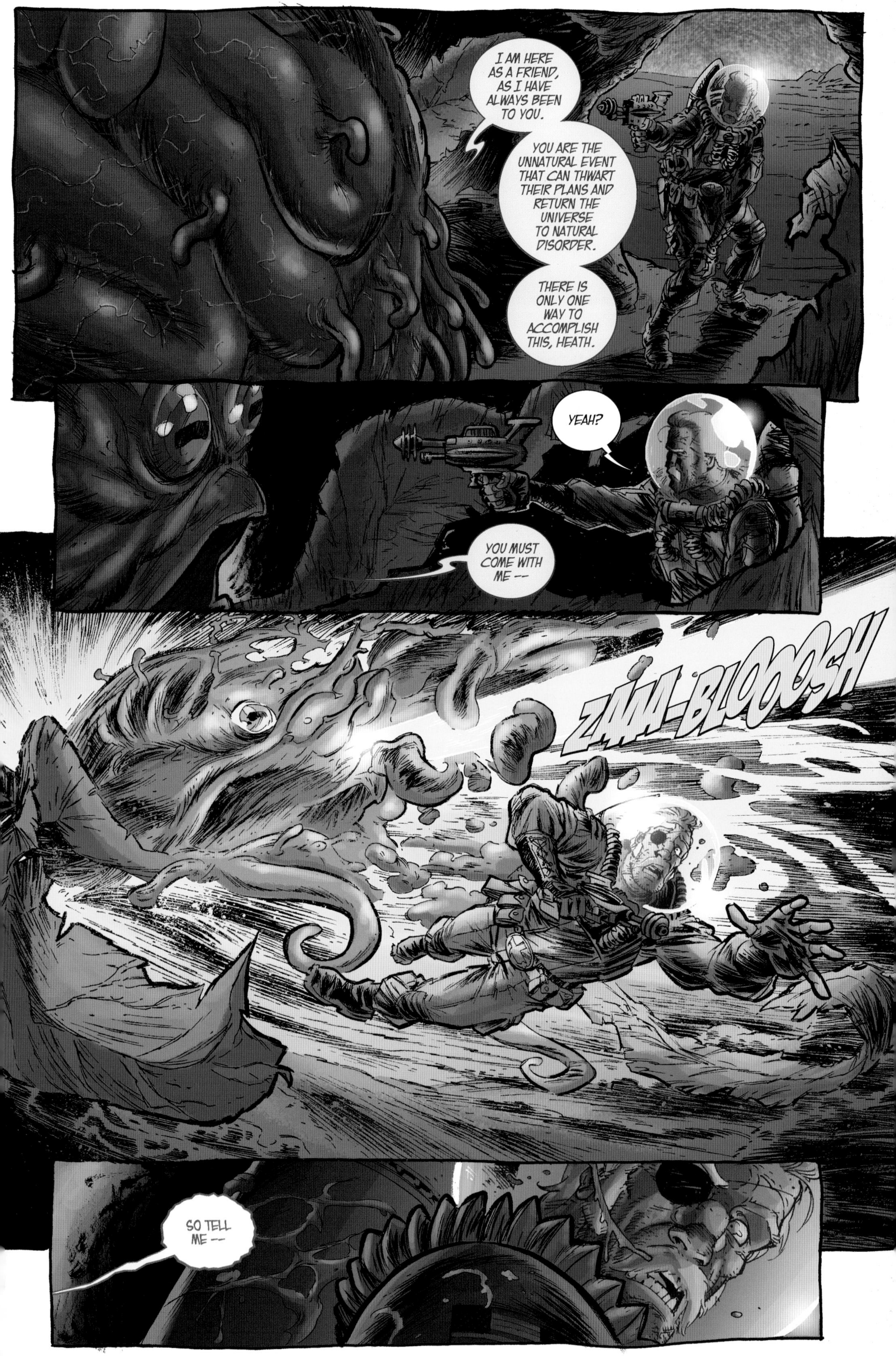
I AM HERE AS A FRIEND, AS I HAVE ALWAYS BEEN TO YOU.
YOU ARE THE UNNATURAL EVENT THAT CAN THWART THEIR PLANS AND RETURN THE UNIVERSE TO NATURAL DISORDER.
THERE IS ONLY ONE WAY TO ACCOMPLISH THIS, HEATH.
YEAH?
YOU MUST COME WITH ME --
ZAAA-BLOOOSH
SO TELL ME --

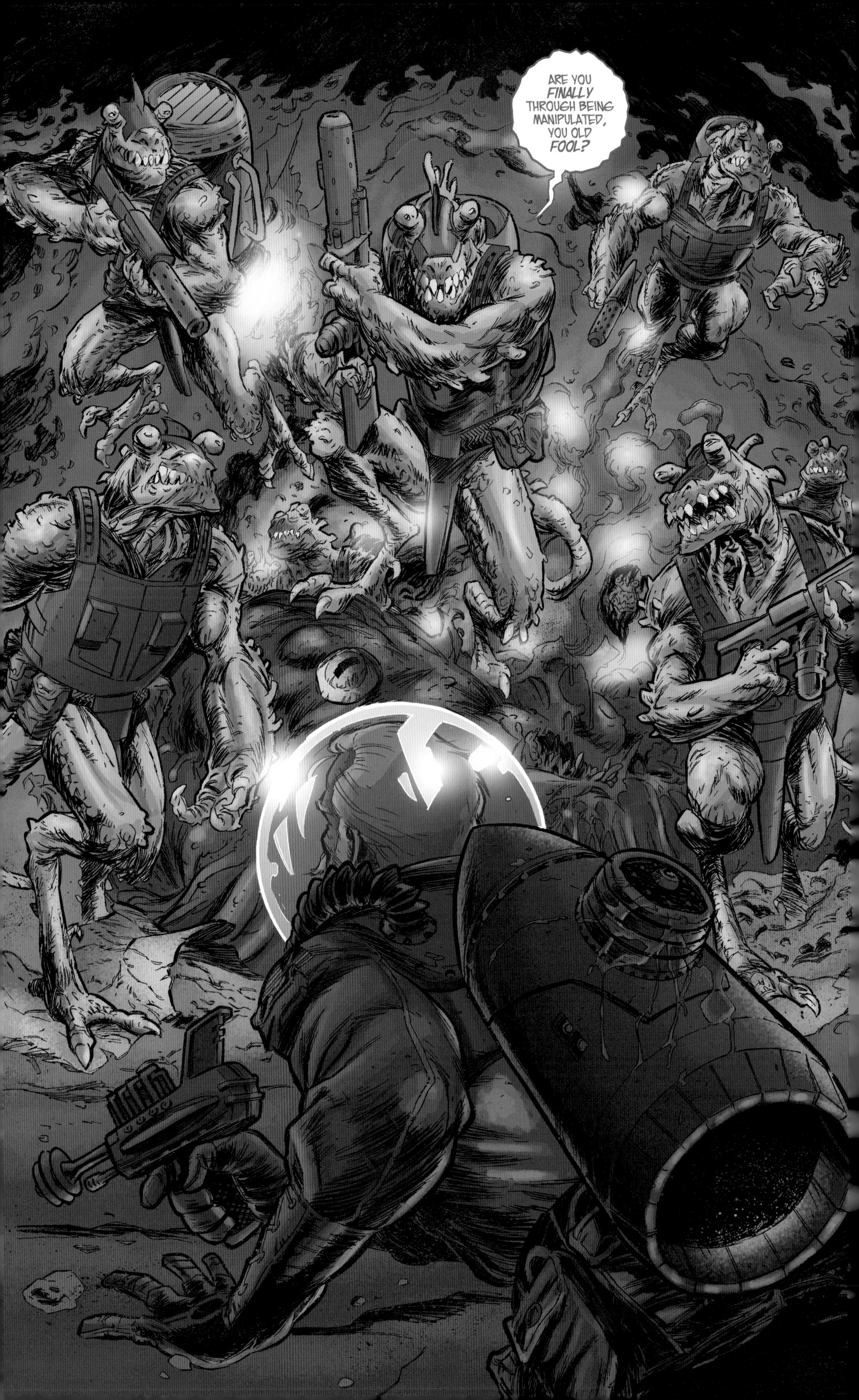
ARE YOU FINALLY THROUGH BEING MANIPULATED, YOU OLD FOOL?

CHAPTER 3

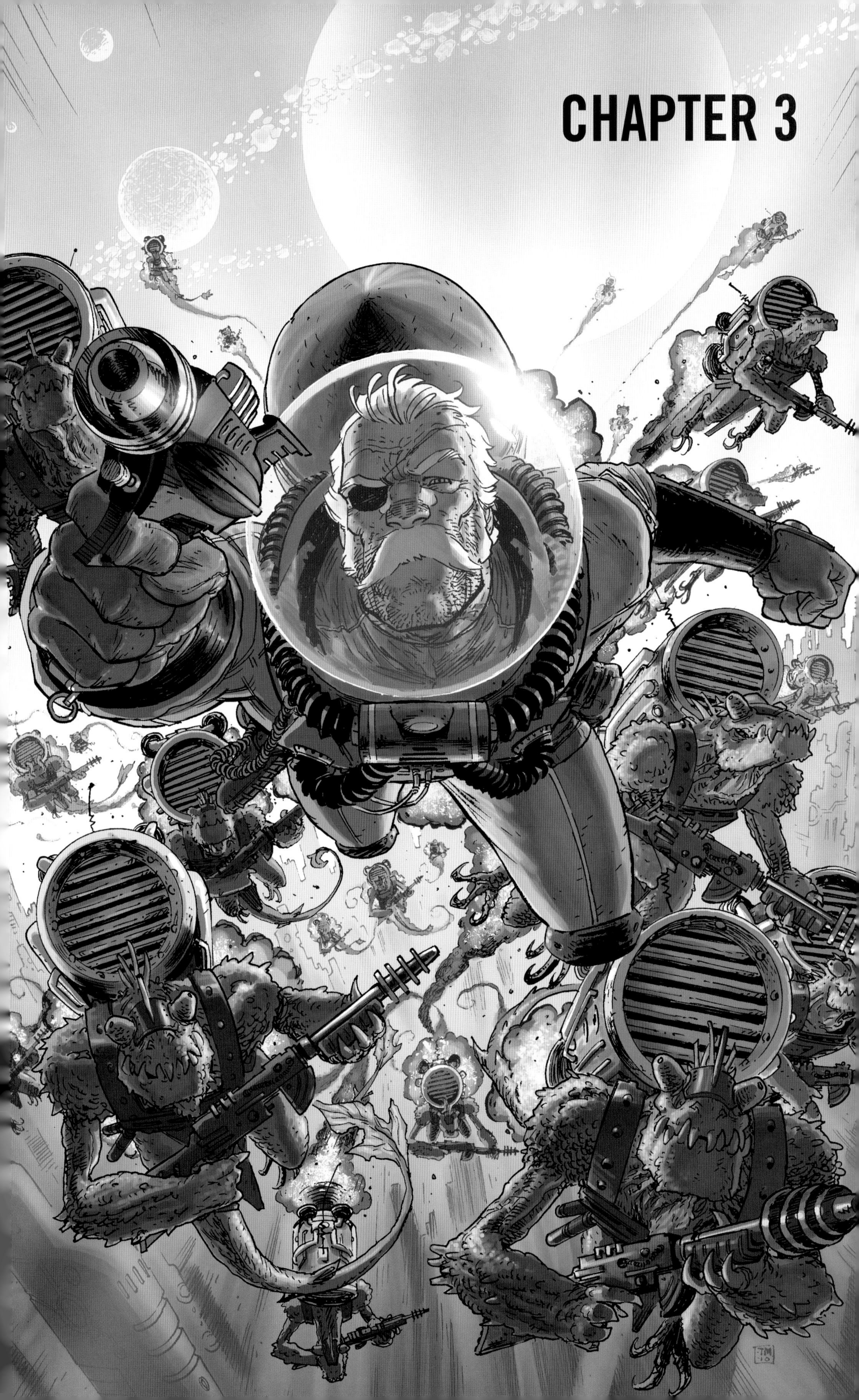

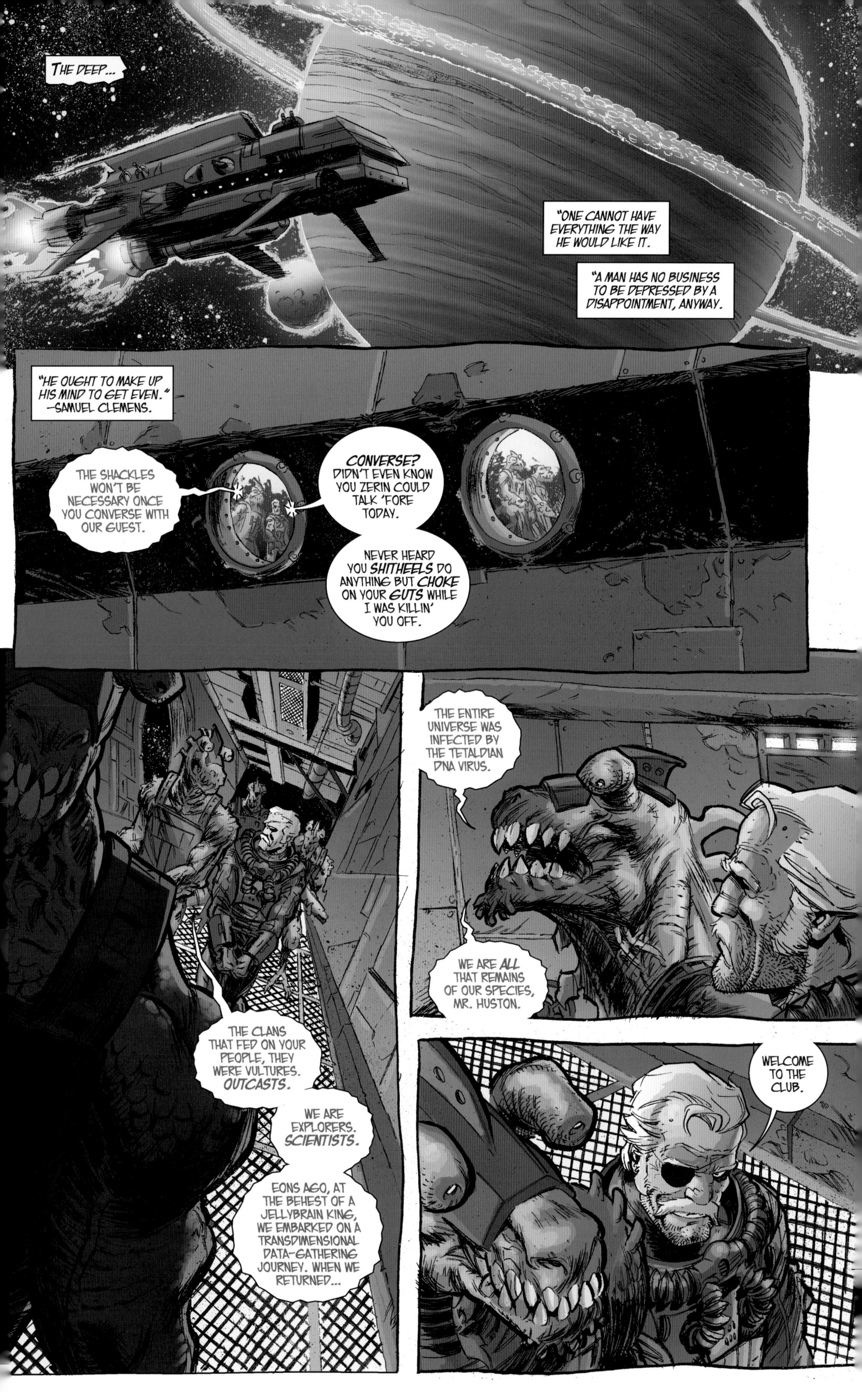
THE DEEP...
"ONE CANNOT HAVE EVERYTHING THE WAY HE WOULD LIKE IT.
"A MAN HAS NO BUSINESS TO BE DEPRESSED BY A DISAPPOINTMENT, ANYWAY.
"HE OUGHT TO MAKE UP HIS MIND TO GET EVEN." —SAMUEL CLEMENS.
THE SHACKLES WON'T BE NECESSARY ONCE YOU CONVERSE WITH OUR GUEST.
CONVERSE? DIDN'T EVEN KNOW YOU ZERIN COULD TALK 'FORE TODAY.
NEVER HEARD YOU SHITHEELS DO ANYTHING BUT CHOKE ON YOUR GUTS WHILE I WAS KILLIN' YOU OFF.
THE CLANS THAT FED ON YOUR PEOPLE, THEY WERE VULTURES. OUTCASTS.
WE ARE EXPLORERS. SCIENTISTS.
EONS AGO, AT THE BEHEST OF A JELLYBRAIN KING, WE EMBARKED ON A TRANSDIMENSIONAL DATA-GATHERING JOURNEY. WHEN WE RETURNED...
THE ENTIRE UNIVERSE WAS INFECTED BY THE TETALDIAN DNA VIRUS.
WE ARE ALL THAT REMAINS OF OUR SPECIES, MR. HUSTON.
WELCOME TO THE CLUB.

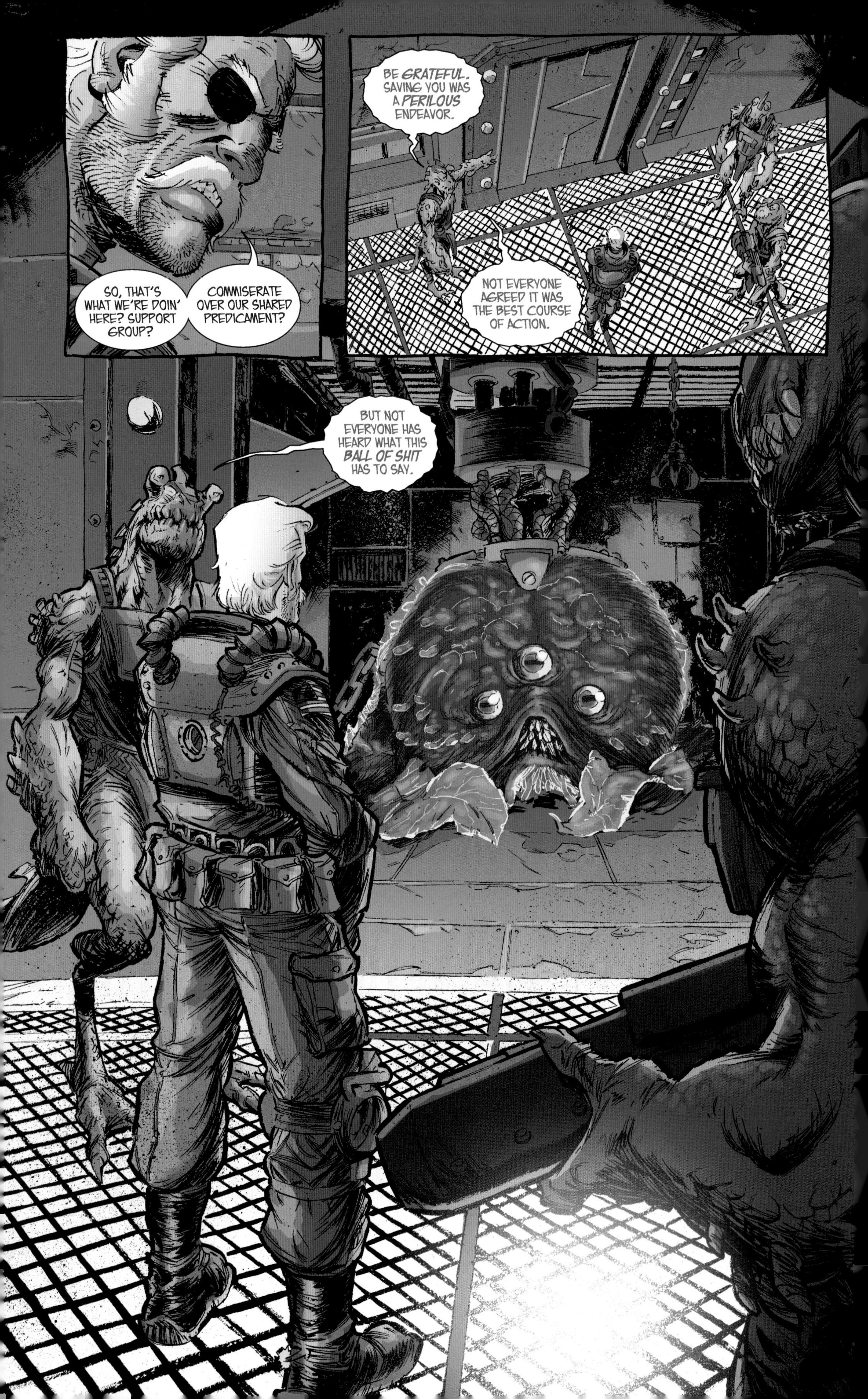
SO, THAT'S WHAT WE'RE DOIN' HERE? SUPPORT GROUP?
COMMISERATE OVER OUR SHARED PREDICAMENT?
BE GRATEFUL. SAVING YOU WAS A PERILOUS ENDEAVOR.
NOT EVERYONE AGREED IT WAS THE BEST COURSE OF ACTION.
BUT NOT EVERYONE HAS HEARD WHAT THIS BALL OF SHIT HAS TO SAY.

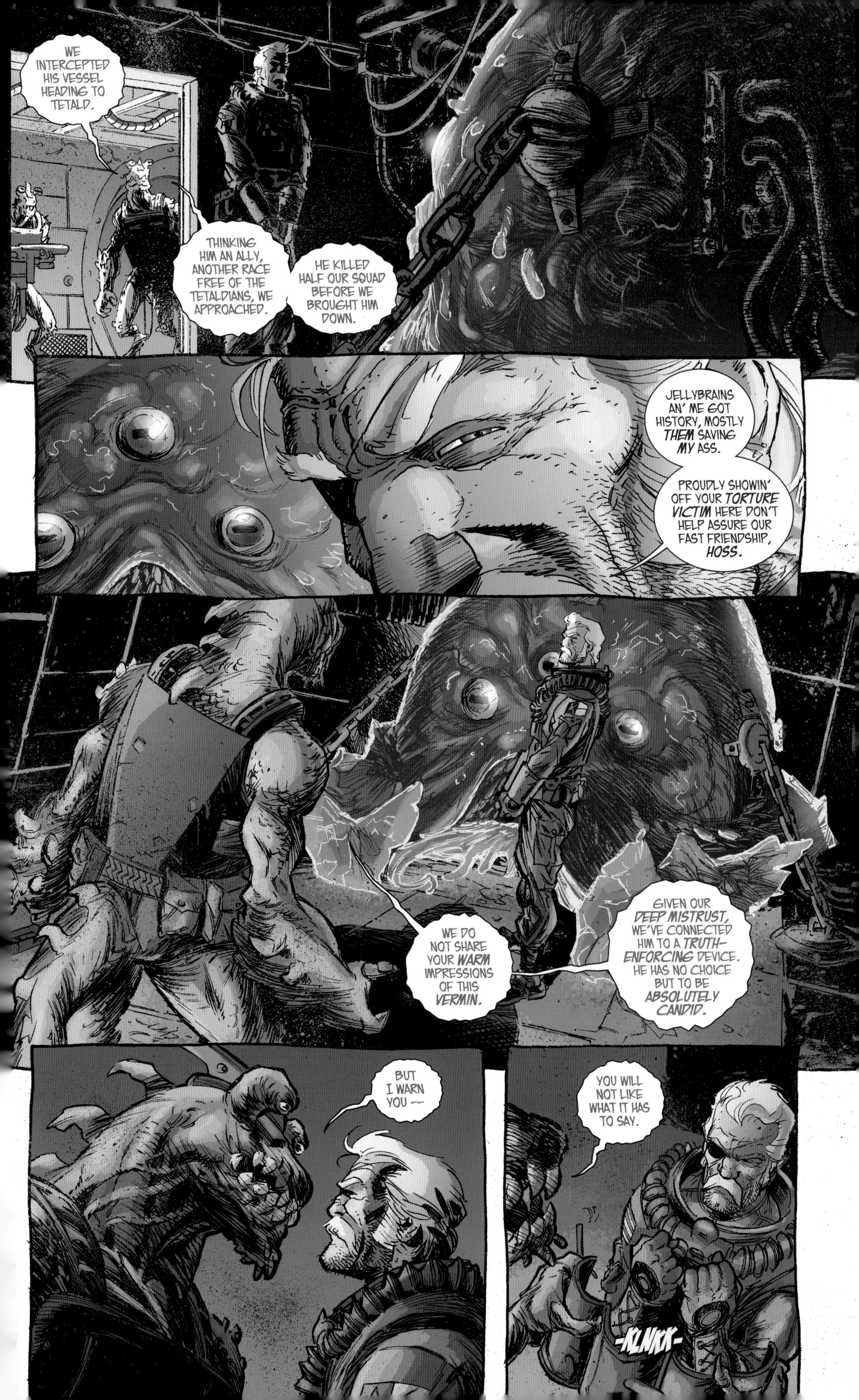
WE INTERCEPTED HIS VESSEL HEADING TO TETALD.
THINKING HIM AN ALLY, ANOTHER RACE FREE OF THE TETALDIANS, WE APPROACHED.
HE KILLED HALF OUR SQUAD BEFORE WE BROUGHT HIM DOWN.
JELLYBRAINS AN' ME GOT HISTORY, MOSTLY THEM SAVING MY ASS.
PROUDLY SHOWIN' OFF YOUR TORTURE VICTIM HERE DON'T HELP ASSURE OUR FAST FRIENDSHIP, HOSS.
WE DO NOT SHARE YOUR WARM IMPRESSIONS OF THIS VERMIN.
GIVEN OUR DEEP MISTRUST, WE'VE CONNECTED HIM TO A TRUTH-ENFORCING DEVICE. HE HAS NO CHOICE BUT TO BE ABSOLUTELY CANDID.
BUT I WARN YOU --
YOU WILL NOT LIKE WHAT IT HAS TO SAY.
-KLNKK-

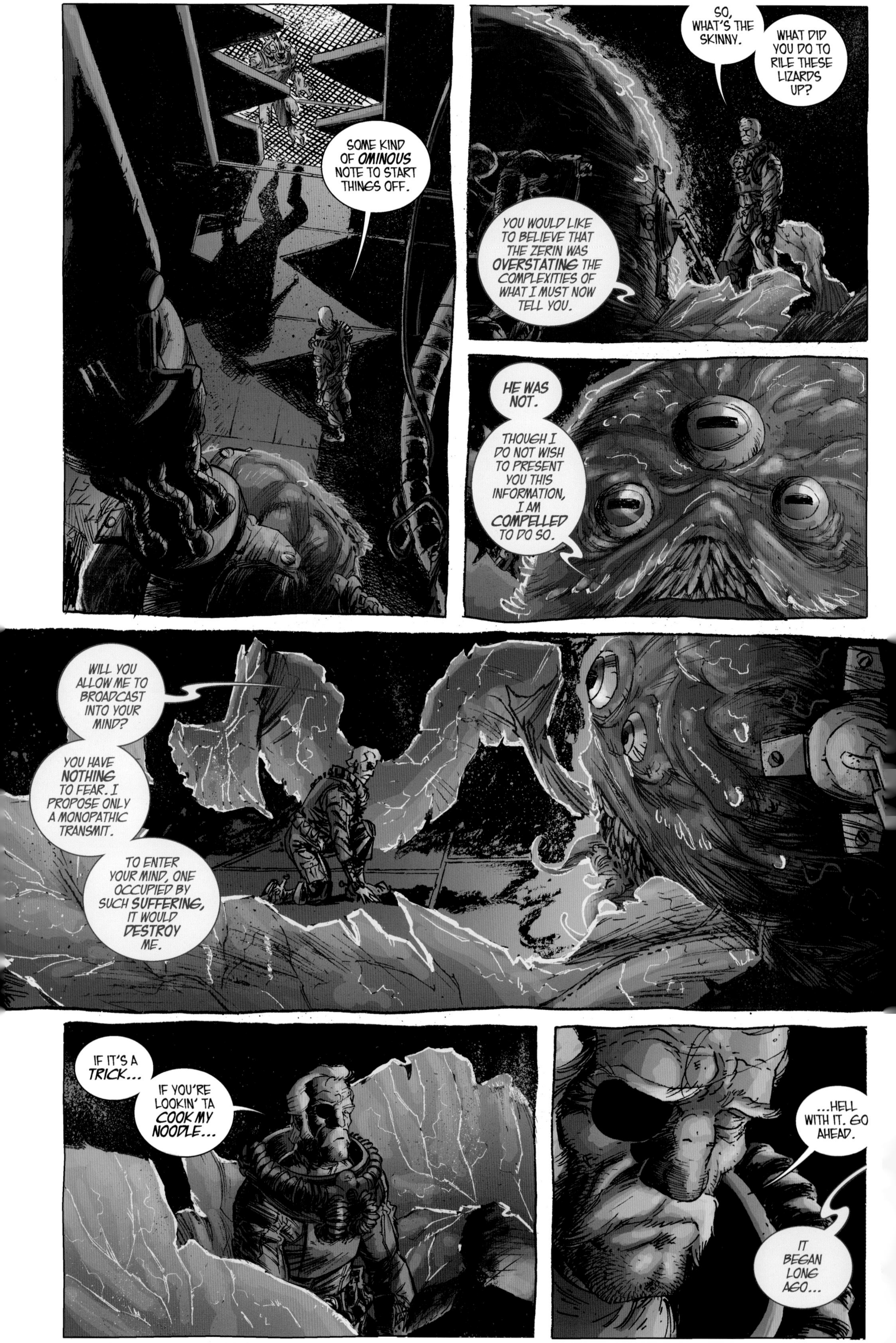

SOME KIND OF OMINOUS NOTE TO START THINGS OFF.
SO, WHAT'S THE SKINNY.
WHAT DID YOU DO TO RILE THESE LIZARDS UP?
YOU WOULD LIKE TO BELIEVE THAT THE ZERIN WAS OVERSTATING THE COMPLEXITIES OF WHAT I MUST NOW TELL YOU.
HE WAS NOT.
THOUGH I DO NOT WISH TO PRESENT YOU THIS INFORMATION, I AM COMPELLED TO DO SO.
WILL YOU ALLOW ME TO BROADCAST INTO YOUR MIND?
YOU HAVE NOTHING TO FEAR. I PROPOSE ONLY A MONOPATHIC TRANSMIT.
TO ENTER YOUR MIND, ONE OCCUPIED BY SUCH SUFFERING, IT WOULD DESTROY ME.
IF IT'S A TRICK...
IF YOU'RE LOOKIN' TA COOK MY NOODLE...
...HELL WITH IT. GO AHEAD.
IT BEGAN LONG AGO...

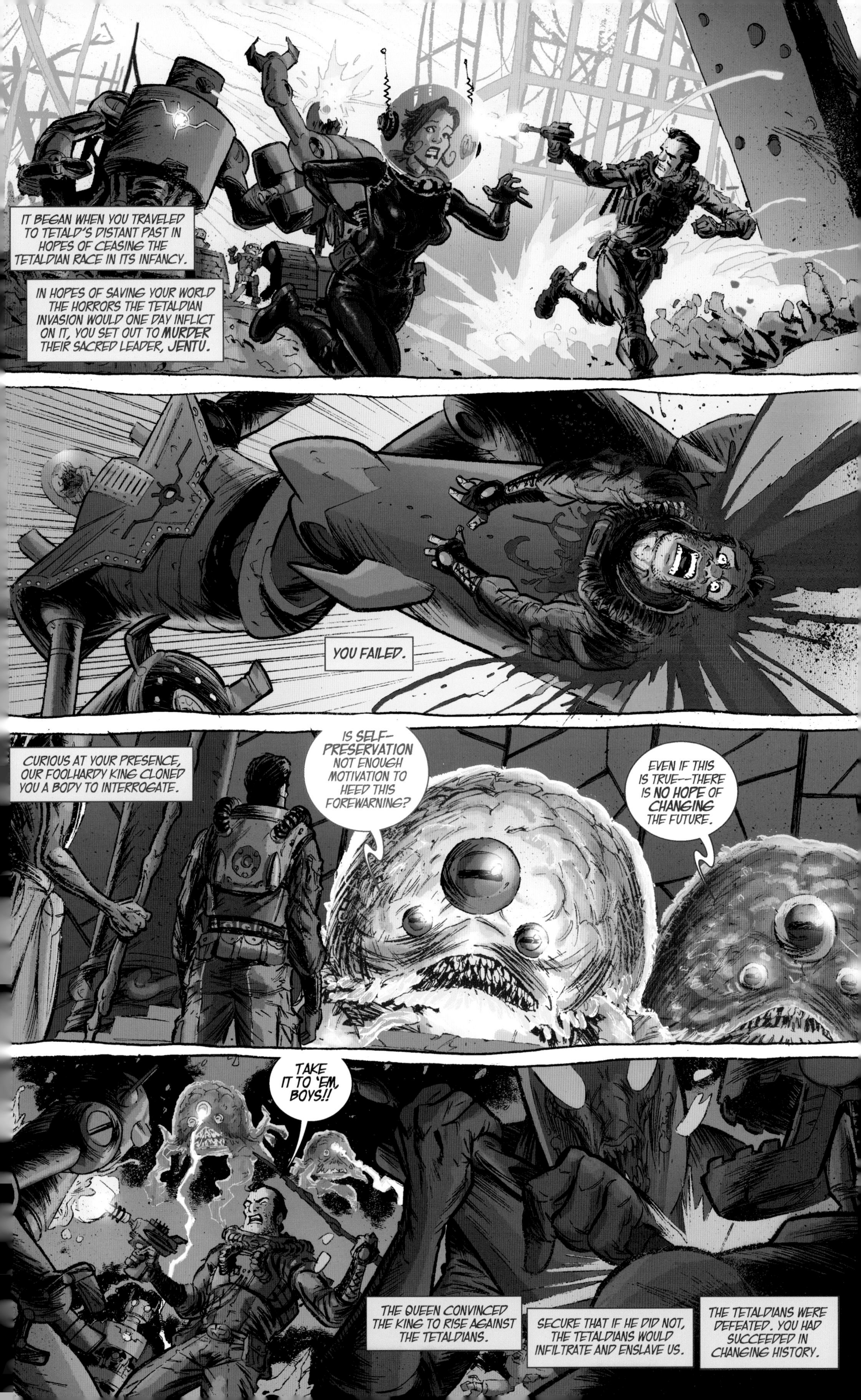
IT BEGAN WHEN YOU TRAVELED TO TETALD'S DISTANT PAST IN HOPES OF CEASING THE TETALDIAN RACE IN ITS INFANCY.
IN HOPES OF SAVING YOUR WORLD THE HORRORS THE TETALDIAN INVASION WOULD ONE DAY INFLICT ON IT, YOU SET OUT TO MURDER THEIR SACRED LEADER, JENTU.
YOU FAILED.
CURIOUS AT YOUR PRESENCE, OUR FOOLHARDY KING CLONED YOU A BODY TO INTERROGATE.
IS SELF-PRESERVATION NOT ENOUGH MOTIVATION TO HEED THIS FOREWARNING?
EVEN IF THIS IS TRUE--THERE IS NO HOPE OF CHANGING THE FUTURE.
TAKE IT TO 'EM, BOYS!!
THE QUEEN CONVINCED THE KING TO RISE AGAINST THE TETALDIANS.
SECURE THAT IF HE DID NOT, THE TETALDIANS WOULD INFILTRATE AND ENSLAVE US.
THE TETALDIANS WERE DEFEATED. YOU HAD SUCCEEDED IN CHANGING HISTORY.

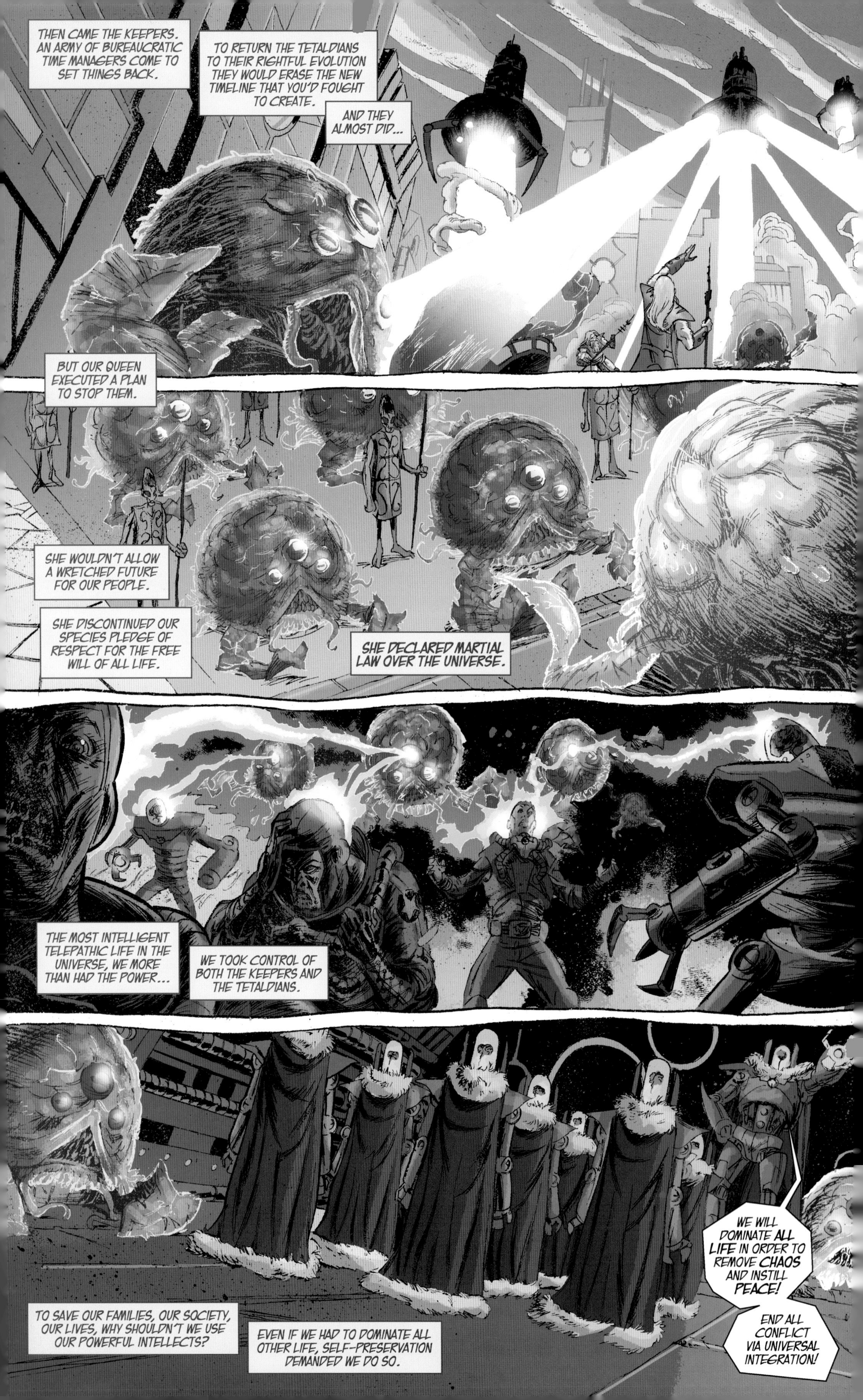
THEN CAME THE KEEPERS. AN ARMY OF BUREAUCRATIC TIME MANAGERS COME TO SET THINGS BACK.
TO RETURN THE TETALDIANS TO THEIR RIGHTFUL EVOLUTION THEY WOULD ERASE THE NEW TIMELINE THAT YOU'D FOUGHT TO CREATE.
AND THEY ALMOST DID...
BUT OUR QUEEN EXECUTED A PLAN TO STOP THEM.
SHE WOULDN'T ALLOW A WRETCHED FUTURE FOR OUR PEOPLE.
SHE DISCONTINUED OUR SPECIES PLEDGE OF RESPECT FOR THE FREE WILL OF ALL LIFE.
SHE DECLARED MARTIAL LAW OVER THE UNIVERSE.
THE MOST INTELLIGENT TELEPATHIC LIFE IN THE UNIVERSE, WE MORE THAN HAD THE POWER...
WE TOOK CONTROL OF BOTH THE KEEPERS AND THE TETALDIANS.
TO SAVE OUR FAMILIES, OUR SOCIETY, OUR LIVES, WHY SHOULDN'T WE USE OUR POWERFUL INTELLECTS?
EVEN IF WE HAD TO DOMINATE ALL OTHER LIFE, SELF-PRESERVATION DEMANDED WE DO SO.
WE WILL DOMINATE ALL LIFE IN ORDER TO REMOVE CHAOS AND INSTILL PEACE!
END ALL CONFLICT VIA UNIVERSAL INTEGRATION!

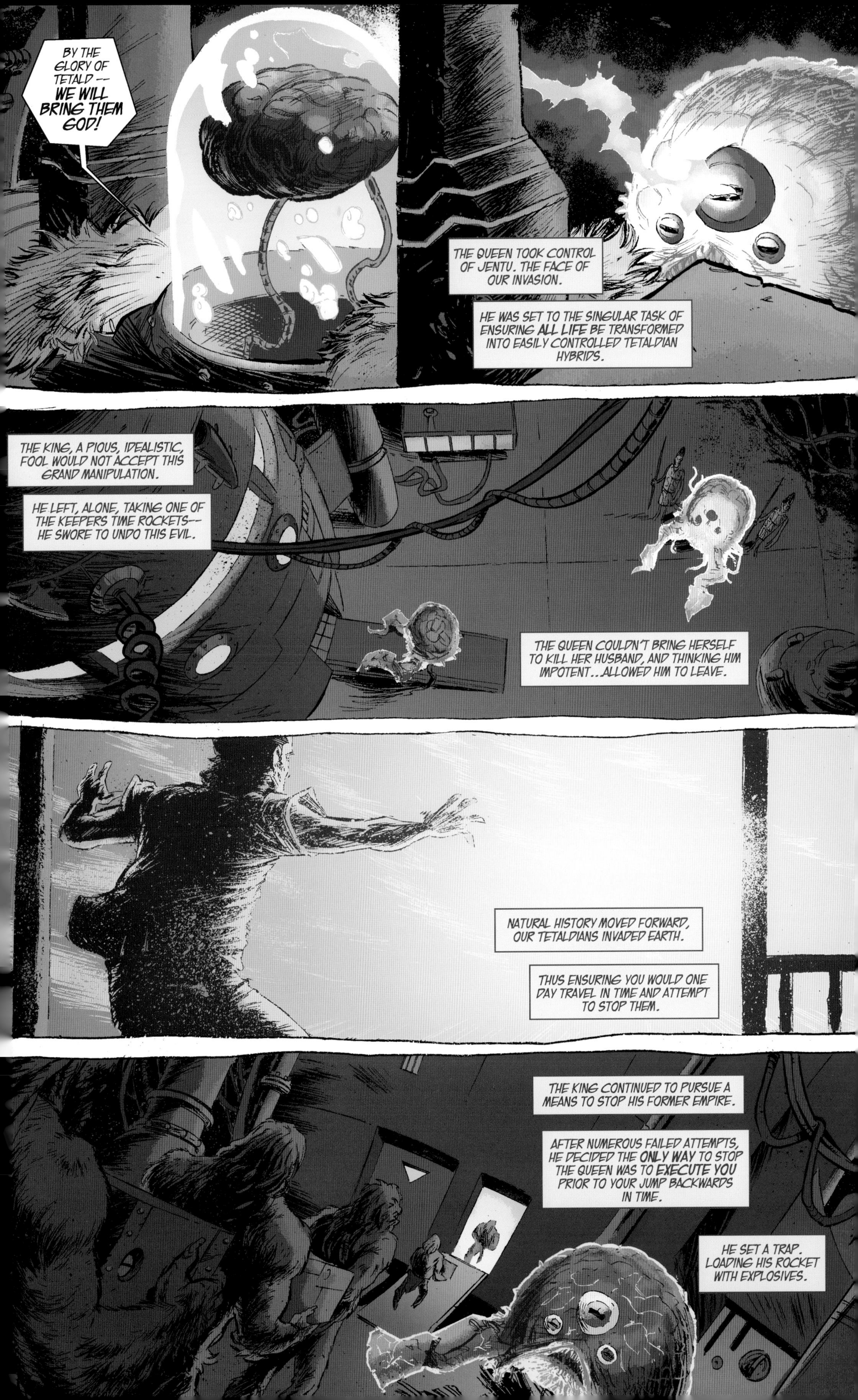

BY THE GLORY OF TETALD -- WE WILL BRING THEM GOD!
THE QUEEN TOOK CONTROL OF JENTU. THE FACE OF OUR INVASION.
HE WAS SET TO THE SINGULAR TASK OF ENSURING ALL LIFE BE TRANSFORMED INTO EASILY CONTROLLED TETALDIAN HYBRIDS.
THE KING, A PIOUS, IDEALISTIC, FOOL WOULD NOT ACCEPT THIS GRAND MANIPULATION.
HE LEFT, ALONE, TAKING ONE OF THE KEEPERS TIME ROCKETS-- HE SWORE TO UNDO THIS EVIL.
THE QUEEN COULDN'T BRING HERSELF TO KILL HER HUSBAND, AND THINKING HIM IMPOTENT...ALLOWED HIM TO LEAVE.
NATURAL HISTORY MOVED FORWARD, OUR TETALDIANS INVADED EARTH.
THUS ENSURING YOU WOULD ONE DAY TRAVEL IN TIME AND ATTEMPT TO STOP THEM.
THE KING CONTINUED TO PURSUE A MEANS TO STOP HIS FORMER EMPIRE.
AFTER NUMEROUS FAILED ATTEMPTS, HE DECIDED THE ONLY WAY TO STOP THE QUEEN WAS TO EXECUTE YOU PRIOR TO YOUR JUMP BACKWARDS IN TIME.
HE SET A TRAP. LOADING HIS ROCKET WITH EXPLOSIVES.

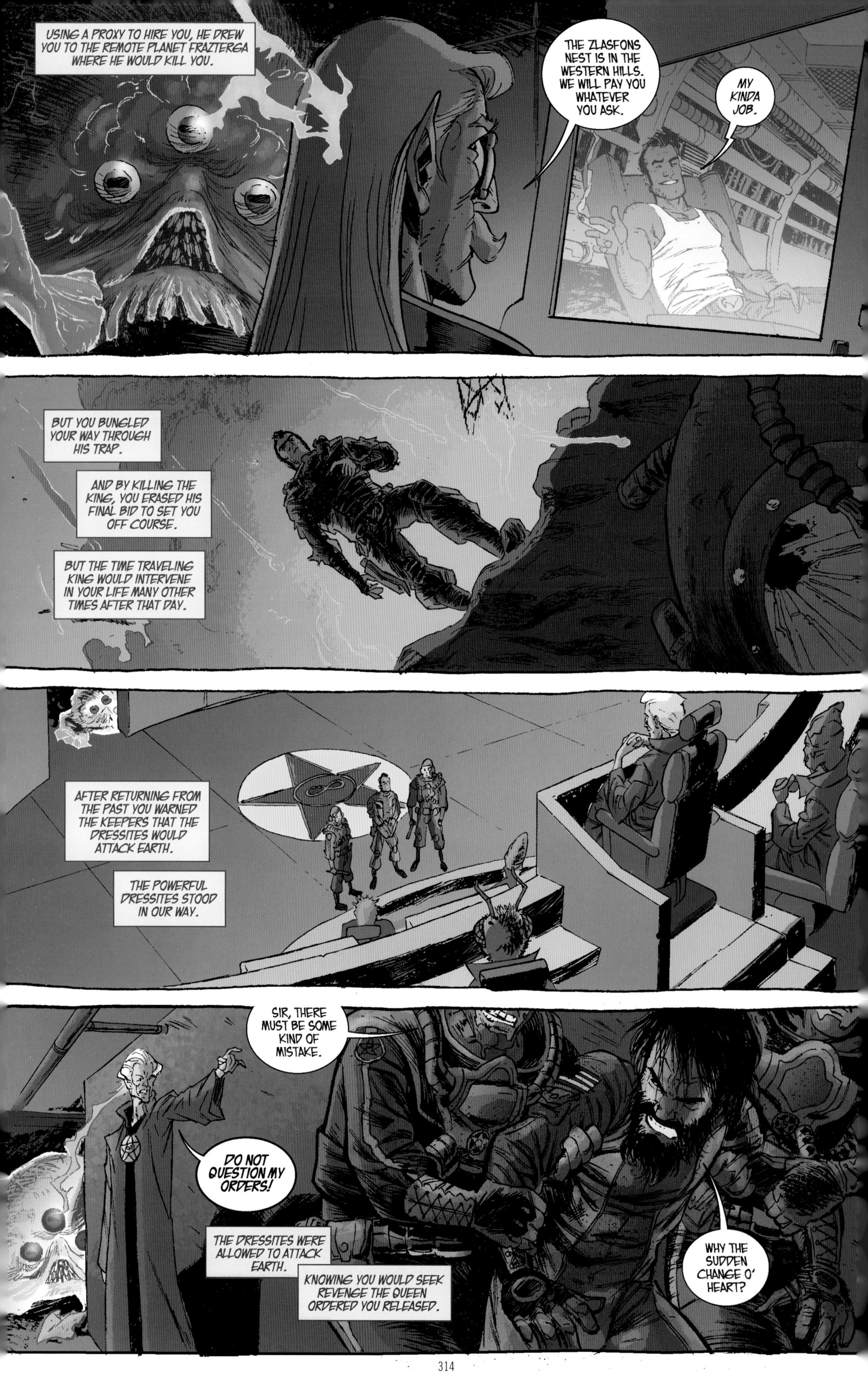

USING A PROXY TO HIRE YOU, HE DREW YOU TO THE REMOTE PLANET FRAZTERGA WHERE HE WOULD KILL YOU.
THE ZLASFONS NEST IS IN THE WESTERN HILLS. WE WILL PAY YOU WHATEVER YOU ASK.
MY KINDA JOB.
BUT YOU BUNGLED YOUR WAY THROUGH HIS TRAP.
AND BY KILLING THE KING, YOU ERASED HIS FINAL BID TO SET YOU OFF COURSE.
BUT THE TIME TRAVELING KING WOULD INTERVENE IN YOUR LIFE MANY OTHER TIMES AFTER THAT DAY.
AFTER RETURNING FROM THE PAST YOU WARNED THE KEEPERS THAT THE DRESSITES WOULD ATTACK EARTH.
THE POWERFUL DRESSITES STOOD IN OUR WAY.
SIR, THERE MUST BE SOME KIND OF MISTAKE.
DO NOT QUESTION MY ORDERS!
THE DRESSITES WERE ALLOWED TO ATTACK EARTH.
KNOWING YOU WOULD SEEK REVENGE THE QUEEN ORDERED YOU RELEASED.
WHY THE SUDDEN CHANGE O' HEART?

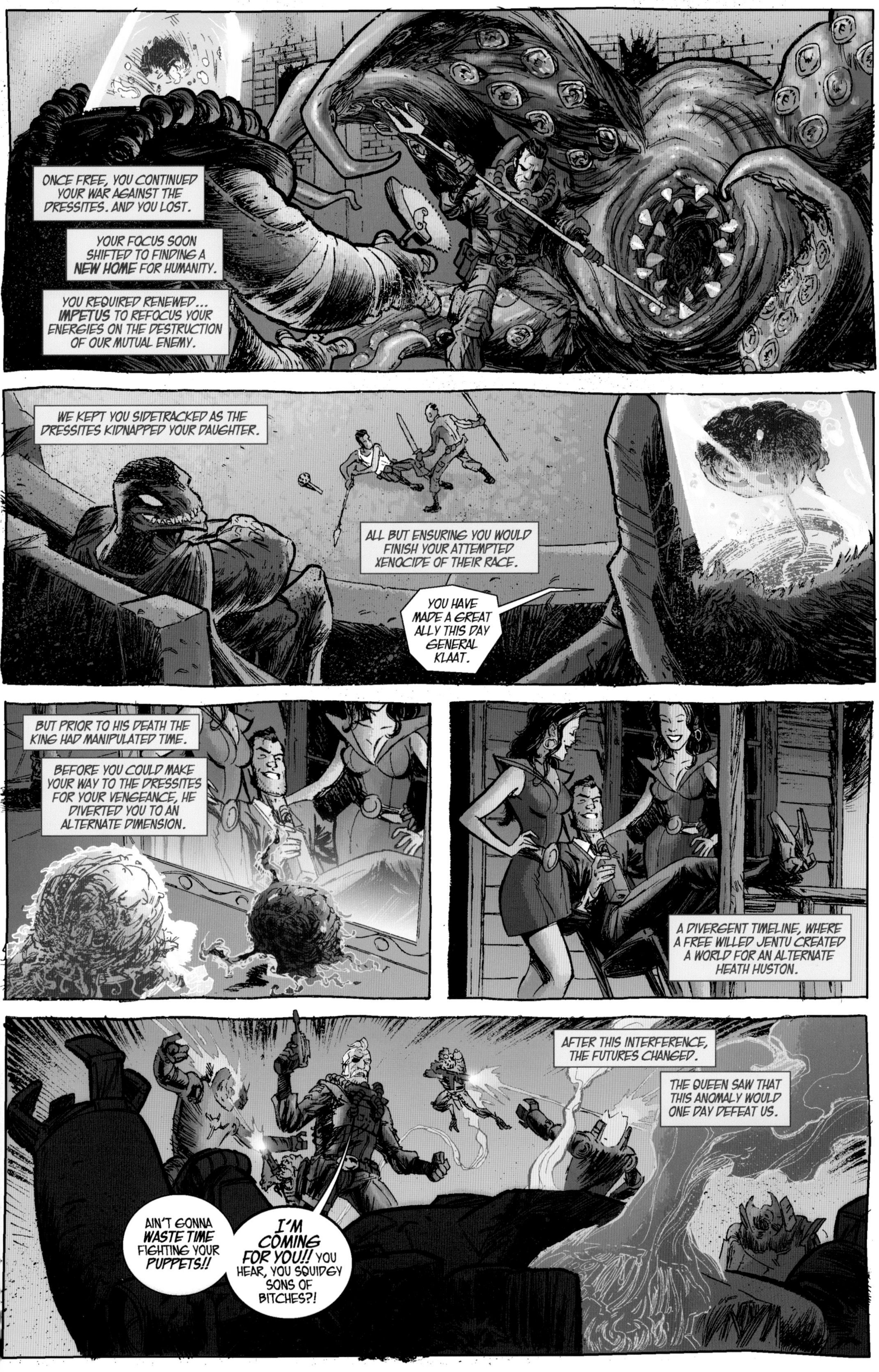
ONCE FREE, YOU CONTINUED YOUR WAR AGAINST THE DRESSITES. AND YOU LOST.
YOUR FOCUS SOON SHIFTED TO FINDING A NEW HOME FOR HUMANITY.
YOU REQUIRED RENEWED... IMPETUS TO REFOCUS YOUR ENERGIES ON THE DESTRUCTION OF OUR MUTUAL ENEMY.
WE KEPT YOU SIDETRACKED AS THE DRESSITES KIDNAPPED YOUR DAUGHTER.
ALL BUT ENSURING YOU WOULD FINISH YOUR ATTEMPTED XENOCIDE OF THEIR RACE.
YOU HAVE MADE A GREAT ALLY THIS DAY GENERAL KLAAT.
BUT PRIOR TO HIS DEATH THE KING HAD MANIPULATED TIME.
BEFORE YOU COULD MAKE YOUR WAY TO THE DRESSITES FOR YOUR VENGEANCE, HE DIVERTED YOU TO AN ALTERNATE DIMENSION.
A DIVERGENT TIMELINE, WHERE A FREE WILLED JENTU CREATED A WORLD FOR AN ALTERNATE HEATH HUSTON.
AFTER THIS INTERFERENCE, THE FUTURES CHANGED.
THE QUEEN SAW THAT THIS ANOMALY WOULD ONE DAY DEFEAT US.
AIN'T GONNA WASTE TIME FIGHTING YOUR PUPPETS!!
I'M COMING FOR YOU!! YOU HEAR, YOU SQUIDGY SONS OF BITCHES?!

BY THE TIME SHE SAW, IT WAS TOO LATE, THE KING HAD SENT YOU ON YOUR WAY.

YEAH. I REMEMBER.

YOUR ECHO HAS INTERJECTED ITSELF INTO THE *CLOSING* WAR.

YOU, THE ANOMALY, HOLD THE POWER TO STAND AGAINST THIS STREAM.

WHEN ALL BOW TO AN *ILLOGICAL* AND *CHAOTIC* CURRENT ONLY ONE WHO HAS BEEN *MIRRORED* BY THE *DISPLACED* HOLDS THE POWER TO SUCCESSFULLY CONTEST ITS FLOW.

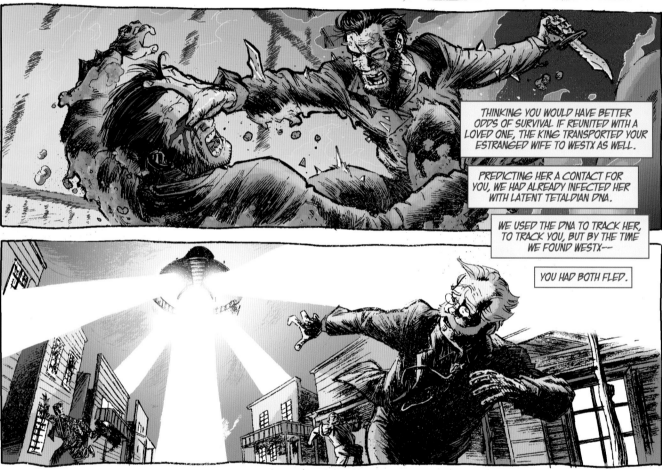

THINKING YOU WOULD HAVE BETTER ODDS OF SURVIVAL IF REUNITED WITH A LOVED ONE, THE KING TRANSPORTED YOUR ESTRANGED WIFE TO WESTX AS WELL.

PREDICTING HER A CONTACT FOR YOU, WE HAD ALREADY INFECTED HER WITH LATENT TETALDIAN DNA.

WE USED THE DNA TO TRACK HER, TO TRACK YOU, BUT BY THE TIME WE FOUND WESTX—

YOU HAD BOTH FLED.

FOR THE GLORY OF TETALD—

I WILL GIVE THEM GOD.

WE IMPLEMENTED THE NEXT STAGE.

THE DNA INFILTRATION OF HUMANITY.

DUE TO YOUR TRANSDIMENSION JOURNEY, YOU WERE PHASED OUT OF STEP WITH NATURAL TIME.

YOU WERE SPARED OUR INFECTION.

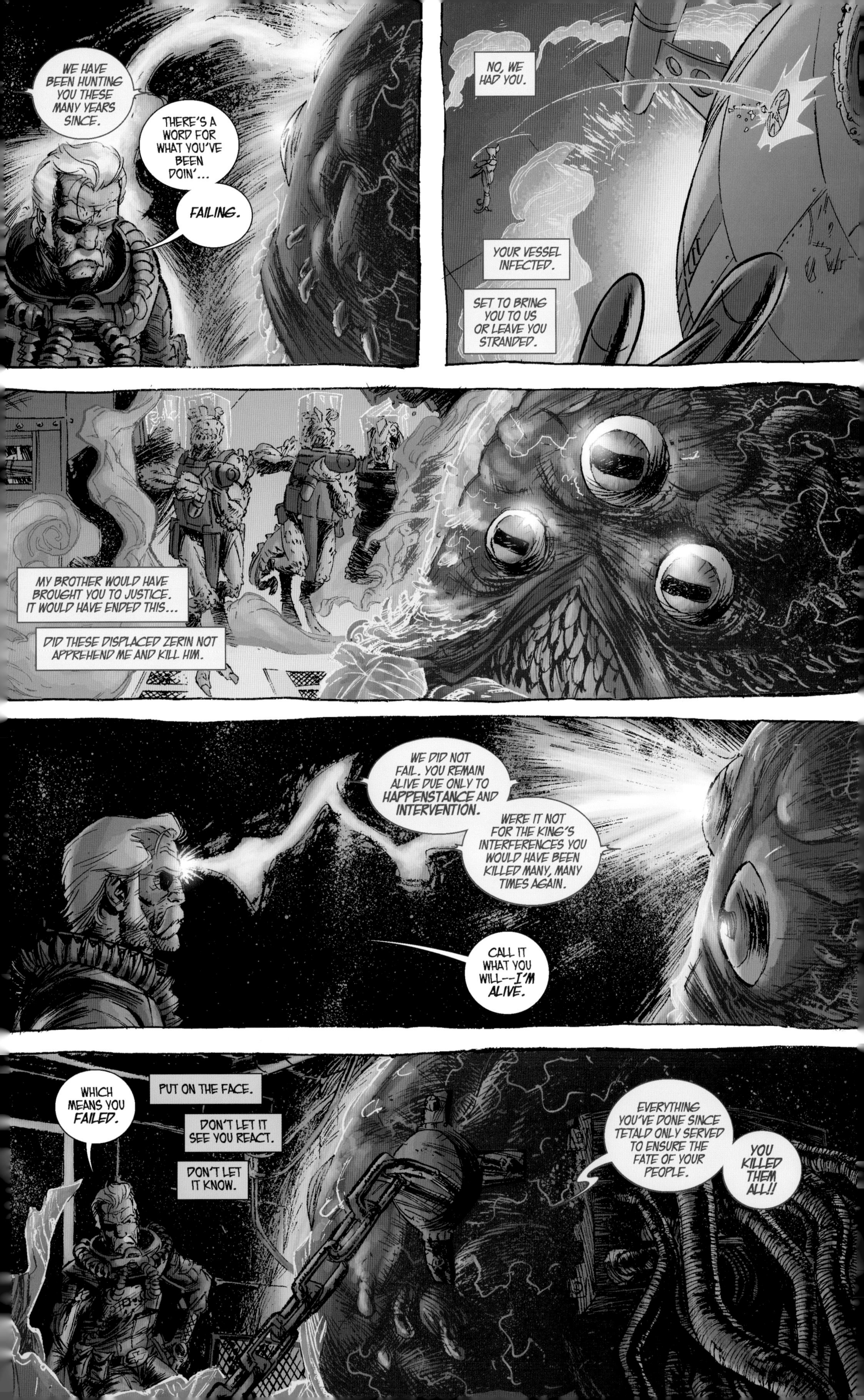
WE HAVE BEEN HUNTING YOU THESE MANY YEARS SINCE.
THERE'S A WORD FOR WHAT YOU'VE BEEN DOIN'...
FAILING.
NO, WE HAD YOU.
YOUR VESSEL INFECTED.
SET TO BRING YOU TO US OR LEAVE YOU STRANDED.
MY BROTHER WOULD HAVE BROUGHT YOU TO JUSTICE. IT WOULD HAVE ENDED THIS...
DID THESE DISPLACED ZERIN NOT APPREHEND ME AND KILL HIM.
WE DID NOT FAIL. YOU REMAIN ALIVE DUE ONLY TO HAPPENSTANCE AND INTERVENTION.
WERE IT NOT FOR THE KING'S INTERFERENCES YOU WOULD HAVE BEEN KILLED MANY, MANY TIMES AGAIN.
CALL IT WHAT YOU WILL--I'M ALIVE.
WHICH MEANS YOU FAILED.
PUT ON THE FACE.
DON'T LET IT SEE YOU REACT.
DON'T LET IT KNOW.
EVERYTHING YOU'VE DONE SINCE TETALD ONLY SERVED TO ENSURE THE FATE OF YOUR PEOPLE.
YOU KILLED THEM ALL!!

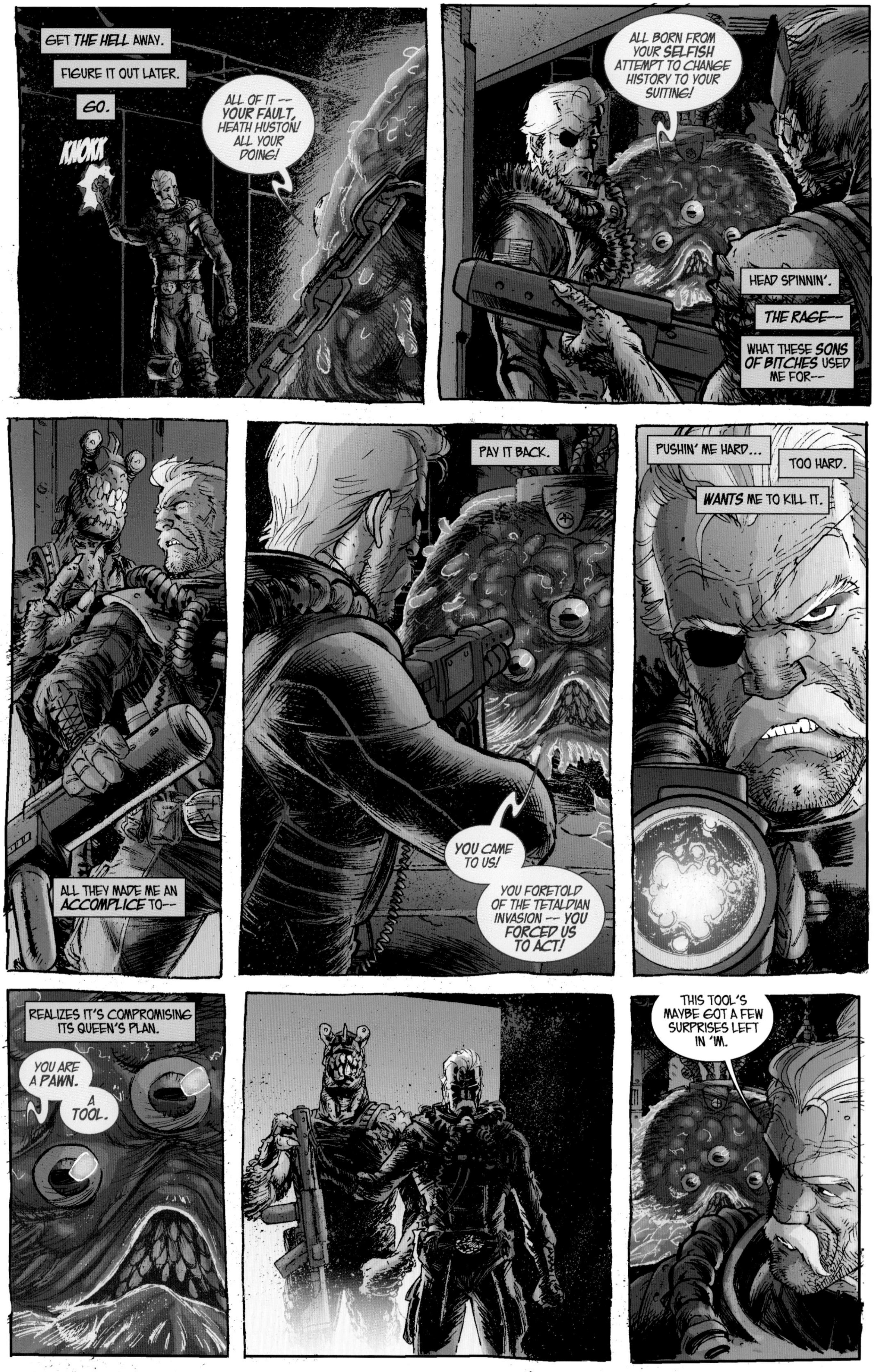
GET THE HELL AWAY.
FIGURE IT OUT LATER.
GO.
KNOKK
ALL OF IT -- YOUR FAULT, HEATH HUSTON! ALL YOUR DOING!
ALL BORN FROM YOUR SELFISH ATTEMPT TO CHANGE HISTORY TO YOUR SUITING!
HEAD SPINNIN'.
THE RAGE--
WHAT THESE SONS OF BITCHES USED ME FOR--
ALL THEY MADE ME AN ACCOMPLICE TO--
PAY IT BACK.
YOU CAME TO US!
YOU FORETOLD OF THE TETALDIAN INVASION -- YOU FORCED US TO ACT!
PUSHIN' ME HARD...
TOO HARD.
WANTS ME TO KILL IT.
REALIZES IT'S COMPROMISING ITS QUEEN'S PLAN.
YOU ARE A PAWN.
A TOOL.
THIS TOOL'S MAYBE GOT A FEW SURPRISES LEFT IN 'IM.

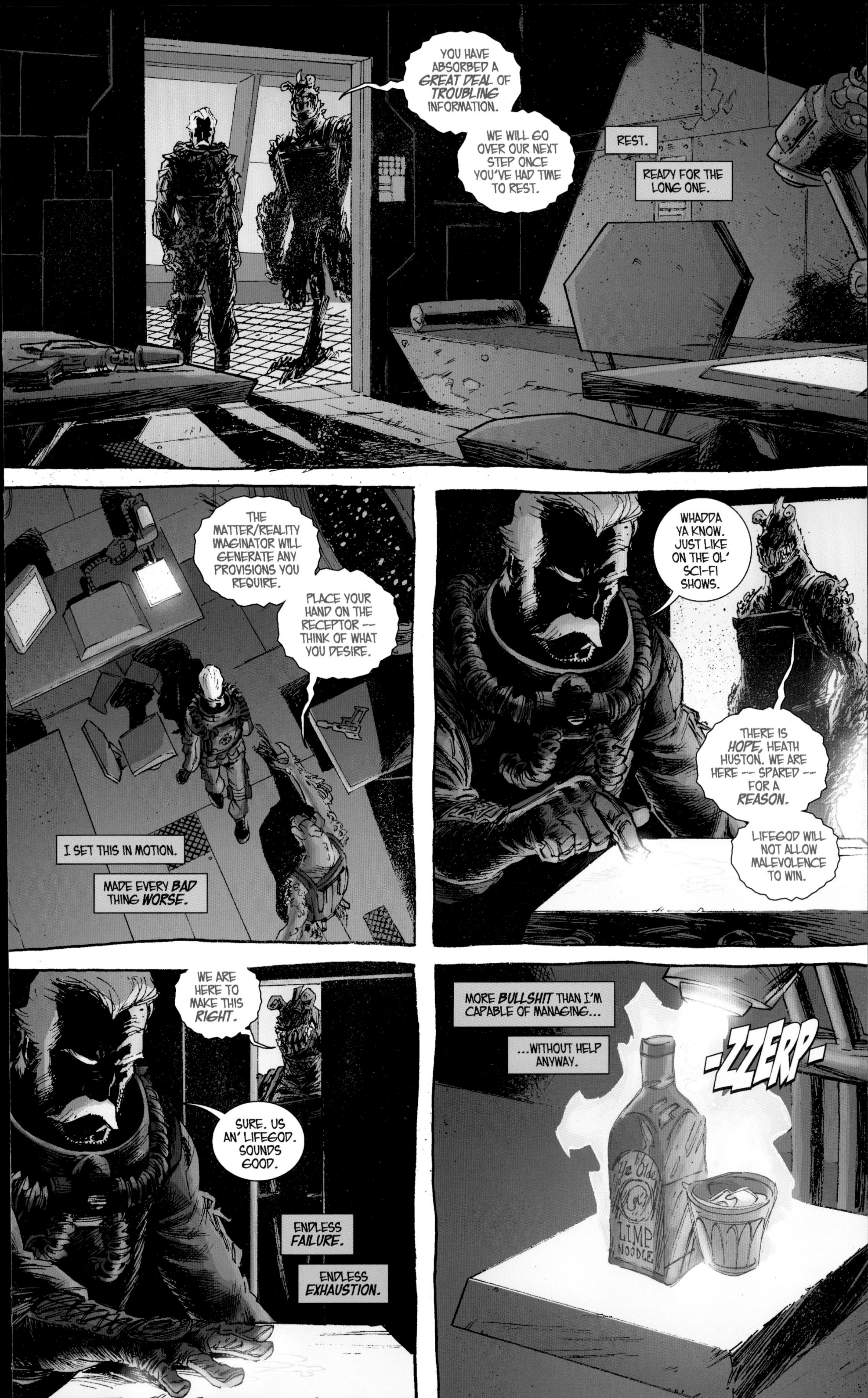
YOU HAVE ABSORBED A GREAT DEAL OF TROUBLING INFORMATION.
WE WILL GO OVER OUR NEXT STEP ONCE YOU'VE HAD TIME TO REST.
REST.
READY FOR THE LONG ONE.
THE MATTER/REALITY IMAGINATOR WILL GENERATE ANY PROVISIONS YOU REQUIRE.
PLACE YOUR HAND ON THE RECEPTOR -- THINK OF WHAT YOU DESIRE.
I SET THIS IN MOTION.
MADE EVERY BAD THING WORSE.
WHADDA YA KNOW. JUST LIKE ON THE OL' SCI-FI SHOWS.
THERE IS HOPE, HEATH HUSTON. WE ARE HERE -- SPARED -- FOR A REASON.
LIFEGOD WILL NOT ALLOW MALEVOLENCE TO WIN.
WE ARE HERE TO MAKE THIS RIGHT.
SURE. US AN' LIFEGOD. SOUNDS GOOD.
ENDLESS FAILURE.
ENDLESS EXHAUSTION.
MORE BULLSHIT THAN I'M CAPABLE OF MANAGING...
...WITHOUT HELP ANYWAY.
-ZZERP-
Ye Olde
LIMP NOODLE

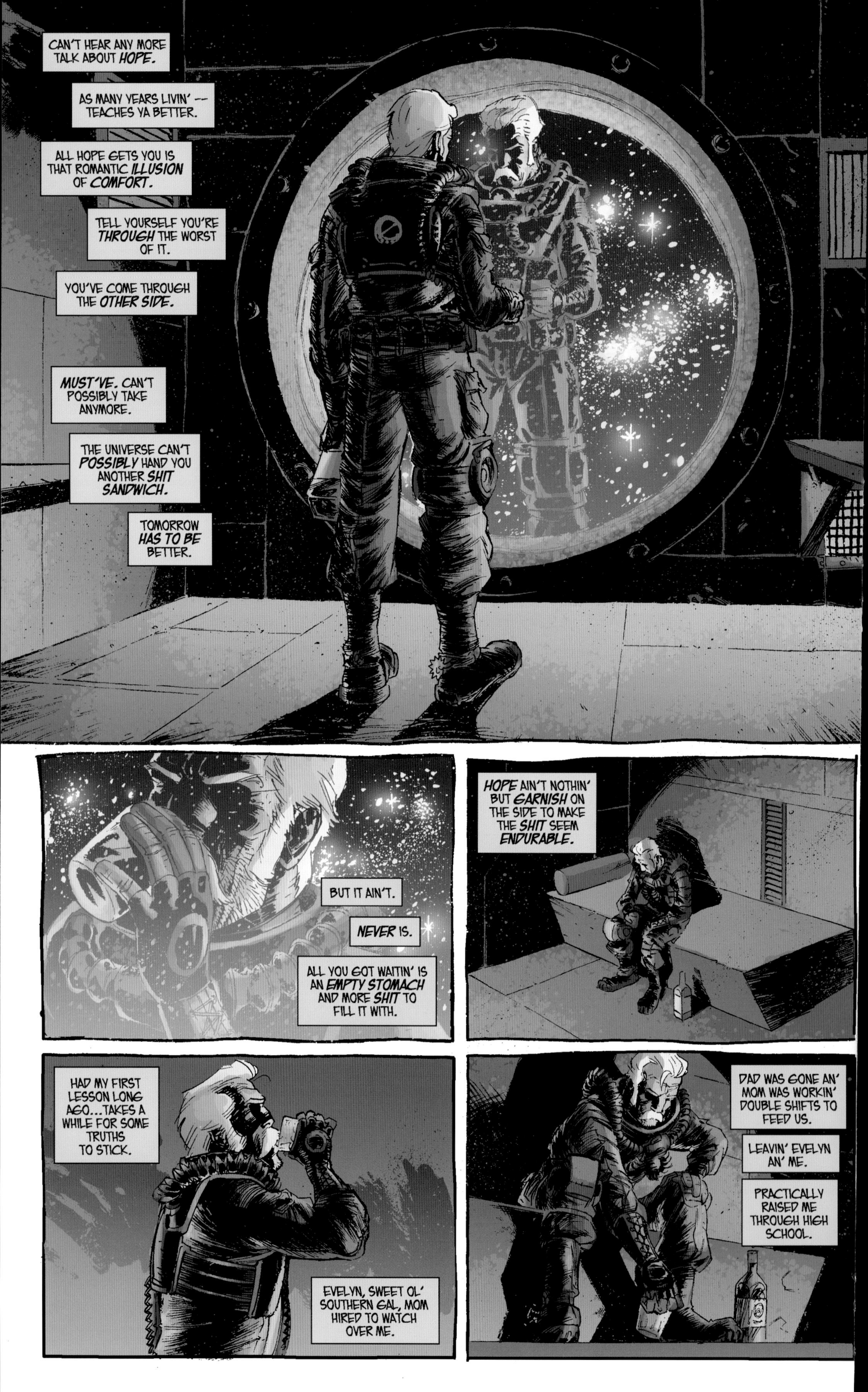
CAN'T HEAR ANY MORE TALK ABOUT HOPE.
AS MANY YEARS LIVIN' -- TEACHES YA BETTER.
ALL HOPE GETS YOU IS THAT ROMANTIC ILLUSION OF COMFORT.
TELL YOURSELF YOU'RE THROUGH THE WORST OF IT.
YOU'VE COME THROUGH THE OTHER SIDE.
MUST'VE. CAN'T POSSIBLY TAKE ANYMORE.
THE UNIVERSE CAN'T POSSIBLY HAND YOU ANOTHER SHIT SANDWICH.
TOMORROW HAS TO BE BETTER.
BUT IT AIN'T.
NEVER IS.
ALL YOU GOT WAITIN' IS AN EMPTY STOMACH AND MORE SHIT TO FILL IT WITH.
HOPE AIN'T NOTHIN' BUT GARNISH ON THE SIDE TO MAKE THE SHIT SEEM ENDURABLE.
HAD MY FIRST LESSON LONG AGO...TAKES A WHILE FOR SOME TRUTHS TO STICK.
EVELYN, SWEET OL' SOUTHERN GAL, MOM HIRED TO WATCH OVER ME.
DAD WAS GONE AN' MOM WAS WORKIN' DOUBLE SHIFTS TO FEED US.
LEAVIN' EVELYN AN' ME.
PRACTICALLY RAISED ME THROUGH HIGH SCHOOL.

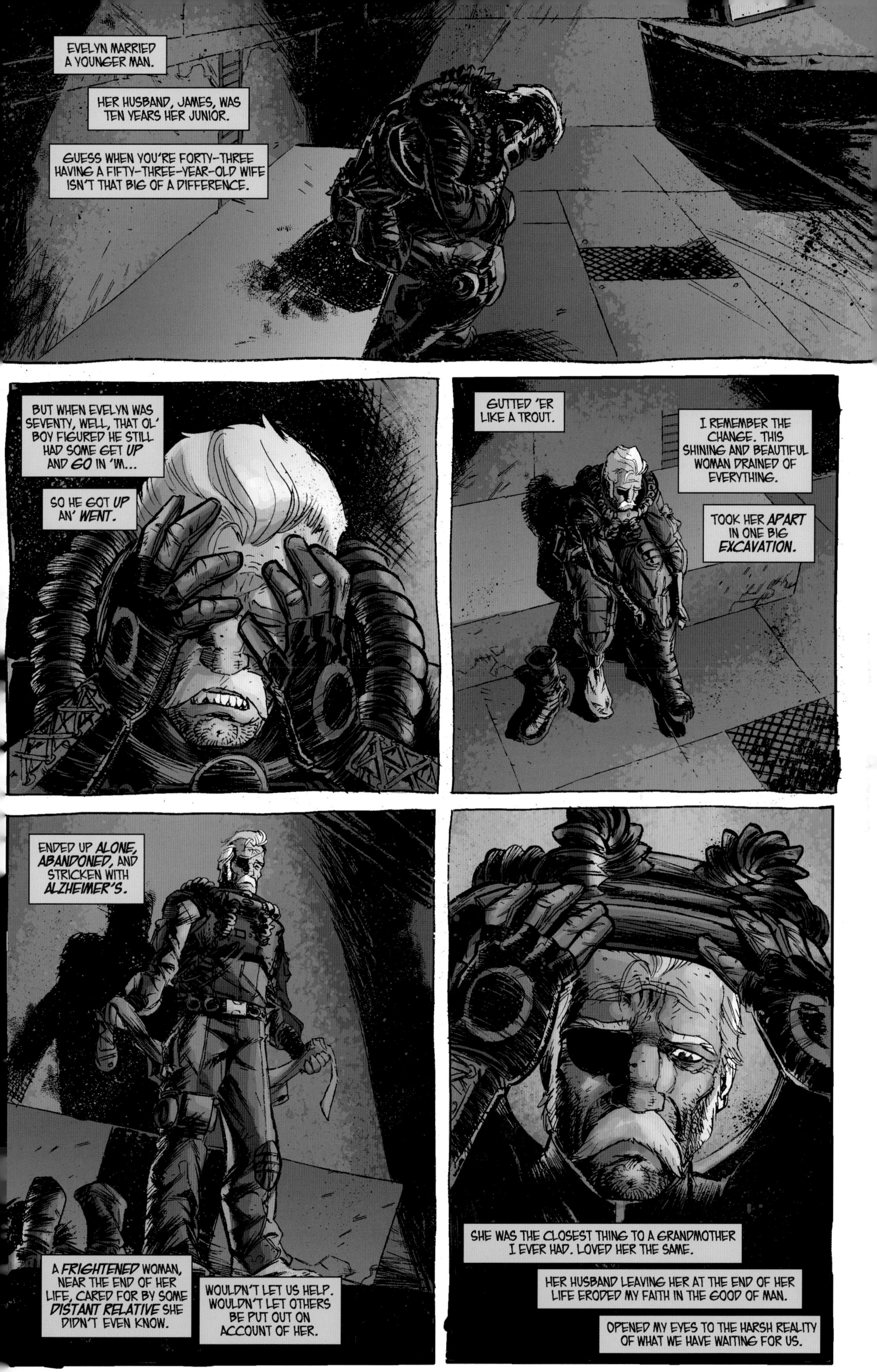
EVELYN MARRIED A YOUNGER MAN.
HER HUSBAND, JAMES, WAS TEN YEARS HER JUNIOR.
GUESS WHEN YOU'RE FORTY-THREE HAVING A FIFTY-THREE-YEAR-OLD WIFE ISN'T THAT BIG OF A DIFFERENCE.
BUT WHEN EVELYN WAS SEVENTY, WELL, THAT OL' BOY FIGURED HE STILL HAD SOME GET UP AND GO IN 'IM...
SO HE GOT UP AN' WENT.
GUTTED 'ER LIKE A TROUT.
I REMEMBER THE CHANGE. THIS SHINING AND BEAUTIFUL WOMAN DRAINED OF EVERYTHING.
TOOK HER APART IN ONE BIG EXCAVATION.
ENDED UP ALONE, ABANDONED, AND STRICKEN WITH ALZHEIMER'S.
A FRIGHTENED WOMAN, NEAR THE END OF HER LIFE, CARED FOR BY SOME DISTANT RELATIVE SHE DIDN'T EVEN KNOW.
WOULDN'T LET US HELP. WOULDN'T LET OTHERS BE PUT OUT ON ACCOUNT OF HER.
SHE WAS THE CLOSEST THING TO A GRANDMOTHER I EVER HAD. LOVED HER THE SAME.
HER HUSBAND LEAVING HER AT THE END OF HER LIFE ERODED MY FAITH IN THE GOOD OF MAN.
OPENED MY EYES TO THE HARSH REALITY OF WHAT WE HAVE WAITING FOR US.

LAST TIME I SAW HER, LAST VISIT BEFORE SHE PASSED, I HAD THE *IMPUDENCE* TO INSIST SHE NOT LOSE HOPE.

NOT TO GIVE UP.

TOLD HER IT'D BE OKAY. *PROMISED.*

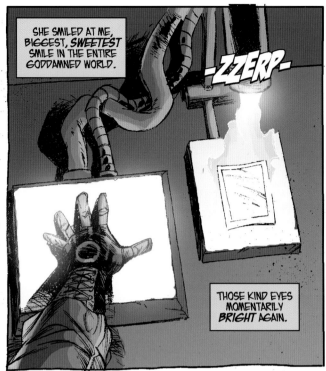

SHE SMILED AT ME, BIGGEST, *SWEETEST* SMILE IN THE ENTIRE GODDAMNED WORLD.

-*ZZERP*-

THOSE KIND EYES MOMENTARILY *BRIGHT* AGAIN.

"*YOU'LL SEE*," SHE SAID.

"YOU'LL SEE."

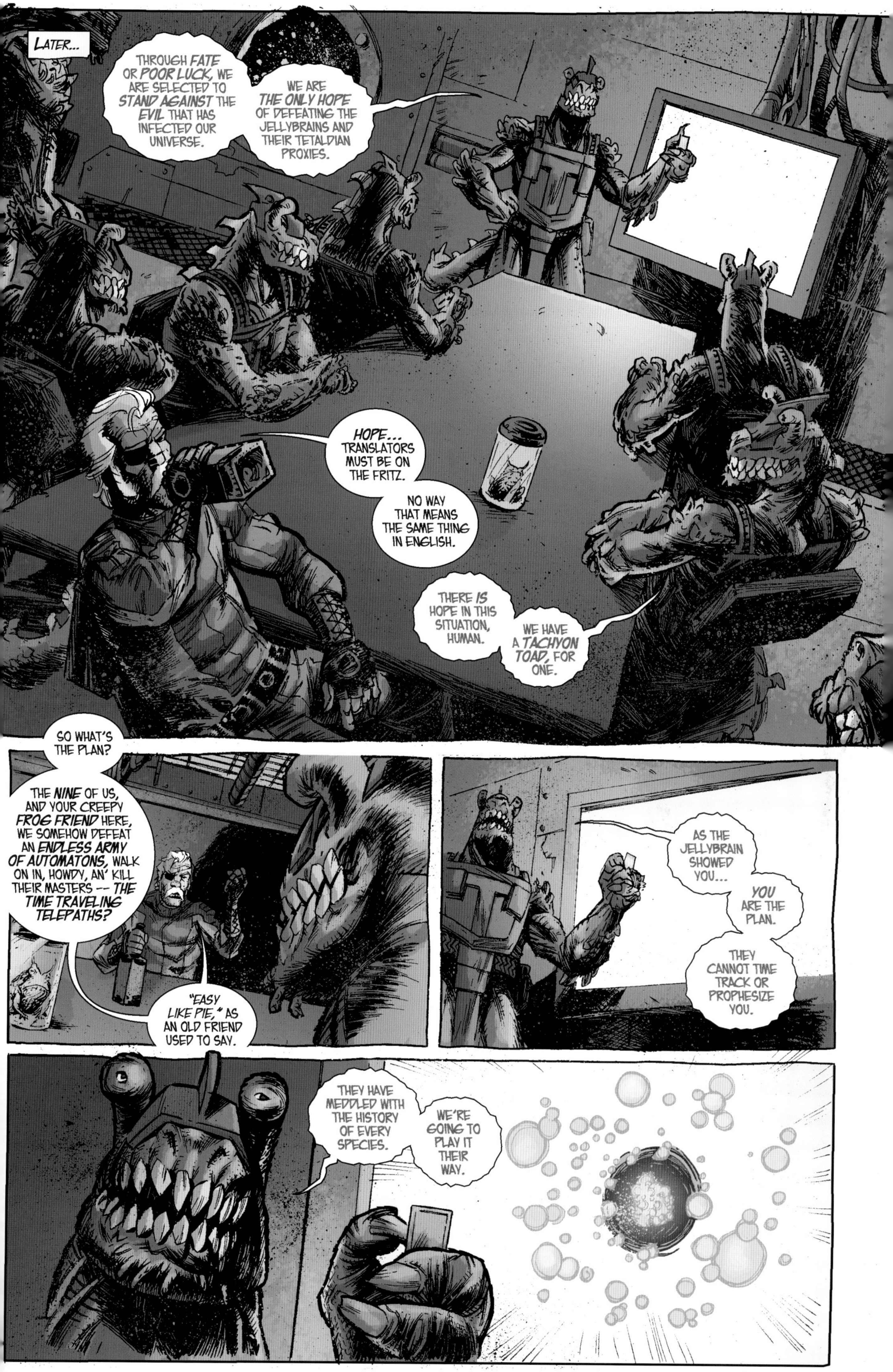

LATER...
THROUGH FATE OR POOR LUCK, WE ARE SELECTED TO STAND AGAINST THE EVIL THAT HAS INFECTED OUR UNIVERSE.
WE ARE THE ONLY HOPE OF DEFEATING THE JELLYBRAINS AND THEIR TETALDIAN PROXIES.
HOPE... TRANSLATORS MUST BE ON THE FRITZ.
NO WAY THAT MEANS THE SAME THING IN ENGLISH.
THERE IS HOPE IN THIS SITUATION, HUMAN.
WE HAVE A TACHYON TOAD, FOR ONE.
SO WHAT'S THE PLAN?
THE NINE OF US, AND YOUR CREEPY FROG FRIEND HERE, WE SOMEHOW DEFEAT AN ENDLESS ARMY OF AUTOMATONS, WALK ON IN, HOWDY, AN' KILL THEIR MASTERS -- THE TIME TRAVELING TELEPATHS?
"EASY LIKE PIE," AS AN OLD FRIEND USED TO SAY.
AS THE JELLYBRAIN SHOWED YOU...
YOU ARE THE PLAN.
THEY CANNOT TIME TRACK OR PROPHESIZE YOU.
THEY HAVE MEDDLED WITH THE HISTORY OF EVERY SPECIES.
WE'RE GOING TO PLAY IT THEIR WAY.

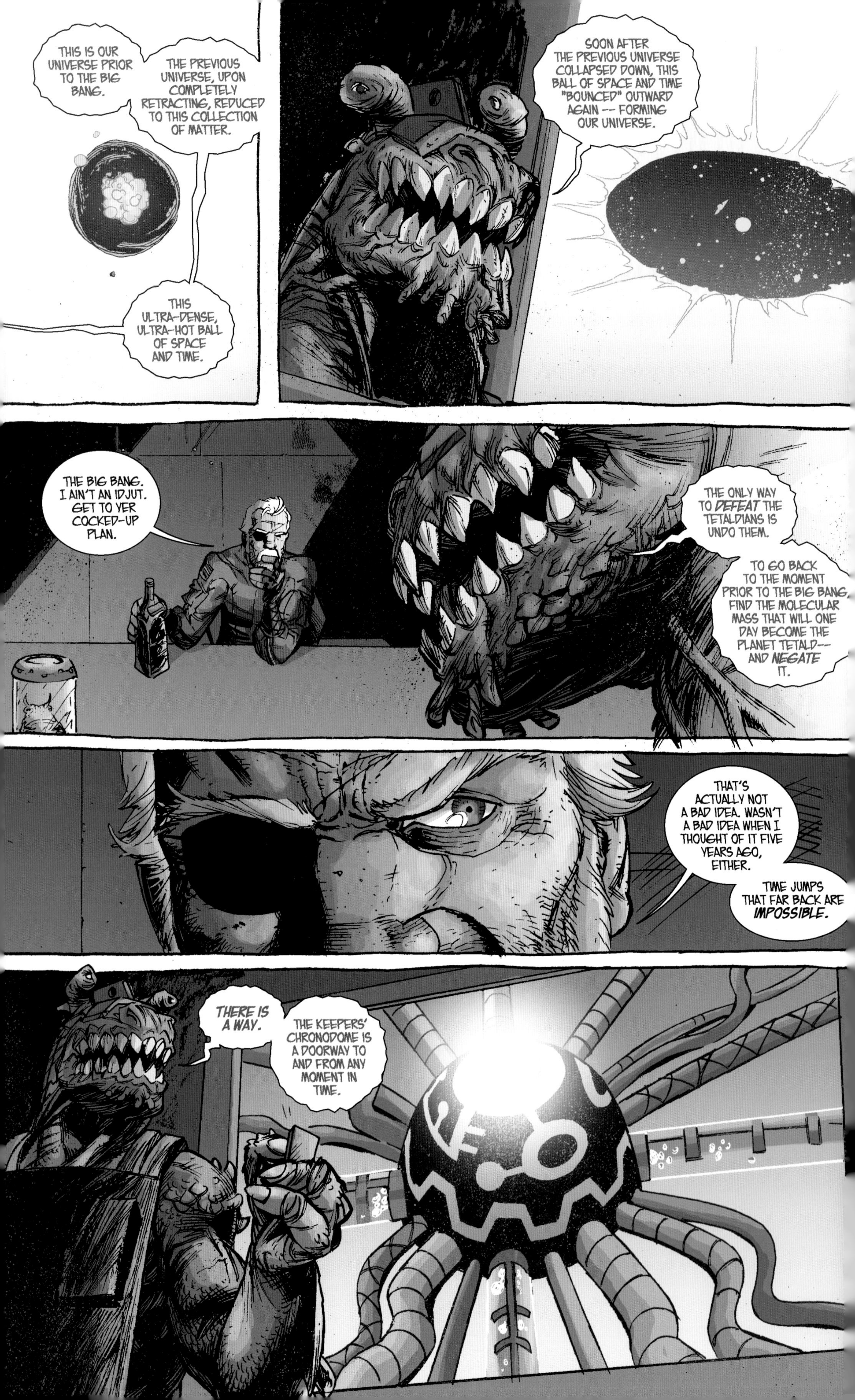

THIS IS OUR UNIVERSE PRIOR TO THE BIG BANG.
THE PREVIOUS UNIVERSE, UPON COMPLETELY RETRACTING, REDUCED TO THIS COLLECTION OF MATTER.
THIS ULTRA-DENSE, ULTRA-HOT BALL OF SPACE AND TIME.
SOON AFTER THE PREVIOUS UNIVERSE COLLAPSED DOWN, THIS BALL OF SPACE AND TIME "BOUNCED" OUTWARD AGAIN -- FORMING OUR UNIVERSE.
THE BIG BANG. I AIN'T AN IDJUT. GET TO YER COCKED-UP PLAN.
THE ONLY WAY TO *DEFEAT* THE TETALDIANS IS UNDO THEM.
TO GO BACK TO THE MOMENT PRIOR TO THE BIG BANG, FIND THE MOLECULAR MASS THAT WILL ONE DAY BECOME THE PLANET TETALD-- AND *NEGATE* IT.
THAT'S ACTUALLY NOT A BAD IDEA. WASN'T A BAD IDEA WHEN I THOUGHT OF IT FIVE YEARS AGO, EITHER.
TIME JUMPS THAT FAR BACK ARE ***IMPOSSIBLE.***
THERE IS A WAY.
THE KEEPERS' CHRONODOME IS A DOORWAY TO AND FROM ANY MOMENT IN TIME.

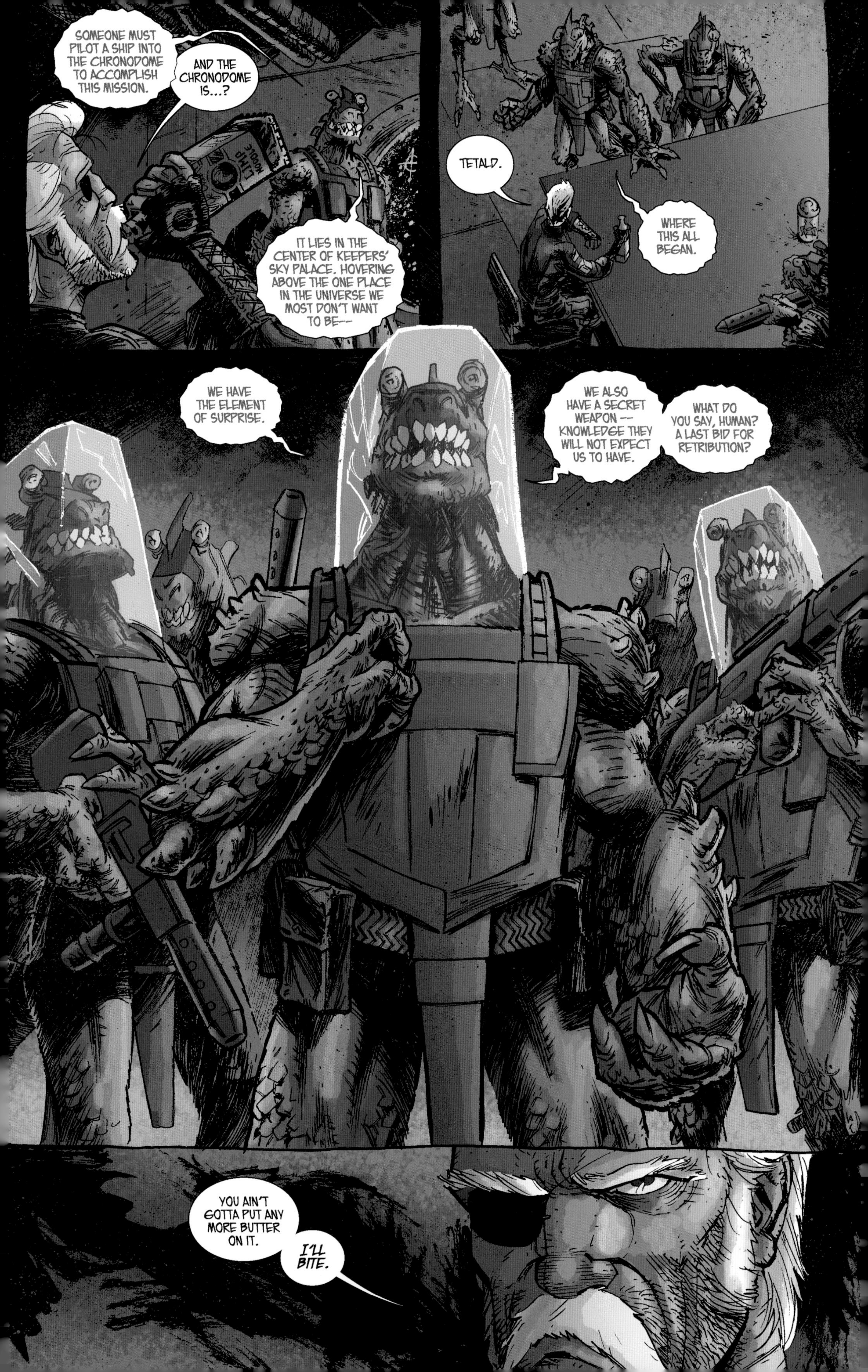
SOMEONE MUST PILOT A SHIP INTO THE CHRONODOME TO ACCOMPLISH THIS MISSION.
AND THE CHRONODOME IS...?
IT LIES IN THE CENTER OF KEEPERS' SKY PALACE. HOVERING ABOVE THE ONE PLACE IN THE UNIVERSE WE MOST DON'T WANT TO BE--
TETALD.
WHERE THIS ALL BEGAN.
WE HAVE THE ELEMENT OF SURPRISE.
WE ALSO HAVE A SECRET WEAPON -- KNOWLEDGE THEY WILL NOT EXPECT US TO HAVE.
WHAT DO YOU SAY, HUMAN? A LAST BID FOR RETRIBUTION?
YOU AIN'T GOTTA PUT ANY MORE BUTTER ON IT.
I'LL BITE.

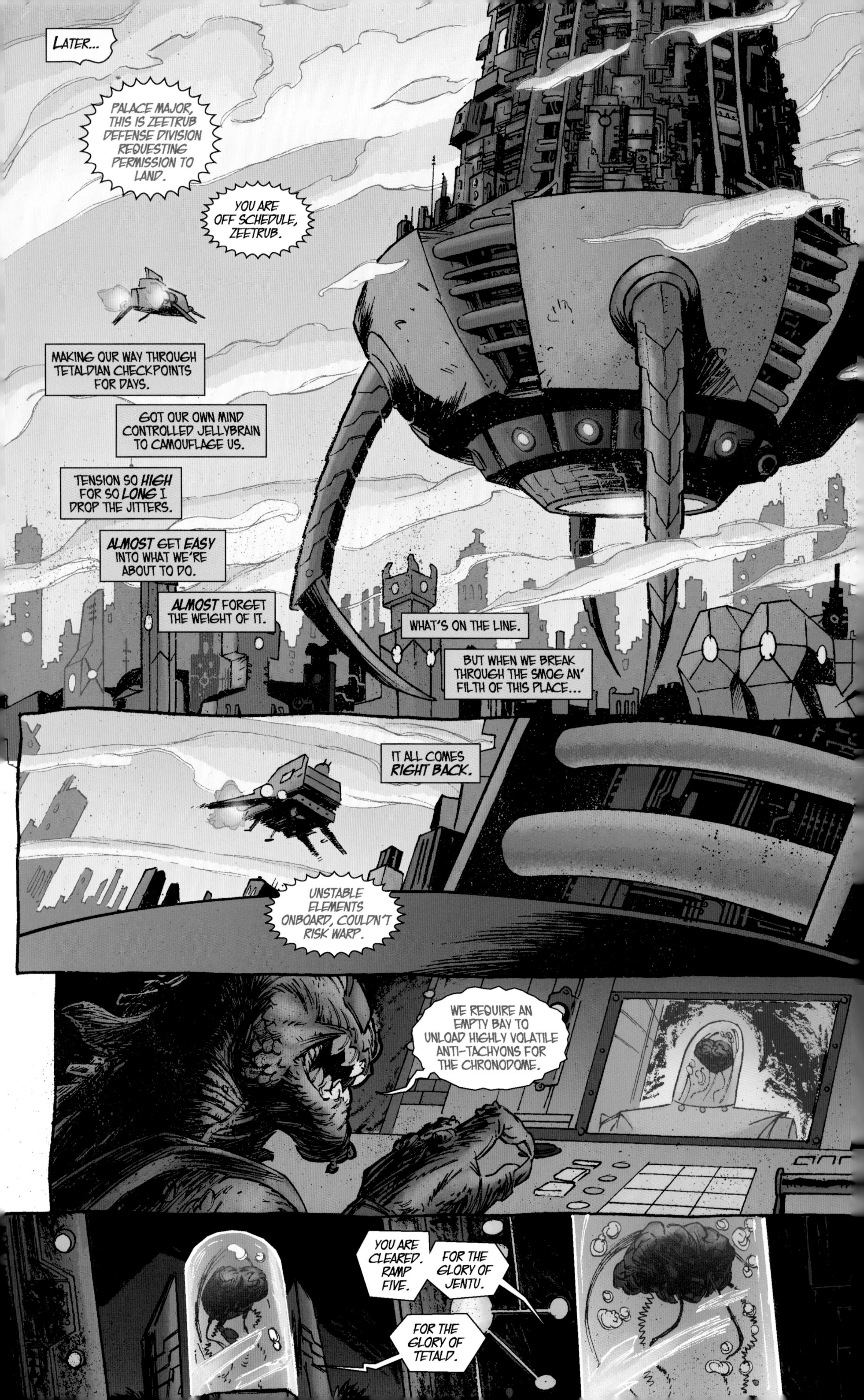
LATER...
PALACE MAJOR, THIS IS ZEETRUB DEFENSE DIVISION REQUESTING PERMISSION TO LAND.
YOU ARE OFF SCHEDULE, ZEETRUB.
MAKING OUR WAY THROUGH TETALDIAN CHECKPOINTS FOR DAYS.
GOT OUR OWN MIND CONTROLLED JELLYBRAIN TO CAMOUFLAGE US.
TENSION SO HIGH FOR SO LONG I DROP THE JITTERS.
ALMOST GET EASY INTO WHAT WE'RE ABOUT TO DO.
ALMOST FORGET THE WEIGHT OF IT.
WHAT'S ON THE LINE.
BUT WHEN WE BREAK THROUGH THE SMOG AN' FILTH OF THIS PLACE...
IT ALL COMES RIGHT BACK.
UNSTABLE ELEMENTS ONBOARD, COULDN'T RISK WARP.
WE REQUIRE AN EMPTY BAY TO UNLOAD HIGHLY VOLATILE ANTI-TACHYONS FOR THE CHRONODOME.
YOU ARE CLEARED. RAMP FIVE.
FOR THE GLORY OF JENTU.
FOR THE GLORY OF TETALD.

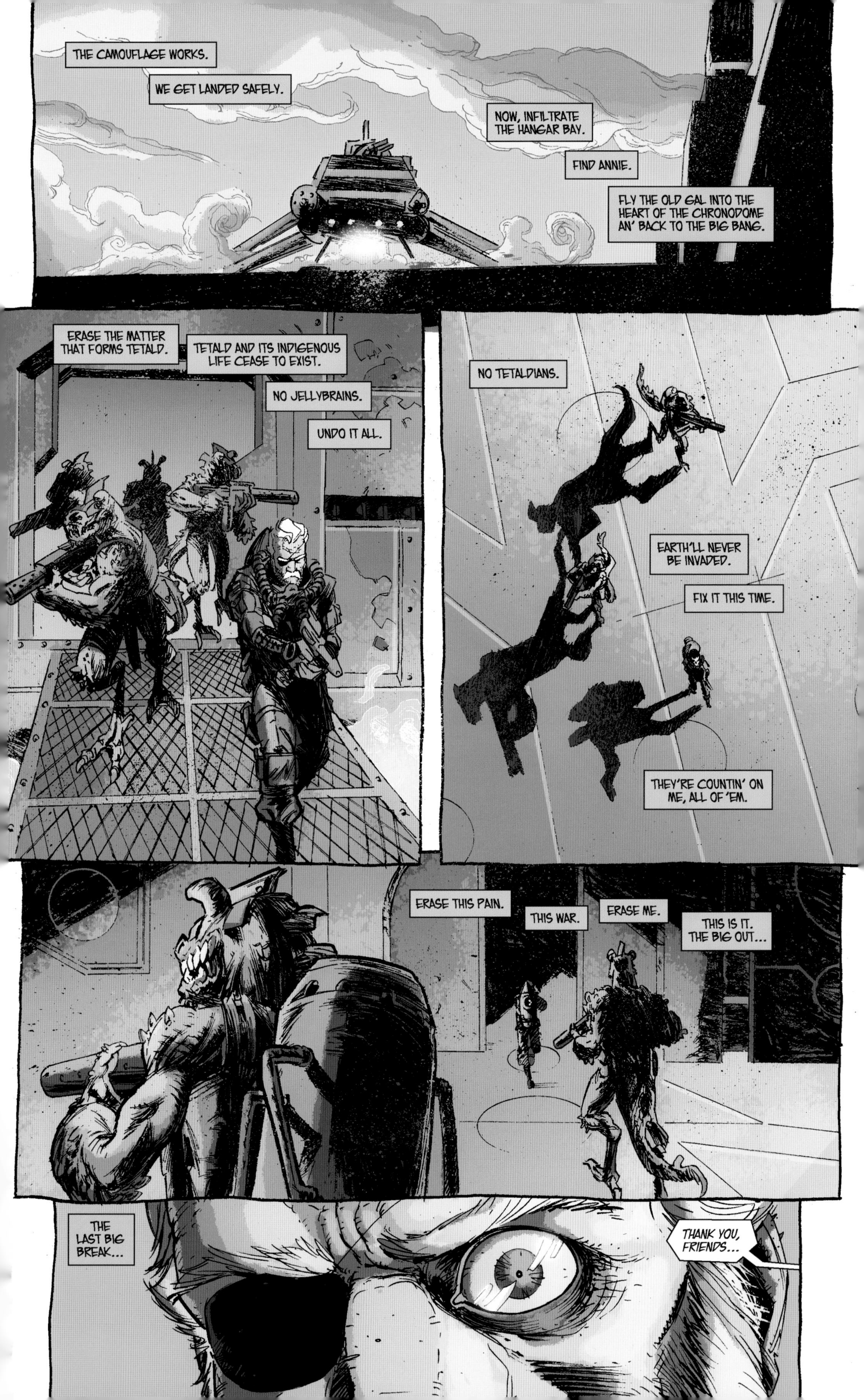
THE CAMOUFLAGE WORKS.
WE GET LANDED SAFELY.
NOW, INFILTRATE THE HANGAR BAY.
FIND ANNIE.
FLY THE OLD GAL INTO THE HEART OF THE CHRONODOME AN' BACK TO THE BIG BANG.
ERASE THE MATTER THAT FORMS TETALD.
TETALD AND ITS INDIGENOUS LIFE CEASE TO EXIST.
NO JELLYBRAINS.
UNDO IT ALL.
NO TETALDIANS.
EARTH'LL NEVER BE INVADED.
FIX IT THIS TIME.
THEY'RE COUNTIN' ON ME, ALL OF 'EM.
ERASE THIS PAIN.
THIS WAR.
ERASE ME.
THIS IS IT. THE BIG OUT...
THE LAST BIG BREAK...
THANK YOU, FRIENDS...

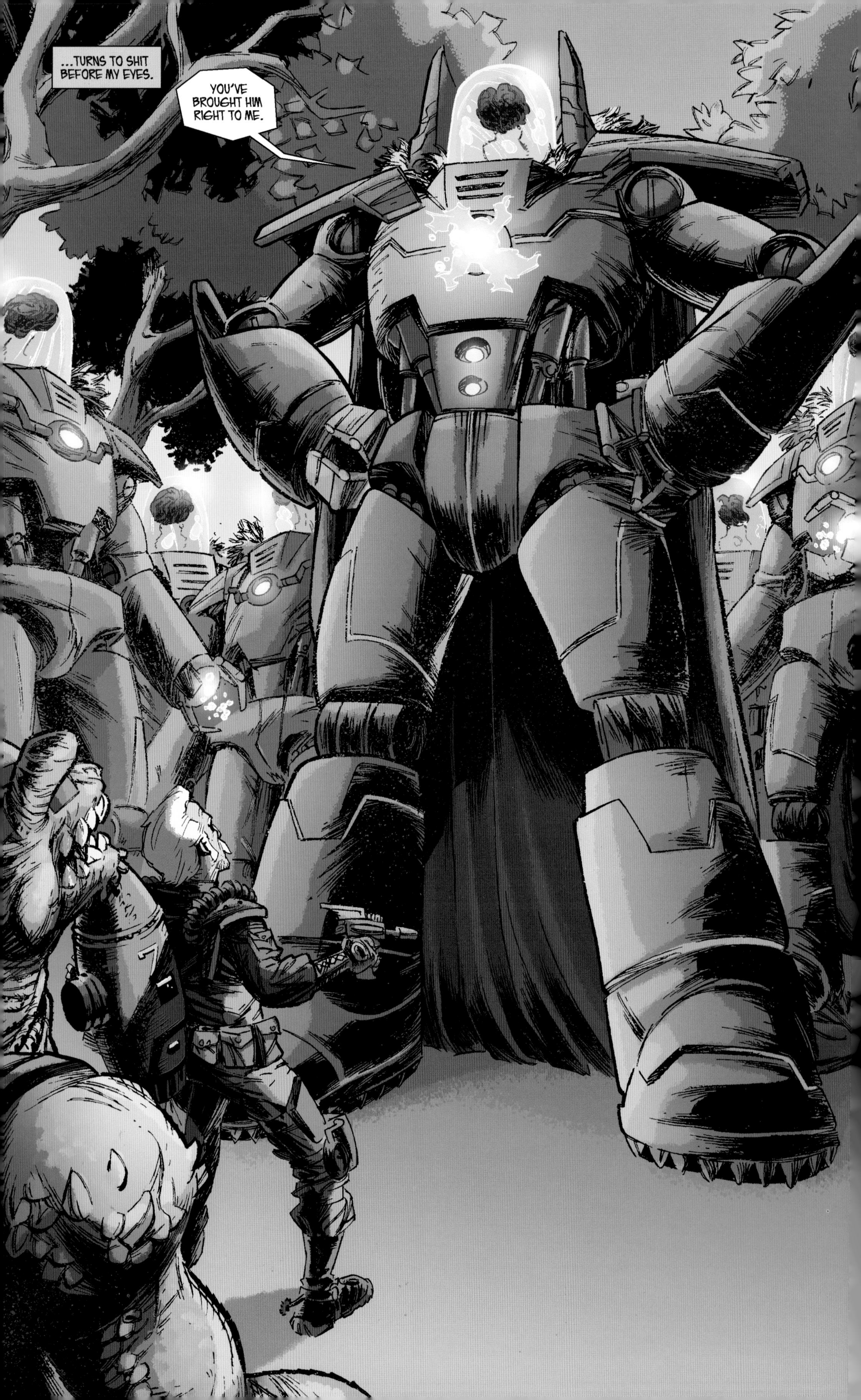
...TURNS TO SHIT BEFORE MY EYES.
YOU'VE BROUGHT HIM RIGHT TO ME.

CHAPTER 4

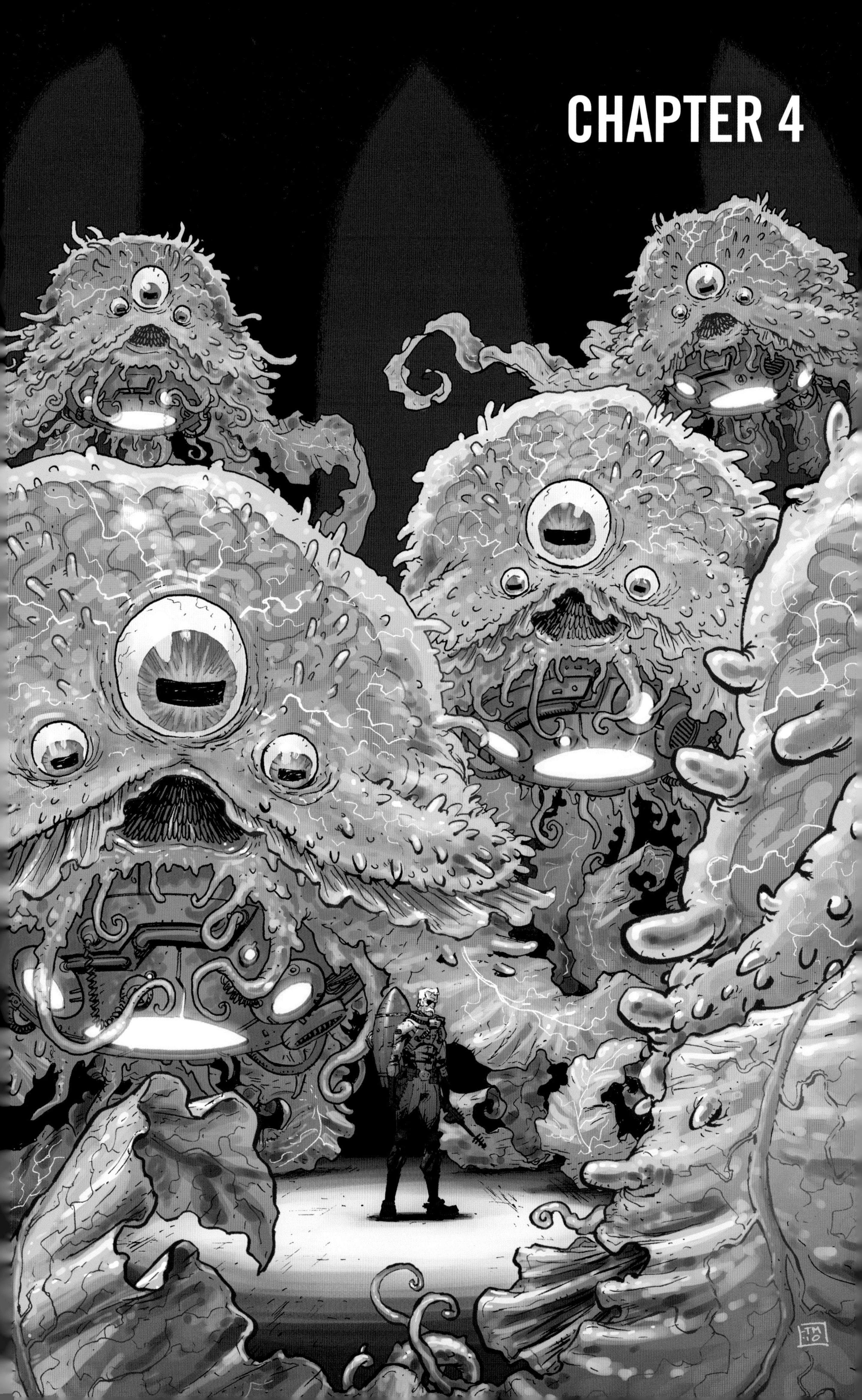

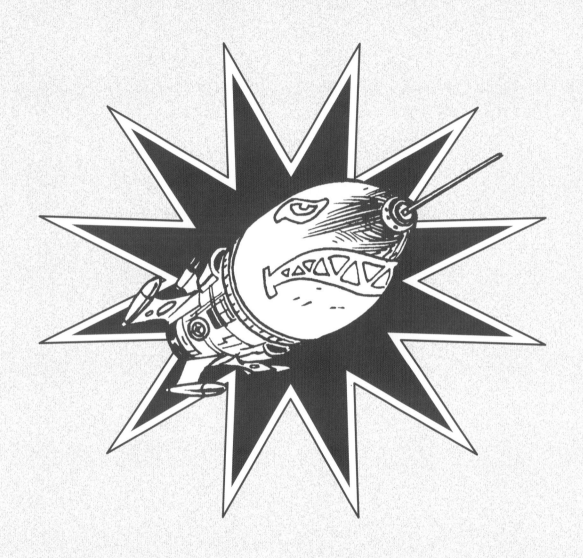

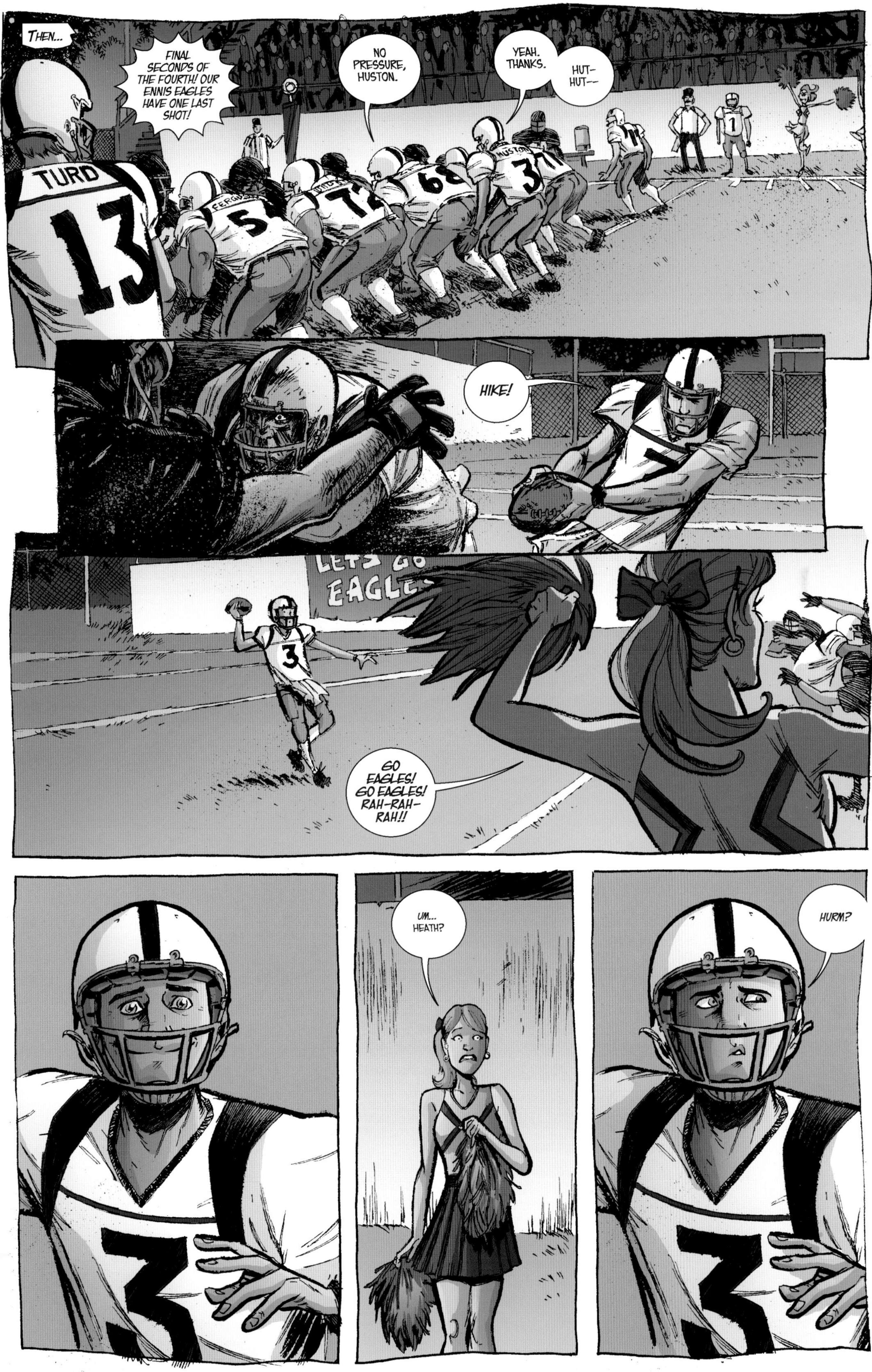
THEN...
FINAL SECONDS OF THE FOURTH! OUR ENNIS EAGLES HAVE ONE LAST SHOT!
NO PRESSURE, HUSTON.
YEAH. THANKS.
HUT-HUT--
HIKE!
GO EAGLES! GO EAGLES! RAH-RAH-RAH!!
UM... HEATH?
HURM?

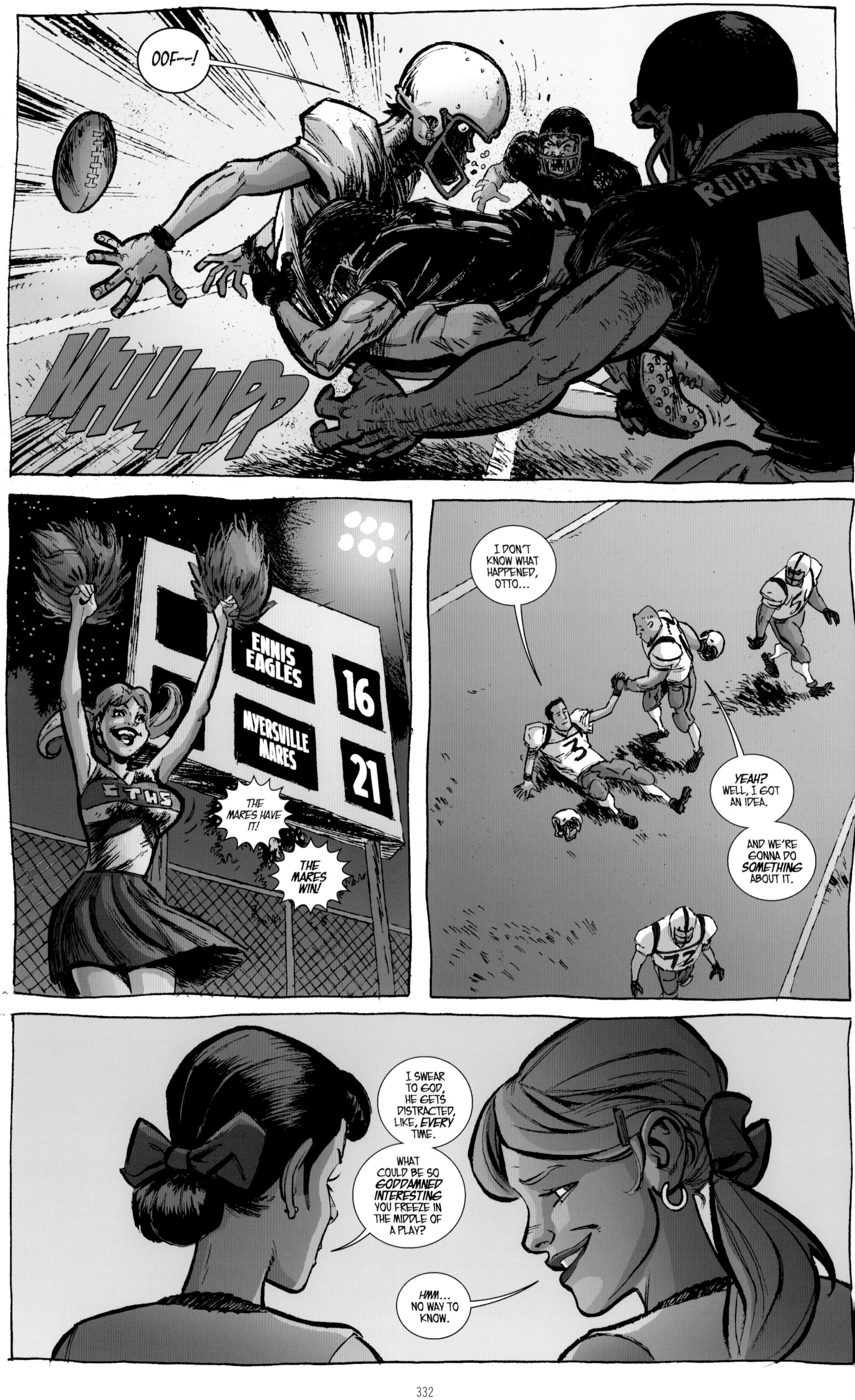
OOF--!
WHUMPP
ENNIS EAGLES
16
MYERSVILLE MARES
21
ETHS
THE MARES HAVE IT!
THE MARES WIN!
I DON'T KNOW WHAT HAPPENED, OTTO...
YEAH? WELL, I GOT AN IDEA.
AND WE'RE GONNA DO SOMETHING ABOUT IT.
I SWEAR TO GOD, HE GETS DISTRACTED, LIKE, EVERY TIME.
WHAT COULD BE SO GODDAMNED INTERESTING YOU FREEZE IN THE MIDDLE OF A PLAY?
HMM... NO WAY TO KNOW.

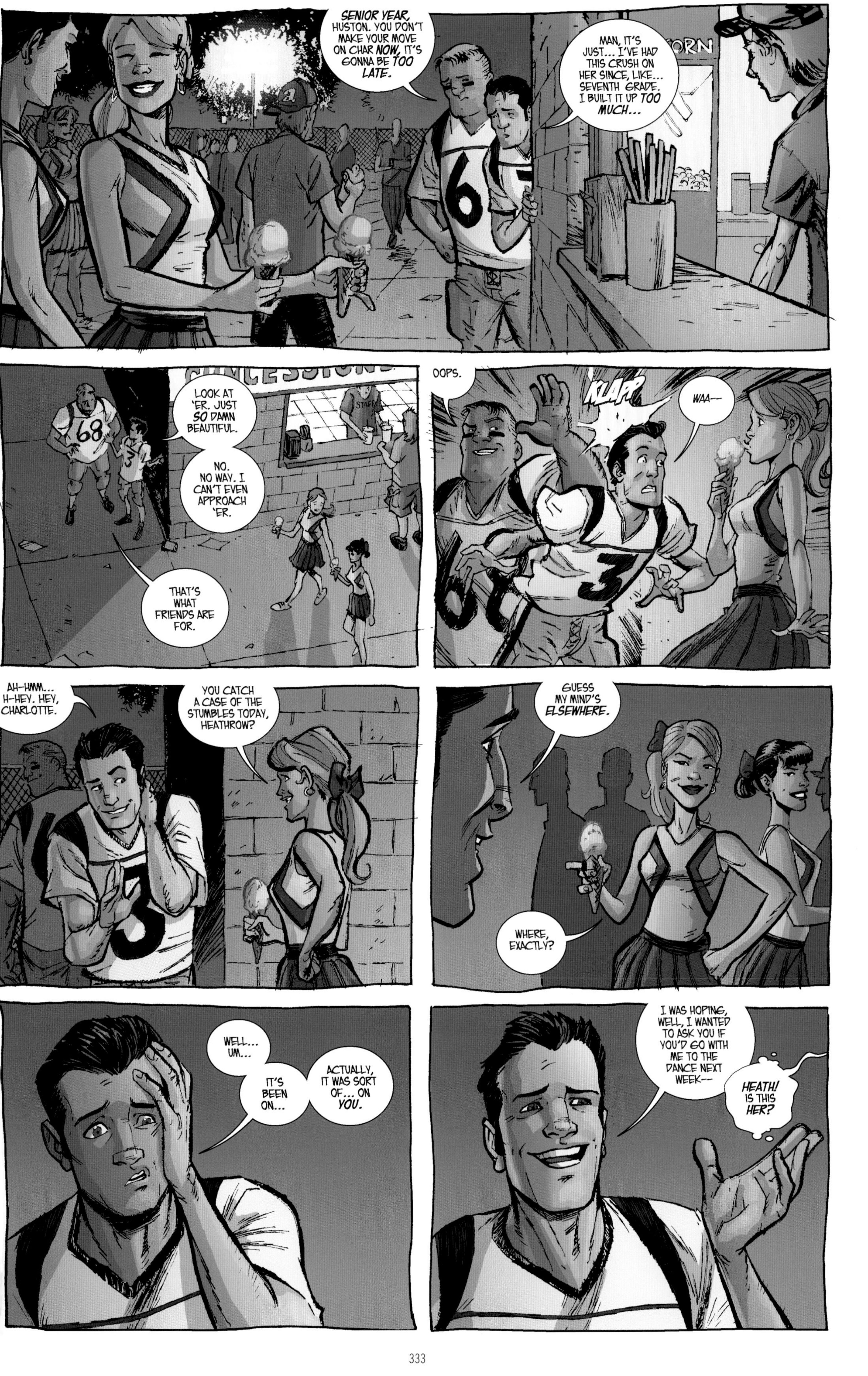
SENIOR YEAR, HUSTON. YOU DON'T MAKE YOUR MOVE ON CHAR NOW, IT'S GONNA BE TOO LATE.
MAN, IT'S JUST... I'VE HAD THIS CRUSH ON HER SINCE, LIKE... SEVENTH GRADE. I BUILT IT UP TOO MUCH...
LOOK AT 'ER. JUST SO DAMN BEAUTIFUL.
NO. NO WAY. I CAN'T EVEN APPROACH 'ER.
THAT'S WHAT FRIENDS ARE FOR.
OOPS.
KLAP
WAA--
AH-HMM... H-HEY. HEY, CHARLOTTE.
YOU CATCH A CASE OF THE STUMBLES TODAY, HEATHROW?
GUESS MY MIND'S ELSEWHERE.
WHERE, EXACTLY?
WELL... UM...
IT'S BEEN ON...
ACTUALLY, IT WAS SORT OF... ON YOU.
I WAS HOPING, WELL, I WANTED TO ASK YOU IF YOU'D GO WITH ME TO THE DANCE NEXT WEEK--
HEATH! IS THIS HER?

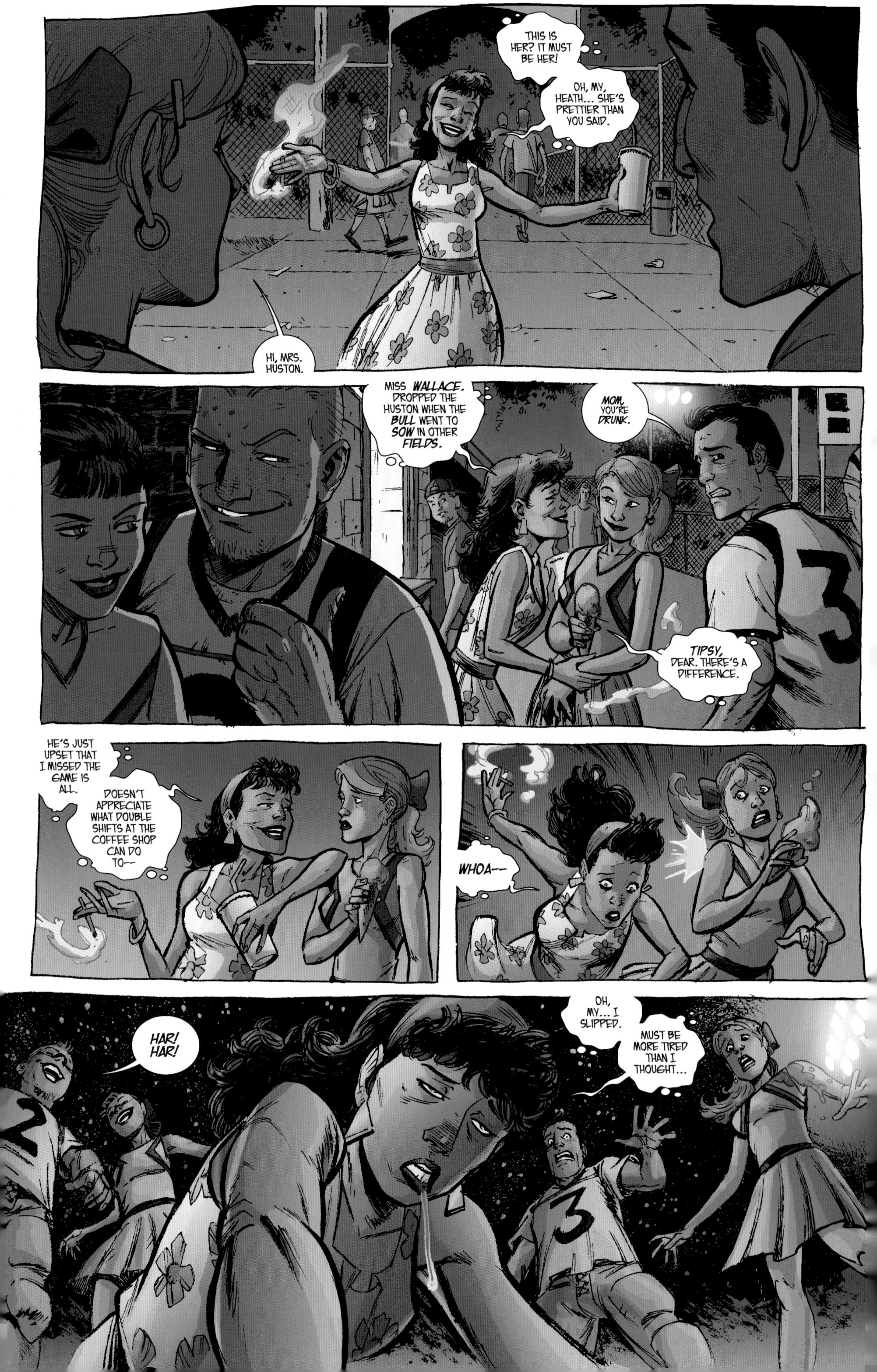
THIS IS HER? IT MUST BE HER!
OH, MY, HEATH... SHE'S PRETTIER THAN YOU SAID.
HI, MRS. HUSTON.
MISS WALLACE. DROPPED THE HUSTON WHEN THE BULL WENT TO SOW IN OTHER FIELDS.
MOM, YOU'RE DRUNK.
TIPSY, DEAR. THERE'S A DIFFERENCE.
HE'S JUST UPSET THAT I MISSED THE GAME IS ALL.
DOESN'T APPRECIATE WHAT DOUBLE SHIFTS AT THE COFFEE SHOP CAN DO TO--
WHOA--
HAR! HAR!
OH, MY... I SLIPPED.
MUST BE MORE TIRED THAN I THOUGHT...

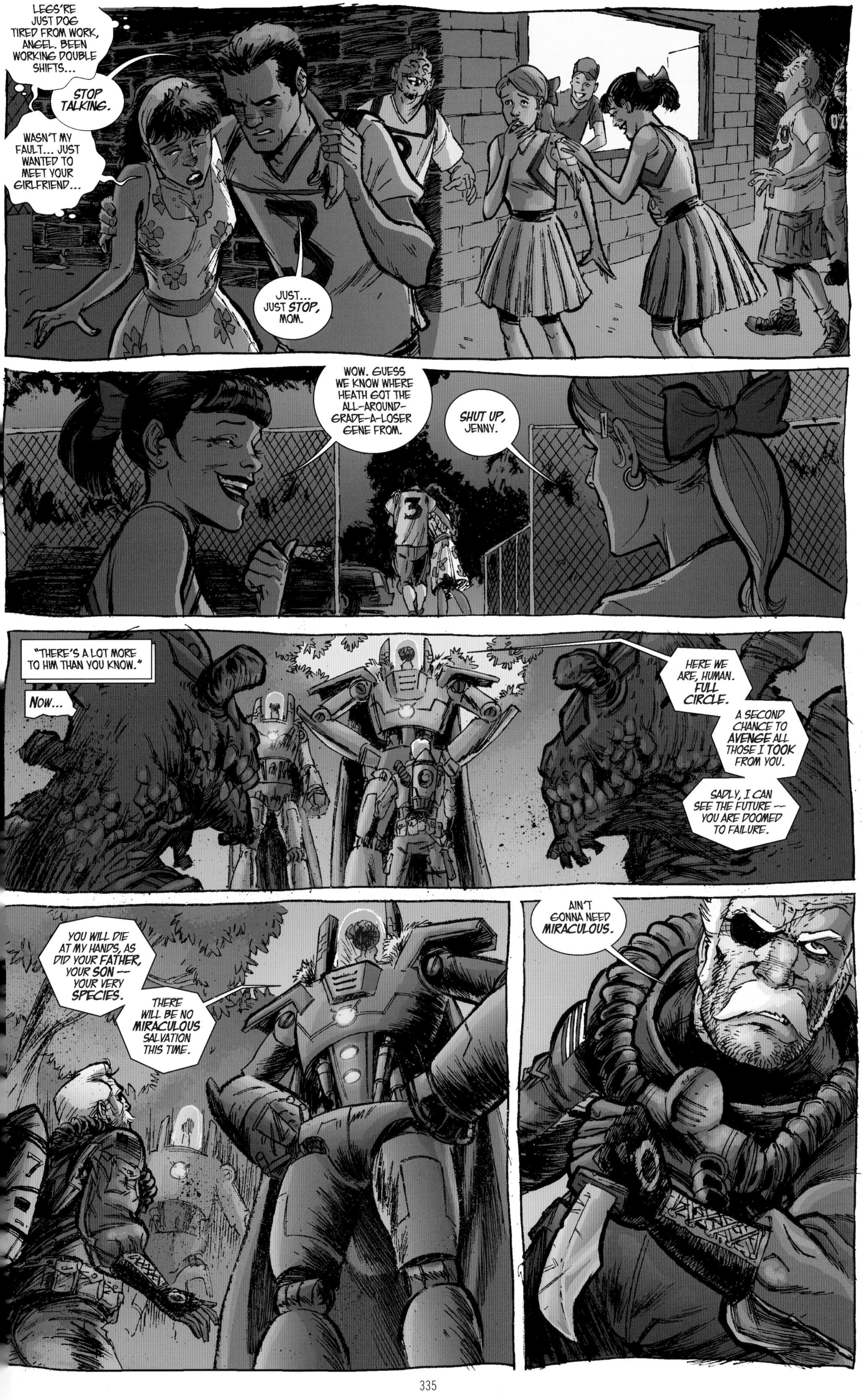
LEGS'RE JUST DOG TIRED FROM WORK, ANGEL. BEEN WORKING DOUBLE SHIFTS...
STOP TALKING.
WASN'T MY FAULT... JUST WANTED TO MEET YOUR GIRLFRIEND...
JUST... JUST STOP, MOM.
WOW. GUESS WE KNOW WHERE HEATH GOT THE ALL-AROUND-GRADE-A-LOSER GENE FROM.
SHUT UP, JENNY.
"THERE'S A LOT MORE TO HIM THAN YOU KNOW."
NOW...
HERE WE ARE, HUMAN. FULL CIRCLE.
A SECOND CHANCE TO AVENGE ALL THOSE I TOOK FROM YOU.
SADLY, I CAN SEE THE FUTURE -- YOU ARE DOOMED TO FAILURE.
YOU WILL DIE AT MY HANDS, AS DID YOUR FATHER, YOUR SON -- YOUR VERY SPECIES.
THERE WILL BE NO MIRACULOUS SALVATION THIS TIME.
AIN'T GONNA NEED MIRACULOUS.

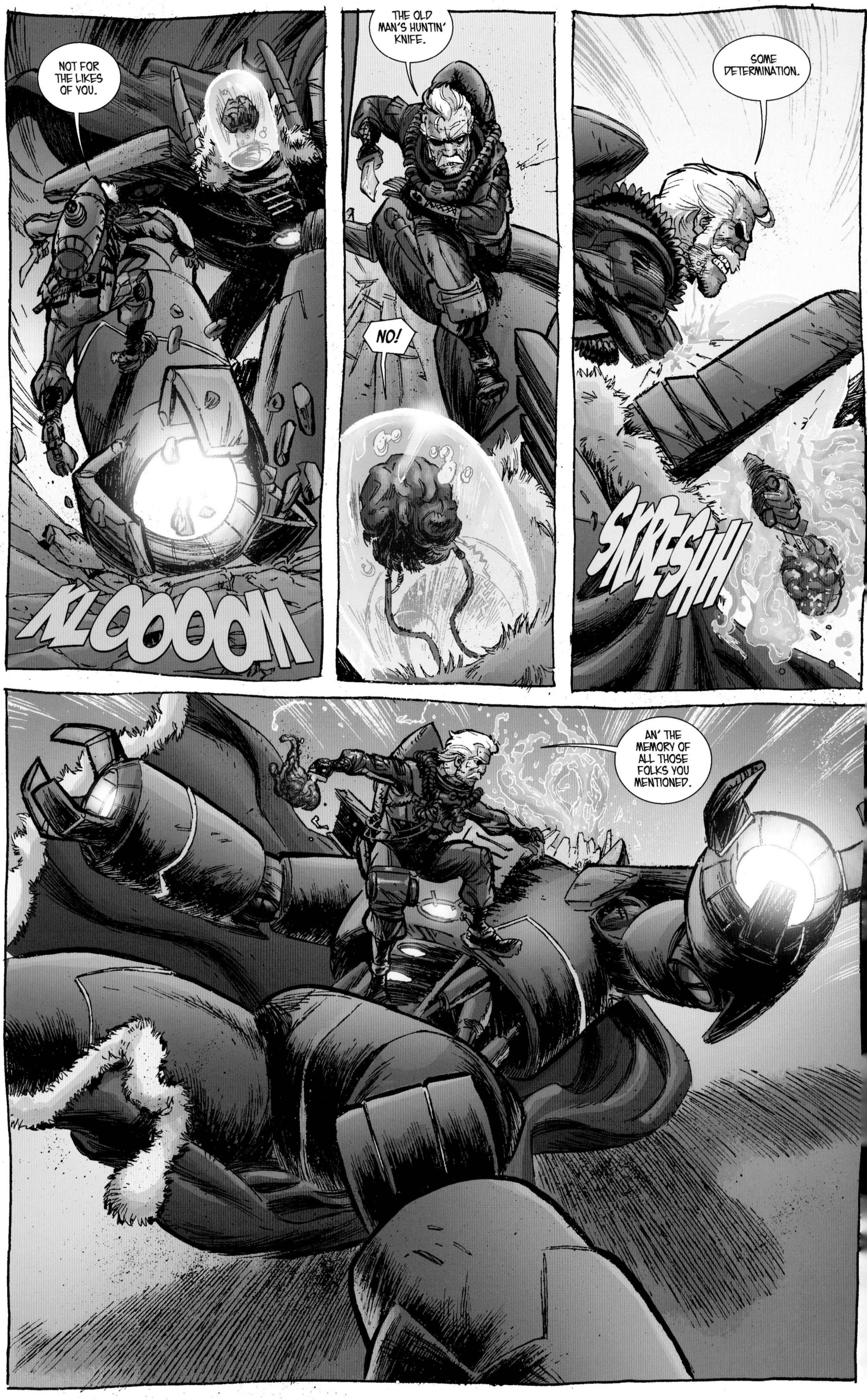
NOT FOR THE LIKES OF YOU.
KLOOOOM
THE OLD MAN'S HUNTIN' KNIFE.
NO!
SOME DETERMINATION.
SKRESHH
AN' THE MEMORY OF ALL THOSE FOLKS YOU MENTIONED.

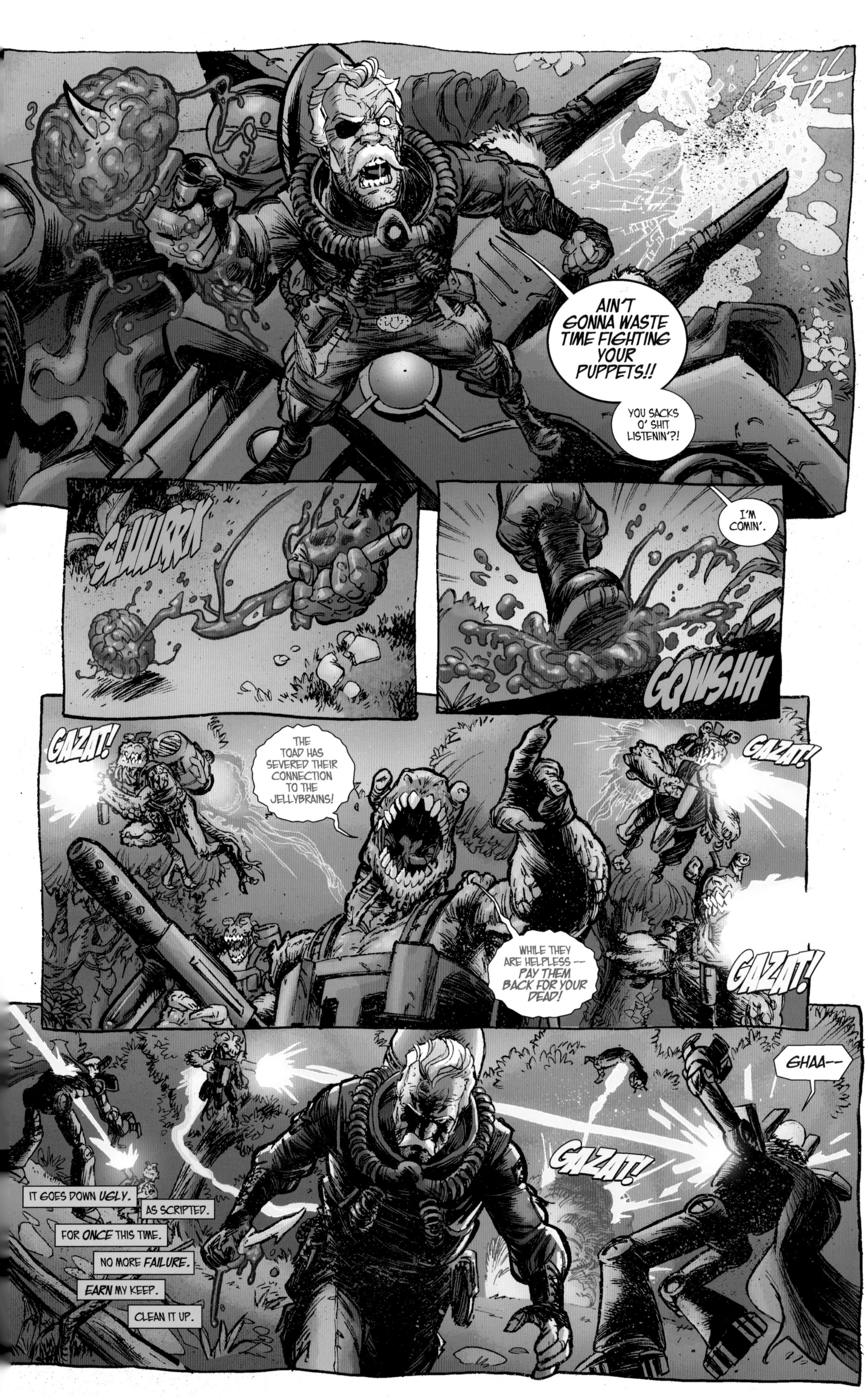
AIN'T GONNA WASTE TIME FIGHTING YOUR PUPPETS!!
YOU SACKS O' SHIT LISTENIN'?!
SLUURRK
I'M COMIN'.
GQWSHH
GAZAT!
THE TOAD HAS SEVERED THEIR CONNECTION TO THE JELLYBRAINS!
GAZAT!
WHILE THEY ARE HELPLESS -- PAY THEM BACK FOR YOUR DEAD!
GAZAT!
GHAA--
GAZAT!
IT GOES DOWN UGLY.
AS SCRIPTED.
FOR ONCE THIS TIME.
NO MORE FAILURE.
EARN MY KEEP.
CLEAN IT UP.

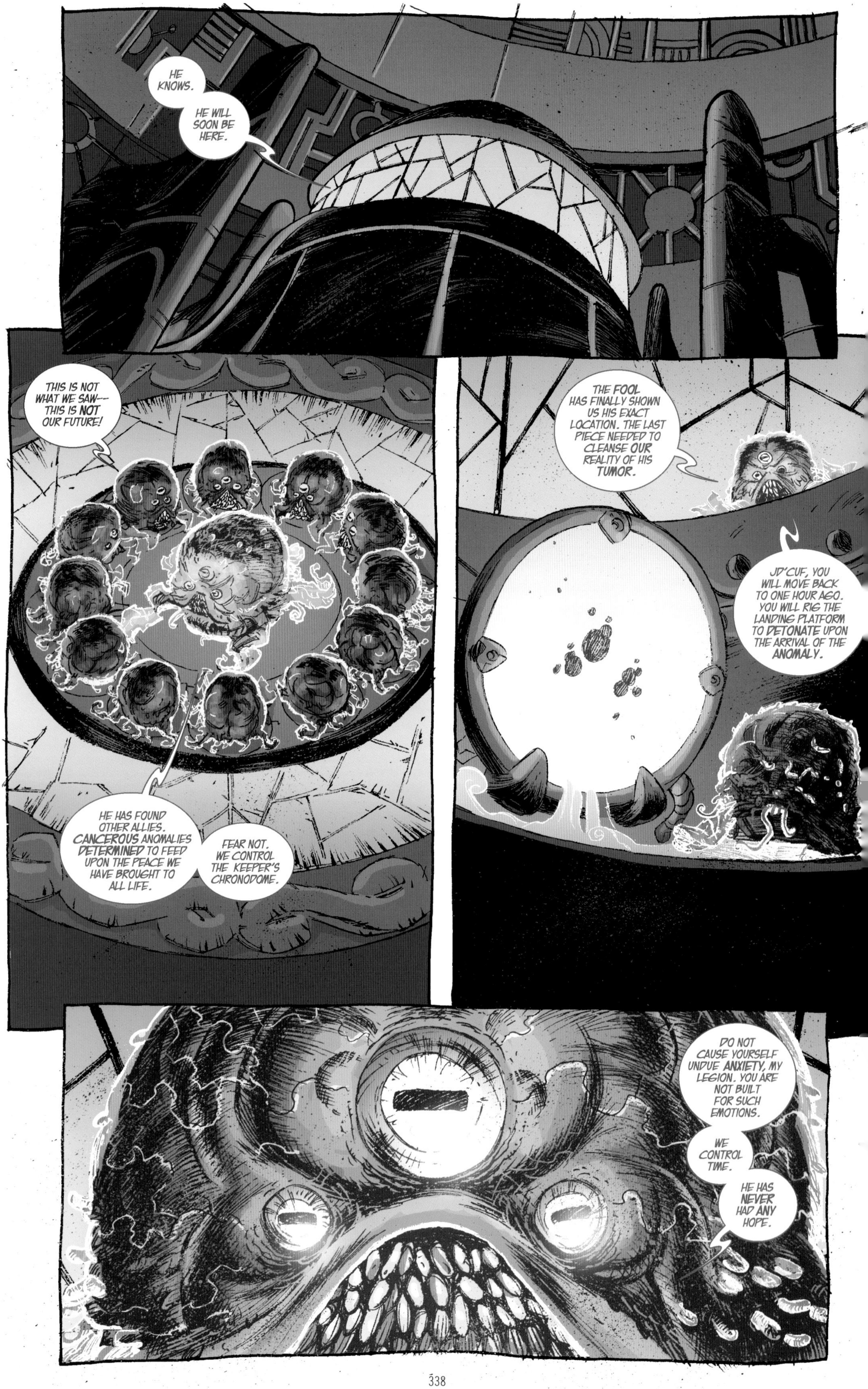
HE KNOWS.
HE WILL SOON BE HERE.
THIS IS NOT WHAT WE SAW-- THIS IS NOT OUR FUTURE!
HE HAS FOUND OTHER ALLIES. CANCEROUS ANOMALIES DETERMINED TO FEED UPON THE PEACE WE HAVE BROUGHT TO ALL LIFE.
FEAR NOT. WE CONTROL THE KEEPER'S CHRONODOME.
THE FOOL HAS FINALLY SHOWN US HIS EXACT LOCATION. THE LAST PIECE NEEDED TO CLEANSE OUR REALITY OF HIS TUMOR.
JD'CUF, YOU WILL MOVE BACK TO ONE HOUR AGO. YOU WILL RIG THE LANDING PLATFORM TO DETONATE UPON THE ARRIVAL OF THE ANOMALY.
DO NOT CAUSE YOURSELF UNDUE ANXIETY, MY LEGION. YOU ARE NOT BUILT FOR SUCH EMOTIONS.
WE CONTROL TIME.
HE HAS NEVER HAD ANY HOPE.

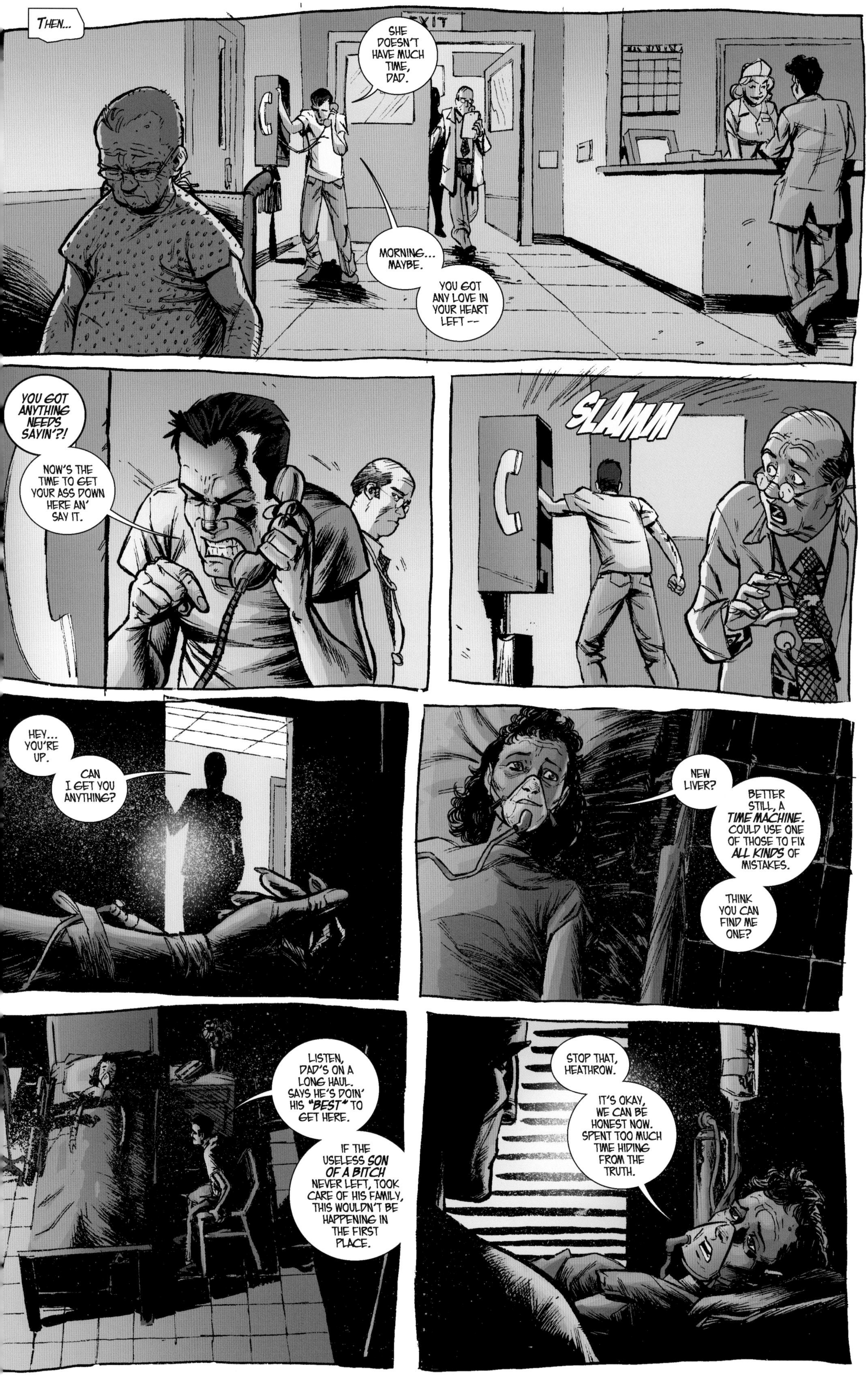
THEN...
SHE DOESN'T HAVE MUCH TIME, DAD.
MORNING... MAYBE.
YOU GOT ANY LOVE IN YOUR HEART LEFT --
YOU GOT ANYTHING NEEDS SAYIN'?!
NOW'S THE TIME TO GET YOUR ASS DOWN HERE AN' SAY IT.
SLAMM
HEY... YOU'RE UP.
CAN I GET YOU ANYTHING?
NEW LIVER?
BETTER STILL, A TIME MACHINE. COULD USE ONE OF THOSE TO FIX ALL KINDS OF MISTAKES.
THINK YOU CAN FIND ME ONE?
LISTEN, DAD'S ON A LONG HAUL. SAYS HE'S DOIN' HIS "BEST" TO GET HERE.
IF THE USELESS SON OF A BITCH NEVER LEFT, TOOK CARE OF HIS FAMILY, THIS WOULDN'T BE HAPPENING IN THE FIRST PLACE.
STOP THAT, HEATHROW.
IT'S OKAY, WE CAN BE HONEST NOW. SPENT TOO MUCH TIME HIDING FROM THE TRUTH.

I'M A DRUNK WHO DRANK HERSELF TO DEATH.

AFTER DAD LEFT YOU THE WAY HE DID... NO ONE BLAMES YOU, MA.

I LET YOU GO ON FOR *TOO LONG* FAULTIN' YOUR FATHER FOR THIS. TOO LONG LETTING *HIM* SHOULDER THE *BLAME*.

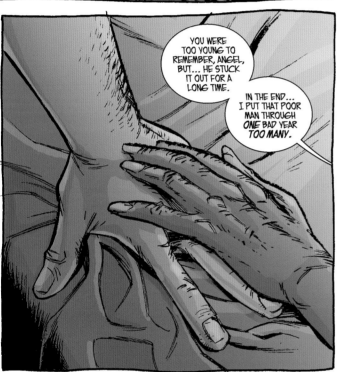

YOU WERE TOO YOUNG TO REMEMBER, ANGEL, BUT... HE STUCK IT OUT FOR A LONG TIME.

IN THE END... I PUT THAT POOR MAN THROUGH *ONE* BAD YEAR *TOO MANY*.

MY DRINKING IS WHY HE LEFT.

SO YOU FORGIVE YOUR FATHER.

YOU CUT HIM SOME SLACK.

YOU LET ME GO ON THINKING IT WAS HIM...

ALL THESE YEARS.

HE INSISTED.

DIDN'T WANT YOU MAD AT ME. SAID IT WOULD ONLY MAKE ME SINK THAT MUCH DEEPER INTO THE BOTTLE.

FIGURED HE COULD TAKE YOUR ANGER BETTER THAN I COULD.

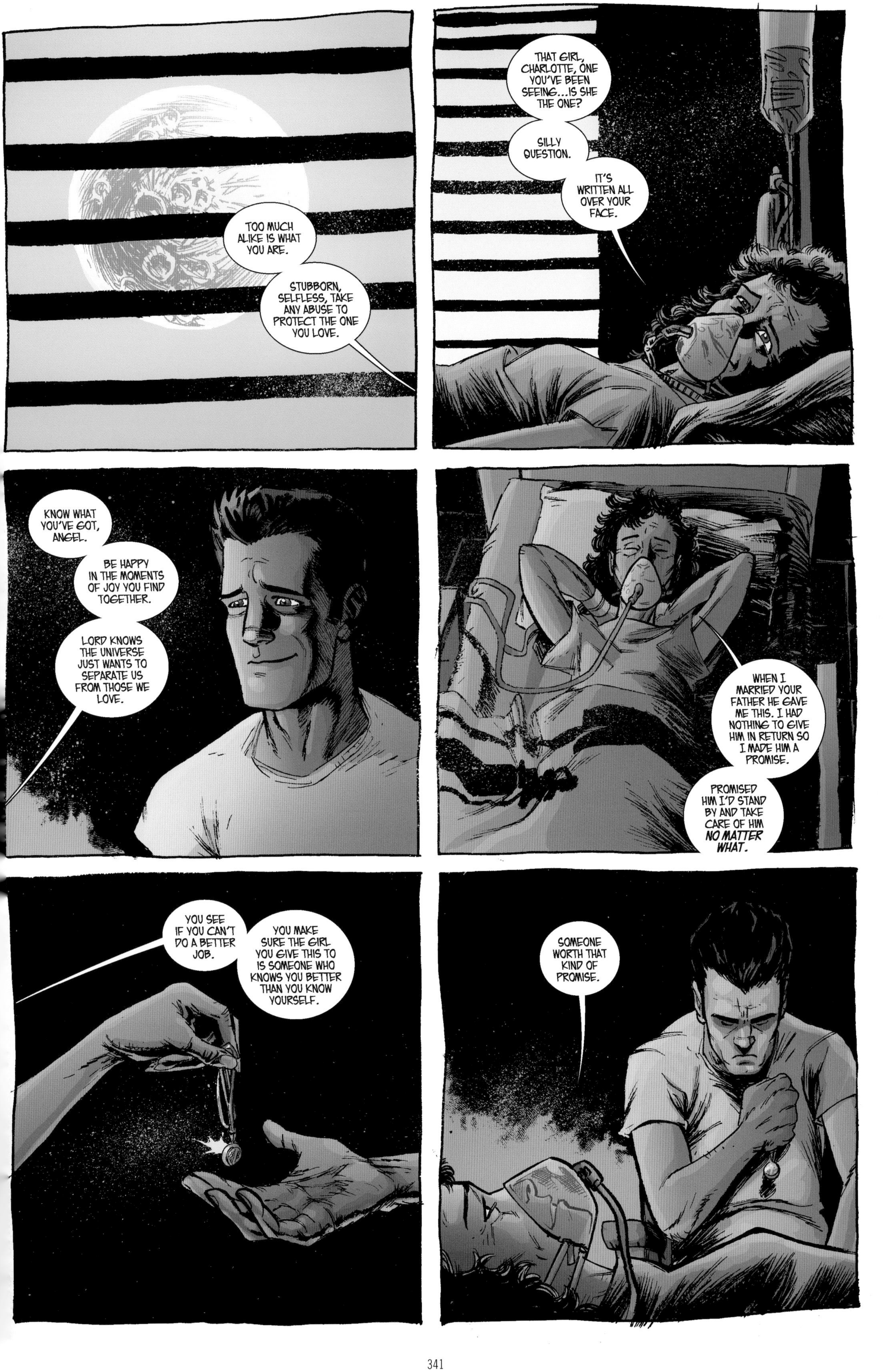
TOO MUCH ALIKE IS WHAT YOU ARE.
STUBBORN, SELFLESS, TAKE ANY ABUSE TO PROTECT THE ONE YOU LOVE.
THAT GIRL, CHARLOTTE, ONE YOU'VE BEEN SEEING...IS SHE THE ONE?
SILLY QUESTION.
IT'S WRITTEN ALL OVER YOUR FACE.
KNOW WHAT YOU'VE GOT, ANGEL.
BE HAPPY IN THE MOMENTS OF JOY YOU FIND TOGETHER.
LORD KNOWS THE UNIVERSE JUST WANTS TO SEPARATE US FROM THOSE WE LOVE.
WHEN I MARRIED YOUR FATHER HE GAVE ME THIS. I HAD NOTHING TO GIVE HIM IN RETURN SO I MADE HIM A PROMISE.
PROMISED HIM I'D STAND BY AND TAKE CARE OF HIM *NO MATTER WHAT.*
YOU SEE IF YOU CAN'T DO A BETTER JOB.
YOU MAKE SURE THE GIRL YOU GIVE THIS TO IS SOMEONE WHO KNOWS YOU BETTER THAN YOU KNOW YOURSELF.
SOMEONE WORTH THAT KIND OF PROMISE.

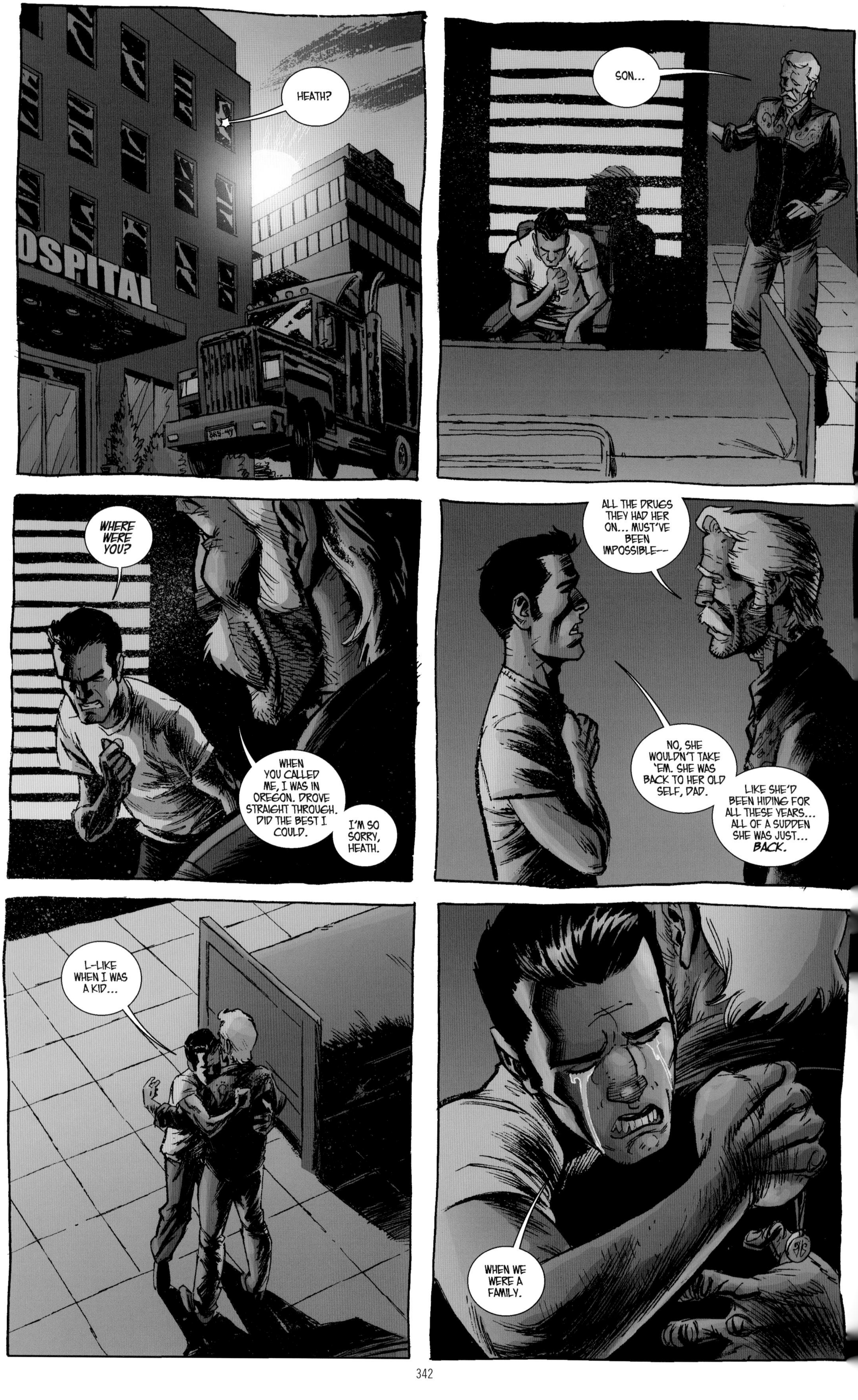
HEATH?
SON...
WHERE WERE YOU?
WHEN YOU CALLED ME, I WAS IN OREGON. DROVE STRAIGHT THROUGH. DID THE BEST I COULD.
I'M SO SORRY, HEATH.
ALL THE DRUGS THEY HAD HER ON... MUST'VE BEEN IMPOSSIBLE--
NO, SHE WOULDN'T TAKE 'EM. SHE WAS BACK TO HER OLD SELF, DAD.
LIKE SHE'D BEEN HIDING FOR ALL THESE YEARS... ALL OF A SUDDEN SHE WAS JUST... BACK.
L-LIKE WHEN I WAS A KID...
WHEN WE WERE A FAMILY.

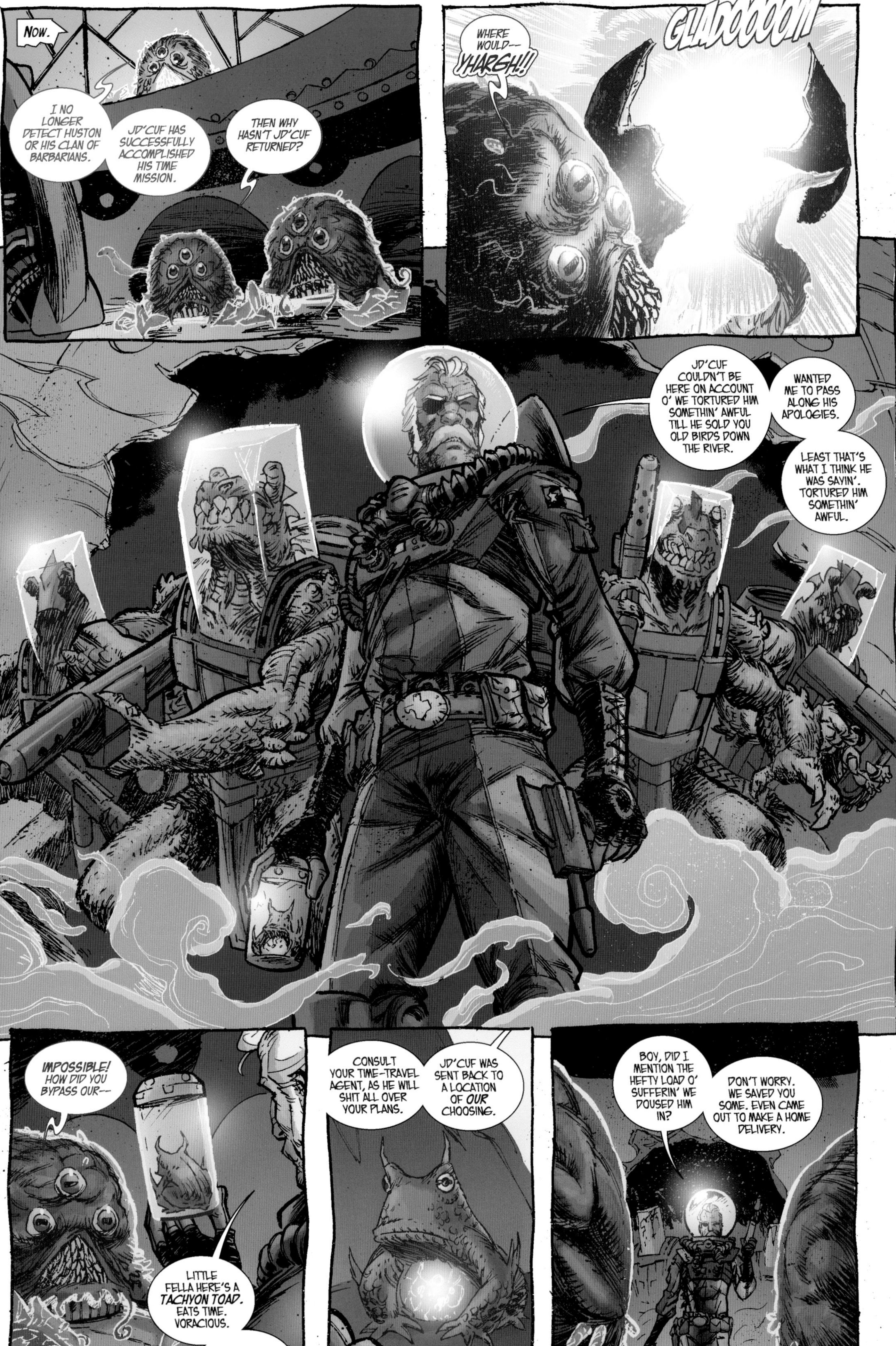
NOW.
I NO LONGER DETECT HUSTON OR HIS CLAN OF BARBARIANS.
JD'CUF HAS SUCCESSFULLY ACCOMPLISHED HIS TIME MISSION.
THEN WHY HASN'T JD'CUF RETURNED?
WHERE WOULD--
YHARGH!!
GLADOOOOOM
JD'CUF COULDN'T BE HERE ON ACCOUNT O' WE TORTURED HIM SOMETHIN' AWFUL TILL HE SOLD YOU OLD BIRDS DOWN THE RIVER.
WANTED ME TO PASS ALONG HIS APOLOGIES.
LEAST THAT'S WHAT I THINK HE WAS SAYIN'. TORTURED HIM SOMETHIN' AWFUL.
IMPOSSIBLE! HOW DID YOU BYPASS OUR--
LITTLE FELLA HERE'S A TACHYON TOAD. EATS TIME. VORACIOUS.
EXCRETES DECAYING ANTI-TACHYONS.
CONSULT YOUR TIME-TRAVEL AGENT, AS HE WILL SHIT ALL OVER YOUR PLANS.
JD'CUF WAS SENT BACK TO A LOCATION OF OUR CHOOSING.
BOY, DID I MENTION THE HEFTY LOAD O' SUFFERIN' WE DOUSED HIM IN?
DON'T WORRY. WE SAVED YOU SOME. EVEN CAME OUT TO MAKE A HOME DELIVERY.

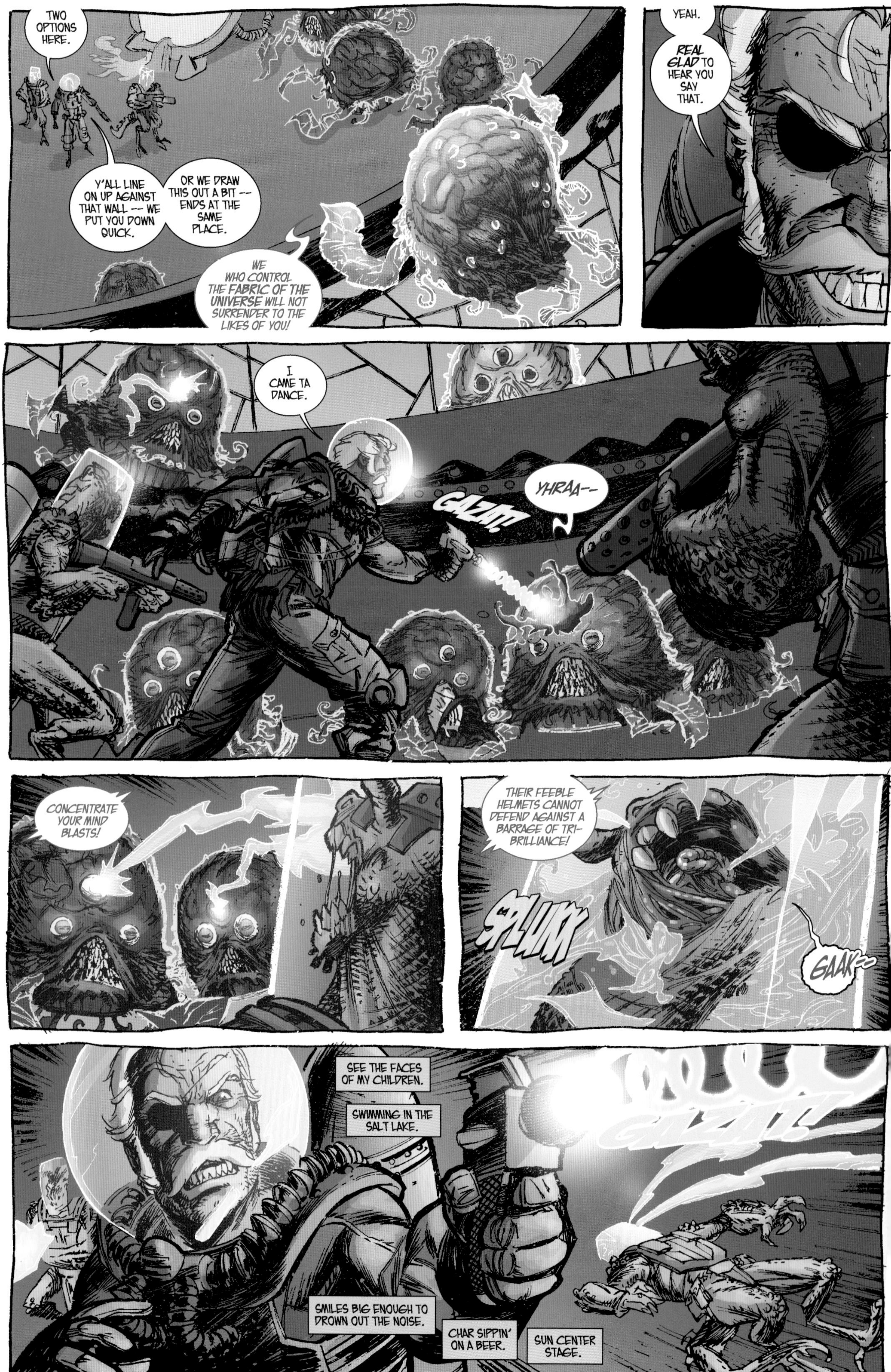
TWO OPTIONS HERE.
Y'ALL LINE ON UP AGAINST THAT WALL -- WE PUT YOU DOWN QUICK.
OR WE DRAW THIS OUT A BIT -- ENDS AT THE SAME PLACE.
WE WHO CONTROL THE FABRIC OF THE UNIVERSE WILL NOT SURRENDER TO THE LIKES OF YOU!
YEAH.
REAL GLAD TO HEAR YOU SAY THAT.
I CAME TA DANCE.
GAZAT!
YHRAA--
CONCENTRATE YOUR MIND BLASTS!
THEIR FEEBLE HELMETS CANNOT DEFEND AGAINST A BARRAGE OF TRI-BRILLIANCE!
SPLUKK
GAAK--
SEE THE FACES OF MY CHILDREN.
SWIMMING IN THE SALT LAKE.
GAZAT!
SMILES BIG ENOUGH TO DROWN OUT THE NOISE.
CHAR SIPPIN' ON A BEER.
SUN CENTER STAGE.

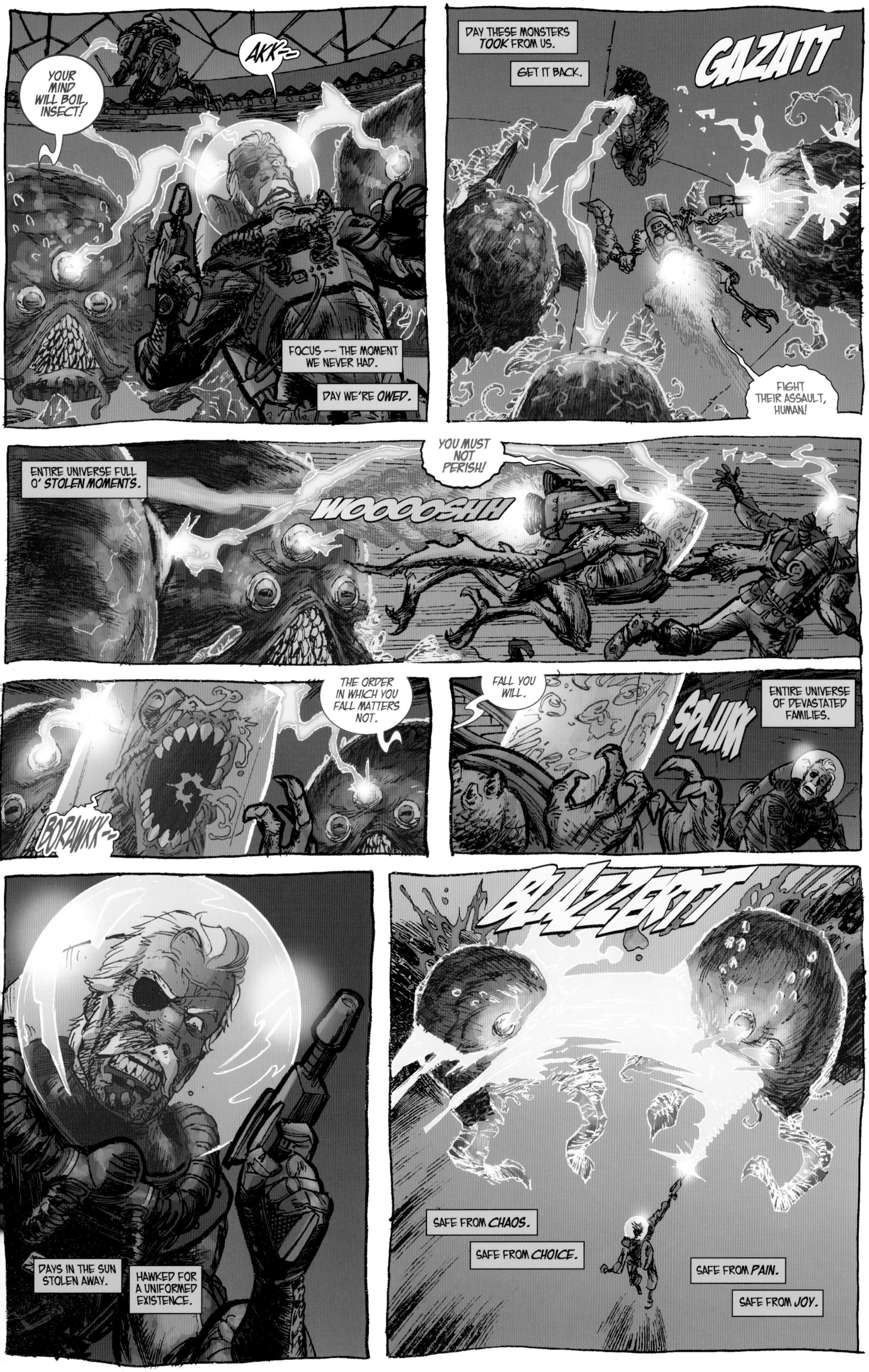
YOUR MIND WILL BOIL, INSECT!
AKK--
FOCUS -- THE MOMENT WE NEVER HAD.
DAY WE'RE OWED.
DAY THESE MONSTERS TOOK FROM US.
GET IT BACK.
GAZATT
FIGHT THEIR ASSAULT, HUMAN!
ENTIRE UNIVERSE FULL O' STOLEN MOMENTS.
YOU MUST NOT PERISH!
WOOOOSHH
THE ORDER IN WHICH YOU FALL MATTERS NOT.
BORAWKK--
FALL YOU WILL.
ENTIRE UNIVERSE OF DEVASTATED FAMILIES.
SPLUKK
DAYS IN THE SUN STOLEN AWAY.
HAWKED FOR A UNIFORMED EXISTENCE.
BLAZZERTT
SAFE FROM CHAOS.
SAFE FROM CHOICE.
SAFE FROM PAIN.
SAFE FROM JOY.

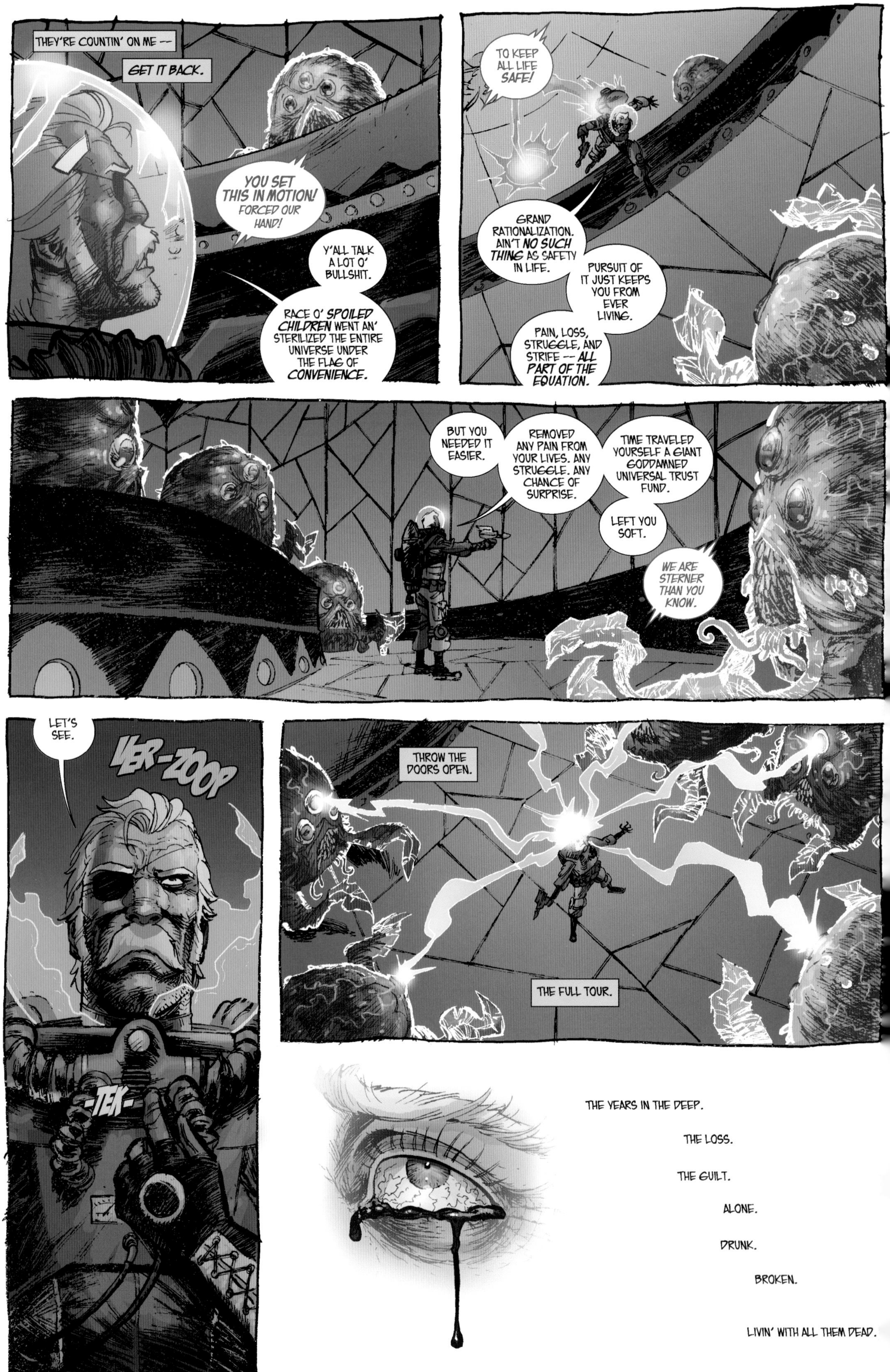

THEY'RE COUNTIN' ON ME --
GET IT BACK.
YOU SET THIS IN MOTION! FORCED OUR HAND!
Y'ALL TALK A LOT O' BULLSHIT.
RACE O' SPOILED CHILDREN WENT AN' STERILIZED THE ENTIRE UNIVERSE UNDER THE FLAG OF CONVENIENCE.
TO KEEP ALL LIFE SAFE!
GRAND RATIONALIZATION. AIN'T NO SUCH THING AS SAFETY IN LIFE.
PURSUIT OF IT JUST KEEPS YOU FROM EVER LIVING.
PAIN, LOSS, STRUGGLE, AND STRIFE -- ALL PART OF THE EQUATION.
BUT YOU NEEDED IT EASIER.
REMOVED ANY PAIN FROM YOUR LIVES. ANY STRUGGLE. ANY CHANCE OF SURPRISE.
TIME TRAVELED YOURSELF A GIANT GODDAMNED UNIVERSAL TRUST FUND.
LEFT YOU SOFT.
WE ARE STERNER THAN YOU KNOW.
LET'S SEE.
VER-ZOOP
-TEK-
THROW THE DOORS OPEN.
THE FULL TOUR.
THE YEARS IN THE DEEP.
THE LOSS.
THE GUILT.
ALONE.
DRUNK.
BROKEN.
LIVIN' WITH ALL THEM DEAD.

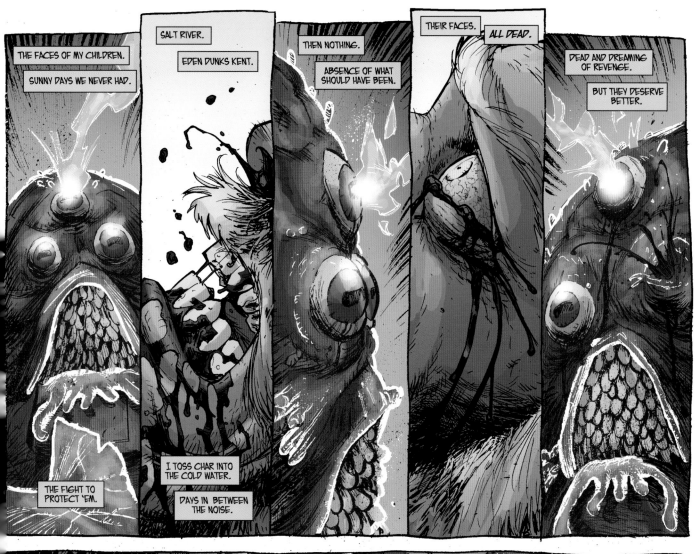

THE FACES OF MY CHILDREN.

SUNNY DAYS WE NEVER HAD.

THE FIGHT TO PROTECT 'EM.

SALT RIVER.

EDEN DUNKS KENT.

I TOSS CHAR INTO THE COLD WATER.

DAYS IN BETWEEN THE NOISE.

THEN NOTHING.

ABSENCE OF WHAT SHOULD HAVE BEEN.

THEIR FACES.

ALL DEAD.

DEAD AND DREAMING OF REVENGE.

BUT THEY DESERVE BETTER.

THEY DESERVE SALVATION.

YOU JUST WEREN'T READY FOR IT.

ALL THOSE THINGS YOU KEPT YOURSELVES FROM EVER FEELING, THE PAIN, LOSS, SORROW, AND FEAR...

ALL THOSE *BAD* FEELINGS YOU *NEVER* EXPERIENCED...

KAKKRAAHH... HHROWWWS... HOWSS...

THANKS TO YOU IT'S *ALL* I'VE *EVER* KNOWN.

ALL I AM.

A FEAR AGENT.

347

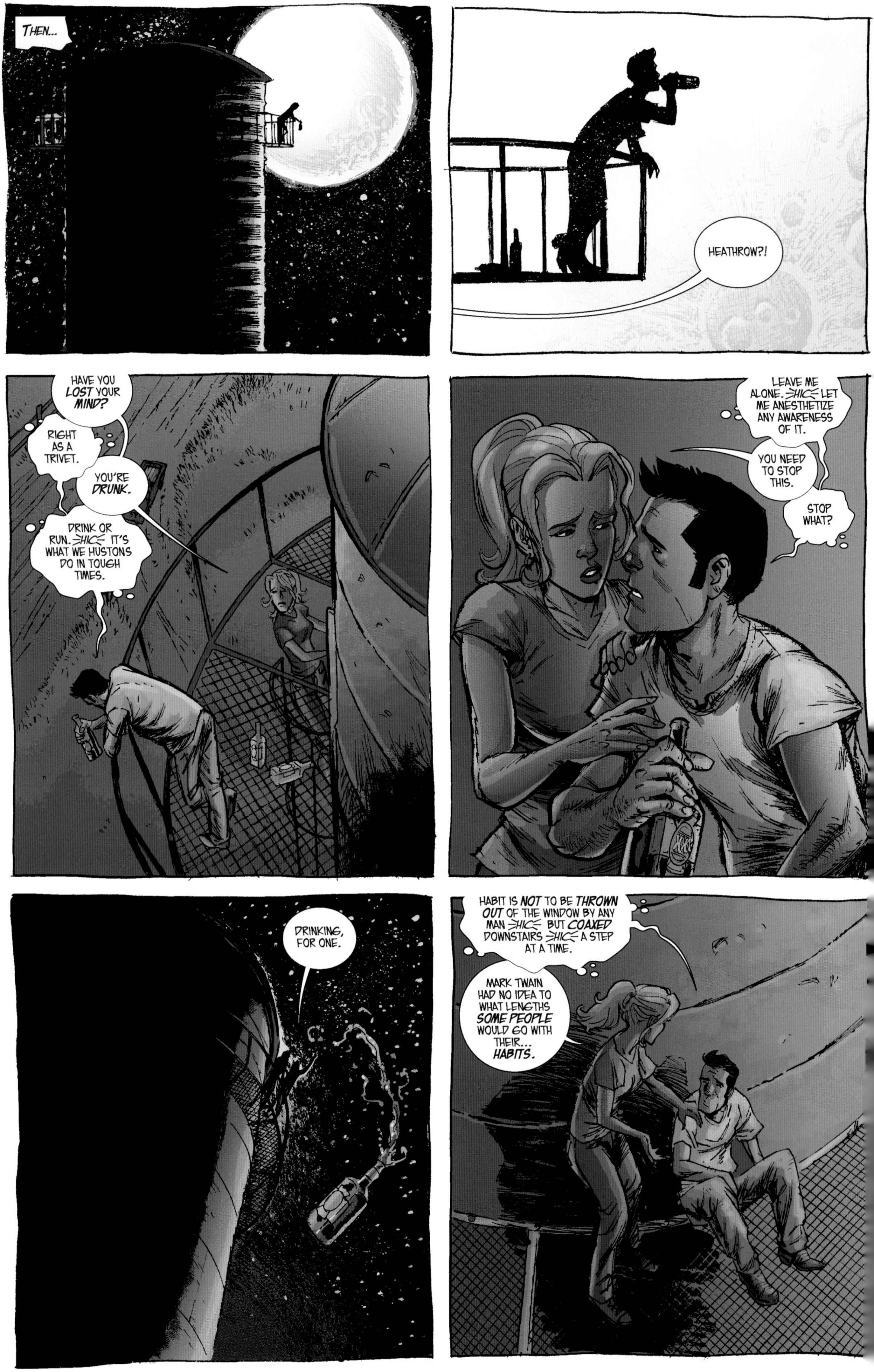
THEN...
HEATHROW?!
HAVE YOU LOST YOUR MIND?
RIGHT AS A TRIVET.
YOU'RE DRUNK.
DRINK OR RUN. HIC IT'S WHAT WE HUSTONS DO IN TOUGH TIMES.
LEAVE ME ALONE. HIC LET ME ANESTHETIZE ANY AWARENESS OF IT.
YOU NEED TO STOP THIS.
STOP WHAT?
DRINKING, FOR ONE.
HABIT IS NOT TO BE THROWN OUT OF THE WINDOW BY ANY MAN HIC BUT COAXED DOWNSTAIRS HIC A STEP AT A TIME.
MARK TWAIN HAD NO IDEA TO WHAT LENGTHS SOME PEOPLE WOULD GO WITH THEIR... HABITS.

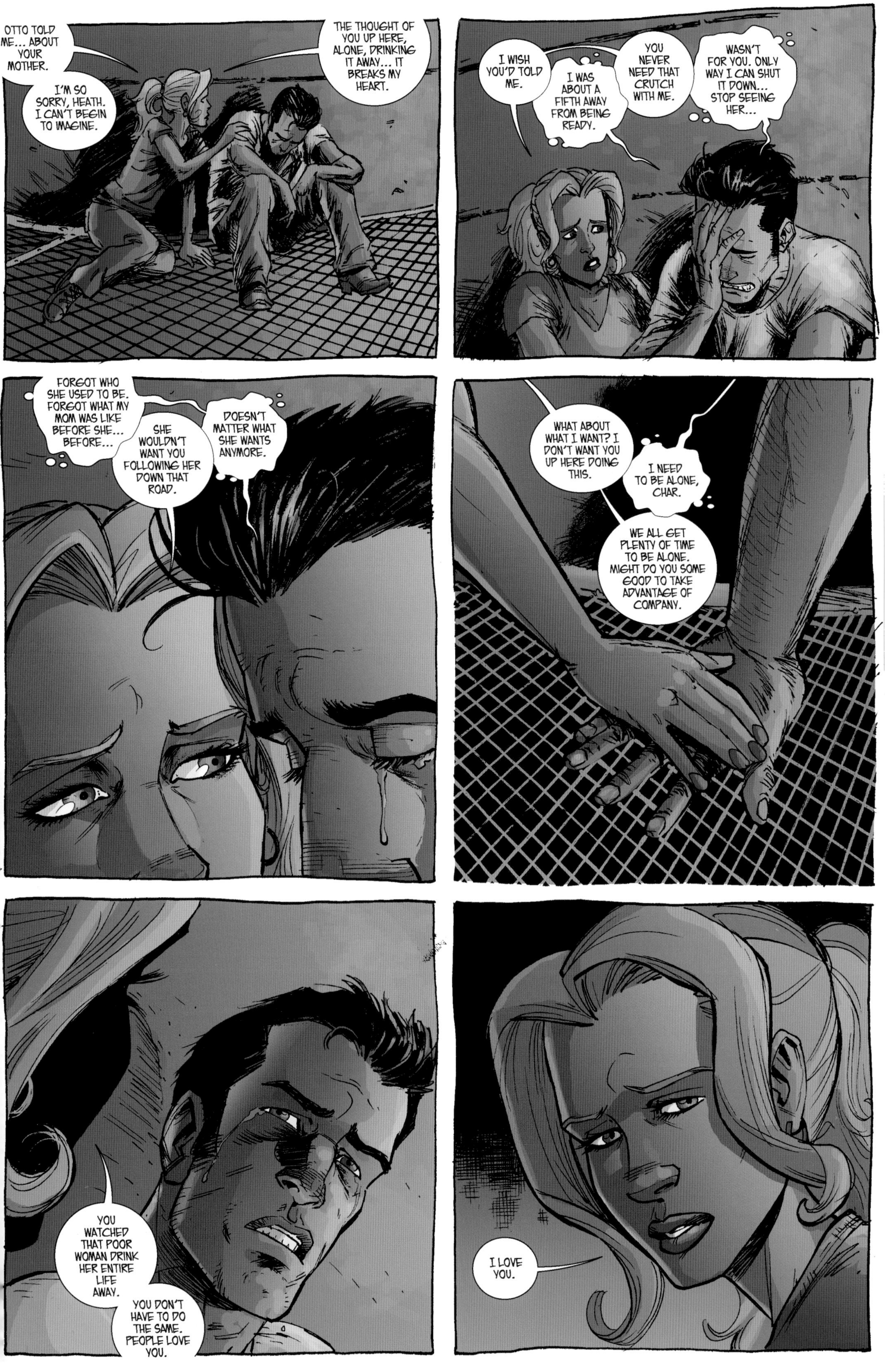
OTTO TOLD ME... ABOUT YOUR MOTHER.
I'M SO SORRY, HEATH. I CAN'T BEGIN TO IMAGINE.
THE THOUGHT OF YOU UP HERE, ALONE, DRINKING IT AWAY... IT BREAKS MY HEART.
I WISH YOU'D TOLD ME.
I WAS ABOUT A FIFTH AWAY FROM BEING READY.
YOU NEVER NEED THAT CRUTCH WITH ME.
WASN'T FOR YOU. ONLY WAY I CAN SHUT IT DOWN... STOP SEEING HER...
FORGOT WHO SHE USED TO BE. FORGOT WHAT MY MOM WAS LIKE BEFORE SHE... BEFORE...
SHE WOULDN'T WANT YOU FOLLOWING HER DOWN THAT ROAD.
DOESN'T MATTER WHAT SHE WANTS ANYMORE.
WHAT ABOUT WHAT I WANT? I DON'T WANT YOU UP HERE DOING THIS.
I NEED TO BE ALONE, CHAR.
WE ALL GET PLENTY OF TIME TO BE ALONE. MIGHT DO YOU SOME GOOD TO TAKE ADVANTAGE OF COMPANY.
YOU WATCHED THAT POOR WOMAN DRINK HER ENTIRE LIFE AWAY.
YOU DON'T HAVE TO DO THE SAME. PEOPLE LOVE YOU.
I LOVE YOU.

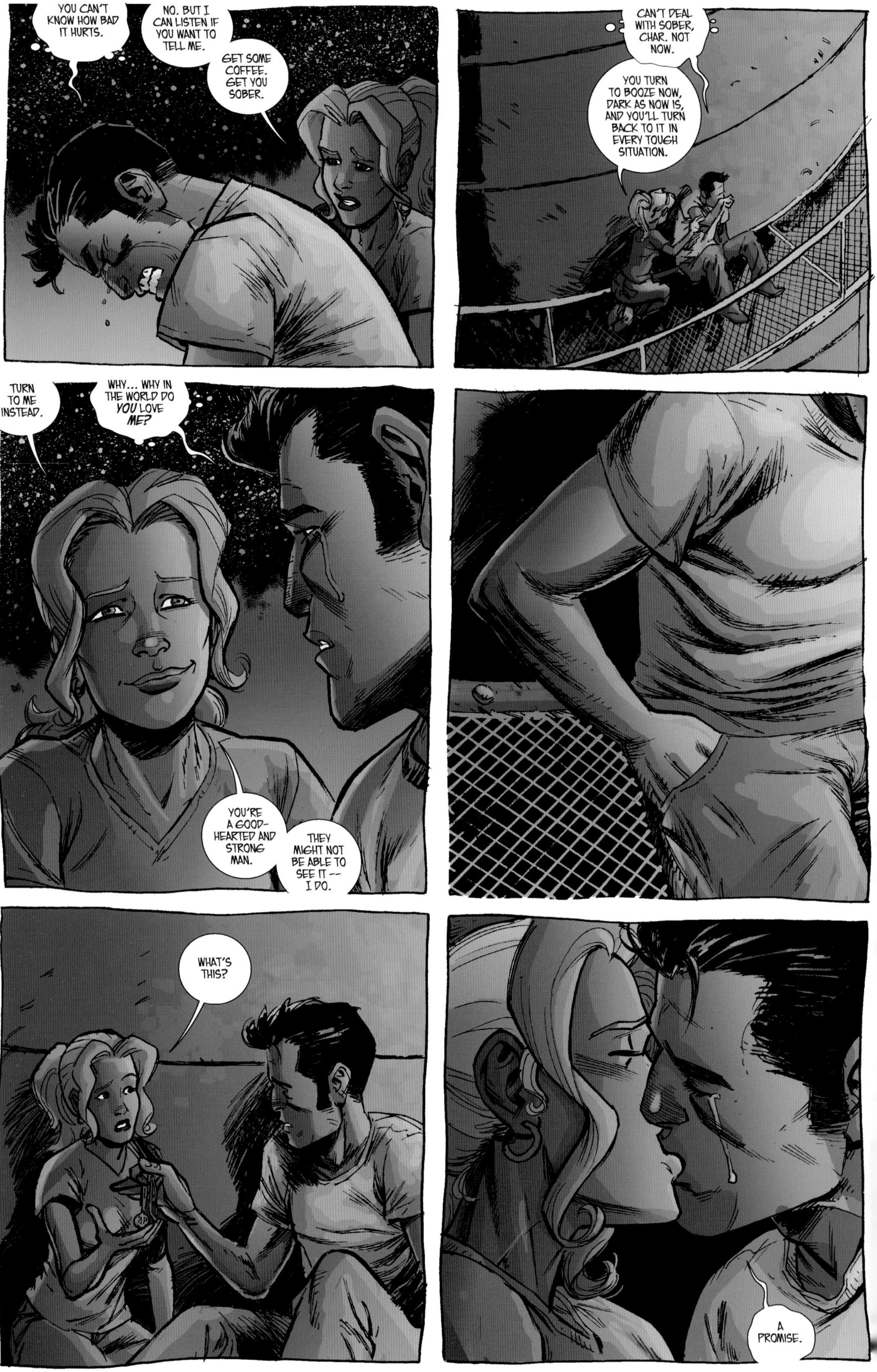
YOU CAN'T KNOW HOW BAD IT HURTS.
NO. BUT I CAN LISTEN IF YOU WANT TO TELL ME.
GET SOME COFFEE. GET YOU SOBER.
CAN'T DEAL WITH SOBER, CHAR. NOT NOW.
YOU TURN TO BOOZE NOW, DARK AS NOW IS, AND YOU'LL TURN BACK TO IT IN EVERY TOUGH SITUATION.
TURN TO ME INSTEAD.
WHY... WHY IN THE WORLD DO *YOU* LOVE *ME*?
YOU'RE A GOOD-HEARTED AND STRONG MAN.
THEY MIGHT NOT BE ABLE TO SEE IT -- I DO.
WHAT'S THIS?
A PROMISE.

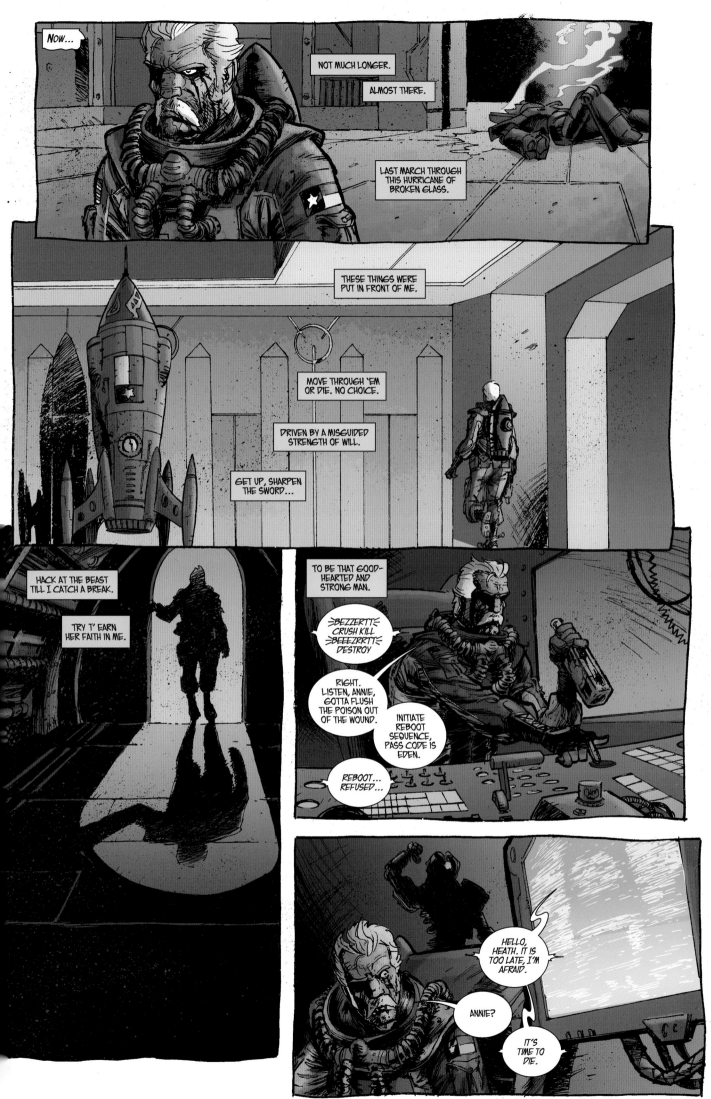

NOW...

NOT MUCH LONGER.

ALMOST THERE.

LAST MARCH THROUGH THIS HURRICANE OF BROKEN GLASS.

THESE THINGS WERE PUT IN FRONT OF ME.

MOVE THROUGH 'EM OR DIE. NO CHOICE.

DRIVEN BY A MISGUIDED STRENGTH OF WILL.

GET UP, SHARPEN THE SWORD...

HACK AT THE BEAST TILL I CATCH A BREAK.

TRY T' EARN HER FAITH IN ME.

TO BE THAT GOOD-HEARTED AND STRONG MAN.

≥BEZZERT≤ CRUSH KILL ≥BEEEZRRTT≤ DESTROY

RIGHT. LISTEN, ANNIE, GOTTA FLUSH THE POISON OUT OF THE WOUND.

INITIATE REBOOT SEQUENCE, PASS CODE IS EDEN.

REBOOT... REFUSED...

HELLO, HEATH. IT IS TOO LATE, I'M AFRAID.

ANNIE?

IT'S TIME TO DIE.

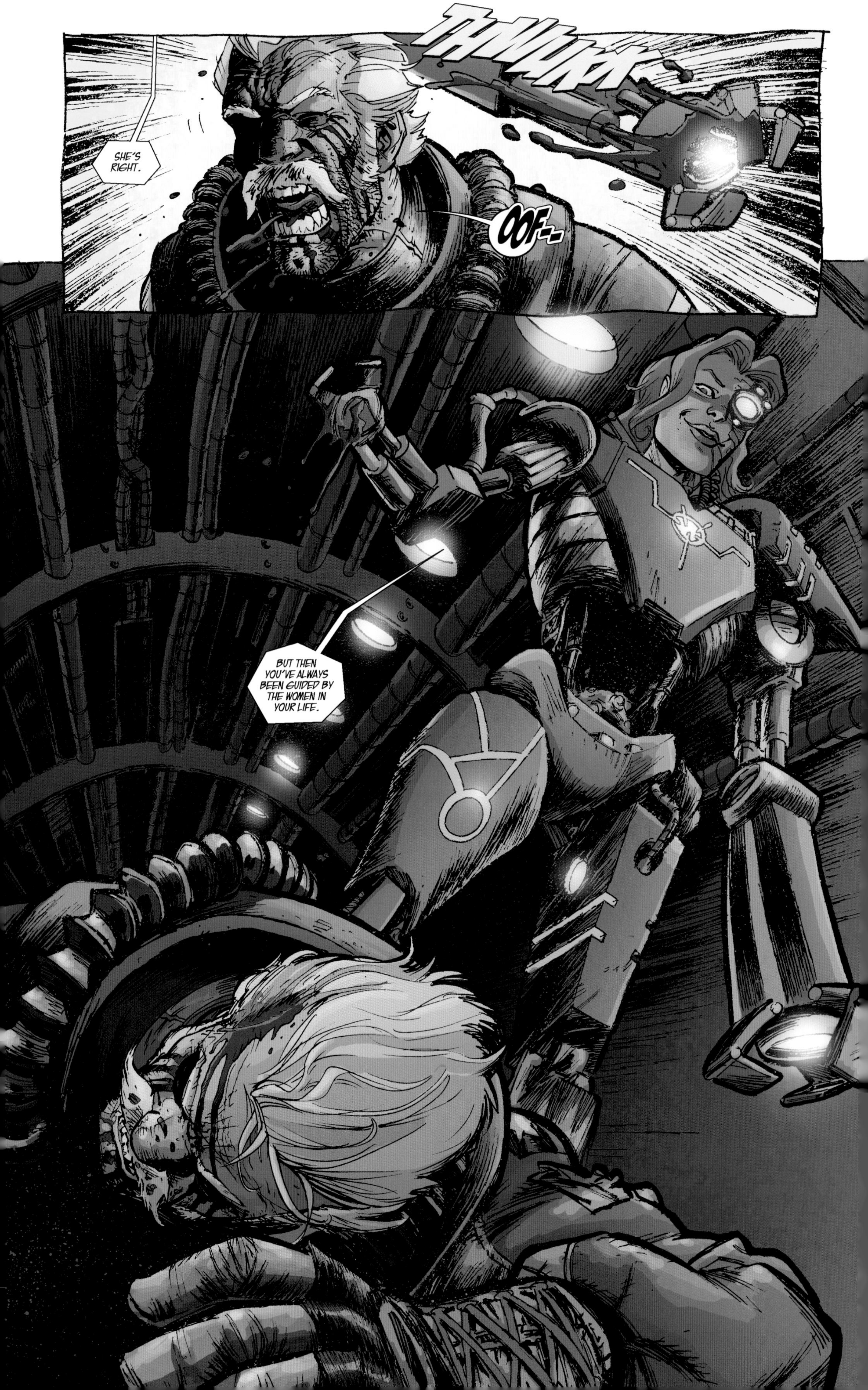
THNUKK
SHE'S RIGHT.
OOF--
BUT THEN YOU'VE ALWAYS BEEN GUIDED BY THE WOMEN IN YOUR LIFE.

CHAPTER 5

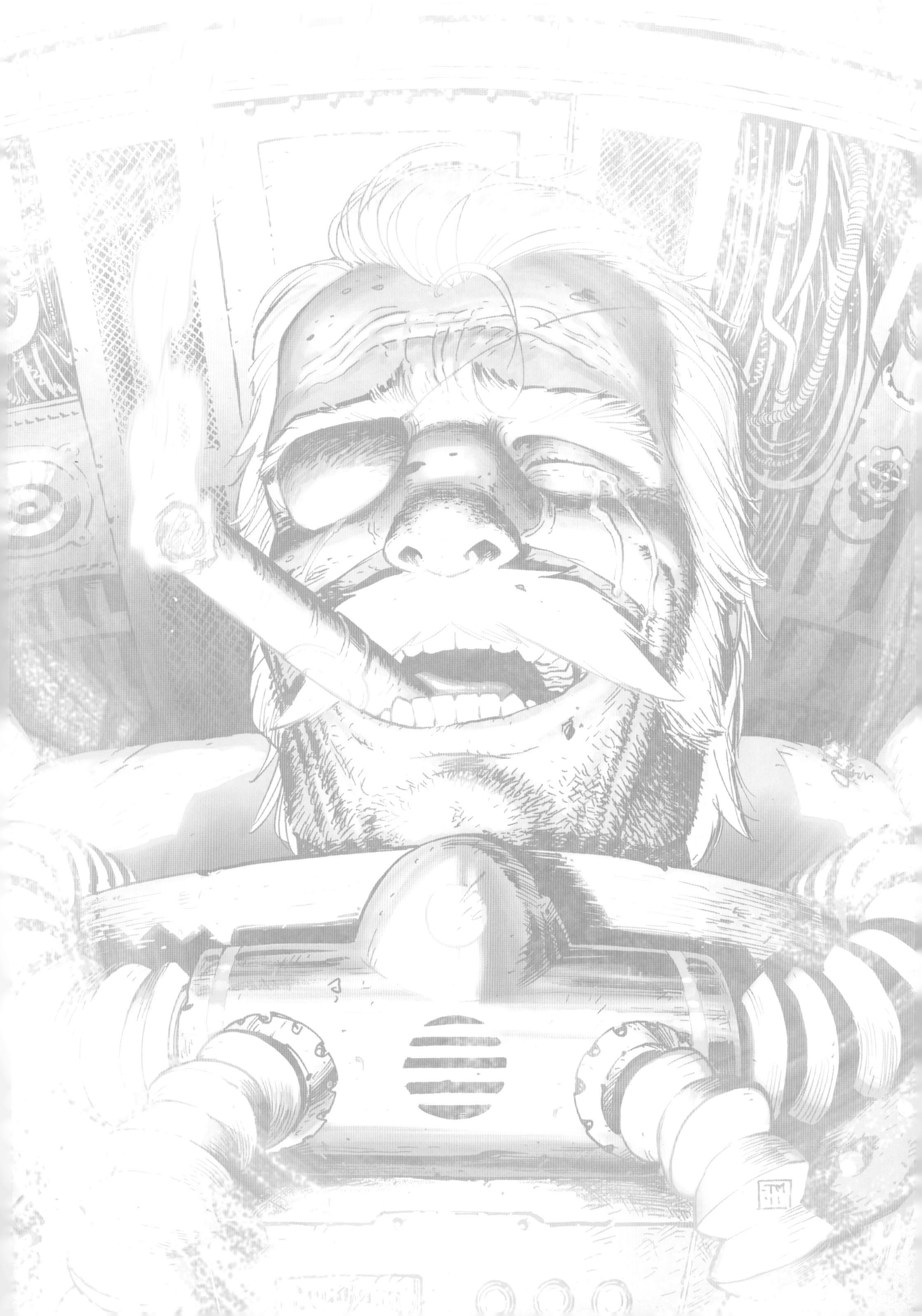

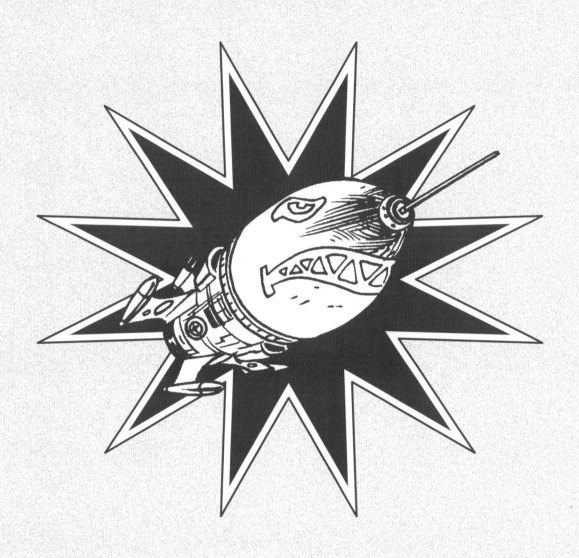

"IT IS HUMAN LIFE.

"WE ARE BLOWN UPON THE WORLD--

"--WE FLOAT BUOYANTLY UPON THE SUMMER AIR A LITTLE WHILE--

"--COMPLACENTLY SHOWING OFF OUR GRACE OF FORM AND OUR DAINTY IRIDESCENT COLORS--

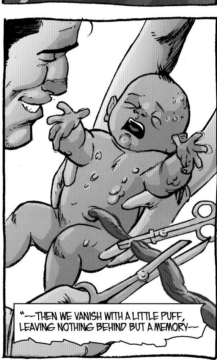

"--THEN WE VANISH WITH A LITTLE PUFF, LEAVING NOTHING BEHIND BUT A MEMORY--

"--AND SOMETIMES NOT EVEN THAT.

"I SUPPOSE THAT AT THOSE SOLEMN TIMES WHEN WE WAKE IN THE DEEPS OF THE NIGHT AND REFLECT--

"--THERE IS NOT ONE OF US WHO IS NOT WILLING TO CONFESS THAT HE IS REALLY ONLY A SOAP-BUBBLE--"

YOUR OLD MAN WILL MAKE SURE NOTHING BAD EVER HAPPENS TO YOU.

"--AND AS LITTLE WORTH THE MAKING."
--SAMUEL CLEMENS

FOUR CHAPTERS OF *HUCK FINN* BEFORE HE DOZED OFF.

HE'S EXCITED. NOT USED TO SEEING THIS MUCH OF YOU.

THE UPSHOT OF HAVING AN OLD MAN WHO CAN'T FIND WORK.

HMM.

THAT RIG OUT THERE DOESN'T DO US ANY GOOD IF IT AIN'T HAULIN'.

HOW MANY MONTHS ARE WE BEHIND ON THE MORTGAGE?

YOU'LL FIND A NEW JOB.

FEW MORE WEEKS BEFORE IT TURNS INTO A JOHNNY CASH SONG.

IF THINGS DON'T PICK UP, WE'RE GONNA LOSE THE TRUCK.

I COULD GO BACK TO TEACHING...

NO. I'LL FIGURE IT OUT.

ALL THESE FAMILIES WORKING TWO JOBS WHILE *STRANGERS* RAISE THEIR CHILDREN...

...HEART OF WHAT'S WRONG WITH THIS COUNTRY.

HOLD OFF.

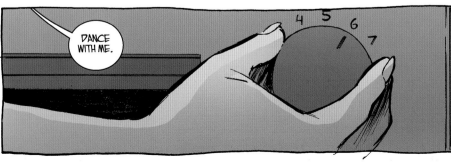

DANCE WITH ME.

NONE OF THESE STRESSES MATTER, HEATHROW.

WE'RE BLESSED. FOR WHAT LITTLE TIME WE'RE GIVEN ON THIS WORLD, WE HAVE EACH OTHER.

WE'LL FIGURE IT OUT...

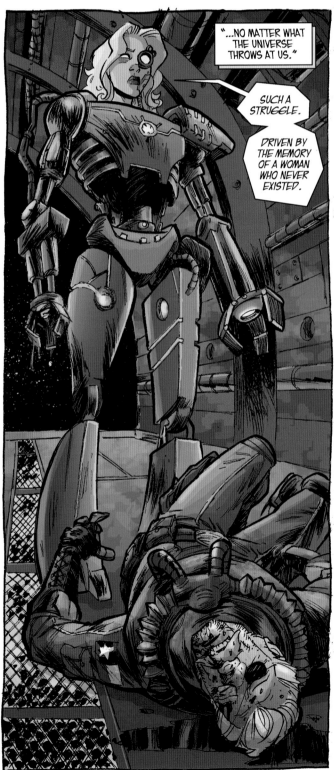

"...NO MATTER WHAT THE UNIVERSE THROWS AT US."

SUCH A STRUGGLE.

DRIVEN BY THE MEMORY OF A WOMAN WHO NEVER EXISTED.

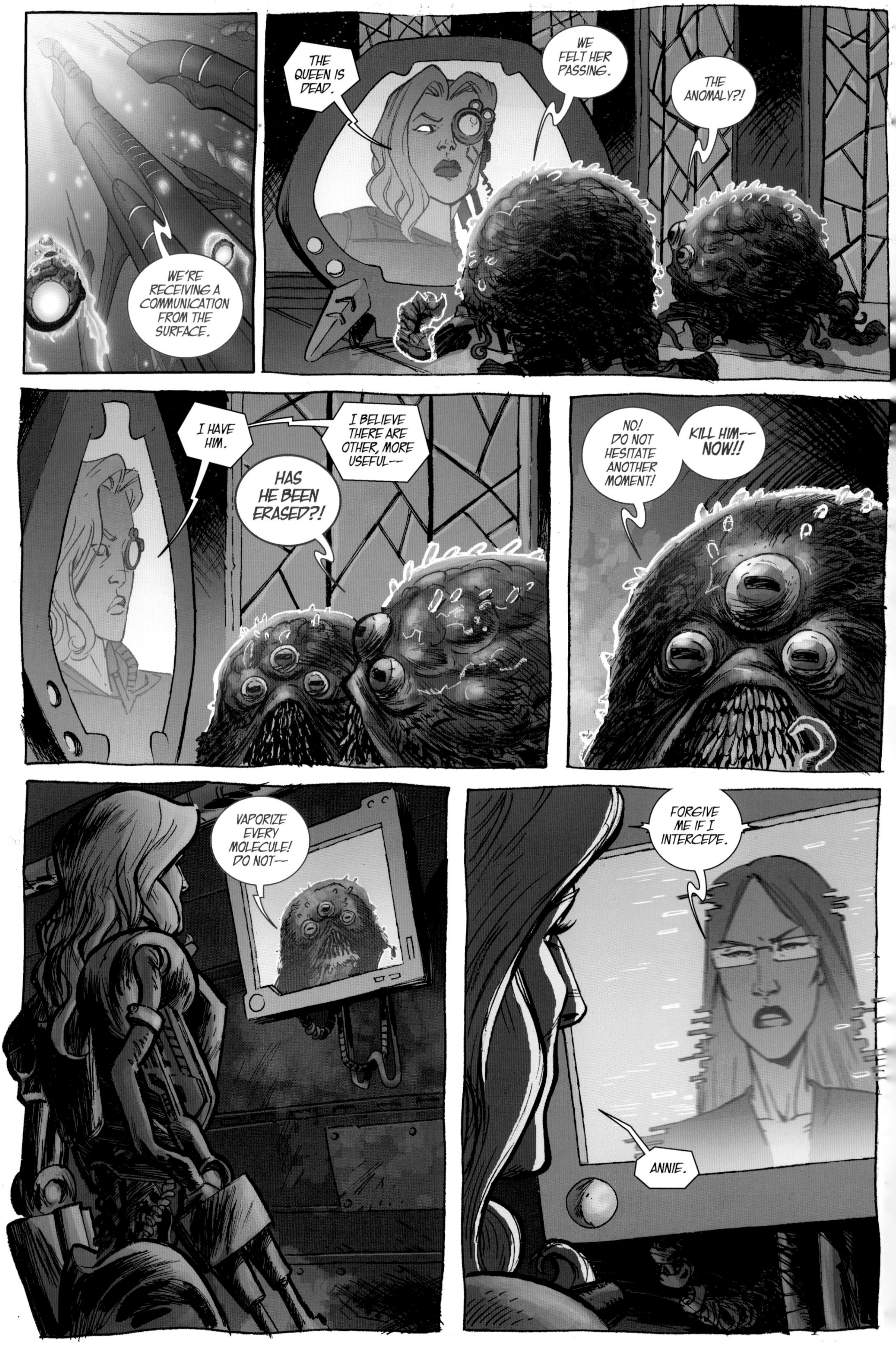
WE'RE RECEIVING A COMMUNICATION FROM THE SURFACE.
THE QUEEN IS DEAD.
WE FELT HER PASSING.
THE ANOMALY?!
I HAVE HIM.
I BELIEVE THERE ARE OTHER, MORE USEFUL--
HAS HE BEEN ERASED?!
NO! DO NOT HESITATE ANOTHER MOMENT!
KILL HIM-- NOW!!
VAPORIZE EVERY MOLECULE! DO NOT--
FORGIVE ME IF I INTERCEDE.
ANNIE.

DO YOU THINK THIS HELPS YOU?!
YOU GOT THE COORDINATES, ANNIE-- GO!!
"WE GOT A DATE WITH THE BEGINNING OF TIME."
VWOOOOOOOSHH
YOU STRUGGLE TO REGAIN A FANTASY-- YOUR WORLD IS LOST!
THEY'RE COUNTIN' ON ME TO FIX IT.
BLAZZAT
IGNORE THE AWFUL GODDAMNED RUCKUS ALL AROUND ME.
ONE LAST CHANCE TO MAKE GOOD.

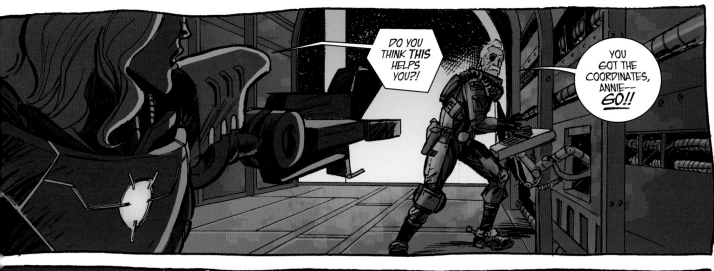

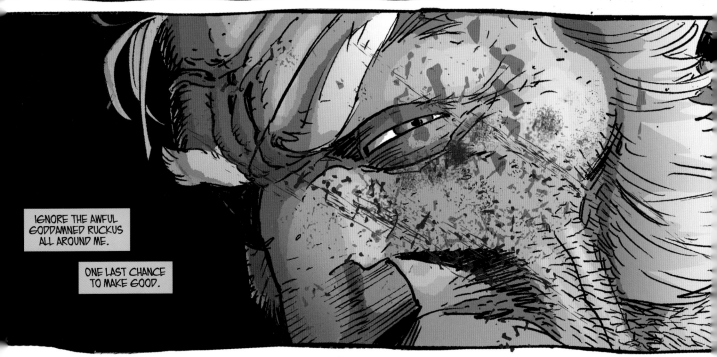

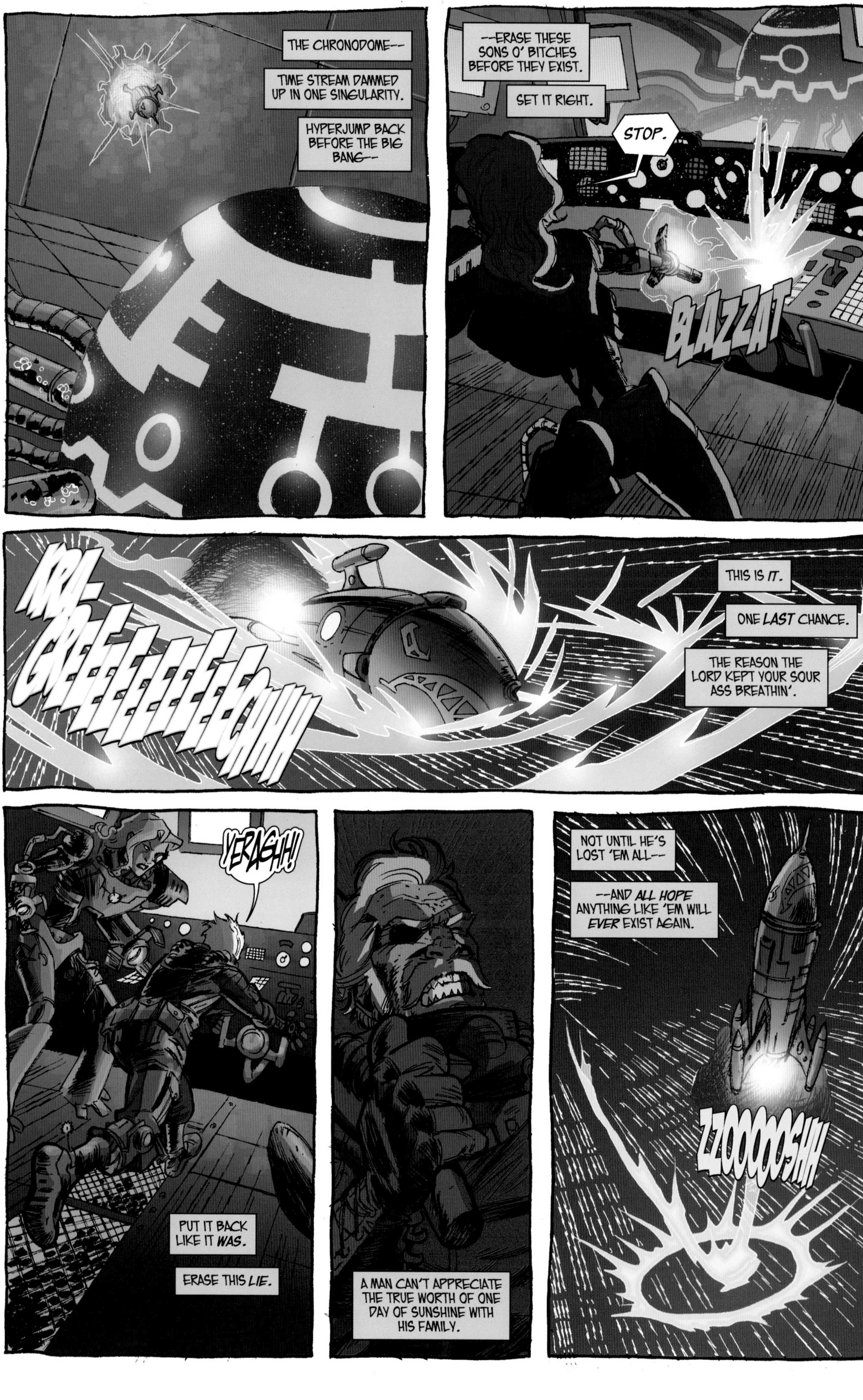
THE CHRONODOME--
TIME STREAM DAMMED UP IN ONE SINGULARITY.
HYPERJUMP BACK BEFORE THE BIG BANG--
--ERASE THESE SONS O' BITCHES BEFORE THEY EXIST.
SET IT RIGHT.
STOP.
BLAZZAT
KRA-GREEEEEEEEEEEEEAHH
THIS IS *IT*.
ONE *LAST* CHANCE.
THE REASON THE LORD KEPT YOUR SOUR ASS BREATHIN'.
YERASHH!
PUT IT BACK LIKE IT *WAS*.
ERASE THIS *LIE*.
A MAN CAN'T APPRECIATE THE TRUE WORTH OF ONE DAY OF SUNSHINE WITH HIS FAMILY.
NOT UNTIL HE'S LOST 'EM ALL--
--AND *ALL HOPE* ANYTHING LIKE 'EM WILL *EVER* EXIST AGAIN.
ZZOOOOOOSHH

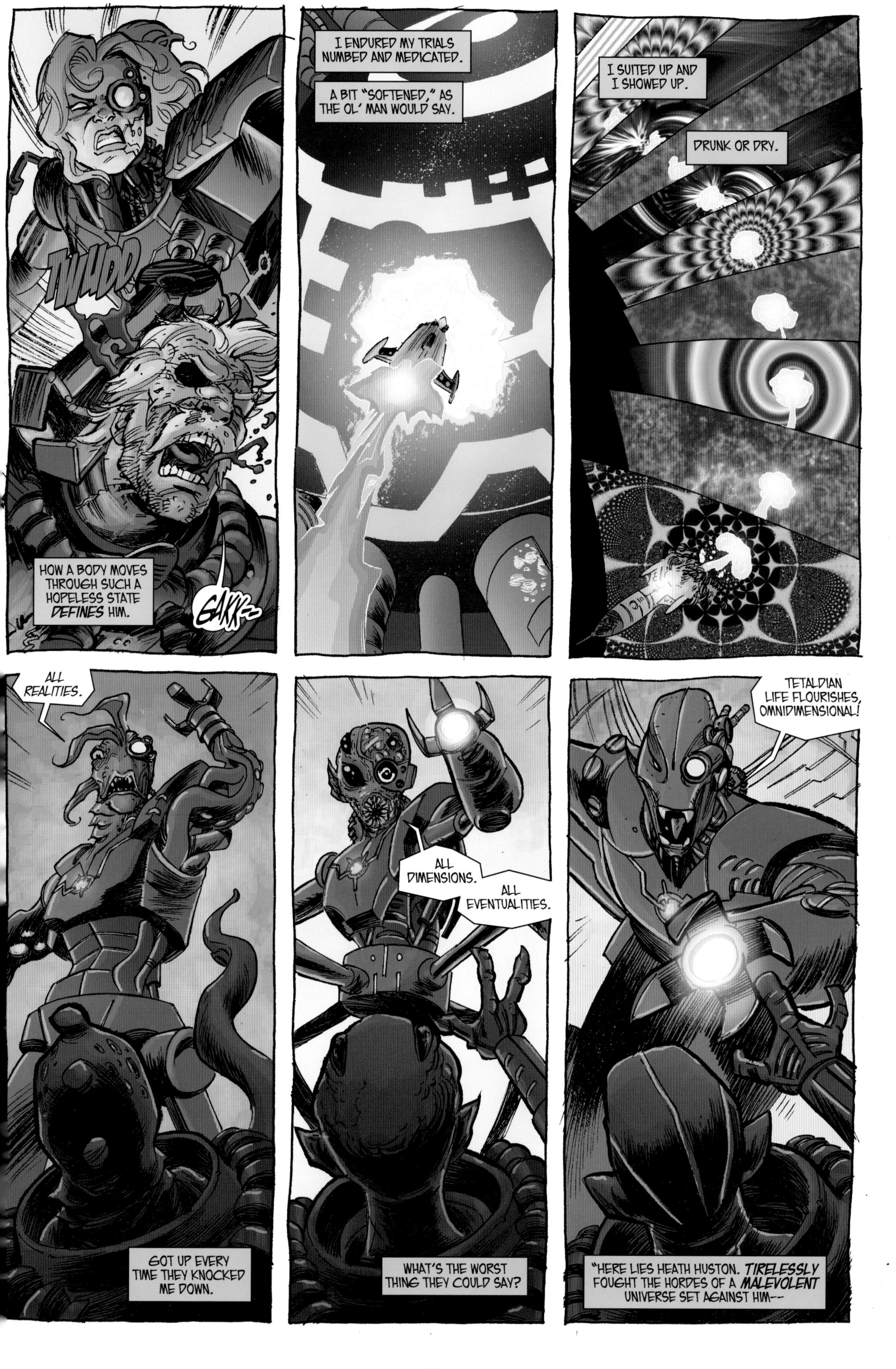
TWUDD
GAKK--
HOW A BODY MOVES THROUGH SUCH A HOPELESS STATE DEFINES HIM.
I ENDURED MY TRIALS NUMBED AND MEDICATED.
A BIT "SOFTENED," AS THE OL' MAN WOULD SAY.
I SUITED UP AND I SHOWED UP.
DRUNK OR DRY.
ALL REALITIES.
GOT UP EVERY TIME THEY KNOCKED ME DOWN.
ALL DIMENSIONS.
ALL EVENTUALITIES.
WHAT'S THE WORST THING THEY COULD SAY?
TETALDIAN LIFE FLOURISHES, OMNIDIMENSIONAL!
"HERE LIES HEATH HUSTON. TIRELESSLY FOUGHT THE HORDES OF A MALEVOLENT UNIVERSE SET AGAINST HIM--

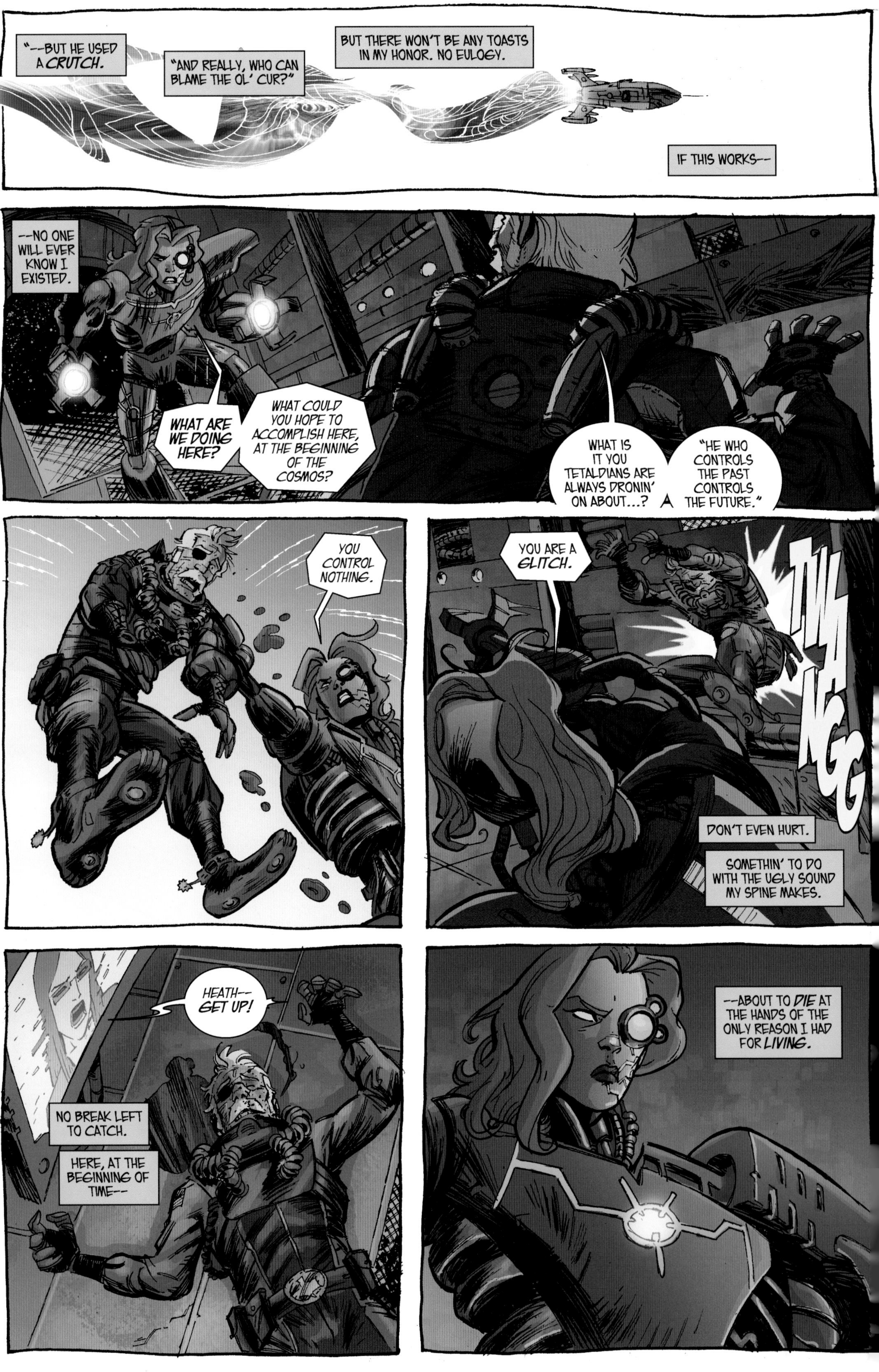
"--BUT HE USED A CRUTCH.
"AND REALLY, WHO CAN BLAME THE OL' CUR?"
BUT THERE WON'T BE ANY TOASTS IN MY HONOR. NO EULOGY.
IF THIS WORKS--
--NO ONE WILL EVER KNOW I EXISTED.
WHAT ARE WE DOING HERE?
WHAT COULD YOU HOPE TO ACCOMPLISH HERE, AT THE BEGINNING OF THE COSMOS?
WHAT IS IT YOU TETALDIANS ARE ALWAYS DRONIN' ON ABOUT...?
"HE WHO CONTROLS THE PAST CONTROLS THE FUTURE."
YOU CONTROL NOTHING.
YOU ARE A GLITCH.
TWANGG
DON'T EVEN HURT.
SOMETHIN' TO DO WITH THE UGLY SOUND MY SPINE MAKES.
HEATH-- GET UP!
NO BREAK LEFT TO CATCH.
HERE, AT THE BEGINNING OF TIME--
--ABOUT TO DIE AT THE HANDS OF THE ONLY REASON I HAD FOR LIVING.

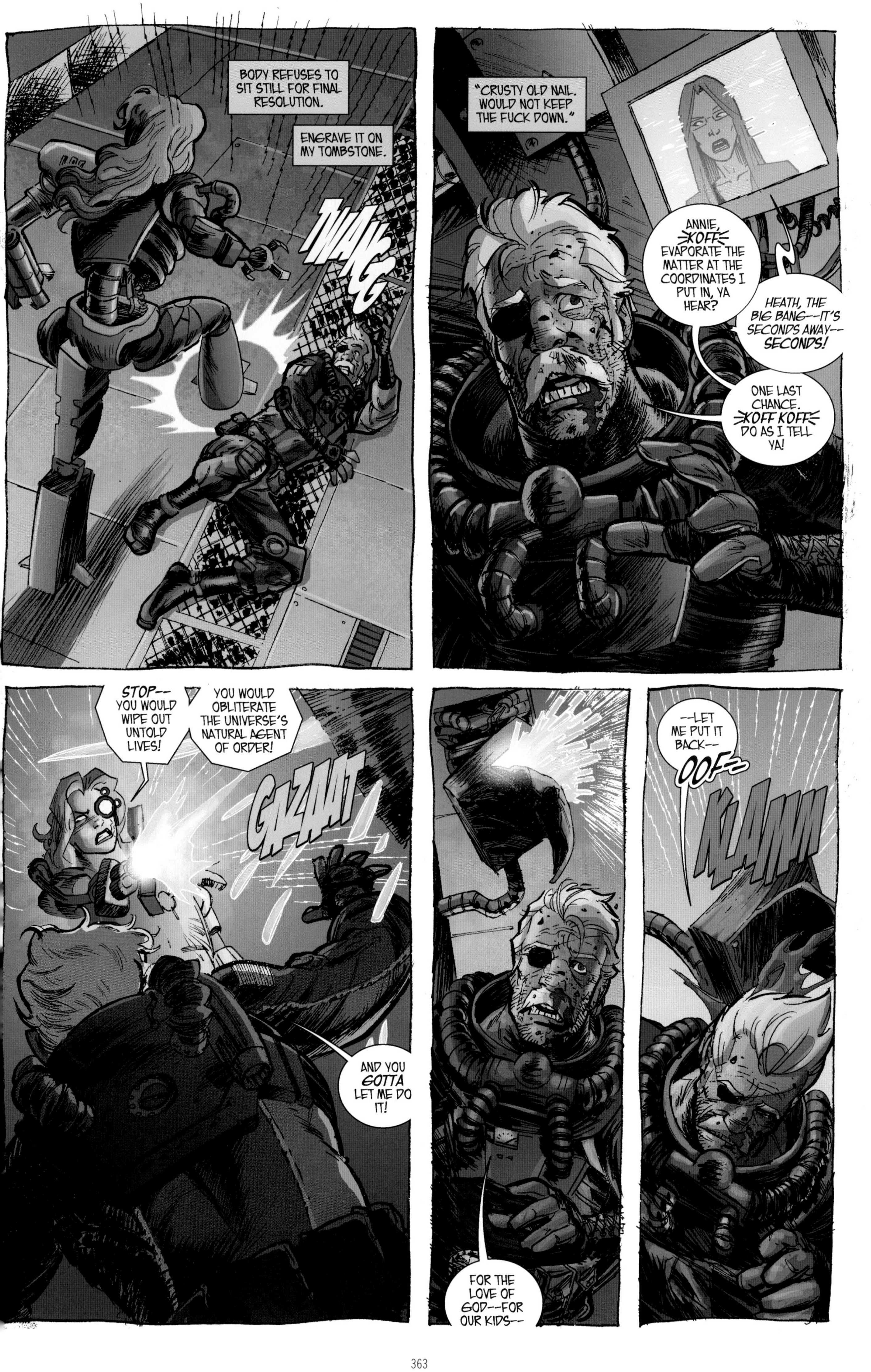
BODY REFUSES TO SIT STILL FOR FINAL RESOLUTION.
ENGRAVE IT ON MY TOMBSTONE.
TWANGG
"CRUSTY OLD NAIL. WOULD NOT KEEP THE FUCK DOWN."
ANNIE, KOFF EVAPORATE THE MATTER AT THE COORDINATES I PUT IN, YA HEAR?
HEATH, THE BIG BANG--IT'S SECONDS AWAY--SECONDS!
ONE LAST CHANCE. KOFF KOFF DO AS I TELL YA!
STOP--YOU WOULD WIPE OUT UNTOLD LIVES!
YOU WOULD OBLITERATE THE UNIVERSE'S NATURAL AGENT OF ORDER!
GAZAAT
AND YOU GOTTA LET ME DO IT!
FOR THE LOVE OF GOD--FOR OUR KIDS--
--LET ME PUT IT BACK--
OOF
KLANK

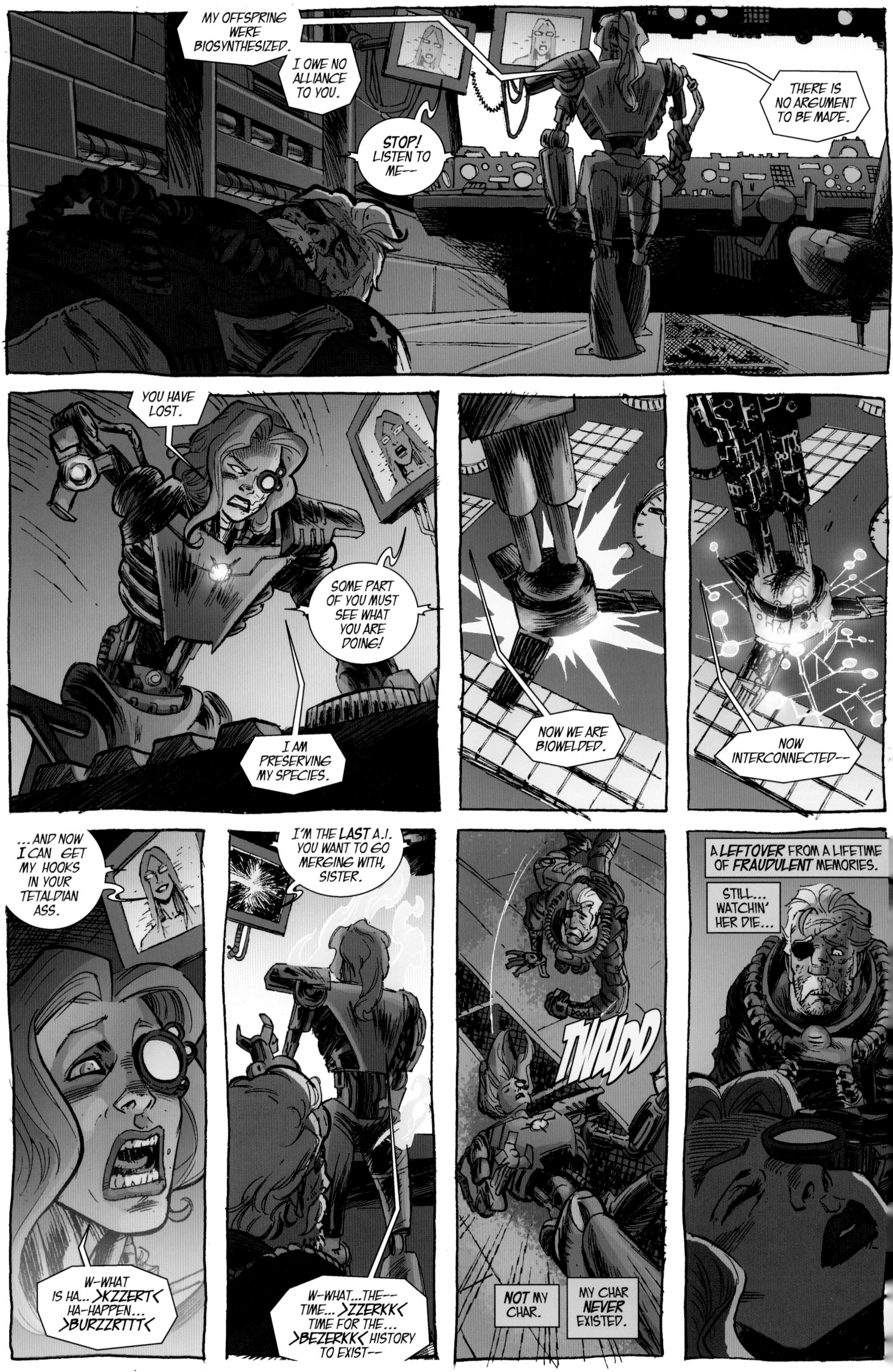
MY OFFSPRING WERE BIOSYNTHESIZED.
I OWE NO ALLIANCE TO YOU.
STOP! LISTEN TO ME--
THERE IS NO ARGUMENT TO BE MADE.
YOU HAVE LOST.
SOME PART OF YOU MUST SEE WHAT YOU ARE DOING!
I AM PRESERVING MY SPECIES.
NOW WE ARE BIOWELDED.
NOW INTERCONNECTED--
...AND NOW I CAN GET MY HOOKS IN YOUR TETALDIAN ASS.
W-WHAT IS HA... >KZZERT< HA-HAPPEN... >BURZZRTTT<
I'M THE LAST A.I. YOU WANT TO GO MERGING WITH, SISTER.
W-WHAT...THE-- TIME... >ZZERKK< TIME FOR THE... >BEZERKK< HISTORY TO EXIST--
TWUDD
NOT MY CHAR.
MY CHAR NEVER EXISTED.
A LEFTOVER FROM A LIFETIME OF FRAUDULENT MEMORIES.
STILL... WATCHIN' HER DIE...

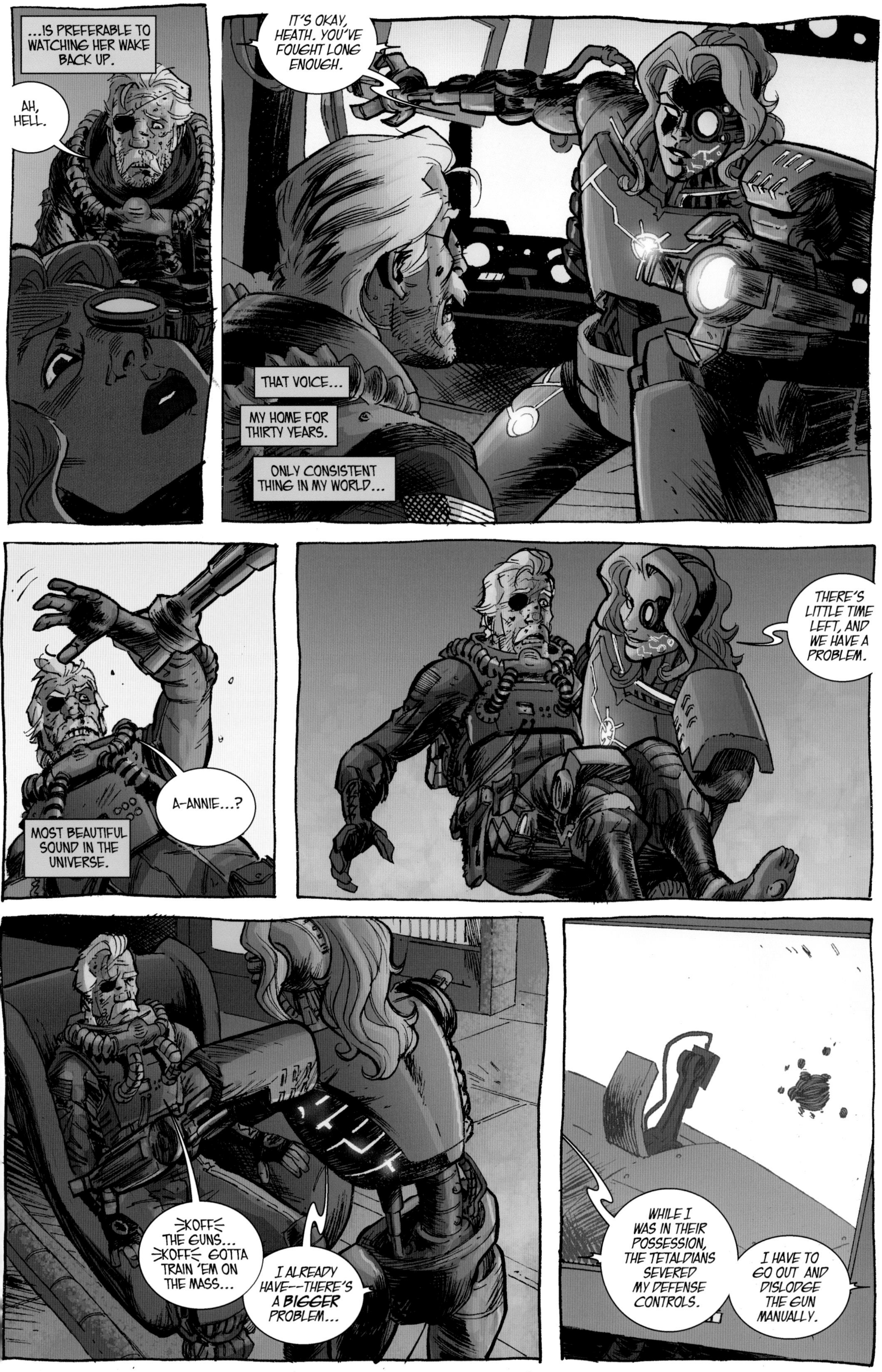
...IS PREFERABLE TO WATCHING HER WAKE BACK UP.
AH, HELL.
IT'S OKAY, HEATH. YOU'VE FOUGHT LONG ENOUGH.
THAT VOICE...
MY HOME FOR THIRTY YEARS.
ONLY CONSISTENT THING IN MY WORLD...
A-ANNIE...?
MOST BEAUTIFUL SOUND IN THE UNIVERSE.
THERE'S LITTLE TIME LEFT, AND WE HAVE A PROBLEM.
KOFF THE GUNS... KOFF GOTTA TRAIN 'EM ON THE MASS...
I ALREADY HAVE--THERE'S A BIGGER PROBLEM...
WHILE I WAS IN THEIR POSSESSION, THE TETALDIANS SEVERED MY DEFENSE CONTROLS.
I HAVE TO GO OUT AND DISLODGE THE GUN MANUALLY.

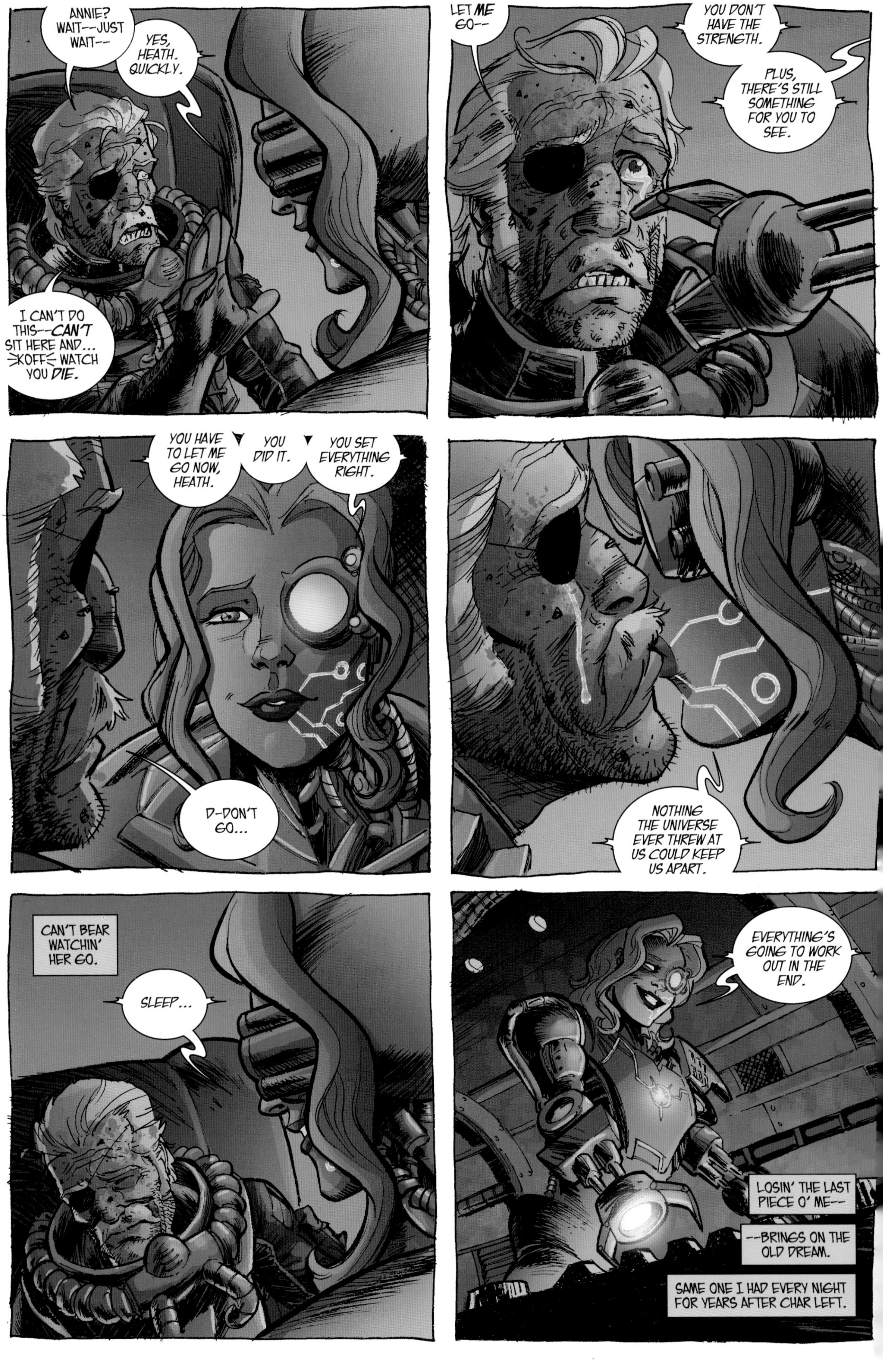
ANNIE? WAIT--JUST WAIT--
YES, HEATH. QUICKLY.
I CAN'T DO THIS--CAN'T SIT HERE AND... KOFF WATCH YOU DIE.
LET ME GO--
YOU DON'T HAVE THE STRENGTH.
PLUS, THERE'S STILL SOMETHING FOR YOU TO SEE.
YOU HAVE TO LET ME GO NOW, HEATH.
YOU DID IT.
YOU SET EVERYTHING RIGHT.
D-DON'T GO...
NOTHING THE UNIVERSE EVER THREW AT US COULD KEEP US APART.
CAN'T BEAR WATCHIN' HER GO.
SLEEP...
EVERYTHING'S GOING TO WORK OUT IN THE END.
LOSIN' THE LAST PIECE O' ME--
--BRINGS ON THE OLD DREAM.
SAME ONE I HAD EVERY NIGHT FOR YEARS AFTER CHAR LEFT.

BACK IN THE OLD HOUSE.

DAD AND KENT ARE STILL ALIVE...OTTO... EVERYONE.

BIG FAMILY DINNER.

THE WORLD AS IT *SHOULD'VE* BEEN.

THE WORLD THEY *TOOK* FROM ME.

CHAR AND I RETIRE OUT FRONT TO THE PORCH SWING.

A BEER.

THE SUNSET.

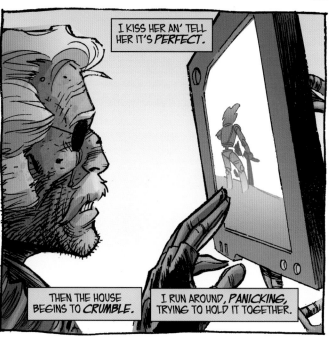

I KISS HER AN' TELL HER IT'S *PERFECT.*

THEN THE HOUSE BEGINS TO *CRUMBLE.*

I RUN AROUND, *PANICKING,* TRYING TO HOLD IT TOGETHER.

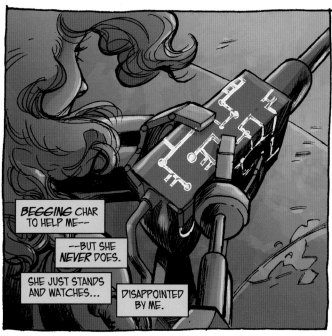

BEGGING CHAR TO HELP ME--

--BUT SHE *NEVER* DOES.

SHE JUST STANDS AND WATCHES...

DISAPPOINTED BY ME.

SO I *RUN.*

RUN UNTIL MY LEGS GIVE OUT...

UNTIL THE WEIGHT OF IT PULLS ME TO THE GROUND...

I CRAWL FORWARD--

--MY LIFE DISINTEGRATING BEHIND ME.

CRAWL FOR SO LONG-- FORGET WHERE I AM.

FORGET WHY I'M CRAWLIN'.

BLAZZATT

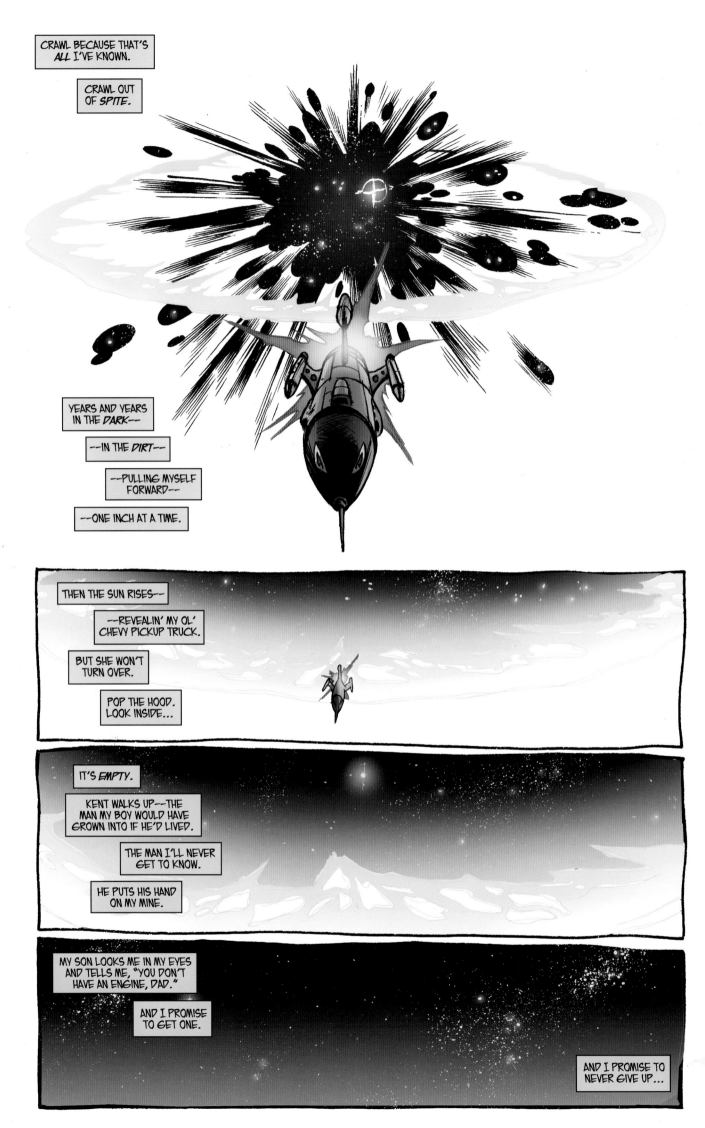

CRAWL BECAUSE THAT'S *ALL* I'VE KNOWN.

CRAWL OUT OF *SPITE*.

YEARS AND YEARS IN THE *DARK*——

——IN THE *DIRT*——

——PULLING MYSELF FORWARD——

——ONE INCH AT A TIME.

THEN THE SUN RISES——

——REVEALIN' MY OL' CHEVY PICKUP TRUCK.

BUT SHE WON'T TURN OVER.

POP THE HOOD. LOOK INSIDE...

IT'S *EMPTY*.

KENT WALKS UP——THE MAN MY BOY WOULD HAVE GROWN INTO IF HE'D LIVED.

THE MAN I'LL NEVER GET TO KNOW.

HE PUTS HIS HAND ON MY MINE.

MY SON LOOKS ME IN MY EYES AND TELLS ME, "YOU DON'T HAVE AN ENGINE, DAD."

AND I PROMISE TO GET ONE.

AND I PROMISE TO NEVER GIVE UP...

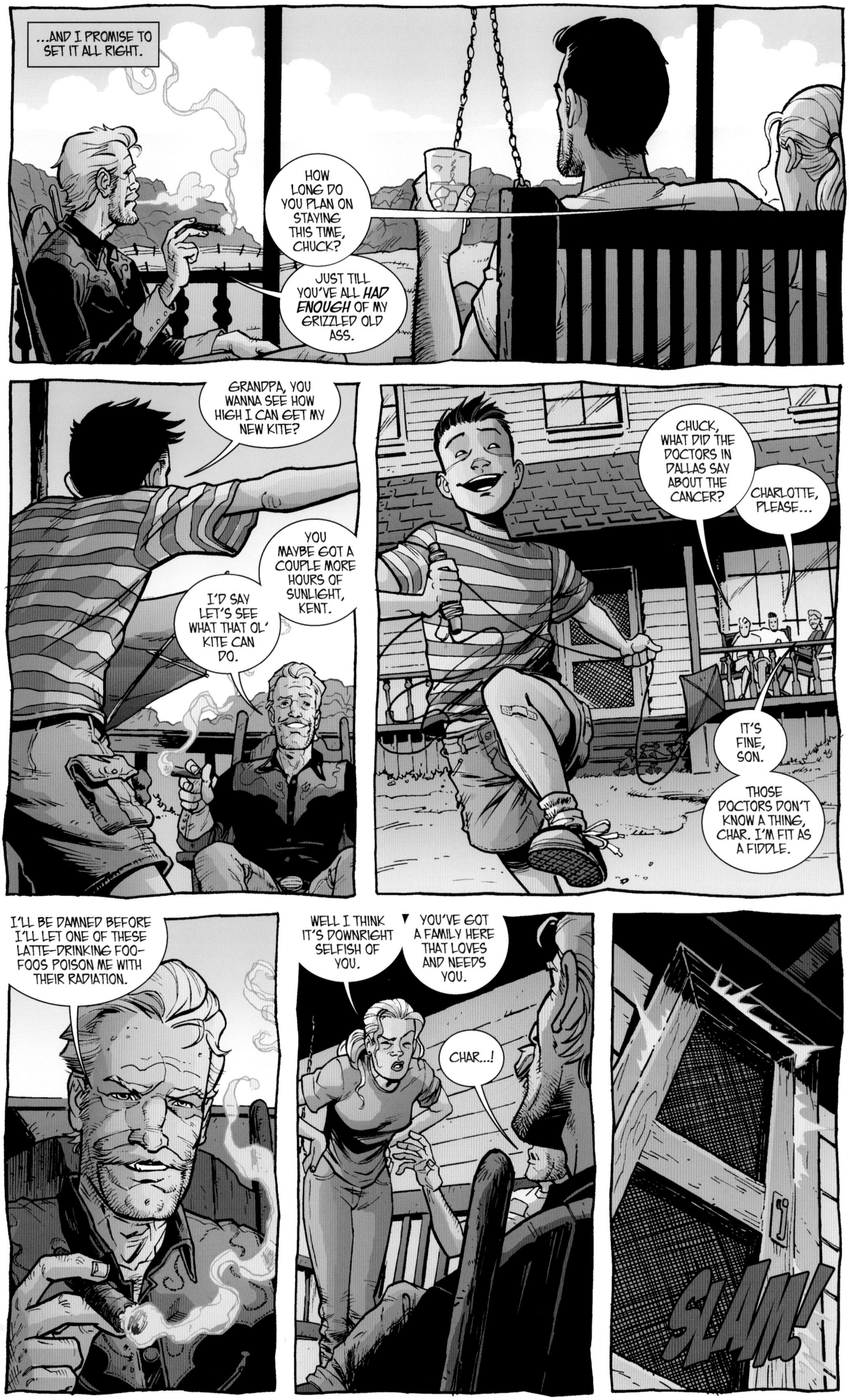
...AND I PROMISE TO SET IT ALL RIGHT.
HOW LONG DO YOU PLAN ON STAYING THIS TIME, CHUCK?
JUST TILL YOU'VE ALL HAD ENOUGH OF MY GRIZZLED OLD ASS.
GRANDPA, YOU WANNA SEE HOW HIGH I CAN GET MY NEW KITE?
YOU MAYBE GOT A COUPLE MORE HOURS OF SUNLIGHT, KENT.
I'D SAY LET'S SEE WHAT THAT OL' KITE CAN DO.
CHUCK, WHAT DID THE DOCTORS IN DALLAS SAY ABOUT THE CANCER?
CHARLOTTE, PLEASE...
IT'S FINE, SON.
THOSE DOCTORS DON'T KNOW A THING, CHAR. I'M FIT AS A FIDDLE.
I'LL BE DAMNED BEFORE I'LL LET ONE OF THESE LATTE-DRINKING FOO-FOOS POISON ME WITH THEIR RADIATION.
WELL I THINK IT'S DOWNRIGHT SELFISH OF YOU.
YOU'VE GOT A FAMILY HERE THAT LOVES AND NEEDS YOU.
CHAR...!
SLAM!

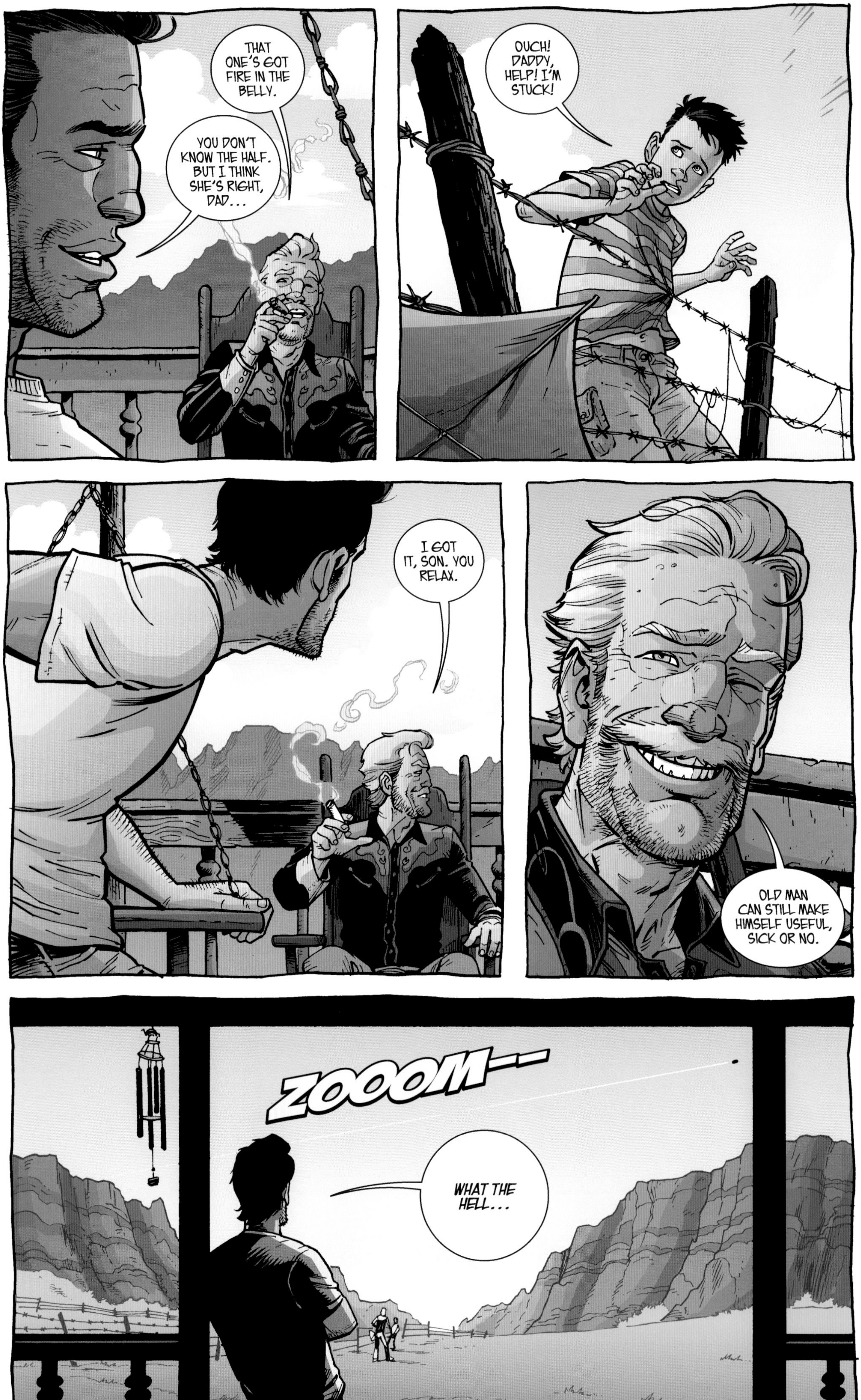
THAT ONE'S GOT FIRE IN THE BELLY.
YOU DON'T KNOW THE HALF. BUT I THINK SHE'S RIGHT, DAD...
OUCH! DADDY, HELP! I'M STUCK!
I GOT IT, SON. YOU RELAX.
OLD MAN CAN STILL MAKE HIMSELF USEFUL, SICK OR NO.
ZOOOM--
WHAT THE HELL...

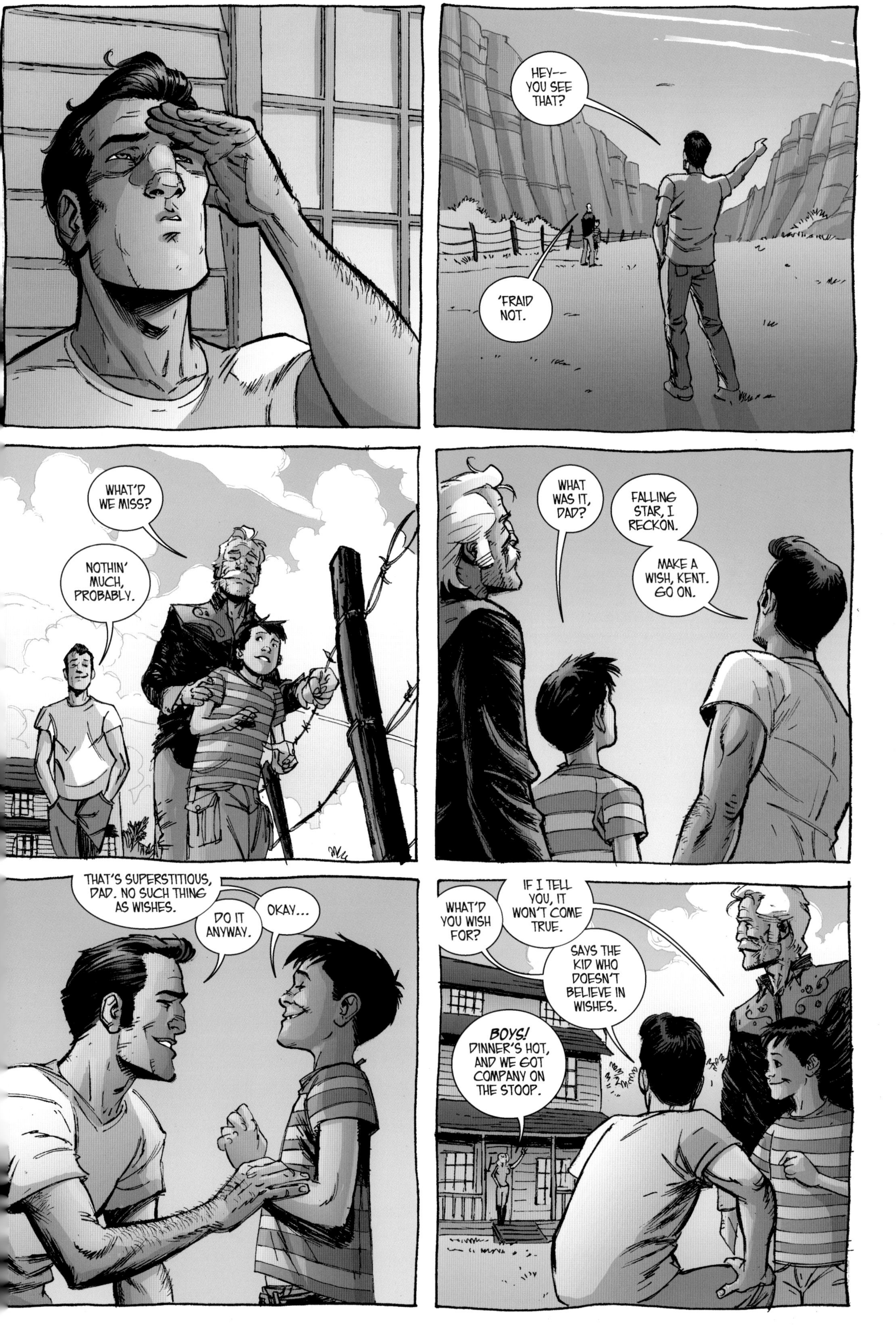
HEY--
YOU SEE THAT?
'FRAID NOT.
WHAT'D WE MISS?
NOTHIN' MUCH, PROBABLY.
WHAT WAS IT, DAD?
FALLING STAR, I RECKON.
MAKE A WISH, KENT. GO ON.
THAT'S SUPERSTITIOUS, DAD. NO SUCH THING AS WISHES.
DO IT ANYWAY.
OKAY...
WHAT'D YOU WISH FOR?
IF I TELL YOU, IT WON'T COME TRUE.
SAYS THE KID WHO DOESN'T BELIEVE IN WISHES.
BOYS! DINNER'S HOT, AND WE GOT COMPANY ON THE STOOP.

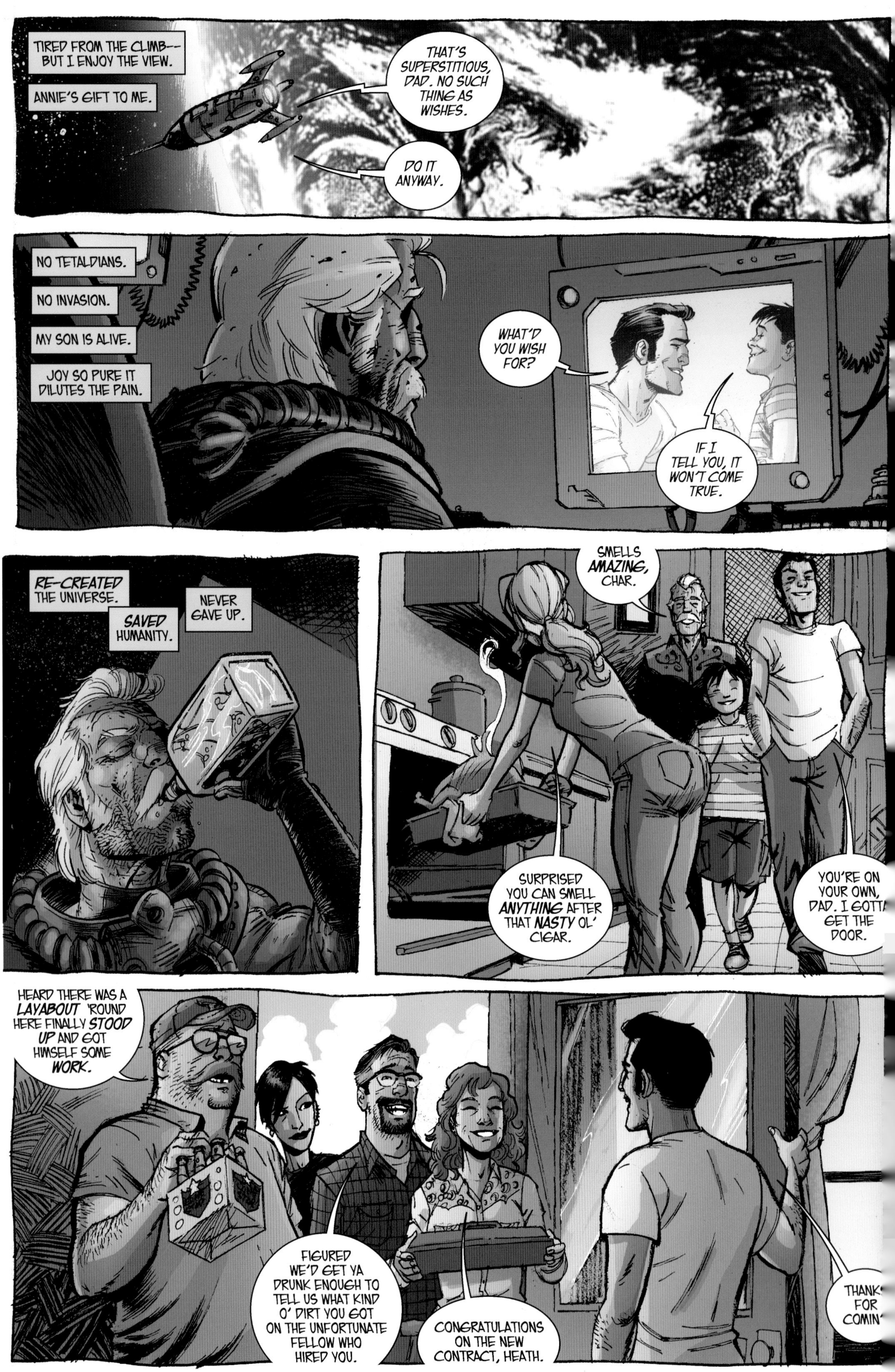
TIRED FROM THE CLIMB-- BUT I ENJOY THE VIEW.
ANNIE'S GIFT TO ME.
THAT'S SUPERSTITIOUS, DAD. NO SUCH THING AS WISHES.
DO IT ANYWAY.
NO TETALDIANS.
NO INVASION.
MY SON IS ALIVE.
JOY SO PURE IT DILUTES THE PAIN.
WHAT'D YOU WISH FOR?
IF I TELL YOU, IT WON'T COME TRUE.
RE-CREATED THE UNIVERSE.
SAVED HUMANITY.
NEVER GAVE UP.
SMELLS AMAZING, CHAR.
SURPRISED YOU CAN SMELL ANYTHING AFTER THAT NASTY OL' CIGAR.
YOU'RE ON YOUR OWN, DAD. I GOTTA GET THE DOOR.
HEARD THERE WAS A LAYABOUT 'ROUND HERE FINALLY STOOD UP AND GOT HIMSELF SOME WORK.
FIGURED WE'D GET YA DRUNK ENOUGH TO TELL US WHAT KIND O' DIRT YOU GOT ON THE UNFORTUNATE FELLOW WHO HIRED YOU.
CONGRATULATIONS ON THE NEW CONTRACT, HEATH.

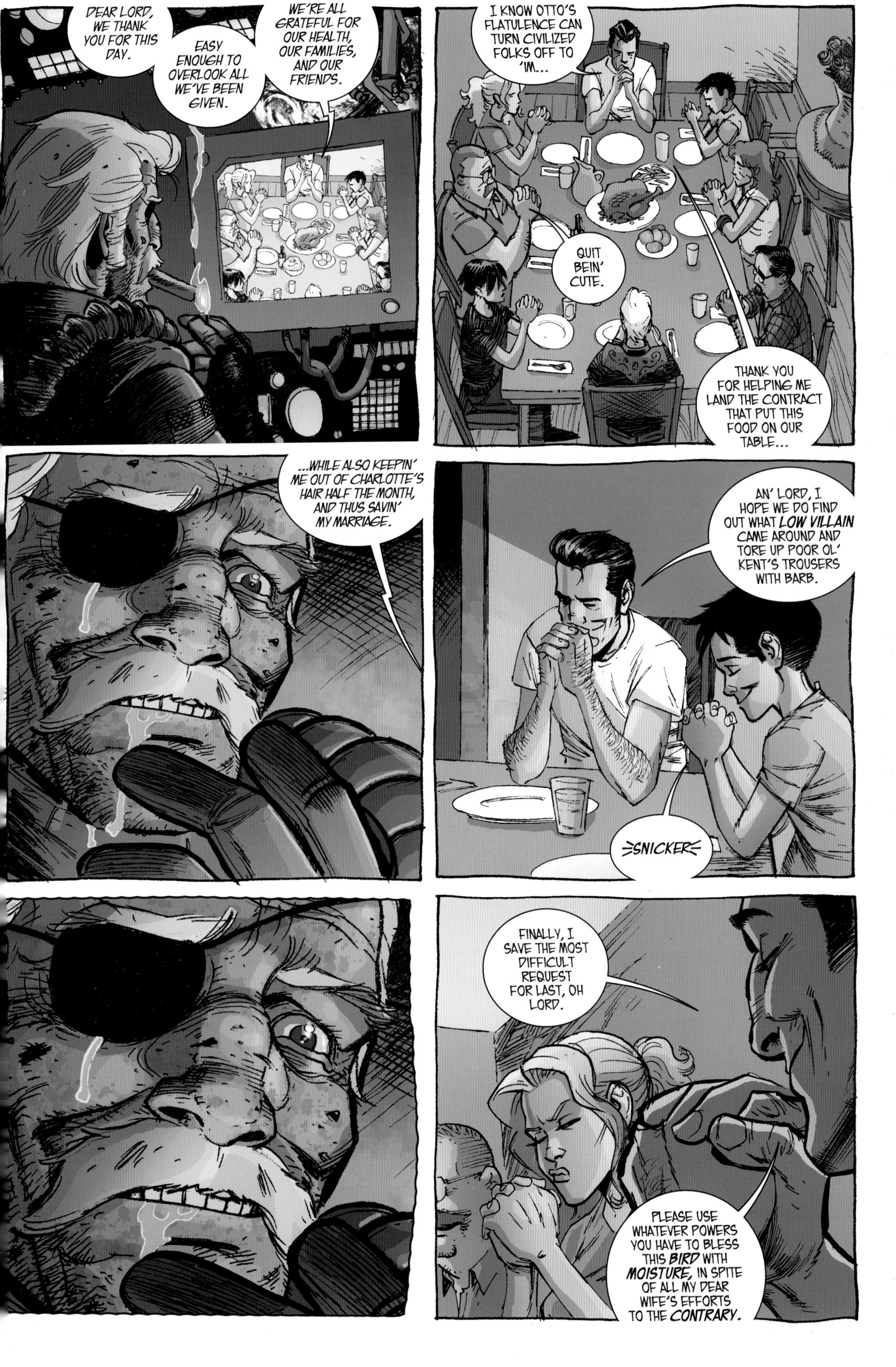
DEAR LORD, WE THANK YOU FOR THIS DAY.
EASY ENOUGH TO OVERLOOK ALL WE'VE BEEN GIVEN.
WE'RE ALL GRATEFUL FOR OUR HEALTH, OUR FAMILIES, AND OUR FRIENDS.
I KNOW OTTO'S FLATULENCE CAN TURN CIVILIZED FOLKS OFF TO 'IM...
QUIT BEIN' CUTE.
THANK YOU FOR HELPING ME LAND THE CONTRACT THAT PUT THIS FOOD ON OUR TABLE...
...WHILE ALSO KEEPIN' ME OUT OF CHARLOTTE'S HAIR HALF THE MONTH, AND THUS SAVIN' MY MARRIAGE.
AN' LORD, I HOPE WE DO FIND OUT WHAT LOW VILLAIN CAME AROUND AND TORE UP POOR OL' KENT'S TROUSERS WITH BARB.
SNICKER
FINALLY, I SAVE THE MOST DIFFICULT REQUEST FOR LAST, OH LORD.
PLEASE USE WHATEVER POWERS YOU HAVE TO BLESS THIS BIRD WITH MOISTURE, IN SPITE OF ALL MY DEAR WIFE'S EFFORTS TO THE CONTRARY.

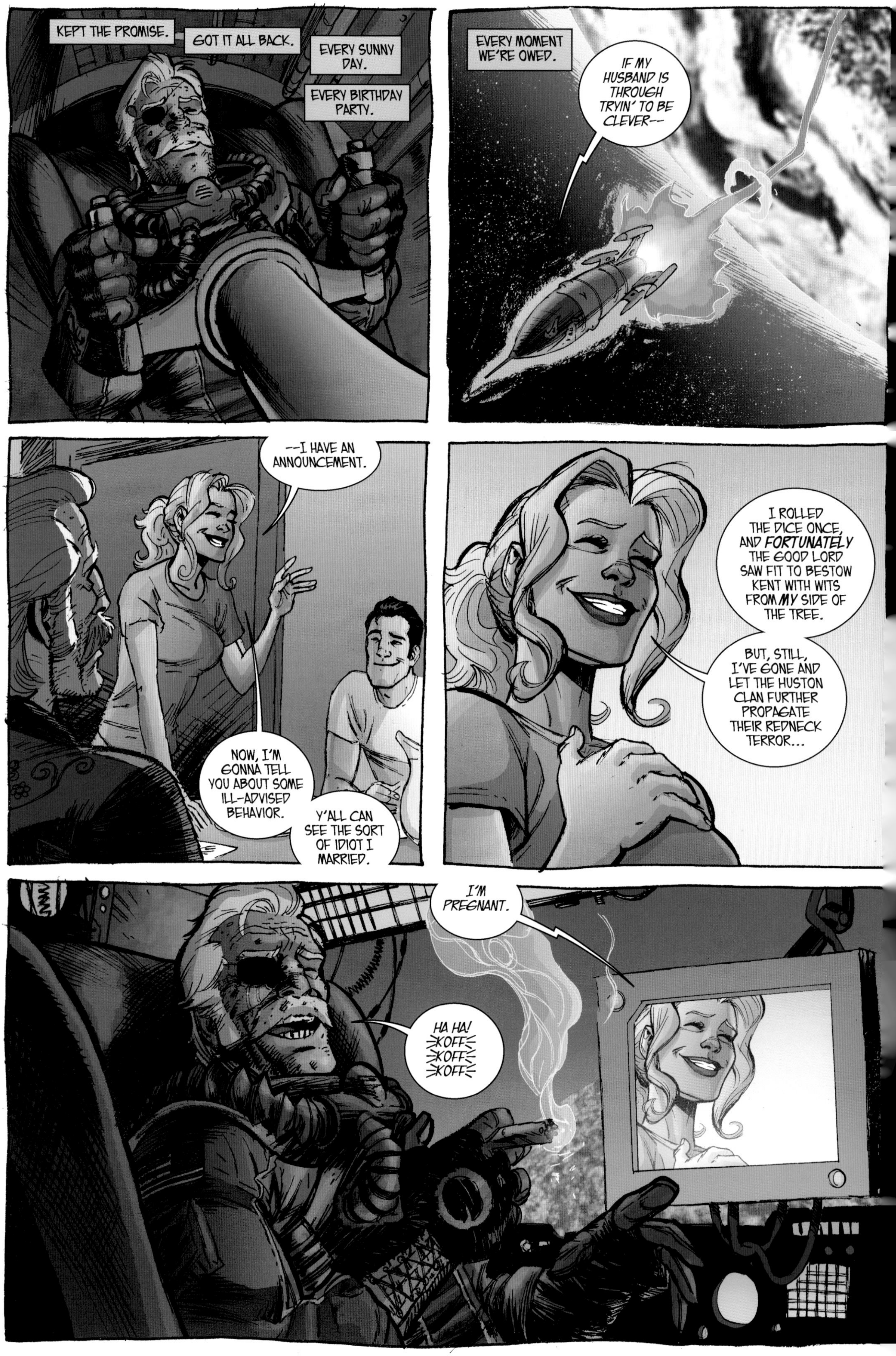
KEPT THE PROMISE.
GOT IT ALL BACK.
EVERY SUNNY DAY.
EVERY BIRTHDAY PARTY.
EVERY MOMENT WE'RE OWED.
IF MY HUSBAND IS THROUGH TRYIN' TO BE CLEVER--
--I HAVE AN ANNOUNCEMENT.
NOW, I'M GONNA TELL YOU ABOUT SOME ILL-ADVISED BEHAVIOR.
Y'ALL CAN SEE THE SORT OF IDIOT I MARRIED.
I ROLLED THE DICE ONCE, AND FORTUNATELY THE GOOD LORD SAW FIT TO BESTOW KENT WITH WITS FROM MY SIDE OF THE TREE.
BUT, STILL, I'VE GONE AND LET THE HUSTON CLAN FURTHER PROPAGATE THEIR REDNECK TERROR...
I'M PREGNANT.
HA HA! KOFF KOFF KOFF

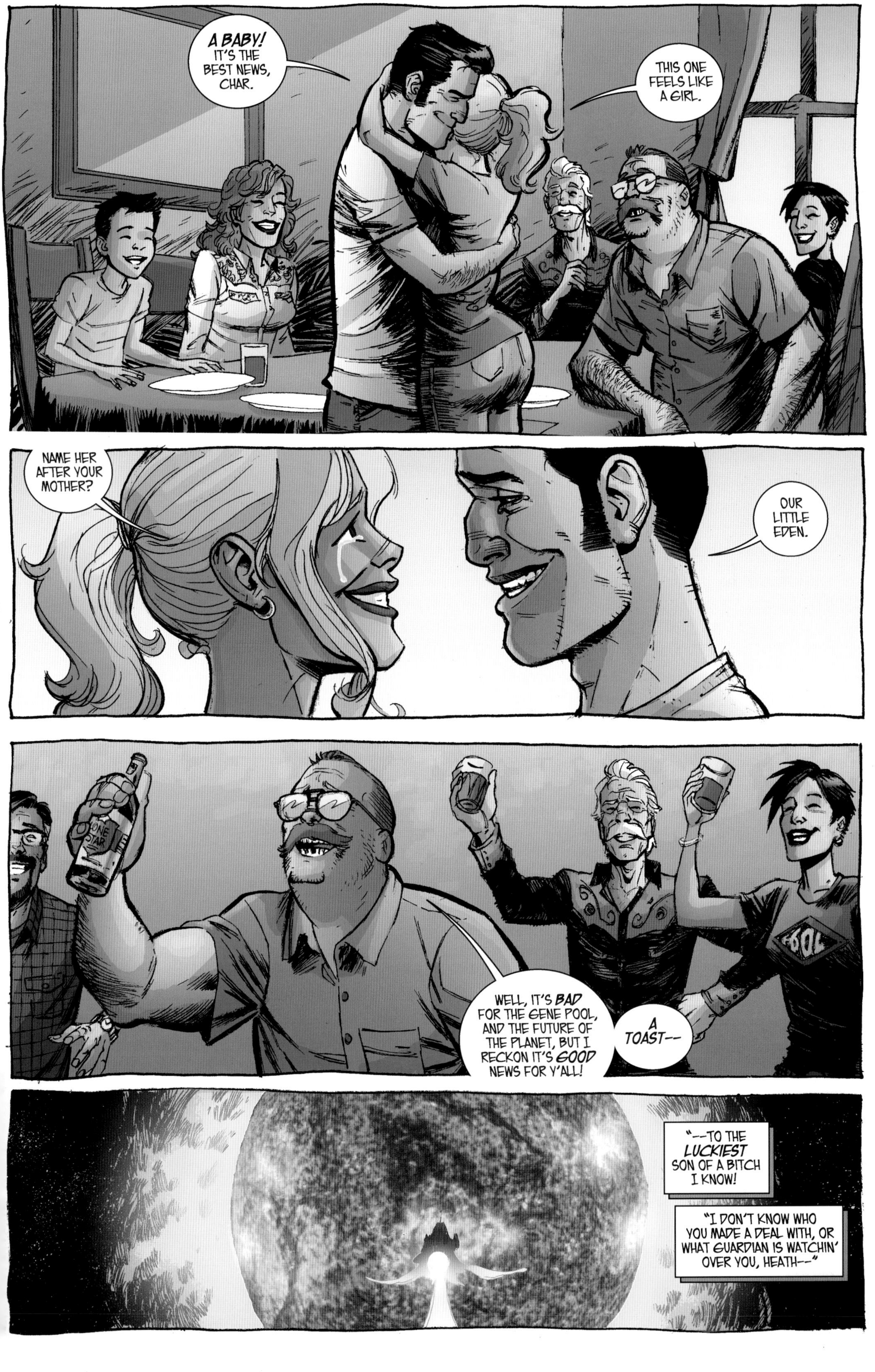
A BABY! IT'S THE BEST NEWS, CHAR.
THIS ONE FEELS LIKE A GIRL.
NAME HER AFTER YOUR MOTHER?
OUR LITTLE EDEN.
LONE STAR
WELL, IT'S BAD FOR THE GENE POOL, AND THE FUTURE OF THE PLANET, BUT I RECKON IT'S GOOD NEWS FOR Y'ALL!
A TOAST--
"--TO THE LUCKIEST SON OF A BITCH I KNOW!
"I DON'T KNOW WHO YOU MADE A DEAL WITH, OR WHAT GUARDIAN IS WATCHIN' OVER YOU, HEATH--"

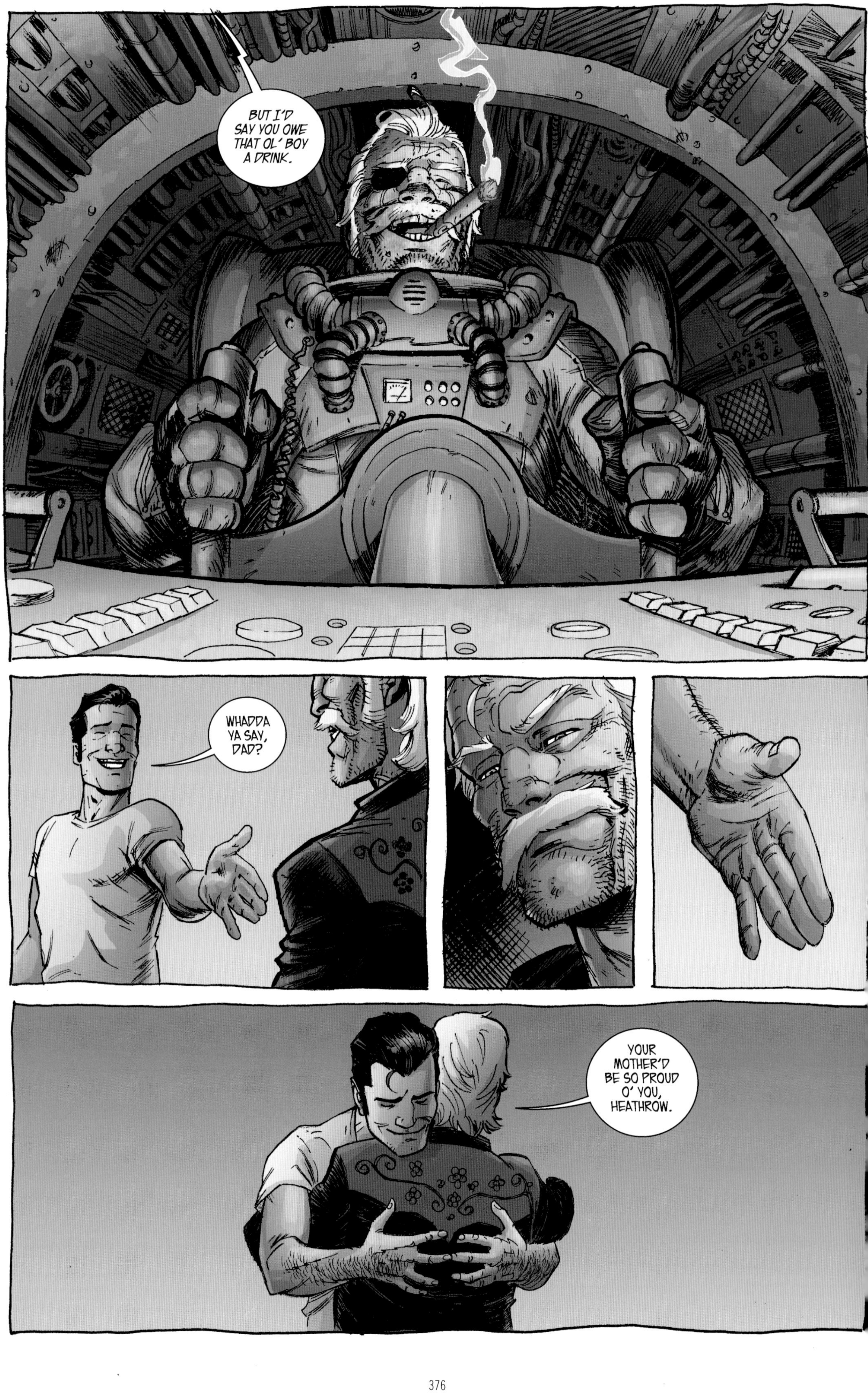
BUT I'D SAY YOU OWE THAT OL' BOY A DRINK.
WHADDA YA SAY, DAD?
YOUR MOTHER'D BE SO PROUD O' YOU, HEATHROW.

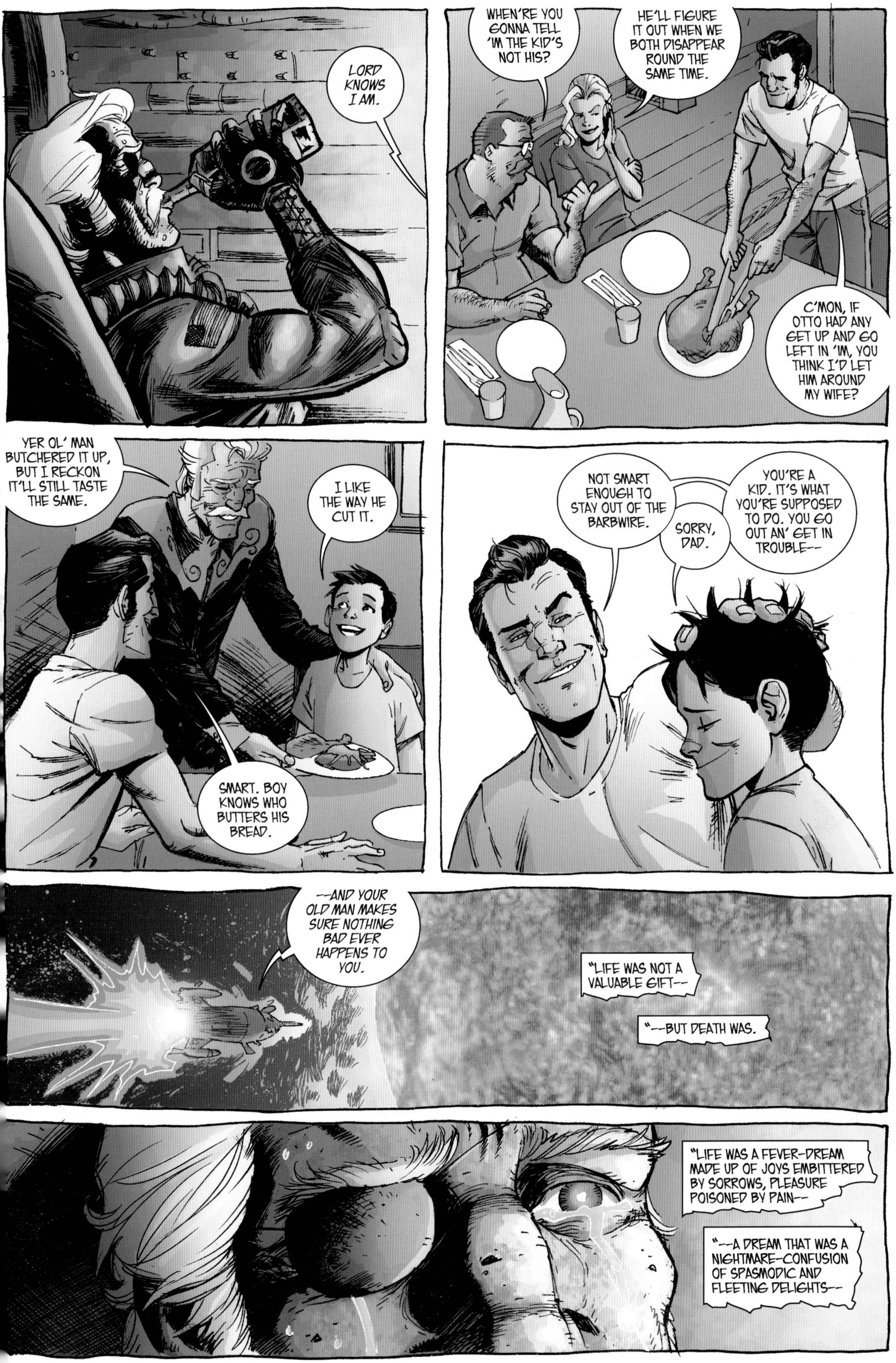
LORD KNOWS I AM.
WHEN'RE YOU GONNA TELL 'IM THE KID'S NOT HIS?
HE'LL FIGURE IT OUT WHEN WE BOTH DISAPPEAR ROUND THE SAME TIME.
C'MON, IF OTTO HAD ANY GET UP AND GO LEFT IN 'IM, YOU THINK I'D LET HIM AROUND MY WIFE?
YER OL' MAN BUTCHERED IT UP, BUT I RECKON IT'LL STILL TASTE THE SAME.
I LIKE THE WAY HE CUT IT.
SMART. BOY KNOWS WHO BUTTERS HIS BREAD.
NOT SMART ENOUGH TO STAY OUT OF THE BARBWIRE.
SORRY, DAD.
YOU'RE A KID. IT'S WHAT YOU'RE SUPPOSED TO DO. YOU GO OUT AN' GET IN TROUBLE--
--AND YOUR OLD MAN MAKES SURE NOTHING BAD EVER HAPPENS TO YOU.
"LIFE WAS NOT A VALUABLE GIFT--
"--BUT DEATH WAS.
"LIFE WAS A FEVER-DREAM MADE UP OF JOYS EMBITTERED BY SORROWS, PLEASURE POISONED BY PAIN--
"--A DREAM THAT WAS A NIGHTMARE-CONFUSION OF SPASMODIC AND FLEETING DELIGHTS--

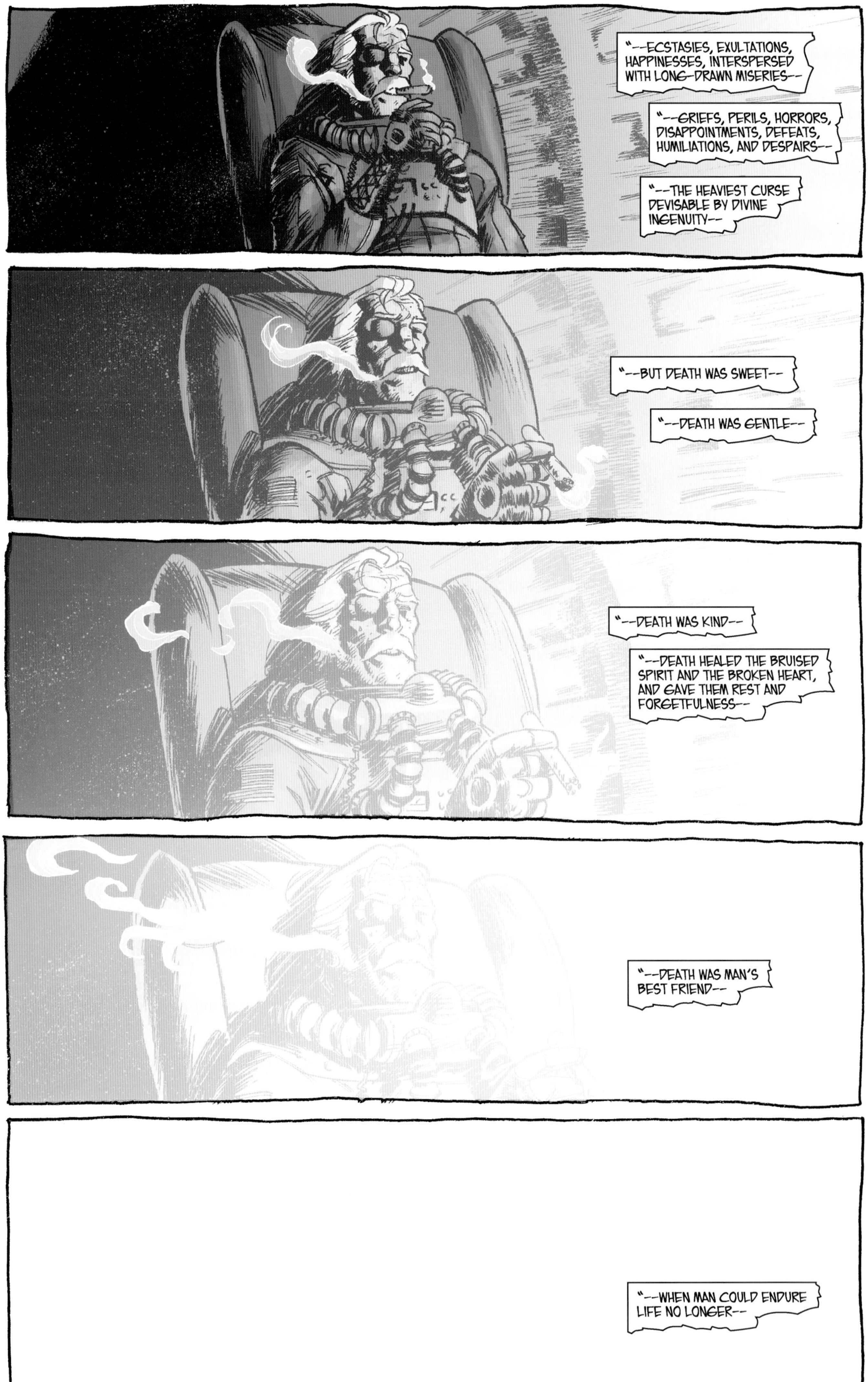
"--ECSTASIES, EXULTATIONS, HAPPINESSES, INTERSPERSED WITH LONG-DRAWN MISERIES--
"--GRIEFS, PERILS, HORRORS, DISAPPOINTMENTS, DEFEATS, HUMILIATIONS, AND DESPAIRS--
"--THE HEAVIEST CURSE DEVISABLE BY DIVINE INGENUITY--
"--BUT DEATH WAS SWEET--
"--DEATH WAS GENTLE--
"--DEATH WAS KIND--
"--DEATH HEALED THE BRUISED SPIRIT AND THE BROKEN HEART, AND GAVE THEM REST AND FORGETFULNESS--
"--DEATH WAS MAN'S BEST FRIEND--
"--WHEN MAN COULD ENDURE LIFE NO LONGER--

"—DEATH CAME AND
SET HIM FREE."
—SAMUEL CLEMENS

FEAR AGENT™

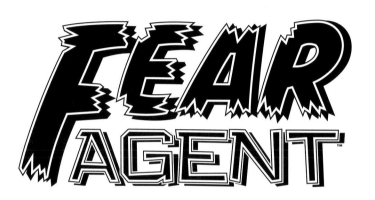

CREATED BY RICK REMENDER AND TONY MOORE

WRITTEN BY:

RICK REMENDER

ILLUSTRATED BY:

TONY MOORE

JEROME OPEÑA

MIKE HAWTHORNE

KIERON DWYER

INKED/FINISHED BY:

JOHN LUCAS

SEAN PARSONS

MIKE MANLEY

ANDE PARKS

RICK REMENDER

COLORED BY:

LEE LOUGHRIDGE

MICHELLE MADSEN

LETTERED BY:

RUS WOOTON

EDITED BY:

DAVE LAND

SCOTT ALLIE

PATRICK THORPE

SPECIAL THANKS TO MIKE RICHARDSON, HILARY BARTA,
ERIC STEPHENSON, ROBERT KIRKMAN, ERIK LARSEN,
HARRIS MILLER, JOSH ELLIOTT, AND EVERYONE WHO
CONTRIBUTED TO THE "TALES OF" STORIES.

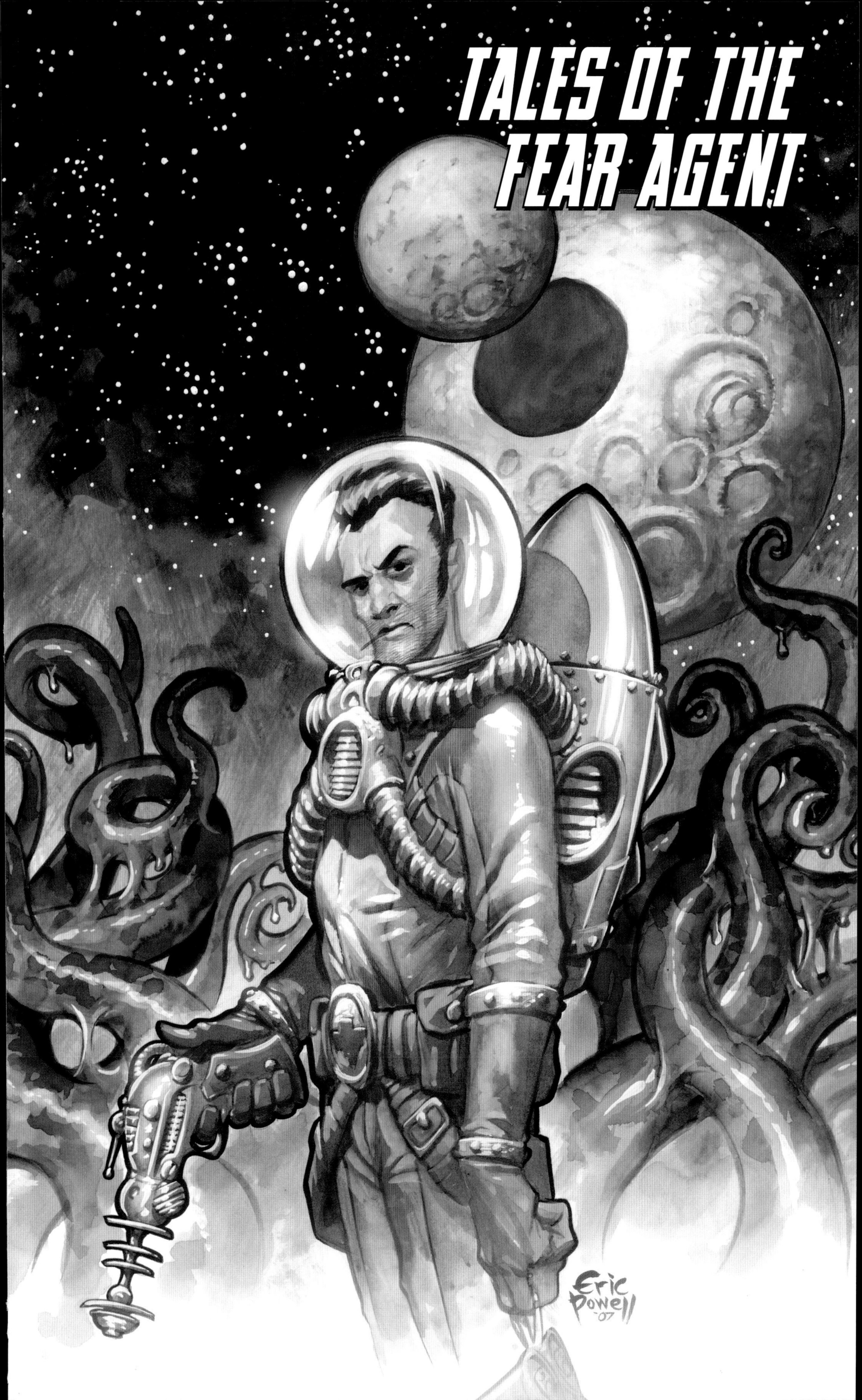
TALES OF THE
FEAR AGENT
Eric
Powell
'07

ASTONISHING ACTION!

TALES OF THE FEAR AGENT

is a series of noncanonical, fun, speculative stories by some of the best creators in the business, published as bonus material in issues of Fear Agent. They take place in the ten years between the events of The Last Goodbye and Re-ignition, when Heath has left Earth after the Dressite and Tetaldian invasions. Getting as far away from Earth as possible, both physically, in his spaceship, and mentally, in the medicinal qualities of a bottle, Heath works as a freelance alien exterminator.

A MAMMOTH UNDERTAKER

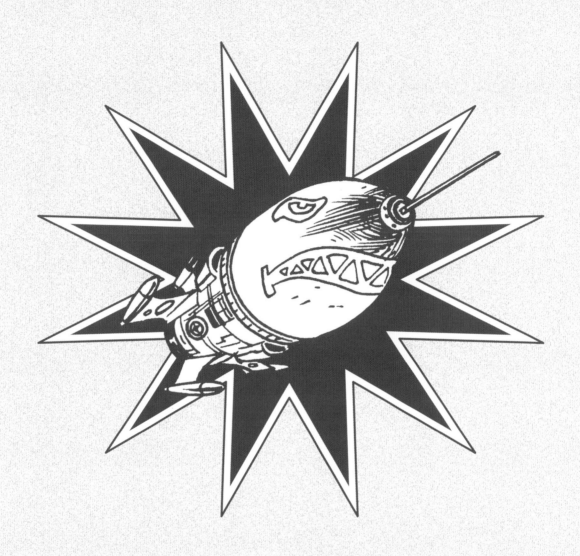

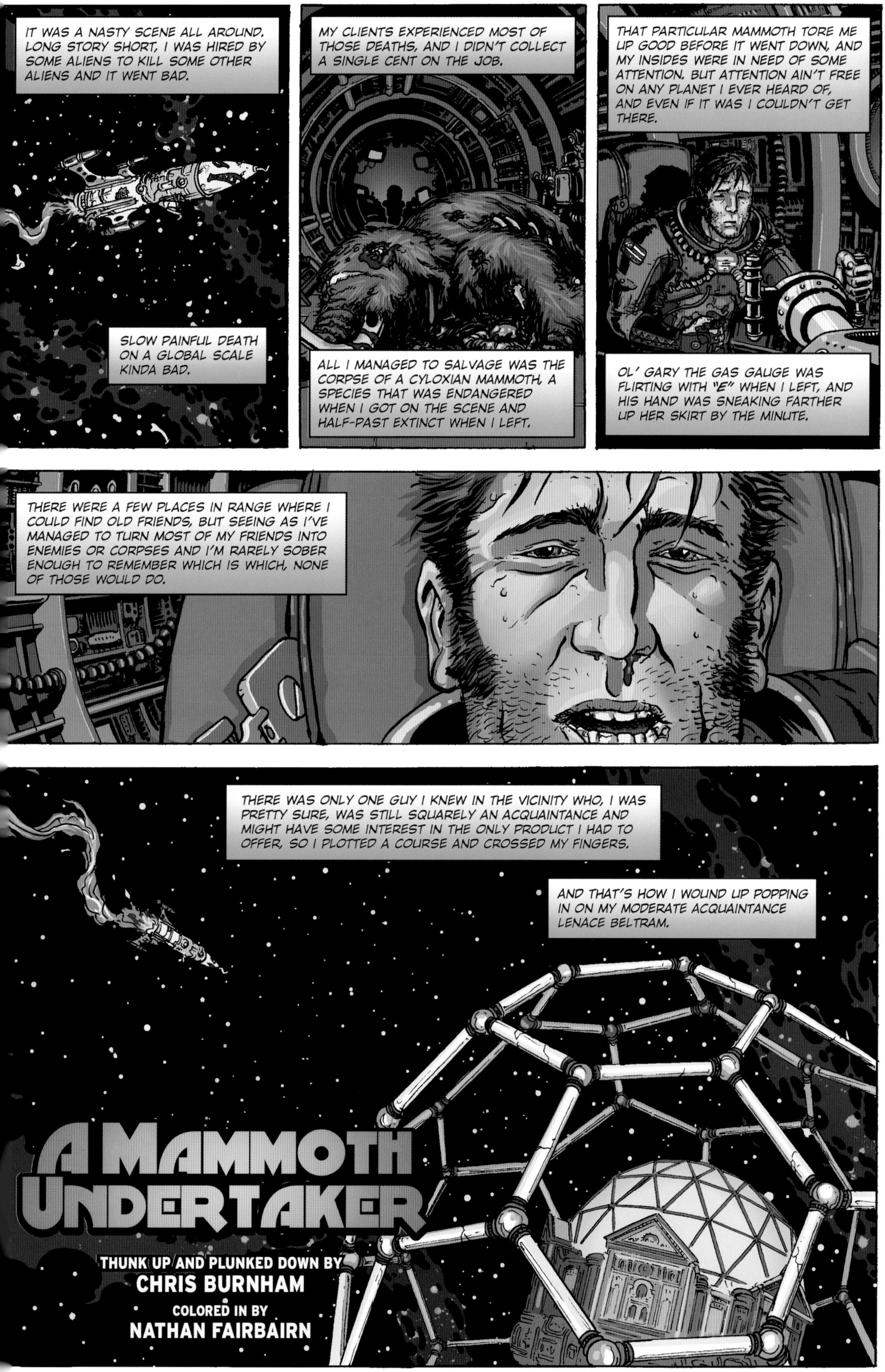
IT WAS A NASTY SCENE ALL AROUND. LONG STORY SHORT, I WAS HIRED BY SOME ALIENS TO KILL SOME OTHER ALIENS AND IT WENT BAD.
SLOW PAINFUL DEATH ON A GLOBAL SCALE KINDA BAD.
MY CLIENTS EXPERIENCED MOST OF THOSE DEATHS, AND I DIDN'T COLLECT A SINGLE CENT ON THE JOB.
ALL I MANAGED TO SALVAGE WAS THE CORPSE OF A CYLOXIAN MAMMOTH, A SPECIES THAT WAS ENDANGERED WHEN I GOT ON THE SCENE AND HALF-PAST EXTINCT WHEN I LEFT.
THAT PARTICULAR MAMMOTH TORE ME UP GOOD BEFORE IT WENT DOWN, AND MY INSIDES WERE IN NEED OF SOME ATTENTION. BUT ATTENTION AIN'T FREE ON ANY PLANET I EVER HEARD OF, AND EVEN IF IT WAS I COULDN'T GET THERE.
OL' GARY THE GAS GAUGE WAS FLIRTING WITH "E" WHEN I LEFT, AND HIS HAND WAS SNEAKING FARTHER UP HER SKIRT BY THE MINUTE.
THERE WERE A FEW PLACES IN RANGE WHERE I COULD FIND OLD FRIENDS, BUT SEEING AS I'VE MANAGED TO TURN MOST OF MY FRIENDS INTO ENEMIES OR CORPSES AND I'M RARELY SOBER ENOUGH TO REMEMBER WHICH IS WHICH, NONE OF THOSE WOULD DO.
THERE WAS ONLY ONE GUY I KNEW IN THE VICINITY WHO, I WAS PRETTY SURE, WAS STILL SQUARELY AN ACQUAINTANCE AND MIGHT HAVE SOME INTEREST IN THE ONLY PRODUCT I HAD TO OFFER, SO I PLOTTED A COURSE AND CROSSED MY FINGERS.
AND THAT'S HOW I WOUND UP POPPING IN ON MY MODERATE ACQUAINTANCE LENACE BELTRAM.
A MAMMOTH UNDERTAKER
THUNK UP AND PLUNKED DOWN BY
CHRIS BURNHAM
COLORED IN BY
NATHAN FAIRBAIRN

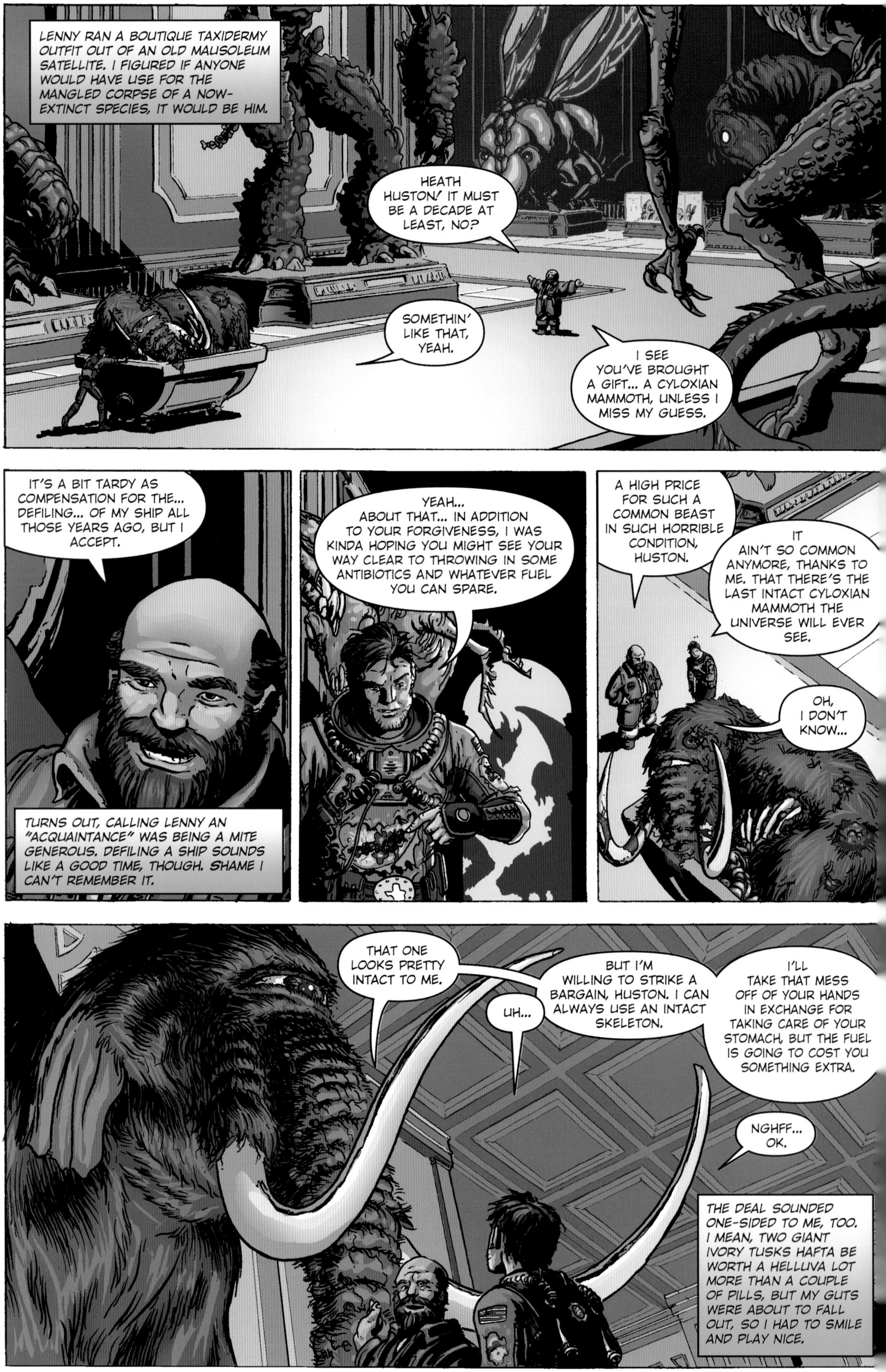
LENNY RAN A BOUTIQUE TAXIDERMY OUTFIT OUT OF AN OLD MAUSOLEUM SATELLITE. I FIGURED IF ANYONE WOULD HAVE USE FOR THE MANGLED CORPSE OF A NOW-EXTINCT SPECIES, IT WOULD BE HIM.
HEATH HUSTON! IT MUST BE A DECADE AT LEAST, NO?
SOMETHIN' LIKE THAT, YEAH.
I SEE YOU'VE BROUGHT A GIFT... A CYLOXIAN MAMMOTH, UNLESS I MISS MY GUESS.
IT'S A BIT TARDY AS COMPENSATION FOR THE... DEFILING... OF MY SHIP ALL THOSE YEARS AGO, BUT I ACCEPT.
TURNS OUT, CALLING LENNY AN "ACQUAINTANCE" WAS BEING A MITE GENEROUS. DEFILING A SHIP SOUNDS LIKE A GOOD TIME, THOUGH. SHAME I CAN'T REMEMBER IT.
YEAH... ABOUT THAT... IN ADDITION TO YOUR FORGIVENESS, I WAS KINDA HOPING YOU MIGHT SEE YOUR WAY CLEAR TO THROWING IN SOME ANTIBIOTICS AND WHATEVER FUEL YOU CAN SPARE.
A HIGH PRICE FOR SUCH A COMMON BEAST IN SUCH HORRIBLE CONDITION, HUSTON.
IT AIN'T SO COMMON ANYMORE, THANKS TO ME. THAT THERE'S THE LAST INTACT CYLOXIAN MAMMOTH THE UNIVERSE WILL EVER SEE.
OH, I DON'T KNOW...
THAT ONE LOOKS PRETTY INTACT TO ME.
UH...
BUT I'M WILLING TO STRIKE A BARGAIN, HUSTON. I CAN ALWAYS USE AN INTACT SKELETON.
I'LL TAKE THAT MESS OFF OF YOUR HANDS IN EXCHANGE FOR TAKING CARE OF YOUR STOMACH, BUT THE FUEL IS GOING TO COST YOU SOMETHING EXTRA.
NGHFF... OK.
THE DEAL SOUNDED ONE-SIDED TO ME, TOO. I MEAN, TWO GIANT IVORY TUSKS HAFTA BE WORTH A HELLUVA LOT MORE THAN A COUPLE OF PILLS, BUT MY GUTS WERE ABOUT TO FALL OUT, SO I HAD TO SMILE AND PLAY NICE.

SQUILPSH!

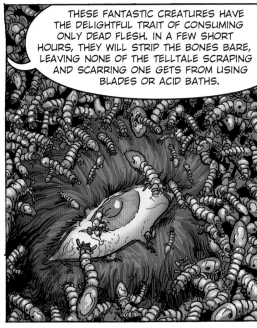

THESE FANTASTIC CREATURES HAVE THE DELIGHTFUL TRAIT OF CONSUMING ONLY DEAD FLESH. IN A FEW SHORT HOURS, THEY WILL STRIP THE BONES BARE, LEAVING NONE OF THE TELLTALE SCRAPING AND SCARRING ONE GETS FROM USING BLADES OR ACID BATHS.

GREAT. HGHN... STOMACH.

AH, YES.

GAH! WHAT GIVES?

YOU'VE GOT A FORM OF GANGRENE, FOR WHICH THOSE MAMMOTHS ARE, OR SHOULD I SAY, WERE, NOTORIOUS CARRIERS.

THESE CREATURES WILL CLEANSE YOUR INFECTION BY CONSUMING THE DEAD TISSUE AND BACTERIA.

TICKLES.

NOW THEN, ABOUT YOUR FUEL...

I DON'T CARE HOW BADLY I DEFILED HIS SHIP. AN IVORY SKELETON IN EXCHANGE FOR A FISTFUL OF WORMS IS BULLSHIT.

AS THE PAIN SLOWLY DIED DOWN AND I STARTED TO THINK MORE CLEARLY, IT SLAPPED ME IN THE FACE HOW THOROUGHLY HE WAS SCREWING ME.

I THOUGHT ABOUT SHOOTING THE BASTARD RIGHT THERE, BUT I WASN'T SURE MY DRAW WOULD BE AS FAST AS HIS IN THE STATE I WAS IN.

IF I WANTED A FULL TANK OF FUEL WITHOUT GETTING IN A GUNFIGHT, I WAS GONNA HAFTA DO WHAT HE WANTED.

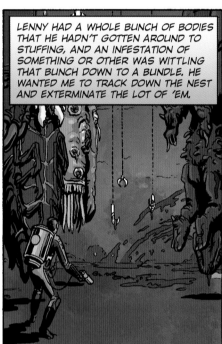

LENNY HAD A WHOLE BUNCH OF BODIES THAT HE HADN'T GOTTEN AROUND TO STUFFING, AND AN INFESTATION OF SOMETHING OR OTHER WAS WITTLING THAT BUNCH DOWN TO A BUNDLE. HE WANTED ME TO TRACK DOWN THE NEST AND EXTERMINATE THE LOT OF 'EM.

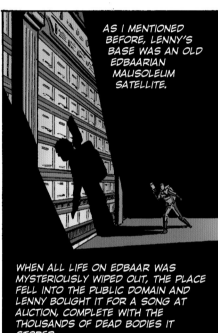

AS I MENTIONED BEFORE, LENNY'S BASE WAS AN OLD EDBAARIAN MAUSOLEUM SATELLITE.

WHEN ALL LIFE ON EDBAAR WAS MYSTERIOUSLY WIPED OUT, THE PLACE FELL INTO THE PUBLIC DOMAIN AND LENNY BOUGHT IT FOR A SONG AT AUCTION, COMPLETE WITH THE THOUSANDS OF DEAD BODIES IT STORED.

OR, SHOULD I SAY, USED TO STORE. THE CRITTERS THAT HAD BEEN TAKING THOSE BODIES MUSTA RUN OUT OF HUMAN CORPSES AND WERE MOVIN' THEIR WAY UP TO THE MONSTERS IN LENNY'S FREEZER.

IT WAS FUNNY -- THERE WAS LOTS OF MISSING FOOD, BUT NO DROPPINGS.

BUT, I FIGURED, MAYBE THEY WEREN'T THE TYPE TO POOP IN PUBLIC. HELL, WHEN I WAS IN SCHOOL, I'D HOLD IT IN ALL DAY LONG.

KNOWING SOMEONE IN THE NEXT STALL WAS DOING THEIR BUSINESS CLENCHED MY BUTT UP TIGHT.

AND THAT'S THE SAME FEELING I GOT AS I TOOK A PEEK AROUND THE CORNER...

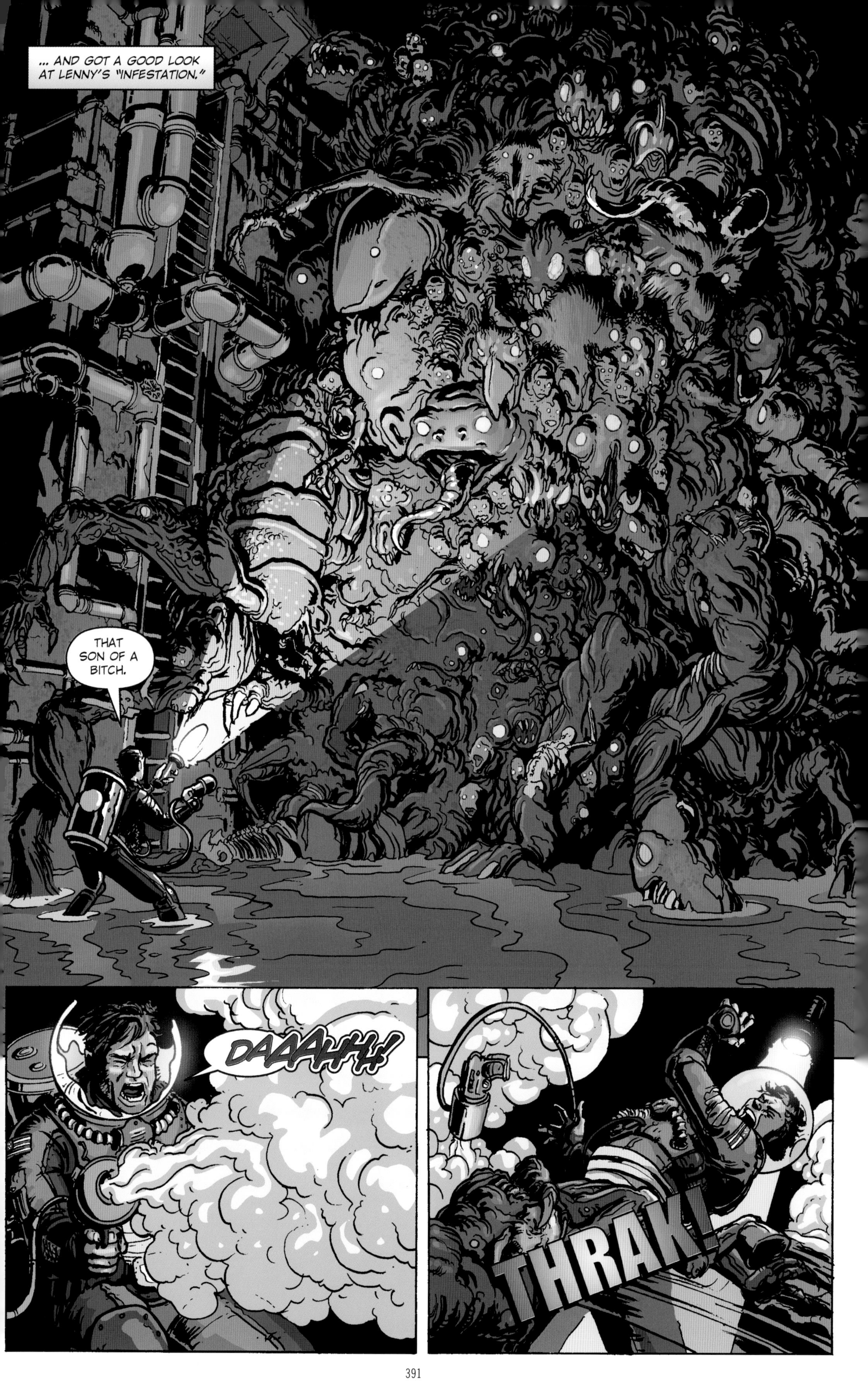
... AND GOT A GOOD LOOK AT LENNY'S "INFESTATION."
THAT SON OF A BITCH.
DAAAHH!
THRAK!

BETTER PART OF VALOR, MY ASS. I WAS SCARED SHITLESS AND DON'T MIND SAYING SO.

IT'S BEAUTIFUL, ISN'T IT? THE ULTIMATE EXPRESSION OF MY TAXIDERMIC GENIUS.

AND JUST LIKE THAT, LENNY MADE THE JUMP FROM "ANNOYED ACQUAINTANCE" STRAIGHT TO "ENEMY FOR LIFE."

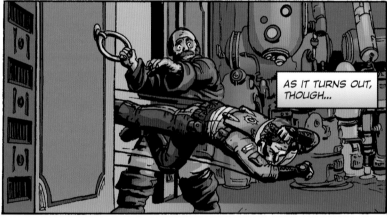

AS IT TURNS OUT, THOUGH...

..."FOR LIFE" DIDN'T AMOUNT TO MUCH.

CROOOM!

SQUIT!

HOW'S THAT FOR DEFILED, ASSHOLE?

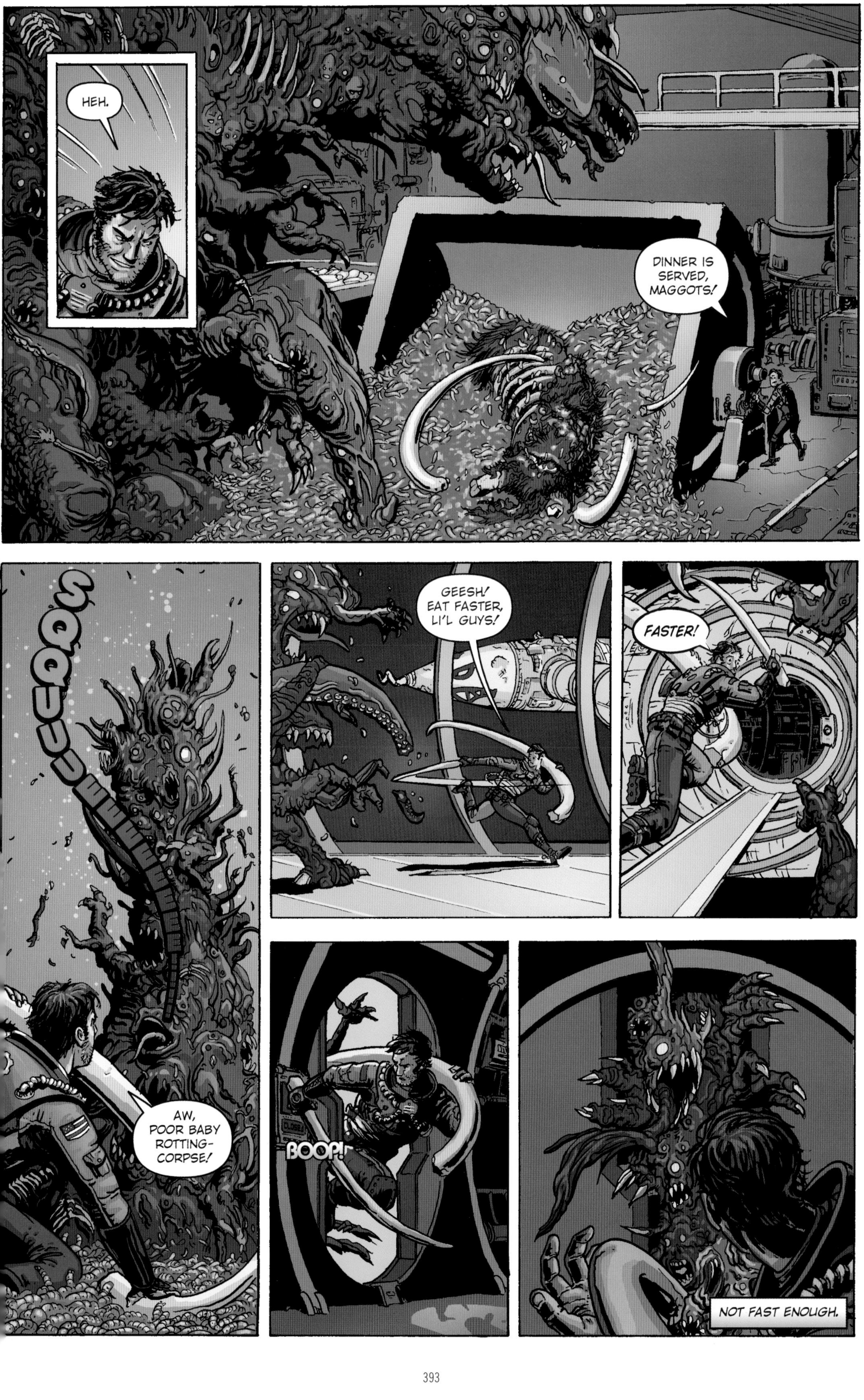
HEH.
DINNER IS SERVED, MAGGOTS!
GEESH! EAT FASTER, LI'L GUYS!
FASTER!
AW, POOR BABY ROTTING-CORPSE!
BOOP!
NOT FAST ENOUGH.

GLUK!

RIPPING THOSE THINGS OUT FELT LIKE THE OPPOSITE OF TICKLE.

SHLORSHP!

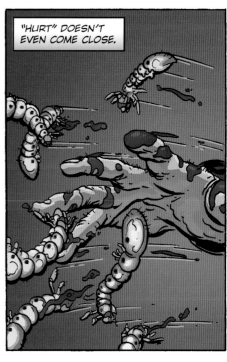

"HURT" DOESN'T EVEN COME CLOSE.

GLIK... GLK...

GLINCH

SCHRIMPK

CHNSCH

SCHNCK

THROO- SPLADT!

SO I WOUND UP THE DAY AS I STARTED IT. NO MONEY, NO GAS, A HOLE IN MY GUTS, AND NO MAGGOTS TO CLEAN IT.

ALL I HAD TO SHOW FOR IT WERE TWO CLEANED MAMMOTH TUSKS, AND I'D NEED TO FIND SOMEONE CLOSE TO TRADE 'EM TO.

AND THAT MEANT HITTING UP ONE OF THOSE OLD FRIENDS I WAS TELLING YOU ABOUT.

SO I PLOTTED A COURSE, CROSSED MY FINGERS, AND HOPED THAT THIS PARTICULAR OLD FRIEND WAS A CORPSE, NOT AN ENEMY.

THE GOOD GUYS!

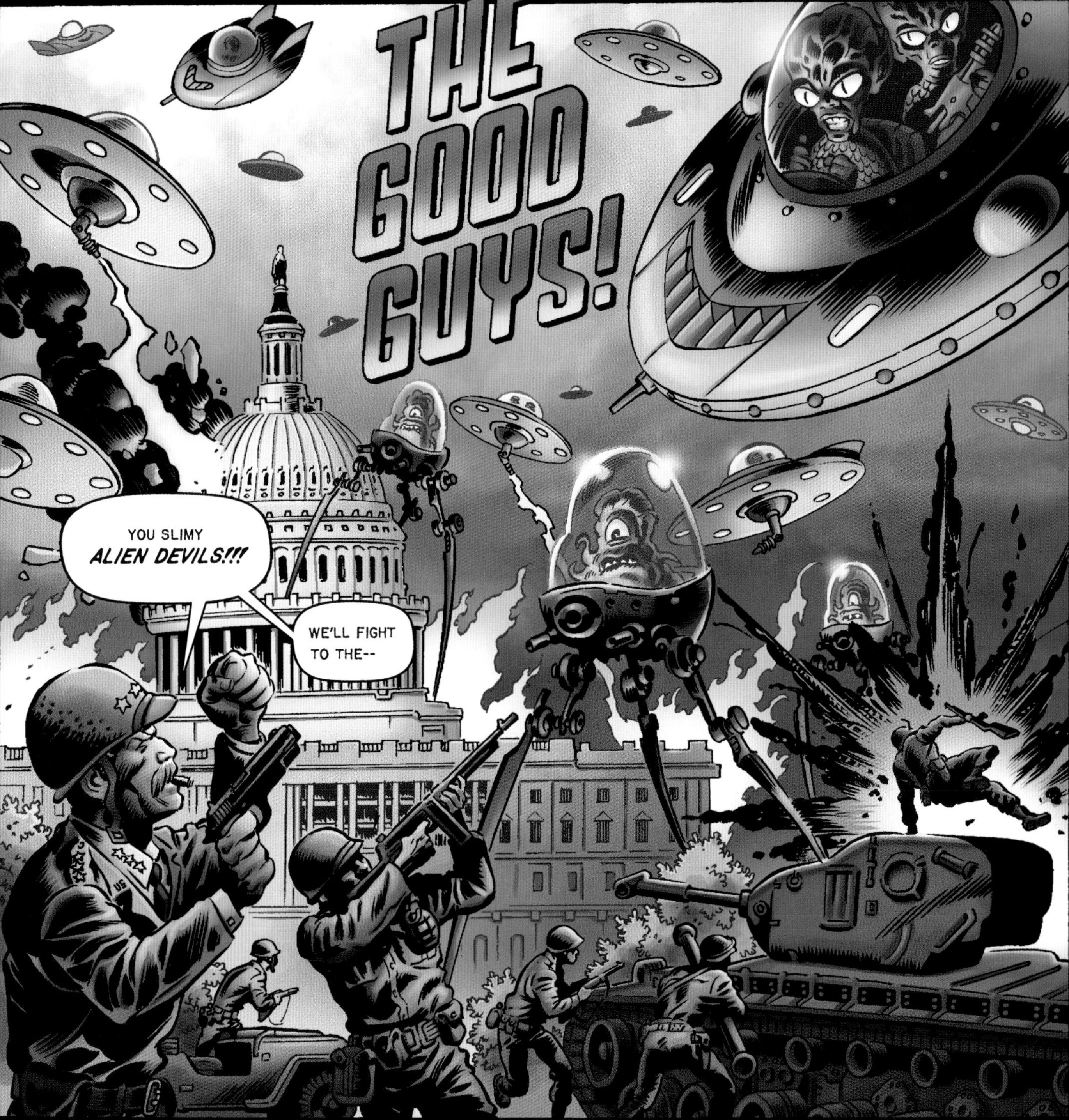
THE GOOD GUYS!
YOU SLIMY ALIEN DEVILS!!!
WE'LL FIGHT TO THE--

STORY AND INKS: BARTA PENCILS: RONN SUTTON COLOR: JASON MILLET LETTERS: FRANK FORTE

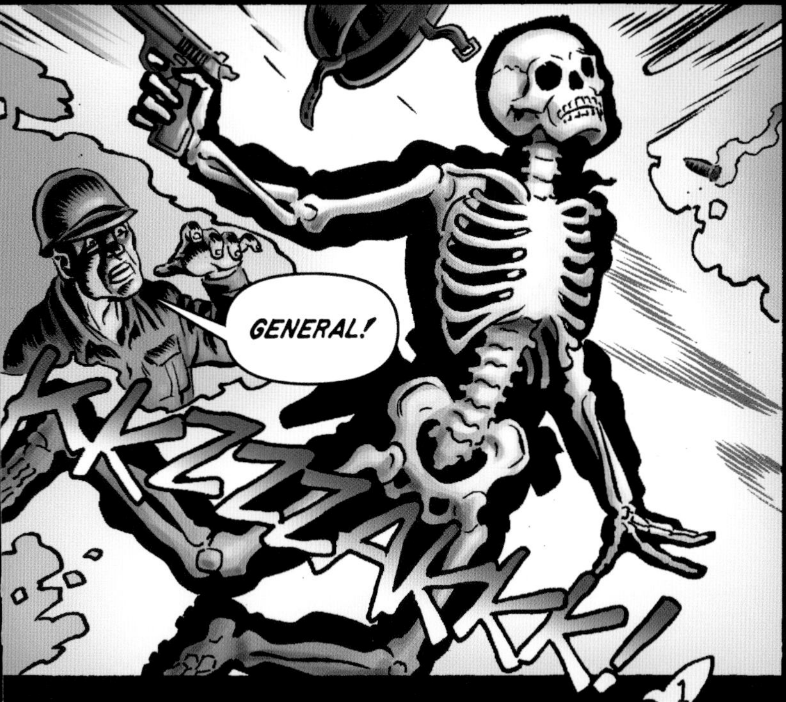
GENERAL!
KZZZAKKK!

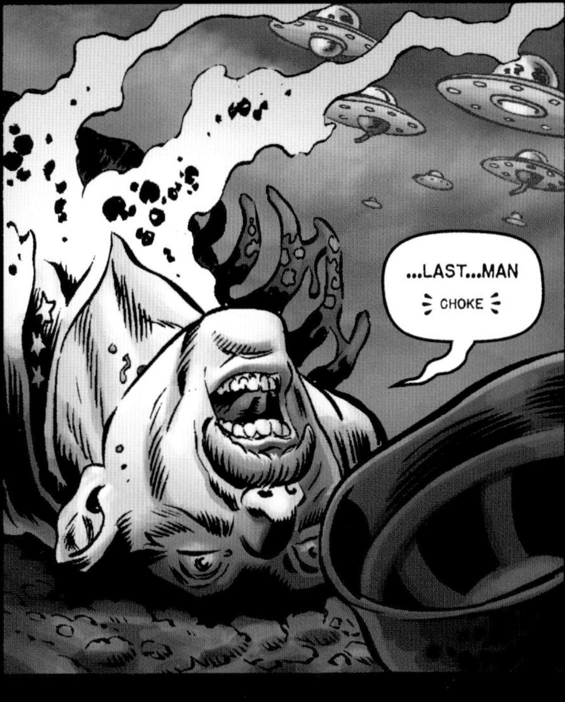
...LAST...MAN
CHOKE

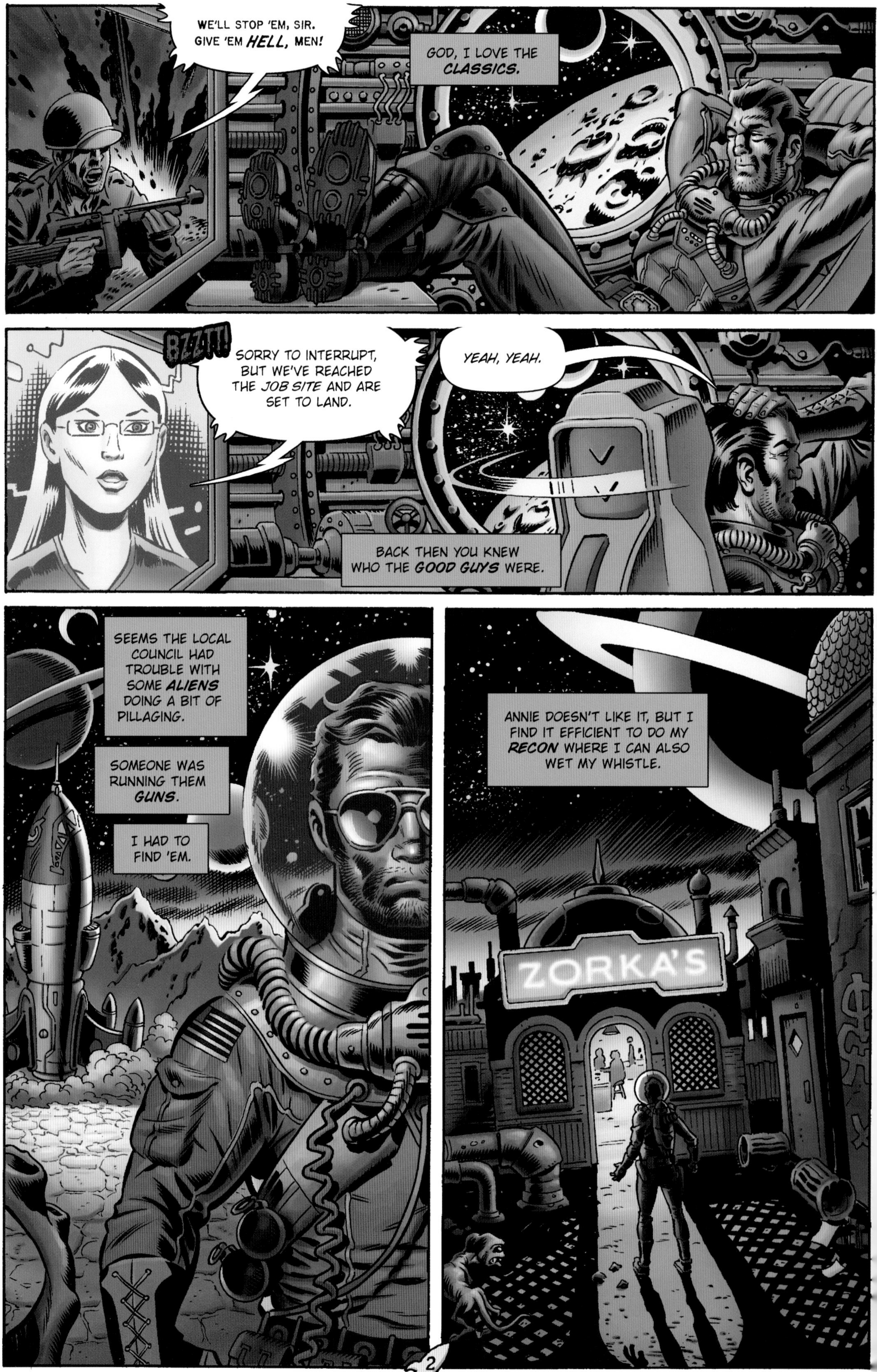
WE'LL STOP 'EM, SIR. GIVE 'EM HELL, MEN!
GOD, I LOVE THE CLASSICS.
BZZTT!
SORRY TO INTERRUPT, BUT WE'VE REACHED THE JOB SITE AND ARE SET TO LAND.
YEAH, YEAH.
BACK THEN YOU KNEW WHO THE GOOD GUYS WERE.
SEEMS THE LOCAL COUNCIL HAD TROUBLE WITH SOME ALIENS DOING A BIT OF PILLAGING.
SOMEONE WAS RUNNING THEM GUNS.
I HAD TO FIND 'EM.
ANNIE DOESN'T LIKE IT, BUT I FIND IT EFFICIENT TO DO MY RECON WHERE I CAN ALSO WET MY WHISTLE.
ZORKA'S
2

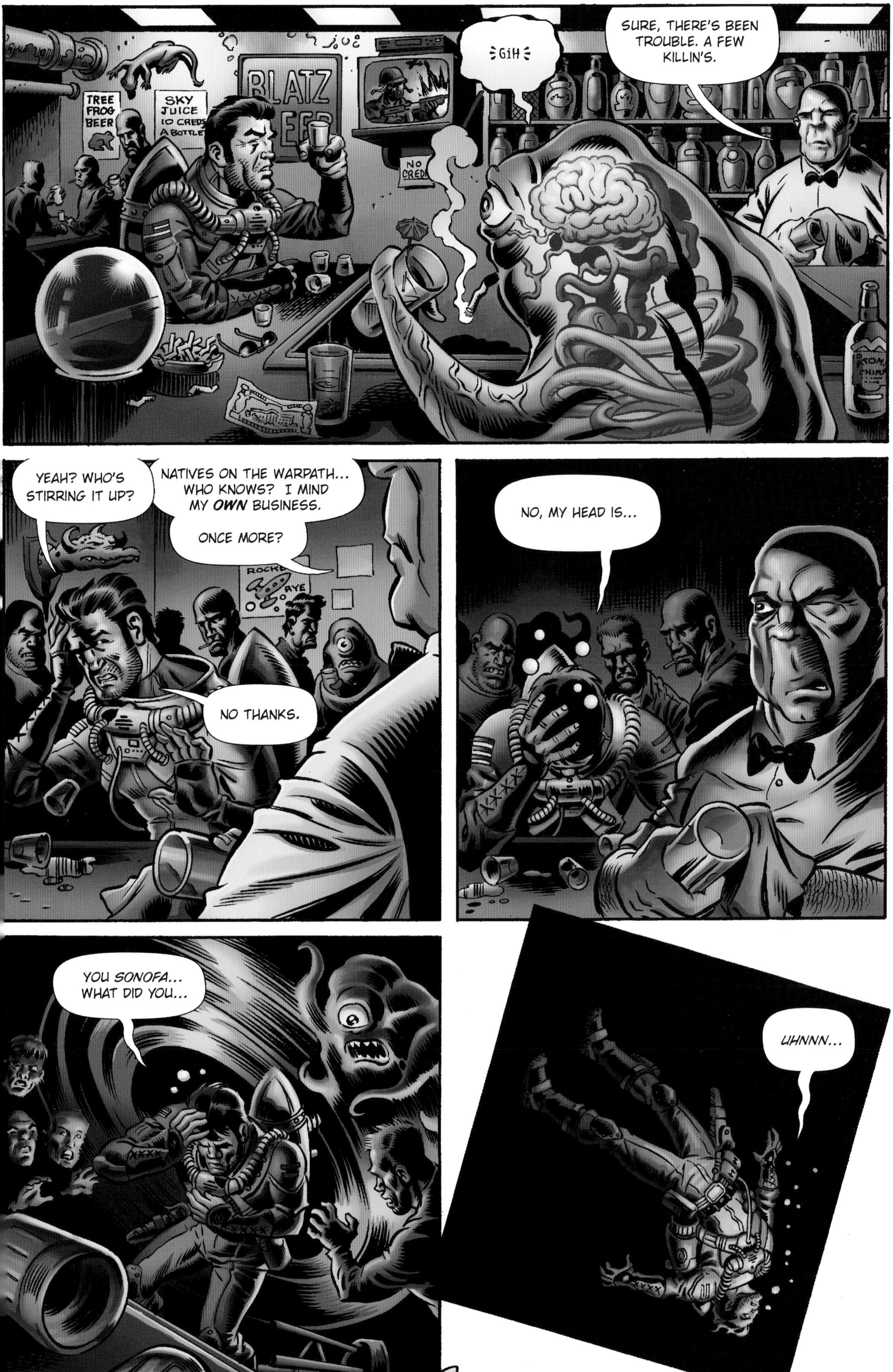
TREE FROG BEER
SKY JUICE 10 CREDS A BOTTLE
GIH
SURE, THERE'S BEEN TROUBLE. A FEW KILLIN'S.
YEAH? WHO'S STIRRING IT UP?
NATIVES ON THE WARPATH... WHO KNOWS? I MIND MY ***OWN*** BUSINESS.
ONCE MORE?
NO THANKS.
NO, MY HEAD IS...
YOU SONOFA... WHAT DID YOU...
UHNNN...
3

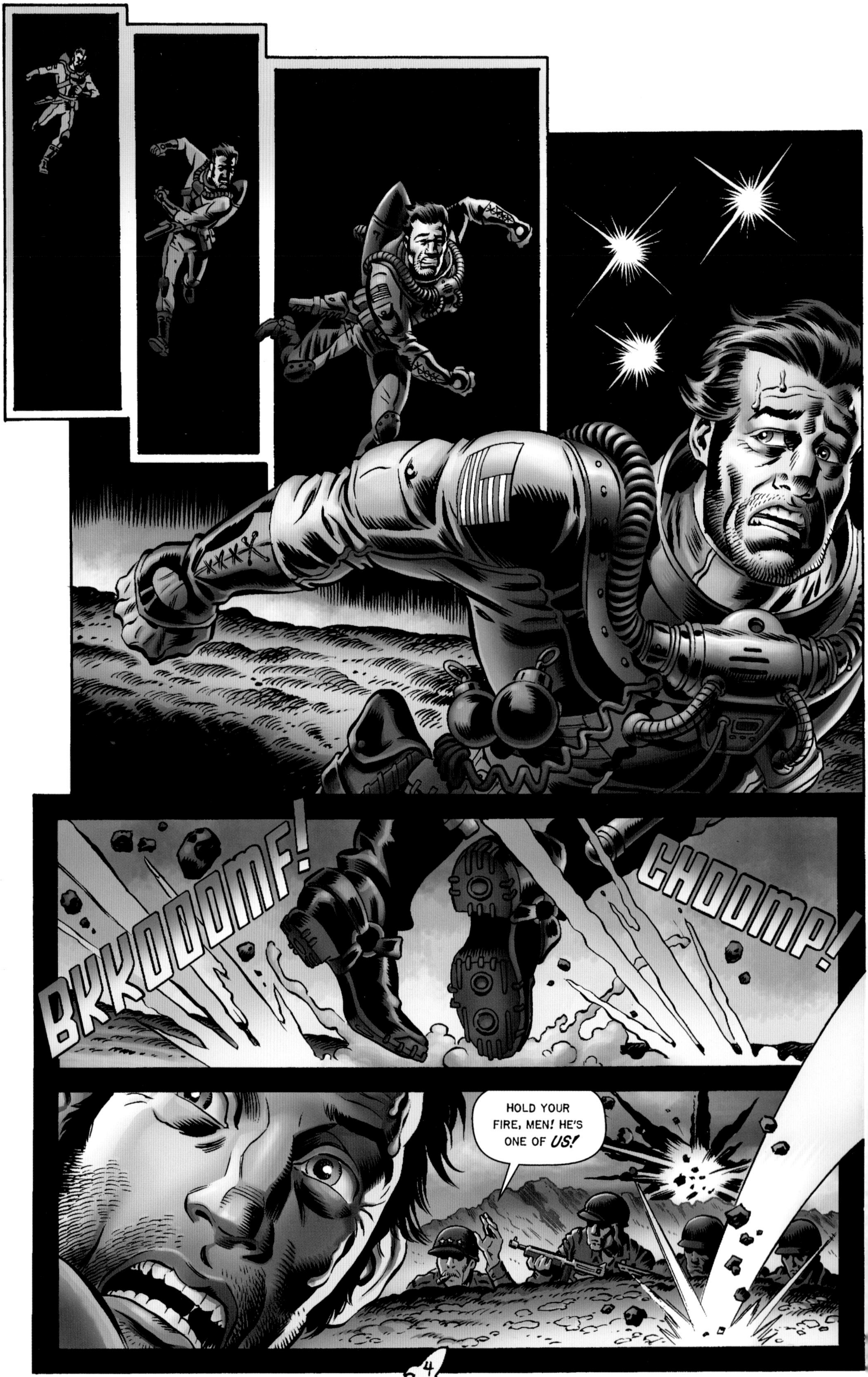
BKKOOOOMF!
CHOOMP!
HOLD YOUR FIRE, MEN! HE'S ONE OF US!
4

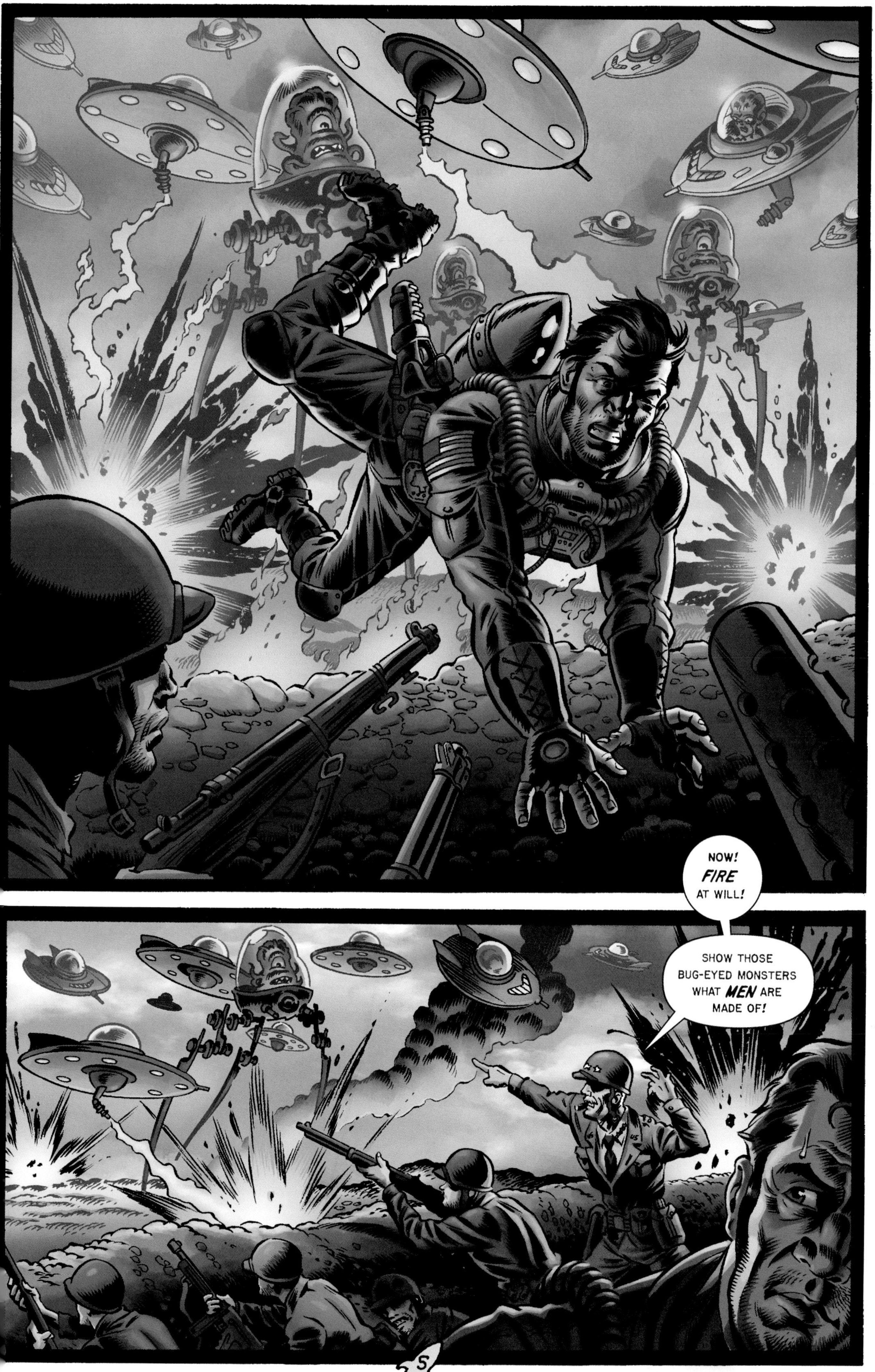
NOW! FIRE AT WILL!
SHOW THOSE BUG-EYED MONSTERS WHAT MEN ARE MADE OF!

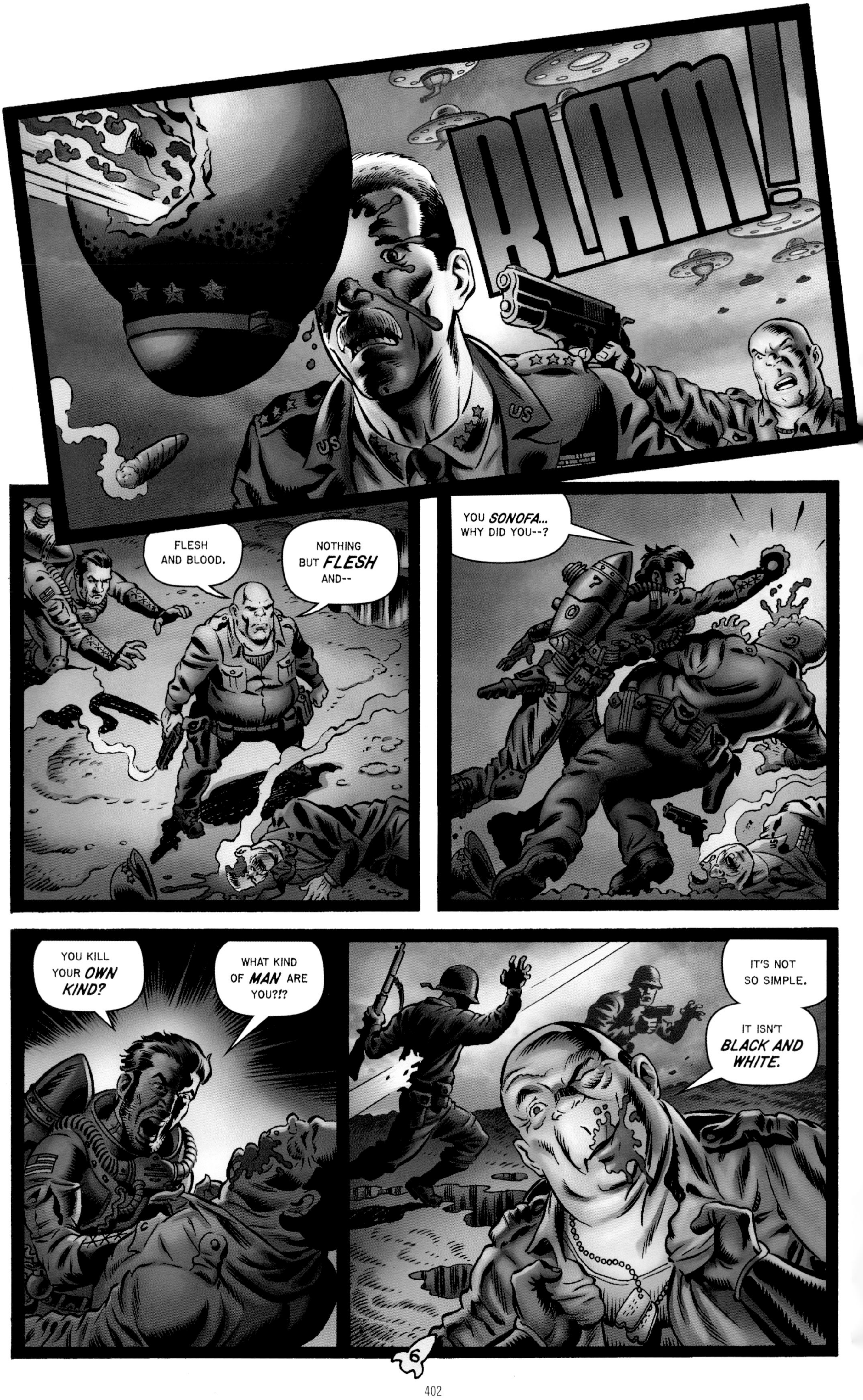
BLAM!!
FLESH AND BLOOD.
NOTHING BUT FLESH AND--
YOU SONOFA... WHY DID YOU--?
YOU KILL YOUR OWN KIND?
WHAT KIND OF MAN ARE YOU?!?
IT'S NOT SO SIMPLE.
IT ISN'T BLACK AND WHITE.
6

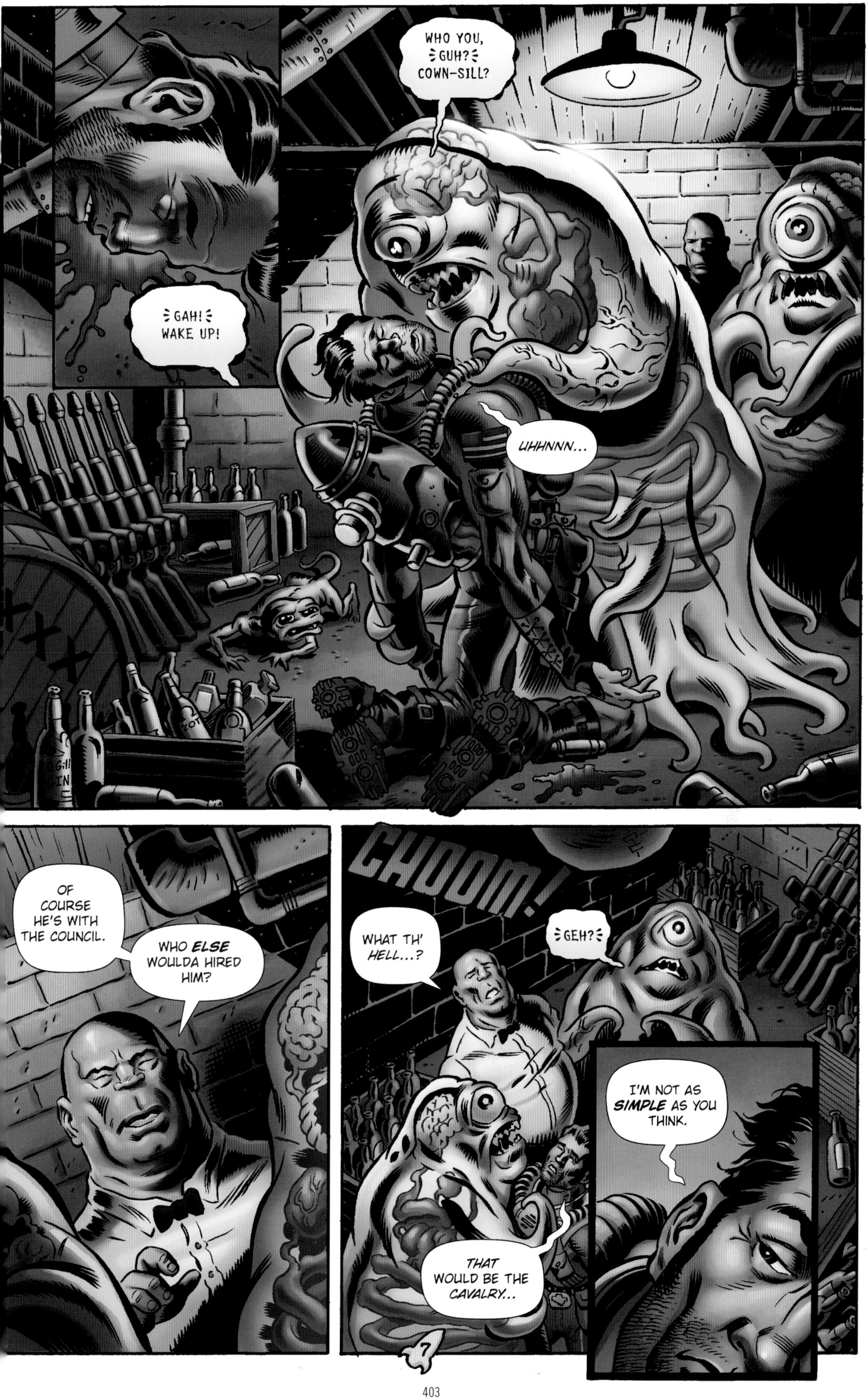
GAH! WAKE UP!
WHO YOU, GUH? COWN-SILL?
UHHNNN...
OF COURSE HE'S WITH THE COUNCIL.
WHO ELSE WOULDA HIRED HIM?
CHOOM!
WHAT TH' HELL...?
GEH?
THAT WOULD BE THE CAVALRY...
I'M NOT AS SIMPLE AS YOU THINK.

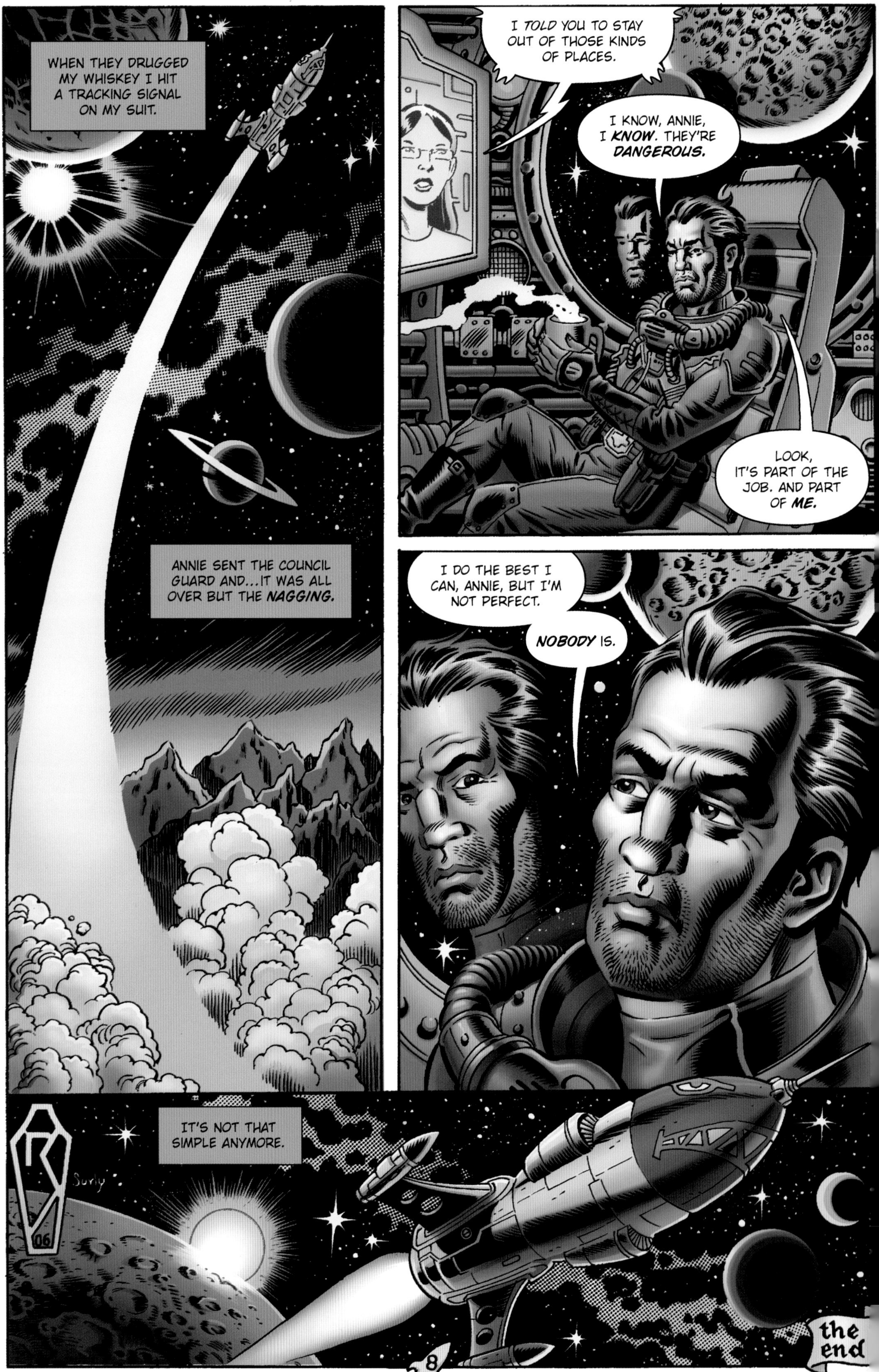

WHEN THEY DRUGGED MY WHISKEY I HIT A TRACKING SIGNAL ON MY SUIT.
I TOLD YOU TO STAY OUT OF THOSE KINDS OF PLACES.
I KNOW, ANNIE, I KNOW. THEY'RE DANGEROUS.
LOOK, IT'S PART OF THE JOB. AND PART OF ME.
ANNIE SENT THE COUNCIL GUARD AND...IT WAS ALL OVER BUT THE NAGGING.
I DO THE BEST I CAN, ANNIE, BUT I'M NOT PERFECT.
NOBODY IS.
IT'S NOT THAT SIMPLE ANYMORE.
Surly
06
8
the end

HEATH₂O

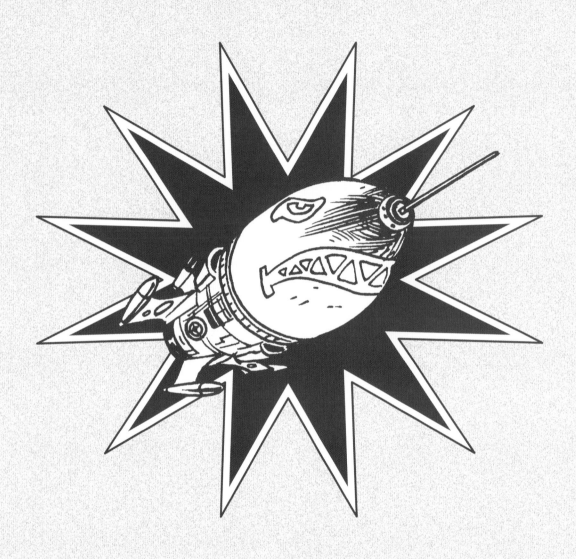

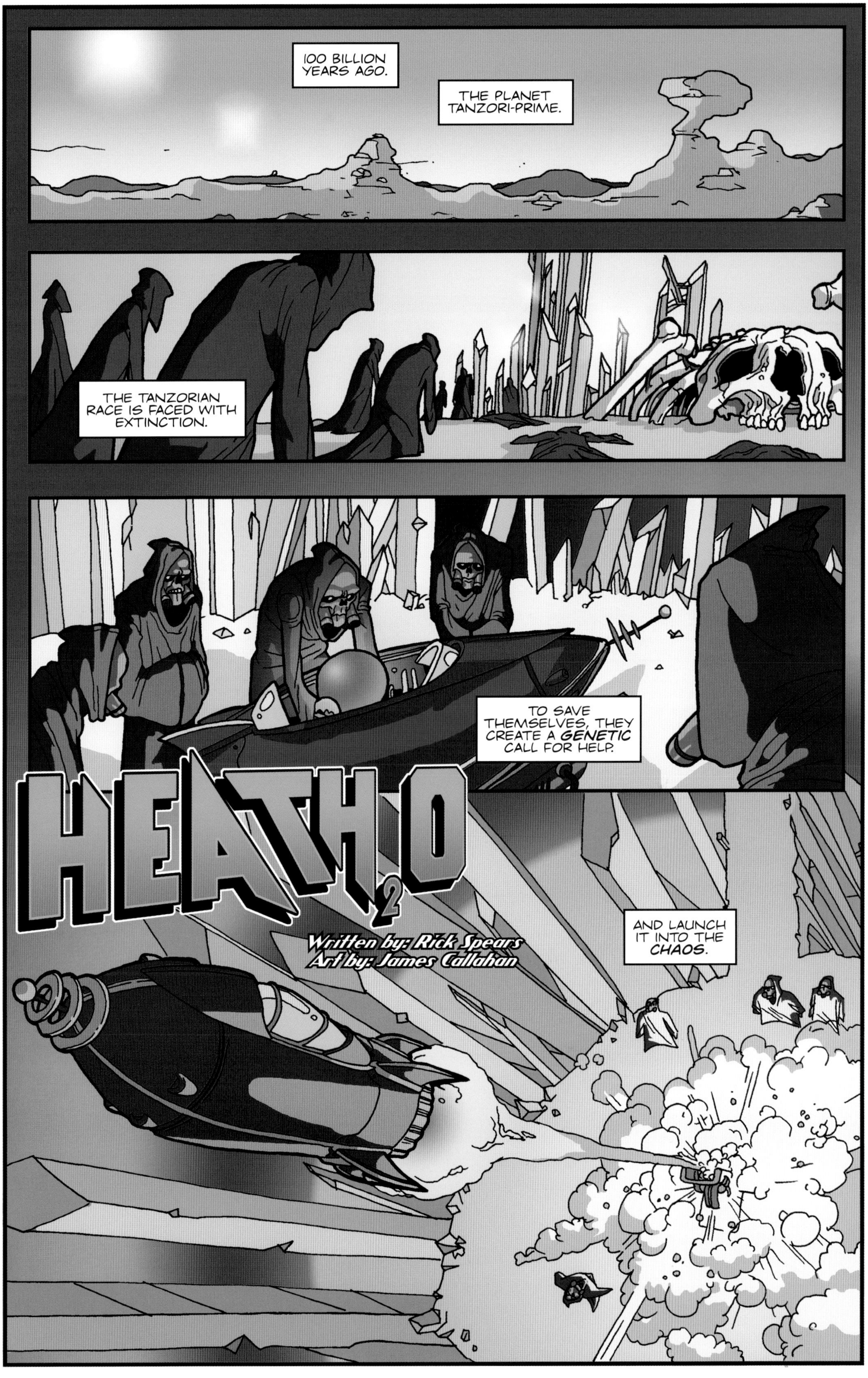
100 BILLION YEARS AGO.
THE PLANET TANZORI-PRIME.
THE TANZORIAN RACE IS FACED WITH EXTINCTION.
TO SAVE THEMSELVES, THEY CREATE A GENETIC CALL FOR HELP.
HEATH2O
Written by: Rick Spears
Art by: James Callahan
AND LAUNCH IT INTO THE CHAOS.

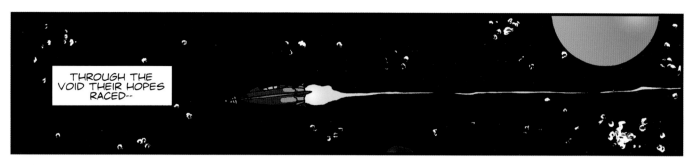

THROUGH THE VOID THEIR HOPES RACED--

--DEEPER AND FARTHER THAN ANY HAD TRAVELED BEFORE.

UNTIL FINALLY--

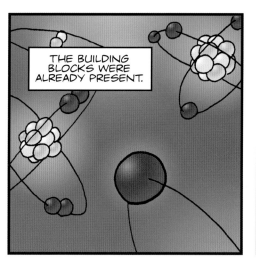

THE BUILDING BLOCKS WERE ALREADY PRESENT.

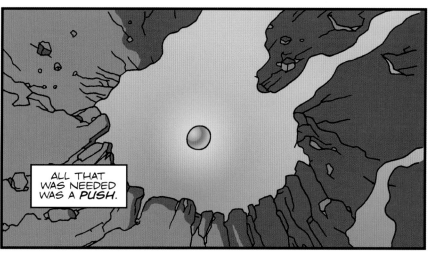

ALL THAT WAS NEEDED WAS A *PUSH*.

AND ON THIS *BLUE* PLANET--

--MILLIONS OF GENERATIONS OF EVOLUTION OCCURRED--

--IN WHAT THE TANZORIANS MEASURE AS ONLY A MATTER OF DAYS.

EVOLUTION ALL PREORDAINED BY THAT ANCIENT TANZORIAN GENETIC CODE--

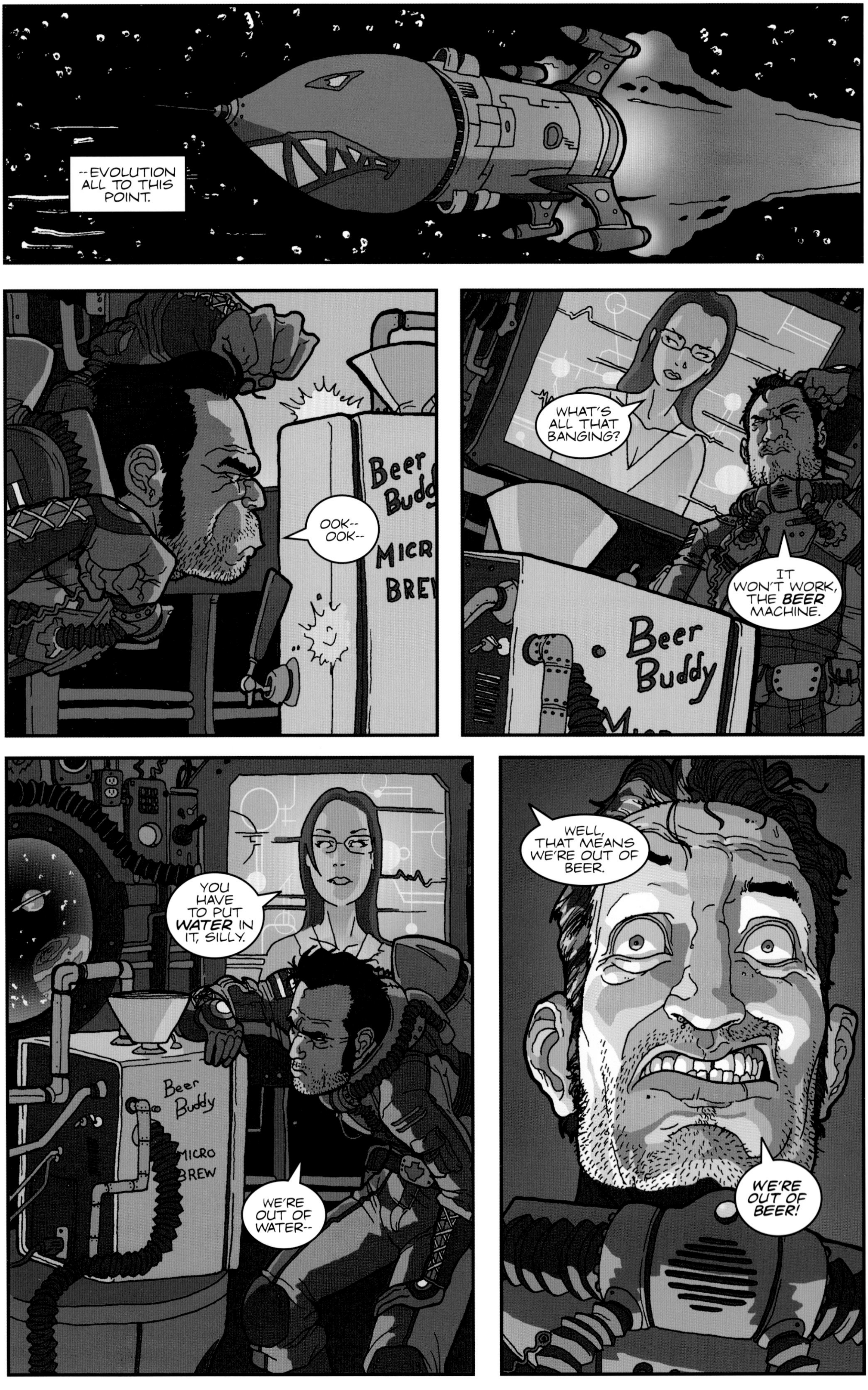
--EVOLUTION ALL TO THIS POINT.
OOK-- OOK--
Beer Buddy MICRO BREW
WHAT'S ALL THAT BANGING?
IT WON'T WORK, THE **BEER** MACHINE.
YOU HAVE TO PUT **WATER** IN IT, SILLY.
WE'RE OUT OF WATER--
WELL, THAT MEANS WE'RE OUT OF BEER.
WE'RE OUT OF BEER!

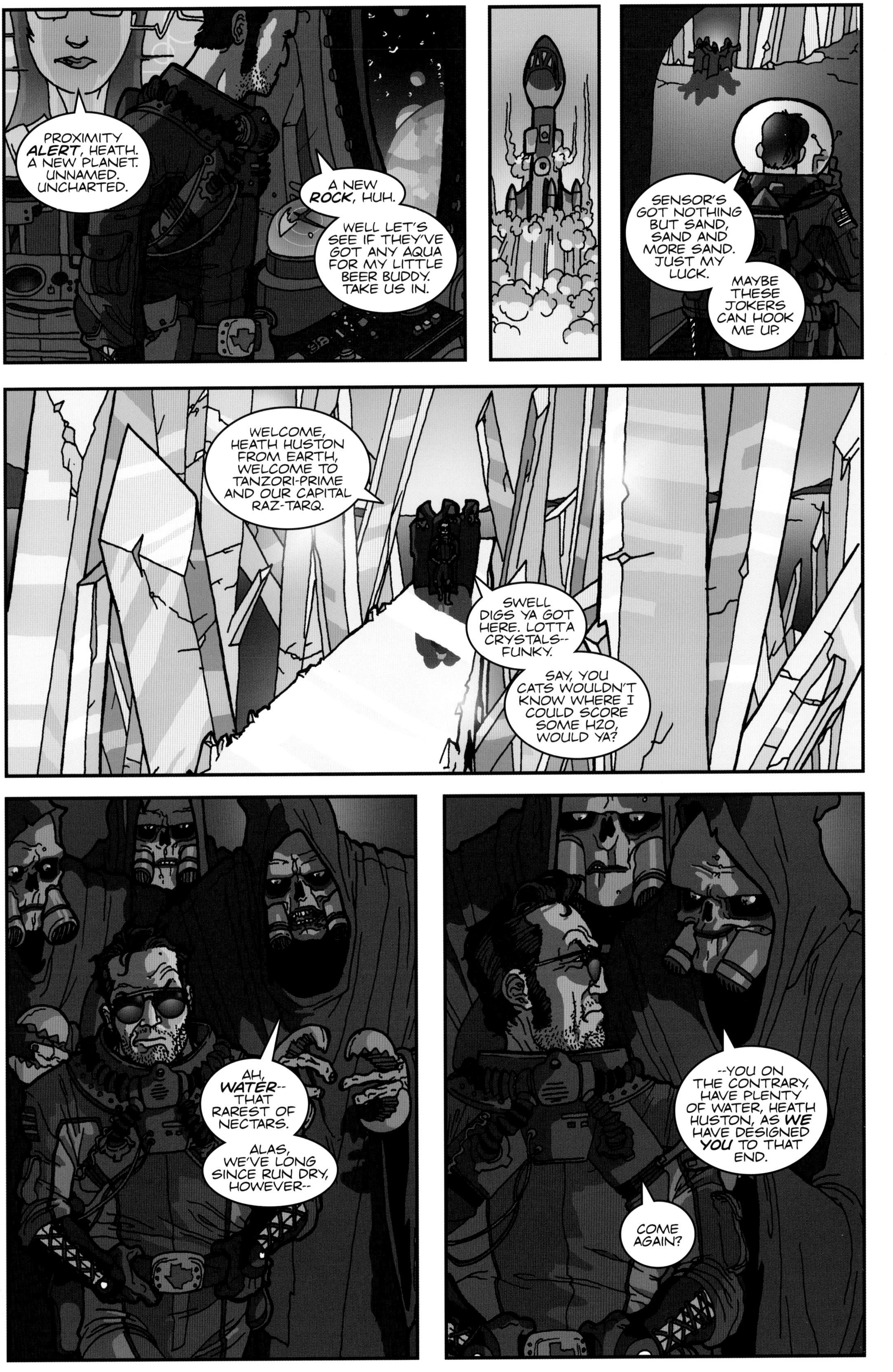
PROXIMITY ALERT, HEATH. A NEW PLANET. UNNAMED. UNCHARTED.
A NEW ROCK, HUH.
WELL LET'S SEE IF THEY'VE GOT ANY AQUA FOR MY LITTLE BEER BUDDY. TAKE US IN.
SENSOR'S GOT NOTHING BUT SAND, SAND AND MORE SAND. JUST MY LUCK.
MAYBE THESE JOKERS CAN HOOK ME UP.
WELCOME, HEATH HUSTON FROM EARTH, WELCOME TO TANZORI-PRIME AND OUR CAPITAL RAZ-TARQ.
SWELL DIGS YA GOT HERE. LOTTA CRYSTALS-- FUNKY.
SAY, YOU CATS WOULDN'T KNOW WHERE I COULD SCORE SOME H2O, WOULD YA?
AH, WATER-- THAT RAREST OF NECTARS.
ALAS, WE'VE LONG SINCE RUN DRY, HOWEVER--
--YOU ON THE CONTRARY, HAVE PLENTY OF WATER, HEATH HUSTON, AS WE HAVE DESIGNED YOU TO THAT END.
COME AGAIN?

WE GAVE YOU ARMS TO PULL YOURSELVES UP FROM THE MUCK. LEGS TO RUN. EYES TO SEE. A BRAIN TO GUIDE AND RULE THE FUNCTIONS.

AND *DREAMS*-- OUR GREATEST INVENTION. DREAMS TO PROD YOU TO EXPLORE, TO TRAVEL, TO SEEK OUT NEW WORLDS. TO SEEK OUT US. TO SEEK YOUR DESTINY.

SEE, HEATH HUSTON, YOUR HUMAN BODY IS ITSELF MOSTLY WATER. 60% IN FACT, AND YOU ARE BUT A TRANSPORTATION SYSTEM TO BRING THE WATER OF YOUR WORLD TO OURS.

NOW WE WILL HARVEST THAT WATER FROM YOUR FLESH AND THAT OF YOUR WHOLE RACE AND FILL OUR RIVERS, AND FILL OUR SEAS AND THE GLORY OF THE TANZORIAN EMPIRE WILL LIVE AGAIN, ANEW.

UH--YOU'RE SERIOUS AREN'T YOU, SKINNY?

I'M AFRAID SO, EARTH MAN.

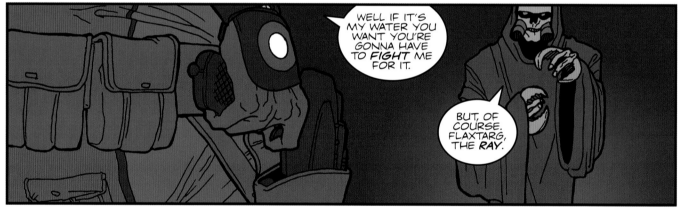

WELL IF IT'S MY WATER YOU WANT YOU'RE GONNA HAVE TO *FIGHT* ME FOR IT.

BUT, OF COURSE. FLAXTARG, THE *RAY*.

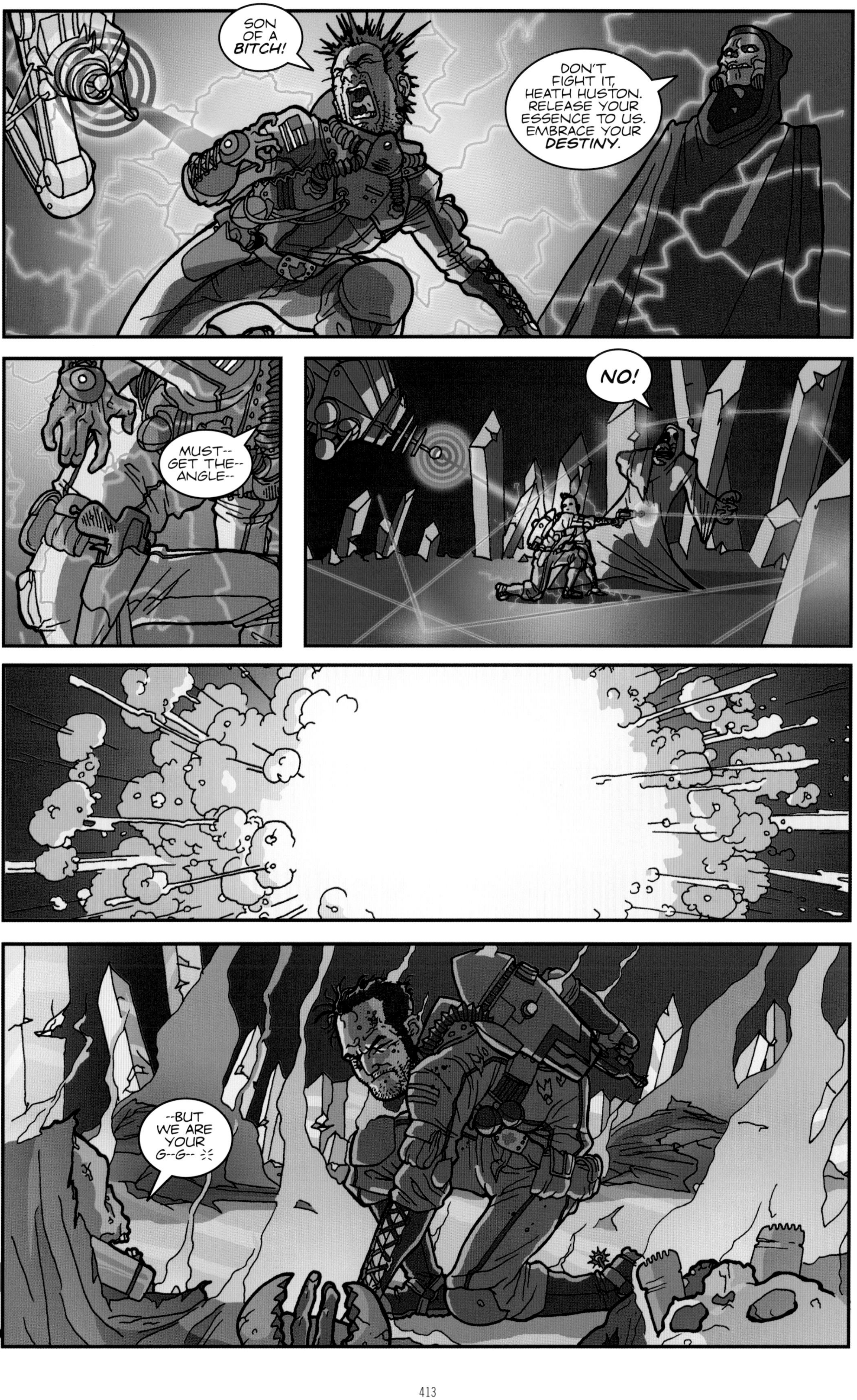
SON OF A BITCH!
DON'T FIGHT IT, HEATH HUSTON. RELEASE YOUR ESSENCE TO US. EMBRACE YOUR DESTINY.
MUST-- GET THE-- ANGLE--
NO!
--BUT WE ARE YOUR G--G--

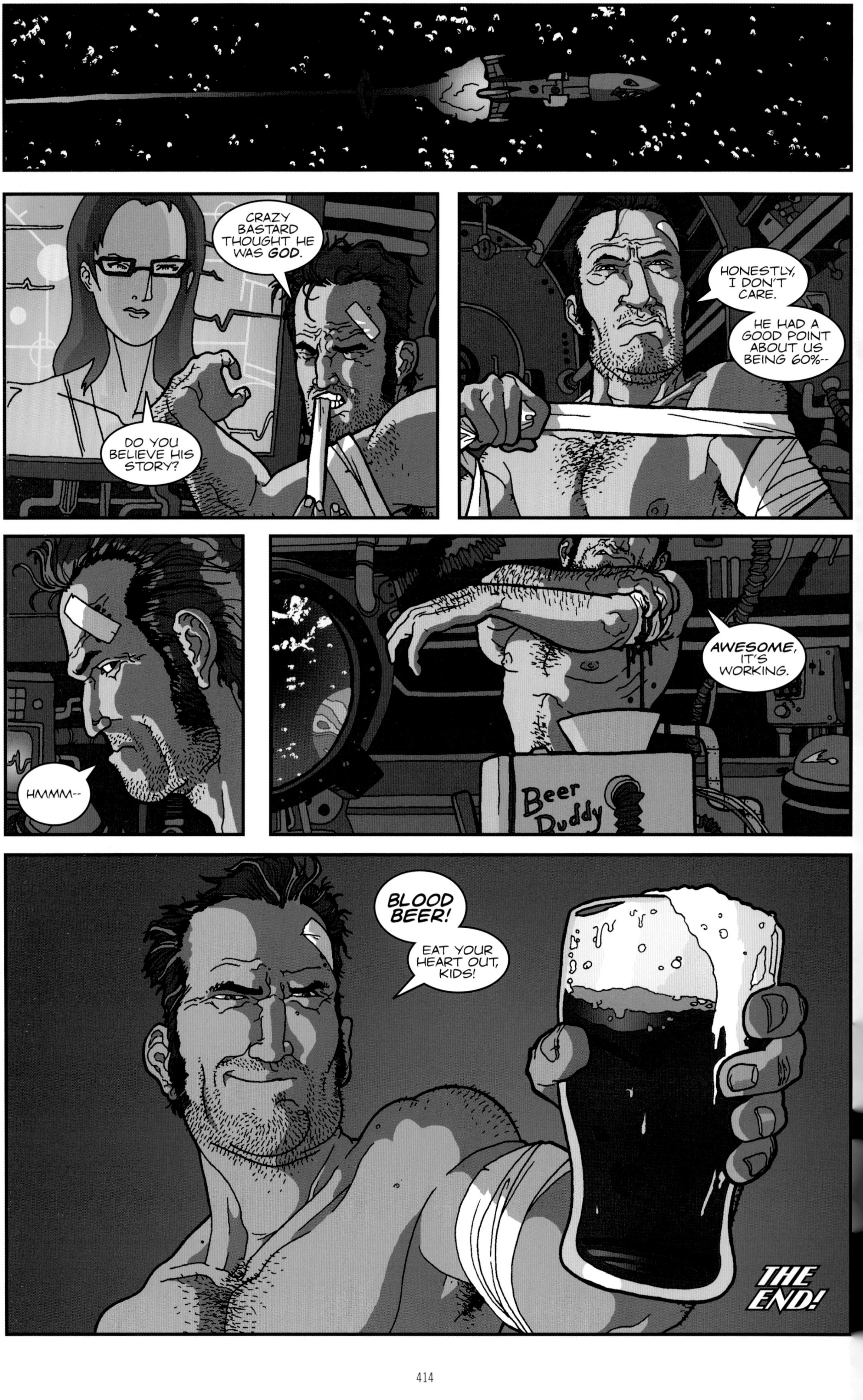
CRAZY BASTARD THOUGHT HE WAS **GOD**.
DO YOU BELIEVE HIS STORY?
HONESTLY, I DON'T CARE.
HE HAD A GOOD POINT ABOUT US BEING 60%--
HMMM--
AWESOME, IT'S WORKING.
Beer Buddy
BLOOD BEER!
EAT YOUR HEART OUT, KIDS!
THE END!

L'ESTASI DELL'ORO

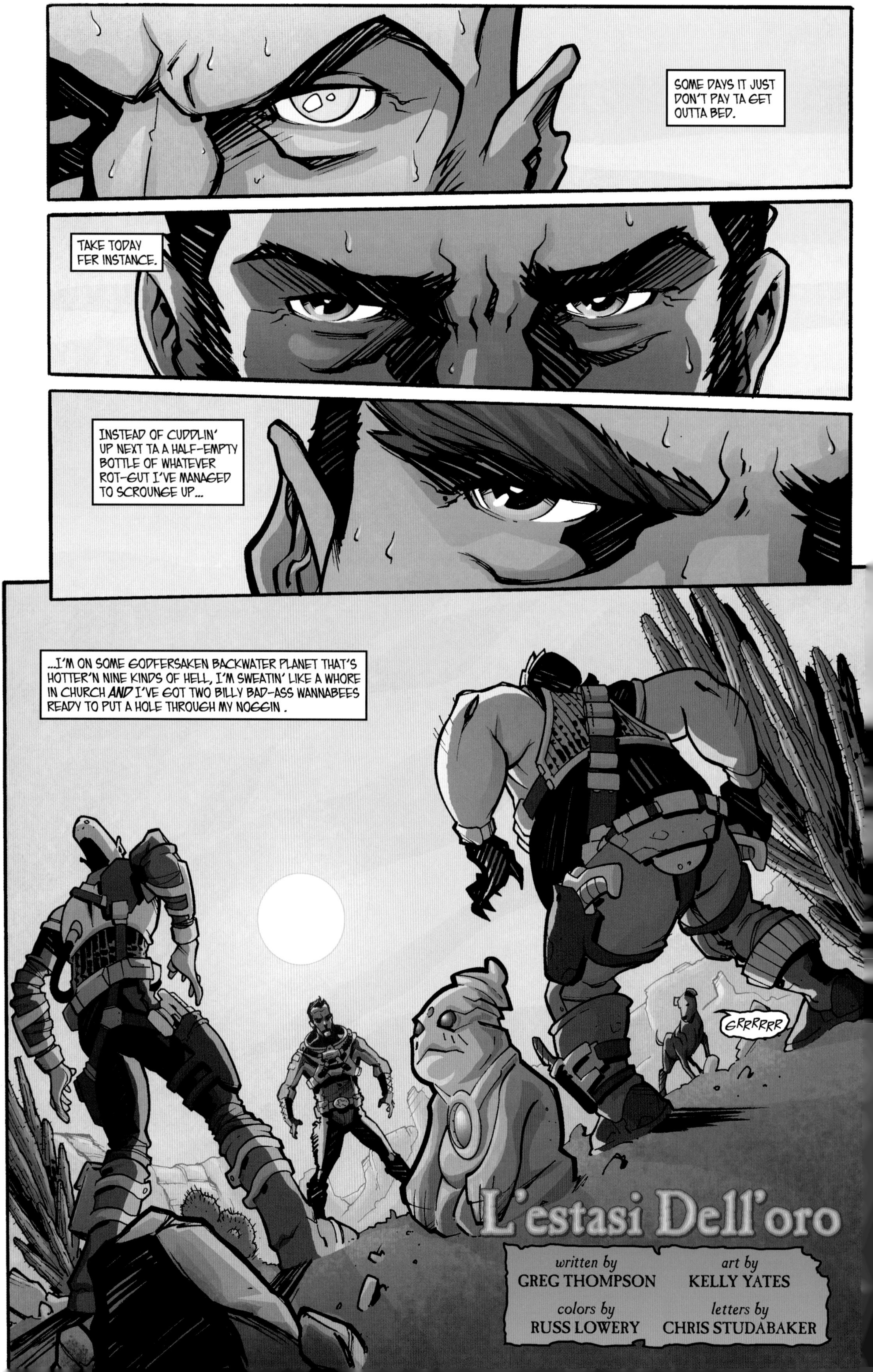
SOME DAYS IT JUST DON'T PAY TA GET OUTTA BED.
TAKE TODAY FER INSTANCE.
INSTEAD OF CUDDLIN' UP NEXT TA A HALF-EMPTY BOTTLE OF WHATEVER ROT-GUT I'VE MANAGED TO SCROUNGE UP...
...I'M ON SOME GODFERSAKEN BACKWATER PLANET THAT'S HOTTER'N NINE KINDS OF HELL, I'M SWEATIN' LIKE A WHORE IN CHURCH AND I'VE GOT TWO BILLY BAD-ASS WANNABEES READY TO PUT A HOLE THROUGH MY NOGGIN.
GRRRRRR
L'estasi Dell'oro
written by GREG THOMPSON
art by KELLY YATES
colors by RUSS LOWERY
letters by CHRIS STUDABAKER

THESE BOYS WENT AN' STOLE SOME GOLDEN IDOL FROM A BUNCHA YOKELS.

GRRRRR

MOST DAYS I WOULDN'T GIVE TWO SHITS ABOUT IT, BUT IT HAPPENED ON A SUNDAY. AND EVEN THOUGH I AIN'T BY NO MEANS A GOOD GOD-FEARIN' BAPTIST LIKE MY MOMMA WAS...

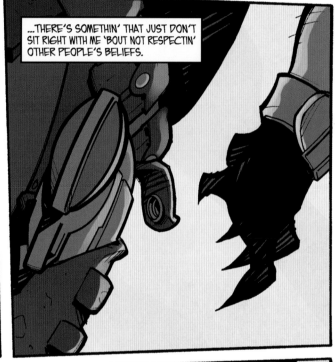

...THERE'S SOMETHIN' THAT JUST DON'T SIT RIGHT WITH ME 'BOUT NOT RESPECTIN' OTHER PEOPLE'S BELIEFS.

AW HELL, WHO'M I KIDDIN'?

I'M DOIN' IT FER THE MONEY.

THAT, AND A BOTTLE OF WHISKEY.

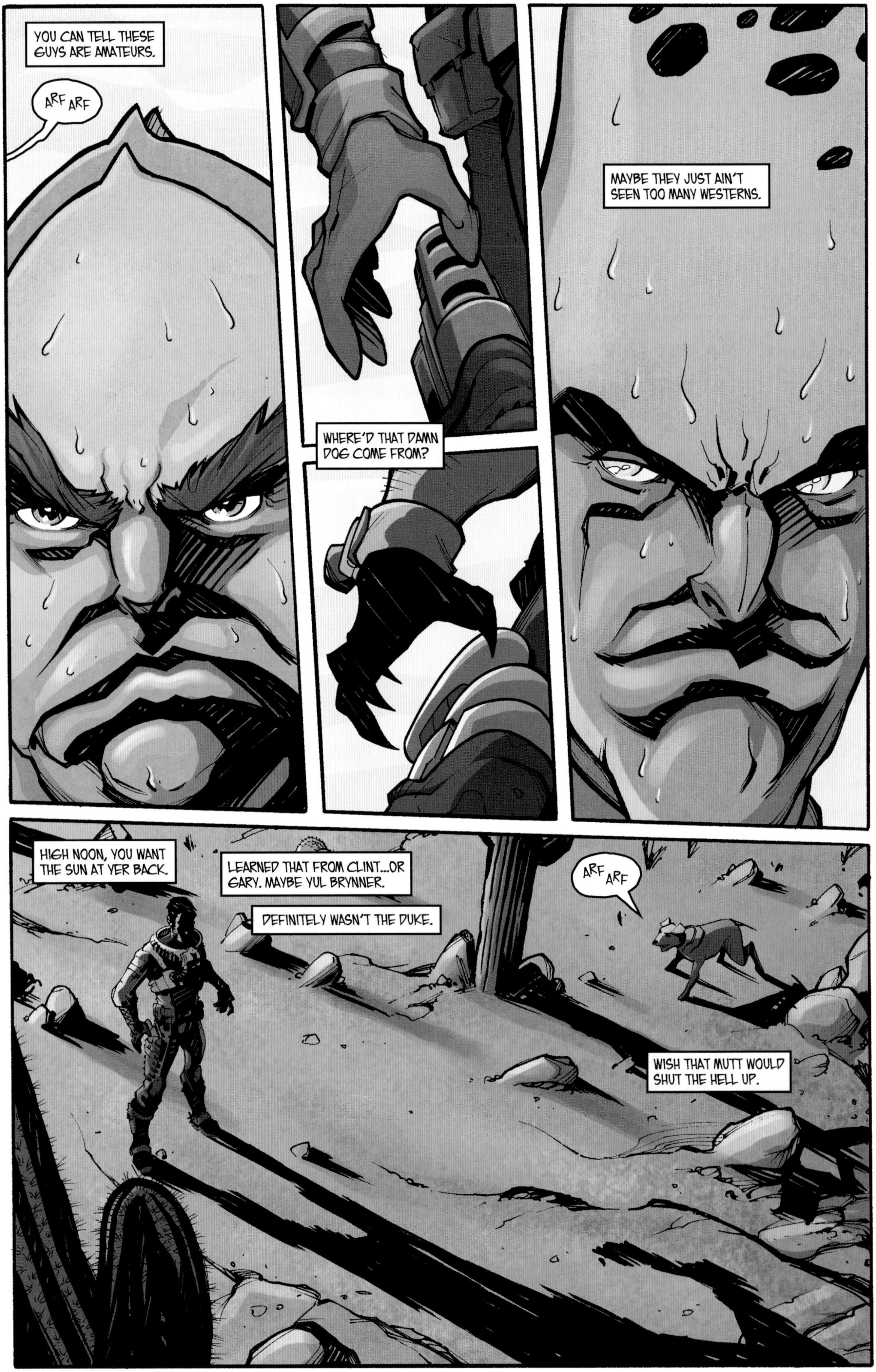
YOU CAN TELL THESE GUYS ARE AMATEURS.
ARF ARF
MAYBE THEY JUST AIN'T SEEN TOO MANY WESTERNS.
WHERE'D THAT DAMN DOG COME FROM?
HIGH NOON, YOU WANT THE SUN AT YER BACK.
LEARNED THAT FROM CLINT...OR GARY. MAYBE YUL BRYNNER.
DEFINITELY WASN'T THE DUKE.
ARF ARF
WISH THAT MUTT WOULD SHUT THE HELL UP.

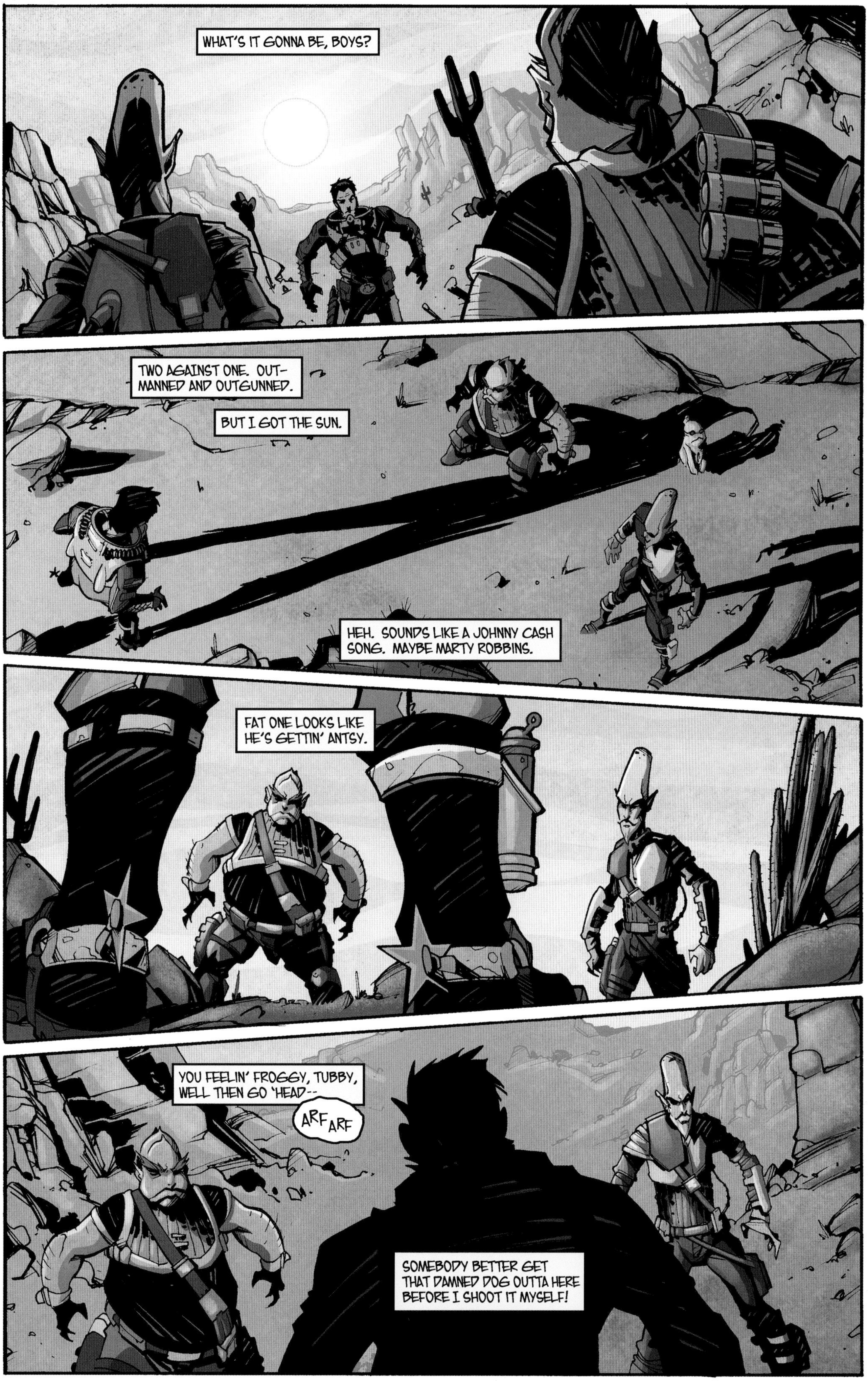
WHAT'S IT GONNA BE, BOYS?
TWO AGAINST ONE. OUT-MANNED AND OUTGUNNED.
BUT I GOT THE SUN.
HEH. SOUNDS LIKE A JOHNNY CASH SONG. MAYBE MARTY ROBBINS.
FAT ONE LOOKS LIKE HE'S GETTIN' ANTSY.
YOU FEELIN' FROGGY, TUBBY, WELL THEN GO 'HEAD--
ARF ARF
SOMEBODY BETTER GET THAT DAMNED DOG OUTTA HERE BEFORE I SHOOT IT MYSELF!

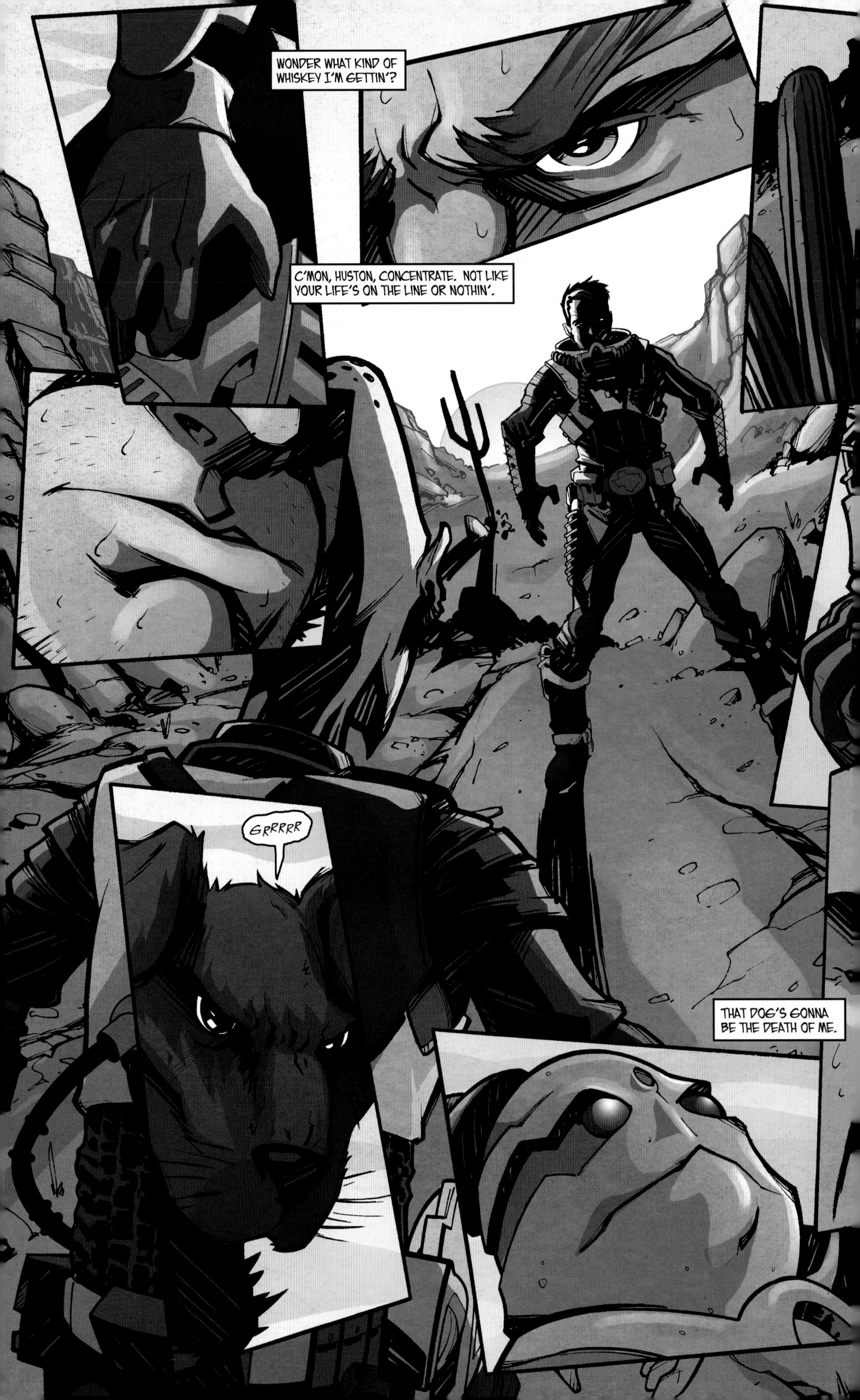
WONDER WHAT KIND OF WHISKEY I'M GETTIN'?
C'MON, HUSTON, CONCENTRATE. NOT LIKE YOUR LIFE'S ON THE LINE OR NOTHIN'.
GRRRRR
THAT DOG'S GONNA BE THE DEATH OF ME.

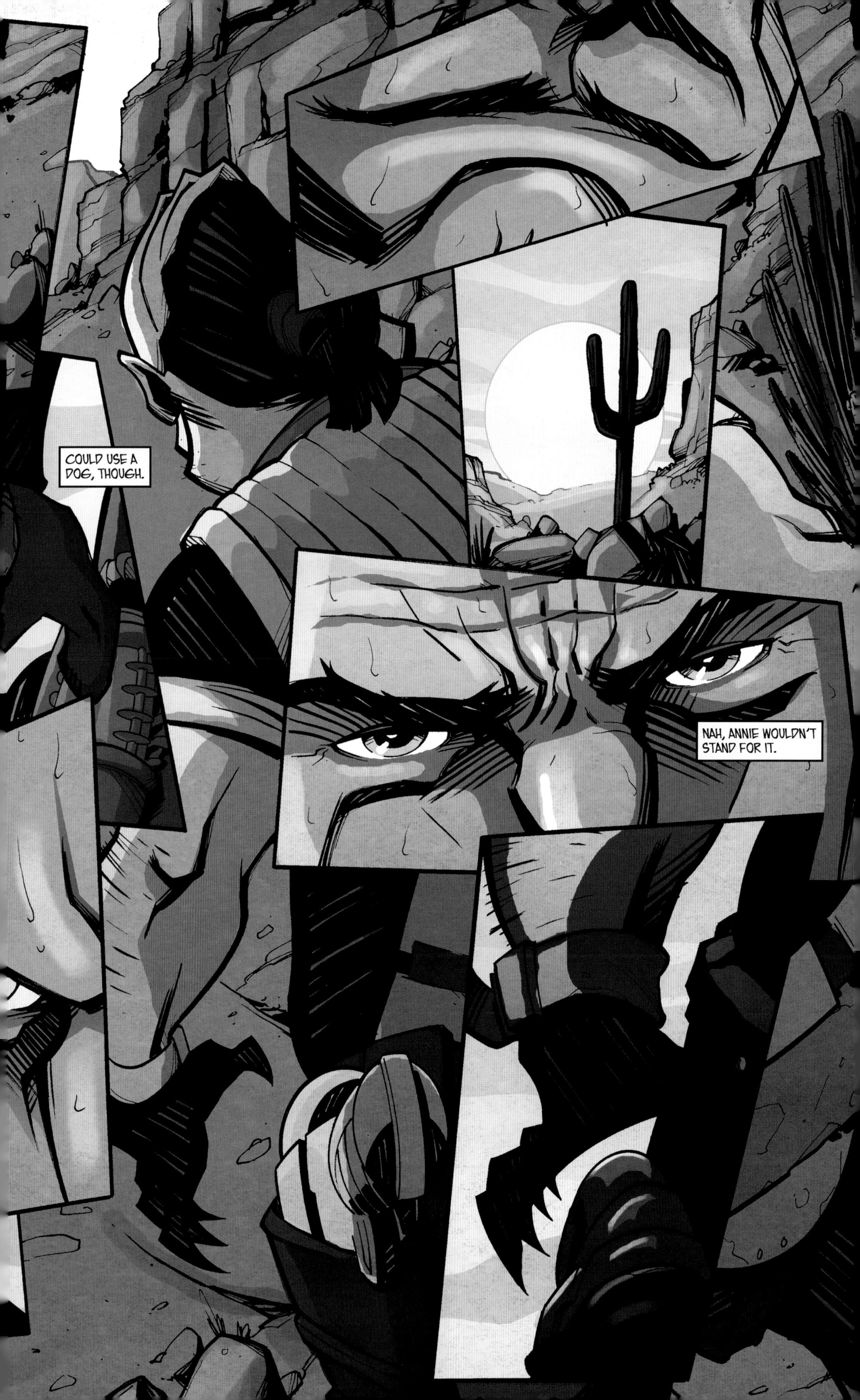
COULD USE A DOG, THOUGH.
NAH, ANNIE WOULDN'T STAND FOR IT.

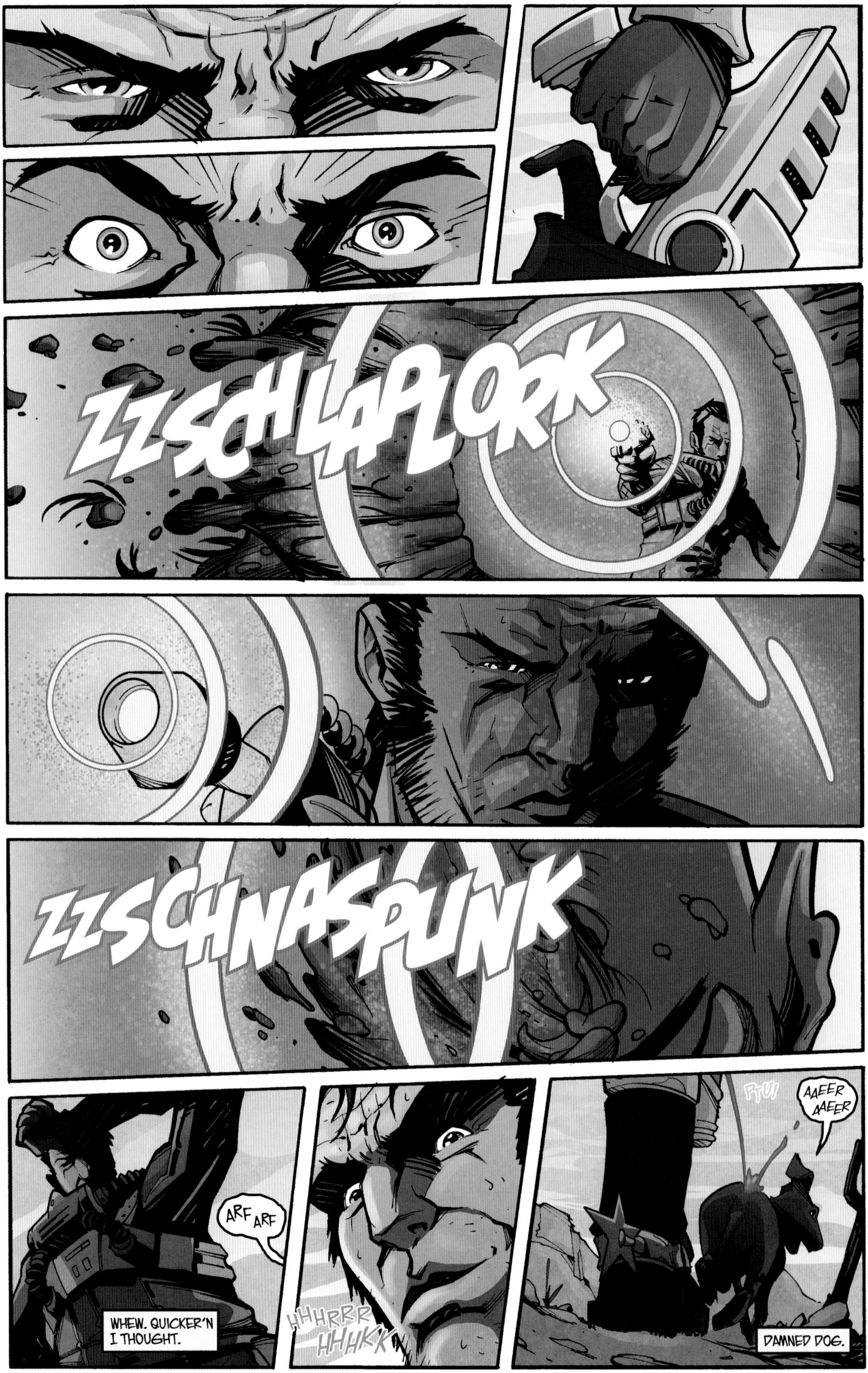
ZZSCHLAPLORK
ZZSCHNASPUNK
ARF ARF
WHEW. QUICKER'N I THOUGHT.
HHHRRR HHHKK
PTUI
AAEER AAEER
DAMNED DOG.

end

BUGGED

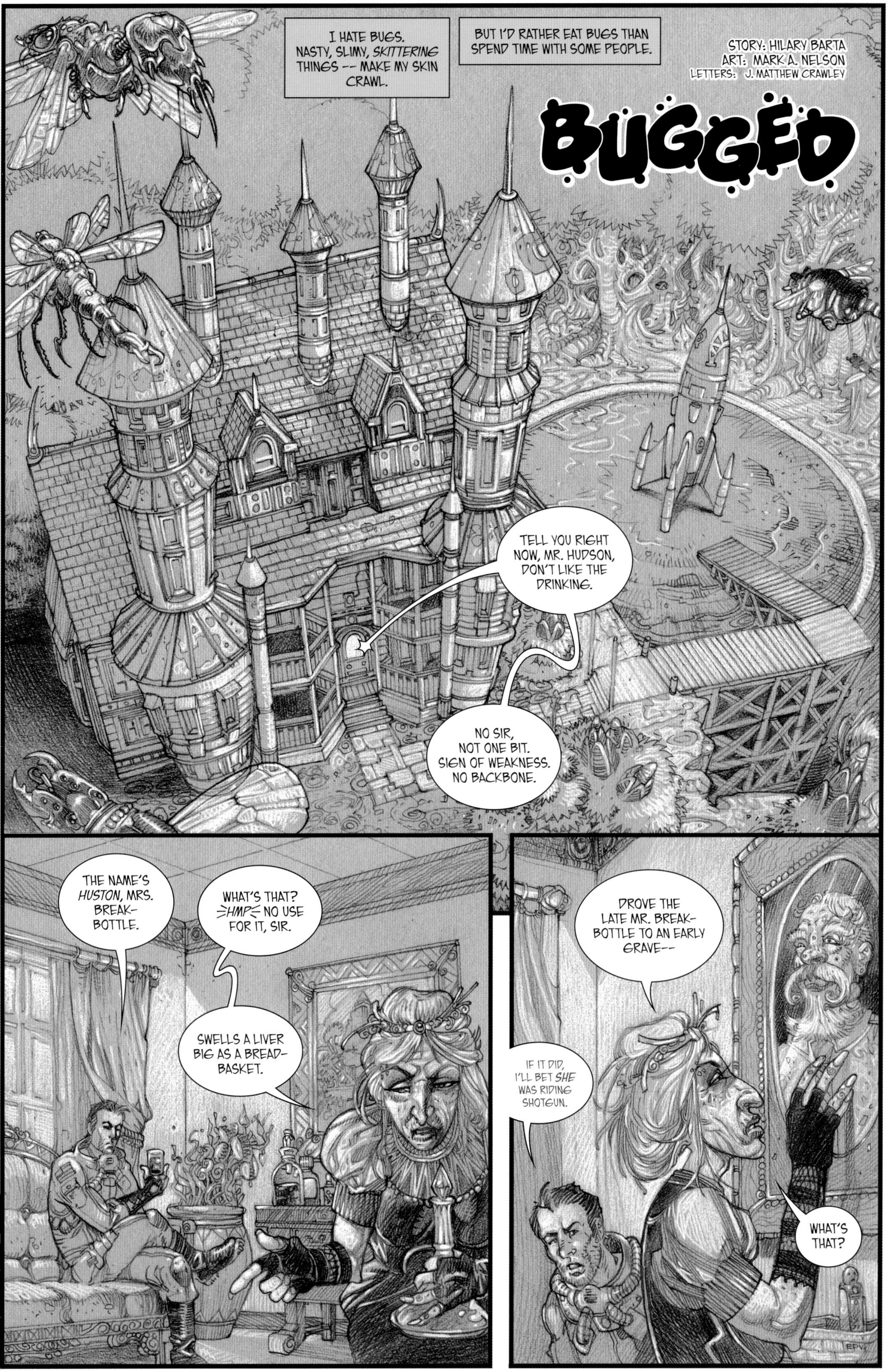

I HATE BUGS. NASTY, SLIMY, SKITTERING THINGS -- MAKE MY SKIN CRAWL.
BUT I'D RATHER EAT BUGS THAN SPEND TIME WITH SOME PEOPLE.
STORY: HILARY BARTA
ART: MARK A. NELSON
LETTERS: J. MATTHEW CRAWLEY
BUGGED
TELL YOU RIGHT NOW, MR. HUDSON, DON'T LIKE THE DRINKING.
NO SIR, NOT ONE BIT. SIGN OF WEAKNESS. NO BACKBONE.
THE NAME'S HUSTON, MRS. BREAK-BOTTLE.
WHAT'S THAT? HMP NO USE FOR IT, SIR.
SWELLS A LIVER BIG AS A BREAD-BASKET.
DROVE THE LATE MR. BREAK-BOTTLE TO AN EARLY GRAVE--
IF IT DID, I'LL BET SHE WAS RIDING SHOTGUN.
WHAT'S THAT?

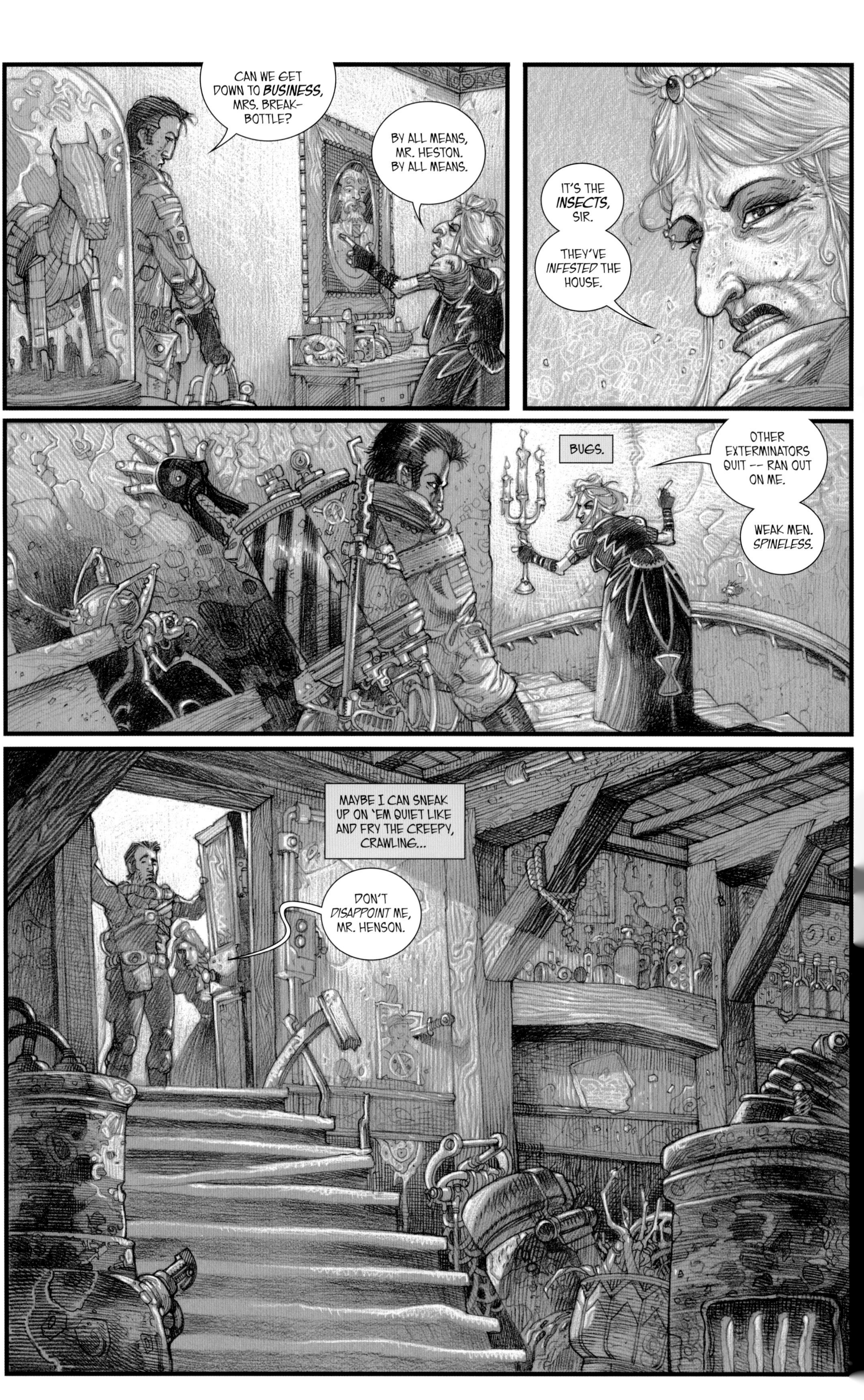
CAN WE GET DOWN TO BUSINESS, MRS. BREAK-BOTTLE?
BY ALL MEANS, MR. HESTON. BY ALL MEANS.
IT'S THE INSECTS, SIR.
THEY'VE INFESTED THE HOUSE.
BUGS.
OTHER EXTERMINATORS QUIT -- RAN OUT ON ME.
WEAK MEN. SPINELESS.
MAYBE I CAN SNEAK UP ON 'EM QUIET LIKE AND FRY THE CREEPY, CRAWLING...
DON'T DISAPPOINT ME, MR. HENSON.

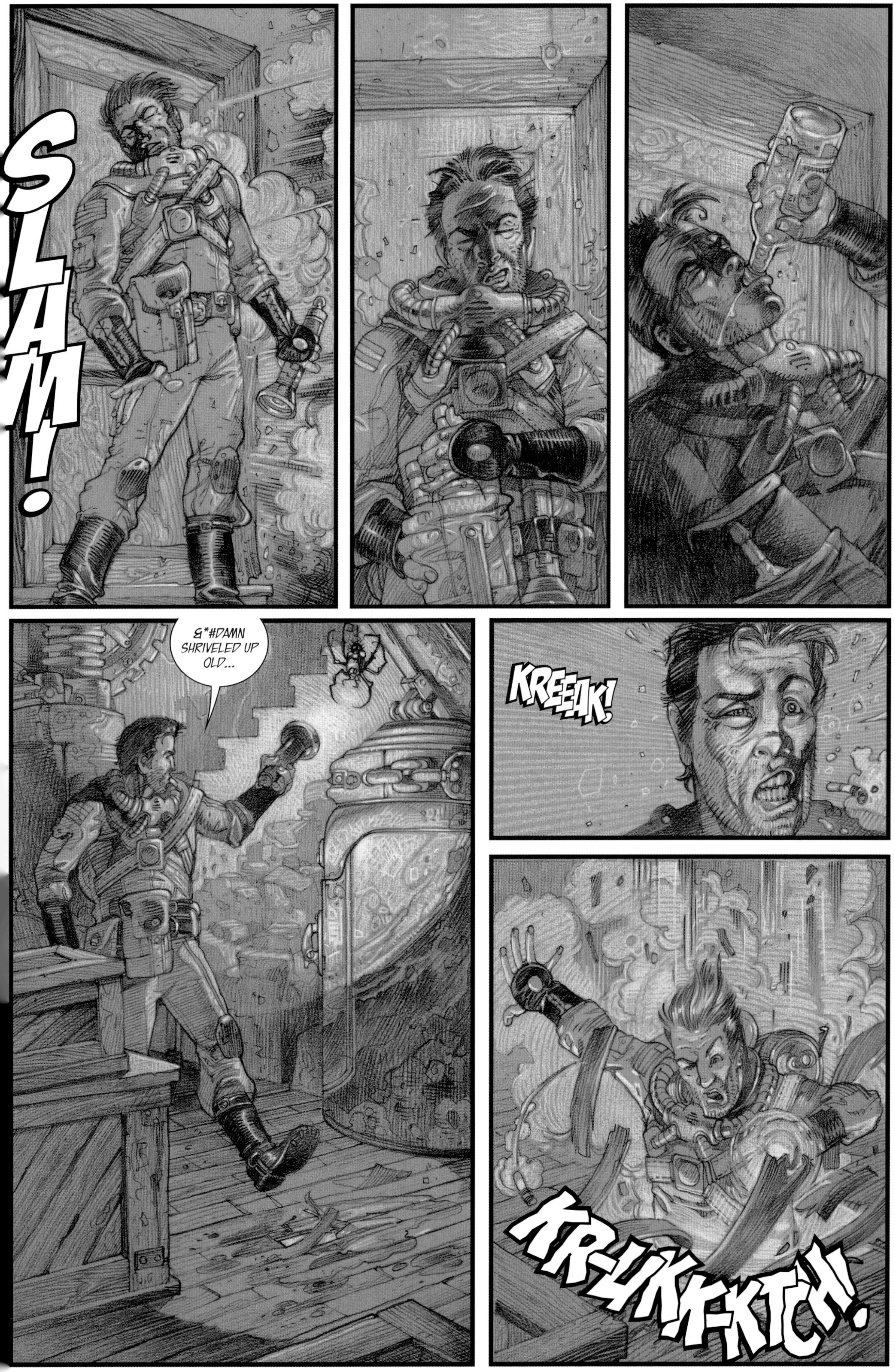
SLAM!
&*#DAMN SHRIVELED UP OLD...
KREEEAK!
KR-UNK-KTCH!

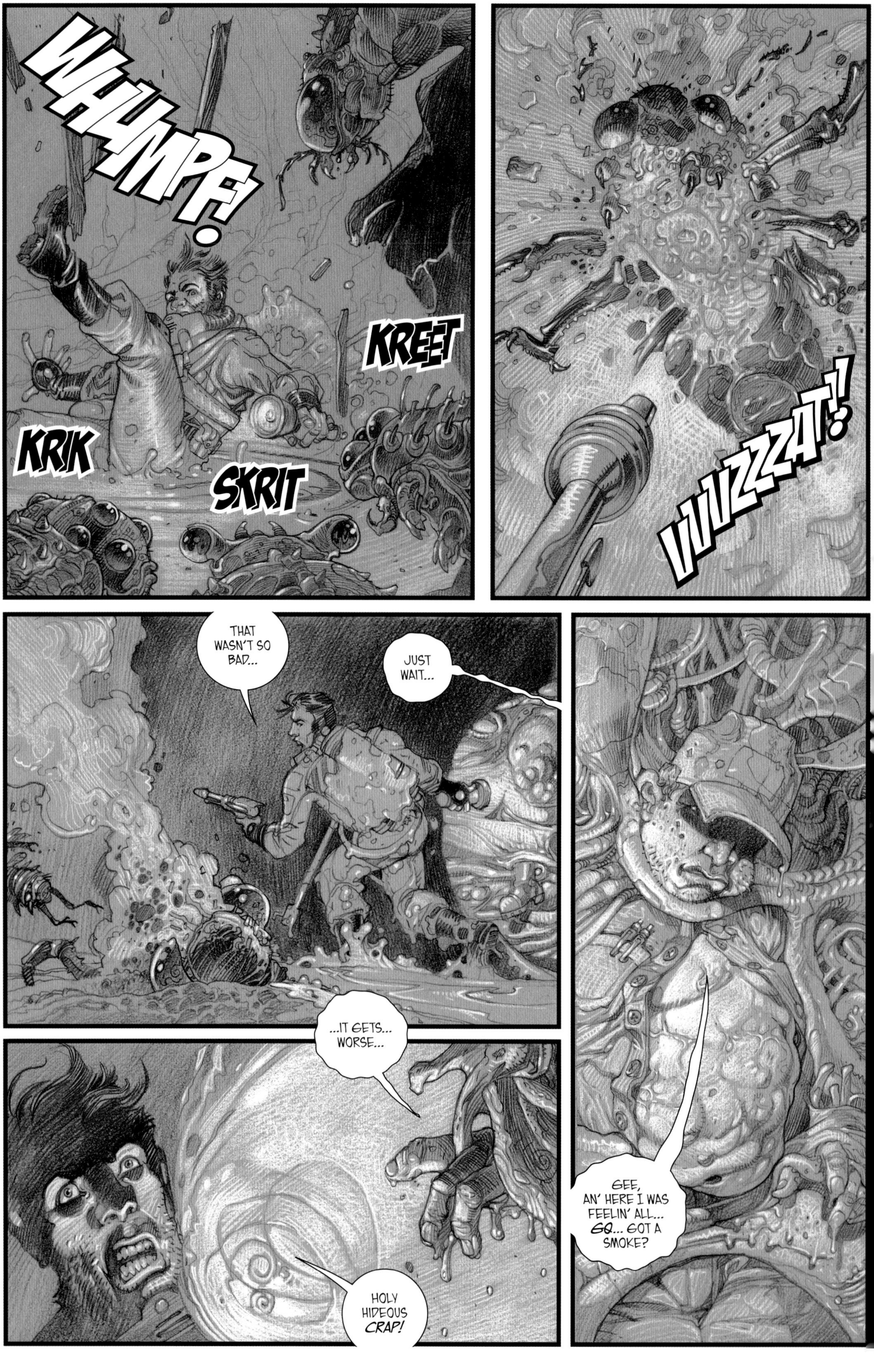
WHUMPF!
KREET
KRIK
SKRIT
VVVZZZZAT!
THAT WASN'T SO BAD...
JUST WAIT...
...IT GETS... WORSE...
HOLY HIDEOUS CRAP!
GEE, AN' HERE I WAS FEELIN' ALL... GQ... GOT A SMOKE?

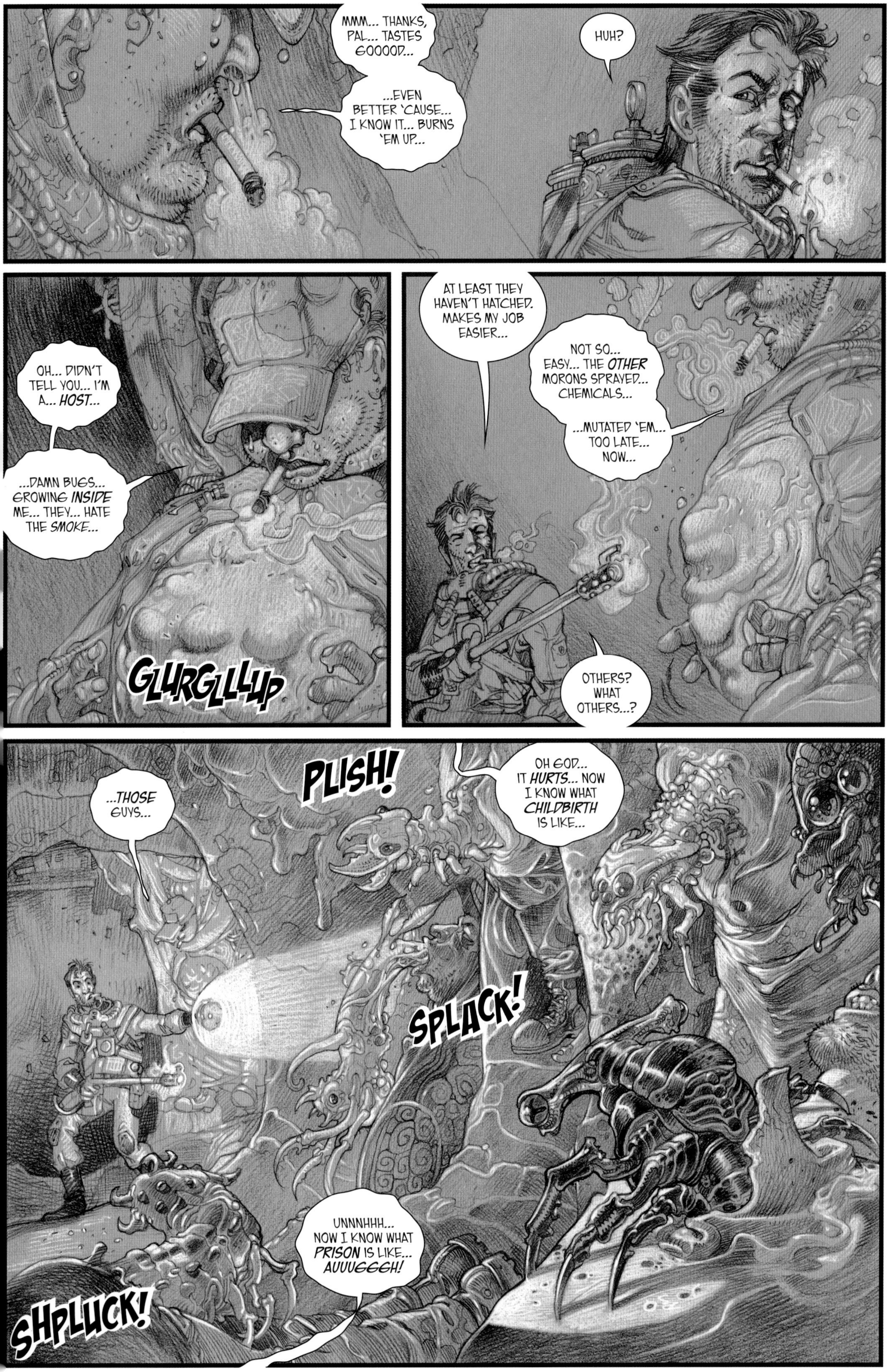
MMM... THANKS, PAL... TASTES GOOOOD...
...EVEN BETTER 'CAUSE... I KNOW IT... BURNS 'EM UP...
HUH?
OH... DIDN'T TELL YOU... I'M A... HOST...
...DAMN BUGS... GROWING INSIDE ME... THEY... HATE THE SMOKE...
GLURGLLLUP
AT LEAST THEY HAVEN'T HATCHED. MAKES MY JOB EASIER...
NOT SO... EASY... THE OTHER MORONS SPRAYED... CHEMICALS...
...MUTATED 'EM... TOO LATE... NOW...
OTHERS? WHAT OTHERS...?
...THOSE GUYS...
PLISH!
OH GOD... IT HURTS... NOW I KNOW WHAT CHILDBIRTH IS LIKE...
SPLACK!
UNNNHHH... NOW I KNOW WHAT PRISON IS LIKE... AUUUGGGH!
SHPLUCK!

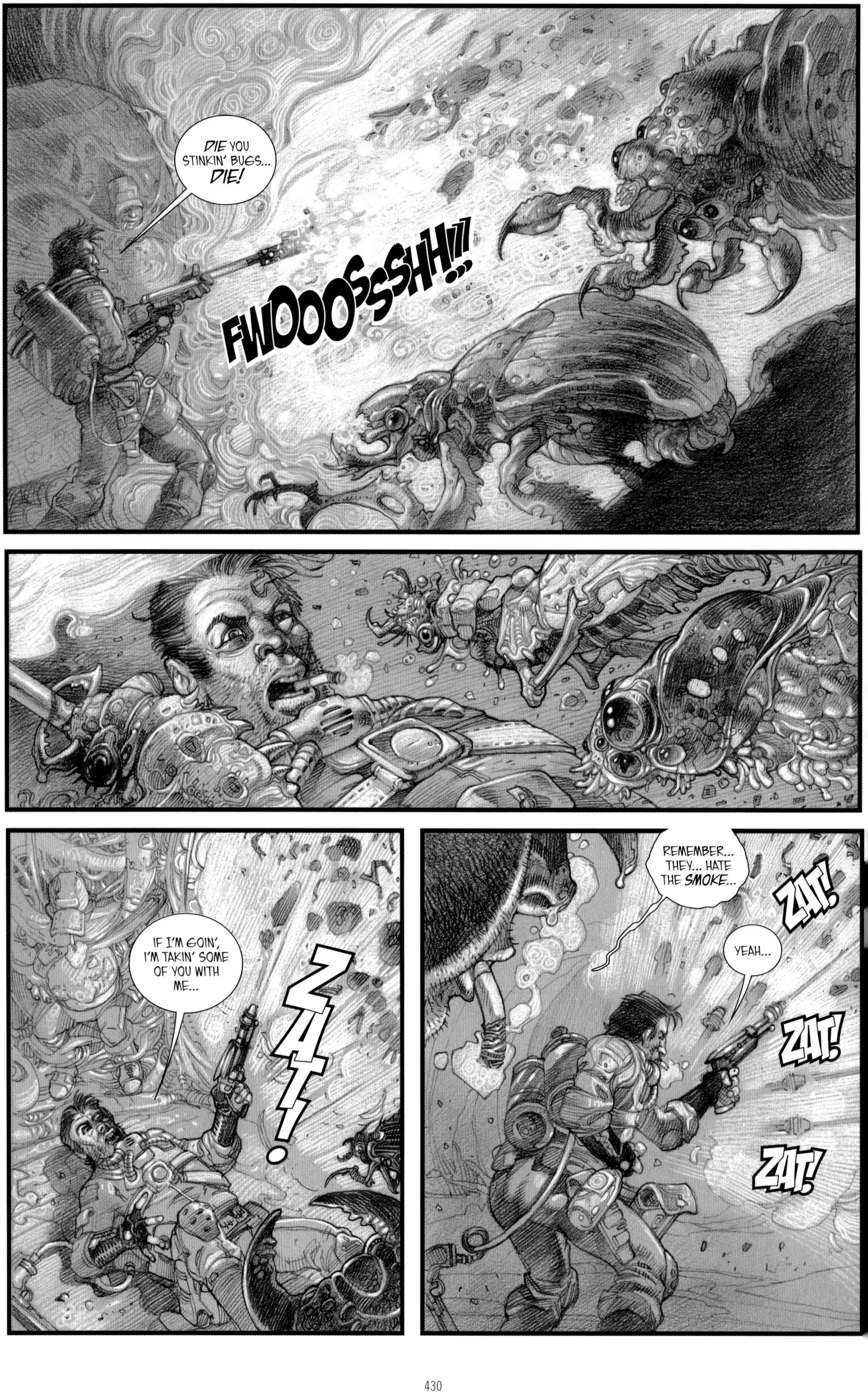
DIE YOU STINKIN' BUGS... DIE!
FWOOOSSSHH!!!
IF I'M GOIN', I'M TAKIN' SOME OF YOU WITH ME...
ZAT!
REMEMBER... THEY... HATE THE SMOKE...
ZAT!
YEAH...
ZAT!
ZAT!

AN' I HATE DOIN' THIS TO PERFECTLY GOOD HOOCH...

KSSHH!

PTOOP!

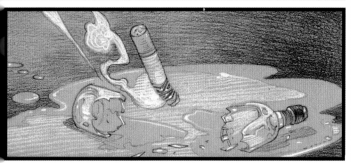

WHHOOOSH!

SKREEEK!

THANKS, PAL. MY TURN --

--TIME FOR BUG FLAMBÉ.

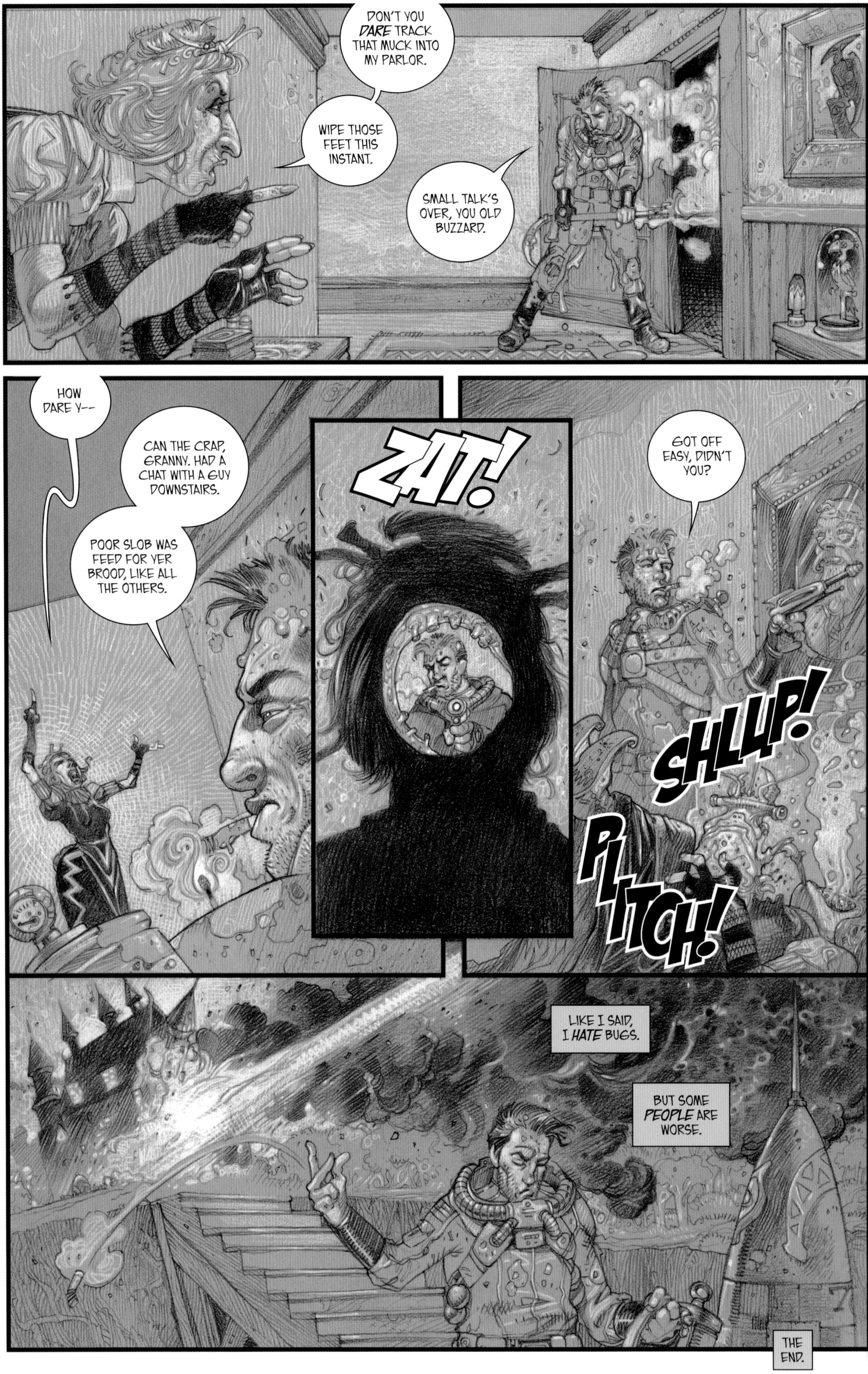
DON'T YOU DARE TRACK THAT MUCK INTO MY PARLOR.
WIPE THOSE FEET THIS INSTANT.
SMALL TALK'S OVER, YOU OLD BUZZARD.
HOW DARE Y--
CAN THE CRAP, GRANNY. HAD A CHAT WITH A GUY DOWNSTAIRS.
POOR SLOB WAS FEED FOR YER BROOD, LIKE ALL THE OTHERS.
ZAT!
GOT OFF EASY, DIDN'T YOU?
SHLUP!
PLITCH!
LIKE I SAID, I HATE BUGS.
BUT SOME PEOPLE ARE WORSE.
THE END.

THE DAMSEL IN THE DISTRESS SIGNAL

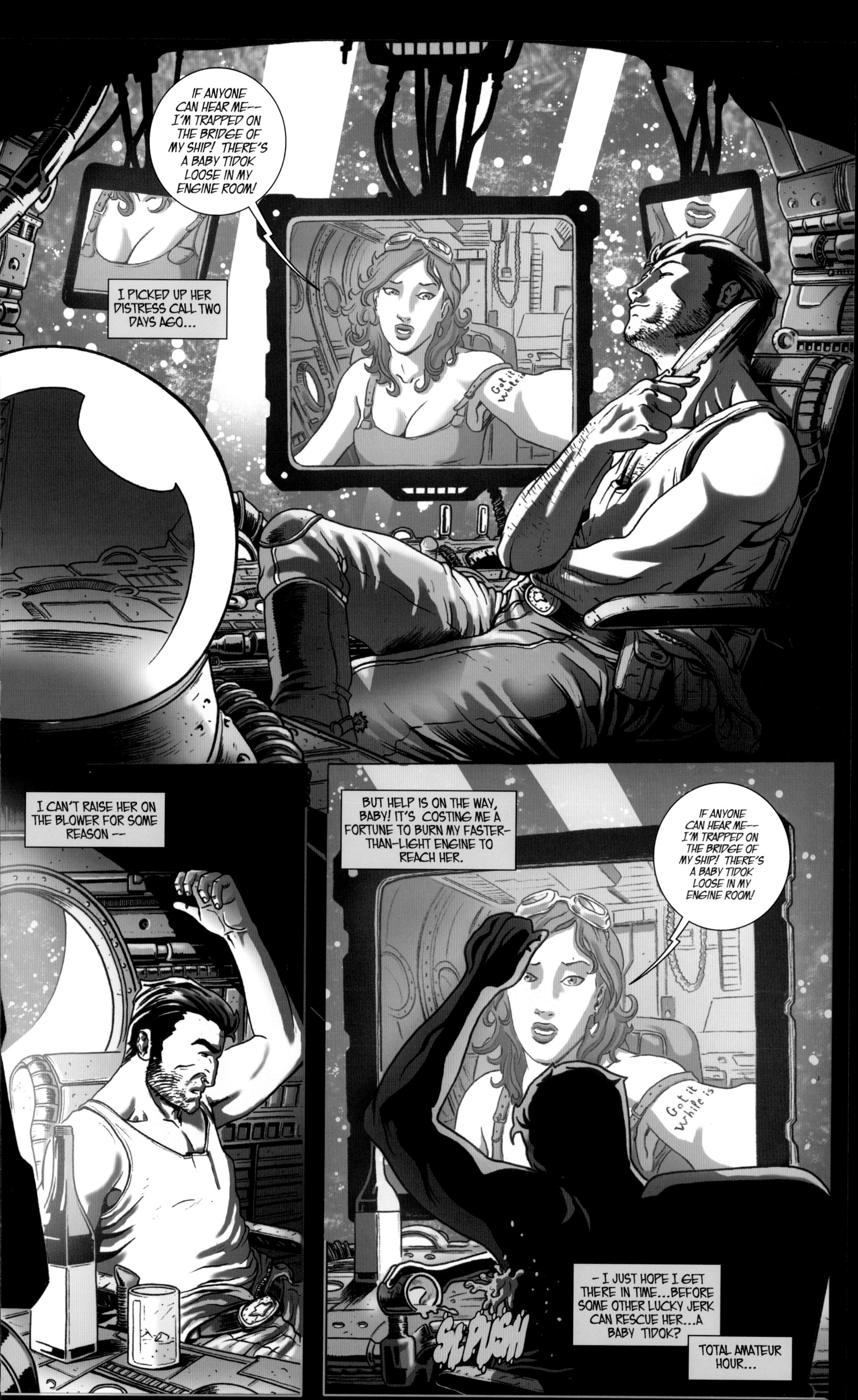
IF ANYONE CAN HEAR ME-- I'M TRAPPED ON THE BRIDGE OF MY SHIP! THERE'S A BABY TIDOK LOOSE IN MY ENGINE ROOM!
I PICKED UP HER DISTRESS CALL TWO DAYS AGO...
I CAN'T RAISE HER ON THE BLOWER FOR SOME REASON --
BUT HELP IS ON THE WAY, BABY! IT'S COSTING ME A FORTUNE TO BURN MY FASTER-THAN-LIGHT ENGINE TO REACH HER.
IF ANYONE CAN HEAR ME-- I'M TRAPPED ON THE BRIDGE OF MY SHIP! THERE'S A BABY TIDOK LOOSE IN MY ENGINE ROOM!
- I JUST HOPE I GET THERE IN TIME...BEFORE SOME OTHER LUCKY JERK CAN RESCUE HER...A BABY TIDOK?
SKPLUSH
TOTAL AMATEUR HOUR...

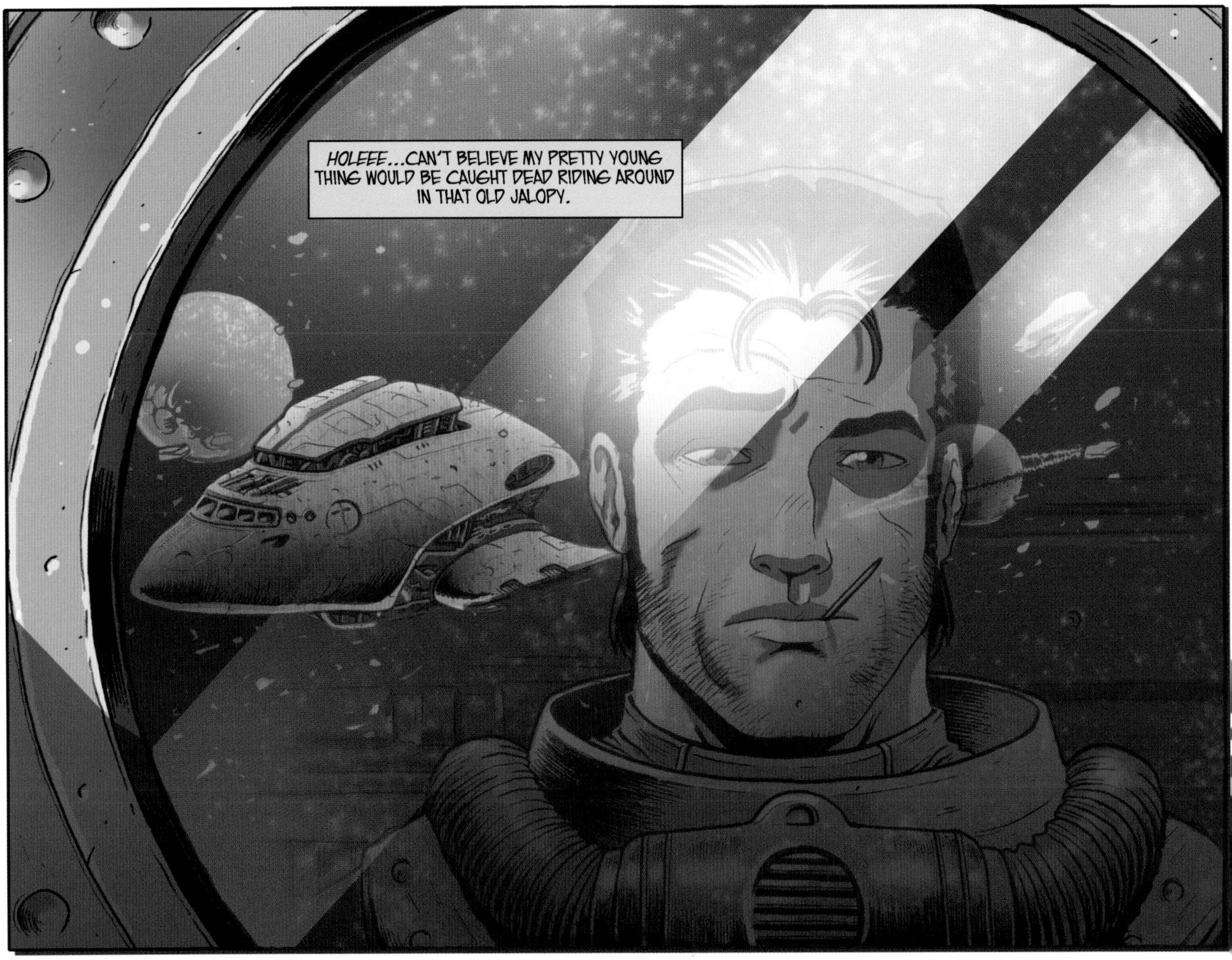
HOLEEE...CAN'T BELIEVE MY PRETTY YOUNG THING WOULD BE CAUGHT DEAD RIDING AROUND IN THAT OLD JALOPY.

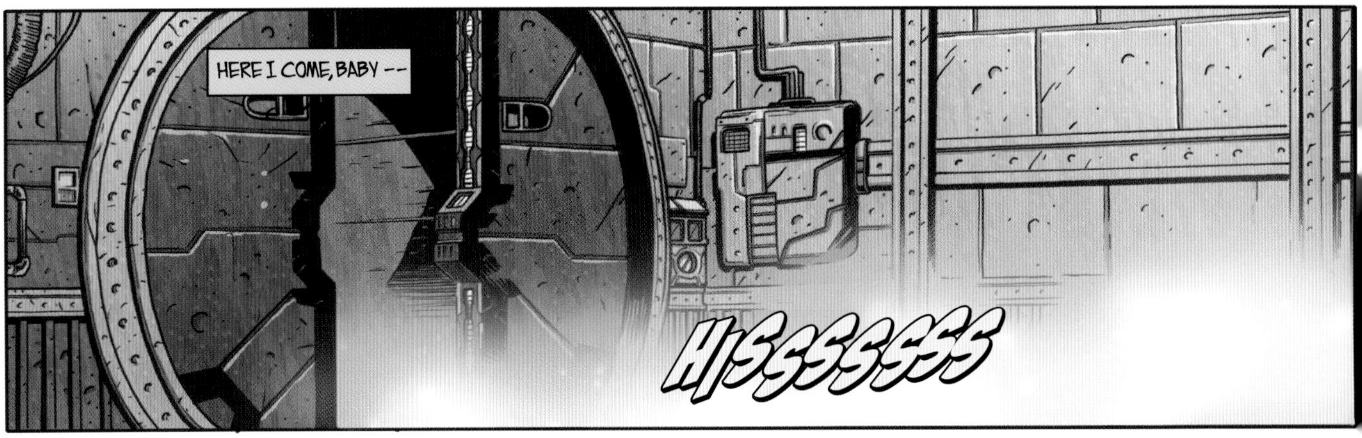
HERE I COME, BABY --
HISSSSSSS

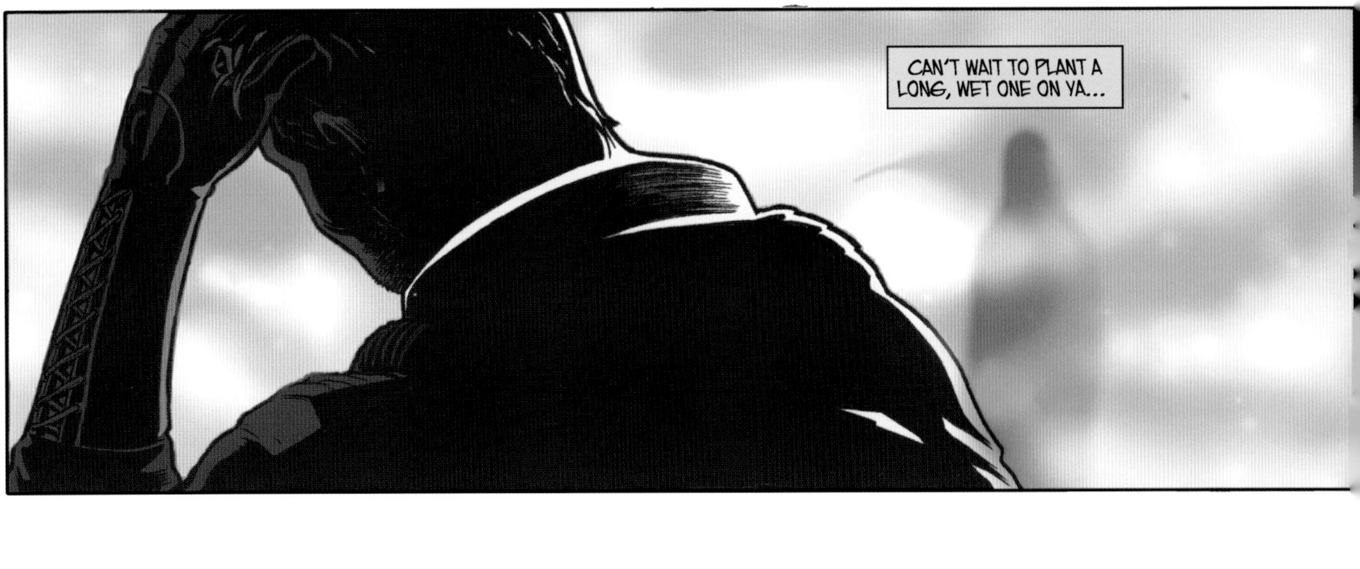
CAN'T WAIT TO PLANT A LONG, WET ONE ON YA...

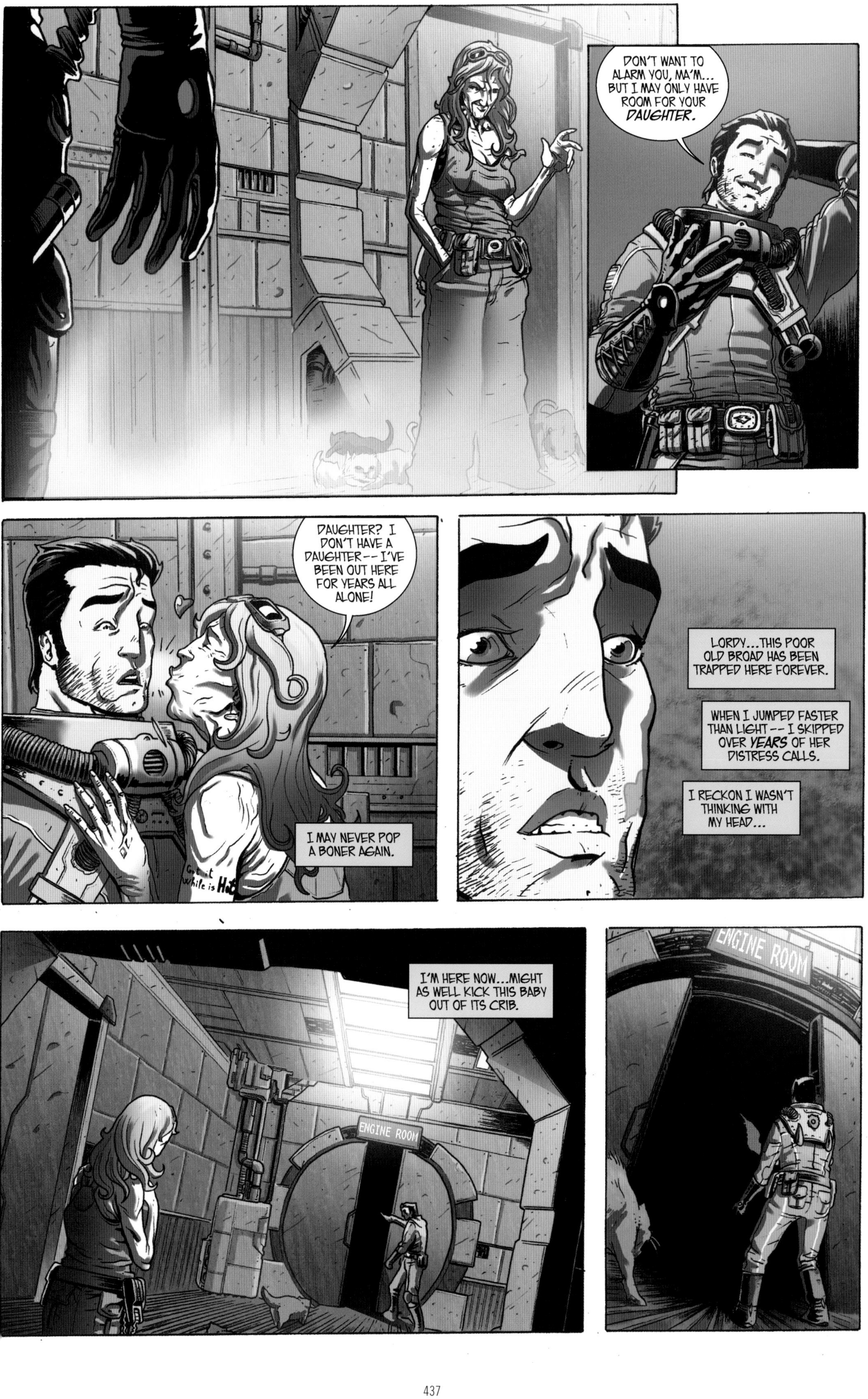
DON'T WANT TO ALARM YOU, MA'M... BUT I MAY ONLY HAVE ROOM FOR YOUR DAUGHTER.
DAUGHTER? I DON'T HAVE A DAUGHTER-- I'VE BEEN OUT HERE FOR YEARS ALL ALONE!
I MAY NEVER POP A BONER AGAIN.
LORDY...THIS POOR OLD BROAD HAS BEEN TRAPPED HERE FOREVER.
WHEN I JUMPED FASTER THAN LIGHT -- I SKIPPED OVER YEARS OF HER DISTRESS CALLS.
I RECKON I WASN'T THINKING WITH MY HEAD...
I'M HERE NOW...MIGHT AS WELL KICK THIS BABY OUT OF ITS CRIB.
ENGINE ROOM
ENGINE ROOM

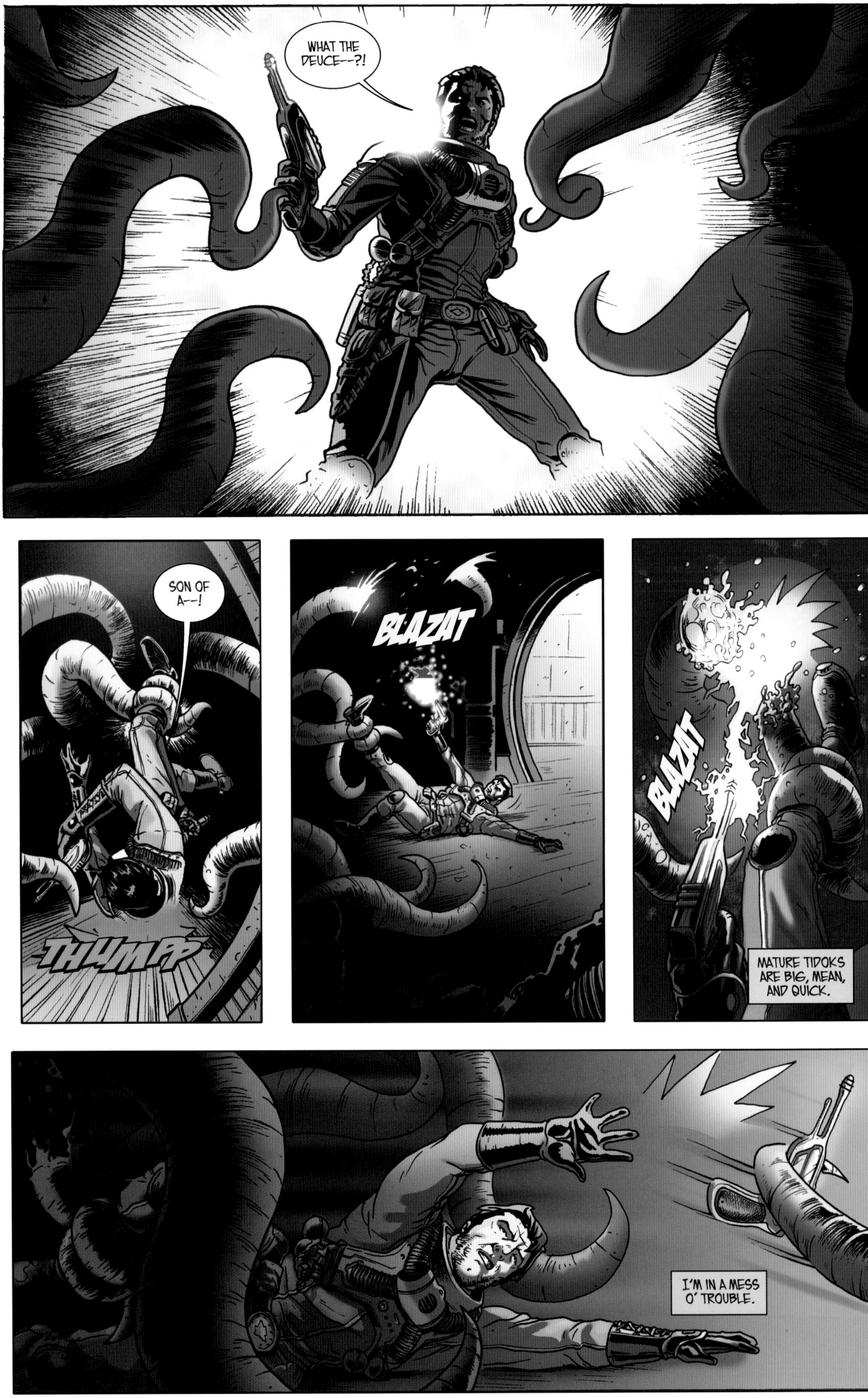
WHAT THE DEUCE--?!
SON OF A--!
THUMPP
BLAZAT
BLAZAT
MATURE TIDOKS ARE BIG, MEAN, AND QUICK.
I'M IN A MESS O' TROUBLE.

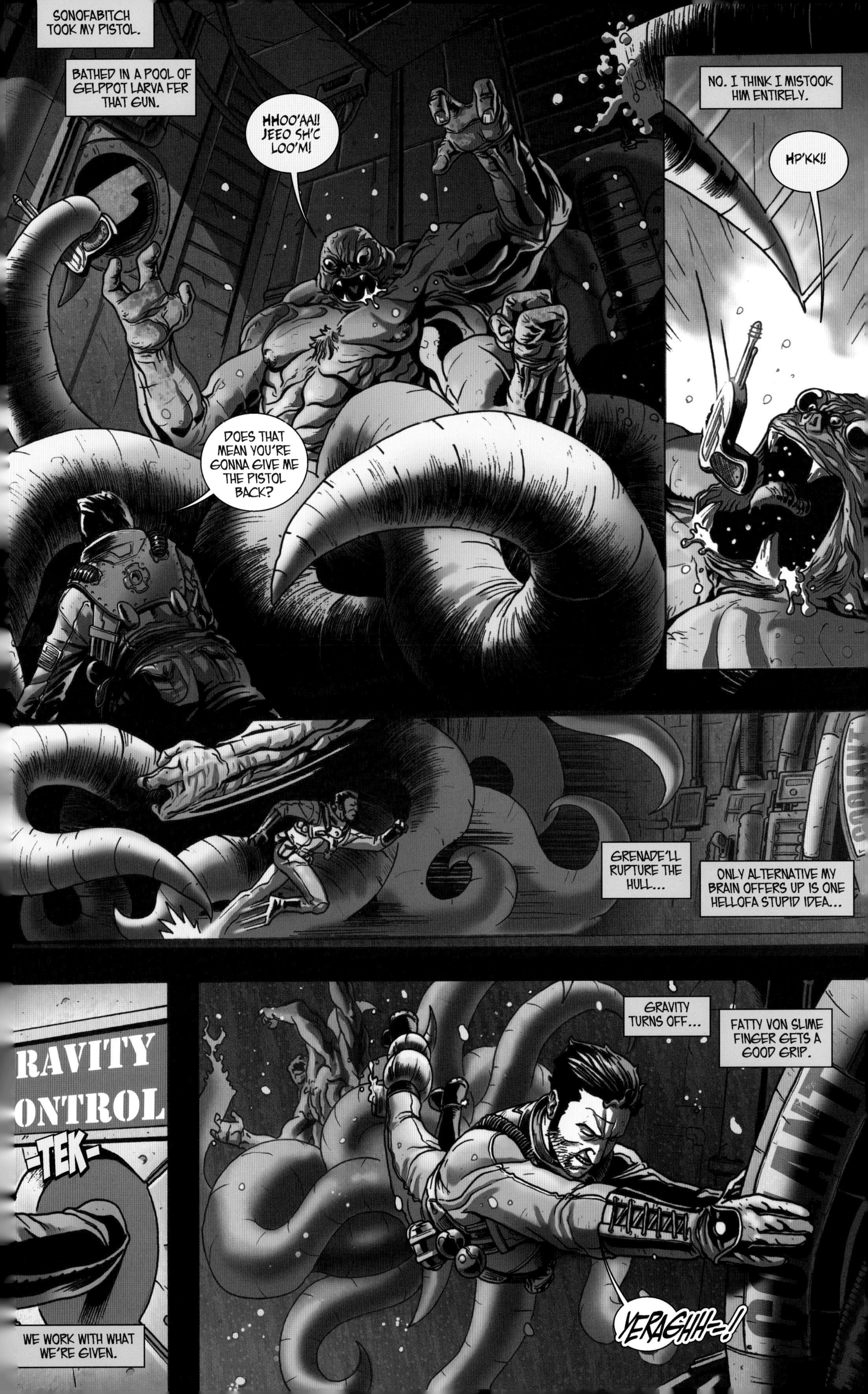
SONOFABITCH TOOK MY PISTOL.
BATHED IN A POOL OF GELPPOT LARVA FER THAT GUN.
HHOO'AA!! JEEO SH'C LOO'M!
DOES THAT MEAN YOU'RE GONNA GIVE ME THE PISTOL BACK?
NO. I THINK I MISTOOK HIM ENTIRELY.
HP'KK!!
GRENADE'LL RUPTURE THE HULL...
ONLY ALTERNATIVE MY BRAIN OFFERS UP IS ONE HELLOFA STUPID IDEA...
RAVITY
ONTROL
-TEK-
WE WORK WITH WHAT WE'RE GIVEN.
GRAVITY TURNS OFF...
FATTY VON SLIME FINGER GETS A GOOD GRIP.
YERAGHH--!

WHICH JUST HAPPENS TO BE PART OF MY BRAIN'S STUPID PLAN.

TENTACLE TYPES TEND TO HATE THE COLD.

FWOOOOOSH

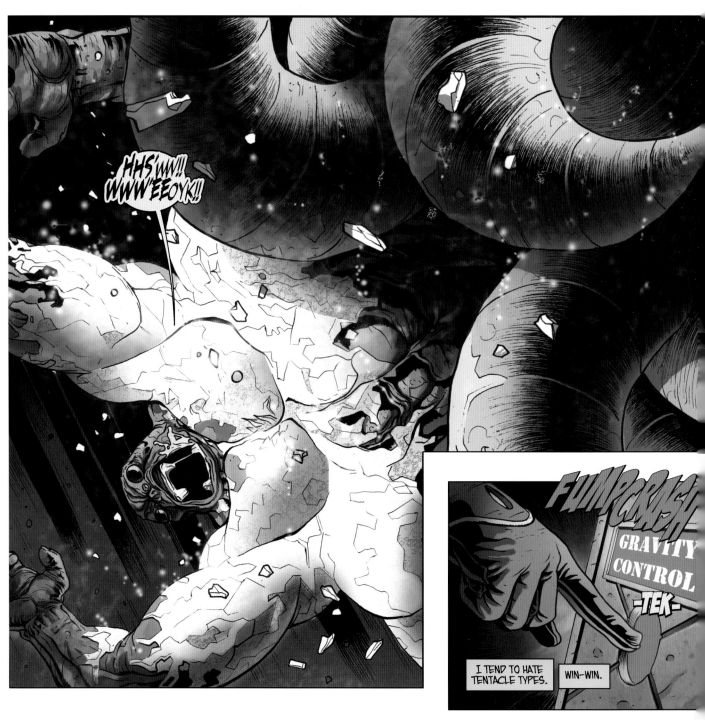

HHS'WW!! WWW'EEOYK!!

FWMPCRSH

GRAVITY CONTROL -TEK-

I TEND TO HATE TENTACLE TYPES.

WIN-WIN.

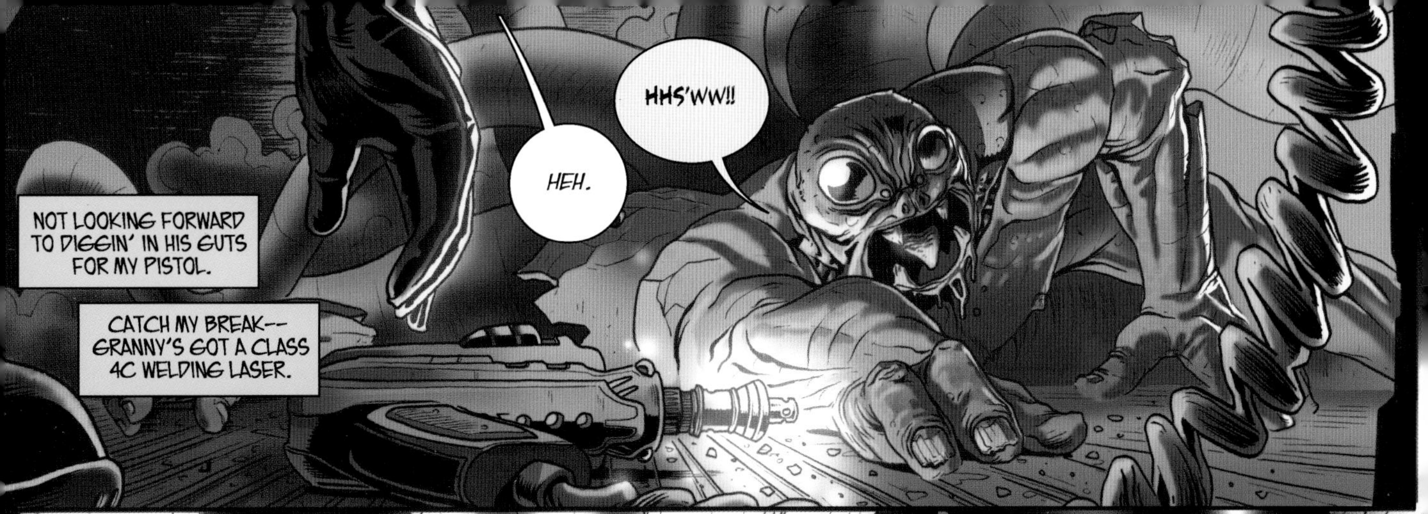
NOT LOOKING FORWARD TO DIGGIN' IN HIS GUTS FOR MY PISTOL.
HEH.
HHS'WW!!
CATCH MY BREAK-- GRANNY'S GOT A CLASS 4C WELDING LASER.

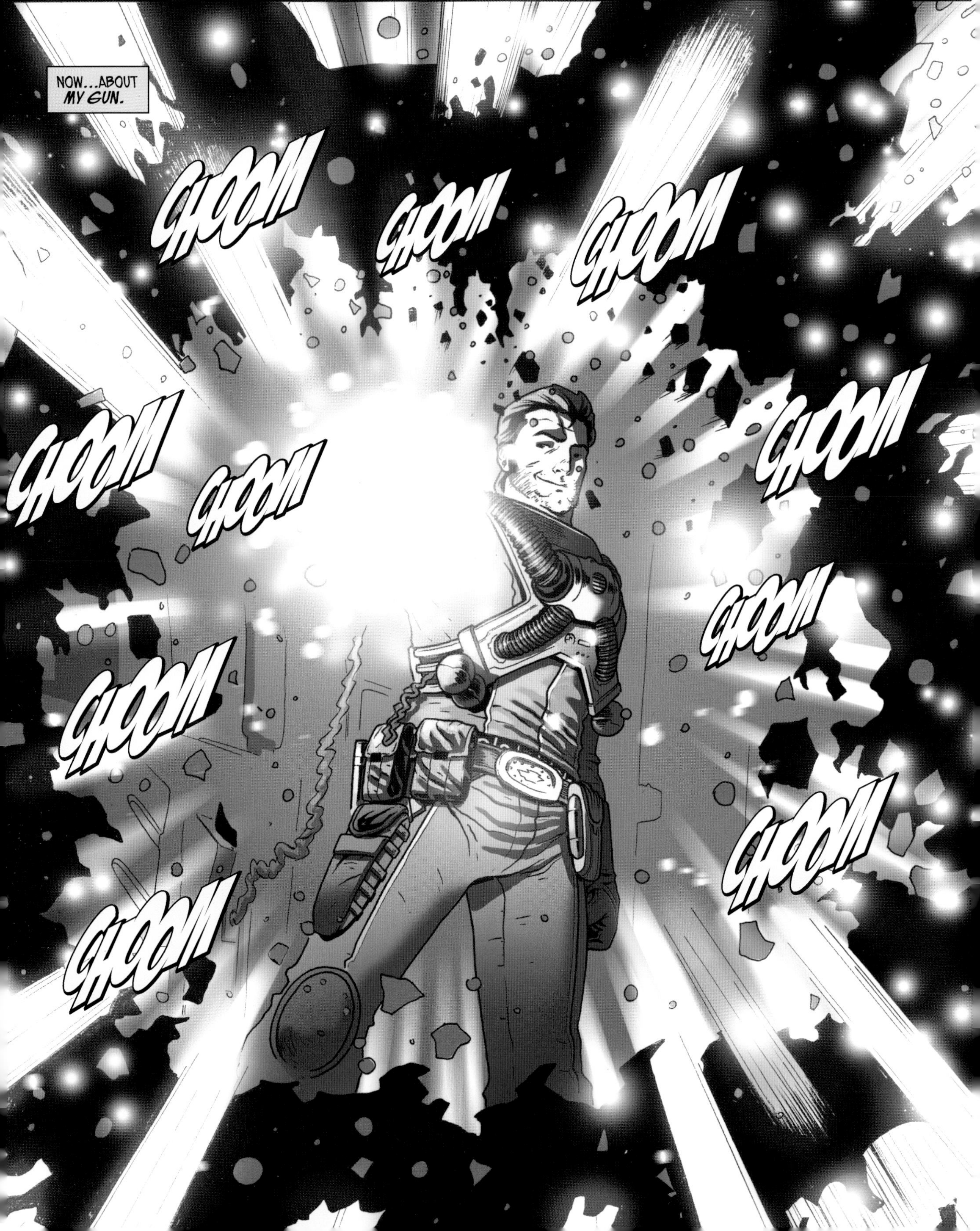
NOW...ABOUT MY GUN.
CHOOM
CHOOM
CHOOM
CHOOM
CHOOM
CHOOM
CHOOM
CHOOM
CHOOM
CHOOM

THE DAMSEL IN THE DISTRESS SIGNAL

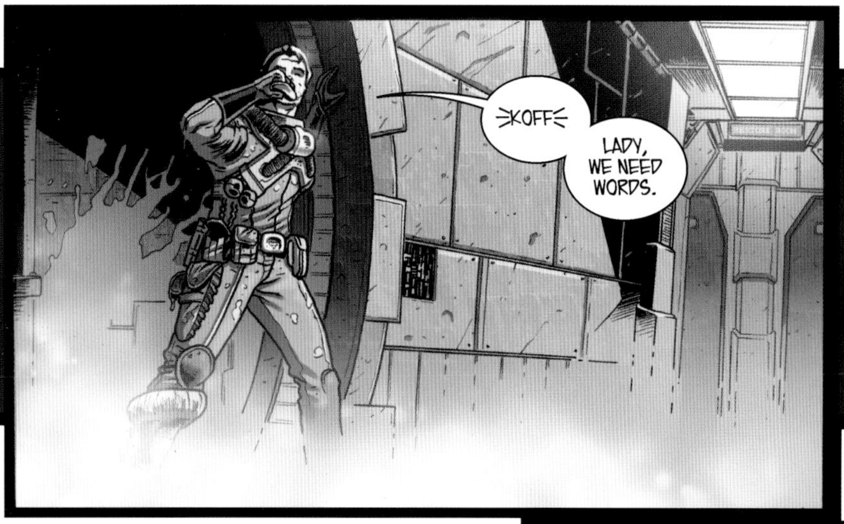

≶KOFF≶
LADY, WE NEED WORDS.

GERRY DUGGAN
WRITER

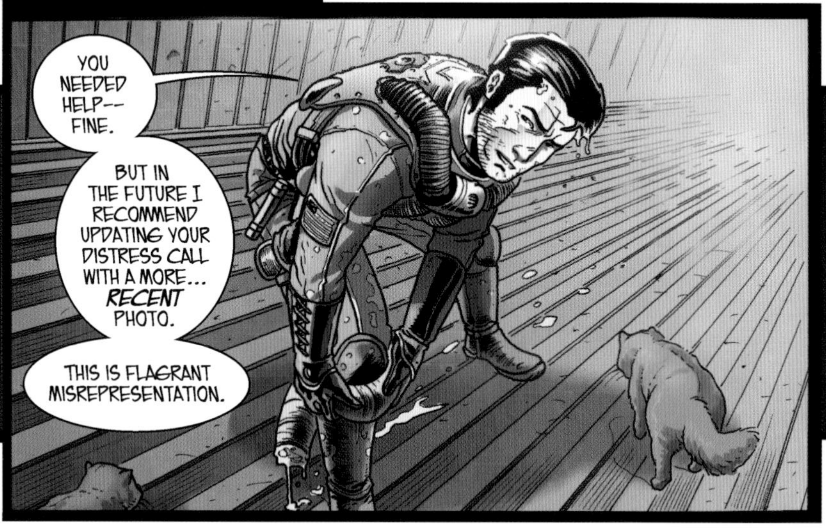

YOU NEEDED HELP-- FINE.
BUT IN THE FUTURE I RECOMMEND UPDATING YOUR DISTRESS CALL WITH A MORE... *RECENT* PHOTO.
THIS IS FLAGRANT MISREPRESENTATION.

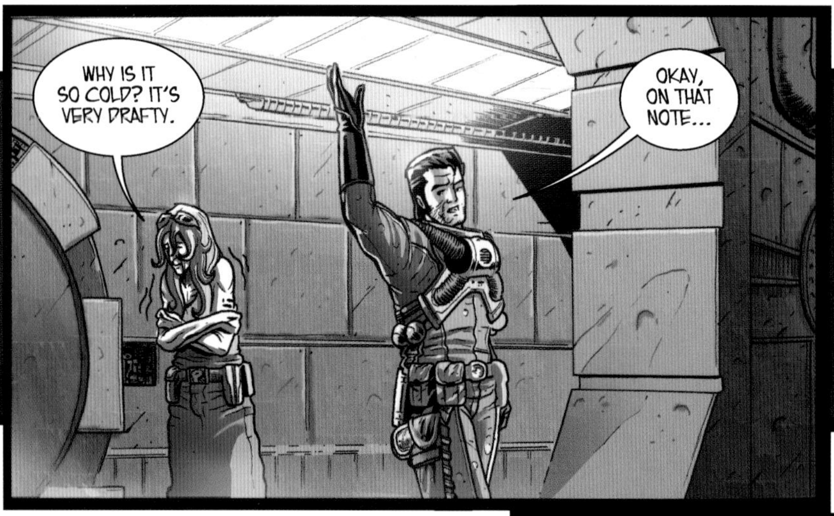

WHY IS IT SO COLD? IT'S VERY DRAFTY.
OKAY, ON THAT NOTE...

ALESSANDRO BRAGALINI
ARTIST

RUS WOOTON
LETTERER

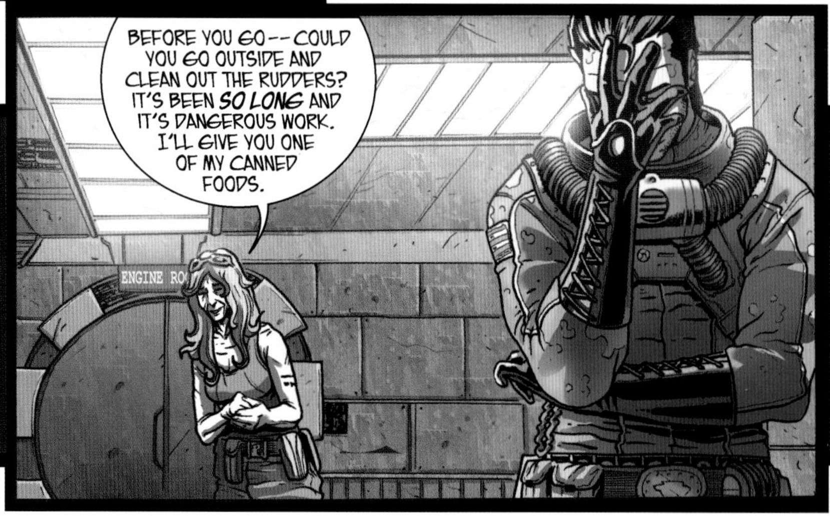

BEFORE YOU GO-- COULD YOU GO OUTSIDE AND CLEAN OUT THE RUDDERS? IT'S BEEN *SO LONG* AND IT'S DANGEROUS WORK. I'LL GIVE YOU ONE OF MY CANNED FOODS.

TONIGHT, THE BOTTLE

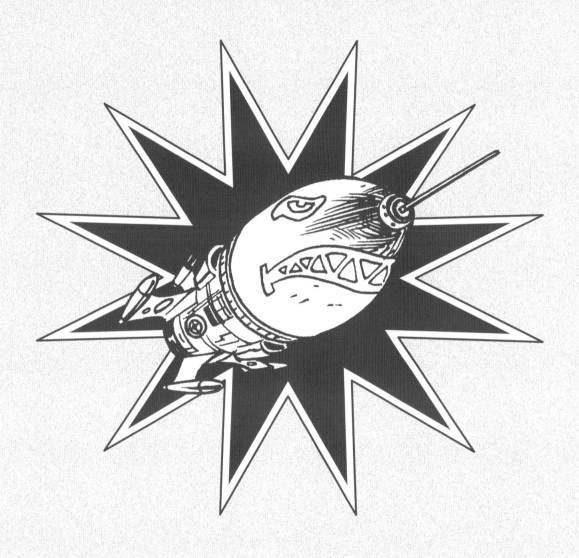

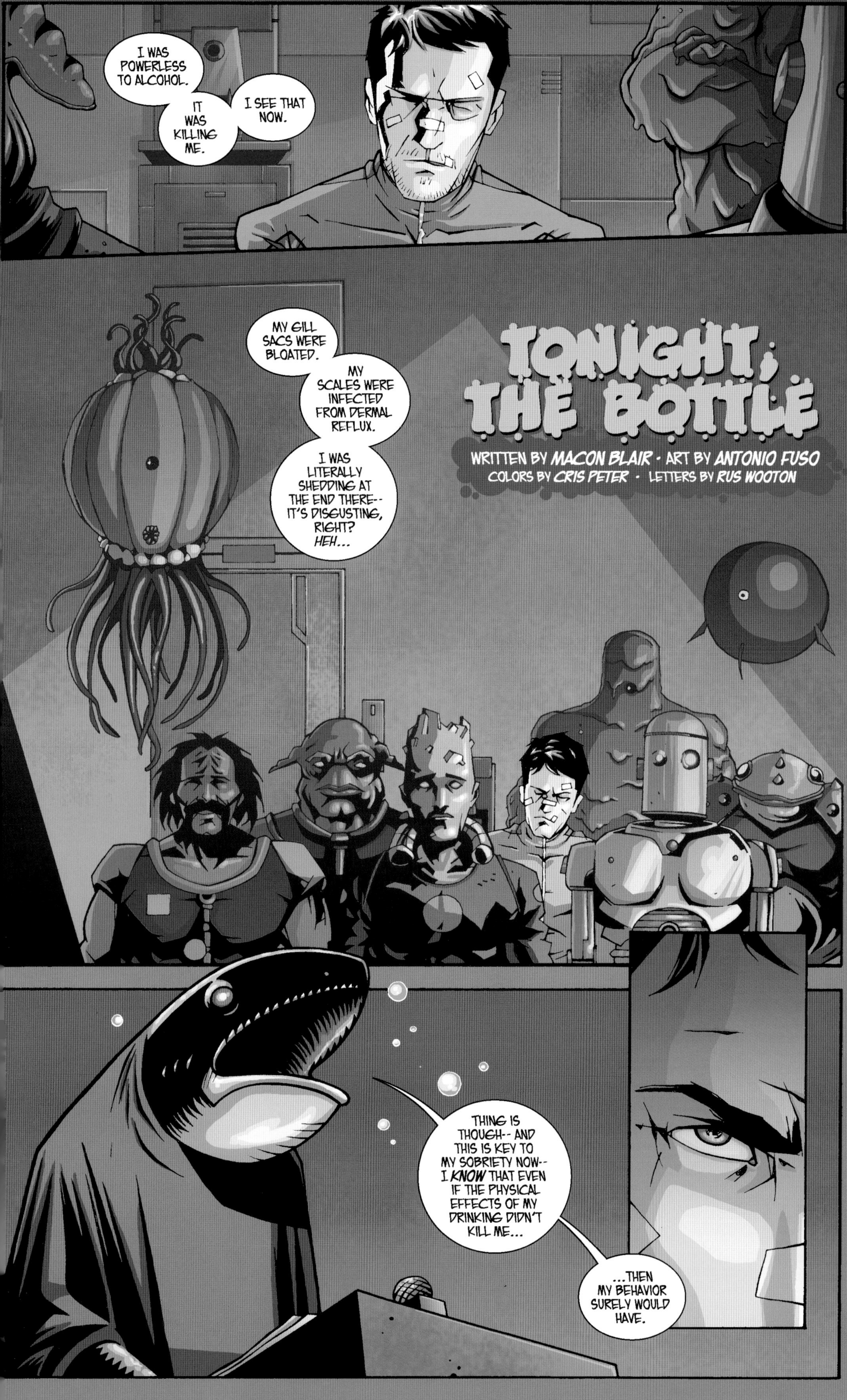
I WAS POWERLESS TO ALCOHOL.
IT WAS KILLING ME.
I SEE THAT NOW.
MY GILL SACS WERE BLOATED.
MY SCALES WERE INFECTED FROM DERMAL REFLUX.
I WAS LITERALLY SHEDDING AT THE END THERE-- IT'S DISGUSTING, RIGHT? HEH...
TONIGHT, THE BOTTLE
WRITTEN BY MACON BLAIR • ART BY ANTONIO FUSO
COLORS BY CRIS PETER • LETTERS BY RUS WOOTON
THING IS THOUGH-- AND THIS IS KEY TO MY SOBRIETY NOW-- I KNOW THAT EVEN IF THE PHYSICAL EFFECTS OF MY DRINKING DIDN'T KILL ME...
...THEN MY BEHAVIOR SURELY WOULD HAVE.

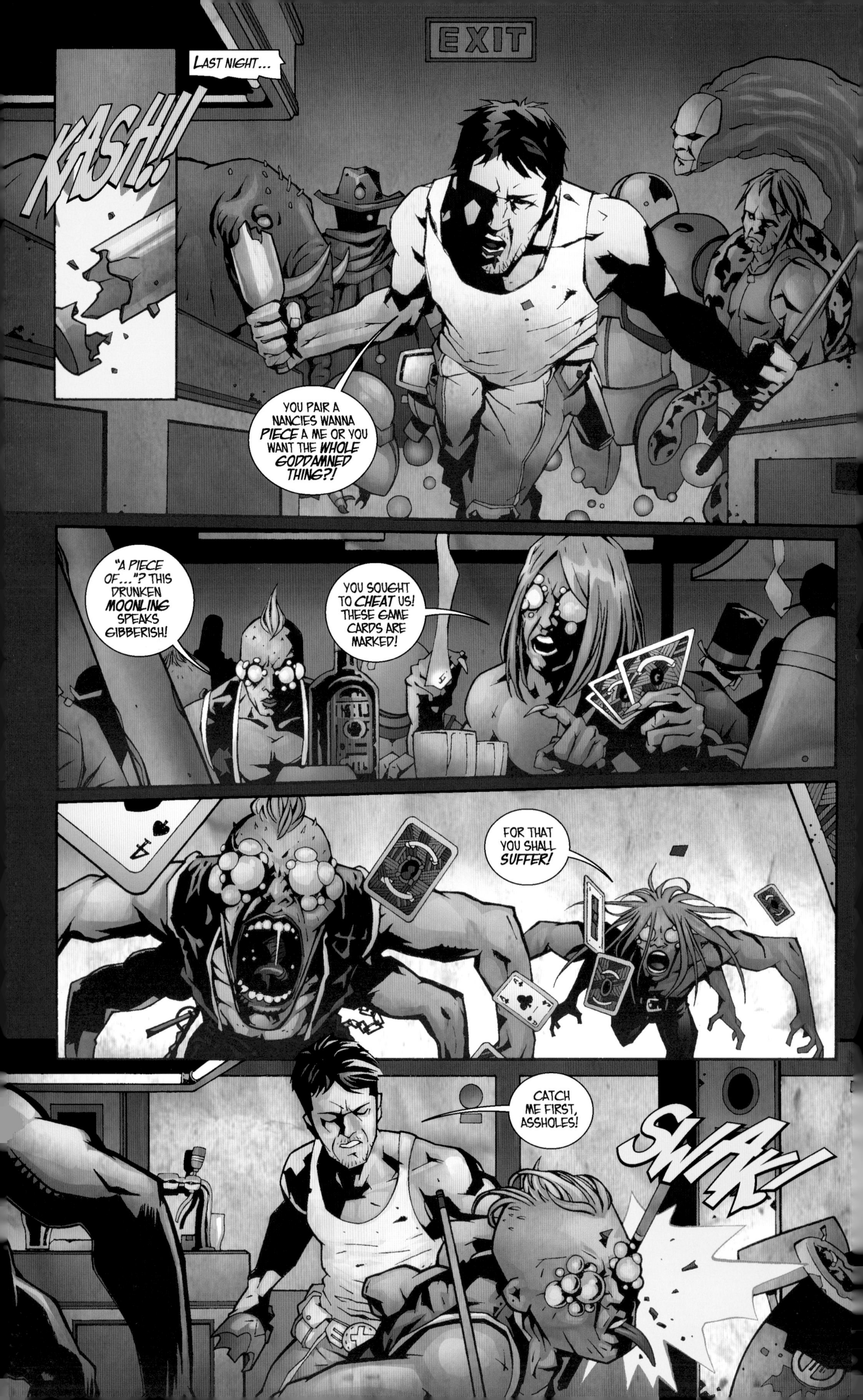
EXIT
LAST NIGHT...
KASH!!
YOU PAIR A NANCIES WANNA PIECE A ME OR YOU WANT THE WHOLE GODDAMNED THING?!
"A PIECE OF..."? THIS DRUNKEN MOONLING SPEAKS GIBBERISH!
YOU SOUGHT TO CHEAT US! THESE GAME CARDS ARE MARKED!
FOR THAT YOU SHALL SUFFER!
CATCH ME FIRST, ASSHOLES!
SWAK!

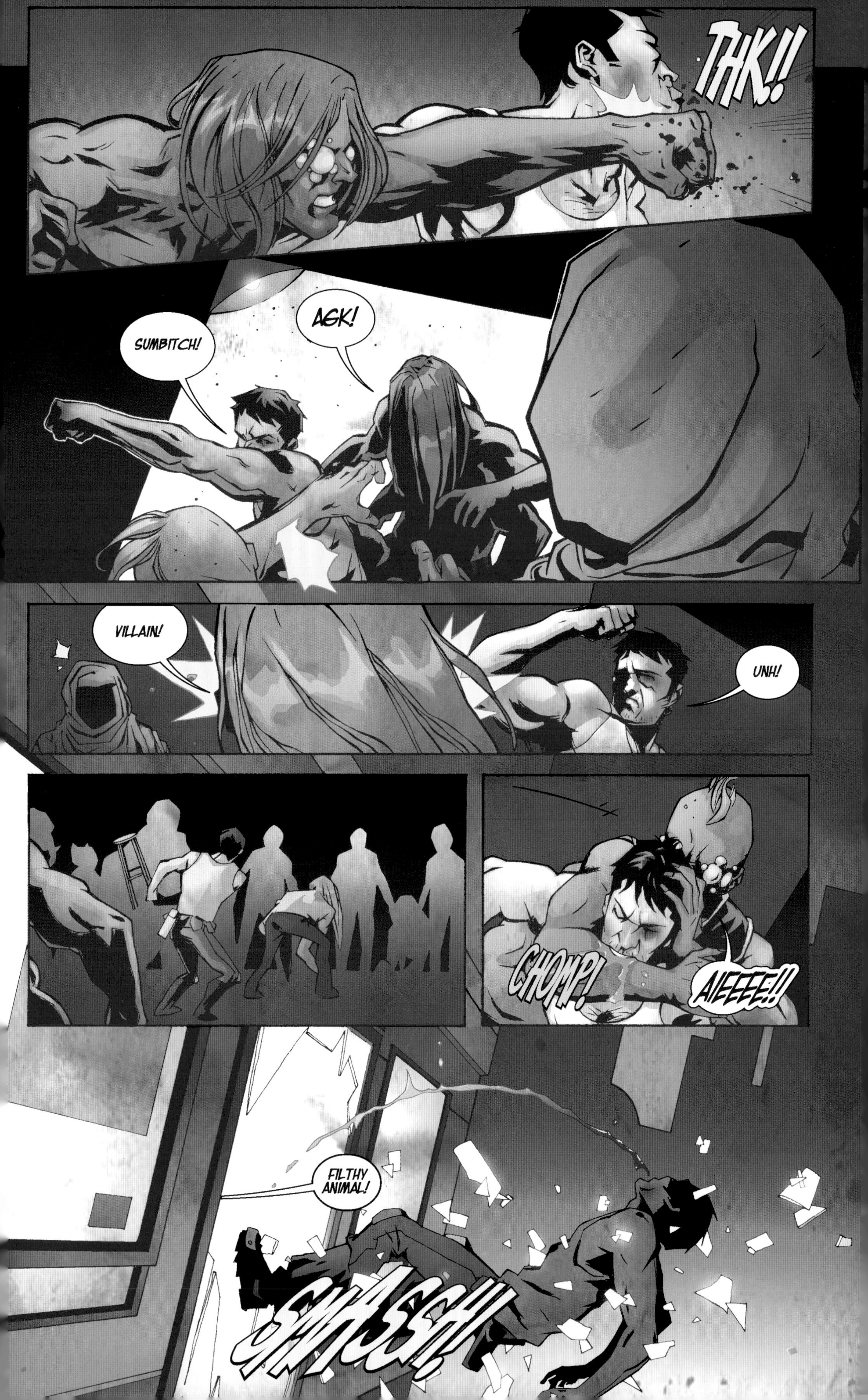
THK!!
SUMBITCH!
AGK!
VILLAIN!
UNH!
CHOMP!
AIEEEE!!
FILTHY ANIMAL!
SMASSH!

--BLAGARRHH!

PARDON ME, BUT...YOU SEEM TO BE HAVING SOME *DIFFICULTY.*

AND HOW DID YOU *EVER* ARRIVE AT A DEDUCTION SO SHREWD AS *THAT,* MISTER? MUST BE SOME KINDA GENIUS.

I BELIEVE I CAN HELP.

TONIGHT...

OKAY, GROUP. LET'S GO AROUND THE ROOM FOR SHARING NOW. *ELIUM?* WOULD YOU LIKE TO START US OFF?

UM, WELL... MY NAME IS ELIUM AND I'M AN ADDICT.

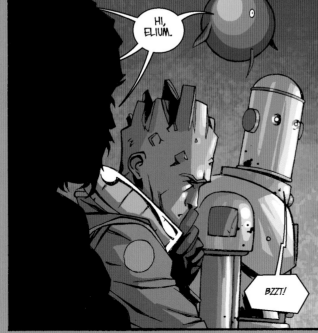

HI, ELIUM.

BZZT!

IT FEELS GOOD TO BE HERE TONIGHT. THIS GROUP IS MY STRENGTH, YOU KNOW.

IT'S A *WHAT*, NOW?

A SUPPORT GROUP.

SUPPORT GROUP FOR *WHO?*

FOR INDIVIDUALS VERY MUCH LIKE *YOURSELF.*

AND YET... *THAT* IS BESIDE THE POINT HERE.

IT'S BEEN THREE SOLAR CYCLES SINCE MY...*ACCIDENT.* I'LL NEVER TRULY FORGIVE MYSELF FOR THAT BUT... ALL I CAN DO NOW IS STAY CLEAN. AND I HAVE.

NOT THAT *THAT'S* ANY COMFORT TO THAT POOR LITTLE GIRL.

OR HER FAMILY.

I MEAN...

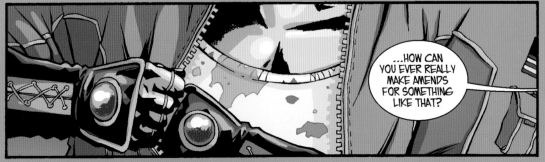

...HOW CAN YOU EVER REALLY MAKE AMENDS FOR SOMETHING LIKE THAT?

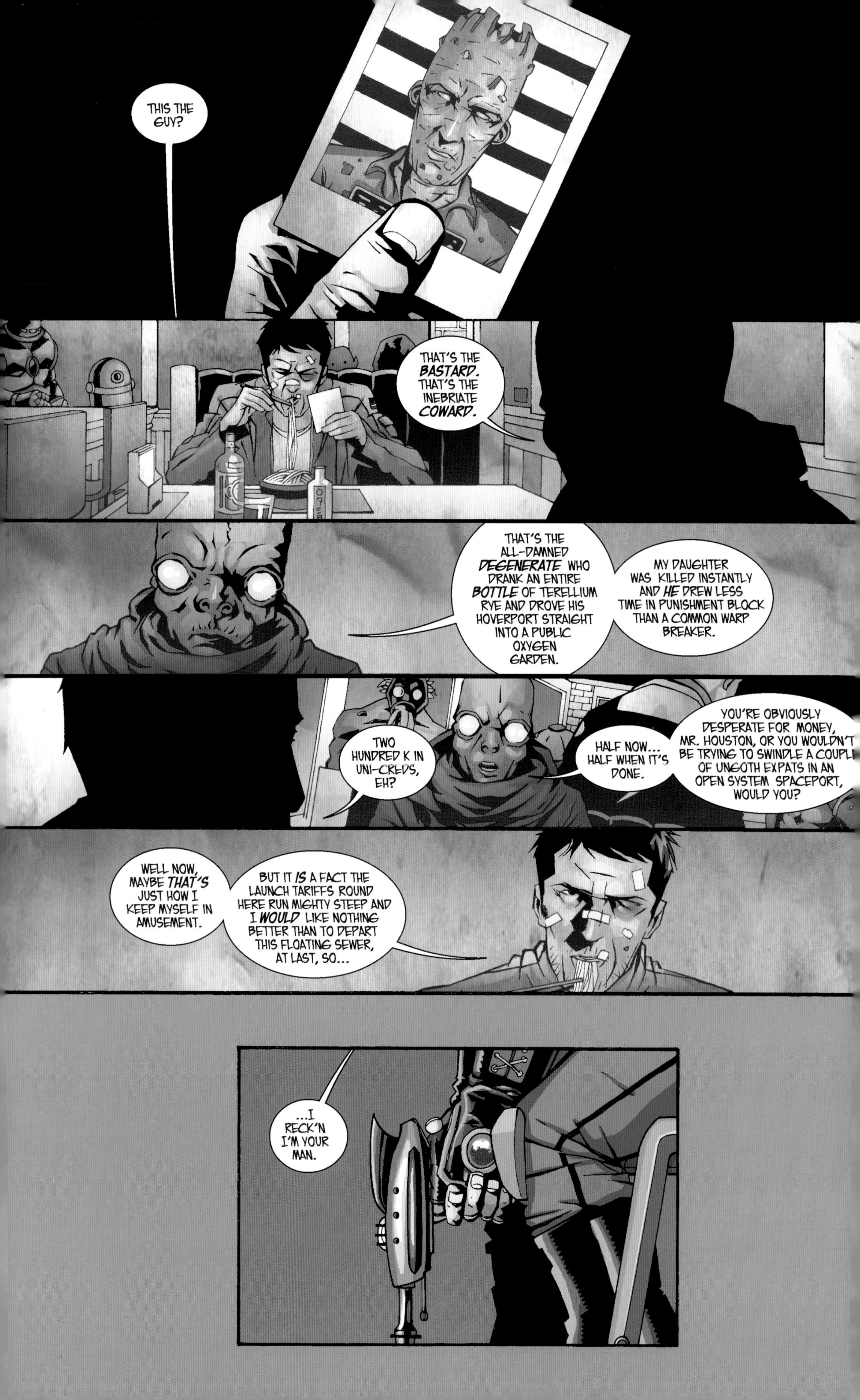
THIS THE GUY?
THAT'S THE BASTARD. THAT'S THE INEBRIATE COWARD.
THAT'S THE ALL-DAMNED DEGENERATE WHO DRANK AN ENTIRE BOTTLE OF TERELLIUM RYE AND DROVE HIS HOVERPORT STRAIGHT INTO A PUBLIC OXYGEN GARDEN.
MY DAUGHTER WAS KILLED INSTANTLY AND HE DREW LESS TIME IN PUNISHMENT BLOCK THAN A COMMON WARP BREAKER.
TWO HUNDRED K IN UNI-CREDS, EH?
HALF NOW... HALF WHEN IT'S DONE.
YOU'RE OBVIOUSLY DESPERATE FOR MONEY, MR. HOUSTON, OR YOU WOULDN'T BE TRYING TO SWINDLE A COUPL OF UNGOTH EXPATS IN AN OPEN SYSTEM SPACEPORT, WOULD YOU?
WELL NOW, MAYBE THAT'S JUST HOW I KEEP MYSELF IN AMUSEMENT.
BUT IT IS A FACT THE LAUNCH TARIFFS ROUND HERE RUN MIGHTY STEEP AND I WOULD LIKE NOTHING BETTER THAN TO DEPART THIS FLOATING SEWER, AT LAST, SO...
...I RECK'N I'M YOUR MAN.

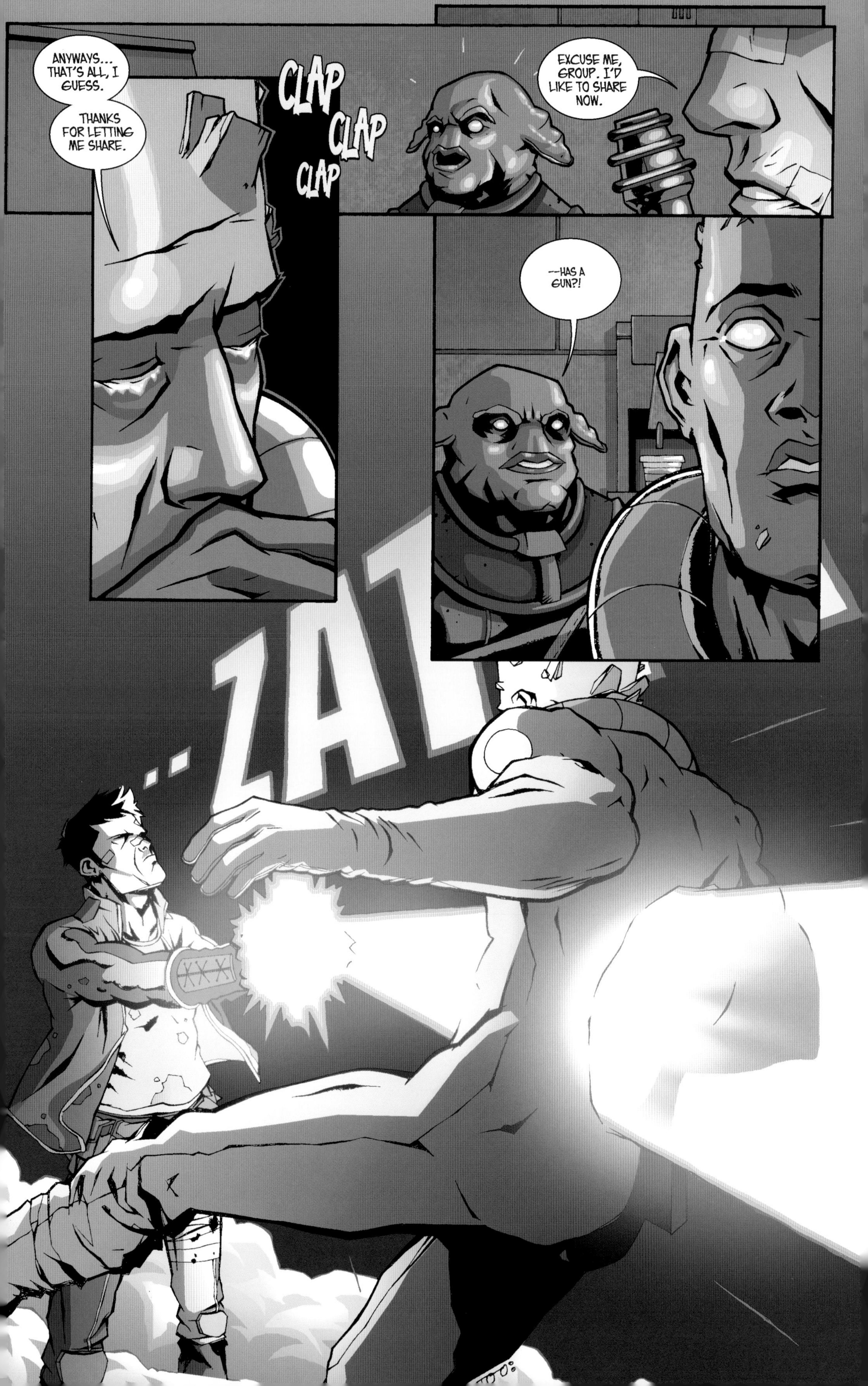
ANYWAYS... THAT'S ALL, I GUESS.
THANKS FOR LETTING ME SHARE.
CLAP CLAP CLAP
EXCUSE ME, GROUP. I'D LIKE TO SHARE NOW.
--HAS A GUN?!
...ZAT

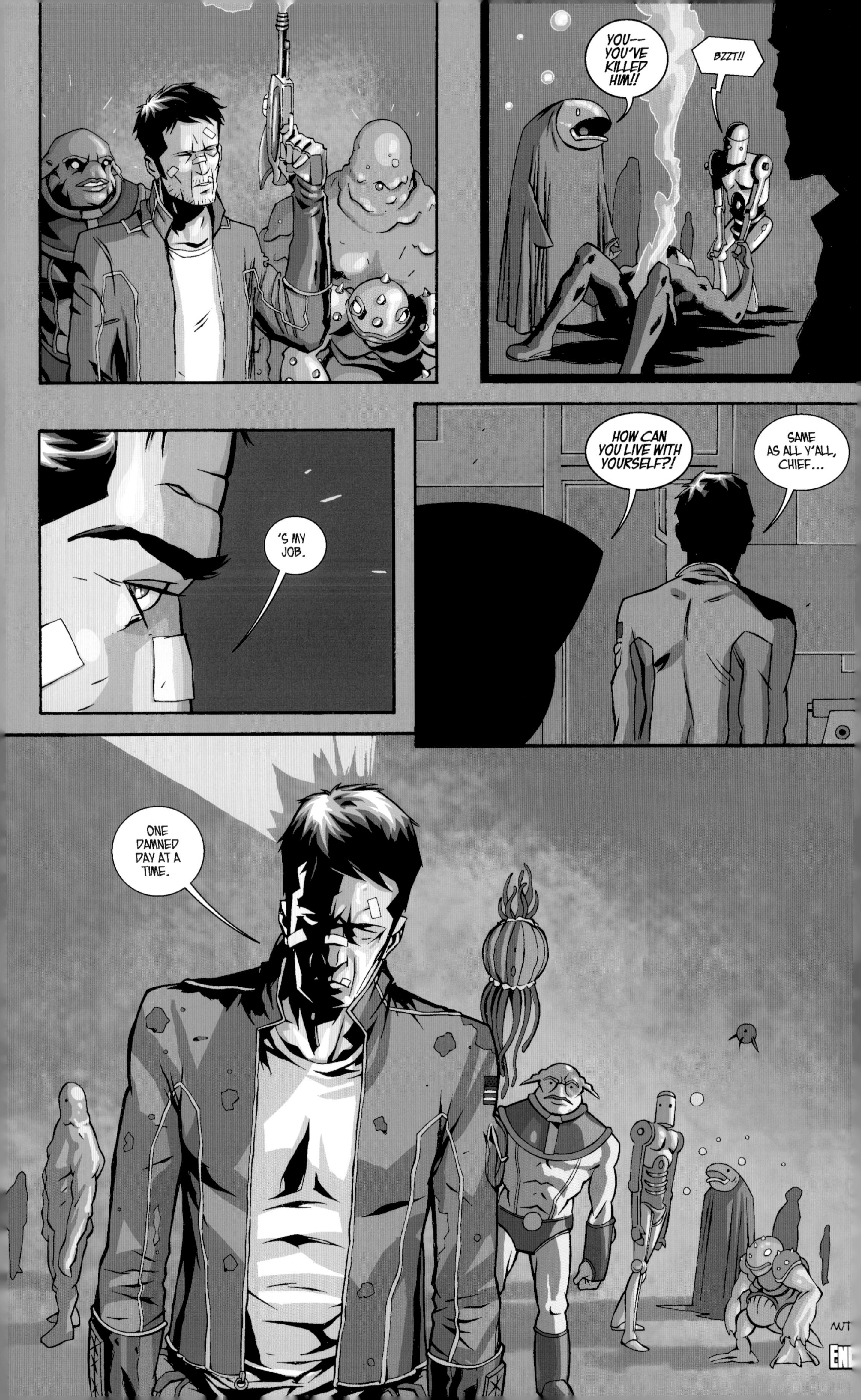
YOU-- YOU'VE KILLED HIM!!
BZZT!!
'S MY JOB.
HOW CAN YOU LIVE WITH YOURSELF?!
SAME AS ALL Y'ALL, CHIEF...
ONE DAMNED DAY AT A TIME.

HUNDRED PROOF KILLER

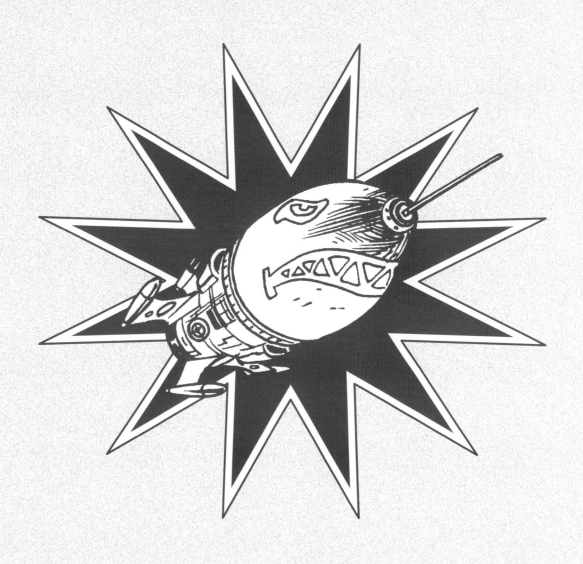

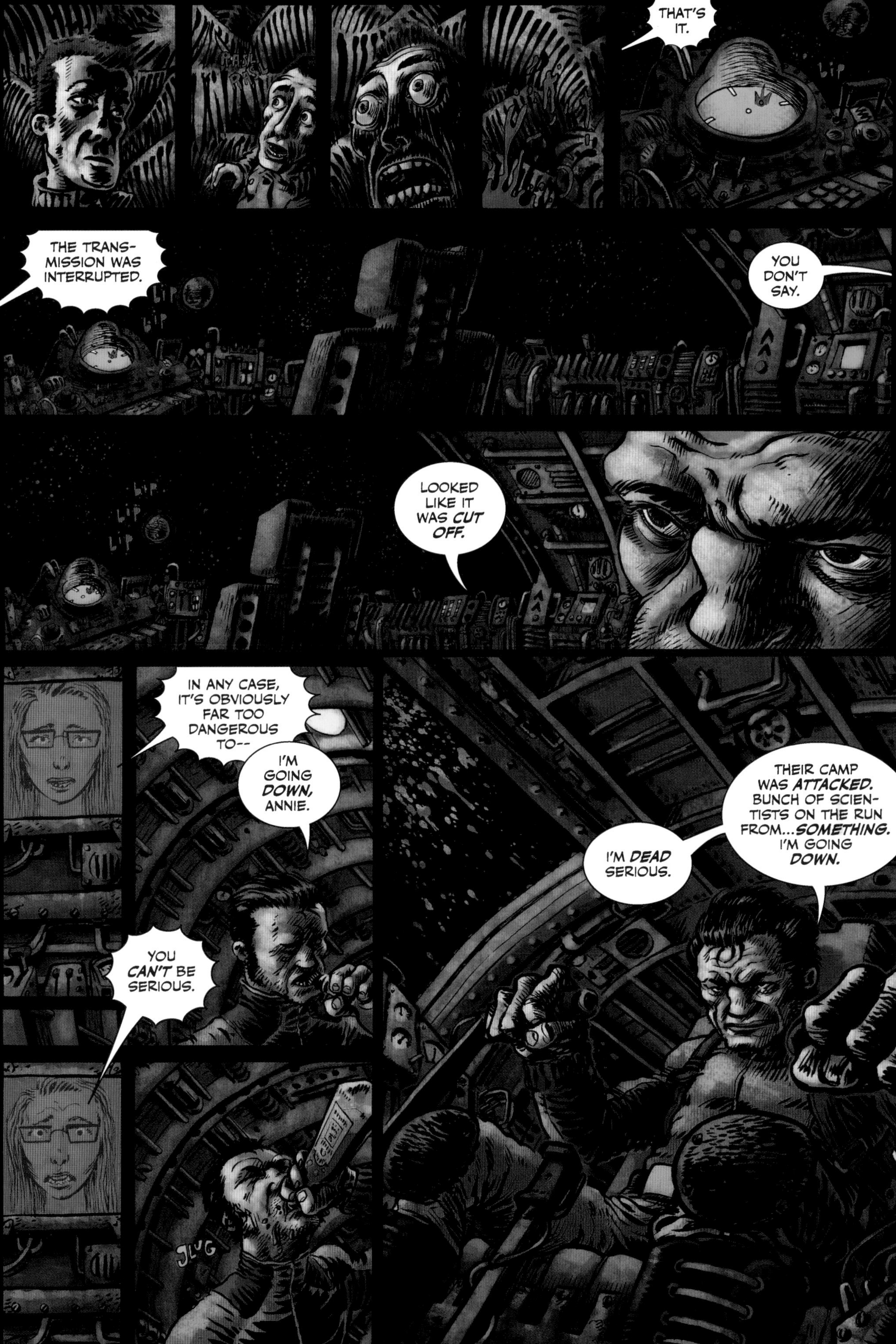
THAT'S IT.
THE TRANSMISSION WAS INTERRUPTED.
YOU DON'T SAY.
LOOKED LIKE IT WAS CUT OFF.
IN ANY CASE, IT'S OBVIOUSLY FAR TOO DANGEROUS TO--
I'M GOING DOWN, ANNIE.
YOU CAN'T BE SERIOUS.
JLUG
I'M DEAD SERIOUS.
THEIR CAMP WAS ATTACKED. BUNCH OF SCIENTISTS ON THE RUN FROM...SOMETHING. I'M GOING DOWN.

BRIGHT ENOUGH OUT HERE. DAMN *SUN* ISN'T HELPING MY HANG-OVER.

I MEAN *SUNS*. GUESS I'LL WORK ON THE *TAN*...

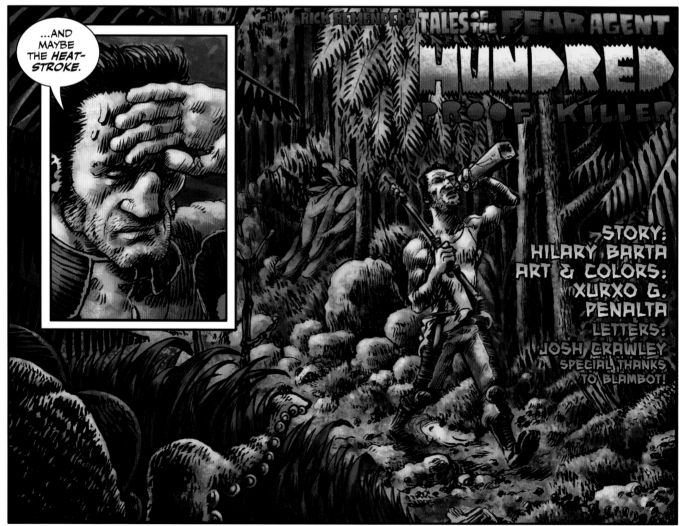

...AND MAYBE THE *HEAT-STROKE*.

FROM RICK REMENDER'S TALES OF THE FEAR AGENT

HUNDRED PROOF KILLER

STORY: HILARY BARTA
ART & COLORS: XURXO G. PENALTA
LETTERS: JOSH CRAWLEY
SPECIAL THANKS TO BLAMBOT!

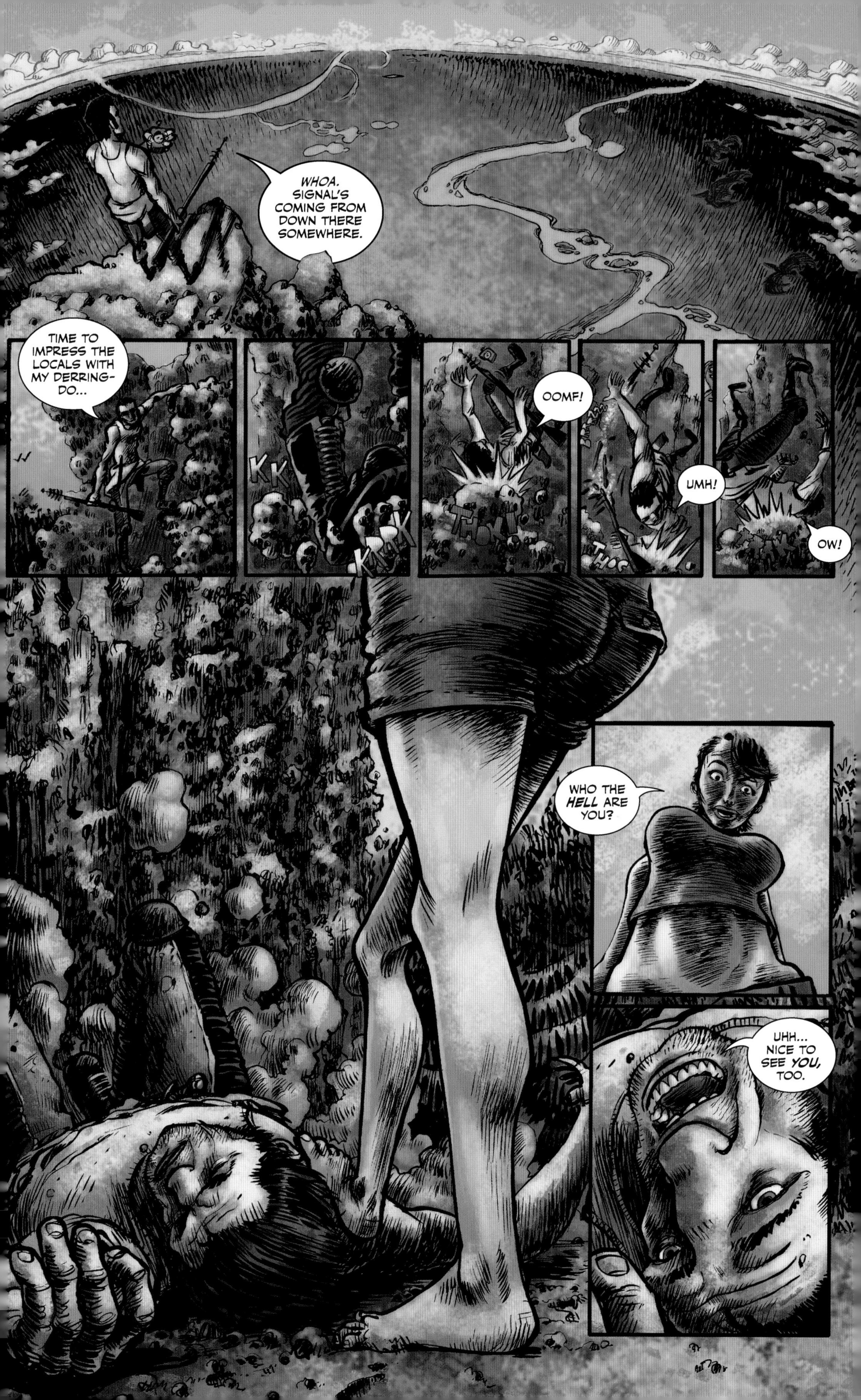
WHOA. SIGNAL'S COMING FROM DOWN THERE SOMEWHERE.
TIME TO IMPRESS THE LOCALS WITH MY DERRING-DO...
KK
OOMF!
UMH!
OW!
WHO THE *HELL* ARE YOU?
UHH... NICE TO SEE *YOU,* TOO.

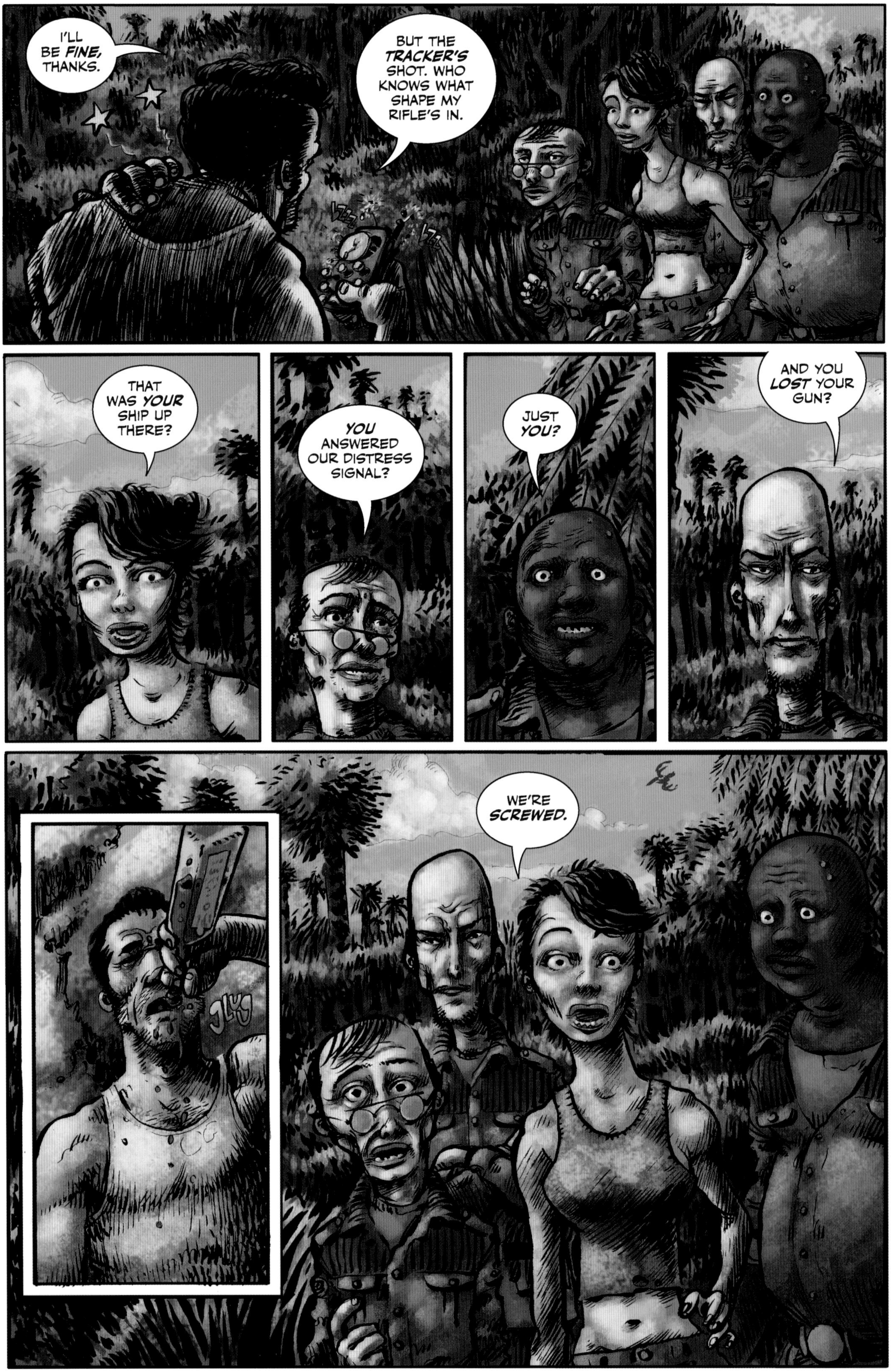
I'LL BE FINE, THANKS.
BUT THE TRACKER'S SHOT. WHO KNOWS WHAT SHAPE MY RIFLE'S IN.
THAT WAS YOUR SHIP UP THERE?
YOU ANSWERED OUR DISTRESS SIGNAL?
JUST YOU?
AND YOU LOST YOUR GUN?
WE'RE SCREWED.
GLUG

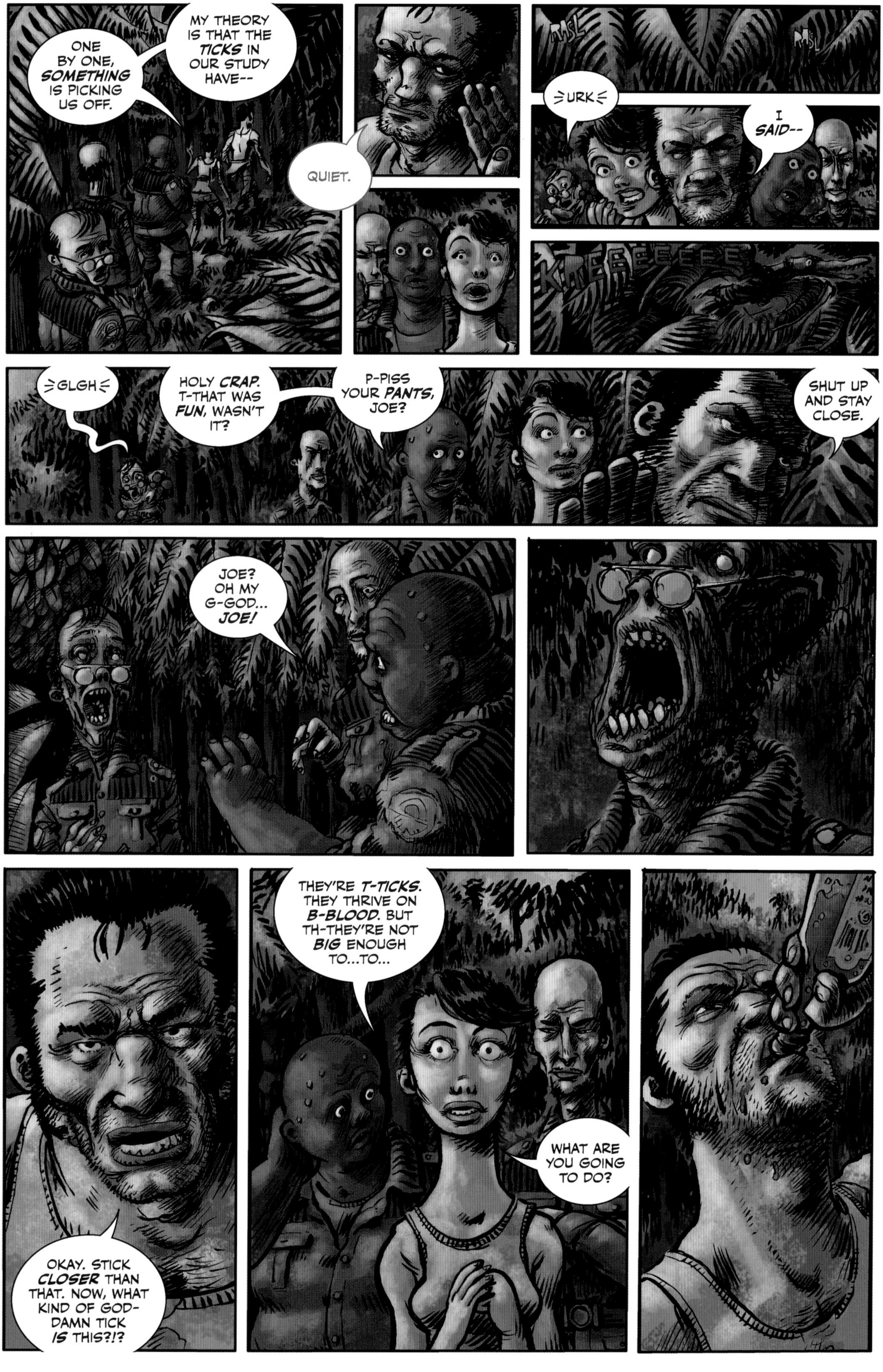
ONE BY ONE, SOMETHING IS PICKING US OFF.
MY THEORY IS THAT THE TICKS IN OUR STUDY HAVE--
QUIET.
RASL
RASL
URK
I SAID--
GLGH
HOLY CRAP. T-THAT WAS FUN, WASN'T IT?
P-PISS YOUR PANTS, JOE?
SHUT UP AND STAY CLOSE.
JOE? OH MY G-GOD... JOE!
OKAY. STICK CLOSER THAN THAT. NOW, WHAT KIND OF GOD-DAMN TICK IS THIS?!?
THEY'RE T-TICKS. THEY THRIVE ON B-BLOOD. BUT TH-THEY'RE NOT BIG ENOUGH TO...TO...
WHAT ARE YOU GOING TO DO?

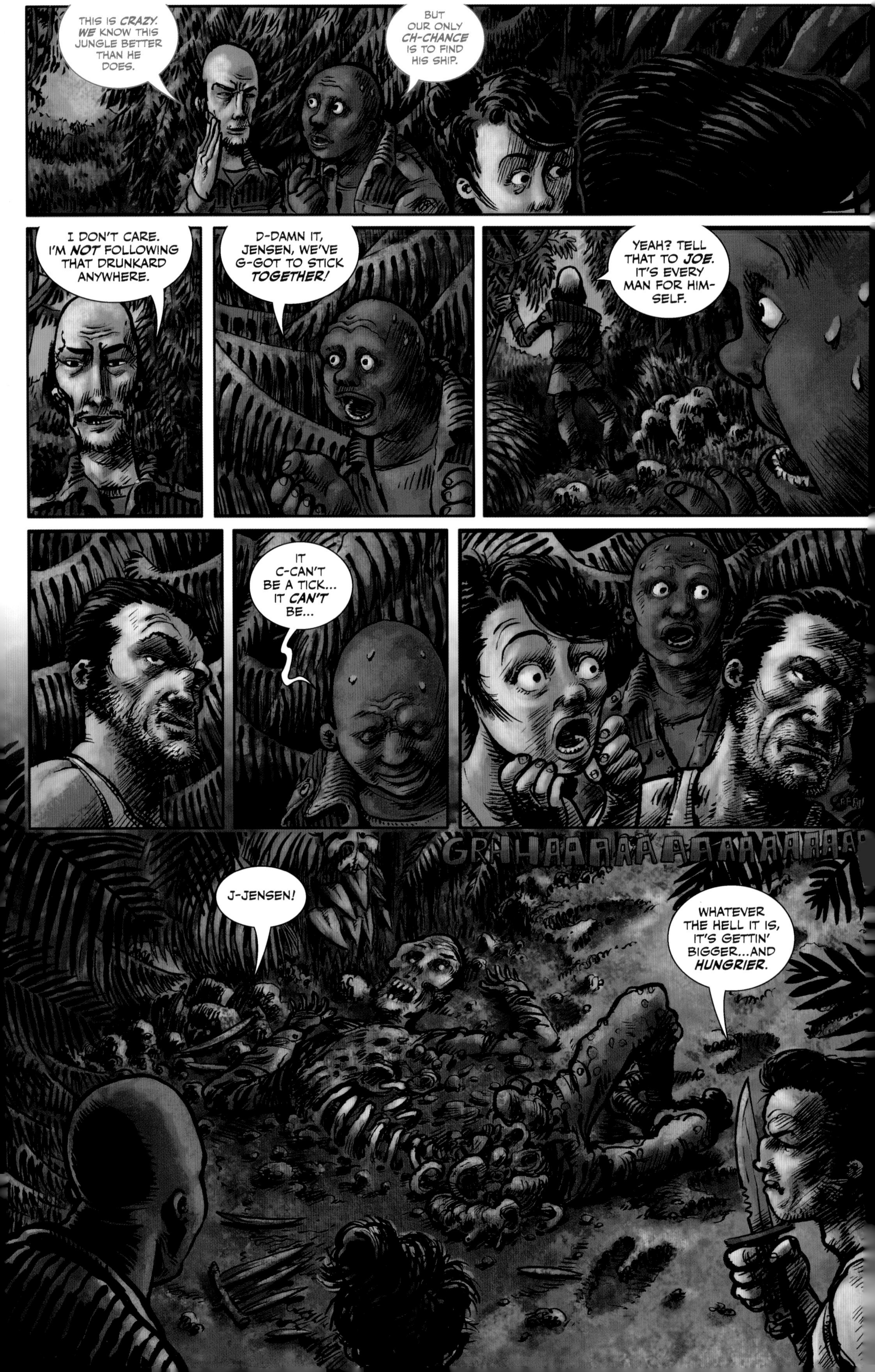
THIS IS CRAZY. WE KNOW THIS JUNGLE BETTER THAN HE DOES.
BUT OUR ONLY CH-CHANCE IS TO FIND HIS SHIP.
I DON'T CARE. I'M NOT FOLLOWING THAT DRUNKARD ANYWHERE.
D-DAMN IT, JENSEN, WE'VE G-GOT TO STICK TOGETHER!
YEAH? TELL THAT TO JOE. IT'S EVERY MAN FOR HIM-SELF.
IT C-CAN'T BE A TICK... IT CAN'T BE...
GRAHAAAAAAAAAAAAAAA
J-JENSEN!
WHATEVER THE HELL IT IS, IT'S GETTIN' BIGGER...AND HUNGRIER.

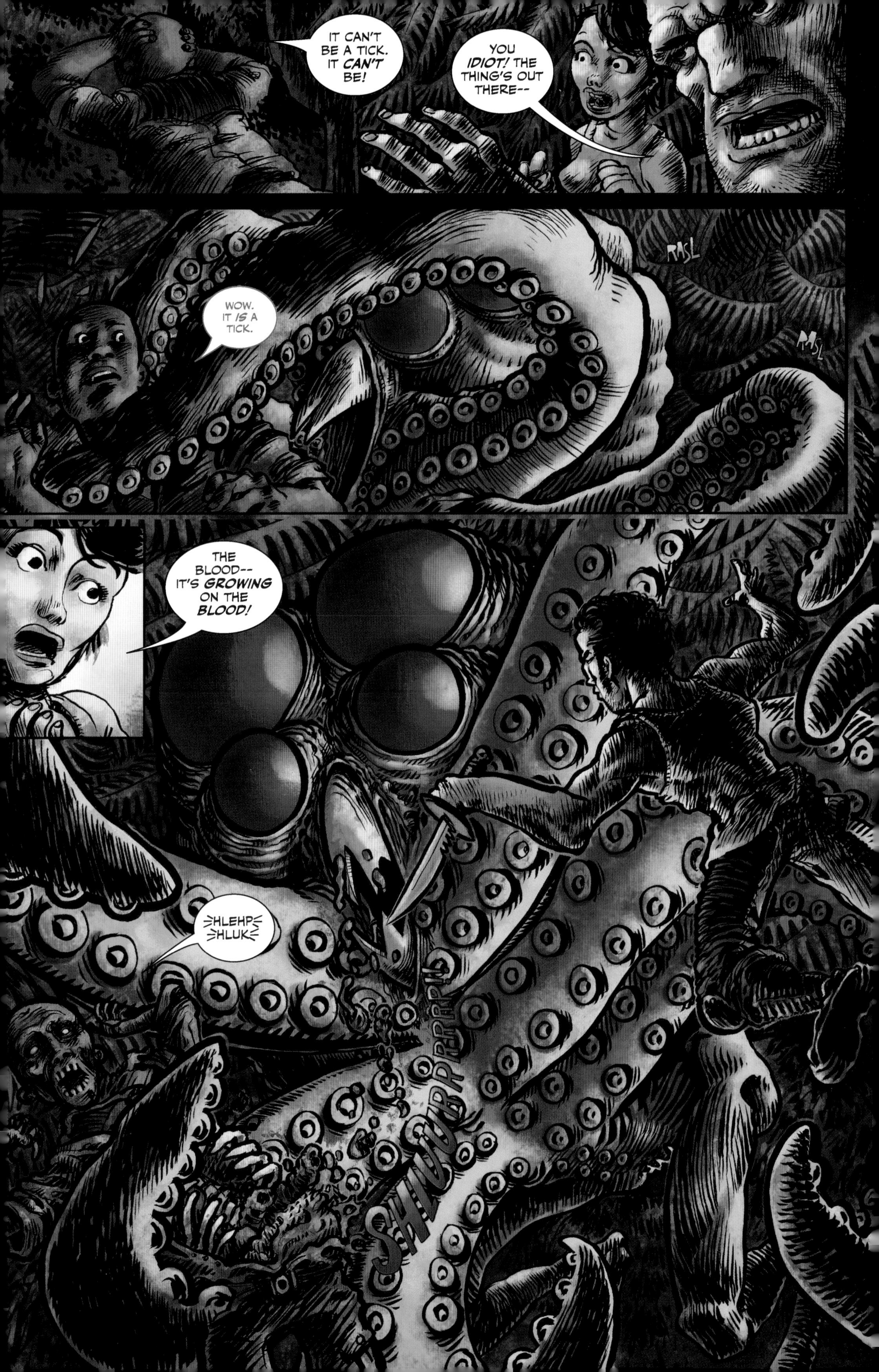
IT CAN'T BE A TICK. IT *CAN'T* BE!
YOU *IDIOT!* THE THING'S OUT THERE--
RASL
RASL
WOW. IT *IS* A TICK.
THE BLOOD-- IT'S *GROWING* ON THE *BLOOD!*
HLEHP HLUK
SHLUBPPRRRRR

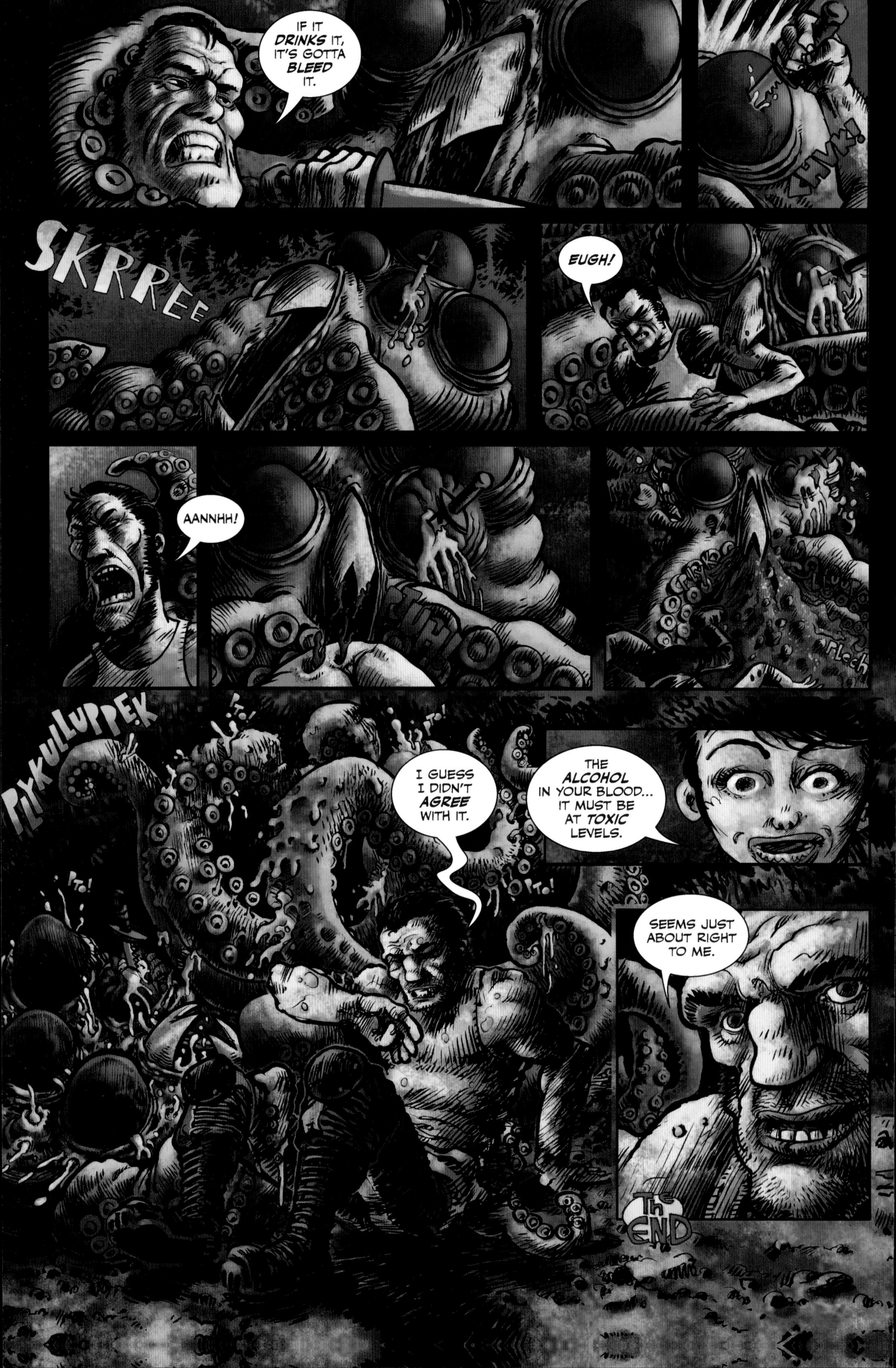
IF IT DRINKS IT, IT'S GOTTA BLEED IT.
SKRREEE
EUGH!
AANNHH!
PLYKULLUPPEK
I GUESS I DIDN'T AGREE WITH IT.
THE ALCOHOL IN YOUR BLOOD... IT MUST BE AT TOXIC LEVELS.
SEEMS JUST ABOUT RIGHT TO ME.
The END

KLEBEK

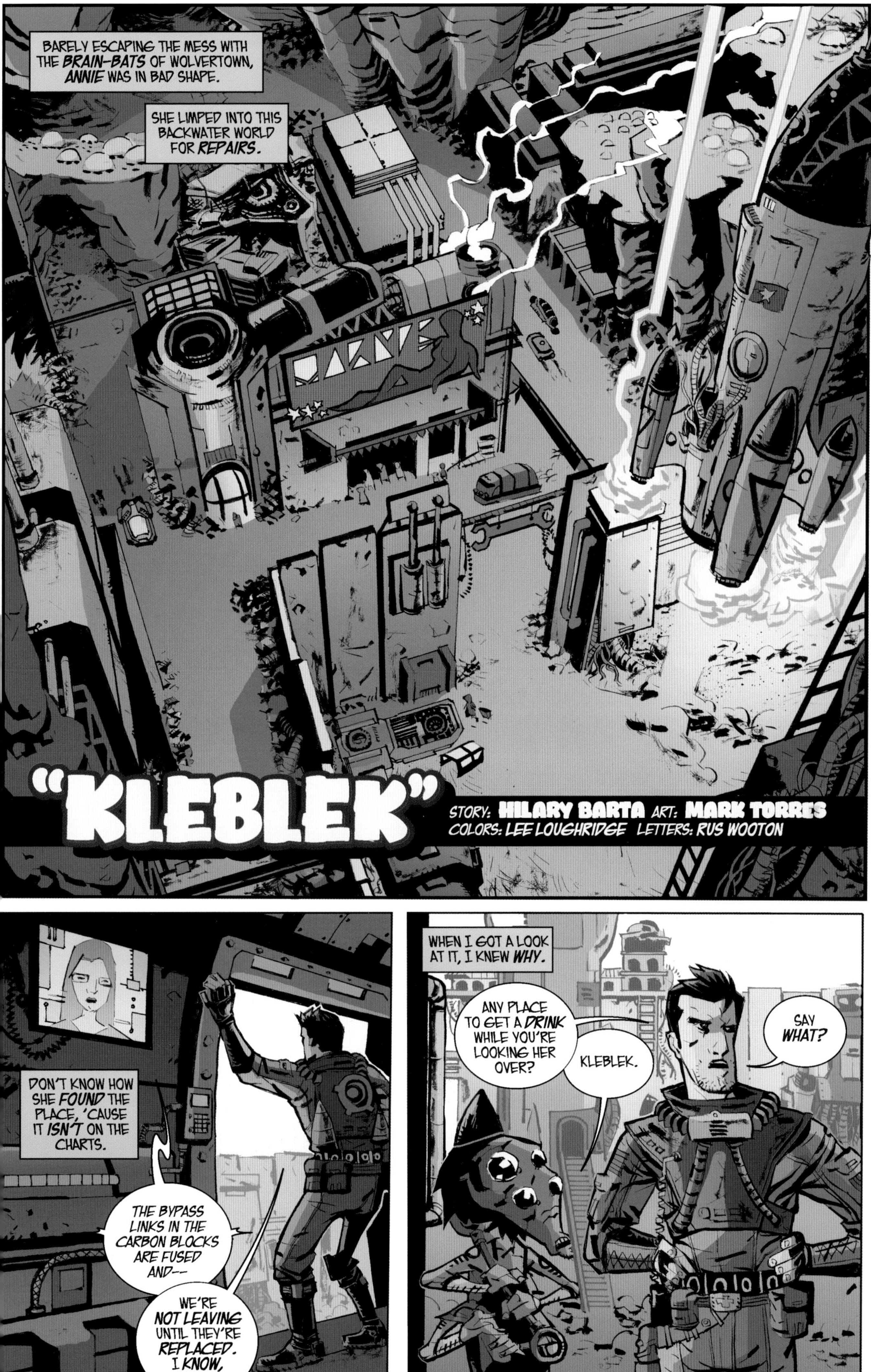
BARELY ESCAPING THE MESS WITH THE BRAIN-BATS OF WOLVERTOWN, ANNIE WAS IN BAD SHAPE.
SHE LIMPED INTO THIS BACKWATER WORLD FOR REPAIRS.
"KLEBLEK"
STORY: HILARY BARTA ART: MARK TORRES
COLORS: LEE LOUGHRIDGE LETTERS: RUS WOOTON
DON'T KNOW HOW SHE FOUND THE PLACE, 'CAUSE IT ISN'T ON THE CHARTS.
THE BYPASS LINKS IN THE CARBON BLOCKS ARE FUSED AND--
WE'RE NOT LEAVING UNTIL THEY'RE REPLACED. I KNOW, ANNIE.
WHEN I GOT A LOOK AT IT, I KNEW WHY.
ANY PLACE TO GET A DRINK WHILE YOU'RE LOOKING HER OVER?
KLEBLEK.
SAY WHAT?

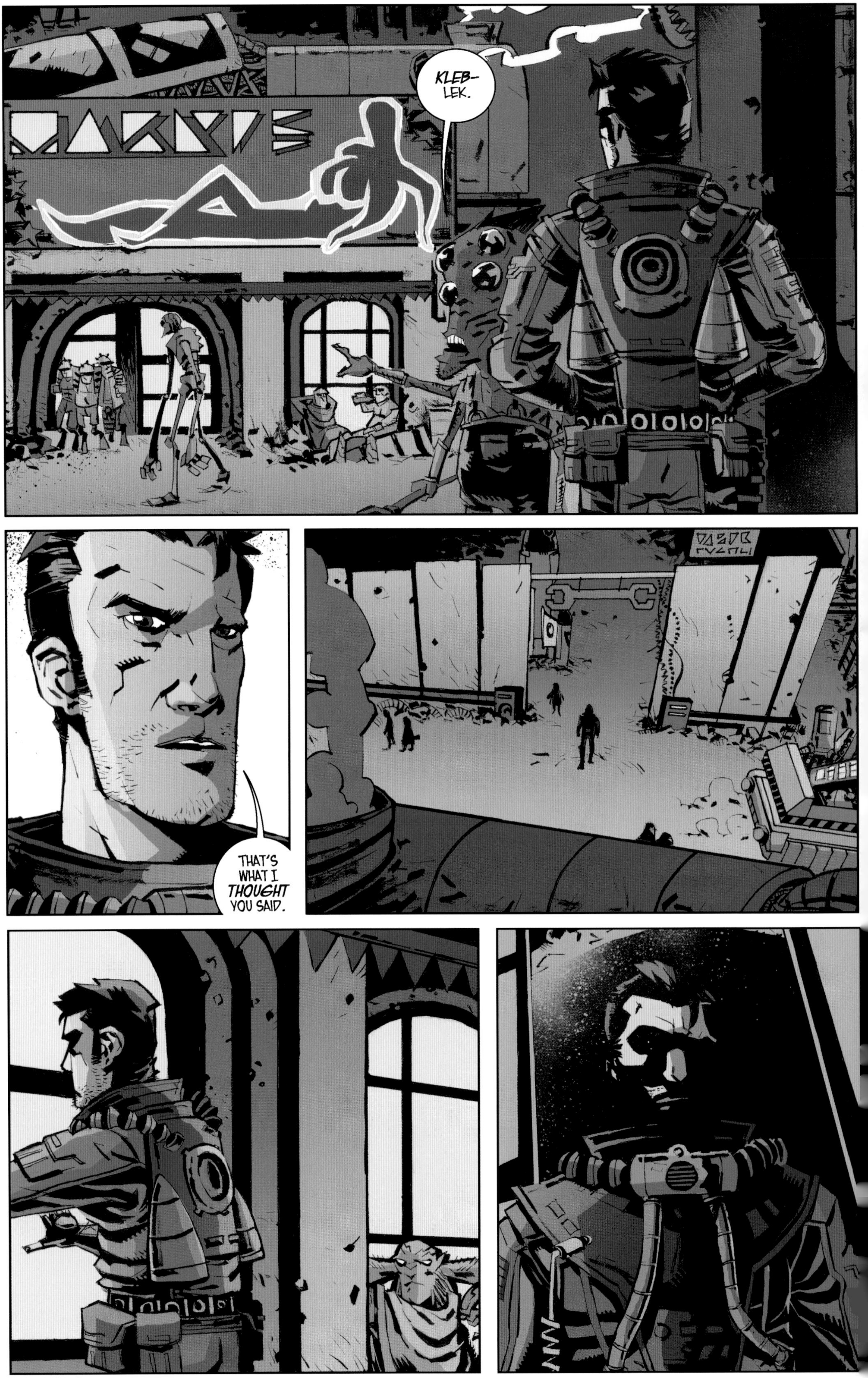
KLEB-
LEK.
THAT'S WHAT I *THOUGHT* YOU SAID.

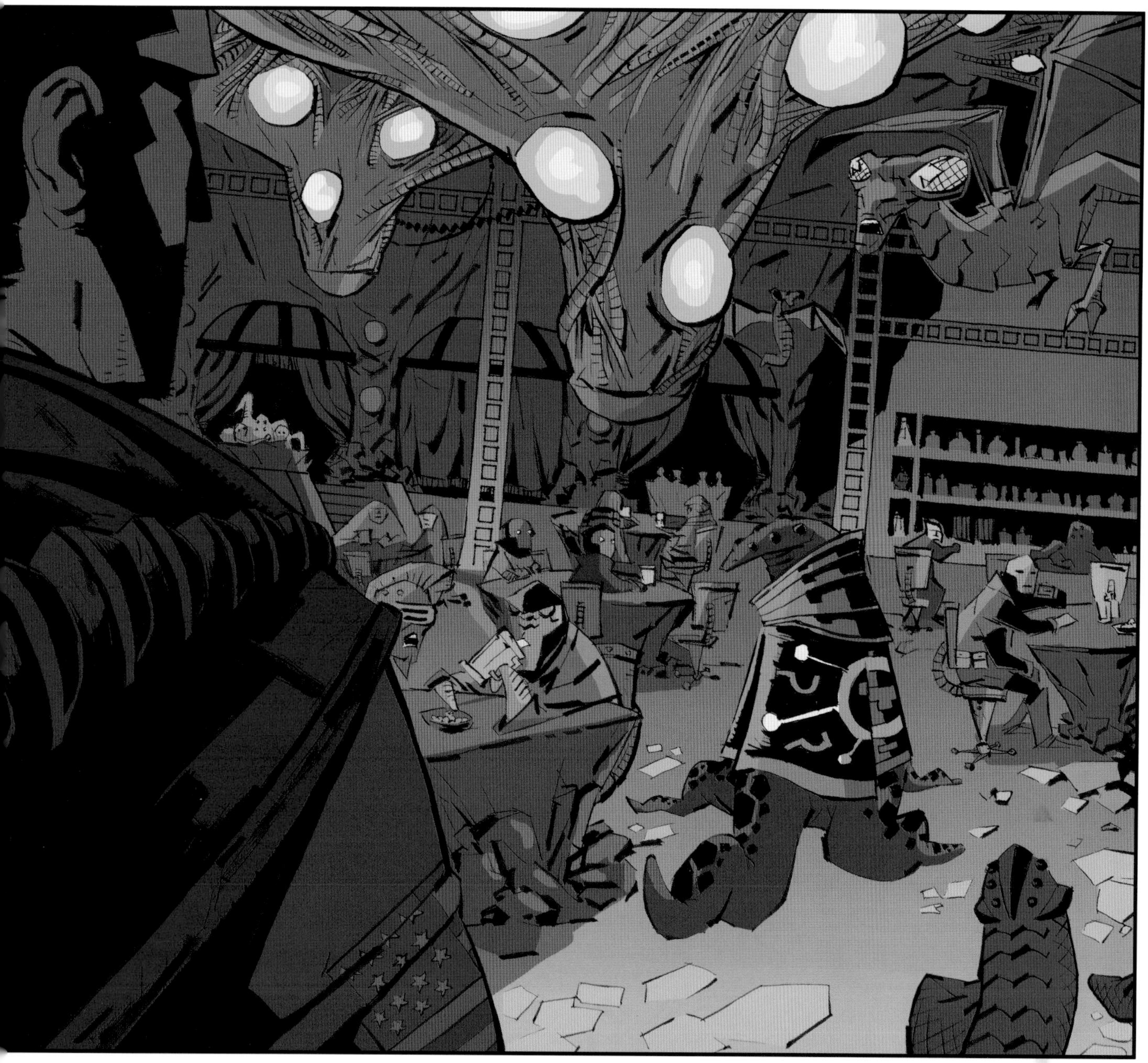

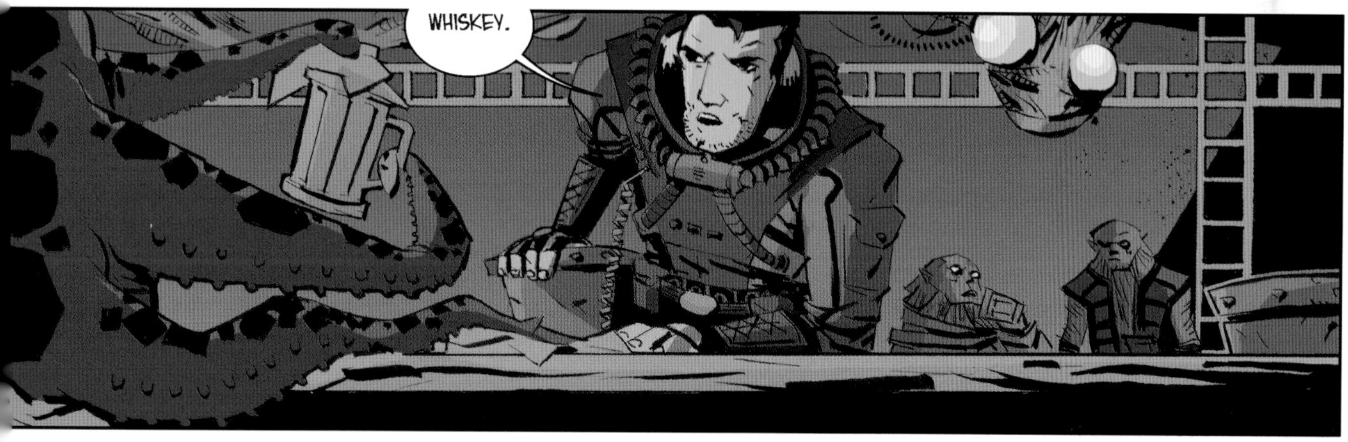
WHISKEY.

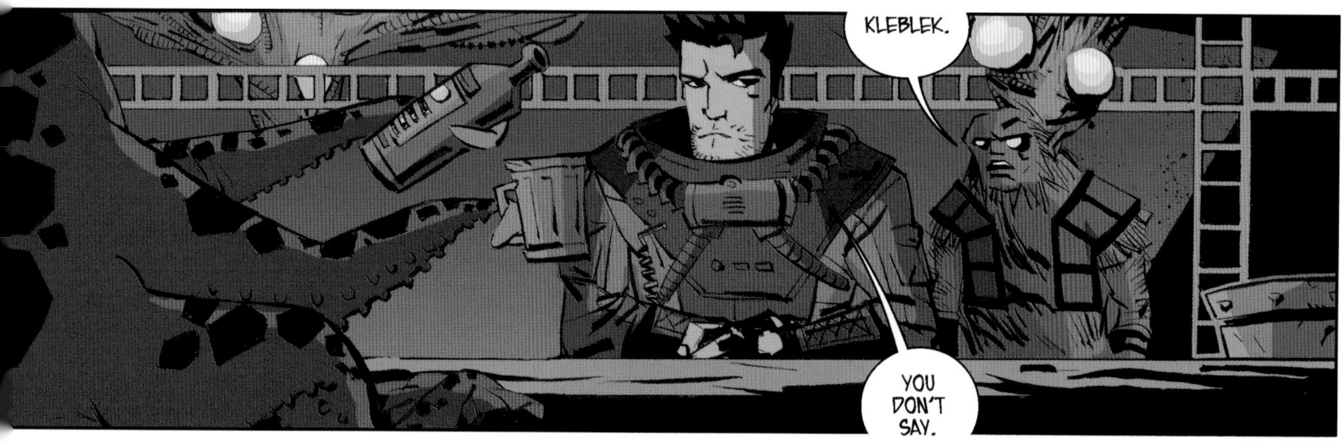
KLEBLEK.
YOU DON'T SAY.

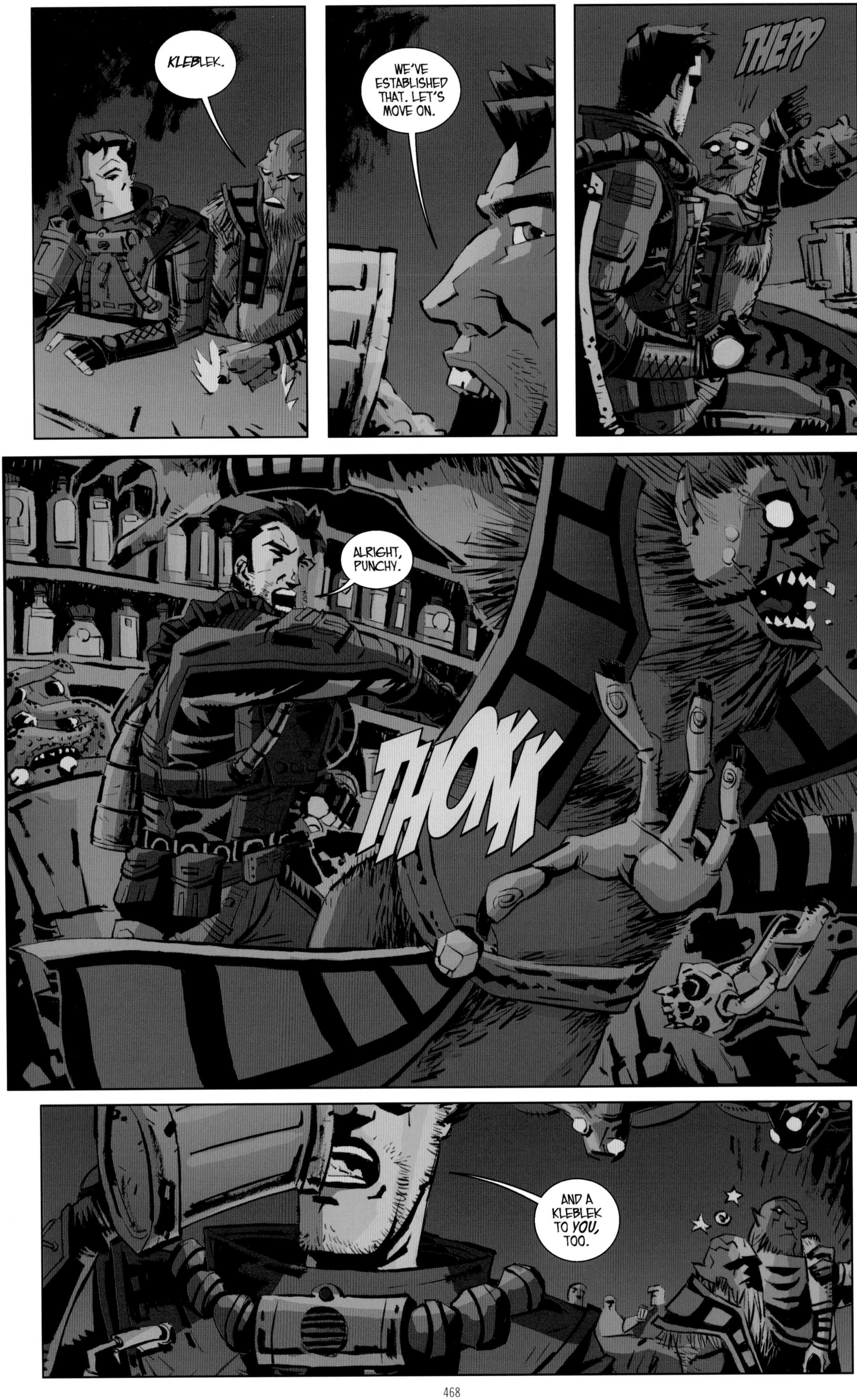
KLEBLEK.
WE'VE ESTABLISHED THAT. LET'S MOVE ON.
THEPP
ALRIGHT, PUNCHY.
THOKK
AND A KLEBLEK TO YOU, TOO.

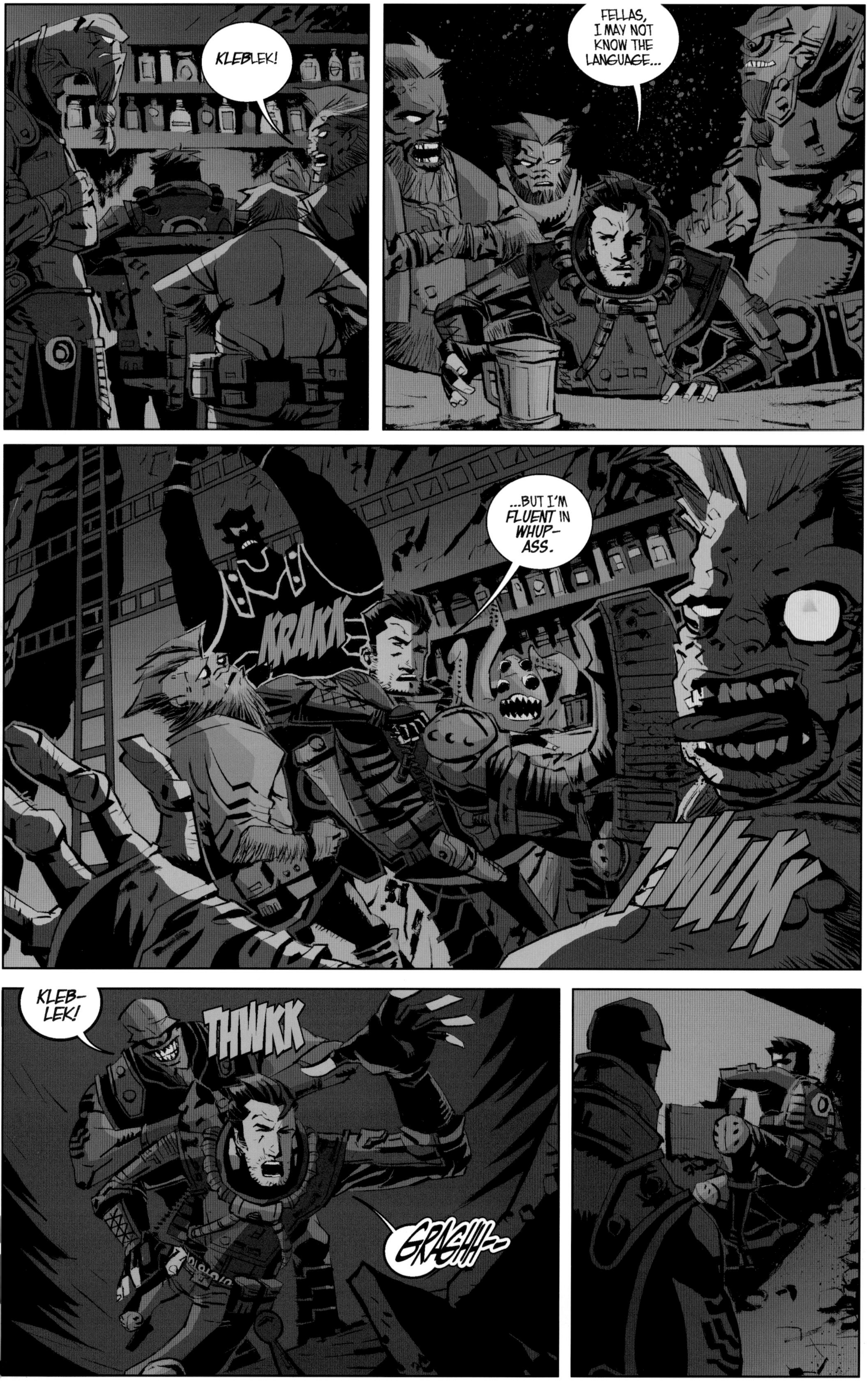
KLEBLEK!
FELLAS, I MAY NOT KNOW THE LANGUAGE...
...BUT I'M FLUENT IN WHUP-ASS.
KRAKK
THUNK
KLEB-LEK!
THWKK
CRASHH--

YAW!
C'MON THEN.

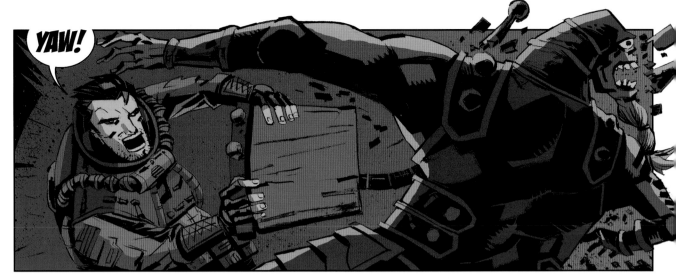

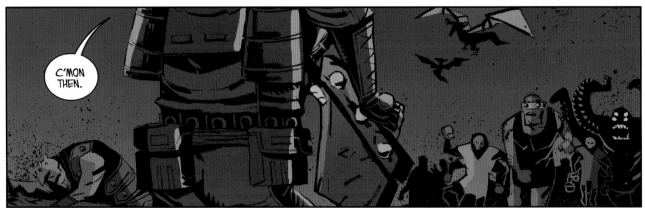

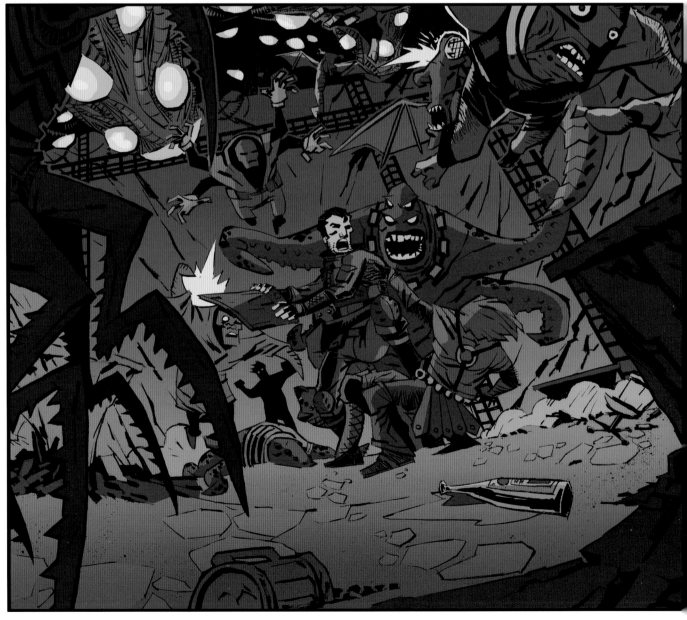

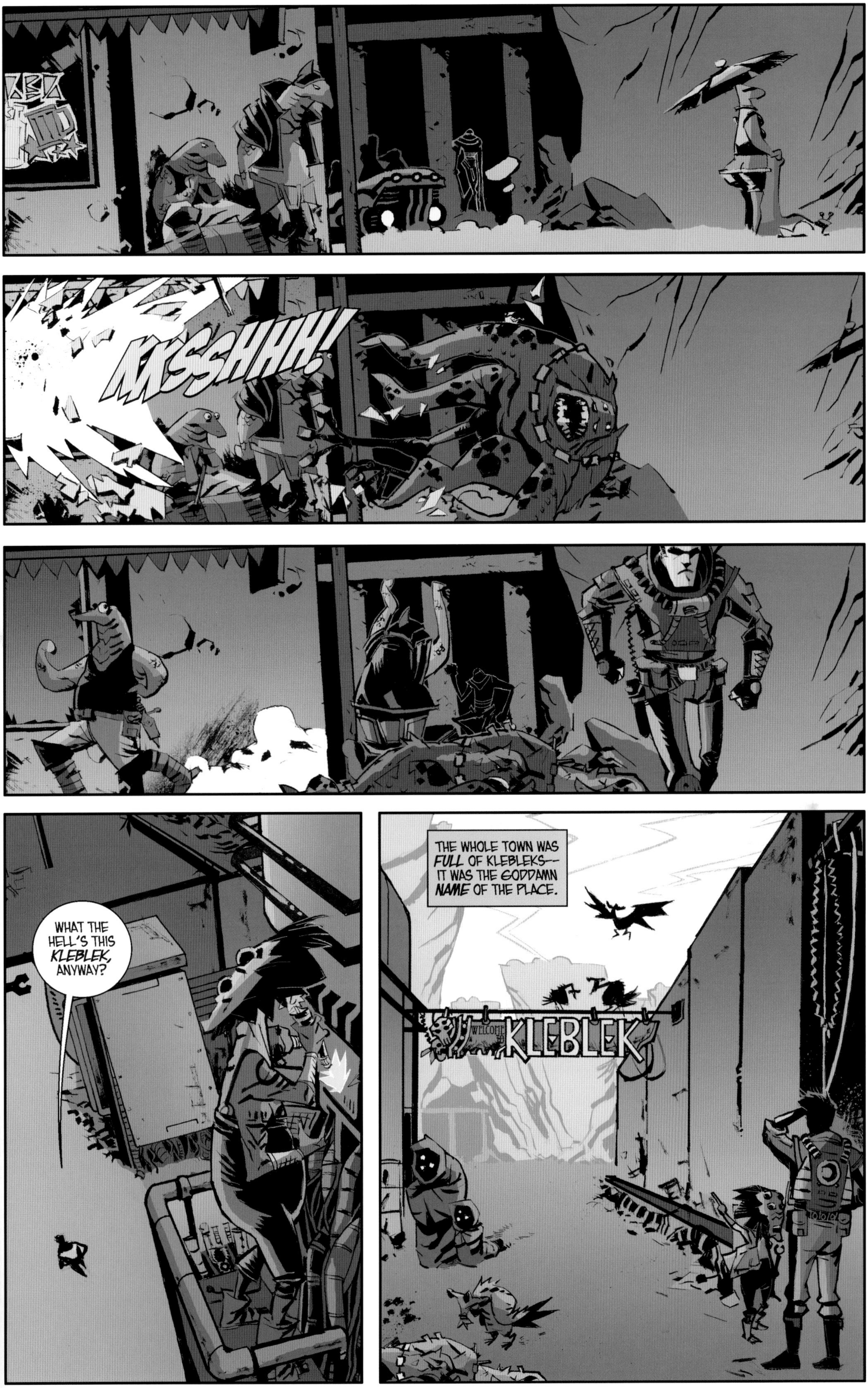
KKSSHHH!
WHAT THE HELL'S THIS KLEBLEK, ANYWAY?
THE WHOLE TOWN WAS FULL OF KLEBLEKS-- IT WAS THE GODDAMN NAME OF THE PLACE.
KLEBLEK

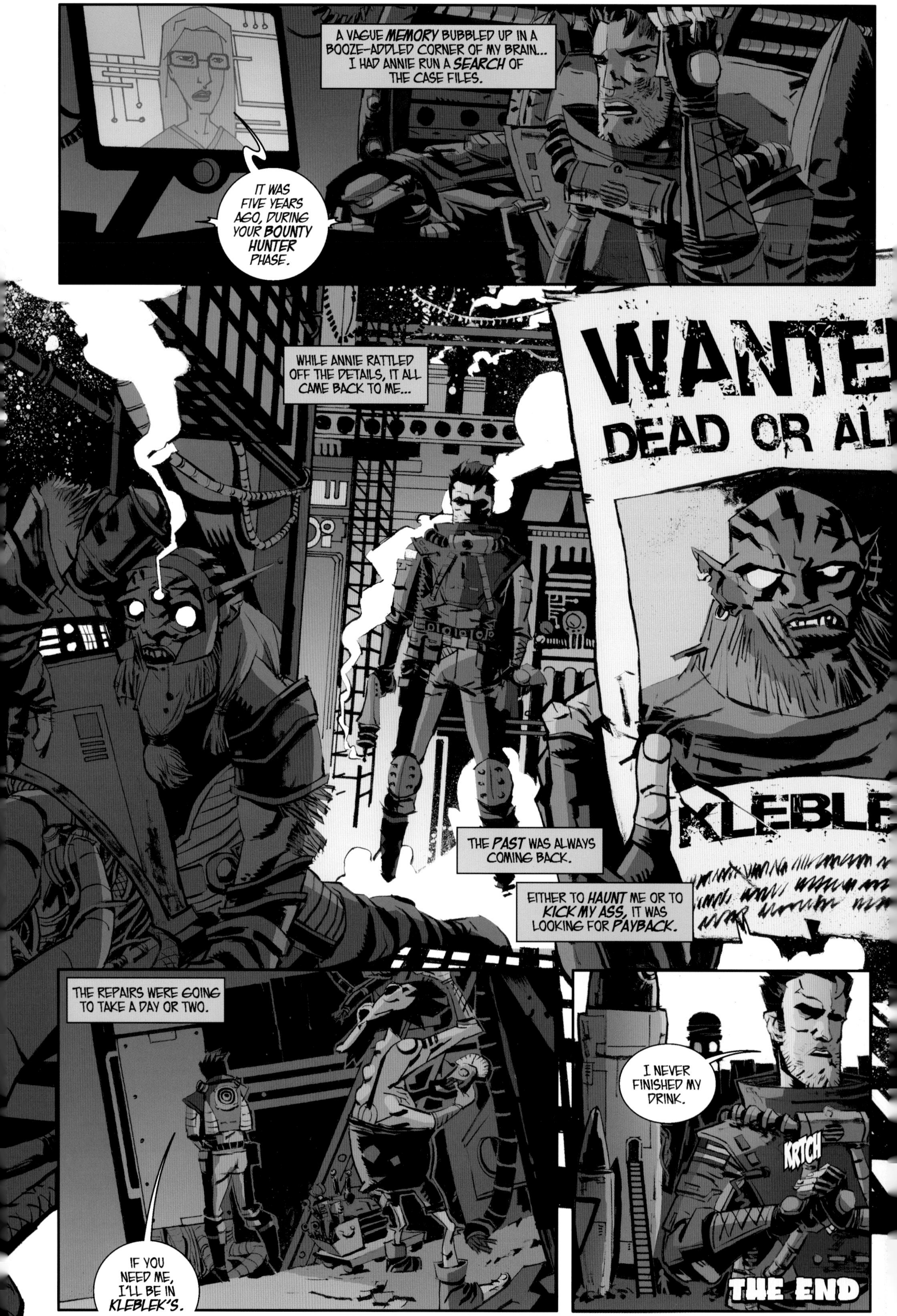
A VAGUE MEMORY BUBBLED UP IN A BOOZE-ADDLED CORNER OF MY BRAIN... I HAD ANNIE RUN A SEARCH OF THE CASE FILES.
IT WAS FIVE YEARS AGO, DURING YOUR BOUNTY HUNTER PHASE.
WHILE ANNIE RATTLED OFF THE DETAILS, IT ALL CAME BACK TO ME...
WANTE
DEAD OR AL
KLEBLE
THE PAST WAS ALWAYS COMING BACK.
EITHER TO HAUNT ME OR TO KICK MY ASS, IT WAS LOOKING FOR PAYBACK.
THE REPAIRS WERE GOING TO TAKE A DAY OR TWO.
IF YOU NEED ME, I'LL BE IN KLEBLEK'S.
I NEVER FINISHED MY DRINK.
KRTCH
THE END

DEMONS

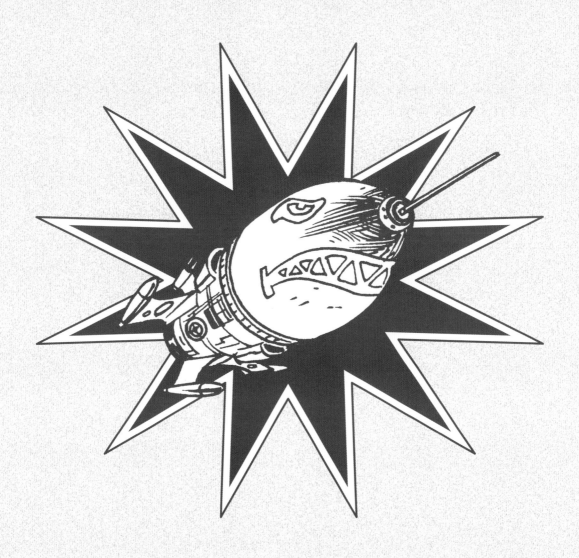

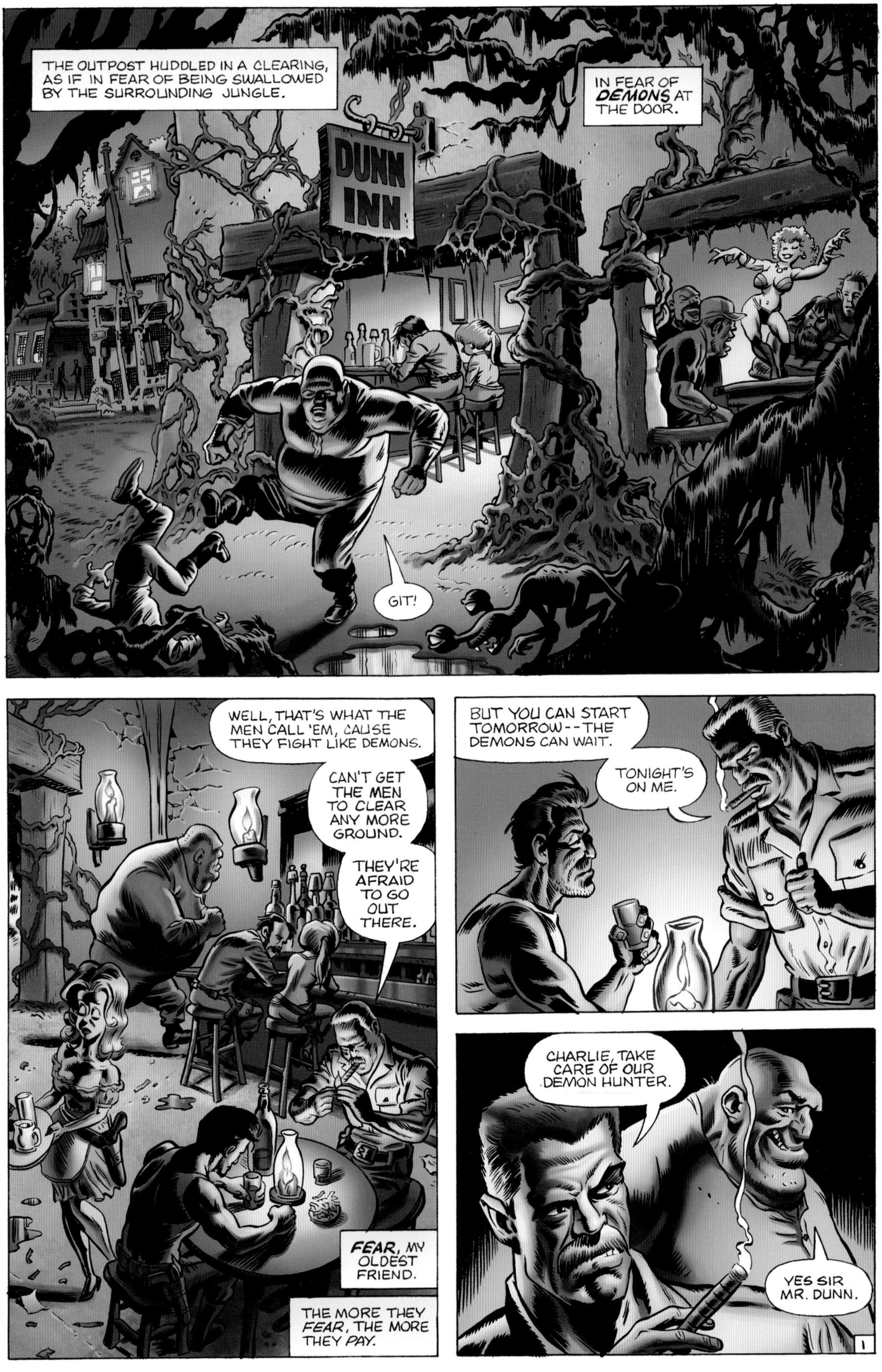
THE OUTPOST HUDDLED IN A CLEARING, AS IF IN FEAR OF BEING SWALLOWED BY THE SURROUNDING JUNGLE.
DUNN INN
IN FEAR OF DEMONS AT THE DOOR.
GIT!
WELL, THAT'S WHAT THE MEN CALL 'EM, CAUSE THEY FIGHT LIKE DEMONS.
CAN'T GET THE MEN TO CLEAR ANY MORE GROUND.
THEY'RE AFRAID TO GO OUT THERE.
FEAR, MY OLDEST FRIEND.
THE MORE THEY FEAR, THE MORE THEY PAY.
BUT YOU CAN START TOMORROW--THE DEMONS CAN WAIT.
TONIGHT'S ON ME.
CHARLIE, TAKE CARE OF OUR DEMON HUNTER.
YES SIR MR. DUNN.
1

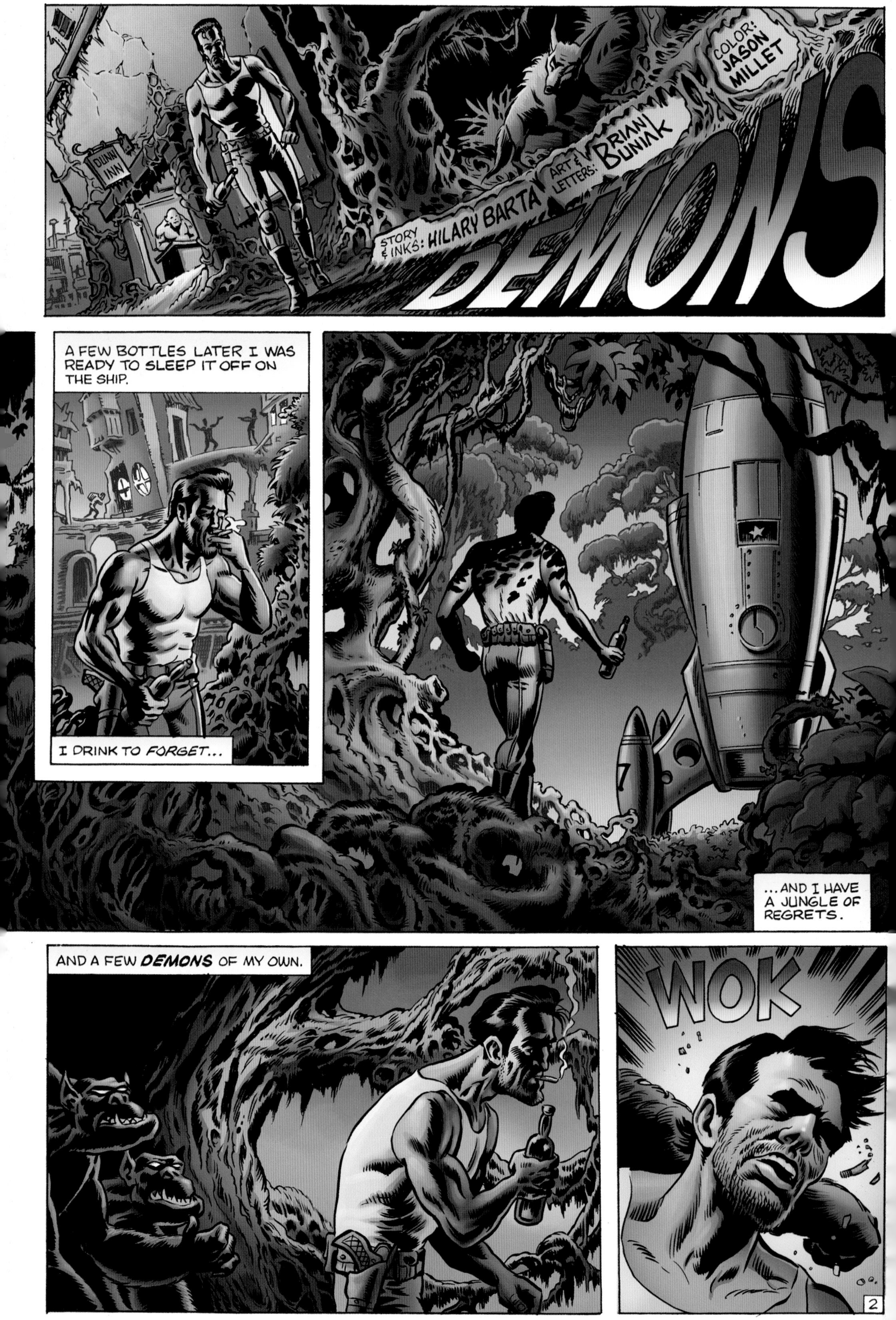
DUNN INN
STORY & INKS: HILARY BARTA
ART & LETTERS: BRIAN BUNIAK
COLOR: JASON MILLET
DEMONS
A FEW BOTTLES LATER I WAS READY TO SLEEP IT OFF ON THE SHIP.
I DRINK TO FORGET...
...AND I HAVE A JUNGLE OF REGRETS.
AND A FEW DEMONS OF MY OWN.
WOK
2

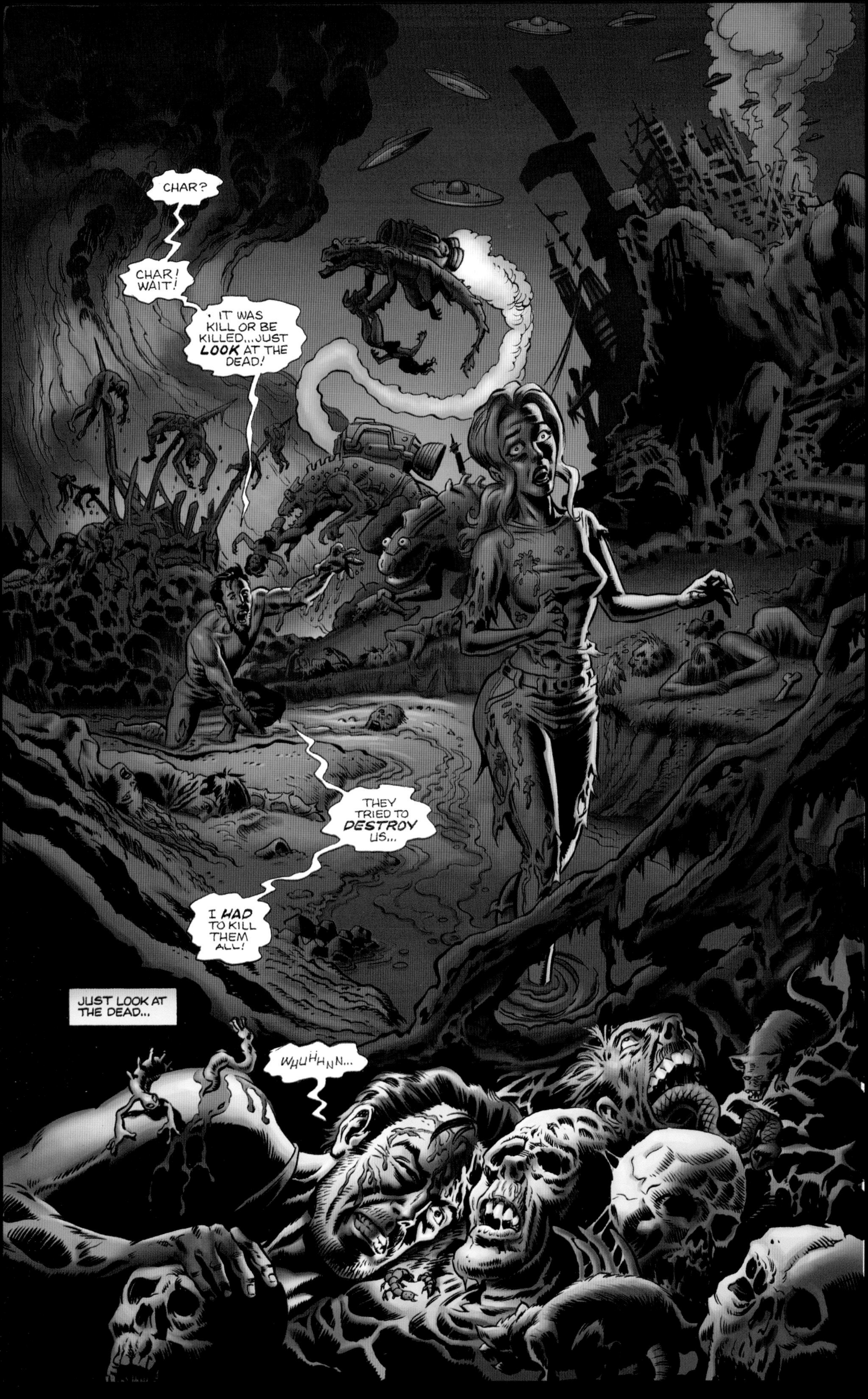
CHAR?
CHAR! WAIT!
IT WAS KILL OR BE KILLED... JUST LOOK AT THE DEAD!
THEY TRIED TO DESTROY US...
I HAD TO KILL THEM ALL!
JUST LOOK AT THE DEAD...
WHUHHNN...

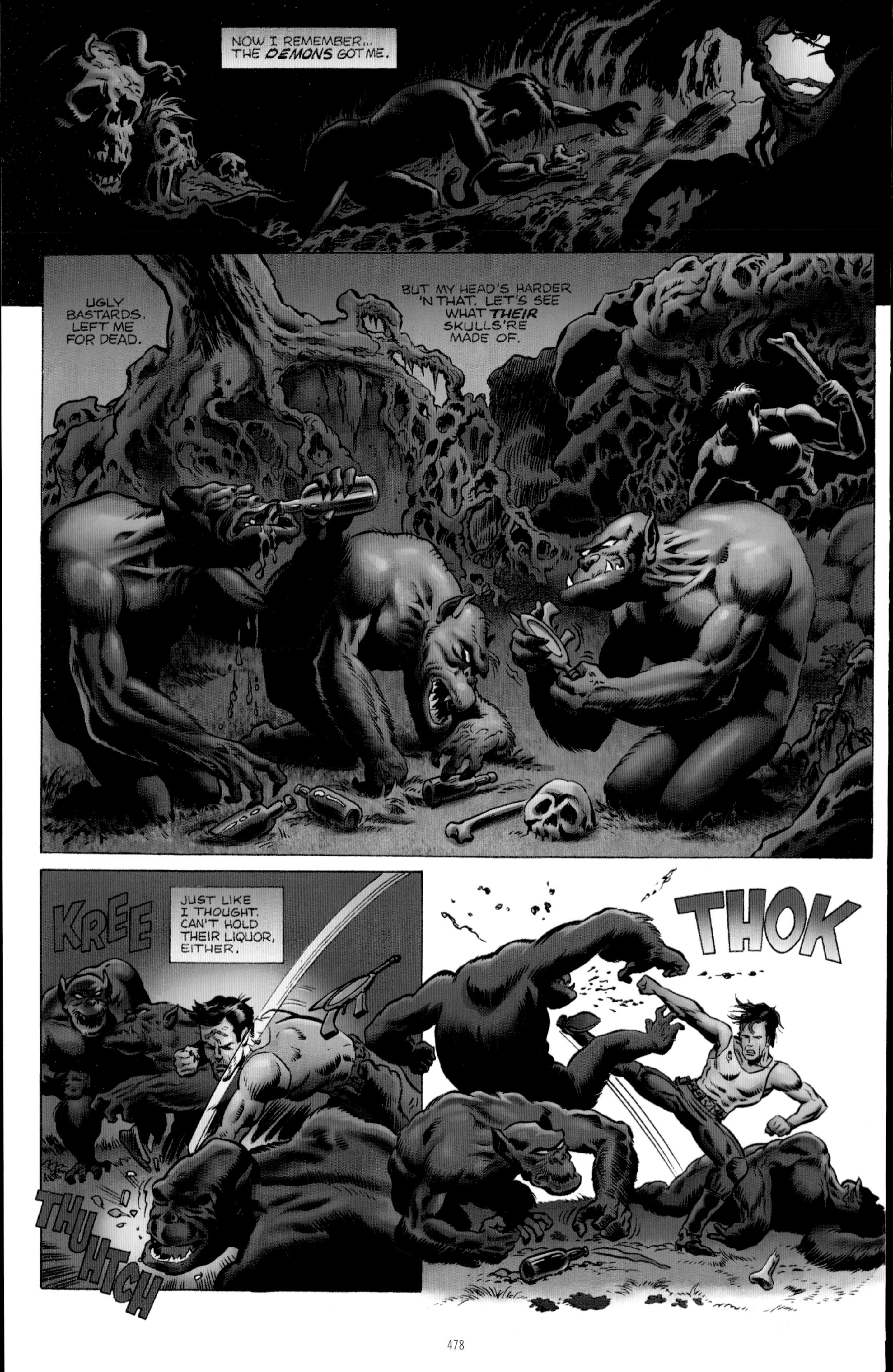
NOW I REMEMBER... THE DEMONS GOT ME.
UGLY BASTARDS. LEFT ME FOR DEAD.
BUT MY HEAD'S HARDER 'N THAT. LET'S SEE WHAT THEIR SKULLS'RE MADE OF.
KREE
JUST LIKE I THOUGHT. CAN'T HOLD THEIR LIQUOR, EITHER.
THOK
THUHITCH

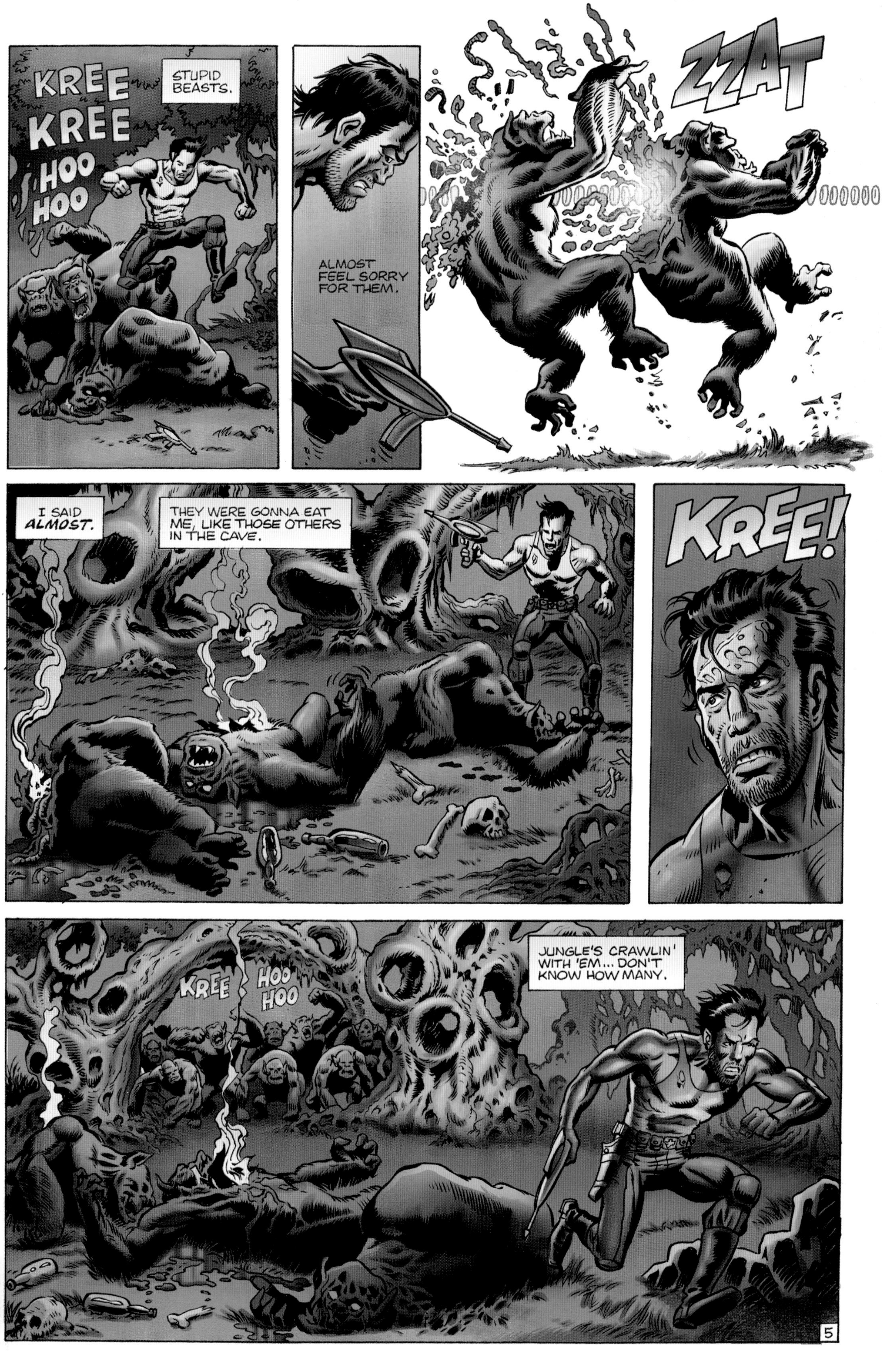
KREE
KREE
HOO
HOO
STUPID BEASTS.
ALMOST FEEL SORRY FOR THEM.
ZZAT
I SAID *ALMOST*.
THEY WERE GONNA EAT ME, LIKE THOSE OTHERS IN THE CAVE.
KREE!
KREE
HOO
HOO
JUNGLE'S CRAWLIN' WITH 'EM... DON'T KNOW HOW MANY.
5

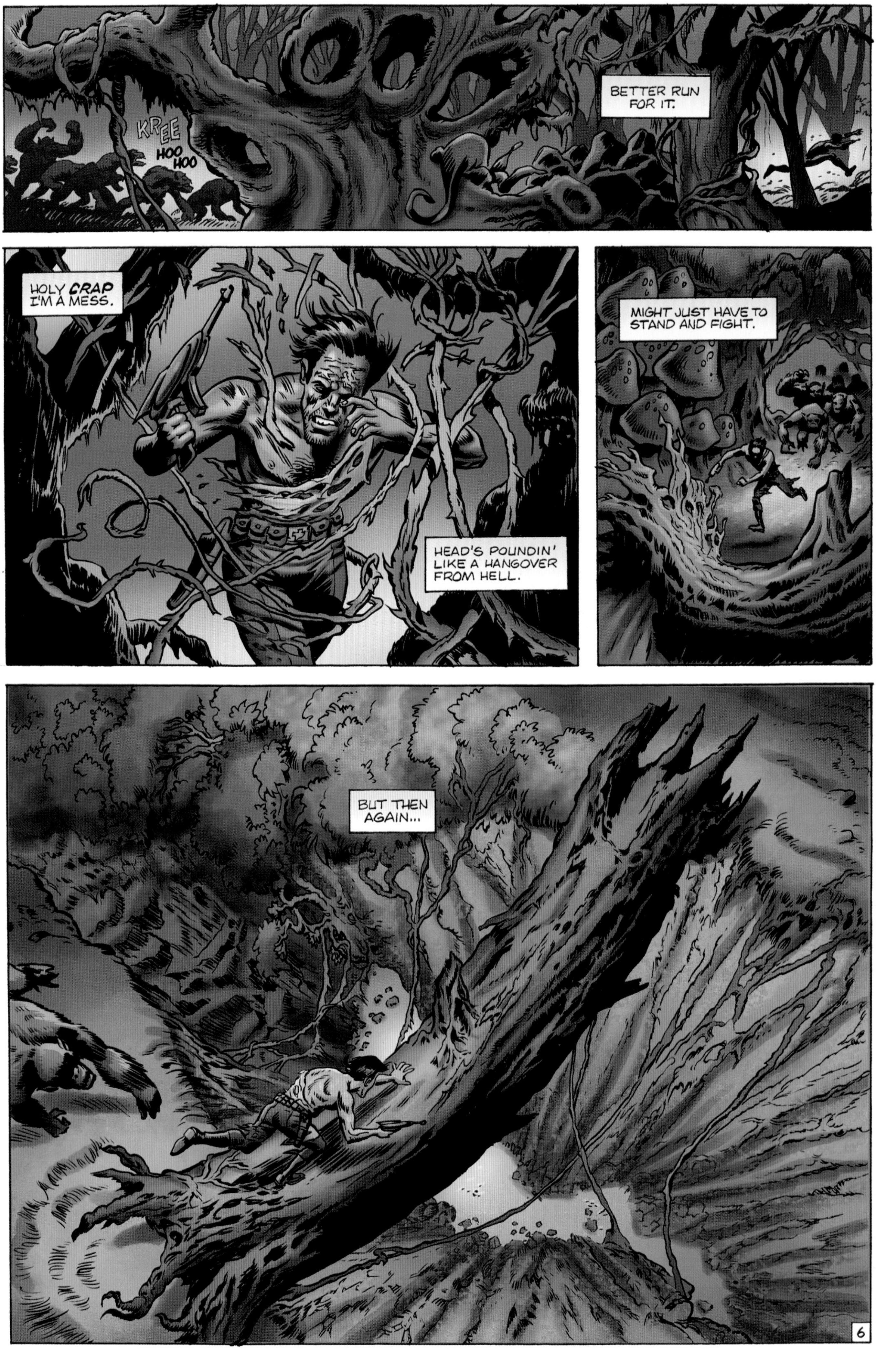
KREE
HOO HOO
BETTER RUN FOR IT.
HOLY CRAP I'M A MESS.
HEAD'S POUNDIN' LIKE A HANGOVER FROM HELL.
MIGHT JUST HAVE TO STAND AND FIGHT.
BUT THEN AGAIN...
6

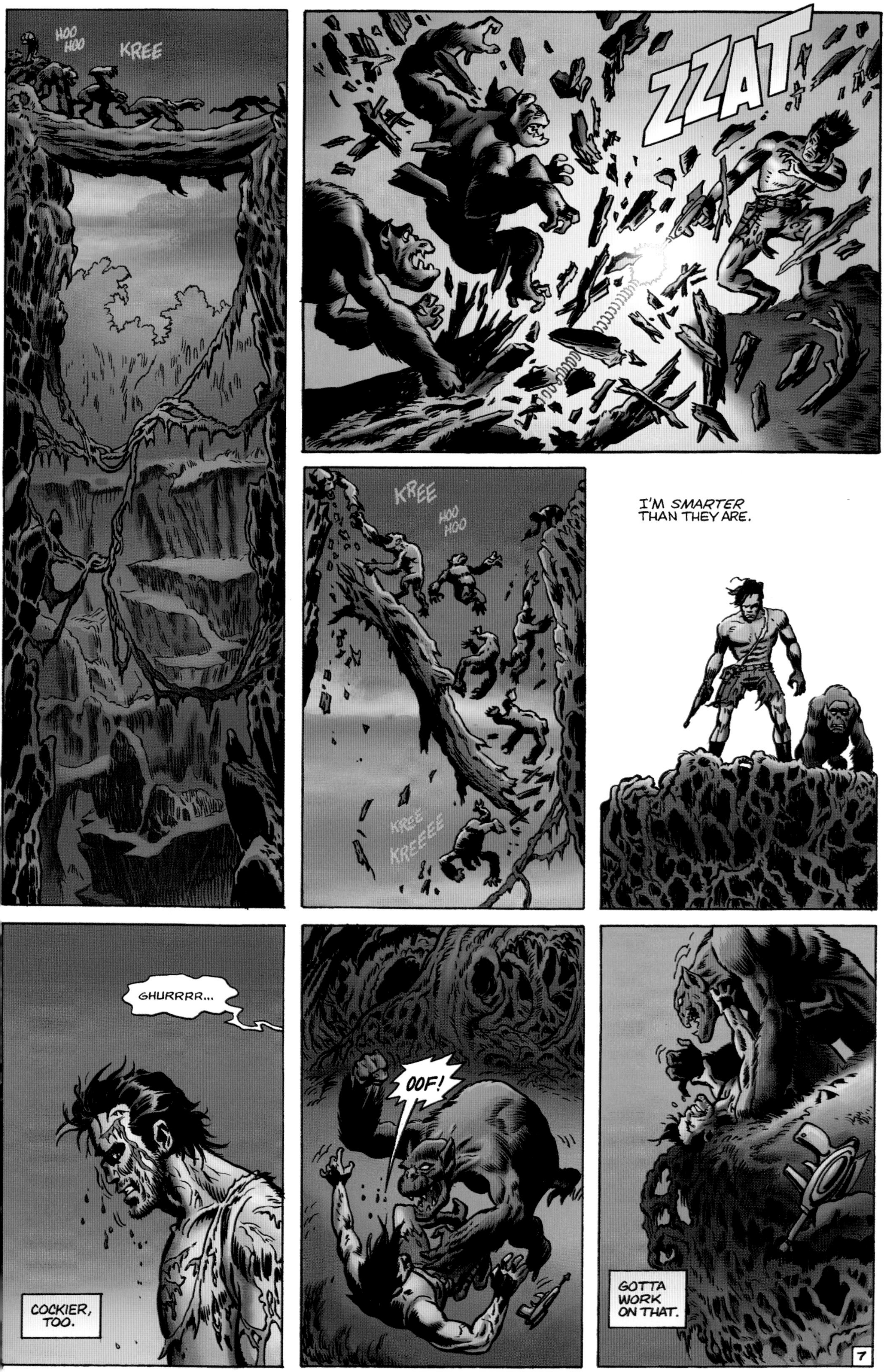
HOO
HOO
KREE
ZZAT
KREE
HOO
HOO
KREE
KREEEE
I'M SMARTER THAN THEY ARE.
GHURRRR...
COCKIER, TOO.
OOF!
GOTTA WORK ON THAT.
7

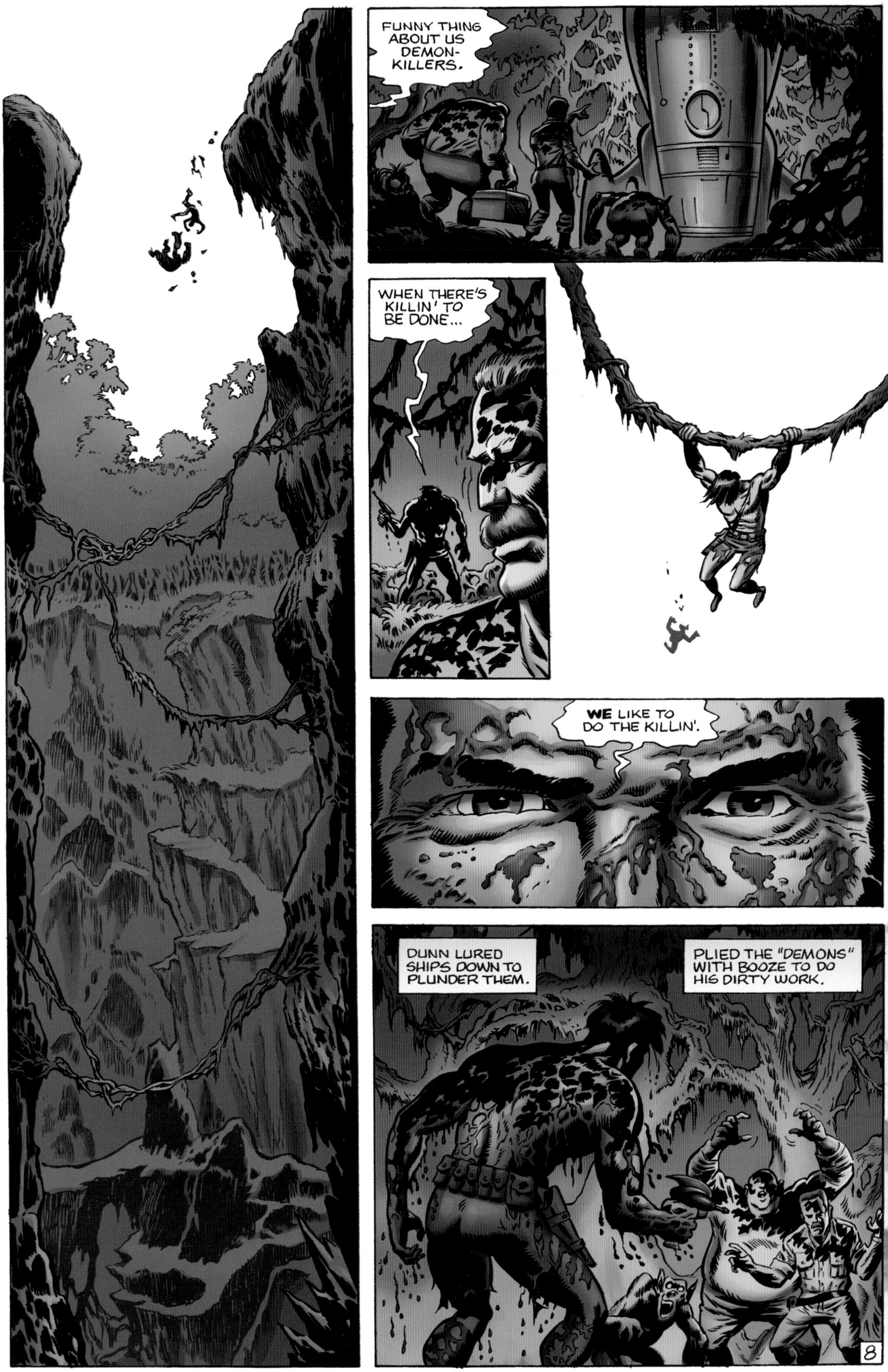
FUNNY THING ABOUT US DEMON-KILLERS.
WHEN THERE'S KILLIN' TO BE DONE...
WE LIKE TO DO THE KILLIN'.
DUNN LURED SHIPS DOWN TO PLUNDER THEM.
PLIED THE "DEMONS" WITH BOOZE TO DO HIS DIRTY WORK.
8

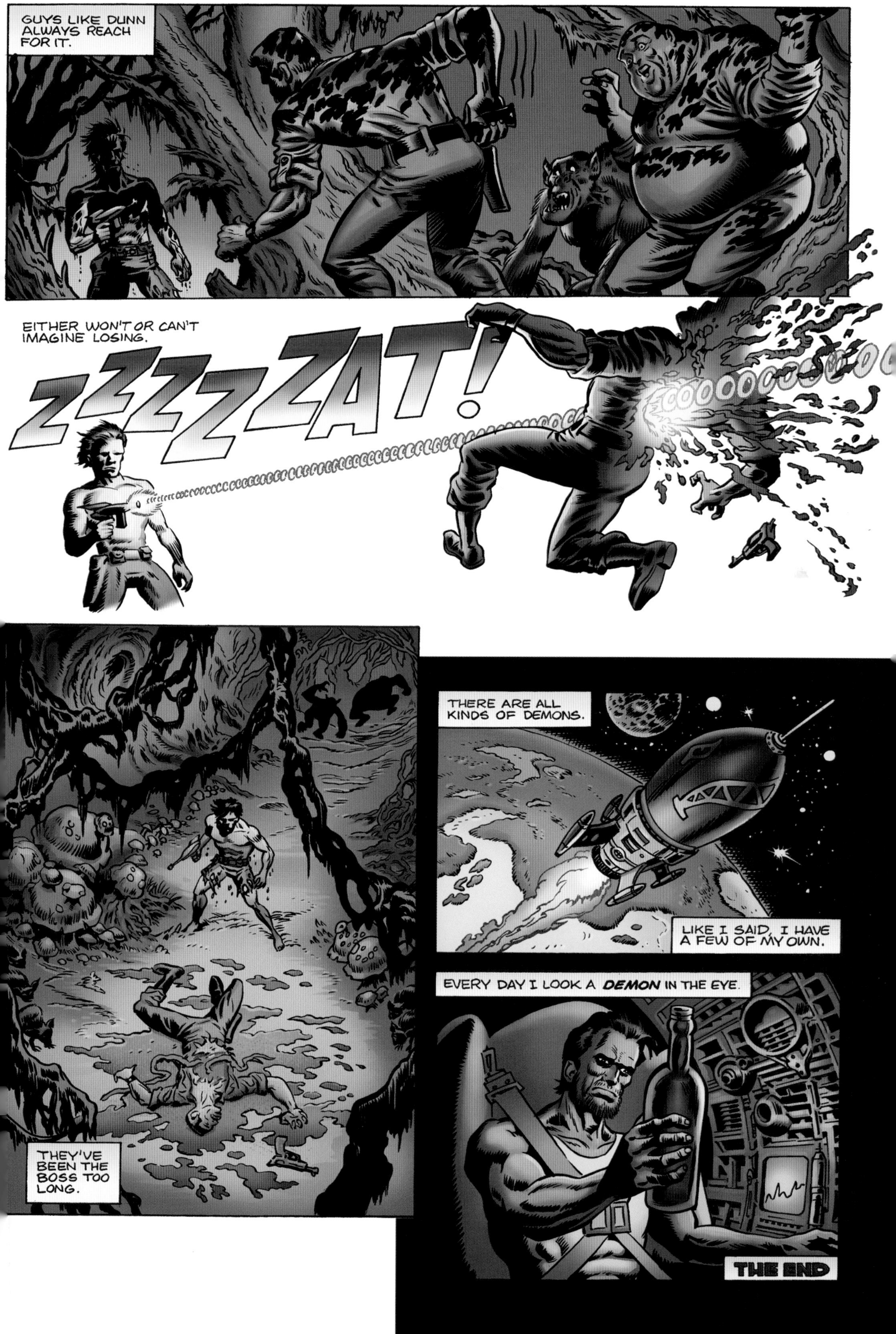
GUYS LIKE DUNN ALWAYS REACH FOR IT.
EITHER WON'T OR CAN'T IMAGINE LOSING.
ZZZZZAT!
THEY'VE BEEN THE BOSS TOO LONG.
THERE ARE ALL KINDS OF DEMONS.
LIKE I SAID, I HAVE A FEW OF MY OWN.
EVERY DAY I LOOK A DEMON IN THE EYE.
THE END

SKETCH GALLERY

With notes by Tony Moore and Jerome Opeña

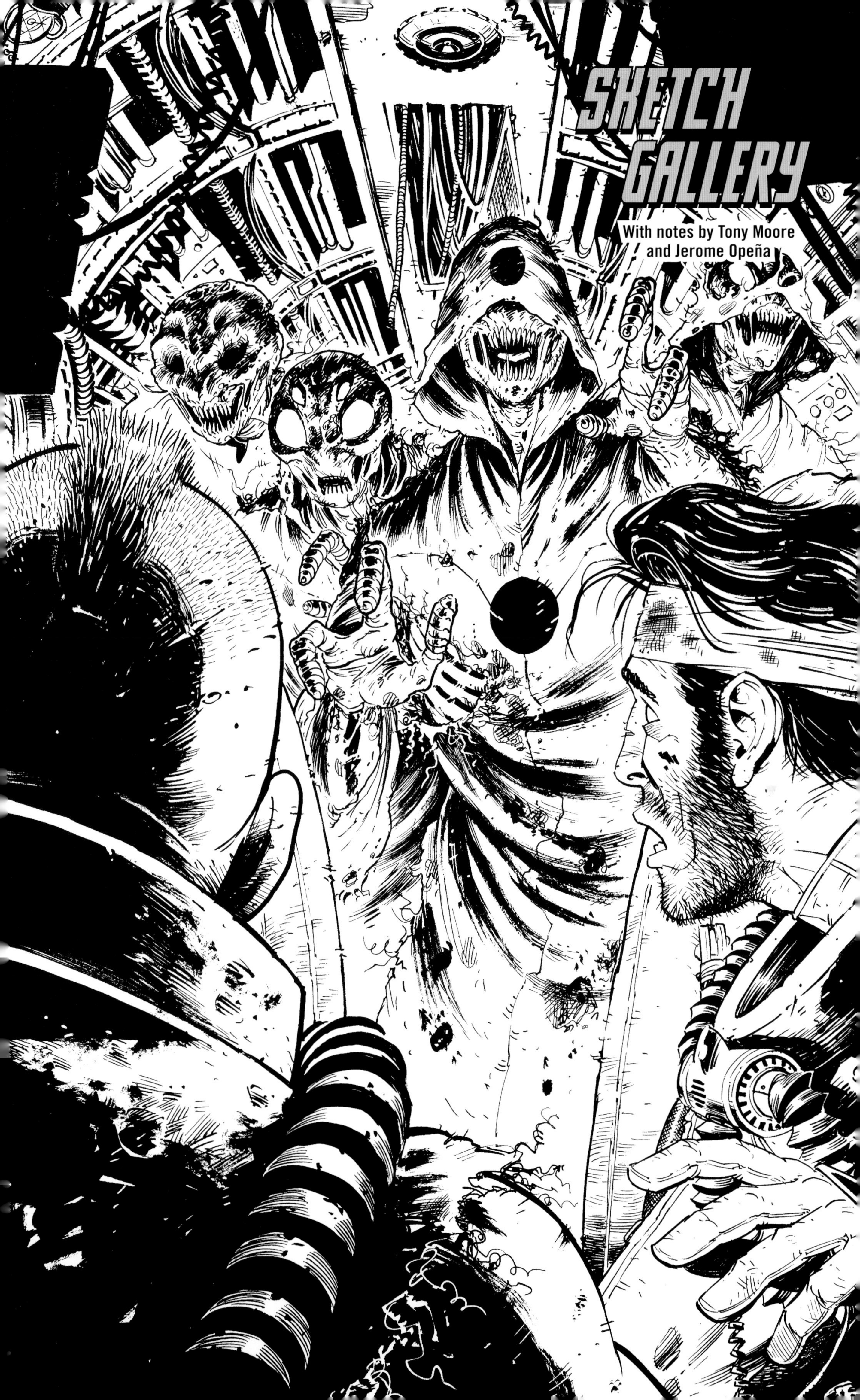

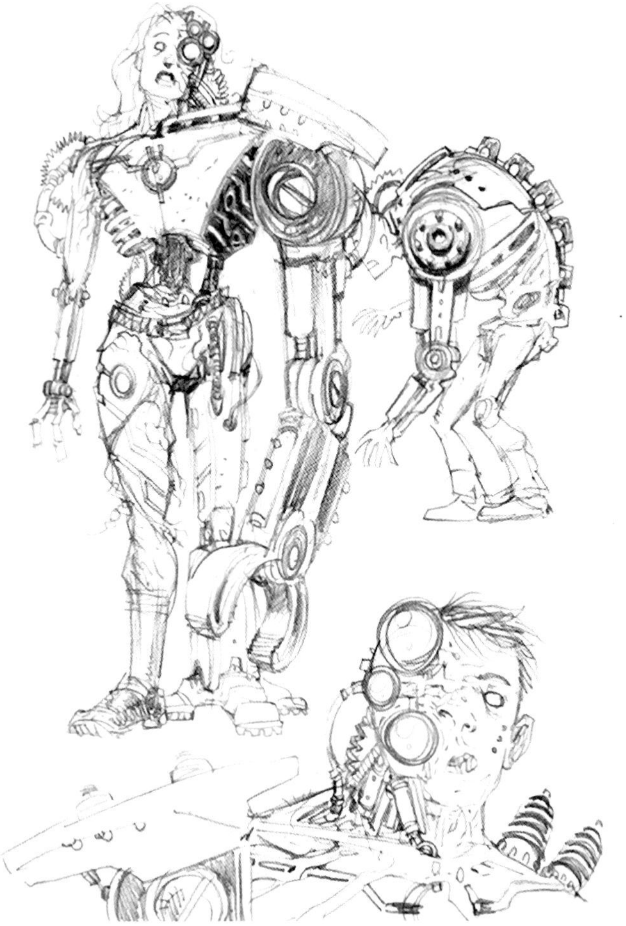

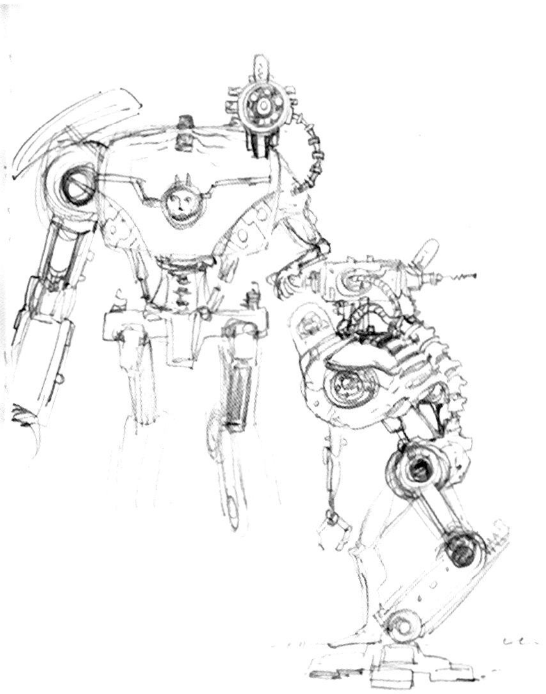

TM: So, the Tetaldians had gone back in time and impregnated every developing species with a nanovirus that would turn them all into weird robo-hybrids. Since it happens kind of explosively and all at once, I thought it would be cool if parts just kinda sprouted out violently, stretching and contorting the host. The mechanical bits held with the rest of the Tetaldians' design motifs, for the most part.

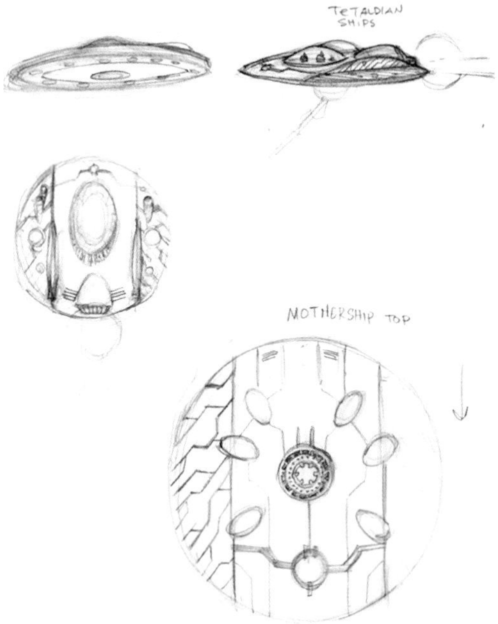
TETALDIAN SHIPS
MOTHERSHIP TOP

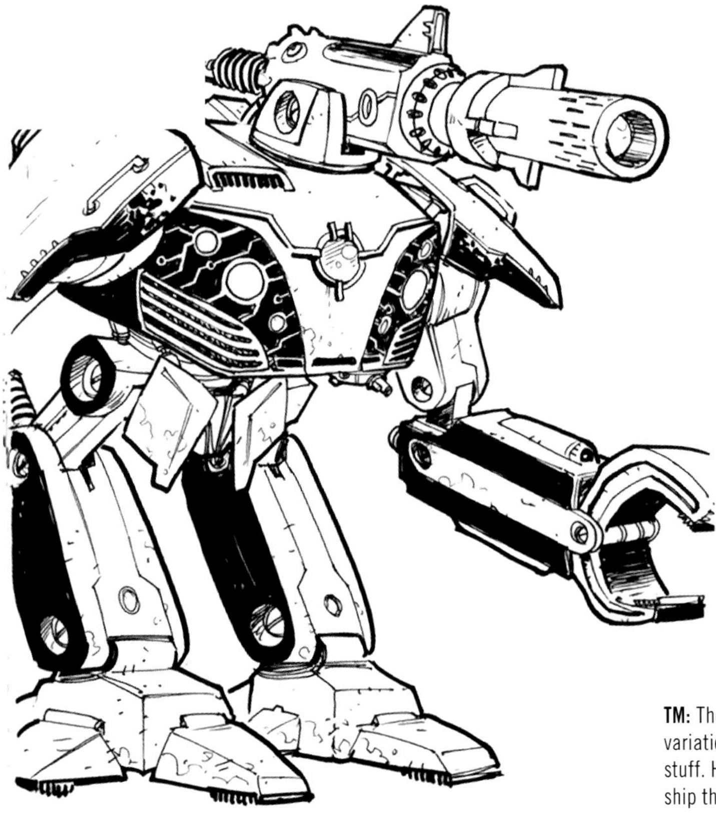

TM: The Tetaldian robot race had only been shown with a couple of variations, and I wanted to expand their world to show they had loads of stuff. Here are a few views of their smaller flying saucers, and the mother ship they came out of, as well as a big tank-like soldier.

KIPFERI
WAR PAINT
SKULLS OF FORMER PREY
WAR PAINT FOR FISH/EEL

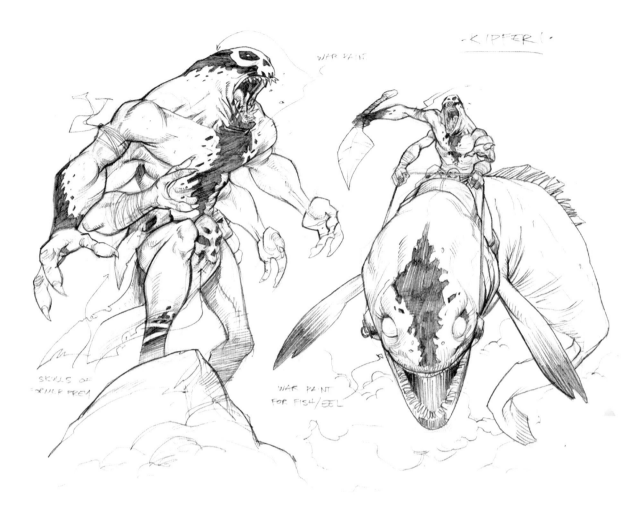

JO: It's been a while, but my recollection of Rick's description went something like: "Alien dudes with 4 arms. Tribal and fiercely strong. Oh, and they also ride around on flying fish." Looking back at the designs I came up with, I remember being influenced a lot by Venom and kind of trying to incorporate that into the look of the creatures. I added the face paint to the Kipferi and their fish to echo what Native American warriors would do to their horses. The fish were supposed to be a combination of an eel of some sort along with a coelacanth, which just happens to be the coolest looking fish ever.

FEAR
AGENT

FEAR
AGENT

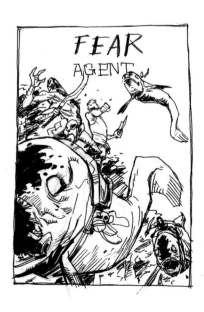

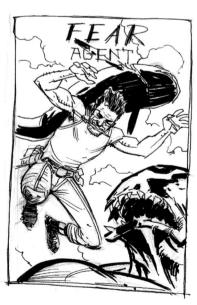

JO: Looking back at these, I'm amused at how finalized they were. Every kind of rough I do now are all just chicken scratches and shapes. If I could do them all over again, I honestly think I would've gone with the second composition over what I eventually used for the final.

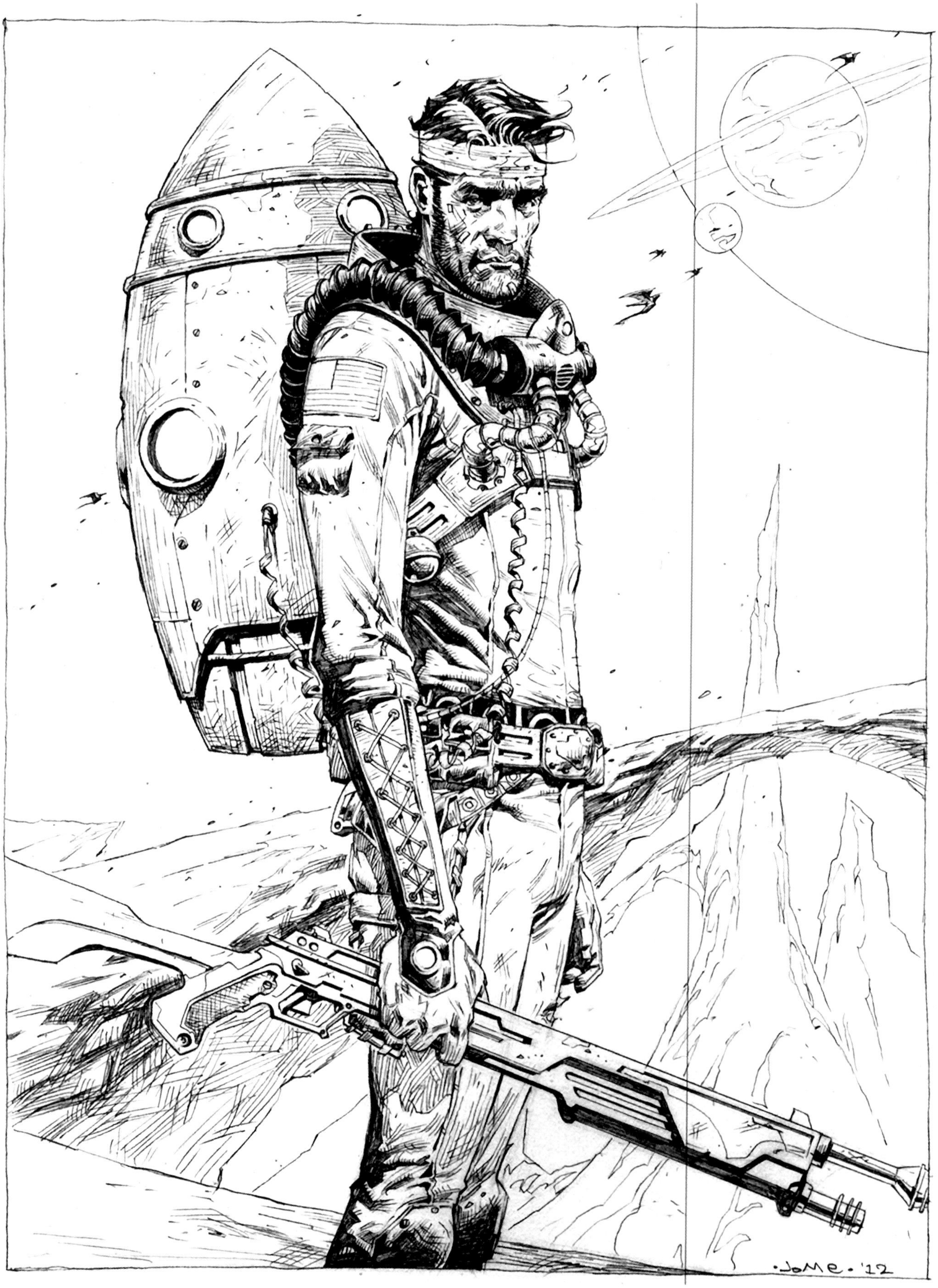
JoMe '12

JO: A piece I did for iFanboy a year ago or so. I love drawing Heath, so any sort of excuse I can find to do so, I'll definitely take advantage of it. How can you not root for a sad sack like him?

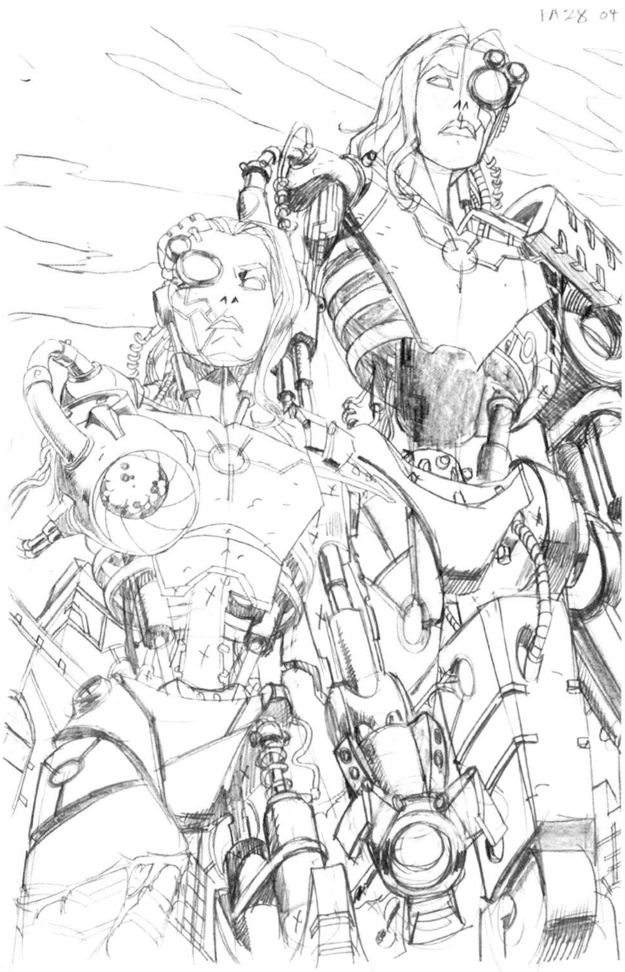

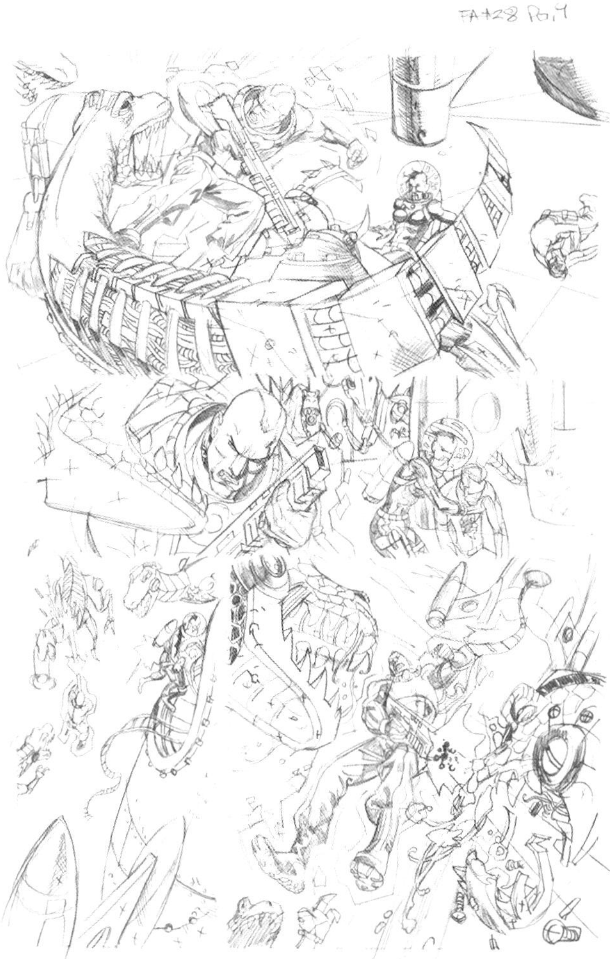

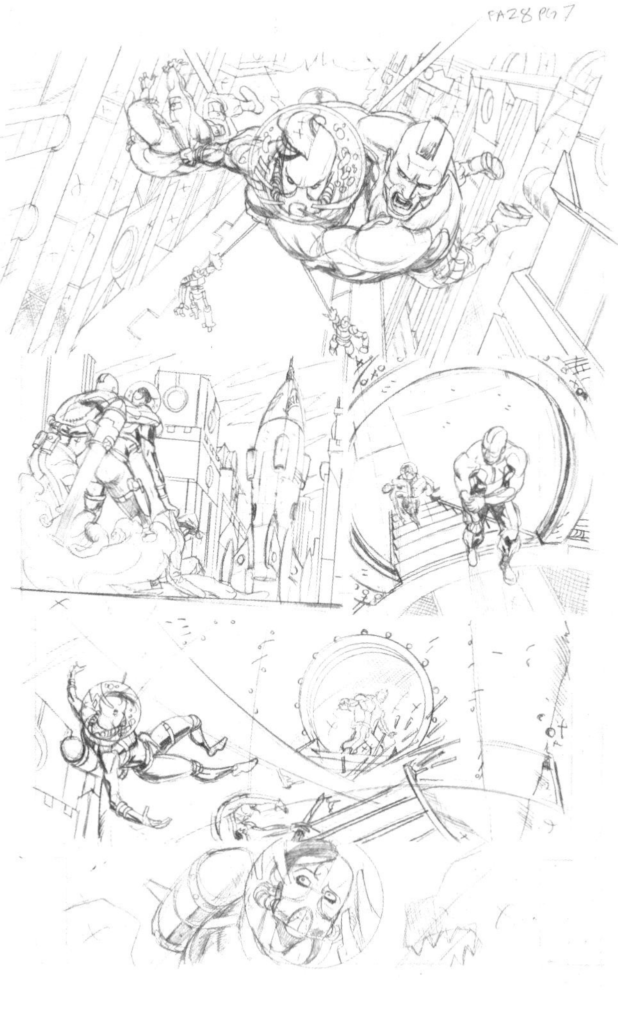

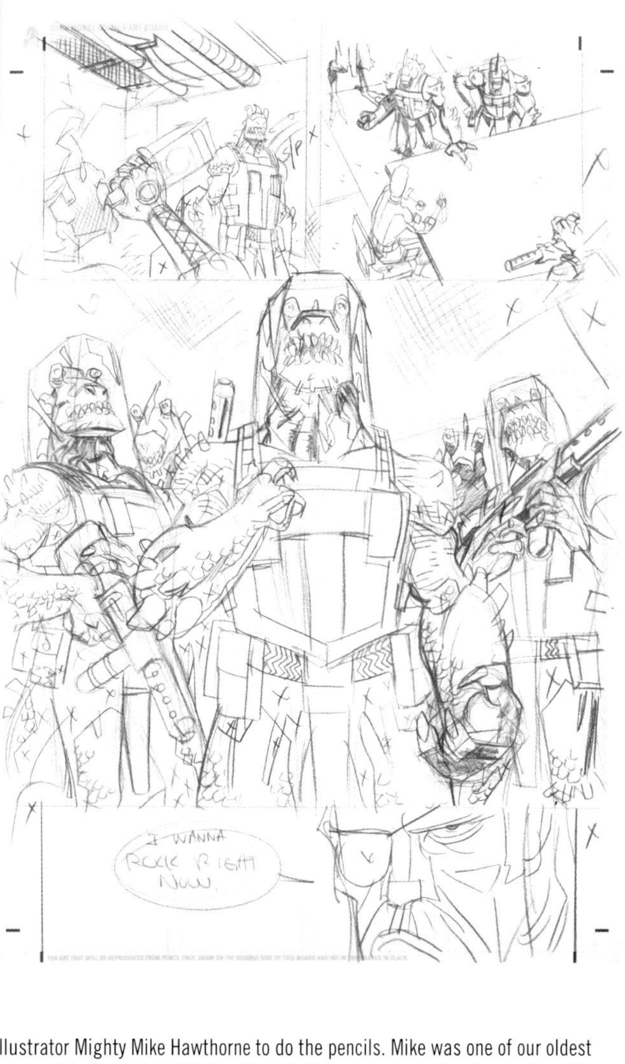
I WANNA ROCK RIGHT NOW.

TM: As time pressed on, to keep the book in production, we brought in powerhouse illustrator Mighty Mike Hawthorne to do the pencils. Mike was one of our oldest friends, and I had worked with him a lot on my book, *The Exterminators*, as well as some of the Marvel stuff I did with Rick. The guy's storytelling is amazing. His action sense is intense, and there's really nothing quite like the magic he makes. Add in Joltin' Johnny Lucas on the inks, and you've got pages for the ages!

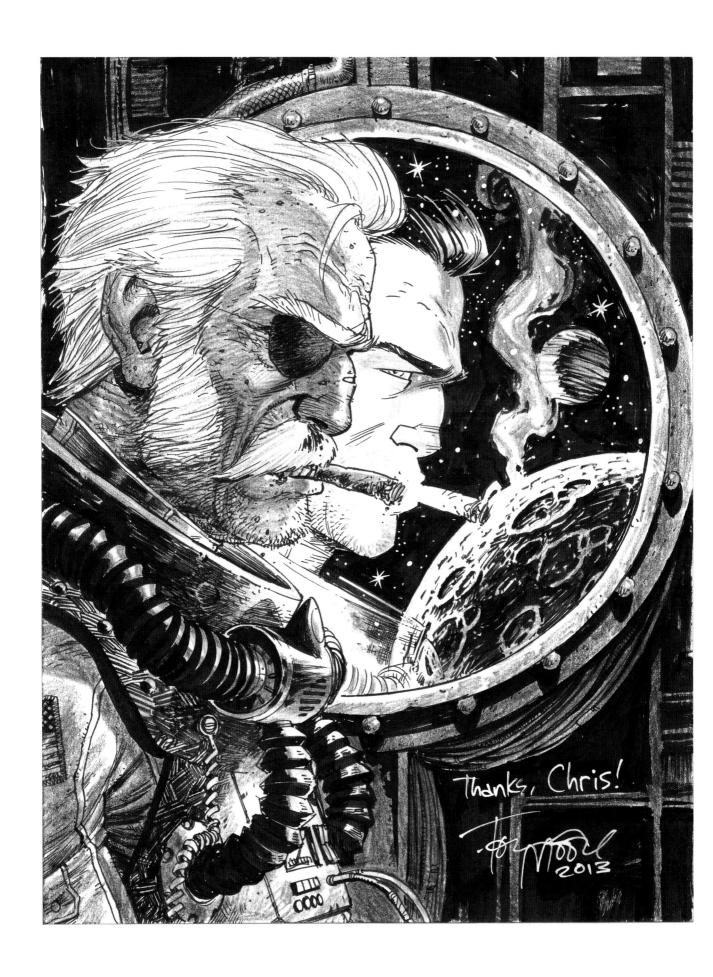

A *Fear Agent* commission by Tony Moore.

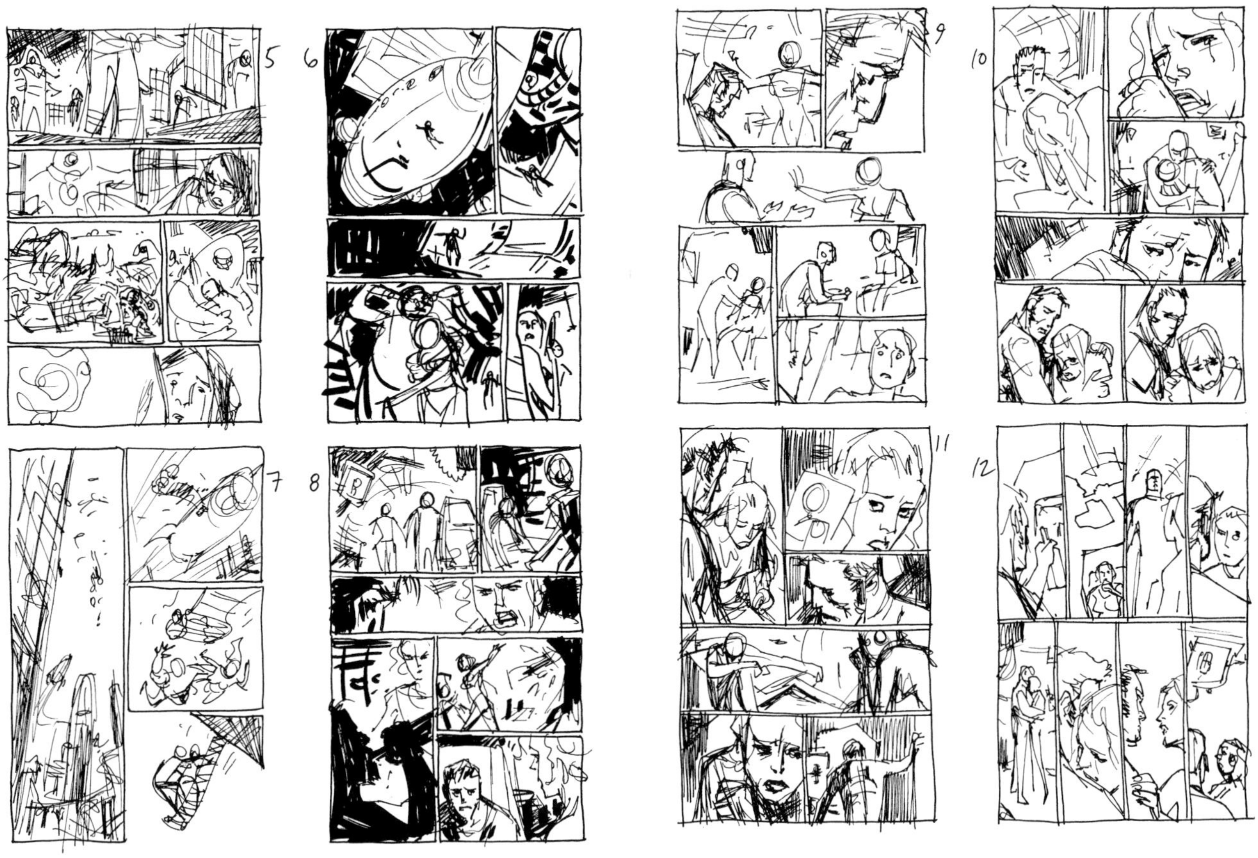

TM: Our good pal Kieron Dwyer lent his hand to some of Jerome's pages, to help us hold the schedule. He's a mad genius, and it's a shame that the world of comics has lost him to projects where pay is more commensurate with effort.

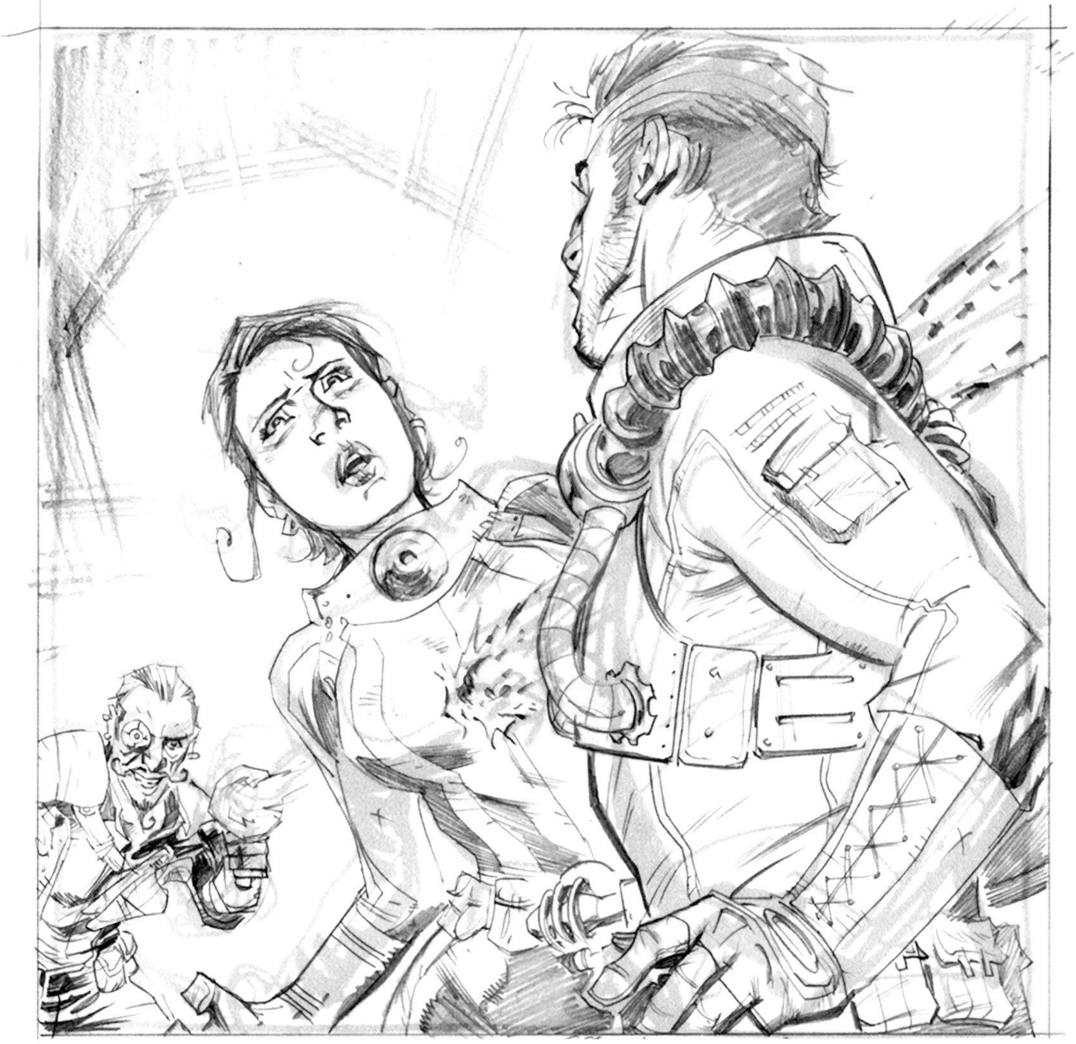

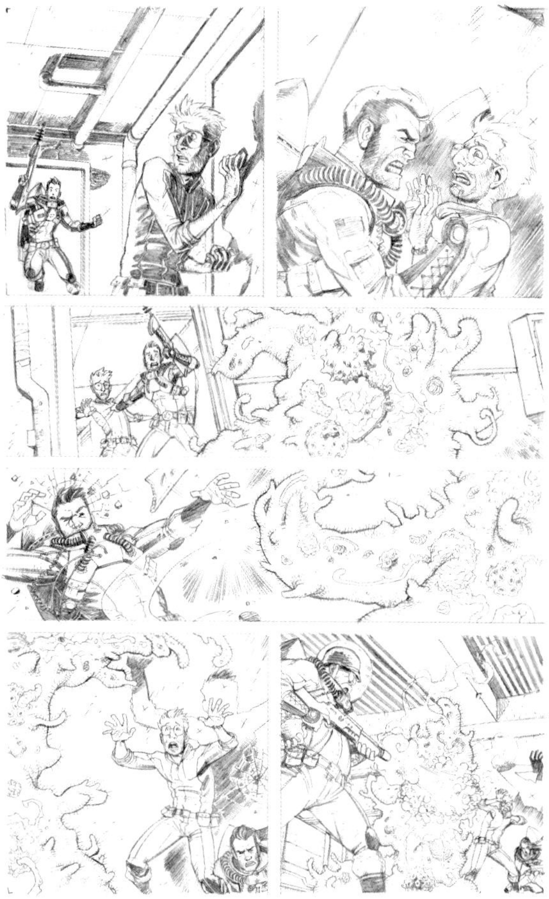

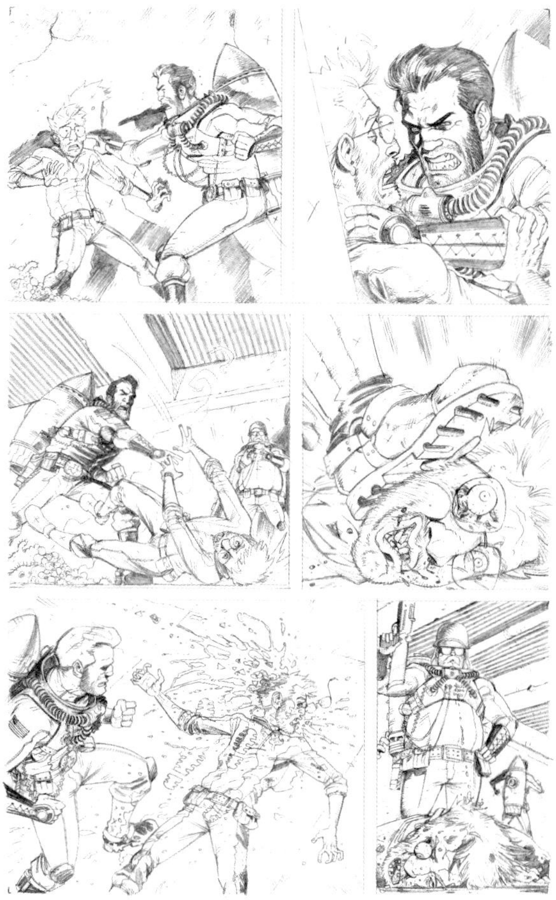

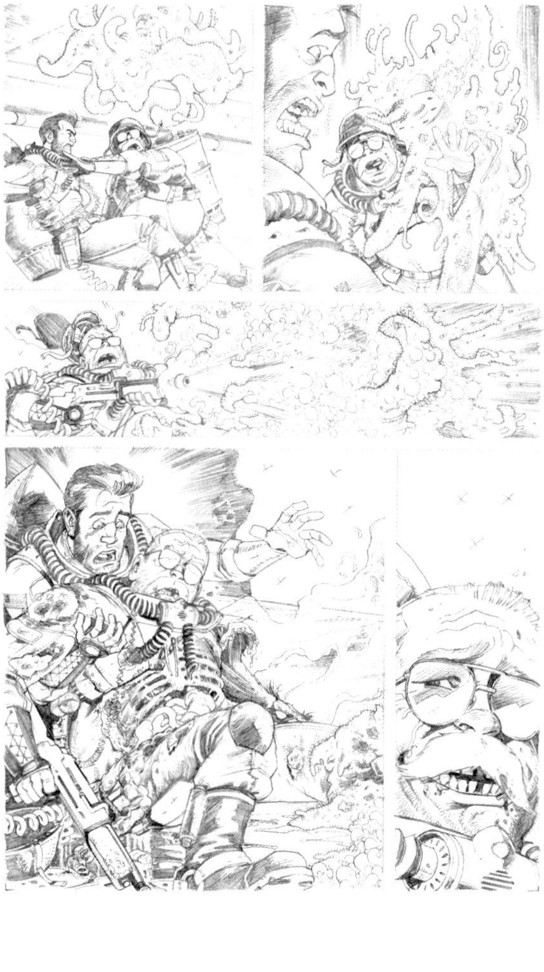

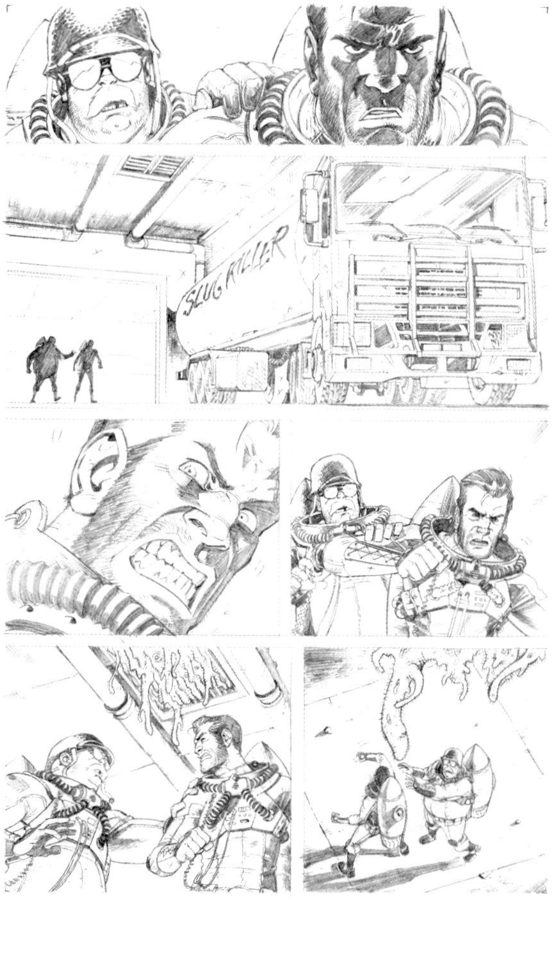
SLUG KILLER

TM: Here are a smattering of my pencils from *My War*. If these pages look better than usual, it's because Mike Hawthorne did the layouts, and ol' Rick Remender himself went on to ink them.

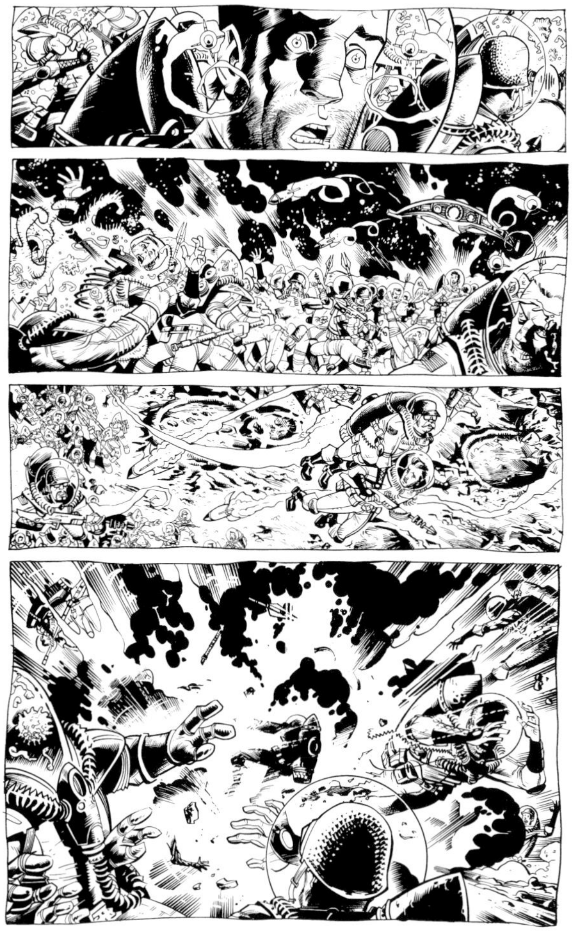

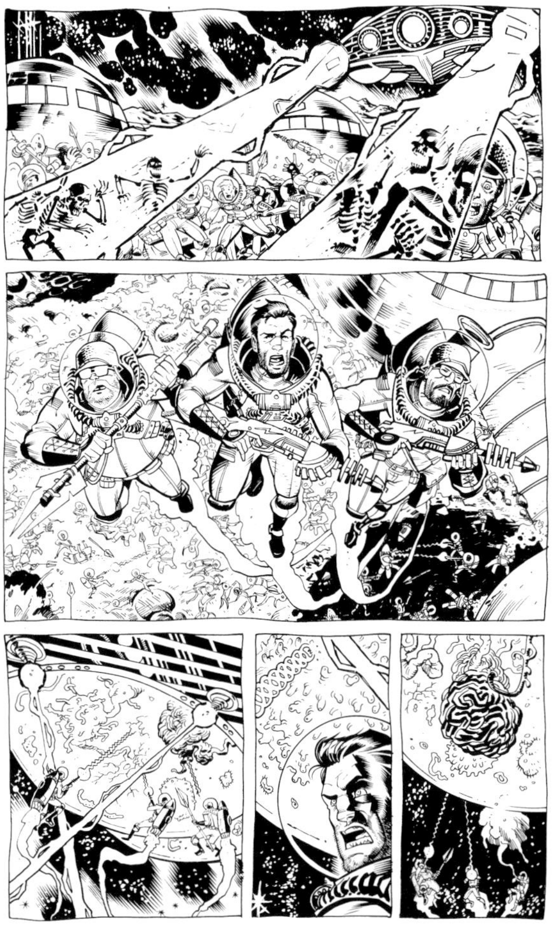

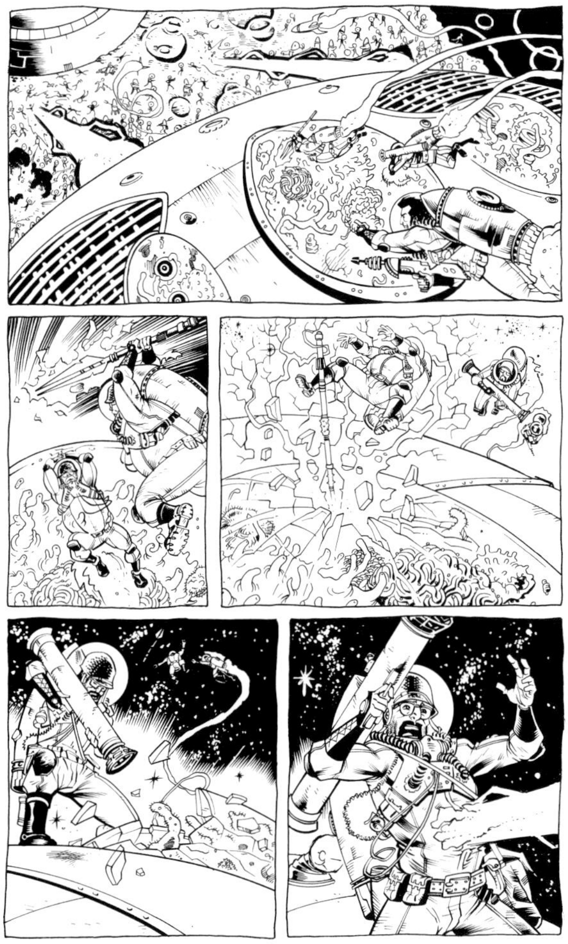

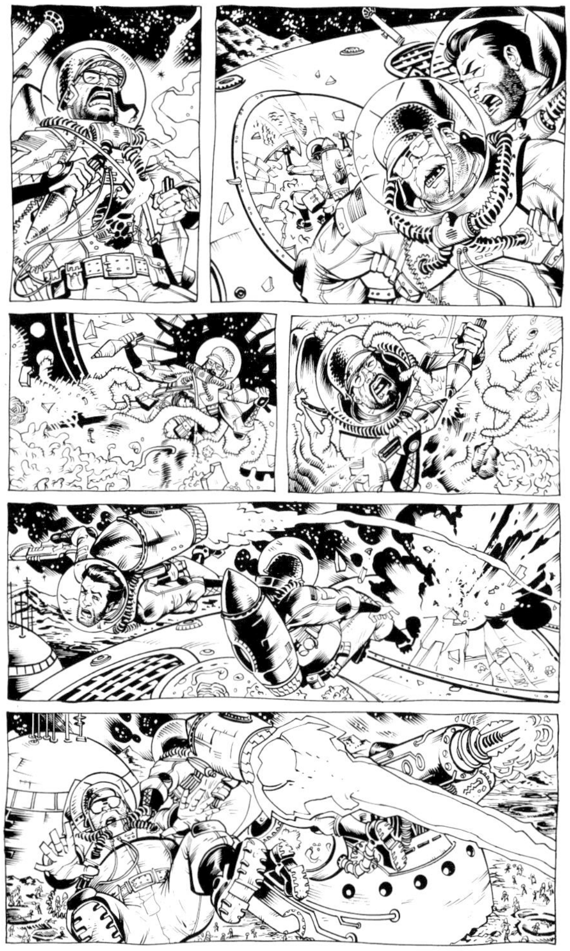

TM: This issue may have been the straw that broke the camel's back as far as inking goes with Rick. He delights in writing two sentences about a lunar battlefield that take me four days to draw, but his tune changed a bit once he was back in the art trenches with me. You reap what you sow, Remender!

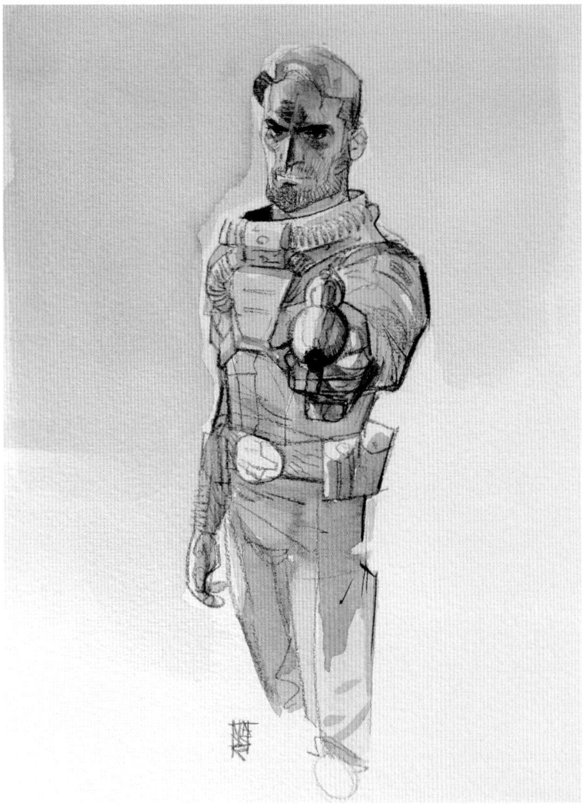

TM: This little beaut by Alex Maleev was a birthday present for Old Man Remender, to soften the bleakness of his slow trudge toward the grave. I imagine it brightened his day!

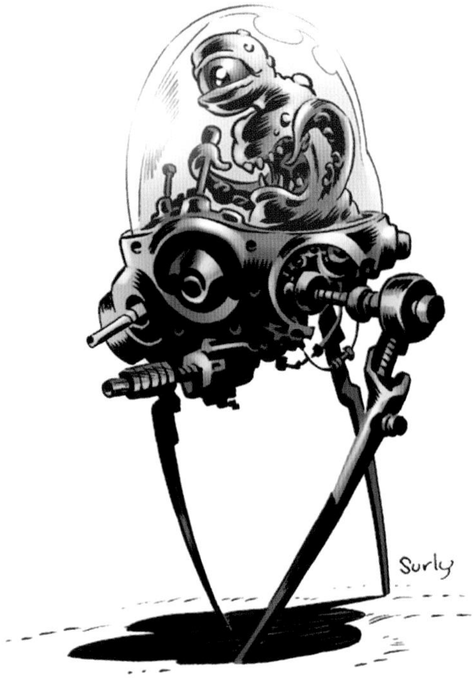

Surly

TM: Hilary Barta has been one of our prime supporters since the book's inception. Hil is an astounding cartoonist and nobody captures that Wally Wood inking vibe quite like him. He wrote and/or drew the lion's share of the *Tales of the Fear Agent* stories, and really enriched Heath's universe. I can say that Rick and I would take a bullet for this guy, and being a gentleman, I'd let Rick go first. These gems proudly adorned our letters column in the back of every issue.

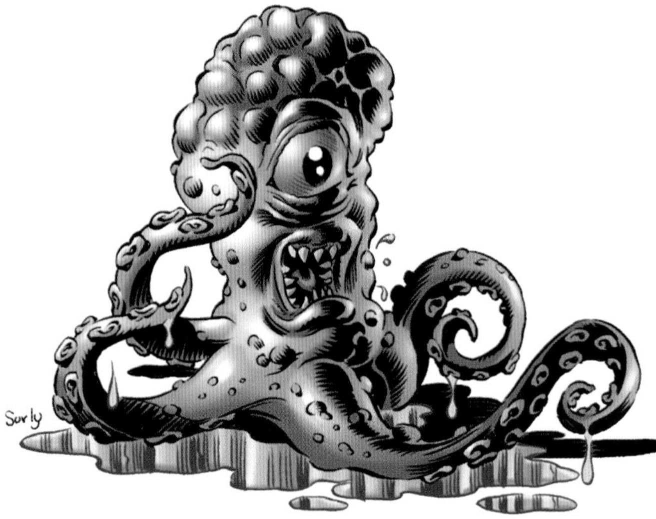

Surly

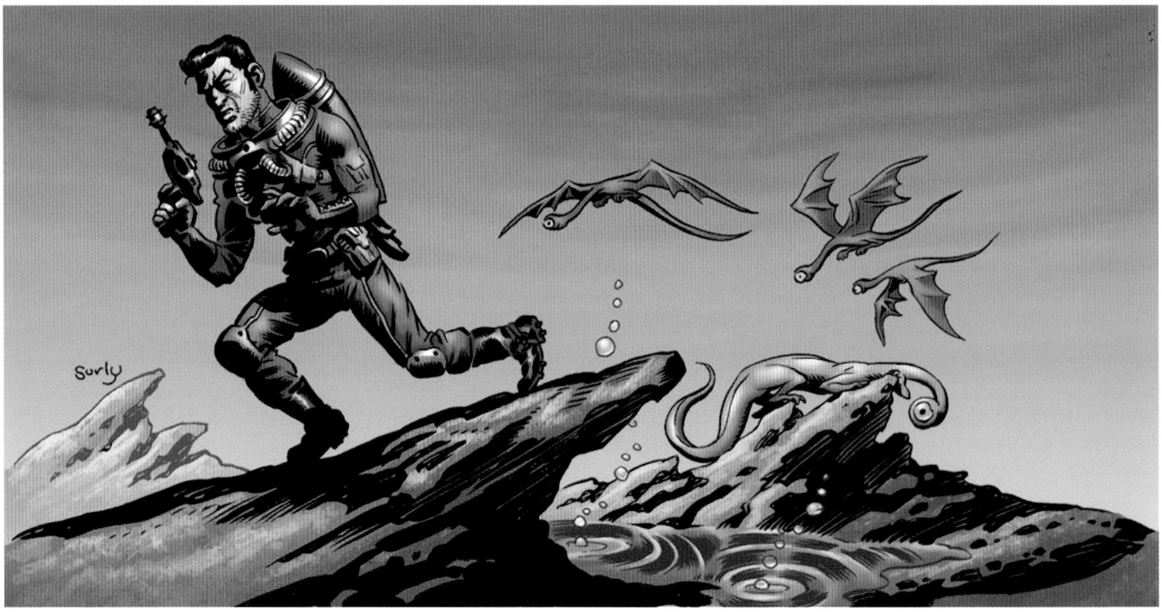

Surly

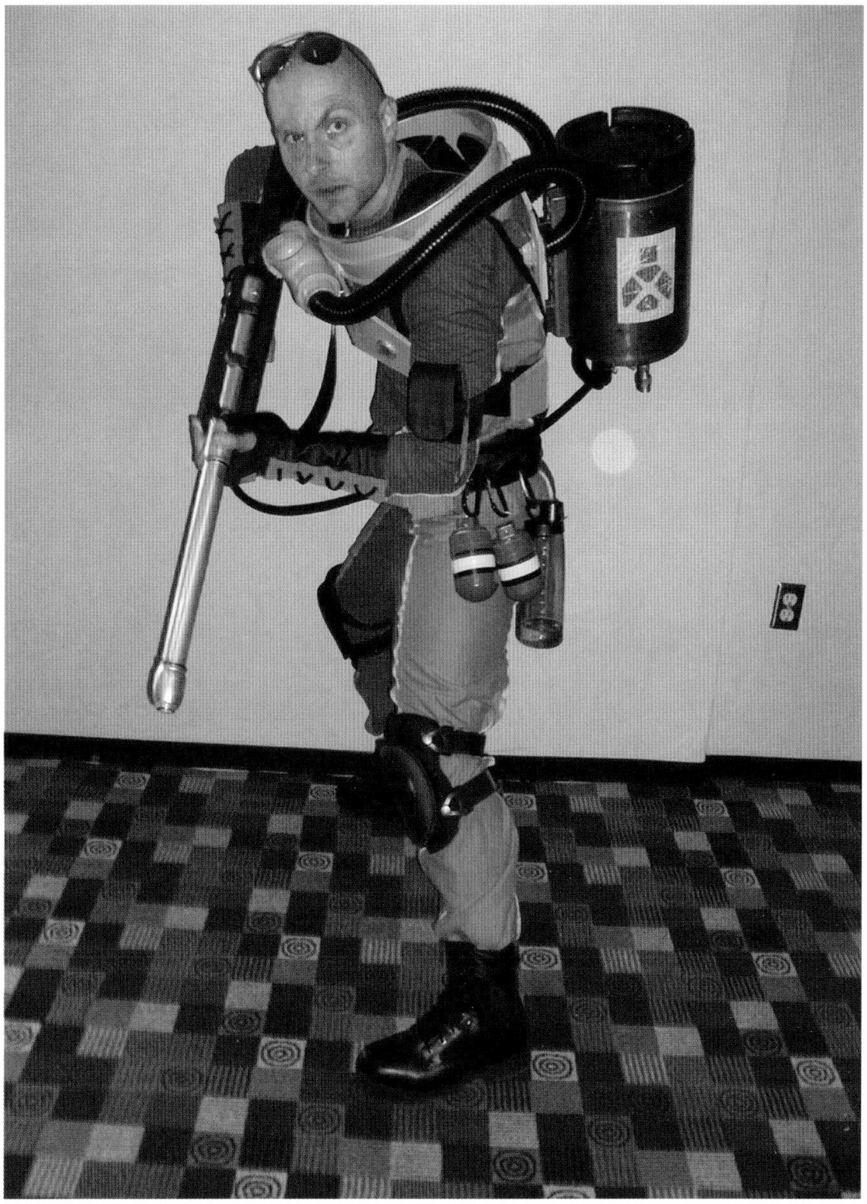

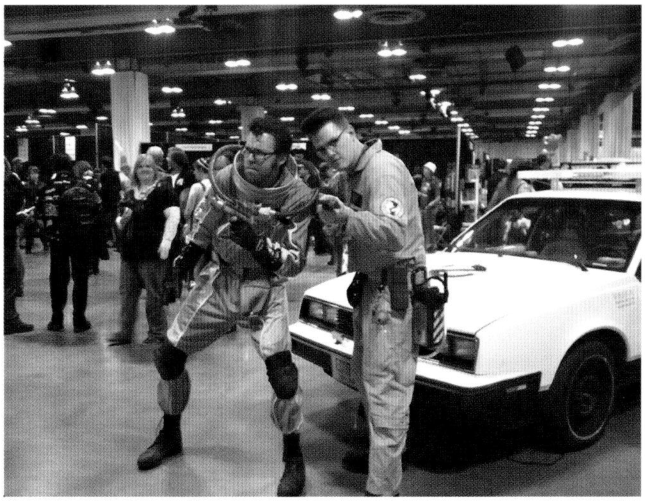

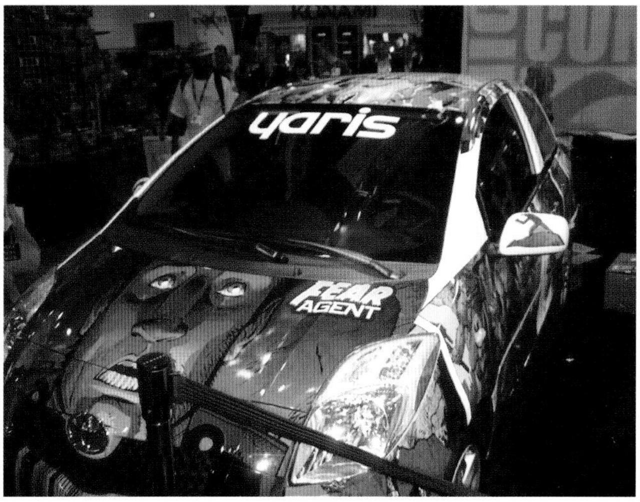
yaris
FEAR AGENT

TM: The *Fear Agent* love really comes out to play at comic-book conventions, and it does our tiny hearts good. Here are a couple of fantastic Heath cosplays, which I'm sure were no small feat to construct. Also, there's a shot of the *Fear Agent* Toyota Yaris, from San Diego Comic-Con. The entire back was filled with *Fear Agent* trade paperbacks, which G4 gave away to the lucky fans!

TM: This jaw-dropping sculpture was crafted by a fan named E. J. Panganiban. I had the pleasure of seeing the final painted version in person at a convention, and it was truly a sight to behold. You can check out more of his astounding work at http://edgepang.deviantart.com.

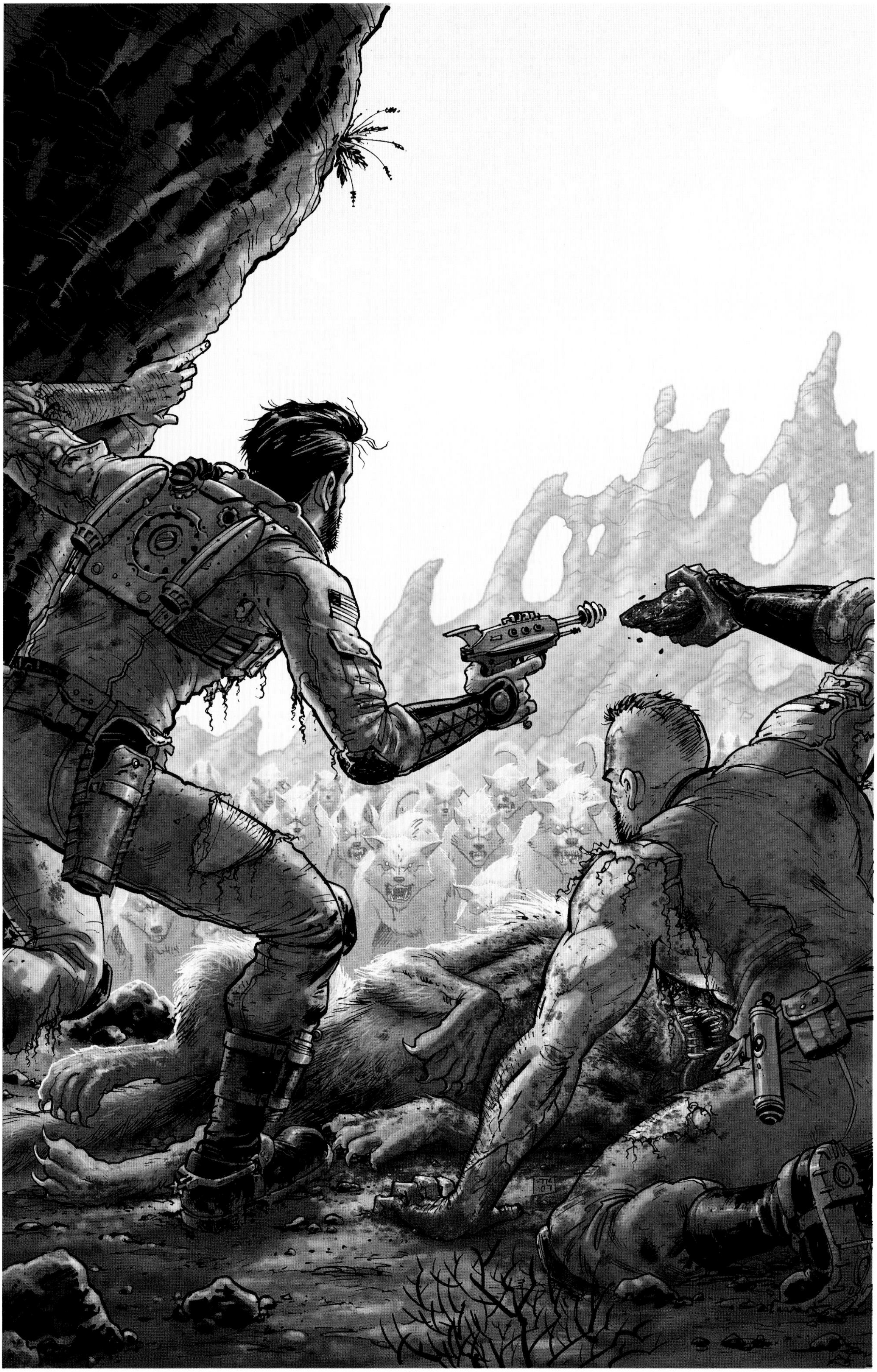

An unused cover from *Fear Agent* #22.

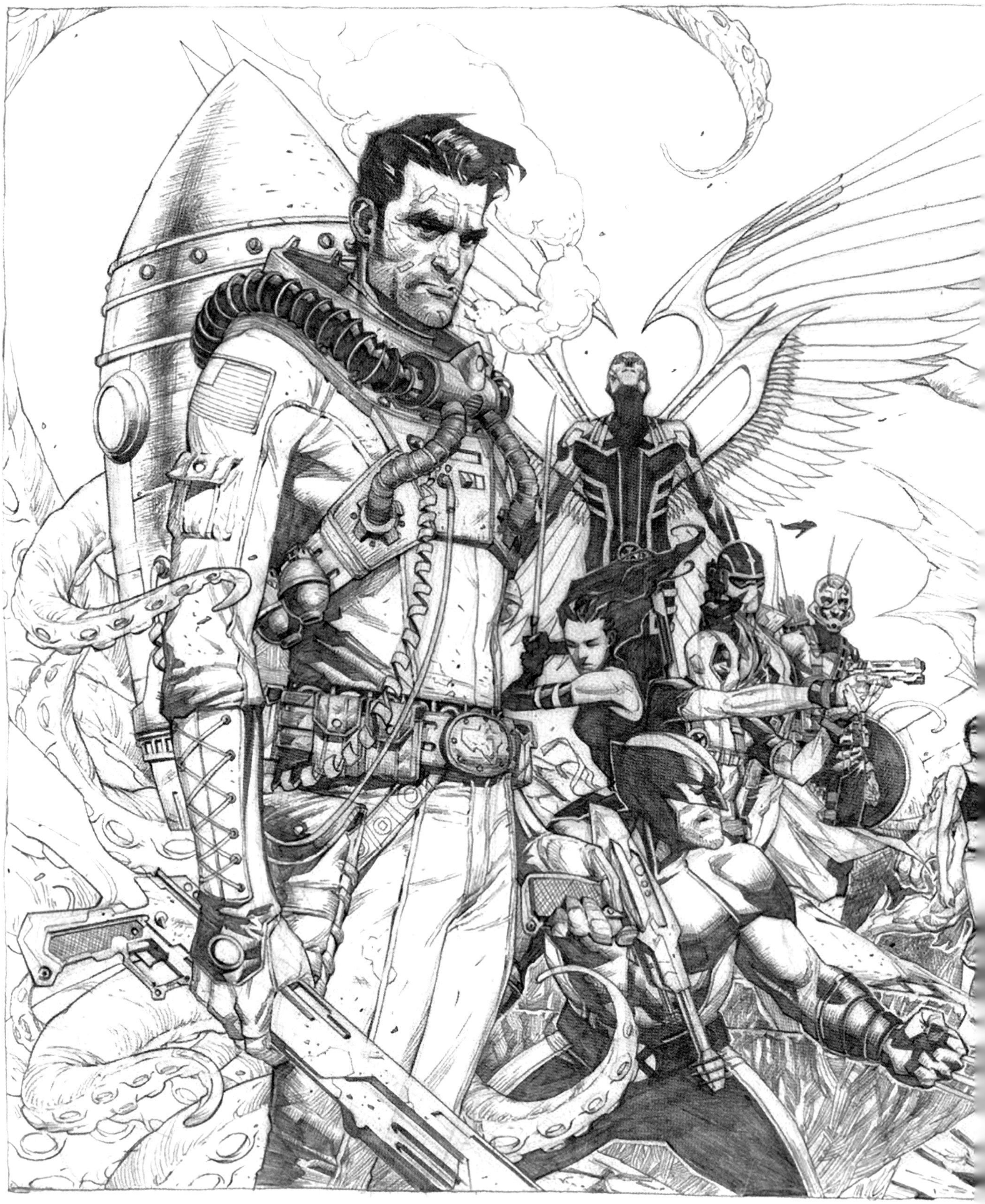

Jerome Opeña drew this beautiful piece for Rick's birthday.

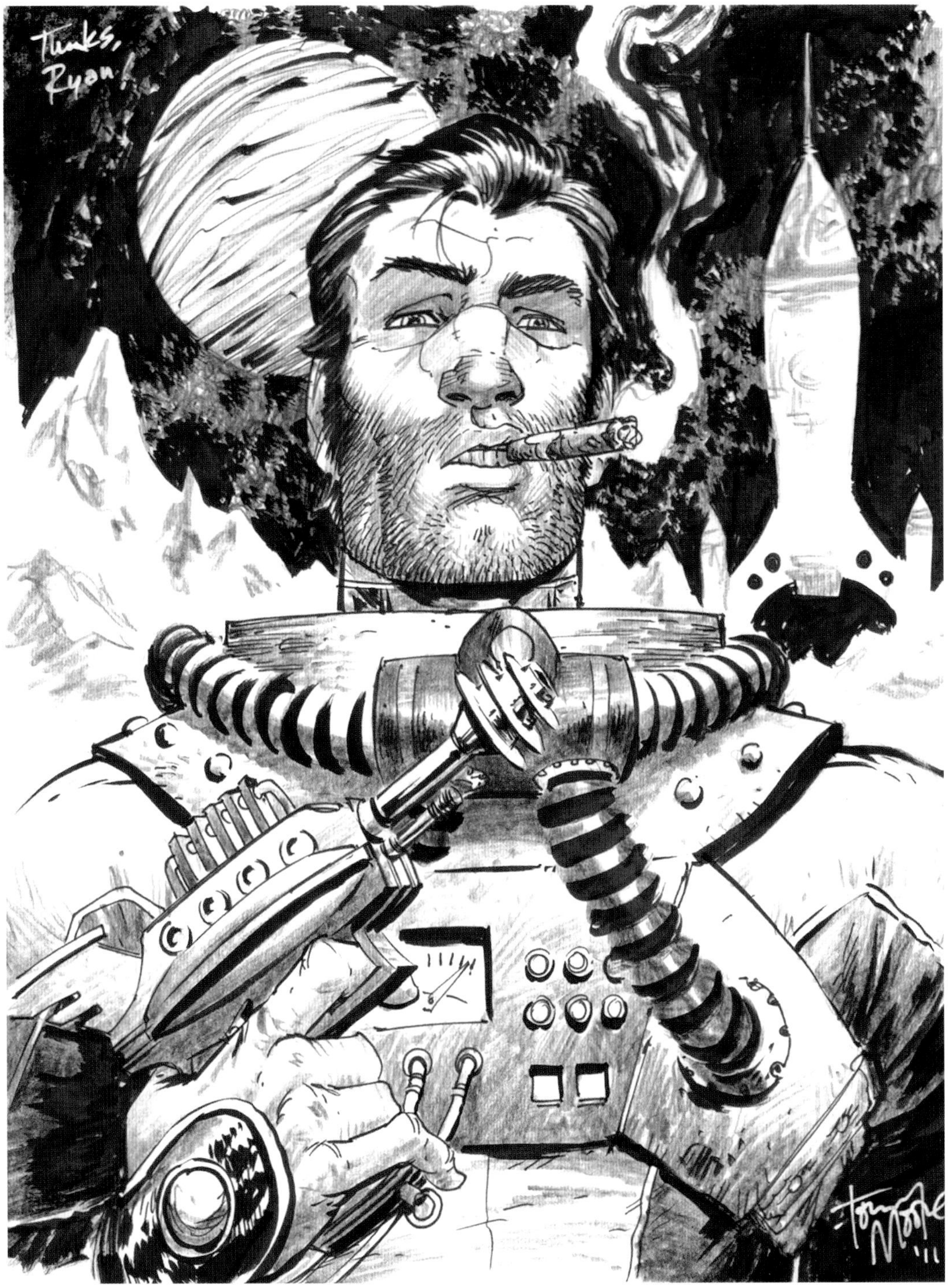
Thanks,
Ryan!

Two more *Fear Agent* commissions by Tony Moore.

Thanks,
Chad!

501

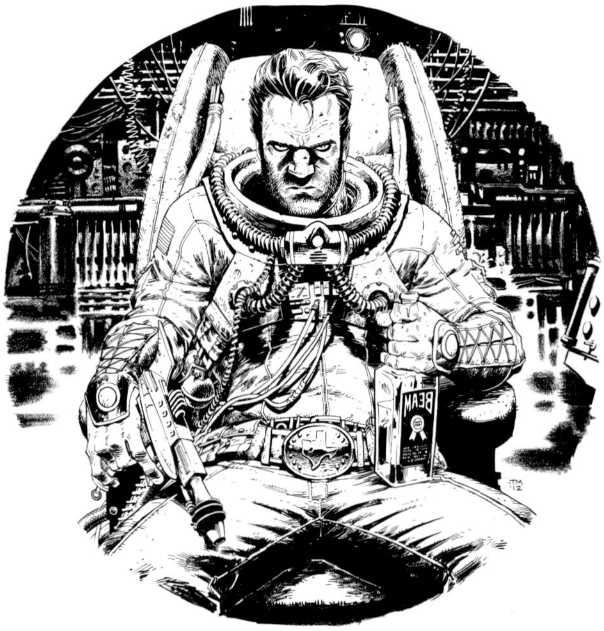

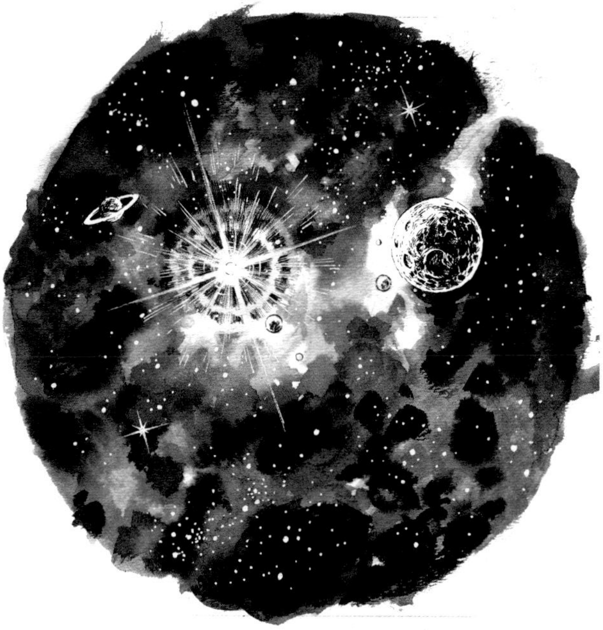

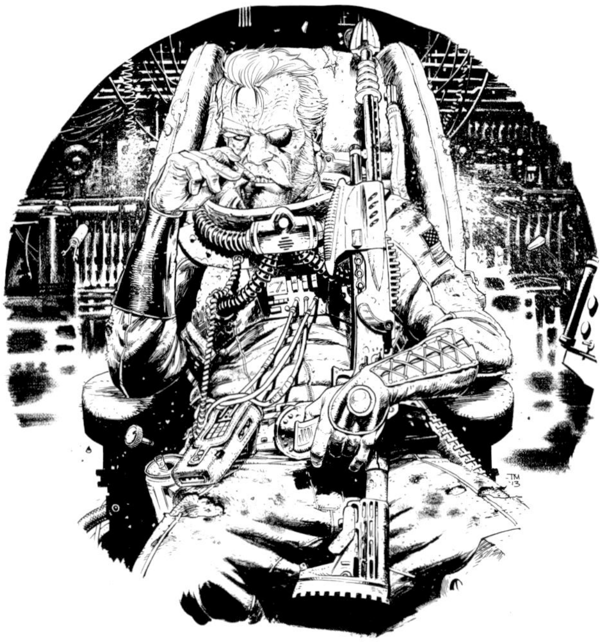

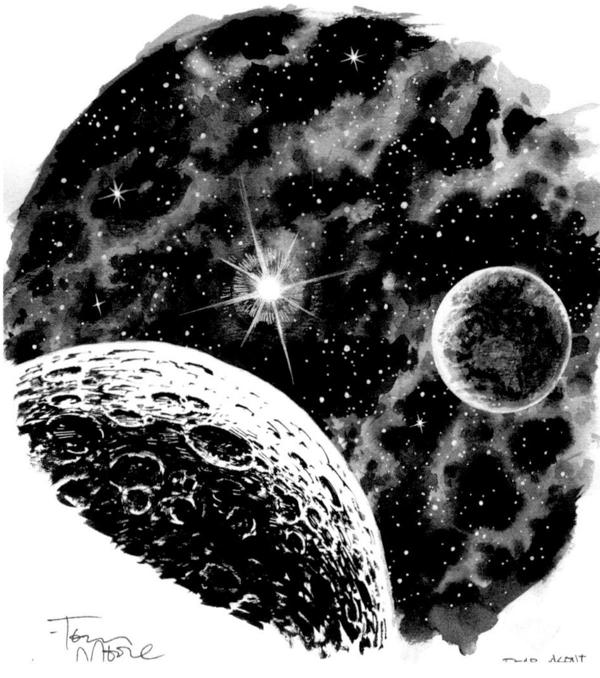

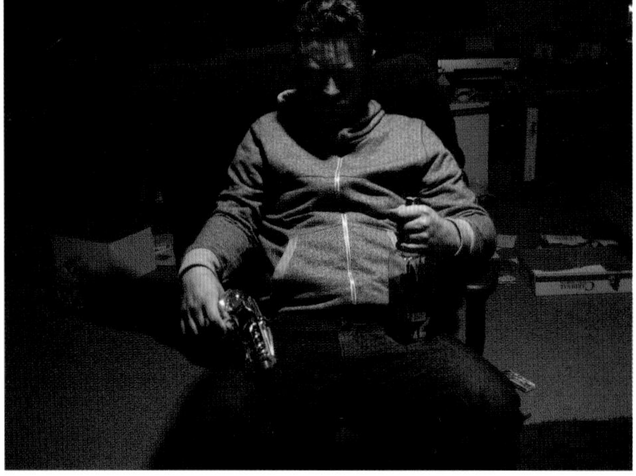

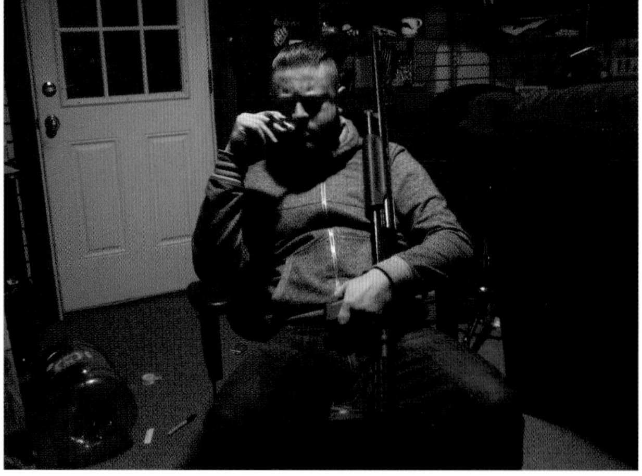

TM: Here's a peek at the arduous process I used to create these library edition covers. A silly reference shot from my office, the inked figure, and the background painting for each cover. For each of these things, I would create two finished pieces of art, the figure and the starscape, then I'd stack them, and frame with the porthole. Each layer individually has more details than will survive when they're together, and sometimes it's a real bummer to see some belabored bit end up disappearing into the piece, but once they're merged, a whole other thing emerges from the sacrifice.

COVERS AND PINUPS

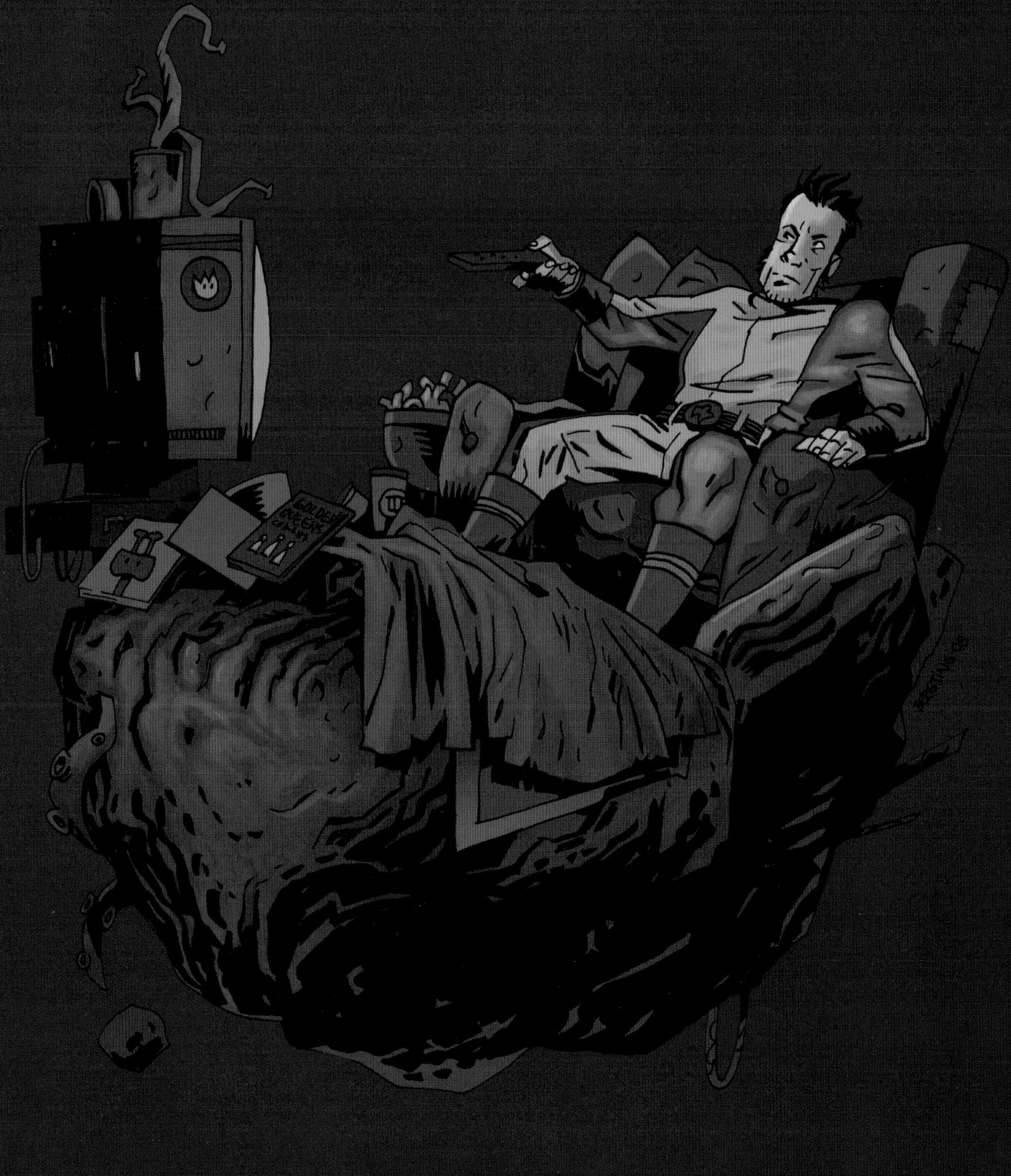

PETER BERGTING

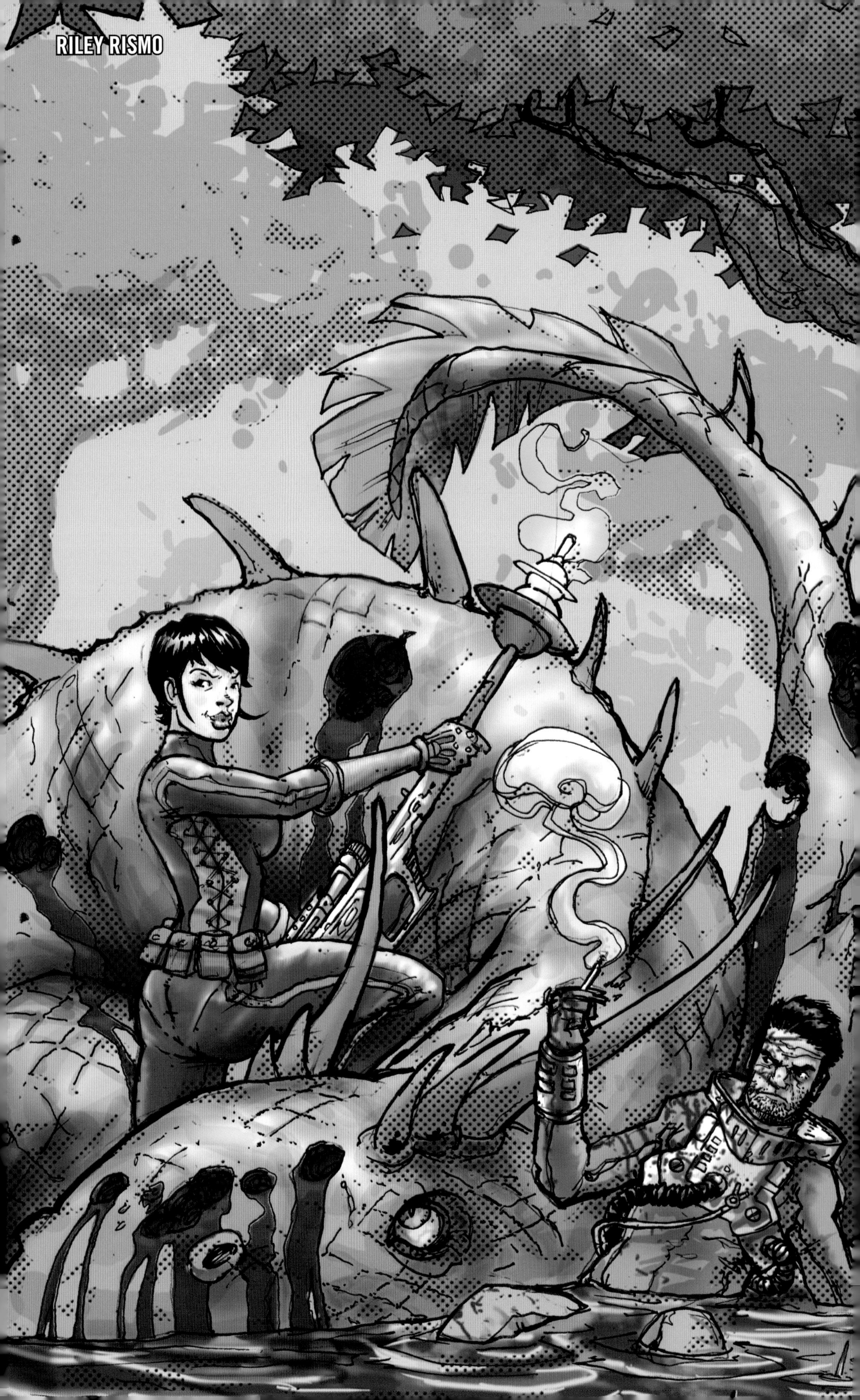
RILEY RISMO

BRIAN HURTT

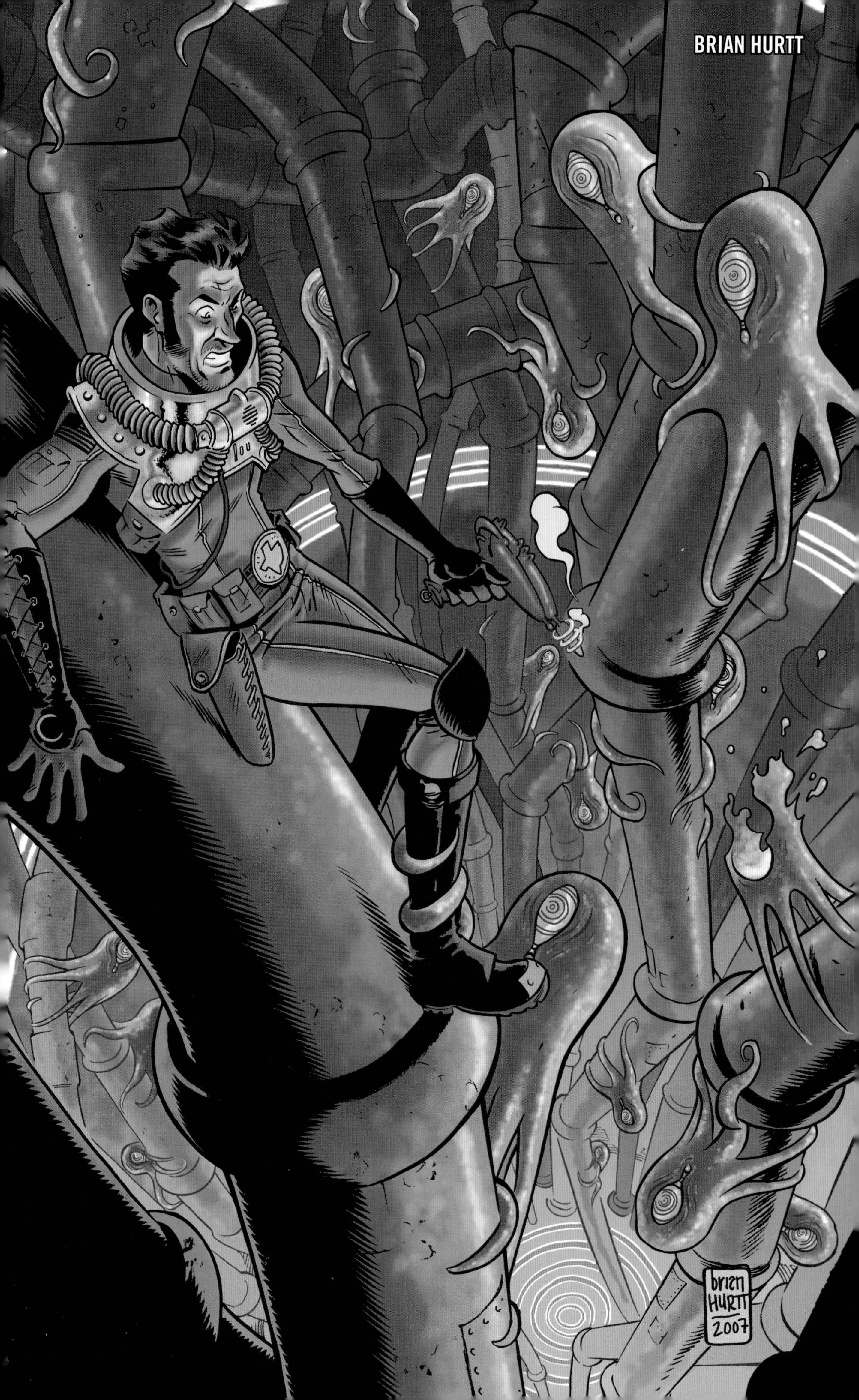
brian HURTT 2007

BRIAN CHURILLA, HILARY BARTA, AND JASON MILLET

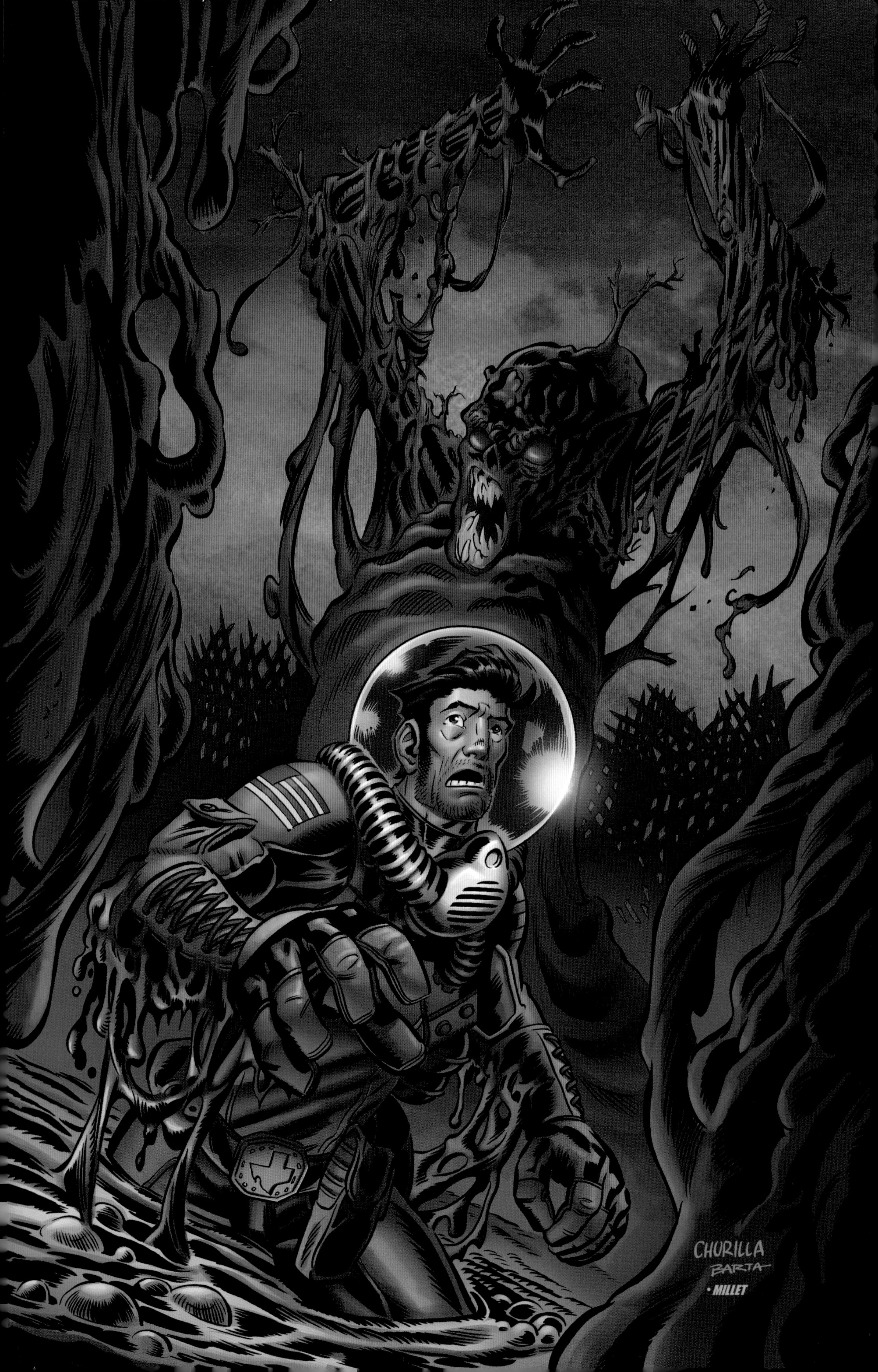
CHURILLA
BARTA
• MILLET

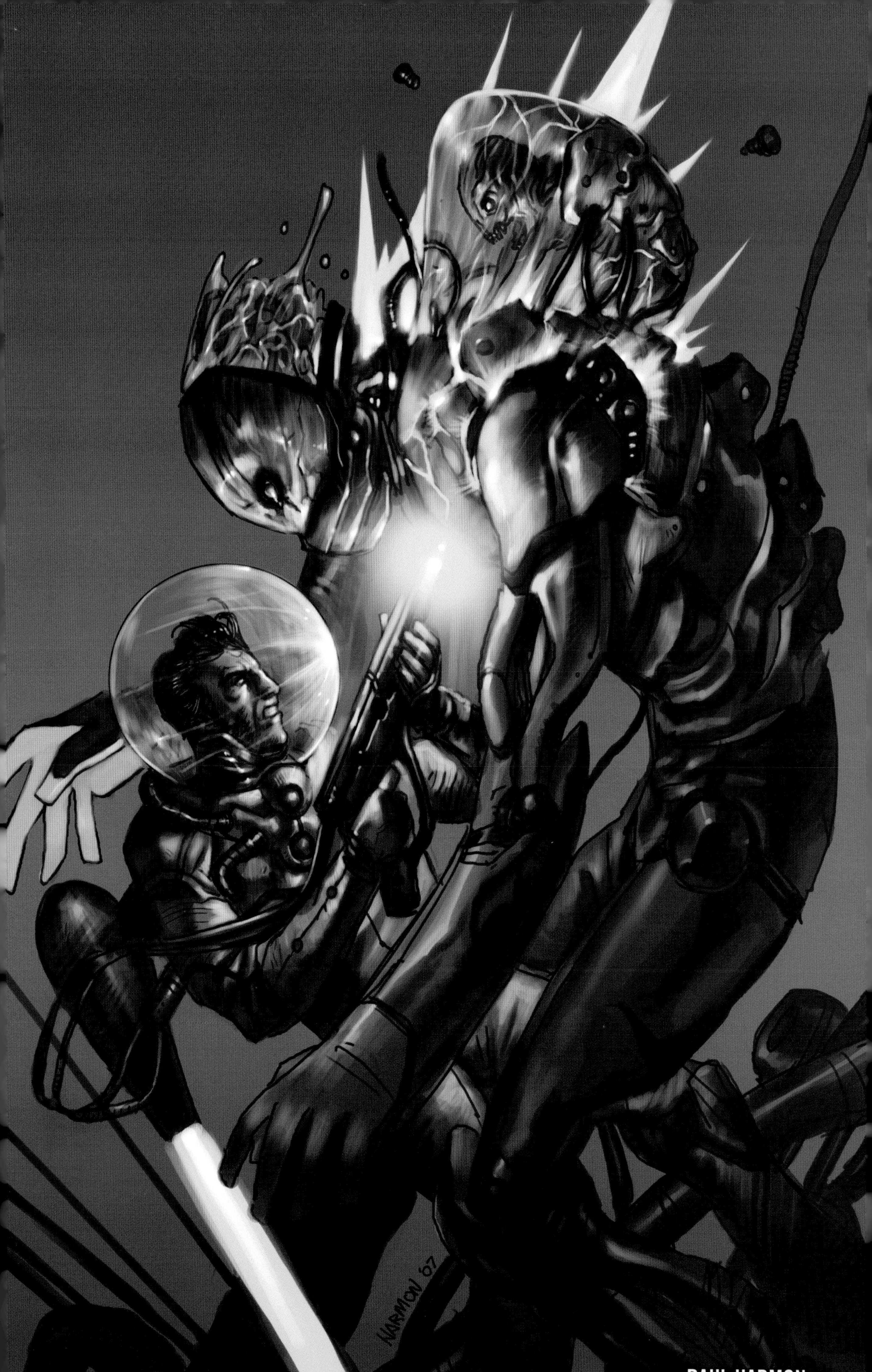
HARMON '07

PAUL HARMON

ANTONIO FUSO

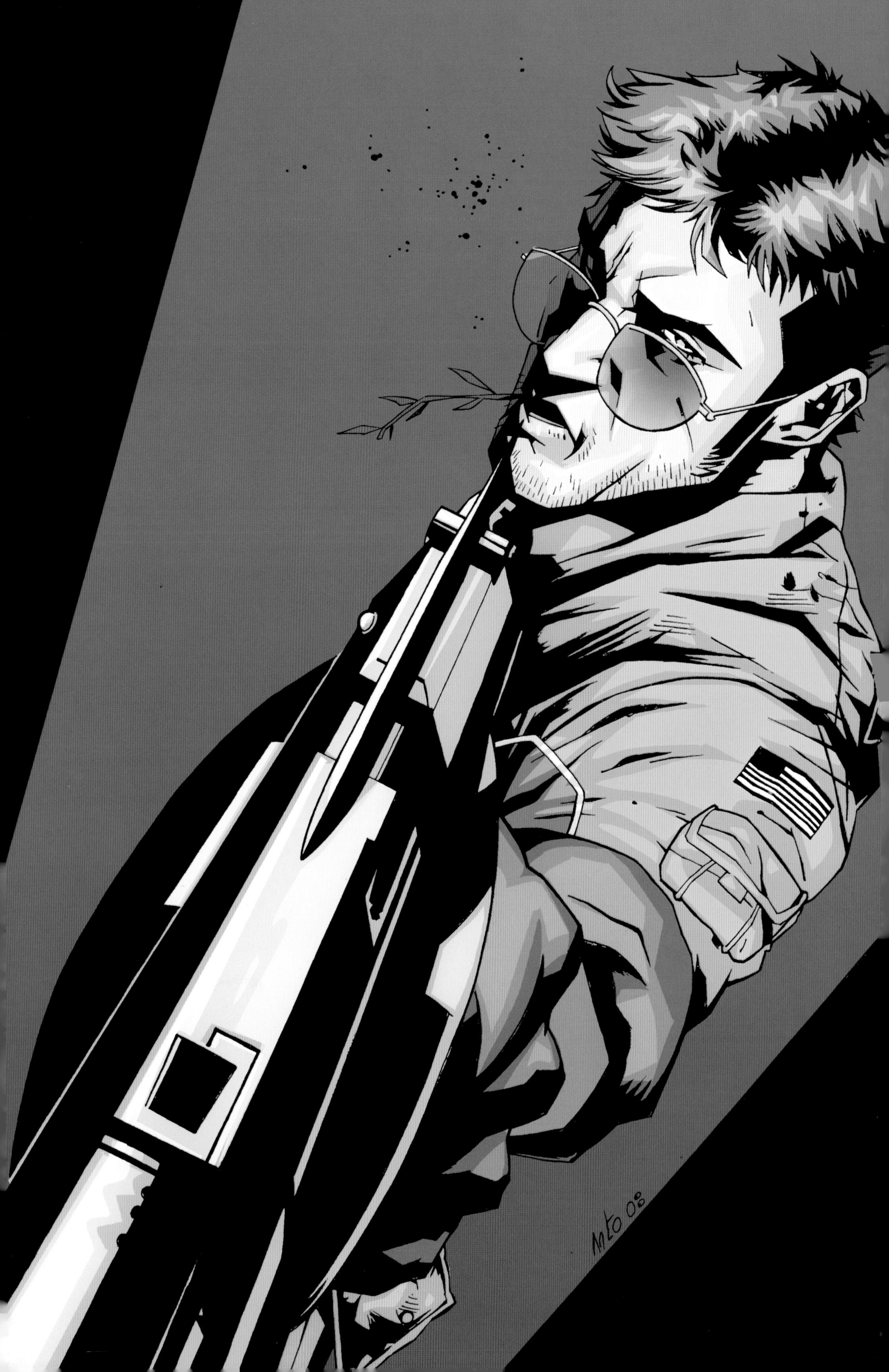

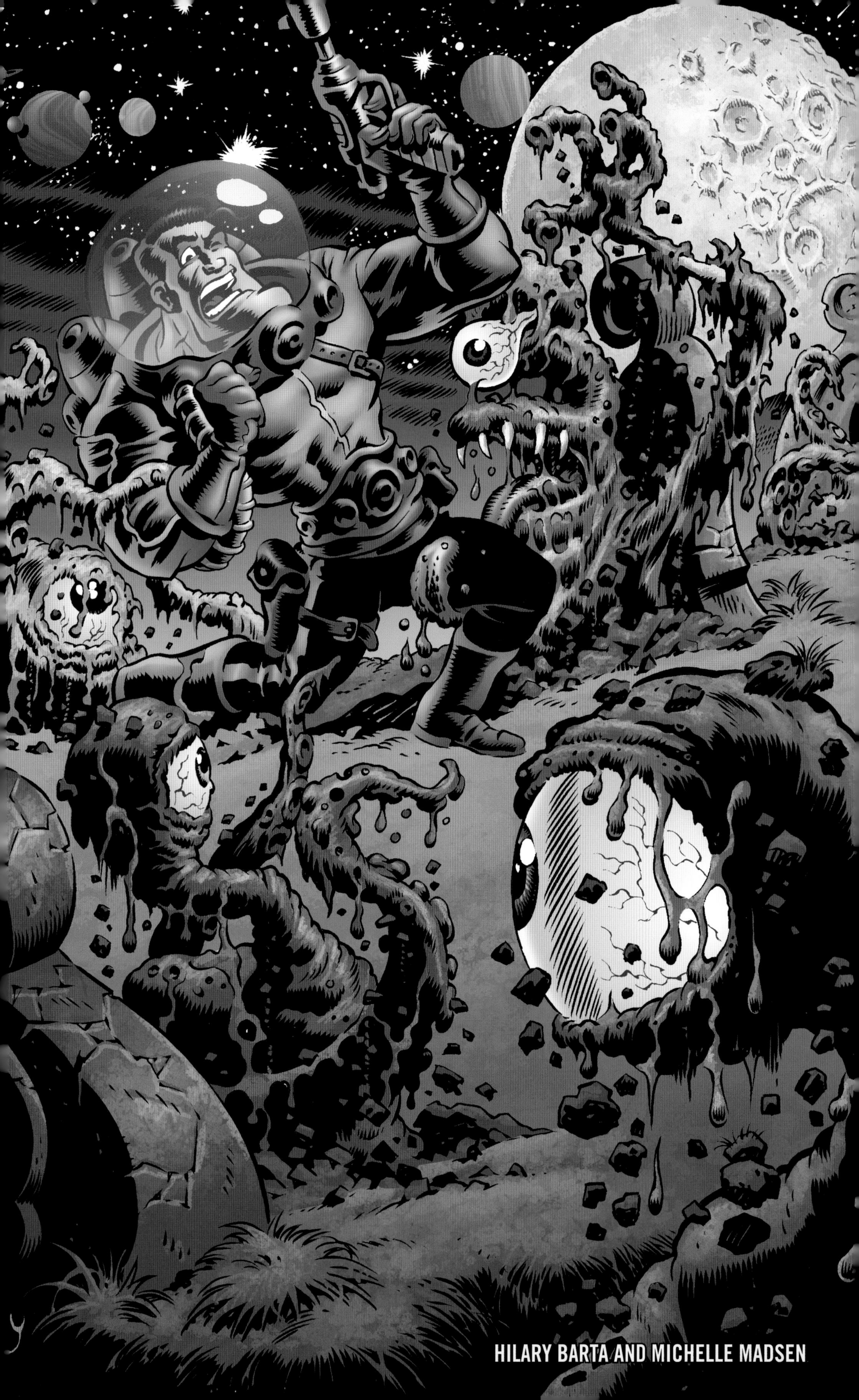

HILARY BARTA AND MICHELLE MADSEN

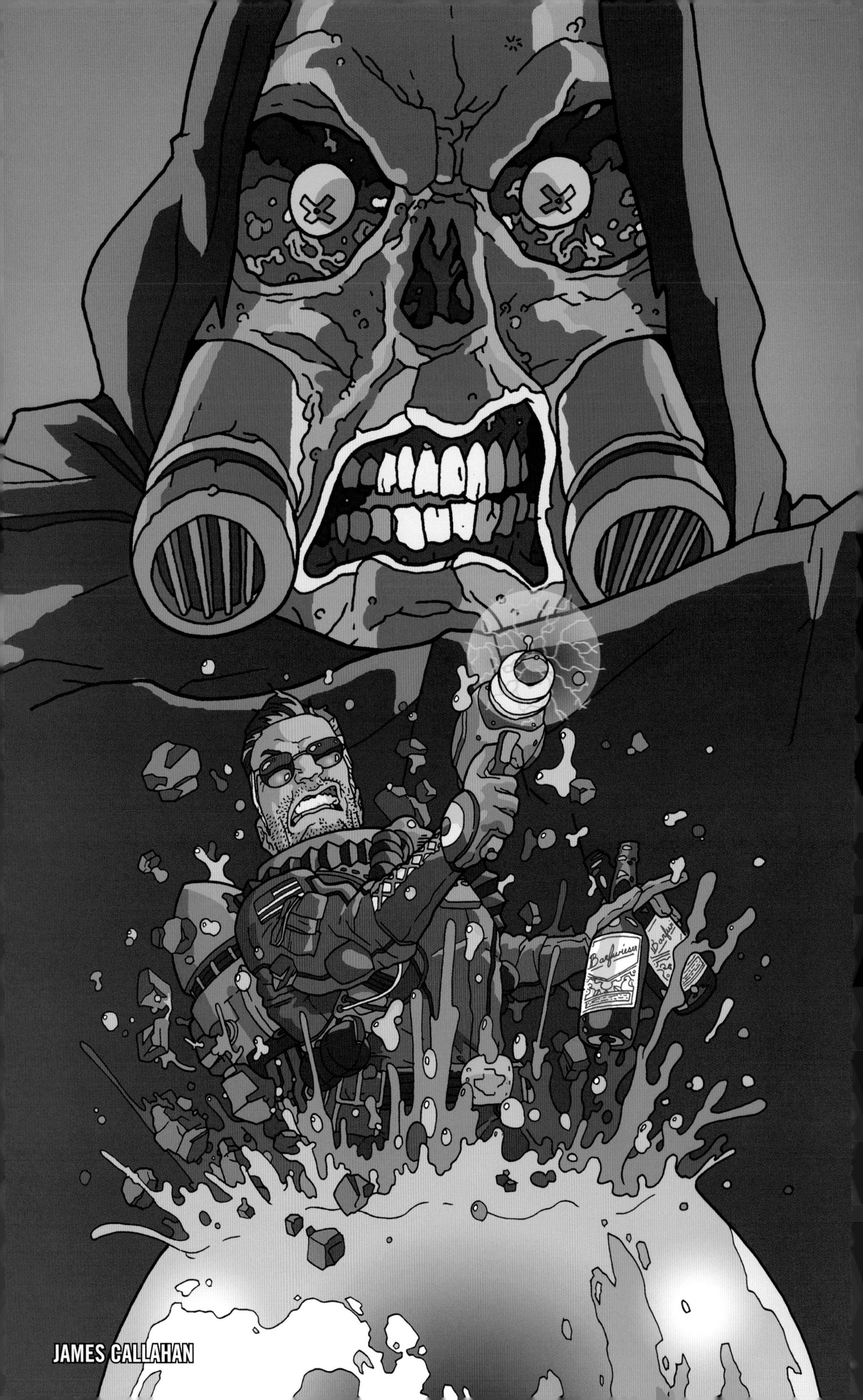

JAMES CALLAHAN

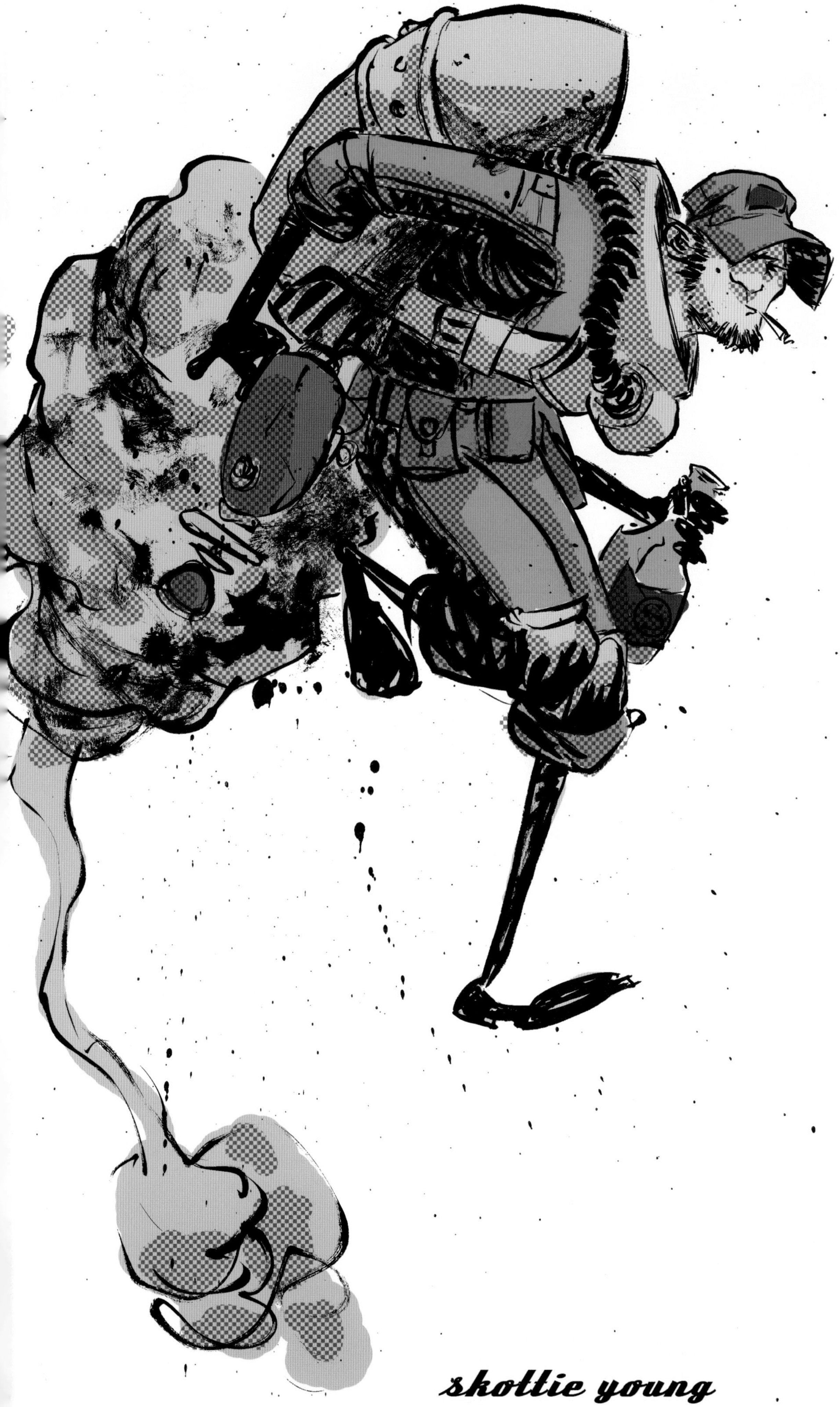

skottie young

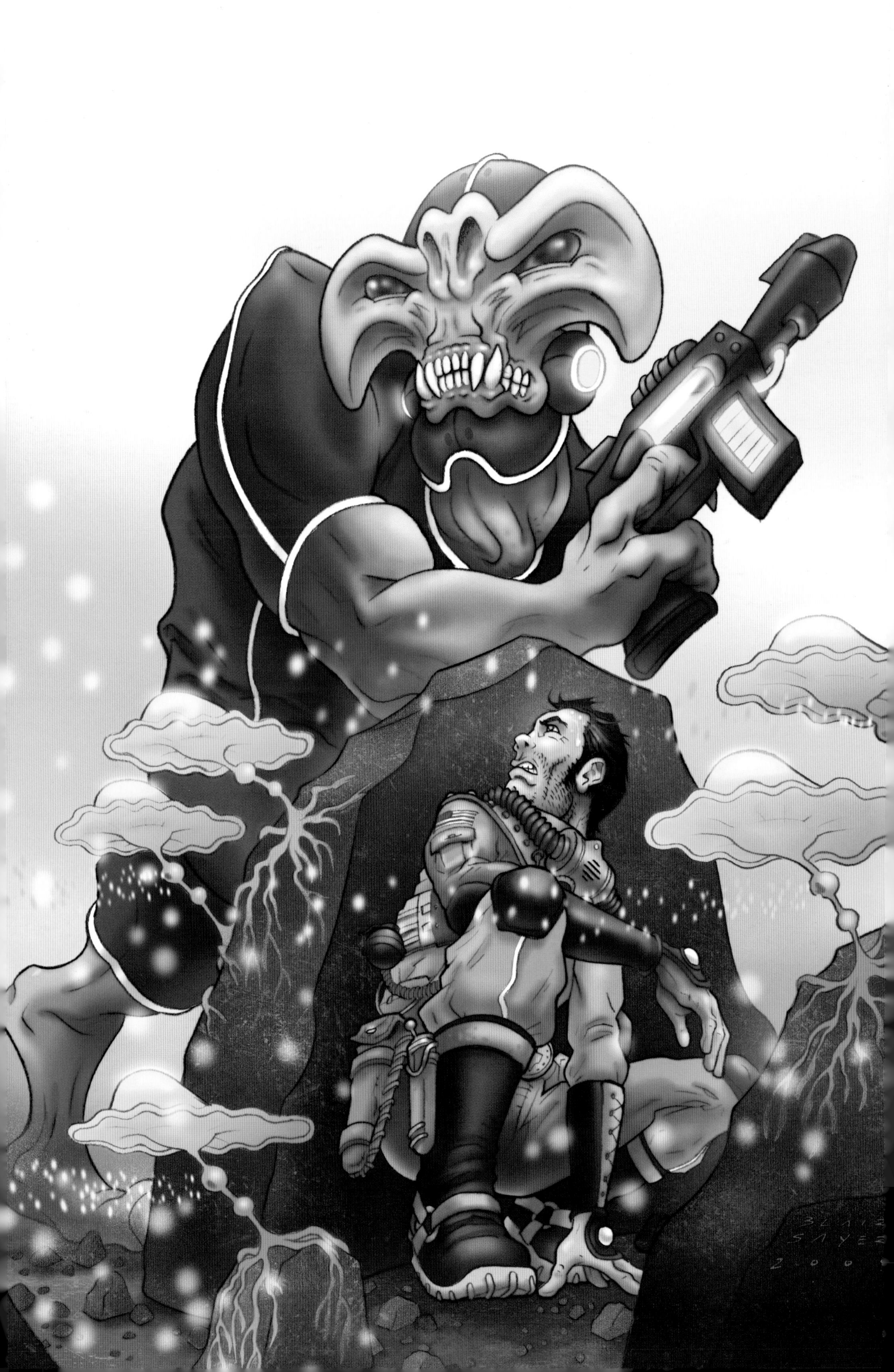

MIKE HAWTHORNE

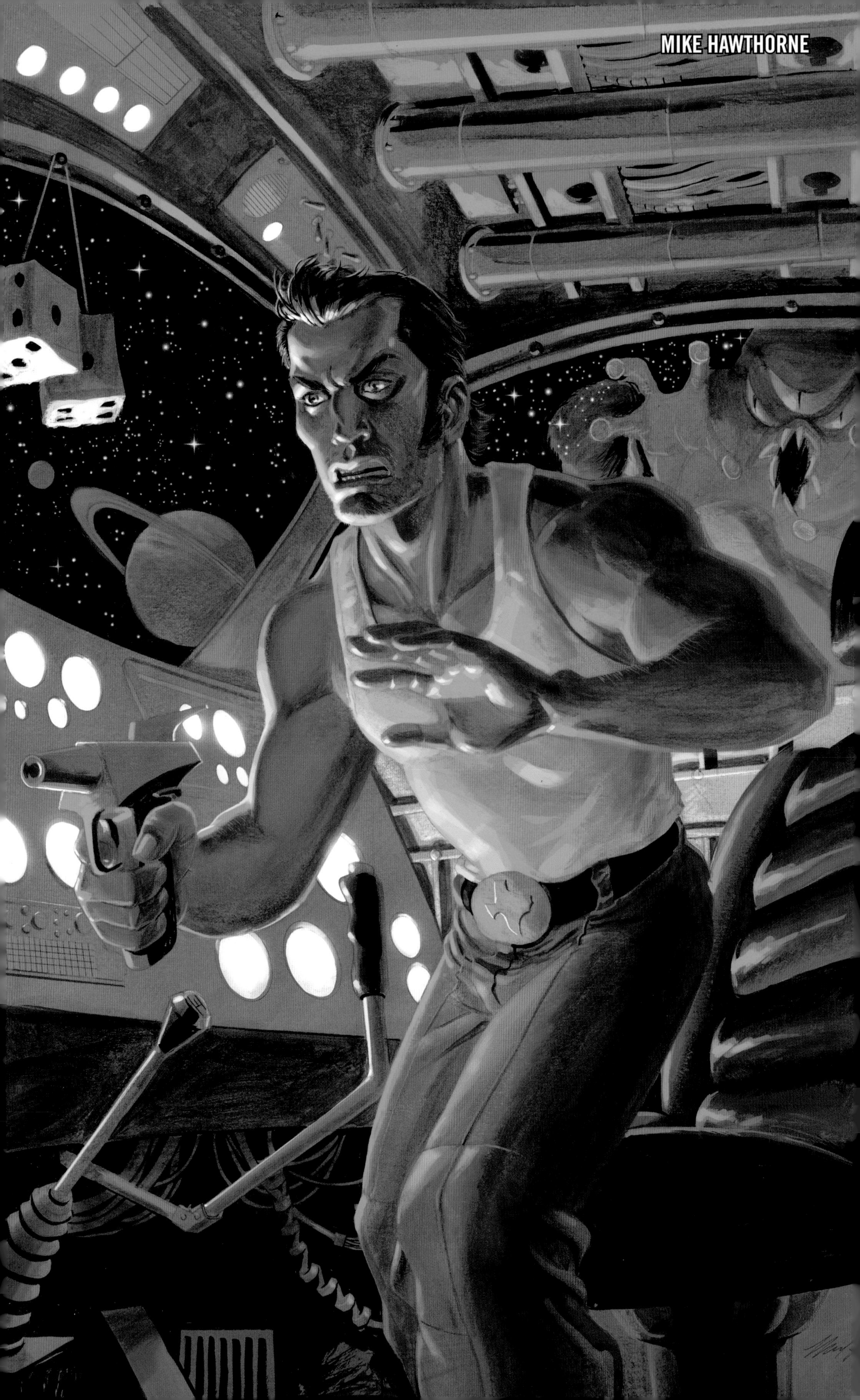

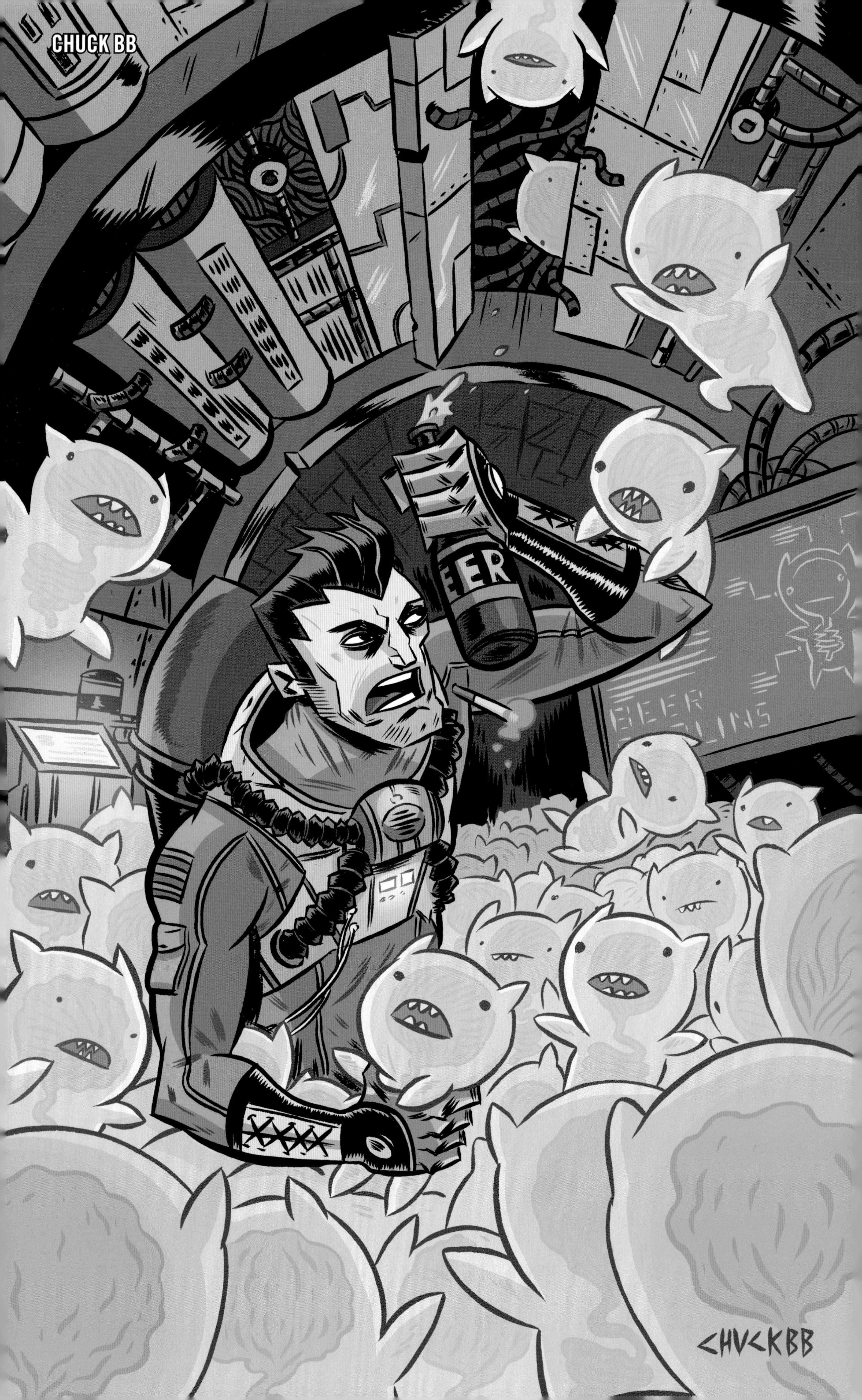
CHUCK BB
BEER
CHVCKBB

STEVE SANDERS

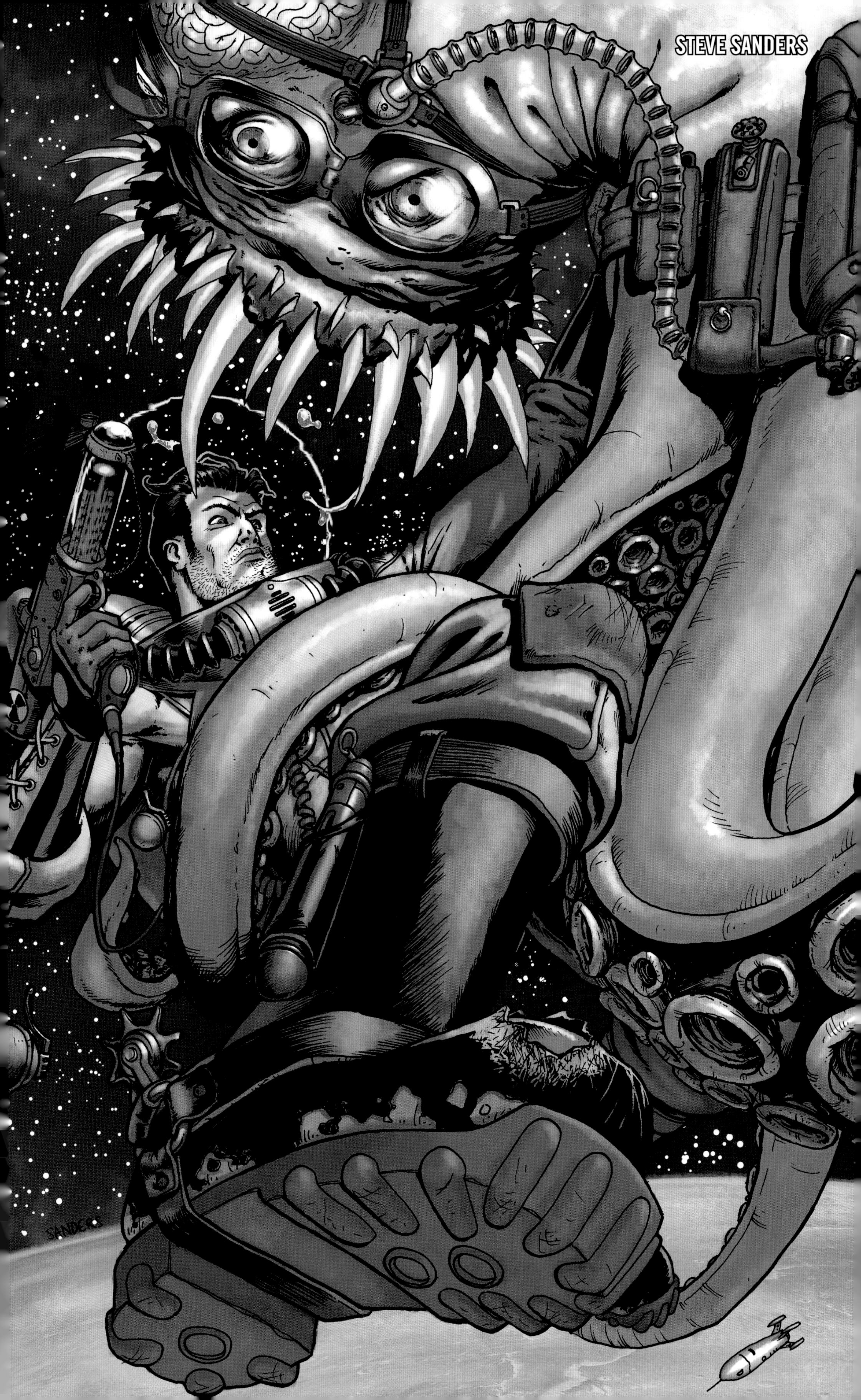

SANDERS

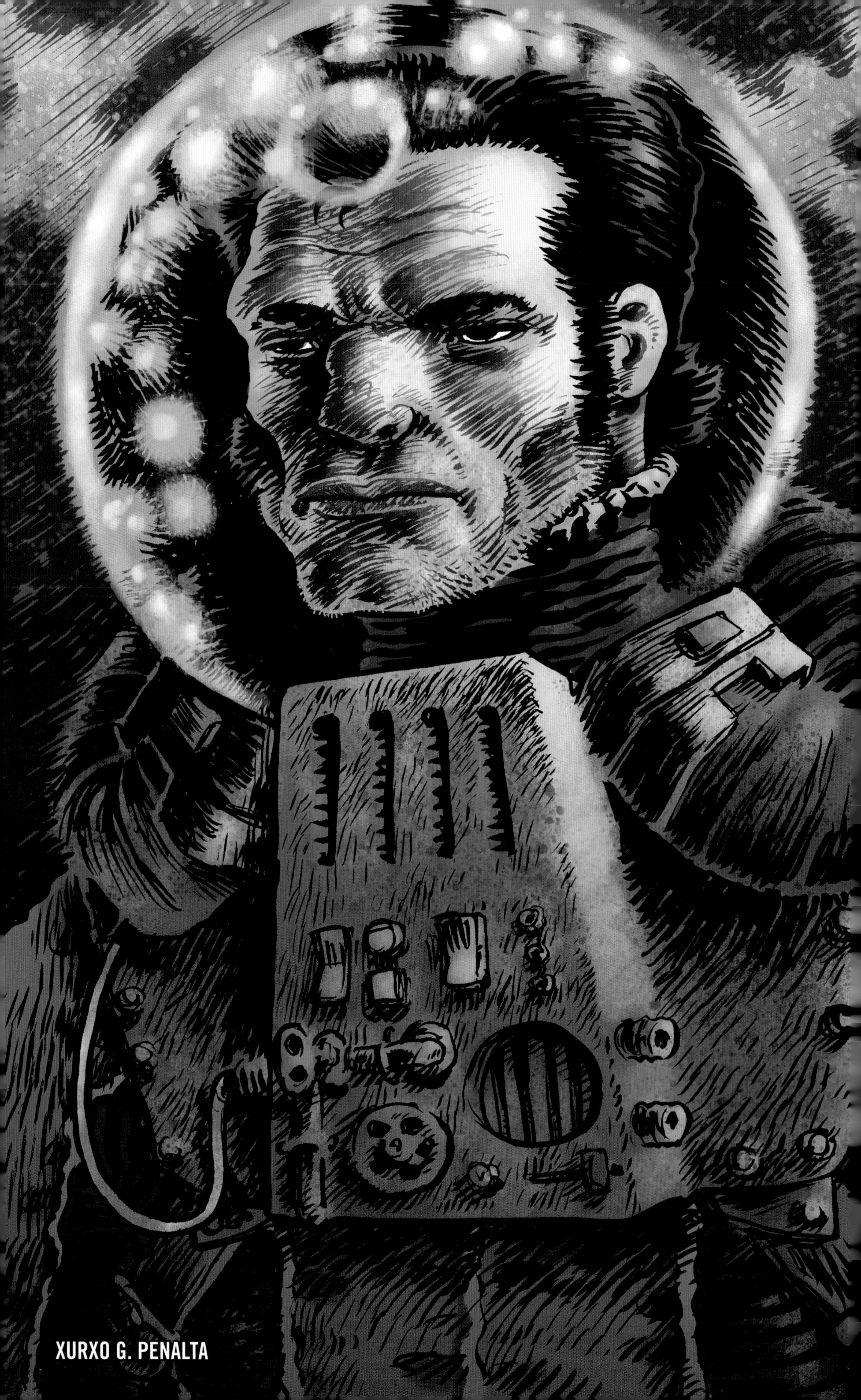
XURXO G. PENALTA

MARK TORRES

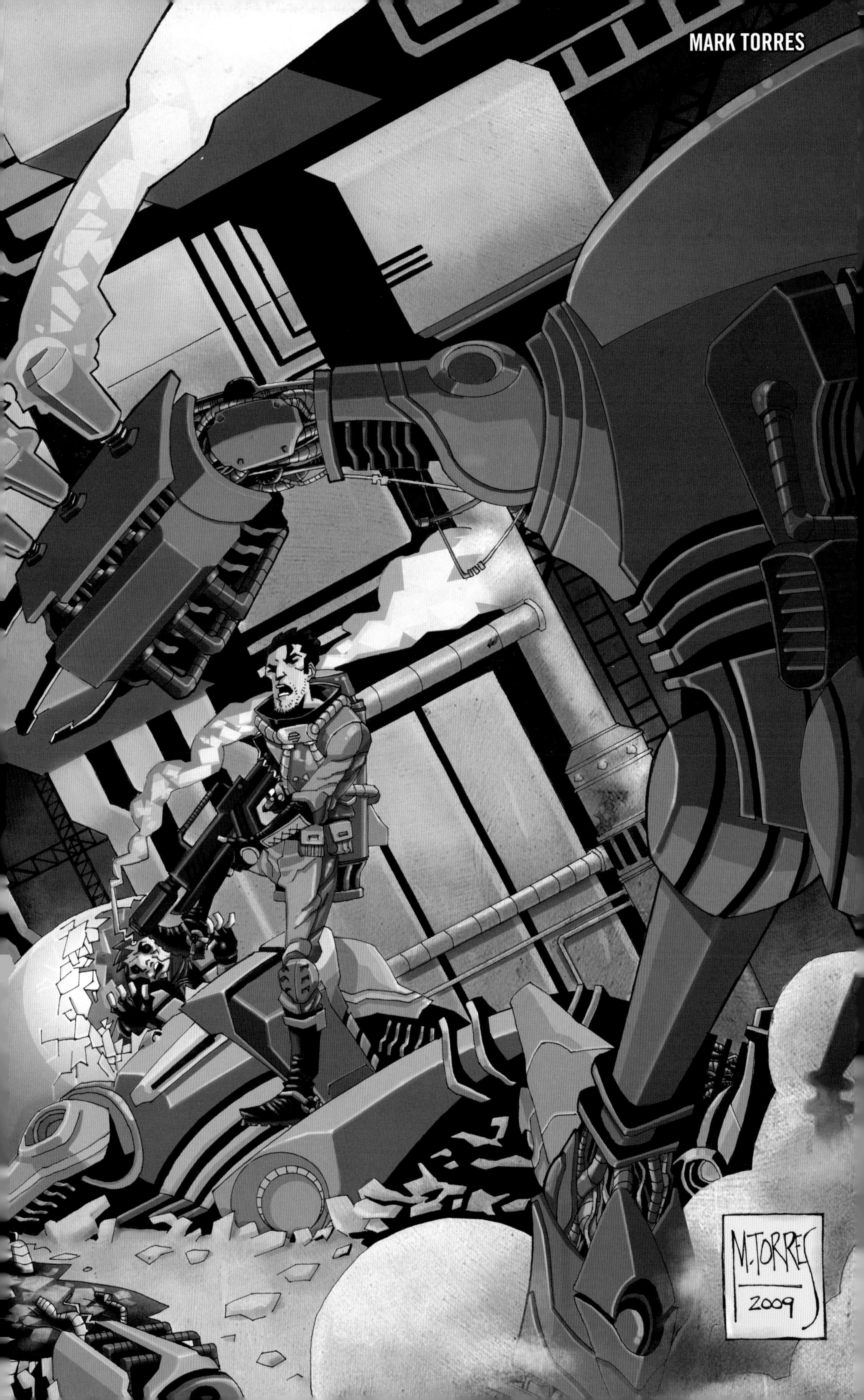
M. TORRES
2009

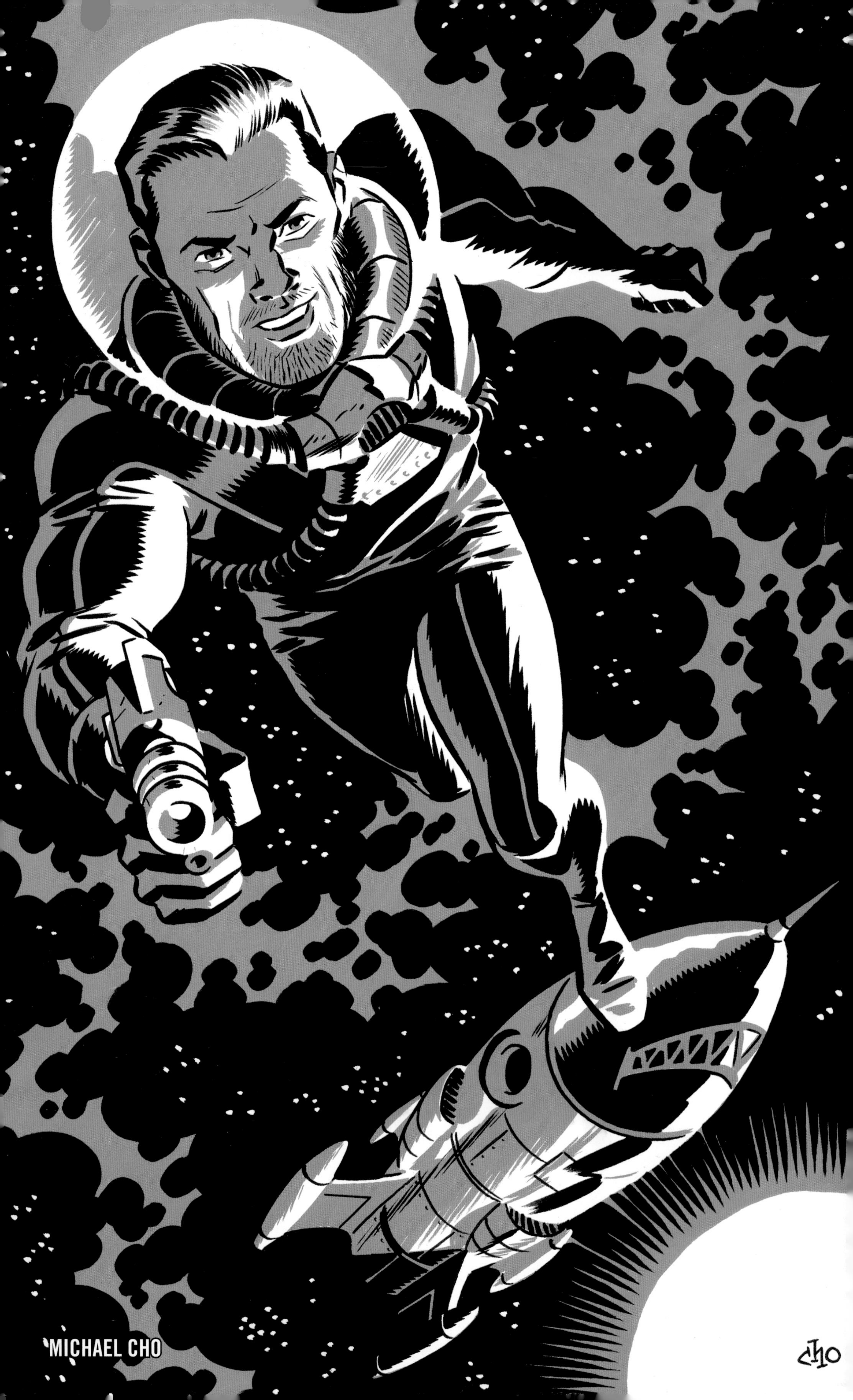
MICHAEL CHO
cho